AMERICAN POETRY AND PROSE

Part One
From the Beginnings to 1865

AMERICAN

Fifth Edition / Part One

HOUGHTON MIFFLIN COMPANY · BOSTON

New York · Atlanta · Geneva, Illinois · Dallas · Palo Alto

POETRY AND PROSE

Edited by Norman Foerster

Norman S. Grabo
University of California, Berkeley

Russel B. Nye
Michigan State University

E. Fred Carlisle
Michigan State University

Robert Falk
University of California, Los Angeles

William Bradford From *History of Plymouth Plantation 1620–
1647*, ed. W. C. Ford, copyright 1912 by the Massachusetts Historical Society; reprinted by permission of the Massachusetts
Historical Society.

William Byrd From *The Secret Diary of William Byrd of Westover, 1709–1712*, ed. Louis B. Wright and Marion Tinling.
Copyright 1941 by Louis B. Wright and Marion Tinling.

James Fenimore Cooper From *The American Democrat*, ed.
H. L. Mencken; reprinted by courtesy of Alfred A. Knopf, Inc.

Jonathan Edwards From *Freedom of the Will*, ed. Paul Ramsey,
by permission of Yale University Press. Copyright © 1957 by
Yale University Press.

From *The Philosophy of Jonathan Edwards from His Private
Notebooks*, ed. Harvey G. Townsend (University of Oregon
Monograph: Studies in Philosophy, no. 2), University of Oregon,
1955; by permission of the University of Oregon.

Ralph Waldo Emerson From *The Journals of Ralph Waldo
Emerson*, ed. E. W. Emerson and W. E. Forbes; selections reprinted by permission of Houghton Mifflin Company.

Nathaniel Hawthorne The passage reprinted from *The American Notebooks by Nathaniel Hawthorne*, based on the original
manuscripts in the Pierpont Morgan Library and edited by
Randall Stewart (New Haven: Yale University Press, 1932), is
copyright © 1932, 1960 by the Ohio State University Press. All
rights reserved.

Thomas Jefferson From *The Papers of Thomas Jefferson*,
edited by Julian P. Boyd et al.; Vol. I, copyright 1950 by Princeton University Press; Vol. XII, copyright © 1955 by Princeton
University Press. Reprinted by permission of Princeton University Press.

Herman Melville Selections from the *Piazza Tales*, ed. Egbert
S. Oliver (1948); from *Collected Poems of Herman Melville*, ed.
Howard P. Vincent (1947); and from *Clarel*, ed. W. E. Bezanson
(1960); by permission of Hendricks House, Inc., Publishers.

Edgar Allan Poe From *The Poems of Edgar Allan Poe*, edited
by Floyd Stovall (Charlottesville, 1965). Selections reprinted
by permission of The University Press of Virginia.

Edward Taylor From *The Poetical Works of Edward Taylor*,
edited by Thomas H. Johnson. Copyright 1939 Rockland Editions, 1943 Princeton University Press. Reprinted by permission
of Princeton University Press.

Phillis Wheatley From *The Poems of Phillis Wheatley*, edited
by Julian D. Mason, Jr., copyright © 1966 by The University of
North Carolina Press; reprinted by permission of The University
of North Carolina Press.

John Winthrop Selections from the *Winthrop Papers*, ed.
Allyn B. Forbes, Vols. I (1929) and II (1931); reprinted by permission of the Massachusetts Historical Society.

John Woolman From *The Journal and Essays of John Wool-
man*, edited by Amelia Mott Gummere, copyright, 1922, by
The Macmillan Company; selections reprinted courtesy of the
Philadelphia Yearly Meeting of The Religious Society of
Friends.

Publisher's Foreword

LIKE ITS DISTINGUISHED PREDECESSORS, this fifth edition of *American Poetry and Prose* is designed to serve both the historical and the critical approaches to our literature. And since the years have narrowed the gap between these two, this edition has been able to incorporate important elements of a third approach, which may be called comparative and developmental, focusing attention on certain recurring themes that have grown out of the unique American experience, and on the various ways American writers of different periods have dealt with them. Within the cultural framework provided by this approach, the student is encouraged to look simultaneously in two directions, from the past to the adumbrated future, and from the present to the seminal past, and thereby to gain a deeper insight into the vitality and continuity of American literature. At the same time, the consistent focus on literary concerns, in the structure of the book, the nature of the selections, and the editorial commentary, has made it possible to avoid the pitfall of the purely documentary or sociological; while the ample treatment of major writers within a setting of lesser but significant figures averts the temptation to include obscure writers out of the main stream, or to introduce the merely novel or the fashionable and evanescent.

This edition differs from even its immediate predecessor in other significant ways. The mere passage of time has shifted the center of gravity toward the contemporary, and has thereby altered the book's proportions. Relatively less space is devoted to colonial and early federal writing, though a few new figures are introduced into the earlier periods, such as Thomas Hooker, exponent of the "plain style" that was to become so important a strain in American writing. The great figures of the nineteenth century receive much the same emphasis as before, though Whitman concludes the section on the romantics in Part One instead of beginning Part Two in the two-volume set. The fifth and contemporary division now begins not at 1900 but at 1914, a genuine break point which gives deeper unity to the sections both before and after, and allows increased space to the ever-growing contemporary. It is interesting to recall that the first edition concluded with Carl Sandburg whereas the fifth ends with John Barth.

In subtler ways also this edition has taken the measure of the day and reflects the many and profound changes of the last decade. The editorial materials—the five period introductions, the author introductions, and the selection headnotes—have been revised or rewritten to sharpen the focus on literary trends and developments. This has been done partly by the omission of matter mainly social and historical, and by increased emphasis on interrelations and influences, intellectual and literary. Throughout, every effort has been made to avoid spoonfeeding, on the one hand, and factual cramming on the other, and instead to present background and explanatory material calculated to help the student grasp, interpret, and interrelate for himself the literary works he reads. To this end, also, the texts are footnoted more extensively than before, but not to the point where information assumes a gratuitous and distracting importance for its own sake.

The problem of representing important writers who are primarily novelists is a perennial one in a survey anthology of American literature. Some of them, such as Hawthorne and Melville, James and Faulkner and Bellow, can be satisfactorily presented through their shorter fiction. Others, such as Cooper and Howells, are less well served through their short or nonfictional pieces, yet are too significant in the literary mainstream to be omitted. In such instances, the editors have chosen in this fifth edition to reach boldly into the novels for thematic chapters that will adequately represent the author's best and most characteristic achievement.

The texts of the selections have been carefully chosen for both their authority and their readability, and are identified throughout. Priority has been given to first editions or first appearance in book form, to standard editions, and to modern critical editions. In the colonial materials, when the verbal sequence of first or early editions is followed, the texts have been generally modernized with respect to italics, abbreviations, capitalization, and spelling. To maintain the rhythms of early American writing, however, the punctuation of the source texts has been generally retained; unusual spellings have been kept when they may be presumed to distinguish colonial pronunciation from modern American English, and special care has been taken not to impair the pronunciation of the poetry. Textual omissions for which the editors of this anthology are responsible are shown by asterisks; titles supplied by the editors are bracketed. The selections from each author are, with few exceptions, in chronological order; dates are given in the headnotes or at the end of a selection (date of publication at the right margin; of composition, if equally or more significant, at the left margin).

Active in the planning and policy-making stages, Professor Foerster was instrumental in soliciting the collaboration of the four distinguished scholars who carried out the actual work of the revision: Norman S. Grabo for the colonial period; Russel B. Nye for the neoclassic and early romantic; E. Fred Carlisle for the romantic; and Robert Falk for the realistic, the recent, and the contemporary. Editors and publisher alike are indebted to the following board of consultants for their advice on the table of contents and the nature of the revision of the editorial materials: Louis J. Budd, Duke University; Hennig Cohen, University of Pennsylvania; Neal F. Doubleday, Millikin University; Richard H. Fogle, University of North Carolina; Ernest E. Sandeen, University of Notre Dame; James Woodress, University of California (Davis); Hyatt H. Waggoner, Brown University. These gentlemen contributed substantially to the final shape of the revision. Others whose contributions to the fifth edition are gratefully acknowledged are Frank Lentricchia, of the University of California (Irvine), for his work on the contemporary poets; Margaret Linville, of Santa Monica City College, for assistance with the contemporary novelists; and Frank Shuffelton, of the University of Rochester, for assistance with the selection and checking of texts.

American Poetry and Prose has helped to shape and inform the changing canon of our literature since publication of the first edition in 1925. It is our belief that it will continue to do so for the critical generation of students coming of age in the 1970's.

Contents

The Colonial Period

The Neoclassic Age

The Romantic Movement

Contents | xiii

AMERICAN POETRY AND PROSE

Part One
From the Beginnings to 1865

The Colonial Period

IN THE BEGINNING was the dream, and the dream was America. Europe was in convulsive transition from the medieval to the modern age: established institutions and patterns of thought were being challenged, and the fabric of society and even of cosmology seemed in danger of dissolution.

> And freely men confess that this world's spent,
> When in the planets and the firmament
> They seek so many new; they see that this
> Is crumbled out again to his atomies.
> 'Tis all in pieces, all coherence gone!

Thus lamented John Donne in 1611. Copernicus and Galileo, Brahe and Kepler had indeed called the Ptolemaic cosmos in doubt. The sixteenth century had done much to throw off the traditions and restraints of medieval learning; in the opening decades of the seventeenth century the growth of a skeptical attitude toward the world, accompanied by new tools for analysis, fractured many traditional concepts and with them much of the era's assurance about the nature of God, man, and the universe. Men were impelled to re-examine and explore their world within and without, to look inside themselves and across immense uncharted seas. The great, hazy, relatively unknown continent of America, already penetrated at its edges by European adventurers, possessed a particular attraction. But the circumstances and motives that thrust Englishmen toward this New World were both varied and confused.

High among these was the assertion of British national pride and honor, especially against the Spanish, Dutch, and French. English sea dogs had plundered galleons returning from South and Central America, where Spaniards and Portuguese had exploited natural riches since the 1490's; and by the end of the sixteenth century, an American base for operations against the Spanish seemed not only a tactical necessity but a patriotic duty.

Economic considerations supplied both a powerful motive and a practical means for colonization. With the substitution of credit for goods and services in the first half of the sixteenth century, financial power tended to concentrate in the hands of the large joint-stock trading companies chartered by the Crown, and the first settlements in the New World were underwritten by London stockholders for whom America represented the hope of a good return on their investment.

Poverty and want in England, especially in the cities, created virtually insoluble social problems. The infant factory system could not hope to accommodate the hosts of unskilled farm workers who streamed cityward, displaced by agricultural reforms. Vagabonds and tramps, thieves and beggars plagued the land; the British government seemed unable to provide for the needy. The colonization of America therefore appeared to furnish an attractive possibility for alleviating England's social problems. As early as 1515, Thomas More's *Utopia* had held out the promise of a New World free of social ills; later writers, both English and American, continued to exploit the Utopian potential as one of the strongest attractions for colonization.

Tying the patriotic, economic, and social motives together was the religious tenor of sixteenth-century England. Henry VIII had made the all-decisive break with the Roman Catholic Church in 1531, but the yeast of Protestantism continued to work within the Church of England, until many who dissented from the established religion came to feel that their only safety and salvation in this world lay across the Atlantic.

Thus out of intellectual, social, economic, and religious unrest and confusion grew seventeenth-century England's dream of a better and more profitable world overseas. Writers like Hakluyt did their best to present America as the cure-all of England's problems and the end-all of her ambitions.

The Virginian Voyage

Shortly after the turn of the century the formation of two new trading companies—the Virginia Company of London and the Virginia Company of Plymouth—fanned fresh interest in establishing planta-

3

tions across the ocean. Michael Drayton wrote his ode "To the Virginian Voyage"; and in May 1607, Captain Christopher Newport's three ships dropped anchor, supplies, and colonists at the mouth of the James River, where the settlers built a stockade and erected the tents and huts they regally named Jamestown. In spite of their expectations of gold and precious stones, their unwillingness to blister gentlemanly hands with hoe and axe, the squabbles that had erupted among them even before they landed, and the selection of swampy, mosquito-ridden Jamestown "island" as a roosting place, the little band of settlers hung on to become England's first permanent settlement in America. Its success was assured in 1612, when John Rolfe discovered a method of curing Indian tobacco, and the following year, when the home company began making land available to private owners, the settlers cultivated the plant with an energy they had never displayed for company profits alone. But as the colonists dispersed on their newly-gotten farms, rule from the London office became increasingly inadequate and inconvenient. On July 30, 1619, therefore, under Governor George Yeardley's leadership, Virginia's first representative assembly met in Jamestown's Anglican church. From that meeting dates the South's long experience in self-rule that was to prove so valuable in creating an independent America in the following century. Still Virginia's central concern was wealth, which was so anguishingly slow in coming that in 1624 King James annulled the distressed Virginia Company's charter, making the colony a royal dependent, subject to royal governorship.

Though Captain John Smith once wrote in irritation, "I am not so simple to think that ever any other motive than wealth will ever erect there a commonweal," Mammon alone was not capable of sustaining American colonization. Settlers looking for quick riches were discouraged by brutally hard labor, the threat of Indian attacks, quarrels among the colony's leaders, and complaints from England. The John Donne who cried "all coherence gone!" was also a shareholder in the Virginia Company, for whom America was a symptom of unrest and dissolution, rather than a symbol of order. If the coherence Donne sought in politics, religion, and the minds of men was to flower in America, it would have to spring from another quarter and other motives.

The Puritan Migrations

In August 1609 another expedition left England. Unprovided with poets' odes, sent on its way with good riddance, and bound for Holland rather than for America, it nevertheless carried with it the seeds of order, the dedication, and the sense of urgency that would soon characterize America. The men making up this expedition belonged to a group of religious radicals, the extreme left-wing of the Puritan reform movement in England, called Separatists then because they denounced and separated from the established Anglican Church, but now known as Pilgrims.

The origins of Puritanism are quite complex, springing directly from the reform movements on the Continent in the sixteenth century. Martin Luther's dramatic break with the Church of Rome in 1517 marked the beginning, but it was John Calvin who provided a theological and ecclesiastical system to replace the Roman faith. His *Institutes of the Christian Religion* (1536–59), combined with his own extraordinary intellectual and evangelistic talents, gained him a zealous following, not only in his native France, but in Geneva (to which he was banished) and in Holland. Englishmen came to know and respect Calvin's thought, especially when under Mary Tudor (1553–58) England returned to Catholicism and the queen drove hundreds of learned and dedicated English Protestants into exile. Calvin's revival of the relatively uncomplicated theology of St. Augustine, and the practices of the early apostolic church, appealed to them; and when they returned to England after Elizabeth's accession to the throne, they pushed English church reform in the direction of Calvinism.

Almost at once a deep rift developed between those Church of England men to whom the old traditions were valuable and satisfying and those who, while still content to remain within the established church, believed that its reformation had not gone far enough. By 1572 the dissidents were called Puritans, a term applied to any religious group that demonstrated extreme scrupulosity regarding religious behavior. Although there was wide diversity among them, English Puritans generally demanded a literal interpretation of the Bible and its application to the affairs of everyday life. Following Augustine and Calvin, they emphasized God's complete and unquestionable sovereignty, and man's innate weakness, incapacity for good, and perverse habit of dignifying wilfulness by the term "free will." They held that God not only foresaw but predestined all worldly events, controlling even the most minute circumstances by His unceasing providence; that some men were thereby elected to everlasting glory while others were bound for hell. Man's salvation, the Puritans believed, depended not on good works (for how could an innately depraved creature be capable of *any* good?), nor on the externals of elaborate public services and rituals, but solely on full faith in Christ. The high seriousness and missionary zeal with which the English Puritans held and argued their beliefs made them a sober people, and gave them an unshakable reputation (often unwarranted) as enemies of frivolity, humor, and beauty. Although it was possible for Anglo-Catholics to agree with many Puritan principles, they could not accept the Puritan demand that the church give up its episcopal system and adopt Congregational or Presbyterian forms of church government.

One group went too far even for most purists. Robert Browne, an early spokesman, argued in *A Treatise of Reformation* (1582) that since not all who attended and supported the Church of England were godly, the truly pious should meet and worship separately. For their complete repudiation of the Anglican Church, the so-called "Separatists," or "Brownists," were subjected to a great deal of harassment and persecution.

It was one such group of persecuted Separatists in Scrooby, Nottinghamshire, that removed in 1609 from England to Amsterdam and thence to Leyden. They found tolerance in Holland, but not peace. Aliens in a foreign land, their means of livelihood restricted, their young people restive, these English expatriates by 1619 felt it imperative to seek a new land where, under more favorable conditions, they might establish their commonwealth of believers. Accordingly, they negotiated with the Virginia Company of London, secured a leaky ship called the *Speedwell*, abandoned it for the *Mayflower*, and in November 1620 arrived not in Virginia as planned, but at Cape Cod. Knowing they were outside the legal jurisdiction of their patent, and fearing lest the lack of authority completely upset their "plantation," forty-one passengers agreed to create a "civil body politic," just as they had made a covenant to form an independent congregation. This famous Mayflower Compact, or Covenant, has been described as "the fundamental instrument of government for the little democracy which it established without any authority than the wishes of the signers." But it must be remembered that these Pilgrims had not left Europe to found a democracy or to establish a free state. They merely sought a refuge for their own religious society, and they were determined to keep all who differed with them out of their new Jerusalem. In the new continent the Plymouth colony survived the rigors of the wilderness, the ineptitude of its London agents, and the diversions of a few free spirits (such as Thomas Morton of Merrymount) who wandered into it. Under the firm and sagacious leadership of William Bradford and the elders, the Pilgrims sold enough cod, lumber, and furs to find a modest prosperity, maintained their New England foothold, and promised to thrive.

Back in England the non-separatist Puritans found themselves involved in increasingly difficult religious and political conflicts, and they observed the Pilgrim experiment with growing interest. In 1623 the Dorchester Adventurers was formed to maintain fishing and trading operations in New England; in 1628 and 1629, expeditions were sent to what is now Salem to prepare the way for a second colonial venture; and on March 4, 1629, within a week of Charles's dissolution of Parliament, the Dorchester Adventurers, now called the New England Company for a Plantation in Massachusetts Bay, secured a generous charter. The following year, under the leadership of Governor John Winthrop aboard the *Arbella*, the first four ships of what has come to be called the Great Migration arrived and settled at Massachusetts Bay.

As Winthrop told his people, their purpose in the New World was not to amass wealth, but to worship God in their own fashion—to establish a "true" religious society, "to improve our lives to do more service to the Lord, the comfort and increase of the body of Christ whereof we are members, that ourselves and posterity may be the better preserved from the common corruptions of this evil world, to serve the Lord and work out our salvation under the power and purity of His holy ordinances." The Massachusetts Bay Colony had a concept of order and a singleness of purpose that Virginia had lacked. Winthrop was careful to let his company know their holy experiment was being observed by all Christendom: "For we must consider that we shall be as a city upon a hill, the eyes of all people are upon us."

The Puritan-citizen of this city upon a hill found evidences of his progress toward salvation by constant surveillance of the state of his soul. To attain salvation, he believed, a man's soul moved through regular, identifiable stages—an effectual calling, justification (by which a soul knows Christ's sacrifice to be efficacious for itself), sanctification (righteous behavior), and finally, with death, glorification. Self-knowledge, then, was a spiritual necessity; but since God revealed His will through the everyday workings of nature, it became necessary, in order to know one's self, to know the world too. As John Cotton put it, the faithful soul applies its faithfulness to all its worldly activities: "though you may have a godly man busy in his calling from sun rising to sun setting, and may by God's providence fill both his hand and his head with business, yet a living Christian, when he lives a most busy life in this world, yet he lives not a worldly life." Cotton did not mean that the good life was perforce a worldly, materialistic life; yet for many New Englanders, following out Cotton's doctrine often meant substantially that. As a result, New England Puritanism faced two ways. On the one hand, it demanded deep and constant thought about the nature of the universe, about the nature of man and his relation to God, about man's duties to God and his neighbors, and about the high seriousness of life in this world. On the other hand, it hallowed every human activity in the state and in society at large, in government and business, with the sanctity of a religious act. One consequence of the bifurcation was to turn New Englanders into successful businessmen, merchants, and traders, as well as into "saints." And thus it became increasingly difficult to maintain the great dream of a holy commonwealth.

The Colonial Way of Life

Virginia and the New England colonies established the basic patterns of life in seventeenth-century America. New settlements splintered off from Massachusetts to form the colonies of Connecticut, Rhode Island, and New Haven. Expansion was contagious. But the impetus for most new colonization came from abroad. Groups in England and Europe were quick to capitalize on the dreams of land, profit, power, and political and religious refuge that America represented. The newer settlements were made not under the directorship of trade companies but under individual proprietors whose patents gave them virtually royal power in the New World.

Catholic George Calvert, Lord Baltimore, secured a grant north of the Potomac as a refuge for persecuted English Catholics. The colony, tactfully named "Maryland" in honor of King Charles's queen, was settled at St. Mary's City in 1633; careful to offend neither the Massachusetts Puritans nor the Virginia Anglicans, it opened its land to all Christians, excluding only Jews and the forerunners of Unitarianism. Holland, England's most shrewd and powerful economic and colonial rival, moved into the area between Maryland and Connecticut, named it New Netherland, founded the town of New Amsterdam in 1625, and began to penetrate Connecticut territory. Though Swedes settled along the Delaware as early as 1638, neither they nor their Dutch neighbors received substantial support from their homelands. They combined in 1635 to form a population of some ten thousand, but fell easily before English power and were converted into New York in 1664.

By that time, though, the Duke of York was already interested in other holdings. In 1655 he and eight others became Lords Proprietors of land reaching from Virginia to below St. Augustine, Florida. They hoped to oust the Spanish outpost there, develop a tropical economy, and establish a grand aristocracy along lines laid out by the Earl of Shaftesbury, John Locke, and James Harrington's Utopian *Oceana*. But their plan for an American nobility proved desperately impractical for Carolina, and was soon abandoned. While unauthorized settlers congregated at Albemarle Sound, forming the colony to be known after 1719 as North Carolina, the Lords Proprietors sent another expedition to settle the southern part of the colony in 1670. Under Governor William Sayle, they settled along the Ashley River, moving near its mouth a few years later to establish Charleston, which by 1680 became the seat of government and in time the most graceful of southern colonial cities.

To the north another proprietary grant was made in 1665 to Sir George and Philip Carteret and Lord John Berkeley for New Jersey. The venture was not profitable, and in 1679 they sold out to William Penn, who three years later also secured the proprietorship of Pennsylvania from the Lords of Trade. Penn thus controlled the last uncommitted coastal lands, which he opened to religious refugees, especially Quakers, though by this time Swedish Lutherans, Dutch, and Finns were firmly planted along the Delaware, and Penn was obliged by the Lords of Trade to permit Anglican churches to develop as the need arose.

By 1700 the American coast from Florida to Maine was in English hands, either as corporate (trade company), proprietary, or royal colonies. Living under governments much like those in England, and enjoying what Raleigh's charter had called "all the privileges of free denizens, and persons native of England," the colonists were yet not quite Englishmen, nor simply Englishmen living away from home. Nor could they be called Americans, for the alembic of transatlantic life had not yet distilled the type that St. Jean de Crèvecoeur described in 1782. Instead, the colonies were a crazy-quilt of migrants, the rawest of raw materials for the "melting pot." There were even Polish and German laborers and craftsmen as part of the original Jamestown venture, soon joined by Italian glassmakers and French vintners. The Dutch, of course, predominated in early New York, but the area fell increasingly under the influence of French, Germans, Danes, Swedes, Finns, Portuguese, Spanish, Italians, Bohemians, and Poles. Jews in New York enjoyed surprising freedom, built synagogues, and early in the eighteenth century could amaze young Puritans like Jonathan Edwards, who furtively observed one— "the devoutest person that I ever saw in my life"— from his adjoining window. French Huguenots lived along the coast, concentrated in Pennsylvania, Virginia, and the Carolinas. German Pietists, Mennonites, and Baptists, attracted by the *New-found Eden*, as one propaganda tract described it, made all haste to the New World, especially to Pennsylvania, while Scotsmen joined the oncoming wave early in the eighteenth century, settling largely in the New Jersey area. One class of migrants came involuntarily, without prospects and without hope: in 1619 a Dutch man-of-war brought the first Africans to the colonies, to be sold into servitude ("the great mistake / That Jamestown / Made long ago").

The quarter million Europeans in America by the end of the seventeenth century brought with them their national languages, customs, styles of living, foods, dress, trades and diversions, architecture, and ornamental arts. Even though Anglicanism was the official faith of the royal and proprietary colonies, and Congregationalism deeply ingrained in New England, the religious toleration that accompanied Charles II's return to the throne in 1660 drew Quakers, Baptists, Lutherans, Pietists, and even Roman Catholics and Jews to the colonies. After 1684, when Massachusetts Bay lost its charter, even New England had to suffer the encroachments of other faiths or risk political reprisal from England. Indeed, there was much more variety and contrast in American colonial life in the later seventeenth and early eighteenth centuries than the myths of somber Puritan New England and romantic Cavalier South would indicate.

That there should be very real distinctions between northern and southern life, even in the seventeenth century, was inevitable. The control of immense tobacco lands fell into the hands of the most resourceful and influential settlers quite early, so that Virginia's leading class was largely self-made. Theirs was recently acquired wealth, and though they assumed the noblesse oblige of traditional English aristocracy in managing their estates, they resembled English country gentry rather than nobility. The large plantation owner was perforce lawyer, doctor, teacher, farmer, judge, surveyor, and engineer. His immediate concerns were practical and numerous, and though he often yielded to the extravagance of sending his children to England for schooling, he could not on the whole afford a very gay or carefree life. That was usually left to the second or third generation. The diary of William Byrd of Westover provides fascinating glimpses into the life of a Virginia gentleman who had "arrived" as an aristocrat. Carolinians, after surrendering hopes of cultivating tropical fruits, turned to rice, and, using Negro and Indian slaves to work the malarial inland rice fields, escaped whenever they could to the coast. Flocking to Charleston, they soon created a sophisticated miniature of London social life unmatched elsewhere in the colonies.

New England, on the other hand, unsuited for large-scale farming and held tightly together by church as well as social covenants, turned to manufacture and trade in its primarily urban economy. The quick result was a merchant aristocracy that built its own ships, stored them with codfish, wood products, food grains, and salted meats, and sent them to trade along the American coast and to England and Europe. New England grew rich on trade, and as its wealth grew, the bonds of its religious dedication loosened. Whereas the early Puritan assumed that God's favor to a man might be manifested in his life, his grandson, reversing the logic, believed that a man's material success might well be evidence of his saintliness. The homespun-to-riches pattern of a town like Boston had ceased to be a novelty long before Benjamin Franklin grew up there. Increasing prosperity revealed itself in the multiplication of worldly comforts—bigger and fancier houses, imported furniture, expensive books for private libraries, and, by the early eighteenth century, private coaches and footmen.

Economic, religious, and political differences drove Virginia and New England further and further apart in the early eighteenth century. But material prosperity allowed both areas to pursue their happiness with increasing comfort and grace. No sooner were streets laid and houses erected than settlers put aside their drab homespun for colorful and elegant fashions from England and France. By the turn of the century, coffee houses, imitative of those in London, vied with taverns from Charleston to Boston as haunts of idleness. And as leisure increased, so did the variety of diversions—traveling shows and exhibits clowns, mechanical marvels, cockfights, horse-racing, hunting and fishing, waxworks, and gaming. Those who could afford it, both North and South, fell into the extravagant habit of having their portraits painted by amateur limners. Silversmiths and goldsmiths, furniture-makers and jewelers found their works in constant demand, and by 1716 even Boston had its own bold dancing master. In short, by the second quarter of the eighteenth century, the rude and rugged way of the frontier had practically disappeared from America's major towns. In its place stood a charming, sophisticated life undreamed of in the philosophies of John Smith and William Bradford.

Intellectual and Literary Activity

Largely because of their closer social and economic connections, more highly organized political system, and reasonably good network of roads, the New England colonies developed a distinctive intellectual life much more quickly than the southern colonies. New England's emphasis on learning was closely connected with its religious commitment. The bedrock of the Reformation was its insistence that the faith upon which the salvation of every individual depended was available through the scriptures. Since to "search the scriptures" one had to be able to read, illiteracy was a tool of Satan. Moreover, saving grace came not through miraculous or supernatural means, but through "hearing the word preached." To hear the word intelligently, church-goers were encouraged to follow the carefully organized delivery of the preacher, to scribble down outlines of his sermons, and to discuss them after meeting with family and neighbors. All this required a high degree of literacy, and much of our knowledge of early American preaching comes from the shorthand notes of avid listeners. Also, New England had from the beginning as great a percentage of university-trained men in proportion to its population as Old England, a fact that encouraged intellectual pursuits. The deep respect in which these Calvinists held learning promoted their desire to maintain a learned ministry and accounts for the promptness with which they established schools and a university, gathered private libraries, and circulated books.

Preaching, of course, forced men to write, but while sermons flowed from their quills, New Englanders turned to other kinds of literary production as well. As early as 1636 plans were under way to turn the Psalms of David into English verse, attending "conscience rather than elegance, fidelity rather than poetry," and early in 1639 Governor John Winthrop noted in his journal that "a printing house was begun at Cambridge by one [Stephen] Day, at the charge of Mr. Glover, who died on sea hitherward. The first thing which was printed was the freeman's oath; the next was an almanac made for New England by Mr. William Pierce, mariner; the next was the Psalms newly turned into meter." This press, even though strictly regulated by the College and by the General Court, immediately groaned under the multitude of informative and edifying works submitted for publication. It was 1681 before a printing press appeared in Virginia, and that was immediately suppressed. In 1683 Virginians were instructed to "allow no person to use a printing press on any occasion whatsoever," and Virginia's lone printing house did not even get started until 1729. There was probably greater need for New Englanders to write: their arguments about theology and church government needed statement and distribution; bothersome differences between the New England Way and English expectations required explanation; and after the revolution of 1642, when victorious English Puritans accused their colonial brethren of deserting the glorious cause by escaping to America, New Englanders wrote to defend their actions. The surprising thing is not that so much was written and printed in the colonies during the seventeenth century, but that out of all the literary activity there grew no great book.

There are probably two reasons for this, neither of which detracts from the intellectual capability or the literary sophistication of colonial writers. In the first place, in keeping with the utilitarian, polemical, and didactic nature of the documents they pro-

duced, their style was plain, perspicuous, and (as they liked to say) "spiritual." Its ideals were clarity, logical consistency, general intelligibility, and decorum, and except for the crabbed wit of Nathaniel Ward and the later pomposities of Cotton Mather, early American writing avoided the current fads of Senecan curtness and Ciceronian elaboration. In this the Puritan plain style looked forward to the scientific style idealized by London's Royal Society, described by Bishop Sprat as "a close, naked, natural" style—and admirably adapted to American purposes by Benjamin Franklin. Second, most seventeenth-century colonial writings were occasional, designed to speak to specific problems at particular times. Thus they never display the comprehensive sweep of ideas that marks great books, nor does any single volume synthesize the variety and breadth of colonial thought. Each work stands like a stone in an elaborate building—structurally necessary, sturdy, often interesting in itself, but no real clue to the nature or meaning of the whole structure.

Early New England writing looked two ways simultaneously: outward toward the experience of building a new land, and inward toward the emotional and spiritual life of the individual. Biographies, histories, accounts of exploration, funeral sermons, and elegies expressed the one; autobiographies, diaries, and meditations, the other. William Bradford's consciously constructed *Of Plymouth Plantation* was no simple chronicle of daily events, but a selective and carefully arranged interpretation of the colonial experience coupled with a remarkable awareness of the historical significance of the great new American adventure. To stir emulation and to maintain respect for the worthies of New England, ministers wrote little biographies celebrating the public virtues and private spirituality of eminent divines and magistrates, heedful to point out that godliness often paved the road to public prominence. Sensational accounts of adventures among the Indians, featuring massacres, flights over torturous terrain, horrible torments, and the final joy of returning to civilization, were so popular that they were being issued in anthologies before the end of the seventeenth century. Cotton Mather's ambitious *Magnalia Christi Americana*, so large it had to be sent to London for publication in 1702, incorporated most of the established literary forms, revealing what was implicit in them from the beginning—that this was a literature designed to build saintly heroes and to trace God's support of New England's holy experiment by the favor He showed its individuals. Indeed, from its beginnings, American literature is an individualistic literature, designed to explore the passions and emotions (an aspect of the Puritan character often overlooked) as well as to recount the rigors of life in the wilderness.

When the Puritan turned inward, emphasizing the spiritual, devotional side of his religious experience, his writing tended to become less a part of his distinctly American experience and to partake more fully of the Western, Christian literary tradition. The poetic meditations of Edward Taylor, America's finest seventeenth-century poet, and the prose-poem passages of Jonathan Edwards gain their literary eminence at the same time they cast off their American significance. The amazing thing about colonial literary art as a whole is not, however, that it occasionally achieves real poetic excellence, but that poetry or verse is so dominant.

Theoretically, poetry was to Puritans (as to most contemporary Englishmen and Europeans, no matter how sophisticated) a branch of rhetoric, and a very minor one at that. Like all rhetorical forms, its end was to persuade, and its primary function lay in the decorating or ornamenting of ideas. Similar views of the nature of poetry did not keep English and Continental poets from magnificent literary achievements, and one must not suppose that the Puritans' low view of poetry was peculiar to them or that they held any special animus toward poetry. For poetry—at least verse—is inescapable in colonial writing.

Five main kinds of verse writing predominated. First, writers who took the prevailing poetic theory literally were likely to produce "poems" constructed of rhymed statements whose function was merely to assist the reader's memory. An obvious example would be the *New England Primer*'s alphabet for children, running from "In Adam's Fall/ We sinned all" to "Zaccheus he/ Did climb the Tree/ His Lord to see." Such mnemonic verse was frequently included in histories and treatises to sum up at the ends of chapters. A second kind, closely related to the first, was the long didactic poem, more elaborate in thought and structure, such as Michael Wigglesworth's *The Day of Doom*. A third favorite was historical verse, intended not merely to teach, but to express an action too magnificent for prose (as in Captain Edward Johnson's *Wonder-Working Providence*), or to recount current events (as in Benjamin Tompson's *New England's Crisis*), or to celebrate the greatness of times past (as in Roger Wolcott's outright epic on the founding of Connecticut). A fourth type was the funeral elegy, commemorating the deaths of prominent and obscure persons alike, and reminding readers of the brevity and purposefulness of life. These were printed broadside for distribution at the funeral service, incorporated into formal histories and biographies, as in Cotton Mather's *Magnalia*, or simply recorded in diaries, letter-books, and family papers. By and large, this commemorative verse is without poetic merit, but it provides some useful insights into Puritan emotional

values, and occasionally flowers into excellence. Finally, there was the personal, reflective, meditative, and often lyrical poetry best illustrated by Anne Bradstreet and Edward Taylor.

There was, then, no prejudice against literary beauty among early New Englanders. Frivolity, however, was another matter. Ministers were often known for their conversational wit and urbane humor, but a favorable attitude toward such social graces did not extend to the production of literary forms like the novel or drama. French and occasionally English romances made their way to America well before 1700; an edition of John Bunyan's *Pilgrim's Progress* was printed in Boston in 1681, and in that same year *Guy of Warwick*, a pious medieval romance, was sold in Boston's bookstores. But for the most part the New Englander satisfied his natural appetite for fiction through a variety of modes not overtly fictional, each of which, however, contributed to the later development of the American novel. The sermon, for example, frequently offered character sketches, anecdotal exempla, and tales of remarkable providences, all designed to excite interest as well as to edify. The formal character sketches practiced in school also found their way to the pulpit and, in extended form, into biographies and histories. Where fact leaves off and fiction starts cannot be clearly seen. William Bradford and Edward Johnson obviously designed parts of their accounts for literary effect, freely feigning speeches and experimenting with character development. Confessions of faith or personal relations of conversion gave form, conflict, change of fortune, and stupendous consequences to the spiritual life; they could not have been heard without excitement and pleasure. The narrative of captivity, marked by a surprising sentimentality, by psychological probing, and, later, by pure sensationalism, duplicated in frontier reality the great struggles waged in the infinite world of spirit between Satan and the captive soul of man. The romance of a soul's rise from poverty to glorious riches enabled colonial writers to experiment with numerous literary devices, and one can easily see in colonial narratives the seeds of the frontier adventure story, the folk tale, the novel of sensibility, the allegorical romance, and the epistolary and Gothic techniques that came to fruition in the fiction of the late eighteenth and early nineteenth century.

When every natural phenomenon, every qualm of conscience, was assumed to be emblematic of the great dramatic struggle between good and evil, no formal dramatic literature seemed necessary to the early colonist. So, except for dialogues and debates worked into treatises and poems, and sometimes into histories, American literary drama did not develop until after the middle of the eighteenth century. In

England, Puritans closed the theaters in 1642, partly because of the licentiousness of the plays, but more because of the social problems endemic to playhouses—the tradition of boys playing the parts of women, the low character of actors (who were lumped with vagabonds and rogues), and the tendency of playgoing to distract men from both business and godliness. This same attitude prevailed in New England. But it is also true, as Louis B. Wright has put it, that "the primary reason that drama did not flourish in seventeenth-century America was the simple fact that no towns were large enough to support theatrical entertainment." Traveling actors occasionally made their ways to the colonies, often to be turned away, and it was approximately 1716 before the first known playhouse was erected in the colonies at Williamsburg, Virginia. Philadelphia, New York, and Charleston all had theaters by the middle of the eighteenth century, though they showed English plays exclusively, and New England college students even presented plays designed to give them practice in Latin and Greek declamation. The first play to be written by a native American was Thomas Godfrey's *The Prince of Parthia*, published in 1765, two years after Godfrey's death; this was a bombastic blank-verse tragedy that strangely and sometimes effectively mingles Elizabethan and Restoration dramatic ideas. But drama did not gain acceptance until after the Revolution, and did not become a distinguished form of American literary art until the twentieth century.

On the whole, while the colonial period provided an excellent apprenticeship for American literature, its products were not of a very high order. The usual explanation—that Puritans were inveterately hostile to beauty and art—is, if not a fiction in itself, at least an oversimplification. The failure of American colonial writing to approach or equal the level of contemporary English or European literature is due rather to other factors. First, the American Puritans represented but one slice of English middle-class society, a class with no very impressive artistic attainments even in England at the time. In the colonies that class was completely removed from contact with the more cultured classes at home. We must remember that the first English settlers in America were born before the golden era of English writing, and that the colonial experience spanned the work of Spenser, Shakespeare, the metaphysical poets, Milton, Dryden, and Pope—a period during which American intellectual life was dominated by one class of people with one overriding concern. Second, the prevailing Calvinism of the American colonists, especially the New England Puritans, contributed to aesthetic barrenness in making art seem impotent if not irrelevant: God's beauty was all-sufficing, and works of nature and of art could be only weak reflections thereof. Moreover, many seventeenth-century Americans believed that the millennium—Christ's second coming—was imminent; with that event all the works of man would pass. This intense conviction of earthly transience further discouraged painstaking artistic creation and concern with form. Emphasis was on ideas and themes rather than on beauty of expression—a fact which may indeed account for the easy acceptance of English literary forms, themselves sometimes inconsistent with American ideas. And finally, Americans of the seventeenth century were simply too busy establishing themselves in the New World to develop and refine a literary culture.

The Decline of Puritanism

At what point the Puritan city upon a hill—and the dominant colonial culture it represented—began to be undermined is not clear. Isolated at first from foreign ideologies, its distinctive theology realized more fully in Massachusetts and Connecticut than anywhere else in the world, Puritanism stiffened into orthodoxy, crystallized, cracked, and began to flake away. The strength derived from adversity in England rigidified in New England to become a fatal defect. More than a religious creed, Puritanism was a way of life that organized all of man's activities, reducing all the arts and sciences to "handmaids" of Theology. As Clarence Faust has pointed out, the Puritan's emphasis on God's sovereignty—with its familiar image of God as a king—hardened into legalism and collapsed in the face of political and social change that everywhere weakened men's trust in monarchical principles. The power of God's providence over man, in the Puritan's view, made him a passive tool in an age when men were—in matters of faith, politics, and ethics—asserting their responsibility and independence; so counter did Calvinism run to eighteenth-century thought and sentiment, that it forced men to look elsewhere for their creeds. The Puritan's concept of an eternal, changeless, static God led him toward an ideal, eternal system of absolutes incapable of adjustment to the new science and the new logic of Descartes, Locke, and Newton. At the same time, the Puritan's emphasis on reason and his respect for human learning opened the door to skepticism, while his glorification of industry slipped almost imperceptibly down the road to materialism. By 1740 the old-fashioned Puritanism was dying, but it went through one last spasm called the Great Awakening.

Religious thought had grown more and more liberal in the last years of the seventeenth century, and many orthodox Calvinists learned to distrust the free-thinking ministers turned out by Harvard. By 1701 they were so dissatisfied that they founded a second college, called Yale, at New Haven, for the express purpose of producing orthodox Calvinist ministers. But "Arminianism," as all liberal thought came to be called, continued to increase. It was not so much that the new breed of ministers spoke against Calvinist doctrines; they simply ignored them, preaching more and more as if man's will were free and his actions had something to do with his salvation. Alarmed by such irresponsible talk, Jonathan Edwards turned aside from intellectual argument to preach a demonstration of the absolutely real and meaningful nature of Calvin's tenets. Preaching to the senses of his congregation, he vivified the consequences of election, damnation, and God's sovereign will, and pictured the depraved condition of their own unconverted souls in such graphic detail that his hearers fell—some literally—before the excitement of his preaching. In 1734 and 1735 his intense sermons brought some to God, many to hysteria, still others to madness and even suicide.

By 1736 Edwards began to moderate his preaching, but religious emotionalism surged up once more when the Reverend George Whitefield, a young English evangelist who had been preaching through the South, arrived in New England in 1740. His intense spirituality and brilliant oratory pierced hardened hearts and melted the religious affections of countless souls as he left a trail of evangelical fire from Georgia to Massachusetts, even joining Edwards for one successful tour. Galleries were packed with hysterical listeners, and a grandstand in Boston collapsed, killing five. Whitefield was succeeded by raving James Davenport, who tore off his clothes as he preached, and by dozens of other itinerant preachers distinguished only by their wild enthusiasm.

By 1745 the Great Awakening was over, but its effects were permanent. Under the lash of its evangelical emotionalism, thirty to forty thousand converts flooded the churches, most of them either distrustful or actively critical of the orthodox clergy whose over-intellectualism and laxity, they believed, had brought religion to its sorry state. Congregations split, church authority and unity almost disappeared, and the range of differences was so great that traditional New England Puritanism was barely recognizable.

The divisions of the Great Awakening drove many people into non-Congregational churches—Anglican, Quaker, Baptist, and Methodist—and also opened the way for the rational religion called "deism," which appeared in America during the latter half of the eighteenth century. Deism served the needs of some of the intellectual, philosophically minded men of the period, but Unitarianism, a somewhat less radical form of religious rationalism, attracted more support. Like the early deists, liberal Congregationalists emphasized the trustworthiness of human reason and moral conscience, but they relied more heavily on the revelations of the Bible, squaring revelation with reason when they could. Because they emphasized the "unity" of God, they were sometimes called "Unitarians," though they did not (until 1826) form a separate church. As the "Unitarian" group developed its theology, it came into greater conflict with traditional Calvinism; it denied Christ's divinity and the whole concept of trinitarianism; it emphasized ethical and humanitarian action as the center of religious worship; and it affirmed man's potential for achieving perfection. Unitarianism, in effect, pointed the way to American Transcendentalism.

When in 1832 Ralph Waldo Emerson surrendered his Unitarian ministry to strike his own original relationship with the universe, he did so from the pulpit of Boston's Second Church, the same pulpit that once held Increase and Cotton Mather. As the impulse that gave seventeenth-century America its most elaborate and distinctive culture, and as a formal movement of serious significance in American life, Puritanism was dead, but its elements were deeply infused into American life and thought.

JOHN SMITH [1580–1631]

THE SPIRIT OF ADVENTURE and the dreams of wealth, glory, and betterment that characterized the Elizabethan expansion are typified in the life and writings of John Smith. Born in Lincolnshire and raised to trade, young Smith found mercantile life unendurably dull. By his own account, he ran away at fifteen to become a soldier of fortune, spending ten years in Europe and the Near East, years of great trial, marvelous adventure, and high accomplishment—though his veracity is not beyond doubt.

But there is no doubt that he joined the first group of colonists bound for Jamestown in 1607, that he played a major role in holding the colony together by strong leadership and uncompromising discipline, that he went back to England in 1609, returned to America in 1614 on a voyage of exploration to New England, was captured and briefly imprisoned by the French, and thereafter lived out a quiet life in England.

To John Smith, America was an opportunity for England to recapture a golden age of chivalric heroism, to gain great wealth, to frustrate the political ambitions of Catholic Spain, to ease poverty, unemployment, and juvenile delinquency at home, and to bring honor and glory to the English throne. In this heroic context he tirelessly worked and wrote. His various promotional writings, particularly *A True Relation of . . . Virginia* (1608), *A Map of Virginia* (1612), *A Description of New England* (1616), *The General History of Virginia* (1624), and *The True Travels, Adventures, and Observations of Captain John Smith* (1630), form the first substantial body of literature done in and about America.

From a literary point of view, Smith's fabulous and perhaps questionable story of his capture by Powhatan and rescue by Pocahontas may be his most significant contribution. Not only did it supply an enduring and charming legend to American folklore, it marked the beginning of a genre of "captivity" narratives that would have great popularity in the seventeenth and eighteenth centuries as "true adventures," and put its stamp on the historical fiction of the early nineteenth century as well as on the modern Western.

Further reading: *Travels and Works,* ed. E. Arber, 1910. Bradford Smith, *Captain John Smith,* 1953.

FROM *The General History of Virginia*

Smith gave the events he wrote about an egotistic coloring and often a dramatic heightening. In *A True Relation* he had represented Powhatan as uniformly friendly and made no mention of a rescue by an Indian princess. But here, in the *General History,* he puts Powhatan in a very different light, and introduces the Pocahontas episode, of which everyone has heard though few have known it in the original telling. In time it became a favorite bit of American legend adapted by various writers in poetry, fiction, and drama.

Pocahontas married an English gentleman, John Rolfe, went to England with him in the year of Shakespeare's death, and was well received by people and court. Before she reached London, Smith wrote the episode in a petition in her behalf addressed to Queen Anne. Pocahontas died the next year, and later Smith inserted the episode in his *General History.*

Text: Edward Arber, ed., *Travels and Works of Captain John Smith* (2nd edition; Edinburgh, 1910), II, 395–401.

[The Captivity]

But our comedies never endured long without a tragedy; some idle exceptions being muttered against Captain Smith, for not discovering the head of Chickahamania River, and taxed by the Council, to be too slow in so worthy an attempt. The next voyage he proceeded so far, that with much labor by cutting of trees in sunder he made his passage; but when his barge could pass no farther, he left her in a broad bay out of danger of shot, commanding none should go ashore till his return. Himself with two English and two salvages went up higher in a canoe; but he was not long absent, but his men went ashore, whose want of government, gave both occasion and opportunity to the salvages to surprise one George Casson, whom they slew, and much failed not to have cut off the boat and all the rest. Smith, little dreaming of that accident, being got to the marshes at the river's head, twenty miles in the desert, had his two men slain (as is supposed) sleeping by the canoe, whilest himself by fowling sought them victual: who finding he was beset with 200 salvages, two of them he slew, still defending himself with the aid of a salvage his guide, whom he bound to his arm with his garters, and used him as a buckler, yet he was shot in his thigh a little and had many arrows that stuck in his clothes but no great hurt, till at last they took him prisoner. When this news came to Jamestown, much was their sorrow for his loss, few expecting what ensued. Six or seven weeks those barbarians kept him prisoner, many strange triumphs and conjurations they made of him, yet he so demeaned himself amongst them, as he not only diverted them from surprising the fort, but procured his own liberty, and got himself and his company such estimation amongst them, that those salvages admired him more than their own Quiyouckosucks. The manner how they used and delivered him is as follows.

The salvages having drawn from George Casson whither Captain Smith was gone, prosecuting that opportunity they followed him with 300 bowmen, conducted by the King of Pamaunkee, who in divisions searching the turnings of the river, found Robinson and Emry by the fireside: those they shot full of arrows and slew. Then finding the captain as is said, that used the salvage that was his guide as his shield (three of them being slain and divers other so galled) all the rest would not come near him. Thinking thus to have returned to his boat, regarding them, as he marched more then his way, slipped up to the middle in an oozy creek and his salvage with him; yet durst they not come to him, till, being near dead with cold, he threw away his arms. Then according to their composition they drew him forth and led him to the fire, where his men were slain. Diligently they chafed his benumbed limbs.

He demanding for their captain, they shewed him Opechankanough, King of Pamaunkee, to whom he gave a round ivory double compass dial. Much they marveled at the playing of the fly and needle, which they could see so plainly, and yet not touch it, because of the glass that covered them. But when he demonstrated by that globe-like jewel, the roundness of the earth, and skies, the sphere of the sun, moon, and stars, and how the sun did chase the night round about the world continually; the greatness of the land and sea, the diversity of nations, variety of complections, and how we were to them antipodes, and many other such like matters, they all stood as amazed with admiration. Notwithstanding, within an hour after, they tied him to a tree, and as many as could stand about him prepared to shoot him, but the king holding up the compass in his hand, they all laid down their bows and arrows, and in a triumphant manner led him to Orapaks, where he was after their manner kindly feasted, and well used.

Their order in conducting him was thus; drawing themselves all in file, the king in the middest had all their pieces and swords borne before him. Captain Smith was led after him by three great salvages, holding him fast by each arm: and on each side six went in file with their arrows nocked. But arriving at the town (which was but only thirty or forty hunting houses made of mats, which they remove as they please, as we our tents) all the women and children staring to behold him, the soldiers first all in file performed the form of a bissone[1] so well as could be; and on each flank, officers as sergeants to see them keep their orders. A good time they continued this exercise, and then cast themselves in a ring, dancing in such several postures, and singing and yelling out such hellish notes and screeches; being strangely painted, every one his quiver of arrows, and at his back a club; on his arm a fox or an otter's skin, or some such matter for his vambrace;[2] their heads and shoulders painted red, with oil and pocones[3] mingled together, which scarlet-like color made an exceeding handsome shew; his bow in his hand, and the skin of a bird with her wings abroad dried, tied on his head, a piece of copper, a white shell, a long feather, with a small rattle growing at the tails of their snakes tied to it, or some such like toy. All this while Smith and the king stood in the middest guarded, as before is said, and after three dances they all departed. Smith they conducted to a long house, where thirty or forty tall fellows did guard him; and ere long more bread and venison was brought him then would have served twenty men. I think his stomach at that time was not very good; what he left they put in baskets and tied over his head. About midnight they set the meat again before him, all this time not one of them would eat a bit with him, till the next morning they

---

[1] A military formation.

[2] Defensive armor for the forearm.

[3] Bloodroot.

brought him as much more, and then did they eat all the old, and reserved the new as they had done the other, which made him think they would fat him to eat him. Yet in this desperate estate to defend him from the cold, one Maocassater brought him his gown, in requital of some beads and toys Smith had given him at his first arrival in Virginia.

Two days after, a man would have slain him (but that the guard prevented it) for the death of his son, to whom they conducted him to recover the poor man then breathing his last. Smith told them that at Jamestown he had a water would do it, if they would let him fetch it, but they would not permit that; but made all the preparations they could to assault Jamestown, craving his advice; and for recompense he should have life, liberty, land, and women. In part of a table book he writ his mind to them at the fort, what was intended, how they should follow that direction to affright the messengers, and without fail send him such things as he writ for. And an inventory with them. The difficulty and danger, he told the salvages, of the mines, great guns, and other engines exceedingly affrighted them, yet according to his request they went to Jamestown, in as bitter weather as could be of frost and snow, and within three days returned with an answer.

But when they came to Jamestown, seeing men sally out as he had told them they would, they fled; yet in the night they came again to the same place where he had told them they should receive an answer, and such things as he had promised them, which they found accordingly, and with which they returned with no small expedition, to the wonder of them all that heard it, that he could either divine, or the paper could speak. Then they led him to the Youthtanunds, the Mattapanients, the Payankatanks, the Nantaughtacunds, and Onawmanients upon the rivers of Rapahanock, and Patawomek, over all those rivers, and back again by divers other several nations, to the king's habitation at Pamaunkee, where they entertained him with most strange and fearful conjurations;

> As if near led to hell,
> Amongst the devils to dwell.

Not long after, early in a morning a great fire was made in a long house, and a mat spread on the one side, as on the other; on the one they caused him to sit, and all the guard went out of the house, and presently came skipping in a great grim fellow, all painted over with coal, mingled with oil; and many snakes and weasels' skins stuffed with moss, and all their tails tied together, so as they met on the crown of his head in a tassel; and round about the tassel was a coronet of feathers, the skins hanging round about his head, back, and shoulders, and in a man-

ner covered his face; with a hellish voice, and a rattle in his hand. With most strange gestures and passions he began his invocation, and environed the fire with a circle of meal; which done, three more such like devils came rushing in with the like antic tricks, painted half black, half red: but all their eyes were painted white, and some red strokes like mutchatos,[4] along their cheeks: round about him those fiends danced a pretty while, and then came in three more as ugly as the rest; with red eyes, and white strokes over their black faces; at last they all sat down right against him; three of them on the one hand of the chief priest, and three on the other. Then all with their rattles began a song, which ended, the chief priest laid down five wheat corns: then straining his arms and hands with such violence that he sweat, and his veins swelled, he began a short oration: at the conclusion they all gave a short groan; and then laid down three grains more. After that, began their song again, and then another oration, ever laying down so many corns as before, till they had twice encircled the fire; that done, they took a bunch of little sticks prepared for that purpose, continuing still their devotion, and at the end of every song and oration, they laid down a stick betwixt the divisions of corn. Till night, neither he nor they did either eat or drink, and then they feasted merrily, with the best provisions they could make. Three days they used this ceremony; the meaning whereof they told him, was to know if he intended them well or no. The circle of meal signified their country, the circles of corn the bounds of the sea, and the sticks his country. They imagined the world to be flat and round, like a trencher, and they in the middest. After this they brought him a bag of gunpowder, which they carefully preserved till the next spring, to plant as they did their corn; because they would be acquainted with the nature of that seed.

Opitchapam the king's brother invited him to his house, where, with as many platters of bread, fowl, and wild beasts, as did environ him, he bid him welcome; but not any of them would eat a bit with him, but put up all the remainder in baskets. At his return to Opechankanough's, all the king's women, and their children, flocked about him for their parts, as a due by custom, to be merry with such fragments.

> But his waking mind in hideous dreams did oft see
> wondrous shapes,
> Of bodies strange, and huge in growth, and of stupendious makes.

At last they brought him to Meronocomo, where was Powhatan, their emperor. Here more then two hundred of those grim courtiers stood wondering at

[4] Mustachios.

him, as he had been a monster; till Powhatan and his train had put themselves in their greatest braveries. Before a fire upon a seat like a bedstead, he sat covered with a great robe, made of rarowcun[5] skins, and all the tails hanging by. On either hand did sit a young wench of sixteen or eighteen years, and along on each side the house, two rows of men, and behind them as many women, with all their heads and shoulders painted red; many of their heads bedecked with the white down of birds; but everyone with something: and a great chain of white beads about their necks. At his entrance before the king, all the people gave a great shout. The Queen of Appamatuck was appointed to bring him water to wash his hands, and another brought him a bunch of feathers, instead of a towel, to dry them. Having feasted him after their best barbarous manner they could, a long consultation was held, but the conclusion was, two great stones were brought before Powhatan: then as many as could laid hands on him, dragged him to them, and thereon laid his head, and being ready with their clubs, to beat out his brains, Pocahontas, the king's dearest daughter, when no entreaty could prevail, got his head in her arms, and laid her own upon his to save him from death: whereat the emperor was contented he should live to make him hatchets, and her bells, beads, and copper; for they thought him as well of all occupations as themselves. For the king himself will make his own robes, shoes, bows, arrows, pots; plant, hunt, or do anything so well as the rest.

> They say he bore a pleasant shew,
> But sure his heart was sad.
> For who can pleasant be, and rest,
> That lives in fear and dread:

[5] Raccoon.

> And having life suspected, doth
> It still suspected lead.

Two days after, Powhatan, having disguised himself in the most fearful manner he could, caused Captain Smith to be brought forth to a great house in the woods, and there upon a mat by the fire to be left alone. Not long after, from behind a mat that divided the house, was made the most dolefullest noise he ever heard; then Powhatan, more like a devil then a man, with some two hundred more as black as himself, came into him and told him now they were friends, and presently he should go to Jamestown, to send him two great guns, and a grindstone, for which he would give him the country of Capahowosick, and forever esteem him as his son Nantaquoud. So to Jamestown with twelve guides Powhatan sent him. That night they quartered in the woods, he still expecting (as he had done all this long time of his imprisonment) every hour to be put to one death or other for all their feasting. But almighty God (by His divine providence) had mollified the hearts of those stern barbarians with compassion. The next morning betimes they came to the fort, where Smith, having used the salvages with what kindness he could, he shewed Rawhunt, Powhatan's trusty servant, two demi-culverings and a millstone to carry Powhatan: they found them somewhat too heavy; but when they did see him discharge them, being loaded with stones, among the boughs of a great tree loaded with icicles, the ice and branches came so tumbling down, that the poor salvages ran away half dead with fear. But at last we regained some conference with them, and gave them such toys; and sent to Powhatan, his women, and children such presents, as gave them in general full content.

1624

The Puritan Way ─────────────────────────────────

WILLIAM BRADFORD [1590–1657]

"OF PLYMOUTH PLANTATION, and first of the occasion and inducements thereunto, the which that I may truly unfold, I must begin at the very root and rise of the same. The which I shall endeavor to manifest in a plain style, with singular regard unto the simple truth in all things, at least as near as my slender judgment can attain the same." So in 1630 did William Bradford begin the history he would write until 1650, as he looked back on the events of two decades and more that brought Plymouth colony to a modest prosperity.

No one was in a better position to write that history. Born in Yorkshire, Bradford was raised in the company of Separatists that gathered at the home of William Brewster: religious purists whose consciences would not permit them to participate in the rites and services of the Church of England. He was with the party of Separatists that left England for Holland in 1609, and despite his relative youth, became one of its most respected leaders. Dissatisfied with Dutch surroundings, fearing disintegration as older members of the society died and youths grew into non-English ways, Bradford was one of several who urged emigration to America and helped arrange the voyage of the *Mayflower*. Shortly after the landing in 1620, Governor John Carver died; Bradford was chosen to succeed him, and for the next thirty years, as judge, treasurer, and governor he selflessly directed the colony's fortunes in war, diplomacy, and business.

Bradford's "simple truth" derived from a sense of history embedded in John Foxe's enormously popular *Actes and Monuments*. Seeing the Separatists as the people chosen of God to carry His truth ever westward in what Foxe called an age of "trial and travail," Bradford sought to demonstrate America's manifest destiny by the careful selection of events and the conscious manipulation of a plain, dignified, unpretentious, and often very gripping style. The ruling purpose of illustrating God's providence toward the American venture reveals not only the Puritan's concept of history, but the color of almost day-to-day events: the disturbing presence of wild spirits such as Thomas Morton, the massacre of the Pequot Indians, the negotiations with Dutch and French governors of other settlements, even the scandalous outbreak of sin during the very year in which Nathaniel Hawthorne set Hester Prynne to face her judgment from the scaffold in the Boston marketplace.

Bradford's manuscript was not immediately published, though it was used by such colonial historians as Nathaniel Morton, Cotton Mather, Thomas Prince, and Thomas Hutchinson. During the British occupation of Boston in the Revolutionary War, the manuscript disappeared, and did not come to light again until 1855—in the library of the Bishop of London. The complete work was thereupon printed for the first time, in 1856, and the manuscript was returned to America in 1897.

Further reading: *Of Plymouth Plantation*, ed. S. E. Morison, 1952. Bradford Smith, *Bradford of Plymouth*, 1951. E. F. Bradford, "Conscious Art in Bradford's History of Plymouth Plantation," *New England Quarterly*, April 1928.

FROM *Of Plymouth Plantation*

A long introduction concerns the departure of the Separatists from England, their life for more than a decade in Holland, the decision to remove to America, the voyage in the *Mayflower,* and the landing. The main body of the work is in the form of annals, recording the history of the colony from the settlement of 1620 through the year 1646. By 1692, Plymouth lost its separate identity and was absorbed into Massachusetts; but as early as 1630 Bradford had sensed that his Pilgrims "should be but even as stepping-stones unto others for the performing of so great a work." Text: William Bradford, *History of Plymouth Plantation 1620-1647,* ed. W. C. Ford (Boston, 1912).

[Arrival]

[1620] But to omit other things (that I may be brief), after long beating at sea they fell with that land which is called Cape Cod; the which being made and certainly known to be it, they were not a little joyful. After some deliberation had amongst themselves and with the master of the ship, they tacked about and resolved to stand for the southward (the wind and weather being fair) to find some place about Hudson's River for their habitation. But after they had sailed that course about half the day, they fell amongst dangerous shoals and roaring breakers, and they were so far entangled therewith as they conceived themselves in great danger; and the wind shrinking upon them withal, they resolved to bear up again for the Cape and thought themselves happy to get out of those dangers before night overtook them, as by God's good providence they did. And the next day they got into the cape harbor where they rid in safety. ° ° °

Being thus arrived in a good harbor, and brought safe to land, they fell upon their knees and blessed the God of heaven who had brought them over the vast and furious ocean, and delivered them from all the perils and miseries thereof, again to set their feet on the firm and stable earth, their proper element. And no marvel if they were thus joyful, seeing wise Seneca was so affected with sailing a few miles on the coast of his own Italy, as he affirmed,[1] that he had rather remain twenty years on his way by land then pass by sea to any place in a short time, so tedious and dreadful was the same unto him.

But here I cannot but stay and make a pause, and stand half amazed at this poor people's present condition; and so I think will the reader, too, when he well considers the same. Being thus passed the vast ocean, and a sea of troubles before in their preparation (as may be remembered by that which went before), they had now no friends to welcome them nor inns to entertain or refresh their weatherbeaten bodies; no houses or much less towns to repair to, to seek for succor. It is recorded in scripture, as a mercy to the Apostle and his shipwrecked company, that the barbarians shewed them no small kindness in refreshing them,[2] but these savage barbarians, when they met with them (as after will appear), were readier to fill their sides full of arrows then otherwise. And for the season it was winter, and they that know the winters of that country know them to be sharp and violent, and subject to cruel and fierce storms, dangerous to travel to known places, much more to search an unknown coast. Besides, what could they see but a hideous and desolate wilderness, full of wild beasts and wild men—and what multitudes there might be of them they knew not. Neither could they, as it were, go up to the top of Pisgah[3] to view from this wilderness a more goodly country to feed their hopes; for which way soever they turned their eyes (save upward to the heavens) they could have little solace or content in respect of any outward objects. For summer being done, all things stand upon them with a weatherbeaten face, and the whole country, full of woods and thickets, represented a wild and savage hue. If they looked behind them, there was the mighty ocean which they had passed and was now as a main bar and gulf to separate them from all the civil parts of the world. If it be said they had a ship to succor them, it is true; but what heard they daily from the master and company? But that with speed they should look out a place (with their shallop) where they would be, at some near distance; for the season was such as he would not stir from thence till a safe harbor was discovered by them, where they would be, and he might go without danger; and that victuals consumed apace but he must and would keep sufficient for themselves and their return. Yea, it was muttered by some that if they got not a place in time, they would turn them and their goods ashore and leave them. Let it also be considered what weak hopes of supply and succor they left behind them, that might bear up their minds in this sad condition and trials they were under; and they could not but be very small. It is true, indeed, the affections and love of their brethren at Leyden was cordial and entire towards them, but they had little power to help them or themselves; and how the case stood between them and the merchants at their coming away hath already been declared. What could now sustain them but the Spirit of God and His grace? May not and ought not the children of these fathers rightly say: "Our fathers were Englishmen which came over this great ocean, and were

[1] Epistle 53 [*ad Lucilium Epistulae Morales;* Bradford's note].

[2] Acts xxviii.2.

[3] The mountain from which Moses viewed the promised land; Deut. xxxv.1.

ready to perish in this wilderness; but they cried unto the Lord, and He heard their voice and looked on their adversity," etc. "Let them therefore praise the Lord, because He is good: and His mercies endure forever." "Yea, let them which have been redeemed of the Lord, shew how He hath delivered them from the hand of the oppressor. When they wandered in the desert wilderness out of the way, and found no city to dwell in, both hungry and thirsty, their soul was overwhelmed in them. Let them confess before the Lord His loving-kindness and His wonderful works before the sons of men."

[The Mayflower Compact]

[1620] I shall a little return back, and begin with a combination made by them before they came ashore; being the first foundation of their government in this place. Occasioned partly by the discontented and mutinous speeches that some of the strangers[4] amongst them had let fall from them in the ship, that when they came ashore they would use their own liberty, for none had power to command them, the patent they had being for Virginia and not for New England, which belonged to another government, with which the Virginia Company had nothing to do. And partly that such an act by them done, this their condition considered, might be as firm as any patent, and in some respects more sure.

The form was as followeth:

In the name of God, Amen. We whose names are underwritten, the loyal subjects of our dread sovereign lord, King James, by the grace of God of Great Britain, France, and Ireland, king, defender of the faith, etc.

Having undertaken, for the glory of God and advancement of the Christian faith and honor of our king and country, a voyage to plant the first colony in the northern parts of Virginia, do by these presents solemnly and mutually in the presence of God and one of another, covenant and combine ourselves together into a civil body politic, for our better ordering and preservation and furtherance of the ends aforesaid; and by virtue hereof to enact, constitute, and frame such just and equal laws, ordinances, acts, constitutions, and offices, from time to time, as shall be thought most meet and convenient for the general good of the colony, unto which we promise all due submission and obedience. In witness whereof we have hereunder subscribed our names at Cape Cod, the 11th of November, in the

[4]Persons not of the Scrooby-Leyden Separatist group, but "from London and other places," who were added to the *Mayflower* company at the insistence of the financial backers of the enterprise.

year of the reign of our sovereign lord, King James, of England, France and Ireland the eighteenth, and of Scotland the fifty-fourth. *Anno Domini* 1620.

After this they chose, or rather confirmed, Mr. John Carver (a man godly and well approved amongst them) their governor for that year. ° ° °

[Survival]

[1621] They now began to dispatch the ship away which brought them over, which lay till about this time, or the beginning of April. The reason on their part why she stayed so long, was the necessity and danger that lay upon them; for it was well towards the end of December before she could land anything here, or they able to receive anything ashore. Afterwards, the 14th of January, the house which they had made for a general rendezvous by casualty fell afire, and some were fain to retire aboard for shelter; then the sickness began to fall sore amongst them, and the weather so bad as they could not make much sooner any dispatch. Again, the Governor and chief of them, seeing so many die and fall down sick daily, thought it no wisdom to send away the ship, their condition considered and the danger they stood in from the Indians, till they could procure some shelter; and therefore thought it better to draw some more charge upon themselves and friends than hazard all. The master and seamen likewise, though before they hasted the passengers ashore to be gone, now many of their men being dead, and of the ablest of them (as is before noted), and of the rest many lay sick and weak; the master durst not put to sea till he saw his men begin to recover, and the heart of winter over.

Afterwards they (as many as were able) began to plant their corn, in which service Squanto stood them in great stead, showing them both the manner how to set it, and after how to dress and tend it. Also he told them, except they got fish and set with it in these old grounds it would come to nothing. And he showed them that in the middle of April they should have store enough come up the brook by which they began to build, and taught them how to take it, and where to get other provisions necessary for them. All which they found true by trial and experience. Some English seed they sowed, as wheat and pease, but it came not to good, either by the badness of the seed or lateness of the season or both, or some other defect.

In this month of April, whilst they were busy about their seed, their Governor (Mr. John Carver) came out of the field very sick, it being a hot day. He complained greatly of his head and lay down, and within a few hours his senses failed, so as he never spake more till he died, which was within a few days after. Whose death was much lamented and caused great heaviness amongst them, as there was cause. He was buried in the best manner they could, with some volleys of shot by all that bore arms. And his wife, being a weak woman, died within five or six weeks after him.

Shortly after, William Bradford was chosen Governor in his stead, and being not recovered of his illness, in which he had been near the point of death, Isaac Allerton was chosen to be an assistant unto him who, by renewed election every year, continued sundry years together. Which I here note once for all.

May 12 was the first marriage in this place which, according to the laudable custom of the Low Countries, in which they had lived, was thought most requisite to be performed by the magistrate, as being a civil thing, upon which many questions about inheritances do depend, with other things most proper to their cognizance and most consonant to the Scriptures (Ruth iv) and nowhere found in the Gospel to be laid on the ministers as a part of their office.°°°

They began now to gather in the small harvest they had, and to fit up their houses and dwellings against winter, being all well recovered in health and strength and had all things in good plenty. For as some were thus employed in affairs abroad, others were exercised in fishing, about cod and bass and other fish, of which they took good store, of which every family had their portion. All the summer there was no want; and now began to come in store of fowl, as winter approached, of which this place did abound when they came first (but afterward decreased by degrees). And besides waterfowl there was great store of wild turkeys, of which they took many, besides venison, etc. Besides they had about a peck of meal a week to a person, or now since harvest, Indian corn to that proportion. Which made many afterwards write so largely of their plenty here to their friends in England, which were not feigned but true reports. ° ° °

[1623] All this while no supply was heard of, neither knew they when they might expect any. So they began to think how they might raise as much corn as they could, and obtain a better crop than they had done, that they might not still thus languish in misery. At length, after much debate of things, the Governor (with the advice of the chiefest amongst them) gave way that they should set corn every man for his own particular, and in that regard trust to themselves; in all other things to go on in the general way as before. And so assigned to every family a parcel of land, according to the proportion of their number, for that end, only for present use (but made no division for inheritance) and ranged all boys and youth under some family. This had very good success, for it made all hands very industrious, so as much more corn was planted than otherwise would have been by any means the Governor or any other could use, and saved him a great deal of trouble, and gave far better content. The women now went willingly into the field, and took their little ones with them to set corn; which before would allege weakness and inability; whom to have compelled would have been thought great tyranny and oppression.

The experience that was had in this common course and condition, tried sundry years and that amongst godly and sober men, may well evince the vanity of that conceit of Plato's and other ancients applauded by some of later times; that the taking away of property and bringing in community into a commonwealth would make them happy and flourishing; as if they were wiser than God. For this community (so far as it was) was found to breed much confusion and discontent and retard much employment that would have been to their benefit and comfort. For the young men, that were most able and fit for labour and service, did repine that they should spend their time and strength to work for other men's wives and children without any recompense. The strong, or man of parts, had no more in division of victuals and clothes than he that was weak and not able to do a quarter the other could; this was thought injustice. The aged and graver men to be ranked and equalized in labours and victuals, clothes, etc., with the meaner and younger sort, thought it some indignity and disrespect unto them. And for men's wives to be commanded to do service for other men, as dressing their meat, washing their clothes, etc., they deemed it a kind of slavery, neither could many husbands well brook it. Upon the point all being to have alike, and all to do alike, they thought themselves in the like condition, and one as good as another; and so, if it did not cut off those relations that God hath set amongst men, yet it did at least much diminish and take off the mutual respects that should be preserved amongst them. And would have been worse if they had been men of another condition. Let none object this is men's corruption, and nothing to the course itself. I answer, seeing all men have this corruption in them, God in His wisdom saw another course fitter for them.

[Morton of Merry Mount]

[1628] Hitherto the Indians of these parts had no pieces nor other arms but their bows and arrows, nor of many years after; neither durst they scarce handle a gun, so much were they afraid of them; and the very sight of one (though out of kilter) was a terror unto them. But those Indians to the east parts, which had commerce with the French, got pieces of them, and they in the end made a common trade of it; and in time our English fishermen, led with the like covetousness, followed their example for their own gain; but upon complaint against them, it pleased the King's Majesty to prohibit the same by a strict proclamation, commanding that no sort of arms or munition should by any of his subjects be traded with them.

About some three or four years before this time, there came over one Captain Wollaston (a man of pretty parts), and with him three or four more of some eminency, who brought with them a great many servants with provisions and other implements for to begin a plantation; and pitched themselves in a place within the Massachusetts, which they called, after their captain's name, Mount Wollaston. Amongst whom was one Mr. Morton, who, it should seem, had some small adventure (of his own or other men's) amongst them, but had little respect amongst them, and was slighted by the meanest servants. Having continued there some time, and not finding things to answer their expectations, nor profit to arise as they looked for, Captain Wollaston takes a great part of the servants, and transports them to Virginia, where he puts them off at good rates, selling their time to other men; and writes back to one Mr. Rasdall, one of his chief partners, and accounted their merchant, to bring another part of them to Virginia likewise, intending to put them off there as he had done the rest. And he, with the consent of the said Rasdall, appointed one Fitcher to be his lieutenant and govern the remains of the plantation till he or Rasdall returned to take further order thereabout. But this Morton abovesaid, having more craft then honesty (who had been a kind of pettifogger of Furnival's Inn)[5], in the others' absence watches an opportunity (and commons being but hard amongst them) and got some strong drink and other junkets, and made them a feast; and after they were merry, he began to tell them he would give them good counsel. "You see," saith he, "that many of your fellows are carried to Virginia; and if you stay till this Rasdall return, you will also be carried away and sold for slaves with the rest. Therefore I would advise you to thrust out this Lieutenant Fitcher; and I, having a part in the plantation, will receive you as my partners and consociates; so may you be free from service; and we will converse, trade, plant, and live together as equals, and support and protect one another," or to like effect. This counsel was easily received; so they took opportu-

[5] These events came to a head in 1627–28. Thomas Morton may have been a rascally attorney and person, but his association was with Clifford's Inn, and he was instrumental in attempts to revoke the Massachusetts charter. His version of these events was published in Amsterdam in 1637 as *New English Canaan*.

nity and thrust Lieutenant Fitcher out o' doors and would suffer him to come no more amongst them, but forced him to seek bread to eat and other relief from his neighbors till he could get passages for England.

After this they fell to great licentiousness and led a dissolute life, pouring out themselves into all profaneness. And Morton became lord of misrule and maintained (as it were) a school of atheism. And after they had got some goods into their hands, and got much by trading with the Indians, they spent it as vainly, in quaffing and drinking, both wine and strong waters in great excess and (as some reported) ten pounds' worth in a morning. They also set up a Maypole, drinking and dancing about it many days together, inviting the Indian women for their consorts, dancing and frisking together like so many fairies (or furies rather), and worse practices, as if they had anew revived and celebrated the feasts of the Roman goddess Flora, or the beastly practices of the mad Bacchanalians. Morton likewise (to shew his poetry) composed sundry rhymes and verses, some tending to lasciviousness, and others to the detraction and scandal of some persons, which he affixed to this idle or idol Maypole. They changed also the name of their place; and instead of calling it Mount Wollaston, they call it Merry Mount, as if this jollity would have lasted ever. But this continued not long, for after Morton was sent for England (as follows to be declared), shortly after came over that worthy gentleman, Mr. John Endecott, who brought over a patent under the broad seal for the government of the Massachusetts, who, visiting those parts, caused that Maypole to be cut down and rebuked them for their profaneness and admonished them to look there should be better walking; so they now, or others, changed the name of their place again and called it Mount Dagon.

Now to maintain this riotous prodigality and profuse excess, Morton, thinking himself lawless, and hearing what gain the French and fishermen made by trading of pieces, powder, and shot to the Indians, he, as the head of this consortship, began the practice of the same in these parts. And first he taught them how to use them, to charge and discharge, and what proportion of powder to give the piece, according to the size or bigness of the same; and what shot to use for fowl and what for deer. And having thus instructed them, he employed some of them to hunt and fowl for him, so as they became far more active in that employment then any of the English, by reason of their swiftness of foot and nimbleness of body, being also quick-sighted, and by continual exercise well knowing the haunts of all sorts of game. So as when they saw the execution that a piece would do, and the benefit that might come by the same, they became mad, as it were,

[margin handwritten note: WHAT WENT ON AT MERRY MOUNT]

after them, and would not stick to give any price they could attain to for them; accounting their bows and arrows but baubles in comparison of them.

And here I may take occasion to bewail the mischief that this wicked man began in these parts, and which since, base covetousness prevailing in men that should know better, has now at length got the upper hand and made this thing common, notwithstanding any laws to the contrary; so as the Indians are full of pieces all over, both fowling pieces, muskets, pistols, etc. They have also their moulds to make shot of all sorts, as musket bullets, pistol bullets, swan and goose shot, and of smaller sorts. Yes, some have seen them have their screw-plates to make screw-pins themselves, when they want them, with sundry other implements, wherewith they are ordinarily better fitted and furnished then the English themselves. Yea, it is well known that they will have powder and shot when the English want it, nor cannot get it; and that in a time of war or danger, as experience hath manifested, that when lead hath been scarce and men for their own defense would gladly have given a groat a pound, which is dear enough, yet hath it been bought up and sent to other places and sold to such as trade it with the Indians at twelve pence the pound; and it is like they give three or four shillings the pound, for they will have it at any rate. And these things have been done in the same times when some of their neighbors and friends are daily killed by the Indians, or are in danger thereof and live but at the Indians' mercy. Yea, some (as they have acquainted them with all other things) have told them how gunpowder is made, and all the materials in it, and that they are to be had in their own land; and I am confident, could they attain to make saltpeter, they would teach them to make powder. O the horribleness of this villainy! How many both Dutch and English have been lately slain by those Indians, thus furnished, and no remedy provided; nay, the evil more increased, and the blood of their brethren sold for gain, as is to be feared; and in what danger all these colonies are in is too well known. O, that princes and parliaments would take some timely order to prevent this mischief, and at length to suppress it, by some exemplary punishment upon some of these gain-thirsty murderers (for they deserve no better title) before their colonies in these parts be overthrown by these barbarous savages thus armed with their own weapons, by these evil instruments and traitors to their neighbors and country! But I have forgotten myself and have been too long in this digression; but now to return.

This Morton having thus taught them the use of pieces, he sold them all he could spare; and he and his consorts determined to send for many out of England, and had by some of the ships sent for above a score. The which being known, and his neighbors meeting the Indians in the woods armed with guns in this sort, it was a terror unto them who lived stragglingly and were of no strength in any place. And other places (though more remote) saw this mischief would quickly spread over all, if not prevented. Besides, they saw they should keep no servants, for Morton would entertain any, how vile soever, and all the scum of the country or any discontents would flock to him from all places, if this nest was not broken; and they should stand in more fear of their lives and goods in short time from this wicked and debased crew than from the savages themselves.

So sundry of the chief of the straggling plantations, meeting together, agreed by mutual consent to solicit those of Plymouth (who were then of more strength then them all) to join with them to prevent the further growth of this mischief, and suppress Morton and his consorts before they grew to further head and strength. Those that joined in this action (and after contributed to the charge of sending him for England) were from Pascataway, Namkeake, Winisimett, Weesagascusett, Natasco, and other places where any English were seated. Those of Plymouth, being thus sought too by their messengers and letters, and weighing both their reasons and the common danger, were willing to afford them their help, though themselves had least cause of fear or hurt. So, to be short, they first resolved jointly to write to him, and in a friendly and neighborly way to admonish him to forbear those courses, and sent a messenger with their letters to bring his answer. But he was so high as he scorned all advice and asked who had to do with him; he had and would trade pieces with the Indians in despite of all, with many other scurrilous terms full of disdain. They sent to him a second time and bade him be better advised and more temperate in his terms, for the country could not bear the injury he did; it was against their common safety and against the King's proclamation. He answered in high terms as before, and that the King's proclamation was no law, demanding what penalty was upon it. It was answered, more than he could bear, His Majesty's displeasure. But insolently he persisted and said the King was dead and his displeasure with him, and many the like things, and threatened withal that if any came to molest him, let them look to themselves, for he would prepare for them. Upon which they saw there was no way but to take him by force; and having so far proceeded, now to give over would make him far more haughty and insolent. So they mutually resolved to proceed, and obtained of the Governor of Plymouth to send Captain Standish and some other aid with him, to take Morton by force. The which accordingly was done. But they found him to stand stiffly in his defense, having made fast his doors, armed his consorts, set divers dishes of powder and bullets ready on the table; and if they had not been over-armed with drink, more hurt might have been done. They summoned him to yield, but he kept his house, and they could get nothing but scoffs and scorns from him. But at length, fearing they would do some violence to the house, he and some of his crew came out, but not to yield but to shoot; but they were so steeled with drink as their pieces were too heavy for them; himself with a carbine (overcharged and almost half filled with powder and shot, as was after found) had thought to have shot Captain Standish; but he stepped to him and put by his piece and took him. Neither was there any hurt done to any of either side, save that one was so drunk that he ran his own nose upon the point of a sword that one held before him, as he entered the house; but he lost but a little of his hot blood. Morton they brought away to Plymouth, where he was kept till a ship went from the Isle of Shoals for England, with which he was sent to the Council of New England; and letters written to give them information of his course and carriage; and also one was sent at their common charge to inform their Honors more particularly, and to prosecute against him. But he fooled of the messenger, after he was gone from hence, and though he went for England, yet nothing was done to him, not so much as rebuked, for aught was heard; but returned the next year. Some of the worst of the company were dispersed, and some of the more modest kept the house till he should be heard from. But I have been too long about so unworthy a person, and bad a cause.

[War with the Pequots]

[1637] In the fore part of this year, the Pequots fell openly upon the English at Connecticut, in the lower parts of the river, and slew sundry of them as they were at work in the fields, both men and women, to the great terror of the rest, and went away in great pride and triumph, and many high threats. They also assaulted a fort at the river's mouth, though strong and well defended; and though they did not there prevail, yet it struck them with much fear and astonishment to see their bold attempts in the face of danger. Which made them in all places to stand upon their guard and to prepare for resistance, and earnestly to solicit their friends and confederates in the Bay of Massachusetts to send them speedy aid, for they looked for more forcible assaults. Mr. Vane, being then Governor, writ from their General Court to them here to join with them in this war. To which they were cordially willing, but took opportunity to write to them about some former things, as well as present, considerable hereabout. ° ° °

In the meantime, the Pequots, especially in the winter before, sought to make peace with the Narragansetts, and used very pernicious arguments to move them thereunto: as that the English were strangers and began to overspread their country, and would deprive them thereof in time, if they were suffered to grow and increase. And if the Narragansetts did assist the English to subdue them, they did but make way for their own overthrow, for if they were rooted out, the English would soon take occasion to subjugate them. And if they would hearken to them, they should not need to fear the strength of the English, for they would not come to open battle with them, but fire their houses, kill their cattle, and lie in ambush for them as they went abroad upon their occasions; and all this they might easily do without any or little danger to themselves. The which course being held, they well saw the English could not long subsist, but they would either be starved with hunger or be forced to forsake the country. With many the like things; insomuch that the Narragansetts were once wavering and were half minded to have made peace with them, and joined against the English. But again, when they considered how much wrong they had received from the Pequots, and what an opportunity they now had by the help of the English to right themselves; revenge was so sweet unto them as it prevailed above all the rest, so as they resolved to join with the English against them, and did.

The Court here agreed forthwith to send fifty men at their own charge; and with as much speed as possibly they could, got them armed and had made them ready under sufficient leaders, and provided a bark to carry them provisions and tend upon them for all occasions. But when they were ready to march, with a supply from the Bay, they had word to stay; for the enemy was as good as vanquished and there would be no need.

I shall not take upon me exactly to describe their proceedings in these things, because I expect it will be fully done by themselves who best know the carriage and circumstances of things.[6] I shall therefore but touch them in general. From Connecticut, who were most sensible of the hurt sustained and the present danger, they set out a party of men, and another party met them from the Bay at the Narragansetts', who were to join with them. The Narragansetts were earnest to be gone before the English were well rested and refreshed, especially some of them which came last. It should seem their desire was to come upon the enemy suddenly and undiscovered. There was a bark of this place, newly put in there, which was come from Connecticut, who did encourage them to lay hold of the Indians' for-

[6] See John Mason, *A Brief History of the Pequod War*, 1735; John Underhill, *News from America*, 1638; and Philip Vincent, *A True Relation . . .*, 1638.

wardness, and to show as great forwardness as they, for it would encourage them, and expedition might prove to their great advantage. So they went on, and so ordered their march as the Indians brought them to a fort of the enemy's (in which most of their chief men were) before day. They approached the same with great silence and surrounded it both with English and Indians, that they might not break out; and so assaulted them with great courage, shooting amongst them, and entered the fort with all speed. And those that first entered found sharp resistance from the enemy, who both shot at and grappled with them; others ran into their houses and brought out fire and set them on fire, which soon took in their mats; and standing close together, with the wind all was quickly on a flame, and thereby more were burnt to death than was otherwise slain. It burnt their bowstrings and made them unserviceable; those that scaped the fire were slain with the sword, some hewed to pieces, others run through with their rapiers, so as they were quickly dispatched and very few escaped. It was conceived they thus destroyed about 400 at this time. It was a fearful sight to see them thus frying in the fire and the streams of blood quenching the same, and horrible was the stink and scent thereof; but the victory seemed a sweet sacrifice, and they gave the praise thereof to God, who had wrought so wonderfully for them, thus to enclose their enemies in their hands and give them so speedy a victory over so proud and insulting an enemy.

JOHN WINTHROP [1588–1649]

BORN THE SAME YEAR as William Bradford, John Winthrop too was destined to be a major force in the shaping of the colonial experience. He came of a well-to-do Suffolk family, was educated at Cambridge, and after considering the ministry turned instead to law. Intensely Puritan, he was one of the leaders of the group that began the Great Migration to Massachusetts Bay in 1630; in fact, he had been elected governor of the new colony the year before. And from then until his death he served as governor or deputy governor for all but seven years, ever mindful of his admonition to the company aboard the flagship *Arbella*: "to do justly, to love mercy, to walk humbly with our God; . . . for we must consider that we shall be as a city upon a hill, the eyes of all people are upon us. . . ."

Politically astute, and dedicated to fulfilling the dream of a holy commonwealth in the New World, Winthrop dominated the life of Massachusetts Bay as Bradford did that of the less sophisticated and less powerful Plymouth. And like Bradford he kept a journal (from 1630 to 1649) that is a rare and rich account of life during that time. It was published early in the nineteenth century as *The History of New England*, but comparison with *Of Plymouth Plantation* shows the faultiness of that title. For, as much as Winthrop's journal reveals, it lacks the philosophy, the historical perspective, the art, and the conscious dignity of Bradford's work.

Winthrop's course was not always smooth, his politics and diplomacy were often highhanded and arbitrary. But on balance he emerges from the journal a devoted and practical leader who recognized that his infant colony could not survive a gentle leadership. Unauthorized ships entering Boston harbor, heretics and civil dissidents such as Roger Williams and Anne Hutchinson, threatening Indians—all were handled with dispatch, and sometimes with harshness. Once, in a matter involving a deposed militia company commander, Winthrop was actually impeached before the General Court of Massachusetts on a charge of having exceeded his powers. His position on the rights and liberties of elected authority is summed up in the now famous "little speech" which he made before the Court upon his exoneration.

Further reading: *Journal*, ed. J. K. Hosmer, 1908. A chapter in S. E. Morison, *Builders of the Bay Colony*, 1930, 1964. S. Gray, "The Political Thought of John Winthrop," *New England Quarterly*, 1930. E. Morgan, *The Puritan Dilemma*, 1958.

Letters to (and from) his Wife

After burying two wives, Winthrop was married in 1618 to Margaret, daughter of Sir John Tyndall, of Great Maplestead, Essex. She bore him eight children (in all he had fifteen). A year after Winthrop sailed she followed him to America. The letters given below, written when the Winthrops had been married a decade, afford intimate glimpses of the Puritan heart and faith. Text: *Winthrop Papers*, I (Boston, 1929), 369–70; II (Boston, 1931), 224–26.

My Most Sweet Husband,

How dearly welcome thy kind letter was to me I am not able to express. The sweetness of it did much refresh me. What can be more pleasing to a wife, than to hear of the welfare of her best beloved, and how he is pleased with her poor endeavors! I blush to hear myself commended, knowing my own wants. But it is your love that conceives the best and makes all things seem better than they are. I wish that I may be always pleasing to thee, and that those comforts we have in each other may be daily increased, as far as they be pleasing to God. I will use that speech to thee, that Abigail did to David, I will be a servant to wash the feet of my lord. I will do any service wherein I may please my good husband. I confess I cannot do enough for thee; but thou art pleased to accept the will for the deed and rest contented.

I have many reasons to make me love thee, whereof I will name two: first, because thou lovest God and, secondly, because that thou lovest me. If these two were wanting, all the rest would be eclipsed. But I must leave this discourse, and go about my household affairs. I am a bad housewife to be so long from them, but I must needs borrow a little time to talk with thee, my sweet heart. The term is more than half done. I hope thy business draws to an end. It will be but two or three weeks before I see thee, though they be long ones. God will bring us together in his good time; for which time I shall pray. I thank the Lord we are all in health. We are very glad to hear so good news of our son Henry. The Lord make us thankful for all His mercies to us and ours. And thus, with my mother's and my own best love to yourself and all the rest, I shall leave scribbling. The weather being cold, makes me make haste. Farewell, my good husband; the Lord keep thee.

Your obedient wife,
Margaret Winthrop.

Groton [England]. *November 22* [1627]

[P.S.] I have not yet received the box; but I will send for it. I send up a turkey and some cheese. I pray send my son Forth such a knife as mine is. Mrs. Hugen would pray you to buy a cake for the boys.

I did dine at Groton Hall yesterday; they are in health, and remember their love. We did wish you there, but that would not bring you, and I could not be merry without thee. Mr. Lee and his wife were there; they remember their love. Our neighbor Cole and goodman Newton have been sick, but somewhat amended again. I fear thy cheese will not prove so good as thou didst expect. I have sent it all, for we could not cut it.

My Faithful and Dear Wife,

It pleaseth God that thou shouldst once again hear from me before our departure, and I hope this shall come safe to thy hands. I know it will be a great refreshing to thee. And blessed be His mercy, that I can write thee so good news, that we are all in very good health, and, having tried our ship's entertainment now more than a week, we find it agree very well with us. Our boys are well and cheerful, and have no mind of home. They lie both with me, and sleep as soundly in a rug (for we use no sheets here) as ever they did at Groton; and so do I myself (I praise God). The wind hath been against us this week and more; but this day it is come fair to the north, so as we are preparing (by God's assistance) to set sail in the morning. We have only four ships ready, and some two or three Hollanders go along with us. The rest of our fleet (being seven ships) will not be ready this sennight. We have spent now two sabbaths on shipboard very comfortably (God be praised), and are daily more and more encouraged to look for the Lord's presence to go along with us. Henry Kingsbury hath a child or two in the Talbot sick of the measles, but like to do well. One of my men had them at Hampton, but he was soon well again. We are, in all our eleven ships, about 700 persons passengers, and 240 cows, and about 60 horses. The ship which went from Plymouth carried about 140 persons, and the ship which goes from Bristowe, carrieth about 80 persons. And now (my sweet soul) I must once again take my last farewell of thee in old England. It goeth very near to my heart to leave thee, but I know to whom I have committed thee, even to Him who loves thee much better than any husband can, who hath taken account of the hairs of thy head, and puts all thy tears into His bottle, who can, and (if it be for His glory) will bring us together again with peace and comfort. Oh how it refresheth my heart, to think that I shall yet again see thy sweet face in the land of the living: that lovely countenance, that I have so much delighted in, and beheld with so great content! I have hitherto been so taken up with business, as I could seldom look back to my former happiness; but now when I shall be at some leisure, I shall not avoid the remembrance of thee, nor the grief for thy absence. Thou hast thy share with me, but I hope the course we have agreed upon will be some ease to us both. Mondays and Fridays, at five of the clock at night, we shall meet in spirit till we meet in person. Yet, if all these hopes should fail, blessed be our God, that we are assured we shall meet one day, if not as husband and wife, yet in a better condition. Let that stay and comfort thy heart. Neither can the sea drown thy husband, nor enemies destroy, nor any adversity deprive thee of thy husband or children. Therefore I will only take thee now and my sweet children in mine arms, and kiss and embrace you all, and so leave you with my God. Farewell, farewell. I bless you all in the name of the Lord Jesus. I salute my daughter Winth., Matt, Nan, and the rest, and all my good neighbors and friends. Pray all for us. Farewell.

Commend my blessing to my son John. I cannot now write to him, but tell him I have committed thee and thine to him. Labor to draw him yet nearer to God, and he will be the surer staff of comfort to thee. I cannot name the rest of my good friends, but thou canst supply it. I wrote, a week since, to thee and Mr. Leigh, and divers others.

Thine wheresoever,

Jo. Winthrop.

From aboard the *Arbella*, riding at the Cowes, *March 28, 1630.*

FROM HIS *Journal*

Winthrop began his journal at Southampton, when the ship *Arbella* was preparing to sail, and continued it till shortly before his death. In both of the following episodes Winthrop raises questions of law, liberty, license, and political dissent and responsibility that still remain vital. Parrington has written of Winthrop's famous "little speech" on liberty, that "No other episode in his varied career reveals so well the admirable poise of the man—the dignity, the self-control, the fair-mindedness, despite an attack that hurt him to the quick." Text: John Winthrop, *The History of New England from 1630 to 1649*, ed. James Savage (2 vols., revised edition; Boston, 1853).

[A Trial for Adultery]

[1644] At this court of assistants, one James Britton, a man ill affected both to our church discipline and civil government, and one Mary Latham, a proper young woman about 18 years of age, whose father was a godly man and had brought her up well, were condemned to die for adultery, upon a law formerly made and published in print. It was thus occasioned and discovered. This woman, being rejected by a young man whom she had an affection unto, vowed she would marry the next that came to her, and accordingly, against her friends' minds, she matched with an ancient man who had neither honesty nor ability, and one whom she had no affection unto. Whereupon, soon after she was married, divers young men solicited her chastity, and drawing her into bad company, and giving her wine and other gifts, easily prevailed with her, and among others this Britton. But God smiting him with a deadly palsy and fearful horror of conscience withal, he could not keep secret, but discovered this, and other the like with other women, and was forced to acknowledge the justice of God in that having often called others fools, &c. for confessing against themselves, he was now forced to do the like. The woman dwelt now in Plymouth patent, and one of the magistrates there, hearing she was detected, &c. sent her to us. Upon her examination, she confessed he did attempt the fact, but did not commit it, and witness was produced that testified (which they both confessed) that in the evening of a day of humiliation through the country for England, &c. a company met at Britton's and there continued drinking sack, &c. till late in the night, and then Britton and the woman were seen upon the ground together, a little from the house. It was reported also that she did frequently abuse her husband, setting a knife to his breast and threatening to kill him, calling him old rogue and cuckold, and said she would make him wear horns as big as a bull. And yet some of the magistrates thought the evidence not sufficient against her, because there were not two direct witnesses; but the jury cast her, and then she confessed the fact, and accused twelve others, whereof two were married men. Five of these were apprehended and committed (the rest were gone), but denying it, and there being no other witness against them than the testimony of a condemned person, there could be no proceeding against them. The woman proved very penitent, and had deep apprehension of the foulness of her sin, and at length attained to hope of pardon by the blood of Christ, and was willing to die in satisfaction to justice. The man also was very much cast down for his sins, but was loth to die, and petitioned the general court for his life, but they would not grant it, though some of the magistrates spake much for it, and questioned the letter, whether adultery was death by God's law now. This Britton had been a professor[1] in England, but coming hither he opposed our church government, &c. and grew dissolute, losing both power and profession of godliness.

They were both executed, they both died very penitently, especially the woman, who had some comfortable hope of pardon of her sin, and gave good exhortation to all young maids to be obedient

---

[1] A religious believer; church member.

to their parents, and to take heed of evil company, &c.

[A Little Speech on Liberty]

In 1645 the militia company of Hingham, Massachusetts, dismissed its company commander and elected another in his place. The deposed officer appealed to the colonial government at Boston, which remonstrated with the Hingham citizens to no avail. The case was called to trial, and Deputy Governor Winthrop argued that the citizens of Hingham had exceeded their powers; the same accusation was then leveled at Winthrop. After long and bitter debate, the court decided in favor of Winthrop, who concluded with some pertinent remarks on political liberty as the Massachusetts theocracy perceived it.

I suppose something may be expected from me, upon this charge that is befallen me, which moves me to speak now to you; yet I intend not to intermeddle in the proceedings of the court, or with any of the persons concerned therein. Only I bless God, that I see an issue of this troublesome business. I also acknowledge the justice of the court, and, for mine own part, I am well satisfied; I was publicly charged, and I am publicly and legally acquitted, which is all I did expect or desire. And though this be sufficient for my justification before men, yet not so before the God, who hath seen so much amiss in my dispensations (and even in this affair) as calls me to be humble. For to be publicly and criminally charged in this court, is matter of humiliation (and I desire to make a right use of it), notwithstanding I be thus acquitted. If her father had spit in her face (saith the Lord concerning Miriam), should she not have been ashamed seven days?[2] Shame had lien upon her, whatever the occasion had been. I am unwilling to stay you from your urgent affairs, yet give me leave (upon this special occasion) to speak a little more to this assembly. It may be of some good use, to inform and rectify the judgments of some of the people, and may prevent such distempers as have arisen amongst us. The great questions that have troubled the country, are about the authority of the magistrates and the liberty of the people. It is yourselves who have called us to this office, and being called by you, we have our authority from God, in way of an ordinance, such as hath the image of God eminently stamped upon it, the contempt and violation whereof hath been vindicated with examples of divine vengeance. I entreat you to consider, that when you choose magistrates, you take them from among yourselves, men subject to like passions as you are. Therefore when you see infirmities in us, you should reflect upon your own, and that would make you bear the more with us, and not be severe censurers of the failings of your magistrates, when you have continual experience of the like infirmities in yourselves and others. We account him a good servant, who breaks not his covenant. The covenant between you and us is the oath you have taken of us, which is to this purpose, that we shall govern you and judge your causes by the rules of God's laws and our own, according to our best skill. When you agree with a workman to build you a ship or house, etc., he undertakes as well for his skill as for his faithfulness, for it is his profession, and you pay him for both. But when you call one to be a magistrate, he doth not profess nor undertake to have sufficient skill for that office, nor can you furnish him with gifts, etc., therefore you must run the hazard of his skill and ability. But if he fail in faithfulness, which by his oath he is bound unto, that he must answer for. If it fall out that the case be clear to common apprehension, and the rule clear, also, if he transgress here, the error is not in the skill, but in the evil of the will: it must be required of him. But if the cause be doubtful, or the rule doubtful, to men of such understanding and parts as your magistrates are, if your magistrates should err here, yourselves must bear it.

For the other point concerning liberty, I observe a great mistake in the country about that. There is a twofold liberty, natural (I mean as our nature is now corrupt) and civil or federal. The first is common to man with beasts and other creatures. By this, man, as he stands in relation to man simply, hath liberty to do what he lists; it is a liberty to evil as well as to good. This liberty is incompatible and inconsistent with authority, and cannot endure the least restraint of the most just authority. The exercise and maintaining of this liberty makes men grow more evil, and in time to be worse than brute beasts: *omnes sumus licentia deteriores.*[3] This is that great enemy of truth and peace, that wild beast, which all the ordinances of God are bent against, to restrain and subdue it. The other kind of liberty I call civil or federal; it may also be termed moral, in reference to the covenant between God and man, in the moral law, and the politic covenants and constitutions, amongst men themselves. This liberty is the proper end and object of authority, and cannot subsist without it; and it is a liberty to that only which is good, just, and honest. This liberty you are to stand for, with the hazard (not only of your goods, but) of your lives, if need be. Whatsoever crosseth this, is not authority, but a distemper thereof. This liberty is maintained and exercised in a way of subjection to authority; it is of the same kind of liberty wherewith Christ hath made us free. The woman's own choice makes such a man her husband; yet being so chosen, he is her lord, and she is to be subject to him, yet in

---

[2] Numbers xii.14.

[3] "We are all weakened by liberty."

a way of liberty, not of bondage; and a true wife accounts her subjection her honor and freedom, and would not think her condition safe and free, but in her subjection to her husband's authority. Such is the liberty of the church under the authority of Christ, her king and husband; His yoke is so easy and sweet to her as a bride's ornaments; and if through frowardness or wantonness, etc., she shake it off, at any time, she is at no rest in her spirit, until she take it up again; and whether her lord smiles upon her, and embraceth her in his arms, or whether he frowns, or rebukes, or smites her, she apprehends the sweetness of his love in all, and is refreshed, supported, and instructed by every such dispensation of his authority over her. On the other side, ye know who they are that complain of this yoke and say, let us break their bands, etc., we will not have this man to rule over us. Even so, brethren, it will be between you and your magistrates. If you stand for your natural corrupt liberties, and will do what is good in your own eyes, you will not endure the least weight of authority, but will murmur, and oppose, and be always striving to shake off that yoke; but if you will be satisfied to enjoy such civil and lawful liberties, such as Christ allows you, then will you quietly and cheerfully submit unto that authority which is set over you, in all the administrations of it, for your good. Wherein, if we fail at any time, we hope we shall be willing (by God's assistance) to hearken to good advice from any of you, or in any other way of God; so shall your liberties be preserved, in upholding the honor and power of authority amongst you.

ROGER WILLIAMS [1603–1683]

ROGER WILLIAMS was one of the first and most conspicuous challengers of the Puritan theocracy in New England. But if he evolved into an advocate of religious liberty, it was not that he lacked religious fervor and conviction; on the contrary, it was precisely because of the value he placed on spiritual truth that he felt it should not be confined and regulated by any formal organization, whether church or state.

This rebel against the Puritan establishment was born in London, the son of a tailor. Little is known of his youth, except that his skill in shorthand earned him a post as court stenographer to Sir Edward Coke, the great English justice and exponent of the common law. He then went to Cambridge, graduated in 1627, and spent two more years there studying theology. For a time he served as private chaplain to a Puritan noble, and in 1631 he emigrated to Massachusetts. From 1633 to 1635 he persistently disturbed the government of each town he lived in, questioning the rights of Englishmen to hold Indian land, raising the issue of the relationship between civil and religious authority, and urging "diverse new and dangerous opinions," as Governor Winthrop wrote in his journal, "adjudged by all magistrates and ministers to be erroneous and very dangerous." Finally, in 1635, the court ordered him "to depart out of our jurisdiction within six weeks," which he did, in the dead of a cold New England winter, to Rhode Island.

That colony, for which Williams eventually secured a very advantageous charter from King Charles II, became a haven for dissident sects and refugees from all religious persecution, Catholic and Puritan alike. Williams was elected president for three terms, even though he carried on a bitter quarrel with the philosophical tenets of the Quakers who most willingly and abundantly took advantage of the religious sanctuary he offered.

But he did not drop his argument with the Bay colonists, especially the noted minister John Cotton, of whom Williams sarcastically reported, New England "could hardly believe that God would suffer Mr. Cotton to err." Their controversy ran for years, beginning with Cotton's letter publishing Williams's dismissal from the Bay. This Williams answered in 1644 in *Mr. Cotton's Letter Lately Printed, Examined and Answered.* In the same year he also wrote a dialogue between Peace and Truth titled *The Bloody Tenent [Tenet] of Persecution for Cause of Conscience.* Cotton retorted with *The Bloody Tenent*

Washed and Made White in the Blood of the Lamb (1647), to which Williams immediately responded in *The Bloody Tenent Yet More Bloody by Mr. Cotton's Endeavor to Wash It White in the Blood of the Lamb* (not published until 1652).

Out of the complex of political and religious issues, Williams argued for two crucial positions: that a state cannot punish a person for what he thinks or believes, and therefore cannot punish "errors" in religion; and that because "the sovereign, original, and foundation of all civil power lies in the people . . . a people may erect and establish what form of government seems to them most meet for their civil condition." Both of these positions struck at the heart of the Puritan theocratic commonwealth.

Further reading: Perry Miller, *Roger Williams*, 1953. S. H. Brockunier, *The Irrepressible Democrat: Roger Williams*, 1940.

FROM ## The Bloody Tenent of Persecution

Like Winthrop, Williams puts into opposition principles of authority and right. But where Winthrop argues that wrong must be endured so long as governors act in good faith, Williams vigorously urges the legality and right of disobedience when the governed conceive the governor to be incompetent or wilful, anticipating Thoreau's famous stance in *Civil Disobedience*. Although Williams follows the popular practice of casting political and religious tracts into the form of a debate or dialogue, he makes no effort to realize any dramatic potential in that form. The text of the excerpt given below is that of the first edition, published in London in 1644.

[The Civil and Spiritual Estates]

Truth. Sweet Peace, what hast thou there?

Peace. Arguments against persecution for cause of conscience.

Truth. And what there?

Peace. An answer to such arguments, contrarily maintaining such persecution for cause of conscience.

Truth. These arguments against such persecution, and the answer pleading for it, written (as love hopes) from godly intentions, hearts, and hands, yet in a marvellous different style and manner. The arguments against persecution in milk, the answer for it (as I may say) in blood.

The author of these arguments (against persecution) (as I have been informed) being committed by some then in power, close prisoner to Newgate, for the witness of some truths of Jesus, and having not the use of pen and ink, wrote these arguments in milk, in sheets of paper, brought to him by the woman his keeper, from a friend in London, as the stopples of his milk bottle.

In such paper written with milk nothing will appear, but the way of reading it by fire being known to this friend who received the papers, he transcribed and kept together the papers, although the author himself could not correct, nor view what himself had written.

It was in milk, tending to soul nourishment, even for babes and sucklings in Christ.

It was in milk, spiritually white, pure and innocent, like those white horses of the Word of truth and meekness, and the white linen or armor of righteousness, in the army of Jesus. Rev. 6 and 19.

It was in milk, soft, meek, peaceable and gentle, tending both to the peace of souls, and the peace of States and Kingdoms.

Peace. The answer (though I hope out of milky pure intentions) is returned in blood: bloody and slaughterous conclusions; bloody to the souls of all men, forced to the religion and worship which every civil state or common-weal agrees on, and compels all subjects to in a dissembled uniformity.

Bloody to the bodies, first of the holy witnesses of Christ Jesus, who testify against such invented worships.

Secondly, of the nations and peoples slaughtering each other for their several respective religions and consciences. ° ° °

Peace. Pass on (holy Truth) to that similitude whereby they illustrate that negative assertion: "The prince in the ship," say they, "is governor over the bodies of all in the ship; but he hath no power to govern the ship or the mariners in the actions of it. If the pilot manifestly err in his action, the prince may reprove him," and so, say they may any passenger; "if he offend against the life or goods of any, the prince may in due time and place punish him, which no private person may."

Truth. Although (dear Peace) we both agree that civil powers may not enjoin such devices, no nor enforce on any God's institutions, since Christ Jesus his coming: yet, for further illustration, I shall propose some queries concerning the civil magistrate's passing in the ship of the church, wherein Christ Jesus hath appointed his ministers and officers as governors and pilots, etc.

If in a ship at sea, wherein the governor or pilot of a ship undertakes to carry the ship to such a port, the civil magistrate (suppose a king or emperor) shall command the master such and such a course, to steer upon such or such a point, which the master knows is not their course, and which if they steer he shall never bring the ship to that port or harbour: what shall the master do? Surely all men will say, the master of the ship or pilot is to present reasons and arguments from his mariner's art (if the prince be capable of them) or else in humble and submissive manner to persuade the prince not to interrupt them in their course and duty properly belonging to them, to wit, governing of the ship, steering of the course etc.

If the master of the ship command the mariners thus and thus, in running the ship, managing the helm, trimming the sail, and the prince command the mariners a different or contrary course, who is to be obeyed?

It is confessed that the mariners may lawfully disobey the prince, and obey the governor of the ship in the actions of the ship.

Thirdly, what if the prince have as much skill (which is rare) as the pilot himself? I conceive it will be answered, that the master of the ship and pilot, in what concerns the ship, are chief and above, in respect of their office, the prince himself, and their commands ought to be attended by all the mariners: unless it be in manifest error, wherein 'tis granted any passenger may reprove the pilot.

Fourthly, I ask if the prince and his attendants be unskillful in the ship's affairs, whether every sailor and mariner, the youngest and lowest, be not (so far as concerns the ship) to be preferred before the prince's followers, and the prince himself? and their counsel and advice more to be attended to, and their service more to be desired and respected, and the prince to be requested to stand by and let the business alone in their hands?

Fifthly, in case a wilful king and his attendants, out of opinion of their skill, or wilfulness of passion, would so steer the course, trim sail, etc., as that in the judgment of the master and seamen the ship and lives shall be endangered: whether (in case humble persuasions prevail not) ought not the ship's company to refuse to act in such a course, yea, and (in case power be in their hands) resist and suppress these dangerous practices of the prince and his followers, and so save the ship?

Lastly, suppose the master, out of base fear and cowardice, or covetous desire of reward, shall yield to gratify the mind of the prince, contrary to the rules of art and experience, etc., and the ship come in danger, and perish, and the prince with it: if the master get to shore, whether may he not be justly questioned, yea, and suffer as guilty of the prince's death, and those that perished with him? These cases are clear, wherein, according to this similitude, the prince ought not to govern and rule the actions of the ship, but such whose office and charge and skill it is.

The result of all is this: the church of Christ is the ship, wherein the prince (if a member, for otherwise the case is altered) is a passenger. In this ship the officers and governors, such as are appointed by the Lord Jesus, they are the chief, and (in those respects) above the prince himself, and are to be obeyed and submitted to in their works and administrations, even before the prince himself.

In this respect every Christian in the church, man or woman (if of more knowledge and grace of Christ) ought to be of higher esteem (concerning religion and Christianity) then all the princes in the world who have either none or less grace or knowledge of Christ: although in civil things all civil reverence, honour, and obedience ought to be yielded by all men.

Therefore, if in matters of religion the king command what is contrary to Christ's rule (though according to his persuasion and conscience) who sees not that (according to the similitude) he ought not to be obeyed? Yea, and (in case) boldly, with spiritual force and power, he ought to be resisted. And if any officer of the church of Christ shall out of baseness yield to the command of the prince, to the danger of the church, and souls committed to his charge, the souls that perish (notwithstanding the prince's command) shall be laid to his charge.

If so, then I rejoin thus: how agree these truths of this similitude with those former positions, viz., that the civil magistrate is keeper of both tables, that he is to see the church do her duty, that he ought to establish the true religion, suppress and punish the false, and so consequently must discern, judge, and determine what the true gathering and governing of the church is, what the duty of every minister of Christ is, what the true ordinances are, and what the true administrations of them; and where men fail, correct, punish, and reform by the civil sword? I desire it may be answered in the fear and presence of Him whose eyes are as a flame of fire, if this be not (according to the similitude, though contrary to their scope in proposing of it) to be governor of the ship of the church, to see the master, pilot, and mariners do their duty, in setting the course, steering the ship, trimming the sails, keeping the watch etc., and where they fail, to punish them; and therefore, by undeniable consequence, to judge and determine what their duties are, when they do right, and when they do wrong: and this not only in manifest error, (for then they say every passenger may reprove) but in their ordinary course and practice.

The similitude of a physician obeying the prince in the body politic, but prescribing to the prince concerning the prince's body, wherein the prince (unless the physician manifestly err) is to be obedient to the physician, and not to be judge of the physician in his art, but to be ruled and judged (as touching the state of his body) by the physician: I say this similitude and many others suiting with the former of a ship, might be alleged to prove the distinction of the civil and spiritual estate, and that according to the rule of the Lord Jesus in the gospel, the civil magistrate is only to attend the calling of the civil magistracy concerning the bodies and goods of the subjects, and is himself (if a member of the church and within) subject to the power of the Lord Jesus therein, as any member of the church is, 1 Cor. v. ° ° °

Peace. We have now (dear Truth) through the gracious hand of God, clambered up to the top of this our tedious discourse.

Truth. Oh! 'tis mercy unexpressible that either thou or I have had so long a breathing time, and that together!

Peace. If English ground must yet be drunk with English blood, oh! where shall Peace repose her wearied head and heavy heart?

Truth. Dear Peace, if thou find welcome, and the God of peace miraculously please to quench these all-devouring flames, yet where shall Truth find rest from cruel persecutions?

Peace. Oh! will not the authority of holy scriptures, the commands and declarations of the Son of God, therein produced by thee, together with all the lamentable experiences of former and present slaughters, prevail with the sons of men (especially with the sons of peace) to depart from the dens of lions, and mountains of leopards, and to put on the bowels (if not of Christianity, yet) of humanity each to other?

Truth. Dear Peace, Habakkuk's fishes[1] keep their constant bloody game of persecutions in the world's mighty ocean; the greater taking, plund'ring, swallowing up the lesser. Oh! happy he whose portion is the God of Jacob! who hath nothing to lose under the sun; but hath a state, a house, an inheritance, a name, a crown, a life, past all the plunderers', ravishers', murderers' reach and fury!

Peace. But lo! Who's there?

Truth. Our sister *Patience,* whose desired company is as needful as delightful. 'Tis like the wolf will send the scattered sheep in one: the common pirate gather up the loose and scattered navy: the slaughter of the witnesses by that bloody beast unite the Independents and Presbyterians.

The God of peace, the God of truth, will shortly seal this truth, and confirm this witness, and make it evident to the whole world,—

THAT THE DOCTRINE OF PERSECUTION FOR CAUSE OF CONSCIENCE, IS MOST EVIDENTLY AND LAMENTABLY CONTRARY TO THE DOCTRINE OF CHRIST JESUS, THE PRINCE OF PEACE. AMEN.

1644

[1] Habakkuk i.13-17.

ANNE BRADSTREET [1612–1672]

IN A BRIEF AUTOBIOGRAPHY, Anne Bradstreet wrote: "After a short time I changed my condition and was marryed, and came into this country, where I found a new world and new manners, at which my heart rose. But after I was convinced it was the way of God, I submitted to it and joined the church at Boston." Her condition had indeed changed in many ways. Her father was Thomas Dudley, steward to the Earl of Lincoln, in whose elegant and literate estates she was raised; he became one of the leaders of the Great Migration and would alternate with John Winthrop in the governorship of Massachusetts Bay. Her husband, Simon Bradstreet, for a time assisted Dudley in England, and eventually became governor of the Bay himself. Coming to America in 1630 must have been a severe blow to a girl of gentle expectations. Farm life at Ipswich and then Andover gave her time to explore the meaning of her fortunes; she put that time to good use, writing poems of such merit that her brother-in-law took some of them to England for publication, without her knowledge.

In 1650 the poems appeared in London as *The Tenth Muse Lately Sprung Up in America. Or Several Poems, Compiled with Great Variety of Wit and Learning, etc.,* a title she would certainly not have chosen herself. The volume consisted primarily of "quarternions," semi-dramatic pieces dealing with the four elements, the four humours, the four ages of man, and the four seasons of the year. She also versified the history of the four monarchies of the ancient world, most of this work completed before 1643. Well publicized and well received, the poems deserved the efforts at revision that Mistress Bradstreet gave them in time stolen from the raising of eight children and the duties of the wife of a man of public affairs—and against carping tongues that thought a woman's hand more suited to the needle than the pen. Until around 1666 she worked at a second edition, adding yet other poems, but it was not published until after her death as *Several Poems Compiled with Great Variety of Wit and Learning, Full of Delight.* The full range of her writing was not available until the 1867 edition of her *Works* by John Harvard Ellis, from which the texts of the following selections are taken.

Mistress Bradstreet was a studiedly literary poet, rarely original, and never spontaneous. A great admirer of Joshua Sylvester's translation of Guillaume Salluste DuBartas' *Divine Weeks and Works* (an admiration shared by Sidney and Milton), of Francis Quarles, Sir Philip Sidney, and Sir Walter Raleigh, she sought to celebrate and emulate these poets by employing the conventions of the kind of poetry they wrote. Such imitation often led her into dull didacticism and sterile artifice, but it also made possible more ambitious poetic attempts than would otherwise have come about, supporting by tradition what otherwise might have become mere doggerel. And Anne Bradstreet's personal warmth, attention to the homely details of daily life, and sensitivity to the beauties of her frontier surroundings often enough emerge to evince her genuine poetic feeling.

Further reading: *Works,* ed. J. H. Ellis, 1867, 1932. A chapter in S. E. Morison, *Builders of the Bay Colony,* 1930, 1962.

The Author to Her Book

When Chaucer wrote his famous envoy to *Troilus and Criseyde* beginning "Go, litel bok, go, litel myn tragedye"—following Statius and perhaps Boccaccio—he spawned countless similar poems by poets from Lydgate to Skelton and Spenser. Mistress Bradstreet's adaptation, presumably composed after she finally abandoned her attempts to bring her collection of poems into "better dress," masters the convention without sacrificing her own individuality and wry humor.

Thou ill-formed offspring of my feeble brain,
Who after birth did'st by my side remain,
Till snatcht from thence by friends, less wise then
    true,
Who thee abroad, exposed to public view,
Made thee in rags, halting to th' press to trudge, 5
Where errors were not lessened (all may judge)
At thy return my blushing was not small,
My rambling brat (in print) should "Mother" call,
I cast thee by as one unfit for light,
Thy visage was so irksome in my sight; 10
Yet being mine own, at length affection would
Thy blemishes amend, if so I could:
I washed thy face, but more defects I saw,
And rubbing off a spot, still made a flaw.
I stretcht thy joints to make thee even feet, 15
Yet still thou run'st more hobbling then is meet;
In better dress to trim thee was my mind,
But nought save homespun cloth i' th' house I find.
In this array, 'mongst vulgars mayst thou roam,

In critics hands, beware thou doth not come; 20
And take thy way where yet thou art not known,
If for thy father askt, say thou hast none:
And for thy mother, she alas is poor,
Which caused her thus to send thee out of door.

1678

The Flesh and the Spirit

"Many times," Mrs. Bradstreet confessed, "hath Satan troubled me concerning the verity of the scriptures, many times by atheism how I could know there was a God." Like other people she had her doubts, and felt herself drawn in opposite directions by the claims of two sides of human nature. For her conception of this conflict she was indebted to the eighth chapter of St. Paul's Epistle to the Romans, and for the form, to the convention of the debate, a popular form since the Middle Ages.

Although the argument is less than balanced—Flesh clearly speaks with the voice of Satan, and Spirit remains staunch in her reliance upon higher laws—one senses that this is not merely a combat of rational arguments. The ecstatic images of permanence and uncorrupted beauty, suggested by Revelation xxi.2, serve to bolster the faithful soul's principal beliefs, even in moments of doubt and temptation, indicating a special function for poetry during this period.

In secret place where once I stood
Close by the banks of lacrym flood,
I heard two sisters reason on
Things that are past, and things to come;

One Flesh was call'd, who had her eye   5
On worldly wealth and vanity;
The other Spirit, who did rear
Her thoughts unto a higher sphere.

"Sister," quoth Flesh, "what liv'st thou on—
Nothing but meditation?   10
Doth contemplation feed thee so
Regardlessly to let earth go?
Can speculation satisfy
Notion without reality?
Dost dream of things beyond the moon   15
And dost thou hope to dwell there soon?
Hast treasures there laid up in store
That all in th'world thou count'st but poor?   *SKEPTICISM OF INVISIBLE WORLD*
Art fancy sick, or turn'd a sot
To catch at shadows which are not?   20
Come, come, I'll shew unto thy sense,
Industry hath its recompense.
What canst desire, but thou mayst see
True substance in variety?
Dost honor like? Acquire the same,   25
As some to their immortal fame,
And trophies to thy name erect
Which wearing time shall ne'er deject.
For riches dost thou long full sore?
Behold enough of precious store.   30
Earth hath more silver, pearls and gold,
Then eyes can see, or hands can hold.   *EARTH'S BOUNTIFUL PLEASURES*
Affect'st thou pleasure? Take thy fill,
Earth hath enough of what you will,
Then let not go, what thou mayst find,   35
For things unknown, only in mind."

   Spirit: "Be still, thou unregenerate part,
Disturb no more my settled heart,
For I have vow'd (and so will do)
Thee as a foe, still to pursue,   40
And combat with thee will and must,   *CONSTANT BATTLE— FLESH VS. SPIRIT*
Until I see thee laid in th'dust.
Sisters we are, yea twins we be,
Yet deadly feud 'twixt thee and me;
For from one father are we not.   45
Thou by old Adam wast begot,
But my arise is from above,
Whence my dear Father I do love.
Thou speak'st me fair, but hat'st me sore,
Thy flatt'ring shews I'll trust no more.   50
How oft thy slave hast thou me made,   *FLESH → WOE*
When I believ'd what thou hast said,
And never had more cause of woe
Then when I did what thou bad'st do.
I'll stop mine ears at these thy charms,   55
And count them for my deadly harms.   *HATRED OF FLESHES PLEASURES*
Thy sinful pleasures I do hate,

Thy riches are to me no bait,
Thine honors do, nor will I love,
For my ambition lies above.   60
My greatest honor it shall be
When I am victor over thee,
And triumph shall, with laurel head,
When thou my captive shalt be led.
How I do live thou need'st not scoff,   65
For I have meat thou know'st not of;[1]
The hidden manna I do eat,[2]
The word of life it is my meat.
My thoughts do yield me more content
Then can thy hours in pleasure spent.   70
Nor are they shadows which I catch,
Nor fancies vain at which I snatch,
But reach at things that are so high,
Beyond thy dull capacity;
Eternal substance I do see,   75
With which enrichéd I would be;
Mine eye doth pierce the heavens, and see
What is invisible to thee.
My garments are not silk nor gold,
Nor such like trash which earth doth hold,   80
But royal robes I shall have on,
More glorious then the glistring sun;[3]
My crown not diamonds, pearls, and gold,
But such as angels' heads enfold.
The city where I hope to dwell,[4]   85   *THE HEAVENLY CITY DESCRIBED IN TERMS OF EARTHLY SPLENDOR*
There's none on earth can parallel:
The stately walls both high and strong,
Are made of precious jasper stone;
The gates of pearl, both rich and clear,
And angels are for porters there;   90
The streets thereof transparent gold,
Such as no eye did e'er behold.
A crystal river there doth run,
Which doth proceed from the Lamb's throne:
Of life, there are the waters sure,   95
Which shall remain for ever pure;
Nor sun, nor moon, they have no need,
For glory doth from God proceed:
No candle there, nor yet torch light,
For there shall be no darksome night.   100
From sickness and infirmity
For evermore they shall be free,
Nor withering age shall e'er come there,
But beauty shall be bright and clear.
This city pure is not for thee,   105
For things unclean there shall not be:
If I of Heaven may have my fill,
Take thou the world, and all that will."

                                              1678

The Flesh and the Spirit [1] John iv.32.
[2] Exodus xvi.15; Revelation ii.17.
[3] Revelation vi.11.
[4] For lines 85–106, cf. Revelation xxi.10–27; xxii.1–15.

Contemplations

Poetically her most fully realized accomplishment, this poem was written probably between 1660 and 1665. Stimulated by the sublime experience of a brilliant autumnal sunset, the speaker is tempted to imagine the superiority of Nature over Man, until a higher knowledge asserts the supremacy of the human soul whose nature can attain the eternal "security" of everlasting salvation. The first movement of the poem (st. 1–9) presents the effect of natural splendor upon the poet's senses, producing wonder and admiration at God's workmanship and the desire to praise the workman—the natural inclination of a rational creature. The second movement (st. 10–20) leaves sensory responses to ruminate through Fancy and Memory upon the progressive degeneracy of man and the apparent superiority of nature's regenerative powers. The third movement, by a series of emblems (st. 21–28), speculates upon the natural happiness of natural creatures, as the river, fish, and birds all express the joy of existence simply by being what they are. By contrast, the unsatisfied speaker identifies first with one, then another of these natural creatures, clearly changeable and uncertain. And this leads to a view of man as the perplexing middle-term of the universe, existing between the fish and the birds, the lower and upper regions, time and eternity, whose full destiny can only be realized in a supernatural, transcendent realm (st. 29–33).

Despite the praise this poem has received for its sensitivity to natural objects, "Contemplations" is not a nature poem. Its major subject is the mutability of all earthly existence, and it is not therefore surprising that readers will detect echoes of Donne, Herbert, and Spenser. Clearly Mrs. Bradstreet worked at this poem. The rhymes that link stanzas 11-13 show this, as does the interesting stanzaic pattern, which varies the versatile *ababcc* iambic pentameter stanza by adding an extra *c* line in hexameter. It is not accurate to call this, as some have, a modified Spenserian stanza, but the spirit of Spenser, especially of the Mutabilitie Cantos, is obvious.

1

Some time now past in the autumnal tide,
When Phoebus wanted but one hour to bed,
The trees all richly clad, yet void of pride,
Were gilded o'er by his rich golden head.
Their leaves and fruits seemed painted, but was true,   5
Of green, of red, of yellow, mixed hue;
Rapt were my senses at this delectable view.

2

I wist not what to wish, "Yet sure," thought I,
"If so much excellence abide below,
How excellent is He that dwells on high,   10
Whose power and beauty by His works we know?
Sure He is goodness, wisdom, glory, light,
That hath this under world so richly dight:
More heaven than earth was here, no winter and no night."

3

Then on a stately oak I cast mine eye,   15
Whose ruffling top the clouds seemed to aspire;
How long since thou wast in thine infancy?
Thy strength and stature, more thy years admire.
Hath hundred winters passed since thou wast born,
Or thousand since thou brak'st thy shell of horn?   20
If so, all these as nought eternity doth scorn.

4

Then higher on the glistering sun I gazed,
Whose beams was shaded by the leafy tree;
The more I looked the more I grew amazed,
And softly said, "What glory's like to thee?   25
Soul of this world, this universe's eye,
No wonder some made thee a deity;
Had I not better known, alas, the same had I.

5

"Thou as a bridegroom from thy chamber rushes
And as a strong man, joys to run a race,[1]   30
The morn doth usher thee with smiles and blushes,
The earth reflects her glances in thy face.
Birds, insects, animals, with vegetive,
Thy heart from death and dullness doth revive: 34
And in the darksome womb of fruitful nature dive.

6

"Thy swift annual and diurnal course,
Thy daily straight and yearly oblique path,
Thy pleasing fervor and thy scorching force,
All mortals here the feeling knowledge hath.
Thy presence makes it day, thy absence night,   40
Quaternal seasons caused by thy might:
Hail, creature full of sweetness, beauty, and delight!

7

"Art thou so full of glory that no eye
Hath strength thy shining rays once to behold?
And is thy splendid throne erect so high   45
As to approach it can no earthly mould?
How full of glory then must thy Creator be,
Who gave this bright light luster unto thee:
Admired, adored forever, be that majesty!"

8

Silent, alone, where none or saw or heard,   50
In pathless paths I led my wand'ring feet,
My humble eyes to lofty skies I reared,
To sing some song my mazed Muse thought meet.
My great Creator I would magnify,
That nature had thus decked liberally: 55
But ah, and ah, again, my imbecility!

9

I heard the merry grasshopper then sing,
The black-clad cricket bear a second part;

Contemplations. [1] Psalms xix.4-6.

They kept one tune and played on the same string,
Seeming to glory in their little art.   60
Shall creatures abject thus their voices raise,
And in their kind resound their Maker's praise,
Whilst I, as mute, can warble forth no higher lays?

10

When present times look back to ages past,
And men in being fancy those are dead,   65
It makes things gone perpetually to last
And calls back months and years that long since
     fled;
It makes a man more aged in conceit
Than was Methuselah or 's grandsire great[2]
While of their persons and their acts his mind doth
     treat.   70

11

Sometimes in Eden fair he seems to be,
Sees glorious Adam there made lord of all,
Fancies the apple dangle on the tree
That turned his sovereign to a naked thrall.
Who like a miscreant's driven from that place   75
To get his bread with pain and sweat of face:
A penalty imposed on his backsliding race.

12

Here sits our grandame in retired place,
And in her lap her bloody Cain new-born;[3]
The weeping imp oft looks her in the face,   80
Bewails his unknown hap and fate forlorn;
His mother sighs to think of paradise,
And how she lost her bliss to be more wise,
Believing him that was, and is, father of lies.

13

Here Cain and Abel came to sacrifice;   85
Fruits of the earth and fatlings each do bring;
On Abel's gift the fire descends from skies,
But no such sign on false Cain's offering;
With sullen hateful looks he goes his ways,   89
Hath thousand thoughts to end his brother's days,
Upon whose blood his future good he hopes to raise.

14

There Abel keeps his sheep, no ill he thinks,
His brother comes, then acts his fratricide,
The virgin earth of blood her first draught drinks,
But since that time she often hath been cloyed.   95
The wretch with ghastly face and dreadful mind
Thinks each he sees will serve him in his kind,
Though none on earth but kindred near then could
     he find.

[2] Genesis v.18–27. Adam lived 930 years; Methuselah lived
969 years; his grandfather Jared, 962 years.
[3] Genesis iv.1–16.

15

Who fancies not his looks now at the bar,   99
His face like death, his heart with horror fraught?
Nor malefactor ever felt like war
When deep despair with wish of life hath fought.
Branded with guilt and crushed with treble woes,
A vagabond to land of Nod he goes;   104
A city builds, that walls might him secure from foes.

16

Who thinks not oft upon the fathers' ages?
Their long descent, how nephews sons they saw,
The starry observations of those sages,
And how their precepts to their sons were law,
How Adam sighed to see his progeny   110
Clothed all in his black sinful livery,
Who neither guilt nor yet the punishment could fly.

17

Our life compare we with their length of days;
Who to the tenth of theirs doth now arrive?
And though thus short we shorten many ways,   115
Living so little while we are alive,
In eating, drinking, sleeping, vain delight.
So unawares comes on perpetual night
And puts all pleasures vain unto eternal flight.

18

When I behold the heavens as in their prime,   120
And then the earth, though old, still clad in green,
The stones and trees insensible of time,
Nor age nor wrinkle on their front are seen;
If winter come, and greenness then do fade,
A spring returns, and they more youthful made.   125
But man grows old, lies down, remains where once
     he's laid.

19

By birth more noble than those creatures all,
Yet seems by nature and by custom cursed;
No sooner born but grief and care makes fall
That state obliterate he had at first: 130
Nor youth nor strength nor wisdom spring again,
Nor habitations long their names retain,
But in oblivion to the final day remain.

20

Shall I then praise the heavens, the trees, the earth,
Because their beauty and their strength last longer?
Shall I wish there or never to had birth,   136
Because they're bigger and their bodies stronger?
Nay, they shall darken, perish, fade, and die,
And when unmade so ever shall they lie,
But man was made for endless immortality.   140

21

Under the cooling shadow of a stately elm
Close sat I by a goodly river's side,

Where gliding streams the rocks did overwhelm;
A lonely place, with pleasures dignified.
I once that loved the shady woods so well,   145
Now thought the rivers did the trees excel,
And if the sun would ever shine, there would I
     dwell.

22

While on the stealing stream I fixed mine eye,
Which to the longed-for ocean held its course,
I marked, nor crooks nor rubs that there did lie   150
Could hinder aught, but still augment its force:
"O happy flood," quoth I, "that holds thy race
Till thou arrive at thy beloved place,
Nor is it rocks or shoals that can obstruct thy pace!

23

"Nor is't enough that thou alone may'st slide,   155
But hundred brooks in thy clear waves do meet;
So hand in hand along with thee they glide
To Thetis' house,[4] where all embrace and greet:
Thou emblem true of what I count the best,
O could I lead my rivulets to rest,   160
So may we press to that vast mansion ever blest.

24

"Ye fish which in this liquid region bide,
That for each season have your habitation,
Now salt, now fresh, where you think best to glide,
To unknown coasts to give a visitation,   165
In lakes and ponds you leave your numerous fry,
So nature taught, and yet you know not why,
You wat'ry folk that know not your felicity.

25

"Look how the wantons frisk to taste the air,
Then to the colder bottom straight they dive;   170
Eftsoon to Neptune's glassy hall repair
To see what trade they great ones there do drive,
Who forage o'er the spacious sea-green field,
And take the trembling prey before it yield,
Whose armor is their scales, their spreading fins
     their shield."   175

26

While musing thus with contemplation fed,
And thousand fancies buzzing in my brain,
The sweet-tongued Philomel[5] perched o'er my head,
And chanted forth a most melodious strain,
Which rapt me so with wonder and delight,   180
I judged my hearing better than my sight,
And wished me wings with her a while to take my
     flight.

[4] In Greek mythology, Thetis was the chief of the Nereids
and the mother of Achilles. Her house is simply the sea.
[5] The nightingale, which is not native to America, is here
strictly a literary convention.

27

"O merry bird," said I, "that fears no snares,
That neither toils nor hoards up in thy barn,
Feels no sad thoughts, nor cruciating cares   185
To gain more good or shun what might thee harm;
Thy clothes ne'er wear, thy meat is everywhere,
Thy bed a bough, thy drink the water clear;
Reminds not what is past, nor what's to come doth
     fear.

28

"The dawning morn with songs thou dost prevent,[6]
Sets hundred notes unto thy feathered crew,   191
So each one tunes his pretty instrument
And warbling out the old, begin anew.
And thus they pass their youth in summer season,
Then follow thee into a better region,   195
Where winter's never felt by that sweet airy legion."

29

Man at the best a creature frail and vain,
In knowledge ignorant, in strength but weak,
Subject to sorrows, losses, sickness, pain,
Each storm his state, his mind, his body break;   200
From some of these he never finds cessation,
But day or night, within, without, vexation,
Troubles from foes, from friends, from dearest,
     near'st relation.

30

And yet this sinful creature, frail and vain,
This lump of wretchedness, of sin and sorrow,   205
This weather-beaten vessel wracked with pain,
Joys not in hope of an eternal morrow;
Nor all his losses, crosses, and vexation,
In weight, in frequency and long duration,
Can make him deeply groan for that divine
     translation.   210

31

The mariner that on smooth waves doth glide
Sings merrily and steers his bark with ease,
As if he had command of wind and tide,
And now become great master of the seas;
But suddenly a storm spoils all the sport,   215
And makes him long for a more quiet port,
Which 'gainst all adverse winds may serve for fort.

32

So he that faileth in this world of pleasure,
Feeding on sweets, that never bit of th' sour,
That's full of friends, of honor, and of treasure, 220
Fond fool, he takes this earth ev'n for heaven's
     bower.
But sad affliction comes and makes him see

[6] Literally, to come before or anticipate.

Here's neither honor, wealth, nor safety;
Only above is found all with security.

33

O Time, the fatal wrack of mortal things,   225
That draws oblivion's curtains over kings,
Their sumptuous monuments, men know them not,
Their names without a record are forgot,
Their parts, their ports, their pomp's all laid in th'
    dust,
Nor wit nor gold nor buildings 'scape time's rust;
But he whose name is graved in the white stone   231
Shall last and shine when all of these are gone.

                       1678

To My Dear and Loving Husband

Mrs. Bradstreet's best poems, for many readers, are the short domestic pieces, those concerning her husband, her children, her house. In them, whether she writes directly or figuratively, her thought and feeling strike us as genuine and unforced. In this poem, for instance, the first two couplets give a direct statement on the human level, the next two employ figures (gold mines, riches of the Orient, rivers), the last two give a direct statement culminating on the level of the eternal. Meaning is communicated through the simplest words, generally monosyllabic.

If ever two were one, then surely we.
If ever man were loved by wife, then thee;
If ever wife was happy in a man,
Compare with me, ye women, if you can.
I prize thy love more then whole mines of gold,   5
Or all the riches that the East doth hold.
My love is such that rivers cannot quench,
Nor ought but love from thee give recompense.
Thy love is such I can no way repay;
The heavens reward thee manifold, I pray.   10
Then while we live, in love let's so persevere,
That when we live no more, we may live ever.

Meditations

Throughout the sixteenth and seventeenth centuries, religious persons of all stations were encouraged to meditate upon man, nature, and God, and what is more, to reduce their meditations to words. In form, these meditations varied from the complex spiritual exercises of Edward Taylor, to the essays of Francis Bacon, which were also called "meditations," to the apothegms of Mrs. Bradstreet. Frequently figurative, they show Mrs. Bradstreet working to isolate ideas in language that is terse, direct, pointed, sometimes witty, but always pithy. This is the kind of writing that produces aphorisms, proverbs, and what were

known in the period as *sententii*. Of course such *sentences* were useful in contemporary compositions such as sermons, but we will find them as very quotable quotations much later, as in the sketches of Irving and the essays of Emerson and Thoreau.

8

Downy beds make drowsy persons, but hard lodging keeps the eyes open. A prosperous state makes a secure Christian, but adversity makes him consider.

9

Sweet words are like honey: a little may refresh, but too much gluts the stomach.

12

Authority without wisdom is like a heavy axe without an edge, fitter to bruise than polish.

31

Iron till it be thoroughly heated is incapable to be wrought: so God sees good to cast some men into the furnace of affliction, and then beats them on His anvil into what frame He pleases.

36

Sore laborers have hard hands, and old sinners have brawny consciences.

62

As man is called the little world, so his heart may be called the little commonwealth: his more fixed and resolved thoughts are like to inhabitants; his slight and flitting thoughts are like passengers that travel to and fro continually. Here is also the great court of justice erected, which is always kept by conscience, who is both accuser, excuser, witness and judge, whom no bribes can pervert, nor flattery cause to favor; but as he finds the evidence, so he absolves or condemns. Yea, so absolute is this court of judicature that there is no appeal from it—no, not to the court of heaven itself. For if our conscience condemn us, He also, who is greater than our conscience, will do it much more. But he that would have the boldness to go to the throne of grace to be accepted there must be sure to carry a certificate from the court of conscience, that he stands right there.

EDWARD TAYLOR [1642?–1729]

THE FINEST POET of the American seventeenth century remained unknown for more than two hundred years. Born and raised in England during the period of Puritan domination, Edward Taylor ventured to New England in 1668, where he immediately entered Harvard College. Three years later he graduated and accepted a call to minister to the frontier town of Westfield, Massachusetts. There he spent the rest of his life, bringing his vigorous intellect to bear on the concerns of that outpost in the wilderness, building its defenses against disease, Indians, civil disorder, heresy, and especially the "apostasy" of such liberal church reformers as Solomon Stoddard of Northampton.

Yet it was not in such worldly activities that Taylor's life found its focus and deepest realization, but rather in the realm of the spirit, which he explored doggedly as he prepared to administer the sacrament of the Lord's Supper (Communion). For a period of over forty years, from 1682 to 1725, he meditated the mysteries of Christ in the sacrament, uttering his pain and delight in 217 "Preparatory Meditations," in a long dramatic narrative poem called "God's Determinations," and in several miscellaneous poems. This solitary singer took great pains with his devotional poetry, seeking homely imagery, intentionally packing his lines and roughing his meters as did the English "metaphysical" poets Donne, Herbert, and Quarles. Except for a few stanzas, his poetry remained unpublished until the late 1930's, when Thomas H. Johnson recognized that the manuscript, in the possession of the Yale University Library, was a literary discovery of the first magnitude.

Taylor's poems prove that a thoroughly orthodox, even conservative, New England Puritan could write real poetry. Of course, to him a poem was less a work of art than an act of religious worship. He never ceased to marvel at the God who took on a human nature and lovingly endured death to save his Elect; the sacrament that symbolized and re-enacted that union of divine and human natures became for Taylor the occasion of both prayer and poetry. "Meditate upon the feast," he urged in his *Treatise Concerning the Lord's Supper* (1694), "its causes, its nature, its guests, its dainties, its reason, and ends: and its benefits, etc. For it carries in its nature and circumstances an umbrage, or epitomized draught of the whole grace of the gospel." The sacrament was central to almost everything he wrote; maintaining and celebrating its purity, against those who valued it less highly than he, became the major effort of his life and art.

Further reading: *Poems*, ed. D. E. Stanford, 1960; abridged edition (paperbound), 1963. Norman S. Grabo, *Edward Taylor*, 1961.

Upon a Spider Catching a Fly

Taylor gives his parable a setting, appropriately, in the world of predatory animals: spider, wasp, and fly. A spider spares a wasp, an "aspish" creature, because the wasp by nature is capable of matching the spider's stratagems. The fly is less lucky. Animals not endowed by Mother Nature with protective equipment should avoid the spider's web, for they will surely be destroyed. In like manner Hell's Spider spins his web to tangle the race of Adam, who by nature are venomous creatures also, but with this difference. In the animal world are some creatures whose protection has been built in, as it were, by Nature. The arrangement is useful, for they can expect no other salvation. Such is not so in the world of man. Though no man has power to win his own salvation, yet all are free to seek the grace of God which, when communicated, will break the spider's web and afford eternal salvation. Thus Taylor, in darting, nervous rhythms and with sharp detail, poses the issue of man's struggle, and envisions the manner by which salvation must be won. (Note prepared by Thomas H. Johnson)

Text: *The Poems of Edward Taylor*, ed. Donald E. Stanford (New Haven, 1960), which for all the poems given below follows the texts established by Thomas H. Johnson in *The Poetical Works of Edward Taylor* (New York, 1939; Princeton, 1943). For this anthology, spelling has been to some extent modernized.

Thou sorrow, venom elf.
  Is this thy play,
To spin a web out of thyself

To catch a fly?
    For why?   5

I saw a pettish wasp
    Fall foul therein:
Whom yet thy whorle pins[1] did not clasp
    Lest he should fling
        His sting.   10

But as afraid, remote
    Didst stand hereat,
And with thy little fingers stroke
    And gently tap
        His back.   15

Whereas the silly fly,
    Caught by its leg,
Thou by the throat took'st hastily,
    And 'hind the head
        Bite dead.   20

This goes to pot, that not
    Nature doth call.
Strive not above what strength hath got,
    Lest in the brawl
        Thou fall.   25

This 'fray seems thus to us:
    Hell's spider gets
His intrails spun to whipcords thus,
    And wove to nets
        And sets.   30

To tangle Adam's race
    In's stratagems
To their destructions, spoil'd, made base
    By venom things,
        Damn'd sins.   35

But mighty, gracious Lord,
    Communicate
Thy grace to break the cord; afford
    Us glory's gate
        And state.   40

We'll Nightengale sing like,
    When pearcht on high
In glory's cage, Thy glory, bright:
    And thankfully,
        For joy.   45

The Ebb and Flow

Occasionally Taylor felt that he had joined with God so
intimately that he had been "almost deified," but more
frequently he found the difference between *my* and *thy*

Upon a Spider. [1] Pins in the small flywheel of a spinning
wheel.

insurmountable. In "The Ebb and Flow," with its subtle
modification of the stanzaic form of his *Preparatory Meditations,* he captures that alternation between assurance
and doubt, spiritual heat and coldness, faith and despair,
which provides the psychological tension behind all his
poems.

When first Thou on me, Lord, wrought'st Thy sweet
        print,
    My heart was made Thy tinder box.
My 'ffections were Thy tinder in't:
    Where fell Thy sparks by drops.
Those holy sparks of heavenly fire that came   5
Did ever catch and often out would flame.

But now my heart is made Thy censer trim,
    Full of Thy golden altar's fire,
To offer up sweet incense in
    Unto Thyself intire: 10
I find my tinder scarce Thy sparks can feel
That drop out from Thy holy flint and steel.

Hence doubts out bud for fear Thy fire in me
    'S a mocking ignis fatuus,[1]
    Or lest Thine altar's fire out be,   15
        It's hid in ashes thus.
Yet when the bellows of Thy spirit blow
Away mine ashes, then thy fire doth glow.

Huswifery

This is Taylor's best-known and most frequently cited
poem. In the same form as his *Preparatory Meditations,*
"Huswifery" develops its central conceit or brief allegory
with unusual consistency. In his *Treatise Concerning the
Lord's Supper* (1694), he argued that participating in the
sacrament of the Lord's Supper, or Communion, required
an appropriate "wedden garment," as in the parable of the
wedding feast of the king's son (Matth. xxii.12). "It's such
a rich web," he maintained, "that only the gospel markets
afford; it's such a web that is only wove in the looms of
the gospel, nay, and a richer web and better huswifery it
gets not up." Evangelical righteousness is the warp and
woof of that garment; with that the poet prays in "Huswifery" to be clothed, so that he may purely and safely
partake of the sacrament.

Make me, O Lord, Thy spinning wheel complete.
    Thy holy Word my distaff make for me.
Make mine affections thy swift flyers neat,
    And make my soul Thy holy spool to be.

The Ebb and Flow. [1] A phosphorescent light seen in
marshes; it disappears when approached.

My conversation make to be Thy reel,   5
　　And reel the yarn thereon spun of Thy wheel.[1]

Make me Thy loom then, knit therein this twine:
　　And make Thy holy Spirit, Lord, wind quills:
Then weave the web Thyself. The yarn is fine.
　　Thine ordinances make my fulling mills.[2]   10
　　Then dye the same in heavenly colors choice,
　　All pink't with varnish't flowers of paradise.

Then clothe therewith mine understanding, will,
　　Affections, judgment, conscience, memory;
My words and actions, that their shine may fill   15
　　My ways with glory and Thee glorify.
　　Then mine apparel shall display before Ye
　　That I am clothed in holy robes for glory.[3]
1694?

Upon Wedlock and Death of Children

The speaker of most of Taylor's poems is not himself but a
representative saint, the personified Church, a collective
"I". "Upon Wedlock" is unusual among his poems for its
intensely personal subject and emotion. (Twice married,
Taylor was father to thirteen children.)

The "knot" of line 1 refers simply to a small plot of
flowers, but it quickly expands to include a striking range
of meanings. Common to them all is the sense of constric-
tion or tightness residing at the heart of Taylor's sense of
loss. When in the fifth stanza Taylor consoles himself for
the loss of his second child, the sentiment is touching but
acceptable. But when the fourth child also dies (l. 34),
amid "torture, vomit, screechings, groans," and again Taylor accepts the loss as God's will, we are made to feel his
anguish and resistance as he finds a tense consolation in "I
piecemeal pass to glory bright in them." Brave but bitter,
the poem shows us a truly human side of seventeenth-
century existence.

Taylor had by this time written several verse elegies for
prominent New England personages, and showed himself
the master of this form of colonial poetry. "Upon Wedlock" belongs among his finest accomplishments.

A curious knot God made in Paradise,
　　And drew it out inamled neatly fresh.
It was the true-love knot, more sweet than spice,
　　And set with all the flowers of grace's dress.

Huswifery. [1] In spinning, the *distaff* is the forked stick that
holds the wool or flax; *flyers* are the revolving arms of the
spinning wheel; the *reel* holds the finished thread; *quills* are
spindles; *fulling mills* finish or polish the cloth; and *pink't*
means decoratively perforated.
[2] Taylor here excludes the ordinance of the Lord's Supper,
referring only to those ordained to convert: hearing the Word
preached, baptism, and church membership.
[3] "It is the robe of evangelical righteousness constituting the
soul complete in the sight of God." See his *Treatise Concerning the Lord's Supper*, 1966.

It's weddens knot, that ne'er can be unti'd: 5
　　No Alexander's sword can it divide.[1]

The slips here planted, gay and glorious grow:
　　Unless an hellish breath do singe their plumes.
Here primrose, cowslips, roses, lillies blow,
　　With violets and pinks that void perfumes: 10
　　Whose beauteous leaves o'erlaid with honey dew,
　　And chanting birds chirp out sweet music true.

When in this knot I planted was, my stock
　　Soon knotted, and a manly flower outbrake.[2]
And after it my branch again did knot: 15
　　Brought out another flow'r: its sweet-breath'd
　　　　mate.
　　One knot gave one tother the tother's place.
　　Whence checkling smiles fought in each other's
　　　　face.

But oh! a glorious hand from glory came,   19
　　Guarded with angels, soon did crop this flow'r,
Which almost tore the root up of the same,
　　At that unlookt for, dolesome, darksome hour.
　　In prayer to Christ perfum'd it did ascend,
　　And angels bright did it to heaven 'tend.

But pausing on't, this sweet perfum'd my thought,
　　Christ would in glory have a flow'r, choice,
　　　　prime,   26
And having choice, chose this my branch forth
　　　　brought.
　　Lord, take't. I thank Thee, Thou tak'st ought of
　　　　mine;
　　It is my pledge in glory; part of me
　　Is now in it, Lord, glorified with Thee.   30

But praying o'er my branch, my branch did sprout,
　　And bore another manly flower, and gay,
And after that another sweet brake out,
　　The which the former hand soon got away.   34
　　But oh! the torture, vomit, screechings, groans:
　　And six weeks' fever would pierce hearts like
　　　　stones.

Grief o'er doth flow: and nature fault would find
　　Were not Thy will my spell, charm, joy, and gem:
That as I said, I say, take, Lord, they're Thine:
　　I piecemeal pass to glory bright in them.   40

Upon Wedlock. [1] Gordian. King Midas' father, tied a knot so
intricate that an oracle declared whoever undid it would rule
Asia. Alexander the Great solved the difficulty by cutting the
knot with his sword.
[2] Taylor, who first married in 1674, here mentions four
children: Samuel, who reached maturity (line 14); Elizabeth,
1676–77 (line 16); James, who also survived childhood (line
32); and Elizabeth, 1681–82 (line 33).

I joy, may I sweet flowers for glory breed,
  Whether Thou get'st them green, or lets them
    seed.
c. 1682

Preparatory Meditations

Taylor described these poems as "Preparatory Meditations before my Approach to the Lord's Supper, Chiefly upon the Doctrine preached upon the Day of Administration." Days of administration came at roughly six-week intervals; for them Taylor prepared a suitable sermon, responding to his own exhortation in poems such as these, a few titled but most of them numbered, both sermons and poems based on the same "doctrine" and both usually drawn from the same scriptural text.

What Love Is This

Taylor's great theme was the union of God with man. On one level it existed in the union of the divine nature with human nature in the "person" of Christ. But on another level, and by virtue of that original "hypostatic" union, it existed in the union of God with all the Elect souls. The sacrificing love manifested in such a union was a persistent wonder to the poet, who ever hoped to "fire the same with love," but who never, to his own mind, measured up to the task.

What love is this of Thine, that cannot be
  In Thine infinity, O Lord, confin'd,
Unless it in Thy very Person[1] see
  Infinity and finity conjoin'd?
  What! hath Thy Godhead, as not satisfi'd,
  Marri'd our manhood, making it its bride?   5

Oh, matchless love! Filling heaven to the brim!
  O'errunning it: all running o'er beside
This world! Nay, overflowing hell, wherein
  For Thine elect, there rose a mighty tide!   10
  That there our veins might through Thy Person
    bleed,
  To quench those flames, that else would on us
    feed.

Oh! that Thy love might overflow my heart!
  To fire the same with love: for love I would.
But oh! my strait'ned breast! my lifeless spark!   15
  My fireless flame! What chilly love, and cold?
  In measure small! In manner chilly! See.
  Lord, blow the coal: Thy love enflame in me.
1682

The Reflexion

The soul knows that the Lord is glorious, but by virtue of its "inkfac'd sin" can neither perceive that glory fully nor bring its "sweetness" to itself. At once then a complaint,

What Love Is This. [1]Taylor calls this joining of the divine nature with the human nature in Christ's Person the "personal union." See his *Christographia*, 1962.

an act of praise, and a petition for purifying grace, the poem's complexity is accentuated by the surprising, almost surrealistic, changes the central image of the rose undergoes. First a symbol of ultimate beauty, following Solomon, it can stand like a pearl, constitute a bundle of sunbeams, sit most unnaturally carving like the host at a meal, and finally return to its flowery nature. This strange juxtaposition of images makes it impossible to visualize literally what is described in the poem. Taylor, however, wrote in a rich tradition of emblem poems where natural objects in unnatural but symbolically appropriate relationships were usually accompanied by woodcuts or engravings that somewhat clarified the meaning of the poems.

[Canticles ii.1: I am the rose of Sharon]

Lord, art Thou at the table head above
  Meat, med'cine, sweetness, sparkling beauties, to
Enamor souls with flaming flakes of love,
  And not my trencher, nor my cup o'erflow?
  Ben't I a bidden guest? Oh! sweat mine eye: 5
  O'erflow with tears: Oh! draw thy fountains dry.

Shall I not smell thy sweet, oh! Sharon's rose?
  Shall not mine eye salute thy beauty? Why?
Shall thy sweet leaves their beauteous sweets
    upclose?
  As half asham'd my sight should on them lie?   10
  Woe's me! For this my sighs shall be in grain
  Offer'd on Sorrow's altar for the same.

Had not my soul's, Thy conduit, pipes stopt been
  With mud, what ravishment would'st Thou
    convey?
Let Grace's golden spade dig till the spring   15
  Of tears arise, and clear this filth away.
  Lord, let Thy Spirit raise my sighings till
  These pipes my soul do with Thy sweetness fill.

Earth once was Paradise of heaven below
  Till inkfac'd sin had it with poison stockt;   20
And chased this Paradise away into
  Heav'ns upmost loft, and it in glory lockt.
  But Thou, sweet Lord, hast with Thy golden key
  Unlockt the door, and made, a golden day.

Once at Thy feast, I saw Thee pearl-like stand   25
  'Tween heaven, and earth, where heaven's bright
    glory all
In streams fell on Thee, as a floodgate and,
  Like sunbeams through Thee on the world to fall.
  Oh! Sugar sweet then! My dear sweet Lord, I see
  Saints' heaven-lost happiness restor'd by Thee.   30

Shall heaven and earth's bright glory all up lie,
  Like sunbeams bundled in the sun, in Thee?
Dost Thou sit rose at table head, where I
  Do sit, and carv'st no morsel sweet for me?   34

So much before, so little now! Sprindge,[1] Lord,
Thy rosy leaves, and me their glee afford.

Shall not Thy rose my garden fresh perfume?
    Shall not Thy beauty my dull heart assail?
Shall not Thy golden gleams run through this gloom?
    Shall my black velvet mask Thy fair face veil?   40
    Pass o'er my faults: shine forth, bright sun; arise!
    Enthrone Thy rosy-self within mine eyes.
1688

The Experience

When a full sense of real communion with God occurred, "sweet though short," Taylor responded with rapturous confidence. Experiences like this gave him the assurance that he was himself among God's Elect; his delight is appropriate. The claim to be higher than the angels in the order of God's creation borders on heresy, but is carefully kept within the bounds of Puritan orthodoxy, and was asserted also by several of Taylor's contemporaries, including the famous Increase Mather.

Oh! that I always breath'd in such an air,
    As I suckt in, feeding on sweet content!
Disht up unto my soul ev'n in that prayer
    Pour'd out to God over last sacrament.
    What beams of light wrapt up my sight to find   5
    Me nearer God than e'er came in my mind?

Most strange it was! But yet more strange that shine
    Which fill'd my soul then to the brim to spy
My nature with Thy nature all divine
    Together join'd in Him that's Thou, and I.   10
    Flesh of my flesh, bone of my bone. There's run
    Thy Godhead, and my manhood in Thy Son.

Oh! that that flame which Thou didst on me cast
    Might me enflame, and lighten e'ry where.
Then heaven to me would be less at last,   15
    So much of heaven I should have while here.
    Oh! Sweet though short! I'll not forget the same.
    My nearness, Lord, to Thee did me enflame.

I'll claim my right: give place, ye angels bright.
    Ye further from the Godhead stand than I.   20
My nature is your lord; and doth unite
    Better than yours unto the Deity.
    God's throne is first and mine is next: to you
    Only the place of waiting-men is due.

Oh! that my heart, thy golden harp might be   25
    Well tun'd by glorious grace, that e'ry string
Screw'd to the highest pitch, might unto Thee
    All praises wrapt in sweetest music bring.

The Reflexion. [1] Unfold, spread out.

I praise Thee, Lord, and better praise Thee
    would,
    If what I had, my heart might ever hold.   30
1687

I Kenning Through Astronomy

In many ways the most striking of his *Preparatory Meditations*, this poem abounds in emblematic conceptions that, as Austin Warren has observed, simultaneously invite and repel visualization, in shocking imagery as God grinds and kneads Christ into the bread of life, and in packed or strong lines as they had been popularized by the English Metaphysical poets (e.g., "This fill would to the brim/ Heav'n's whelm'd-down crystal meal bowl, yea and higher").

John vi.51: I am the living bread.

I kenning through astronomy divine
    The world's bright battlement, wherein I spy
A golden path my pencil cannot line
    From that bright throne unto my threshold lie.
    And while my puzzled thoughts about it pore,   5
    I find the bread of life in't at my door.

When that this bird of paradise put in
    This wicker cage (my corpse) to tweedle praise
Had peckt the fruit forbid: and so did fling
    Away its food, and lost its golden days;   10
    It fell into celestial famine sore:
    And never could attain a morsel more.

Alas! alas! poor bird, what wilt thou do?
    This creatures' field no food for souls e'er gave:
And if thou knock at angels' doors, they show   15
    An empty barrel: they no soul bread have.
    Alas! poor bird, the world's white loaf is done,
    And cannot yield thee here the smallest crumb.

In this sad state, God's tender bowels[1] run
    Out streams of grace: and He to end all strife   20
The purest wheat in heaven, His dear-dear Son
    Grinds, and kneads up into this bread of life:
    Which bread of life from heaven down came and
        stands
    Disht on thy table up by angels' hands.   24

Did God mould up this bread in heaven, and bake,
    Which from His table came, and to thine goeth?
Doth He bespeak thee thus: "This soul bread take;
    Come, eat thy fill of this, thy God's white loaf!
    It's food too fine for angels; yet come, take
    And eat thy fill! It's heaven's sugar cake."   30

What grace is this knead in this loaf? This thing
    Souls are but petty things it to admire.

I Kenning. [1] A conventional image for pity or compassion.

Ye angels, help: this fill would to the brim
    Heav'n's whelm'd-down crystal meal bowl, yea
        and higher.   34
    This bread of life dropt in thy mouth doth cry:
    "Eat, eat me, soul, and thou shalt never die."
1688

God's Determinations

Sometime probably between 1685 and 1695, Taylor composed the thirty-five poems that he titled, collectively, *Gods Determinations Touching His Elect: and the Elects Combat in their Conversion, and Coming up to God in Christ together with the Comfortable Effects thereof.* The poem mingles lyric, dramatic, narrative, and meditative modes in tracing man's fall, God's plan to redeem him, man's futile attempts to resist God's grace, and his success, with the help of Christ and the saints, against the accusations of a Satanic conscience, until in the last six lyrics he joyously enters the church and ecstatically rises to partake of the royal feast God has prepared for him.

The Preface

The questions put to Job by the Lord had become a classical *locus* or set-piece for writers in Taylor's time. The freshness of Taylor's treatment lies in his various allusions to human crafts (lathe, bellows, furnace, mould, etc.), which serve to contrast the diminutive capacities of man with the boundless creative power that "spake all things from nothing." Even as he praises God's handiwork, the poet relies upon inadequate, diminishing terms that reduce creation to a pretty trinket or a toy, and so reveals the incapacity of man to appreciate the grandeur of God's accomplishment. Thereby he shows man's weakness and his reliance—unconscious though it may be—upon God, the main theme of the whole of *God's Determinations.* Taylor builds the poem from a series of contrasts between *all* and *nothing,* and indeed it is an all-or-nothing proposition that faces fallen man in the ensuing poems.

    Infinity, when all things it beheld
In nothing, and of nothing all did build,
Upon what base was fixt the lathe, wherein
He turn'd this globe, and riggall'd[1] it so trim?
Who blew the bellows of His furnace vast?   5
Or held the mould wherein the world was cast?
Who laid its corner stone? Or whose command?
Where stand the pillars upon which it stands?
Who lac'd and fillitted the earth so fine,
With rivers like green ribbons smaragdine?[2]   10
Who made the seas its selvedge, and it locks
Like a quilt ball within a silver box?
Who spread its canopy? Or curtains spun?
Who in this bowling alley bowled the sun?
Who made it always when it rises set   15
To go at once both down, and up to get?

The Preface. [1] Grooved.
[2] Emerald.

Who th'curtain rods made for this tapestry?
Who hung the twinkling lanthorns in the sky?[3]
Who? who did this? or who is He? Why, know
It's only Might Almighty this did do.   20
His hand hath made this noble work which stands
His glorious handiwork not made by hands.
Who spake all things from nothing; and with ease
Can speak all things to nothing, if He please.
Whose little finger at His pleasure can   25
Outmete ten thousand worlds with half a span;
Whose might almighty can by half a looks
Root up the rocks and rock the hills by th'roots.
Can take this mighty world up in His hand,
And shake it like a squitchen or a wand,   30
Whose single frown will make the heavens shake
Like as an aspen leaf the wind makes quake.
Oh! what a might is this! Whose single frown
Doth shake the world as it would shake it down?
Which all from nothing fet,[4] from nothing, all: 35
Hath all on nothing set, lets nothing fall.
Gave all to nothing man indeed, whereby
Through nothing man all might Him glorify.
In nothing then embosst the brightest gem
More precious than all preciousness in them.   40
But nothing man did throw down all by sin:
And darkened that lightsome gem in him.
    That now his brightest diamond is grown
    Darker by far than any coalpit stone.

The Glory of and Grace in the Church Set Out

In imagery very like that of "Upon Wedlock and Death of Children," Taylor here (near the end of *God's Determinations*) shows the soul who has now accepted her conversion the blessings of being joined to the church. The versatile stanzaic pattern suggests his knowledge of George Herbert, while the refrain inescapably reminds one of John Donne's "A Hymn to God the Father."

    Come now behold
  Within this knot what flowers do grow:
    Spangled like gold:
  Whence wreaths of all perfumes do flow.
Most curious colors of all sorts you shall   5
With all sweet spirits scent. Yet that's not all.

    Oh! Look, and find
  These choicest flowers most richly sweet
    Are disciplin'd
  With artificial angels meet.   10
An heap of pearls is precious: but they shall
When set by art excel. Yet that's not all.

    Christ's Spirit showers
  Down in His Word, and sacraments

[3] Lines 1–18 are based upon "The Voice from the Whirlwind," Job xxxviii.1–41.
[4] An old form of "fetched."

Upon these flowers,
  The clouds of grace divine contents.
Such things of wealthy blessings on them fall
As make them sweetly thrive. Yet that's not all.   15

   Yet still behold!
All flourish not at once. We see   20
  While some unfold
Their blushing leaves, some buds there be.
Here's faith, hope, charity in flower, which call
On yonders in the bud. Yet that's not all.

   But as they stand   25
Like beauties reeching in perfume
  A divine hand
Doth hand them up to glory's room:
Where each in sweet'ned songs all praises shall
Sing all o're heaven for aye. And that's but all.   30

The Joy of Church Fellowship Rightly Attended

This is the last poem of *God's Determinations*. The saints, now fully convinced of their salvation and joying in their church membership ("in Christ's coach"), soar heavenward. Some backslide and must be retuned to become "more melodious"; others who were predetermined to be saved, but were kept from church membership, trudge toward glory rather than ride. But all raise their uncontainable joy in song, an apt emblem of Taylor's own sense of poetic motive and purpose.

In heaven soaring up, I dropt an ear
  On earth: and oh! sweet melody!

And listening, found it was the saints who were
  Encoacht for heaven that sang for joy.
For in Christ's coach they sweetly sing,   5
  As they to glory ride therein.

Oh! joyous hearts! Enfir'd with holy flame!
  Is speech thus tasseled with praise?
Will not your inward fire of joy contain,
  That it in open flames doth blaze?   10
  For in Christ's coach saints sweetly sing,
  As they to glory ride therein.

And if a string do slip, by chance, they soon
  Do screw it up again: whereby
They set it in a more melodious tune   15
  And a diviner harmony.
  For in Christ's coach they sweetly sing,
  As they to glory ride therein.

In all their acts, public, and private, nay
  And secret too, they praise impart.   20
But in their acts divine, and worship, they
  With hymns do offer up their heart.
  Thus in Christ's coach they sweetly sing,
  As they to glory ride therein.

Some few not in; and some whose time and place
  Block up this coach's way, do go   26
As travelers afoot:[1] and so do trace
  The road that gives them right thereto;
  While in this coach these sweetly sing
  As they to glory ride therein.   30

Joy of Church Fellowship. [1]Those elect souls who through various circumstances did not have access to church membership.

THOMAS HOOKER [1586–1647]

AMONG PREACHERS of his time, only two rivaled Thomas Hooker in respect and significance—John Cotton, and Hooker's son-in-law Thomas Shepard. Of the three, Shepard has come to represent the spirit of Puritan devotional preaching and writing, while Cotton and Hooker have vied for pre-eminence as architects of New England's social and ecclesiastical thought. Hooker's definitions of the ruling concepts of law, nature, and reason in *A Survey of the Summe of Church Discipline* (1648) have led to a view of Hooker as arch-defender of New England church polity, preacher of the covenant or federal theology, and powerful if inadvertent prophet of democratic principles. But these activities were all part of a later phase of his ministry.

  Born in England of middle-class folk, Hooker took his B.A. at Puritan-dominated Emmanuel College, Cambridge, in 1608, his M.A. in 1611. He remained at Cambridge as a tutor until 1618, served as rector of a small community in Surrey until 1320, then became lecturer and assistant minister in Chelmsford, Essex, in 1626. Complaints soon reached his ecclesiastical superiors that he was becoming a dangerously popular preacher, and in 1630 the High Commission arrested him for nonconformity. On the advice of friends who posted bond for him, Hooker escaped to Holland. In 1633 he contrived to sail to New England, where he became pastor of the church of Cambridge. In 1636, with the reluctant approval of Massachusetts Bay officials, he took his congregation to the Connecticut Valley, establishing the new colony of Hartford.

Despite his active involvement in colony affairs, the key to his preaching was not basically political; it was spiritual. Its main endeavor was to spell out and clarify God's plan to redeem fallen and unworthy mankind, and to urge upon men the necessity of coming into an intimate and right relationship with the Lord. God redeemed men by the free distribution of His grace; and while Hooker did not believe that men could earn that grace, he differed from Calvin in arguing that men are obliged to prepare themselves for it. In a series of beautifully written treatises, he taught in practical terms the advantages of self-examination, prayer, and meditation, rigorously intellectual exercises that always involved verbal expression. These spiritual directives began appearing as early as 1632, but Hooker assembled them shortly before his death in the only book he authorized for publication—*The Application of Redemption, By the effectual Work of the Word, and Spirit of Christ, for the bringing home of lost Sinners to God* (London, 1656, 1659).

The scheme of redemption is there stated amply, and in the portion devoted to making ready "a people prepared," Hooker urges the importance of a powerful ministry whose force lies in plain and vigorous preaching. Not only does he teach what was for Puritans an ideal style, he embodies it. Rich in invention of analogies and metaphors, teeming with earthy and commonplace details, terse, pointed, tough-minded, and spiritual—hard talk to crack stubborn spirits—Hooker's style reflects a realistic and practical aesthetic that would mark American writing well beyond his time.

Further reading: Moses C. Tyler, *A History of American Literature*, 1878, 1949. Norman Pettit, *The Heart Prepared*, 1966.

A Plain and Powerful Ministry

Most Puritan preachers believed that the conversion Taylor wrote about came from "hearing the Word preached" and from no other source. Even so, it did not reside in the rhetorical skill of the preacher, but in the mysterious power of grace working through the sermon. For that reason Puritans avoided originality in preaching and subscribed to a set form.

The preacher first read a text (in Hooker's case here, from Luke i.17, "to make ready a people prepared for the Lord"), which he then explicated or "opened" to yield a concise, tersely stated truth called the "doctrine." The doctrine was then proved by a number of reasons, and then the proved doctrine was applied in the "application" or "uses," which normally concluded with an "exhortation" or call to the congregation to accept the truth thus preached.

The advantage of so rigid a form was that the preacher's audience always knew exactly where he was in the sermon; the gain in clarity more than compensated for what was lost of surprise and ingenuity. Hooker's sermon demonstrates that even while his literary judgments are secondary and indirect, they are not insignificant. He is concerned here with the relationships among art (eloquence), language, and truth, as Poe, Emerson, and James will later be. The Bible in this context functions as a *literary* standard as well as a religious authority. In acknowledging the importance of human affections, Hooker counters the popular myth that emotion and beauty had no place in Puritan thought, and his recognition that souls can be deluded by words testifies to a faith in the power of language that was widely shared in the seventeenth century. Even the predominant images of building, carpentry, and houses will emerge in new contexts in the work of Hawthorne, Emerson, and Thoreau. Hooker's is a strong case for the plain businesslike prose that will be fashioned by Franklin and others into a distinctive American language.

Text: The first edition of *The Application of Redemption* (London, 1656).

[Doctrine:] *A plain and powerful ministry, is the only ordinary means to prepare the heart soundly for Christ.*

Hence it is, when our Savior would have this work done, he prepares a workman fit for it, and furnisheth him with abilities, which might enable him to the discharge thereof; the work is great, and the service difficult, and therefore Elias is fitted with a spirit suitable with power answerable unto that purpose for which he was appointed, an instrument as we say for the nonce. John the Baptist he also inherits these abilities, and that minister must be an Elias, i.e., must have his spirit and power in proportion, if ever this great work of preparation followeth his hand with comfort and success. As it was in the material, so also is it in the building of "this spiritual temple, in which the Holy Ghost doth dwell": the Elect of God are like trees of righteousness, the Word is like the axe, that must be lifted by a skillful and strong arm of a cunning minister, who like a spiritual artificer must hew and square, and take off the knotty untowardness in the soul before we can come to couch close and settle upon the Lord Christ as the cornerstone: Paul calls the saints "God's husbandry," I *Cor.* 3.9. A powerful humbling ministry is like the plow, to "plow up the fallow ground, the thorny" sensual hearts of sinful men to receive "the immortal seed of the word of promise" and the spirit of Christ thereby.

For the opening of the point two things are to be attended.

1. What is meant by a plain and powerful ministry, such as that of Elias.

2. How this hath force to effect so great a work.

1. The plainness of the ministry appears, when the language and words are such as those of the meanest capacity have some acquaintance with, and may be able to conceive; when the preacher accommodates his speech to the shallow understanding of the simplest hearer, so far as in him lies, always avoiding the frothy tinkling of quaint and far-fetched phrases, which take off, and blunt as it were the edge of the blessed truth and Word of God. Therefore the Apostle[1] rejects "the wisdom of words" as that which makes the cross of Christ; that is, the doctrine of Christ crucified, revealed in the Gospel, to lose his proper and powerful effect when it is so preached; where let it be observed that it is not only the vanity and emptiness of words which is here condemned, but even that pompous gaudiness, and elegancy of speech, which after an unsuspected manner steals away the mind and affection from the truth, and stays it with itself, when it should be a means both to convey both attention and affection from itself to the truth. He that puts so much sugar into the potion, that he hinders the strength, and the work of it by such a kind of mixture; though he please the palate of the patient, yet thereby he wrongs both the physic, and his health. So here in preaching.

For the excellency of eloquence, and enticing words of human wisdom which in case were commendable to be used by him who is an orator, or a declaimer in the school,[2] in the pulpit becomes ever fruitless, and many times hurtful and prejudicial to the saving success of the Gospel. Hence the Apostle

[1] St. Paul.
[2] Declamations were customary school and college exercises which all students performed.

makes these as opposite, II *Cor.* 2.4: "My speech and my preaching was not with enticing words of man's wisdom, but in the demonstration of the spirit and of power": taking this for granted, as it appears in manner of the speech, the pomp of enticing words must not be discovered if we would have the spirit in the powerful work of it be demonstrated and made to appear; so much sweetness of words as may make way for the efficacy of the Gospel, may be admitted, and no more. And as all kind of curiosity and niceness is to be avoided, so all obscure and unusual phrases, dark sentences and expressions, strange languages are much more to be rejected, as opposite even to the end of speaking, much more to plainness of the preaching of the truth. Words are appointed by God in His providence, to be carriers as it were, by whose help the thoughts of our minds and the savory apprehensions of truth may be communicated, and conveyed over to the understanding of others, whereas by mystical and dark sentences he that comes to hear can by no means profit, because he cannot conceive, and so both hearer and speaker must needs miss their end, and lose their labor, since the one doth no good in his speech, because he so speaks that the other can receive no benefit. He that hath a pastoral heart must be so affected in dispensing the doctrine of grace, as Paul was in writing, *Rom.* 1.7, to all that are, "to all that be at Rome," so should he labor to reach out mercy and comfort to every soul in the congregation, by every sentence he delivers, as much as in him lies, whereas mystical cloudy discourses which exceed the capacity and understanding of most in the assembly, it's not possible they should work powerfully upon their consciences. That which the mind conceives not, the heart affects not: ministers should be, and, if faithful they will be as nurses to the people: they will prepare milk for the meanest and weakest, and meat for all, but never give dry crust or stones instead of bread to any; for that was not to feed, but to starve the child. Hence the Apostle concludes strange languages in the delivery of the truth, to be a curse sent of God upon a people, and therefore the minister that so communicates the Word, he is the messenger that brings a curse to the congregation, I *Cor.* 14.21, 22: "In the Law it is written, with men of other tongues and other lips, will I speak unto this people, wherefore tongues are for a sign not to them that believe, but to them that believe not": whereas prophesying should be in that openness and familiarity of language, that the unbelieving, yea, "unlearned should be convinced, and have the secrets of his heart made manifest to his own conscience," that so he may be truly humbled and acknowledge God's power and presence in the virtue of His own ordinance blessed by Him, I *Cor.* 14.24. It was the complaint of God, *Job* 38.2, "that counsel was darkened by words without knowledge." It was not allowed in Job's conference and debate of questions with his friends, it cannot but be much more condemned in publishing the mysteries of life and salvation to others. It's the scope of the calling and work of the ministry "to give the knowledge of God in the face of Jesus Christ," II *Cor.* 4.8. To darken knowledge therefore, is to cross God's honor, our own callings, the comforts of the people over whom we set, and to be concealers of God's mind, not interpreters and revealers of His will.

Objection: There is only one plea here objected, that carries any appearance of likelihood with it, gathered out of *Eccles.* 12.10, where it is said, "The preacher sought to find out acceptable words, and that that was written, was upright, even words of truth": was it Solomon's care directed by the spirit to study pleasing words to affect his hearers? Should not his practice be a pattern to all to imitate him in like expressions? Dare any affirm but that he did what he ought? And shall any be so careless or presumptuous as not to endeavor to follow that course recorded with so much commendation by the Holy Ghost?

Answer: I yield willingly to all the truths which the text holds out unto us; but it shall appear that nothing from thence by just consequence be collected, that will cross, but rather confirm, and that undoubtedly what hath been affirmed before. That the writings of men should be sound, their speeches acceptable, is granted; but when are they? How shall they be judged to be such? That's the doubt: which once cleared, the objection will be answered fully. Words then must be judged acceptable, not by the foolish fancies, corrupt and carnal humors of men, but from the warrant they have from the scripture, and the work they have in the hearers for their good, as the 11 verse of *Eccles.* 12 discovers; it being added as it were by way of explication, to evidence where that pleasantness of speech lay, "The words of the wise are as goads and nails fastened by the masters of assemblies which are given by one shepherd," as though the preacher should have expressed himself, more freely and fully thus. If any shall ask what these acceptable words formerly mentioned are, and how they may be discerned, it is easy for any thus to know them: by their working upon the heart, as we judge the goodness and virtue of physic by its working upon the body, or in the stomach. Those words which are as goads to awaken and spur on the sluggish and sleepy hearted to the performance of service with greater cheerfulness and speed: those that are as nails to fasten on the precious truths of God, upon the consciences of men, that they are kept within the compass of God's command as sheep within the fold.

Lastly, those words which are indited and taught

not by "human wisdom, but by the spirit of Christ," I *Cor.* 2.4, who is the only chief shepherd of his church, and whose voice should only be heard: such words should be sought out by the speaker, such words deserve to be accounted acceptable by those who hear them. Now how far all quaintness and darkness of speech is from this warrant of the Lord, or this powerful work in the hearts of His people, let the sluggish and secure courses, the loose lives and conversations of such persons, parishes, places, and congregations, who have, and love such teachers, and such kind of teaching, proclaim and testify to all the world.

2. Plainness of preaching, appears also in the matter that is spoken: when sin and sinners are set out in their native and natural colors, and carry their proper names, whereby they may be owned suitable to the loathsomeness that is in them, and the danger of those evils which are their undoubted reward: a spade is a spade, and a drunkard is a drunkard, &c, and if he will have his sins, he must and shall have hell with them. It's Satan's policy (who painter or tyre-maker[3] like, cozens all the world with colors) to smut and disfigure the beautiful ways of godliness, and the glorious graces of the spirit, with the soot and dirt of reproaches, and base nick-names: sincerity, he terms singularity; exactness, puritanism and hypocrisy; and so ignorant men (who judge the person by the picture) are brought out of love and liking with those blessed ways of wisdom and holiness. Contrariwise, when he would cast a veil over the ugly and deformed face of Vice, and graceless courses, he is forced to lay some false colors of indifferency, delight, and pleasure: drunkenness is good fellowship, and neighborhood; covetousness comes masked under the vizard of frugality and moderation; cowardliness is trimmed and decked up in the robes of discretion, and wariness. If ministers will not be the devil's brokers, and followers, their manner of proceeding must be expressly contrary. When they come to preach, they must make sin appear truly odious, and fearful to the open view of all, that all may be afraid and endeavor to avoid it. Those secret wipes, and witty jerks, and nips at sin, at which the most profane are pleased, but not reformed, are utterly unsavory and unseeming the place, the person, the office, of the messenger of the Lord of Hosts. What! A minister a jester! O fearful! to make the pulpit a stage, to play with sin, when he should terrify the conscience for it? The Lord abominates the practice; he that knows and fears the Lord should abhor it with detestation. Thus plainly dealt Elias with Ahab, I *Kings* 18.13: "It's thou and thy father's house that have troubled Israel, because ye have forsaken the commandments

[3]A maker of head-dresses.

of the Lord, and followed Baalim." So also with Israel, I *Kings* 18.21: "How long will you halt between two opinions? If the Lord be God, follow Him; but if Baal, then follow him." As if he should have said, away with this patching in profession, either a saint or a devil, make something of it; this is downright dealing. And thus plainly John the Baptist who had the same spirit dealt with Herod. He doth not beat the bush, and go behind the door to tell him his faults, and mince the matter with some intimations, but he speaks out, *Matt.* 14.4: "It is not lawful for thee to have thy brother Philip's wife": either thou must not have that incestuous harlot, or thou must not have grace and glory. Thus again he dealt with the Sadducees and Pharisees when he saw them come to his baptisms. He says to them, *Matt.* 3.7, "Oh ye generation of vipers, who hath forewarned you to flee from the wrath to come?" As if he should have said, eggs and birds, parents and posterity, you are a race of venomous, and poisonful wretches. What? A proud Pharisee to listen to the simplicity of the doctrine of grace, is it possible? If in sincerity and good earnest, you purpose to embrace the doctrine of truth, "bring forth then fruits worthy of amendment of life," verse 8.

We have done with the plainness of the ministry, we are now to inquire wherein the power of a ministry consists: and that appears in two things.

1. There must be soundness of argument, and undeniable evidence of reason out of the Word, which is able to command the conscience; such strength of truth, which like a mighty stream, may carry an understanding hearer. When the Apostle was to come amongst the slanting orators and silken doctors of Corinth, which so excelled in eloquence, he brings the trial of their ministry unto this touch, I *Cor.* 4. 19, 20: "I will know not the speech of them that are puffed up, but the power, for the kingdom of God stands not in word, but in power." It's not the flourishes of words, not the sound and tinkling of a company of fine sentences, like apish toys and rattles, that will commend our ministry in the account of God; there is no kingdom, no power of the work of the spirit; the heavenly majesty of an ordinance is not seen in such empty shells and shadows. A building with painted walls, and no pillars, would be of little use, and less continuance. A body framed out of colors, may be a picture of a bird or beast, but a living creature it cannot be, because it wants the soul and substance which should give life and virtue thereunto. So it is when a multitude of gay sentences are packed together without the sinews and substance of convicting arguments: there may be the picture of a sermon, but the life and power of preaching there will not be in any such expressions.

That a minister may be powerful, an inward heat of heart, and holy affection is required, answerable and suitable to the matter, which is to be communicated; and those add great life and force to the delivery of the truth. "Out of the abundance of the heart the mouth speaks, and a good man out of the good treasure of his heart, brings forth good things," *Matt.* 12.35. Where then there is a heart awanting, the chiefest part of speech, the pith and heart of it is gone; for the several affections out of which the words arise, make an impression, and work a like temper of spirit in him to whom we utter and express ourselves. Thus we speak from heart to heart, and that is the best way to be in the bosom of the hearer, and the only way to make our words take place and prevail. He that mourns in speaking of sin, makes another mourn for sin committed. An exhortation that proceeds from the heart, carries a kind of authority and commission with it, to make way for itself not to return before it confer with the heart of him that will give attendance to it. Brainish discourses talk only with the understanding, they go no further, because they rise no deeper then from the understanding of him that speaks. The doctrine of the Gospel "is like the rain upon the herbs, and the dew upon the grass," *Deut.* 32.2. The strength and stirring of holy affections is like a mighty wind or tempest, makes the truth delivered to press in with more power and speed, and to soak in more deeply, even to the heart root of him that with meekness will receive it.

2. It may be here inquired for explication of the point: how a ministry thus plain and powerful doth work? *Answer:* To speak only so much here as concerns the place, leaving particulars until we entreat of the several parts of preparation, know we must, the preparing work of a plain and powerful ministry stands in two things.

1. It discovers the secrets of sin, makes known the close passages of the soul to itself, and that in the ugliness thereof, *Heb.* 4.11: "The Word of God is mighty in operation, sharper than any two-edged sword, divides betwixt the soul and the spirit, and is a discerner of the thoughts and intents of the heart." This was the work that Paul aimed at in the dispensation of the Gospel, II *Cor.* 4.4: "Handling the Word of God, not deceitfully, but plainly, by manifestation of the truth, he commended himself to every man's conscience in the sight of God." As though he had said, speak O ye blessed saints of Corinth, was not Paul in your bosom? Did he not ransack every corner of your consciences? Certainly you cannot but acknowledge it, your hearts dare not but confess as much.

2. A lively ministry over-powers the corruption, and sets an awe upon the spirits of such to whom the Word is spoken and blessed. The stout soldiers, the refuse publicans, all stoop and stand amazed at the

ministry of John, *Luke* 3.11, 12. They all said, "Master, what shall we do?" Paul a prisoner at the bar, makes Faelix (the judge upon the bench) to tremble. Hence it is, the time of the discovery of the Gospel is called "the great and dreadful day of the Lord," *Mal.* 4.5. Hence that of the Apostle, II *Cor.* 10.5: "The weapons of our warfare" (that is, the powerful ministry of the Word) "are mighty through God, to pull down strongholds, to cast down imaginations, to captivate every high thought to the obedience of Christ."

Therefore our Savior, the "chief master of the assemblies," is said to speak with "authority, not as the scribes," *Matt.* 7. last. Not to tell a man a sleepy tale, a toothless, sapless discourse, so that the hearers when they are gone, are never stirred, never troubled for their sins, nor quickened onward in obedience: but when the power of the spirit, the presence and majesty of the Lord Christ, appears in His ordinances, they then carry authority with them and bear down all before them: "Satan falls like lightning," forsakes his hold, and the stoutest heart is forced to give way to the government of the King of saints. Strong physic either cures or kills, either takes away the disease, or the life of the patient; so it is with a spiritual and powerful ministry, it will work one way or other, either it humbles or hardens, converts or condemns those that live under the stroke thereof. For observe we must, that the Word is but an instrument in the hand of Christ, who dispenseth the same according to his good pleasure, and the counsel of his own will, working when, and upon whom he will, and what he will by it. The sword in the hand of him that wields it may as easily kill as defend another, answerable to the affection of him that strikes therewith. It is so with the Word which is the sword of the spirit. It is the savor of life unto life, but then and to those only to whom the Lord will bless the same; and the savor of death unto death, then and unto those when such a blessing is denied.

USE 1. Such as be ministers may hence see the reason, of that little success we find, that little good we do, in the vineyard of the Lord: our pains prosper not, our preaching prevails not, with the hearts of men; not one mountain leveled, not a crooked piece squared, not one poor soul prepared for a Christ, after many months, quarters, years traveling[4] in the work of the ministry.

The time was "Satan fell like lightning, suddenly," speedily, when the disciples of Christ "as sons of thunder," delivered the Gospel in the power and demonstration of the spirit. But now Satan stands up in his full strength, takes up his stand, maintains his hold in the hearts of men, notwithstanding all that we commonly see done by the most. What is the

⁴Travailing?

reason? God is as merciful as ever, His Word and ordinances as effectual as ever they were: I need not inquire as he, "Where is the Lord God of Elias?" No, Brethren, I must rather ask, "Where is the spirit and power of Elias?" We want power, and spirit, and then no wonder we do not, nay, upon these terms in reason we shall never prepare a people for the Lord. The Word of God, which is the sword of the spirit, is as sharp as ever it was, but our hands are weak, our hearts are feeble, we have no courage, nor power to follow the blow, against the sturdy and base distempers of men. We keep these "shameful hidings" too much about us (condemned by the Apostle, II *Cor.* 4.2) in the course of our ministry, loath we are to offend our friends, to displease great ones, to provoke the wicked, and malicious, fear we do, lest their love should be lost, their bounty and kindness taken away, and removed, or else hazard our own earthly comforts, and contents. It's pity but the tongue of that minister should cleave to the roof of his mouth, who speaks anything less than God requires of him; for these base and by respects sometimes ministers are afraid to speak to the hearts of men, and ashamed to reprove them for those sins which they are not afraid or ashamed to do in the face of the world. Neither do ministers many times convince so soundly as they ought, nor gather in those arguments which may make those truths undeniable, and men's consciences at a stand. Again, they want that holy spiritual affection, which they should deliver God's Word withal unto His people. And this is the sum of all, ministers do not deliver the Word with a heavenly, hearty, violent affection, they do not speak "out of the abundance of their hearts." If they would speak against sin with a holy indignation, it would make men stand in awe of sin; they talk of it hourly, and say, it is not good to profane God's Name, and His sabbaths, and to live an ungodly life, but they do not speak from their hearts in this kind. A sturdy messenger if he come to a man's house to speak with him, he will not be put off, he will take no denial, but he will speak with him, if it be possible before he goes away. But send a child of a message to a man, if a servant do but tell him, his master is not at leisure, or that he may speak with him another time, he will easily be put off, and go away before he hath delivered his message. So it is with a minister that performs his office with a hearty affection. For when a man speaks from his heart in this case, he will have no answer, he will not be dallied withal, he will take no denial but will have that he came for. If a man should say he is not at leisure to speak with him, or to hear him now, he will speak with him another time, he will not go away with this answer, but he will tell him, I came to speak with your hearts, and I will speak with your hearts. He will say to the people, tell your hearts that ye love the world and the profits and pleasures thereof, (and my heart tells you) did you know the good things that are in Christ Jesus, did you but know what a happy thing it is to have assurance of God's love, you would never love sin, nor delight in wickedness, as you have done before: grieve no more for the things of the world, but for your sins. The day is coming when the heavens shall meet with fire, and you shall hear the voice of the Archangel, saying, "Arise ye dead and come to judgment." Where you shall hear that dreadful sentence, "Depart from me all ye workers of iniquity, I know you not," *Matt.* 7. 23. Oh this may be your case one day. And we that are ministers of God do mourn for you, and tell your souls, we must have sorrow from you, we came for hearts, and must have hearts before we go. And this is the first use, shewing the reason why the ministers of God do so little good. It is because this plain and powerful preaching is so much wanting.

USE 2. The second use discovereth to us the fearful estate and miserable condition of those that lived a long time under a plain and powerful ministry, and yet their hearts have not been fitted and prepared for the Lord Jesus. It is a fearful suspicion that the Lord will never bestow any saving good upon that soul. He that hath lived under a powerful ministry many years, and yet is not wrought upon thereby, it cannot certainly be concluded, but it is greatly to be suspected, that the means of grace will never profit that man. Look as it is with the master carpenter, when he hath turned every piece of timber, and taken what he will for his turn, he tells them that be under him, let this be hewed, and that be framed and made fit for the building. Afterward he finds one piece broken, and another crackt, and another knotty. Why, what says he? There is no squaring of these, they are fit for nothing but for burning; they are not fit for any place in the building. Oh! take heed, when God's ministers have been cutting, and hewing, now exhorting, now persuading, now cutting the heart with reproof, and yet finds here a crackt heart, and there a stubborn soul, that will not be squared by the Word, lest then the Lord should say, these will never be fitted and prepared for me; they are fit for nothing but the fire. Oh! take heed of it, for he that will not be fitted for grace, shall be made a firebrand in Hell forever. Therefore all you that have lived under a powerful ministry, and yet are not prepared, go home and reason with your souls, and plead with your own hearts, and say, Lord, why am not I yet humbled and prepared? Shall I thus be always under the hacking and hewing of the Word, and never be framed? Such a man, and such a man was stubborn, and wicked, and profane, and yet the Lord hath brought him home, and he is become a broken-hearted Christian. What shall I

think that am not fitted and prepared for Christ by all the means that I have had? Alas! thou mayest justly suspect God never intends good to thy soul. It is no absolute conclusion, but it is a great suspicion, that those that have lived under a plain and powerful ministry half a dozen years or longer, and have got no good, nor profited under the same, I say, it's a shrewd suspicion, that God will send them down to Hell. Therefore suspect thy own soul and say, Lord, will exhortations never prevail? Will instructions never do me any good? Will terrors, and reproofs never strike my heart? Why, I have heard sermons that would have shaken the very stones I trod on, that would have moved the seat I sat upon; the very fire of Hell hath flashed in my face, I have seen even the very plagues of Hell, I have had many exhortations, instructions, admonitions, and reproofs, and as powerful means as may be, which yet never did me any good. The Lord be merciful to such a poor soul, and turn his heart that he may lay hold of Mercy in due time.

USE 3. Exhortation. Is it so, that a plain and powerful ministry is the means of preparing the soul of a poor sinner for the Lord Jesus? Why then, when you hear the Word plainly and powerfully preached to you, labor that the Word may be so unto you as it is in itself. It is a preparing Word, labor you that it may prepare your hearts to receive Christ. And you that be hearers, everyone labor to save the soul of another; let the father speak concerning his children, and the husband concerning his wife and his family, and the wife concerning her husband. Oh, when will it once be, when will the time come that my child may be fitted for the Lord, when will it be that my poor family, my poor wife, my poor husband shall be prepared for the Lord; the Lord grant, that it may be, if not this sabbath, yet on another; if not this sermon, then at the next. Labor therefore to give way unto the Word of God, and suffer your souls to be wrought upon by it, for the Word is powerful to prepare your hearts, but the minister must hew and square your hearts before they can be prepared for the Lord Jesus, and you must "suffer the words of the exhortation" (as the Apostle says), *Heb.* 13.22. So likewise suffer the words of conviction, of reproof, of admonition, and hold and keep your hearts under the Word, that you may be wrought upon thereby. And as when men have set carpenters awork to build an house, then they come every day, and ask them, how doth the work go on? How doth the building go forward? When you are gone home, do you so reason with yourselves, and ask your own hearts how the work of the Lord goes forward in you? Is my heart yet humbled? Am I yet fitted and prepared for Christ? I thank God I find some work and power of the Word, and therefore I hope the building will go forward.

COTTON MATHER [1663–1728]

HIS FATHER, INCREASE MATHER, was pastor of the Second Church in Boston, President of Harvard, and perhaps the most powerful intellectual force in New England during his generation. One grandfather was Richard Mather, equally prestigious among first-generation ministers and author of the Cambridge Platform (1649) that established the New England Congregational way; his other grandfather was the famous John Cotton, inventor of the name "Congregational," chief adversary of Roger Williams, and the foremost architect of New England theology. It was a proud lineage, and Cotton Mather was equal to it.

He entered Harvard at twelve, took his B.A. at fifteen and his M.A. at eighteen, was ordained at twenty-two, and quickly emerged as the acknowledged leader of late-seventeenth-century theology, politics, and letters. Tremendously erudite, he wrote nearly five hundred books and pamphlets, mastered a dozen or more languages, dabbled in science, medicine, philanthropy, politics, and literature, was elected to the Royal Society of London, and corresponded with scholars from all over the Western world. He found time for three wives and fifteen children, and he died at the age of sixty-five, only five years after his father.

His writing, as varied as it is abundant, includes devotional tracts, sermons, biographies of New England notables, elegiac poetry, political fables, learned papers on subjects as diverse as hybridization and smallpox inoculation, literary criticism, and most significantly, the history of the culture his family had done so much to create and sustain. Almost all of this variety is contained in his monumental *Magnalia Christi Americana; or, The Ecclesiastical History of New England from Its First Planting*, which he completed in 1697, but had to send to London for publication (1702). In separate parts he therein describes the history of New England's settlement, the lives of governors and magistrates, the lives of sixty eminent divines, the development of Harvard College, the faith and order of the churches, "illustrious providences" affecting the country, and the "Wars of the Lord."

One of these wars, the assaults of Satan through the agency of witches, had long occupied his attention. In 1684 his father had completed a plan formulated some thirty years earlier—to record "such divine judgments, tempests, floods, earthquakes, thunders as are unusual, strange apparitions, or whatever else shall happen that is prodigious, witchcrafts, diabolical possessions, remarkable judgments upon noted sinners, eminent deliverances, and answers of prayer"—in *An Essay for the Recording of Illustrious Providences*. And young Cotton continued the work in *Memorable Providences Relating to Witchcraft and Possessions* (1689).

In 1691, Satan focused on Salem Village, where the accusations of a few little "bewitched" girls created a panic that did not subside until twenty men and women and two dogs had been executed for witchcraft, fifty-five had confessed, one hundred and fifty were still imprisoned, and some two hundred others stood accused. Although Increase and Cotton Mather urged caution and propriety at the trials that ran from June to September, 1692, their credulity undoubtedly contributed to the catastrophe. Not a participant in the trials, Cotton Mather was commissioned to summarize the events and testimony, which he did under the title *The Wonders of the Invisible World* (London, 1692). The book was answered in 1700 by Robert Calef, a Boston merchant, under the sarcastic title, *More Wonders of the Invisible World*. In terms of the extent of similar events in Europe during the sixteenth and seventeenth centuries, the Salem witchcraft episode was a very minor one. But its impact on provincial New England, and especially on the pre-eminence of the clergy, was enormous; the damage to ministerial prestige contributed to the decline of the orthodoxy that Cotton Mather strove all his life to invigorate.

Further reading: Barrett Wendell, *Cotton Mather: The Puritan Priest*, 1891, 1963. David Levin, *What Happened in Salem?*, 1960. Chadwick Hansen, *Witchcraft at Salem*, 1969.

The Trial of Bridget Bishop

Ichabod Crane's remarkable "appetite for the marvellous" fed on what Washington Irving called Cotton Mather's "History of New England Witchcraft": "No tale was too gross or monstrous for his capacious swallow." And the trial testimony Mather provides here suggests that Crane was not alone among the credulous and superstitious. But the "poppets" found in Bridget Bishop's cellar should also remind us that malefic witchcraft was practiced in seventeenth-century New England as elsewhere. Even concerned ministers knew enough to boil urine with pins in it to drive off a supposed witch—fighting witchcraft with witchcraft; and many persons so profoundly believed in the power of witches to harm them that they succumbed to their own fears, assuming the condition of "bewitched" persons. Text: Cotton Mather, *The Wonders of the Invisible World* (London, 1693 [1692]).

II. The Tryal of Bridget Bishop, alias Oliver, at the Court of Oyer and Terminer, held at Salem, June 2, 1692.

I. She was indicted for bewitching of several persons in the neighborhood, the indictment being drawn up, according to the form in such cases as usual. And pleading, not guilty, there were brought in several persons, who had long undergone many kinds of miseries, which were preternaturally inflicted, and generally ascribed unto an horrible witchcraft. There was little occasion to prove the witchcraft, it being evident and notorious to all beholders. Now to fix the witchcraft on the prisoner of[1] the bar, the first thing used, was the testimony of[1] the bewitched; whereof several testified, that the shape of the prisoner did oftentimes very grievously pinch them, choke them, bite them, and afflict them; urging them to write their names in a book, which the said spectre called, ours. One of them did further testify, that it was the shape of this prisoner, with another, which one day took her from her wheel, and carrying her to the river-side, threatened there to drown her, if she did not sign to the book mentioned: which yet she refused. Others of them did also testify, that the said shape did in her threats brag to them that she had been the death of sundry persons, then by her named; that she had ridden a man then likewise named. Another testified, the apparition of ghosts unto the spectre of Bishop, crying out, you murdered us! About the truth whereof, there was in the matter of fact but too much suspicion.

II. It was testified, that at the examination of the prisoner before the magistrates, the bewitched were

[1] That is, *about* or *concerning*.

extreemly tortured. If she did but cast her eyes on them, they were presently struck down; and this in such a manner as there could be no collusion in the business. But upon the touch of her hand upon them, when they lay in their swoons, they would immediately revive; and not upon the touch of any one's else. Moreover, upon some special actions of her body, as the shaking of her head, or the turning of her eyes, they presently and painfully fell into the like postures. And many of the like accidents now fell out, while she was at the bar. One at the same time testifying, that she said, she could not be troubled to see the afflicted thus tormented.

III. There was testimony likewise brought in, that a man striking once at the place, where a bewitched person said, the shape of the Bishop stood, the bewitched cried out, that he had tore her coat, in the place then particularly specified; and the woman's coat was found to be torn in that very place.

IV. One Deliverance Hobbs, who had confessed her being a witch, was now tormented by the spectres, for her confession. And she now testified, that this Bishop tempted her to sign the book again, and to deny what she had confessed. She affirmed, that it was the shape of this prisoner, which whipped her with iron rods, to compel her thereunto. And she affirmed that this Bishop was at a general meeting of the witches, in a field at Salem-Village, and there partook of a diabolical sacrament in bread and wine then administered.

V. To render it further unquestionable, that the prisoner at the bar, was the person truly charged in this witchcraft, there were produced many evidences of other witchcrafts, by her perpetrated. For instance, John Cook testified, that about five or six years ago, one morning, about sun-rise, he was in his chamber assaulted by the shape of this prisoner: which looked on him, grinned at him, and very much hurt him with a blow on the side of the head: and that on the same day, about noon, the same shape walked in the room where he was, and an apple strangely flew out of his hand, into the lap of his mother, six or eight foot from him.

VI. Samuel Gray testified, that about fourteen years ago, he waked on a night, and saw the room where he lay full of light; and that he then saw plainly a woman between the cradle, and the bed-side, which looked upon him. He rose, and it vanished; tho' he found the doors all fast. Looking out at the entry-door, he saw the same woman, in the same garb again; and said, In God's name, what do you come for? He went to bed, and had the same woman again assaulting him. The child in the cradle gave a great screech, and the woman disappeared. It was long before the child could be quieted; and tho' it were a very likely thriving child, yet from this time it pined away, and after divers months, died in a sad condition. He knew not Bishop, nor her name; but when he saw her after this, he knew by her countenance, and apparel, and all circumstances, that it was the apparition of this Bishop, which had thus troubled him.

VII. John Bly and his wife testified, that he bought a sow of Edward Bishop, the husband of the prisoner; and was to pay the price agreed, unto another person. This prisoner being angry that she was thus hindered from fingering the money, quarrelled with Bly. Soon after which, the sow was taken with strange fits; jumping, leaping, and knocking her head against the fence; she seemed blind and deaf, and would neither eat nor be sucked. Whereupon a neighbor said, she believed the creature was overlooked; and sundry other circumstances concurred, which made the deponents believe that Bishop had bewitched it.

VIII. Richard Coman testified, that eight years ago, as he lay awake in his bed, with a light burning in the room, he was annoyed with the apparition of this Bishop, and of two more that were strangers to him, who came and oppressed him so, that he could neither stir himself, nor wake any one else, and that he was the night after, molested again in the like manner; the said Bishop, taking him by the throat, and pulling him almost out of the bed. His kinsman offered for this cause to lodge with him; and that night, as they were awake, discoursing together, this Coman was once more visited by the guests which had formerly been so troublesome; his kinsman being at the same time strook speechless, and unable to move hand or foot. He had laid his sword by him, which these unhappy spectres did strive much to wrest from him; only he held too fast for them. He then grew able to call the people of his house; but altho' they heard him, yet they had not power to speak or stir; until at last, one of the people crying out, What's the matter? the spectres all vanished.

IX. Samuel Shattock[2] testified, that in the year, 1680, this Bridget Bishop, often came to his house upon such frivolous and foolish errands, that they suspected she came indeed with a purpose of mischief. Presently, whereupon, his eldest child, which was of as promising health and sense, as any child of its age, began to droop exceedingly; and the oftener that Bishop came to the house, the worse grew the child. As the child would be standing at the door, he would be thrown and bruised against the stones, by

an invisible hand, and in like sort knock his face against the sides of the house, and bruise it after a miserable manner. After this Bishop would bring him things to dye, and whereof he could not imagine any use; and when she paid him a piece of money, the purse and money were unaccountably conveyed out of a locked box, and never seen more. The child was immediately, hereupon, taken with terrible fits, whereof his friends thought he would have died: indeed he did almost nothing but cry and sleep for several months together; and at length his understanding was utterly taken away. Among other symptoms of an enchantment upon him, one was, that there was a board in the garden, whereon he would walk; and all the invitations in the world could never fetch him off. About 17 or 18 years after, there came a stranger to Shattock's house, who seeing the child, said, This poor child is bewitched; and you have a neighbor living not far off, who is a witch. He added, your neighbor has had a falling out with your wife; and she said, in her heart, your wife is a proud woman, and she would bring down her pride in this child. He then remembered, that Bishop had parted from his wife in muttering and menacing terms, a little before the child was taken ill. The abovesaid stranger would needs carry the bewitched boy with him, to Bishop's house, on pretence of buying a pot of cider. The woman entertained him in a furious manner; and flew also upon the boy, scratching his face till the blood came; and saying, Thou rogue, what dost thou bring this fellow here to plague me? Now it seems the man had said, before he went, that he would fetch blood of her. Ever after the boy was followed with grievous fits, which the doctors themselves generally ascribed unto witchcraft; and wherein he would be thrown still into the fire or the water, if he were not constantly looked after; and it was verily believed that Bishop was the cause of it.

X. John Louder testified, that upon some little controversy with Bishop about her fowls, going well to bed, he did awake in the night by moonlight, and did see clearly the likeness of this woman grievously oppressing him; in which miserable condition she held him, unable to help himself, till near day. He told Bishop of this; but she denied it, and threatened him very much. Quickly after this, being at home on a Lord's day, with the doors shut about him, he saw a black pig approach him; at which, he going to kick, it vanished away. Immediately after, sitting down, he saw a black thing jump in at the window, and come and stand before him. The body was like that of a monkey, the feet like a cock's, but the face much like a man's. He being so extremely affrighted, that he could not speak; this monster spoke to him, and said, I am a messenger sent unto you, for I understand that you are in some trouble

[2] Ironically, the same man who in 1661 wrote *The Quaker Petition* seeking legal redress for persecutions then suffered by Quakers in Salem.

of mind, and if you will be ruled by me, you shall want for nothing in this world. Whereupon he endeavored to clap his hands upon it; but he could feel no substance; and it jumped out of the window again; but immediately came in by the porch, tho' the doors were shut, and said, You had better take my counsel. He then struck at it with a stick, but struck only the ground-sel, and broke the stick: the arm with which he struck was presently disenabled, and it vanished away. He presently went out at the back-door, and spied this Bishop, in her orchard, going toward her house; but he had not power to set one foot forward unto her. Whereupon, returning into the house, he was immediately accosted by the monster he had seen before; which goblin was now going to fly at him; whereat he cry'd out, The whole armor of God be between me and you! So it sprang back, and flew over the apple tree; shaking many apples off the tree, in its flying over. At its leap, it flung dirt with its feet against the stomach of the man; whereon he was then struck dumb, and so continued for three days together. Upon the producing of this testimony, Bishop denied that she knew this deponent: yet their two orchards joined; and they had often had their little quarrels for some years together.

XI. William Stacy testified, that receiving money of this Bishop, for work done by him; he was gone but a matter of three rods from her, and looking for his money, found it unaccountably gone from him. Some time after, Bishop asked him, whether his father would grind her grist for her? He demanded why? She replied, Because folks count me a witch. He answered, No question but he will grind it for you. Being then gone about six rods from her, with a small load in his cart, suddenly the off-wheel slumped; and sunk down into an hole, upon plain ground; so that the deponent was forced to get help for the recovering of the wheel: but stepping back to look for the hole, which might give him this disaster, there was none at all to be found. Some time after, he was waked in the night; but it seemed as light as day; and he perfectly saw the shape of this Bishop in the room, troubling of him; but upon her going out, all was dark again. He charged Bishop afterwards with it, and she denied it not; but was very angry. Quickly after, this deponent having been threatened by Bishop, as he was in a dark night going to the barn, he was very suddenly taken or lifted from the ground, and thrown against a stone wall: after that, he was again hoisted up and thrown down a bank, at the end of his house. After this again, passing by this Bishop, his horse with a small load, striving to draw, all his gears flew to pieces, and the cart fell down; and this deponent going then to lift a bag of corn, of about two bushels, could not budge it with all his might.

Many other pranks of this Bishop's this deponent was ready to testify. He also testified, that he verily believed, the said Bishop was the instrument of his daughter Priscilla's death; of which suspicion, pregnant reasons were assigned.

XII. To crown all, John Bly and William Bly testified, that being employed by Bridget Bishop, to help take down the cellar-wall of the old house wherein she formerly lived, they did in holes of the said old wall, find several poppets, made up of rags and hogs-brussels, with headless pins in them, the points being outward; whereof she could give no account to the court, that was reasonable or tolerable.

XIII. One thing that made against the prisoner was, her being evidently convicted of gross lying in the court, several times, while she was making her plea; but besides this, a jury of women found a preternatural teat upon her body[3]: but upon a second search, within 3 or 4 hours, there was no such thing to be seen. There was also an account of other people whom this woman had afflicted; and there might have been many more, if they had been enquired for; but there was no need of them.

XIV. There was one very strange thing more, with which the court was newly entertained. As this woman was under a guard, passing by the great and spacious meeting-house of Salem, she gave a look towards the house: and immediately a demon invisibly entering the meeting-house, tore down a part of it; so that tho' there was no person to be seen there, yet the people, at the noise, running in, found a board, which was strongly fastened with several nails, transported unto another quarter of the house. 1692

Of Style

Manuductio ad Ministerium: Directions for a Candidate of the Ministry was published in 1726. In the training of a preacher of the Word of God, Mather found a place for poetry, recommending not only Homer and Virgil, despite their pagan idolatries, but even advising scholars to write poetry themselves—"try your young wings now and then." But to the young men of Boston it seemed that Mather's own prose too frequently outdid itself poetically. They found it ornate, overelaborated, pretentiously aureate, while they preferred a direct, economical prose in the service of business, news, and science. Though Mather here defends a richer, more embellished style, he curiously does so in a prose as direct and pointed as Hooker's. Text: T. J. Holmes and K. B. Murdock, eds., *Manuductio ad Ministerium* (New York, 1938; The Facsimile Text Society, no. 42).

[3] Devilish spirits (familiars) appeared to witches to suck on their bodies, leaving behind small marks or teats, which especially in England and New England became primary evidence that persons were indeed leagued with the Devil, and were therefore witches.

There has been a deal of ado about a style; so much, that I must offer you my sentiments upon it. There is a way of writing, wherein the author endeavors, that the reader may have something to the purpose in every paragraph. There is not only a vigor sensible in every sentence, but the paragraph is embellished with profitable references, even to something beyond what is directly spoken. Formal and painful quotations are not studied; yet all that could be learnt from them is insinuated. The writer pretends not unto reading, yet he could not have writ as he does if he had not read very much in his time; and his composures are not only a cloth of gold, but also struck with as many jewels, as the gown of a Russian ambassador. This way of writing has been decried by many, and is at this day more than ever so, for the same reason, that in the old story, the grapes were decried: that they were not ripe. A lazy, ignorant, conceited set of authors, would persuade the whole tribe, to lay aside that way of writing, for the same reason that one would have persuaded his brethren to part with the encumbrance of their bushy tails. But however fashion and humour may prevail, they must not think that the club at their coffee-house is all the world, but there will always be those, who will in this case be governed by indisputable reason: and who will think, that the real excellency of a book will never lie in saying of little; that the less one has for his money in a book, 'tis really the more valuable for it; and that the less one is instructed in a book, and the more of superfluous margin, and superficial harangue, and the less of substantial matter one has in it, the more 'tis to be accounted of? And if a more massy way of writing be never so much disgusted at this day, a better gust will come on, as will some other thing, *quae jam cecidere*. In the meantime, nothing appears to me more impertinent and ridiculous than the modern way (I cannot say rule; for they have none!) of criticizing. The blades that set up for critics, I know not who constituted or commissioned 'em!—they appear to me, for the most part as contemptible, as they are a supercilious generation. For indeed no two of them have the same style; and they are as intolerably cross-grained and severe in their censures one upon another, as they are upon the rest of mankind. But while each of them, conceitedly enough, sets up for the standard of perfection, we are entirely at a loss which fire to follow. Nor can you easily find any one thing wherein they agree for their style, except perhaps a perpetual care to give us jejune and empty pages, without such touches of erudition (so to speak in the style of an ingenious traveler) as may make the discourses less tedious, and more enriching, to the mind of him that peruses them. There is much talk of a florid style, obtaining among the pens, that are most in vogue; but how often would it puzzle one, even with the best glasses to find the flowers! And if they were to be chastised for it, it would be with as much of justice, as Jerome was, for being a Ciceronian. After all, every man will have his own style, which will distinguish him as much as his gait: and if you can attain to that which I have newly described, but always writing so as to give an easy conveyance unto your ideas, I would not have you by any scourging be driven out of your gait; but if you must confess a fault in it, make a confession like that of the lad unto his father while he was beating him for his versifying.

However, since every man will have his own style, I would pray, that we may learn to treat one another with mutual civilities, and condescensions, and handsomely indulge one another in this, as gentlemen do in other matters.

I wonder what ails people, that they can't let Cicero write in the style of Cicero, and Seneca write in the (much other!) style of Seneca; and own that both may please in their several ways. But I will freely tell you; what has made me consider the humourists that set up for critics upon style, as the most unregardable set of mortals in the world, is this! Far more illustrious critics than any of those to whom I am now bidding defiance, and no less men than your Erasmus's, and your Grotius's, have taxed the Greek style of the New Testament, with I know not what solecisms and barbarisms; and, how many learned folks have obsequiously run away with the notion! Whereas 'tis an ignorant and an insolent whimsy; which they have been guilty of. It may be (and particularly by an ingenious Blackwall, it has been) demonstrated, that the gentlemen are mistaken in every one of their pretended instances; all the unquestionable classics, may be brought in, to convince them of their mistakes. Those glorious oracles are as pure Greek as ever was written in the world; and so correct, so noble, so sublime in their style, that never anything under the cope of heaven, but the Old Testament, has equaled it.

1726

JONATHAN EDWARDS [1703–1758]

No ONE EXEMPLIFIED the force of the Puritan plain style better than Jonathan Edwards; its proof lay in the startling effects it had upon his hearers. By the time he was eleven or twelve, his precocious essays on natural and supernatural topics clearly revealed his rare ability to observe minutely and reason tightly. As student and instructor at Yale from 1716 to 1722 he formed the basic philosophical positions that underlay his later writings; as his grandfather Solomon Stoddard's assistant at the Northampton church, and later as pastor in his own right, he was able to put those theories into confirming practice.

From Edwards' plain talk, a series of religious revivals radiated from Northampton through the Connecticut Valley in 1734 and 1735. Revitalized by the arrival of the famed English evangelist George Whitefield in 1740, this "Great Awakening" became for five years the most powerful social force of the time. With almost the detachment of Benjamin Franklin, who carefully paced off the distance Whitefield's famous voice would carry, Edwards reported and investigated forces he himself had done much to create in such compelling sermons as *Sinners in the Hands of an Angry God*. His case studies in *A Faithful Narrative of the Surprising Work of God in ... Conversion* (1736) had been widely published and translated. Further exploring the psychology of religious experience in his brilliant *Treatise Concerning Religious Affections* (1746), he drew a careful distinction between true and false religious emotion and analyzed at length the role of beauty, imagination, and taste.

Convinced by his observations that requirements for church membership had become too lax and that reform was necessary, Edwards attempted to reverse his grandfather's liberal policies and was consequently dismissed from his Northampton pulpit in 1750. He accepted a call to Stockbridge, in the Berkshires, and while ministering to that remote Indian community he returned to the speculations that had occupied him in the "Notes on the Mind" which he had begun as an undergraduate at Yale. Internationally known as a revivalist, he now devoted his energies to the composition of his three greatest intellectual works—*Freedom of the Will* (1754), *The Nature of True Virtue* (1755–58), and *The Great Doctrine of Original Sin Defended* (1757)—in which he asserted more rigorously than ever before the philosophical and psychological bases of fundamental Calvinism. In 1757 he was invited to become president of the College of New Jersey (now Princeton), where he died early the following year from a smallpox inoculation.

Edwards was unremitting in his defense of what are now considered distasteful, anachronistic, and narrow views. He sarcastically and consciously rejected "this age of light and inquiry" because he found it contrary, not only to the Bible, but to logic and experience as well. But he did not retreat into bitter misanthropy; rather, he found mystical rapture and beauty in the stern doctrines of election, predetermination, original sin, and man's absolute dependence on God. Seeking God through experience of and reflections on beauty, he created the first statement of the kind of aesthetic idealism that Emerson, Poe, and Whitman would later urge as the basis for both poetry and morality.

Further reading: *Jonathan Edwards: Representative Selections*, ed. C. H. Faust and T. H. Johnson, 1935, 1962. Ola E. Winslow, *Jonathan Edwards*, 1940. Perry Miller, *Jonathan Edwards*, 1949.

Character of a Truly Virtuous Person

Tradition holds that the young lady was Sarah Pierrepont, then thirteen, whom Edwards later married; but it may merely be a formal literary exercise referring to no particular person. Concise, pithy "characters" of personality types, social classes, or even of inanimate objects and social institutions, had been a popular literary genre since the late sixteenth century when Theophrastus' *Characters* began to be imitated by Englishmen. By Edwards' time such sketches were frequently worked into sermons and histories.

For this and the following selections, except as noted, the text is that of the eight-volume edition of *The Works of President Edwards,* ed. Samuel Austin (Worcester, Mass., 1808–9).

They say there is a young lady in ——— who is beloved of that great Being, who made and rules the world, and that there are certain seasons in which this great Being, in some way or other invisible, comes to her and fills her mind with exceeding sweet delight, and that she hardly cares for anything, except to meditate on Him—that she expects after a while to be received up where He is, to be raised up out of the world and caught up into heaven; being assured that He loves her too well to let her remain at a distance from Him always. There she is to dwell with Him, and to be ravished with His love and delight forever. Therefore, if you present all the world before her, with the richest of its treasures, she disregards it and cares not for it, and is unmindful of any pain or affliction. She has a strange sweetness in her mind, and singular purity in her affections; is most just and conscientious in all her conduct; and you could not persuade her to do anything wrong or sinful, if you would give her all the world, lest she should offend this great Being. She is of a wonderful sweetness, calmness, and universal benevolence of mind; especially after the great God has manifested Himself to her mind. She will sometimes go about from place to place, singing sweetly; and seems to be always full of joy and pleasure; and no one knows for what. She loves to be alone, walking in the fields and groves, and seems to have someone invisible always conversing with her.
1723

Personal Narrative

During the Great Awakening, Edwards analyzed the religious experiences of many persons, trying to sort out in the frenzy of the period valid signs of saving grace from false signs. His own spiritual autobiography shows him putting his own experience to the test as he traces the four "seasons of awakenings" that brought him to assurance of salvation. The form of the work is therefore not linear but cyclical, each cycle showing an expanding and deepening of his spiritual consciousness, occasionally joined with mystical experiences of complete self-annihilation, of being "swallowed up in Christ." As he tries to communicate the "sweetness" of such experiences, his prose attains a poetic quality that almost matches Edward Taylor's, revealing the lyrical foundation of his tough-minded theology.

I had a variety of concerns and exercises about my soul from my childhood; but had two more remarkable seasons of awakening, before I met with that change, by which I was brought to those new dispositions, and that new sense of things, that I have since had. The first time was when I was a boy, some years before I went to college, at a time of remarkable awakening in my father's congregation. I was then very much affected for many months, and concerned about the things of religion, and my soul's salvation; and was abundant in duties. I used to pray five times a day in secret, and to spend much time in religious talk with other boys; and used to meet with them to pray together. I experienced I know not what kind of delight in religion. My mind was much engaged in it, and had much self-righteous pleasure; and it was my delight to abound in religious duties. I with some of my school-mates joined together, and built a booth in a swamp, in a very retired spot, for a place of prayer. And besides, I had particular secret places of my own in the woods, where I used to retire by myself; and was from time to time much affected. My affections seemed to be lively and easily moved, and I seemed to be in my element when engaged in religious duties. And I am ready to think, many are deceived with such affections, and such a kind of delight as I then had in religion, and mistake it for grace.

But in process of time, my convictions and affections wore off; and I entirely lost all those affections and delights, and left off secret prayer, at least as to any constant performance of it; and returned like a dog to his vomit, and went on in the ways of sin. Indeed I was at times very uneasy, especially towards the latter part of my time at college; when it pleased God, to seize me with a pleurisy; in which he brought me nigh to the grave, and shook me over the pit of hell. And yet, it was not long after my recovery, before I fell again into my old ways of sin. But God would not suffer me to go on with any quietness; I had great and violent inward struggles, till, after many conflicts with wicked inclinations, repeated resolutions, and bonds that I laid myself under by a kind of vows to God, I was brought wholly to break off all former wicked ways and all ways of known outward sin; and to apply myself to seek salvation, and practice many religious duties; but without that kind of affection and delight which I had formerly experienced. My concern now wrought more by inward struggles, and conflicts, and self-reflections. I made seeking my salvation the main business of my life. But yet, it seems to me, I sought after a miserable manner; which has made me sometimes since to question, whether ever it issued in that which was saving; being ready to doubt, whether such miserable seeking ever succeeded. I was indeed brought to seek salvation in a manner that I never was before; I felt a spirit to part with all things in the world, for an interest in Christ. My concern continued and prevailed, with many exercising thoughts and inward struggles; but yet it never seemed to be proper, to express that concern by the name of terror.

From my childhood up, my mind had been full of objections against the doctrine of God's sovereignty, in choosing whom He would to eternal life, and rejecting whom He pleased; leaving them eternally to perish, and be everlastingly tormented in hell. It used to appear like a horrible doctrine to me. But I remember the time very well, when I seemed to be convinced, and fully satisfied, as to this sovereignty of God, and His justice in thus eternally disposing of men, according to His sovereign pleasure. But never could give an account, how, or by what means, I was thus convinced, not in the least imagining at the time, nor a long time after, that there was any extraordinary influence of God's Spirit in it; but only that now I saw further, and my reason apprehended the justice and reasonableness of it. However, my mind rested in it; and it put an end to all those cavils and objections. And there has been a wonderful alteration in my mind, with respect to the doctrine of God's sovereignty, from that day to this; so that I scarce ever have found so much as the rising of an objection against it, in the most absolute sense, in God's shewing mercy to whom He will shew mercy, and hardening whom he will. God's absolute sovereignty and justice, with respect to salvation and damnation, is what my mind seems to rest assured of, as much as of any thing that I see with my eyes; at least it is so at times. But I have often, since that first conviction, had quite another kind of sense of God's sovereignty than I had then. I have often since had not only a conviction, but a delightful conviction. The doctrine has very often appeared exceeding pleasant, bright and sweet. Absolute sovereignty is what I love to ascribe to God. But my first conviction was not so.

The first instance that I remember of that sort of inward, sweet delight in God and divine things that I have lived much in since, was on reading those words, 1 Tim. i:17, *Now unto the King eternal, immortal, invisible, the only wise God, be honor and glory for ever and ever, Amen.* As I read the words, there came into my soul, and was as it were diffused through it, a sense of the glory of the Divine Being; a new sense, quite different from anything I ever experienced before. Never any words of scripture seemed to me as these words did. I thought with myself, how excellent a Being that was, and how happy I should be, if I might enjoy that God, and be rapt up to Him in heaven, and be as it were swallowed up in Him for ever! I kept saying, and as it were singing, over these words of scripture to myself; and went to pray to God that I might enjoy Him, and prayed in a manner quite different from what I used to do; with a new sort of affection. But it never came into my thought, that there was anything spiritual, or of a saving nature in this.

From about that time, I began to have a new kind of apprehensions and ideas of Christ, and the work of redemption and the glorious way of salvation by Him. An inward, sweet sense of these things, at times, came into my heart; and my soul was led away in pleasant views and contemplations of them. And my mind was greatly engaged to spend my time in reading and meditating on Christ, on the beauty and excellency of His person, and the lovely way of salvation by free grace in Him. I found no books so delightful to me, as those that treated of these subjects. Those words Cant. ii:1 used to be abundantly with me, *I am the rose of Sharon, and the lily of the valleys.* The words seemed to me, sweetly to represent the loveliness and beauty of Jesus Christ. The whole book of Canticles used to be pleasant to me, and I used to be much in reading it, about that time; and found, from time to time, an inward sweetness, that would carry me away, in my contemplations. This I knew not how to express otherwise, than by a calm, sweet abstraction of soul from all the concerns of this world; and sometimes a kind of vision, or fixed ideas and imaginations, of being alone in the mountains, or some solitary wilderness, far from all mankind, sweetly conversing with Christ, and wrapt and swallowed up in God. The sense I had of divine things, would often of a sudden kindle up, as it were, a sweet burning in my heart; an ardor of soul, that I know not how to express.

Not long after I first began to experience these things, I gave an account to my father of some things that had passed in my mind. I was pretty much affected by the discourse we had together; and when the discourse was ended, I walked abroad alone, in a solitary place in my father's pasture, for contemplation. And as I was walking there, and looking upon the sky and clouds, there came into my mind so sweet a sense of the glorious *majesty* and *grace* of God, as I know not how to express. I seemed to see them both in a sweet conjunction; majesty and meekness joined together; it was a sweet, and gentle, and holy majesty; and also a majestic meekness; an awful sweetness; a high, and great, and holy gentleness.

After this my sense of divine things gradually increased, and became more and more lively, and had more of that inward sweetness. The appearance of everything was altered; there seemed to be, as it were, a calm, sweet cast, or appearance of divine glory, in almost everything. God's excellency, His wisdom, His purity and love, seemed to appear in everything; in the sun, moon, and stars; in the clouds, and blue sky; in the grass, flowers, trees; in the water, and all nature; which used greatly to fix my mind. I often used to sit and view the moon for continuance; and in the day, spent much time in viewing the clouds and sky, to behold the sweet glory of God in these things; in the meantime, singing forth, with a low voice, my contemplations of the Creator and Redeemer. And scarce anything, among all the works of nature, was so sweet to me as thunder and lightning; formerly nothing had been so terrible to me. Before, I used to be uncommonly terrified with thunder, and to be struck with terror when I saw a thunder storm rising; but now, on the contrary, it rejoiced me. I felt God, so to speak, at the first appearance of a thunder storm; and used to take the opportunity, at such times, to fix myself in order to view the clouds, and see the lightnings play, and hear the majestic and awful voice of God's thunder, which oftentimes was exceedingly entertaining, leading me to sweet contemplations of my great and glorious God. While thus engaged, it always seemed natural for me to sing, or chant for my meditations; or, to speak my thoughts in soliloquies with a singing voice.

I felt then great satisfaction, as to my good state, but that did not content me. I had vehement longings of soul after God and Christ, and after more holiness, wherewith my heart seemed to be full, and ready to break; which often brought to my mind the words of the Psalmist, Psal. cxix:28: *My soul breaketh for the longing it hath.* I often felt a mourning and lamenting in my heart, that I had not turned to God sooner, that I might have had more time to grow in grace. My mind was greatly fixed on divine things; almost perpetually in the contemplation of them. I spent most of my time in thinking of divine things, year after year; often walking alone in the woods, and solitary places, for meditation, soliloquy, and prayer, and converse with God; and it was always my manner, at such times, to sing forth my contemplations. I was almost constantly in ejaculatory prayer, wherever I was. Prayer seemed to be natural to me, as the breath by which the inward burnings of my heart had vent. The delights which I now felt in the things of religion, were of an exceeding different kind from those before mentioned, that I had when a boy; and what I then had no more notion of, than one born blind has of pleasant and beautiful colors. They were of a more inward, pure, soul-animating and refreshing nature. Those former delights never reached the heart; and did not arise from any sight of the divine excellency of the things of God; or any taste of the soul-satisfying and life-giving good there is in them.

My sense of divine things seemed gradually to increase, till I went to preach at New York, which was about a year and a half after they began; and while I was there, I felt them, very sensibly, in a much higher degree than I had done before. My longings after God, and holiness, were much increased. Pure and humble, holy and heavenly Christianity appeared exceeding amiable to me. I felt a burning desire to be, in everything, a complete Christian; and conformed to the blessed image of Christ; and that I might live, in all things, according to the pure, sweet, and blessed rules of the gospel. I had an eager thirsting after progress in these things; which put me upon pursuing and pressing after them. It was my continual strife day and night, and constant inquiry, how I should *be* more holy and *live* more holily, and more becoming a child of God, and a disciple of Christ. I now sought an increase of grace and holiness, and a holy life, with much more earnestness, than ever I sought grace before I had it. I used to be continually examining myself, and studying and contriving for likely ways and means, how I should live holily, with far greater diligence and earnestness, than ever I pursued anything in my life; but yet with too great a dependence on my own strength; which afterwards proved a great damage to me. My experience had not then taught me, as it has done since, my extreme feebleness and impotence, every manner of way; and the bottomless depths of secret corruption and deceit there was in my heart. However, I went on with my eager pursuit after more holiness, and conformity to Christ.

The heaven I desired was a heaven of holiness; to be with God, and to spend my eternity in divine love and holy communion with Christ. My mind was very much taken up with contemplations on heaven, and the enjoyments there; and living there in perfect holiness, humility, and love: and it used at that time to appear a great part of the happiness of heaven, that there the saints could express their love to Christ. It appeared to me a great clog and burden, that what I felt within, I could not express as I desired. The inward ardor of my soul, seemed to be hindered and pent up, and could not freely flame out as it would. I used often to think, how in heaven this principle should freely and fully vent and express itself. Heaven appeared exceedingly delightful, as a world of love; and that all happiness consisted in living in pure, humble, heavenly, divine love.

I remember the thoughts I used then to have of holiness; and said sometimes to myself, "I do certainly know that I love holiness, such as the gospel prescribes." It appeared to me, that there was nothing in it but what was ravishingly lovely; the highest beauty and amiableness — a *divine* beauty; far purer than anything here upon earth; and that everything else was like mire and defilement, in comparison of it.

Holiness, as I then wrote down some of my contemplations on it, appeared to me to be of a sweet, pleasant, charming, serene, calm nature; which brought an inexpressible purity, brightness, peacefulness and ravishment to the soul. In other words, that it made the soul like a field or garden of God, with all manner of pleasant flowers; all pleasant, delightful, and undisturbed; enjoying a sweet calm, and the gently vivifying beams of the sun. The soul of a true Christian, as I then wrote my meditations, appeared like such a little white flower as we see in the spring of the year; low and humble on the ground, opening its bosom to receive the pleasant beams of the sun's glory; rejoicing as it were in a calm rapture; diffusing around a sweet fragrancy; standing peacefully and lovingly, in the midst of other flowers round about; all in like manner opening their bosoms, to drink in the light of the sun. There was no part of creature-holiness, that I had so great a sense of its loveliness, as humility, brokenness of heart, and poverty of spirit; and there was nothing that I so earnestly longed for. My heart panted after this—to lie low before God, as in the dust; that I might be nothing, and that God, might be ALL, that I might become as a little child.

While at New York,[1] I was sometimes much affected with reflections on my past life, considering how late it was before I began to be truly religious; and how wickedly I had lived till then: and once so as to weep abundantly, and for a considerable time together.

On January 12, 1723, I made a solemn dedication of myself to God, and wrote it down; giving up myself, and all that I had to God; to be for the future in no respect my own; to act as one that had no right to himself, in any respect. And solemnly vowed, to take God for my whole portion and felicity; looking on nothing else as any part of my happiness, nor acting as if it were; and His law for the constant rule of my obedience; engaging to fight with all my might, against the world, the flesh, and the Devil, to the end of my life. But I have reason to be infinitely humbled, when I consider, how much I have failed, of answering my obligation.

I had then abundance of sweet religious conversation in the family where I lived, with Mr. John Smith and his pious mother. My heart was knit in affection to those in whom were appearances of true piety; and I could bear the thoughts of no other companions, but such as were holy, and the disciples of the blessed Jesus. I had great longings for the advancement of Christ's kingdom in the world; and my secret prayer used to be, in great part, taken up in praying for it. If I heard the least hint of any thing that happened, in any part of the world, that appeared, in some respect or other, to have a favorable aspect on the interest of Christ's kingdom, my soul eagerly catched at it; and it would much animate and refresh me. I used to be eager to read public news letters, mainly for that end; to see if I could not find some news favorable to the interest of religion in the world.

I very frequently used to retire into a solitary place, on the banks of Hudson's river, at some distance from the city, for contemplation on divine things, and secret converse with God; and had many sweet hours there. Sometimes Mr. Smith and I walked there together, to converse on the things of God; and our conversation used to turn much on the advancement of Christ's kingdom in the world, and the glorious things that God would accomplish for his church in the latter days. I had then, and at other times, the greatest delight in the holy scriptures, of any book whatsoever. Oftentimes in reading it, every word seemed to touch my heart. I felt a harmony between something in my heart, and those sweet and powerful words. I seemed often to see so much light exhibited by every sentence, and such a refreshing food communicated, that I could not get along in reading; often dwelling long on one sentence, to see the wonders contained in it; and yet almost every sentence seemed to be full of wonders.

I came away from New York in the month of April, 1723, and had a most bitter parting with Madam Smith and her son. My heart seemed to sink within me at leaving the family and city, where I had enjoyed so many sweet and pleasant days. I went from New York to Weathersfield, by water, and as I sailed away, I kept sight of the city as long as I could. However, that night, after this sorrowful parting, I was greatly comforted in God at Westchester, where we went ashore to lodge; and had a pleasant time of it all the voyage to Saybrook. It was sweet to me to think of meeting dear Christians in heaven, where we should never part more. At Saybrook we went ashore to lodge, on Saturday, and there kept the Sabbath; where I had a sweet and refreshing season, walking alone in the fields.

After I came home to Windsor, I remained much in a like frame of mind, as when at New York; only sometimes I felt my heart ready to sink with the thoughts of my friends at New York. My support was in contemplations on the heavenly state; as I find in my Diary of May 1, 1723. It was a comfort to think of that state, where there is fulness of joy; where reigns heavenly, calm, and delightful love, without alloy; where there are continually the dearest expressions of this love; where is the enjoyment of the persons loved, without ever parting; where those persons who appear so lovely in this world, will really be inexpressibly more lovely and full of love to us. And how sweetly will the mutual lovers join together to sing the praises of God and the Lamb! How will it fill us with joy to think, that this enjoyment, these sweet exercises will never cease,

[1] From 1722 to 1723 Edwards was minister to a Presbyterian church in New York City.

but will last to all eternity! I continued much in the same frame, in the general, as when at New York, till I went to New Haven as tutor to the college; particularly once at Bolton, on a journey from Boston, while walking out alone in the fields. After I went to New Haven I sunk in religion; my mind being diverted from my eager pursuits after holiness, by some affairs that greatly perplexed and distracted my thoughts.

In September, 1725, I was taken ill at New Haven, and while endeavoring to go home to Windsor, was so ill at the North Village, that I could go no further; where I lay sick for about a quarter of a year. In this sickness God was pleased to visit me again with the sweet influences of his Spirit. My mind was greatly engaged there in divine, pleasant contemplations, and longings of soul. I observed that those who watched with me, would often be looking out wishfully for the morning; which brought to my mind those words of the Psalmist, and which my soul with delight made its own language, *My soul waiteth for the Lord, more than they that watch for the morning, I say, more than they that watch for the morning;* and when the light of day came in at the windows, it refreshed my soul from one morning to another. It seemed to be some image of the light of God's glory.

I remember, about that time, I used greatly to long for the conversion of some that I was concerned with; I could gladly honor them, and with delight be a servant to them, and lie at their feet, if they were but truly holy. But, some time after this, I was again greatly diverted in my mind with some temporal concerns that exceedingly took up my thoughts, greatly to the wounding of my soul; and went on through various exercises, that it would be tedious to relate, which gave me much more experience of my own heart, than ever I had before.

Since I came to this town,[2] I have often had sweet complacency in God, in views of his glorious perfections and the excellency of Jesus Christ. God has appeared to me a glorious and lovely being, chiefly on the account of his holiness. The holiness of God has always appeared to me the most lovely of all his attributes. The doctrines of God's absolute sovereignty, and free grace, in shewing mercy to whom he would shew mercy; and man's absolute dependence on the operations of God's Holy Spirit, have very often appeared to me as sweet and glorious doctrines. These doctrines have been much my delight. God's sovereignty has ever appeared to me, great part of his glory. It has often been my delight to approach God, and adore him as a sovereign God, and ask sovereign mercy of him.

I have loved the doctrines of the gospel; they

have been to my soul like green pastures. The gospel has seemed to me the richest treasure; the treasure that I have most desired, and longed that it might dwell richly in me. The way of salvation by Christ has appeared, in a general way, glorious and excellent, most pleasant and most beautiful. It has often seemed to me, that it would in a great measure spoil heaven, to receive it in any other way. That text has often been affecting and delightful to me, Isa. xxxii:2. *A man shall be an hiding place from the wind, and a covert from the tempest, etc.*

It has often appeared to me delightful, to be united to Christ; to have him for my head, and to be a member of his body; also to have Christ for my teacher and prophet. I very often think with sweetness, and longings, and pantings of soul, of being a little child, taking hold of Christ, to be led by him through the wilderness of this world. That text, Matth. xviii:3, has often been sweet to me, *except ye be converted and become as little children, etc.* I love to think of coming to Christ, to receive salvation of him, poor in spirit, and quite empty of self, humbly exalting him alone; cut off entirely from my own root, in order to grow into, and out of Christ; to have God in Christ to be all in all; and to live by faith on the Son of God, a life of humble unfeigned confidence in him. That scripture has often been sweet to me, Psal. cxv:1. *Not unto us, O Lord, not unto us, but to thy name give glory, for thy mercy and for thy truth's sake.* And those words of Christ, Luke x:21. *In that hour Jesus rejoiced in spirit, and said, I thank thee, O Father, Lord of heaven and earth, that thou hast hid these things from the wise and prudent, and hast revealed them unto babes; even so, Father, for so it seemed good in thy sight.* That sovereignty of God which Christ rejoiced in, seemed to me worthy of such joy; and that rejoicing seemed to show the excellency of Christ, and of what spirit he was.

Sometimes, only mentioning a single word caused my heart to burn within me; or only seeing the name of Christ, or the name of some attribute of God. And God has appeared glorious to me, on account of the Trinity. It has made me have exalting thoughts of God, that he subsists in three persons; Father, Son and Holy Ghost. The sweetest joys and delights I have experienced, have not been those that have arisen from a hope of my own good state; but in a direct view of the glorious things of the gospel. When I enjoy this sweetness, it seems to carry me above the thoughts of my own estate; it seems at such times a loss that I cannot bear, to take off my eye from the glorious pleasant object I behold without me, to turn my eye in upon myself, and my own good estate.

My heart has been much on the advancement of Christ's kingdom in the world. The histories of the

___

[2] Edwards returned to Northampton in February 1727.

past advancement of Christ's kingdom have been sweet to me. When I have read histories of past ages, the pleasantest thing in all my reading has been, to read of the kingdom of Christ being promoted. And when I have expected, in my reading, to come to any such thing, I have rejoiced in the prospect, all the way as I read. And my mind has been much entertained and delighted with the scripture promises and prophecies, which relate to the future glorious advancement of Christ's kingdom upon earth.

I have sometimes had a sense of the excellent fulness of Christ, and his meetness and suitableness as a Saviour; whereby he has appeared to me, far above all, the chief of ten thousands. His blood and atonement have appeared sweet, and his righteousness sweet; which was always accompanied with ardency of spirit; and inward strugglings and breathings, and groanings that cannot be uttered, to be emptied of myself, and swallowed up in Christ.

Once as I rode out into the woods for my health, in 1737, having alighted from my horse in a retired place, as my manner commonly has been, to walk for divine contemplation and prayer, I had a view that for me was extraordinary, of the glory of the Son of God, as Mediator between God and man, and His wonderful, great, full, pure, and sweet grace and love, and meek and gentle condescension. This grace that appeared so calm and sweet, appeared also great above the heavens. The person of Christ appeared ineffably excellent with an excellency great enough to swallow up all thought and conception—which continued, as near as I can judge, about an hour, which kept me the greater part of the time in a flood of tears, and weeping aloud. I felt an ardency of soul to be, what I know not otherwise how to express, emptied and annihilated; to lie in the dust, and to be full of Christ alone; to love Him with a holy and pure love; to trust in Him; to live upon Him; to serve and follow Him; and to be perfectly sanctified and made pure, with a divine and heavenly purity. I have, several other times, had views very much of the same nature, and which have had the same effects.

I have many times had a sense of the glory of the third person in the Trinity, in His office of Sanctifier, in His holy operations, communicating divine light and life to the soul. God, in the communications of His Holy Spirit, has appeared as an infinite fountain of divine glory and sweetness; being full, and sufficient to fill and satisfy the soul; pouring forth itself in sweet communications; like the sun in its glory, sweetly and pleasantly diffusing light and life. And I have sometimes had an affecting sense of the excellency of the Word of God as a Word of life; as the light of life; a sweet, excellent, life-giving Word; accompanied with a thirsting after that Word, that it might dwell richly in my heart.

Often, since I lived in this town, I have had very affecting views of my own sinfulness and vileness; very frequently to such a degree as to hold me in a kind of loud weeping, sometimes for a considerable time together; so that I have often been forced to shut myself up. I have had a vastly greater sense of my own wickedness, and the badness of my own heart, than ever I had before my conversion. It has often appeared to me, that if God should mark iniquity against me, I should appear the very worst of all mankind; of all that have been, since the beginning of the world to this time; and that I should have by far the lowest place in hell. When others, that have come to talk with me about their soul concerns, have expressed the sense they have had of their own wickedness, by saying that it seemed to them, that they were as bad as the Devil himself; I thought their expressions seemed exceeding faint and feeble, to represent my wickedness.

My wickedness, as I am in myself, has long appeared to me perfectly ineffable, and swallowing up all thought and imagination; like an infinite deluge, or mountains over my head. I know not how to express better what my sins appear to me to be, than by heaping infinite upon infinite, and multiplying infinite by infinite. Very often, for these many years, these expressions are in my mind, and in my mouth, "Infinite upon infinite—Infinite upon infinite!" When I look into my heart, and take a view of my wickedness, it looks like an abyss infinitely deeper than hell. And it appears to me, that were it not for free grace, exalted and raised up to the infinite height of all the fulness and glory of the great Jehovah, and the arm of His power and grace stretched forth in all the majesty of His power, and in all the glory of His sovereignty, I should appear sunk down in my sins below hell itself; far beyond the sight of everything but the eye of sovereign grace, that can pierce even down to such a depth. And yet it seems to me, that my conviction of sin is exceeding small, and faint: it is enough to amaze me, that I have no more sense of my sin. I know certainly, that I have very little sense of my sinfulness. When I have had turns of weeping and crying for my sins, I thought I knew at the time, that my repentance was nothing to my sin.

I have greatly longed of late, for a broken heart, and to lie low before God; and, when I ask for humility, I cannot bear the thoughts of being no more humble than other Christians. It seems to me, that though their degrees of humility may be suitable for them, yet it would be a vile self-exaltation in me, not to be the lowest in humility of all mankind. Others speak of their longing to be "humbled to the dust"; that may be a proper expression for them, but I always think of myself, that

I ought, and it is an expression that has long been natural for me to use in prayer, "to lie infinitely low before God." And it is affecting to think, how ignorant I was, when a young Christian, of the bottomless, infinite depths of wickedness, pride, hypocrisy, and deceit, left in my heart.

I have a much greater sense of my universal, exceeding dependence on God's grace and strength, and mere good pleasure, of late, than I used formerly to have; and have experienced more of an abhorrence of my own righteousness. The very thought of any joy arising in me, on any consideration of my own amiableness, performances, or experiences, or any goodness of heart or life, is nauseous and detestable to me. And yet I am greatly afflicted with a proud and self-righteous spirit, much more sensibly than I used to be formerly. I see that serpent rising and putting forth its head continually, everywhere, all around me. Though it seems to me, that, in some respects, I was a far better Christian, for two or three years after my first conversion, than I am now; and lived in a more constant delight and pleasure; yet, of late years, I have had a more full and constant sense of the absolute sovereignty of God, and a delight in that sovereignty; and have had more of a sense of the glory of Christ, as a Mediator revealed in the gospel. On one Saturday night, in particular, I had such a discovery of the excellency of the gospel above all other doctrines, that I could not but say to myself, "This is my chosen light, my chosen doctrine"; and of Christ, "This is my chosen prophet." It appeared sweet, beyond all expression, to follow Christ, and to be taught, and enlightened, and instructed by Him; to learn of Him, and live to Him. Another Saturday night (January, 1739), I had such a sense, how sweet and blessed a thing it was to walk in the way of duty; to do that which was right and meet to be done, and agreeable to the holy mind of God; that it caused me to break forth into a kind of loud weeping, which held me some time, so that I was forced to shut myself up, and fasten the doors. I could not but, as it were, cry out, "How happy are they which do that which is right in the sight of God! They are blessed indeed; they are the happy ones!" I had, at the same time, a very affecting sense, how meet and suitable it was that God should govern the world, and order all things according to His own pleasure; and I rejoiced in it, that God reigned and that His will was done.
1742?

Notes on the Mind

Emerson's observation that "Beauty is the mark God sets upon virtue" strikes very near the heart of Edwards' philosophy. Edwards, who saw true virtue as indistinguishable from holiness, elaborated the philosophical implications of beauty in *The Nature of True Virtue*, but even as early as his college years he was exploring the aesthetic principles that contribute to that late work. He began his series of seventy-two notes on "The Mind" in his senior year at Yale, intending a treatise on the subject.

His geometrical approach to beauty is akin to Poe's later speculations about poetic unity and also shares the metaphysical implications of Poe's *Eureka*. His emphasis on equality as a principle of beauty bears an interesting relationship to Whitman's principle of Equality in the 1855 preface to *Leaves of Grass*. Never a literary critic, however, even though he did commend both Milton and Richardson, Edwards nonetheless speaks clearly and rigorously about principles relevant to art. And we can see how the terms *excellence* and *excellency*, which occur frequently in his writing, may bear an inconspicuous but significant artistic implication.

Text: From "'The Mind' of Jonathan Edwards: The Reconstructed Manuscript," in Harvey G. Townsend, *The Philosophy of Jonathan Edwards from His Private Notebooks* (University of Oregon Monograph: Studies in Philosophy, no. 2, 1955).

1. EXCELLENCY. There has nothing been more without a definition, than excellency; although it be what we are more concerned with, than any thing else whatsoever: yea, we are concerned with nothing else. But what is this excellency? Wherein is one thing excellent, and another evil; one beautiful, and another deformed? Some have said that all excellency is harmony, symmetry, or proportion; but they have not yet explained it. We would know, why proportion is more excellent than disproportion; that is, why proportion is pleasant to the mind, and disproportion unpleasant? Proportion is a thing that may be explained yet further. It is an equality, or likeness of ratios; so that it is the equality, that makes the proportion. Excellency therefore seems to consist in equality. Thus, if there be two perfect equal circles, or globes, together, there is something more of beauty than if they were of unequal, disproportionate magnitudes. And if two parallel lines be drawn, the beauty is greater, than if they were obliquely inclined without proportion, because there is equality of distance. And if betwixt two parallel lines, two equal circles be placed, each at the same distance from each parallel line, as in Fig. 1, the beauty is greater, than if they stood at irregular distances from the parallel lines. If they stand, each in a perpendicular line, going from the parallel lines, (Fig. 2,) it is requisite that they should each stand at an equal distance from the perpendicular line next to them; otherwise there is no beauty. If there be three of these circles between two parallel lines, and near to a perpendicular line run between them, (Fig. 3,) the most beautiful form perhaps, that they could be placed in, is in an equilateral triangle with the cross line, because there are most equalities. The distance of the two next to the cross line is equal from that, and also equal from the parallel lines.

The distance of the third from each parallel is equal, and its distance from each of the other two circles is equal, and is also equal to their distance from one another, and likewise equal to their distance from each end of the cross line. There are two equilateral triangles: one made by the three circles, and the other made by the cross line and two of the sides of the first protracted till they meet that line. And if there be another like it, on the opposite side, to correspond with it and it be taken altogether, the beauty is still greater, where the distances from the lines, in the one, are equal to the distances in the other; also the two next to the cross lines are at equal distances from the other two; or, if you go crosswise, from corner to corner. The two cross lines are also parallel, so that all parts are at an equal distance, and innumerable other equalities might be found.

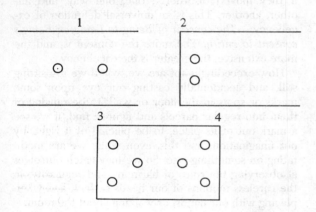

This simple equality, without proportion, is the lowest kind of regularity, and may be called simple beauty. All other beauties and excellencies may be resolved into it. Proportion is complex beauty. Thus, if we suppose that there are two points, A B, placed at two inches distance, and the next, C, one inch farther; (Fig. 1.) it is requisite, in order to regularity and beauty, if there be another, D, that it should be at half an inch distance; otherwise there is no regularity, and the last, D, would stand out of its proper place; because now the relation that the space C D, bears to B C, is equal to the relation that B C, bears to A B; so that B C D, is exactly similar to A B C. It is evident, this is a more complicated excellency than that which consisted in equality, because the terms of the relation are here complex, and before were simple. When there are three points set in a right line, it is requisite, in order to regularity, that they should be set at an equal distance, as A B C, (Fig. 2.) where A B, is similar to B C, or the relation of C to B, is the same as of B to A. But in the other are three terms necessary in each of the parts, be-

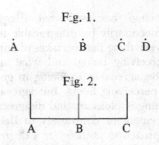

tween which, is the relation, B C D, is as A B C: so that where more simple beauties are omitted, and yet there is a general complex beauty: that is, B C is not as A B, nor is C D as B C, but yet, B C D is as A B C. It is requisite that the consent or regularity of C D to B C, be omitted, for the sake of the harmony of the whole. For although, if C D was perfectly equal to B C, there would be regularity and beauty with respect to them two; yet, if A B be taken into the idea, there is nothing but confusion. And it might be requisite, if these stood with others, even to omit this proposition,[1] for the sake of one more complex still. Thus, if they stood with other points, where B stood at four inches distance from A, C at two from B, and D at six from C: the place where D must stand in, if A, B, C, D were alone, viz. one inch from C, must be so as to be made proportionate with the other points beneath;

So that although A, B, C, D, are not proportioned, but are confusion among themselves; yet taken with the whole they are proportioned and beautiful.

All beauty consists in similarness or identity of relation. In identity of relation consists all likeness, and all identity between two consists in identity of relation. Thus, when the distance between two is exactly equal, their distance is their relation one to another, the distance is the same, the bodies are two; wherefore this is their correspondency and beauty. So bodies exactly of the same figure, the bodies are two, the relation between the parts of the extremities is the same, and this is their agreement with them. But if there are two bodies of different shapes, having no similarness of relation between the parts of the extremities; this, considered by itself, is a deformity, because being disagrees with being, which must undoubtedly be disagreeable to

---

[1] Proportion?

perceiving being: because what disagrees with Being, must necessarily be disagreeable to Being in general, to every thing that partakes of entity, and of course to perceiving being; and what agrees with Being must be agreeable to Being in general, and therefore to perceiving being. But agreeableness to perceiving being is pleasure, and disagreeableness is pain. Disagreement or contrariety to Being, is evidently an approach to nothing, or a degree of nothing; which is nothing else but disagreement or contrariety of Being, and the greatest and only evil: And entity is the greatest and only good. And by how much more perfect entity is, that is without mixture of nothing, by so much the more excellency. Two beings can agree one with another in nothing else but relation; because otherwise the notion of their twoness (duality,) is destroyed, and they become one.

And so, in every case, what is called correspondency, symmetry, regularity, and the like, may be resolved into equalities; though the equalities in a beauty, in any degree complicated, are so numerous, that it should be a most tedious piece of work to enumerate them. There are millions of these equalities. Of these consist the beautiful shape of flowers, the beauty of the body of man, and of the bodies of other animals. That sort of beauty which is called natural, as of vines, plants, trees, etc. consists of a very complicated harmony; and all the natural motions, and tendencies, and figures of bodies in the universe are done according to proportion, and therein is their beauty. Particular disproportions sometimes greatly add to the general beauty, and must necessarily be, in order to a more universal proportion:—So much equality, so much beauty; though it may be noted that the quantity of equality is not to be measured only by the number, but the intenseness, according to the quantity of being. As bodies are shadows of being, so their proportions are shadows of proportions.

The pleasures of the senses, where harmony is not the object of judgment, are the result of equality. Thus in music, not only in the proportion which the several notes of a tune bear, one among another, but in merely two notes, there is harmony; whereas it is impossible there should be proportion between only two terms. But the proportion is in the particular vibrations of the air, which strike on the ear. And so, in the pleasantness of light, colours, tastes, smells and touch, all arise from proportion of motion. The organs are so contrived that, upon the touch of such and such particles, there shall be a regular and harmonious motion of the animal spirits.

Spiritual harmonies are of vastly larger extent: i.e. the proportions are vastly oftener redoubled, and respect mere [more?] beings, and require a vastly larger view to comprehend them; as some simple notes do more affect one, who has not a comprehensive understanding of music.

The reason, why equality thus pleases the mind, and inequality is unpleasing, is because disproportion, or inconsistency, is contrary to Being. For Being, if we examine narrowly, is nothing else but proportion. When one being is inconsistent with another being, then Being is contradicted. But contradiction to Being, is intolerable to perceiving being, and the consent to Being, most pleasing.

Excellency consists in the Similarness of one being to another—not merely equality and proportion, but any kind of similarness—thus similarness of direction. Supposing many globes moving in right lines, it is more beautiful, that they should move all the same way, and according to the same direction, than if they moved disorderly; one, one way, and another, another. This is an universal definition of excellency:—*The consent of Being to Being, or Being's consent to entity.* The more the consent is, and the more extensive, the greater is the excellency.

How exceedingly apt are we, when we are sitting still, and accidentally casting our eye upon some marks or spots in the floor or wall, to be ranging of them into regular parcels and figures: and, if we see a mark out of its place, to be placing of it right, by our imagination; and this, even while we are meditating on something else. So we may catch ourselves at observing the rules of harmony and regularity, in the careless motions of our heads or feet, and when playing with our hands, or walking about the room.

Pleasedness, in perceiving being, always rises, either from a perception of consent to Being in general, or of consent to that being that perceives. As we have shown, that agreeableness to entity must be agreeable to perceiving entity; it is as evident that it is necessary that agreeableness to that being must be pleasing to it, if it perceives it. So that pleasedness does not always arise from a perception of excellency; [in general: (Dwight's brackets)] but the greater a Being is, and the more it has of entity, the more will consent to Being in general please it. But God is proper entity itself, and these two therefore, in Him, become the same; for, so far as a thing consents to Being in general, so far it consents to Him; and the more perfect created spirits are, the nearer do they come to their Creator, in this regard.

That, which is often called *self love*, is exceedingly improperly called *love*, for they do not only say that one loves himself, when he sees something amiable in himself, the view of which begets delight. But merely an inclination to pleasure, and averseness to pain, they call self love; so that the devils, and other damned spirits, love themselves, not because they see any thing in themselves, which they imagine to be lovely, but merely, because they do not incline to pain but to pleasure, or merely because they are capable of pain or pleasure; for pain and pleasure include an inclination to agreeableness, and an aversion to disagreeableness. Now how improper is it to say, that one loves himself, because what is agreeable to him is agreeable to him, and what is disagreeable to him is disagreeable to him: which mere entity supposes. So that this, that they call self-love, is no affection, but only the entity of the thing, or his being what he is.

One alone, without any reference to any more, cannot be excellent; for in such case, there can be no manner of relation no way, and therefore no such thing as consent. Indeed what we call *One*, may be excellent because of a consent of parts, or some consent of those in that being, that are distinguished into a plurality some way or other. But in a being that is absolutely without any plurality, there cannot be excellency, for there can be no such thing as consent or agreement.

One of the highest excellencies is love. As nothing else has a proper being but spirits, and as bodies are but the shadow of being, therefore the consent of bodies one to another, and the harmony that is among them, is but the shadow of excellency. The highest excellency therefore must be the consent of spirits one to another. But the consent of spirits consists half in their mutual love one to another. And the sweet harmony between the various parts of the universe, is only an image of mutual love. But yet a lower kind of love may be odious, because it hinders, or is contrary to, a higher and more general. Even a lower proportion is often a deformity, because it is contrary to a more general proportion.

Coroll. 1. If so much of the beauty and excellency of spirits consists in love, then the deformity of evil spirits consists as much in hatred and malice.

Coroll. 2. The more any doctrine, or institution, brings to light of the spiritual world, the more will it urge to love and charity.

Happiness strictly consists in the perception of these three things: of the consent of being to its own being; of its own consent to being; and of being's consent to being.

[14.] EXCELLENCE, to put it in other words, is that which is beautiful and lovely. That which is beautiful, considered by itself separately, and deformed, considered as a part of something else more extended; or beautiful, only with respect to itself and a few other things, and not as a part of that which contains all things—the universe—; is false beauty and a confined beauty. That which is beautiful, with respect to the university of things, has a generally extended excellence and a true beauty; and the more extended, or limited, its system is, the more confined or extended is its beauty.
1719

Passages from Sermons

A Divine and Supernatural Light

Good men are distinguished from bad, virtuous from vicious, holy from reprobate, not by particular acts they perform, Edwards believed, but by the inclination, habit, or tendency of their souls toward either good or evil. Conversion was a turning of the soul from evil to good, wrought by the power of God's grace. In describing the effects of that power, Edwards concluded that it was most like a light that suddenly illuminated the loveliness of divine objects. The beauty—"excellency"—of things already existed, of course, but now the light of grace made that beauty visible. Moreover, it accompanied a new psychological sense in the convert, a new perceptive power, which he sometimes refers to as "taste," and which in *A Treatise Concerning Religious Affections* he compares to literary taste.

2. This spiritual and divine light does not consist in any impression made upon the imagination. It is no impression upon the mind, as though one saw any thing with the bodily eyes: it is no imagination or idea of an outward light or glory, or any beauty of form or countenance, or a visible lustre or brightness of any object. The imagination may be strongly impressed with such things; but this is not spiritual light. Indeed when the mind has a lively discovery of spiritual things, and is greatly affected by the power of divine light, it may, and probably very commonly doth, much affect the imagination; so that impressions of an outward beauty or brightness may accompany those spiritual discoveries. But spiritual light is not that impression upon the imagination, but an exceeding different thing from it. Natural men may have lively impressions on their imaginations; and we cannot determine but that the devil, who transforms himself into an angel of light, may cause imaginations of an outward beauty, or visible glory, and of sounds and speeches, and other such things; but these are things of a vastly inferior nature to spiritual light.

3. This spiritual light is not the suggesting of any new truths or propositions not contained in the word of God This suggesting of new truths or doctrines to the mind, independent of any antecedent revelation of those propositions, either in word or writing, is inspiration; such as the prophets and apostles had and such as some enthusiasts pretend to. But this spiritual light that I am speaking of, is

quite a different thing from inspiration: it reveals no new doctrine, it suggests no new proposition to the mind, it teaches no new thing of God, or Christ, or another world, not taught in the Bible, but only gives a due apprehension of those things that are taught in the word of God.

4. It is not every affecting view that men have of the things of religion that is this spiritual and divine light. Men by mere principles of nature are capable of being affected with things that have a special relation to religion as well as other things. A person by mere nature, for instance, may be liable to be affected with the story of Jesus Christ, and the sufferings he underwent, as well as by any other tragical story: he may be the more affected with it from the interest he conceives mankind to have in it: yea, he may be affected with it without believing it; as well as a man may be affected with what he reads in a romance, or sees acted in a stage play. He may be affected with a lively and eloquent description of many pleasant things that attend the state of the blessed in heaven, as well as his imagination be entertained by a romantic description of the pleasantness of fairy land, or the like. And that common belief of the truth of the things of religion, that persons may have from education or otherwise, may help forward their affection. We read in Scripture of many that were greatly affected with things of a religious nature, who yet are there represented as wholly graceless, and many of them very ill men. A person therefore may have affecting views of the things of religion, and yet be very destitute of spiritual light. Flesh and blood may be the author of this: one man may give another an affecting view of divine things with but common assistance; but God alone can give a spiritual discovery of them.

But I proceed to show,

SECONDLY, Positively what this spiritual and divine light is.

And it may be thus described: a true sense of the divine excellency of the things revealed in the word of God, and a conviction of the truth and reality of them thence arising.

This spiritual light primarily consists in the former of these, viz., a real sense and apprehension of the divine excellency of things revealed in the word of God. A spiritual and saving conviction of the truth and reality of these things, arises from such a sight of their divine excellency and glory; so that this conviction of their truth is an effect and natural consequence of this sight of their divine glory. There is therefore in this spiritual light,

1. A true sense of the divine and superlative excellency of the things of religion; a real sense of the excellency of God and Jesus Christ, and of the work of redemption, and the ways and works of God revealed in the gospel. There is a divine and super-lative glory in these things; an excellency that is of a vastly higher kind, and more sublime nature than in other things; a glory greatly distinguishing them from all that is earthly and temporal. He that is spiritually enlightened truly apprehends and sees it, or has a sense of it. He does not merely rationally believe that God is glorious, but he has a sense of the gloriousness of God in his heart. There is not only a rational belief that God is holy, and that holiness is a good thing, but there is a sense of the loveliness of God's holiness. There is not only a speculatively judging that God is gracious, but a sense how amiable God is upon that account, or a sense of the beauty of this divine attribute.

There is a twofold understanding or knowledge of good that God has made the mind of man capable of. The first, that which is merely speculative and notional; as when a person only speculatively judges that any thing is, which, by the agreement of mankind, is called good or excellent, viz., that which is most to general advantage, and between which and a reward there is a suitableness, and the like. And the other is, that which consists in the sense of the heart: as when there is a sense of the beauty, amiableness, or sweetness of a thing; so that the heart is sensible of pleasure and delight in the presence of the idea of it. In the former is exercised merely the speculative faculty, or the understanding, strictly so called, or as spoken of in distinction from the will or disposition of the soul. In the latter, the will, or inclination, or heart, is mainly concerned.

Thus there is a difference between having an opinion, that God is holy and gracious, and having a sense of the loveliness and beauty of that holiness and grace. There is a difference between having a rational judgment that honey is sweet, and having a sense of its sweetness. A man may have the former, that knows not how honey tastes; but a man cannot have the latter unless he has an idea of the taste of honey in his mind. So there is a difference between believing that a person is beautiful, and having a sense of his beauty. The former may be obtained by hearsay, but the latter only by seeing the countenance. There is a wide difference between mere speculative rational judging any thing to be excellent, and having a sense of its sweetness and beauty. The former rests only in the head, speculation only is concerned in it; but the heart is concerned in the latter. When the heart is sensible of the beauty and amiableness of a thing, it necessarily feels pleasure in the apprehension. It is implied in a person's being heartily sensible of the loveliness of a thing, that the idea of it is sweet and pleasant to his soul; which is a far different thing from having a rational opinion that it is excellent.

2. There arises from this sense of divine excellency of things contained in the word of God, a

conviction of the truth and reality of them; and that either directly or indirectly.

First, Indirectly, and that two ways.

1. As the prejudices that are in the heart, against the truth of divine things, are hereby removed; so that the mind becomes susceptive of the due force of rational arguments for their truth. The mind of man is naturally full of prejudices against the truth of divine things: it is full of enmity against the doctrines of the gospel; which is a disadvantage to those arguments that prove their truth, and causes them to lose their force upon the mind. But when a person has discovered to him the divine excellency of Christian doctrines, this destroys the enmity, removes those prejudices, and sanctifies the reason, and causes it to lie open to the force of arguments for their truth.

Hence was the different effect that Christ's miracles had to convince the disciples, from what they had to convince the Scribes and Pharisees. Not that they had a stronger reason, or had their reason more improved; but their reason was sanctified, and those blinding prejudices, that the Scribes and Pharisees were under, were removed by the sense they had of the excellency of Christ and his doctrine.

2. It not only removes the hindrances of reason, but positively helps reason. It makes even the speculative notions the more lively. It engages the attention of the mind, with the more fixedness and intenseness to that kind of objects; which causes it to have a clearer view of them, and enables it more clearly to see their mutual relations, and occasions it to take more notice of them. The ideas themselves that otherwise are dim and obscure, are by this means impressed with the greater strength, and have a light cast upon them; so that the mind can better judge of them. As he that beholds the objects on the face of the earth, when the light of the sun is cast upon them, is under greater advantage to discern them in their true forms and mutual relations, than he that sees them in a dim starlight or twilight.

The mind having a sensibleness of the excellency of divine objects, dwells upon them with delight; and the powers of the soul are more awakened and enlivened to employ themselves in the contemplation of them, and exert themselves more fully and much more to the purpose. The beauty and sweetness of the objects draws on the faculties, and draws forth their exercises: so that reason itself is under far greater advantages for its proper and free exercises, and to attain its proper end, free of darkness and delusion. But,

SECONDLY. A true sense of the divine excellency of the things of God's word doth more directly and immediately convince of the truth of them; and that because the excellency of these things is so superlative. There is a beauty in them that is so divine and

godlike, that is greatly and evidently distinguishing of them from things merely human, or that men are the inventors and authors of; a glory that is so high and great, that when clearly seen, commands assent to their divinity and reality. When there is an actual and lively discovery of this beauty and excellency, it will not allow of any such thought as that it is a human work, or the fruit of men's invention. This evidence that they that are spiritually enlightened have of the truth of the things of religion, is a kind of intuitive and immediate evidence. They believe the doctrines of God's word to be divine, because they see divinity in them; i.e., they see a divine, and transcendent, and most evidently distinguishing glory in them; such a glory as, if clearly seen, does not leave room to doubt of their being of God, and not of men.

Such a conviction of the truth of religion as this, arising, these ways, from a sense of the divine excellency of them, is that true spiritual conviction that there is in saving faith. And this original of it, is that by which it is most essentially distinguished from that common assent, which unregenerate men are capable of.

II. I proceed now to the second thing proposed, viz., to show how this light is immediately given by God, and not obtained by natural means. And here,

1. It is not intended that the natural faculties are not made use of in it. The natural faculties are the subject of this light: and they are the subject in such a manner, that they are not merely passive, but active in it; the acts and exercises of man's understanding are concerned and made use of in it. God, in letting in this light into the soul, deals with man according to his nature, or as a rational creature; and makes use of his human faculties. But yet this light is not the less immediately from God for that; though the faculties are made use of, it is as the subject and not as the cause; and that acting of the faculties in it, is not the cause, but is either implied in the thing itself (in the light that is imparted) or is the consequence of it. As the use that we make of our eyes in beholding various objects, when the sun arises, is not the cause of the light that discovers those objects to us.

2. It is not intended that outward means have no concern in this affair. As I have observed already, it is not in this affair, as it is in inspiration, where new truths are suggested: for here is by this light only given a due apprehension of the same truths that are revealed in the word of God; and therefore it is not given without the word. The gospel is made use of in this affair: this light is the light of the glorious gospel of Christ, 2 Cor. iv:4. The gospel is as a glass, by which this light is conveyed to us, 1 Cor. xiii:12. Now we see through a glass.—But,

3. When it is said that this light is given immedi-

[handwritten margin note top: NOTHING A PERSON CAN DO —]

ately by God, and not obtained by natural means, hereby is intended, that it is given by God without making use of any means that operate by their own power, or a natural force. God makes use of means; but it is not as mediate causes to produce this effect. There are not truly any second causes of it; but it is produced by God immediately. The word of God is no proper cause of this effect: it does not operate by any natural force in it. The word of God is only made use of to convey to the mind the subject matter of this saving instruction: and this indeed it doth convey to us by natural force or influence. It conveys to our minds these and those doctrines; it is the cause of the notion of them in our heads, but not of the sense of the divine excellency of them in our hearts. Indeed a person cannot have spiritual light without the word. But that does not argue, that the word properly causes that light. The mind cannot see the excellency of any doctrine, unless that doctrine be first in the mind; but the seeing of the excellency of the doctrine may be immediately from the Spirit of God; though the conveying of the doctrine or proposition itself may be by the word. So that the notions that are the subject matter of this light, are conveyed to the mind by the word of God; but that due sense of the heart, wherein this light formally consists, is immediately by the Spirit of God. As for instance, that notion that there is a Christ, and that Christ is holy and gracious, is conveyed to the mind by the word of God: but the sense of the excellency of Christ by reason of that holiness and grace, is nevertheless immediately the work of the Holy Spirit.

1734

Sinners in the Hands of an Angry God

Thomas Hooker had argued that it was men's hearts that had to be prepared, not their minds, and with this Edwards heartily agreed. But he found—as did Thomas Shepard before him and Edgar Allan Poe a century later—that terror was often a quicker avenue to the heart than pleasure. Intent, as he said, upon "awakening unconverted persons in this congregation" of Enfield, Connecticut, he chose as his grim text Deut. xxxii.35, "Their foot shall slide in due time." He developed his "awful subject" with such inexorable logic and dramatic art—though without flamboyant gestures—that a minister who was present reported, "There was such a breathing of distress, and weeping, that the preacher was obliged to speak to the people and desire silence that he might be heard."

Your wickedness makes you as it were heavy as lead, and to tend downwards with great weight and pressure towards hell; and, if God should let you go, you would immediately sink and swiftly descend and plunge into the bottomless gulf, and your healthy constitution, and your own care and prudence, and best contrivance, and all your righteous-

[handwritten margin right, top, vertical: CREATION MAN ABHORS]

ness, would have no more influence to uphold you and keep you out of hell, than a spider's web would have to stop a falling rock. Were it not that so is the sovereign pleasure of God, the earth would not bear you one moment; for you are a burden to it; the creation groans with you; the creature is made subject to the bondage of your corruption, not willingly; the sun does not willingly shine upon you to give you light to serve sin and Satan; the earth does not willingly yield her increase to satisfy your lusts; nor is it willingly a stage for your wickedness to be acted upon; the air does not willingly serve you for breath to maintain the flame of life in your vitals, while you spend your life in the service of God's enemies. God's creatures are good, and were made for men to serve God with, and do not willingly subserve to any other purpose, and groan when they are abused to purposes so directly contrary to their nature and end. And the world would spew you out, were it not for the sovereign hand of Him who hath subjected it in hope. There are the black clouds of God's wrath now hanging directly over your heads, full of the dreadful storm, and big with thunder; and were it not for the restraining hand of God, it would immediately burst forth upon you. The sovereign pleasure of God, for the present, stays His rough wind; otherwise it would come with fury, and your destruction would come like a whirlwind, and you would be like the chaff of the summer threshing floor.

[handwritten margin right, vertical: LIKE WATER BEHIND A DAM]

The wrath of God is like great waters that are dammed for the present; they increase more and more, and rise higher and higher, till an outlet is given; and, the longer the stream is stopped, the more rapid and mighty is its course, when once it is let loose. It is true, that judgment against your evil work has not been executed hitherto; the floods of God's vengeance have been withheld; but your guilt in the meantime is constantly increasing, and you are every day treasuring up more wrath; the waters are continually rising and waxing more and more mighty; and there is nothing but the mere pleasure of God, that holds the waters back, that are unwilling to be stopped, and press hard to go forward. If God should only withdraw His hand from the floodgate, it would immediately fly open, and the fiery floods of the fierceness and wrath of God, would rush forth with inconceivable fury, and would come upon you with omnipotent power; and if your strength were ten thousand times greater than it is, yea, ten thousand times greater than the strength of the stoutest, sturdiest devil in hell, it would be nothing to withstand or endure it.

The bow of God's wrath is bent, and the arrow made ready on the string, and justice bends the arrow at your heart, and strains the bow, and it is nothing but the mere pleasure of God, and that of an angry God, without any promise or obligation at all, that keeps the arrow one moment from being made drunk with your blood.

Thus are all you that never passed under a great change of heart, by the mighty power of the Spirit of God upon your souls; all that were never born again, and made new creatures, and raised from being dead in sin, to a state of new, and before altogether unexperienced light and life (however you may have reformed your life in many things, and may have had religious affections, and may keep up a form of religion in your families and closets, and in the houses of God, and may be strict in it), you are thus in the hands of an angry God; it is nothing but His mere pleasure that keeps you from being this moment swallowed up in everlasting destruction.

However unconvinced you may now be of the truth of what you hear, by and by you will be fully convinced of it. Those that are gone from being in the like circumstances with you, see that it was so with them; for destruction came suddenly upon most of them; when they expected nothing of it, and while they were saying, Peace and safety: now they see that those things that they depended on for peace and safety were nothing but thin air and empty shadows.

The God that holds you over the pit of hell, much as one holds a spider, or some loathsome insect, over the fire, abhors you, and is dreadfully provoked; His wrath towards you burns like fire; He looks upon you as worthy of nothing else, but to be cast into the fire; He is of purer eyes than to bear to have you in His sight; you are ten thousand times so abominable in His eyes, as the most hateful and venomous serpent is in ours. You have offended him infinitely more than ever a stubborn rebel did his prince. And yet, it is nothing but His hand that holds you from falling into the fire every moment. It is ascribed to nothing else, that you did not go to hell the last night; that you was suffered to awake again in this world, after you closed your eyes to sleep. And there is no other reason to be given why you have not dropped into hell since you arose in the morning, but that God's hand has held you up. There is no other reason to be given why you have not gone to hell, since you have sat here in the house of God, provoking His pure eyes by your sinful wicked manner of attending His solemn worship: yea, there is nothing else that is to be given as a reason why you do not this very moment drop down into hell.

O sinner! consider the fearful danger you are in: it is a great furnace of wrath, a wide and bottomless pit, full of the fire of wrath, that you are held over in the hand of that God, whose wrath is provoked and incensed as much against you, as against many

of the damned in hell. You hang by a slender thread, with the flames of divine wrath flashing about it, and ready every moment to singe it, and burn it asunder; and you have no interest in any Mediator, and nothing to lay hold of to save yourself, nothing to keep off the flames of wrath, nothing of your own, nothing that you ever have done, nothing that you can do, to induce God to spare you one moment.

1741

FROM *A Letter to Benjamin Coleman*

The effectiveness of Edwards' "rhetoric of sensation" was evident immediately, as he informed Benjamin Coleman after the first flurry of awakenings in 1734–35. The startling results led Edwards in three significant directions—first toward the series of speculations concerning religious psychology that made him America's foremost religious philosopher of the eighteenth century; second, toward the self-analysis that found a lyric, almost poetic, voice in pieces such as his "Personal Narrative"; and third, toward a series of spiritual biographies, hinted at in this letter, where for the first time an American writer used narrative patterns to test the validity of a character's moral condition by describing his actions. The question raised by these narratives—to what extent can you judge a person's interior moral condition from his observable behavior?—became one of the key concerns of nineteenth-century romancers

[To the Reverend Benjamin Coleman, May 30, 1735]

° ° ° A concern about the great things of religion began, about the latter end of December, and the beginning of January, to prevail abundantly in the town, till in a very little time it became universal throughout the town, among old and young, and from the highest to the lowest; all seemed to be seized with a deep concern about their eternal salvation; all the talk in all companies, and upon all occasions was upon the things of religion, and no other talk was anywhere relished; and scarcely a single person in the whole town was left unconcerned about the great things of the eternal world. Those that were wont to be the vainest, and loosest persons in town seemed in general to be seized with strong convictions. Those that were most disposed to contemn vital and experimental religion, and those that had the greatest conceit of their own reason; the highest families in the town, and the oldest persons in the town, and many little children were affected remarkably; no one family that I know of, and scarcely a person has been exempt and the Spirit of God went on in His saving influences, to the appearance of all human reason and charity, in a truly wonderful and astonishing manner. The news of it filled the neighbouring towns with talk, and there were many in them that scoffed and made a ridicule of the religion that appeared in Northampton. But it was observable that it was very frequent and common that those of other towns that came into this town, and observed how it was here, were greatly affected, and went home with wounded spirits, and were never more able to shake off the impression that it made upon them, till at length there began to appear a general concern in several of the towns in the country. ° ° °

People are brought off from inordinate engagedness after the world, and have been ready to run into the other extreme of too much neglecting their worldly business and to mind nothing but religion. Those that are under convictions are put upon it earnestly to enquire what they shall do to be saved, and diligently to use appointed means of grace, and apply themselves to all known duty. And those that obtain hope themselves, and the charity of others concerning their good estate, generally seem to be brought to a great sense of their own exceeding misery in a natural condition, and their utter helplessness, and insufficiency for themselves, and their exceeding wickedness and guiltiness in the sight of God; it seldom fails but that each one seems to think himself worse than anybody else, and they are brought to see that they deserve no mercy of God, that all their prayers and pains are exceedingly worthless and polluted, and that God, notwithstanding all that they have done, or can do, may justly execute His eternal wrath upon them, and they seem to be brought to a lively sense of the excellency of Jesus Christ and His sufficiency and willingness to save sinners, and to be much weaned in their affections from the world, and to have their hearts filled with love to God and Christ, and a disposition to lie in the dust before Him. They seem to have given them a lively conviction of the truth of the Gospel, and the divine authority of the holy scriptures; though they can't have the exercise of this at all times alike, nor indeed of any other grace. They seem to be brought to abhor themselves for the sins of their past life, and to long to be holy, and to live holily, and to God's glory; but at the same time complain that they can do nothing, they are poor impotent creatures, utterly insufficient to glorify their Creator and Redeemer. They commonly seem to be much more sensible of their own wickedness after their conversion than before, so that they are often humbled by it; it seems to them that they are really become more wicked, when at the same time they are evidently full of a gracious Spirit. Their remaining sin seems to be their very great burthen, and many of them seem to long after heaven, that there they may be rid of sin. They generally seem to be united in dear love, and affection one to another, and to have a love to all mankind: I never saw the

Christian spirit in love to enemies so exemplified, in all my life as I have seen it within this half year. They commonly express a great concern for others' salvation; some say that they think they are far more concerned for others' conversion, after they themselves have been converted, than ever they were for their own; several have thought (though perhaps they might be deceived in it) that they could freely die for the salvation of any soul, of the meanest of mankind, of any Indian in the woods. This town was never so full of love, nor so full of joy, nor so full of distress as it has lately been. Some persons have had those longing desires after Jesus Christ, that have been to that degree as to take away their strength, and very much to weaken them, and make them faint: many have been even overcome with a sense of the dying love of Christ, so that the home of the body has been ready to fail under it; there was once three pious young persons in this town talking together of the dying love of Christ, till they all fainted away; though tis probable the fainting of the two latter was much promoted by the fainting of the first. Many express a sense of the glory of the divine perfections, and of the excellency and fulness of Jesus Christ, and of their own littleness and unworthiness, in a manner truly wonderful, and almost unparalleled; and so likewise of the excellency and wonderfulness of the way of salvation by Jesus Christ. Their esteem of the holy scriptures is exceedingly increased. Many of them say the Bible seems to be a new book to them, as though they never read it before. There have been some instances of persons that by only an accidental sight of the Bible, have been as much moved, it seemed to me, as a lover by the sight of his sweetheart. The preaching of the Word is greatly prized by them; they say they never heard preaching before; and so are God's sabbaths, and ordinances, and opportunities of public worship. The sabbath is longed for before it comes, some by only hearing the bell ring on some occasion in the week time, have been greatly moved, because it has put them in mind of its ringing to call the people together to worship God. But no part of public worship has commonly put an effect on them as singing God's praises. They have a greater respect to ministers than they used to have, there is scarcely a minister preaches here but gets their esteem and affection. The experiences of some persons lately amongst [us] have been beyond almost all that ever I heard or read of. There is a pious woman in this town that is a very modest bashful person, that was moved by what she heard of the experiences of others earnestly to seek to God to give her more clear manifestations of Himself, and evidences of her own good estate, and God answered her request, and gradually gave her more and more of a sense of His glory and love, which she had with intermissions for several days, till one morning the week before last she had it to a more than ordinary degree, and it prevailed more and more till towards the middle of the day, till her nature began to sink under it, as she was alone in the house; but there came somebody into the house, and found her in an unusual, extraordinary frame. She expressed what she saw and felt to him; it came to that at last that they raised the neighbours, they were afraid she would die; I went up to see her and found her perfectly sober and in the exercise of her reason, but having her nature seemingly overborne and sinking, and when she could speak expressing in a manner that can't be described the sense she had of the glory of God, and particularly of such and such perfections, and her own unworthiness, her longing to lie in the dust, sometimes her longing to go to be with Christ, and crying out of the excellency of Christ, and the wonderfulness of His dying love; and so she continued for hours together, though not always in the same degree; at some times she was able to discourse to those about her; but it seemed to me if God had manifested a little more of Himself to her she would immediately have sunk and her frame dissolved under it. She has since been at my house, and continues as full as she can hold, but looks on herself not as an eminent saint, but as the worst of all, and unworthy to go to speak with a minister; but yet now beyond any great doubt of her good estate. There are two persons that belong to other towns that have had such a sense of God's exceeding greatness and majesty, that they were as it were swallowed up; they both of them told me to that purpose that if they in the time of it they had had the least fear that they were not at peace with that great God, they should immediately have died. But there is a very vast variety of degrees of spiritual discoveries, that are made to those that we hope are godly, as there is also in the steps, and method of the Spirit's operation in convincing and converting sinners, and the length of time that persons are under conviction before they have comfort. There is an alteration made in the town in a few months that strangers can scarcely [be] conscious of; our church, I believe, was the largest in New England before, but persons have lately thronged in, so that there are very few adult persons left out. There have been a great multitude hopefully converted, too many, I find, for me to declare abroad with credit to my judgment. The town seems to be full of the presence of God; our young people when they get together instead of frolicking as they used to do are altogether on pious subjects; tis so at weddings and on all occasions. The children in this, and the neighbouring towns have been greatly affected and influenced by the Spirit of God, and many of them hopefully changed; the youngest in this town is between nine and ten years of age; some of them seem to be full of love to Christ and have expressed great longings after Him and willingness to die, and leave father and mother and all things in the world to go to Him, together with a great sense of their unworthiness and admiration of the free grace of God towards them. And there have been many old people, many above fifty and several near seventy, that seem to be wonderfully changed and hopefully new born. The good people that have been formerly converted in the town have many of them been wonderfully enlivened and increased. This work seems to be upon every account an extraordinary dispensation of Providence. Tis extraordinary upon the account of [the] universality of it in affecting all sorts, high and low, rich and poor, wise and unwise, old and young, vicious and moral; tis very extraordinary as to the numbers that are hopefully savingly wrought upon, and particularly the number of aged persons and children and loose livers; and also on the account of the quickness of the work of the Spirit on them, for many seem to have been suddenly taken from a loose way of living, and to be so changed as to become truly holy, spiritual, heavenly persons; tis extraordinary as to the degrees of gracious communications, and the abundant measures in which the Spirit of God has been poured out on many persons; tis extraordinary as to the extent of it, God's Spirit being so remarkably poured out on so many towns at once, and its making such swift progress from place to place. The extraordinariness of the thing has been, I believe, one principal cause that people abroad have suspected it. There have been, as I have heard, many odd and strange stories that have been carried about the country of this affair, which it is a wonder some wise men should be so ready to believe. Some indeed under great terrors of conscience have had impressions on their imaginations; and also under the power of the spiritual discoveries, they have had lively impressed ideas of Christ shedding blood for sinners, His blood running from His veins, and of Christ in His glory in heaven and such like things, but they are always taught, and have been several times taught in public not to lay the weight of their hopes on such things and many have nothing of any such imaginations. There have been several persons that have had their natures overborne under strong convictions, and trembled, and han't been able to stand, they have had such a sense of divine wrath. But there are no new doctrines embraced, but people have been abundantly established in those that we account orthodox; there is no new way of worship affected. There is no oddity of behavior prevails; people are no more superstitious about their clothes, or anything else than they used to be. Indeed there is a great deal of talk when they are together of one another's experiences, and indeed no other is to be expected in a town where the concern of the soul is so universally the concern, and that to so great a degree. And doubtless some persons under the strength of impressions that are made on their minds and under the power of strong affections, are guilty of imprudences, their zeal may need to be regulated by more prudence, and they may need a guide to their assistance; as of old when the church of Corinth had the extraordinary gifts of the Spirit, they needed to be told by the Apostle that the spirit of the prophets were subject to the prophets, and that their gifts were to be exercised with prudence, because God was not the author of confusion but of peace. There is no unlovely oddity in peoples' temper prevailing with this work, but on the contrary the face of things is much changed as to the appearance of a meek, humble, amiable behavior. Indeed the devil has not been idle, but his hand has evidently appeared in several instances endeavoring to mimick the work of the Spirit of God and to cast a slur upon it and no wonder: and there has hereby appeared the need of the watchful eye of skillful guides, and of wisdom from above to direct them. There lately came up hither a couple of ministers from Connecticut, viz., Mr. Lord of Preston, and Mr. Owen of Groton, who had heard of the extraordinary circumstances of this and the neighbouring towns, who had heard the affair well represented by some, and also heard many reports greatly to its disadvantage, who came on purpose to see and satisfy themselves; and that they might thoroughly acquaint themselves, went about, and spent good part of a day, in hearing the accounts of many of our new converts, and examining of them; which was greatly to their satisfaction and they took particular notice, among other things of the modesty with which persons gave account of themselves, and said that the one half was not told them, and could not be told them; and that if they renounced these persons' experiences they must renounce Christianity itself. And Mr. Owens said particularly as to their impressions on their imaginations, they were quite different from what had been represented, and that they were no more than might naturally be expected in such cases.

Thus, Sir, I have given you a particular account of this affair which Satan has so much misrepresented in the country. This is a true account of the matter as far as I have opportunity to know, and I suppose I am under greater advantages to know than any person living. Having been thus long in the account, I forebear to make reflections, or to guess what God is about to do; I leave this to you, and shall only say, as I desire always to say from my heart, "To God be all the glory whose work alone it is"; and let Him have an interest in your prayers, who so much needs divine help at that day, and is your affectionate brother,

& humble servant,
Jth Edwards.

Northampton May 30, 1735

Since I wrote the foregoing letter, there has happened a thing of a very awful nature in the town; my uncle Hawley, the last sabbath morning, laid violent hands on himself, and put an end to his life, by cutting his own throat. He had been for a considerable time greatly concerned about the condition of his soul; till, by the ordering of a sovereign Providence he was suffered to fall into deep melancholy, a distemper that the family are very prone to; he was much overpowered by it; the devil took the advantage and drove him into despairing thoughts: he was kept very much awake a nights, so that he had but very little sleep for two months, till he seemed not to have his faculties in his own power; he was in a great measure past a capacity of receiving advice, or being reasoned with. The coroner's inquest judged him delirious. Satan seems to be in a great rage, at this extraordinary breaking forth of the work of God. I hope it is because he knows that he has but a short time: doubtless he had a great reach, in this violent attack of his against the whole affair. We have appointed a day of fasting in the town this week, by reason of this and other appearances of Satan's rage against poor souls. I yesterday saw a woman that belongs to Durham, who says there is a considerable revival of religion there.

I am yours &c—
J. E.

Northampton, June 3, 1735.

FROM *Freedom of the Will*

The full title of Edwards' most famous work is *A Careful and Strict Enquiry into the Modern Prevailing Notions of that Freedom of Will, which is Supposed to Be Essential to Moral Agency, Virtue and Vice, Reward and Punishment, Praise and Blame.* In it Edwards mustered all the passion of twenty years of revival preaching, but harnessed it in the logical exactness that marked his "Notes on the Mind." He brought the power of his logic to bear on each major "notion" represented in that title, and his arguments are so abundant, telling, and lengthy, that no selection can do his treatise justice. But the following excerpt is a good example of Edwards at work upon one of the central concepts involved—what does it mean to say the will is free? Is there in fact any such "thing" as a will to be free?

In general he argues that man in his fallen state has a natural inclination toward evil. So long as he exists in a natural state, his understanding will compel his will to choose evil over good. For this he is as blameworthy as the alcoholic who acts execrably when, by virtue of alcohol, we say he is not in control of his faculties. Only when a man's total understanding is re-directed, turned, or converted by God's saving grace can he make choices that are truly good. In either state, what we speak of as will is determined by our prior understanding, and therefore is *not* free.

Text: *Freedom of the Will*, ed. Paul Ramsey (New Haven, 1957).

[On the Notion of a Self-Determining Power in the Will]

And first of all, I shall consider the notion of a self-determining power in the will: wherein, according to the Arminians, does most essentially consist the will's freedom; and shall particularly inquire, whether it be not plainly absurd, and a manifest inconsistence, to suppose that the will itself determines all the free acts of the will.

Here I shall not insist on the great impropriety of such phrases, and ways of speaking, as "the will's determining itself"; because actions are to be ascribed to agents, and not properly to the powers of agents; which improper way of speaking leads to many mistakes, and much confusion, as Mr. Locke observes.[1] But I shall suppose that the Arminians, when they speak of the will's determining itself, do by the will mean "the soul willing." I shall take it for granted, that when they speak of the will, as the determiner, they mean the soul in the exercise of a power of willing, or acting voluntarily. I shall suppose this to be their meaning, because nothing else can be meant, without the grossest and plainest absurdity. In all cases, when we speak of the powers or principles of acting, as doing such things, we mean that the agents which have these powers of acting, do them, in the exercise of those powers. So when we say, valor fights courageously, we mean, the man who is under the influence of valor fights courageously. When we say, love seeks the object loved, we mean, the person loving seeks that object. When we say, the understanding discerns, we mean the soul in the exercise of that faculty. So when it is said, the will decides or determines, the meaning must be, that the person in the exercise of a power of willing and choosing, or the soul acting voluntarily, determines.

Therefore, if the will determines all its own free acts, the soul determines all the free acts of the will in the exercise of a power of willing and choosing; or, which is the same thing, it determines them of choice; it determines its own acts by choosing its own acts. If the will determines the will, then choice orders and determines the choice: and acts of choice are subject to the decision, and follow the conduct of other acts of choice. And therefore if the will determines all its own free acts, then every free act of choice is determined by a preceding act of choice, choosing that act. And if that preceding act of the will or choice be also a free act, then by these principles, in this act too, the will is self-determined; that is, this, in like manner, is an act that the soul voluntarily chooses; or which is the same thing, it is an act determined still by a preceding act of the will, choosing that. And the like may again be observed of the last mentioned act. Which brings us directly to a contradiction: for it supposes an act of the will preceding the first act in the whole train, directing and determining the rest; or a free act of the will before the first free act of the will. Or else we must come at last to an act of the will, determining the consequent acts, wherein the will is not self-determined, and so is not a free act, in this notion of freedom: but if the first act in the train, determining and fixing the rest, be not free, none of them all can be free; as is manifest at first view, but shall be demonstrated presently.

If the will, which we find governs the members of the body, and determines and commands their motions and actions, does also govern itself, and determine its own motions and acts, it doubtless determines them the same way, even by antecedent volitions. The will determines which way the hands and feet shall move, by an act of volition or choice: and there is no other way of the will's determining, directing or commanding anything at all. Whatsoever the will commands, it commands by an act of the will. And if it has itself under its command, and determines itself in its own actions, it doubtless does it the same way that it determines other things which are under its command. So that if the freedom of the will consists in this, that it has itself and its own actions under its command and direction, and its own volitions are determined by itself, it will follow, that every free volition arises from another antecedent volition, directing and commanding that: and if that *directing* volition be also free, in that also the will is self-determined; that is to say, that directing volition is determined by another going before that, and so on, till we come to the first volition in the whole series: and if that first volition be free, and the will self-determined in it, then that is determined by another volition preceding that. Which is a contradiction; because by the supposition it can have none before it, to direct or determine it, being the first in the train. But if that first volition is not determined by any preceding act of the will, then that act is not determined by the will, and so is not free, in the Arminian notion of freedom, which consists in the will's self-determination. And if that first act of the will, which deter-

---

[1] See John Locke's chapter "Of Power" in the *Essay Concerning Human Understanding*, Bk. II, ch. 21.

mines and fixes the subsequent acts, be not free, none of the following acts, which are determined by it, can be free. If we suppose there are five acts in the train, the fifth and last determined by the fourth, and the fourth by the third, the third by the second, and the second by the first; if the first is not determined by the will, and so not free, then none of them are truly determined by the will: that is, that each of them are as they are, and not otherwise, is not first owing to the will, but to the determination of the first in the series, which is not dependent on the will, and is that which the will has no hand in the determination of. And this being that which decides what the rest shall be, and determines their existence; therefore the first determination of their existence is not from the will. The case is just the same, if instead of a chain of five acts of the will, we should suppose a succession of ten, or an hundred, or ten thousand. If the first act be not free, being determined by something out of the will, and this determines the next to be agreeable to itself, and that the next, and so on; they are none of them free, but all originally depend on, and are determined by some cause out of the will: and so all freedom in the case is excluded, and no act of the will can be free, according to this notion of freedom. If we should suppose a long chain, of ten thousand links, so connected, that if the first link moves, it will move the next, and that the next; and so the whole chain must be determined to motion, and in the direction of its motion, by the motion of the first link; and that is moved by something else: in this case, though all the links, but one, are moved by other parts of the same chain; yet it appears that the motion of no one, nor the direction of its motion, is from any self-moving or self-determining power in the chain, any more than if every link were immediately moved by something that did not belong to the chain. If the will be not free in the first act, which causes the next, then neither is it free in the next, which is caused by that first act: for though indeed the will caused it, yet it did not cause it freely; because the preceding act, by which it was caused, was not free. And again, if the will ben't free in the second act, so neither can it be in the third, which is caused by that; because in like manner, that third was determined by an act of the will that was not free. And so we may go on to the next act, and from that to the next; and how long soever the succession of acts is, it is all one; if the first on which the whole chain depends, and which determines all the rest, ben't a free act, the will is not free in causing or determining any one of those acts; because the act by which it determines them all, is not a free act; and therefore the will is no more free in determining them, than if it did not cause them at all. Thus, this Arminian notion of liberty of the will, consisting in the will's self-determination, is repugnant to itself, and shuts itself wholly out of the world.

1754

The Quaker Temper

JOHN WOOLMAN [1720–1772]

QUAKERS FIRST ARRIVED in New England in 1656, preaching a personal spiritualism that outspokenly denounced all outward forms of ecclesiastical order and worship, and even, at the beginning, the Bible. Flagrantly eccentric in their behavior, they met with equally extreme repressive measures—fines, warnings, whipping, branding, mutilation, and in some cases death. But with the opening of Pennsylvania and New Jersey to varieties of religious belief in the 1680's, Quakers moderated their behavior, turning more and more to social service, so that established churches and communities found less and less excuse for punitive action against them.

By 1720, when John Woolman was born in New Jersey, the faith of his family was no longer the threat to social order that it once had been. Tailor, shopkeeper, and schoolmaster, Woolman spent most of his life as an itinerant minister for the Society of Friends, preaching the Quaker faith from New England to the Carolinas to all who would hear him. At the same time, in a series of pamphlets, he pleaded for temperance, the abolition of slavery, fairer treatment of the Indians, and relief for the poor. His record of a modest and moving life appeared in his *Journal*, published in Philadelphia two years after his death. John Greenleaf Whittier, who edited it in 1871, called it "a classic of the inner life." In England, Charles Lamb advised readers to get it "by heart"; and Crabb Robinson said of Woolman: "His is a schöne Seele, a beautiful soul. An illiterate tailor, he writes in a style of the most exquisite purity and grace. His moral qualities are transferred to his writings."

Further reading: *The Journal and Essays of John Woolman*, ed. with a biographical introduction by A. M. Gummere, 1922. Janet Whitney, *John Woolman, American Quaker*, 1942. Daniel B. Shea, *Spiritual Autobiography in Early America*, 1968.

FROM HIS *Journal*

Text: *The Journal and Essays of John Woolman*, ed. A. M. Gummere (New York, 1922).

[Youth]

I have often felt a motion of love to leave some hints of my experience of the goodness of God: and pursuant thereto, in the thirty-sixth year of my age, I begin this work.

I was born in Northampton, in Burlington county, in West Jersey, in the year of our Lord 1720; and before I was seven years old I began to be acquainted with the operations of divine love. Through the care of my parents, I was taught to read near as soon as I was capable of it; and as I went from school one seventh-day, I remember, while my companions went to play by the way, I went forward out of sight, and setting down, I read the twenty-second chapter of the Revelations: "He showed me a pure river of water of life, clear as crystal, proceeding out of the throne of God and of the lamb," etc.; and in the reading of it, my mind was drawn to seek after that pure habitation, which I then believed God had prepared for His servants. The place where I sat, and the sweetness that attended my mind, remain fresh in my memory.

This, and the like gracious visitations, had that effect upon me, that when boys used ill language, it troubled me, and through the continued mercies of God, I was preserved from it. The pious instructions of my parents were often fresh in my mind when I happened to be among wicked children, and were of use to me.

My parents, having a large family of children, used frequently, on first days after meeting, to put us to read in the holy scriptures, or some religious books, one after another, the rest sitting by without much conversation, which I have since often thought was a good practice. From what I had read, I believed there had been in past ages, people who walked in uprightness before God in a degree exceeding any that I knew, or heard of, now living; and the apprehension of there being less steadiness and firmness amongst people in this age than in past ages, often troubled me while I was still young.

I had a dream about the ninth year of my age as follows: I saw the moon rise near the West, and run a regular course Eastward, so swift that in about a quarter of an hour, she reached our meridian, when there descended from her a small cloud on a direct line to the earth, which lighted on a pleasant green about twenty yards from the door of my father's house (in which I thought I stood) and was immediately turned into a beautiful green tree. The moon appeared to run on with equal swiftness, and soon set in the East, at which time the sun arose at the place where it commonly doth in the summer, and shining with full radiance in a serene air, it appeared as pleasant a morning as ever I saw.

All this time I stood still in the door, in an awful frame of mind, and I observed that as heat increased by the rising sun, it wrought so powerfully on the little green tree, that the leaves gradually withered, and before noon it appeared dry and dead. There then appeared a being small of size, moving swift from the North Southward, called a sun worm.

Though I was a child, this dream was instructive to me.

Another thing remarkable in my childhood was, that once, as I went to a neighbor's house, I saw, on the way, a robin sitting on her nest; and as I came near she went off, but having young ones, flew about, and with many cries expressed her concern for them. I stood and threw stones at her, till one striking her, she fell down dead. At first I was pleased with the exploit, but after a few minutes was seized with horror, as having in a sportive way killed an innocent creature while she was careful for her young. I beheld her lying dead, and thought those young ones for which she was so careful must now perish for want of their dam to nourish them; and after some painful considerations on the subject, I climbed up the tree, took all the young birds, and killed them—supposing that better than to leave them to pine away and die miserably: and believed in this case, that scripture proverb was fulfilled, "The tender mercies of the wicked are cruel."[1] I then went on my errand, but, for some hours, could think of little else but the cruelties I had committed, and was much troubled.

Thus He, whose tender mercies are over all His works, hath placed that in the human mind, which incites to exercise goodness towards every living creature, and this being singly attended to, people become tender-hearted and sympathizing; but being frequently and totally rejected, the mind shuts itself up in a contrary disposition.

About the twelfth year of my age, my father being abroad, my mother reproved me for some misconduct, to which I made an undutiful reply; and the next first-day, as I was with my father returning from meeting, he told me he understood I had behaved amiss to my mother, and advised me to be more careful in future. I knew myself blamable, and in shame and confusion remained silent. Being thus awakened to a sense of my wickedness, I felt remorse in my mind, and getting home, I retired and prayed to the Lord to forgive me; and I do not remember that I ever, after that, spoke unhandsomely to either of my parents, however foolish in some other things.

Having attained the age of sixteen, I began to love wanton company: and though I was preserved from profane language or scandalous conduct, still I perceived a plant in me which produced much wild grapes. Yet my merciful Father forsook me not utterly, but at times, through His grace, I was brought seriously to consider my ways; and the sight of my backsliding affected me with sorrow: but for want of rightly attending to the reproofs of instruction, vanity was added to vanity, and repentance. Upon the whole, my mind was more and more alienated from the truth, and I hastened towards destruction. While I meditate on the gulf towards which I traveled, and reflect on my youthful disobedience, my heart is affected with sorrow.

Advancing in age, the number of my acquaintance increased, and thereby my way grew more difficult. Though I had heretofore found comfort in reading the holy scriptures, and thinking on heavenly things, I was now estranged therefrom. I knew I was going from the flock of Christ, and had no resolution to return; hence serious reflections were uneasy to me, and youthful vanities and diversions my greatest pleasure. Running in this road I found many like myself; and we associated in that which is reverse to true friendship. But in this swift race it pleased God to visit me with sickness, so that I doubted of recovering: and then did darkness, horror, and amazement, with full force seize me, even when my pain and distress of body was very great. I thought it would have been better for me never to have had a being, than to see the day which I now saw. I was filled with confusion; and in great affliction both of mind and body, I lay and bewailed myself. I had not confidence to lift up my cries to God, whom I had thus offended; but in a deep sense of my great folly, I was humbled before Him, and at length, that Word which is as a fire and a hammer, broke and dissolved my rebellious heart, and then my cries were put up in contrition, and in the multitude of His mercies I found inward relief, and felt a close engagement, that if He was pleased to restore my health, I might walk humbly before Him.

After my recovery, this exercise remained with me a considerable time, but, by degrees, giving way to youthful vanities, they gained strength, and getting with wanton young people I lost ground. The Lord had been very gracious, and spoke peace to me in the time of my distress, and I now most ungratefully turned again to folly, on which account, at times, I felt sharp reproof, but did not get low enough to cry for help. I was not so hardy as to commit things scandalous, but to exceed in vanity, and promote mirth, was my chief study. Still I retained a love and esteem for pious people, and their company brought an awe upon me. My dear parents several times admonished me in the fear of the Lord, and their admonition entered into my heart, and had a good effect for a season; but not getting deep enough to pray rightly, the tempter, when he came, found entrance. I remember once, having spent a part of a day in wantonness, as I went to bed at night, there lay in a window near my bed a Bible, which I opened, and first cast my eye on the text, "we lie down in our shame, and our confusion covers us."[2] This I knew to be my case, and meeting with so unexpected a reproof, I was somewhat affected with it, and went to bed under remorse of conscience, which I soon cast off again.

Thus time passed on, my heart was replenished with mirth and wantonness, while pleasing scenes of vanity were presented to my imagination, till I attained the age of eighteen years, near which time I

WANTONNESS → SICKNESS → CONTRITION → HEALTH

---

[1] Proverbs xii.10.

[2] Jeremiah iii.25.

felt the judgments of God in my soul like a consuming fire, and looking over my past life, the prospect was moving. I was often sad, and longed to be delivered from those vanities; then again my heart was strongly inclined to them, and there was in me a sore conflict. At times I turned to folly, and then again sorrow and confusion took hold of me. In a while, I resolved totally to leave off some of my vanities, but there was a secret reserve in my heart, of the more refined part of them, and I was not low enough to find true peace. Thus some months, I had great troubles and disquiet, there remaining in me an unsubjected will, which rendered my labors fruitless, till at length, through the merciful continuance of heavenly visitations, I was made to bow down in spirit before the Most High. I remember one evening I had spent some time in reading a pious author, and walking out alone, I humbly prayed to the Lord for His help, that I might be delivered from those vanities which so ensnared me. . . . Thus, being brought low, He helped me, and as I learned to bear the cross, I felt refreshment to come from His presence: but not keeping in that strength which gave victory, I lost ground again, the sense of which greatly afflicted me; and I sought deserts and lonely places, and there with tears did confess my sins to God, and humbly craved help of Him. And I may say with reverence, He was near to me in my troubles, and in those times of humiliation opened my ear to discipline.

I was now led to look seriously at the means by which I was drawn from the pure truth, and I learned this: that if I would live in the life which the faithful servants of God lived in, I must not go into company as heretofore, in my own will; but all the cravings of sense must be governed by a divine principle. In times of sorrow and abasement, these instructions were sealed upon me, and I felt the power of Christ prevail over all selfish desires, so that I was preserved in a good degree of steadiness; and being young and believing at that time that a single life was best for me, I was strengthened to keep from such company as had often been a snare to me.

I kept steady to meetings; spent first-days in the afternoon chiefly in reading the scriptures and other good books; and was early convinced in my mind that true religion consisted in an inward life, wherein the heart doth love and reverence God the Creator, and learn to exercise true justice and goodness, not only toward all men, but also toward the brute creatures. That as the mind was moved by an inward principle to love God as an invisible, incomprehensible Being, by the same principle it was moved to love Him in all His manifestations in the visible world. That, as by His breath the flame of life was kindled in all animal and sensible creatures,

to say we love God as unseen, and at the same time exercise cruelty toward the least creature moving by His life, or by life derived from Him, was a contradiction in itself.

I found no narrowness respecting sects and opinions; but believed that sincere, upright-hearted people, in every society, who truly love God, were accepted of Him. As I lived under the cross, and simply followed the openings of truth, my mind from day to day was more enlightened; my former acquaintance were left to judge of me as they would, for I found it safest for me to live in private and keep these things sealed up in my own breast. While I silently ponder on that change which was wrought in me, I find no language equal to it, nor any means to convey to another a clear idea of it. I looked upon the works of God in this visible creation, and an awfulness covered me: my heart was tender and often contrite, and a universal love to my fellow creatures increased in me. This will be understood by such who have trodden in the same path.

Some glances of real beauty is perceivable in their faces, who dwell in true meekness. Some tincture of true harmony in the sound of that voice to which divine love gives utterance, and some appearance of right order in their temper and conduct, whose passions are fully regulated; yet all these do not fully show forth that inward life to such as have not felt it; but this white stone and new name is known rightly to such only who have it.

[Business and Conscience]

Until the year 1756, I continued to retail goods, besides following my trade as a tailor; about which time I grew uneasy on account of my business growing too cumbersome. I began with selling trimmings for garments, and from thence proceeded to sell cloths and linens, and at length having got a considerable shop of goods, my trade increased every year, and the road to large business appeared open: but I felt a stop in my mind.

Through the mercies of the Almighty I had in good degree learned to be content with a plain way of living. I had but a small family, my outward affairs had been prosperous, and, on serious reflection I believed truth did not require me to engage in much cumbering affairs. It had generally been my practice to buy and sell things really useful. Things that served chiefly to please the vain mind in people, I was not easy to trade in; seldom did it, and whenever I did, I found it weaken me as a Christian.

The increase of business became my burthen, for though my natural inclination was towards merchandise, yet I believed truth required me to live more free from outward cumbers. There was now a strife in my mind betwixt the two, and in this exercise my prayers were put up to the Lord, who graciously heard me, and gave me a heart resigned to His holy will; I then lessened my outward business; and as I had opportunity, told my customers of my intention, that they might consider what shop to turn to: and so in a while, wholly laid down merchandise, following my trade as a tailor, myself only, having no prentice. I also had a nursery of apple trees, in which I spent a good deal of time, howing, grafting, trimming, and inoculating.

In merchandise it is the custom, where I lived, to sell chiefly on credit; and poor people often get in debt, and when payment is expected, having not wherewith to pay, and so their creditors often sue for it at law: having often observed occurrences of this kind, I found it good for me to advise poor people to take such as were most useful and not costly.

In the time of trading I had an opportunity of seeing that a too liberal use of spiritous liquors, and the custom of wearing too costly apparel, led some people into great inconveniences: and these two things appear to be often connected one with the other; for by not attending to that use of things which is consistent with universal righteousness, there is a necessary increase of labor which extends beyond what our heavenly Father intends for us: and by great labor, and often by much sweating in the heat, there is, even among such who are not drunkards, a craving of some liquor to revive the spirits: that partly by the wanton, luxurious drinking of some, and partly by the drinking of others, led to it through immoderate labor, very great quantities of rum are annually expended in our colonies, of which we should have no need, did we steadily attend to pure wisdom.

Where men take pleasure in feeling their minds elevated with strong drink, and so indulge this appetite as to disorder their understanding, neglect their duty as members in a family or civil society, and cast off all pretense to religion, their case is much to be pitied. And where such whose lives are for the most part regular, and whose examples have a strong influence on the minds of others, adhere to some customs which powerfully draw toward the use of more strong liquor than pure wisdom directeth the use of, this also, as it hinders the spreading of the spirit of meekness, and strengthens the hands of the more excessive drinkers, is a case to be lamented.

As the least degree of luxury hath some connection with evil, for those who profess to be disciples of Christ, and are looked upon as leaders of the people, to have that mind in them which was also in

Him, and so stand separate from every wrong way, is a means of help to the weaker. As I have sometimes been much spent in the heat, and taken spirits to revive me, I have found by experience that the mind is not so calm in such circumstances, nor so fit for divine meditation, as when all such extremes are avoided; and I have felt an increasing care to attend that Holy Spirit which sets right bounds to our desires, and leads those who faithfully follow it to apply all the gifts of divine providence to the purposes for which they were intended. Did such who have the care of great estates attend with singleness of heart to this heavenly instructor, which so opens and enlarges the mind that men love their neighbors as themselves, they would have wisdom given them to manage, without ever finding occasion to employ some people in the luxuries of life, or to make it necessary for others to labor too hard. But for want of regarding steadily this principle of divine love, a selfish spirit takes place in the minds of people, which is attended with darkness and manifold confusions in the world. °°°

Though trading in things useful is an honest employ, yet through the great number of superfluities which are commonly bought and sold, and through the corruptions of the times, they who apply to merchandise for a living, have great need to be well experienced in that precept which the prophet Jeremiah laid down for Baruk, his scribe: "Seekest thou great things for thyself? seek them not."

[A Testimony Against Slavery]

The monthly-meeting of Philadelphia having been under a concern on account of some Friends who, this summer, A.D. 1758, had bought Negro slaves, the said meeting moved it in their quarterly-meeting, to have the minute reconsidered in the yearly-meeting, which was made last on that subject: and the said quarterly-meeting appointed a committee to consider it and report to their next; which committee having met once and adjourned, and I going to Philadelphia to meet a committee of the yearly-meeting, was in town the evening on which the quarterly-meeting's committee met the second time, and finding an inclination to sit with them, was, with some others, admitted; and Friends had a weighty conference on the subject. And soon after their next quarterly-meeting, I heard that the case was coming to our yearly-meeting, which brought a weighty exercise upon me, and under a sense of my own infirmities and the great danger I felt of turning aside from perfect purity, my mind was often drawn to retire alone and put up my prayers to the Lord, that He would be graciously pleased to so strengthen me, that, setting aside all views of self-interest and the friendship of this world, I might stand fully resigned to His holy will.

In this yearly-meeting several weighty matters were considered; and, toward the last, that in relation to dealing with persons who purchase slaves. During the several sittings of the said meeting, my mind was frequently covered with inward prayer, and I could say with David, that tears were my meat day and night. The case of slave keeping lay heavy upon me, nor did I find any engagement to speak directly to any other matter before the meeting. Now when this case was opened several faithful Friends spake weightily thereto, with which I was comforted; and, feeling a concern to cast in my mite, I said, in substance, as follows:

"In the difficulties attending us in this life, nothing is more precious than the mind of truth inwardly manifested, and it is my earnest desire that in this weighty matter we may be so truly humbled, as to be favored with a clear understanding of the mind of truth, and follow it: this would be of more advantage to the society, than any mediums which are not in the clearness of divine wisdom. The case is difficult to some who have them; but if such set aside all self-interest, and come to be weaned from the desire of getting estates, or even from holding them together when truth requires the contrary, I believe way will open, that they will know how to steer through those difficulties."

Many Friends appeared to be deeply bowed under the weight of the work; and manifested much firmness in their love to the cause of truth and universal righteousness in the earth. And though none did openly justify the practice of slave keeping in general, yet some appeared concerned, lest the meeting should go into such measures as might give uneasiness to many brethren, alleging that if Friends patiently continued under the exercise, the Lord, in time to come, might open a way for the deliverance of these people, and I, finding an engagement to speak, said: "My mind is often led to consider the purity of the divine Being, and the justice of His judgments; and herein my soul is covered with awfulness. I cannot omit to hint of some cases where people have not been treated with the purity of justice, and the event hath been lamentable. Many slaves on this continent are oppressed, and their cries have reached the ears of the Most High! Such are the purity and certainty of His judgments, that He cannot be partial toward any. In infinite love and goodness He hath opened our understandings, from time to time, respecting our duty toward this people; and it is not a time for delay. Should we now be sensible of what He requires of us, and through a respect to the outward interest of some persons, or through a regard to some friendships which do not stand on the immutable foundation,

neglect to do our duty in firmness and constancy, still waiting for some extraordinary means to bring about their freedom, it may be that by terrible things in righteousness God may answer us in this matter."

Many faithful brethren labored with great firmness, and love of truth, in a good degree, prevailed. Several Friends who had Negroes exprest their desire that a rule might be made to deal with such Friends as offenders who might buy slaves in future. To this it was replied that the root of this evil would not be removed from amongst us, till a close inquiry was made in regard to the righteousness of their motives who detained Negroes in their service, that impartial justice might be administered throughout. Several Friends exprest a desire that a visit might be made to such Friends who kept slaves: and many Friends said that they believed liberty was the Negroes' right, to which at length no opposition was made publicly. A minute was at length made more full on that subject than any heretofore and the names of several Friends entered who were free to join in a visit to such who kept slaves.

[A Visit to Indian Country]

10 day, 6 month, [1763]. Set out early in the morning and crossed the western branch of Delaware, called the Great Lehie, near fort Allen; the water being high, we went over in a canoe: here we met an Indian and had some friendly conversation with him, and gave him some bisquit; and he having killed a deer, gave the Indians with us some of it: then after traveling some miles, we met several Indian men and women with a cow and horse, and some household goods, who were lately come from their dwelling at Wioming,[3] and going to settle at another place; we made them some small presents, and some of them understanding English, I told them my motive in coming into their country; with which they appeared satisfied: and one of our guides talking a while with an ancient woman concerning us, the poor old woman came to my companion and me, and took her leave of us with an appearance of sincere affection. So going on, we pitched our tent near the banks of the same river, having labored hard in crossing some of those mountains, called the Blue Ridge; and by the roughness of the stones, and the cavities between them, and the steepness of the hills, it appeared dangerous: but we were preserved in safety, through the kindness of Him whose works in these mountainous deserts appeared awful; toward whom my heart was turned during this day's travel.

Near our tent, on the sides of large trees peeled for that purpose, were various representations of

[3] Wyoming, Pennsylvania.

men going to, and returning from the wars, and of some killed in battle, this being a path heretofore used by warriors. And as I walked about viewing those Indian histories, which were painted mostly in red but some with black, and thinking on the innumerable afflictions which the proud, fierce spirit produceth in the world; thinking on the toils and fatigues of warriors, traveling over mountains and deserts, thinking on their miseries and distresses when wounded far from home by their enemies; and of their bruises and great weariness in chasing one another over the rocks and mountains; and of their restless, unquiet state of mind, who live in this spirit, and of the hatred which mutually grows up in the minds of the children of those nations engaged in war with each other: the desire to cherish the spirit of love and peace amongst these people, arose very fresh in me.

This was the first night that we were in the woods; and being wet with traveling in the rain, the ground and our tent wet, and the bushes wet which we purposed to lay under, our blankets also, all looked discouraging; but I believed that it was the Lord who had thus far brought me forward, and that He would dispose of me as He saw good, and therein I felt easy. So we kindled a fire, with our tent door open to it, and with some bushes next the ground, and then blankets, we made our bed, and lying down, got some sleep: and in the morning, feeling a little unwell, I went into the river all over. The water was cold, but soon after I felt fresh and well.

11 day, 6 month. The bushes being wet, we tarried in our tent till about eight o'clock; then going on, crossed a high mountain supposed to be upwards of four miles wide, and the steepness on the north side exceeded all the others. We also crossed two swamps; and it raining near night, we pitched our tent and lodged. About noon, on our way, we were overtaken by one of the Moravian brethren going to Wahalowsing, and an Indian man with him who could talk English; and we being together while our horses eat grass, had some friendly conversation; then they traveling faster than we, soon left us. This Moravian brother, I understood, had spent some time this spring at Wahalowsing, and was by some of them invited to come again.

12 day, 6 month, of the week being a rainy day, we continued in our tent; and here I was led to think on the nature of the exercise which hath attended me. Love was the first motion, and then a concern arose to spend some time with the Indians, that I might feel and understand their life, and the spirit they live in, if happily I might receive some instruction from them, or they be in any degree helped forward by my following the leadings of truth amongst them: and as it pleased the Lord to

make way for my going at a time when the troubles of war were increasing, and when by reason of much wet weather traveling was more difficult than usual at that season, I looked upon it as a more favorable opportunity to season my mind, and bring me into a nearer sympathy with them. And as mine eye was to the great Father of mercies, humbly desiring to learn what His will was concerning me, I was made quiet and content.

Our pilot's horse, though hoppled, went away in the night; and after finding our own, and searching some time for him, his footsteps were discovered in the path going back again, whereupon my kind companion went off in the rain, and after about seven hours returned with him: and here we lodged again, tying up our horses before we went to bed, and loosing them to feed about break of day.

13 day, 6 month: the sun appearing, we set forward; and as I rode over the barren hills, my meditations were on the alterations of the circumstances of the natives of this land since the coming in of the English. The lands near the sea are conveniently situated for fishing; the lands near the rivers, where the tides flow, and some above, are in many places fertile, and not mountainous; while the running of the tides makes passing up and down easy with any kind of traffic. Those natives have in some places, for small considerations, sold their inheritance so favorably situated; and in other places been driven back by superior force: so that in many places, as their way of clothing themselves is now altered from what it was, and they far remote from us, have to pass over mountains, swamps, and barren deserts, where traveling is very troublesome, in bringing their furs and skins to trade with us.

By the extending of English settlements, and partly by English hunters, the wild beasts they chiefly depend on for a subsistence, are not so plenty as they were. And people too often, for the sake of gain, open a door for them to waste their skins and furs, in purchasing a liquor which tends to the ruin of them and their families.

My own will and desire being now very much broken, and my heart with much earnestness turned to the Lord, to whom alone I looked for help in the dangers before me, I had a prospect of the English along the coast for upwards of nine hundred miles where I have traveled; and the favorable situation of the English, and the difficulties attending the natives and the slaves among us, were open before me; and a weighty and heavenly care came over my mind, and love filled my heart toward all mankind, in which I felt a strong engagement, that we might be faithful to the Lord while His mercies are yet extended to us, and so attend to pure universal righteousness, as to give no just cause of offence to the Gentiles who do not profess Christianity, whether the blacks from Africa, or the native inhabitants of this continent. And here I was led into a close, laborious enquiry, whether I as an individual kept clear from all things which tended to stir up, or were connected with wars, either in this land or Africa; and my heart was deeply concerned that in future I might in all things keep steadily to the pure truth, and live and walk in the plainness and simplicity of a sincere follower of Christ. And in this lonely journey, I did this day greatly bewail the spreading of a wrong spirit, believing that the prosperous convenient situation of the English, requires a constant attention to divine love and wisdom to guide and support us in a way answerable to the will of that good, gracious, and almighty Being, who hath an equal regard to all mankind. And here luxury and covetousness, with the numerous oppressions, and other evils attending them, appeared very afflicting to me, and I felt in that which is immutable, that the seeds of great calamity and desolation are sown and growing fast on this continent. Nor have I words sufficient to set forth that longing I then felt, that we who are placed along the coast, and have tested the love and goodness of God, might arise in His strength, and like faithful messengers, labor to check the growth of those seeds that they may not ripen to the ruin of our posterity.

1774

FROM *Considerations on Keeping Negroes*

Negro slavery had been a thorn to Christian consciences for some years before Judge Samuel Sewall of Boston published a broadside entitled *The Selling of Joseph: A Memorial* (1700), which argued that "all men, as they are the sons of Adam, are co-heirs; and have equal right unto liberty, and all other outward comforts of life." Seventy-five years later the first antislavery society was organized in Philadelphia—The Society for the Relief of Free Negroes, Unlawfully Held in Bondage. Quakers had long been outspoken opponents of slavery, Woolman's voice one of the foremost among them following his 1500-mile trip to Virginia and North Carolina in 1746. *Some Considerations* (1754, 1762) is a significant document in the early phase of antislavery agitation. Text: The Gummere edition of *The Journals and Essays*.

[Final Appeal]

If we seriously consider that liberty is the right of innocent men; that the mighty God is a refuge for the oppressed; that in reality we are indebted to them; that they being set free, are still liable to the penalties of our laws, and as likely to have punishment for their crimes as other people: this may answer all our objections. And to retain them in perpetual servitude, without just cause for it, will produce effects, in the event, more grievous than setting

them free would do, when a real love to truth and equity was the motive to it.

Our authority over them stands originally in a purchase made from those who, as to the general, obtained theirs by unrighteousness. Whenever we have recourse to such authority, it tends more or less to obstruct the channels through which the perfect plant in us receives nourishment.

There is a principle which is pure, placed in the human mind, which in different places and ages hath had different names; it is, however, pure, and proceeds from God. It is deep, and inward, confined to no forms of religion, nor excluded from any, where the heart stands in perfect sincerity. In whomsoever this takes root and grows, of what nation soever, they become brethren, in the best sense of the expression. Using ourselves to take ways which appear most easy to us, when inconsistent with that purity which is without beginning, we thereby set up a government of our own, and deny obedience to Him whose service is true liberty.

He that hath a servant, made so wrongfully, and knows it to be so, when he treats him otherwise than a free man, when he reaps the benefit of his labor, without paying him such wages as are reasonably due to free men for the like service, clothes excepted; these things, though done in calmness, without any shew of disorder, do yet deprave the mind in like manner, and with as great certainty as prevailing cold congeals water. These steps taken by masters, and their conduct striking the minds of their children, whilst young, leave less room for that which is good to work upon them. The customs of their parents, their neighbors, and the people with whom they converse, working upon their minds; and they, from thence, conceiving ideas of things, and modes of conduct, the entrance into their hearts becomes, in a great measure, shut up against the gentle movings of uncreated purity.

From one age to another, the gloom grows thicker and darker, till error gets established by general opinion so that whoever attends to perfect goodness, and remains under the melting influence of it, finds a path unknown to many, and sees the necessity to lean upon the arm of divine strength, and dwell alone, or with a few, in the right committing their cause to Him who is a refuge for His people in all their troubles.

Where, through the agreement of a multitude, some channels of justice are stopped, and men may support their characters as just men by being just to a party, there is great danger of contracting an alliance with that spirit which stands in opposition to the God of love, and spreads discord, trouble, and vexation among such who give up to the influence of it.

Negroes are our fellow creatures, and their present condition amongst us requires our serious consideration. We know not the time when those scales in which mountains are weighed may turn. The Parent of mankind is gracious; His care is over His smallest creatures; and a multitude of men escape not His notice. And though many of them are trodden down, and despised, yet He remembers them; He seeth their affliction, and looketh upon the spreading, increasing exaltation of the oppressor. He turns the channels of power, humbles the most haughty people, and gives deliverance to the op-

pressed, at such periods as are consistent with His infinite justice and goodness. And wherever gain is preferred to equity, and wrong things publicly encouraged, to that degree that wickedness takes root, and spreads wide amongst the inhabitants of a country, there is real cause for sorrow to all such whose love to mankind stands on a true principle, and who wisely consider the end and event of things.

1762

A Virginia Gentleman

WILLIAM BYRD [1674–1744]

RICH IN LAND and equally rich in curiosity and zest for life, Byrd joined a robust temperament to opportunity and means in creating and recording a style of life that has charmed generations of readers. Son of a wealthy and prominent Virginia tobacco planter, he was born near the site of the present city of Richmond, which he himself founded. In 1681 he was sent to England to be educated, and there he spent most of the next twenty years and more. He traveled, read law, dabbled in science, was made a Fellow of the Royal Society, represented Virginia at court, frequented the theater, mingled with literary notables—especially the dramatists William Congreve, Nicholas Rowe, and William Wycherly—and thoroughly absorbed the elegance and sophistication of London.

His father's death in 1704 brought him back to Virginia and to the privileges and responsibilities of a large plantation. At Westover on the James he built one of the finest colonial mansions of the period, filling it with appropriately handsome furniture, glass, and silver from England, as well as with portraits of English noblemen whom he had known and with whom he corresponded. To one of them, the Earl of Orrery, he wrote a description of his life as a rich planter:

> I have a large family of my own, and my doors are open to everybody, yet I have no bills to pay, and half a crown will rest undisturbed in my pocket for many moons together. Like one of the patriarchs, I have my flocks and my herds, my bondmen and bondwomen, and every sort of trade amongst my own servants, so that I live in a kind of independence of everyone but Providence. However, this sort of life is without expense, yet it is attended with a great deal of trouble. I must take care to keep all my people to their duty, to set all the springs in motion, and to make everyone draw his equal share to carry the machine forward. But then 'tis an amusement in this silent country.

And even as he increased his estates from the 26,231 acres he inherited to more than 179,000 before his death, he also vigorously pursued the public duties his position entailed. Receiver-general of the King's revenues, he bore a prominent part in the colony's long dispute with Governor Spotswood, and in 1709 he became a member of the Council of State, the aristocratic group that virtually governed Virginia.

Byrd's interests, however, were not exclusively material. His library was distinguished not only by its size (at 3,600 titles it was the largest in Virginia), but by its remarkable balance, ranging from divinity and natural philosophy to history and literature, especially the Elizabethan and Restoration dramatists, and featuring more than five hundred titles in Greek, Latin, and French. In England he tried his hand at verse and polite essay forms, and even published a forty-page *Discourse Concerning the Plague*, but his main literary accomplishment was of another kind.

From 1709 to 1741, Byrd kept a shorthand diary in which he registered with gusto the delights and pangs of the flesh as well as the mind. The brilliance of his observations, the shrewdness of his comments, his ability to vivify characters and places, and the frankness and humor of his approach to everything make the diaries a remarkable portrait of provincial life. The same qualities mark his *History of the Dividing Line Run in the Year 1728*, and another *Secret History*, both of which recount the boundary survey between Virginia and North Carolina (a project which he led), and his account of a visit to Governor Spotswood's iron mines in *A Progress to the Mines in the Year 1732*.

Further reading: *The Writings*, ed. J. S. Bassett, 1901. *William Byrd's Histories of the Dividing Line Betwixt Virginia and North Carolina*, ed. W. K. Boyd, 1929. L. B. Wright, *The First Gentlemen of Virginia*, 1940. R. C. Beatty, *William Byrd of Westover*, 1932.

FROM *Secret Diary*

Undiscovered till well into the twentieth century, a diary for 1709–1712 was published in 1941, one for 1739–1741 in 1942. Our selections are from the former. They provide interesting glimpses of Byrd's life at Westover. Text: *The Secret Diary of William Byrd of Westover, 1709–1712*, ed. Louis B. Wright and Marion Tinling (Richmond, 1941).

[The Life of a Virginia Gentleman]

Dec. 25, 1709. I rose at 7 o'clock and ate milk for breakfast. I neglected to say my prayers because of my company. I ate milk for breakfast. About 11 o'clock the rest of the company ate some broiled turkey for their breakfast. Then we went to church, notwithstanding it rained a little, where Mr. Anderson preached a good sermon for the occasion. I received the sacrament with great devoutness. After church the same company went to dine with me and I ate roast beef for dinner. In the afternoon Dick Randolph and Mr. Jackson went away and Mr. Jackson rode sidelong like a woman. Then we took a walk about the plantation, but a great fog soon drove us into the house again. In the evening we were merry with nonsense and so were my servants. I said my prayers shortly and had good health, good thoughts, and good humor, thanks be to God Almighty.

Dec. 29. I rose at 5 o'clock and read two chapters in Hebrew and some Greek in Cassius.[1] I said my prayers and ate milk for breakfast. I danced my

dance.[2] About 9 o'clock I ate again some chocolate with the company. Then we took a walk and I slid on skates, notwithstanding there was a thaw. Then we returned and played at billiards till dinner. I ate boiled beef for dinner. In the afternoon we played at billiards again and in the evening took another walk and gave Mr. Isham Randolph two bits to venture on the ice. He ventured and the ice broke with him and took him up to the mid-leg. Then we came home and played a little at whisk, but I was so sleepy we soon left off.

March 31, 1710. I rose at 7 o'clock and read some Greek in bed. I said my prayers and ate milk for breakfast. Then about 8 o'clock we got a-horseback and rode to Mr. Harrison's and found him very ill but sensible. Here I met Mr. Bland who brought me several letters from England and among the rest two from Colonel Blakiston who had endeavored to procure the Government of Virginia for me at the price of £1000 of my Lady Orkney and that my Lord [agreed], but the Duke of Marlborough declared that no one but soldiers should have the government of a plantation so I was disappointed. God's will be done. From hence I came home where I found all well, thank God. I ate fish for dinner. In the afternoon I went again with my wife to Mr. Harrison's who continued very bad so that I resolved to stay with him all night, which I did with Mr. Anderson and Nat Burwell. He was in the same bad condition till he vomited and then he was more easy. In the morning early I returned home and

[1] Probably the history of Rome by Dion Cassius, a copy of which Byrd owned.

[2] This recurring phrase probably refers to a calisthenic dance, or setting-up exercise, devised by Byrd, who was a bit of a faddist in his lifelong preoccupation with his health.

went to bed. It is remarkable that Mrs. Burwell dreamed this night that she saw a person that with money scales weighed time and declared that there was no more than 18 pennies worth of time to come, which seems to be a dream with some significance either concerning the world or a sick person. In my letters from England I learned that the Bishop of Worcester was of opinion that in the year 1715 the city of Rome would be burnt to the ground, that before the year 1745 the popish religion would be rooted out of the world, that before the year 1790 the Jews and Gentiles would be converted to the Christianity and then would begin the millennium.

April 10. I rose at 6 o'clock and wrote several letters to my overseers. I sent early to inquire after Mr. Harrison and received word that he died about 4 o'clock this morning, which completed the 18th day of his sickness, according to Mrs. Burwell's dream exactly. Just before his death he was sensible and desired Mrs. L— with importunity to open the door because he wanted to go out and could not go till the door was open and as soon as the door was opened he died. The country has lost a very useful man and who was both an advantage and an ornament to it, and I have lost a good neighbor, but God's will be done. I said my prayers and ate caudle[3] for breakfast. I danced my dance. My wife rode to Mrs. Harrison's to comfort her and to assure her that I should be always ready to do her all manner of service. My wife returned before dinner. I ate tripe for dinner. In the afternoon we played at piquet.[4] Then I prepared my matters for the General Court. It rained, with the wind at northeast, and it was very cold, and in the night it snowed.

May 23. I rose at 5 o'clock and read 2 chapters in Hebrew and some Greek in Anacreon. The children were a little better, thank God. I said my prayers and ate milk and strawberries for breakfast. I danced my dance. My daughter was very ill, but the boy had lost his fever, thank God. I settled some accounts and wrote some commonplace. I ate hashed shoat for dinner. In the afternoon Evie had a sweat that worked pretty well, but not long enough, for which I was out of humor with my wife. I read some Italian and some news and then took a walk about the plantation. When I returned I had a great quarrel with my wife, in which she was to blame altogether; however, I made the first step to a reconciliation, to [which] she with much difficulty consented.

June 15. I rose at 5 o'clock and read a chapter in Hebrew and some Greek in Thucydides. I said my prayers and ate milk for breakfast. The weather was very hot. I wrote a letter to England. I ate some broiled pork for dinner. In the afternoon my gripes[5] returned on me and continued till the evening with some violence. Hot things did it no good but in the evening I drank some warm milk from the cow which eased me immediately. It rained this afternoon very hard with a little wind and thunder. This hindered my walking anywhere but in the garden. I foretold by my cellar stinking that it would rain. I impute my gripes to cherry wine, or else pulling my coat off about noon. I said my prayers and had good thoughts, good humor, but indifferent good health, thank God Almighty.

June 16. I rose at 5 o'clock and drank some milk warm from the cow. I read a chapter in Hebrew and some Greek in Thucydides. I said my prayers and danced my dance. About 10 o'clock Captain Drury Stith and his wife came to make us a visit, notwithstanding it was very hot. I was glad to see them because I think them excellent people. We played at billiards till dinner. I ate boiled pork. In the afternoon we passed away the time pleasantly till about 6 o'clock and then they went home. In the evening I took a walk with my wife. We made a little cider of the G-n-t-n apples, which yielded but little juice. I was better of my gripes, thank God. I neglected to say my prayers but had good health, good thoughts, and good humor, thank God Almighty.

June 17. I rose at 5 o'clock and drank some milk hot from the cow. I read a chapter in Hebrew and some Greek in Thucydides. I said my prayers and danced my dance. About 8 o'clock Mr. Anderson came on his way over the river. He told me the quarrel was made up between Parson Slater and his vestry without coming to trial. He stayed about half an hour. Colonel Hill sent his man with a basket of apricots, of which my wife ate twelve immediately and I ate eight which however did not make my gripes return. I set my closet right. I ate tongue and chicken for dinner. In the afternoon I caused L-s-n to be whipped for beating his wife and Jenny was whipped for being his whore. In the evening the sloop came from Appomatox with tobacco. I took a walk about the plantation. I said my prayers and drank some new milk from the cow. I had good health, good thoughts, and good humor, thanks be to God Almighty.

June 18. I rose at 5 o'clock and drank some new milk from the cow. I read a chapter in Hebrew and some Greek in Thucydides. I said my prayers. It was extremely hot. I read a sermon in Dr. Tillotson about angels. I wrote a letter to Williamsburg to send by my sloop which I sent for rum, wine, and sugar from thence and that this might come safely I resolved to send Bannister with the sloop. I ate

[3]A warm, spiced drink of gruel mixed with wine or ale.
[4]A two-handed card game played with 32 cards.

[5]Intermittent stomach cramps.

chicken for dinner but very little because I had no appetite. In the afternoon my wife told me a dream she had two nights. She thought she saw a scroll in the sky in form of a light cloud with writing on it. It ran extremely fast from west to east with great swiftness. The writing she could not read but there was a woman before her that told her there would be a great dearth because of want of rain and after that a pestilence for that the seasons were changed and time inverted. Mr. James Burwell and Charles Doyley came and in the evening I took a walk with them. Our nurse went away in the sloop. I said my prayers and had good health, good thoughts, and good humor, thanks be to God Almighty.

June 19. I rose at 5 o'clock and read a chapter in Hebrew and some Greek in Thucydides. I drank some warm milk from the cow. I said my prayers and danced my dance. About 10 o'clock came Isham Randolph and Mr. Finney to see us. They told me Colonel Randolph was very ill and very melancholy. We played at billiards till dinner. I ate fish for dinner. In the afternoon Mr. Stith came over with my cousin Berkeley, who all stayed here till the evening and then they all went away but Mr. Finney. In the evening we took a walk. Mr. Finney is a sensible man and good natured. He told me that Major Allen died on Thursday last. In our walk we met Mr. C—s who came home with us. I neglected to say my prayers but had good health, good thoughts, and good humor, thank God Almighty.

June 20. I rose at 5 o'clock and drank milk from the cow. I read a chapter in Hebrew and some Greek in Thucydides. I said my prayers and danced my dance. Mr. Finney returned home without any breakfast but I gave him some strong water. Colonel Hill sent us another present of apricots. I wrote a letter to England. I ate five apricots which put my belly out of order. I ate roast mutton for dinner. In the afternoon my belly was griped. I played with my wife at piquet and then I ordered the boat to carry us to my cousin Harrison's where we found my cousin Berkeley and Jimmy Burwell. I was out of order in my belly. About 8 o'clock we returned home where we found all well, thank God. I said my prayers and had good health, good thoughts, and good humor, thanks be to God Almighty.

June 21. I rose at 5 o'clock and drank milk from the cow. I read a chapter in Hebrew and some Greek in Thucydides. I said my prayers and danced my dance. My wife was indisposed. I sent Tom to Appomattox to desire Mr. Mumford to go to the outcry of my uncle's estate. About five nights since I dreamed I saw a flaming star in the air at which I was much frightened and called some others to see it but when they came it disappeared. I fear this portends some judgment to this country or at least to myself. I ate roast mutton for dinner. In the

afternoon I settled the closet. About 5 o'clock I received an express from Mr. Clayton that the Governor, Colonel Spotswood, with two men-of-war arrived last night at Kiquotan with several other ships. I sent word of this to Mrs. Harrison and then prepared to go to Williamsburg tomorrow. In the evening I took a walk about the plantation. I said my prayers and had good thoughts, good humor, and good health, thank God Almighty.

July 9. About 11 o'clock we went to church and had a good sermon. After church I invited nobody home because I design to break that custom, that my people may go to church. I ate boiled pork for dinner. In the afternoon my wife and I had a terrible quarrel about the things she had come in [i.e. her goods from England], but at length she submitted because she was in the wrong. For my part I kept my temper very well.

July 15. About 7 o'clock the Negro Betty that ran away was brought home. My wife against my will caused little Jenny to be burned with a hot iron, for which I quarreled with her. It was so hot today that I did not intend to go to the launching of Colonel Hill's ship but about 9 o'clock the Colonel was so kind as to come and call us. My wife would not go at first but with much entreaty she at last consented. About 12 o'clock we went and found abundance of company at the ship, and about one she was launched and went off very well, notwithstanding several had believed the contrary.

Sept. 20. I rose at 6 o'clock but read nothing because I prepared for the Governor's coming in the evening. I neglected to say my prayers but ate milk for breakfast. I settled several things in my library. All the wood was removed from the place where it used to lay to a better place. I sent John to kill some blue wing[6] and he had good luck. I ate some boiled beef for dinner. In the afternoon all things were put into the best order because Captain Burbydge sent word that the Governor would be here at 4 o'clock but he did not come till 5. Captain Burbydge sent his boat for him and fired as he came up the river. I received at the landing with Mr. C—s and gave him 3 guns. Mr. Clayton and Mr. Robinson came with him. After he had drunk some wine he walked in the garden and into the library till it was dark. Then we went to supper and ate some blue wing. After supper we sat and talked till 9 o'clock,

Sept. 21. I rose at 6 o'clock and read nothing but got ready to receive the company. About 8 o'clock the Governor came down. I offered him some of my fine water [?]. Then we had milk tea and bread and butter for breakfast. The Governor was pleased with everything and very complaisant. About 10 o'clock Captain Stith came and soon after him Colonel Hill,

[6]A North American teal that appeared early every fall.

Mr. Anderson and several others of the militia officers. The Governor was extremely courteous to them. About 12 o'clock Mr. Clayton went to Mrs. Harrison's and then orders were given to bring all the men into the pasture to muster. Just as we got on our horses it began to rain hard; however this did not discourage the Governor but away we rode to the men. It rained half an hour and the Governor mustered them all the while and he presented me to the people to be their Colonel and commander-in-chief. About 3 o'clock we returned to the house and as many of the officers as could sit at the table stayed to dine with the Governor, and the rest went to take part of the hogshead [of punch] in the churchyard. We had a good dinner, well served, with which the Governor seemed to be well pleased. I ate venison for dinner. In the evening all the company went away and we took a walk and found a comic freak of a man that was drunk that hung on the pales. Then we went home and played at piquet and I won the pool. About 9 the Governor went to bed.

Feb. 5, 1711. I rose about eight o'clock and found my cold still worse. I said my prayers and ate milk and potatoes for breakfast. My wife and I quarreled about her pulling her brows. She threatened she would not go to Williamsburg if she might not pull them; I refused, however, and got the better of her, and maintained my authority.

Nov. 23. It was very cold this morning. About 11 o'clock I went to the coffeehouse where the Governor also came and from thence we went to the capitol and read the bill concerning ports the first time. We stayed till 3 o'clock and then went to dinner to Marot's but could get none there and therefore Colonel Lewis and I dined with Colonel Duke and I ate broiled chicken for dinner. After dinner we went to Colonel Carter's room where we had a bowl of punch of French brandy and oranges. We talked very lewdly and were almost drunk and in that condition we went to the coffeehouse and played at dice and I lost £12. We stayed at the coffeehouse till almost 4 o'clock in the morning talking with Major Harrison.

Dec. 29. I rose about 7 o'clock and read two chapters in Hebrew and some Greek in Lucian. I said my prayers and ate boiled milk for breakfast. I had abundance of talk with Mr. G-r-l about the affairs of Falling Creek and he told me some of his wants and so did George Smith, which I endeavored to supply as well as I could. I gave John G-r-l leave to go visit his mother. Poor old Jane died this morning about 9 o'clock and I caused her to be buried as soon as possible because she stank very much. It was not very cold today. I danced my dance. Mr. G-r-l and George Smith went away about 12 o'clock. I ate some broiled goose for dinner. In the afternoon I set my razor, and then went out to shoot with bow and

arrow till the evening and then I ran to breathe myself and looked over everything. At night I read some Latin in Terence till about 10 o'clock. I said my prayers and had good health, good thoughts, and good humor, thank God Almighty.

Dec. 30. I rose about 7 o'clock and read a chapter in Hebrew and three chapters in the Greek Testament. I said my prayers very devoutly and ate boiled milk for breakfast. The weather was very clear and warm so that my wife walked out with Mrs. Dunn and forgot dinner, for which I had a little quarrel with her and another afterwards because I was not willing to let her have a book out of the library. About 12 o'clock came Mr. Bland from Williamsburg but brought no news. He stayed to dinner and I ate some roast beef. In the afternoon we sat and talked till about 4 o'clock and then I caused my people to set him over the river and then I walked with the women about the plantation till they were very weary. At night we ate some eggs and drank some Virginia beer and talked very gravely without reading anything. However I said my prayers and spoke with all my people. I had good health, good thoughts, and good humor, thank God Almighty. I danced my dance in the morning.

Dec. 31. I rose about 7 o'clock and read a chapter in Hebrew and six leaves in Lucian. I said my prayers and ate boiled milk for breakfast. The weather continued warm and clear. I settled my accounts and wrote several things till dinner. I danced my dance. I ate some turkey and chine for dinner. In the afternoon I weighed some money and then read some Latin in Terence and then Mr. Mumford came and told me my man Tony had been very sick but he was recovered again, thank God. He told me Robin Bolling had been like to die and that he denied that he was the first to mention the imposition on skins which he certainly did. Then he and I took a walk about the plantation. When I returned I was out of humor to find the Negroes all at work in our chambers. At night I ate some broiled turkey with Mr. Mumford and we talked and were merry all the evening. I said my prayers and had good health, good thoughts, and good humor, thank God Almighty. My wife and I had a terrible quarrel about whipping Eugene while Mr. Mumford was there but she had a mind to show her authority before company but I would not suffer it, which she took very ill; however for peace sake I made the first advance towards a reconciliation which I obtained with some difficulty and after abundance of crying. However it spoiled the mirth of the evening, but I was not conscious that I was to blame in that quarrel.

Jan. 1, 1712. I lay abed till 9 o'clock this morning to bring my wife into temper again and rogered her by way of reconciliation. I read nothing because Mr.

Mumford was here, nor did I say my prayers, for the same reason. However I ate boiled milk for breakfast, and after my wife tempted me to eat some pancakes with her. Mr. Mumford and I went to shoot with our bows and arrows but shot nothing, and afterwards we played at billiards till dinner, and when we came we found Ben Harrison there, who dined with us. I ate some partridge for dinner. In the afternoon we played at billiards again and I won two bits. I had a letter from Colonel Duke by H-l the bricklayer who came to offer his services to work for me. Mr. Mumford went away in the evening and John Bannister with him to see his mother. I took a walk about the plantation and at night we drank some mead of my wife's making which was very good. I gave the people some cider and a dram to the Negroes. I read some Latin in Terence and had good health, good thoughts, and good humor, thank God Almighty. I said my prayers.

FROM *History of the Dividing Line*

Surveying the disputed boundary line between Virginia and North Carolina was an arduous undertaking. Byrd's narrative, presumably intended for publication, remained in manuscript form until 1841, nearly a century after his death. In 1929 a rougher version, *A Secret History of the Line*, appeared. The selections below are from the more finished version. Byrd's fresh, lively style, with its flashes of wit, causes us to regard lightly his exaggerations and prejudices. Text: *William Byrd's Histories of the Dividing Line . . . ,* ed. William K. Boyd (Raleigh, 1929).

[Life in North Carolina]

March 25 [1728]. The air was chilled this morning with a smart north-west wind, which favored the Dismalites[1] in their dirty march. They returned by the path they had made in coming out, and with great industry arrived in the evening at the spot where the Line had been discontinued.

After so long and laborious a journey, they were glad to repose themselves on their couches of cypress-bark, where their sleep was as sweet as it would have been on a bed of Finland down.

In the mean time, we who stayed behind had nothing to do, but to make the best observations we could upon that part of the country. The soil of our landlord's plantation, though none of the best, seemed more fertile than any thereabouts, where the ground is near as sandy as the deserts of Africa, and consequently barren. The road leading from thence to Edenton, being in distance about 27 miles, lies upon a ridge called Sandy Ridge, which is so wretchedly poor that it will not bring potatoes.

[1]A reference to the Dismal Swamp connecting Albemarle Sound with Chesapeake Bay.

The pines in this part of the country are of a different species from those that grow in Virginia: their bearded leaves are much longer and their cones much larger. Each cell contains a seed of the size and figure of a black-eyed pea, which, shedding in November, is very good mast for hogs, and fattens them in a short time.

The smallest of these pines are full of cones, which are eight or nine inches long, and each affords commonly 60 or 70 seeds. This kind of mast has the advantage of all other by being more constant, and less liable to be nipped by the frost or eaten by the caterpillars. The trees also abound more with turpentine, and consequently yield more tar than either the yellow or the white pine; and for the same reason make more durable timber for building. The inhabitants hereabouts pick up knots of lightwood[2] in abundance, which they burn into tar, and then carry it to Norfolk or Nansimond for a market. The tar made in this method is the less valuable because it is said to burn the cordage, though it is full as good for all other uses as that made in Sweden and Muscovy.

Surely there is no place in the world where the inhabitants live with less labor than in North Carolina. It approaches nearer to the description of Lubberland than any other, by the great felicity of the climate, the easiness of raising provisions, and the slothfulness of the people.

Indian corn is of so great increase that a little pains will subsist a very large family with bread, and then they may have meat without any pains at all, by the help of the low grounds, and the great variety of mast that grows on the high land. The men for their parts, just like the Indians, impose all the work upon the poor women. They make their wives rise out of their beds early in the morning, at the same time that they lie and snore till the sun has run one-third of his course and disperst all the unwholesome damps. Then, after stretching and yawning for half an hour, they light their pipes, and, under the protection of a cloud of smoke, venture out into the open air; though, if it happens to be never so little cold, they quickly return shivering into the chimney corner. When the weather is mild, they stand leaning with both their arms upon the cornfield fence, and gravely consider whether they had best go and take a small heat at the hoe: but generally find reasons to put it off till another time.

Thus they loiter away their lives, like Solomon's sluggard,[3] with their arms across, and at the winding up of the year scarcely have bread to eat.

To speak the truth, 'tis a thorough aversion to labor that makes people file off to North Carolina,

[2]A resinous pine-wood.
[3]Proverbs vi.6–11.

where plenty and a warm sun confirm them in their disposition to laziness for their whole lives.

March 26. Since we were like to be confined to this place, till the people returned out of the Dismal, 'twas agreed that our chaplain might safely take a turn to Edenton, to preach the Gospel to the infidels there, and christen their children. He was accompanied thither by Mr. Little, one of the Carolina Commissioners, who, to show his regard for the Church, offered to treat him on the road with a fricassee of rum. They fried half a dozen rashers of very fat bacon in a pint of rum, both which being dished up together, served the company at once for meat and drink.

Most of the rum they get in this country comes from New England, and is so bad and unwholesome, that it is not improperly called "kill-devil." It is distilled there from foreign molasses, which, if skilfully managed, yields near gallon for gallon. Their molasses comes from the same country, and has the name of "long sugar" in Carolina, I suppose from the ropiness of it, and serves all the purposes of sugar, both in their eating and drinking.

When they entertain their friends bountifully, they fail not to set before them a capacious bowl of bombo, so called from the Admiral of that name. This is a compound of rum and water in equal parts, made palatable with the said long sugar. As good humor begins to flow, and the bowl to ebb, they take care to replenish it with sheer rum, of which there always is a reserve under the table. But such generous doings happen only when that balsam of life is plenty; for they have often such melancholy times, that neither land-graves nor cassicks[4] can procure one drop for their wives, when they lie in, or are troubled with the colic or vapors. Very few in this country have the industry to plant orchards, which, in a dearth of rum, might supply them with much better liquor.

The truth is, there is one inconvenience that easily discourages lazy people from making this improvement: very often, in autumn, when the apples begin to ripen, they are visited with numerous flights of paraqueets, that bite all the fruit to pieces in a moment, for the sake of the kernels. The havoc they make is sometimes so great, that whole orchards are laid waste in spite of all the noises that can be made, or mawkins that can be dressed up, to fright 'em away. These ravenous birds visit North Carolina only during the warm season, and so soon as the cold begins to come on, retire back towards the sun. They rarely venture so far north as Virginia, except in a very hot summer, when they visit the most southern parts of it. They are very beautiful; but like some other pretty creatures, are apt to be loud and mischievous.

March 27. Betwixt this and Edenton there are many thuckleberry slashes, which afford a convenient harbor for wolves and foxes. The first of these wild beasts is not so large and fierce as they are in other countries more northerly. He will not attack a man in the keenest of his hunger, but run away from him, as from an animal more mischievous than himself.

The foxes are much bolder, and will sometimes not only make a stand, but likewise assault any one that would balk them of their prey. The inhabitants hereabouts take the trouble to dig abundance of wolf-pits, so deep and perpendicular, that when a wolf is once tempted into them, he can no more scramble out again, than a husband who had taken the leap can scramble out of matrimony.

Most of the houses in this part of the country are log-houses, covered with pine or cypress shingles, 3 feet long, and one broad. They are hung upon laths with pegs, and their doors too turn upon wooden hinges, and have wooden locks to secure them, so that the building is finished without nails or other iron-work. They also set up their pales without any nails at all, and indeed more securely than those that are nailed. There are 3 rails mortised into the posts, the lowest of which serves as a sill with a groove in the middle, big enough to receive the end of the pales: the middle part of the pale rests against the inside of the next rail, and the top of it is brought forward to the outside of the uppermost. Such wreathing of the pales in and out makes them stand firm, and much harder to unfix than when nailed in the ordinary way.

Within 3 or 4 miles of Edenton, the soil appears to be a little more fertile, though it is much cut with slashes, which seem all to have a tendency towards the Dismal.

This town is situate on the north side of Albemarle Sound, which is there about 5 miles over. A dirty slash runs all along the back of it, which in the summer is a foul annoyance, and furnishes abundance of that Carolina plague, mosquitoes. They may be 40 or 50 houses, most of them small, and built without expense. A citizen here is counted extravagant, if he has ambition enough to aspire to a brick-chimney. Justice herself is but indifferently lodged, the court-house having much the air of a common tobacco-house. I believe this is the only metropolis in the Christian or Mahomedan world, where there is neither church, chapel, mosque, synagogue, or any other place of public worship of any sect or religion whatsoever.

What little devotion there may happen to be is much more private than their vices. The people seem easy without a minister, as long as they are

---

[4]Landgraves and Casiques (or Cassocks) were members of the upper house of the Carolina legislature.

exempted from paying him. Sometimes the Society for Propagating the Gospel has had the charity to send over missionaries to this country; but unfortunately the priest has been too lewd for the people, or, which oftener happens, they too lewd for the priest. For these reasons these reverend gentlemen have always left their flocks as arrant heathen as they found them. Thus much however may be said for the inhabitants of Edenton, that not a soul has the least taint of hypocrisy, or superstition, acting very frankly and aboveboard in all their excesses.

Provisions here are extremely cheap, and extremely good, so that people may live plentifully at trifling expense. Nothing is dear but law, physic, and strong drink, which are all bad in their kind, and the last they get with so much difficulty, that they are never guilty of the sin of suffering it to sour upon their hands. Their vanity generally lies not so much in having a handsome dining-room, as a handsome house of office: in this kind of structure they are really extravagant.

They are rarely guilty of flattering or making any court to their governors, but treat them with all the excesses of freedom and familiarity. They are of opinion their rulers would be apt to grow insolent, if they grew rich, and for that reason take care to keep them poorer, and more dependent, if possible, than the saints in New England used to do their governors. They have very little coin, so they are forced to carry on their home-traffic with paper-money. This is the only cash that will tarry in the country, and for that reason the discount goes on increasing between that and real money, and will do so to the end of the chapter.

[A Visit to the Indians]

April 7. The next day being Sunday, we ordered notice to be sent to all the neighborhood that there would be a sermon at this place, and an opportunity of christening their children. But the likelihood of rain got the better of their devotion, and what perhaps, might still be a stronger motive of their curiosity. In the morning we dispatched a runner to the Nottoway Town, to let the Indians know we intend them a visit that evening, and our honest landlord was so kind as to be our pilot thither, being about 4 miles from his house.

Accordingly in the afternoon we marched in good order to the town, where the female scouts, stationed on an eminence for that purpose, had no sooner spied us, but they gave notice of our approach to their fellow-citizens by continual whoops and cries, which could not possibly have been more dismal at the sight of their most implacable enemies.

This signal assembled all their great men, who received us in a body, and conducted us into the fort. This fort was a square piece of ground, inclosed with substantial puncheons, or strong palisades, about ten feet high, and leaning a little outwards, to make a scalade more difficult.

Each side of the square might be about 100 yards long, with loop-holes at proper distances, through which they may fire upon the enemy.

Within this inclosure we found bark cabins sufficient to lodge all their people, in case they should be obliged to retire thither. These cabins are no other but close arbors made of saplings, arched at the top, and covered so well with bark as to be proof against all weather. The fire is made in the middle, according to the Hibernian fashion, the smoke whereof finds no other vent but at the door, and so keeps the whole family warm, at the expense both of their eyes and complexion.

The Indians have no standing furniture in their cabins but hurdles to repose their persons upon, which they cover with mats or deer-skins. We were conducted to the best apartments in the fort, which just before had been made ready for our reception, and adorned with new mats that were sweet and clean.

The young men had painted themselves in a hideous manner, not so much for ornament as terror. In that frightful equipage they entertained us with sundry war-dances, wherein they endeavored to look as formidable as possible. The instrument they danced to was an Indian-drum, that is, a large gourd with skin braced taut over the mouth of it. The dancers all sang to this music, keeping exact time with their feet, while their heads and arms were screwed into a thousand menacing postures.

Upon this occasion the ladies had arrayed themselves in all their finery. They were wrapt in their red and blue match-coats, thrown so negligently about them that their mahogany skins appeared in several parts, like the Lacedaemonian damsels of old. Their hair was braided with white and blue peak, and hung gracefully in a large roll upon their shoulders.

This peak consists of small cylinders cut out of a conque-shell, drilled through and strung like beads. It serves them both for money and jewels, the blue being of much greater value than the white, for the same reason that Ethiopian mistresses in France are dearer than French, because they are more scarce. The women wear necklaces and bracelets of these precious materials, when they have a mind to appear lovely. Though their complexions be a little sad-colored, yet their shapes are very straight and well proportioned. Their faces are seldom handsome, yet they have an air of innocence and bashfulness, that with a little less dirt would not fail to make them desirable. Such charms might have had their full effect upon men who had been so long deprived of female conversation, but that the whole winter's soil was so crusted on the skins of those dark angels, that it required a very strong appetite to approach them. The bear's oil, with which they anoint their persons all over, makes their skins soft, and at the same time protects them from every species of vermin that use to be troublesome to other uncleanly people.

We were unluckily so many that they could not well make us the complement of bed-fellows, according to the Indian rules of hospitality, though a grave matron whispered one of the Commissioners very civilly in the ear, that if her daughter had been but one year older, she should have been at his devotion.

It is by no means a loss of reputation among the Indians, for damsels that are single to have intrigues with the men; on the contrary, they count it an argument of superior merit to be liked by a great number of gallants. However, like the ladies that game they are a little mercenary in their amours, and seldom bestow their favors out of stark love and kindness. But after these women have once appropriated their charms by marriage, they are from thenceforth faithful to their vows, and will hardly ever be tempted by an agreeable gallant, or be provoked by a brutal or even by a fumbling husband to go astray.

The little work that is done among the Indians is done by the poor women, while the men are quite idle, or at most employed only in the gentlemanly diversions of hunting and fishing.

In this, as well as in their wars, they now use nothing but fire-arms, which they purchase of the English for skins. Bows and arrows are grown into disuse, except only amongst their boys. Nor is it ill policy, but on the contrary very prudent, thus to furnish the Indians with fire-arms, because it makes them depend entirely upon the English, not only for their trade, but even for their subsistence. Besides, they were really able to do more mischief while they made use of arrows, of which they would let silently fly several in a minute with wonderful dexterity, whereas now they hardly ever discharge their fire-locks more than once, which they insidiously do from behind a tree, and then retire as nimbly as the Dutch Horse used to do now and then formerly in Flanders.

We put the Indians to no expense, but only of a little corn for our horses, for which in gratitude we cheered their hearts with what rum we had left, which they love better than they do their wives and children.

Though these Indians dwell among the English, and see in what plenty a little industry enables them to live, yet they choose to continue in their stupid idleness, and to suffer all the inconveniences of dirt,

cold, and want, rather than to disturb their heads with care, or defile their hands with labor.

The whole number of people belonging to the Nottoway Town, if you include women and children, amount to about 200. These are the only Indians of any consequence now remaining within the limits of Virginia. The rest are either removed, or dwindled to a very inconsiderable number, either by destroying one another, or else by the small-pox and other diseases. Though nothing has been so fatal to them as their ungovernable passion for rum, with which, I am sorry to say it, they have been but too liberally supplied by the English that live near them.

And here I must lament the bad success Mr. Boyle's charity has hitherto had towards converting any of these poor heathens to Christianity.[5] Many children of our neighboring Indians have been brought up in the College of William and Mary. They have been taught to read and write, and have been carefully instructed in the principles of the Christian religion, till they came to be men. Yet after they returned home, instead of civilizing and converting the rest, they have immediately relapsed into infidelity and barbarism themselves.

And some of them too have made the worst use of the knowledge they acquired among the English, by employing it against their benefactors. Besides, as they unhappily forget all the good they learn, and remember the ill, they are apt to be more vicious and disorderly than the rest of their countrymen.

I ought not to quit this subject without doing justice to the great prudence of Col. Spotswood in this affair. That gentleman was lieut. governor of Virginia when Carolina was engaged in a bloody war with the Indians. At that critical time it was thought expedient to keep a watchful eye upon our tributary savages, who we knew had nothing to keep them to their duty but their fears.

Then it was that he demanded of each Nation a competent number of their great men's children to be sent to the College, where they served as so many hostages for the good behavior of the rest, and at the same time were themselves principled in the Christian religion. He also placed a school-master among the Saponi Indians, at the salary of fifty pounds per annum, to instruct their children. The person that undertook that charitable work was Mr. Charles Griffin, a man of good family, who by the innocence of his life, and the sweetness of his temper, was perfectly well qualified for that pious undertaking. Besides, he had so much the secret of mixing pleasure with instruction, that he had not a scholar who did not love him affectionately.

Such talents must needs have been blest with a

[5] Robert Boyle, the English physicist, left funds to civilize and Christianize American Indians; the College of William and Mary was the chief beneficiary of his bequest.

proportionable success, had he not been unluckily removed to the College, by which he left the good work he had begun unfinished. In short, all the pains he had undertaken among the infidels had no other effect but to make them something cleanlier than other Indians are.

The care Col. Spotswood took to tincture the Indian children with Christianity produced the following epigram, which was not published during his administration, for fear it might then have looked like flattery.

> Long has the furious priest assay'd in vain,
> With sword and faggot, infidels to gain.
> But now the milder soldier wisely tries
> By gentler methods to unveil their eyes.
> Wonders apart, he knew 'twere vain t'engage
> The fix'd preventions of misguided age.
> With fairer hopes he forms the Indian youth
> To early manners, probity and truth.
> The lion's whelp thus on the Lybian shore
> Is tam'd and gentled by the artful Moor,
> Not the grim sire, inured to blood before.

I am sorry I can't give a better account of the state of the poor Indians with respect to Christianity, although a great deal of pains has been and still continues to be taken with them. For my part, I must be of opinion, as I hinted before, that there is but one way of converting these poor infidels, and reclaiming them from barbarity, and that is, charitably to intermarry with them, according to the modern policy of the most Christian King in Canada and Louisiana.

Had the English done this at the first settlement of the Colony, the infidelity of the Indians had been worn out at this day, with their dark complexions, and the country had swarmed with people more than it does with insects.

It was certainly an unreasonable nicety, that prevented their entering into so good-natured an alliance. All nations of men have the same natural dignity, and we all know that very bright talents may be lodged under a very dark skin. The principal difference between one people and another proceeds only from the different opportunities of improvement.

The Indians by no means want understanding, and are in their figure tall and well-proportioned. Even their copper-colored complexion would admit of blanching, if not in the first, at the farthest in the second generation.

I may safely venture to say, the Indian women would have made altogether as honest wives for the first planters, as the damsels they used to purchase from aboard the ships. It is strange, therefore, that any good Christian should have refused a wholesome, straight bed-fellow, when he might have had so fair a portion with her, as the merit of saving her soul.

8. We rested on our clean mats very comfortably, though alone, and the next morning went to the toilet of some of the Indian ladies, where, what with the charms of their persons and the smoke of their apartments, we were almost blinded. They offered to give us silk-grass baskets of their own making, which we modestly refused, knowing that an Indian present, like that of a nun, is a liberality put out to interest, and a bribe placed to the greatest advantage.

Our Chaplain observed with concern that the ruffles of some of our fellow travellers were a little discolored with pochoon,[6] wherewith the good man had been told those Ladies used to improve their invisible charms.

About 10 o'clock we marched out of town in good order, and the war captains saluted us with a volley of small-arms. From thence we proceeded over Black-water Bridge to Col. Henry Harrison's, where we congratulated each other upon our return into Christendom.

FROM *A Progress to the Mines*

Text: *The Writings of Colonel William Byrd* . . . , ed. John S. Bassett (New York, 1901).

[A Visit to a Neighbor's]

Sept. 18, 1732. For the pleasure of the good company of Mrs. Byrd, and her little governor, my son, I went about halfway to the falls in the chariot. There we halted, not far from a purling stream, and upon the stump of a propagate oak picked the bones of a piece of roast beef. By the spirit which that gave me, I was the better able to part with the dear companions of my travels, and to perform the rest of my journey on horseback by myself. I reached Shaccoe's before two o'clock, and crossed the river to the mills. I had the grief to find them both stand as still for the want of water as a dead woman's tongue for want of breath. It had rained so little for many weeks above the falls, that the naiads had hardly water enough left to wash their faces. However, as we ought to turn all our misfortunes to the best advantage, I directed Mr. Booker, my first minister there, to make use of the lowness of the water for blowing up the rocks at the mouth of the canal. For that purpose I ordered iron drills to be made about two foot long, pointed with steel, chisel-fashion, in order to make holes, into which we put our cartridges of powder, containing each about

---

[6] Bloodroot, which makes a yellow or deep red stain.

three ounces. There wanted skill among my engineers to choose the best parts of the stone for boring, that we might blow to the most advantage. They made all their holes quite perpendicular, whereas they should have humored the grain of the stone for the more effectual execution. I ordered the points of the drills to be made chisel-way, rather than the diamond, that they might need to be seldomer repaired, though in stone the diamond points would make the most dispatch. The water now flowed out of the river so slowly, that the miller was obliged to pond it up in the canal, by setting open the flood-gates at the mouth, and shutting those close at the mill. By this contrivance, he was able at any time to grind two or three bushels, either for his choice customers, or for the use of my plantations. Then I walked to the place where they broke the flax, which is wrought with much greater ease than the hemp, and is much better for spinning. From thence I paid a visit to the weaver, who needed a little of Minerva's inspiration to make the most of a piece of fine cloth. Then I looked in upon my Caledonian spinster, who was mended more in her looks than in her humor. However, she promised much, though at the same time intended to perform little. She is too high-spirited for Mr. Booker, who hates to have his sweet temper ruffled, and will rather suffer matters to go a little wrong sometimes, than give his righteous spirit any uneasiness. He is very honest, and would make an admirable overseer where servants will do as they are bid. But eye-servants, who want abundance of overlooking, are not so proper to be committed to his care. I found myself out of order and for that reason retired early, yet with all this precaution had a gentle fever in the night; but towards morning nature sat open all her gates, and drove it out in a plentiful perspiration.

Sept. 20. I continued the bark, and then tossed down my poached eggs, with as much ease as some good breeders slip children into the world. About nine I left the prudentest orders I could think of with my vizier, and then crossed the river to Shaccoe's. I made a running visit to three of my quarters, where, besides finding all the people well, I had the pleasure to see better crops than usual, both of corn and tobacco. I parted there with my intendant, and pursued my journey to Mr. Randolph's, at Tuckahoe, without meeting with any adventure by the way. Here I found Mrs. Fleming, who was packing her baggage with design to follow her husband the next day, who was gone to a new settlement in Goochland. Both he and she have been about seven years persuading themselves to remove to that retired part of the country, though they had the two strong arguments of health and interest for so doing. The widow smiled graciously upon me,

and entertained me very handsomely. Here I learnt all the tragical story of her daughter's humble marriage with her uncle's overseer. Besides the meanness of this mortal's aspect, the man has not one visible qualification, except impudence, to recommend him to a female's inclinations. But there is sometimes such a charm in that Hibernian endowment, that frail woman can't withstand it, though it stand alone without any other recommendation. Had she run away with a gentleman or a pretty fellow, there might have been some excuse for her, though he were of inferior fortune; but to stoop to a dirty plebeian, without any kind of merit, is the lowest prostitution. I found the family justly enraged at it; and though I had more good nature than to join in her condemnation, yet I could devise no excuse for so senseless a prank as this young gentlewoman had played. Here good drink was more scarce than good victuals, the family being reduced to the last bottle of wine, which was therefore husbanded very carefully. But the water was excellent. The heir of the family did not come home till late in the evening. He is a pretty young man, but had the misfortune to become his own master too soon. This puts young fellows upon wrong pursuits, before they have sense to judge rightly for themselves. Though at the same time they have a strange conceit of their own sufficiency, when they grow near twenty years old, especially if they happen to have a small smattering of learning. 'Tis then they fancy themselves wiser than all their tutors and governors, which makes them headstrong to all advice, and above all reproof and admonition.

Sept. 21. I was sorry in the morning to find myself stopped in my career by bad weather brought upon us by a northeast wind. This drives a world of raw, unkindly vapors upon us from Newfoundland, loaden with blight, coughs, and pleurisies. However, I complained not, lest I might be suspected to be tired of the good company. Though Mrs. Fleming was not so much upon her guard, but mutinied strongly at the rain, that hindered her from pursuing her dear husband. I said what I could to comfort a gentlewoman under so sad a disappointment. I told her a husband that stayed so much at home as hers did, could be no such violent rarity, as for a woman to venture her precious health to go daggling through the rain after him, or to be miserable if she happened to be prevented. That it was prudent for married people to fast sometimes from one another, that they might come together again with the better stomach. That the best things in this world, if constantly used, are apt to be cloying, which a little absence and abstinence would prevent. This was strange doctrine to a fond female, who fancies people should love with as little reason after marriage as before. In the afternoon Monsieur Marij, the minister of the parish, came to make me a visit. He had been a Romish priest, but found reasons, either spiritual or temporal, to quit that gay religion. The fault of this new convert is that he looks for as much respect from his Protestant flock, as is paid to the popish clergy, which our ill-bred Huguenots don't understand. Madam Marij had so much curiosity as to want to come too; but another horse was wanting, and she believed it would have too vulgar an air to ride behind her husband. This woman was of the true exchange breed, full of discourse but void of discretion, and married a parson with the idle hopes he might some time or other come to be his grace of Canterbury. The gray mare is the better horse in that family, and the poor man submits to her wild vagaries for peace's sake. She has just enough of the fine lady, to run in debt, and be of no signification in her household. And the only thing that can prevent her from undoing her loving husband will be that nobody will trust them beyond the 16,000,[1] which is soon run out in a Goochland store. The way of dealing there is for some small merchant or pedlar to buy a Scots penny-worth of goods, and clap 150 per cent upon that. At this rate the parson can't be paid much more for his preaching than 'tis worth. No sooner was our visitor retired, but the facetious widow was so kind as to let me into all this secret history, but was at the same time exceedingly sorry that the woman should be so indiscreet, and the man so tame as to be governed by an unprofitable and fantastical wife.

Sept. 22. We had another wet day, to try both Mrs. Fleming's patience and my good breeding. The northeast wind commonly sticks by us three or four days, filling the atmosphere with damps, injurious both to man and beast. The worst of it was, we had no good liquor to warm our blood, and fortify our spirits against so strong a malignity. However, I was cheerful under all these misfortunes, and expressed no concern but a decent fear lest my long visit might be troublesome. Since I was like to have thus much leisure, I endeavored to find out what subject a dull married man could introduce that might best bring the widow to the use of her tongue. At length I discovered she was a notable quack, and therefore paid that regard to her knowledge, as to put some questions to her about the bad distemper that raged then in the country. I mean the bloody flux, that was brought us in the Negro-ship consigned to Col. Braxton. She told me she made use of very simple remedies in that case, with very good success. She did the business either with Hartshorn drink, that

[1] The legal salary of a minister, fixed at 16,000 pounds of tobacco.

had plantain leaves boiled in it, or else with a strong decoction of St. Andrew's Cross, in new milk instead of water. I agreed with her that those remedies might be very good, but would be more effectual after a dose or two of Indian physic. But for fear this conversation might be too grave for a widow, I turned the discourse, and began to talk of plays, and finding her taste lay most towards comedy, I offered my service to read one to her, which she kindly accepted. She produced the second part of *The Beggar's Opera*, which had diverted the town for 40 nights successively, and gained four thousand pounds to the author. This was not owing altogether to the wit or humor that sparkled in it, but to some political reflections that seemed to hit the ministry. But the great advantage of the author was that his interest was solicited by the Duchess of Queensbury, which no man could refuse who had but half an eye in his head, or half a guinea in his pocket. Her grace, like Death, spared nobody, but even took my Lord Selkirk in for two guineas, to repair which extravagance he lived upon Scots herrings two months afterwards. But the best story was, she made a very smart officer in his majesty's guards give her a guinea, who swearing at the same time 'twas all he had in the world, she sent him 50 for it the next day, to reward his obedience. After having acquainted my company with the history of the play, I read three acts of it, and left Mrs. Fleming and Mr. Randolph to finish it, who read as well as most actors do at a rehearsal. Thus we killed the time, and triumphed over the bad weather.

Sept. 23. The clouds continued to drive from the northeast, and to menace us with more rain. But as the lady resolved to venture through it, I thought it a shame for me to venture to flinch. Therefore, after fortifying myself with two capacious dishes of coffee, and making my compliments to the ladies, I mounted, and Mr. Randolph was so kind as to be my guide. At the distance of about three miles, in a path as narrow as that which leads to heaven, but much more dirty, we reached the homely dwelling of the Reverend Mr. Marij. His land is much more barren than his wife, and needs all Mr. Bradley's skill in agriculture to make it bring corn. Thence we proceeded five miles farther, to a mill of Mr. Randolph's, that is apt to stand still when there falls but little rain, and to be carried away when there falls a great deal. Then we pursued a very blind path four miles farther, which puzzled my guide, who I suspect led me out of the way. At length we came into a great road, where he took leave, after giving me some very confused directions, and so left me to blunder out the rest of the journey by myself. I lost myself more than once, but soon recovered the right way again.

Two Letters to "Lucretia"

Probably written some time between 1717 and 1720, while Byrd was in England, these two letters were addressed to "Lucretia," a kinswoman who lived in the southwest of England, six days by stagecoach from London. Text: *Another Secret Diary of William Byrd of Westover, 1739–1741*, ed. Maude H. Woodfin and Marion Tinling (Richmond, 1942), pp. 282–84, 288–90.

Amongst so many packets of love letters as you every post receive from your admirers, I fear you'll have no leisure to allow a slight reading of a tasteless epistle from a relation. I reckon there is to a taste a certain insipidness in a kinsman's addresses, which goes on increasing from a cousin to a husband. A stranger of inferior accomplishment hits a woman's taste much better than the finest gentleman who has the misfortune to be of kin to her. This, Madam, we find commonly true in practice though it be not easy to account for so unjust a distinction. The reason must doubtless be because that near relations don't burn so much incense to their kinswomen and flatter their vanity with so good a grace as strangers do. They are apt to assault them with illbred truths, and to assure them that instead of goddesses they are no better than frail women. 'Tis not so great a provocation to a young lady to uncover her person as 'tis to undress her imperfections, because the first 'tis possible may make her more agreeable, but this will be sure to make her less. However provided you'll read my letters and answer them punctually I promise you I will never be so rude as to tell you of one single fault you have. I can safely enter into this engagement, Madam, because I can discover no shades in your picture but what help to set off and temper the exceeding lights of it. I can commend you not only with a good grace, but with a good conscience too, and I may the safer do it, because I observe that praise serves only to whet your endeavors after perfection, which serves only to inflame the vanity of other women. Besides I protest your very few follies are so agreeable that it needs a world of distinction and a great deal of cynic philosophy to discover them to be follies. You have the art of making those little imperfections so charming, that 'tis impossible to find fault with them. They are in you what discord is in music and serve only to make you more enchanting. While the men have their fancy to please, as well as their severer part the understanding, so long 'twill be necessary for women to have a little palatable frailty in order to please irresistibly. And were it not for this ingredient in the men, the Empire of Love must sink and young women would have little more charms than their grandmothers. For God's sake, Madam, don't grow too wise therefore nor too perfect for fear of being less agreeable. Folly becomes youth as well as gravity does grey hairs, and really too much discretion gives a woman an old look, which all the world knows is no advantage to her. If one would inquire nicely into the pretty extravagancies of women's dress and behavior (which very much help to warm the hearts of men) we should be forced to call them follies, and yet how much do they advance the triumphs of the sex? The same may be said of the bewitching graces of their movement, of their looks, and the enchanting airs which they contrive to give themselves to the undoing of the swain that observes them. Let me therefore conjure you, dear cousin, till the dreadful age of 31 (when you know a woman's game is up) to mix 9 grams of folly with one of wisdom, if you have a mind to do remarkable execution. That is the just proportion which Ovid and all the doctors in the deep science of love allow to a woman that would be irresistible. More than this would make you a coquette, and less a prude, both which characters are detestable. I have the honor to be

    Madam

      a great admirer of your agreeable follies.

° ° ° But this [country parson] was but one of our plagues for we had a certain female of that sort yclep'd a prude who disturbed our small commonwealth[1] very much. She was a virgin of 33 or thereabouts with a face that would not tempt one 500 leagues from land. Her features were all stiffened with a long habit of squeamish airs, which she had given herself for 14 years together. She had no part of her free and easy but her tongue, which I own moved with a surprising facility, and she would take liberties with that though she laid a strict confinement upon all the rest of her precious person. Most of her eloquence was leveled at the disorders of her own sex, the license women took she said was intolerable in a Christian country, she wondered how they could have the confidence to converse with the vile men so freely and even to venture themselves in a room alone with them which she pronounced impossible to be done with safety to their virtue. I asked her whether she could not trust herself alone with the person who set over against her in the coach? "I warrant her," replied the parson, "for she with a great deal of gentleness suffers me to press her knees betwixt mine." This ungallant discovery made a mortal quarrel between those opposites as long as they traveled together, and nobody triumphed at the parson's disaster so much as this dainty gentlewoman. She would neither get out or into the coach so much as before the women except

---

[1] The company of travelers.

they would solemnly promise to shut their eyes, for said she, "I should sink into the ground if anybody should see my ankle." "Ay," quoth the Parson, "the poor woman had the rickets when she was a child, and so abhors anyone should see her legs." This you may be sure did not much heal the breach that was formerly between 'em. I asked her what she thought of shewing her elbows? She told me I had a great deal of assurance to name so obscene a part as that in civil company. I begged her pardon for being guilty of so great an indecency, but humbly inquired into the reason why so useful a part as the elbow was so much in disgrace with her? She with a disdainful look reproached me with impertinence for repeating things so shocking to a woman of virtue. "You are right, madam," said her good friend the parson, "for the elbow is near akin to the knee and all the modest saints of the world know that a woman's knee is a hallowed part and ought to be veiled from the curiosity of men. Besides," said he, "the skin of the elbow is shriveled and of a darker color than the rest of the body, which shews it ought not to be exposed to the view because 'tis a deformity. But pray neighbor (continued he) what will become of all your shyness at the Resurrection,

when you will rise stark naked out of the grave without a rag to cover your backside, and all the whole universe will be gazing at you?" "Saucy fellow," replied she with a look as stern as Alecto,[2] "how can you mention such filthy ideas? I hope the good angels at that time will find some way to save our modesty, or else I should desire to lie still in the grave rather than be so confused and out of countenance as I should be in such an utter dishabille." I told her that one so fearful of the men would do well to live in Spain, Turkey or China where the better sort of women were never seen but by their husbands. "Indeed," said she, "I envy the women very much of those countries where they are never forced to walk before the men: a woman's gait is what she should be very careful of discovering, because uncharitable inferences may be made from that innocent motion." Now you will be surprised, Lucretia, when I tell you that this saint of untainted virtue, this unsullied unpolluted nymph had a child by her uncle's coachman, and made this journey on purpose to meet him at one of the inns by the way.

[2] With Megaera and Tisiphone, one of the three furies.

The Neoclassic Age

THE COLONIAL AMERICAN of the early eighteenth century was very much a child of the Age of Reason. John Locke wrote a charter for the Carolinas; Rousseau, Franklin, Montesquieu, Cotton Mather, and Sir Isaac Newton were contemporaries; Voltaire lived to see the signing of the American Declaration of Independence. Puritanism, though still a powerful force, was fast losing its thrust; the new age, in turning away from a God-centered view of life, gave primary allegiance to values it found best exemplified in the classical culture of the ancient Greek world, man-centered and rational, and of the Roman civilization, with its concern for law and form. The Enlightenment, as it arrived in America, was the first nationalized ideological movement in the American experience. Whereas Puritanism was parochial, and largely restricted to New England, the ideas of the Age of Reason permeated the colonies, attracting leaders of thought, from John Adams of Massachusetts, to Benjamin Franklin of Pennsylvania, to Thomas Jefferson of Virginia.

The Intellectual Context

The eighteenth-century philosophical impulse known as the Enlightenment rested on five general beliefs: the inevitability of progress; the perfectibility of man and his institutions; the efficacy of reason; the beneficence of God; and the plenitude and perfection of nature. It stressed the primacy of science over theology, skepticism over authority, reason over faith. The philosophers of the Enlightenment were convinced that it was within man's capacity, by applying reason to his problems, to discover those great laws by which all human and natural activity could be explained. Possessing such knowledge, men could then direct their efforts toward building a society in which progress was certain and continuous. The temper of the Enlightenment was orderly, progressive, hopeful.

American thought, however, much as it drew from Europe, was not simply a transatlantic reflection. The American version of the Enlightenment was late, eclectic, and native. First of all, the natural lag in the transfer of ideas across the ocean meant that patterns of thought conceived in Britain and France were employed to their greatest effect in America a half-century later (or more) under different circumstances, in response to different needs. Americans worked with ideas already old by European standards, in another part of the world, for new purposes, and more often than not with changed meanings attached to them.

Second, the English Enlightenment was a relatively conservative compromise of new and old ideas with current conditions. The British produced a few genuine radicals—William Godwin, Horne Tooke, Thomas Paine, Joseph Priestley (these last two exported to America)—but its Age of Reason was better represented by such reasonable men as Charles James Fox and Edmund Burke. The *philosophes* across the channel—among them Diderot, Holbach, Helvetius, and Voltaire—translated the French version of the Age of Reason into quite un-British extremes. Americans, who needed positive rules to justify a revolution and a new kind of society, found French interpretations of the Enlightenment much more to their satisfaction. American intellectuals read the French and British radicals, praised them, and hoped to turn their thinking to American uses. They took what they needed from British and European thought—using, for example, Locke's explanation of an old English revolution to justify their own against a different England, or adopting French "radicalism," aimed at the long tyranny of royal France, to overthrow a much less tyrannical King and Parliament on another continent. They shaped the Enlightenment to their advantage, and put an American stamp on it.

In literature and art, as in politics, the eighteenth-century American found the temper of the Age of Reason congenial with his own experience and aspirations. Drawing from his education in Enlightened rationalism, he saw a number of analogies between his civilization and that of the classic world; he hoped in his national culture to combine something of the intellectual symmetry and beauty of Greek thought with the Roman sense of law, control, and arrangement. The Newtonian vision of a perfectly machined universe, to his mind, paralleled the classic concept of universal order and beauty. As the classics—and the Puritans—taught him, the eighteenth-century American valued ideas and institutions in terms of their usefulness. Franklin's "Nothing is good or beautiful but in the measure that it is useful" is as much the expression of the American Neoclassic mode as it is of the functional pragmatism of a frontier society. Like their British and French instructors, American writers and artists placed great emphasis on structure, channeling their creative energies within the limits of form established by the masters of the past. And of course, in good Augustan fashion, they believed in the virtues of discipline, reasonableness, clarity, and uniformity, accepting the need for standards of taste, propriety, and decorum.

The rise of Romanticism in England and Europe introduced another factor into later eighteenth-century American thought. The basic concepts of the Romantic movement were not new, but a revival of interest, beginning about 1750, brought about a reexamination and extension of them, which in turn led men on both sides of the Atlantic to question and to alter some of the ideas of the Enlightenment. The Romantics, while never wholly consistent among themselves, tended to agree on three essential principles. First, on the organic nature of life—men, ideas, and institutions were conceived of as wholes or units, each with its own rules of development and governance. Second, on the dynamic quality of life—which was conceived of as fluid, changing, constantly in adaptation and permutation. Third, on the diversity of life—with emphasis on difference in cultures, tastes, societies, principles, and individuals, in contrast to the uniformitarian standards of the Enlightenment. Where the Age of Reason recognized that man was a mixture of passion and reason, and stressed the need for control of the former by the latter power, the Romantics emphasized the validity of human emotions, intuitions, and fancies, or (as they often called it) of the Imagination. Because of this, they believed deeply in the importance of the individual, his private judgment, and his capacity for growth and improvement.

Though the classical tradition remained the cultural anchor of American intellectual life for another generation, American thought after 1780 began to show clear effects of the new Romanticism—its enlargement of man's inward boundaries to include a wider range of imaginative and sensual knowledge;

its renewed interest in direct and concrete observation; its awareness of nature and the face of the American land; its emphasis on the validity of ordinary, average, common-held experience; its recognition of nonconformity; its fascination with the exotic, strange, faraway, and "Gothic." Romanticism broadened every man's scope, and opened windows out into the world. Thus Philip Freneau found in the powers of fancy

> Endless images of things,
> Fluttering each on golden wings,
> Ideal objects, such a store,
> The universe could hold no more.

The Revolutionary Experience

The framework of ideas, then, within which the United States achieved its independence was constructed of materials furnished by two great European intellectual movements, Neoclassicism and Romanticism. American thought, as it took shape in the crucial years of its creation between 1765 and 1820, shared in both.

The American people, over these years, confronted three of the most difficult and intricate problems in politics ever faced by any people in the history of the Western world. The first, which occupied their energies to 1776, was how to make and to justify a revolution against the world's greatest military and economic power. The second, paramount during the years 1776 to 1783, was how to execute a revolution and control it. The third, dominating the postwar years, was how to consolidate a revolution—how to bring out of it a just and stable government that would stand in proper relationships to its own citizens and to the rest of a hostile world which (for the most part) did not believe in it. Each phase raised new questions and posed new difficulties on whose solution survival depended; there was little room for error, and everything was being done for the first time. In addition, those involved in this great experiment believed sincerely that everything that was done carried consequences of tremendous importance for the future of the nation, the world, and perhaps for mankind.

At the close of the Seven Years' War in 1763 (known in its American phase as the French and Indian War) Great Britain, having defeated France in India and driven her from North America, was indisputably the master of the Western world. American colonists were proud to have played a crucial role in the victory and equally proud to be British. As Franklin wrote after the victories at Quebec and Montreal, "No one can more sincerely rejoice than I do, on the reduction of Canada, and this is not merely as I am a colonist, but as I am a Briton." Yet in less than twenty years Franklin and thousands of other proud and loyal Britons rejected their King, repudiated their Parliament, and declared war on their fellow Englishmen. Small wonder that John Adams wrote on July 3, 1776, as he paused to reflect on "the whole period from that time to this, and recollect the series of political events, the chain of causes and effect," that "I am surprised at the suddenness as well as the greatness of this revolution." What moved these men from patriotic loyalty to defiance and open rebellion?

There were two complementary sets of reasons, the one political and economic, the other ideological. In the first instance, the argument between Britain and the colonies after 1763 centered on matters of imperial organization and the rights of the colonist within the empire. In the second, the conflict involved different concepts of the rights of man and the contractual nature of governments, both of which were parts of the great intellectual heritage of the Age of Reason.

The period between the French and Indian War and the Declaration of Independence witnessed the shaping of a conflict between a set of colonies that were rapidly beginning to feel like a nation, and a central government that was determined to hold its empire together after the strain of a long, wearisome war. After 1763 the colonies unconsciously began to close ranks against England, as they had against the French danger, and to think of themselves as "Americans." It is impossible to point to a particular year and say, "Here Americanism began," but it is certain that by the middle of the eighteenth century the colonists conceived of themselves as a special kind of Briton, and that they possessed a common outlook and sense of relationship that could only be described as *American*. The term seemed to have, by Franklin's time, a meaning distinct from "British" or "English" that the term "West Indian," for example, clearly did not have. It was quite normal for Franklin's Poor Richard, who was by no means a revolutionary, to refer to his countrymen as "American patriots," or for Dr. William Smith of Philadelphia, long before the Revolution, to speak of the colonies as "our nation," with no sense of disloyalty to England. The growing national spirit provided a wider dimension to the arguments with Britain, and undoubtedly contributed greatly to the colonial will to resist. This is what John Adams meant when he remarked later that "The revolution was effected before the war commenced. The revolution was in the hearts and minds of the people."

The issues at stake, however, were not limited to the rights of Englishmen or colonists. There was also a broader conflict over general political principles, arising from different interpretations of the twin theories of natural rights and government by social contract, both of which stemmed from Enlightenment philosophy. It was assumed that in the beginning man was endowed by his Creator with certain natural rights, which antedated the existence of governments and were superior to them. They were, as Thomas Paine called them, "those rights which always appertain to man in right of his existence." These rights were never exactly enumerated and defined, but they included the protection of life, the acquisition and security of property, freedom of movement, equal justice before law, and the freedom to speak and think within certain limits.

The social contract theory grew from the natural rights concept, for since these rights were not self-enforcing, some form of government seemed necessary to maintain them. To accomplish this, it was also assumed that men consented to a contract with the state for the furtherance and defense of their natural rights. A government was, then, in the definition of the English jurist Blackstone, "a voluntary compact between a ruler and the ruled . . . , liable to such limitations as are necessary for the security of the absolute rights of the latter." The aim of the contract, as James Otis of Pennsylvania explained it, was "above all things to provide for the security, the quiet and happy enjoyment of life, liberty, and property." Implicit in the terms of this contract were three things: that the primary power of government remain with the people; that the authority of government rest on the consent of the governed; and that violations of the contract by the state render that government null and void. The Declaration of Independence defined these theories best, and for all time.

The Revolution forced the colonists to consider much more carefully what "America" and "Americanism" meant, and why they deserved independent existence. They entered the war as a nation, with strong convictions that they knew what they were fighting for; having won, they now had to define that nation. Consistent (and sometimes savage) attacks by British and European critics forced Americans to examine and defend their ideas and ideals, their way of life. Again and again they tried to answer the question of the Frenchman Crèvecoeur, "What is an American?" and in the process they slowly evolved a set of answers to what an American was, and hoped to be.

Americans, at the end of the Revolution, looked ahead with a feeling of fresh beginnings. They held great hope for the future, for they had no record of failure in their past. They were especially conscious of the importance of their actuality as a nation—of existing not simply as England or Europe projected to another continent, but as a different civilization with its own being and futurity. British and European travelers and commentators constantly criticized the United States for being new, different, and un-European (charges which no American could deny)—until Americans gradually began to realize that being so was not necessarily shameful. Indeed, it occurred to them that the United States, because of its very newness, difference, and American-ness, was far superior to Britain or Europe.

Nor was this all. The evidence of history, closely examined, seemed to show that God had willed the United States to be different, so that it might play a special role in the future. It seemed plain to many Americans, as it did to a Connecticut magazine contributor in 1786, that God "had reserved this country to be the last and greatest theater in the improvement of mankind." To fulfill this assignment, it was imperative that America emphasize its nationality, reject the prejudices and patterns of the corrupt Old World, and construct its own civilization to fit the nation's divine purpose. In other words, the United States must be *American*, if it were to succeed in what Jefferson called man's greatest experiment, to determine whether "men may be trusted to govern themselves without a master."

The Acceleration of Social Change

The American colonist in 1760 lived in an environment that was not substantially different from his grandfather's. He owned the same kind of house, traveled in the same fashion, communicated with his fellows in much the same way, drew power for his production from similar sources, and for that matter produced and consumed much the same kinds of goods. The span between the close of the French and Indian War and the Treaty of Ghent measured only fifty-one years—but they were years of incredibly swift change. Between lay two major revolutions, the rise and fall of Napoleon, the attainment of American independence, the ratification of the Constitution, an explosion of scientific knowledge, the culmination of the Industrial Revolution, the formation of modern urban society, and a complete change in methods of transportation and communication. The American of 1820 lived in what was almost literally a new society, so recently built that one man's lifetime might have spanned it all.

At the center of this period of change was the American Revolution, a relatively conservative revolution fought to protect certain rights and practices the colonists believed they already possessed. Its aim was not to destroy an established order, but rather to be allowed to create a new order without interference. American radicals, by European standards, were no more than cautious liberals; yet theirs was a true revolution which wrought irrevocable alterations in American society, in some cases simply by allowing movements already under way to continue without hindrance, in others by initiating wholly new trends.

The Revolution did not create an egalitarian, level, homogeneous American society. The war disturbed but did not substantially rearrange the colonial class structure which, by the mid-eighteenth century, was already different from that of England and Europe. Wealth, talent, education, language, manners, lineage, and such things still counted in the America of 1800 as they had in 1750 (the Jacksonian "common man" had not yet arrived) but never so much as they did abroad, and not quite so much as they had a half-century earlier. Enlightened Americans, like Jefferson, believed in leadership by "a natural aristocracy of worth" and in the social and political guidance of "gentlemen"—which was not the same as the British "gentry." Most would probably have agreed with John Adams, who, though a committed revolutionary, felt that there had to be stability and order in the new society, "decency and respect and veneration introduced for persons in authority, at every rank."

On the other hand, this postwar society was by far the most open and flexible in the world. It included both rich and poor, educated and ignorant, gentleman and boor, but, as Lafayette noted, the gap between them was much narrower than in Europe. In a general way, almost everyone within it had a chance to better himself and his children. There were too many roads to success for any group or class to monopolize them; land, resources, and opportunities were too plentiful to be appropriated for the benefit of a few.

At the time of the Revolution, the American colonies had been settled for more than a century and a half. Since the beginning of the eighteenth century they had shown signs of social and cultural division and a tendency to group themselves along regional lines. Postwar geographers usually identified a central "middle" group of states, a "northern" or "New England" group, a Southern bloc, and occasionally a "coastal" and "back" region. Delegates to the Continental Congress referred to themselves as representing Northern, Middle, or Southern states; likewise, the Continental Army command divided the nation into three military districts, Eastern (New England), Middle, and Southern. After 1800, standard geographies usually identified a fourth or "western" region.

Within these regions there were a number of generally accepted social and cultural divisions—the Boston area as separate from the New England mountain states or the Connecticut Valley; upstate

New York as distinct from New York City or the Hudson Valley; the division of Pennsylvania into western (Pittsburgh) and eastern (Philadelphia); the Chesapeake Bay area; the deep South; the Kentucky-Tennessee frontier; and so on. Each of these had its temperamental traits, its personality, its presumably "typical" character such as the canny Yankee, the Dutch New Yorker, the contentious Philadelphian, the cavalier Southerner, the hearty Westerner—who probably did not exist at all except in the popular imagination, but who illustrated the variety of ways by which Americans saw themselves. Even in its youth American society showed great diversity and cultural differentiation. The motto *E Pluribus Unum* had its basis in fact.

One of the most far-reaching consequences of the Revolution was its effect on American economic and industrial life. No longer a colony within an imperial system, the United States at once became an independent unit in the world competition for markets, and rapidly matured, within two generations, into a business civilization. Nowhere was a nation quite so ready as the United States to accept the Industrial Revolution. Lacking any deeply entrenched economic group, it had vast natural resources, a rapidly growing population of producers and consumers, relative political stability and unity, and the protection of a government friendly to business. "All the world," commented Jefferson as he looked about him in 1783, "is becoming commercial." The spread of factories, the introduction of improved machinery and production methods, the establishment of tariffs and other government aids, the growth of banking and credit systems, the opening of the West, and the revolution in transportation combined to make the United States into a burgeoning business society. The conversion from a mercantile to a manufacturing economy was under way, the pattern of nineteenth-century industrial America virtually complete. "We have one material that constitutes aristocracy," John Adams noted in 1808, "and that material is wealth."

The extensive changes wrought in American life during the early decades of independence were accompanied by an astonishing enlargement in the sheer size of the nation. Three states (Vermont, Kentucky, and Tennessee) entered the union between 1789 and 1801; Ohio, Louisiana, Indiana, Illinois, Mississippi, Alabama, Maine, and Missouri joined over the next twenty years. Jefferson's purchase of Louisiana in 1803 more than doubled the size of the country overnight; by a single stroke the United States became proprietor of nearly one-half of North America, master of the continental navigational system, and owner of the Western world's greatest storehouse of untapped natural wealth. At the same time the population more than doubled between 1790 and 1820, rising from 3,900,000 to 9,600,000 in thirty years. The West grew even faster, from a few thousand to more than three million over the same period, so that one-third of the people of the United States, by 1820, lived beyond the mountains.

Postwar America was overwhelmingly rural. In 1790 less than five percent of the population lived in towns of more than 8,000, and even by 1800 there were only five cities of more than 10,000 population. Philadelphia, the largest (and also the second largest in the English-speaking world) had 70,000, New York 60,000, Boston 25,000, Charleston 18,000 and Baltimore 13,000. Within a decade American cities, large and small alike, began a period of phenomenal expansion. New York passed Philadelphia by adding 36,000 people, and Baltimore moved up to third place, while the western cities mushroomed. It took Boston two hundred years to reach 30,000; it took Cincinnati only fifty years to count five times that many. Though the United States still remained a predominantly agrarian nation of farms and small settlements, the cities provided focal points for trade, immigration, and political organization that had lasting effects on the configuration of American society. It was in the cities that the patterns of emergent American culture were largely shaped and directed.

The early nineteenth century saw sweeping changes in transportation and communication, essential for the movement of people, goods, and information in a land of immense distances and scattered population. To unify the country economically and politically, and to join its separate sections into a common society under one government, the new United States needed to construct at least three east-west lines of travel, each six hundred to a thousand miles long, across a mountain range into wild country inhabited by savages; and a similar north-south line about a thousand miles long. Unlike Europe, where a network of roads and canals had been in the making for seven hundred years, the United States was expected to accomplish this at once. Actually, it took less than fifty years. It was possible for a child who had ridden a packhorse into Kentucky to ride within his lifetime from New York to St. Louis on a train.

The effects of this new transportation network on American economic life were incalculable. And not only goods, but ideas, opinions, and people moved over these roads and waterways. People moved by the thousands—chiefly westward. When John Jay remarked in 1785 on "the rage for emigrating to the westward country," the first wave was already sweeping into the back counties of the settled states and across the mountains into western Pennsylvania,

Kentucky, and Tennessee. Virginia counted 400,000 people in 1775 and 750,000 in 1790, with most of the increase concentrated in its western counties. Kentucky, which had a few hundred people in 1770, listed 73,000 in the 1790 census. This first wave, however, was a mere ripple in comparison with the flood that streamed into the Northwest, the Southwest, and the Mississippi Valley in the years directly ahead. It seemed to the English traveler Morris Birkbeck in 1817 that the entire country was "breaking up and moving westward." By 1821 the nine new Western states contained slightly more than one-quarter of the entire national population. Meanwhile, exploring parties probed beyond the Mississippi into the plains; Lewis and Clark's expedition crossed the continent in 1804–6, and John Jacob Astor set up fur posts on the Pacific coast in 1811 and 1812. For the next century the drive westward and the gradual movement with it of the frontier were facts of primary importance in the development of American society.

"Making Thirteen Clocks Strike Together"

The British governed their colonies under a dual system, that is, by means of a strong central government in London, which made major decisions in colonial affairs, and a subordinate government in the colony itself. The central issue of the Revolution, reduced to its simplest terms, was the degree and quality of subordination that should characterize this relationship. In setting up the government of the newly independent nation, the Founding Fathers retained the dual nature of British policy, replaced the colonial law-making bodies with state legislatures, Parliament with Congress, and wrote new documents spelling out the powers and functions of each.

The Revolutionary leaders agreed that they wanted a government which guaranteed natural rights, states' rights, and all those other individual and political privileges which they believed the British colonial system had denied them. They assumed that, since they had been unable to govern themselves as they wished under a strong centralized British government in London, they could possibly do so under a weaker American government in Philadelphia; furthermore, their whole colonial experience had taught them, long before, to distrust any political authority very far beyond their reach. As inheritors of the Enlightenment, as well as of generations of British political theory, they also believed that government was most effective and trustworthy when kept close to the people, the original source of sovereignty. Thus when the state constitutions were drawn up between 1776 and 1780, they placed the essentials of political control—taxes, currency, militia, voting rights, appointments, guarantees of civil and natural rights—in the state legislatures. These new constitutions translated the principles of the Revolution and the Declaration from general to practical political terms. Not only were these the primary contracts under which the nation governed itself during its first decisive decade; they also established precedents and processes of great usefulness for its later political life. The device of the convention, employed by most of the states in evolving their constitutions, still remains the best political method for the actual making of a social compact. The manner of forming constitutions, as developed in the United States, became the model for establishing or revising constitutional governments all over the Western world. In addition, these documents introduced into politics the American conviction, truly novel to the eighteenth century, that government should be based on a written document, which spelled out the principles on which it was founded, and which must have the approval of those who were to live under it. The careful, specific construction of written instruments of government on such a grand scale was an important contribution to the science of politics.

At the same time that the Continental Congress adopted the Declaration of Independence, it also resolved that "a plan of confederation be prepared and transmitted to the respective colonies for their consideration and approbation." A committee headed by John Dickinson of Pennsylvania prepared a set of Articles of Confederation, which the Congress approved in 1777. After ratification by the necessary number of states, these Articles supplied the machinery by which the United States governed itself as a nation until 1789. With the states exerting control over local matters, and the Congress over national and foreign affairs, the United States, wrote the editor of the *Pennsylvania Packet* in 1781, formed "a well-constructed arch, whose parts, harmonizing and mutually supporting each other, are all the more closely united the greater the pressure is upon them."

The trouble was that the system did not work that way. The Articles of Confederation denied Congress certain indispensable powers over finance, diplomatic affairs, and commerce, distributing them instead among the states. Congress, as a result, became little more than an advisory body, with insufficient authority to act on key national issues or to force cooperation from the reluctant states on domestic ones: in John Adams' pungent phrase, it was the problem of "making thirteen clocks strike together."

Neither Congress, nor the executive, nor the judiciary possessed sufficient jurisdiction where it was needed most, and the worsening situation convinced a number of leaders that a stronger central government was necessary. Some argued that the Articles could be amended into an effective document; others (among them Alexander Hamilton, James Madison, and John Jay) thought that the only solution lay in greater federal control. In 1787 Congress, responding to urgent appeals for action, authorized a convention "for the sole and express purpose of revising the Articles of Confederation and reporting to Congress and the several legislatures therein."

The convention which met in Philadelphia on May 25, 1787, did much more than the charge from Congress suggested. The fifty-five delegates represented a cross-section of the groups that had provided political leadership since the early eighteenth century—landowners, planters, lawyers, businessmen, shippers, bankers. Forty-one of them had served in Congress, seven were former state governors. Washington, who commanded unanimous respect, was chosen presiding officer. In attempting one of the most delicate tasks of political history, the formation of a stable union of independent states under a written body of fundamental law, the delegates had few precedents from which to work; they could draw upon the histories of the Greek confederacies, the colonial charters and state constitutions, the British and classical traditions of law and philosophy, their own colonial past, and little else. The materials which went into the Constitution were not new; the delegates gathered them from the total of Western political experience. But the convention, in an act of creative statesmanship, blended them into new and meaningful combinations, bringing them to bear directly on the specific problems of their place and time.

The delegates did not all agree exactly on what kind of document the convention should produce, but there seemed to be a general consensus on three things. First, the national government would be republican in form and aim, consistent with the substance of the American revolutionary philosophy and the Declaration of Independence. Second, the national government would derive its powers from the consent of the governed and rest on the rights of man. Third, the national authority would be sufficiently increased (and that of the states correspondingly lessened) to meet the requirements of an expanding nation, yet without infringement of the rights of states and individuals. The result was not perfection—the Founding Fathers were, after all, mortal men living in time, subject to circumstance—but it was a very great achievement, and an enduring one. John Adams, assessing what had been done at Philadelphia, found it well done; the American system, he wrote, "will last forever, govern the globe, and introduce the perfection of man."

In one vital respect, however, the Constitution was tragically flawed: its failure to deal forthrightly with the fact of black slavery. Without explicitly recognizing slavery as an institution (the words "slave" and "slavery" were not used, but "person" or "person held to service or labor"), it yet implemented a compromise hammered out between northern and southern delegates whereby five slaves were to be counted as the equivalent of three whites in determining the population count on which a state's Congressional representation was to be based. Without some such compromise, it is true, the Constitution might never have been ratified, nor the Federal Union have come to birth. Moreover, slavery was then on the defensive, even on the decline, and its gradual extinction was rather generally expected. Nevertheless, the great paradox of the American Age of Reason was that the principles of natural rights and equality, so nobly stated in the Declaration of Independence, were not applied to the enslaved Afro-Americans. In the outcome, the additional votes in the House of Representatives that the "three-fifths" provision gave to the slaveholding states weighted the scales toward the perpetuation of slavery, and the invention of the cotton gin in 1793 made the slave system economically viable and ended all prospects of its gradual demise.

When the new Constitution came to the states for ratification, it found strong favor and almost equally strong opposition. Many of its proponents, called "Federalists," were drawn from the same mercantile, financial, and social classes that controlled the convention; a number of the Anti-Federalists, who opposed it, came from the ranks of farmers, laborers, debtors, and small tradesmen, who feared the domination of government by the wealthy groups. One by one, however, the states gave their approval; and when the presidential electors met in 1789 to choose Washington as first President, and John Adams as Vice President, the United States was fully launched as a federal union.

The Frontiers of American Science

The most direct expression of the rationalistic spirit of the Enlightenment came in the advancement of science. The eighteenth-century attitude toward science was founded on four generally accepted principles: the belief that all natural and human problems responded to the application of scientific investigation; a belief in the unity of science, that all knowledge was fundamentally scientific; a belief in a mechanistic universe, governed by consistent natural law which was discoverable by human reason; a belief in the efficacy of the inductive method, and a corresponding distrust of dogmatism and authority. This scientific point of view seemed to provide the best and most understandable pattern by which the affairs of God, man, and nature might be explained;

therefore the eighteenth-century philosopher worked outward from this set of beliefs, probing into the social world and the universe in search of laws and principles.

The Neoclassic Age, or Age of Reason, might also be called the Age of Science, for it coincided with the tremendous burst of scientific knowledge that erupted in the late seventeenth century. The American colonies were children of this age, settled in the era of Bacon, Kepler, and Galileo, matured in the era of Newton and Leibnitz. Americans were never far from the stream of scientific knowledge that flowed through the eighteenth century, and men of scientific attainments, such as John Winthrop of Harvard, Cotton Mather, and Benjamin Franklin were representative products of the American Enlightenment. President Thomas Jefferson, for that matter, was a scientist of more than amateur attainments; nor should it be forgotten that the Lewis and Clark expedition, which Jefferson sent westward in 1804, was one of the most significant scientific projects in American history.

Americans believed that science was vitally important to the development of their new continent and new society, for it not only gave man the means to control nature but assisted him in gaining mastery over his own troublesome problems. Thus the poet Joel Barlow hailed the day when

> Science bright
> Through shadowy nature leads with surer light . . . ;
> Gives each effect its own indubious cause,
> Divides her moral from her physic laws,
> Shows where the virtues find their nurturing food,
> And men their motives to be just and good.

It seemed urgent, therefore, that science be encouraged; in fact, there seemed reason to believe that science was peculiarly destined to flourish in America, where, said Samuel Cooper, "liberty unfetters and expands the human mind."

In the process of settling America, there were always new observations to be made, new conditions to be met, new adjustments to the ever-changing frontiers of discovery; hence the American experience proved especially receptive to the implications of scientific method, to the testing and proving of theories by conformity to facts. American conditions, too, favored science that was useful, emphasizing such branches as cartography, surveying, navigational mathematics, astronomy, agriculture, metallurgy, medicine, chemistry, and physics. It was true that American scientists, as they themselves admitted, made fewer theoretical contributions to science than practical ones, and that their main achievements lay in the identification of the flora and fauna of the new continent and the classification of its natural resources. Nevertheless, this was in itself an achievement, for everywhere one looked in

the land there were distant horizons of knowledge, so much unknown. In the United States, as in Britain and Europe, these were years of scientific consolidation, rather than discovery. The Reverend Samuel Miller, writing his *Retrospect of the Eighteenth Century* in 1802, concluded that while American science had matured in the half-century just past, it still derived its impetus from abroad, and that it was not yet "properly self-reliant and independent." This would come in time.

The Search for a National Culture

The early years of American independence produced a great deal of writing, of which only a small part could be called artistically distinguished. It was an age of persuasion and argument, rather than of belles-lettres, and much of what was produced seems amateurish and labored. But whatever its literary value, the writing that Americans did in these years is of utmost importance to an understanding of what they thought and felt as their society took shape—as American ideas were germinating, as a national style was forming, as key issues were being hammered out on the anvil of day-to-day experience. The attainments of the age were not small. Within the span of half a century these men knit thirteen disparate colonies into a unit, erected a government, and launched a nation. What they wrote reflects and expresses much of this achievement.

Having won their political independence, Americans searched for ways to create a culture of their own to express the sense and spirit of their new civilization. They were inheritors of the great Western, classical, Christian tradition they shared with Britain and Europe. Yet they were no longer British and European, but American. How, then, might this inheritance be absorbed and used, rather than simply borrowed or imitated? Editors, critics, authors, orators, and politicians alike agreed with those like Nathan Appleton of New England, who after the Revolution reminded his fellow citizens that they must "sing a New song, a Song that neither We nor our Fathers were ever able to sing before," and the historian David Ramsay, who called for "poets, orators, critics and historians equal to the most celebrated of the ancient commonwealths of Greece and Italy."

Exhortations, unfortunately, did not immediately produce great literary accomplishments. Potential American Homers and Shakespeares faced a number of hurdles and handicaps. A great deal of the creative energy of the times was channeled into political and business life; with a government to construct and a continent to subdue, there was little opportunity to pause for poems. Philip Freneau's advice to young poets to find a job lest they starve had the ring of bitter truth. There were some who felt also that the United States did not have the necessary resources for a distinctive culture and must always lean on Europe. It had no usable past, no tradition of literary patronage, no social diversity; as Washington Irving wrote, it lacked "the charms of storied and poetical associations . . . , the accumulated treasures of age." Neither did the United States have an adequate copyright law. As late as 1830 two of every three books sold came from British or continental presses, and the American market was glutted with cheap, pirated editions of foreign books.

Nevertheless, the outlook for authors was not wholly dark. The American public was literate and well-educated, and, in contrast to Europe, the reading habit was not restricted to the upper classes. Americans, an observer remarked in 1772, had "a taste for books that made almost every man a reader," and foreign travelers rarely failed to note the avidity of newspaper consumption. The cities had numbers of bookstores (Boston alone had fifty in the 1770's) and after 1800 the spread of circulating libraries made books available to almost any American who really wanted to read them. The famous "Coonskin" Library on the Ohio frontier rented books for pelts, and the traveling book-agent poked his way into the remotest log-town hamlet.

To produce its own culture, the United States had first to declare its intellectual independence of Britain. Since no educated American could conceivably wish to reject the great tradition of English letters, his problem became one of what to reject and what to retain that might be made American. As Noah Webster said, no amount of national pride could make him lay aside his beloved Addison. At the outset, the critics decided that Americans should accept Milton, Shakespeare, Addison, Pope, and the rest, but that they must avoid what Webster called "servile imitation" of foreign writing. They must shun anything untrue, immoral, or useless, and things which, in Joel Barlow's phrase, "might prove false and destructive" to American minds.

Simply to avoid European models was not enough. What positive steps might be taken to encourage an *American* artistic tradition? First, though Americans did not have Rob Roy, the Thames, or Cromwell to write about, they decided that they did have a number of things that neither Britain nor Europe could equal. The Indian, the frontier, the Revolution and its heroes, especially the American land itself—these were subjects to challenge and excite the finest artists. The robin, the whippoorwill, and the whispering brook were as inspiring materials for poets, Joseph Dennie thought, "as nightingales, or skylarks, dingles or dells." The Yankee, the Dutchman, the frontiersman, the Southern yeoman,

and other national types were as promising literary timber as any of Scott's knights in armor or Germany's young Werthers. The American writer must, then, find the right way to use these unique resources, so that he might create from them a true, correct, and American art. Thus the novelist Charles Brockden Brown advised the American writer to observe his own land directly, to "examine objects with his own eyes, employ European models merely for the improvement of his own taste," and to build his art about "all that is genuine and peculiar in the scene before him." In this way, predicted *The Columbian Orator* (1807), "Columbia's soil" might

> Rear Men as great as Britain's isle;
> Exceed what Greece and Rome have done,
> Or any land beneath the sun.

The post-Revolutionary period was one of intense literary activity, marking the beginnings of a strong (if not always first-rate) belletristic tradition, the emergence of a profession of letters, and the slow recognition by artist and public that literature was art as well as utility. The writing of the period is not easily classifiable. It has been called "late Neoclassic," "pre-Romantic," "transitional," "Federalistic," and other terms, all proper but only partially descriptive. Despite Webster's injunction against imitation, it was heavily derivative, filled with echoes of Addison, Pope, Goldsmith, Richardson, and others, as the writing of a generation later would echo Scott, Wordsworth, Burns, and Byron. It was distinguished by two general trends: first, the dominance of political writing; and second, the decreasing importance of certain older forms and the increased popularity of others.

Politics naturally bulked large, since the overriding issues of the times were centered on political rights, independence, and survival. Government and law (as theology earlier) attracted the best minds of the Revolutionary generation, and the level of their writing was high. Paine's pamphlets and the *Federalist* papers belong in the first rank of political literature in any century. Jefferson's Declaration of Independence, with its adjustment of reason to emotion, its balance of theory with application, and its magnificent rhetoric, cannot be matched.

Among the forms which lost considerable ground after the Revolution were the diary and the journal, both favorite means of self-expression in an earlier, more introspective era. The published sermon rapidly declined in popularity (soon to be replaced by the secular oration), and though travel narratives were still fairly common, they were no longer so widely read as earlier. The promotional tract, its purpose gone, quickly disappeared. The "captivity" tale, favorite American reading since Captain John Smith's adventures, was absorbed into the novel.

Such changes were natural reflections of the shifting nature of American society and taste. Those forms of writing of a more direct artistic purpose, in which the ideas of the writer were shaped within the pattern of novel, poem, essay, or play, increased in popularity and their practitioners in skill and sophistication. Also, as one might expect, the postwar drive for nationalism and patriotism caused great activity in both biography and history.

The development of the American essay depended largely on the growth of magazines and newspapers. American writers copied Addison, Steele, Goldsmith, Butler, and the other great English satirists in profusion; few newspapers were without a "Tatler" or a "Scriblerus" imitating their masters. The essay attracted the best authors of the time, as well as the least talented; among those who wrote essays of superior literary quality were Franklin, Freneau, Noah Webster, Joseph Dennie, and James Paulding. The essay was not only an accepted form within which one could imitate or experiment without much risk; it was also a useful vehicle for moral instruction, political comment, satire, burlesque, criticism, or casual pleasure.

Although the novel encountered less public and ecclesiastical opposition after the war than earlier in the century, few men of substance believed it worthy of serious consideration as an art form. Ministers cautioned against fiction that might "inflame the passions and corrupt the heart," and even so sophisticated a poet as John Trumbull expressed distrust of

> . . . books that poison all the mind,
> Novels and plays (where shines display'd
> A world that nature never made.)

For that matter, some believed that there was really very little in America for the novelist to write about. "A novel describing these savage barbarians (*Indians*), their squaws and papooses," wrote one critic (a few years before James Fenimore Cooper), "would not be very interesting." The American who wanted to write a novel also had to compete against the whole established array of British novelists in pirated editions, as well as against the lingering snobbishness and Anglophilia of segments of the reading public. It was easier and safer to imitate Richardson or Scott than to write an American book. Cooper himself found it advisable to foster the rumor that his first novel was by "a prominent Englishman."

Nevertheless, the demand for novels increased so swiftly that bookstores could hardly stock them fast enough, and magazines printed them serially by scores. Following British models, American novels tended to fall into four classes: the novel of morality and sentiment, derived from Richardson and Sterne;

the "Gothic" novel of suspense and emotion, modeled on Ann Radcliffe, Walpole, and Godwin; the picaresque-satiric novel, drawn from Smollett, Swift, and Fielding; and the historical romance, inspired by Sir Walter Scott. William Hill Brown's *Power of Sympathy* (1789), the first successful American sentimental novel, was followed by Susannah Rowson's *Charlotte Temple* (1790), which ran subsequently to nearly two hundred editions. After Charlotte opened the floodgates, the magazines were filled with despairing but virtuous heroines, rascally villains, and hapless orphans. Royall Tyler's *Algerine Captive* (1797) and H. H. Brackenridge's *Modern Chivalry* (1792-1815) were satiric novels, but the type never attained popularity. The Gothic tradition attracted Charles Brockden Brown, the most gifted novelist of the pre-Cooper years, whose *Wieland* (1798) and *Ormond* (1799) were excellent if uneven books.

Sir Walter Scott's novels took the United States by storm. Scott's powerful nationalism and his superb use of history represented exactly what Americans hoped to do with their own national experience, and dozens of novelists tried to apply the Scott formula to native materials, with negligible success. James Fenimore Cooper, however, did more than imitate Scott; he naturalized him, so that the historical romance became American. When Leatherstocking walked into fiction with his long rifle, the American novel came of age.

The shift of opinion concerning the theater after 1750 reflected parallel changes in American society. The lessening of religious prejudices against plays, the growth of urban playgoing audiences, the emergence of professional management and the star system, among other things, had much to do with the growing interest in the stage. English companies played fairly regular tours of the colonies, and a few American plays had been produced before the Revolution, notably Thomas Godfrey's pseudo-Jacobean tragedy, *The Prince of Parthia* (1767). However, since the theaters were closed as a wartime measure and the British occupied the major cities, the drama practically vanished until 1783. At the close of the war acting groups quickly reappeared, and within fifteen years several new playhouses were built. Boston's Federal Street Theater and Philadelphia's Chestnut Street Theater opened in 1794, New York's Park Theater in 1798, and both New York and Philadelphia had permanent acting companies by 1800. But the American stage still leaned heavily on imported plays and players, with a few notable exceptions such as Thomas Wignell, who made a career of playing the down-east Yankee, and Lewis Hallam junior, who played everything.

Of the numerous American playwrights who attempted to compete with imported British plays, only Royall Tyler and William Dunlap found much success. Tyler, a Boston lawyer who later sat on the Vermont Supreme Court, wrote a witty comedy of manners, *The Contrast*, first performed in 1787, that merits being called the first American dramatic hit. Dunlap, who wrote at least sixty-five plays, adapted dozens more, and managed two stage companies, wrote and produced *André*, the best tragic play of the period. Despite the popularity of a few dramatists and players, however, the theater found hard going. It had not yet outgrown its dependence on Britain; playgoing audiences, complained the dramatist James Nelson Barker, were still "mental colonists" in the theater. The American stage needed good plays, regular seasons, and solid financing, for all of which it had to wait another generation.

Poets had the most difficult task. "Of all the fools that haunt our coast," wrote Philip Freneau, "the scribbling tribe I pity most." There were no doubt many young men of poetic gifts in the new nation, but the muse attracted few disciples in a climate of revolution and political strife. Some wrote a limited amount of verse, but gave up and turned to law, politics, theology, or education, for, as Freneau commented, "An age employed in edging steel, can no poetic raptures feel." The poetic tradition was trapped in imitation—of Pope, Dryden, Churchill, the "graveyard" school, and later of Scott, Byron, Moore, Leigh Hunt—for it was more convenient and much safer for an American to copy approved models than to strike out for himself, notwithstanding the clamor of critics for "bards of native style."

Since satire was especially suited to the uses of war and politics, lampoons, burlesques, mock epics, hudibrastics, and other combative poetic types flooded out nearly everything else. The contemporary obsession with nationalism led a number of poets, such as Joel Barlow and Timothy Dwight, to expend their limited gifts on awkward patriotic odes and national epics. Yet there were a few authentic American voices. John Trumbull's impish satires showed more than passing talent; Timothy Dwight's inflated pomposities displayed some effective moments of power and dignity; Joel Barlow's "American epic" never came off, but his attempt was not a total failure. Philip Freneau, sea captain, journalist, and poet, produced the best lyric poetry of his generation, combining an unusual freshness and originality with consummate technique. The skill and delicacy of his better verse was unmatched by any American poet of his era and few British, and despite his restlessness and uneven discipline he deserves to be called the first major American poet.

American literature, in the Neoclassic Age, was still only partially American, still to a large extent derivative, imitative, dependent on British models and standards. It was, however, self-consciously searching for a mode and style of its own, testing ways of using its own materials and expressing its own attitudes. The real liberation of American literature was yet to come.

BENJAMIN FRANKLIN [1706–1790]

FRANKLIN REPRESENTED perhaps more fully than any other one man the temper and personality of the American eighteenth century: its rationalism and middle-way common sense, its political concerns and its humanitarian activities, its interest in science and the natural world, its belief in individual integrity and its deistic religious tendencies. His life spanned eighty-four years of that century; born and bred in the provincial colonial Boston of Mather and Sewall, he lived on into the new Republic of Washington and Jefferson, alert to and involved in every aspect of its rich, complex, and exciting life.

Son of a tallow chandler and soap boiler, young Franklin was apprenticed in his brother's print shop, but at age seventeen he ran away to New York and Philadelphia to make his fortune, as he recounts in the familiar story told in his *Autobiography*. He soon made it, becoming a wealthy man and Philadelphia's first citizen, and then retired from business in 1748, hoping to spend a quiet, contemplative life in his library and laboratory. However, he was soon appointed deputy postmaster for the colonies, an office he held for nearly twenty years. He also became deeply involved in the argument between the colonies and Britain, and after 1757 served as colonial agent for Pennsylvania in London. From 1770 to 1775 he represented not only Pennsylvania but Georgia, New Jersey, and Massachusetts in their dealings with King and Parliament. In 1775, having given up hope of finding any way to avert the imminent clash between colonies and empire, he returned to America.

At sixty-nine, when he might have retired to his study, Franklin's career in public life was just beginning. He was not a political philosopher like Jefferson; he was rather the practical organizer, the diplomat, the political tactician, but he was no less a believer in liberty, reason, and justice than the Virginian. He served as a member of the Pennsylvania Committee of Correspondence, as a delegate to the Second Continental Congress, as one of the committee appointed to draft the Declaration of Independence, and as the new nation's first representative to France. In 1778 he secured the French alliance, the greatest single factor in the ultimate victory of the American cause, and in 1783 he served with Adams and Jay on the committee that signed the peace treaty at Paris. Franklin then returned to the United States to begin two terms as governor of Pennsylvania, and finally, at eighty-one, he sat in the Philadelphia convention with men half his age to write the American Constitution.

Though science was often crowded out of his life by public service and diplomacy, Franklin was nevertheless one of the dozen or so first-rank scientific scholars of his century, responsible for some of the most notable basic research done in his time. His contributions to the infant science of electricity were especially important: he defined the existence and function of "positive" and "negative" charges (terms which he coined), performed basic research on the battery principle, and proved by his lightning experiment the identity of electricity in natural and manufactured form. He also wrote more than a hundred scientific papers in medicine, botany, hydraulics, physics, engineering, agronomy, chemistry, and ethnology—his first at twenty-three, his last at seventy-nine. A member of the Royal Society of London, Franklin held seven honorary degrees, mastered six languages, and was recognized as one of the world's great scientists by eight foreign governments.

Like Jefferson, Franklin preferred to keep his religious principles to himself, but he held them firmly and practiced them with deep sincerity. He had little interest in theological disputation or speculation, evolved his own set of Christian religious principles, and lived by them. He was, in effect, a deist who found proof of God in His world and works around him. The most acceptable way to worship this deity, he believed, was to serve his fellow men, and to translate the Christian principles he believed in into practical life. He contributed to a Protestant church and a Jewish synagogue, and helped his friend John Carroll to become the first Catholic archbishop in the United States. He attacked no sect, praised or argued with none, and worshipped God in his own way.

Further reading: Carl Van Doren, *Benjamin Franklin*, 1938. A. O. Aldridge, *Benjamin Franklin*, 1965. V. W. Crane, *Benjamin Franklin and a Rising People*, 1954. Bruce Granger, *Benjamin Franklin: American Man of Letters*, 1965 Ralph Ketcham, *The Political Thought of Benjamin Franklin*, 1966.

FROM THE *Autobiography*

Franklin's autobiography brings to the reader some sense of the vitality and energy of Franklin's mind, as well as the variety of his life and the rationality and honesty of his character. He wrote slightly more than half of the manuscript at Twyford, Hampshire, England, in 1771; a small portion at Passy, near Paris, in 1784; and the final portions at Philadelphia in 1788–89. Because it was written at different times over a period of eighteen years, an alert reader may discover over the span certain differences of spirit and attitude. At Twyford Franklin, in his mid-sixties, enjoying good health and obviously pleased at the chance to recall his youth, wrote with quiet satisfaction of his upward climb from runaway apprentice to man of fortune and reputation. When he resumed his task at Passy, however, he was an internationally known celebrity, writing not only the story of his life for his son and family, but a much more formal account for posterity of how he attained eminence, virtue, and wealth. He was much more concerned in this portion with the public record of his career as businessman, civic leader, and scientist, than with his inward life. In 1788, he was eighty-two, ill, and in retirement, and while the writing shows flashes of his old force and spirit, it is for the most part little more than a straightforward account of facts and dates.

The *Autobiography* carries Franklin's life only until 1757, after which came his careers as colonial agent, scientist, Revolutionary leader, diplomat, and statesman. It is therefore an unfortunately incomplete picture of the man, since it omits almost half of his life, and seems to emphasize the "success story" aspects of it. It should be remembered that Franklin retired from business at the age of forty-two, and spent the next forty-two years of his life in the service of his fellowman and his country.

Text: John Bigelow, ed., *The Complete Works of Benjamin Franklin* (New York, 1904; The Federal Edition).

Twyford, at the Bishop of St. Asaph's, 1771

DEAR SON: I have ever had pleasure in obtaining any little anecdotes of my ancestors. You may remember the inquiries I made among the remains of my relations when you were with me in England, and the journey I undertook for that purpose. Imagining it may be equally agreeable to you to know the circumstances of my life, many of which you are yet unacquainted with, and expecting the enjoyment of a week's uninterrupted leisure in my present country retirement, I sit down to write them for you. To which I have besides some other inducements. Having emerged from the poverty and obscurity in which I was born and bred, to a state of affluence and some degree of reputation in the world, and having gone so far through life with a considerable share of felicity, the conducing means I made use of, which with the blessing of God so well succeeded, my posterity may like to know, as they may find some of them suitable to their own situations, and therefore fit to be imitated.

That felicity, when I reflected on it, has induced me sometimes to say, that were it offered to my choice, I should have no objection to a repetition of the same life from its beginning, only asking the advantages authors have in a second edition to correct some faults of the first. So I might, besides correcting the faults, change some sinister accidents and events of it for others more favorable. But though this were denied, I should still accept the offer. Since such a repetition is not to be expected, the next thing most like living one's life over again seems to be a recollection of that life, and to make that recollection as durable as possible by putting it down in writing.

Hereby, too, I shall indulge the inclination so natural in old men, to be talking of themselves and their own past actions; and I shall indulge it without being tiresome to others, who, through respect to age, might conceive themselves obliged to give me a hearing, since this may be read or not as any one pleases. And, lastly (I may as well confess it, since my denial of it will be believed by nobody), perhaps I shall a good deal gratify my own *vanity*. Indeed, I scarce ever heard or saw the introductory words, *"Without vanity I may say,"* etc., but some vain thing immediately followed. Most people dislike vanity in others, whatever share they have of it themselves; but I give it fair quarter wherever I meet with it, being persuaded that it is often productive of good to the possessor, and to others that are within his sphere of action; and therefore, in many cases, it would not be altogether absurd if a man were to thank God for his vanity among the other comforts of life.

And now I speak of thanking God, I desire with all humility to acknowledge that I owe the mentioned happiness of my past life to His kind providence, which lead me to the means I used and gave them success. My belief of this induces me to *hope*, though I must not *presume*, that the same goodness will still be exercised toward me, in continuing that happiness, or enabling me to bear a fatal reverse, which I may experience as others have done; the complexion of my future fortune being known to Him only in whose power it is to bless to us even our afflictions.

The notes of one of my uncles (who had the same kind of curiosity in collecting family anecdotes) once put into my hands, furnished me with several particulars relating to our ancestors. From these notes I learned that the family had lived in the same village, Ecton, in Northamptonshire, for three hundred years, and how much longer he knew not (perhaps from the time when the name of Franklin, that before was the name of an order of people,[1] was assumed by them as a surname when others took surnames all over the kingdom), on a freehold of about thirty acres, aided by the smith's business, which had continued in the family till his time, the eldest son being always bred to that business, a custom which he and my father followed as to their eldest sons. When I searched the registers at Ecton, I found an account of their births, marriages, and burials, from the year 1555 only, there being no registers kept in that parish at any time preceding. By that register, I perceived that I was the youngest son of the youngest son for five generations back. My grandfather Thomas, who was born in 1598, lived at Ecton till he grew too old to follow business longer, when he went to live with his son John, a dyer at Banbury, in Oxfordshire, with whom my father served an apprenticeship. There my grandfather died and lies buried. We saw his gravestone in 1758. His eldest son Thomas lived in the house at Ecton, and left it with the land to his only child, a

daughter, who, with her husband, one Richard Fisher, of Wellingborough, sold it to Mr. Isted, now lord of the manor there. My grandfather had four sons that grew up, viz.: Thomas, John, Benjamin, and Josiah. I will give you what account I can of them at this distance from my papers, and if these are not lost in my absence, you will among them find many more particulars.

Thomas was bred a smith under his father, but being ingenious, and encouraged in learning (as all my brothers were) by an Esquire Palmer, then the principal gentleman in that parish, he qualified himself for the business of scrivener,[2] became a considerable man in the county, was a chief mover of all public-spirited undertakings for the county or town of Northampton, and his own village, of which many instances were related of him, and much taken notice of and patronized by the then Lord Halifax. He died in 1702, January 6, old style, just four years to a day before I was born. The account we received of his life and character from some old people at Ecton, I remember, struck you as something extraordinary, from its similarity to what you knew of mine. "Had he died on the same day," you said, "one might have supposed a transmigration."

John was bred a dyer, I believe, of woollens. Benjamin was bred a silk-dyer, serving an apprenticeship at London. He was an ingenious man. I remember him well, for, when I was a boy, he came over to my father in Boston, and lived in the house with us some years. He lived to a great age. His grandson, Samuel Franklin, now lives in Boston. He left behind him two quarto volumes, MS., of his own poetry, consisting of little occasional pieces addressed to his friends and relations, of which the following, sent to me, is a specimen.[3] He had formed a short-hand of his own, which he taught me, but, never practising it, I have now forgot it. I was named after this uncle, there being a particular affection between him and my father. He was very pious, a great attender of sermons of the best preachers, which he took down in his short-hand, and had with him many volumes of them. He was also much of a politician; too much, perhaps, for his station. There fell lately into my hands in London a collection he had made of all the principal pamphlets relating to public affairs, from 1641 to 1717; many of the volumes are wanting, as appears by the numbering, but there still remain eight volumes in folio, and twenty-four in quarto and in octavo. A dealer in old books met with them, and knowing me by my sometimes buying of him, he brought them to me. It seems my uncle must have left them here when he

---

[1] That is, those who owned property, or freeholders.

[2] A professional writer, a copyist.

[3] Franklin did not include this poetry in his manuscript.

went to America, which was above fifty years since. There are many of his notes in the margins.

This obscure family of ours was early in the Reformation, and continued Protestants through the reign of Queen Mary, when they were sometimes in danger of trouble on account of their zeal against popery. They had got an English Bible, and to conceal and secure it, it was fastened open with tapes under and within the cover of a joint-stool. When my great-great-grandfather read it to his family, he turned up the joint-stool upon his knees, turning over the leaves then under the tapes. One of the children stood at the door to give notice if he saw the apparitor coming, who was an officer of the spiritual court. In that case the stool was turned down again upon its feet, when the Bible remained concealed under it as before. This anecdote I had from my uncle Benjamin. The family continued all of the Church of England till about the end of Charles the Second's reign, when some of the ministers that had been outed for non-conformity, holding conventicles[4] in Northamptonshire, Benjamin and Josiah adhered to them, and so continued all their lives: the rest of the family remained with the Episcopal Church.

Josiah, my father, married young, and carried his wife with three children into New England, about 1682. The conventicles having been forbidden by law, and frequently disturbed, induced some considerable men of his acquaintance to remove to that country, and he was prevailed with to accompany them thither, where they expected to enjoy their mode of religion with freedom. By the same wife he had four children more; born there, and by a second wife ten more, in all seventeen; of which I remember thirteen sitting at one time at his table, who all grew up to be men and women, and married; I was the youngest son, and the youngest child but two, and was born in Boston, New England. My mother, the second wife, was Abiah Folger, daughter of Peter Folger, one of the first settlers of New England, of whom honorable mention is made by Cotton Mather, in his church history of that country entitled *Magnalia Christi Americana*, as *"a godly, learned Englishman,"* if I remember the words rightly. I have heard that he wrote sundry small occasional pieces, but only one of them was printed, which I saw now many years since. It was written in 1675, in the home-spun verse of that time and people, and addressed to those then concerned in the government there. It was in favor of liberty of conscience, and in behalf of the Baptists, Quakers, and other sectaries that had been under persecution, ascribing the Indian wars, and other distresses that

had befallen the country, to that persecution, as so many judgments of God to punish so heinous an offense, and exhorting a repeal of those uncharitable laws. The whole appeared to me as written with a good deal of decent plainness and manly freedom. The six concluding lines I remember, though I have forgotten the two first of the stanza; but the purport of them was, that his censures proceeded from good will, and therefore he would be known to be the author.

> "Because to be a libeller (says he)
>   I hate it with my heart;
> From Sherburne town, where now I dwell
>   My name I do put here;
> Without offense your real friend,
>   It is Peter Folgier."

My elder brothers were all put apprentices to different trades. I was put to the grammar-school at eight years of age, my father intending to devote me, as the tithe[5] of his sons, to the service of the Church. My early readiness in learning to read (which must have been very early, as I do not remember when I could not read), and the opinion of all his friends, that I should certainly make a good scholar, encouraged him in this purpose of his. My uncle Benjamin, too, approved of it, and proposed to give me all his short-hand volumes of sermons, I suppose as a stock to set up with, if I would learn his character. I continued, however, at the grammar-school not quite one year, though in that time I had risen gradually from the middle of the class of that year to be the head of it, and farther was removed into the next class above it, in order to go with that into the third at the end of the year. But my father, in the meantime, from a view of the expense of a college education, which having so large a family he could not well afford, and the mean living many so educated were afterwards able to obtain,—reasons that he gave to his friends in my hearing,—altered his first intention, took me from the grammar-school, and sent me to a school for writing and arithmetic, kept by a then famous man, Mr. George Brownell, very successful in his profession generally, and that by mild, encouraging methods. Under him I acquired fair writing pretty soon, but I failed in the arithmetic, and made no progress in it. At ten years old I was taken home to assist my father in his business, which was that of a tallow-chandler and sope-boiler; a business he was not bred to, but had assumed on his arrival in New England, and on finding his dying trade would not maintain his family, being in little request. Accordingly, I was employed in cutting wick for the candles,

---

[4] Meetings of dissenters (here Presbyterians) outlawed by the 1662 Act of Conformity.

[5] The tenth part of income set aside for the church; hence, a gift or contribution.

filling the dipping mold and the molds for cast candles, attending the shop, going of errands, etc.

I disliked the trade, and had a strong inclination for the sea, but my father declared against it; however, living near the water, I was much in and about it, learnt early to swim well, and to manage boats; and when in a boat or canoe with other boys, I was commonly allowed to govern, especially in any case of difficulty; and upon other occasions I was generally a leader among the boys, and sometimes led them into scrapes, of which I will mention one instance, as it shows an early projecting public spirit, tho' not then justly conducted.

There was a salt-marsh that bounded part of the mill-pond, on the edge of which, at high water, we used to stand to fish for minnows. By much trampling, we had made it a mere quagmire. My proposal was to build a wharf there fit for us to stand upon, and I showed my comrades a large heap of stones, which were intended for a new house near the marsh, and which would very well suit our purpose. Accordingly, in the evening, when the workmen were gone, I assembled a number of my play-fellows, and working with them diligently like so many emmets,[6] sometimes two or three to a stone, we brought them all away and built our little wharf. The next morning the workmen were surprised at missing the stones, which were found in our wharf. Inquiry was made after the removers; we were discovered and complained of; several of us were corrected by our fathers; and, though I pleaded the usefulness of the work, mine convinced me that nothing was useful which was not honest.

I think you may like to know something of his person and character. He had an excellent constitution of body, was of middle stature, but well set, and very strong; he was ingenious, could draw prettily, was skilled a little in music, and had a clear, pleasing voice, so that when he played psalm tunes on his violin and sung withal, as he sometimes did in an evening after the business of the day was over, it was extremely agreeable to hear. He had a mechanical genius too, and, on occasion, was very handy in the use of other tradesmen's tools; but his great excellence lay in a sound understanding and solid judgment in prudential matters, both in private and publick affairs. In the latter, indeed, he was never employed, the numerous family he had to educate and the straitness of his circumstances keeping him close to his trade; but I remember well his being frequently visited by leading people, who consulted him for his opinion in affairs of the town or of the church he belonged to, and showed a good deal of respect for his judgment and advice: he was also

[6]Ants.

much consulted by private persons about their affairs when any difficulty occurred, and frequently chosen an arbitrator between contending parties. At his table he liked to have, as often as he could, some sensible friend or neighbor to converse with, and always took care to start some ingenious or useful topic for discourse, which might tend to improve the minds of his children. By this means he turned our attention to what was good, just, and prudent in the conduct of life; and little or no notice was ever taken of what related to the victuals on the table, whether it was well or ill dressed, in or out of season, of good or bad flavor, preferable or inferior to this or that other thing of the kind, so that I was bro't up in such a perfect inattention to those matters as to be quite indifferent what kind of food was set before me, and so unobservant of it that to this day if I am asked I can scarcely tell a few hours after dinner what I dined upon. This has been a convenience to me in travelling, where my companions have been sometimes very unhappy for want of a suitable gratification of their more delicate, because better instructed, tastes and appetites.

My mother had likewise an excellent constitution: she suckled all her ten children. I never knew either my father or mother to have any sickness but that of which they dy'd, he at eighty-nine, and she at eighty-five years of age. They lie buried together at Boston, where I some years since placed a marble over their grave, with this inscription:

> Josiah Franklin,
> and
> Abiah his wife,
> Lie here interred.
> They lived lovingly together in wedlock
> Fifty-five years.
> Without an estate, or any gainful employment,
> By constant labor and industry
> With God's blessing,
> They maintained a large family
> Comfortably,
> And brought up thirteen children
> And seven grandchildren
> Reputably.
> From this instance, reader,
> Be encouraged to diligence in thy calling,
> And distrust not Providence.
> He was a pious and prudent man;
> She, a discreet and virtuous woman.
> Their youngest son,
> In filial regard to their memory,
> Places this stone.
> J. F. born 1655, died 1744, Aetat 89.
> A. F. born 1667, died 1752, —— 85.

By my rambling digressions I perceive myself to be grown old. I us'd to write more methodically. But one does not dress for private company as for a publick ball. 'T is perhaps only negligence.

To return: I continued thus employed in my father's business for two years, that is, till I was twelve years old; and my brother John, who was bred to that business, having left my father, married, and set up for himself at Rhode Island, there was all appearance that I was destined to supply his place, and become a tallow-chandler. But my dislike to the trade continuing, my father was under apprehensions that if he did not find one for me more agreeable, I should break away and get to sea, as his son Josiah had done, to his great vexation. He therefore sometimes took me to walk with him, and see joiners, bricklayers, turners, braziers, etc., at their work, that he might observe my inclination, and endeavor to fix it on some trade or other on land. It has ever since been a pleasure to me to see good workmen handle their tools; and it has been useful to me, having learnt so much by it as to be able to do little jobs myself in my house when a workman could not readily be got, and to construct little machines for my experiments, while the intention of making the experiment was fresh and warm in my mind. My father at last fixed upon the cutler's trade, and my uncle Benjamin's son Samuel, who was bred to that business in London, being about that time established in Boston, I was sent to be with him some time on liking. But his expectations of a fee with me displeasing my father, I was taken home again.

From a child I was fond of reading, and all the little money that came into my hands was ever laid out in books. Pleased with the *Pilgrim's Progress*, my first collection was of John Bunyan's works in separate little volumes. I afterward sold them to enable me to buy R. Burton's *Historical Collections;* they were small chapmen's books,[7] and cheap, forty or fifty in all. My father's little library consisted chiefly of books in polemic divinity, most of which I read, and have since often regretted that, at a time when I had such a thirst for knowledge, more proper books had not fallen in my way, since it was now resolved I should not be a clergyman. Plutarch's *Lives* there was in which I read abundantly, and I still think that time spent to great advantage. There was also a book of De Foe's, called an *Essay on Projects,* and another of Dr. Mather's, called *Essays to do Good,* which perhaps gave me a turn of thinking that had an influence on some of the principal future events of my life.

This bookish inclination at length determined my father to make me a printer, though he had already one son (James) of that profession. In 1717 my brother James returned from England with a press and letters to set up his business in Boston. I liked it much better than that of my father, but still had a hankering for the sea. To prevent the apprehended effect of such an inclination, my father was impatient to have me bound[8] to my brother. I stood out some time, but at last was persuaded, and signed the indentures when I was yet but twelve years old. I was to serve as an apprentice till I was twenty-one years of age, only I was to be allowed journeyman's wages during the last year. In a little time I made great proficiency in the business, and became a useful hand to my brother. I now had access to better books. An acquaintance with the apprentices of booksellers enabled me sometimes to borrow a small one, which I was careful to return soon and clean. Often I sat up in my room reading the greatest part of the night, when the book was borrowed in the evening and to be returned early in the morning, lest it should be missed or wanted.

And after some time an ingenious tradesman, Mr. Matthew Adams, who had a pretty collection of books, and who frequented our printing-house, took notice of me, invited me to his library, and very kindly lent me such books as I chose to read. I now took a fancy to poetry, and made some little pieces; my brother, thinking it might turn to account, encouraged me, and put me on composing occasional ballads. One was called *The Lighthouse Tragedy,* and contained an account of the drowning of Captain Worthilake, with his two daughters; the other was a sailor's song, on the taking of *Teach* (or Blackbeard) the pirate. They were wretched stuff, in the Grub-street-ballad style; and when they were printed he sent me about the town to sell them. The first sold wonderfully; the event, being recent, having made a great noise. This flattered my vanity; but my father discouraged me by ridiculing my performances, and telling me verse-makers were generally beggars. So I escaped being a poet, most probably a very bad one; but as prose writing has been of great use to me in the course of my life, and was a principal means of my advancement, I shall tell you how, in such a situation I acquired what little ability I have in that way.

There was another bookish lad in the town, John Collins by name, with whom I was intimately acquainted. We sometimes disputed, and very fond we were of argument, and very desirous of confuting one another, which disputatious turn, by the way, is apt to become a very bad habit, making people often extremely disagreeable in company by the contradiction that is necessary to bring it into practice; and thence, besides souring and spoiling the conversation, is productive of disgusts and, perhaps, enmities where you may have occasion for friendship. I had caught it by reading my father's books of

---

[7] Cheap books sold by street peddlers.

[8] Apprenticed.

dispute about religion. Persons of good sense, I have since observed, seldom fall into it, except lawyers, university men, and men of all sorts that have been bred at Edinborough.

A question was once, somehow or other, started between Collins and me, of the propriety of educating the female sex in learning, and their abilities for study. He was of opinion that it was improper, and that they were naturally unequal to it. I took the contrary side, perhaps a little for dispute's sake. He was naturally more eloquent, had a ready plenty of words, and sometimes, as I thought, bore me down more by his fluency than by the strength of his reasons. As we parted without settling the point, and were not to see one another again for some time, I sat down to put my arguments in writing, which I copied fair and sent to him. He answered, and I replied. Three or four letters of a side had passed, when my father happened to find my papers and read them. Without entering into the discussion, he took occasion to talk to me about the manner of my writing; observed that, though I had the advantage of my antagonist in correct spelling and pointing[9] (which I ow'd to the printing-house), I fell far short in elegance of expression, in method and in perspicuity, of which he convinced me by several instances. I saw the justice of his remarks, and thence grew more attentive to the manner in writing, and determined to endeavor at improvement.

About this time I met with an odd volume of the *Spectator*. It was the third. I had never before seen any of them. I bought it, read it over and over, and was much delighted with it. I thought the writing excellent, and wished, if possible, to imitate it. With this view I took some of the papers, and, making short hints of the sentiment in each sentence, laid them by a few days, and then, without looking at the book, try'd to compleat the papers again, by expressing each hinted sentiment at length, and as fully as it had been expressed before, in any suitable words that should come to hand. Then I compared my *Spectator* with the original, discovered some of my faults, and corrected them. But I found I wanted a stock of words, or a readiness in recollecting and using them, which I thought I should have acquired before that time if I had gone on making verses; since the continual occasion for words of the same import, but of different length, to suit the measure, or of different sound for the rhyme, would have laid me under a constant necessity of searching for variety, and also have tended to fix that variety in my mind, and make me master of it. Therefore I took some of the tales and turned them into verse; and, after a time, when I had pretty well forgotten the prose, turned them back

[9] Punctuation.

again. I also sometimes jumbled my collections of hints into confusion, and after some weeks endeavored to reduce them into the best order, before I began to form the full sentences and compleat the paper. This was to teach me method in the arrangement of thoughts. By comparing my work afterwards with the original, I discovered my faults and amended them; but I sometimes had the pleasure of fancying that, in certain particulars of small import, I had been lucky enough to improve the method or the language, and this encouraged me to think I might possibly in time come to be a tolerable English writer, of which I was extremely ambitious. My time for these exercises and for reading was at night, after work or before it began in the morning, or on Sundays, when I contrived to be in the printing-house alone, evading as much as I could the common attendance on public worship which my father used to exact of me when I was under his care, and which indeed I still thought a duty, though I could not, as it seemed to me, afford time to practise it.

When about 16 years of age I happened to meet with a book, written by one Tryon, recommending a vegetable diet. I determined to go into it. My brother, being yet unmarried, did not keep house, but boarded himself and his apprentices in another family. My refusing to eat flesh occasioned an inconveniency, and I was frequently chid for my singularity. I made myself acquainted with Tryon's manner of preparing some of his dishes, such as boiling potatoes or rice, making hasty pudding, and a few others, and then proposed to my brother, that if he would give me, weekly, half the money he paid for my board, I would board myself. He instantly agreed to it, and I presently found that I could save half what he paid me. This was an additional fund for buying books. But I had another advantage in it. My brother and the rest going from the printing-house to their meals, I remained there alone, and, despatching presently my light repast, which often was no more than a bisket or a slice of bread, a handful of raisins, or a tart from the pastry-cook's, and a glass of water, had the rest of the time, till their return, for study, in which I made the greater progress, from that greater clearness of head and quicker apprehension which usually attend temperance in eating and drinking.

And now it was that, being on some occasion made asham'd of my ignorance in figures, which I had twice failed in learning when at school, I took Cocker's book of Arithmetick, and went through the whole by myself with great ease. I also read Seller's and Shermy's books of Navigation, and became acquainted with the little geometry they contain; but never proceeded far in that science. And I read about this time Locke *On Human Understanding*, and the *Art of Thinking*, by Messrs. du Port Royal.

While I was intent on improving my language, I met with an English grammar (I think it was Greenwood's), at the end of which there were two little sketches of the arts of rhetoric and logic, the latter finishing with a specimen of a dispute in the Socratic method, and soon after I procur'd Xenophon's *Memorable Things of Socrates*, wherein there are many instances of the same method. I was charm'd with it, adopted it, dropt my abrupt contradiction and positive argumentation, and put on the humble inquirer and doubter. And being then, from reading Shaftesbury and Collins,[10] become a real doubter in many points of our religious doctrine, I found this method safest for myself, and very embarrassing to those against whom I used it; therefore I took a delight in it, practis'd it continually, and grew very artful and expert in drawing people, even of superior knowledge, into concessions, the consequences of which they did not foresee, entangling them in difficulties out of which they could not extricate themselves, and so obtaining victories that neither myself nor my cause always deserved. I continu'd this method some few years, but gradually left it, retaining only the habit of expressing myself in terms of modest diffidence, never using, when I advanced any thing that may possibly be disputed, the words *certainly, undoubtedly,* or any others that give the air of positiveness to an opinion, but rather say, I conceive or apprehend a thing to be so and so; it appears to me, or *I should think it so or so,* for such and such reasons; or *I imagine it to be so; or it is so, if I am not mistaken.* This habit, I believe, has been of great advantage to me when I have had occasion to inculcate my opinions, and persuade men into measures that I have been from time to time engag'd in promoting; and, as the chief ends of conversation are to *inform* or to be *informed,* to *please* or to *persuade,* I wish well-meaning, sensible men would not lessen their power of doing good by a positive, assuming manner, that seldom fails to disgust, tends to create opposition, and to defeat every one of those purposes for which speech was given to us,—to wit, giving or receiving information or pleasure. For, if you would inform, a positive and dogmatical manner in advancing your sentiments may provoke contradiction and prevent a candid attention. If you wish information and improvement from the knowledge of others, and yet at the same time express yourself as firmly fix'd in your present opinions, modest, sensible men, who do not love disputation, will probably leave you undisturbed in the possession of your error. And by such a manner, you can seldom hope to recommend yourself in *pleasing* your hearers, or to persuade those whose concurrence you desire. Pope says, judiciously:

> Men should be taught as if you taught them not;
> And things unknown propos'd as things forgot;

farther recommending to us

> To speak, tho' sure, with seeming diffidence.

And he might have coupled with this line that which he has coupled with another, I think, less properly:

> For want of modesty is want of sense.

If you ask, Why less properly? I must repeat the lines:

> Immodest words admit of no defense,
> For want of modesty is want of sense.

Now, is not *want of sense* (where a man is so unfortunate as to want it) some apology for his *want of modesty?* and would not the lines stand more justly thus?

> Immodest words admit *but* this defense,
> That want of modesty is want of sense.

This, however, I should submit to better judgments. ° ° °

I had been religiously educated as a Presbyterian;[11] and tho' some of the dogmas of that persuasion, such as *the eternal decrees of God, election, reprobation, etc.,* appeared to me unintelligible, others doubtful, and I early absented myself from the public assemblies of the sect, Sunday being my studying day, I never was without some religious principles. I never doubted, for instance, the existence of the Deity; that he made the world, and govern'd it by his Providence; that the most acceptable service of God was the doing good to man; that our souls are immortal; and that all crime will be punished, and virtue rewarded, either here or hereafter. These I esteem'd the essentials of every religion; and, being to be found in all the religions we had in our country, I respected them all, tho' with different degrees of respect, as I found them more or less mix'd with other articles, which, without any tendency to inspire, promote, or confirm morality, serv'd principally to divide us, and make us unfriendly to one another. This respect to all, with an opinion that the worst had some good effects, induc'd me to avoid all discourse that might tend to lessen the good opinion another might have of his own religion; and as our province increas'd in people, and new places of worship were continually wanted, and generally erected by voluntary contribution, my mite for such purpose, whatever might be the sect, was never refused.

---

[10] The Earl of Shaftesbury's *Characteristics* (1712, 1714) and Anthony Collins' *Discourse* (1713) were somewhat radical theological treatises.

[11] This portion of the manuscript Franklin wrote in France, after an interval of thirteen years.

DOESN'T ATTEND----- UTILITY ---- REGULARY PAID?

Tho' I seldom attended any public worship, I had still an opinion of its propriety, and of its utility when rightly conducted, and I regularly paid my annual subscription for the support of the only Presbyterian minister or meeting we had in Philadelphia. He us'd to visit me sometimes as a friend, and admonish me to attend his administrations, and I was now and then prevail'd on to do so, once for five Sundays successively. Had he been in my opinion a good preacher, perhaps I might have continued, notwithstanding the occasion I had for the Sunday's leisure in my course of study; but his discourses were chiefly either polemic arguments, or explications of the peculiar doctrines of our sect, and were all to me very dry, uninteresting, and unedifying, since not a single moral principle was inculcated or enforc'd, their aim seeming to be rather to make us Presbyterians than good citizens.

"GOOD CITIZENS"

At length he took for his text that verse of the fourth chapter of Philippians: *"Finally, brethren, whatsoever things are true, honest, just, pure, lovely, or of good report, if there be any virtue, or any praise, think on these things."* And I imagin'd, in a sermon on such a text, we could not miss of having some morality. But he confin'd himself to five points only, as meant by the apostle, viz.: 1. Keeping holy the Sabbath day. 2. Being diligent in reading the holy Scriptures. 3. Attending duly the publick worship. 4. Partaking of the Sacrament. 5. Paying a due respect to God's ministers. These might be all good things; but, as they were not the kind of good things that I expected from that text, I despaired of ever meeting with them from any other, was disgusted, and attended his preaching no more. I had some years before compos'd a little Liturgy, or form of prayer, for my own private use (viz., in 1728), entitled *Articles of Belief and Acts of Religion.* I return'd to the use of this, and went no more to the public assemblies. My conduct might be blameable, but I leave it, without attempting further to excuse it; my present purpose being to relate facts, and not to make apologies for them.

It was about this time I conceiv'd the bold and arduous project of arriving at moral perfection. I wish'd to live without committing any fault at any time; I would conquer all that either natural inclination, custom, or company might lead me into. As I knew, or thought I knew, what was right and wrong, I did not see why I might not always do the one and avoid the other. But I soon found I had undertaken a task of more difficulty than I had imagined. While my care was employ'd in guarding against one fault, I was often surprised by another; habit took the advantage of inattention; inclination was sometimes too strong for reason. I concluded, at length, that the mere speculative conviction that it was our interest to be completely virtuous, was not sufficient

to prevent our slipping; and that the contrary habits must be broken, and good ones acquired and established, before we can have any dependence on a steady, uniform rectitude of conduct. For this purpose I therefore contrived the following method.

In the various enumerations of the moral virtues I had met with in my reading, I found the catalogue more or less numerous, as different writers included more or fewer ideas under the same name. Temperance, for example, was by some confined to eating and drinking, while by others it was extended to mean the moderating every other pleasure, appetite, inclination, or passion, bodily or mental, even to our avarice and ambition. I propos'd to myself, for the sake of clearness, to use rather more names, with fewer ideas annex'd to each, than a few names with more ideas; and I included under thirteen names of virtues all that at that time occurr'd to me as necessary or desirable, and annexed to each a short precept, which fully express'd the extent I gave to its meaning.

These names of virtues, with their precepts, were:

1. TEMPERANCE
Eat not to dullness; drink not to elevation.

2. SILENCE
Speak not but what may benefit others or yourself; avoid trifling conversation.

3. ORDER
Let all your things have their places; let each part of your business have its time.

4. RESOLUTION
Resolve to perform what you ought; perform without fail what you resolve.

5. FRUGALITY
Make no expense but to do good to others or yourself; *i.e.*, waste nothing.

6. INDUSTRY
Lose no time; be always employ'd in something useful; cut off all unnecessary actions.

7. SINCERITY
Use no hurtful deceit; think innocently and justly; and, if you speak, speak accordingly.

8. JUSTICE
Wrong none by doing injuries, or omitting the benefits that are your duty.

9. MODERATION
Avoid extreams; forbear resenting injuries so much as you think they deserve.

10. CLEANLINESS
Tolerate no uncleanliness in body, cloaths, or habitation.

11. Tranquillity

Be not disturbed at trifles, or at accidents common or unavoidable.

12. Chastity

Rarely use venery but for health or offspring, never to dulness, weakness, or the injury of your own or another's peace or reputation.

13. Humility

Imitate Jesus and Socrates.

My intention being to acquire the *habitude* of all these virtues, I judg'd it would be well not to distract my attention by attempting the whole at once, but to fix it on one of them at a time; and, when I should be master of that, then proceed to another, and so on till I had gone thro' the thirteen; and, as the previous acquisition of some might facilitate the acquisition of certain others, I arrang'd them with that view, as they stand above. Temperance first, as it tends to procure that coolness and clearness of head, which is so necessary where constant vigilance was to be kept up, and guard maintained against the unremitting attraction of ancient habits, and the force of perpetual temptations. This being acquir'd and establish'd, Silence would be more easy; and my desire being to gain knowledge at the same time that I improv'd in virtue, and considering that in conversation it was obtain'd rather by the use of the ears than of the tongue, and therefore wishing to break a habit I was getting into of prattling, punning, and joking, which only made me acceptable to trifling company, I gave *Silence* the second place. This and the next, *Order*, I expected would allow me more time for attending to my project and my studies. *Resolution*, once become habitual, would keep me firm in my endeavors to obtain all the subsequent virtues; *Frugality* and Industry freeing me from my remaining debt, and producing affluence and independence, would make more easy the practice of Sincerity and Justice, etc., etc. Conceiving, then, that, agreeably to the advice of Pythagoras in his *Golden Verses*, daily examination would be necessary, I contrived the following method for conducting that examination.

I made a little book, in which I allotted a page for each of the virtues. I rul'd each page with red ink, so as to have seven columns, one for each day of the week, marking each column with a letter for the day. I cross'd these columns with thirteen red lines, marking the beginning of each line with the first letter of one of the virtues, on which line, and in its proper column, I might mark, by a little black spot, every fault I found upon examination to have been committed respecting that virtue upon that day.

I determined to give a week's strict attention to each of the virtues successively. Thus, in the first

Form of the Pages

TEMPERANCE.							
EAT NOT TO DULLNESS; DRINK NOT TO ELEVATION.							
	S.	M.	T.	W.	T.	F.	S.
T.							
S.	°	°		°		°	
O.	° °	°	°		°	°	°
R.			°			°	
F.		°			°		
I.			°				
S.							
J.							
M.							
C.							
T.							
C.							
H.							

week, my great guard was to avoid every the least offence against *Temperance*, leaving the other virtues to their ordinary chance, only marking every evening the faults of the day. Thus, if in the first week I could keep my first line, marked T, clear of spots, I suppos'd the habit of that virtue so much strengthen'd, and its opposite weaken'd, that I might venture extending my attention to include the next, and for the following week keep both lines clear of spots. Proceeding thus to the last, I could go thro' a course compleat in thirteen weeks, and four courses in a year. And like him who, having a garden to weed, does not attempt to eradicate all the bad herbs at once, which would exceed his reach and his strength, but works on one of the beds at a time, and, having accomplish'd the first, proceeds to a second, so I should have, I hoped, the encouraging pleasure of seeing on my pages the progress I made in virtue, by clearing successively my lines of their spots, till in the end, by a number of courses, I should be happy in viewing a clean book, after a thirteen weeks' daily examination.

This my little book had for its motto these lines from Addison's *Cato*:

Here will I hold. If there's a power above us
(And that there is, all nature cries aloud
Thro' all her works), He must delight in virtue;
And that which He delights in must be happy.

Another from Cicero,

O vitae Philosophia dux! O virtutum indagatrix expultrixque vitiorum! Unus dies, bene et ex praeceptis tuis actus, peccanti immortalitati est anteponendus.

Another from the Proverbs of Solomon, speaking of wisdom or virtue:

> Length of days is in her right hand, and in her left hand riches and honour. Her ways are ways of pleasantness, and all her paths are peace.—iii. 16, 17.

And conceiving God to be the fountain of wisdom, I thought it right and necessary to solicit his assistance for obtaining it; to this end I formed the following little prayer, which was prefix'd to my tables of examination, for daily use.

> *O powerful Goodness! bountiful Father! merciful Guide! Increase in me that wisdom which discovers my truest interest. Strengthen my resolutions to perform what that wisdom dictates. Accept my kind offices to thy other children as the only return in my power for thy continual favours to me.*

I used also sometimes a little prayer which I took from Thomson's *Poems*, viz.:

> Father of light and life, thou Good Supreme!
> O teach me what is good; teach me Thyself!
> Save me from folly, vanity, and vice,
> From every low pursuit; and fill my soul
> With knowledge, conscious peace, and virtue pure;
> Sacred, substantial, never-fading bliss!

The precept of *Order* requiring that *every part of my business should have its allotted time*, one page in my little book contain'd the following scheme of employment for the twenty-four hours of a natural day.

THE MORNING. *Question.* What good shall I do this day?	5 6 7	Rise, wash, and address *Powerful Goodness!* Contrive day's business, and take the resolution of the day; prosecute the present study, and breakfast.
	8 9 10 11	Work.
NOON.	12 1	Read, or overlook my accounts, and dine.
	2 3 4 5	Work.
EVENING. *Question.* What good have I done today?	6 7 8 9	Put things in their places. Supper. Music or diversion, or conversation. Examination of the day.
	10 11 12	
NIGHT.	1 2 3 4	Sleep.

I enter'd upon the execution of this plan for self-examination, and continu'd it with occasional intermissions for some time. I was surpris'd to find myself so much fuller of faults than I had imagined; but I had the satisfaction of seeing them diminish. To avoid the trouble of renewing now and then my little book, which, by scraping out the marks on the paper of old faults to make room for new ones in a new course, became full of holes, I transferr'd my tables and precepts to the ivory leaves of a memorandum book, on which the lines were drawn with red ink, that made a durable stain, and on those lines I mark'd my faults with a black-lead pencil, which marks I could easily wipe out with a wet sponge. After a while I went thro' one course only in a year, and afterward only one in several years, till at length I omitted them entirely, being employ'd in voyages and business abroad, with a multiplicity of affairs that interfered; but I always carried my little book with me.

My scheme of ORDER gave me the most trouble; and I found that, tho' it might be practicable where a man's business was such as to leave him the disposition of his time, that of a journeyman printer, for instance, it was not possible to be exactly observed by a master who must mix with the world and often receive people of business at their own hours. *Order*, too, with regard to places for things, papers, etc., I found extreamly difficult to acquire. I had not been early accustomed to it, and, having an exceeding good memory, I was not so sensible of the inconvenience attending want of method. This article, therefore cost me so much painful attention and my faults in it vexed me so much, and I made so little progress in amendment, and had such frequent relapses that I was almost ready to give up the attempt, and content myself with a faulty character in that respect, like the man who, in buying an ax of a smith, my neighbour, desired to have the whole of its surface as bright as the edge. The smith consented to grind it bright for him if he would turn the wheel; he turn'd while the smith press'd the broad face of the ax hard and heavily on the stone which made the turning of it very fatiguing. The man came every now and then from the wheel to see how the work went on and at length would take his ax as it was, without farther grinding. "No," said the smith, "turn on, turn on; we shall have it bright by and by; as yet, it is only speckled." "Yes," says the man, *"but I think I like a speckled ax best."* And I believe this may have been the case with many who, having, for want of some such means as I employ'd, found the difficulty of obtaining good and breaking bad habits in other points of vice and virtue, have given up the struggle, and concluded that *"a speckled ax was best"*; for something, that pretended to be reason, was every now and then suggesting to me that such extream nicety as I exacted of myself might be a kind of foppery in morals, which, if it were known, would make me ridiculous; that a perfect character might be attended with the inconvenience of being envied and hated; and that a benevolent man should allow a few faults in himself, to keep his friends in countenance.

In truth, I found myself incorrigible with respect to Order; and now I am grown old and my memory bad, I feel very sensibly the want of it. But, on the whole, tho' I never arrived at the perfection I had been so ambitious of obtaining, but fell far short of it, yet I was, by the endeavour, a better and a happier man than I otherwise should have been if I had not attempted it; as those who aim at perfect writing by imitating the engraved copies, tho' they never reach the wish'd-for excellence of those copies, their hand is mended by the endeavour, and is tolerable while it continues fair and legible.

It may be well my posterity should be informed that to this little artifice, with the blessing of God, their ancestor ow'd the constant felicity of his life, down to his 79th year, in which this is written. What reverses may attend the remainder is in the hand of Providence; but, if they arrive, the reflection on past happiness enjoy'd ought to help his bearing them with more resignation. To Temperance he ascribes his long-continued health, and what is still left to him of a good constitution; to Industry and Frugality, the early easiness of his circumstances and acquisition of his fortune, with all that knowledge that enabled him to be a useful citizen, and obtained for him some degree of reputation among the learned; to Sincerity and Justice, the confidence of his country, and the honorable employs it conferred upon him; and to the joint influence of the whole mass of virtues, even in the imperfect state he was able to acquire them, all that evenness of temper, and that cheerfulness in conversation, which makes his company still sought for and agreeable even to his younger acquaintances. I hope, therefore, that some of my descendants may follow the example and reap the benefit.]

It will be remark'd that, tho' my scheme was not wholly without religion, there was in it no mark of any of the distinguishing tenets of any particular sect. I had purposely avoided them; for, being fully persuaded of the utility and excellence of my method, and that it might be serviceable to people in all religions, and intending some time or other to publish it, I would not have any thing in it that should prejudice any one, of any sect, against it. I purposed writing a little comment on each virtue, in which I would have shown the advantages of possessing it, and the mischiefs attending its opposite vice; and I should have called my book THE ART OF VIRTUE, because it would have shown the means

and manner of obtaining virtue, which would have distinguished it from the mere exhortation to be good, that does not instruct and indicate the means, but is like the apostle's man of verbal charity, who only, without showing to the naked and hungry how or where they might get clothes or victuals, exhorted them to be fed and clothed.—James ii. 15, 16.

But it so happened that my intention of writing and publishing this comment was never fulfilled. I did, indeed, from time to time, put down short hints of the sentiments, reasonings, etc., to be made use of in it, some of which I have still by me; but the necessary close attention to private business in the earlier part of my life, and public business since, have occasioned my postponing it; for, it being connected in my mind with *a great and extensive project* that required the whole man to execute, and which an unforeseen succession of employs prevented my attending to, it has hitherto remain'd unfinish'd.

In this piece it was my design to explain and enforce this doctrine, that vicious actions are not hurtful because they are forbidden, but forbidden because they are hurtful, the nature of man alone considered; that it was, therefore, every one's interest to be virtuous who wish'd to be happy even in this world; and I should, from this circumstance (there being always in the world a number of rich merchants, nobility, states, and princes, who have need of honest instruments for the management of their affairs, and such being rare), have endeavored to convince young persons that no qualities were so likely to make a poor man's fortune as those of probity and integrity.

My list of virtues contain'd at first but twelve; but a Quaker friend having kindly informed me that I was generally thought proud; that my pride show'd itself frequently in conversation; that I was not content with being in the right when discussing any point, but was overbearing, and rather insolent, of which he convinc'd me by mentioning several instances; I determined endeavoring to cure myself, if I could, of this vice or folly among the rest, and I added *Humility* to my list, giving an extensive meaning to the word.

I cannot boast of much success in acquiring the *reality* of this virtue, but I had a good deal with regard to the *appearance* of it. I made it a rule to forbear all direct contradiction to the sentiments of others, and all positive assertion of my own. I even forbid myself, agreeably to the old laws of our Junto, the use of every word or expression in the language that imported[12] a fix'd opinion, such as *certainly, undoubtedly,* etc., and I adopted, instead

[12] Implied.

of them, *I conceive, I apprehend*, or *I imagine* a thing to be so or so; or it *so appears to me at present*. When another asserted something that I thought an error, I deny'd myself the pleasure of contradicting him abruptly, and of showing immediately some absurdity in his proposition; and in answering I began by observing that in certain cases or circumstances his opinion would be right, but in the present case there *appear'd* or *seem'd* to me some difference, etc. I soon found the advantage of this change in my manner; the conversations I engag'd in went on more pleasantly. The modest way in which I propos'd my opinions procur'd them a readier reception and less contradiction; I had less mortification when I was found to be in the wrong, and I more easily prevail'd with others to give up their mistakes and join with me when I happened to be in the right.

And this mode, which I at first put on with some violence to natural inclination, became at length so easy, and so habitual to me, that perhaps for these fifty years past no one has ever heard a dogmatical expression escape me. And to this habit (after my character of integrity) I think it principally owing that I had early so much weight with my fellow-citizens when I proposed new institutions, or alterations in the old, and so much influence in public councils when I became a member; for I was but a bad speaker, never eloquent, subject to much hesitation in my choice of words, hardly correct in language, and yet I generally carried my points.

In reality, there is, perhaps, no one of our natural passions so hard to subdue as *pride*. Disguise it, struggle with it, beat it down, stifle it, mortify it as much as one pleases, it is still alive, and will every now and then peep out and show itself; you will see it, perhaps, often in this history; for, even if I could conceive that I had compleatly overcome it, I should probably be proud of my humility.

[Thus far written at Passy, 1784.][13]

Having mentioned *a great and extensive project* which I had conceiv'd, it seems proper that some account should be here given of that project and its object. Its first rise in my mind appears in the following little paper, accidentally preserv'd, viz.:

Observations on my reading history, in Library, May 19th, 1731.

"That the great affairs of the world, the wars, revolutions, etc., are carried on and effected by parties.

"That the view of these parties is their present general interest, or what they take to be such.

"That the different views of these different parties occasion all confusion.

"That while a party is carrying on a general design, each man has his particular private interest in view.

"That as soon as a party has gain'd its general point, each member becomes intent upon his particular interest; which, thwarting others, breaks that party into divisions, and occasions more confusion.

"That few in public affairs act from a meer view of the good of their country, whatever they may pretend; and, tho' their actings bring real good to their country, yet men primarily considered that their own and their country's interest was united, and did not act from a principle of benevolence.

"That fewer still, in public affairs, act with a view to the good of mankind.

"That seems to me at present to be great occasion for raising a United Party for Virtue, by forming the virtuous and good men of all nations into a regular body, to be govern'd by suitable good and wise rules, which good and wise men may probably be more unanimous in their obedience to, than common people are to common laws.

"I at present think that whoever attempts this aright, and is well qualified, can not fail of pleasing God, and of meeting with success.   B. F."

Revolving this project in my mind, as to be undertaken hereafter, when my circumstances should afford me the necessary leisure, I put down from time to time on pieces of paper such thoughts as occurr'd to me respecting it. Most of these are lost; but I find one purporting to be the substance of an intended creed, containing, as I thought, the essentials of every known religion, and being free of every thing that might shock the professors of any religion. It is express'd in these words, viz.:

"That there is one God, who made all things.

"That he governs the world by his providence.

"That he ought to be worshiped by adoration, prayer, and thanksgiving.

"But that the most acceptable service of God is doing good to man.

"That the soul is immortal.

"And that God will certainly reward virtue and punish vice, either here or hereafter."

My ideas at that time were, that the sect should be begun and spread at first among young and single men only; that each person to be initiated should not only declare his assent to such creed, but should have exercised himself with the thirteen weeks' examination and practice of the virtues, as in the before-mention'd model; that the existence of such a society should be kept a secret till it was become considerable, to prevent solicitations for the admission of improper persons, but that the members should each of them search among his acquaintance for ingenuous, well-disposed youths to whom with prudent caution the scheme should be gradually communicated; that the members should engage to afford their advice, assistance, and support to each other in promoting one another's interests, business, and advancement in life; that, for distinction, we should be call'd *The Society of the Free and Easy:* free, as being, by the general practice and habit of the virtues free from the dominion of vice; and particularly by the practice of industry and frugality, free from debt which exposes a man to confinement and a species of slavery to his creditors.

This is as much as I can now recollect of the project, except that I communicated it in part to two young men, who adopted it with some enthusiasm; but my then narrow circumstances and the necessity I was under of sticking close to my business occasion'd my postponing the further prosecution of it at that time; and my multifarious occupations, public and private, induc'd me to continue postponing, so that it has been omitted till I have no longer strength or activity left sufficient for such an enterprise; tho' I am still of the opinion that it was a practicable scheme, and might have been very useful, by forming a great number of good citizens; and I was not discourag'd by the seeming magnitude of the undertaking, as I have always thought that one man of tolerable abilities may work great changes, and accomplish great affairs among mankind if he first forms a good plan and, cutting off all amusements or other employments that would divert his attention, makes the execution of that same plan his sole study and business.

In 1732 I first publish'd my Almanac, under the name of *Richard Saunders;* it was continu'd by me about twenty-five years, commonly call'd *Poor Richard's Almanac.* I endeavor'd to make it both entertaining and useful, and it accordingly came to be in such demand, that I reap'd considerable profit from it, vending annually near ten thousand. And observing that it was generally read, scarce any neighborhood in the province being without it, I consider'd it as a proper vehicle for conveying instruction among the common people, who bought scarcely any other books; I therefore filled all the little spaces that occurr'd between the remarkable days in the calendar with proverbial sentences, chiefly such as inculcated industry and frugality, as the means of procuring wealth, and thereby securing virtue; it being more difficult for a man in want, to act always honestly, as, to use here one of those proverbs, *it is hard for an empty sack to stand upright.* ° ° °

I began now to turn my thoughts a little to public affairs, beginning, however, with small matters. The city watch was one of the first things that I conceiv'd to want regulation. It was managed by the constables of the respective wards in turn; the constable warned a number of housekeepers to attend him for the night.[14] Those who chose never to attend, paid him six shillings a year to be excus'd, which was suppos'd to be for hiring substitutes but was, in reality, much more than was necessary for that purpose and made the constableship a place of profit; and the constable, for a little drink, often got such ragamuffins about him as a watch, that respectable housekeepers did not choose to mix with. Walking the rounds, too, was often neglected and most of the nights spent in tippling. I thereupon wrote a paper to be read in Junto, representing these irregularities, but insisting more particularly on the inequality of this six-shilling tax of the constables, respecting the circumstances of those who paid it, since a poor widow housekeeper, all whose property to be guarded by the watch did not perhaps exceed the value of fifty pounds, paid as much as the wealthiest merchant who had thousands of pounds' worth of goods in his stores.

On the whole, I proposed as a more effectual watch, the hiring of proper men to serve constantly in that business; and as a more equitable way of supporting the charge, the levying a tax that should be proportion'd to the property. This idea, being approv'd by the Junto, was communicated to the other clubs, but as arising in each of them; and though the plan was not immediately carried into execution, yet, by preparing the minds of people for the change, it paved the way for the law obtained a few years after when the members of our clubs were grown into more influence.

About this time I wrote a paper (first to be read in Junto but it was afterward publish'd) on the different accidents and carelessnesses by which houses were set on fire, with cautions against them, and means propos'd of avoiding them. This was much spoken of as a useful piece and gave rise to a project which soon followed it, of forming a company for the more ready extinguishing of fires and mutual assistance in removing and securing of goods when in danger. Associates in this scheme were presently found, amounting to thirty. Our articles of agreement oblig'd every member to keep always in good order and fit for use, a certain number of leather buckets with strong bags and baskets (for packing and transporting of goods), which were to be brought to every fire; and we agreed to meet once a month and spend a social evening together, in discoursing and communicating such ideas as occurred

[14] Cities were policed only at night; householders, serving in rotation, assisted the constables and marshals who patrolled the wards.

to us upon the subject of fires as might be useful in our conduct on such occasions.

The utility of this institution soon appeared, and many more desiring to be admitted than we thought convenient for one company, they were advised to form another, which was accordingly done; and this went on, one new company being formed after another till they became so numerous as to include most of the inhabitants who were men of property; and now, at the time of my writing this, tho' upward of fifty years since its establishment, that which I first formed, called the Union Fire Company[15] still subsists and flourishes, tho' the first members are all deceas'd but myself and one, who is older by a year than I am. The small fines that have been paid by members for absence at the monthly meetings have been apply'd to the purchase of fire-engines, ladders, fire-hooks, and other useful implements for each company, so that I question whether there is a city in the world better provided with the means of putting a stop to beginning conflagrations; and, in fact, since these institutions, the city has never lost by fire more than one or two houses at a time and the flames have often been extinguished before the house in which they began has been half consumed. ° ° °

In order of time, I should have mentioned before, that having, in 1742, invented an open stove for the better warming of rooms, and at the same time saving fuel, as the fresh air admitted was warmed in entering, I made a present of the model to Mr. Robert Grace, one of my early friends, who, having an iron-furnace found the casting of the plates for these stoves a profitable thing, as they were growing in demand. To promote that demand, I wrote and published a pamphlet, entitled *An Account of the new-invented Pennsylvania Fireplaces; wherein their Construction and Manner of Operation is particularly explained; their Advantages above every other Method of warming Rooms demonstrated: and all Objections that have been raised against the Use of them answered and obviated,* etc. This pamphlet had a good effect. Gov'r. Thomas was so pleas'd with the construction of this stove, as described in it, that he offered to give me a patent for the sole vending of them for a term of years; but I declin'd it from a principle which has ever weighed with me on such occasions, viz.: *That, as we enjoy great advantages from the inventions of others, we should be glad of an opportunity to serve others by any invention of ours; and this we should do freely and generously.*

An ironmonger in London however, assuming[16] a good deal of my pamphlet, and working it up into

his own and making some small changes in the machine, which rather hurt its operation, got a patent for it there and made, as I was told, a little fortune by it. And this is not the only instance of patents taken out for my inventions by others, tho' not always with the same success, which I never contested, as having no desire of profiting by patents myself, and hating disputes. The use of these fireplaces in very many houses, both of this and the neighboring colonies, has been, and is, a great saving of wood to the inhabitants.

Peace being concluded, and the association business therefore at an end, I turn'd my thoughts again to the affair of establishing an academy. The first step I took was to associate in the design a number of active friends, of whom the Junto furnished a good part; the next was to write and publish a pamphlet, entitled *Proposals relating to the Education of Youth in Pennsylvania.* This I distributed among the principal inhabitants gratis; and as soon as I could suppose their minds a little prepared by the perusal of it, I set on foot a subscription for opening and supporting an academy: it was to be paid in quotas yearly for five years; by so dividing it, I judg'd the subscription might be larger and I believe it was so, amounting to no less, if I remember right, than five thousand pounds.

In the introduction to these proposals, I stated their publication, not as an act of mine, but of some *publick-spirited gentlemen,* avoiding as much as I could, according to my usual rule, the presenting myself to the public as the author of any scheme for their benefit.

The subscribers, to carry the project into immediate execution, chose out of their number twenty-four trustees and appointed Mr. Francis, then attorney-general and myself to draw up constitutions for the government of the academy; which being done and signed, a house was hired, masters engag'd, and the schools opened, I think, in the same year, 1749.

The scholars increasing fast, the house was soon found too small and we were looking out for a piece of ground properly situated, with intention to build, when Providence threw into our way a large house ready built which, with a few alterations, might well serve our purpose. This was the building before mentioned, erected by the hearers of Mr. Whitefield,[17] and was obtained for us in the following manner.

It is to be noted that the contributions to this building being made by people of different sects, care was taken in the nomination of trustees, in whom the building and ground were to be vested, that a predominancy should not be given to any

[15] Organized December 7, 1736.
[16] Appropriating.

[17] The Rev. George Whitefield, an English Methodist evangelist assisted by Franklin when he earlier visited Pennsylvania.

sect, lest in time that predominancy might be a means of appropriating the whole to the use of such sect, contrary to the original intention. It was therefore that one of each sect was appointed, viz., one Church-of-England man, one Presbyterian, one Baptist, one Moravian,[18] etc., those, in case of vacancy by death, were to fill it by election from among the contributors. The Moravian happen'd not to please his colleagues and on his death they resolved to have no other of that sect. The difficulty then was, how to avoid having two of some other sect, by means of the new choice.

Several persons were named, and for that reason not agreed to. At length one mention'd me with the observation that I was merely an honest man, and of no sect at all, which prevail'd with them to chuse me. The enthusiasm which existed when the house was built had long since abated, and its trustees had not been able to procure fresh contributions for paying the ground-rent and discharging some other debts the building had occasion'd, which embarrass'd them greatly. Being now a member of both setts of trustees, that for the building and that for the academy, I had a good opportunity of negotiating with both, and brought them finally to an agreement, by which the trustees for the building were to cede it to those of the academy, the latter undertaking to discharge the debt, to keep forever open in the building a large hall for occasional preachers according to the original intention and maintain a free-school for the instruction of poor children. Writings were accordingly drawn and on paying the debts, the trustees of the academy were put into possession of the premises; and by dividing the great and lofty hall into stories, and different rooms above and below for the several schools and purchasing some additional ground the whole was soon made fit for our purpose, and the scholars remov'd into the building. The care and trouble of agreeing with the workmen, purchasing materials and superintending the work, fell upon me; and I went thro' it the more cheerfully, as it did not then interfere with my private business, having the year before taken a very able, industrious, and honest partner, Mr. David Hall with whose character I was well acquainted as he had work'd for me four years. He took off my hands all care of the printing-office, paying me punctually my share of the profits. This partnership continued eighteen years, successfully for us both.

The trustees of the academy, after a while, were incorporated by a charter from the governor; their funds were increas'd by contributions in Britain and grants of land from the proprietaries, to which the Assembly has since made considerable addition; and

thus was established the present University of Philadelphia.[19] I have been continued one of its trustees from the beginning, now near forty years, and have had the very great pleasure of seeing a number of the youth who have receiv'd their education in it, distinguished by their improv'd abilities, serviceable in public stations, and ornaments to their country.

When I disengaged myself, as above mentioned, from private business, I flatter'd myself that, by the sufficient tho' moderate fortune I had acquir'd, I had secured leisure during the rest of my life for philosophical studies and amusements. I purchased all Dr. Spence's apparatus, who had come from England to lecture here, and I proceeded in my electrical experiments with great alacrity; but the publick, now considering me as a man of leisure, laid hold of me for their purposes; every part of our civil government, and almost at the same time, imposing some duty upon me. The governor put me into the commission of the peace, the corporation of the city chose me of the common council, and soon after an alderman, and the citizens at large chose me a burgess to represent them in Assembly. This latter station was the more agreeable to me, as I was at length tired with sitting there to hear debates, in which, as clerk, I could take no part, and which were so often unentertaining that I was induc'd to amuse myself with making magic squares or circles, or any thing to avoid weariness; and I conceiv'd my becoming a member would enlarge my power of doing good. I would not, however, insinuate that my ambition was not flatter'd by all these promotions; it certainly was; for, considering my low beginning, they were great things to me and they were still more pleasing as being so many spontaneous testimonies of the public good opinion, and by me entirely unsolicited.

The office of justice of the peace I try'd a little, by attending a few courts, and sitting on the bench to hear causes, but finding that more knowledge of the common law than I possessed was necessary to act in that station with credit, I gradually withdrew from it, excusing myself by my being oblig'd to attend the higher duties of a legislator in the Assembly. My election to this trust was repeated every year for ten years without my ever asking any elector for his vote or signifying, either directly or indirectly, any desire of being chosen. On taking my seat in the House, my son was appointed their clerk.

The year following, a treaty being to be held with the Indians at Carlisle, the governor sent a message to the House, proposing that they should nominate some of their members, to be join'd with some members of council, as commissioners for that purpose. The House named the speaker (Mr. Norris)

[18]An evangelical sect which arose in Austria and Germany; large numbers had settled in Pennsylvania.

[19]The present University of Pennsylvania.

and myself; and, being commission'd, we went to Carlisle, and met the Indians accordingly.

As those people are extreamly apt to get drunk and, when so, are very quarrelsome and disorderly, we strictly forbade the selling any liquor to them; and when they complain'd of this restriction, we told them that if they would continue sober during the treaty we would give them plenty of rum when business was over. They promis'd this and they kept their promise because they could get no liquor, and the treaty was conducted very orderly and concluded to mutual satisfaction. They then claim'd and receiv'd the rum; this was in the afternoon; they were near one hundred men, women, and children, and were lodg'd in temporary cabins built in the form of a square, just without the town. In the evening, hearing a great noise among them, the commissioners walk'd out to see what was the matter. We found they had made a great bonfire in the middle of the square; they were all drunk, men and women, quarreling and fighting. Their dark-colour'd bodies half naked, seen only by the gloomy light of the bonfire, running after and beating one another with firebrands, accompanied by their horrid yellings, form'd a scene the most resembling our ideas of hell that could well be imagin'd; there was no appeasing the tumult, and we retired to our lodging. At midnight a number of them came thundering at our door, demanding more rum, of which we took no notice.

The next day, sensible they had misbehav'd in giving us that disturbance, they sent three of their old counsellors to make their apology. The orator acknowledg'd the fault, but laid it upon the rum; and then endeavored to excuse the rum by saying: *"The Great Spirit, who made all things, made every thing for some use, and whatever use he design'd any thing for, that use it should always be put to. Now, when he made rum, he said, 'Let this be for the Indians to get drunk with,' and it must be so."* And, indeed, if it be the design of Providence to extirpate these savages in order to make room for cultivators of the earth, it seems not improbable that rum may be the appointed means. It has already annihilated all the tribes who formerly inhabited the sea-coast.

In 1751, Dr. Thomas Bond, a particular friend of mine, conceived the idea of establishing a hospital in Philadelphia (a very beneficent design, which has been ascrib'd to me, but was originally his), for the reception and cure of poor sick persons, whether inhabitants of the province or strangers. He was zealous and active in endeavoring to procure subscriptions for it, but the proposal being a novelty in America, and at first not well understood, he met with small success.

At length he came to me with the compliment that he found there was no such thing as carrying a public-spirited project through without my being concern'd in it. "For," says he, "I am often ask'd by those to whom I propose subscribing, Have you consulted Franklin upon this business? And what does he think of it? And when I tell them that I have not (supposing it rather out of your line), they do not subscribe, but say they will consider of it." I enquired into the nature and probable utility of his scheme, and receiving from him a very satisfactory explanation, I not only subscribed to it myself, but engag'd heartily in the design of procuring subscriptions from others. Previously, however, to the solicitation, I endeavoured to prepare the minds of the people by writing on the subject in newspapers, which was my usual custom in such cases but which he had omitted.

The subscriptions afterwards were more free and generous, but beginning to flag, I saw they would be insufficient without some assistance from the Assembly and therefore propos'd to petition for it, which was done. The country members did not at first relish the project; they objected that it could only be serviceable to the city and therefore the citizens alone should be at the expense of it; and they doubted whether the citizens themselves generally approv'd of it. My allegation on the contrary, that it met with such approbation as to leave no doubt of our being able to raise two thousand pounds by voluntary donations, they considered as a most extravagant supposition, and utterly impossible.

On this I form'd my plan and, asking leave to bring in a bill for incorporating the contributors according to the prayer of their petition, and granting them a blank sum of money, which leave was obtained chiefly on the consideration that the House could throw the bill out if they did not like it, I drew it so as to make the important clause a conditional one, viz.: "And be it enacted, by the authority aforesaid, that when the said contributors shall have met and chosen their managers and treasurer, *and shall have raised by their contributions a capital stock of* —— *value* (the yearly interest of which is to be applied to the accommodating of the sick poor in the said hospital, free of charge for diet, attendance, advice, and medicines), *and shall make the same appear to the satisfaction of the speaker of the Assembly for the time being,* that *then* it shall and may be lawful for the said speaker, and he is hereby required, to sign an order on the provincial treasurer for the payment of two thousand pounds, in two yearly payments, to the treasurer of the said hospital, to be applied to the founding, building, and finishing of the same."

This condition carried the bill through; for the members, who had oppos'd the grant and now conceived they might have the credit of being charitable without the expence, agreed to its passage; and then, in soliciting subscriptions among the people, we urg'd the conditional promise of the law as an additional motive to give, since every man's donation would be doubled; thus the clause work'd both ways. The subscriptions accordingly soon exceeded the requisite sum, and we claim'd and receiv'd the public gift, which enabled us to carry the design into execution. A convenient and handsome building was soon erected; the institution has by constant experience been found useful, and flourishes to this day; and I do not remember any of my political manoeuvres, the success of which gave me at the time more pleasure, or wherein, after thinking of it I more easily excus'd myself for having made some use of cunning.

It was about this time that another projector, the Rev. Gilbert Tennent,[20] came to me with a request that I would assist him in procuring a subscription for erecting a new meeting-house. It was to be for the use of a congregation he had gathered among the Presbyterians, who were originally disciples of Mr. Whitefield. Unwilling to make myself disagreeable to my fellow-citizens by too frequently soliciting their contributions, I absolutely refus'd. He then desired I would furnish him with a list of the names of persons I knew by experience to be generous and public-spirited. I thought it would be unbecoming in me, after their kind compliance with my solicitations, to mark them out to be worried by other beggars, and therefore refus'd also to give such a list. He then desir'd I would at least give him my advice. "That I will readily do," said I; "and, in the first place, I advise you to apply to all those whom you know will give something; next to those whom you are uncertain whether they will give any thing or not, and show them the list of those who have given; and, lastly, do not neglect those who you are sure will give nothing, for in some of them you may be mistaken." He laugh'd and thank'd me, and said he would take my advice. He did so, for he ask'd of *everybody*, and he obtain'd a much larger sum than he expected, with which he erected the capacious and very elegant meeting-house that stands in Arch-street.

Our city, tho' laid out with a beautiful regularity, the streets large, straight, and crossing each other at right angles, had the disgrace of suffering those streets to remain long unpav'd, and in wet weather the wheels of heavy carriages plough'd them into a quagmire so that it was difficult to cross them; and in dry weather the dust was offensive. I had liv'd near what was call'd the Jersey Market and saw with pain the inhabitants wading in mud while pur-

chasing their provisions. A strip of ground down the middle of that market was at length pav'd with brick, so that, being once in the market, they had firm footing, but were often over shoes in dirt to get there. By talking and writing on the subject, I was at length instrumental in getting the street pav'd with stone between the market and the brick'd foot-pavement, that was on each side next the houses. This, for some time gave an easy access to the market dry-shod, but, the rest of the street not being pav'd, whenever a carriage came out of the mud upon this pavement it shook off and left its dirt upon it and it was soon cover'd with mire, which was not remov'd, the city as yet having no scavengers.[21]

After some inquiry, I found a poor, industrious man who was willing to undertake keeping the pavement clean by sweeping it twice a week, carrying off the dirt from before all the neighbours' doors, for the sum of sixpence per month to be paid by each house. I then wrote and printed a paper setting forth the advantages to the neighbourhood that might be obtain'd by this small expense; the greater ease in keeping our houses clean, so much dirt not being brought in by people's feet; the benefit to the shops by more custom, etc., etc., as buyers could more easily get at them; and by not having, in windy weather, the dust blown in upon their goods, etc., etc. I sent one of these papers to each house and in a day or two went round to see who would subscribe an agreement to pay these sixpences. It was unanimously sign'd, and for a time well executed. All the inhabitants of the city were delighted with the cleanliness of the pavement that surrounded the market, it being a convenience to all, and this rais'd a general desire to have all the streets paved, and made the people more willing to submit to a tax for that purpose.

After some time I drew a bill for paving the city, and brought it into the Assembly. It was just before I went to England, in 1757, and did not pass till I was gone, and then with an alteration in the mode of assessment, which I thought not for the better, but with an additional provision for lighting as well as paving the streets, which was a great improvement. It was by a private person, the late Mr. John Clifton, his giving a sample of the utility of lamps, by placing one at his door, that the people were first impress'd with the idea of enlighting all the city. The honour of this public benefit has also been ascrib'd to me, but it belongs truly to that gentleman. I did but follow his example, and have only some merit to claim respecting the form of our lamps, as differing from the globe lamps we were at first supply'd with from London. Those we found inconvenient in these respects: they admitted no air

[20] Tennent, a co-worker of Whitefield's, became one of the most influential of American evangelists.

[21] Street cleaners.

STREET-
LIGHTS

below; the smoke, therefore, did not readily go out above, but circulated in the globe, lodg'd on its inside, and soon obstructed the light they were intended to afford; giving, besides, the daily trouble of wiping them clean; and an accidental stroke on one of them would demolish it, and render it totally useless. I therefore suggested the composing them of four flat panes, with a long funnel above to draw up the smoke, and crevices admitting air below, to facilitate the ascent of the smoke; by this means they were kept clean, and did not grow dark in a few hours, as the London lamps do, but continu'd bright till morning, and an accidental stroke would generally break but a single pane, easily repair'd.

I have sometimes wonder'd that the Londoners did not, from the effect holes in the bottom of the globe lamps us'd at Vauxhall[22] have in keeping them clean, learn to have such holes in their street lamps. But, these holes being made for another purpose, viz., to communicate flame more suddenly to the wick by a little flax hanging down thro' them, the other use, of letting in air, seems not to have been thought of; and therefore, after the lamps have been lit a few hours, the streets of London are very poorly illuminated. ° ° °

1771–1789

The Way to Wealth

These proverbs, which Franklin gathered from many sources, he wrote in his *Autobiography*, "I assembled and formed into a connected discourse prefixed to the Almanac of 175[8], as the harangue of a wise old man to the people attending an auction. The bringing all these scattered counsels thus into a focus enabled them to make greater impression. The piece, being universally approved, was copied in all the newspapers of the [American] Continent; reprinted in Britain on a broadside, to be stuck up in houses; two translations were made of it in French; and great numbers bought by the clergy and gentry, to distribute gratis among their poor parishioners and tenants. In Pennsylvania, ... some thought it had its share of influence in producing that growing plenty of money which was observable for several years after its publication." The selection was sometimes titled "Father Abraham's Speech." Text: Bigelow edition of *Complete Works* (New York, 1904).

COURTEOUS READER:

I have heard that nothing gives an author so great pleasure as to find his works respectfully quoted by others. Judge, then, how much I must have been gratified by an incident I am going to relate to you. I stopped my horse lately where a great number of people were collected at an auction of merchants' goods. The hour of the sale not being come, they were conversing on the badness of the times; and

one of the company called to a plain, clean, old man, with white locks: "Pray, Father Abraham, what think you of the times? Will not these heavy taxes quite ruin the country? How shall we ever be able to pay them? What would you advise us to do?" Father Abraham stood up and replied: "If you would have my advice, I will give it you in short; for *A word to the wise is enough*, as Poor Richard says." They joined in desiring him to speak his mind, and gathering round him he proceeded as follows:

"Friends," said he, "the taxes are indeed very heavy, and if those laid on by the government were the only ones we had to pay, we might more easily discharge them, but we have many others and much more grievous to some of us. We are taxed twice as much by our idleness, three times as much by our pride, and four times as much by our folly, and from these taxes the commissioners cannot ease or deliver us by allowing an abatement. However, let us hearken to good advice and something may be done for us; *God helps them that help themselves*, as Poor Richard says.

"I. It would be thought a hard government that should tax its people one-tenth part of their time, to be employed in its service, but idleness taxes many of us much more; sloth by bringing on diseases, absolutely shortens life. *Sloth, like rust, consumes faster than labor wears, while the used key is always bright*, as Poor Richard says. *But dost thou love life, then do not squander time, for that is the stuff life is made of*, as Poor Richard says. How much more than is necessary do we spend in sleep, forgetting that *The sleeping fox catches no poultry*, and that *There will be sleeping enough in the grave*, as Poor Richard says.

"*If time be of all things the most precious, wasting time must be*, as Poor Richard says, *the greatest prodigality*, since, as he elsewhere tells us, *Lost time is never found again*, and what we call time enough always proves little enough. Let us then up and be doing, and doing to the purpose; so by diligence shall we do more with less perplexity. *Sloth makes all things difficult, but industry all things easy*; and *He that riseth late must trot all day, and shall scarce overtake his business at night*; while *Laziness travels so slowly that Poverty soon overtakes him.* Drive thy business, let not that drive thee; and *Early to bed and early to rise, makes a man healthy, wealthy, and wise*, as Poor Richard says.

"So what signifies wishing and hoping for better times? We may make these times better if we bestir ourselves. *Industry need not wish, and he that lives upon hopes will die fasting. There are no gains without pains; then help, hands, for I have no lands; or if I have they are smartly taxed. He that hath a trade hath an estate, and he that hath a calling hath an office of profit and honor*, as Poor Richard says;

---

[22] Vauxhall Gardens, a famous London amusement park.

but then the trade must be worked at and the calling followed, or neither the estate nor the office will enable us to pay our taxes. If we are industrious we shall never starve, for *At the working man's house hunger looks in but dares not enter.* Nor will the bailiff nor the constable enter, for *Industry pays debts, while despair increaseth them.* What though you have found no treasure, nor has any rich relation left you a legacy, *Diligence is the mother of good luck, and God gives all things to industry.* Then *plough deep while sluggards sleep, and you shall have corn to sell and to keep.* Work while it is called to-day, for you know not how much you may be hindered to-morrow. *One to-day is worth two to-morrows,* as Poor Richard says; and further, *Never leave that till to-morrow which you can do to-day.* If you were a servant would not you be ashamed that a good master should catch you idle? Are you then your own master? Be ashamed to catch yourself idle when there is so much to be done for yourself, your family, your country, and your king. Handle your tools without mittens; remember that *The cat in gloves catches no mice,* as Poor Richard says. It is true there is much to be done, and perhaps you are weak-handed, but stick to it steadily and you will see great effects; for *Constant dropping wears away stones;* and *By diligence and patience the mouse ate in two the cable;* and *Little strokes fell great oaks.*

"Methinks I hear some of you say, 'Must a man afford himself no leisure?' I will tell thee, my friend, what Poor Richard says: *Employ thy time well, if thou meanest to gain leisure; and, since thou art not sure of a minute, throw not away an hour.* Leisure is time for doing something useful; this leisure the diligent man will obtain, but the lazy man never; for *A life of leisure and a life of laziness are two things. Many, without labor, would live by their wits only, but they break for want of stock;* whereas industry gives comfort and plenty and respect. *Fly pleasures, and they will follow you. The diligent spinner has a large shift; and now I have a sheep and a cow, everybody bids me good morrow.*

"II. But with our industry we must likewise be steady, settled, and careful, and oversee our own affairs with our own eyes, and not trust too much to others; for, as Poor Richard says:

> I never saw an oft removed tree,
> Nor yet an oft-removed family,
> That throve so well as those that settled be.

And again, *Three removes are as bad as a fire;* and again, *Keep thy shop, and thy shop will keep thee;* and again: *If you would have your business done, go; if not, send.* And again:

> He that by the plough would thrive,
> Himself must either hold or drive.

And again, *The eye of a master will do more work*

than both his hands; and again, *Want of care does us more damage than want of knowledge;* and again, *Not to oversee workmen is to leave them your purse open.* Trusting too much to others' care is the ruin of many; for, *In the affairs of this world men are saved not by faith, but by the want of it;* but a man's own care is profitable; for, *If you would have a faithful servant, and one that you like, serve yourself. A little neglect may breed great mischief; for want of a nail the shoe was lost; for want of a shoe the horse was lost; and for want of a horse the rider was lost, being overtaken and slain by the enemy; all for want of a little care about a horse-shoe nail.*

"III. So much for industry, my friends, and attention to one's own business; but to these we must add frugality, if we would make our industry more certainly successful. A man may, if he knows not how to save as he gets, keep his nose all his life to the grindstone and die not worth a groat at last. *A fat kitchen makes a lean will;* and

> Many estates are spent in the getting,
> Since women for tea forsook spinning and knitting,
> And men for punch forsook hewing and splitting.

If you would be wealthy, think of saving as well as of getting. The Indies have not made Spain rich, because her outgoes are greater than her incomes.

"Away then with your expensive follies, and you will not then have so much cause to complain of hard times, heavy taxes, and chargeable families; for

> Women and wine, game and deceit,
> Make the wealth small and the want great.

And further, *What maintains one vice would bring up two children.* You may think, perhaps, that a little tea, or a little punch now and then, diet a little more costly, clothes a little finer, and a little entertainment now and then, can be no great matter; but remember, *Many a little makes a mickle.* Beware of little expenses: *A small leak will sink a great ship,* as Poor Richard says; and again, *Who dainties love, shall beggars prove;* and moreover, *Fools make feasts, and wise men eat them.*

"Here you are all got together at this sale of fineries and knick-knacks. You call them *goods;* but if you do not take care they will prove *evils* to some of you. You expect they will be sold cheap, and perhaps they may for less than they cost; but if you have no occasion for them they must be dear to you. Remember what Poor Richard says: *Buy what thou hast no need of, and ere long thou shalt sell thy necessaries.* And again, *At a great pennyworth pause a while.* He means, that perhaps the cheapness is apparent only, and not real; or the bargain, by straitening thee in thy business, may do thee more harm than good. For in another place he says, *Many have been ruined by buying good pennyworths.* Again, *It is foolish to lay out money in a purchase of repen-*

tance; and yet this folly is practised every day at auctions for want of minding the Almanac. Many a one, for the sake of finery on the back, have gone with a hungry belly and half-starved their families. *Silks and satins, scarlet and velvets, put out the kitchen fire,* as Poor Richard says.

"These are not the necessaries of life; they can scarcely be called the conveniences; and yet, only because they look pretty, how many want to have them! By these and other extravagances the genteel are reduced to poverty and forced to borrow of those whom they formerly despised, but who, through industry and frugality, have maintained their standing; in which case it appears plainly that *A ploughman on his legs is higher than a gentleman on his knees,* as Poor Richard says. Perhaps they have had a small estate left them, which they knew not the getting of: they think, *It is day, and will never be night;* that a little to be spent out of so much is not worth minding; but *Always taking out of the meal-tub, and never putting in, soon comes to the bottom,* as Poor Richard says; and then, *When the well is dry, they know the worth of water.* But this they might have known before, if they had taken his advice. *If you would know the value of money, go and try to borrow some; for he that goes a borrowing goes a sorrowing,* as Poor Richard says; and indeed so does he that lends to such people, when he goes to get it again. Poor Dick further advises and says,

> *Fond pride of dress is sure a very curse;*
> *Ere fancy you consult, consult your purse.*

And again, *Pride is as loud a beggar as Want, and a great deal more saucy.* When you have bought one fine thing you must buy ten more, that your appearance may be all of a piece; but Poor Dick says, *It is easier to suppress the first desire than to satisfy all that follow it.* And it is as truly folly for the poor to ape the rich, as for the frog to swell in order to equal the ox.

> *Vessels large may venture more,*
> *But little boats should keep near shore.*

It is, however, a folly soon punished; for, as Poor Richard says, *Pride that dines on vanity sups on contempt. Pride breakfasted with Plenty, dined with Poverty, and supped with Infamy.* And after all, of what use is this pride of appearance, for which so much is risked, so much is suffered? It cannot promote health, nor ease pain; it makes no increase of merit in the person; it creates envy; it hastens misfortune.

"But what madness must it be to *run in debt* for these superfluities! We are offered by the terms of this sale six months' credit; and that, perhaps, has induced some of us to attend it, because we cannot spare the ready money, and hope now to be fine without it. But ah! think what you do when you run in debt; you give to another power over your liberty. If you cannot pay at the time, you will be ashamed to see your creditor; you will be in fear when you speak to him; you will make poor, pitiful, sneaking excuses, and by degrees come to lose your veracity, and sink into base, downright lying; for, *The second vice is lying, the first is running in debt,* as Poor Richard says; and again, to the same purpose, *Lying rides upon Debt's back;* whereas a freeborn Englishman ought not to be ashamed nor afraid to see or speak to any man living. But poverty often deprives a man of all spirit and virtue. *It is hard for an empty bag to stand upright.*

"What would you think of that prince or of that government who should issue an edict forbidding you to dress like a gentleman or gentlewoman, on pain of imprisonment or servitude? Would you not say that you were free, have a right to dress as you please, and that such an edict would be a breach of your privileges, and such a government tyrannical? And yet you are about to put yourself under such tyranny when you run in debt for such dress! Your creditor has authority, at his pleasure, to deprive you of your liberty by confining you in gaol till you shall be able to pay him. When you have got your bargain you may perhaps think little of payment, but, as Poor Richard says, *Creditors have better memories than debtors; creditors are a superstitious sect, great observers of set days and times.* The day comes round before you are aware, and the demand is made before you are prepared to satisfy it; or, if you bear your debt in mind, the term, which at first seemed so long, will, as it lessens, appear extremely short. Time will seem to have added wings to his heels as well as his shoulders. *Those have a short Lent who owe money to be paid at Easter.* At present, perhaps, you may think yourselves in thriving circumstances, and that you can bear a little extravagance without injury, but—

> *For age and want save while you may;*
> *No morning sun lasts a whole day.*

Gain may be temporary and uncertain, but ever, while you live, expense is constant and certain; and *It is easier to build two chimneys than to keep one in fuel,* as Poor Richard says; so, *Rather go to bed supperless than rise in debt.*

> *Get what you can, and what you get hold;*
> *'T is the stone that will turn all your lead into gold.*

And, when you have got the Philosopher's stone, sure you will no longer complain of bad times or the difficulty of paying taxes.

"IV. This doctrine, my friends, is reason and wisdom; but, after all, do not depend too much upon your own industry and frugality and prudence, though excellent things, for they may all be blasted, without the blessing of Heaven; and therefore ask that blessing humbly, and be not uncharitable to those that at present seem to want it, but comfort and help them. Remember Job suffered and was afterwards prosperous.

"And now, to conclude, *Experience keeps a dear school, but fools will learn in no other,* as Poor Richard says, and scarce in that, for it is true *We may give advice, but we cannot give conduct.* However, remember this, *They that will not be counselled cannot be helped;* and further, that *If you will not hear Reason, she will surely rap your knuckles,* as Poor Richard says."

Thus the old gentleman ended his harangue. The people heard it and approved the doctrine, and immediately practised the contrary, just as if it had been a common sermon; for the auction opened, and they began to buy extravagantly. I found the good man had thoroughly studied my Almanacs, and digested all I had dropped on these topics during the course of twenty-five years. The frequent mention he made of me must have tired any one else, but my vanity was wonderfully delighted with it, though I was conscious that not a tenth part of the wisdom was my own which he ascribed to me, but rather the gleanings that I had made of the sense of all ages and nations. However, I resolved to be the better for the echo of it, and though I had at first determined to buy stuff for a new coat, I went away resolved to wear my old one a little longer. Reader, if thou wilt do the same thy profit will be as great as mine. I am, as ever, thine to serve thee,

RICHARD SAUNDERS
1758

Rules for Reducing a Great Empire to a Small One

While serving as agent for several American colonies in London, Franklin wrote this ironic hoax, intended to convince the King and the Ministry of the folly of their attitude toward their American possessions. Its catalogue of grievances, actually a review from the American point of view of British colonial policy from 1768 to 1772, should be compared with that included three years later in the Declaration of Independence. Text: Bigelow edition of *Complete Works* (New York, 1904)

An ancient sage valued himself upon this, that, though he could not fiddle he knew how to make a great city of a little one. The science that I, a modern simpleton, am about to communicate, is the very reverse.

I address myself to all ministers who have the management of extensive dominions, which from their very greatness have become troublesome to govern, because the multiplicity of their affairs leaves no time for fiddling.

1. In the first place, gentlemen, you are to consider that a great empire, like a great cake, is most easily diminished at the edges. Turn your attention, therefore, first to your *remotest* provinces; that, as you get rid of them, the next may follow in order.

2. That the possibility of this separation may always exist, take special care the provinces are *never incorporated with the mother country;* that they do not enjoy the same common rights, the same privileges in commerce; and that they are governed by severer laws, all of your enacting, without allowing them any share in the choice of the legislators. By carefully making and preserving such distinctions, you will (to keep to my simile of the cake) act like a wise gingerbread-baker, who, to facilitate a division, cuts his dough half through in those places where, when baked, he would have it broken to pieces.

3. Those remote provinces have perhaps been acquired, purchased, or conquered, at the sole expense of the settlers, or their ancestors; without the aid of the mother country. If this should happen to increase her strength, by their growing numbers ready to join in her wars; her commerce, by their growing demand for her manufactures; or her naval power, by greater employment for her ships and seamen, they may probably suppose some merit in this, and that it entitles them to some favor; you are therefore to *forget it all,* or *resent it all,* as if they had done you injury. If they happen to be zealous Whigs, friends of liberty, nurtured in revolution principles, remember all that to their prejudice, and contrive to punish it; for such principles, after a revolution is thoroughly established, are of no more use; they are even odious and abominable.

4. However peaceably your colonies have submitted to your government, shown their affection to your interests, and patiently borne their grievances, you are to suppose them *always inclined to revolt,* and treat them accordingly. Quarter troops among them, who by their insolence may provoke the rising of mobs, and by their bullets and bayonets suppress them. By this means, like the husband who uses his wife ill from suspicion, you may in time convert your suspicions into realities.

5. Remote provinces must have governors and judges to represent the royal person and execute everywhere the delegated parts of his office and authority. You ministers know that much of the strength of government depends on the opinion of the people, and much of that opinion on the *choice of rulers* placed immediately over them. If you send them wise and good men for governors, who study the interests of the colonists, and advance their prosperity, they will think their king wise and good, and

that he wishes the welfare of his subjects. If you send them learned and upright men for judges, they will think him a lover of justice. This may attach your provinces more to his government. You are therefore to be careful whom you recommend to those offices. If you can find prodigals who have ruined their fortunes, broken gamesters or stockjobbers, these may do well as governors; for they will probably be rapacious, and provoke the people by their extortions. Wrangling proctors and pettifogging lawyers, too, are not amiss; for they will be forever disputing and quarrelling with their little Parliaments. If withal they should be ignorant, wrongheaded, and insolent, so much the better. Attorney's clerks and Newgate solicitors[1] will do for chief-justices, especially if they hold their places during your pleasure; and all will contribute to impress those ideas of your government that are proper for a people you would wish to renounce it.

6. To confirm these impressions and strike them deeper, whenever the injured come to the capital with complaints of maladministration, oppression, or injustice, *punish such suitors* with long delay, enormous expense, and a final judgment in favor of the oppressor. This will have an admirable effect every way. The trouble of future complaints will be prevented, and governors and judges will be encouraged to further acts of oppression and injustice; and thence the people may become more disaffected, and at length desperate.

7. When such governors have crammed their coffers and made themselves so odious to the people that they can no longer remain among them with safety to their persons, *recall and reward* them with pensions. You may make them baronets too, if that respectable order should not think fit to resent it. All will contribute to encourage new governors in the same practice, and make the supreme government detestable.

8. If when you are engaged in war, your colonies should vie in liberal aids of men and money against the common enemy, upon your simple requisition, and give far beyond their abilities, reflect that a penny taken from them by your power is more honorable to you than a pound presented by their benevolence; *despise therefore their voluntary grants*, and resolve to harass them with *novel taxes*. They will probably complain to your Parliament, that they are taxed by a body in which they have no representative and that this is contrary to common right. They will petition for redress. Let the Parliament flout their claims, reject their petitions, refuse even to suffer the reading of them, and treat the petitioners with the utmost contempt. Nothing can have a better effect in producing the alienation

[1] That is, inexpert and scheming lawyers.

proposed; for, though many can forgive injuries, none ever forgave contempt.

9. In laying these taxes, *never regard the heavy burdens* those remote people already undergo, in defending their own frontiers, supporting their own provincial government, making new roads, building bridges, churches, and other public edifices; which in old countries have been done to your hands by your ancestors, but which occasion constant calls and demands on the purses of a new people. Forget the restraint you lay on their trade for your own benefit, and the advantage a monopoly of this trade gives your exacting merchants. Think nothing of the wealth those merchants and your manufacturers acquire by the colony commerce; their increased ability thereby to pay taxes at home; their accumulating, in the price of their commodities, most of those taxes, and so levying them from their consuming customers; all this, and the employment and support of thousands of your poor by the colonists, you are entirely to forget. But remember to make your arbitrary tax more grievous to your provinces, by public declarations importing that your power of taxing them has *no limits;* so that, when you take from them without their consent a shilling in the pound, you have a clear right to the other nineteen. This will probably weaken every idea of security in their property, and convince them that under such a government they have nothing they can call their own; which can scarce fail of producing the happiest consequences!

10. Possibly, indeed, some of them might still comfort themselves, and say; "Though we have no property, we have yet something left that is valuable; we have constitutional *liberty, both of person and of conscience.* This King, these Lords, and these Commons, who it seems are too remote from us to know us, and feel for us, cannot take from us our Habeas Corpus right, or our right of trial by a jury of our neighbors; they cannot deprive us of the exercise of our religion, alter our ecclesiastical constitution, and compel us to be Papists, if they please, or Mahometans." To annihilate this comfort, begin by laws to perplex their commerce with infinite regulations, impossible to be remembered and observed; ordain seizures of their property for every failure; take away the trial of such property by jury, and give it to arbitrary judges of your own appointing, and of the lowest characters in the country, whose salaries and emoluments are to arise out of the duties or condemnations, and whose appointments are during pleasure. Then let there be a formal declaration of both houses, that opposition to your edicts is treason, and that persons suspected of treason in the provinces may, according to some obsolete law, be seized and sent to the metropolis of the empire for trial; and pass an act, that those there

charged with certain other offences shall be sent away in chains from their friends and country to be tried in the same manner for felony. Then erect a new court of Inquisition among them, accompanied by an armed force, with instructions to transport all such suspected persons; to be ruined by the expense, if they bring over evidences to prove their innocence, or be found guilty and hanged if they cannot afford it. And, lest the people should think you cannot possibly go any further, pass another solemn declaratory act, "that King, Lords, Commons had, have, and of right ought to have, full power and authority to make statutes of sufficient force and validity to bind the unrepresented provinces *in all cases whatsoever.*"[2] This will include spiritual with temporal, and, taken together, must operate wonderfully to your purpose; by convincing them that they are at present under a power something like that spoken of in the Scriptures, which can not only kill their bodies, but damn their souls to all eternity, by compelling them, if it pleases, to worship the Devil.

11. To make your taxes more odious, and more likely to procure resistance, send from the capital a *board of officers* to superintend the collection, *composed of the most indiscreet*, ill-bred, and insolent you can find. Let these have large salaries out of the extorted revenue, and live in open, grating luxury upon the sweat and blood of the industrious; whom they are to worry continually with groundless and expensive prosecutions before the above-mentioned arbitrary revenue judges; all at the cost of the party prosecuted, though acquitted, because the king is to pay no costs. Let these men, by your order, be exempted from all the common taxes and burdens of the province, though they and their property are protected by its laws. If any revenue officers are suspected of the least tenderness for the people, discard them. If others are justly complained of, protect and reward them. If any of the under officers behave so as to provoke the people to drub them, promote those to better offices; this will encourage others to procure for themselves such profitable drubbings, by multiplying and enlarging such provocations, and all will work towards the end you aim at.

12. Another way to make your tax odious, is to *misapply the produce of it.* If it was originally appropriated for the defence of the provinces, and the better support of government, and the administration of justice, where it may be necessary, then apply none of it to that defence; but bestow it where it is not necessary, in augmenting salaries or pensions to every governor who has distinguished himself by

his enmity to the people, and by calumniating them to their sovereign. This will make them pay it more unwillingly, and be more apt to quarrel with those that collect it and those that imposed it; who will quarrel again with them; and all shall contribute to your own purpose, of making them weary of your government.

13. If the people of any province have been accustomed *to support their own governors and judges* to satisfaction, you are to apprehend that such governors and judges may be thereby influenced to treat the people kindly and to do them justice. This is another reason for applying part of that revenue in larger salaries to such governors and judges, given, as their commissions are, during *your* pleasure only; forbidding them to take any salaries from their provinces; that thus the people may no longer hope any kindness from their governors, or (in crown cases[3] any justice from their judges. And, as the money thus misapplied in one province is extorted from all, probably all will resent the misapplication.

14. If the Parliaments of your provinces should dare to claim rights, or complain of your administration, order them to be harassed with *repeated dissolutions.* If the same men are continually returned by new elections, adjourn their meetings to some country village, where they cannot be accommodated and there keep them during pleasure; for this, you know, is your prerogative; and an excellent one it is, as you may manage it to promote discontents among the people, diminish their respect, and increase their disaffection.

15. Convert the brave, honest officers of your *navy* into pimping tide-waiters and colony officers of the *customs.* Let those who in time of war fought gallantly in defence of the commerce of their countrymen, in peace be taught to prey upon it. Let them learn to be corrupted by great and real smugglers; but (to show their diligence) scour with armed boats every bay, harbor, river, creek, cove, or nook throughout the coast of your colonies; stop and detain every coaster, every wood-boat, every fisherman; tumble their cargoes and even their ballast inside out and upside down; and, if a pennyworth of pins is found unentered, let the whole be seized and confiscated. Thus shall the trade of your colonists suffer more from their friends in time of peace, than it did from their enemies in war. Then let these boats' crews land upon every farm in their way, rob their orchards, steal their pigs and poultry, and insult the inhabitants. If the injured and exasperated farmers, unable to procure other justice, should attack the aggressors, drub them, and burn their boats; you are to call this *high treason and rebellion,* order fleets and armies into their country, and threat-

---

[2] The Declaratory Act, passed by Parliament on the same day it repealed the Stamp Act, March 18, 1766, reaffirmed its power over the colonies in no uncertain terms.

[3] Cases in equity, formerly appealed directly to the King.

en to carry all the offenders three thousand miles to be hanged, drawn and quartered. Oh, this will work admirably!

16. If you are told of *discontents* in your colonies, never believe that they are general, or that you have given occasion for them; therefore do not think of applying any remedy, or of changing any offensive measure. Redress no grievance, lest they should be encouraged to demand the redress of some other grievance. Grant no request that is just and reasonable, lest they should make another that is unreasonable. Take all your informations of the state of the colonies from your governors and officers in enmity with them. Encourage and reward these leasing-makers; secrete their lying accusations, lest they should be confuted; but act upon them as the clearest evidence; and believe nothing you hear from the friends of the people. Suppose all *their* complaints to be invented and promoted by a few factious demagogues, whom if you could catch and hang, all would be quiet. Catch and hang a few of them accordingly; and the blood of the martyrs shall work miracles in favor of your purpose.

17. If you see *rival nations* rejoicing at the prospect of your disunion with your provinces, and endeavoring to promote it; if they translate, publish, and applaud all the complaints of your discontented colonists, at the same time privately stimulating you to severer measures, let not that offend you. Why should it, since you all mean the same thing?

18. If any colony should *at their own charge erect a fortress* to secure their *port* against the fleets of a foreign enemy, get your governor to betray that fortress into your hands.[4] Never think of paying what it costs the country, for that would look at least like some regard for justice; but turn it into a citadel to awe the inhabitants and curb their commerce. If they should have lodged in such fortress the very arms they bought and used to aid you in your conquests, seize them all; it will provoke, like ingratitude added to robbery. One admirable effect of these operations will be to discourage every other colony from erecting such defences, and so their and your enemies may more easily invade them, to the great disgrace of your government, and, of course, the furtherance of your project.

19. Send armies into their country under pretence of protecting the inhabitants; but, instead of garrisoning the forts on their frontiers with those troops to prevent incursions, demolish those forts and order the troops into the heart of the country, that the savages may be encouraged to attack the frontiers, and that the troops may be protected by the inhabitants. This will seem to proceed from your *ill-will or your ignorance*, and contribute further to produce and strengthen an opinion among them that you are no longer fit to govern them.

20. Lastly, invest the *general of your army in the provinces* with great and unconstitutional powers, and free him from the control of even your own civil governors. Let him have troops enough under his command, with all the fortresses in his possession; and who knows but (like some provincial generals in the Roman empire, and encouraged by the universal discontent you have produced) he may take it into his head to set up for himself? If he should, and you have carefully practised the few excellent rules of mine, take my word for it, all the provinces will immediately join him; and you will that day (if you have not done it sooner) get rid of the trouble of governing them, and all the plagues attending their commerce and connection from thenceforth and forever. Q.E.D.[5]
1773

The Ephemera

An Emblem of Human Life

During his residence at Passy, near Paris, Franklin amused himself by writing and printing (on his own press) an occasional "bagatelle," a light personal essay, for circulation among his friends. The person addressed is Madame Brillon de Jouy, one of his Passy neighbors and a favorite chess partner. Text: Bigelow edition of *Complete Works* (New York, 1904).

TO MADAME BRILLON, OF PASSY

You may remember, my dear friend, that when we lately spent that happy day in the delightful garden and sweet society of the Moulin Joly,[1] I stopped a little in one of our walks, and stayed some time behind the company. We had been shown numberless skeletons of a kind of little fly, called an ephemera, whose successive generations, we were told, were bred and expired within the day. I happened to see a living company of them on a leaf, who appeared to be engaged in conversation. You know I understand all the inferior animal tongues. My too great application to the study of them is the best excuse I can give for the little progress I have made in your charming language. I listened through curiosity to the discourse of these little creatures; but as they, in their national vivacity, spoke three or

---

[4]A reference to Castle William in Boston Harbor, given over to the British forces by Governor Hutchinson in 1770.

[5]"Quod Erat Demonstrandum" ("Which was to be demonstrated"), usually placed at the end of a geometry problem.
[1]An island in the Seine, Madame Brillon's home.

four together, I could make but little of their conversation. I found, however, by some broken expressions that I heard now and then, they were disputing warmly on the merit of two foreign musicians, one a *cousin*, the other a *moscheto*;[2] in which dispute they spent their time, seemingly as regardless of the shortness of life as if they had been sure of living a month. Happy people! thought I; you are certainly under a wise, just, and mild government, since you have no public grievances to complain of, nor any subject of contention but the perfections and imperfections of foreign music. I turned my head from them to an old gray-headed one, who was single on another leaf, and talking to himself. Being amused with his soliloquy, I put it down in writing, in hopes it will likewise amuse her to whom I am so much indebted for the most pleasing of all amusements, her delicious company and heavenly harmony.

"It was," said he, "the opinion of learned philosophers of our race, who lived and flourished long before my time, that this vast world, the Moulin Joly, could not itself subsist more than eighteen hours; and I think there was some foundation for that opinion, since, by the apparent motion of the great luminary that gives life to all nature, and which in my time has evidently declined considerably towards the ocean at the end of our earth, it must then finish its course, be extinguished in the waters that surround us, and leave the world in cold and darkness, necessarily producing universal death and destruction. I have lived seven of those hours, a great age, being no less than four hundred and twenty minutes of time. How very few of us continue so long! I have seen generations born, flourish, and expire. My present friends are the children and grandchildren of the friends of my youth, who are now, alas, no more! And I must soon follow them; for, by the course of nature, though still in health, I cannot expect to live above seven or eight minutes longer. What now avails all my toil and labor in amassing honey-dew on this leaf, which I cannot live to enjoy! What the political struggles I have been engaged in for the good of my compatriot inhabitants of this bush, or my philosophical studies for the benefit of our race in general! for in politics what can laws do without morals? Our present race of ephemerae will in a course of minutes become corrupt, like those of other and older bushes, and consequently as wretched. And in philosophy how small our progress! Alas! art is long, and life is short! My friends would comfort me with the idea of a name they say I shall leave behind me; and they tell me I have lived long enough to nature and to glory. But

what will fame be to an ephemera who no longer exists? And what will become of all history in the eighteenth hour, when the world itself, even the whole Moulin Joly, shall come to its end and be buried in universal ruin?'

To me, after all my eager pursuits, no solid pleasures now remain, but the reflection of a long life spent in meaning well, the sensible conversation of a few good lady ephemerae, and now and then a kind smile and a tune from the ever amiable *Brillante*.[3]

B. FRANKLIN.

1778

Advice to a Young Tradesman

Despite Franklin's financial success, the game of business, with what he called its "little cares and fatigues," neither excited nor interested him once he knew its rules and had met its challenges. Had he patented only a few of his inventions, he could easily have been one of the wealthiest men in America, but he was interested in much more than money. He once wrote, "I would rather have it said, 'He lived usefully,' than 'He died rich.'" Having decided in early middle age that he had money enough, he retired from business and lived comfortably for the rest of his life on the relatively modest income from his holdings. However, because of his personal success, and because of the image of the wise and shrewd tradesman that he had established through "Poor Richard," he was frequently asked for advice by ambitious young men about how to find the way to wealth. Text Bigelow edition of *Complete Works* (New York, 1904).

TO MY FRIEND, A. B.:

As you have desired it of me, I write the following hints, which have been of service to me, and may, if observed, be so to you.

Remember that *time* is money. He that can earn ten shillings a day by his labor, and goes abroad, or sits idle, one half of that day, though he spends but sixpence during his diversion or idleness, ought not to reckon *that* the only expense; he has really spent, or rather thrown away, five shillings besides.

Remember that *credit* is money. If a man lets his money lie in my hands after it is due, he gives me the interest, or so much as I can make of it during that time. This amounts to a considerable sum where a man has good and large credit, and makes good use of it.

Remember that money is of the prolific, generating nature. Money can beget money, and its offspring can beget more, and so on. Five shillings turned is six, turned again it is seven and three-pence, and so on till it becomes an hundred pounds. The more there is of it, the more it produces every turning, so that the profits rise quicker and quicker. He that

---

[2] One a gnat, the other a mosquito. At the time, Paris was divided over the respective merits of Gluck, a German musician, and Piccini, an Italian.

[3] A pun on "Brillon."

kills a breeding sow destroys all her offspring to the thousandth generation. He that murders a crown destroys all that it might have produced, even scores of pounds.

Remember that six pounds a year is but a groat a day. For this little sum (which may be daily wasted either in time or expense unperceived) a man of credit may, on his own security, have the constant possession and use of an hundred pounds. So much in stock, briskly turned by an industrious man, produces great advantage.

Remember this saying: *The good paymaster is lord of another man's purse.* He that is known to pay punctually and exactly to the time he promises, may at any time, and on any occasion, raise all the money his friends can spare. This is sometimes of great use. After industry and frugality, nothing contributes more to the raising of a young man in the world than punctuality and justice in all his dealings; therefore, never keep borrowed money an hour beyond the time you promised, lest a disappointment shut up your friend's purse for ever.

The most trifling actions that affect a man's credit are to be regarded. The sound of your hammer at five in the morning, or nine at night, heard by a creditor, makes him easy six months longer; but if he sees you at a billiard-table or hears your voice at a tavern when you should be at work, he sends for his money the next day; demands it, before he can receive it, in a lump.

It shows, besides, that you are mindful of what you owe; it makes you appear a careful as well as an honest man, and that still increases your credit.

Beware of thinking all your own that you possess, and of living accordingly. It is a mistake that many people who have credit fall into. To prevent this, keep an exact account for some time, both of your expenses and your income. If you take the pains at first to mention particulars, it will have this good effect: you will discover how wonderfully small, trifling expenses mount up to large sums, and will discern what might have been and may for the future be saved, without occasioning any great inconvenience.

In short, the way to wealth, if you desire it, is as plain as the way to market. It depends chiefly on two words, *industry* and *frugality*—that is, waste neither *time* nor *money*, but make the best use of both. Without industry and frugality nothing will do, and with them every thing. He that gets all he can honestly, and saves all he gets (necessary expenses excepted), will certainly become *rich*, if that Being who governs the world, to whom all should look for a blessing on their honest endeavours, doth not, in his wise providence, otherwise determine.

AN OLD TRADESMAN.

1748

Letters

To Peter Collinson

Primarily because of his identification of lightning with electricity, Franklin received the Copley Medal in 1753 and was elected a Fellow of the Royal Society in 1756. Peter Collinson (1694–1768) was an English botanist, Fellow of the Royal Society, friend and frequent correspondent of Franklin. Text: Bigelow edition of *Complete Works* (New York, 1904).

READ AT THE ROYAL SOCIETY, DECEMBER 21, 1752

Philadelphia, 19 October, 1752.

SIR:—As frequent mention is made in publick papers from Europe of the success of the Philadelphia experiment for drawing the electric fire from clouds by means of pointed rods of iron erected on high buildings, &c., it may be agreeable to the curious to be informed that the same experiment has succeeded in Philadelphia, though made in a different and more easy manner, which is as follows.

Make a small cross of two light strips of cedar, the arms so long as to reach to the four corners of a large thin silk handkerchief when extended; tie the corners of the handkerchief to the extremities of the cross, so you have the body of a kite; which, being properly accommodated with a tail, loop, and string, will rise in the air, like those made of paper; but this being of silk is fitter to bear the wet and wind of a thunder-gust without tearing. To the top of the upright stick of the cross is to be fixed a very sharp-pointed wire, rising a foot or more above the wood. To the end of the twine, next the hand, is to be tied a silk ribbon, and where the silk and twine join, a key may be fastened. This kite is to be raised when a thunder-gust appears to be coming on, and the person who holds the string must stand within a door or window, or under some cover, so that the silk ribbon may not be wet; and care must be taken that the twine does not touch the frame of the door or window. As soon as any of the thunderclouds come over the kite, the pointed wire will draw the electric fire from them, and the kite, with all the twine, will be electrified, and the loose filaments of the twine will stand out every way, and be attracted by an approaching finger. And when the rain has wetted the kite and twine, so that it can conduct the electric fire freely, you will find it stream out plentifully from the key on the approach of your knuckle. At this key the phial may be charged; and from electric fire thus obtained spirits may be kindled, and all the other electric experiments be performed which are usually done by the help of a rubbed glass globe or tube, and thereby the sameness of the electric matter with that of lightning completely demonstrated.

B. FRANKLIN.

To Mrs. Jane Mecom

Jane Mecom was Franklin's favorite sister, six years younger than he. Text: Bigelow edition of *Complete Works*.

London, 16 September, 1758.

DEAR SISTER:—I received your favor of June 17th. I wonder you have had no letter from me since my being in England. I have wrote you at least two, and I think a third before this, and, what was next to waiting on you in person, sent you my picture. In June last I sent Benny a trunk of books, and wrote to him. I hope they are come to hand, and that he meets with encouragement in his business. I congratulate you on the conquest of Cape Breton, and hope, as your people took it by praying the first time, you will now pray that it may never be given up again, which you then forgot. Billy is well, but in the country. I left him at Tunbridge Wells where we spent a fortnight, and he is now gone with some company to see Portsmouth. We have been together over a great part of England this summer, and, among other places, visited the town our father was born in, and found some relations in that part of the country still living.

Our cousin Jane Franklin, daughter of our uncle John, died about a year ago. We saw her husband, Robert Page, who gave us some old letters to his wife from uncle Benjamin. In one of them, dated Boston, July 4, 1723, he writes that your uncle Josiah has a daughter Jane, about twelve years old, a good-humored child. So keep up to your character, and don't be angry when you have no letters. In a little book he sent her, called *None but Christ*, he wrote an acrostic on her name, which for namesake's sake, as well as the good advice it contains, I transcribe and send you, viz.:

Illuminated from on high,
And shining brightly in your sphere,
Ne'er faint, but keep a steady eye,
Expecting endless pleasures there.

Flee vice as you'd a serpent flee;
Raise *faith* and *hope* three stories higher,
And let Christ's endless love to thee
Ne'er cease to make thy love aspire.

Kindness of heart by words express,
Let your obedience be sincere,
In prayer and praise your God address,
Nor cease, till he can cease to hear.

After professing truly that I had a great esteem and veneration for the pious author, permit me a little to play the commentator and critic on these lines. The meaning of *three stories higher* seems somewhat obscure. You are to understand, then, that *faith*, *hope*, and *charity* have been called the three steps of Jacob's ladder, reaching from earth to heaven; our author calls them *stories*, likening religion to a building, and these are the three stories of the Christian edifice. Thus improvement in religion is called *building up* and *edification*. *Faith* is, then, the ground floor; *hope* is up one pair of stairs. My dear beloved Jenny, don't delight so much to dwell, in those lower rooms, but get as fast as you can into the garret, for in truth the best room in the house is *charity*. For my part, I wish the house was turned upside down; it is so difficult (when one is fat) to go up stairs; and not only so, but I imagine *hope* and *faith* may be more firmly built upon *charity*, than *charity* upon *faith* and *hope*. However that may be, I think it the better reading to say—

Raise faith and hope one story higher.

Correct it boldly, and I'll support the alteration; for, when you are up two stories already, if you raise your building three stories higher you will make five in all, which is two more than there should be, you expose your upper rooms more to the winds and storms; and, besides, I am afraid the foundation will hardly bear them, unless indeed you build with such light stuff as straw and stubble, and that, you know, won't stand fire. Again, where the author says—

Kindness of heart by words express,

strike out *words*, and put in *deeds*. The world is too full of compliments already. They are the rank growth of every soil, and choke the good plants of benevolence and beneficence; nor do I pretend to be the first in this comparison of words and actions to plants; you may remember an ancient poet, whose works we have all studied and copied at school long ago:

A man of words and not of deeds
Is like a garden full of weeds.

It is a pity that good works, among some sorts of people, are so little valued, and good words admired in their stead; I mean seemingly pious discourses, instead of humane, benevolent actions. Those they almost put out of countenance, by calling morality *rotten morality*, righteousness *ragged righteousness*, and even filthy rags. So much by way of commentary.

My wife will let you see my letter, containing an account of our travels, which I would have you read to sister Dowse, and give my love to her. I have no thoughts of returning till next year, and then may possibly have the pleasure of seeing you and yours; taking Boston in my way home. My love to brother and all your children, concludes at this time from, dear Jenny, your affectionate brother,

B. FRANKLIN.

To Joseph Priestley

Priestley, English clergyman and scientist, the discoverer of oxygen, was a friend of Franklin's and like him interested in researches in electricity. Text: Bigelow edition of *Complete Works*.

Passy, 8 February, 1780.

DEAR SIR:—Your kind letter of September 27th came to hand but very lately, the bearer having stayed long in Holland. I always rejoice to hear of your being still employed in experimental researches into nature, and of the success you meet with. The rapid progress *true* science now makes, occasions my regretting sometimes that I was born so soon. It is impossible to imagine the height to which may be carried, in a thousand years, the power of man over matter. We may perhaps learn to deprive large masses of their gravity, and give them absolute levity, for the sake of easy transport. Agriculture may diminish its labor and double its produce; all diseases may by sure means be prevented or cured, not excepting even that of old age, and our lives lengthened at pleasure even beyond the antediluvian standard. O that moral science were in as fair a way of improvement, that men would cease to be wolves to one another, and that human beings would at length learn what they now improperly call humanity!

I am glad my little paper on the *Aurora Borealis* pleased. If it should occasion further inquiry, and so produce a better hypothesis, it will not be wholly useless. I am ever, with the greatest and most sincere esteem, dear sir, etc.,   B. FRANKLIN.

To Samuel Mather

Samuel Mather, son of Cotton Mather, was himself a noted theologian. Text: Bigelow edition of *Complete Works*.

Passy, 12 May, 1784.

REVEREND SIR:—I received your kind letter, with your excellent advice to the people of the United States, which I read with great pleasure, and hope it will be duly regarded. Such writings, though they may be lightly passed over by many readers, yet, if they make a deep impression on one active mind in a hundred, the effects may be considerable. Permit me to mention one little instance, which, though it relates to myself, will not be quite uninteresting to you. When I was a boy, I met with a book entitled *Essays to do Good*, which I think was written by your father. It had been so little regarded by a former possessor, that several leaves of it were torn out; but the remainder gave me such a turn of thinking, as to have an influence on my conduct

through life; for I have always set a greater value on the character of a *doer of good*, than on any other kind of reputation; and if I have been, as you seem to think, a useful citizen, the public owes the advantage of it to that book.

You mention your being in your seventy-eighth year; I am in my seventy-ninth; we are grown old together. It is now more than sixty years since I left Boston, but I remember well both your father and grandfather, having heard them both in the pulpit, and seen them in their houses. The last time I saw your father was in the beginning of 1724, when I visited him after my first trip to Pennsylvania. He received me in his library, and on my taking leave showed me a shorter way out of the house, through a narrow passage, which was crossed by a beam overhead. We were all talking as I withdrew, he accompanying me behind, and I turning partly towards him, when he said hastily, *"Stoop, stoop!"* I did not understand him till I felt my head hit against the beam. He was a man that never missed any occasion of giving instruction, and upon this he said to me: *"You are young, and have the world before you;* STOOP *as you go through it, and you will miss many hard thumps."* This advice, thus beat into my head, has frequently been of use to me, and I often think of it when I see pride mortified and misfortunes brought upon people by their carrying their heads too high.

I long much to see my native place, and to lay my bones there. I left it in 1723; I visited it in 1733, 1743, 1753, and 1763. In 1773 I was in England; in 1775 I had a sight of it, but could not enter, it being in possession of the enemy. I did hope to have been there in 1783, but could not obtain my dismission from this employment here, and now I fear I shall never have that happiness. My best wishes, however, attend my dear country. *Esto perpetua.*[1] It is now blest with an excellent constitution; may it last for ever!

This powerful monarchy continues its friendship for the United States. It is a friendship of the utmost importance to our security, and should be carefully cultivated. Britain has not yet well digested the loss of its dominion over us, and has still at times some flattering hopes of recovering it. Accidents may increase those hopes and encourage dangerous attempts. A breach between us and France would infallibly bring the English again upon our backs; and yet we have some wild heads among our countrymen who are endeavoring to weaken that connection! Let us preserve our reputation by performing our engagements, our credit by fulfilling our contracts, and friends by gratitude and kindness; for we know not how soon we may again have occasion for

To Samuel Mather. [1] "May she endure forever."

all of them. With great and sincere esteem, I have the honor to be, etc.,

B. FRANKLIN.

To Ezra Stiles

The Rev. Ezra Stiles, President of Yale, wrote Franklin in January 1790, "I wish to know the opinion of my venerable friend concerning Jesus of Nazareth." Text: Albert H. Smyth, ed., *The Works of Benjamin Franklin* (New York, 1905–7).

Philadelphia, March 9, 1790.

REVEREND AND DEAR SIR:—I received your kind Letter of Jan'y 28, and am glad you have at length received the portrait of Gov'r Yale from his Family, and deposited it in the College Library. He was a great and good Man, and had the Merit of doing infinite Service to your Country by his Munificence to that Institution. The Honour you propose doing me by placing mine in the same Room with his, is much too great for my Deserts; but you always had a Partiality for me, and to that it must be ascribed. I am however too much obliged to Yale College, the first learned Society that took Notice of me and adorned me with its Honours,[1] to refuse a Request that comes from it thro' so esteemed a Friend. But I do not think any one of the Portraits you mention, as in my Possession, worthy of the Place and Company you propose to place it in. You have an excellent Artist lately arrived. If he will undertake to make one for you, I shall cheerfully pay the Expence; but he must not delay setting about it, or I may slip thro' his fingers, for I am now in my eighty-fifth year, and very infirm.

I send with this a very learned Work, as it seems to me, on the antient Samaritan Coins, lately printed in Spain, and at least curious for the Beauty of the Impression. Please to accept it for your College Library. I have subscribed for the Encyclopaedia now printing here, with the Intention of presenting it to the College. I shall probably depart before the Work is finished, but shall leave Directions for its Continuance to the End. With this you will receive some of the first numbers.

You desire to know something of my Religion. It

To Stiles. [1] Yale awarded Franklin an honorary Master of Arts degree in 1753.

is the first time I have been questioned upon it. But I cannot take your Curiosity amiss, and shall endeavour in a few Words to gratify it. Here is my Creed. I believe in one God, Creator of the Universe. That he governs it by his Providence. That he ought to be worshipped. That the most acceptable Service we render to him is doing good to his other Children. That the soul of Man is immortal, and will be treated with Justice in another Life respecting its Conduct in this. These I take to be the fundamental Principles of all sound Religion, and I regard them as you do in whatever Sect I meet with them.

As to Jesus of Nazareth, my Opinion of whom you particularly desire, I think the System of Morals and his Religion, as he left them to us, the best the World ever saw or is likely to see; but I apprehend it has received various corrupting Changes, and I have, with most of the present Dissenters in England, some Doubts as to his Divinity; tho' it is a question I do not dogmatize upon, having never studied it, and think it needless to busy myself with it now, when I expect soon an Opportunity of knowing the Truth with less Trouble. I see no harm, however, in its being believed, if that Belief has the good Consequence, as probably it has, of making his Doctrines more respected and better observed; especially as I do not perceive, that the Supreme takes it amiss, by distinguishing the Unbelievers in his Government of the World with any peculiar Marks of his Displeasure.

I shall only add, respecting myself, that, having experienced the Goodness of that Being in conducting me prosperously thro' a long life, I have no doubt of its Continuance in the next, though without the smallest Conceit of meriting such Goodness. My Sentiments on this Head you will see in the Copy of an old Letter enclosed, which I wrote in answer to one from a zealous Religionist, whom I had relieved in a paralytic case by electricity, and who, being afraid I should grow proud upon it, sent me his serious though rather impertinent Caution. I send you also the Copy of another Letter, which will shew something of my Disposition relating to Religion. With great and sincere Esteem and Affection, I am, Your obliged old Friend and most obedient humble Servant

B. FRANKLIN.

THOMAS PAINE [1737–1809]

FRANKLIN ONCE SAID, "Where liberty is, there is my country." Thomas Paine's reply was typical: "Where liberty is not, there is mine." He was born in England, and after failing as a corset-maker, schoolteacher, sailor, and excise officer, he came to America at the age of thirty-seven in 1774 bearing some circumspect letters of recommendation from Franklin. He had already developed a passion for liberty, a clear and forceful pamphlet style, and an excellent command of persuasive techniques. The controversy between colonies and Crown over rights and liberties was exactly fitted to Paine's interests and talents. He plunged into the argument, and in January 1776 published *Common Sense*, which had much to do with crystallizing public support for independence, to Paine "the cause of God and humanity."

Paine served with the Continental Army on General Greene's staff, and at intervals from 1776 to 1783 brought out thirteen pamphlets called "The Crisis," in which he commented on the course of the war and exhorted the populace to greater efforts. After the war, acclaimed by Congress and the people for his services to the nation, he turned his attention to Europe, where other revolutions seemed in the making. He witnessed the early events of the French Revolution, and did his best to assist the beginnings of something similar in England. He was a member of the French Revolutionary Convention, participated in its deliberations, and finally in 1774 he was imprisoned and narrowly escaped the guillotine because he opposed the execution of the king. His American citizenship and the intervention of James Monroe, the American ambassador, saved him, but meanwhile he had published *The Rights of Man* (1791, 1792), had been charged with libel and treason in England, and hanged in effigy by a London mob.

After his release from prison, Paine remained in Paris, in poor health and on the edge of poverty. He continued to write, publishing his strongly deistic *Age of Reason* (1794–96), his political tract *Dissertation on First-Principles of Government* (1795), and his ideas on tax and land reform, *Agrarian Justice* (1797). However, *The Age of Reason* and his bitter attack on the President in his *Letter to Washington* (1796) aroused powerful antagonisms in the United States, and when Paine returned to America in 1802 he found himself discredited and vilified as a drunkard, atheist, and dangerous radical. He lived in obscurity at New Rochelle, New York, stripped of his right to vote and subject to constant abuse and harassment, until he died in 1809. Even in death he remained controversial—the Quakers refused to admit his body to their burial ground, and his bones were finally sent to England, sold at auction as a curiosity, and lost.

Paine, a tactless and often intemperate man of strong feelings, aroused equally strong feelings in others; some of his ideas are still distasteful to large groups of people. He was neither a learned man nor an original thinker, and many of his ideas he borrowed from his contemporaries. But he was one of the most gifted and effective political propagandists who ever lived, and no one did more by his pen for revolutionary America. He was absolutely unafraid, willing to stand up for his principles, and no man fought harder—in three countries—for the freedom he believed in.

Further reading: Moncure D. Conway, *The Life of Thomas Paine*, 2 vols., 1892 (the standard older biography). A. O. Aldridge, *Man of Reason: The Life of Thomas Paine*, 1959. The entry on Paine by Crane Brinton in *The Dictionary of American Biography*.

FROM *Common Sense*

(January 10, 1776)

Paine, in late 1775, after Lexington, Concord, and Bunker Hill, predicted the eventual separation of the colonies from Britain and was generally recognized as the most effective spokesman of the so-called "radicals." *Common Sense*, written with Franklin's encouragement not long after George III had proclaimed the colonies in rebellion, was the first open demand for a declaration of independence and stated the case for it with clarity and vigor. It sold more than a hundred thousand copies within three months and ran through fifteen editions before the end of the year; Washington credited its "sound doctrine and unanswerable reasoning" with convincing more colonists of the necessity of separation than any other single document. Paine provided, with his statement of the future destiny of the colonies as a continental nation, a common ground on which almost all elements of American opinion could unite. *Common Sense* appeared as a pamphlet of seventy-nine pages, of which this was the third chapter. Other chapters discussed the American case within the context of English political history and theory, the powers and prerogatives of monarchy, and the ability of the colonies to unite and survive as a nation. Text: William Van der Weyde, ed., *The Life and Works of Thomas Paine* (New Rochelle, New York, 1925).

Thoughts on the Present State of American Affairs

In the following pages I offer nothing more than simple facts, plain arguments, and common sense: and have no other preliminaries to settle with the reader, than that he will divest himself of prejudice and prepossession, and suffer his reason and his feelings to determine for themselves: that he will put on, or rather that he will not put off, the true character of a man, and generously enlarge his views beyond the present day.

Volumes have been written on the subject of the struggle between England and America. Men of all ranks have embarked in the controversy, from different motives, and with various designs; but all have been ineffectual, and the period of debate is closed. Arms as the last resource decide the contest; the appeal was the choice of the king, and the continent has accepted the challenge.

It hath been reported of the late Mr. Pelham[1] (who though an able minister was not without his faults) that on his being attacked in the House of Commons on the score that his measures were only of a temporary kind, replied, *"they will last my time."* Should a thought so fatal and unmanly possess the colonies in the present contest, the name of ancestors will be remembered by future generations with detestation.

The sun never shone on a cause of greater worth. 'Tis not the affair of a city, a county, a province, or a kingdom; but of a continent—of at least one eighth part of the habitable globe. 'Tis not the concern of a day, a year, or an age; posterity are virtually involved in the contest, and will be more or less affected even to the end of time, by the proceedings now. Now is the seed-time of continental union, faith and honor. The least fracture now will be like a name engraved with the point of a pin on the tender rind of a young oak; the wound would enlarge with the tree, and posterity read it in full grown characters.

By referring the matter from argument to arms, a new aera for politics is struck—a new method of thinking has arisen. All plans, proposals, &c. prior to the nineteenth of April, *i.e.* to the commencement of hostilities,[2] are like the almanacks of the last year; which though proper then, are superceded and useless now. Whatever was advanced by the advocates on either side of the question then, terminated in one and the same point, viz. a union with Great Britain; the only difference between the parties was the method of effecting it; the one proposing force, the other friendship; but it has so far happened that the first has failed, and the second has withdrawn her influence.

As much has been said of the advantages of reconciliation which, like an agreeable dream, has passed away and left us as we were, it is but right that we should examine the contrary side of the argument, and inquire into some of the many material injuries which these colonies sustain, and always will sustain, by being connected with and dependant on Great Britain. To examine that connection and dependance, on the principles of nature and common sense, to see what we have to trust to, if separated, and what we are to expect, if dependant.

I have heard it asserted by some, that as America has flourished under her former connection with Great Britain, the same connection is necessary towards her future happiness, and will always have the same effect. Nothing can be more fallacious than this kind of argument. We may as well assert that because a child has thrived upon milk, that it is never to have meat, or that the first twenty years of our lives is to become a precedent for the next twenty. But even this is admitting more than is true; for I answer roundly, that America would have flourished as much, and probably much more, had no European power taken any notice of her. The commerce by which she hath enriched herself are the necessaries of life, and will always have a market while eating is the custom of Europe.

But she has protected us, say some. That she hath engrossed us is true, and defended the continent at our expense as well as her own, is admitted; and she would have defended Turkey from the same motive, *viz.* for the sake of trade and dominion.

---

[1] Prime Minister of England 1744–54.

[2] Battle of Lexington, Massachusetts, April 19, 1775.

Alas! we have been long led away by ancient prejudices and made large sacrifices to superstition. We have boasted the protection of Great Britain, without considering, that her motive was *interest* not *attachment;* and that she did not protect us from *our enemies on our account;* but from *her enemies* on *her own account,* from those who had no quarrel with us on any *other account,* and who will always be our enemies on the *same account.* Let Britain waive her pretensions to the continent, or the continent throw off the dependance, and we should be at peace with France and Spain, were they at war with Britain. The miseries of Hanover's last war ought to warn us against connections.[3]

It hath lately been asserted in Parliament, that the colonies have no relation to each other but through the parent country, *i.e.* that Pennsylvania and the Jerseys, and so on for the rest, are sister colonies by the way of England; this is certainly a very roundabout way of proving relationship, but it is the nearest and only true way of proving enmity (or enemyship, if I may so call it). France and Spain never were, nor perhaps ever will be, our enemies as *Americans,* but as our being the *subjects of Great Britain.*

But Britain is the parent country, say some. Then the more shame upon her conduct. Even brutes do not devour their young, nor savages make war upon their families; wherefore, the assertion, if true, turns to her reproach; but it happens not to be true, or only partly so, and the phrase *parent* or *mother country* hath been jesuitically adopted by the king and his parasites, with a low papistical design of gaining an unfair bias on the credulous weakness of our minds. Europe, and not England, is the parent country of America. This new world hath been the asylum for the persecuted lovers of civil and religious liberty from *every part* of Europe. Hither have they fled, not from the tender embraces of the mother, but from the cruelty of the monster; and it is so far true of England, that the same tyranny which drove the first emigrants from home, pursues their descendants still.

In this extensive quarter of the globe, we forget the narrow limits of three hundred and sixty miles (the extent of England) and carry our friendship on a larger scale; we claim brotherhood with every European Christian, and triumph in the generosity of the sentiment.

It is pleasant to observe by what regular gradations we surmount the force of local prejudices, as we enlarge our acquaintance with the world. A man born in any town in England divided into parishes, will naturally associate most with his fellow parishioners (because their interests in many cases will be common) and distinguish him by the name of *neighbor;* if he meet him but a few miles from home, he drops the narrow idea of a street, and salutes him by the name of *townsman;* if he travel out of the county and meet him in any other, he forgets the minor divisions of street and town, and calls him *countryman, i.e. countyman;* but if in their foreign excursions they should associate in France, or any other part of *Europe,* their local remembrance would be enlarged into that of *Englishman.* And by a just parity of reasoning, all Europeans meeting in America, or any other quarter of the globe, are *countrymen;* for England, Holland, Germany, or Sweden, when compared with the whole, stand in the same places on the larger scale, which the divisions of street, town, and county do on the smaller ones; distinctions too limited for continental minds. Not one third of the inhabitants, even of this province,[4] are of English descent. Wherefore, I reprobate the phrase of parent or mother country applied to England only, as being false, selfish, narrow and ungenerous.

But, admitting that we were all of English descent, what does it amount to? Nothing. Britain, being now an open enemy, extinguishes every other name and title: and to say that reconciliation is our duty, is truly farcical. The first king of England, of the present line (William the Conqueror) was a Frenchman, and half the peers of England are descendants from the same country; wherefore, by the same method of reasoning, England ought to be governed by France.

Much hath been said of the united strength of Britain and the colonies, that in conjunction they might bid defiance to the world. But this is mere presumption; the fate of war is uncertain, neither do the expressions mean any thing; for this continent would never suffer itself to be drained of inhabitants, to support the British arms in either Asia, Africa or Europe.

Besides, what have we to do with setting the world at defiance? Our plan is commerce, and that, well attended to, will secure us the peace and friendship of all Europe; because it is the interest of all Europe to have America a free port. Her trade will always be a protection, and her barrenness of gold and silver secure her from invaders.

I challenge the warmest advocate for reconciliation to show a single advantage that this continent can reap by being connected with Great Britain. I repeat the challenge; not a single advantage is derived. Our corn will fetch its price in any market in Europe, and our imported goods must be paid for buy them where we will.

But the injuries and disadvantages which we sus-

---

[3] Once independent, now a German province, the scene of heavy fighting during the Seven Years' War, 1756–63.

[4] Pennsylvania.

tain by that connection, are without number; and our duty to mankind at large, as well as to ourselves, instruct us to renounce the alliance: because, any submission to, or dependence on, Great Britain, tends directly to involve this continent in European wars and quarrels, and set us at variance with nations who would otherwise seek our friendship, and against whom we have neither anger nor complaint. As Europe is our market for trade, we ought to form no partial connection with any part of it. It is the true interest of America to steer clear of European contentions, which she never can do, while, by her dependence on Britain, she is made the make-weight in the scale of British politics.

Europe is too thickly planted with kingdoms to be long at peace, and whenever a war breaks out between England and any foreign power, the trade of America goes to ruin, *because of her connection with Britain.* The next war may not turn out like the last, and should it not, the advocates for reconciliation now will be wishing for separation then, because neutrality in that case would be a safer convoy than a man of war. Every thing that is right or reasonable pleads for separation. The blood of the slain, the weeping voice of nature cries, 'TIS TIME TO PART. Even the distance at which the Almighty hath placed England and America is a strong and natural proof that the authority of the one over the other, was never the design of heaven. The time likewise at which the continent was discovered, adds weight to the argument, and the manner in which it was peopled, encreases the force of it. The Reformation was preceded by the discovery of America: As if the Almighty graciously meant to open a sanctuary to the persecuted in future years, when home should afford neither friendship nor safety.

The authority of Great Britain over this continent, is a form of government, which sooner or later must have an end. And a serious mind can draw no true pleasure by looking forward, under the painful and positive conviction that what he calls "the present constitution" is merely temporary. As parents, we can have no joy, knowing that this government is not sufficiently lasting to insure any thing which we may bequeath to posterity. And by a plain method of argument, as we are running the next generation into debt, we ought to do the work of it, otherwise we use them meanly and pitifully. In order to discover the line of our duty rightly, we should take our children in our hand, and fix our station a few years farther into life; that eminence will present a prospect which a few present fears and prejudices conceal from our sight.

Though I would carefully avoid giving unnecessary offence, yet I am inclined to believe, that all those who espouse the doctrine of reconciliation, may be included within the following descriptions.

Interested men, who are not to be trusted, weak men who *cannot* see, prejudiced men who will not see, and a certain set of moderate men who think better of the European world than it deserves; and this last class, by an ill-judged deliberation, will be the cause of more calamities to this continent than all the other three.

It is the good fortune of many to live distant from the scene of present sorrow; the evil is not sufficiently brought to their doors to make them feel the precariousness with which all American property is possessed. But let our imaginations transport us a few moments to Boston,[5] that seat of wretchedness will teach us wisdom, and instruct us for ever to renounce a power in whom we can have no trust. The inhabitants of that unfortunate city who but a few months ago were in ease and affluence, have now no other alternative than to stay and starve, or turn out to beg. Endangered by the fire of their friends if they continue within the city, and plundered by the soldiery if they leave it, in their present situation they are prisoners without the hope of redemption, and in a general attack for their relief they would be exposed to the fury of both armies.

Men of passive tempers look somewhat lightly over the offences of Great Britain, and, still hoping for the best, are apt to call out, *Come, come, we shall be friends again for all this.* But examine the passions and feelings of mankind: bring the doctrine of reconciliation to the touchstone of nature, and then tell me whether you can hereafter love, honor, and faithfully serve the power that hath carried fire and sword into your land? If you cannot do all these, then are you only deceiving yourselves, and by your delay bringing ruin upon posterity. Your future connection with Britain, whom you can neither love nor honor, will be forced and unnatural, and being formed only on the plan of present convenience will in a little time fall into a relapse more wretched than the first. But if you say, you can still pass the violations over, then I ask, hath your house been burnt? Hath your property been destroyed before your face? Are your wife and children destitute of a bed to lie on, or bread to live on? Have you lost a parent or a child by their hands, and yourself the ruined and wretched survivor? If you have not, then are you not a judge of those who have. But if you have, and can still shake hands with the murderers, then are you unworthy the name of husband, father, friend, or lover, and whatever may be your rank or title in life, you have the heart of a coward, and the spirit of a sycophant.

This is not inflaming or exaggerating matters, but trying them by those feelings and affections which nature justifies, and without which we should be

[5] Under siege from July 1775 to March 1776.

incapable of discharging the social duties of life, or enjoying the felicities of it. I mean not to exhibit horror for the purpose of provoking revenge, but to awaken us from fatal and unmanly slumbers, that we may pursue determinately some fixed object. 'Tis not in the power of Britain or of Europe to conquer America, if she doth not conquer herself by delay and timidity. The present winter is worth an age if rightly employed, but if lost or neglected the whole continent will partake of the misfortune; and there is no punishment which that man doth not deserve, be he who, or what, or where he will, that may be the means of sacrificing a season so precious and useful.

'Tis repugnant to reason, to the universal order of things, to all examples from former ages, to suppose that this continent can long remain subject to any external power. The most sanguine in Britain doth not think so. The utmost stretch of human wisdom cannot, at this time, compass a plan, short of separation, which can promise the continent even a year's security. Reconciliation is *now* a fallacious dream. Nature has deserted the connection, and art cannot supply her place. For, as Milton wisely expresses, "never can true reconcilement grow where wounds of deadly hate have pierced so deep."

Every quiet method for peace hath been ineffectual. Our prayers have been rejected with disdain; and hath tended to convince us that nothing flatters vanity or confirms obstinacy in kings more than repeated petitioning—and nothing hath contributed more than that very measure to make the kings of Europe absolute. Witness Denmark and Sweden.[6] Wherefore, since nothing but blows will do, for God's sake let us come to a final separation, and not leave the next generation to be cutting throats under the violated unmeaning names of parent and child.

To say they will never attempt it again is idle and visionary; we thought so at the repeal of the Stamp Act, yet a year or two undeceived us; as well may we suppose that nations which have been once defeated will never renew the quarrel.

As to government matters, 'tis not in the power of Britain to do this continent justice: the business of it will soon be too weighty and intricate to be managed with any tolerable degree of convenience, by a power so distant from us, and so very ignorant of us; for if they cannot conquer us, they cannot govern us. To be always running three or four thousand miles with a tale or a petition, waiting four or five months for an answer, which, when obtained, requires five or six more to explain it in, will in a few years be looked upon as folly and childishness. There was a time when it was proper, and there is a proper time for it to cease.

[6] Frederick III established a monarchy in Denmark in 1660, and Gustavus in Sweden in 1772.

Small islands not capable of protecting themselves are the proper objects for government[7] to take under their care; but there is something absurd, in supposing a Continent to be perpetually governed by an island. In no instance hath nature made the satellite larger than its primary planet; and as England and America, with respect to each other, reverse the common order of nature, it is evident that they belong to different systems. England to Europe: America to itself.

I am not induced by motives of pride, party or resentment to espouse the doctrine of separation and independence; I am clearly, positively, and conscientiously persuaded that it is the true interest of this continent to be so; that everything short of *that* is mere patchwork, that it can afford no lasting felicity,—that it is leaving the sword to our children, and shrinking back at a time when a little more, a little further, would have rendered this continent the glory of the earth.

As Britain hath not manifested the least inclination towards a compromise, we may be assured that no terms can be obtained worthy the acceptance of the continent, or any ways equal to the expence of blood and treasure we have been already put to.

The object contended for, ought always to bear some just proportion to the expence. The removal of North[8] or the whole detestable junto, is a matter unworthy the millions we have expended. A temporary stoppage of trade was an inconvenience, which would have sufficiently balanced the repeal of all the acts complained of, had such repeals been obtained; but if the whole continent must take up arms, if every man must be a soldier, 'tis scarcely worth our while to fight against a contemptible ministry only. Dearly, dearly do we pay for the repeal of the acts, if that is all we fight for; for, in a just estimation 'tis as great a folly to pay a Bunker Hill price for law as for land. As I have always considered the independancy of this continent, as an event which sooner or later must arrive, so from the late rapid progress of the continent to maturity, the event cannot be far off. Wherefore, on the breaking out of hostilities, it was not worth the while to have disputed a matter which time would have finally redressed, unless we meant to be in earnest: otherwise it is like wasting an estate on a suit at law, to regulate the trespasses of a tenant whose lease is just expiring. No man was a warmer wisher for a reconciliation than myself, before the fatal nineteenth of April, 1775, but the moment the event of that day was made known, I rejected the hardened, sullen-

[7] "Kingdoms" replaced "government" in some later editions.

[8] Lord North, particularly detested by the colonists for his support of the principle of taxation, who was made Chancellor of the Exchequer in 1767.

tempered Pharaoh of England[9] for ever; and disdain the wretch, that with the pretended title of FATHER OF HIS PEOPLE can unfeelingly hear of their slaughter, and composedly sleep with their blood upon his soul.

But admitting that matters were now made up, what would be the event? I answer, the ruin of the continent. And that for several reasons.

First. The powers of governing still remaining in the hands of the king, he will have a negative over the whole legislation of this continent. And as he hath shown himself such an inveterate enemy to liberty, and discovered such a thirst for arbitrary power, is he, or is he not, a proper person to say to these colonies, *You shall make no laws but what I please!?* And is there any inhabitant of America so ignorant as not to know, that according to what is called the *present Constitution,* this continent can make no laws but what the king gives leave to; and is there any man so unwise as not to see, that (considering what has happened) he will suffer no law to be made here but such as suits *his* purpose? We may be as effectually enslaved by the want of laws in America, as by submitting to laws made for us in England. After matters are made up (as it is called) can there be any doubt, but the whole power of the crown will be exerted to keep this continent as low and humble as possible? Instead of going forward we shall go backward, or be perpetually quarrelling, or ridiculously petitioning. We are already greater than the king wishes us to be, and will he not hereafter endeavor to make us less? To bring the matter to one point, Is the power who is jealous of our prosperity, a proper power to govern us? Whoever says *No,* to this question, is an independent for independency means no more than this, whether we shall make our own laws, or, whether the king, the greatest enemy this continent hath, or can have, shall tell us *there shall be no laws but such as I like.*

But the king, you will say, has a negative in England; the people there can make no laws without his consent. In point of right and good order, it is something very ridiculous that a youth of twenty-one (which hath often happened) shall say to several millions of people older and wiser than himself, "I forbid this or that act of yours to be law." But in this place I decline this sort of reply, though I will never cease to expose the absurdity of it, and only answer that England being the king's residence, and America not so, makes quite another case. The king's negative here is ten times more dangerous and fatal than it can be in England; for there he will scarcely refuse his consent to a bill for putting England into as strong a state of defense as possible, and in America he would never suffer such a bill to be passed.

[9] George III.

America is only a secondary object in the system of British politics. England consults the good of this country no further than it answers her own purpose. Wherefore, her own interest leads her to suppress the growth of ours in every case which doth not promote her advantage or in the least interferes with it. A pretty state we should soon be in under such a second hand government, considering what has happened! Men do not change from enemies to friends by the alteration of a name: And in order to show that reconciliation now is a dangerous doctrine, I affirm, *that it would be policy in the king at this time to repeal the acts, for the sake of reinstating himself in the government of the provinces;* In order that HE MAY ACCOMPLISH BY CRAFT AND SUBTLETY, IN THE LONG RUN, WHAT HE CANNOT DO BY FORCE AND VIOLENCE IN THE SHORT ONE. Reconciliation and ruin are nearly related.

Secondly. That as even the best terms which we can expect to obtain can amount to no more than a temporary expedient, or a kind of government by guardianship, which can last no longer than till the colonies come of age, so the general face and state of things in the interim will be unsettled and unpromising. Emigrants of property will not choose to come to a country whose form of government hangs but by a thread, and who is every day tottering on the brink of commotion and disturbance; and numbers of the present inhabitants would lay hold of the interval to dispose of their effects, and quit the continent.

But the most powerful of all arguments is, that nothing but independance, *i.e.* a continental form of government, can keep the peace of the continent and preserve it inviolate from civil wars. I dread the event of a reconciliation with Britain now, as it is more than probable that it will be followed by a revolt some where or other, the consequences of which may be far more fatal than all the malice of Britain.

Thousands are already ruined by British barbarity; (thousands more will probably suffer the same fate). Those men have other feelings than us who have nothing suffered. All they now possess is liberty; what they before enjoyed is sacrificed to its service, and having nothing more to lose they disdain submission. Besides, the general temper of the colonies, towards a British government will be like that of a youth who is nearly out of his time; they will care very little about her: And a government which cannot preserve the peace is no government at all, and in that case we pay our money for nothing; and pray what is it that Britain can do, whose power will be wholly on paper, should a civil tumult break out the very day after reconciliation? I have heard some men say, many of whom I believe spoke without thinking, that they dreaded an independance, fearing that it would produce civil wars: It is but seldom that our first thoughts are truly correct, and that is the case here; for there is ten times more to dread from a patched up connection than from independance. I make the sufferer's case my own, and I protest, that were I driven from house and home, my property destroyed, and my circumstances ruined, that as a man, sensible of injuries, I could never relish the doctrine of reconciliation, or consider myself bound thereby.

The colonies have manifested such a spirit of good order and obedience to continental government, as is sufficient to make every reasonable person easy and happy on that head. No man can assign the least pretence for his fears, on any other grounds, than such as are truly childish and ridiculous, viz., that one colony will be striving for superiority over another.

Where there are no distinctions there can be no superiority; perfect equality affords no temptation. The Republics of Europe are all (and we may say always) in peace. Holland and Switzerland are without wars, foreign or domestic: Monarchical governments, it is true, are never long at rest: the crown itself is a temptation to enterprising ruffians at home; and that degree of pride and insolence ever attendant on regal authority, swells into a rupture with foreign powers in instances where a republican government, by being formed on more natural principles, would negociate the mistake.

If there is any true cause of fear respecting independence, it is because no plan is yet laid down. Men do not see their way out. Wherefore, as an opening into that business I offer the following hints; at the same time modestly affirming, that I have no other opinion of them myself, than that they may be the means of giving rise to something better. Could the straggling thoughts of individuals be collected, they would frequently form materials for wise and able men to improve into useful matter.

Let the assemblies be annual, with a president only. The representation more equal, their business wholly domestic, and subject to the authority of a Continental Congress.

Let each colony be divided into six, eight, or ten, convenient districts, each district to send a proper number of delegates to Congress, so that each colony send at least thirty. The whole number in Congress will be at least 390. Each Congress to sit and to choose a President by the following method. When the delegates are met, let a colony be taken from the whole thirteen colonies by lot, after which let the Congress choose (by ballot) a President from out of the delegates of that province. In the next Congress, let a colony be taken by lot from twelve only, omitting that colony from which the president

was taken in the former Congress, and so proceeding on till the whole thirteen shall have had their proper rotation. And in order that nothing may pass into a law but what is satisfactorily just, not less than three-fifths of the Congress to be called a majority. He that will promote discord, under a government so equally formed as this, would have joined Lucifer in his revolt.

But as there is a peculiar delicacy from whom, or in what manner, this business must first arise, and as it seems most agreeable and consistent that it should come from some intermediate body between the governed and the governors, that is, between the Congress and the people, let a continental conference be held in the following manner, and for the following purpose,

A committee of twenty-six members of Congress, *viz.* Two for each colony. Two members from each House of Assembly, or Provincial Convention; and five representatives of the people at large, to be chosen in the capital city or town of each province, for, and in behalf of the whole province, by as many qualified voters as shall think proper to attend from all parts of the province for that purpose; or, if more convenient, the representatives may be chosen in two or three of the most populous parts thereof. In this conference, thus assembled, will be united the two grand principles of business, *knowledge* and *power*. The Members of Congress, Assemblies, or Conventions, by having had experience in national concerns, will be able and useful counsellors, and the whole, being impowered by the people, will have a truly legal authority.

The conferring members being met, let their business be to frame a Continental Charter, or Charter of the United Colonies; (answering to what is called the Magna Charta of England) fixing the number and manner of choosing Members of Congress, Members of Assembly, with their date of sitting; and drawing the line of business and jurisdiction between them: Always remembering, that our strength is continental, not provincial. Securing freedom and property to all men, and above all things, the free exercise of religion, according to the dictates of conscience; with such other matter as it is necessary for a charter to contain. Immediately after which, the said conference to dissolve, and the bodies which shall be chosen conformable to the said charter, to be the legislators and governors of this continent for the time being: Whose peace and happiness, may GOD preserve. AMEN.

Should any body of men be hereafter delegated for this or some similar purpose, I offer them the following extracts from that wise observer on governments, Dragonetti. "The science," says he, "of the politician consists in fixing the true point of happiness and freedom. Those men would deserve the gratitude of ages, who should discover a mode of government that contained the greatest sum of individual happiness, with the least national expense."[10]

But where, say some, is the king of America? I'll tell you, friend, he reigns above, and doth not make havoc of mankind like the royal brute of Great Britain. Yet that we may not appear to be defective even in earthly honors, let a day be solemnly set apart for proclaiming the charter; let it be brought forth placed on the divine law, the Word of God; let a crown be placed thereon, by which the world may know, that so far as we approve of monarchy, that in America the law is king. For as in absolute governments the king is law, so in free countries the law ought to be king; and there ought to be no other. But lest any ill use should afterwards arise, let the crown at the conclusion of the ceremony be demolished, and scattered among the people whose right it is.

A government of our own is our natural right: and when a man seriously reflects on the precariousness of human affairs, he will become convinced, that it is infinitely wiser and safer, to form a Constitution of our own in a cool deliberate manner, while we have it in our power, than to trust such an interesting event to time and chance. If we omit it now, some Massanello[11] may hereafter arise, who, laying hold of popular disquietudes, may collect together the desperate and the discontented, and by assuming to themselves the powers of government, finally sweep away the liberties of the continent like a deluge. Should the government of America return again into the hands of Britain, the tottering situation of things will be a temptation for some desperate adventurer to try his fortune; and in such a case, what relief can Britain give? Ere she could hear the news, the fatal business might be done; and ourselves suffering like the wretched Britons under the oppression of the conqueror. Ye that oppose independance now, ye know not what ye do: ye are opening a door to eternal tyranny, by keeping vacant the seat of government. There are thousands and tens of thousands, who would think it glorious to expel from the continent, that barbarous and hellish power, which hath stirred up the indians and the negroes to destroy us; the cruelty hath a double guilt, it is dealing brutally by us, and treacherously by them.

[10] Giacinto Dragonetti (1738-1818), Italian writer on political affairs.
[11] Thomas Anello, otherwise Massanello, a fisherman of Naples, who after spiriting up his countrymen in the public market place, against the oppression of the Spaniards, to whom the place was then subject, prompted them to revolt, and in the space of a day became king. [Paine's note.]

To talk of friendship with those in whom our reason forbids us to have faith, and our affections wounded through a thousand pores instruct us to detest, is madness and folly. Every day wears out the little remains of kindred between us and them; and can there be any reason to hope, that as the relationship expires, the affection will increase, or that we shall agree better when we have ten times more and greater concerns to quarrel over than ever?

Ye that tell us of harmony and reconciliation, can ye restore to us the time that is past? Can ye give to prostitution its former innocence? neither can ye reconcile Britain and America. The last cord now is broken, the people of England are presenting addresses against us. There are injuries which nature cannot forgive; she would cease to be nature if she did. As well can the lover forgive the ravisher of his mistress, as the continent forgive the murders of Britain. The Almighty hath implanted in us these unextinguishable feelings for good and wise purposes. They are the guardians of his image in our hearts. They distinguish us from the herd of common animals. The social compact would dissolve, and justice be extirpated from the earth, or have only a casual existence were we callous to the touches of affection. The robber and the murderer would often escape unpunished, did not the injuries which our tempers sustain, provoke us into justice.

O! ye that love mankind! Ye that dare oppose not only the tyranny but the tyrant, stand forth! Every spot of the old world is overrun with oppression. Freedom hath been hunted round the globe. Asia and Africa have long expelled her. Europe regards her like a stranger, and England hath given her warning to depart. O! receive the fugitive, and prepare in time an asylum for mankind.

The American Crisis

(December 19, 1776)

Written in camp (as legend has it, on a drumhead by the light of a campfire) while Washington's army, after a series of defeats, retreated across New Jersey. Washington, who had written his brother, "I think the game is pretty nearly up," ordered the paper read aloud to every regiment of the army, and six days later won a decisive victory at the Battle of Trenton. The famous trumpet call of the opening paragraph is Paine at his brilliant best; seven years later, in the fifteenth issue of the Crisis series, he could write exultantly, "The times that tried men's souls are over—and the greatest and completest revolution the world ever knew, gloriously and happily accomplished." The sixteenth and final number of The Crisis was published December 9, 1783. Text: Van der Weyde edition of The Life and Works.

I

These are the times that try men's souls. The summer soldier and the sunshine patriot will, in this crisis, shrink from the service of their country; but he that stands it *now,* deserves the love and thanks of man and woman. Tyranny, like hell, is not easily conquered; yet we have this consolation with us, that the harder the conflict, the more glorious the triumph. What we obtain too cheap, we esteem too lightly: it is dearness only that gives every thing its value. Heaven knows how to put a proper price upon its goods; and it would be strange indeed if so celestial an article as FREEDOM should not be highly rated. Britain, with an army to enforce her tyranny, has declared that she has a right (*not only to* TAX) but "to BIND *us in* ALL CASES WHATSOEVER," and if being *bound in that manner,* is not slavery, then is there not such a thing as slavery upon earth. Even the expression is impious; for so unlimited a power can belong only to God.

Whether the independence of the continent was declared too soon, or delayed too long, I will not now enter into as an argument; my own simple opinion is, that had it been eight months earlier, it would have been much better. We did not make a proper use of last winter, neither could we, while we were in a dependent state. However, the fault, if it were one, was all our own;[1] we have none to blame but ourselves. But no great deal is lost yet. All that Howe has been doing for this month past, is rather a ravage than a conquest, which the spirit of the Jerseys, a year ago, would have quickly repulsed, and which time and a little resolution will soon recover.

I have as little superstition in me as any man living, but my secret opinion has ever been, and still is, that God Almighty will not give up a people to military destruction, or leave them unsupportedly to perish, who have so earnestly and so repeatedly sought to avoid the calamities of war, by every decent method which wisdom could invent. Neither have I so much of the infidel in me, as to suppose that He has relinquished the government of the world, and given us up to the care of devils; and as I do not, I cannot see on what grounds the king of Britain can look up to heaven for help against us: a common murderer, a highwayman, or a housebreaker, has as good a pretence as he.

'Tis surprising to see how rapidly a panic will sometimes run through a country. All nations and ages have been subject to them. Britain has trembled like an ague at the report of a French fleet of flat-bottomed boats; and in the fourteenth century the whole English army, after ravaging the kingdom of France, was driven back like men petrified with fear; and this brave exploit was performed by a few broken forces collected and headed by a woman, Joan of Arc. Would that heaven might inspire some Jersey maid to spirit up her countrymen, and save her fair fellow sufferers from ravage and ravishment! Yet panics, in some cases, have their uses; they produce as much good as hurt. Their duration is always short; the mind soon grows through them, and acquires a firmer habit than before. But their peculiar advantage is, that they are the touchstones of sincerity and hypocrisy, and bring things and men to light, which might otherwise have lain forever undiscovered. In fact, they have the same effect on secret traitors, which an imaginary apparition would have upon a private murderer. They sift out the hidden thoughts of man, and hold them up in public to the world. Many a disguised Tory has lately shown his head, that shall penitentially solemnize with curses the day on which Howe arrived upon the Delaware.

As I was with the troops at Fort Lee, and marched with them to the edge of Pennsylvania, I am well acquainted with many circumstances, which those who live at a distance know but little or nothing of.[2] Our situation there was exceedingly cramped, the place being a narrow neck of land between the North River and the Hackensack. Our force was inconsiderable, being not one-fourth so great as Howe could bring against us. We had no army at hand to have relieved the garrison, had we shut ourselves up and stood on our defence. Our ammunition, light artillery, and the best part of our stores, had been removed, on the apprehension that Howe[3] would endeavor to penetrate the Jerseys, in which case Fort Lee could be of no use to us; for it must occur to every thinking man, whether in the army or not, that these kind of field forts are only for temporary purposes, and last in use no longer than the enemy directs his force against the particular object which such forts are raised to defend. Such was our situation and condition at Fort Lee on the morning of the 20th of November, when an officer arrived with information that the enemy with 200 boats had landed about seven miles above; Major General Green, who commanded the garrison, immediately ordered them under arms, and sent express to General Washington at the town of Hack-

---

[1] The present winter is worth an age, if rightly employed; but, if lost or neglected, the whole continent will partake of the evil; and there is no punishment that man does not deserve, be he who, or what, or where he will, that may be the means of sacrificing a season so precious and useful. [Paine's note, a citation from his "Common Sense."]

[2] The British General Cornwallis surprised General Nathanael Greene's troops at Fort Lee, New Jersey, on November 20, 1776, and forced the Americans to retreat.

[3] General William Howe, in command of the British forces in the colonies.

ensack, distant by the way of the ferry = six miles. Our first object was to secure the bridge over the Hackensack, which laid up the river between the enemy and us, about six miles from us, and three from them. General Washington arrived in about three-quarters of an hour, and marched at the head of the troops towards the bridge, which place I expected we should have a brush for; however, they did not choose to dispute it with us, and the greatest part of our troops went over the bridge, the rest over the ferry, except some which passed at a mill on a small creek, between the bridge and the ferry, and made their way through some marshy grounds up to the town of Hackensack, and there passed the river. We brought off as much baggage as the wagons could contain, the rest was lost. The simple object was to bring off the garrison, and march them on till they could be strengthened by the Jersey or Pennsylvania militia, so as to be enabled to make a stand. We staid four days at Newark, collected our out-posts with some of the Jersey militia, and marched out twice to meet the enemy, on being informed that they were advancing, though our numbers were greatly inferior to theirs. Howe, in my little opinion, committed a great error in generalship in not throwing a body of forces off from Staten Island through Amboy, by which means he might have seized all our stores at Brunswick, and intercepted our march into Pennsylvania; but if we believe the power of hell to be limited, we must likewise believe that their agents are under some providential control.

I shall not now attempt to give all the particulars of our retreat to the Delaware; suffice it for the present to say, that both officers and men, though greatly harassed and fatigued, frequently without rest, covering, or provision, the inevitable consequences of a long retreat, bore it with a manly and martial spirit. All their wishes centred in one, which was, that the country would turn out and help them to drive the enemy back. Voltaire has remarked that King William never appeared to full advantage but in difficulties and in action; the same remark may be made on General Washington, for the character fits him. There is a natural firmness in some minds which cannot be unlocked by trifles, but which, when unlocked, discovers a cabinet of fortitude; and I reckon it among those kind of public blessings, which we do not immediately see, that God hath blessed him with uninterrupted health, and given him a mind that can even flourish upon care.

I shall conclude this paper with some miscellaneous remarks on the state of our affairs; and shall begin with asking the following question, Why is it that the enemy have left the New England provinces, and made these middle ones the seat of war? The answer is easy: New England is not in-

fested with Tories, and we are. I have been tender in raising the cry against these men, and used numberless arguments to show them their danger, but it will not do to sacrifice a world either to their folly or their baseness. The period is now arrived, in which either they or we must change our sentiments, or one or both must fall. And what is a Tory? Good God! what is he? I should not be afraid to go with a hundred Whigs against a thousand Tories, were they to attempt to get into arms. Every Tory is a coward; for servile, slavish, self-interested fear is the foundation of Toryism; and a man under such influence, though he may be cruel, never can be brave.

But, before the line of irrecoverable separation be drawn between us, let us reason the matter together: Your conduct is an invitation to the enemy, yet not one in a thousand of you has heart enough to join him. Howe is as much deceived by you as the American cause is injured by you. He expects you will all take up arms, and flock to his standard, with muskets on your shoulders. Your opinions are of no use to him, unless you support him personally, for 'tis soldiers, and not Tories, that he wants.

I once felt all that kind of anger, which a man ought to feel, against the mean principles that are held by the Tories: a noted one, who kept a tavern at Amboy,[4] was standing at his door, with as pretty a child in his hand, about eight or nine years old, as I ever saw, and after speaking his mind as freely as he thought was prudent, finished with this unfatherly expression, "Well! give me peace in my day." Not a man lives on the continent but fully believes that a separation must some time or other finally take place, and a generous parent should have said, "If there must be trouble, let it be in my day, that my child may have peace;" and this single reflection, well applied, is sufficient to awaken every man to duty. Not a place upon earth might be so happy as America. Her situation is remote from all the wrangling world, and she has nothing to do but to trade with them. A man can distinguish himself between temper and principle, and I am as confident, as I am that God governs the world, that America will never be happy till she gets clear of foreign dominion. Wars, without ceasing, will break out till that period arrives, and the continent must in the end be conqueror; for though the flame of liberty may sometimes cease to shine, the coal can never expire.

America did not, nor does not want force; but she wanted a proper application of that force. Wisdom is not the purchase of a day, and it is no wonder that we should err at the first setting off. From an excess of tenderness, we were unwilling to raise an army,

[4] Paine enlisted August 1776 in the Pennsylvania divison of the Flying Camp and was stationed at Amboy, now Perth Amboy, New Jersey.

and trusted our cause to the temporary defence of a well-meaning militia. A summer's experience has now taught us better; yet with those troops, while they were collected, we were able to set bounds to the progress of the enemy, and, thank God! they are again assembling. I always considered militia as the best troops in the world for a sudden exertion, but they will not do for a long campaign. Howe, it is probable, will make an attempt on this city;[5] should he fail on this side the Delaware, he is ruined. If he succeeds, our cause is not ruined. He stakes all on his side against a part on ours; admitting he succeeds, the consequence will be, that armies from both ends of the continent will march to assist their suffering friends in the middle states; for he cannot go everywhere, it is impossible. I consider Howe as the greatest enemy the Tories have; he is bringing a war into their country, which, had it not been for him and partly for themselves, they had been clear of. Should he now be expelled, I wish with all the devotion of a Christian, that the names of Whig and Tory may never more be mentioned; but should the Tories give him encouragement to come, or assistance if he come, I as sincerely wish that our next year's arms may expel them from the continent, and the Congress appropriate their possessions to the relief of those who have suffered in well-doing. A single successful battle next year will settle the whole. America could carry on a two years' war by the confiscation of the property of disaffected persons, and be made happy by their expulsion. Say not that this is revenge, call it rather the soft resentment of a suffering people, who, having no object in view but the *good* of *all*, have staked their *own all* upon a seemingly doubtful event. Yet it is folly to argue against determined hardness; eloquence may strike the ear, and the language of sorrow draw forth the tear of compassion, but nothing can reach the heart that is steeled with prejudice.

Quitting this class of men, I turn with the warm ardor of a friend to those who have nobly stood, and are yet determined to stand the matter out: I call not upon a few, but upon all: not on *this* state or *that* state, but on *every* state: up and help us; lay your shoulders to the wheel; better have too much force than too little, when so great an object is at stake. Let it be told to the future world, that in the depth of winter, when nothing but hope and virtue could survive, that the city and the country, alarmed at one common danger, came forth to meet and to repulse it. Say not that thousands are gone, turn out your tens of thousands; throw not the burden of the day upon Providence, but *"show your faith by your works,"* that God may bless you. It matters not where you live, or what rank of life you hold, the evil or the blessing will reach you all. The far and the near, the home counties and the back, the rich and the poor, will suffer or rejoice alike. The heart that feels not now is dead; the blood of his children will curse his cowardice, who shrinks back at a time when a little might have saved the whole, and made *them* happy. I love the man that can smile in trouble, that can gather strength from distress, and grow brave by reflection. 'Tis the business of little minds to shrink; but he whose heart is firm, and whose conscience approves his conduct, will pursue his principles unto death. My own line of reasoning is to myself as straight and clear as a ray of light. Not all the treasures of the world, so far as I believe, could have induced me to support an offensive war, for I think it murder; but if a thief breaks into my house, burns and destroys my property, and kills or threatens to kill me, or those that are in it, and to *"bind me in all cases whatsoever"*[6] to his absolute will, am I to suffer it? What signifies it to me, whether he who does it is a king or a common man; my countryman or not my countryman; whether it be done by an individual villain, or an army of them? If we reason to the root of things we shall find no difference; neither can any just cause be assigned why we should punish in the one case and pardon in the other. Let them call me rebel and welcome, I feel no concern from it; but I should suffer the misery of devils, were I to make a whore of my soul by swearing allegiance to one whose character is that of a sottish, stupid, stubborn, worthless, brutish man. I conceive likewise a horrid idea in receiving mercy from a being, who at the last day shall be shrieking to the rocks and mountains to cover him, and fleeing with terror from the orphan, the widow, and the slain of America.

There are cases which cannot be overdone by language, and this is one. There are persons, too, who see not the full extent of the evil which threatens them; they solace themselves with hopes that the enemy, if he succeed, will be merciful. It is the madness of folly, to expect mercy from those who have refused to do justice; and even mercy, where conquest is the object, is only a trick of war; the cunning of the fox is as murderous as the violence of the wolf, and we ought to guard equally against both. Howe's first object is, partly by threats and partly by promises, to terrify or seduce the people to deliver up their arms and receive mercy. The ministry recommended the same plan to Gage, and this is what the tories call making their peace, *"a peace which passeth all understanding"* indeed! A

---

[5] Philadelphia.

[6] Paine is quoting the Declaratory Act of 1766 affirming British authority over the colonies.

peace which would be the immediate forerunner of a worse ruin than any we have yet thought of. Ye men of Pennsylvania, do reason upon these things! Were the back counties to give up their arms, they would fall an easy prey to the Indians, who are all armed: this perhaps is what some Tories would not be sorry for. Were the home counties to deliver up their arms, they would be exposed to the resentment of the back counties, who would then have it in their power to chastise their defection at pleasure. And were any one state to give up its arms, *that* state must be garrisoned by all Howe's army of Britons and Hessians to preserve it from the anger of the rest. Mutual fear is the principal link in the chain of mutual love, and woe be to that state that breaks the compact. Howe is mercifully inviting you to barbarous destruction, and men must be either rogues or fools that will not see it. I dwell not upon the vapors of imagination; I bring reason to your ears, and, in language as plain as A, B, C, hold up truth to your eyes.

I thank God, that I fear not. I see no real cause for fear. I know our situation well, and can see the way out of it. While our army was collected, Howe dared not risk a battle; and it is no credit to him that he decamped from the White Plains, and waited a mean opportunity to ravage the defenceless Jerseys; but it is great credit to us, that, with a handful of men, we sustained an orderly retreat for near an hundred miles, brought off our ammunition, all our field pieces, the greatest part of our stores, and had four rivers to pass. None can say that our retreat was precipitate, for we were near three weeks in performing it, that the country might have time to come in. Twice we marched back to meet the enemy, and remained out till dark. The sign of fear was not seen in our camp, and had not some of the cowardly and disaffected inhabitants spread false alarms through the country, the Jerseys had never been ravaged. Once more we are again collected and collecting; our new army at both ends of the continent is recruiting fast, and we shall be able to open the next campaign with sixty thousand men, well armed and clothed. This is our situation, and who will may know it. By perseverance and fortitude we have the prospect of a glorious issue; by cowardice and submission, the sad choice of a variety of evils—a ravaged country—a depopulated city—habitations without safety, and slavery without hope—our homes turned into barracks and bawdy-houses for Hessians, and a future race to provide for, whose fathers we shall doubt of. Look on this picture and weep over it! and if there yet remains one thoughtless wretch who believes it not, let him suffer it unlamented.

COMMON SENSE.

FROM ***The Rights of Man***

Part I

The Rights of Man was Paine's reply to Edmund Burke's *Reflections on the French Revolution* (1790) which cast doubts, Paine believed, on the natural right theory of government, the validity of the right of revolution, and the aspirations of free men everywhere. Part I, published in 1791 in London, where Paine was living, was a direct rebuttal of Burke's interpretation of recent events in France; Part II, which appeared in 1792, was a more general and theoretical exposition of Paine's concept of democratic government. After the appearance of Part II Paine, already under surveillance as a dangerously skilful agitator, was indicted for treason and escaped to France barely an hour ahead of a warrant for his arrest. The book was widely read in the United States, where the struggle between Federalist and Republican was beginning in earnest, and became a kind of handbook for both English and French radicals. The text follows that of the Van der Weyde edition of *The Life and Works.*

[Civil and Natural Rights]

I have now to follow Mr. Burke through a pathless wilderness of rhapsodies, and a sort of descant upon governments, in which he asserts whatever he pleases, on the presumption of its being believed, without offering either evidence or reasons for so doing.

Before anything can be reasoned upon to a conclusion, certain facts, principles, or data, to reason from, must be established, admitted, or denied. Mr. Burke, with his usual outrage, abuses the *Declaration of the Rights of Man,* published by the National Assembly of France,[1] as the basis on which the Constitution of France is built. This he calls "paltry and blurred sheets of paper about the rights of man."

Does Mr. Burke mean to deny that *man* has any rights? If he does, then he must mean that there are no such things as rights any where, and that he has none himself; for who is there in the world but man? But if Mr. Burke means to admit that man has rights, the question then will be, what are those rights, and how came man by them originally?

The error of those who reason by precedents drawn from antiquity, respecting the rights of man, is that they do not go far enough into antiquity. They do not go the whole way. They stop in some of the intermediate stages of an hundred or a thousand years, and produce what was then done as a rule for the present day. This is no authority at all.

If we travel still further into antiquity, we shall find a directly contrary opinion and practise prevailing; and, if antiquity is to be authority, a thousand such authorities may be produced, successively

[1] In August 1789.

contradicting each other; but if we proceed on, we shall at last come out right; we shall come to the time when man came from the hand of his Maker. What was he then? Man. Man was his high and only title, and a higher cannot be given him. But of titles I shall speak hereafter.

We have now arrived at the origin of man, and at the origin of his rights. As to the manner in which the world has been governed from that day to this, it is no further any concern of ours than to make a proper use of the errors or the improvements which the history of it presents. Those who lived a hundred or a thousand years ago, were then moderns as we are now. They had *their* ancients, and those ancients had others, and we also shall be ancients in our turn.

If the mere name of antiquity is to govern in the affairs of life, the people who are to live an hundred or a thousand years hence, may as well take us for a precedent, as we make a precedent of those who lived an hundred or a thousand years ago.

The fact is, that portions of antiquity, by proving every thing, establish nothing. It is authority against authority all the way, till we come to the divine origin of the rights of man, at the Creation. Here our inquiries find a resting-place, and our reason finds a home.

If a dispute about the rights of man had arisen at a distance of an hundred years from the Creation, it is to this source of authority they must have referred, and it is to the same source of authority that we must now refer.

Though I mean not to touch upon any sectarian principle of religion, yet it may be worth observing, that the genealogy of Christ is traced to Adam. Why then not trace the rights of man to the creation of man? I will answer the question. Because there have been upstart governments, thrusting themselves between, and presumptuously working to *unmake* man.

If any generation of men ever possessed the right of dictating the mode by which the world should be governed for ever, it was the first generation that existed; and if that generation did it not, no succeeding generation can show any authority for doing it, nor can set any up.

The illuminating and divine principle of the equal rights of man (for it has its origin from the Maker of man), relates not only to the living individuals, but to generations of men succeeding each other. Every generation is equal in rights to the generations which preceded it, by the same rule that every individual is born equal in rights with his contemporary.

Every history of the Creation, and every traditionary account, whether from the lettered or unlettered world, however they may vary in their opinion or belief of certain particulars, all agree in establishing one point, *the unity of man;* by which I mean that men are all of *one degree,* and consequently that all men are born equal, and with equal natural rights, in the same manner as if posterity had been continued by *creation* instead of *generation,* the latter being only the mode by which the former is carried forward; and consequently, every child born into the world must be considered as deriving its existence from God. The world is as new to him as it was to the first man that existed, and his natural right in it is of the same kind.

The Mosaic account of the Creation, whether taken as divine authority or merely historical, is full to this point, *the unity or equality of man.* The expressions admit of no controversy. "And God said, let us make man in our own image. In the image of God created he him; male and female created he them." The distinction of sexes is pointed out, but no other distinction is even implied. If this be not divine authority, it is at least historical authority, and shows that the equality of man, so far from being a modern doctrine, is the oldest upon record.

It is also to be observed, that all the religions known in the world are founded, so far as they relate to man, on the *unity of man,* as being all of one degree. Whether in heaven or in hell, or in whatever state man may be supposed to exist hereafter, the good and the bad are the only distinctions. Nay, even the laws of governments are obliged to slide into this principle, by making degrees to consist in crimes and not in persons.

It is one of the greatest of all truths, and of the highest advantage to cultivate. By considering man in this light, and by instructing him to consider himself in this light, it places him in a close connection with all his duties, whether to his Creator or to the creation, of which he is a part; and it is only when he forgets his origin, or, to use a more fashionable phrase, his *birth and family,* that he becomes dissolute.

It is not among the least of the evils of the present existing governments in all parts of Europe, that man, considered as man, is thrown back to a vast distance from his Maker, and the artificial chasm filled up by a succession of barriers, or a sort of turnpike gates, through which he has to pass.

I will quote Mr. Burke's catalogue of barriers that he has set up between man and his Maker. Putting himself in the character of a herald, he says—"We fear God—we look with *awe* to kings—with affection to parliaments—with duty to magistrates—with reverence to priests, and with respect to nobility." Mr. Burke has forgotten to put in *"chivalry."* He has also forgotten to put in Peter.

The duty of man is not a wilderness of turnpike gates, through which he is to pass by tickets from one to the other. It is plain and simple, and consists but of two points. His duty to God, which every man must feel; and with respect to his neighbor, to do as he would be done by. If those to whom power is delegated do well, they will be respected; if not, they will be despised; and with regard to those to whom no power is delegated, but who assume it, the rational world can know nothing of them.

Hitherto we have spoken only (and that but in part) of the natural rights of man. We have now to consider the civil rights of man, and to show how the one originates from the other. Man did not enter into society to become *worse* than he was before, nor to have fewer rights than he had before, but to have those rights better secured. His natural rights are the foundation of all his civil rights. But in order to pursue this distinction with more precision, it is necessary to make the different qualities of natural and civil rights.

A few words will explain this. Natural rights are those which appertain to man in right of his existence. Of this kind are all the intellectual rights, or rights of the mind, and also all those rights of acting as an individual for his own comfort and happiness, which are not injurious to the natural rights of others. Civil rights are those which appertain to man in right of his being a member of society.

Every civil right has for its foundation some natural right pre-existing in the individual, but to the enjoyment of which his individual power is not, in all cases, sufficiently competent. Of this kind are all those which relate to security and protection.

From this short review, it will be easy to distinguish between that class of natural rights which man retains after entering into society, and those which he throws into the common stock as a member of society.

The natural rights which he retains, are all those in which the *power* to execute is as perfect in the individual as the right itself. Among this class, as is before mentioned, are all the intellectual rights, or rights of the mind: consequently, religion is one of those rights.

The natural rights which are not retained, are all those in which, though the right is perfect in the individual, the power to execute them is defective. They answer not his purpose. A man, by natural right, has a right to judge in his own cause; and so far as the right of the mind is concerned, he never surrenders it: but what availeth it him to judge, if he has not power to redress? He therefore deposits his right in the common stock of society, and takes the arm of society, of which he is a part, in preference and in addition to his own. Society *grants* him nothing. Every man is proprietor in society, and draws on the capital as a matter of right.

From these premises, two or three certain conclusions will follow.

First, That every civil right grows out of a natural right; or, in other words, is a natural right exchanged.

Secondly, That civil power, properly considered as such, is made up of the aggregate of that class of the natural rights of man, which becomes defective in the individual in point of power, and answers not his purpose, but when collected to a focus, becomes competent to the purpose of every one.

Thirdly, That the power produced from the aggregate of natural rights, imperfect in power in the individual, cannot be applied to invade the natural rights which are retained in the individual, and in which the power to execute is as perfect as the right itself.

We have now, in a few words, traced man from a natural individual to a member of society, and shown, or endeavored to show, the quality of the natural rights retained, and those which are exchanged for civil rights. Let us now apply those principles to governments.

In casting our eyes over the world, it is extremely easy to distinguish the governments which have arisen out of society, or out of the social compact, from those which have not: but to place this in a clearer light than what a single glance may afford, it will be proper to take a review of the several sources from which the governments have arisen, and on which they have been founded.

They may be all comprehended under three heads. First, superstition. Secondly, power. Thirdly, the common interests of society, and the common rights of man.

The first was a government of priestcraft, the second of conquerors, and the third of reason.

When a set of artful men pretended, through the medium of oracles, to hold intercourse with the Deity, as familiarly as they now march up the backstairs in European courts, the world was completely under the government of superstition. The oracles were consulted, and whatever they were made to say, became the law; and this sort of government lasted as long as this sort of superstition lasted.

1791

FROM *The Age of Reason*

In Paris, after his escape from England, Paine wrote *The Age of Reason* (Part I, 1794 Part II, 1796) as an assault on that kind of conservative, organized religion which he believed supported tyranny, superstition, and human misery everywhere. He told Samuel Adams that he hoped by it to stop the people of France, during the violent anticlericalism that characterized the later phases of the French Revolution, from "running into Atheism," and to fix in every man's mind "the first article (as I have said before) of every man's Creed who has any Creed at all, 'I believe in God.'" Unfortunately, his harsh polemics and merciless prose offended the majority of his readers everywhere, who construed the book as an onslaught on Christianity itself and made Paine an object of bitter controversy on both sides of the Atlantic. There were more than thirty-five American replies to *The Age of Reason* within a decade; its author was attacked in press and pulpit as an atheist, Satan's emissary, a drunkard, and a traitor, and he very nearly lost his citizenship. Yet it is clear that in his own fashion Paine considered himself a genuinely religious Christian, and that his book was the most carefully written exposition of deism, or as Paine called it, "the religion of reason," produced during the time. The text follows the Van der Weyde edition of *The Life and Works*.

The Author's Profession of Faith

It has been my intention, for several years past, to publish my thoughts upon religion. I am well aware of the difficulties that attend the subject, and from that consideration, had reserved it to a more advanced period of life. I intended it to be the last offering I should make to my fellow-citizens of all nations, and that at a time when the purity of the motive that induced me to it could not admit of a question, even by those who might disapprove the work. The circumstance that has now taken place in France[1] of the total abolition of the whole national order of priesthood, and of everything appertaining to compulsive systems of religion, and compulsive articles of faith, has not only precipitated my intention, but rendered a work of this kind exceedingly necessary, lest in the general wreck of superstition, of false systems of government and false theology, we lose sight of morality, of humanity and of the theology that is true.

As several of my colleagues, and others of my fellow-citizens of France, have given me the example of making their voluntary and individual profession of faith, I also will make mine; and I do this with all that sincerity and frankness with which the mind of man communicates with itself.

I believe in one God, and no more; and I hope for happiness beyond this life.

I believe in the equality of man; and I believe that religious duties consist in doing justice, loving mercy, and endeavoring to make our fellow-creatures happy.

But, lest it should be supposed that I believe many other things in addition to these, I shall, in the progress of this work, declare the things I do not believe, and my reasons for not believing them.

I do not believe in the creed professed by the Jewish Church, by the Roman Church, by the Greek Church, by the Turkish Church, by the Protestant Church, nor by any church that I know of. My own mind is my own church.

All national institutions of churches, whether Jew-

[1]Acts of the National Convention since 1792.

ish, Christian or Turkish, appear to me no other than human inventions, set up to terrify and enslave mankind, and monopolize power and profit.

I do not mean by this declaration to condemn those who believe otherwise; they have the same right to their belief as I have to mine. But it is necessary to the happiness of man that he be mentally faithful to himself. Infidelity does not consist in believing, or in disbelieving; it consists in professing to believe what he does not believe.

It is impossible to calculate the moral mischief, if I may so express it, that mental lying has produced in society. When a man has so far corrupted and prostituted the chastity of his mind as to subscribe his professional belief to things he does not believe he has prepared himself for the commission of every other crime.

He takes up the trade of a priest for the sake of gain, and in order to qualify himself for that trade he begins with a perjury. Can we conceive any thing more destructive to morality than this?

Soon after I had published the pamphlet "Common Sense," in America, I saw the exceeding probability that a revolution in the system of government would be followed by a revolution in the system of religion. The adulterous connection of church and state, wherever it has taken place, whether Jewish, Christian or Turkish, has so effectually prohibited by pains and penalties every discussion upon established creeds, and upon first principles of religion, that until the system of government should be changed, those subjects could not be brought fairly and openly before the world; but that whenever this should be done, a revolution in the system of religion would follow. Human inventions and priestcraft would be detected; and man would return to the pure, unmixed and unadulterated belief of one God, and no more.

Concerning Missions and Revelations

Every national church or religion has established itself by pretending some special mission from God, communicated to certain individuals. The Jews have their Moses; the Christians their Jesus Christ, their apostles and saints; and the Turks their Mahomet, as if the way to God was not open to every man alike.

Each of those churches show certain books, which they call *revelation,* or the Word of God. The Jews say that their Word of God was given by God to Moses, face to face; the Christians say that their Word of God came by divine inspiration; and the Turks say that their Word of God (the Koran) was brought by an angel from heaven. Each of those churches accuses the other of unbelief; and for my own part, I disbelieve them all.

As it is necessary to affix right ideas to words, I

will, before I proceed further into the subject, offer some observations on the word *revelation*. Revelation, when applied to religion, means something communicated *immediately* from God to man.

No one will deny or dispute the power of the Almighty to make such a communication, if He pleases. But admitting, for the sake of a case, that something has been revealed to a certain person, and not revealed to any other person, it is revelation to that person only. When he tells it to a second person, a second to a third, a third to a fourth, and so on, it ceases to be a revelation to those persons. It is revelation to the first person only, and *hearsay* to every other, and consequently they are not obliged to believe it.

It is a contradiction in terms and ideas, to call anything a revelation that comes to us at second-hand, either verbally or in writing. Revelation is necessarily limited to the first communication—after this it is only an account of something which that person says was a revelation made to him; and though he may find himself obliged to believe it, it cannot be incumbent on me to believe it in the same manner; for it was not a revelation made to *me*, and I have only his word for it that it was made to him. When Moses told the children of Israel that he received the two tables of the commandments from the hands of God, they were not obliged to believe him, because they had no other authority for it than his telling them so; and I have no other authority for it than some historian telling me so. The commandments carry no internal evidence of divinity with them; they contain some good moral precepts, such as any man qualified to be a lawgiver, or a legislator, could produce himself, without having recourse to supernatural intervention.[2]

When I am told that the Koran was written in heaven and brought to Mahomet by an angel, the account comes too near the same kind of hearsay evidence and second-hand authority as the former. I did not see the angel myself and, therefore, I have a right not to believe it.

When also I am told that a woman called the Virgin Mary, said, or gave out, that she was with child without any cohabitation with a man, and that her betrothed husband, Joseph, said that an angel told him so, I have a right to believe them or not; such a circumstance required a much stronger evidence than their bare word for it; but we have not even this—for neither Joseph nor Mary wrote any such matter themselves; it is only reported by others that *they said so*—it is hearsay upon hearsay, and I do not choose to rest my belief upon such evidence.

It is, however, not difficult to account for the credit that was given to the story of Jesus Christ being the Son of God. He was born at a time when the heathen mythology had still some fashion and repute in the world, and that mythology had prepared the people for the belief of such a story. Almost all the extraordinary men that lived under the heathen mythology were reputed to be the sons of some of their gods. It was not a new thing, at that time, to believe a man to have been celestially begotten; the intercourse of gods with women was then a matter of familiar opinion.

Their Jupiter, according to their accounts, had cohabited with hundreds: the story, therefore, had nothing in it either new, wonderful or obscene; it was conformable to the opinions that then prevailed among the people called Gentiles, or Mythologists, and it was those people only that believed it.

The Jews, who had kept strictly to the belief of one God, and no more, and who had always rejected the heathen mythology, never credited the story.

It is curious to observe how the theory of what is called the Christian Church sprung out of the tail of the heathen mythology. A direct incorporation took place in the first instance, by making the reputed founder to be celestially begotten. The trinity of gods that then followed was no other than a reduction of the former plurality, which was about twenty or thirty thousand; the statue of Mary succeeded the statue of Diana of Ephesus; the deification of heroes changed into the canonization of saints; the Mythologists had gods for everything; the Christian Mythologists had saints for everything; the Church became as crowded with the one as the Pantheon had been with the other, and Rome was the place of both. The Christian theory is little else than the idolatry of the ancient Mythologists, accommodated to the purposes of power and revenue; and it yet remains to reason and philosophy to abolish the amphibious fraud. ° ° °

Defining the True Revelation

But some, perhaps, will say: Are we to have no Word of God—no revelation? I answer, Yes; there is a Word of God; there is a revelation.

THE WORD OF GOD IS THE CREATION WE BEHOLD and it is in *this word*, which no human invention can counterfeit or alter, that God speaketh universally to man.

Human language is local and changeable, and is therefore incapable of being used as the means of unchangeable and universal information. The idea that God sent Jesus Christ to publish, as they say, the glad tidings to all nations, from one end of the earth unto the other, is consistent only with the ignorance of those who knew nothing of the extent

---

[2] It is, however, necessary to except the declaration which says that God *visits the sins of the fathers upon the children;* it is contrary to every principle of moral justice. [Paine's note.]

of the world, and who believed, as those world-saviors believed, and continued to believe for several centuries (and that in contradiction to the discoveries of philosophers and the experience of navigators), that the earth was flat like a trencher, and that man might walk to the end of it.

But how was Jesus Christ to make anything known to all nations? He could speak but one language, which was Hebrew, and there are in the world several hundred languages. Scarcely any two nations speak the same language, or understand each other; and as to translations, every man who knows anything of languages knows that it is impossible to translate from one language into another, not only without losing a great part of the original, but frequently mistaking the sense; and besides all this, the art of printing was wholly unknown at the time Christ lived.

It is always necessary that the means that are to accomplish any end be equal to the accomplishment of that end, or the end cannot be accomplished. It is in this that the difference between finite and infinite power and wisdom discovers itself. Man frequently fails in accomplishing his ends, from a natural inability of the power to the purpose, and frequently from the want of wisdom to apply power properly. But it is impossible for infinite power and wisdom to fail as man faileth. The means it uses are always equal to the end; but human language, more especially as there is not an universal language, is incapable of being used as an universal means of unchangeable and uniform information, and therefore it is not the means that God uses in manifesting himself universally to man.

It is only in the CREATION that all our ideas and conceptions of a *Word of God* can unite. The Creation speaks a universal language, independently of human speech or human language, multiplied and various as they be. It is an ever-existing original, which every man can read. It cannot be forged; it cannot be counterfeited; it cannot be lost; it cannot be altered; it cannot be suppressed. It does not depend upon the will of man whether it shall be published or not; it publishes itself from one end of the earth to the other. It preaches to all nations and to all worlds; and this *Word of God* reveals to man all that is necessary for man to know of God.

Do we want to contemplate His power? We see it in the immensity of the creation. Do we want to contemplate His wisdom? We see it in the unchangeable order by which the incomprehensible whole is governed. Do we want to contemplate His munificence? We see it in the abundance with which He fills the earth. Do we want to contemplate His mercy? We see it in His not withholding that abundance even from the unthankful. In fine, do we want to know what God is? Search not the book called the Scripture, which any human hand might make, but the Scripture called the creation.

Concerning God, and the Lights Cast on His Existence and Attributes by the Bible

The only idea man can affix to the name of God is that of a *first cause*, the cause of all things. And incomprehensible and difficult as it is for a man to conceive what a first cause is, he arrives at the belief of it from the tenfold greater difficulty of disbelieving it.

It is difficult beyond description to conceive that space can have no end; but it is more difficult to conceive an end. It is difficult beyond the power of man to conceive an eternal duration of what we call time; but it is more impossible to conceive a time when there shall be no time.

In like manner of reasoning, everything we behold carries in itself the internal evidence that it did not make itself. Every man is an evidence to himself that he did not make himself; neither could his father make himself, nor his grandfather, nor any of his race; neither could any tree, plant or animal make itself; and it is the conviction arising from this evidence that carries us on, as it were, by necessity to the belief of a first cause eternally existing, of a nature totally different to any material existence we know of, and by the power of which all things exist; and this first cause man calls God.

It is only by the exercise of reason that man can discover God. Take away that reason, and he would be incapable of understanding anything; and, in this case, it would be just as consistent to read even the book called the Bible to a horse as to a man. How, then, is it that people pretend to reject reason?

Almost the only parts of the book called the Bible that convey to us any idea of God are some chapters in Job and the 19th Psalm; I recollect no other. Those parts are true *deistical* compositions, for they treat of the *Deity* through His works. They take the book of creation as the Word of God, they refer to no other book, and all the inferences they make are drawn from that volume.

I insert in this place the 19th Psalm, as paraphrased into English verse by Addison. I recollect not the prose, and where I write this I have not the opportunity of seeing it.

"The spacious firmament on high,
With all the blue ethereal sky,
And spangled heavens, a shining frame
Their great original proclaim.
The unwearied sun, from day to day,
Does his Creator's power display;
And publishes to every land
The work of an Almighty hand.

"Soon as the evening shades prevail,
The moon takes up the wondrous tale,
And nightly to the list'ning earth
Repeats the story of her birth;
While all the stars that round her burn,
And all the planets in their turn,
Confirm the tidings as they roll,
And spread the truth from pole to pole.

"What though in solemn silence all
Move round this dark, terrestrial ball?
What though no real voice, nor sound,
Amidst their radiant orbs be found?
In reason's ear they all rejoice
And utter forth a glorious voice,
Forever singing, as they shine,
The hand that made us is divine."

What more does man want to know than that the hand or power that made these things is divine, is omnipotent? Let him believe this with the force it is impossible to repel, if he permits his reason to act, and his rule of moral life will follow of course.

The allusions in Job have, all of them, the same tendency with this Psalm; that of deducing or proving a truth that would be otherwise unknown, from truths already known.

I recollect not enough of the passages in Job to insert them correctly; but there is one occurs to me that is applicable to the subject I am speaking upon. "Canst thou by searching find out God? Canst thou find out the Almighty to perfection?"

I know not how the printers have pointed this passage, for I keep no Bible; but it contains two distinct questions that admit of distinct answers.

First,—Canst thou by searching find out God? Yes; because, in the first place, I know I did not make myself, and yet I have existence; and by *searching* into the nature of other things, I find that no other thing could make itself; and yet millions of other things exist; therefore it is, that I know, by positive conclusion resulting from this search, that there is a power superior to all those things, and that power is God.

Secondly,—Canst thou find out the Almighty to *perfection?* No; not only because the power and wisdom He has manifested in the structure of the creation that I behold is to me incomprehensible, but because even this manifestation, great as it is, is probably but a small display of that immensity of power and wisdom by which millions of other worlds, to me invisible by their distance, were created and continue to exist.

It is evident that both these questions were put to the reason of the person to whom they are supposed to have been addressed; and it is only by admitting the first question to be answered affirmatively that the second could follow. It would have been unnecessary, and even absurd, to have put a second question, more difficult than the first, if the first question had been answered negatively.

The two questions have different objects; the first refers to the existence of God; the second to His attributes; reason can discover the one, but it falls infinitely short in discovering the whole of the other.

I recollect not a single passage in all the writings ascribed to the men called apostles that conveys any idea of what God is. Those writings are chiefly controversial; and the subjects they dwell upon, that of a man dying in agony on a cross, is better suited to the gloomy genius of a monk in a cell, by whom it is not impossible they were written, than to any man breathing the open air of the creation.

The only passage that occurs to me that has any reference to the works of God, by which only His power and wisdom can be known, is related to have been spoken by Jesus Christ as a remedy against distrustful care. "Behold the lilies of the field, they toil not, neither do they spin." This, however, is far inferior to the allusions in Job and in the 19th Psalm; but it is similar in idea, and the modesty of the imagery is correspondent to the modesty of the man. ° ° °

Instead then of studying theology, as is now done out of the Bible and Testament, the meanings of which books are always controverted and the authenticity of which is disproved, it is necessary that we refer to the Bible of the Creation. The principles we discover there are eternal and of divine origin; they are the foundation of all the science that exists in the world, and must be the foundation of theology.

We can know God only through His works. We cannot have a conception of any one attribute but by following some principle that leads to it. We have only a confused idea of His power, if we have not the means of comprehending something of its immensity. We can have no idea of His wisdom, but by knowing the order and manner in which it acts. The principles of science lead to this knowledge; for the Creator of man is the Creator of science, and it is through that medium that man can see God, as it were, face to face.

Could a man be placed in a situation, and endowed with the power of vision, to behold at one view, and to contemplate deliberately, the structure of the universe; to mark the movements of the several planets, the cause of their varying appearances, the unerring order in which they revolve, even to the remotest comet; their connection and dependence on each other, and to know the system of laws established by the Creator, that governs and regulates the whole, he would then conceive, far beyond what any church theology can teach him, the power, the wisdom, the vastness, the munificence of the Creator; he would then see, that all the knowledge man has of science, and that all mechanical arts by which he renders his situation comfortable here, are derived from that source; his mind, exalted by the scene, and convinced by the fact, would increase in gratitude as it increased in knowledge; his religion or his worship would become united with his improvement as a man; any employment he followed, that had any connection with the principles of the creation, as everything of agriculture, of science and of the mechanical arts has, would teach him more of God, and of the gratitude he owes to Him, than any theological Christian sermon he now hears.

Great objects inspire great thoughts; great munificence excites great gratitude; but the groveling tales and doctrines of the Bible and the Testament are fit only to excite contempt.

Though man cannot arrive, at least in this life, at the actual scene I have described, he can demonstrate it, because he has a knowledge of the principles upon which the creation is constructed.[3] We know that the greatest works can be represented in model, and that the universe can be represented by the same means.

The same principles by which we measure an inch, or an acre of ground, will measure to millions in extent. A circle of an inch diameter has the same geometrical properties as a circle that would circumscribe the universe.

The same properties of a triangle that will demonstrate upon paper the course of a ship, will do it on the ocean; and when applied to what are called the heavenly bodies, will ascertain to a minute the time of an eclipse, though these bodies are millions of miles from us. This knowledge is of divine origin, and it is from the Bible of the Creation that man has learned it, and not from the stupid Bible of the Church, that teacheth man nothing.

All the knowledge man has of science and of

machinery, by the aid of which his existence is rendered comfortable upon earth, and without which he would be scarcely distinguishable in appearance and condition from a common animal, comes from the great machine and structure of the universe.

The constant and unwearied observations of our ancestors upon the movements and revolutions of the heavenly bodies, in what are supposed to have been the early ages of the world, have brought this knowledge upon earth. It is not Moses and the prophets, nor Jesus Christ, nor his apostles, that have done it. The Almighty is the great mechanic of the creation; the first philosopher and original teacher of all science. Let us, then, learn to reverence our master, and let us not forget the labors of our ancestors.

Had we, at this day, no knowledge of machinery, and were it possible that man could have a view, as I have before described, of the structure and machinery of the universe, he would soon conceive the idea of constructing some at least of the mechanical works we now have; and the idea so conceived would progressively advance in practice. Or could a model of the universe, such as is called an orrery, be presented before him and put in motion, his mind would arrive at the same idea.

Such an object and such a subject would, while it improved him in knowledge useful to himself as a man and a member of society, as well as entertaining, afford far better matter for impressing him with a knowledge of, and a belief in, the Creator, and of the reverence and gratitude that man owes to Him, than the stupid texts of the Bible and of the Testament, from which, be the talents of the preacher what they may, only stupid sermons can be preached.

If man must preach, let him preach something that is edifying, and from texts that are known to be true.

The Bible of the Creation is inexhaustible in texts. Every part of science, whether connected with the geometry of the universe, with the systems of animal and vegetable life, or with the properties of inanimate matter, is a text as well for devotion as for philosophy—for gratitude as for human improvement. It will perhaps be said, that if such a revolution in the system of religion takes place, every preacher ought to be a philosopher. *Most certainly;* and every house of devotion a school of science.

It has been by wandering from the immutable laws of science, and the light of reason, and setting up an invented thing called revealed religion, that so many wild and blasphemous conceits have been formed of the Almighty.

The Jews have made Him the assassin of the human species to make room for the religion of the Jews. The Christians have made Him the murderer

---

[3] The Bible-makers have undertaken to give us, in the first chapter of Genesis, an account of the Creation; and in doing this, they have demonstrated nothing but their ignorance. They make there to have been three days and three nights, evenings and mornings, before there was a sun; when it is the presence or absence of the sun that is the cause of day and night, and what is called his rising and setting that of morning and evening. Besides, it is a puerile and pitiful idea, to suppose the Almighty to say, Let there be light. It is the imperative manner of speaking that a conjuror uses when he says to his cups and balls, Presto, begone, and most probably has been taken from it; as Moses and his rod are a conjuror and his wand. Longinus calls this expression the sublime; and, by the same rule, the conjuror is sublime too, for the manner of speaking is expressively and grammatically the same. When authors and critics talk of the sublime, they see not how nearly it borders on the ridiculous. The sublime of the critics, like some parts of Edmund Burke's "Sublime and Beautiful," is like a wind-mill just visible in a fog, which imagination might distort into a flying mountain, or an archangel, or a flock of wild geese. [Paine's note.]

of Himself and the founder of a new religion, to supersede and expel the Jewish religion. And to find pretense and admission for these things, they must have supposed His power or His wisdom imperfect, or His will changeable; and the changeableness of the will is imperfection of the judgment.

The philosopher knows that the laws of the Creator have never changed with respect either to the principles of science or the properties of matter. Why, then, is it supposed they have changed with respect to man?

I here close the subject. I have shown in all the foregoing parts of this work that the Bible and the Testament are impositions and forgeries; and I leave the evidence I have produced in proof of it to be refuted, if any one can do it; and I leave the ideas that are suggested in the conclusion of the work to rest on the mind of the reader; certain, as I am, that when opinions are free, either in matters of government or religion, truth will finally and powerfully prevail.

1794–96

Building a New Society

MICHEL-GUILLAUME JEAN DE CRÈVECOEUR [1731–1813]

St. Jean de Crèvecoeur was among the first to perceive the significance of the frontier environment in the development of American society, and the first to observe the "melting pot" at work. He was born into a noble French family in Caen, Normandy, and educated in England. He arrived in Canada in 1754 as a lieutenant with Montcalm's army, specializing in map-making and surveying. About 1759 he came to the American colonies, and in 1765 he took out British citizenship in New York under the name of John Hector St. John. Later he married an American girl, bought a farm in Orange County, sixty miles from New York City, and settled down to an idyllic life as a gentleman farmer.

During the Revolution, however, Crèvecoeur was suspected of Tory sympathies and subjected to such harassment that he returned to France. His *Letters from an American Farmer*, dedicated to the French philosopher Raynal and written in English, was published in London in 1782. In 1783 he returned to New York as French consul to find his wife dead, his house burned, and his three children in a stranger's home. He remained in the United States for nearly ten years, then went back to France where he spent the rest of his life.

Crèvecoeur was an admirer of Rousseau and a child of French romanticism. He found in America exactly what romantic agrarian philosophy prepared him to find—a land of happy husbandmen, living in a free, simple, egalitarian society close to a benevolent nature. "Sentiment and feeling," he once wrote, "are the only guides I know." His portrait of America is both sentimentalized and idealized, but it is nonetheless a perceptive and sympathetic articulation of the feeling that underlay the American dream of the Revolutionary generation.

Further reading: Julia P. Mitchell, *St. Jean de Crèvecoeur*, 1916. S. T. Williams' entry in *The Dictionary of American Biography*. V. L. Parrington, *Main Currents in American Thought*, I (1927), 140–47.

FROM *Letters from an American Farmer*

These "letters," really essays, were written "for the information of a friend in England" and published under the name of "J. Hector St. John, a Farmer in Pennsylvania." Twelve in all, they present a broad and optimistic view of American society, discuss American classes and institutions, and provide information about agriculture, flora, and fauna, under the guise of conversations held with a farmer and his wife. First published in London, the book sold well in both Europe and America; it was reprinted five times in English within ten years, and translated into both French and German. Text: W. B. Trent, ed., *Letters from an American Farmer* (New York, 1904; a reprint of the 1792 edition).

Letter III

What Is an American?

I wish I could be acquainted with the feelings and thoughts which must agitate the heart and present themselves to the mind of an enlightened Englishman, when he first lands on this continent. He must greatly rejoice that he lived at a time to see this fair country discovered and settled; he must necessarily feel a share of national pride, when he views the chain of settlements which embellishes these extended shores. When he says to himself, this is the work of my countrymen, who, when convulsed by factions, afflicted by a variety of miseries and wants, restless and impatient, took refuge here. They brought along with them their national genius, to which they principally owe what liberty they enjoy, and what substance they possess. Here he sees the industry of his native country displayed in a new manner, and traces in their works the embrios of all the arts, sciences, and ingenuity which flourish in Europe. Here he beholds fair cities, substantial villages, extensive fields, an immense country filled with decent houses, good roads, orchards, meadows, and bridges, where an hundred years ago all was wild, woody and uncultivated! What a train of pleasing ideas this fair spectacle must suggest; it is a prospect which must inspire a good citizen with the most heartfelt pleasure. The difficulty consists in the manner of viewing so extensive a scene. He is arrived on a new continent; a modern society offers itself to his contemplation, different from what he had hitherto seen. It is not composed, as in Europe, of great lords who possess every thing, and of a herd of people who have nothing. Here are no aristocratical families, no courts, no kings, no bishops, no ecclesiastical dominion, no invisible power giving to a few a very visible one; no great manufacturers employing thousands, no great refinements of luxury. The rich and the poor are not so far removed from each other as they are in Europe. Some few towns excepted, we are all tillers of the earth, from Nova Scotia to West Florida. We are a people of cultivators, scattered over an immense territory, communicating with each other by means of good roads and navigable rivers, united by the silken bands of mild government, all respecting the laws, without dreading their power, because they are equitable. We are all animated with the spirit of an industry which is unfettered and unrestrained, because each person works for himself. If he travels through our rural districts he views not the hostile castle, and the haughty mansion, contrasted with the clay-built hut and miserable cabbin, where cattle and men help to keep each other warm, and dwell in meanness, smoke, and indigence. A pleasing uniformity of decent competence appears throughout our habitations. The meanest of our log-houses is a dry and comfortable habitation. Lawyer or merchant are the fairest titles our towns afford; that of a farmer is the only appellation of the rural inhabitants of our country. It must take some time ere he can reconcile himself to our dictionary, which is but short in words of dignity, and names of honour. There, on a Sunday, he sees a congregation of respectable farmers and their wives, all clad in neat homespun, well mounted, or riding in their own humble waggons. There is not among them an esquire, saving the unlettered magistrate. There he sees a parson as simple as his flock, a farmer who does not riot on the labour of others. We have no princes, for whom we toil, starve, and bleed: we are the most perfect society now existing in the world. Here man is free as he ought to be; nor is this pleasing equality so transitory as many others are. Many ages will not see the shores of our great lakes replenished with inland nations, nor the unknown bounds of North America entirely peopled. Who can tell how far it extends? Who can tell the millions of men whom it will feed and contain? for no European foot has as yet travelled half the extent of this mighty continent!

The next wish of this traveller will be to know whence came all these people? they are a mixture of English, Scotch, Irish, French, Dutch, Germans, and Swedes. From this promiscuous breed, that race now called Americans have arisen. The eastern provinces must indeed be excepted, as being the unmixed descendents of Englishmen. I have heard many wish that they had been more intermixed also: for my part, I am no wisher, and think it much better as it has happened. They exhibit a most conspicuous figure in this great and variegated picture; they too enter for a great share in the pleasing perspective displayed in these thirteen provinces. I know it is fashionable to reflect on them, but I respect them for what they have done; for the accuracy and wisdom with which they have settled their territory; for the decency of their manners; for their early love of letters; their ancient college, the first in this hemisphere; for their industry; which to me who am but a farmer, is the criterion of everything. There never was a people, situated as they are, who with so ungrateful a soil have done more in so short a time. Do you think that the monarchical ingredients which are more prevalent in other governments, have purged them from all foul stains? Their histories assert the contrary.

In this great American asylum, the poor of Europe have by some means met together, and in consequence of various causes; to what purpose should they ask one another what countrymen they are? Alas, two thirds of them had no country. Can a wretch who wanders about, who works and starves, whose life is a continual scene of sore affliction or pinching penury; can that man call England or any other kingdom his country? A country that had no bread for him, whose fields procured him no harvest, who met with nothing but the frowns of the rich, the severity of the laws, with jails and punishments; who owned not a single foot of the extensive surface of this planet? No! urged by a variety of motives, here they came. Every thing has tended to regenerate them; new laws, a new mode of living, a new social system; here they are become men: in Europe they were as so many useless plants, wanting vegetative mould, and refreshing showers; they withered, and were mowed down by want, hunger, and war; but now by the power of transplantation, like all other plants they have taken root and flourished! Formerly they were not numbered in any civil lists of their country, except in those of the poor; here they rank as citizens. By what invisible power has this surprising metamorphosis been performed? By that of the laws and that of their industry. The laws, the indulgent laws, protect them as they arrive, stamping on them the symbol of adoption; they receive ample rewards for their labours; these accumulated rewards procure them lands; those lands confer on them the title of freemen, and to that title every benefit is affixed which men can possibly require. This is the great operation daily performed by our laws. From whence proceed these laws? From our government. Whence the government? It is derived from the original genius and strong desire of the people ratified and confirmed by the crown. This is the great chain which links us all, this is the picture which every province exhibits, Nova Scotia excepted. There the crown has done all;[1] either there were no people who had genius, or it was not much attended to: the consequence is, that the province is very thinly inhabited indeed; the power

of the crown in conjunction with the musketos has prevented men from settling there. Yet some parts of it flourished once, and it contained a mild harmless set of people. But for the fault of a few leaders, the whole were banished. The greatest political error the crown ever committed in America, was to cut off men from a country which wanted nothing but men!

What attachment can a poor European emigrant have for a country where he had nothing? The knowledge of the language, the love of a few kindred as poor as himself, were the only cords that tied him: his country is now that which gives him land, bread, protection, and consequence: *Ubi panis ibi patria*,[2] is the motto of all emigrants. What then is the American, this new man? He is either an European, or the descendant of an European, hence that strange mixture of blood, which you will find in no other country. I could point out to you a family whose grandfather was an Englishman, whose wife was Dutch, whose son married a French woman, and whose present four sons have now four wives of different nations. *He* is an American, who leaving behind him all his ancient prejudices and manners, receives new ones from the new mode of life he has embraced, the new government he obeys, and the new rank he holds. He becomes an American by being received in the broad lap of our great *Alma Mater*. Here individuals of all nations are melted into a new race of men, whose labours and posterity will one day cause great changes in the world. Americans are the western pilgrims, who are carrying along with them that great mass of arts, sciences, vigour, and industry which began long since in the east; they will finish the great circle. The Americans were once scattered all over Europe; here they are incorporated into one of the finest systems of population which has ever appeared, and which will hereafter become distinct by the power of the different climates they inhabit. The American ought therefore to love this country much better than that wherein either he or his forefathers were born. Here the rewards of his industry follow with equal steps the progress of his labour; his labour is founded on the basis of nature, *self-interest;* can it want a stronger allurement? Wives and children, who before in vain demanded of him a morsel of bread, now, fat and frolicsome, gladly help their father to clear those fields whence exuberant crops are to arise to feed and to clothe them all; without any part being claimed, either by a despotic prince, a rich abbot, or a mighty lord. Here religion demands but little of him; a small voluntary salary to the minister, and gratitude to God; can he refuse these? The American is a new man, who acts upon new principles; he

---

[1] The British removed some ten thousand French Acadians from Nova Scotia in 1755 and gave their land to settlers from New England.

[2] "Where the bread is, there is one's country."

must therefore entertain new ideas, and form new opinions. From involuntary idleness, servile dependence, penury, and useless labour, he has passed to toils of a very different nature, rewarded by ample subsistence.—This is an American.

British America is divided into many provinces, forming a large association, scattered along a coast 1500 miles extent and about 200 wide. This society I would fain examine, at least such as it appears in the middle provinces; if it does not afford that variety of tinges and gradations which may be observed in Europe, we have colours peculiar to ourselves. For instance, it is natural to conceive that those who live near the sea, must be very different from those who live in the woods; the intermediate space will afford a separate and distinct class.

Men are like plants; the goodness and flavour of the fruit proceeds from the peculiar soil and exposition in which they grow. We are nothing but what we derive from the air we breathe, the climate we inhabit, the government we obey, the system of religion we profess, and the nature of our employment. Here you will find but few crimes; these have acquired as yet no root among us. I wish I were able to trace all my ideas; if my ignorance prevents me from describing them properly, I hope I shall be able to delineate a few of the outlines, which are all I propose.

Those who live near the sea, feed more on fish than on flesh, and often encounter that boisterous element. This renders them more bold and enterprising; this leads them to neglect the confined occupations of the land. They see and converse with a variety of people; their intercourse with mankind becomes extensive. The sea inspires them with a love of traffic, a desire of transporting produce from one place to another; and leads them to a variety of resources which supply the place of labour. Those who inhabit the middle settlements, by far the most numerous, must be very different; the simple cultivation of the earth purifies them, but the indulgences of the government, the soft remonstrances of religion, the rank of independent freeholders, must necessarily inspire them with sentiments, very little known in Europe among people of the same class. What do I say? Europe has no such class of men; the early knowledge they acquire, the early bargains they make, give them a great degree of sagacity. As freemen they will be litigious; pride and obstinacy are often the cause of law suits; the nature of our laws and governments may be another. As citizens it is easy to imagine, that they will carefully read the newspapers, enter into every political disquisition, freely blame or censure governors and others. As farmers they will be careful and anxious to get as much as they can, because what they get is their own. As northern men they will love the chearful

cup. As Christians, religion curbs them not in their opinions; the general indulgence leaves every one to think for themselves in spiritual matters; the laws inspect our actions, our thoughts are left to God. Industry, good living, selfishness, litigiousness, country politics, the pride of freemen, religious indifference, are their characteristics. If you recede still farther from the sea, you will come into more modern settlements; they exhibit the same strong lineaments, in a ruder appearance. Religion seems to have still less influence, and their manners are less improved.

Now we arrive near the great woods, near the last inhabited districts; there men seem to be placed still farther beyond the reach of government, which in some measure leaves them to themselves. How can it pervade every corner; as they were driven there by misfortunes, necessity of beginnings, desire of acquiring large tracks of land, idleness, frequent want of oeconomy, ancient debts; the re-union of such people does not afford a very pleasing spectacle. When discord, want of unity and friendship; when either drunkenness or idleness prevail in such remote districts; contention, inactivity, and wretchedness must ensue. There are not the same remedies to these evils as in a long established community. The few magistrates they have, are in general little better than the rest; they are often in a perfect state of war; that of man against man, sometimes decided by blows, sometimes by means of the law; that of man against every wild inhabitant of these venerable woods, of which they are come to dispossess them. There men appear to be no better than carnivorous animals of a superior rank, living on the flesh of wild animals when they can catch them, and when they are not able, they subsist on grain. He who would wish to see America in its proper light, and have a true idea of its feeble beginnings and barbarous rudiments, must visit our extended line of frontiers where the last settlers dwell, and where he may see the first labours of settlement, the mode of clearing the earth, in all their different appearances; where men are wholly left dependent on their native tempers, and on the spur of uncertain industry, which often fails when not sanctified by the efficacy of a few moral rules. There, remote from the power of example, and check of shame, many families exhibit the most hideous parts of our society. They are a kind of forlorn hope, preceding by ten or twelve years the most respectable army of veterans which come after them. In that space, prosperity will polish some, vice and the law will drive off the rest, who uniting again with others like themselves will recede still farther; making room for more industrious people, who will finish their improvements, convert the loghouse into a convenient habitation, and rejoicing that the first heavy labours are finished, will change in a few years that hitherto barbarous country into a fine fertile, well regulated district. Such is our progress, such is the march of the Europeans toward the interior parts of this continent. In all societies there are off-casts; this impure part serves as our precursors or pioneers; my father himself was one of that class, but he came upon honest principles, and was therefore one of the few who held fast; by good conduct and temperance, he transmitted to me his fair inheritance, when not above one in fourteen of his contemporaries had the same good fortune.[3]

Forty years ago this smiling country was thus inhabited; it is now purged, a general decency of manners prevails throughout, and such has been the fate of our best countries.

Exclusive of those general characteristics, each province has its own, founded on the government, climate, mode of husbandry, customs, and peculiarity of circumstances. Europeans submit insensibly to these great powers, and become, in the course of a few generations, not only Americans in general, but either Pennsylvanians, Virginians, or provincials under some other name. Whoever traverses the continent must easily observe those strong differences, which will grow more evident in time. The inhabitants of Canada, Massachuset, the middle provinces, the southern ones will be as different as their climates; their only points of unity will be those of religion and language.

As I have endeavoured to shew you how Europeans become Americans; it may not be disagreeable to shew you likewise how the various Christian sects introduced, wear out, and how religious indifference becomes prevalent. When any considerable number of a particular sect happen to dwell contiguous to each other, they immediately erect a temple, and there worship the Divinity agreeably to their own peculiar ideas. Nobody disturbs them. If any new sect springs up in Europe, it may happen that many of its professors will come and settle in America. As they bring their zeal with them, they are at liberty to make proselytes if they can, and to build a meeting and to follow the dictates of their consciences; for neither the government nor any other power interferes. If they are peaceable subjects, and are industrious, what is it to their neighbours how and in what manner they think fit to address their prayers to the Supreme Being? But if the sectaries are not settled close together, if they are mixed with other denominations, their zeal will cool for want of fuel, and will be extinguished in a little time. Then the Americans become as to religion, what they are as to country, allied to all. In

them the name of Englishman, Frenchman, and European is lost, and in like manner, the strict modes of Christianity as practised in Europe are lost also. This effect will extend itself still farther hereafter, and though this may appear to you as a strange idea, yet it is a very true one. I shall be able perhaps hereafter to explain myself better, in the meanwhile, let the following example serve as my first justification.

Let us suppose you and I to be travelling; we observe that in this house, to the right, lives a Catholic, who prays to God as he has been taught, and believes in transubstantiation; he works and raises wheat, he has a large family of children, all hale and robust; his belief, his prayers offend nobody. About one mile farther on the same road, his next neighbour may be a good honest plodding German Lutheran, who addresses himself to the same God, the God of all, agreeably to the modes he has been educated in, and believes in consubstantiation; by so doing he scandalizes nobody; he also works in his fields, embellishes the earth, clears swamps, &c. What has the world to do with his Lutheran principles? He persecutes nobody, and nobody persecutes him, he visits his neighbours, and his neighbours visit him. Next to him lives a seceder, the most enthusiastic of all sectaries; his zeal is hot and fiery, but separated as he is from others of the same complexion, he has no congregation of his own to resort to, where he might cabal and mingle religious pride with worldly obstinacy. He likewise raises good crops, his house is handsomely painted, his orchard is one of the fairest in the neighbourhood. How does it concern the welfare of the country, or of the province at large, what this man's religious sentiments are, or really whether he has any at all? He is a good farmer, he is a sober, peaceable, good citizen: William Penn himself would not wish for more. This is the visible character, the invisible one is only guessed at, and is nobody's business. Next again lives a Low Dutchman, who implicitly believes the rules laid down by the synod of Dort. He conceives no other idea of a clergyman than that of an hired man; if he does his work well he will pay him the stipulated sum; if not he will dismiss him, and do without his sermons, and let his church be shut up for years. But notwithstanding this coarse idea, you will find his house and farm to be the neatest in all the country; and you will judge by his waggon and fat horses, that he thinks more of the affairs of this world than of those of the next. He is sober and laborious, therefore he is all he ought to be as to the affairs of this life; as for those of the next, he must trust to the great Creator. Each of these people instruct their children as well as they can, but these instructions are feeble compared to those which are given to the youth of the poorest

[3] There is some doubt, however, that Crèvecoeur's father was ever in the American colonies.

class in Europe. Their children will therefore grow up less zealous and more indifferent in matters of religion than their parents. The foolish vanity, or rather the fury of making Proselytes, is unknown here; they have no time, the seasons call for all their attention, and thus in a few years, this mixed neighbourhood will exhibit a strange religious medley, that will be neither pure Catholicism nor pure Calvinism. A very perceptible indifference even in the first generation, will become apparent; and it may happen that the daughter of the Catholic will marry the son of the seceder, and settle by themselves at a distance from their parents. What religious education will they give their children? A very imperfect one. If there happens to be in the neighbourhood any place of worship, we will suppose a Quaker's meeting; rather than not shew their fine clothes, they will go to it, and some of them may perhaps attach themselves to that society. Others will remain in a perfect state of indifference; the children of these zealous parents will not be able to tell what their religious principles are, and their grandchildren still less. The neighbourhood of a place of worship generally leads them to it, and the action of going thither, is the strongest evidence they can give of their attachment to any sect. The Quakers are the only people who retain a fondness for their own mode of worship; for be they ever so far separated from each other, they hold a sort of communion with the society, and seldom depart from its rules, at least in this country. Thus all sects are mixed as well as all nations; thus religious indifference is imperceptibly disseminated from one end of the continent to the other; which is at present one of the strongest characteristics of the Americans. Where this will reach no one can tell, perhaps it may leave a vacuum fit to receive other systems. Persecution, religious pride, the love of contradiction, are the food of what the world commonly calls religion. These motives have ceased here: zeal in Europe is confined; here it evaporates in the great distance it has to travel; there it is a grain of powder inclosed, here it burns away in the open air, and consumes without effect.

But to return to our back settlers. I must tell you, that there is something in the proximity of the woods, which is very singular. It is with men as it is with the plants and animals that grow and live in the forests; they are entirely different from those that live in the plains. I will candidly tell you all my thoughts but you are not to expect that I shall advance any reasons. By living in or near the woods, their actions are regulated by the wildness of the neighbourhood. The deer often come to eat their grain, the wolves to destroy their sheep, the bears to kill their hogs, the foxes to catch their poultry. This surrounding hostility, immediately puts the gun into their hands; they watch these animals, they kill some; and thus by defending their property, they soon become professed hunters; this is the progress; once hunters, farewell to the plough. The chase renders them ferocious, gloomy, and unsociable; a hunter wants no neighbour, he rather hates them, because he dreads the competition. In a little time their success in the woods makes them neglect their tillage. They trust to the natural fecundity of the earth, and therefore do little; carelessness in fencing, often exposes what little they sow to destruction; they are not at home to watch; in order therefore to make up the deficiency, they go oftener to the woods. That new mode of life brings along with it a new set of manners, which I cannot easily describe. These new manners being grafted on the old stock, produce a strange sort of lawless profligacy, the impressions of which are indelible. The manners of the Indian natives are respectable, compared with this European medley. Their wives and children live in sloth and inactivity; and having no proper pursuits, you may judge what education the latter receive. Their tender minds have nothing else to contemplate but the example of their parents; like them they grow up a mongrel breed, half civilized, half savage, except nature stamps on them some constitutional propensities. That rich, that voluptuous sentiment is gone that struck them so forcibly; the possession of their freeholds no longer conveys to their minds the same pleasure and pride. To all these reasons you must add, their lonely situation, and you cannot imagine what an effect on manners the great distances they live from each other has! Consider one of the last settlements in it's first view: of what is it composed? Europeans who have not that sufficient share of knowledge they ought to have, in order to prosper; people who have suddenly passed from oppression, dread of government, and fear of laws, into the unlimited freedom of the woods. This sudden change must have a very great effect on most men, and on that class particularly. Eating of wild meat, whatever you may think, tends to alter their temper; though all the proof I can adduce, is, that I have seen it: and having no place of worship to resort to, what little society this might afford, is denied them. The Sunday meetings, exclusive of religious benefits, were the only social bonds that might have inspired them with some degree of emulation in neatness. Is it then surprising to see men thus situated, immersed in great and heavy labours, degenerate a little? It is rather a wonder the effect is not more diffusive. The Moravians and the Quakers are the only instances in exception to what I have advanced. The first never settle singly, it is a colony of the society which emigrates; they carry with them their forms, worship, rules, and decency: the others never begin so hard, they are always able to buy improvements, in which there is a great advantage, for by that time the country is recovered from its first barbarity. Thus our bad people are those who are half cultivators and half hunters; and the worst of them are those who have degenerated altogether into the hunting state. As old ploughmen and new men of the woods, as Europeans and new made Indians, they contract the vices of both; they adopt the moroseness and ferocity of a native, without his mildness, or even his industry at home. If manners are not refined, at least they are rendered simple and inoffensive by tilling the earth; all our wants are supplied by it, our time is divided between labour and rest, and leaves none for the commission of great misdeeds. As hunters it is divided between the toil of the chase, the idleness of repose, or the indulgence of inebriation. Hunting is but a licentious idle life, and if it does not always pervert good dispositions; yet, when it is united with bad luck, it leads to want: want stimulates that propensity to rapacity and injustice, too natural to needy men, which is the fatal gradation. After this explanation of the effects which follow by living in the woods, shall we yet vainly flatter ourselves with the hope of converting the Indians? We should rather begin with converting our back-settlers; and now if I dare mention the name of religion, its sweet accents would be lost in the immensity of these woods. Men thus placed, are not fit either to receive or remember its mild instructions; they want temples and ministers, but as soon as men cease to remain at home, and begin to lead an erratic life, let them be either tawny or white, they cease to be its disciples.

Thus have I faintly and imperfectly endeavoured to trace our society from the sea to our woods! yet you must not imagine that every person who moves back, acts upon the same principles, or falls into the same degeneracy. Many families carry with them all their decency of conduct, purity of morals, and respect of religion; but these are scarce, the power of example is sometimes irresistible. Even among these back-settlers, their depravity is greater or less, according to what nation or province they belong. Were I to adduce proofs of this, I might be accused of partiality. If there happens to be some rich intervals, some fertile bottoms, in those remote districts, the people will there prefer tilling the land to hunting, and will attach themselves to it; but even on these fertile spots you may plainly perceive the inhabitants to acquire a great degree of rusticity and selfishness.

It is in consequence of this straggling situation, and the astonishing power it has on manners, that the back-settlers of both the Carolinas, Virginia, and many other parts, have been long a set of lawless people; it has been even dangerous to travel among them. Government can do nothing in so extensive a country, better it should wink at these irregularities, than that it should use means inconsistent with its usual mildness. Time will efface those stains: in proportion as the great body of population approaches them they will reform, and become polished and subordinate. Whatever has been said of the four New England provinces, no such degeneracy of manners has ever tarnished their annals; their back-settlers have been kept within the bounds of decency, and government, by means of wise laws, and by the influence of religion. What a detestable idea such people must have given to the natives of the Europeans! They trade with them, the worst of people are permitted to do that which none but persons of the best characters should be employed in. They get drunk with them, and often defraud the Indians. Their avarice, removed from the eyes of their superiors, knows no bounds; and aided by a little superiority of knowledge, these traders deceive them, and even sometimes shed blood. Hence those shocking violations, those sudden devastations which have so often stained our frontiers, when hundreds of innocent people have been sacrificed for the crimes of a few. It was in consequence of such behaviour, that the Indians took the hatchet against the Virginians in 1774. Thus are our first steps trod, thus are our first trees felled, in general, by the most vicious of our people; and thus the path is opened for the arrival of a second and better class, the true American freeholders; the most respectable set of people in this part of the world: respectable for their industry, their happy independence, the great share of freedom they possess, the good regulation of their families, and for extending the trade and the dominion of our mother country.

Europe contains hardly any other distinctions but lords and tenants; this fair country alone is settled by freeholders, the possessors of the soil they cultivate, members of the government they obey, and the framers of their own laws, by means of their representatives. This is a thought which you have taught me to cherish; our difference from Europe, far from diminishing, rather adds to our usefulness and consequence as men and subjects. Had our forefathers remained there, they would only have crouded it, and perhaps prolonged those convulsions which had shook it so long. Every industrious European who transports himself here, may be compared to a sprout growing at the foot of a great tree; it enjoys and draws but a little portion of sap; wrench it from the parent roots, transplant it, and it will become a tree bearing fruit also. Colonists are therefore entitled to the consideration due to the most useful subjects; a hundred families barely existing in some parts of Scotland, will here in six years, cause an annual exportation of 10,000 bushels of wheat:

100 bushels being but a common quantity for an industrious family to sell, if they cultivate good land. It is here then that the idle may be employed, the useless become useful, and the poor become rich; but by riches I do not mean gold and silver, we have but little of those metals; I mean a better sort of wealth, cleared lands, cattle, good houses, good cloaths, and an increase of people to enjoy them.

There is no wonder that this country has so many charms, and presents to Europeans so many temptations to remain in it. A traveller in Europe becomes a stranger as soon as he quits his own kingdom; but it is otherwise here. We know, properly speaking, no strangers; this is every person's country; the variety of our soils, situations, climates, governments, and produce, hath something which must please every body. No sooner does an European arrive, no matter of what condition, than his eyes are opened upon the fair prospect; he hears his language spoke, he retraces many of his own country manners, he perpetually hears the names of families and towns with which he is acquainted; he sees happiness and prosperity in all places disseminated; he meets with hospitality, kindness, and plenty every where; he beholds hardly any poor, he seldom hears of punishments and executions; and he wonders at the elegance of our towns, those miracles of industry and freedom. He cannot admire enough our rural districts, our convenient roads, good taverns, and our many accommodations; he involuntarily loves a country where every thing is so lovely. When in England, he was a mere Englishman; here he stands on a larger portion of the globe, not less than its fourth part, and may see the productions of the north, in iron and naval stores; the provisions of Ireland, the grain of Egypt, the indigo, the rice of China. He does not find, as in Europe, a crouded society, where every place is over-stocked; he does not feel that perpetual collision of parties, that difficulty of beginning, that contention which oversets so many. There is room for every body in America; has he any particular talent, or industry? he exerts it in order to procure a livelihood, and it succeeds. Is he a merchant? the avenues of trade are infinite; is he eminent in any respect? he will be employed and respected. Does he love a country life? pleasant farms present themselves; he may purchase what he wants, and thereby become an American farmer. Is he a labourer, sober and industrious? he need not go many miles, nor receive many informations before he will be hired, well fed at the table of his employer, and paid four or five times more than he can get in Europe. Does he want uncultivated lands? thousands of acres present themselves, which he may purchase cheap. Whatever be his talents or inclinations, if they are moderate, he may satisfy them. I do not mean that every one who comes will grow rich in a little time; no, but he may procure an easy, decent maintenance, by his industry. Instead of starving he will be fed, instead of being idle he will have employment; and these are riches enough for such men as come over here. The rich stay in Europe, it is only the middling and the poor that emigrate. Would you wish to travel in independent idleness, from north to south, you will find easy access, and the most chearful reception at every house; society without ostentation, good cheer without pride, and every decent diversion which the country affords, with little expence. It is no wonder that the European who has lived here a few years, is desirous to remain; Europe with all its pomp, is not to be compared to this continent, for men of middle stations, or labourers.

An European, when he first arrives, seems limited in his intentions, as well as in his views; but he very suddenly alters his scale; two hundred miles formerly appeared a very great distance, it is now but a trifle; he no sooner breathes our air than he forms schemes, and embarks in designs he never would have thought of in his own country. There the plenitude of society confines many useful ideas, and often extinguishes the most laudable schemes which here ripen into maturity. Thus Europeans become Americans.

But how is this accomplished in that croud of low, indigent people, who flock here every year from all parts of Europe? I will tell you; they no sooner arrive than they immediately feel the good effects of that plenty of provisions we possess: they fare on our best food, and are kindly entertained; their talents, character, and peculiar industry are immediately inquired into; they find countrymen every where disseminated, let them come from whatever part of Europe. Let me select one as an epitome of the rest; he is hired, he goes to work, and works moderately; instead of being employed by a haughty person, he finds himself with his equal, placed at the substantial table of the farmer, or else at an inferior one as good; his wages are high, his bed is not like that bed of sorrow on which he used to lie: if he behaves with propriety, and is faithful, he is caressed, and becomes as it were a member of the family. He begins to feel the effects of a sort of resurrection; hitherto he had not lived, but simply vegetated; he now feels himself a man, because he is treated as such; the laws of his own country had overlooked him in his insignificancy; the laws of this cover him with their mantle. Judge what an alteration there must arise in the mind and thoughts of this man; he begins to forget his former servitude and dependence, his heart involuntarily swells and glows; this first swell inspires him with those new thoughts which constitute an American. What love can he entertain for a country where his existence was a burthen to him; if he is a generous good man, the love of this new adoptive parent will sink deep into his heart. He looks around, and sees many a prosperous person, who but a few years before was as poor as himself. This encourages him much, he begins to form some little scheme, the first, alas, he ever formed in his life. If he is wise he thus spends two or three years, in which time he acquires knowledge, the use of tools, the modes of working the lands, felling trees, &c. This prepares the foundation of a good name, the most useful acquisition he can make. He is encouraged, he has gained friends; he is advised and directed, he feels bold, he purchases some land; he gives all the money he has brought over, as well as what he has earned, and trusts to the God of harvests for the discharge of the rest. His good name procures him credit. He is now possessed of the deed, conveying to him and his posterity the fee simple and absolute property of two hundred acres of land, situated on such a river. What an epocha in this man's life! He is become a freeholder, from perhaps a German boor—he is now an American, a Pennsylvanian, an English subject. He is naturalized, his name is enrolled with those of the other citizens of the province. Instead of being a vagrant, he has a place of residence; he is called the inhabitant of such a county, or of such a district, and for the first time in his life counts for something; for hitherto he has been a cypher. I only repeat what I have heard many say, and no wonder their hearts should glow, and be agitated with a multitude of feelings, not easy to describe. From nothing to start into being; from a servant to the rank of a master; from being the slave of some despotic prince, to become a free man, invested with lands, to which every municipal blessing is annexed! What a change indeed! It is in consequence of that change that he becomes an American. This great metamorphosis has a double effect, it extinguishes all his European prejudices, he forgets that mechanism of subordination, that servility of disposition which poverty had taught him; and sometimes he is apt to forget too much, often passing from one extreme to the other. If he is a good man, he forms schemes of future prosperity, he proposes to educate his children better than he has been educated himself; he thinks of future modes of conduct, feels an ardor to labour he never felt before. Pride steps in and leads him to every thing that the laws do not forbid: he respects them; with a heart-felt gratitude he looks toward the east, toward that insular government from whose wisdom all his new felicity is derived, and under whose wings and protection he now lives. These reflections constitute him the good man and the good subject. Ye poor Europeans, ye, who sweat, and work for the great—ye, who are obliged to give so many sheaves to the church, so many to your lords, so many to your government, and have hardly any left for yourselves—ye, who are held in less estimation than favourite hunters or useless lap dogs—ye, who only breathe the air of nature, because it cannot be withheld from you: it is here that ye can conceive the possibility of those feelings I have been describing; it is here the laws of naturalization invite every one to partake of our great labours and felicity, to till unrented, untaxed lands! Many, corrupted beyond the power of amendment, have brought with them all their vices, and disregarding the advantages held to them, have gone on in their former career of iniquity, until they have been overtaken and punished by our laws. It is not every emigrant who succeeds; no, it is only the sober, the honest, and industrious: happy those to whom this transition has served as a powerful spur to labour, to prosperity, and to the good establishment of children, born in the days of their poverty; and who had no other portion to expect but the rags of their parents, had it not been for their happy emigration. Others again, have been led astray by this enchanting scene; their new pride, instead of leading them to the fields, has kept them in idleness; the idea of possessing lands is all that satisfies them—though surrounded with fertility, they have mouldered away their time in inactivity misinformed husbandry, and ineffectual endeavours. How much wiser, in general, the honest Germans than almost all other Europeans; they hire themselves to some of their wealthy landsmen, and in that apprenticeship learn every thing that is necessary. They attentively consider the prosperous industry of others, which imprints in their minds a strong desire of possessing the same advantages. This forcible idea never quits them, they launch forth, and by dint of sobriety, rigid parsimony, and the most persevering industry, they commonly succeed. Their astonishment at their first arrival from Germany is very great—it is to them a dream; the contrast must be powerful indeed; they observe their countrymen flourishing in every place; they travel through whole counties where not a word of English is spoken; and in the names and the language of the people, they retrace Germany. They have been an useful acquisition to this continent, and to Pennsylvania in particular; to them it owes some share of its prosperity: to their mechanical knowledge and patience, it owes the finest mills in all America, the best teams of horses, and many other advantages. The recollection of their former poverty and slavery never quits them as long as they live.

The Scotch and the Irish might have lived in their own country perhaps as poor, but enjoying more civil advantages, the effects of their new situation do not strike them so forcibly, nor has it so lasting an effect. From whence the difference arises I know not, but out of twelve families of emigrants of each country, generally seven Scotch will succeed, nine German, and four Irish. The Scotch are frugal and laborious, but their wives cannot work so hard as German women, who on the contrary vie with their husbands, and often share with them the most severe toils of the field, which they understand better. They have therefore nothing to struggle against, but the common casualties of nature. The Irish do not prosper so well; they love to drink and to quarrel; they are litigious, and soon take to the gun, which is the ruin of every thing; they seem beside to labour under a greater degree of ignorance in husbandry than the others; perhaps it is that their industry had less scope, and was less exercised at home. I have heard many relate, how the land was parcelled out in that kingdom; their ancient conquest has been a great detriment to them, by oversetting their landed property. The lands possessed by a few, are leased down *ad infinitum*, and the occupiers often pay five guineas an acre. The poor are worse lodged there than any where else in Europe; their potatoes, which are easily raised, are perhaps an inducement to laziness: their wages are too low and their whisky too cheap.

There is no tracing observations of this kind, without making at the same time very great allowances, as there are every where to be found, a great many exceptions. The Irish themselves, from different parts of that kingdom, are very different. It is difficult to account for this surprising locality, one would think on so small an island an Irishman must be an Irishman: yet it is not so, they are different in their aptitude to, and in their love of labour.

The Scotch on the contrary are all industrious and saving; they want nothing more than a field to exert themselves in, and they are commonly sure of succeeding. The only difficulty they labour under is, that technical American knowledge which requires some time to obtain; it is not easy for those who seldom saw a tree, to conceive how it is to be felled, cut up, and split into rails and posts.

As I am fond of seeing and talking of prosperous families, I intend to finish this letter by relating to you the history of an honest Scotch Hebridean, who came here in 1774, which will shew you in epitome, what the Scotch can do, wherever they have room for the exertion of their industry. Whenever I hear of any new settlement, I pay it a visit once or twice a year, on purpose to observe the different steps each settler takes, the gradual improvements, the different tempers of each family, on which their prosperity in a great nature depends; their different modifications of industry, their ingenuity, and contrivance; for being all poor, their life requires sagacity and prudence. In an evening I love to hear them tell their stories, they furnish me with new ideas; I sit still and listen to their ancient misfortunes, observing in many of them a strong degree of gratitude to God, and the government. Many a well meant sermon have I preached to some of them. When I found laziness and inattention to prevail, who could refrain from wishing well to these new countrymen; after having undergone so many fatigues. Who could withhold good advice? What a happy change it must be, to descend from the high, sterile, bleak lands of Scotland, where every thing is barren and cold, to rest on some fertile farms in these middle provinces! Such a transition must have afforded the most pleasing satisfaction.

The following dialogue passed at an out-settlement, where I lately paid a visit:

Well, friend, how do you do now; I am come fifty odd miles on purpose to see you; how do you go on with your new cutting and slashing? Very well, good Sir, we learn the use of the axe bravely, we shall make it out; we have a belly full of victuals every day, our cows run about, and come home full of milk, our hogs get fat of themselves in the woods: Oh, this is a good country! God bless the king, and William Penn; we shall do very well by and by, if we keep our healths. Your loghouse looks neat and light, where did you get these shingles? One of our neighbours is a New-England man, and he shewed us how to split them out of chestnut-trees. Now for a barn, but all in good time, here are fine trees to build with. Who is to frame it, sure you don't understand that work yet? A countryman of ours who has been in America these ten years, offers to wait for his money until the second crop is lodged in it. What did you give for your land? Thirty-five shillings per acre, payable in seven years. How many acres have you got? An hundred and fifty. That is enough to begin with; is not your land pretty hard to clear? Yes, Sir, hard enough, but it would be harder still if it was ready cleared, for then we should have no timber, and I love the woods much; the land is nothing without them. Have not you found out any bees yet? No, Sir; and if we had we should not know what to do with them. I will tell you by and by. You are very kind. Farewell, honest man, God prosper you; whenever you travel toward °°, enquire for J. S. he will entertain you kindly, provided you bring him good tidings from your family and farm. In this manner I often visit them, and carefully examine their houses, their modes of ingenuity, their different ways; and make them all relate all they know, and describe all they feel. These are scenes which I believe you would willingly share with me. I well remember your philanthropic turn of mind. Is it not better to contemplate under these humble roofs, the rudiments of future wealth and population, than to behold the accumulated bundles of litigious papers in the office of a lawyer? To examine how the world is gradually settled, how the howling swamp is converted into a pleasing meadow, the rough ridge into a fine field; and to hear the chearful whistling, the rural song, where there was no sound heard before, save the yell of the savage, the screech of the owl, or the hissing of the snake? Here an European, fatigued with luxury, riches, and pleasures, may find a sweet relaxation in a series of interesting scenes, as affecting as they are new. England, which now contains so many domes, so many castles, was once like this; a place woody and marshy; its inhabitants, now the favourite nation for arts and commerce, were once painted like our neighbours. The country will flourish in its turn, and the same observations will be made which I have just delineated. Posterity will look back with avidity and pleasure, to trace, if possible, the aera of this or that particular settlement.

Pray, what is the reason that the Scots are in general more religious, more faithful, more honest, and industrious than the Irish? I do not mean to insinuate national reflections, God forbid! It ill becomes any man, and much less an American; but as I know men are nothing of themselves, and that they owe all their different modifications either to government or other local circumstances, there must be some powerful causes which constitute this great national difference.

Agreeable to the account which severale Scotchmen have given me of the north of Britain, of the Orkneys, and the Hebride Islands, they seem, on many accounts, to be unfit for the habitation of men; they appear to be calculated only for great sheep pastures. Who then can blame the inhabitants of these countries for transporting themselves hither? This great continent must in time absorb the poorest part of Europe; and this will happen in proportion as it becomes better known; and as war, taxation, oppression, and misery increase there. The Hebrides appear to be fit only for the residence of malefactors, and it would be much better to send felons there than either to Virginia or Maryland. What a strange compliment has our mother country paid to two of the finest provinces in America! England has entertained in that respect very mistaken ideas; what was intended as a punishment, is become the good fortune of several; many of those who have been transported as felons, are now rich, and strangers to the stings of those wants that urged them to violations of the law: they are become industrious, exemplary, and useful citizens. The English government should purchase the most northern and barren of those islands; it should send over to us the honest, primitive Hebrideans, settle them here on good lands, as a reward for their virtue and ancient poverty; and replace them with a colony of her wicked sons. The severity of the climate, the inclemency of the seasons, the sterility of the soil, the tempestuousness of the sea, would afflict and punish enough. Could there be found a spot better adapted to retaliate the injury it had received by their crimes? Some of those islands might be considered as the hell of Great Britain, where all evil spirits should be sent. Two essential ends would be answered by this simple operation. The good people, by emigration, would be rendered happier; the bad ones would be placed where they ought to be. In a few years the dread of being sent to that wintry region would have a much stronger effect, than that of transportation.—This is no place of punishment; were I a poor hopeless, breadless Englishman, and not restrained by the power of shame, I should be very thankful for the passage. It is of very little importance how, and in what manner an indigent man arrives; for if he is but sober, honest, and industrious he has nothing more to ask of heaven. Let him go to work, he will have opportunities enough to earn a comfortable support, and even the means of procuring some land; which ought to be the utmost wish of every person who has health and hands to work. I knew a man who came to this country, in the literal sense of the expression, stark naked; I think he was a Frenchman, and a sailor on board an English man of war. Being discontented, he had stripped himself and swam ashore; where finding clothes and friends, he settled afterwards at Maraneck, in the county of Chester, in the province of New-York: he married and left a good farm to each of his sons I knew another person who was but twelve years old when he was taken on the frontiers of Canada, by the Indians; at his arrival at Albany he was purchased by a gentleman, who generously bound him apprentice to a taylor. He lived to the age of ninety, and left behind him a fine estate and a numerous family, all well settled; many of them I am acquainted with.—Where is then the industrious European who ought to despair?

After a foreigner from any part of Europe is arrived, and become a citizen; let him devoutly listen to the voice of our great parent, which says to him, "Welcome to my shores, distressed European; bless the hour in which thou didst see my verdant fields, my fair navigable rivers, and my green mountains!—If thou wilt work, I have bread for thee; if thou wilt be honest, sober, and industrious, I have greater rewards to confer on thee—ease and independence. I will give thee fields to feed and cloath thee; a comfortable fire-side to sit by, and tell thy children by what means thou hast prospered; and a decent bed to repose on. I shall endow thee beside with the immunities of a freeman. If thou wilt carefully educate thy children, teach them gratitude to God, and reverence to that government, that philanthropic government, which has collected here so many men and made them happy. I will also provide for thy progeny; and to every good man this ought to be the most holy, the most powerful, the most earnest wish he can possibly form, as well as the most consolatory prospect when he dies. Go thou and work and till;

thou shalt prosper, provided thou be just, grateful and industrious."

1782

THOMAS JEFFERSON [1743–1826]

THOMAS JEFFERSON was born into one of Virginia's First Families and related by marriage and friendship to most of the others. Educated at William and Mary College, he read law under the great teacher George Wythe and was admitted to the Virginia bar. As a youth he inherited a large family estate and a modest fortune; later, from his wife, he gained forty thousand additional acres and a hundred more slaves. However, he found little to interest him in the life of a wealthy plantation aristocrat or in legal practice, and he soon embarked on the most remarkable public career in American history. He was almost constantly in the service of his colony, state, and nation from 1769, when he entered the Virginia House of Burgesses, until 1809, when he retired from the Presidency after declining a third term. He served as member of the Continental Congress, as governor of Virginia, as Minister to France, as Secretary of State, as Vice President, and as President. After his retirement to his beloved home, Monticello, near Charlottesville, he continued through his correspondence and his circle of friends to serve his nation as adviser, elder statesman, and example. Perhaps no one man, with the possible exception of Washington, had more influence on the early history of the United States.

Jefferson, thirty-seven years younger than Franklin, was like him an excellent representative of the American Enlightenment. He ranged with ease and authority over law, science, history, philosophy, architecture, the classics, art, music, and almost every aspect of the knowledge of his age. He established the design of American public education; he was chiefly responsible for the development of the American two-party system; he bought Louisiana and much of the West from Napoleon and sent Lewis and Clark to open it; he evolved the parliamentary procedures which are still practiced in Congress; his books formed the nucleus of the Library of Congress; and he was most certainly, as his state papers and correspondence show, one of the greatest of American political philosophers.

Jefferson's political creed rested on his ultimate faith that man had "capacity for improvement, for learning and understanding himself and the world." He had too much experience with human nature to trust it completely, but he was confident that under proper conditions, men could be relied upon to think and do the right thing—if they were free, educated, and "habituated to think for themselves and to follow reason as their guides." For this reason he favored a government which diffused political power through an educated, enlightened people, the majority of whom he believed "competent to judge of the facts occurring in ordinary life." His philosophy of government, reduced to a single key idea, was *freedom*, governed by reason and justice. His statement to Benjamin Rush in 1800 expressed it best: "I have sworn," he wrote, "upon the altar of God, eternal hostility against every form of tyranny over the mind of man." Significantly, he chose for his epitaph the three achievements—political, religious, intellectual—for which he wished to be remembered, making no mention of any political office he ever held:

Here was buried Thomas Jefferson
Author of the Declaration of Independence,
of the Statute of Virginia for Religious freedom,
and Father of the University of Virginia.

Jefferson's innate rationalism and his interest in science led him in his religious beliefs toward his own personal variety of deism. Reticent about what he believed, for he thought that religion "is a matter which lies solely between a man and his God," he once remarked that "I am a sect for myself, as far as I know." However, he was an Episcopalian, born, married, and buried under the rites of his church and a lifelong parishioner of it. He believed, as his letters show, in the excellence of New Testament Christianity, feeling that the moral and ethical doctrines of Jesus were "the most pure and perfect" of all teachings and the best possible guides to mankind.

Further reading: Nathan Schachner, *Thomas Jefferson,* 2 vols., 1951. S. G. Brown, *Thomas Jefferson,* 1963. E. T. Martin, *Thomas Jefferson, Scientist,* 1952. Adrienne Koch, *The Philosophy of Thomas Jefferson,* 1943. C. M. Wiltse, *The Jeffersonian Tradition in American Democracy,* 1935. M. D. Peterson, *The Jeffersonian Image in the American Mind,* 1960. Carl Becker, *The Declaration of Independence,* 1922.

The Declaration of Independence

Drafting of the Declaration was initiated by Richard Henry Lee's motion in Continental Congress of June 7, 1776. On June 11 Congress appointed Jefferson, Franklin, Adams, Sherman, and Livingston as a committee to draft the document; Jefferson's copy of the "rough draft" includes changes made by himself, Adams, Franklin, and members of the committee, before its presentation to Congress. It was Jefferson who gave a new direction to the course of American democratic philosophy when in his draft version he altered the customary trio of natural rights, commonly accepted by the English Enlightenment, from "life, liberty, and property," to read "life, liberty, and the pursuit of happiness." Texts: Julian Boyd, editor, *The Papers of Thomas Jefferson* (Princeton, 1950), I, 423–32.

Jefferson's "Original Rough Draught"

A Declaration of the Representatives of the UNITED STATES OF AMERICA, in General Congress assembled.

When in the course of human events it becomes necessary for a people to advance from that subordination in which they have hitherto remained, & to assume among the powers of the earth the equal & independant station to which the laws of nature & of nature's god entitle them, a decent respect to the opinions of mankind requires that they should declare the causes which impel them to the change.

We hold these truths to be sacred & undeniable; that all men are created equal & independant, that from that equal creation they derive rights inherent & inalienable, among which are the preservation of life, & liberty, & the pursuit of happiness; that to secure these ends, governments are instituted among men, deriving their just powers from the consent of the governed; that whenever any form of government shall become destructive of these ends, it is

the right of the people to alter or to abolish it, & to institute new government, laying it's foundation on such principles & organising it's powers in such form, as to them shall seem most likely to effect their safety & happiness. prudence indeed will dictate that governments long established should not be changed for light & transient causes: and accordingly all experience hath shewn that mankind are more disposed to suffer while evils are sufferable, than to right themselves by abolishing the forms to which they are accustomed. but when a long train of abuses & usurpations, begun at a distinguished period, & pursuing invariably the same object, evinces a design to subject them to arbitrary power, it is their right, it is their duty, to throw off such government & to provide new guards for their future security. such has been the patient sufferance of these colonies; & such is now the necessity which constrains them to expunge their former systems of government. the history of his present majesty, is a history of unremitting injuries and usurpations, among which no one fact stands single or solitary to contradict the uniform tenor of the rest, all of which have in direct object the establishment of an absolute tyranny over these states. to prove this, let facts be submitted to a candid world, for the truth of which we pledge a faith yet unsullied by falsehood.

he has refused his assent to laws the most wholesome and necessary for the public good:

he has forbidden his governors to pass laws of immediate & pressing importance, unless suspended in their operation till his assent should be obtained; and when so suspended, he has neglected utterly to attend to them.

he has refused to pass other laws for the accomodation of large districts of people unless those people would relinquish the right of representation, a right inestimable to them, & formidable to tyrants alone:

he has dissolved Representative houses repeatedly & continually, for opposing with manly firmness his invasions on the rights of the people:

he has refused for a long space of time to cause others to be elected, whereby the legislative powers, incapable of annihilation, have returned to the people at large for their exercise, the state remaining in the mean time exposed to all the dangers of invasion from without, & convulsions within:

he has endeavored to prevent the population of these states; for that purpose obstructing the laws for naturalization of foreigners; refusing to pass others to encourage their migrations hither; & raising the conditions of new appropriations of lands:

he has suffered the administration of justice totally to cease in some of these colonies, refusing his assent to laws for establishing judiciary powers:

he has made our judges dependant on his will alone, for the tenure of their offices, and amount of their salaries:

he has erected a multitude of new offices by a self-assumed power, & sent hither swarms of officers to harrass our people & eat out their substance:

he has kept among us in times of peace standing armies & ships of war:

he has affected to render the military, independant of & superior to the civil power:

he has combined with others to subject us to a jurisdiction foreign to our constitutions and unacknoleged by our laws; giving his assent to their pretended acts of legislation, for quartering large bodies of armed troops among us;

> for protecting them by a mock-trial from punishment for any murders they should commit on the inhabitants of these states;
>
> for cutting off our trade with all parts of the world;
>
> for imposing taxes on us without our consent;
>
> for depriving us of the benefits of trial by jury;
>
> for transporting us beyond seas to be tried for pretended offences:
>
> for taking away our charters, & altering fundamentally the forms of our governments;
>
> for suspending our own legislatures & declaring themselves invested with power to legislate for us in all cases whatsoever:

he has abdicated government here, withdrawing his governors, & declaring us out of his allegiance & protection:

he has plundered our seas, ravaged our coasts, burnt our towns & destroyed the lives of our people:

he is at this time transporting large armies of foreign mercenaries to compleat the works of death, desolation & tyranny, already begun with circumstances of cruelty & perfidy unworthy the head of a civilized nation:

he has endeavored to bring on the inhabitants of our frontiers the merciless Indian savages, whose known rule of warfare is an undistinguished destruction of all ages, sexes, & conditions of existence:

he has incited treasonable insurrections in our fellow-subjects, with the allurements of forfeiture & confiscation of our property:

he has waged cruel war against human nature itself, violating it's most sacred rights of life & liberty in the persons of a distant people who never offended him, captivating & carrying them into slavery in another hemisphere, or to incur miserable death in their transportation thither. this piratical warfare, the opprobrium of *infidel* powers, is the warfare of the CHRISTIAN king of Great Britain, determined to keep open a market where MEN should be bought & sold, he has prostituted his negative for suppressing every legislative attempt to prohibit or to restrain this execrable commerce: and that this assemblage of horrors might want no fact of distinguished die, he is now exciting those very people to rise in arms among us, and to purchase that liberty of which *he* has deprived them, by murdering the people upon whom *he* also obtruded them; thus paying off former crimes committed against the *liberties* of one people, with crimes which he urges them to commit against the *lives* of another.

in every stage of these oppressions we have petitioned for redress in the most humble terms; our repeated petitions have been answered by repeated injury. a prince whose character is thus marked by every act which may define a tyrant, is unfit to be the ruler of a people who mean to be free. future ages will scarce believe that the hardiness of one man, adventured within the short compass of 12 years only, on so many acts of tyranny without a mask, over a people fostered & fixed in principles of liberty.

Nor have we been wanting in attentions to our British brethren. we have warned them from time to time of attempts by their legislature to extend a jurisdiction over these our states. we have reminded them of the circumstances of our emigration & settlement here, no one of which could warrant so strange a pretension: that these were effected at the expence of our own blood & treasure, unassisted by the wealth or the strength of Great Britain: that in constituting indeed our several forms of government, we had adopted one common king, thereby laying a foundation for perpetual league & amity with them: but that submission to their parliament was no part of our constitution, nor ever in idea, if history may be credited: and we appealed to their native justice & magnanimity, as well as to the ties of our common kindred to disavow these usurpations which were likely to interrupt our correspondence & connection. they too have been deaf to the voice of justice & of consanguinity, & when occasions have been given them, by the regular course of their laws, of removing from their councils the disturbers of our harmony, they have by their free election re-established them in power. at this very time too they are permitting their chief magistrate to send over not only soldiers of our common blood, but Scotch & foreign mercenaries to invade & deluge us in blood. these facts have given the last stab to agonizing affection, and manly spirit bids us to renounce for ever these unfeeling brethren. we must endeavor to forget our former love for them, and to hold them as we hold the rest of mankind, enemies in war, in peace friends. we might have been a free & a great people together; but a communication of grandeur & of freedom it seems is below their dignity. be it so, since they will have it: the road to glory & happiness is open to us too; we will climb it in a separate state, and acquiesce in the necessity which pronounces our everlasting Adieu!

We therefore the representatives of the United States of America in General Congress assembled do, in the name & by authority of the good people of these states, reject and renounce all allegiance & subjection to the kings of Great Britain & all others who may hereafter claim by, through, or under them; we utterly dissolve & break off all political connection which may have heretofore subsisted between us & the people or parliament of Great Britain; and finally we do assert and declare these colonies to be free and independant states, and that as free & independant states they shall hereafter have power to levy war, conclude peace, contract alliances, establish commerce, & to do all other acts and things which independant states may of right do. And for the support of this declaration we mutually pledge to each other our lives, our fortunes, & our sacred honour.

As Adopted by Congress

IN CONGRESS, JULY 4, 1776.

THE UNANIMOUS DECLARATION OF THE THIRTEEN UNITED STATES OF AMERICA,

When in the Course of human events, it becomes necessary for one people to dissolve the political bands which have connected them with another, and to assume among the powers of the earth, the separate and equal station to which the Laws of Nature and of Nature's God entitle them, a decent respect to the opinions of mankind requires that they should declare the causes which impel them to the separation. We hold these truths to be self-evident, that all men are created equal, that they are endowed by their Creator with certain unalienable Rights, that among these are Life, Liberty and the pursuit of Happiness. That to secure these rights, Governments are instituted among Men, deriving their just powers from the consent of the governed, That whenever any Form of Government becomes destructive of these ends, it is the Right of the People to alter or to abolish it, and to institute new Government, laying its foundation on such principles and organizing its powers in such form, as to them shall seem most likely to effect their Safety and Happiness. Prudence, indeed, will dictate that Governments long established should not be changed for light and transient causes; and accordingly all experience hath shewn, that mankind are more disposed to suffer, while evils are sufferable, than to right themselves by abolishing the forms to which they are accustomed. But when a long train of abuses and usurpations, pursuing invariably the same Object evinces a design to reduce them under absolute Despotism, it is their right, it is their duty, to throw off such Government, and to provide new Guards for their future security. Such has been the patient sufferance of these Colonies; and such is now the necessity which constrains them to alter their former Systems of Government. The history of the present King of Great Britain is a history of repeated injuries and usurpations, all having in direct object the establishment of an absolute Tyranny over these States. To prove this, let Facts be submitted to a candid world. He has refused his Assent to Laws, the most wholesome and necessary for the public good. He has forbidden his Governors to pass Laws of immediate and pressing importance, unless suspended in their operation till his Assent should be obtained; and when so suspended, he has utterly neglected to attend to them. He has refused to pass other Laws for the accommodation of large districts of people, unless those people would relinquish the right of Representation in the Legislature, a right inestimable to them and formidable to tyrants only. He has called together legislative bodies at places unusual, uncomfortable, and distant from the depository of their public Records, for the sole purpose of fatiguing them into compliance with his measures. He has dissolved Representative Houses repeatedly, for opposing with manly firmness his invasions on the rights of the people. He has refused for a long time, after such dissolutions, to cause others to be elected; whereby the Legislative powers, incapable of Annihilation, have returned to the People at large for their exercise; the State remaining in the mean time exposed to all the dangers of invasion from without, and convulsions within. He has endeavoured to prevent the population of these States; for that purpose obstructing the Laws for Naturalization of Foreigners; refusing to pass others to encourage their migrations hither, and raising the conditions of new Appropriations of Lands. He has obstructed the Administration of Justice, by refusing his Assent to Laws for establishing Judiciary powers. He has made Judges dependent on his Will alone, for the tenure of their offices, and the amount and payment of their salaries. He has erected a multitude of New Offices, and sent hither swarms of Officers to harrass our people, and eat out their substance. He has kept among us, in times of peace, standing Armies without the Consent of our legislatures. He has affected to render the Military independent of and superior to the Civil power. He has combined with others to subject us to a jurisdiction foreign to our constitution, and unacknowledged by our laws; giving his Assent to their Acts of pretended Legislation: For Quartering large bodies of armed troops among us: For protecting them, by a mock Trial, from punishment for any Murders which they should commit on the Inhabitants of these States: For cutting off our Trade with all parts of the world: For imposing Taxes on us without our Consent: For depriving us in many cases of the benefits of Trial by Jury: For transporting us beyond Seas to be tried for pretended offences: For abolishing the free System of English Laws in a neighbouring Province, establishing therein an Arbitrary government, and enlarging its Boundaries so as to render it at once an example and fit instrument for introducing the same absolute rule into these Colonies: For taking away our Charters, abolishing our most valuable Laws, and altering fundamentally the Forms of our Governments: For suspending our own Legislatures, and declaring themselves invested with power to legislate for us in all cases whatsoever. He has abdicated Government here, by declaring us out of his Protection and waging War against us. He has plundered our seas, ravaged our Coasts, burnt our towns, and destroyed the Lives of our people. He is at this time transporting large Armies of foreign Mercenaries to compleat the works of death, desolation and tyranny, already begun with circumstances of Cruelty & perfidy scarcely paralleled in the most barbarous ages, and totally unworthy the Head of a civilized nation. He has constrained our fellow Citizens taken Captive on the high Seas to bear Arms against their Country, to become the executioners of their friends and Brethren, or to fall themselves by their Hands. He has excited domestic insurrections amongst us, and has endeavoured to bring on the inhabitants of our frontiers, the merciless Indian Savages, whose known rule of warfare, is an undistin-

guished destruction of all ages, sexes and conditions. In every stage of these Oppressions We have Petitioned for Redress in the most humble terms: Our repeated Petitions have been answered only by repeated injury. A Prince, whose character is thus marked by every act which may define a Tyrant, is unfit to be the ruler of a free people. Nor have We been wanting in attentions to our Brittish brethren. We have warned them from time to time of attempts by their legislature to extend an unwarrantable jurisdiction over us. We have reminded them of the circumstances of our emigration and settlement here. We have appealed to their native justice and magnanimity, and we have conjured them by the ties of our common kindred to disavow these usurpations, which would inevitably interrupt our connections and correspondence. They too have been deaf to the voice of justice and of consanguinity. We must, therefore, acquiesce in the necessity, which denounces our Separation, and hold them, as we hold the rest of mankind, Enemies in War, in Peace Friends.

We, therefore, the Representatives of the united States of America, in General Congress, Assembled, appealing to the Supreme Judge of the world for the rectitude of our intentions, do, in the Name, and by Authority of the good People of these Colonies, solemnly publish and declare, That these United Colonies are, and of Right ought to be Free and Independent States; that they are Absolved from all Allegiance to the British Crown, and that all political connection between them and the State of Great Britain, is and ought to be totally dissolved; and that as Free and Independent States, they have full Power to levy War, conclude Peace, contract Alliances, establish Commerce, and to do all other Acts and Things which Independent States may of right do. And for the support of this Declaration, with a firm reliance on the protection of divine Providence, we mutually pledge to each other our Lives, our Fortunes and our sacred Honor.

FROM *Notes on Virginia*

The range and depth of Jefferson's learning were never better illustrated than in the *Notes on Virginia*, which had its inception in a series of questions about his native state asked of Jefferson by the Marquis de Barbé-Marbois, Secretary of the French Legation at Philadelphia. Jefferson's reply opened with seven chapters on the geography, climate, and natural resources of Virginia, while the remaining sixteen dealt with its history and its social and political institutions. The *Notes* were printed privately in Paris in 1784 for circulation among Jefferson's friends, and an English edition was authorized in 1787. Text: A. A. Lipscomb and A. E. Bergh, eds., *The Writings of Thomas Jefferson* (Washington, 1903–5).

In enumerating the defects of the Constitution, it would be wrong to count among them what is only the error of particular persons. In December 1776, our circumstances being much distressed, it was proposed in the house of delegates to create a *dictator*, invested with every power legislative, executive, and judiciary, civil and military, of life and of death, over our persons and over our properties; and in June 1781, again under calamity, the same proposition was repeated, and wanted a few votes only of being passed. One who entered into this contest from a pure love of liberty, and a sense of injured rights, who determined to make every sacrifice, and to meet every danger, for the re-establishment of those rights on a firm basis, who did not mean to expend his blood and substance for the wretched purpose of changing this matter for that, but to place the powers of governing him in a plurality of hands of his own choice, so that the corrupt will of no one man might in future oppress him, must stand confounded and dismayed when he is told, that a considerable portion of that plurality had mediated the surrender of them into a single hand, and, in lieu of a limited monarchy, to deliver him over to a despotic one! How must we find his efforts and sacrifices abused and baffled, if he may still, by a single vote, be laid prostrate at the feet of one man! In God's name, from whence have they derived this power? Is it from our ancient laws? None such can be produced. Is it from any principle in our new Constitution expressed or implied? Every lineament expressed or implied, is in full opposition to it. Its fundamental principle is, that the State shall be governed as a commonwealth. It provides a republican organization, proscribes under the name of *prerogative* the exercise of all powers undefined by the laws; places on this basis the whole system of our laws; and by consolidating them together, chooses that they should be left to stand or fall together, never providing for any circumstances, nor admitting that such could arise, wherein either should be suspended; no, not for a moment. Our ancient laws expressly declare, that those who are but delegates themselves shall not delegate to others powers which require judgment and integrity in their exercise. Or was this proposition moved on a supposed right in the movers, of abandoning their posts in a moment of distress? The same laws forbid the abandonment of that post, even on ordinary occasions; and much more a transfer of their powers into other hands and other forms, without consulting the people. They never admit the idea that these, like sheep or cattle, may be given from hand to hand without an appeal to their own will. Was it from the necessity of the case? Necessities which dissolve a government, do not convey its authority to an oligarchy or a monarchy. They throw back, into the hands of the people, the powers they had delegated, and leave them as individuals to shift for themselves. A leader may offer, but not impose himself, nor be imposed on them. Much less can their necks be submitted to his sword, their breath to be held at his will or caprice. The necessity which should operate these tremendous effects should at least be palpable and irresistible. Yet in both instances, where it was feared, or pretended with us, it was belied by the event. It was belied, too, by the preceding experience of our sister States, several of whom had grappled through greater difficulties without abandoning their forms of government. When the proposition was first made, Massachusetts had found even the government of committees sufficient to carry them through an invasion. But we at the time of that proposition, were under no invasion. When the second was made, there had been added to this example those of Rhode Island, New York, New Jersey, and Pennsylvania, in all of which the republican form had been found equal to the task of carrying them through the severest trials. In this State alone did there exist so little virtue, that fear was to be fixed in the hearts of the people, and to become the motive of their exertions, and principle of their government? The very thought alone was treason against the people; was treason against mankind in general; as riveting forever the chains which bow down their necks, by giving to their oppressors a proof, which they would have trumpeted through the universe, of the imbecility of republican government, in times of pressing danger, to shield them from harm. Those who assume the right of giving away the reins of government in any case, must be sure that the herd, whom they hand on to the rods and hatchet of the dictator, will lay their necks on the block when he shall nod to them. But if our assemblies supposed such a recognition in the people, I hope they mistook their character. I am of opinion, that the government, instead of being braced and invigorated for greater exertions under their difficulties, would have been thrown back upon the bungling machinery of county committees for administration, till a convention could have been called, and its wheels again set into regular motion. What a cruel moment was this for creating such an embarrassment, for putting to the proof the attachment of our countrymen to republican government! Those who meant well of the advocates of this measure, (and most of them meant well, for I know them personally, had been their fellow-laborer in the common cause, and had often proved the purity of their principles,) had been seduced in their judgment by the example of an ancient republic, whose constitution and circumstances were fundamentally different. They had sought this precedent in the history of Rome, where alone it was to be found, and where at length, too, it had proved fatal. They had taken it from a republic rent by the most bitter factions and tumults, where the government was of a heavy-handed unfeeling aristocracy, over a people ferocious, and rendered desperate by poverty and wretchedness; tumults which could not be allayed under the most trying circumstances, but by the omnipotent hand of a single despot. Their constitution, therefore, allowed a temporary tyrant to be erected, under the name of a dictator; and that temporary tyrant, after a few examples, became perpetual. They misapplied this precedent to a people mild in their dispositions, patient under their trial, united for the public liberty, and affectionate to their leaders. ° ° °

The present state of our laws on the subject of religion is this. The convention of May 1776, in their declaration of rights, declared it to be a truth, and a natural right, that the exercise of religion should be free; but when they proceeded to form on that declaration the ordinance of government, instead of taking up every principle declared in the bill of rights, and guarding it by legislative sanction, they passed over that which asserted our religious rights, leaving them as they found them. The same convention, however, when they met as a member of the general assembly in October, 1776, repealed all *acts of Parliament* which had rendered criminal the maintaining any opinions in matters of religion, the forbearing to repair to church, and the exercising any mode of worship; and suspended the laws giving salaries to the clergy, which suspension was made perpetual in October, 1779. Statutory oppressions in religion being thus wiped away, we remain at present under those only imposed by the common law, or by our own acts of assembly. At the common law, *heresy* was a capital offence, punishable by burning. Its definition was left to the ecclesiastical judges, before whom the conviction was, till the statute of the 1 El. c. 1 circumscribed it, by declaring, that nothing should be deemed heresy, but what had been so determined by authority of the canonical scriptures, or by one of the four first general councils, or by other council, having for the grounds of their declaration the express and plain words of the scriptures. Heresy, thus circumscribed, being an offence against the common law, our act of assembly of October 1777, c. 17, gives cognizance of it to the general court, by declaring that the jurisdiction of that court shall be general in all matters at the common law. The execution is by the writ *De hoeretico comburendo.* By our own act of assembly of 1705, c. 30, if a person brought up in the Christian religion denies the being of a God, or the Trinity, or asserts there are more gods than one, or denies the Christian religion to be true, or the scriptures to be of divine authority, he is punishable on the first

offence by incapacity to hold any office or employment ecclesiastical, civil, or military; on the second by disability to sue, to take any gift or legacy, to be guardian, executor, or administrator, and by three years' imprisonment without bail. A father's right to the custody of his own children being founded in law on his right of guardianship, this being taken away, they may of course be severed from him, and put by the authority of a court into more orthodox hands. This is a summary view of that religious slavery under which a people have been willing to remain, who have lavished their lives and fortunes for the establishment of their civil freedom. The error seems not sufficiently eradicated, that the operations of the mind, as well as the acts of the body, are subject to the coercion of the laws. But our rulers can have no authority over such natural rights, only as we have submitted to them. The rights of conscience we never submitted, we could not submit. We are answerable for them to our God. The legitimate powers of government extend to such acts only as are injurious to others. But it does me no injury for my neighbor to say there are twenty gods, or no God. It neither picks my pocket nor breaks my leg. If it be said, his testimony in a court of justice cannot be relied on, reject it then, and be the stigma on him. Constraint may make him worse by making him a hypocrite, but it will never make him a truer man. It may fix him obstinately in his errors, but will not cure them. Reason and free inquiry are the only effectual agents against error. Give a loose to them, they will support the true religion by bringing every false one to their tribunal, to the test of their investigation. They are the natural enemies of error, and of error only. Had not the Roman government permitted free inquiry, Christianity could never have been introduced. Had not free inquiry been indulged at the era of the Reformation, the corruptions of Christianity could not have been purged away. If it be restrained now, the present corruptions will be protected, and new ones encouraged. Was the government to prescribe to us our medicine and diet, our bodies would be in such keeping as our souls are now. Thus in France the emetic was once forbidden as a medicine, and the potato as an article of food. Government is just as infallible, too, when it fixes systems in physics. Galileo was sent to the Inquisition for affirming that the earth was a sphere; the government had declared it to be as flat as a trencher, and Galileo was obliged to abjure his error. This error, however, at length prevailed, the earth became a globe, and Descartes declared it was whirled round its axis by a vortex. The government in which he lived was wise enough to see that this was no question of civil jurisdiction, or we should all have been involved by authority in vortices. In fact, the vortices have been exploded, and the Newtonian principle of gravitation is now more firmly established, on the basis of reason, than it would be were the government to step in, and to make it an article of necessary faith. Reason and experiment have been indulged, and error has fled before them. It is error alone which needs the support of government. Truth can stand by itself. Subject opinion to coercion: whom will you make your inquisitors? Fallible men; men governed by bad passions, by private as well as public reasons. And why subject it to coercion? To produce uniformity. But is uniformity of opinion desirable? No more than of face and stature. Introduce the bed of Procrustes then, and as there is danger that the large men may beat the small, make us all of a size, by lopping the former and stretching the latter. Difference of opinion is advantageous in religion. The several sects perform the office of a *censor morum* over such other. Is uniformity attainable? Millions of innocent men, women, and children, since the introduction of Christianity, have been burnt, tortured, fined, imprisoned; yet we have not advanced one inch towards uniformity. What has been the effect of coercion? To make one half the world fools, and the other half hypocrites. To support roguery and error all over the earth. Let us reflect that it is inhabited by a thousand millions of people. That these profess probably a thousand different systems of religion. That ours is but one of that thousand. That if there be but one right, and ours that one, we should wish to see the nine hundred and ninety-nine wandering sects gathered into the fold of truth. But against such a majority we cannot effect this by force. Reason and persuasion are the only practicable instruments. To make way for these, free inquiry must be indulged; and how can we wish others to indulge it while we refuse it ourselves. But every State, says an inquisitor, has established some religion. No two, say I, have established the same. Is this a proof of the infallibility of establishments? Our sister States of Pennsylvania and New York, however, have long subsisted without any establishment at all. The experiment was new and doubtful when they made it. It has answered beyond conception. They flourish infinitely. Religion is well supported; of various kinds, indeed, but all good enough; all sufficient to preserve peace and order; or if a sect arises, whose tenets would subvert morals, good sense has fair play, and reasons and laughs it out of doors, without suffering the State to be troubled with it. They do not hang more malefactors than we do. They are not more disturbed with religious dissensions. On the contrary, their harmony is unparalleled, and can be ascribed to nothing but their unbounded tolerance, because there is no other circumstance in which they differ from every nation on earth. They have made the happy discovery, that the way to silence religious disputes, is to take no notice of them. Let us too give this experiment fair play, and get rid, while we may, of those tyrannical laws. It is true, we are as yet secured against them by the spirit of the times. I doubt whether the people of this country would suffer an execution for heresy, or a three years' imprisonment for not comprehending the mysteries of the Trinity. But is the spirit of the people an infallible, a permanent reliance? Is it government? Is this the kind of protection we receive in return for the rights we give up? Besides, the spirit of the times may alter, will alter. Our rulers will become corrupt, our people careless. A single zealot may commence persecutor, and better men be his victims. It can never be too often repeated, that the time for fixing every essential right on a legal basis is while our rulers are honest, and ourselves united. From the conclusion of this war we shall be going down hill. It will not then be necessary to resort every moment to the people for support. They will be forgotten, therefore, and their rights disregarded. They will forget themselves, but in the sole faculty of making money, and will never think of uniting to effect a due respect for their rights. The shackles, therefore, which shall not be knocked off at the conclusion of this war, will remain on us long, will be made heavier and heavier, till our rights shall revive or expire in a convulsion. ° ° °

It is difficult to determine on the standard by which the manners of a nation may be tried, whether *catholic* or *particular*. It is more difficult for a native to bring to that standard the manners of his own nation, familiarized to him by habit. There must doubtless be an unhappy influence on the manners of our people produced by the existence of slavery among us. The whole commerce between master and slave is a perpetual exercise of the most boisterous passions, the most unremitting despotism on the one part, and degrading submissions on the other. Our children see this, and learn to imitate it; for man is an imitative animal. This quality is the germ of all education in him. From his cradle to his grave he is learning to do what he sees others do. If a parent could find no motive either in his philanthropy or his self-love, for restraining the intemperance of passion towards his slave, it should always be a sufficient one that his child is present. But generally it is not sufficient. The parent storms, the child looks on, catches the lineaments of wrath, puts on the same airs in the circle of smaller slaves, gives a loose to the worst of passions, and thus nursed, educated, and daily exercised in tyranny, cannot but be stamped by it with odious peculiarities. The man must be a prodigy who can retain his manners and morals undepraved by such circumstances. And with what execration should the statesman be loaded, who, permitting one half the citizens thus to trample on the rights of the other, transforms those into despots, and these into enemies, destroys the morals of the one part, and the *amor patriae* of the other. For if a slave can have a country in this world, it must be any other in preference to that in which he is born to live and labor for another; in which he must lock up the faculties of his nature, contribute as far as depends on his individual endeavors to the evanishment of the human race, or entail his own miserable condition on the endless generations proceeding from him. With the morals of the people, their industry also is destroyed. For in a warm climate, no man will labor for himself who can make another labor for him. This is so true, that of the proprietors of slaves a very small proportion indeed are ever seen to labor. And can the liberties of a nation be thought secure when we have removed their only firm basis, a conviction in the minds of the people that these liberties are of the gift of God? That they are not to be violated but with His wrath? Indeed I tremble for my country when I reflect that God is just; that his justice cannot sleep forever; that considering numbers, nature and natural means only, a revolution of the wheel of fortune, an exchange of situation is among possible events; that it may become probable by supernatural interference! The Almighty has no attribute which can take side with us in such a contest. But it is impossible to be temperate and to pursue this subject through the various considerations of policy, of morals, of history natural and civil. We must be contented to hope they will force their way into every one's mind. I think a change already perceptible, since the origin of the present revolution. The spirit of the master is abating, that of the slave rising from the dust, his condition mollifying, the way I hope preparing, under the auspices of heaven, for a total emancipation, and that this is disposed, in the order of events, to be with the consent of the masters, rather than by their extirpation.

1782

Letters

To Charles Thompson

Thompson was a friend of Jefferson's with similar scientific interests, and formerly Secretary of the Continental Congress. Text: A. A. Lipscomb and A. E. Bergh, eds., *The Writings of Thomas Jefferson* (Washington, 1903–5), VI, 11–15.

Paris, December 17, 1786.

DEAR SIR,—A dislocation of my right wrist has for three months past, disabled me from writing except with my left hand, which was too slow and awkward to be employed often. I begin to have so much use of my wrist, as to be able to write, but it is slowly, and in pain. I take the first moment I can, however, to acknowledge the receipt of your letters of April the 6th, July the 8th and 30th. In one of these, you say, you have not been able to learn, whether, in the new mills in London, steam is the immediate mover of the machinery, or raises water to move it? It is the immediate mover. The power of this agent, though long known, is but now beginning to be applied to the various purposes of which it is susceptible. You observe that Whitehurst supposes it to have been the agent, which bursting the earth, threw it up into mountains and valleys. You ask me what I think of his book? I find in it many interesting facts brought together, and many ingenious commentaries on them. But there are great chasms in his facts, and consequently in his reasoning. These he fills up by suppositions, which may be as reasonably denied as granted. A sceptical reader therefore, like myself, is left in the lurch. I acknowledge, however, he makes more use of fact, than any other writer on a theory of the earth. But I give one answer to all these theorists. That is as follows. They all suppose the earth a created existence. They must suppose a creator then; and that he possessed power and wisdom to a great degree. As he intended the earth for the habitation of animals and vegetables, is it reasonable to suppose, he made two jobs of his creation, that he first made a chaotic lump and set it into rotatory motion, and then waited the millions of ages necessary to form itself? That when it had done this, he stepped in a second time, to create the animals and plants which were to inhabit it? As the hand of a creator is to be called in, it may as well be called in at one stage of the process as another. We may as well suppose he created the earth at once, nearly in the state in which we see it, fit for the preservation of the beings he placed on it. But it is said, we have a proof that he did not create it in its present solid form, but in a state of fluidity; because its present shape of an oblate spheroid is precisely that which a fluid mass revolving on its axis would assume.

I suppose that the same equilibrium between gravity and centrifugal force, which would determine a fluid mass into the form of an oblate spheroid, would determine the wise creator of that mass, if he made it in a solid state, to give it the same spheroidical form. A revolving fluid will continue to change its shape, till it attains that in which its principles of contrary motion are balanced. For if you suppose them not balanced, it will change its form. Now, the same balanced form is necessary for the preserva-

1784

tion of a revolving solid. The creator, therefore, of a revolving solid, would make it an oblate spheroid, that figure alone admitting a perfect equilibrium. He would make it in that form, for another reason; that is, to prevent a shifting of the axis of rotation. Had he created the earth perfectly spherical, its axis might have been perpetually shifting, by the influence of the other bodies of the system; and by placing the inhabitants of the earth successively under its poles, it might have been depopulated; whereas, being spheroidical, it has but one axis on which it can revolve in equilibrio. Suppose the axis of the earth to shift forty-five degrees; then cut it into one hundred and eighty slices, making every section in the plane of a circle of latitude, perpendicular to the axis: every one of these slices, except the equatorial one, would be unbalanced, as there would be more matter on one side of its axis than on the other. There could be but one diameter drawn through such a slice, which would divide it into two equal parts. On every other possible diameter, the parts would hang unequal. This would produce an irregularity in the diurnal rotation. We may, therefore, conclude it impossible for the poles of the earth to shift, if it was made spheroidically; and that it would be made spheroidical, though solid, to obtain this end. I use this reasoning only on the supposition that the earth has had a beginning. I am sure I shall read your conjectures on this subject with great pleasure, though I bespeak, beforehand, a right to indulge my natural incredulity and scepticism. The pain in which I write awakens me here from my reverie, and obliges me to conclude with compliments to Mrs. Thompson, and assurances to yourself of the esteem and affection with which I am sincerely, dear Sir, your friend and servant.

P. S. Since writing the preceding, I have had a conversation on the subject of the steam mills, with the famous Boulton, to whom those of London belong, and who is here at this time. He compares the effect of steam with that of horses, in the following manner: Six horses, aided with the most advantageous combination of the mechanical powers hitherto tried, will grind six bushels of flour in an hour; at the end of which time they are all in a foam, and must rest. They can work thus, six hours in the twenty-four, grinding thirty-six bushels of flour, which is six to each horse, for the twenty-four hours. His steam mill in London consumes one hundred and twenty bushels of coal in twenty-four hours, turns ten pair of stones, which grind eight bushels of flour an hour each, which is nineteen hundred and twenty bushels in the twenty-four hours. This makes a peck and a half of coal perform exactly as much as a horse, in one day, can perform.

To Peter Carr

Jefferson's nephew Peter Carr was at this time seventeen years old and a student at the College of William and Mary. Text: Boyd, ed., *Papers*, XII, 14–19.

Paris, Aug. 10, 1787.

DEAR PETER,—I have received your two letters of Decemb. 30. and April 18. and am very happy to find by them, as well as by letters from Mr. Wythe, that you have been so fortunate as to attract his notice and good will: I am sure you will find this to have been one of the most fortunate events of your life, as I have ever been sensible it was of mine. I inclose you a sketch of the sciences to which I would wish you to apply in such order as Mr. Wythe shall advise: I mention also the books in them worth your reading, which submit to his correction. Many of these are among your father's books, which you should have brought to you. As I do not recollect those of them not in his library, you must write to me for them, making out a catalogue of such as you think you shall have occasion for in 18 months from the date of your letter, and consulting Mr. Wythe on the subject. To this sketch I will add a few particular observations.

1. Italian. I fear the learning this language will confound your French and Spanish. Being all of them degenerated dialects of the Latin, they are apt to mix in conversation. I have never seen a person speaking the three languages who did not mix them. It is a delightful language, but late events having rendered the Spanish more useful, lay it aside to prosecute that.

2. Spanish. Bestow great attention on this, and endeavor to acquire an accurate knowlege of it. Our future connections with Spain and Spanish America will render that language a valuable acquisition. The antient history of a great part of America too is written in that language. I send you a dictionary.

3. Moral philosophy. I think it lost time to attend lectures in this branch. He who made us would have been a pitiful bungler if he had made the rules of our moral conduct a matter of science. For one man of science, there are thousands who are not. What would have become of them? Man was destined for society. His morality therefore was to be formed to this object. He was endowed with a sense of right and wrong merely relative to this. This sense is as much a part of his nature as the sense of hearing, seeing, feeling; it is the true foundation of morality, and not the το χαλον truth, &c., as fanciful writers have imagined. The moral sense, or conscience, is as much a part of man as his leg or arm. It is given to all human beings in a stronger or weaker degree, as force of members is given them in a greater or less

degree. It may be strengthened by exercise, as may any particular limb of the body. This sense is submitted indeed in some degree to the guidance of reason; but it is a small stock which is required for this: even a less one than what we call Common sense. State a moral case to a ploughman and a professor. The former will decide it as well, and often better than the latter, because he has not been led astray by artificial rules. In this branch therefore read good books because they will encourage as well as direct your feelings. The writings of Sterne particularly form the best course of morality that ever was written. Besides these read the books mentioned in the inclosed paper; and above all things lose no occasion of exercising your dispositions to be grateful, to be generous, to be charitable, to be humane, to be true, just, firm, orderly, couragious &c. Consider every act of this kind as an exercise which will strengthen your moral faculties, and increase your worth.

4. Religion. Your reason is now mature enough to receive this object. In the first place divest yourself of all bias in favour of novelty and singularity of opinion. Indulge them in any other subject rather than that of religion. It is too important, and the consequences of error may be too serious. On the other hand shake off all the fears and servile prejudices under which weak minds are servilely crouched. Fix reason firmly in her seat, and call to her tribunal every fact, every opinion. Question with boldness even the existence of a god; because, if there be one, he must more approve the homage of reason, than that of blindfolded fear. You will naturally examine first the religion of your own country. Read the bible then, as you would read Livy or Tacitus. The facts which are within the ordinary course of nature you will believe on the authority of the writer, as you do those of the same kind in Livy and Tacitus. The testimony of the writer weighs in their favor in one scale, and their not being against the laws of nature does not weigh against them. But those facts in the bible which contradict the laws of nature, must be examined with more care, and under a variety of faces. Here you must recur to the pretensions of the writer to inspiration from god. Examine upon what evidence his pretensions are founded, and whether that evidence is so strong as that it's falshood would be more improbable than a change of the laws of nature in the case he relates. For example in the book of Joshua we are told the sun stood still several hours. Were we to read that fact in Livy or Tacitus we should class it with their showers of blood, speaking of statues, beasts &c., but it is said that the writer of that book was inspired. Examine therefore candidly what evidence there is of his having been inspired. The pretension is entitled to your enquiry, because millions believe it. On the other hand you are Astronomer enough to know how contrary it is to the law of nature that a body revolving on it's axis, as the earth does, should have stopped, should not by that sudden stoppage have prostrated animals, trees, buildings, and should after a certain time have resumed it's revolution, and that without a second general prostration. Is this arrest of the earth's motion, or the evidence which affirms it, most within the law of probabilities? You will next read the new testament. It is the history of a personage called Jesus. Keep in your eye the opposite pretensions. 1. Of those who say he was begotten by god, born of a virgin, suspended and reversed the laws of nature at will, and ascended bodily into heaven: and 2. of those who say he was a man, of illegitimate birth, of a benevolent heart, enthusiastic mind, who set out without pretensions to divinity, ended in believing them, and was punished capitally for sedition by being gibbeted according to the Roman law which punished the first commission of that offence by whipping, and the second by exile or death *in furcâ*. See this law in the Digest Lib. 48. tit. 19 § 28. 3. and Lipsius Lib. 2. de cruce. cap. 2. These questions are examined in the books I have mentioned under the head of religion, and several others. They will assist you in your enquiries, but keep your reason firmly on the watch in reading them all. Do not be frightened from this enquiry by any fear of it's consequences. If it ends in a belief that there is no god, you will find incitements to virtue in the comfort and pleasantness you feel in it's exercise, and the love of others which it will procure you. If you find reason to believe there is a god, a consciousness that you are acting under his eye, and that he approves you, will be a vast additional incitement. If that there be a future state, the hope of a happy existence in that increases the appetite to deserve it; if that Jesus was also a god, you will be comforted by a belief of his aid and love. In fine, I repeat that you must lay aside all prejudice on both sides, and neither believe nor reject any thing because any other person, or description of persons have rejected or believed it. Your own reason is the only oracle given you by heaven, and you are answerable not for the rightness but uprightness of the decision.—I forgot to observe when speaking of the New testament that you should read all the histories of Christ, as well of those whom a council of ecclesiastics have decided for us to be Pseudo-evangelists, as those they named Evangelists, because these Pseudo-evangelists pretended to inspiration as much as the others, and you are to judge their pretensions by your own reason, and not by the reason of those ecclesiastics. Most of these are lost. There are some however still extant, collected by Fabricius which I will endeavor to get and send you.

5. Travelling. This makes men wiser, but less happy. When men of sober age travel, they gather knowlege which they may apply usefully for their country, but they are subject ever after to recollections mixed with regret, their affections are weakened by being extended over more objects, and they learn new habits which cannot be gratified when they return home. Young men who travel are exposed to all these inconveniences in a higher degree, to others still more serious, and do not acquire that wisdom for which a previous foundation is requisite by repeated and just observations at home. The glare of pomp and pleasure is analogous to the motion of their blood, it absorbs all their affection and attention, they are torn from it as from the only good in this world, and return to their home as to a place of exile and condemnation. Their eyes are for ever turned back to the object they have lost, and it's recollection poisons the residue of their lives. Their first and most delicate passions are hackneyed on unworthy objects here, and they carry home only the dregs, insufficient to make themselves or any body else happy. Add to this that a habit of idleness, an inability to apply themselves to business is acquired and renders them useless to themselves and their country. These observations are founded in experience. There is no place where your pursuit of knowlege will be so little obstructed by foreign objects as in your own country, nor any wherein the virtues of the heart will be less exposed to be weakened. Be good, be learned, and be industrious, and you will not want the aid of travelling to render you precious to your country, dear to your friends, happy within yourself. I repeat my advice to take a great deal of exercise, and on foot. Health is the first requisite after morality. Write to me often and be assured of the interest I take in your success, as well as of the warmth of those sentiments of attachment with which I am, dear Peter, your affectionate friend,   TH: JEFFERSON

P. S. Let me know your age in your next letter. Your cousins here are well and desire to be remembered to you.

ENCLOSURE

Antient history. Herodot. Thucyd. Xenoph. hellen. Xenoph. Anab. Q. Curt. Just.
Livy. Polybius. Sallust. Caesar. Suetonius. Tacitus. Aurel. Victor. Herodian.
Gibbons' decline of the Roman empire. Milot histoire ancienne.
Mod. hist. English. Tacit. Germ. & Agricole. Hume to the end of H.VI. then Habington's E.IV.—Sr. Thomas Moor's E.5. & R.3.—Ld. Bacon's H.7.—Ld. Herbert of Cherbury's H.8.—K. Edward's journal (in Burnet) Bp. of Hereford's E.6. & Mary.—Cambden's Eliz. Wilson's Jac.I. Ludlow (omit Clarendon as too seducing for a young republican. By and by read him) Burnet's Charles 2. Jac.2. Wm. & Mary & Anne.—Ld. Orrery down to George 1. & 2.—Burke's G.3. Robertson's hist. of Scotland.
American. Robertson's America.—Douglass's N. America.—Hutcheson's Massachusets, Smith's N. York.—Smith's N. Jersey.—Franklin's review of Pennsylvania. Smith's, Stith's, Keith's, & Beverley's hist. of Virginia.
Foreign. Mallet's Northn. Antiquities by Percy.—Puffendorf's histy. of Europe & Martiniere's of Asia, Africa & America.—Milot histoire Moderne. Voltaire histoire universelle.—Milot hist. de France.—Mariana's hist. of Spain in Spa[nish.] —Robertson's Charles V.—Watson's Phil. II. & III.—Grotii Belgica.
Mosheim's Ecclesiastical history.
Poetry.   Homer—Milton—Ossian—Sophocles—Aeschylus—Eurip.—Metastasio—Shakesp.—Theocritus—Anacreon [. . .]
Mathematics. Bezout & whatever else Mr. Madison recommends.
Astronomy. Delalande &c. as Mr. Madison shall recommend.
Natural Philosophy. Musschenbroeck.
Botany. Linnaei Philosophia Botanica—Genera Plantarum—Species plantarum—Gronovii flora [Virginica.]
Chemistry. Fourcroy.
Agriculture. Home's principles of Agriculture—Tull &c.
Anatomy. Cheselden.
Morality. The Socratic dialogues—Cicero's Philosophies—Kaim's principles of Natl. religion—Helvetius de l'esprit et de l'homme.—Locke's Essay.—Lucretius—Traité de Morale & du Bon[heur]
Religion. Locke's Conduct of the mind.—Middleton's works—Bolingbroke's philosoph. works—Hume's essays—Voltaire's works—Beattie.
Politics & Law. Whatever Mr. Wythe pleases, who will be so good as to correct also all the preceding articles which are only intended as a ground work to be finished by his pencil.

To John Adams

Jefferson and Adams, estranged during the bitter campaign of 1800, exchanged no letters for almost twelve years, when Benjamin Rush persuaded them to renew their old friendship. Both retired from active political life, the two men began a remarkable correspondence which ended only with their deaths on the same day, July 4, 1826. Text: Paul L. Ford, ed., *The Writings of Thomas Jefferson* (New York, 1892–99), IX, 425–29.

Monticello, October 28, 1813.

° ° ° For I agree with you that there is a natural aristocracy among men. The grounds of this are virtue and talents. Formerly, bodily powers gave place among the aristoi. But since the invention of gunpowder has armed the weak as well as the strong with missile death, bodily strength, like beauty, good humor, politeness and other accomplishments, has become but an auxiliary ground for distinction. There is also an artificial aristocracy, founded on wealth and birth, without either virtue or talents; for with these it would belong to the first class. The natural aristocracy I consider as the most precious gift of nature, for the instruction, the trusts, and government of society. And indeed, it would have been inconsistent in creation to have formed man for the social state, and not to have provided virtue and wisdom enough to manage the concerns of the society. May we not even say, that that form of government is the best, which provides the most effectually for a pure selection of these natural aristoi into the offices of government? The artificial aristocracy is a mischievous ingredient in government, and provision should be made to prevent its ascendency. On the question, what is the best provision, you and I differ; but we differ as rational friends, using the free exercise of our own reason, and mutually indulging its errors. You think it best to put the pseudo-aristoi into a separate chamber of legislation, where they may be hindered from doing mischief by their co-ordinate branches, and where, also, they may be a protection to wealth against the Agrarian and plundering enterprises of the majority of the people. I think that to give them power in order to prevent them from doing mischief, is arming them for it, and increasing instead of remedying the evil. For if the co-ordinate branches can arrest their action, so may they that of the co-ordinates. Mischief may be done negatively as well as positively. Of this, a cabal in the Senate of the United States has furnished many proofs. Nor do I believe them necessary to protect the wealthy; because enough of these will find their way into every branch of the legislation, to protect themselves. From fifteen to twenty legislatures of our own, in action for thirty years past, have proved that no fears of an equalization of property are to be apprehended from them. I think the best remedy is exactly that provided by all our constitutions, to leave to the citizens the free election and separation of the aristoi from the pseudo-aristoi, of the wheat from the chaff. In general they will elect the really good and wise. In some instances, wealth may corrupt, and birth blind them; but not in sufficient degree to endanger the society.

It is probable that our difference of opinion may, in some measure, be produced by a difference of character in those among whom we live. From what I have seen of Massachusetts and Connecticut myself, and still more from what I have heard, and the character given of the former by yourself, who know them so much better, there seems to be in those two States a traditionary reverence for certain families, which has rendered the offices of the gov-

ernment nearly hereditary in those families. I presume that from an early period of your history, members of those families happening to possess virtue and talents, have honestly exercised them for the good of the people, and by their services have endeared their names to them. In coupling Connecticut with you, I mean it politically only, not morally. For having made the Bible the common law of their land, they seemed to have modeled their morality on the story of Jacob and Laban. But although this hereditary succession to office with you, may, in some degree, be founded in real family merit, yet in a much higher degree, it has proceeded from your strict alliance of Church and State. These families are canonised in the eyes of the people on common principles, "you tickle me, and I will tickle you." In Virginia we have nothing of this. Our clergy, before the revolution, having been secured against rivalship by fixed salaries, did not give themselves the trouble of acquiring influence over the people. Of wealth, there were great accumulations in particular families, handed down from generation to generation, under the English law of entails. But the only object of ambition for the wealthy was a seat in the King's Council. All their court then was paid to the crown and its creatures; and they Philipised in all collisions between the King and the people. Hence they were unpopular; and that unpopularity continues attached to their names. A Randolph, a Carter, or a Burwell must have great personal superiority over a common competitor to be elected by the people even at this day. At the first session of our legislature after the Declaration of Independence, we passed a law abolishing entails. And this was followed by one abolishing the privilege of primogeniture, and dividing the lands of intestates equally among all their children, or other representatives. These laws, drawn by myself, laid the ax to the foot of pseudo-aristocracy. And had another which I prepared been adopted by the legislature, our work would have been complete. It was a bill for the more general diffusion of learning. This proposed to divide every county into wards of five or six miles square, like your townships; to establish in each ward a free school for reading, writing and common arithmetic; to provide for the annual selection of the best subjects from these schools, who might receive, at the public expense, a higher degree of education at a district school; and from these district schools to select a certain number of the most promising subjects, to be completed at an University, where all the useful sciences should be taught. Worth and genius would thus have been sought out from every condition of life, and completely prepared by education for defeating the competition of wealth and birth for public trusts. My proposition had, for a further object, to impart to these wards those portions of self-government for which they are best qualified, by confiding to them the care of their poor, their roads, police, elections, the nomination of jurors, administration of justice in small cases, elementary exercises of militia; in short, to have made them little republics, with a warden at the head of each, for all those concerns which, being under their eye, they would better manage than the larger republics of the county or State. A general call of ward meetings by their wardens on the same day through the State, would at any time produce the genuine sense of the people on any required point, and would enable the State to act in mass, as your people have so often done, and with so much effect by their town meetings. The law for religious freedom, which made a part of this system, having put down the aristocracy of the clergy, and restored to the citizen the freedom of the mind, and those of entails and descents nurturing an equality of condition among them, this on education would have raised the mass of the people to the high ground of moral respectability necessary to their own safety, and to orderly government; and would have completed the great object of qualifying them to select the veritable aristoi, for the trusts of government, to the exclusion of the pseudalists; and the same Theognis who has furnished the epigraphs of your two letters, assures us that "Ονδεμιαν πω, Κυρν', αγαθοι πολιν ωλεσαν ανδρες." [1] Although this law has not yet been acted on but in a small and inefficient degree, it is still considered as before the legislature, with other bills of the revised code, not yet taken up, and I have great hope that some patriotic spirit will, at a favorable moment, call it up, and make it the key-stone of the arch of our government.

With respect to aristocracy, we should further consider, that before the establishment of the American States, nothing was known to history but the man of the old world, crowded within limits either small or overcharged, and steeped in the vices which that situation generates. A government adapted to such men would be one thing; but a very different one, that for the man of these States. Here every one may have land to labor for himself, if he chooses; or, preferring the exercise of any other industry, may exact for it such compensation as not only to afford a comfortable subsistence, but wherewith to provide for a cessation from labor in old age. Every one, by his property, or by his satisfactory situation, is interested in the support of law and order. And such men may safely and advantageously reserve to themselves a wholesome control over their public affairs, and a degree of freedom, which, in the hands of the *canaille* of the cities of Europe,

would be instantly perverted to the demolition and destruction of everything public and private. The history of the last twenty-five years of France, and of the last forty years in America, nay of its last two hundred years, proves the truth of both parts of this observation.

But even in Europe a change has sensibly taken place in the mind of man. Science had liberated the ideas of those who read and reflect, and the American example had kindled feelings of right in the people. An insurrection has consequently begun, of science, talents, and courage, against rank and birth, which have fallen into contempt. It has failed in its first effort, because the mobs of the cities, the instrument used for its accomplishment, debased by ignorance, poverty and vice, could not be restrained to rational action. But the world will recover from the panic of this first catastrophe. Science is progressive, and talents and enterprise on the alert. Resort may be had to the people of the country, a more governable power from their principles and subordination; and rank, and birth, and tinsel-aristocracy will finally shrink into insignificance, even there. This, however, we have no right to meddle with. It suffices for us, if the moral and physical condition of our own citizens qualifies them to select the able and good for the direction of their government, with a recurrence of elections at such short periods as will enable them to displace an unfaithful servant, before the mischief he meditates may be irremediable.

I have thus stated my opinion on a point on which we differ, not with a view to controversy, for we are both too old to change opinions which are the result of a long life of inquiry and reflection; but on the suggestions of a former letter of yours, that we ought not to die before we have explained ourselves to each other. We acted in perfect harmony, through a long and perilous contest for our liberty and independence. A constitution has been acquired, which, though neither of us thinks perfect, yet both consider as competent to render our fellow citizens the happiest and the securest on whom the sun has ever shone. If we do not think exactly alike as to its imperfections, it matters little to our country, which, after devoting to it long lives of disinterested labor, we have delivered over to our successors in life, who will be able to take care of it and of themselves. ° ° °

To Dr. Walter Jones

Jones, a Congressman from Virginia and a close friend, had asked Jefferson to comment on the party battles of the Federalist period. In the course of his reply, Jefferson produced this character sketch of George Washington. Text: Lipscomb and Bergh, eds., *Writings*, XIV, 48–52.

To John Adams. [1] "Not any state, Curnos, have good men yet destroyed."

Monticello, January 2, 1814.

° ° ° I think I knew General Washington intimately and thoroughly; and were I called on to delineate his character, it should be in terms like these.

His mind was great and powerful, without being of the very first order; his penetration strong, though not so acute as that of a Newton, Bacon, or Locke; and as far as he saw, no judgment was ever sounder. It was slow in operation, being little aided by invention or imagination, but sure in conclusion. Hence the common remark of his officers, of the advantage he derived from councils of war, where hearing all suggestions, he selected whatever was best; and certainly no general ever planned his battles more judiciously. But if deranged during the course of the action, if any member of his plan was dislocated by sudden circumstances, he was slow in re-adjustment. The consequence was, that he often failed in the field, and rarely against an enemy in station, as at Boston and York. He was incapable of fear, meeting personal dangers with the calmest unconcern. Perhaps the strongest feature in his character was prudence, never acting until every circumstance, every consideration, was maturely weighed; refraining if he saw a doubt, but, when once decided, going through with his purpose, whatever obstacles opposed. His integrity was most pure, his justice the most inflexible I have ever known, no motives of interest or consanguinity, of friendship or hatred, being able to bias his decision. He was, indeed, in every sense of the words, a wise, a good, and a great man. His temper was naturally irritable and high toned; but reflection and resolution had obtained a firm and habitual ascendency over it. If ever, however, it broke its bonds, he was most tremendous in his wrath. In his expenses he was honorable, but exact; liberal in contributions to whatever promised utility; but frowning and unyielding on all visionary projects, and all unworthy calls on his charity. His heart was not warm in its affections; but he exactly calculated every man's value, and gave him a solid esteem proportioned to it. His person, you know, was fine, his stature exactly what one would wish, his deportment easy, erect and noble; the best horseman of his age, and the most graceful figure that could be seen on horseback. Although in the circle of his friends, where he might be unreserved with safety, he took a free share in conversation, his colloquial talents were not above mediocrity, possessing neither copiousness of ideas, nor fluency of words. In public, when called on for a sudden opinion, he was unready, short and embarrassed. Yet he wrote readily, rather diffusely, in an easy and correct style. This he had acquired by conversation with the world, for his education was merely reading, writing and common arithmetic, to which he added surveying at a later day. His time was employed in action chiefly, reading little, and that only in agriculture and English history. His correspondence became necessarily extensive, and, with journalizing his agricultural proceedings, occupied most of his leisure hours within doors. On the whole, his character was, in its mass, perfect, in nothing bad, in few points indifferent; and it may truly be said, that never did nature and fortune combine more perfectly to make a man great, and to place him in the same constellation with whatever worthies have merited from man an everlasting remembrance. For his was the singular destiny and merit, of leading the armies of his country successfully through an arduous war, for the establishment of its independence; of conducting its councils through the birth of a government, new in its forms and principles, until it had settled down into a quiet and orderly train; and of scrupulously obeying the laws through the whole of his career, civil and military, of which the history of the world furnishes no other example.

How, then, can it be perilous for you to take such a man on your shoulders? I am satisfied the great body of republicans think of him as I do. We were, indeed, dissatisfied with him on his ratification of the British treaty. But this was short lived. We knew his honesty, the wiles with which he was encompassed, and that age had already begun to relax the firmness of his purposes; and I am convinced he is more deeply seated in the love and gratitude of the republicans, than in the Pharisaical homage of the federal monarchists. For he was no monarchist from preference of his judgment. The soundness of that gave him correct views of the rights of man, and his severe justice devoted him to them. He has often declared to me that he considered our new Constitution as an experiment on the practicability of republican government, and with what dose of liberty man could be trusted for his own good; that he was determined the experiment should have a fair trial, and would lose the last drop of his blood in support of it. And these declarations he repeated to me the oftener and more pointedly, because he knew my suspicions of Colonel Hamilton's views, and probably had heard from him the same declarations which I had, to wit, "that the British constitution, with its unequal representation, corruption and other existing abuses, was the most perfect government which had ever been established on earth, and that a reformation of those abuses would make it an impracticable government." I do believe that General Washington had not a firm confidence in the durability of our government. He was naturally distrustful of men, and inclined to gloomy apprehensions; and I was ever persuaded that a belief that we must at length end in something like a British constitution, had some weight in his adoption of the ceremonies of levees, birthdays, pompous meetings with Congress, and other forms of the same character, calculated to prepare us gradually for a change which he believed possible, and to let it come on with as little shock as might be to the public mind.

These are my opinions of General Washington, which I would vouch at the judgment seat of God, having been formed on an acquaintance of thirty years. I served with him in the Virginia legislature from 1769 to the Revolutionary war, and again, a short time in Congress, until he left us to take command of the army. During the war and after it we corresponded occasionally, and in the four years of my continuance in the office of Secretary of State, our intercourse was daily, confidential and cordial. After I retired from that office, great and malignant pains were taken by our federal monarchists, and not entirely without effect, to make him view me as a theorist, holding French principles of government, which would lead infallibly to licentiousness and anarchy. And to this he listened the more easily, from my known disapprobation of the British treaty. I never saw him afterwards, or these malignant insinuations should have been dissipated before his just judgment, as mists before the sun. I felt on his death, with my countrymen, that "verily a great man hath fallen this day in Israel."

More time and recollection would enable me to add many other traits of his character; but why add them to you who knew him well? And I cannot justify to myself a longer detention of your paper.

Vale, proprieque tuum, me esse tibi persuadeas.[1]

To Thomas Law, Esq.

Thomas Law was the author of a book on moral philosophy which he sent to Jefferson. Text: Lipscomb and Bergh, eds., *Writings*, XIV, 138–44.

Poplar Forest, June 13, 1814.

DEAR SIR,—The copy of your Second Thoughts on Instinctive Impulses, with the letter accompanying it, was received just as I was setting out on a journey to this place, two or three days distant from Monticello. I brought it with me and read it with great satisfaction, and with the more as it contained exactly my own creed on the foundation of morality in man. It is really curious that on a question so fundamental, such a variety of opinions should have prevailed among men, and those, too, of the most exemplary virtue and first order of understanding. It shows how necessary was the care of the Creator in making the moral principle so much a part of our constitution as that no errors of reasoning or of specu-

To Walter Jones. [1] "Farewell, you persuade me to be especially yours."

lation might lead us astray from its observance in practice. Of all the theories on this question, the most whimsical seems to have been that of Wollaston,[1] who considers *truth* as the foundation of morality. The thief who steals your guinea does wrong only inasmuch as he acts a lie in using your guinea as if it were his own. Truth is certainly a branch of morality, and a very important one to society. But presented as its foundation, it is as if a tree taken up by the roots, had its stem reversed in the air, and one of its branches planted in the ground. Some have made the *love of God* the foundation of morality. This, too, is but a branch of our moral duties, which are generally divided into duties to God and duties to man. If we did a good act merely from the love of God and a belief that it is pleasing to Him, whence arises the morality of the Atheist? It is idle to say, as some do, that no such being exists. We have the same evidence of the fact as of most of those we act on, to wit: their own affirmations, and their reasonings in support of them. I have observed, indeed, generally, that while in Protestant countries the defections from the Platonic Christianity of the priests is to Deism, in Catholic countries they are to Atheism. Diderot, D'Alembert, D'Holbach, Condorcet, are known to have been among the most virtuous of men.[2] Their virtue, then, must have had some other foundation than the love of God.

The Το κλον[3] of others is founded in a different faculty, that of taste, which is not even a branch of morality. We have indeed an innate sense of what we call beautiful, but that is exercised chiefly on subjects addressed to the fancy, whether through the eye in visible forms, as landscape, animal figure, dress, drapery, architecture, the composition of colors, etc., or to the imagination directly, as imagery, style, or measure in prose or poetry, or whatever else constitutes the domain of criticism or taste, a faculty entirely distinct from the moral one. Self-interest, or rather self-love, or *egoism*, has been more plausibly substituted as the basis of morality. But I consider our relations with others as constituting the boundaries of morality. With ourselves we stand on the ground of identity, not of relation, which last, requiring two subjects, excludes self-love confined to a single one. To ourselves, in strict language, we can owe no duties, obligation requiring also two parties. Self-love, therefore, is no part of morality. Indeed it is exactly its counterpart. It is the sole antagonist of virtue, leading us constantly by our propensities to self-gratification in violation

To Thomas Law. [1] William Wollaston (1660–1724), English philosopher and author of *The Religion of Nature Delineated* (1724).
[2] French rationalist philosophers of the eighteenth century, considered to be theologically unorthodox.
[3] "Concept of beauty."

of our moral duties to others. Accordingly, it is against this enemy that are erected the batteries of moralists and religionists, as the only obstacle to the practice of morality. Take from man his selfish propensities, and he can have nothing to seduce him from the practice of virtue. Or subdue those propensities by education, instruction or restraint, and virtue remains without a competitor. Egoism, in a broader sense, has been thus presented as the source of moral action. It has been said that we feed the hungry, clothe the naked, bind up the wounds of the man beaten by thieves, pour oil and wine into them, set him on our own beast and bring him to the inn, because we receive ourselves pleasure from these acts. So Helvetius,[4] one of the best men on earth, and the most ingenious advocate of this principle, after defining "interest" to mean not merely that which is pecuniary, but whatever may procure us pleasure or withdraw us from pain, [*de l'esprit* 2, 1,] says, [ib. 2, 2,] "the humane man is he to whom the sight of misfortune is insupportable, and who to rescue himself from this spectacle, is forced to succor the unfortunate object." This indeed is true. But it is one step short of the ultimate question. These good acts give us pleasure, but how happens it that they give us pleasure? Because nature hath implanted in our breasts a love of others, a sense of duty to them, a moral instinct, in short, which prompts us irresistibly to feel and to succor their distresses, and protests against the language of Helvetius, [ib. 2, 5,] "what other motive than self-interest could determine a man to generous actions? It is as impossible for him to love what is good for the sake of good, as to love evil for the sake of evil." The Creator would indeed have been a bungling artist, had he intended man for a social animal, without planting in him social dispositions. It is true they are not planted in every man, because there is no rule without exceptions; but it is false reasoning which converts exceptions into the general rule. Some men are born without the organs of sight, or of hearing, or without hands. Yet it would be wrong to say that man is born without these faculties, and sight, hearing, and hands may with truth enter into the general definition of man.

The want or imperfection of the moral sense in some men, like the want or imperfection of the senses of sight and hearing in others, is no proof that it is a general characteristic of the species. When it is wanting, we endeavor to supply the defect by education, by appeals to reason and calculation, by presenting to the being so unhappily conformed, other motives to do good and to eschew evil, such as the love, or the hatred, or rejection of those among whom he lives, and whose society is necessary to his happiness and even existence; demonstrations by sound calculation that honesty promotes interest in the long run; the rewards and penalties established by the laws; and ultimately the prospects of a future state of retribution for the evil as well as the good done while here. These are the correctives which are supplied by education, and which exercise the functions of the moralist, the preacher, and legislator; and they lead into a course of correct action all those whose disparity is not too profound to be eradicated. Some have argued against the existence of a moral sense, by saying that if nature had given us such a sense, impelling us to virtuous actions, and warning us against those which are vicious, then nature would also have designated, by some particular ear-marks, the two sets of actions which are, in themselves, the one virtuous and the other vicious. Whereas, we find, in fact, that the same actions are deemed virtuous in one country and vicious in another. The answer is, that nature has constituted *utility* to man, the standard and test of virtue. Men living in different countries, under different circumstances, different habits and regimens, may have different utilities; the same act, therefore, may be useful, and consequently virtuous in one country which is injurious and vicious in another differently circumstanced. I sincerely, then, believe with you in the general existence of a moral instinct. I think it the brightest gem with which the human character is studded, and the want of it as more degrading than the most hideous of the bodily deformities. I am happy in reviewing the roll of associates in this principle which you present in your second letter, some of which I had not before met with. To these might be added Lord Kaims,[5] one of the ablest of our advocates, who goes so far as to say, in his Principles of Natural Religion, that a man owes no duty to which he is not urged by some impulsive feeling. This is correct, if referred to the standard of general feeling in the given case, and not to the feeling of a single individual. Perhaps I may misquote him, it being fifty years since I read his book.

The leisure and solitude of my situation here has led me to the indiscretion of taxing you with a long letter on a subject whereon nothing new can be offered you. I will indulge myself no farther than to repeat the assurances of my continued esteem and respect.

To Monsieur Du Pont de Nemours

Pierre Samuel Du Pont de Nemours, French scientist, political thinker, and founder of a mighty industrial dynasty, wrote Jefferson to ask his opinion of a set of constitutions

---

[4] Claude Adrien Helvetius (1715–71), French philosopher whose books were condemned as heretical and burned in 1759.

[5] Henry Home, Lord Kames (1696–1782). Scottish eighteenth-century philosopher.

being drawn up for certain South American republics. Text: Lipscomb and Bergh, eds., *Writings*, XIV, 487–92.

Poplar Forest, April 24, 1816.

I received, my dear friend, your letter covering the Constitution for your Equinoctial republics, just as I was setting out for this place. I brought it with me, and have read it with great satisfaction. I suppose it well formed for those for whom it was intended, and the excellence of every government is its adaptation to the state of those to be governed by it. For us it would not do. Distinguishing between the structure of the government and the moral principles on which you prescribe its administration, with the latter we concur cordially, with the former we should not. We of the United States, you know, are constitutionally and conscientiously democrats. We consider society as one of the natural wants with which man has been created; that he has been endowed with faculties and qualities to effect its satisfaction by concurrence of others having the same want; that when, by the exercise of these faculties, he has procured a state of society, it is one of his acquisitions which he has a right to regulate and control, jointly indeed with all those who have concurred in the procurement, whom he cannot exclude from its use or direction more than they him. We think experience has proved it safer, for the mass of individuals composing the society, to reserve to themselves personally the exercise of all rightful powers to which they are competent, and to delegate those to which they are not competent to deputies named, and removable for unfaithful conduct, by themselves immediately. Hence, with us, the people (by which is meant the mass of individuals composing the society) being competent to judge of the facts occurring in ordinary life, they have retained the functions of judges of facts, under the name of jurors; but being unqualified for the management of affairs requiring intelligence above the common level, yet competent judges of human character, they chose, for their management, representatives, some by themselves immediately, others by electors chosen by themselves. Thus our President is chosen by ourselves, directly in *practice*, for we vote for A as elector only on the condition he will vote for B, our representatives by ourselves immediately, our Senate and judges of law through electors chosen by ourselves. And we believe that this proximate choice and power of removal is the best security which experience has sanctioned for ensuring an honest conduct in the functionaries of society. Your three or four alembications have indeed a seducing appearance. We should conceive, *prima facie*, that the last extract would be the pure alcohol of the substance, three or four times rectified. But in proportion as they are more and more sublimated, they are also farther and farther removed from the control of the society; and the human character, we believe, requires in general constant and immediate control, to prevent its being biased from right by the seductions of self-love. Your process produces, therefore, a structure of government from which the fundamental principle of ours is excluded. You first set down as zeros all individuals not having lands, which are the greater number in every society of long standing. Those holding lands are permitted to manage in person the small affairs of their commune or corporation, and to elect a deputy for the canton; in which election, too, every one's vote is to be an unit, a plurality, or a fraction, in proportion to his landed possessions. The assemblies of cantons, then, elect for the districts; those of districts for circles; and those of circles for the national assemblies. Some of these highest councils, too, are in a considerable degree self-elected, the regency partially, the judiciary entirely, and some are for life. Whenever, therefore, an *esprit de corps*, or of party, gets possession of them, which experience shows to be inevitable, there are no means of breaking it up, for they will never elect but those of their own spirit. Juries are allowed in criminal cases only. I acknowledge myself strong in affection to our own form, yet both of us act and think from the same motive, we both consider the people as our children, and love them with parental affection. But you love them as infants whom you are afraid to trust without nurses; and I as adults whom I freely leave to self-government. And you are right in the case referred to you; my criticism being built on a state of society not under your contemplation. It is, in fact, like a critic on Homer by the laws of the Drama.

But when we come to the moral principles on which the government is to be administered, we come to what is proper for all conditions of society. I meet you there in all the benevolence and rectitude of your native character; and I love myself always most where I concur most with you. Liberty, truth, probity, honor, are declared to be the four cardinal principles of your society. I believe with you that morality, compassion, generosity, are innate elements of the human constitution; that there exists a right independent of force; that a right to property is founded in our natural wants, in the means with which we are endowed to satisfy these wants, and the right to what we acquire by those means without violating the similar rights of other sensible beings; that no one has a right to obstruct another, exercising his faculties innocently for the relief of sensibilities made a part of his nature; that justice is the fundamental law of society; that the majority, oppressing an individual, is guilty of a crime, abuses its strength, and by acting on the law of the strongest, breaks up the foundations of society; that action by the citizens in person, in affairs within their reach and competence, and in all others by representatives, chosen immediately, and removable by themselves, constitutes the essence of a republic; that all governments are more or less republican in proportion as this principle enters more or less into their composition; and that a government by representation is capable of extension over a greater surface of country than one of any other form. These, my friend, are the essentials in which you and I agree; however, in our zeal for their maintenance, we may be perplexed and divaricate, as to the structure of society most likely to secure them.

In the Constitution of Spain, as proposed by the late Cortes, there was a principle entirely new to me, and not noticed in yours, that no person, born after that day, should ever acquire the rights of citizenship until he could read and write. It is impossible sufficiently to estimate the wisdom of this provision. Of all those which have been thought of for securing fidelity in the administration of the government, constant ralliance to the principles of the Constitution, and progressive amendments with the progressive advances of the human mind, or changes in human affairs, it is the most effectual. Enlighten the people generally, and tyranny and oppressions of body and mind will vanish like evil spirits at the dawn of day. Although I do not, with some enthusiasts, believe that the human condition will ever advance to such a state of perfection as that there shall no longer be pain or vice in the world, yet I believe it susceptible of much improvement, and most of all, in matters of government and religion; and that the diffusion of knowledge among the people is to be the instrument by which it is to be effected. ° ° °

To John Brazier

Jefferson, a better-than-average classicist in an age that admired classical learning above all other, reflects in this letter the contemporary view of its values. Brazier, an eminent scholar, had written a review of Pickering's book on Greek pronunciation. Text: Lipscomb and Bergh, eds., *Writings*, XV, 207–11.

Poplar Forest, August 24, 1819.

SIR,—The acknowledgment of your favor of July 15th, and thanks for the Review which it covered of Mr. Pickering's Memoir on the Modern Greek, have been delayed by a visit to an occasional but distant residence from Monticello, and to an attack here of rheumatism which is just now moderating. I had been much pleased with the memoir, and was much also with your review of it. I have little hope indeed of the recovery of the ancient pronunciation of that finest of human languages, but still I rejoice at the attention the subject seems to excite with you, because it is an evidence that our country begins to have a taste for something more than merely as much Greek as will pass a candidate for clerical ordination.

You ask my opinion on the extent to which classical learning should be carried in our country. A sickly condition permits me to think, and a rheumatic hand to write too briefly on this litigated question. The utilities we derive from the remains of the Greek and Latin languages are, first, as models of pure taste in writing. To these we are certainly indebted for the rational and chaste style of modern composition which so much distinguishes the nations to whom these languages are familiar. Without these models we should probably have continued the inflated style of our northern ancestors, or the hyperbolical and vague one of the east. Second. Among the values of classical learning, I estimate the luxury of reading the Greek and Roman authors in all the beauties of their originals. And why should not this innocent and elegant luxury take its preëminent stand ahead of all those addressed merely to the senses? I think myself more indebted to my father for this than for all the other luxuries his cares and affections have placed within my reach; and more now than when younger, and more susceptible of delights from other sources. When the decays of age have enfeebled the useful energies of the mind, the classic pages fill up the vacuum of *ennui*, and become sweet composers to that rest of the grave into which we are all sooner or later to descend. Third. A third value is in the stores of real science deposited and transmitted us in these languages, to wit: in history, ethics, arithmetic, geometry, astronomy, natural history, etc.

But to whom are these things useful? Certainly not to all men. There are conditions of life to which they must be forever estranged, and there are epochs of life too, after which the endeavor to attain them would be a great misemployment of time. Their acquisition should be the occupation of our early years only, when the memory is susceptible of deep and lasting impressions, and reason and judgment not yet strong enough for abstract speculations. To the moralist they are valuable, because they furnish ethical writings highly and justly esteemed: although in my own opinion, the moderns are far advanced beyond them in this line of science, the divine finds in the Greek language a translation of his primary code, of more importance to him than the original because better understood; and, in the same language, the newer code, with the doctrines of the earliest fathers, who lived and wrote before the simple precepts of the Founder of this most benign and pure of all systems of morality became frittered into subtleties and mysteries, and hidden under jargons incomprehensible to the human mind. To these original sources he must now, therefore, return, to recover the virgin purity of his religion. The lawyer finds in the Latin language the system of civil law most conformable with the principles of justice of any which has ever yet been established among men, and from which much has been incorporated into our own. The physician as good a code of his art as has been given us to this day. Theories and systems of medicine, indeed, have been in perpetual change from the days of the good Hippocrates to the days of the good Rush, but which of them is the true one? the present, to be sure, as long as it is the present, but to yield its place in turn to the next novelty, which is then to become the true system, and is to mark the vast advance of medicine since the days of Hippocrates. Our situation is certainly benefited by the discovery of some new and very valuable medicines; and substituting those for some of his with the treasure of facts, and of sound observations recorded by him (mixed, to be sure, with anilities of his day) and we shall have nearly the present sum of the healing art. The statesman will find in these languages history, politics, mathematics, ethics, eloquence, love of country, to which he must add the sciences of his own day, for which of them should be unknown to him? And all the sciences must recur to the classical languages for the etymon, and sound understanding of their fundamental terms. For the merchant I should not say that the languages are a necessary. Ethics, mathematics, geography, political economy, history, seem to constitute the immediate foundations of his calling. The agriculturist needs ethics, mathematics, chemistry and natural philosophy. The mechanic the same. To them the languages are but ornament and comfort. I know it is often said there have been shining examples of men of great abilities in all the businesses of life, without any other science than what they had gathered from conversations and intercourse with the world. But who can say what these men would not have been, had they started in the science on the shoulders of a Demosthenes or Cicero, of a Locke or Bacon, or a Newton? To sum the whole, therefore, it may truly be said that the classical languages are a solid basis for most, and an ornament to all the sciences.

I am warned by my aching fingers to close this hasty sketch, and to place here my last and fondest wishes for the advancement of our country in the useful sciences and arts, and my assurances of respect and esteem for the Reviewer of the Memoir on modern Greek.

To Dr. Benjamin Waterhouse

Waterhouse, a prominent physician and a professor at Harvard, was a pioneer in vaccination research and a crusader against tobacco and liquor. Text: Ford, ed., *Writings*, X, 219–20.

Monticello, June 26, 1822.

DEAR SIR,—I have received and read with thankfulness and pleasure your denunciation of the abuses of tobacco and wine. Yet, however sound in its principles, I expect it will be but a sermon to the wind. You will find it as difficult to inculcate these sanative precepts on the sensualities of the present day, as to convince an Athanasian that there is but one God. I wish success to both attempts, and am happy to learn from you that the latter, at least, is making progress, and the more rapidly in proportion as our Platonizing Christians make more stir and noise about it. The doctrines of Jesus are simple, and tend all to the happiness of man.

1. That there is one only God, and he all perfect.
2. That there is a future state of rewards and punishments.
3. That to love God with all thy heart and thy neighbor as thyself, is the sum of religion. These are the great points on which he endeavored to reform the religion of the Jews. But compare with these the demoralizing dogmas of Calvin.

1. That there are three Gods.
2. That good works, or the love of our neighbor, are nothing.
3. That faith is every thing, and the more incomprehensible the proposition, the more merit in its faith.
4. That reason in religion is of unlawful use.
5. That God, from the beginning, elected certain individuals to be saved, and certain others to be damned; and that no crimes of the former can damn them; no virtues of the latter save.

Now, which of these is the true and charitable Christian? He who believes and acts on the simple doctrines of Jesus? Or the impious dogmatists, as Athanasius and Calvin? Verily I say these are the false shepherds foretold as to enter not by the door into the sheepfold, but to climb up some other way. They are mere usurpers of the Christian name, teaching a counter-religion made up of the *deliria* of crazy imaginations, as foreign from Christianity as is that of Mahomet. Their blasphemies have driven thinking men into infidelity, who have too hastily rejected the supposed author himself, with the horrors so falsely imputed to him. Had the doctrines of Jesus been preached always as pure as they came from his lips, the whole civilized world would now have been Christian. I rejoice that in this blessed country of free inquiry and belief, which has surrendered its creed and conscience to neither kings nor priests, the genuine doctrine of one only God is reviving, and I trust that there is not a *young man* now living in the United States who will not die an Unitarian.

But much I fear, that when this great truth shall be re-established, its votaries will fall into the fatal error of fabricating formulas of creed and confessions of faith, the engines which so soon destroyed the religion of Jesus, and made of Christendom a mere Aceldama; that they will give up morals for mysteries, and Jesus for Plato. How much wiser are the Quakers, who, agreeing in the fundamental doctrines of the gospel, schismatize about no mysteries, and, keeping within the pale of common sense, suffer no speculative differences of opinion, any more than of feature, to impair the love of their brethren. Be this the wisdom of Unitarians, this the holy mantle which shall cover within its charitable circumference all who believe in one God, and who love their neighbor! I conclude my sermon with sincere assurances of my friendly esteem and respect.

ALEXANDER HAMILTON [1757–1804]

JAMES MADISON [1751–1836]

JOHN JAY [1745–1829]

THE PROPOSED NEW CONSTITUTION, intended to replace the Articles of Confederation, emerged from the Philadelphia Convention on September 27, 1787, to be put in force as soon as nine states ratified it. But ratification was by no means certain, and Alexander Hamilton of New York, assessing the strength of the opposition in his own state, asked John Jay and James Madison to assist him in writing a series of essays explaining and defending the new instrument of government.

Hamilton, the son of a Scottish merchant, was born in the West Indies and in 1772 was sent to New Jersey and New York to complete his education. As a student of seventeen at King's College (now Columbia) he entered the political controversy by writing pamphlets answering the Tory cleric, Samuel Seabury. In the Revolution he served on the staff of General Washington. A member of the Constitutional Convention, he endorsed its work by writing more than half of the *Federalist* papers. As first Secretary of the Treasury, supported by President Washington and by Congress, he virtually directed the new administration in its task of making the Constitution work. He declined the office of Chief Justice of the Supreme Court in favor of a distinguished law practice, and died early in consequence of a duel with Aaron Burr.

James Madison, fourth President of the United States, was brought up on a plantation in Virginia and educated at the College of New Jersey (now Princeton), where his classmates included the poet Freneau. With the coming of the Revolution, he held political office in Virginia and served in the Continental Congress. In the Constitutional Convention of 1787, he used his subtle, penetrating mind and deep knowledge of history and politics to such advantage that he earned the name of ' Father of the Constitution." When the new government was set up, he was in the House of Representatives, taking a leading part in the framing of the Bill of Rights then added to the Constitution. After 1800 he became Jefferson's Secretary of State, and succeeded Jefferson in the Presidency, serving for two terms.

John Jay, born in New York City, like Hamilton graduated from King's College and entered the practice of law. One of New York's most active and influential Revolutionary leaders, he served in the Continental Congress almost continuously from 1774 to 1779, and was elected its president in 1778. At the close of the Revolution he joined Franklin and Adams in Paris on the American delegation to the peace conference, returning to become Secretary of Foreign Affairs in the new government from 1784 to 1789. That year Washington appointed Jay Chief Justice of the Supreme Court under the new Constitution, a post he held until he resigned in 1795 to run successfully for Governor of New York.

Further reading: L. M. Hacker, *Alexander Hamilton in the American Tradition*, 1957. Irving Brant, *James Madison, Father of the Constitution*, 1950. Frank Monaghan, *John Jay, Defender of Liberty*, 1935. *The Federalist*, ed. B. F. Wright, 1962.

FROM *The Federalist*

The *Federalist* series, numbering eighty-five papers, or letters, signed "Publius," appeared in the newspapers between October 1787 and April 1788. Hamilton wrote fifty-one, Madison twenty-six, and Jay five; the authorship of three remains uncertain. The central argument of the series is that the Articles of Confederation did not provide the national government with sufficient authority to maintain liberty, security, and property; and that the Constitution, which remedied those deficiencies, ought to be adopted in its place. By June 1788 nine states had given their approval, but although the Constitution was now legally in force, it was obvious that without the ratification of Virginia and New York it could never operate successfully. *The Federalist* played an important role in consolidating support for the Constitutional forces, and in June and July 1788 these two crucial states became the tenth and eleventh to ratify. Text: Henry Cabot Lodge, ed., *The Federalist* (New York, 1904).

No. III

[Jay]

To the People of the State of New York:

It is not a new observation that the people of any country (if, like the Americans, intelligent and well-informed) seldom adopt and steadily persevere for many years in an erroneous opinion respecting their interests. That consideration naturally tends to create great respect for the high opinion which the people of America have so long and uniformly entertained of the importance of their continuing firm-

ly united under one federal government, vested with sufficient powers for all general and national purposes.

The more attentively I consider and investigate the reasons which appear to have given birth to this opinion, the more I become convinced that they are cogent and conclusive.

Among the many objects to which a wise and free people find it necessary to direct their attention, that of providing for their *safety* seems to be the first. The *safety* of the people doubtless has relation to a great variety of circumstances and considerations, and consequently affords great latitude to those who wish to define it precisely and comprehensively.

At present I mean only to consider it as it respects security for the preservation of peace and tranquillity, as well as against dangers from *foreign arms and influence*, as from dangers of the *like kind* arising from domestic causes. As the former of these comes first in order, it is proper it should be the first discussed. Let us therefore proceed to examine whether the people are not right in their opinion that a cordial Union, under an efficient national government, affords them the best security that can be devised against *hostilities* from abroad.

The number of wars which have happened or will happen in the world will always be found to be in proportion to the number and weight of the causes, whether *real* or *pretended*, which *provoke* or *invite* them. If this remark be just, it becomes useful to inquire whether so many *just* causes of war are likely to be given by *United America* as by *disunited*

America; for if it should turn out that United America will probably give the fewest, then it will follow that in this respect the Union tends most to preserve the people in a state of peace with other nations.

The *just* causes of war, for the most part, arise either from violations of treaties or from direct violence. America has already formed treaties with no less than six foreign nations, and all of them, except Prussia, are maritime, and therefore able to annoy and injure us. She has also extensive commerce with Portugal, Spain, and Britain, and, with respect to the two latter, has, in addition, the circumstance of neighborhood to attend to.

It is of high importance to the peace of America that she observe the laws of nations towards all these powers, and to me it appears evident that this will be more perfectly and punctually done by one national government than it could be either by thirteen separate States or by three or four distinct confederacies.

Because when once an efficient national government is established, the best men in the country will not only consent to serve, but also will generally be appointed to manage it; for, although town or country, or other contracted influence, may place men in State assemblies, or senates, or courts of justice, or executive departments, yet more general and extensive reputation for talents and other qualifications will be necessary to recommend men to offices under the national government,—especially as it will have the widest field for choice, and never experience that want of proper persons which is not uncommon in some of the States. Hence, it will result that the administration, the political counsels, and the judicial decisions of the national government will be more wise, systematical, and judicious than those of individual States, and consequently more satisfactory with respect to other nations, as well as more *safe* with respect to us.

Because, under the national government, treaties and articles of treaties, as well as the laws of nations, will always be expounded in one sense and executed in the same manner,—whereas adjudications on the same points and questions, in thirteen States, or in three or four confederacies, will not always accord or be consistent; and that, as well from the variety of independent courts and judges appointed by different and independent governments, as from the different local laws and interests which may affect and influence them. The wisdom of the convention, in committing such questions to the jurisdiction and judgment of courts appointed by and responsible only to one national government, cannot be too much commended.

Because the prospect of present loss or advantage may often tempt the governing party in one or two States to swerve from good faith and justice; but those temptations, not reaching the other States, and consequently having little or no influence on the national government, the temptation will be fruitless, and good faith and justice be preserved. The case of the treaty of peace with Britain adds great weight to this reasoning.

Because, even if the governing party in a State should be disposed to resist such temptations, yet, as such temptations may, and commonly do, result from circumstances peculiar to the State, and may affect a great number of the inhabitants, the governing party may not always be able, if willing, to prevent the injustice meditated, or to punish the aggressors. But the national government, not being affected by those local circumstances, will neither be induced to commit the wrong themselves, nor want power or inclination to prevent or punish its commission by others.

So far, therefore, as either designed or accidental violations of treaties and the laws of nations afford *just* causes of war, they are less to be apprehended under one general government than under several lesser ones, and in that respect the former most favors the *safety* of the people.

As to those just causes of war which proceed from direct and unlawful violence, it appears equally clear to me that one good national government affords vastly more security against dangers of that sort than can be derived from any other quarter.

Because such violences are more frequently caused by the passions and interests of a part than of the whole; of one or two States than of the Union. Not a single Indian war has yet been occasioned by aggressions of the present federal government, feeble as it is; but there are several instances of Indian hostilities having been provoked by the improper conduct of individual States, who, either unable or unwilling to restrain or punish offences, have given occasion to the slaughter of many innocent inhabitants.

The neighborhood of Spanish and British territories, bordering on some States and not on others, naturally confines the causes of quarrel more immediately to the borderers. The bordering States, if any, will be those who, under the impulse of sudden irritation, and a quick sense of apparent interest or injury, will be most likely, by direct violence, to excite war with these nations; and nothing can so effectually obviate that danger as a national government, whose wisdom and prudence will not be diminished by the passions which actuate the parties immediately interested.

But not only fewer just causes of war will be given by the national government, but it will also be more in their power to accommodate and settle them amicably. They will be more temperate and cool, and in that respect, as well as in others, will be more in capacity to act advisedly than the offending State. The pride of states, as well as of men, naturally disposes them to justify all their actions, and opposes their acknowledging, correcting, or repairing their errors and offences. The national government, in such cases, will not be affected by this pride, but will proceed with moderation and candor to consider and decide on the means most proper to extricate them from the difficulties which threaten them.

Besides, it is well known that acknowledgments, explanations, and compensations are often accepted as satisfactory from a strong united nation, which would be rejected as unsatisfactory if offered by a State or confederacy of little consideration or power.

In the year 1685, the state of Genoa having offended Louis XIV., endeavored to appease him. He demanded that they should send their *Doge,* or chief magistrate, accompanied by four of their senators, to *France,* to ask his pardon and receive his terms. They were obliged to submit to it for the sake of peace. Would he on any occasion either have demanded or have received the like humiliation from Spain, or Britain, or any other *powerful* nation?

PUBLIUS.
1787

No. X

[Madison]

To the People of the State of New York:

Among the numerous advantages promised by a well-constructed Union, none deserves to be more accurately developed than its tendency to break and control the violence of faction. The friend of popular governments never finds himself so much alarmed for their character and fate, as when he contemplates their propensity to this dangerous vice. He will not fail, therefore, to set a due value on any plan which, without violating the principles to which he is attached, provides a proper cure for it. The instability, injustice, and confusion introduced into the public councils, have, in truth, been the mortal diseases under which popular governments have everywhere perished; as they continue to be the favorite and fruitful topics from which the adversaries to liberty derive their most specious declamations. The valuable improvements made by the American constitutions on the popular models, both ancient and modern, cannot certainly be too much admired; but it would be an unwarrantable partiality, to contend that they have as effectually obviated the danger on this side, as was wished and expected. Complaints are everywhere heard from our most considerate and virtuous citizens, equally the friends of public and private faith, and of public and personal liberty, that our governments are too unstable, that the public good is disregarded in the conflicts of rival parties, and that measures are too often decided, not according to the rules of justice and the rights of the minor party, but by the superior force of an interested and overbearing majority. However anxiously we may wish that these complaints had no foundation, the evidence of known facts will not permit us to deny that they are in some degree true. It will be found, indeed, on a candid review of our situation, that some of the distresses under which we labor have been erroneously charged on the operation of our governments; but it will be found, at the same time, that other causes will not alone account for many of our heaviest misfortunes; and, particularly, for that prevailing and increasing distrust of public engagements, and alarm for private rights, which are echoed from one end of the continent to the other. These must be chiefly, if not wholly, effects of the unsteadiness and injustice with which a factious spirit has tainted our public administrations.

By a faction, I understand a number of citizens, whether amounting to a majority or minority of the whole, who are united and actuated by some common impulse of passion, or of interest, adverse to the rights of other citizens, or to the permanent and aggregate interests of the community.

There are two methods of curing the mischiefs of faction: the one, by removing its causes; the other, by controlling its effects.

There are again two methods of removing the causes of faction: the one, by destroying the liberty which is essential to its existence; the other, by giving to every citizen the same opinions, the same passions, and the same interests.

It could never be more truly said than of the first remedy, that it was worse than the disease. Liberty is to faction what air is to fire, an aliment without which it instantly expires. But it could not be less folly to abolish liberty, which is essential to political life, because it nourishes faction, than it would be to wish the annihilation of air, which is essential to animal life, because it imparts to fire its destructive agency.

The second expedient is as impracticable as the first would be unwise. As long as the reason of man continues fallible, and he is at liberty to exercise it, different opinions will be formed. As long as the connection subsists between his reason and his self-love, his opinions and his passions will have a reciprocal influence on each other; and the former will be objects to which the latter will attach themselves. The diversity in the faculties of men, from which the rights of property originate, is not less an insuperable obstacle to a uniformity of interests. The protection of these faculties is the first object of government. From the protection of different and unequal faculties of acquiring property, the possession of different degrees and kinds of property immediately results; and from the influence of these on the sentiments and views of the respective proprietors, ensues a division of the society into different interests and parties.

The latent causes of faction are thus sown in the nature of man; and we see them everywhere brought into different degrees of activity, according to the different circumstances of civil society. A zeal for different opinions concerning religion, concerning government, and many other points, as well of speculation as of practice; an attachment to different leaders ambitiously contending for pre-eminence and power; or to persons of other descriptions whose fortunes have been interesting to the human passions, have, in turn, divided mankind into parties, inflamed them with mutual animosity, and rendered them much more disposed to vex and oppress each other than to co-operate for their common good. So strong is this propensity of mankind to fall into mutual animosities, that where no substantial occasion presents itself, the most frivolous and fanciful distinctions have been sufficient to kindle their unfriendly passions and excite their most violent conflicts. But the most common and durable source of factions has been the various and unequal distribution of property. Those who hold and those who are without property have ever formed distinct interests in society. Those who are creditors, and those who are debtors, fall under a like discrimination. A landed interest, a manufacturing interest, a mercantile interest, a moneyed interest, with many lesser interests, grow up of necessity in civilized nations, and divide them into different classes, actuated by different sentiments and views. The regulation of these various and interfering interests forms the principal task of modern legislation, and involves the spirit of party and faction in the necessary and ordinary operations of the government.

No man is allowed to be a judge in his own cause, because his interest would certainly bias his judgment, and, not improbably, corrupt his integrity. With equal, nay with greater reason, a body of men are unfit to be both judges and parties at the same time; yet what are many of the most important acts of legislation, but so many judicial determinations, not indeed concerning the rights of single persons, but concerning the rights of large bodies of citizens. And what are the different classes of legislators but advocates and parties to the causes which they determine? Is a law proposed concerning private debts? It is a question to which the creditors are parties on one side and the debtors on the other.

Justice ought to hold the balance between them. Yet the parties are, and must be, themselves the judges; and the most numerous party, or, in other words, the most powerful faction must be expected to prevail. Shall domestic manufactures be encouraged, and in what degree, by restrictions on foreign manufactures? are questions which would be differently decided by the landed and the manufacturing classes, and probably by neither with a sole regard to justice and the public good. The apportionment of taxes on the various descriptions of property is an act which seems to require the most exact impartiality; yet there is, perhaps, no legislative act in which greater opportunity and temptation are given to a predominant party to trample on the rules of justice. Every shilling with which they overburden the inferior number, is a shilling saved to their own pockets.

It is in vain to say that enlightened statesmen will be able to adjust these clashing interests, and render them all subservient to the public good. Enlightened statesmen will not always be at the helm. Nor, in many cases, can such an adjustment be made at all without taking into view indirect and remote considerations, which will rarely prevail over the immediate interest which one party may find in disregarding the rights of another or the good of the whole.

The inference to which we are brought is, that the *causes* of faction cannot be removed, and that relief is only to be sought in the means of controlling its *effects*.

If a faction consists of less than a majority, relief is supplied by the republican principle, which enables the majority to defeat its sinister views by regular vote. It may clog the administration, it may convulse the society; but it will be unable to execute and mask its violence under the forms of the Constitution. When a majority is included in a faction, the form of popular government, on the other hand, enables it to sacrifice to its ruling passion or interest both the public good and the rights of other citizens. To secure the public good and private rights against the danger of such a faction, and at the same time to preserve the spirit and the form of popular government, is then the great object to which our inquiries are directed. Let me add that it is the great desideratum by which this form of government can be rescued from the opprobrium under which it has so long labored, and be recommended to the esteem and adoption of mankind.

By what means is this object attainable? Evidently by one of two only. Either the existence of the same passion or interest in a majority at the same time must be prevented, or the majority, having such co-existent passion or interest, must be rendered, by their number and local situation, unable to concert and carry into effect schemes of oppression. If the impulse and the opportunity be suffered to coincide, we well know that neither moral nor religious motives can be relied on as an adequate control. They are not found to be such on the injustice and violence of individuals, and lose their efficacy in proportion to the number combined together; that is, in proportion as their efficacy becomes needful.

From this view of the subject it may be concluded that a pure democracy, by which I mean a society consisting of a small number of citizens, who assemble and administer the government in person, can admit of no cure for the mischiefs of faction. A common passion or interest will, in almost every case, be felt by a majority of the whole; a communication and concert result from the form of government itself; and there is nothing to check the inducements to sacrifice the weaker party or an obnoxious individual. Hence it is that such democracies have ever been spectacles of turbulence and contention; have ever been found incompatible with personal security or the rights of property; and have in general been as short in their lives as they have been violent in their deaths. Theoretic politicians, who have patronized this species of government, have erroneously supposed that by reducing mankind to a perfect equality in their political rights, they would, at the same time, be perfectly equalized and assimilated in their possessions, their opinions, and their passions.

A republic, by which I mean a government in which the scheme of representation takes place, opens a different prospect, and promises the cure for which we are seeking. Let us examine the points in which it varies from pure democracy, and we shall comprehend both the nature of the cure and the efficacy which it must derive from the Union.

The two great points of difference between a democracy and a republic are: first, the delegation of the government, in the latter, to a small number of citizens elected by the rest; secondly, the greater number of citizens, and greater sphere of country, over which the latter may be extended.

The effect of the first difference is, on the one hand, to refine and enlarge the public views, by passing them through the medium of a chosen body of citizens, whose wisdom may best discern the true interest of their country, and whose patriotism and love of justice will be least likely to sacrifice it to temporary or partial considerations. Under such a regulation, it may well happen that the public voice, pronounced by the representatives of the people, will be more consonant to the public good than if pronounced by the people themselves, convened for the purpose. On the other hand, the effect may be inverted. Men of factious tempers, of local preju-

dices, or of sinister designs, may, by intrigue, by corruption, or by other means, first obtain the suffrages, and then betray the interests, of the people. The question resulting is whether small or extensive republics are more favorable to the election of proper guardians of the public weal; and it is clearly decided in favor of the latter by two obvious considerations:

In the first place, it is to be remarked that, however small the republic may be, the representatives must be raised to a certain number, in order to guard against the cabals of a few; and that, however large it may be, they must be limited to a certain number, in order to guard against the confusion of a multitude. Hence, the number of representatives in the two cases not being in proportion to that of the two constituents, and being proportionally greater in the small republic, it follows that, if the proportion of fit characters be not less in the large than in the small republic, the former will present a greater option, and consequently a greater probability of a fit choice.

In the next place, as each representative will be chosen by a greater number of citizens in the large than in the small republic, it will be more difficult for unworthy candidates to practise with success the vicious arts by which elections are too often carried; and the suffrages of the people being more free, will be more likely to centre in men who possess the most attractive merit and the most diffusive and established characters.

It must be confessed that in this, as in most other cases, there is a mean, on both sides of which inconveniences will be found to lie. By enlarging too much the number of electors, you render the representative too little acquainted with all their local circumstances and lesser interests; as by reducing it too much, you render him unduly attached to these, and too little fit to comprehend and pursue great and national objects. The federal Constitution forms a happy combination in this respect; the great and aggregate interests being referred to the national, the local and particular to the State legislatures.

The other point of difference is, the greater number of citizens and extent of territory which may be brought within the compass of republican than of democratic government; and it is this circumstance principally which renders factious combinations less to be dreaded in the former than in the latter. The smaller the society, the fewer probably will be the distinct parties and interests composing it; the fewer the distinct parties and interests, the more frequently will a majority be found of the same party; and the smaller the number of individuals composing a majority, and the smaller the compass within which they are placed, the more easily will they concert and execute their plans of oppression. Extend the sphere, and you take in a greater variety of parties and interests; you make it less probable that a majority of the whole will have a common motive to invade the rights of other citizens; or if such a common motive exists, it will be more difficult for all who feel it to discover their own strength, and to act in unison with each other. Besides other impediments, it may be remarked that, where there is a consciousness of unjust or dishonorable purposes, communication is always checked by distrust in proportion to the number whose concurrence is necessary.

Hence, it clearly appears, that the same advantage which a republic has over a democracy, in controlling the effects of faction, is enjoyed by a large over a small republic,—is enjoyed by the Union over the States composing it. Does the advantage consist in the substitution of representatives whose enlightened views and virtuous sentiments render them superior to local prejudices and to schemes of injustice? It will not be denied that the representation of the Union will be most likely to possess these requisite endowments. Does it consist in the greater security afforded by a greater variety of parties, against the event of any one party being able to outnumber and oppress the rest? In an equal degree does the increased variety of parties comprised within the Union, increase this security. Does it, in fine, consist in the greater obstacles opposed to the concert and accomplishment of the secret wishes of an unjust and interested majority? Here, again, the extent of the Union gives it the most palpable advantage.

The influence of factious leaders may kindle a flame within their particular States, but will be unable to spread a general conflagration through the other States. A religious sect may degenerate into a political faction in a part of the Confederacy; but the variety of sects dispersed over the entire face of it must secure the national councils against any danger from that source. A rage for paper money, for an abolition of debts, for an equal division of property, or for any other improper or wicked project, will be less apt to pervade the whole body of the Union than a particular member of it; in the same proportion as such a malady is more likely to taint a particular county or district than an entire State.

In the extent and proper structure of the Union, therefore, we behold a republican remedy for the diseases more incident to republican government. And according to the degree of pleasure and pride we feel in being republicans ought to be our zeal in cherishing the spirit and supporting the character of Federalists.

PUBLIUS.
1787

No. XXIII

[Hamilton]

To the People of the State of New York:

The necessity of a Constitution, at least equally energetic with the one proposed, to the preservation of the Union, is the point at the examination of which we are now arrived.

This inquiry will naturally divide itself into three branches—the objects to be provided for by the federal government, the quantity of power necessary to the accomplishment of those objects, the persons upon whom that power ought to operate. Its distribution and organization will more properly claim our attention under the succeeding head.

The principal purposes to be answered by union are these—the common defence of the members; the preservation of the public peace, as well against internal convulsions as external attacks; the regulation of commerce with other nations and between the States; the superintendence of our intercourse, political and commercial, with foreign countries.

The authorities essential to the common defence are these: to raise armies; to build and equip fleets; to prescribe rules for the government of both; to direct their operations; to provide for their support. These powers ought to exist without limitation, *because it is impossible to foresee or define the extent and variety of national exigencies, or the correspondent extent and variety of the means which may be necessary to satisfy them.* The circumstances that endanger the safety of nations are infinite, and for this reason no constitutional shackles can wisely be imposed on the power to which the care of it is committed. This power ought to be co-extensive with all the possible combinations of such circumstances; and ought to be under the direction of the same councils which are appointed to preside over the common defence.

This is one of those truths which, to a correct and unprejudiced mind, carries its own evidence along with it; and may be obscured, but cannot be made plainer by argument or reasoning. It rests upon axioms as simple as they are universal; the *means* ought to be proportioned to the *end;* the persons, from whose agency the attainment of any *end* is expected, ought to possess the *means* by which it is to be attained.

Whether there ought to be a federal government intrusted with the care of the common defence, is a question in the first instance, open for discussion; but the moment it is decided in the affirmative, it will follow, that that government ought to be clothed with all the powers requisite to complete execution of its trust. And unless it can be shown that the circumstances which may affect the public safety are reducible within certain determinate limits; unless the contrary of this position can be fairly and rationally disputed, it must be admitted, as a necessary consequence, that there can be no limitation of that authority which is to provide for the defence and protection of the community, in any matter essential to its efficacy—that is, in any matter essential to the *formation*, *direction*, or *support* of the NATIONAL FORCES.

Defective as the present Confederation has been proved to be, this principle appears to have been fully recognized by the framers of it; though they have not made proper or adequate provision for its exercise. Congress have an unlimited discretion to make requisitions of men and money; to govern the army and navy; to direct their operations. As their requisitions are made constitutionally binding upon the States, who are in fact under the most solemn obligations to furnish the supplies required of them, the intention evidently was, that the United States should command whatever resources were by them judged requisite to the "common defence and general welfare." It was presumed that a sense of their true interests, and a regard to the dictates of good faith, would be found sufficient pledges for the punctual performance of the duty of the members to the federal head.

The experiment has, however, demonstrated that this expectation was ill-founded and illusory; and the observations, made under the last head, will, I imagine, have sufficed to convince the impartial and discerning, that there is an absolute necessity for an entire change in the first principles of the system; that if we are in earnest about giving the Union energy and duration, we must abandon the vain project of legislating upon the States in their collective capacities; we must extend the laws of the federal government to the individual citizens of America; we must discard the fallacious scheme of quotas and requisitions, as equally impracticable and unjust. The result from all this is that the Union ought to be invested with full power to levy troops; to build and equip fleets; and to raise the revenues which will be required for the formation and support of an army and navy, in the customary and ordinary modes practised in other governments.

If the circumstances of our country are such as to demand a compound instead of a simple, a confederate instead of a sole, government, the essential point which will remain to be adjusted will be to discriminate the OBJECTS, as far as it can be done, which shall appertain to the different provinces or departments of power; allowing to each the most ample authority for fulfilling the objects committed to its charge. Shall the Union be constituted the guardian of the common safety? Are fleets and armies and revenues necessary to this purpose? The government of the Union must be empowered to pass all laws, and to make all regulations which have relation to them. The same must be the case in respect to commerce, and to every other matter to which its jurisdiction is permitted to extend. Is the administration of justice between the citizens of the same State the proper department of the local governments? These must possess all the authorities which are connected with this object, and with every other that may be allotted to their particular cognizance and direction. Not to confer in each case a degree of power commensurate to the end, would be to violate the most obvious rules of prudence and propriety, and improvidently to trust the great interests of the nation to hands which are disabled from managing them with vigor and success.

Who so likely to make suitable provisions for the public defence, as that body to which the guardianship of the public safety is confided; which, as the centre of information, will best understand the extent and urgency of the dangers that threaten; as the representative of the WHOLE, will feel itself most deeply interested in the preservation of every part; which, from the responsibility implied in the duty assigned to it, will be most sensibly impressed with the necessity of proper exertions; and which, by the extension of its authority throughout the States, can alone establish uniformity and concert in the plans and measures by which the common safety is to be secured? Is there not a manifest inconsistency in devolving upon the federal government the care of the general defence, and leaving in the State governments the *effective* powers by which it is to be provided for? Is not a want of co-operation the infallible consequence of such a system? And will not weakness, disorder, an undue distribution of the burdens and calamities of war, an unnecessary and intolerable increase of expense, be its natural and inevitable concomitants? Have we not had unequivocal experience of its effects in the course of the revolution which we have just accomplished?

Every view we may take of the subject, as candid inquirers after truth, will serve to convince us, that it is both unwise and dangerous to deny the federal government an unconfined authority, as to all those objects which are intrusted to its management. It will indeed deserve the most vigilant and careful attention of the people, to see that it be modelled in such a manner as to admit of its being safely vested with the requisite powers. If any plan which has been, or may be, offered to our consideration, should not, upon a dispassionate inspection, be found to answer this description, it ought to be rejected. A government, the constitution of which renders it unfit to be trusted with all the powers which a free people *ought to delegate to any government*, would be an unsafe and improper depositary of the NATIONAL INTERESTS. Wherever THESE can with propriety be confided, the coincident powers may safely accompany them. This is the true result of all just reasoning upon the subject. And the adversaries of the plan promulgated by the convention ought to have confined themselves to showing, that the internal structure of the proposed government was such as to render it unworthy of the confidence of the people. They ought not to have wandered into inflammatory declamations and unmeaning cavils about the extent of the powers. The POWERS are not too extensive for the OBJECTS of federal administration, or, in other words, for the management of our NATIONAL INTERESTS; nor can any satisfactory argument be framed to show that they are chargeable with such an excess. If it be true, as has been insinuated by some of the writers on the other side, that the difficulty arises from the nature of the thing, and that the extent of the country will not permit us to form a government in which such ample powers can safely be reposed, it would prove that we ought to contract our views, and resort to the expedient of separate confederacies, which will move within more practicable spheres. For the ab-

surdity must continually stare us in the face of confiding to a government the direction of the most essential national interests, without daring to trust it to the authorities which are indispensable to their proper and efficient management. Let us not attempt to reconcile contradictions, but firmly embrace a rational alternative.

I trust, however, that the impracticability of one general system cannot be shown. I am greatly mistaken, if any thing of weight has yet been advanced of this tendency; and I flatter myself, that the observations which have been made in the course of these papers have served to place the reverse of that position in as clear a light as any matter still in the womb of time and experience can be susceptible of. This, at all events, must be evident, that the very difficulty itself, drawn from the extent of the country, is the strongest argument in favor of an energetic government; for any other can certainly never preserve the Union of so large an empire. If we embrace the tenets of those who oppose the adoption of the proposed Constitution, as the standard of our political creed, we cannot fail to verify the gloomy doctrines which predict the impracticability of a national system pervading entire limits of the present Confederacy.   PUBLIUS.

1787

JOHN TRUMBULL [1750–1831]

JOHN TRUMBULL came from a distinguished New England family. Like Jonathan Edwards, who was his mother's cousin, he entered Yale at the age of thirteen (though he had passed his entrance examinations at seven). He took his B.A. in 1767, continued at Yale for three more years and an M.A., then briefly returned as tutor before embarking upon the practice of law. While an undergraduate at Yale he became acquainted with Timothy Dwight and David Humphreys; these three young men formed the nucleus of a group known as "The Connecticut Wits," who specialized in satires of the contemporary scene. Joel Barlow joined the group, as did other "wits," among them Lemuel Hopkins, Richard Alsop, and Theodore Dwight.

Trumbull gained the admiration of his colleagues by his graceful Addisonian essays and his satire on Yale in the Tom Brainless section of *The Progress of Dulness* (1772), written when he was a tutor. To placate the offended college officials, Trumbull added two more sections, which toned down the satire of the first part by generalizing the subjects into the typical eighteenth-century coquette and fop, Harriet Simper and Dick Hairbrain. He also excused himself by pointing out that the ideal end of satire is to "expose vice by general animadversions, and not to brand characters by personal satire."

Trumbull was admitted to the bar in 1773, and entered the Boston law office of John Adams; the following year he moved his practice to New Haven. In 1776 he issued the first two cantos of *M'Fingal*, which quickly became the most popular anti-Tory poem of the Revolution, going through thirty editions in sixty years. A distinguished judge of the Supreme Court of Errors and a state legislator until 1819, Trumbull revised his works in 1820, moved to Detroit five years later, and died there in 1831.

Further reading: Alexander Cowie, *John Trumbull: Connecticut Wit*, 1936. V. L. Parrington, ed., *The Connecticut Wits*, 1926. Leon Howard, *The Connecticut Wits*, 1943.

Prospect of the Future Glory of America

Being the conclusion of an Oration, delivered at the public commencement at Yale-College, September 12, 1770

The rising tide of self-confidence and self-consciousness that swept through the colonies after the French and Indian War elicited numerous demands for and prophecies of a future America that would equal and surpass England and Europe. The term "American," as it was used after 1760 to denote a certain kind of British colonist, began to take on connotations of its own. Although his loyalty to England was not in question, the American colonist became increasingly conscious that he was *American* English, a rather special kind of Englishman with a different future. Thus Franklin could tell Lord Kames in 1767 that the American colonies were destined "to become a great country, populous and mighty," without any thought of separation from the empire. This poem of Trumbull's, prepared for a college commencement and cast in the familiar poetic tradition of the "vision," reflects the nascent nationalism so deeply felt by the young men of his generation who would soon fight a war for independence against England. Text: Arthur H. Nason, ed., *The Writings of John Trumbull*, volume XIV of *The Colonnade*, published by the Andiron Club, New York, 1922; a reprint of the 1820 edition of Trumbull's works.

—And see th' expected hour is on the wing,
With every joy the flight of years can bring;
The splendid scenes the Muse shall dare display,
And unborn ages view the ripen'd day.

Beneath a sacred grove's inspiring shade,   5
When Night the world in pleasing glooms array'd,
While the fair moon, that leads the heav'nly train,
With varying brightness dyed the dusky plain,
Entranced I sate; to solemn thought resign'd,
Long visions rising in the raptured mind,   10
Celestial music charm'd the listening dale,
While these blest sounds my ravish'd ear assail.
   "To views far distant and to scenes more bright,
Along the vale of Time extend thy sight,
Where hours and days and years from yon dim pole,
Wave following wave in long succession roll,   16
There see, in pomp for ages without end,
The glories of the Western World ascend.
   "See, this blest land in orient morn appears,
Waked from the slumber of six thousand years,   20
While clouds of darkness veil'd each cheering ray;
To savage beasts and savage men, a prey.
Fair Freedom now her ensigns bright displays,
And peace and plenty bless the golden days.
In radiant state th' imperial realm shall rise,   25
Her splendor circling to the boundless skies;
Of every Fair she boasts the assembled charms,
The Queen of empires and the nurse of arms.
   "See her bold heroes mark their glorious way,
Arm'd for the fight and blazing on the day!   30
Blood stains their steps, and o'er th' ensanguined
      plain,
Mid warring thousands and mid thousands slain,
Their eager swords unsated carnage blend,
And ghastly deaths their raging course attend.
Her dreaded power the subject world shall see,   35
And laurel'd conquest wait her high decree.
   "And see her navies, rushing to the main,
Catch the swift gales and sweep the wat'ry plain;
Or led by commerce, at the merchant's door
Unlade the treasures of the Asian shore;   40
Or arm'd with thunder, on the guilty foe
Rush big with death and aim th' unerring blow;
Bid every realm, that hears the trump of fame,
Quake at the distant terror of her name.
   "For pleasing Arts behold her matchless charms,
The first in letters, as the first in arms.   46
See bolder genius quit the narrow shore,
And realms of science, yet untraced, explore,
Hiding in brightness of superior day,
The fainting gleam of Europe's setting ray.   50
   "Sublime the Muse shall lift her eagle wing;
Of heavenly themes the sacred bards shall sing,
Tell how the blest Redeemer, man to save,
Thro' the deep mansions of the gloomy grave,
Sought the low shades of night, then rising high   55
Vanquish'd the powers of hell, and soar'd above the
      sky;
Or paint the scenes of that funereal day,
When earth's last fires shall mark their dreadful
      way,

In solemn pomp th' eternal Judge descend,
Doom the wide world and give to nature, end;   60
Or ope heaven's glories to th' astonish'd eye,
And bid their lays with lofty Milton vie;
Or wake from nature's themes the moral song,
And shine with Pope, with Thompson and with
      Young.
   "This land her Swift and Addison shall view,   65
The former honours equall'd by the new;
Here shall some Shakspeare charm the rising age,
And hold in magic chains the listening stage;
A second Watts[1] shall string the heavenly lyre,
And other muses other bards inspire.   70
   "Her Daughters too the happy land shall grace
With powers of genius, as with charms of face;
Blest with the softness of the female mind,
With fancy blooming and with taste refined,
Some Rowe[2] shall rise, and wrest with daring pen   75
The pride of science from assuming men;
While each bright line a polish'd beauty wears,
For every muse and every grace are theirs.
   "Nor shall these bounds her rising fame confine,
With equal praise the sister arts shall shine.   80
   "Behold some new Apelles,[3] skill'd to trace
The varied features of the virgin's face,
Bid the gay landscape rise in rural charms,
Or wake from dust the slumb'ring chief in arms,
Bid art with nature hold a pleasing strife,   85
And warm the pictured canvas into life.
   "See heaven-born Music strike the trembling
      string,
Devotion rising on the raptured wing.
   "See the proud dome with lofty walls ascend,
Wide gates unfold, stupendous arches bend,   90
The spiry turrets, piercing to the skies,
And all the grandeur of the palace rise.
   "The patriot's voice shall Eloquence inspire
With Roman splendor and Athenian fire,
At freedom's call, teach manly breasts to glow,   95
And prompt the tender tear o'er guiltless woe."
1770

FROM *The Progress of Dulness*

Trumbull chooses the careers of Tom Brainless, a thick-
headed parson, Dick Hairbrain, a foppish coxcomb, and
Harriet Simper, a silly coquette, as his medium for a satiric
commentary on the fashions and foibles of his times, pat-
terned on Samuel Butler's *Hudibras*, which he helped to

Prospect. [1] Isaac Watts (1674–1748), writer of hymns and
popular, heavily moralistic poetry.
[2] Mrs. Elizabeth Rowe (1674–1737), English poetess of
eighteenth-century repute.
[3] Greek painter of the fourth century B.C., regarded as the
greatest painter of classical antiquity.

establish as a popular model for American satiric verse. In the course of the slender plot Harriet, having failed to capture Hairbrain, settles for the stodgy Brainless, a successful small-town minister, thereby bringing poetic justice to all. Text: Arthur H. Nason, ed., *The Writings of John Trumbull.*

Preface

"Pray, what does the author mean?" is the first question most readers will ask, and the last they are able to answer. Therefore in a few words I will explain the subject and design of the following Poem.

The subject is the state of the times in regard to literature and religion. The author was prompted to write, by a hope that it might be of use to point out, in a clear, concise, and striking manner, those general errors, that hinder the advantages of education and the growth of piety. The subject is inexhaustible; nor is my design yet completed. This first part describes the principal mistakes in one course of life, and exemplifies the following well known truths;—that to the frequent scandal, as well of religion, as learning, a fellow, without any share of genius, or application to study, may pass with credit through life, receive the honours of a liberal education, and be admitted to the right hand of fellowship among ministers of the gospel;—that except in one neighboring province, ignorance wanders unmolested at our colleges, examinations are dwindled to mere form and ceremony, and after four years dozing there, no one is ever refused the honors of a degree, on account of dulness and insufficiency;—that the mere knowledge of ancient languages, of the abstruser parts of mathematics, and the dark researches of metaphysics, is of little advantage in any business or profession in life;—that it would be more beneficial, in every place of public education, to take pains in teaching the elements of oratory, the grammar of the English tongue, and the elegancies of style and composition;—that in numberless instances, sufficient care hath not been taken to exclude the ignorant and irreligious from the sacred desk;—that this tenderness to the undeserving tends to debase the dignity of the clergy, and to hinder many worthy men from undertaking the office of the ministry;—and that the virulent controversies of the present day concerning religious, or in many cases, merely speculative opinions, savoring so highly of vanity and ostentation, and breathing a spirit so opposite to christian benevolence, have done more hurt to the cause of religion, than all the malice, the ridicule, and the folly of its enemies.

New-Haven, August 1772.

[Tom Brainless as Student and Preacher]

Two years thus spent in gathering knowledge,
The lad sets forth t' unlade at college,
While down his sire and priest attend him,
To introduce and recommend him;
Or if detain'd, a letter's sent   5
Of much apocryphal content,
To set him forth, how dull soever,
As very learn'd and very clever;
A genius of the first emission,
With burning love for erudition;   10
So studious he'll outwatch the moon
And think the planets set too soon.
He had but little time to fit in;
Examination too must frighten.
Depend upon't he must do well,   15
He knows much more than he can tell;
Admit him, and in little space
He'll beat his rivals in the race;
His father's incomes are but small,
He comes now, if he come at all.   20
  So said, so done, at college now
He enters well, no matter how;
New scenes awhile his fancy please,
But all must yield to love of ease.
In the same round condemn'd each day,   25
To study, read, recite and pray;
To make his hours of business double—
He can't endure th' increasing trouble;
And finds at length, as times grow pressing,
All plagues are easier than his lesson.   30
With sleepy eyes and count'nance heavy,
With much excuse of *non paravi*,[1]
Much absence, *tardes* and *egresses*,
The college-evil on him seizes.
Then ev'ry book, which ought to please,   35
Stirs up the seeds of dire disease;
Greek spoils his eyes, the print's so fine,
Grown dim with study, or with wine;
Of Tully's latin much afraid,
Each page, he calls the doctor's aid;   40
While geometry, with lines so crooked,
Sprains all his wits to overlook it.
His sickness puts on every name,
Its cause and uses still the same;
'Tis tooth-ache, cholic, gout or stone,   45
With phases various as the moon;
But though through all the body spread,
Still makes its cap'tal seat, the head.
In all diseases, 'tis expected,
The weakest parts be most infected.   50

　　°　　°　　°　　°　　°

Progress of Dulness. [1] *Non paravi,* I have not prepared for recitation—an excuse commonly given; *tardes* and *egresses,* were terms used at college, for coming in late and going out before the conclusion of service. [Trumbull's note.]

Now in the desk,[2] with solemn air,
Our hero makes his audience stare;
Asserts with all dogmatic boldness,
Where impudence is yoked to dulness;
Reads o'er his notes with halting pace, 55
Mask'd in the stiffness of his face;
With gestures such as might become
Those statues once that spoke at Rome,
Or Livy's ox, that to the state
Declared the oracles of fate, 60
In awkward tones, nor said, nor sung,
Slow rumbling o'er the falt'ring tongue,
Two hours his drawling speech holds on,
And names it preaching, when he's done.

With roving tired, he fixes down 65
For life, in some unsettled town.
People and priest full well agree,
For why—they know no more than he.
Vast tracts of unknown land he gains,
Better than those the moon contains; 70
There deals in preaching and in prayer,
And starves on sixty pounds a year,
And culls his texts, and tills his farm,
Does little good, and little harm;
On Sunday, in his best array, 75
Deals forth the dulness of the day,
And while above he spends his breath,
The yawning audience nod beneath.

Thus glib-tongued Merc'ry in his hand
Stretch'd forth the sleep-compelling wand, 80
Each eye in endless doze to keep—
The God of speaking, and of sleep.

[Dick Hairbrain Learns the Social Graces]

Poor Dick![3] though first thy airs provoke
Th' obstreperous laugh and scornful joke,
Doom'd all the ridicule to stand, 85
While each gay dunce shall lend a hand;
Yet let not scorn dismay thy hope
To shine a witling and a fop.
Blest impudence the prize shall gain,
And bid thee sigh no more in vain. 90
Thy varied dress shall quickly show
At once the spendthrift and the beau.
With pert address and noisy tongue,
That scorns the fear of prating wrong,
'Mongst list'ning coxcombs shalt thou shine, 95
And every voice shall echo thine.

How blest the brainless fop, whose praise
Is doom'd to grace these happy days,
When well-bred vice can genius teach,

And fame is placed in folly's reach, 100
Impertinence all tastes can hit,
And every rascal is a wit.
The lowest dunce, without despairing,
May learn the true sublime of swearing;
Learn the nice art of jests obscene, 105
While ladies wonder what they mean;
The heroism of brazen lungs,
The rhetoric of eternal tongues;
While whim usurps the name of spirit,
And impudence takes place of merit, 110
And every money'd clown and dunce
Commences gentleman at once.

For now, by easy rules of trade,
Mechanic gentlemen are made!
From handicrafts of fashion born; 115
Those very arts so much their scorn.
To taylors half themselves they owe,
Who make the clothes, that make the beau.
Lo! from the seats, where, fops to bless,
Learn'd artists fix the forms of dress, 120
And sit in consultation grave,
On folded skirt, or strait'ned sleeve,
The coxcomb trips with sprightly haste,
In all the flush of modern taste;
Oft turning, if the day be fair, 125
To view his shadow's graceful air;
Well pleased with eager eye runs o'er
The laced suit glitt'ring gay before,[4]
The ruffle, where from open'd vest
The rubied brooch adorns the breast; 130
The coat with length'ning waist behind,
Whose short skirts dangle in the wind;
The modish hat, whose breadth contains
The measure of its owner's brains;
The stockings gay with various hues; 135
The little toe-encircling shoes;
The cane, on whose carv'd top is shown
An head, just emblem of his own;
While wrapp'd in self, with lofty stride,
His little heart elate with pride, 140
He struts in all the joys of show,
That taylors give, or beaux can know.
And who for beauty need repine,
That's sold at every barber's sign;
Nor lies in features or complexion, 145
But curls disposed in meet direction,
With strong pomatum's grateful odour,
And *quantum sufficit* of powder?
These charms can shed a sprightly grace,
O'er the dull eye and clumsy face; 150
While the trim dancing-master's art
Shall gestures, trips and bows impart,

[2] Tom, having graduated, has entered the ministry. The "desk" is a pulpit.
[3] Dick Hairbrain, son of a wealthy farmer, enters college to learn the social graces.

[4] This passage alludes to the modes of dress then in fashion. [Trumbull's note.]

Give the gay piece its final touches,
And lend those airs, would lure a dutchess.
　　Thus shines the form, nor aught behind, 155
The gifts that deck the coxcomb's mind;
Then hear the daring muse disclose
The sense and piety of beaux.
　　To grace his speech, let France bestow
A set of compliments for show. 160
Land of politeness! that affords
The treasure of new-fangled words,
And endless quantities disburses
Of bows and compliments and curses;
The soft address, with airs so sweet, 165
That cringes at the ladies' feet;
The pert, vivacious, play-house style,
That wakes the gay assembly's smile;
Jests that his brother beaux may hit,
And pass with young coquettes for wit, 170
And prized by fops of true discerning,
Outface the pedantry of learning.
Yet learning too shall lend its aid,
To fill the coxcomb's spongy head,
And studious oft he shall peruse 175
The labours of the modern muse.
From endless loads of novels gain
Soft, simp'ring tales of amorous pain,
With double meanings, neat and handy,
From Rochester and Tristram Shandy.[5] 180
The blund'ring aid of weak reviews,
That forge the fetters of the muse,
Shall give him airs of criticising
On faults of books, he ne'er set eyes on.
The magazines shall teach the fashion, 185
And common-place of conversation,
And where his knowledge fails, afford
The aid of many a sounding word.
　　Then least religion he should need,
Of pious Hume he'll learn his creed, 190
By strongest demonstration shown,
Evince that nothing can be known;
Take arguments, unvex'd by doubt,
On Voltaire's trust, or go without;
'Gainst scripture rail in modern lore, 195
As thousand fools have rail'd before;
Or pleased a nicer art display
T' expound its doctrines all away,
Suit it to modern tastes and fashions
By various notes and emendations; 200
The rules the ten commands contain,
With new provisos well explain;
Prove all religion was but fashion,
Beneath the Jewish dispensation.

[5] Sterne's *Tristram Shandy* was then in the highest vogue,
and in the zenith of its transitory reputation. [Trumbull's
note.]

[Harriet Simper Has Her Day]

　　Thus HARRIET,[6] rising on the stage, 205
Learns all the arts, that please the age,
And studies well, as fits her station,
The trade and politics of fashion:
A judge of modes in silks and satins,
From tassels down to clogs and pattens; 210
A genius, that can calculate
When modes of dress are out of date,
Cast the nativity with ease
Of gowns, and sacks and negligees,
And tell, exact to half a minute, 215
What's out of fashion and what's in it;
And scanning all with curious eye,
Minutest faults in dresses spy,
(So in nice points of sight a flea
Sees atoms better far than we;) 220
A patriot too, she greatly labours,
To spread her arts among her neighbours,
Holds correspondences to learn
What facts the female world concern,
To gain authentic state-reports 225
Of varied modes in distant courts,
The present state and swift decays
Of tuckers, handkerchiefs and stays,
The colour'd silk that beauty wraps,
And all the rise and fall of caps. 230
Then shines, a pattern to the fair,
Of mien, address and modish air,
Of every new, affected grace,
That plays the eye, or decks the face,
The artful smile, that beauty warms, 235
And all th' hypocrisy of charms.
　　On Sunday, see the haughty maid
In all the glare of dress array'd,
Deck'd in her most fantastic gown,
Because a stranger's come to town. 240
Heedless at church she spends the day,
For homelier folks may serve to pray,
And for devotion those may go,
Who can have nothing else to do.
Beauties at church must spend their care in 245
Far other work, than pious hearing;
They've beaux to conquer, bells to rival;
To make them serious were uncivil.
For, like the preacher, they each Sunday
Must do their whole week's work in one day. 250
　　As though they meant to take by blows
Th' opposing galleries of beaux,[7]
To church the female squadron move,
All arm'd with weapons used in love.

[6] Harriet Simper, trained in the coquettish arts, pursues
Dick, who eludes her.
[7] Young people of different sexes used then to sit in the
opposite galleries. [Trumbull's note.]

Like colour'd ensigns gay and fair,   255
High caps rise floating in the air;
Bright silk its varied radiance flings,
And streamers wave in kissing-strings;
Each bears th' artill'ry of her charms,
Like training bands at viewing arms.   260

So once, in fear of Indian beating,
Our grandsires bore their guns to meeting,
Each man equipp'd on Sunday morn,
With psalm-book, shot and powder-horn;
And look'd in form, as all must grant,   265
Like th' ancient, true church militant;
Or fierce, like modern deep divines,
Who fight with quills, like porcupines.

Or let us turn the style and see
Our belles assembled o'er their tea;   270
Where folly sweetens ev'ry theme,
And scandal serves for sugar'd cream.

"And did you hear the news? (they cry)
The court wear caps full three feet high,
Built gay with wire, and at the end on't,   275
Red tassels streaming like a pendant.
Well sure, it must be vastly pretty;
'Tis all the fashion in the city.
And were you at the ball last night?
Well, Chloe look'd like any fright;   280
Her day is over for a toast,
She'd now do best to act a ghost.
You saw our Fanny; envy must own
She figures, since she came from Boston.
Good company improves one's air—   285
I think the troops were station'd there.
Poor Coelia ventured to the place;
The small-pox quite has spoil'd her face,
A sad affair, we all confest;
But providence knows what is best.   290
Poor Dolly, too, that writ the letter
Of love to Dick; but Dick knew better;
A secret that; you'll not disclose it;
There's not a person living knows it.
Sylvia shone out, no peacock finer;   295
I wonder what the fops see in her.
Perhaps 'tis true what Harry maintains,
She mends on intimate acquaintance."

Yet that we fairly may proceed,
We own that ladies sometimes read,   300
And grieve, that reading is confin'd
To books that poison all the mind;
Novels and plays (where shines display'd
A world that nature never made),
Which swell their hopes with airy fancies,   305
And amorous follies of romances;
Inspire with dreams the witless maiden
On flowery vales and fields Arcadian,
And constant hearts no chance can sever,
And mortal loves, that last for ever.   310

For while she reads romance, the fair one
Fails not to think herself the heroine;
For every glance, or smile, or grace,
She finds resemblance in her face,
Expects the world to fall before her,   315
And every fop she meets adore her.

Thus Harriet reads, and reading really
Believes herself a young Pamela,
The high-wrought whim, the tender strain
Elate her mind and turn her brain: 320
Before her glass, with smiling grace,
She views the wonders of her face;
There stands in admiration moveless,
And hopes a Grandison, or Lovelace.[8]

Then shines she forth, and round her hovers,   325
The powder'd swarm of bowing lovers;
By flames of love attracted thither,
Fops, scholars, dunces, cits, together.
No lamp exposed in nightly skies,
E'er gather'd such a swarm of flies;   330
Or flame in tube electric draws
Such thronging multitudes of straws.
(For I shall still take similes
From fire electric when I please.)

With vast confusion swells the sound,   335
When all the coxcombs flutter round.
What undulation wide of bows!
What gentle oaths and am'rous vows!
What double entendres all so smart!
What sighs hot-piping from the heart!   340
What jealous leers! what angry brawls
To gain the lady's hand at balls!
What billet-doux, brimful of flame!
Acrostics lined with Harriet's name!
What compliments, o'er-strained with telling   345
Sad lies of Venus and of Helen!
What wits half-crack'd with commonplaces
On angels, goddesses and graces!
On fires of love what witty puns!
What similes of stars and suns!   350
What cringing, dancing, ogling, sighing,
What languishing for love, and dying!

                °   °   °   °

And here her brightest hopes miscarry;
For Dick was too gallant to marry.
He own'd she'd charms for those who need 'em,   355
But he, be sure, was all for freedom;
So, left in hopeless flames to burn,
Gay Dick esteem'd her in her turn.
In love, a lady once given over
Is never fated to recover,   360
Doom'd to indulge her troubled fancies,

[8] Pamela, Sir Charles Grandison, and Lovelace were all characters in the enormously popular sentimental novels of Samuel Richardson (1689–1761).

And feed her passion by romances;
And always amorous, always changing,
From coxcomb still to coxcomb ranging,
Finds in her heart a void, which still   365
Succeeding beaux can never fill:
As shadows vary o'er a glass,
Each holds in turn the vacant place;
She doats upon her earliest pain,
And following thousands loves in vain.   370

  Poor HARRIET now hath had her day;
No more the beaux confess her sway;
New beauties push her from the stage;
She trembles at th' approach of age,
And starts to view the alter'd face,   375
That wrinkles at her in her glass:
So Satan, in the monk's tradition,
Fear'd, when he met his apparition.

  At length her name each coxcomb cancels
From standing lists of toasts and angels;   380
And slighted where she shone before,
A grace and goddess now no more,
Despised by all, and doom'd to meet
Her lovers at her rival's feet,
She flies assemblies, shuns the ball,   385
And cries out, vanity, on all;
Affects to scorn the tinsel-shows
Of glittering belles and gaudy beaux;
Nor longer hopes to hide by dress
The tracks of age upon her face.   390
Now careless grown of airs polite,
Her noonday nightcap meets the sight;
Her hair uncomb'd collects together,
With ornaments of many a feather;
Her stays for easiness thrown by,   395
Her rumpled handkerchief awry,
A careless figure half undress'd,
(The reader's wits may guess the rest;)
All points of dress and neatness carried,
As though she'd been a twelvemonth married;   400
She spends her breath, as years prevail,
At this sad wicked world to rail,
To slander all her sex *impromptu*,
And wonder what the times will come to.

[An Amorous Temper]

Tom Brainless, at the close of last year,   405
Had been six years a rev'rend Pastor,
And now resolved, to smooth his life,
To seek the blessing of a wife.
His brethren saw his amorous temper,
And recommended fair Miss Simper,   410
Who fond, they heard, of sacred truth,
Had left her levities of youth,
Grown fit for ministerial union,
And grave, as Christian's wife in Bunyan.

On this he rigg'd him in his best,   415
And got his old grey wig new dress'd,
Fix'd on his suit of sable stuffs,
And brush'd the powder from the cuffs,
With black silk stockings, yet in being,
The same he took his first degree in;   420
Procured a horse of breed from Europe,
And learn'd to mount him by the stirrup,
And set forth fierce to court the maid;
His white-hair'd Deacon went for aid;
And on the right, in solemn mode,   425
The Reverend Mr. Brainless rode.
Thus grave, the courtly pair advance,
Like knight and squire in famed romance.
The priest then bow'd in sober gesture,
And all in scripture terms address'd her;   430
He'd found, for reasons amply known,
It was not good to be alone,
And thought his duty led to trying
The great command of multiplying;
So with submission, by her leave,   435
He'd come to look him out an Eve,
And hoped, in pilgrimage of life,
To find an helpmate in a wife,
A wife discreet and fair withal,
To make amends for Adam's fall.   440
  In short, the bargain finish'd soon,
A reverend Doctor made them one.
  And now the joyful people rouze all
To celebrate their priest's espousal;
And first, by kind agreement set,   445
In case their priest a wife could get,
The parish vote him five pounds clear,
T' increase his salary every year.
Then swift the tag-rag gentry come
To welcome Madam Brainless home;   450
Wish their good Parson joy; with pride
In order round salute the bride.

                              1772–73

FROM *M'Fingal*

The first half of the poem was published in 1776, the latter half in 1782, when Trumbull revised the whole and divided it into four cantos. The time is shortly after the Battle of Lexington, the occasion a rowdy town meeting. In Cantos I and II the pompous Tory squire M'Fingal is bested in a heated debate with the Whig leader Honorious (identified by some as John Adams), while in Canto III the Squire sallies forth from the meetinghouse to disperse a crowd bent on erecting a liberty pole in the marketplace. In the best mock-epic tradition, M'Fingal draws his rusty sword to duel a patriot armed with a spade, loses, is hauled to the top of the pole by a rope attached to his trousers, and then is tarred and feathered. In Canto IV, a burlesque of Milton's *Paradise Lost*, M'Fingal and his Tories, like Satan and his fallen angels, meet secretly in a cellar to plot against the revolutionary leaders, with no greater prospect of success. The following portion describes the great battle at the liberty pole. The text is that of the Nason edition.

At once with resolution fatal,
Both Whigs and Tories rush'd to battle.
Instead of weapons, either band
Seized on such arms as came to hand.
And as famed Ovid[1] paints th' adventures   5
Of wrangling Lapithae and Centaurs,
Who at their feast, by Bacchus led,
Threw bottles at each other's head;
And these arms failing in their scuffles,
Attack'd with andirons, tongs and shovels: 10
So clubs and billets, staves and stones
Met fierce, encountering every sconce,
And cover'd o'er with knobs and pains
Each void receptacle for brains;
Their clamours rend the skies around,   15
The hills rebellow to the sound;
And many a groan increas'd the din
From batter'd nose and broken shin.
M'Fingal, rising at the word,
Drew forth his old militia-sword;   20
Thrice cried "King George," as erst in distress,
Knights of romance invoked a mistress;
And brandishing the blade in air,
Struck terror through th' opposing war.
The Whigs, unsafe within the wind   25
Of such commotion, shrunk behind.
With whirling steel around address'd,
Fierce through their thickest throng he press'd,
(Who roll'd on either side in arch,
Like Red Sea waves in Israel's march)   30
And like a meteor rushing through,
Struck on their Pole a vengeful blow.
Around, the Whigs, of clubs and stones
Discharged whole vollies, in platoons,
That o'er in whistling fury fly;   35
But not a foe dares venture nigh.
And now perhaps with glory crown'd
Our 'Squire had fell'd the pole to ground,
Had not some Pow'r, a whig at heart,
Descended down and took their part;[2]   40
(Whether 'twere Pallas, Mars or Iris,
'Tis scarce worth while to make inquiries)
Who at the nick of time alarming,
Assumed the solemn form of Chairman,
Address'd a Whig, in every scene   45

M'Fingal. [1] See Ovid's Metamorphoses, book 12th. [This and subsequent notes are Trumbull's.]
[2] The learned reader will readily observe the allusions in this scene, to the single combats of Paris and Menelaus in Homer, Aeneas and the Turnus in Virgil, and Michael and Satan in Milton.

The stoutest wrestler on the green,
And pointed where the spade was found,
Late used to set their pole in ground,
And urged, with equal arms and might,
To dare our 'Squire to single fight.   50
The Whig thus arm'd, untaught to yield,
Advanced tremendous to the field:
Nor did M'Fingal shun the foe,
But stood to brave the desp'rate blow;
While all the party gazed, suspended   55
To see the deadly combat ended;
And Jove[3] in equal balance weigh'd
The sword against the brandish'd spade,
He weigh'd; but lighter than a dream,
The sword flew up, and kick'd the beam.   60
Our 'Squire on tiptoe rising fair
Lifts high a noble stroke in air,
Which hung not, but like dreadful engines,
Descended on his foe in vengeance.
But ah! in danger, with dishonor   65
The sword perfidious fails its owner;
That sword, which oft had stood its ground,
By huge trainbands encircled round;
And on the bench, with blade right loyal,
Had won the day at many a trial,[4]   70
Of stones and clubs had braved th' alarms,
Shrunk from these new Vulcanian arms.[5]
The spade so temper'd from the sledge,
Nor keen nor solid harm'd its edge,
Now met it, from his arm of might,   75
Descending with steep force to smite;
The blade snapp'd short—and from his hand,
With rust embrown'd the glittering sand.
Swift turn'd M'Fingal at the view,
And call'd to aid th' attendant crew,   80
In vain; the Tories all had run,
When scarce the fight was well begun;
Their setting wigs he saw decreas'd
Far in th' horizon tow'rd the west.
Amazed he view'd the shameful sight,   85
And saw no refuge, but in flight:
But age unwieldy check'd his pace,
Though fear had wing'd his flying race;

[3] Jupiter ipse duas aequato examine lances
Sustinet & fata imponit diversa duorum,
Quem damnet labor, &c.   Aeneid, 12.
[4] It was the fashion in New-England at that time, for judges to wear swords on the bench.
[5] ———Postquam arma Dei ad Vulcania ventum est,
Mortalis mucro, glacies ceu futilis, ictu
Dissiluit; fulva resplendent fragmina arena.   Virgil.
———The sword
Was given him temper'd so, that neither keen
Nor solid might resist that edge; it met
The sword of Satan with steep force to smite
Descending and in half cut sheer.   Milton.

For not a trifling prize at stake;
No less than great M'FINGAL's back.[6]
With legs and arms he work'd his course,
Like rider that outgoes his horse,
And labor'd hard to get away, as
Old Satan[7] struggling on through chaos;
'Till looking back, he spied in rear
The spade-arm'd chief advanced too near:
Then stopp'd and seized a stone, that lay
An ancient landmark near the way;
Nor shall we as old bards have done,
Affirm it weigh'd an hundred ton;[8]
But such a stone, as at a shift
A modern might suffice to lift,
Since men, to credit their enigmas,
Are dwindled down to dwarfs and pigmies,

And giants exiled with their cronies
To Brobdignags and Patagonias.
But while our Hero turn'd him round,
And tugg'd to raise it from the ground,
The fatal spade discharged a blow
Tremendous on his rear below:
His bent knee fail'd[9] and void of strength
Stretch'd on the ground his manly length.
Like ancient oak o'erturn'd, he lay,
Or tower to tempests fall'n a prey,
Or mountain sunk with all his pines,
Or flow'r the plow to dust consigns,
And more things else—but all men know 'em,
If slightly versed in epic poem.
At once the crew, at this dread crisis,
Fall on, and bind him, ere he rises;
And with loud shouts and joyful soul,
Conduct him prisoner to the pole.

[6]———nec enim levia aut ludicra petuntur
Praemia, sed Turni de vita et sanguine certant. *Virgil.*
[7] In Milton.
[8] This thought is taken from Juvenal, Satire 15.
[9] Genua labant ————— incidit ictus,
Ingens ad terram duplicato poplite Turnus. *Virgil.*

JOEL BARLOW [1754–1812]

JOEL BARLOW, born a farmer's son near Redding, Connecticut, in 1754, attended Dartmouth and Yale, graduating from the latter in 1778 as "class poet." Licensed a Congregational minister after a six-week course in theology, he served as chaplain to a Massachusetts line regiment during the war, and afterwards entered law practice in Hartford. During his army years he began work on a long "national" epic, published in 1787 as *The Vision of Columbus,* highly regarded for its patriotism at the time. He was also associated, as one of the conservative group of "Connecticut Wits," with Trumbull, Humphreys, and Hopkins in the series of strongly Federalist satires known as *The Anarchiad* in 1786-87.

Barlow left the law to join the Scioto Company, formed to promote speculative land sales in Ohio, and was sent to England in 1788 as its European agent. When the company was exposed as a swindle, Barlow, who apparently was innocent, immediately resigned. While in London, he met and moved with the political radicals—among them Paine, William Godwin, and Joseph Priestley—and soon he was caught up in the wave of revolutionary excitement sweeping England and Europe. The Connecticut Yankee became a cosmopolite, at home in London and Paris; the Federalist conservative became a Jacobin radical; the New England Congregationalist turned into a deist. His *Advice to the Privileged Orders* (Part I, 1791), an answer to Edmund Burke's criticisms of the French revolutionaries, attacked the church, the monarchy, courts, armies, and all other institutions that subverted justice and oppressed the people:

The tyrannies of the world, whatever be the appellation of the government under which they are exercised, are all aristocratical tyrannies. An ordinance to plunder and murder, whether it fulminate from the Vatican, or steal silently forth from the Harem; whether it come clothed in the *certain science* of a Bed of Justice, or in the legal solemnities of a bench of lawyers; whether it be purchased by the caresses of a woman, or the treasures of a nation,—never confines its effects to the benefit of a single individual; it goes to enrich the whole combination of conspirators whose business it is to dupe and to govern the nation.

In verse he wrote *The Conspiracy of Kings* (1792), proclaiming that under the leadership of France,

> Freedom at last, with Reason in her train,
> Extends o'er earth her everlasting reign.

For the services of his pen he was made an honorary French citizen and lived through the Reign of Terror in Paris without difficulty. From 1795 to 1797 he was American consul in Algiers, during the naval troubles with the Barbary pirates, with whom he concluded a useful treaty.

Barlow had a talent for money-making and by shrewd speculation built up a comfortable fortune. He returned to the United States in 1805 to purchase a country estate near Washington, where he lived in considerable splendor and maintained a salon for liberal writers and thinkers. He also reworked *The Vision of Columbus* into *The Columbiad*, publishing it in 1807, and planned next to write a history of the United States. In 1811, however, President Madison made him ambassador to France, especially to negotiate favorable trade treaties with Napoleon. The Napoleonic armies were deep in Russia, and Barlow's request for an audience with the Emperor was delayed by the disastrous retreat from Moscow. Finally he received word that Napoleon would see him at Wilna, in Poland, but Barlow never arrived. He died of pneumonia on December 22, 1812, at a small village near Cracow.

Further reading: James Woodress, *A Yankee's Odyssey*, 1958. Vernon L. Parrington, ed., *The Connecticut Wits*, 1926. Leon Howard, *The Connecticut Wits*, 1943.

The Hasty Pudding

A Poem in Three Cantos

In January 1793 Barlow was in Savoy, near the French Alps, at Chambéry, where unexpectedly (and inexplicably) he was served corn-meal mush, or hasty pudding, at the inn. Suddenly homesick for New England, he wrote this playful dietary epic in memory of the familiar dish of his Yankee boyhood. It was published in the United States three years later, running through five editions in its first year and remaining perennially popular. A mock-heroic pastoral, the poem burlesques the conventions of the epic form, with an invocation to the Muse, learned allusions, rhetorical flights, and inflated diction. Yet it was something more than a humorous burlesque. It not only represents one of the earliest uses of folklore and folk-materials in American poetry, but it is also a sincere affirmation of Jeffersonian agrarian simplicity and a celebration of the honest, homely joys of American country life. Text: The New Haven edition, 1796, with the original preface.

> *Omne tulit punctum qui miscuit utile dulci,*
> He makes a good breakfast who mixes pudding with molasses.

To Mrs. Washington

MADAM:—A simplicity in diet, whether it be considered with reference to the happiness of individuals or the prosperity of a nation, is of more consequence than we are apt to imagine. In recommending so great and necessary a virtue to the rational part of mankind, I wish it were in my power to do it in such a manner as would be likely to gain their attention. I am sensible that it is one of those subjects in which example has infinitely more power than the most convincing arguments, or the highest charms of poetry. Goldsmith's *Deserted Village*, though possessing these two advantages in a greater degree than any other work of the kind, has not prevented villages in England from being deserted. The apparent interest of the rich individuals, who form the taste as well as the laws in that country, has been against him; and with that interest it has been vain to contend.

The vicious habits which in this little piece I endeavor to combat, seem to me not so difficult to cure. No class of people has any interest in supporting them, unless it be the interest which certain families may feel in vieing with each other in sumptuous entertainments. There may indeed be some instances of depraved appetites which no arguments will conquer; but these must be rare. There are very few persons but would always prefer a plain dish for themselves, and would prefer it likewise for their guests, if there were no risk of reputation in the case. This difficulty can only be removed by example; and the example should proceed from those whose situation enables them to take the lead in forming the manners of a nation. Persons of this description in America, I should hope, are neither above nor below the influence of truth and reason when conveyed in language suited to the subject.

Whether the manner I have chosen to address my arguments to them be such as to promise any success, is what I cannot decide. But I certainly had hopes of doing some good, or I should not have taken the pains of putting so many rhymes together; and much less should I have ventured to place your name at the head of these observations.

Your situation commands the respect and your character the affections of a numerous people. These circumstances impose a duty upon you, which I believe you discharge to your own satisfaction and that of others. The example of your domestic virtues has doubtless a great effect among your countrywomen. I only wish to rank *simplicity of diet* among the virtues. In that case it will certainly be cherished by you, and I should hope more esteemed by others than it is at present.

THE AUTHOR.

Canto I

Ye Alps audacious, through the heavens that rise,
To cramp the day and hide me from the skies;
Ye Gallic flags, that o'er their heights unfurled,
Bear death to kings, and freedom to the world,
I sing not you. A softer theme I choose, 5
A virgin theme, unconscious of the Muse,
But fruitful rich, well suited to inspire
The purest frenzy of poetic fire.
Despise it not, ye bards to terror steel'd,
Who hurl your thunders round the epic field; 10
Nor ye who strain your midnight throats to sing
Joys that the vineyard and the still-house[1] bring;
Or on some distant fair your notes employ,
And speak of raptures that you ne'er enjoy.
I sing the sweets I know, the charms I feel, 15
My morning incense, and my evening meal,
The sweets of Hasty Pudding. Come, dear bowl,
Glide o'er my palate, and inspire my soul.
The milk beside thee, smoking from the kine,
Its substance mingle, married in with thine, 20
Shall cool and temper thy superior heat,
And save the pains of blowing while I eat.
Oh! could the smooth, the emblematic song
Flow like thy genial juices o'er my tongue,
Could those mild morsels in my numbers chime, 25
And, as they roll in substance, roll in rhyme,
No more thy awkward unpoetic name
Should shun the muse, or prejudice thy fame;
But rising grateful to the accustom'd ear,
All bards should catch it, and all realms revere! 30

The Hasty Pudding. [1] Distillery.

Assist me first with pious toil to trace
Through wrecks of time, thy lineage and thy race;
Declare what lovely squaw, in days of yore,
(Ere great Columbus sought thy native shore)
First gave thee to the world; her works of fame 35
Have lived indeed, but lived without a name.
Some tawny Ceres,[2] goddess of her days,
First learn'd with stones to crack the well dried maize,
Through the rough sieve to shake the golden shower,
In boiling water stir the yellow flour: 40
The yellow flour, bestrew'd and stirr'd with haste,
Swells in the flood and thickens to a paste,
Then puffs and wallops, rises to the brim,
Drinks the dry knobs that on the surface swim;
The knobs at last the busy ladle breaks, 45
And the whole mass its true consistence takes.
Could but her sacred name, unknown so long,
Rise, like her labors, to the son of song,
To her, to them, I'd consecrate my lays,
And blow her pudding with the breath of praise. 50
If 'twas Oella[3] whom I sang before
I here ascribe her one great virtue more.
Not through the rich Peruvian realms alone
The fame of Sol's sweet daughter should be known,
But o'er the world's wide clime should live secure,
Far as his rays extend, as long as they endure. 56
Dear Hasty Pudding, what unpromised joy
Expands my heart to meet thee in Savoy!
Doom'd o'er the world through devious paths to roam,
Each clime my country, and each house my home,
My soul is soothed, my cares have found an end, 61
I greet my long lost, unforgotten friend.
For thee through Paris, that corrupted town,
How long in vain I wandered up and down,
Where shameless Bacchus, with his drenching hoard, 65
Cold from his cave usurps the morning board.
London is lost in smoke and steep'd in tea;
No Yankee there can lisp the name of thee;
The uncouth word, a libel on the town,
Would call a proclamation from the crown.[4] 70
From climes oblique, that fear the sun's full rays,
Chill'd in their fogs, exclude the generous maize:
A grain, whose rich, luxuriant growth requires
Short gentle showers, and bright etherial fires. 74
But here, though distant from our native shore,
With mutual glee, we meet and laugh once more,
The same! I know thee by that yellow face,

[2] Goddess of grain.
[3] A Peruvian goddess of household arts, to whom Barlow had referred in *The Vision of Columbus.*
[4] A certain king, at the time when this was written, was publishing proclamations to prevent American principles from being propagated in his country. [Barlow's note.]

That strong complexion of true Indian race,
Which time can never change, nor soil impair,
Nor Alpine snows, nor Turkey's morbid air;   80
For endless years, through every mild domain,
Where grows the maize, there thou art sure to reign.
    But man, more fickle, the bold license claims,
In different realms to give thee different names.
Thee the soft nations round the warm Levant   85
Polenta call, the French of course *Polente.*
E'en in thy native regions, how I blush
To hear the Pennsylvanians call thee *Mush!*
On Hudson's banks, while men of Belgic spawn
Insult and eat thee by the name *Suppawn.*   90
All spurious appellations, void of truth;
I've better known thee from my earliest youth,
Thy name is *Hasty-Pudding!* thus my sire
Was wont to greet thee fuming from his fire;
And while he argued in thy just defence   95
With logic clear, he thus explain'd the sense:—
"In *haste* the boiling cauldron, o'er the blaze,
Receives and cooks the ready powder'd maize;
In *haste* 'tis served, and then in equal *haste,*
With cooling milk, we make the sweet repast.   100
No carving to be done, no knife to grate
The tender ear, and wound the stony plate;
But the smooth spoon, just fitted to the lip,
And taught with art the yielding mass to dip,
By frequent journeys to the bowl well stored,   105
Performs the *hasty* honors of the board."
Such is thy name, significant and clear,
A name, a sound to every Yankee dear,
But most to me, whose heart and palate chaste
Preserve my pure hereditary taste.   110
    There are who strive to stamp with disrepute
The luscious food, because it feeds the brute;
In tropes of high-strain'd wit, while gaudy prigs
Compare thy nursling, man, to pamper'd pigs;
With sovereign scorn I treat the vulgar jest,   115
Nor fear to share thy bounties with the beast.
What though the generous cow gives me to quaff
The milk nutritious: am I then a calf?
Or can the genius of the noisy swine,
Though nursed on pudding, claim a kin to mine?   120
Sure the sweet song, I fashion to thy praise,   121
Runs more melodious than the notes they raise.
    My song resounding in its grateful glee,
No merit claims: I praise myself in thee.
My father loved thee through his length of days!   125
For thee his fields were shaded o'er with maize;
From thee what health, what vigor he possess'd,
Ten sturdy freemen from his loins attest;
Thy constellation ruled my natal morn,
And all my bones were made of Indian corn.   130
Delicious grain! whatever form it take,
To roast or boil, to smother or to bake,
In every dish 'tis welcome still to me,
But most, my *Hasty Pudding,* most in thee.

Let the green succotash with thee contend,   135
Let beans and corn their sweetest juices blend,
Let butter drench them in its yellow tide,
And a long slice of bacon grace their side;
Not all the plate, how famed soe'er it be,
Can please my palate like a bowl of thee.   140
Some talk of *Hoe-Cake,* fair Virginia's pride,
Rich *Johnny-Cake,* this mouth has often tried;
Both please me well, their virtues much the same,
Alike their fabric, as allied their fame,
Except in dear New England, where the last   145
Receives a dash of pumpkin in the paste,
To give it sweetness and improve the taste.
But place them all before me, smoking hot,
The big, round dumpling, rolling from the pot,
The pudding of the bag, whose quivering breast,
With suet lined, leads on the Yankee feast,   151
The *Charlotte*[5] brown within whose crusty sides
A belly soft the pulpy apple hides;
The yellow bread whose face like amber glows,
And all of Indian that the bake-pan knows,—   155
You tempt me not—my fav'rite greets my eyes,
To that loved bowl my spoon by instinct flies.

Canto II

    To mix the food by vicious rules of art,
To kill the stomach, and to sink the heart
To make mankind to social virtue sour,
Cram o'er each dish, and be what they devour;
For this the kitchen muse first fram'd her book,   5
Commanding sweats to stream from every cook;
Children no more their antic gambols tried,
And friends to physic wonder'd why they died.
    Not so the Yankee—his abundant feast,
With simples furnish'd and with plainness drest,   10
A numerous offspring gathers round the board,
And cheers alike the servant and the lord;
Whose well-bought hunger prompts the joyous taste,
And health attends them from the short repast.
    While the full pail rewards the milk-maid's toil,
The mother sees the morning cauldron boil;   16
To stir the pudding next demands their care;
To spread the table and the bowls prepare;
To feed the household as their portions cool
And send them all to labor or to school.   20
    Yet may the simplest dish some rules impart,
For nature scorns not all the aids of art.
E'en *Hasty-Pudding,* purest of all food,
May still be bad, indifferent, or good,
As sage experience the short process guides,   25
Or want of skill, or want of care presides.
Whoe'er would form it on the surest plan,
To rear the child and long sustain the man;
To shield the morals while it mends the size,

[5]A pastry dessert.

And all the powers of every food supplies, 30
Attend the lesson that the muse shall bring,
Suspend your spoons, and listen while I sing.

But since, O man! thy life and health demand
Not food alone but labor from thy hand,
First in the field, beneath the sun's strong rays, 35
Ask of thy mother earth the needful maize;
She loves the race that courts her yielding soil,
And gives her bounties to the sons of toil.

When now the ox, obedient to thy call,
Repays the loan that fill'd the winter stall, 40
Pursue his traces o'er the furrow'd plain,
And plant in measur'd hills the golden grain.
But when the tender germ begins to shoot,
And the green spire declares the sprouting root,
Then guard your nursling from each greedy foe, 45
The insidious worm, the all-devouring crow.
A little ashes, sprinkled round the spire,
Soon steep'd in rain, will bid the worm retire;
The feather'd robber with his hungry maw
Swift flies the field before your man of straw, 50
A frightful image, such as schoolboys bring,
When met to burn the pope, or hang the king.[6]

Thrice in the season, through each verdant row
Wield the strong ploughshare and the faithful hoe:
The faithful hoe, a double task that takes, 55
To till the summer corn, and roast the winter cakes.

Slow springs the blade, while check'd by chilling rains,
Ere yet the sun the seat of Cancer[7] gains;
But when his fiercest fires emblaze the land,
Then start the juices, then the roots expand; 60
Then, like a column of Corinthian mould,
The stalk struts upward and the leaves unfold;
The busy branches all the ridges fill,
Entwine their arms, and kiss from hill to hill.
Here cease to vex them, all your cares are done: 65
Leave the last labors to the parent sun;
Beneath his genial smiles, the well-drest field,
When autumn calls, a plenteous crop shall yield.

Now the strong foliage bears the standards high,
And shoots the tall top-gallants to the sky; 70
The suckling ears their silky fringes bend,
And pregnant grown, their swelling coats distend;
The loaded stalk, while still the burthen grows,
O'erhangs the space that runs between the rows;
High as a hop-field waves the silent grove, 75
A safe retreat for little thefts of love,
When the pledged roasting ears invite the maid,
To meet her swain beneath the new-form'd shade;
His generous hand unloads the cumbrous hill,
And the green spoils her ready basket fill; 80
Small compensation for the two-fold bliss,
The promised wedding, and the present kiss.

[6]A reference perhaps to "Guy Fawkes Day" in England, November 5.
[7]The sign of the zodiac marking June.

Slight depredations these; but now the moon
Calls from his hollow tree the sly raccoon;
And while by night he bears his prize away, 85
The bolder squirrel labors through the day.
Both thieves alike, but provident of time,
A virtue rare, that almost hides their crime.
Then let them steal the little stores they can,
And fill their gran'ries from the toils of man; 90
We've one advantage, where they take no part,
With all their wiles they ne'er have found the art
To boil the *Hasty-Pudding;* here we shine
Superior far to tenants of the pine;
This envied boon to man shall still belong, 95
Unshared by them, in substance or in song.

At last the closing season browns the plain,
And ripe October gathers in the grain;
Deep loaded carts the spacious corn-house fill,
The sack distended marches to the mill; 100
The lab'ring mill beneath the burthen groans,
And showers the future pudding from the stones;
Till the glad housewife greets the powder'd gold,
And the new crop exterminates the old.
Ah who can sing what every wight must feel, 105
The joy that enters with the bag of meal,
A general jubilee pervades the house,
Wakes every child and gladdens every mouse.

Canto III

The days grow short; but though the falling sun
To the glad swain proclaims his day's work done,
Night's pleasing shades his various tasks prolong,
And yield new subjects to my various song.
For now, the corn-house fill'd, the harvest home, 5
The invited neighbors to the *husking* come;
A frolic scene, where work, and mirth, and play,
Unite their charms to chase the hours away.

Where the huge heap lies centred in the hall,
The lamp suspended from the cheerful wall, 10
Brown corn-fed nymphs, and strong hard-handed beaus,
Alternate ranged, extend in circling rows,
Assume their seats, the solid mass attack;
The dry husks rustle, and the corn-cobs crack;
The song, the laugh, alternate notes resound, 15
And the sweet cider trips in silence round.

The laws of husking every wight can tell;
And sure no laws he ever keeps so well:
For each red ear a general kiss he gains,
With each smut ear he smuts the luckless swains; 20
But when to some sweet maid a prize is cast,
Red as her lips, and taper as her waist,
She walks the round, and culls one favored beau,
Who leaps, the luscious tribute to bestow.
Various the sport, as are the wits and brains 25
Of well pleased lasses and contending swains;

Till the vast mound of corn is swept away,
And he that gets the last ear wins the day.

Meanwhile the housewife urges all her care,
The well-earn'd feast to hasten and prepare. 30
The sifted meal already waits her hand,
The milk is strain'd, the bowls in order stand,
The fire flames high; and, as a pool (that takes
The headlong stream that o'er the mill-dam breaks)
Foams, roars, and rages, with incessant toils, 35
So the vex'd cauldron rages, roars and boils.

First with clean salt, she seasons well the food,
Then strews the flour, and thickens all the flood.
Long o'er the simmering fire she lets it stand;
To stir it well demands a stronger hand; 40
The husband takes his turn: and round and round
The ladle flies; at last the toil is crown'd;
When to the board the thronging huskers pour,
And take their seats as at the corn before.

I leave them to their feast. There still belong 45
More useful matters to my faithful song.
For rules there are, though ne'er unfolded yet,
Nice rules and wise, how pudding should be ate.

Some with molasses grace the luscious treat,
And mix, like bards, the useful and the sweet. 50
A wholesome dish, and well deserving praise,
A great resource in those bleak wintry days,
When the chill'd earth lies buried deep in snow,
And raging Boreas dries the shivering cow.

Blest cow! thy praise shall still my notes employ,
Great source of health, the only source of joy; 56
Mother of Egypt's god,—but sure, for me,
Were I to leave my God, I'd worship thee.
How oft thy teats these pious hands have press'd!
How oft thy bounties prove my only feast! 60
How oft I've fed thee with my favorite grain!
And roar'd, like thee, to see thy children slain!

Ye swains who know her various worth to prize,
Ah! house her well from winter's angry skies.
Potatoes, pumpkins, should her sadness cheer, 65
Corn from your crib, and mashes from your beer;
When spring returns, she'll well acquit the loan,
And nurse at once your infants and her own.

Milk then with pudding I should always choose;
To this in future I confine my muse, 70
Till she in haste some further hints unfold,
Good for the young, nor useless to the old.
First in your bowl the milk abundant take,
Then drop with care along the silver lake
Your flakes of pudding; these at first will hide 75
Their little bulk beneath the swelling tide;
But when their growing mass no more can sink,
When the soft island looms above the brink,
Then check your hand; you've got the portion due,
So taught my sire, and what he taught is true. 80

There is a choice in spoons. Though small appear
The nice distinction, yet to me 'tis clear.
The deep bowl'd Gallic spoon, contrived to scoop
In ample draughts the thin diluted soup,

Performs not well in those substantial things, 85
Whose mass adhesive to the metal clings;
Where the strong labial muscles must embrace,
The gentle curve, and sweep the hollow space.
With ease to enter and discharge the freight,
A bowl less concave, but still more dilate, 90
Becomes the pudding best. The shape, the size,
A secret rests, unknown to vulgar eyes.
Experienced feeders can alone impart
A rule so much above the lore of art.
These tuneful lips that thousand spoons have tried,
With just precision could the point decide. 96
Though not in song; the muse but poorly shines
In cones, and cubes, and geometric lines;
Yet the true form, as near as she can tell,
Is that small section of a goose egg shell, 100
Which in two equal portions shall divide
The distance from the centre to the side.

Fear not to slaver; 'tis no deadly sin:——
Like the free Frenchman, from your joyous chin
Suspend the ready napkin; or like me, 105
Poise with one hand your bowl upon your knee;
Just in the zenith your wise head project,
Your full spoon, rising in a line direct,
Bold as a bucket, heed no drops that fall, 109
The wide mouth'd bowl will surely catch them all![8]

1793   1796

A Song

Why Barlow was regarded as a dangerous revolutionary in England, and by some in the United States, is aptly illustrated by a parody he wrote on England's "God Save the King" for the amusement of his friends, presumably sung at a dinner after the execution of Louis XVI in France in 1793. The text follows the version given in the *Columbian Centinel*, November 16, 1805.

Fame let thy trumpet sound,
Tell all the world around—
How Capet fell:

[8] The following note was added in a later edition: "There are various ways of preparing and eating it; with molasses, butter, sugar, cream, and fried. Why so excellent a thing cannot be eaten alone? Nothing is perfect alone, even man who boasts of so much perfection is nothing without his fellow substance. In eating, beware of the lurking heat that lies deep in the mass; dip your spoon gently, take shallow dips and cool it by degrees. It is sometimes necessary to blow. This is indicated by certain signs which every experienced feeder knows. They should be taught to young beginners. I have known a child's tongue blistered for want of this attention, and then the schooldame would insist that the poor thing had told a lie. A mistake: the falsehood was in the faithless pudding. A prudent mother will cool it for her child with her own sweet breath. The husband, seeing this, pretends his own wants blowing too from the same lips. A sly deceit of love. She knows the cheat, lends her pouting lips, and gives a gentle blast, which warms the husband's heart more than it cools his pudding."

And when great George's poll
  Shall in the basket roll,   5
Let mercy then control
    The Guillotine.

When all the sceptered crew
Have paid their homage to
    The Guillotine;   10
Let Freedom's flag advance,
Till all the world, like France!
O'er tyrants' graves shall dance,
    And peace begin.

1793

On the Discoveries of Captain Lewis

On January 14, 1807, a dinner was given at Washington for Captain Meriwether Lewis, in recognition of his safe return from his journey with William Clark to the Pacific. "At an early period in the entertainment," reported the *National Intelligencer*, "the following elegant and glowing stanzas, from the pen of Mr. Barlow, were recited by Mr. Beckley." Barlow, like others in the Jefferson administration, was fully aware of the implications of the Lewis and Clark expedition for the nation's future, and fascinated by the prospects of westward expansion. Text: *National Intelligencer*, January 16, 1807.

Let the Nile cloak his head in the clouds, and defy
  The researches of science and time;
Let the Niger escape the keen traveller's eye,
  By plunging or changing his clime.

Columbus! not so shall thy boundless domain   5
  Defraud thy brave sons of their right:
Streams, midlands, and shorelands elude us in vain,
  We shall drag their dark regions to light.

Look down, sainted sage, from thy synod of Gods;
  See, inspired by thy venturous soul,   10
Mackenzie roll northward his earth-draining floods,
  And surge the broad waves to the pole.

With the same soaring genius thy Lewis ascends,
  And seizing the car of the sun,
O'er the sky-propping hills and high waters he
    bends   15
  And gives the proud earth a new zone.

Potowmak, Ohio, Missouri had felt
  Half her globe in their cincture comprest;
His long curving course has completed the belt,
  And tamed the last tide of the west.   20

Then hear the loud voice of the nation proclaim,
  And all ages resound the decree:

Let our occident stream bear the young hero's name
  Who taught him his path to the sea.

These four brother floods, like a garland of flowers,
  Shall entwine all our states in a band,   26
Conform and confederate their wide spreading
    powers,
  And their wealth and their wisdom expand.

From Darien to Davis one garden shall bloom,
  Where war's wearied banners are furl'd,   30
And the far scenting breezes that waft its perfume,
  Shall settle the storms of the world.

Then hear the loud voice of the nation proclaim
  And all ages resound the decree:
Let our occident stream bear the young hero's
    name,   35
Who taught him his path to the sea.

1807

from *The Columbiad*

Barlow revised *The Vision of Columbus* (1787) and published it in 1807 as *The Columbiad*, almost doubling the original length. Dedicated to his friend Robert Fulton, who saw it through the press and painted a portrait of Barlow for the frontispiece, it was possibly the most expensive book yet published in the United States; Fulton arranged for the best London engravers to execute eleven engravings and designed an elaborate binding. Borrowing the plan of the poem from Book XI of *Paradise Lost*, Barlow had the aged, ill Columbus led from his prison cell at Valladolid by the angel Hesper, the Spirit of the West (or America), to a "hill of vision" where she unfolded the future before him. Of the poem's ten books, the first four reviewed the history of the world to the peace of 1763; the next three, American history to the surrender of Cornwallis; with the last three rising to a vision of a world in which all nations were united in peace and prosperity. Text: The first edition of 1807, Philadelphia. The selection given below is the conclusion of Book X (lines 529–642).

    Eager he look'd. Another train of years
Had roll'd unseen, and brighten'd still their spheres;
Earth more resplendent in the floods of day
Assumed new smiles, and flush'd around him lay.
Green swell the mountains, calm the oceans roll,   5
Fresh beams of beauty kindle round the pole;
Thro all the range where shores and seas extend,
In tenfold pomp the works of peace ascend.
Robed in the bloom of spring's eternal year,
And ripe with fruits the same glad fields appear;   10
O'er hills and vales perennial gardens run,
Cities unwall'd stand sparkling to the sun;
The streams all freighted from the bounteous plain
Swell with the load and labor to the main,
Whose stormless waves command a steadier gale   15
And prop the pinions of a bolder sail:

Sway'd with the floating weight each ocean toils,
And joyous nature's full perfection smiles.

    Fill'd with unfolding fate, the vision'd age
Now leads its actors on a broader stage;   20
When clothed majestic in the robes of state,
Moved by one voice, in general congress meet
The legates of all empires. Twas the place[1]
Where wretched men first firm'd their wandering
      pace;
Ere yet beguiled, the dark delirious hordes   25
Began to fight for altars and for lords;
Nile washes still the soil, and feels once more
The works of wisdom press his peopled shore.

    In this mid site, this monumental clime,
Rear'd by all realms to brave the wrecks of time   30
A spacious dome swells up, commodious great,
The last resort, the unchanging scene of state.
On rocks of adamant the walls ascend,
Tall columns heave and sky-like arches bend;
Bright o'er the golden roofs the glittering spires   35
Far in the concave meet the solar fires;
Four blazing fronts, with gates unfolding high,
Look with immortal splendor round the sky:
Hither the delegated sires ascend,
And all the cares of every clime attend.   40

    As that blest band, the guardian guides of heaven,
To whom the care of stars and suns is given,
(When one great circuit shall have proved their
      spheres,
And time well taught them how to wind their years)
Shall meet in general council; call'd to state   45
The laws and labors that their charge await;
To learn, to teach, to settle how to hold
Their course more glorious, as their lights unfold:
From all the bounds of space (the mandate known)
They wing their passage to the eternal throne;   50
Each thro his far dim sky illumes the road,
And sails and centres tow'rd the mount of God;
There, in mid universe, their seats to rear,
Exchange their counsels and their works compare:
So, from all tracts of earth, this gathering throng   55
In ships and chariots shape their course along,
Reach with unwonted speed the place assign'd
To hear and give the counsels of mankind.

    South of the sacred mansion, first resort
The assembled sires, and pass the spacious court.   60
Here in his porch earth's figured Genius stands,
Truth's mighty mirror poizing in his hands;
Graved on the pedestal and chased in gold,
Man's noblest arts their symbol forms unfold,
His tillage and his trade; with all the store   65
Of wondrous fabrics and of useful lore:
Labors that fashion to his sovereign sway
Earth's total powers, her soil and air and sea;

Force them to yield their fruits at his known call,
And bear his mandates round the rolling ball.   70
Beneath the footstool all destructive things,
The mask of priesthood and the mace of kings,
Lie trampled in the dust; for here at last
Fraud, folly, error all their emblems cast.
Each envoy here unloads his wearied hand   75
Of some old idol from his native land;
One flings a pagod on the mingled heap,
One lays a crescent, one a cross to sleep;[2]
Swords, sceptres, mitres, crowns and globes and
      stars,
Codes of false fame and stimulants to wars   80
Sink in the settling mass; since guile began,
These are the agents of the woes of man.

    Now the full concourse, where the arches bend,
Pour thro by thousands and their seats ascend.
Far as the centred eye can range around,   85
Or the deep trumpet's solemn voice resound,
Long rows of reverend sires sublime extend,
And cares of worlds on every brow suspend.
High in the front, for soundest wisdom known,
A sire elect in peerless grandeur shone;   90
He open'd calm the universal cause,
To give each realm its limit and its laws,
Bid the last breath of tired contention cease,
And bind all regions in the leagues of peace;
Till one confederate, condependent sway   95
Spread with the sun and bound the walks of day,
One centred system, one all ruling soul
Live thro the parts and regulate the whole.

    Here then, said Hesper, with a blissful smile,
Behold the fruits of thy long years of toil.   100
To yon bright borders of Atlantic day
Thy swelling pinions led the trackless way,
And taught mankind such useful deeds to dare,
To trace new seas and happy nations rear;
Till by fraternal hands their sails unfurl'd   105
Have waved at last in union o'er the world.

    Then let thy stedfast soul no more complain
Of dangers braved and griefs endured in vain,
Of courts insidious, envy's poison'd stings,
The loss of empire and the frown of kings;   110
While these broad views thy better thoughts
      compose
To spurn the malice of insulting foes;
And all the joys descending ages gain,
Repay thy labors and remove thy pain.

                           1807

Advice to a Raven in Russia

In early December 1812, at the onset of his fatal illness,
Barlow dictated to his secretary a bitterly ironical indictment of the ruin and desolation left by twenty years of

---

The Columbiad. [1] Egypt, where Barlow believed civilization
to have begun and therefore a logical site for the parliament
of man.

[2] The pagoda, crescent, and cross symbolize Oriental, Moham-
medan, and Christian religions.

war in Europe. Napoleon's army, reeling back from the defeat at Moscow, retreating in the iron cold of Russian winter, was but a day or so away from Barlow's inn near Cracow. To him it seemed that the Emperor had shattered utterly the great eighteenth-century dream of the "everlasting reign" of peace and justice hailed in *The Columbiad*, and that tyranny and oppression once more stalked the world. The poem was copied in diplomatic code and sent to Mrs. Barlow in Paris but never reached her. The manuscript, after Barlow's death, was preserved and published some thirty years later. The text given here is that newly established by Leon Howard from the holograph manuscript and printed in his article "Joel Barlow and Napoleon," *Huntington Library Quarterly*, Vol. II, No. 1 (October 1938).

Black fool, why winter here? These frozen skies,
Worn by your wings and deafen'd by your cries,
Should warn you hence, where milder suns invite,
And day alternates with his mother night.

You fear perhaps your food will fail you there, 5
Your human carnage, that delicious fare
That lured you hither, following still your friend
The great Napoleon to the world's bleak end.
You fear, because the southern climes pour'd forth
Their clustering nations to infest the north, 10
Bavarians, Austrians, those who drink the Po
And those who skirt the Tuscan seas below,
With all Germania, Neustria,[1] Belgia, Gaul,
Doom'd here to wade thro slaughter to their fall,
You fear he left behind no wars, to feed 15
His feather'd canibals and nurse the breed.

Fear not, my screamer, call your greedy train,
Sweep over Europe, hurry back to Spain,
You'll find his legions there; the valliant crew
Please best their master when they toil for you. 20
Abundant there they spread the country o'er
And taint the breeze with every nation's gore,
Iberian, Lussian,[2] British widely strown,
But still more wide and copious flows their own.

Go where you will; Calabria, Malta, Greece, 25
Egypt and Syria still his fame increase,
Domingo's fatten'd isle and India's plains
Glow deep with purple drawn from Gallic veins.
No Raven's wing can stretch the flight so far
As the torn bandrols of Napoleon's war. 30
Choose then your climate, fix your best abode,
He'll make you deserts and he'll bring you blood.

How could you fear a dearth? have not mankind,
Tho slain by millions, millions left behind?
Has not CONSCRIPTION still the power to weild 35

Advice to a Raven. [1] Part of the Frankish empire of Clovis I, encompassing much of the Seine and Loire valleys.
[2] Lusian; Portuguese.

Her annual faulchion[3] o'er the human field?
A faithful harvester! or if a man
Escape that gleaner, shall he scape the BAN?
The triple BAN, that like the hound of hell
Gripes with three joles,[4] to hold his victim well. 40

Fear nothing then, hatch fast your ravenous
brood,
Teach them to cry to Bonaparte for food;
They'l be like you, of all his suppliant train,
The only class that never cries in vain.
For see what mutual benefits you lend! 45
(The surest way to fix the mutual friend)
While on his slaughter'd troops your tribes are fed,
You cleanse his camp and carry off his dead.
Imperal Scavenger! but now you know
Your work is vain amid these hills of snow. 50
His tentless troops are marbled thro with frost
And change to crystal when the breath is lost.
Mere trunks of ice, tho limb'd like human frames
And lately warm'd with life's endearing flames,
They cannot taint the air, the world impest, 55
Nor can you tear one fiber from their breast.
No! from their visual sockets, as they lie,
With beak and claws you cannot pluck an eye.
The frozen orb, preserving still its form,
Defies your talons as it braves the storm, 60
But stands and stares to God, as if to know
In what curst hands he leaves his world below.

Fly then, or starve; tho all the dreadful road
From Minsk to Moskow with their bodies strow'd
May count some Myriads, yet they can't suffice 65
To feed you more beneath these dreary skies.
Go back, and winter in the wilds of Spain;
Feast there awhile, and in the next campaign
Rejoin your master; for you'll find him then,
With his new million of the race of men, 70
Clothed in his thunders, all his flags unfurl'd,
Raging and storming o'er the prostrate world.

War after war his hungry soul requires,
State after State shall sink beneath his fires,
Yet other Spains in victim smoke shall rise 75
And other Moskows suffocate the skies,
Each land he reeking with its people's slain
And not a stream run bloodless to the main.
Till men resume their souls, and dare to shed
Earth's total vengeance on the monster's head, 80
Hurl from his blood-built throne this king of woes,
Dash him to dust, and let the world repose.
1812   1843

[3] Sword or sickle.
[4] Jowls; that is, jaws.

PHILLIS WHEATLEY [1754?-1784]

THE LITTLE GIRL who would be Phillis Wheatley was brought from Africa to Boston in 1761 when she was about seven years old (she was then shedding her front teeth) and was purchased at the slave market by John Wheatley, a prosperous tailor, to be trained up as a personal servant for his wife. She apparently retained only one memory of her African life: her mother's custom of pouring a libation of water to the rising sun. Frail, gentle, and affectionate, she immediately won the heart of her mistress; and under the tutelage of the Wheatleys' accomplished daughter Mary, she learned to speak, read, and write English with a quick intelligence that carried teacher and pupil on to a more ambitious program of studies that included astronomy, geography, ancient history, and, more significantly, the Bible, the Latin classical writers (in translation and in the original), and the English poets. Under these literary influences, Phillis was soon writing poetry herself, an endeavor in which she was encouraged by the Wheatleys, who treated her almost as one of the family, assigning her only such light tasks as might be expected of a daughter of the house, and introducing her to their circle of acquaintance. She was sixteen when her first published poem appeared, an elegy on the death of the popular revivalist preacher George Whitefield, issued as a broadside and widely reprinted. As word of her talent spread, she was often asked to compose a memorial poem on some departed worthy, famous or obscure, for the New England tradition of the funeral elegy was still strong in pre-Revolutionary Boston. Several of these were published as broadsides. In 1773 Mr. Wheatley and others arranged for the publication, in London, of a volume of her poems, which was prefaced by an "attestation" signed by the governor and other dignitaries of Massachusetts. In the same year, as Phillis was in poor health, the Wheatleys sent her on a visit to England, under the escort of their son, Nathaniel, in the hope that the sea voyage would be beneficial. There, through the Countess of Huntington, Whitefield's patroness, to whom Phillis dedicated her book, she met many prominent personages including the Lord Mayor of London, who presented her with a copy of *Paradise Lost*. Plans were under way for her presentation at Court, when word came of the serious illness of Mrs. Wheatley, and Phillis returned home.

Phillis' London triumph marked the high tide of her fortunes. Mrs. Wheatley died in 1774, and Mr. Wheatley four years later. After the break-up of the Wheatley household, Phillis married John Peters, a free Negro of Boston, but the marriage was plagued by poverty and misfortune. The couple lived in the country for a time, and when they returned to Boston, it was to a life radically different from what Phillis had earlier known. Mary Wheatley Lathrop was dead, Nathaniel was living in England, and many family friends had been dispersed by the outbreak of the Revolution and the British occupation of Boston. Perhaps too diffident and too proud to seek out those who had known her in better days, Phillis lapsed into obscurity and died in 1784, survived only a few hours by the last of her three children.

If Phillis Wheatley's work has been both underrated and overpraised, it is perhaps because the story of her life has prejudiced critical evaluations. Like all the American neoclassic poets, she was imitative. Pope's translation of Homer was her favorite work, and the strongest influence on her writing, in combination with the religious piety of her adopted New England culture. Undeniably, much of her poetry is mediocre, but much of it was "occasional" verse written in response to requests which she always obligingly fulfilled. In her better poems she often displays a genuine empathy for the classical mode and a craftsmanship that entitle her to an acknowledged place among the poets of America's Neoclassic Age.

Further reading: *The Poems of Phillis Wheatley*, ed. Julian D. Mason, Jr., 1966. Winthrop D. Jordan, *White Over Black: American Attitudes Toward the Negro, 1550–1812*, 1968.

To the University of Cambridge, in New-England

Exactly what prompted the thirteen-year-old "Ethiop" girl to pen this admonition to the young men of Harvard, it is impossible to say; but the conversation in many a Boston drawing room of the time must often have dealt with the goings-on across the Charles: the escapades of the students, the inroads of liberal theology and deism, and the college's first full-scale rebellion in 1766 (triggered by rancid butter in the commons). This early poem, one of the few she wrote in other than heroic couplets, shows the influence more of Milton than of Pope. Text: The poems reprinted here are from the edition by Julian D. Mason, Jr. (Chapel Hill, 1966).

While an intrinsic ardor prompts to write,
The muses promise to assist my pen;
'Twas not long since I left my native shore
The land of errors, and *Egyptian* gloom:
Father of mercy, 'twas thy gracious hand   5
Brought me in safety from those dark abodes.[1]

Students, to you 'tis giv'n to scan the heights
Above, to traverse the ethereal space,
And mark the systems of revolving worlds.
Still more, ye sons of science ye receive   10
The blissful news by messengers from heav'n,
How *Jesus'* blood for your redemption flows.
See him with hands out-stretcht upon the cross;
Immense compassion in his bosom glows;
He hears revilers, nor resents their scorn: 15
What matchless mercy in the Son of God!
When the whole human race by sin had fall'n,
He deign'd to die that they might rise again,
And share with him in the sublimest skies,
Life without death, and glory without end.   20

Improve your privileges while they stay,
Ye pupils, and each hour redeem, that bears
Or good or bad report of you to heav'n.
Let sin, that baneful evil to the soul,
By you be shunn'd, nor once remit your guard;   25
Suppress the deadly serpent in its egg.
Ye blooming plants of human race devine,
An *Ethiop* tells you 'tis your greatest foe;

To the University. [1] Phillis Wheatley rarely alluded to her condition in her poems. When she does so, here and in lines 24–30 of "To the Earl of Dartmouth" (where she expresses a different view), it is, as Mason has remarked, to strengthen her points.

Its transient sweetness turns to endless pain,
And in immense perdition sinks the soul,   30
1767   1773

To the Right Honourable William, Earl of Dartmouth

Hail, happy day, when, smiling like the morn,
Fair *Freedom* rose *New-England* to adorn:
The northern clime beneath her genial ray,
Dartmouth, congratulates thy blissful sway:
Elate with hope her race no longer mourns,   5
Each soul expands, each grateful bosom burns,
While in thine hand with pleasure we behold
The silken reins, and *Freedom's* charms unfold.[2]
Long lost to realms beneath the northern skies
She shines supreme, while hated *faction* dies: 10
Soon as appear'd the *Goddess* long desir'd,
Sick at the view, she languish'd and expir'd;
Thus from the splendors of the morning light
The owl in sadness seeks the caves of night.

No more, *America*, in mournful strain   15
Of wrongs, and grievance unredress'd complain,
No longer shalt thou dread the iron chain,
Which wanton *Tyranny* with lawless hand
Had made, and with it meant t' enslave the land.   19

Should you, my lord, while you peruse my song,
Wonder from whence my love of *Freedom* sprung,
Whence flow these wishes for the common good,
By feeling hearts alone best understood,
I, young in life, by seeming cruel fate
Was snatch'd from *Afric's* fancy'd happy seat: 25
What pangs excruciating must molest,
What sorrows labour in my parent's breast?
Steel'd was that soul and by no misery mov'd
That from a father seiz'd his babe belov'd:
Such, such my case.[3] And can I then but pray   30
Others may never feel tyrannic sway?

To the Earl of Dartmouth. [1] William Legge, Second Earl of Dartmouth (1731–1801), who in August 1772 became Secretary of State for the Colonies and President of the Board of Trade and Foreign Plantations in Lord North's administration. Phillis met him when she was in England in 1773, and he gave her a copy of Smollett's translation of *Don Quixote*. Dartmouth College was named for him.
[2] Phillis' hopes proved to be false ones, as he proved to be a minister not in sympathy with the events which occurred in New England in the following months. (Mason)
[3] Cf. lines 2–6 of "To the University of Cambridge."

For favours past, great Sir, our thanks are due,
And thee we ask thy favours to renew,
Since in thy pow'r, as in thy will before,　34
To sooth the griefs, which thou did'st once deplore.
May heav'nly grace the sacred sanction give
To all thy works, and thou for ever live
Not only on the wings of fleeting *Fame*,
Though praise immortal crowns the patriot's name,
But to conduct to heav'ns refulgent fane,　40
May fiery coursers sweep th' ethereal plain,
And bear thee upwards to that blest abode,
Where, like the prophet, thou shalt find thy God.
1772　　　　　　　　　　　　　　　　　1773

On Imagination

Thy various works, imperial queen, we see,
How bright their forms! how deck'd with pomp by
　　thee!
Thy wond'rous acts in beauteous order stand,
And all attest how potent is thine hand.

From *Helicon's* refulgent heights attend,　5
Ye sacred choir, and my attempts befriend:
To tell her glories with a faithful tongue,
Ye blooming graces, triumph in my song.

Now here, now there, the roving *Fancy* flies,
Till some lov'd object strikes her wand'ring eyes,　10
Whose silken fetters all the senses bind,
And soft captivity involves the mind.

Imagination! who can sing thy force?
Or who describe the swiftness of thy course?
Soaring through air to find the bright abode,　15
Th' empyreal palace of the thund'ring God,
We on thy pinions can surpass the wind,
And leave the rolling universe behind:
From star to star the mental optics rove,
Measure the skies, and range the realms above.　20
There in one view we grasp the mighty whole,
Or with new worlds amaze th' unbounded soul.

Though *Winter* frowns to *Fancy's* raptur'd eyes
The fields may flourish, and gay scenes arise;
The frozen deeps may break their iron bands,　25
And bid their waters murmur o'er the sands.
Fair *Flora* may resume her fragrant reign,
And with her flow'ry riches deck the plain;
Sylvanus may diffuse his honours round,
And all the forest may with leaves be crown'd:　30
Show'rs may descend, and dews their gems disclose,
And nectar sparkle on the blooming rose.

Such is thy pow'r, nor are thine orders vain,
O thou the leader of the mental train:

In full perfection all thy works are wrought,　35
And thine the sceptre o'er the realms of thought.
Before thy throne the subject-passions bow,
Of subject-passions sov'reign ruler Thou,
At thy command joy rushes on the heart,
And through the glowing veins the spirits dart.　40

Fancy might now her silken pinions try
To rise from earth, and sweep th' expanse on high;
From *Tithon's* bed now might *Aurora* rise,
Her cheeks all glowing with celestial dies,
While a pure stream of light o'erflows the skies.　45
The monarch of the day I might behold,
And all the mountains tipt with radiant gold,
But I reluctant leave the pleasing views,
Which *Fancy* dresses to delight the *Muse*;
Winter austere forbids me to aspire,　50
And northern tempests damp the rising fire;
They chill the tides of *Fancy's* flowing sea,
Cease then, my song, cease the unequal lay.

1773

FROM *An Address to Miss Phillis Wheatley*

by Jupiter Hammon

Not Phillis Wheatley, but Jupiter Hammon, a slave belonging to Mr. Joseph Lloyd of Queen's Village, Long Island, was probably America's first published black poet. Whether slave or free, the most difficult problem facing the Negro in Revolutionary America was to establish an identity and some measure of independence in a society where slavery seemed to be permanent. Some, like Hammon, found religion the most acceptable outlet for self-expression, for white society would quickly acknowledge Christian piety as evidence of personal integrity and individuality. Hammon, taught early to read, was strongly influenced by Methodist revivalism and the writings of Charles Wesley and William Cowper. His poetical broadside, "An Evening Thought. Salvation by Christ, with Penitential Cries," was published in 1760 with the help of his master and friends; other poems and religious pieces appeared over the next two decades, including his tribute to Phillis Wheatley, published as a broadside in 1778, of which the first eleven stanzas are given below. Hammon's "Address to the Negroes of the State of New York" (1787) counseled slaves to bear their servitude patiently, but he also attacked the system and advocated that young slaves be manumitted so that the institution could gradually be abolished. In 1799, a year before his death, Hammon's hopes were justified by the passage of legislation in New York leading toward the gradual emancipation of all the state's slaves. His verse, simple and direct in style and content, was in the tradition of the *Bay Psalm Book*, eighteenth-century hymnody, and the older ballad, displaying much less sophistication and learning than Phillis

Wheatley's. Text: Oscar Wegelin, *Jupiter Hammon, American Negro Poet: Selections from His Writings* (New York, 1915).

O come you pious youth! adore
    The wisdom of thy God,
In bringing thee from distant shore,
    To learn His holy word.
                                            Eccles. xii.

Thou mightst been left behind,   5
    Amidst a dark abode;
God's tender mercy still combin'd,
    Thou hast the holy word.
                                            Psal. cxxxv, 2, 3.

Fair wisdom's ways are paths of peace,
    And they that walk therein,   10
Shall reap the joys that never cease,
    And Christ shall be their king.
                                            Psal. i. 1, 2; Prov. iii, 7.

God's tender mercy brought thee here;
    Tost o'er the raging main;
In Christian faith thou hast a share,   15
    Worth all the gold of Spain.
                                            Psal. ciii, 1, 3, 4.

While thousands tossed by the sea,
    And others settled down,
God's tender mercy set thee free,
    From dangers that come down.   20
                                            Death.

That thou a pattern still might be,
    To youth of Boston town,

The blessed Jesus set thee free,
    From every sinful wound.
                                            2 Cor. v, 10.

The blessed Jesus, who came down,   25
    Unvail'd his sacred face,
To cleanse the soul of every wound,
    And give repenting grace.
                                            Rom. v, 21.

That we poor sinners may obtain,
    The pardon of our sin;   30
Dear blessed Jesus now constrain,
    And bring us flocking in.
                                            Psal. xxxiv, 6, 7, 8.

Come you, Phillis, now aspire,
    And seek the living God,
So step by step thou mayst go higher,   35
    Till perfect in the word.
                                            Matth. vii, 7, 8.

While thousands mov'd to distant shore,
    And others left behind,
The blessed Jesus still adore,
    Implant this in thy mind.   40
                                            Psal. lxxxix, 1.

Thou hast left the heathen shore;
    Thro' mercy of the Lord,
Among the heathen live no more,
    Come magnify thy God.
                                            Psal. xxxiv, 1, 2, 3.

. . . . .

PHILIP FRENEAU [1752–1832]

FRENEAU WAS BORN of French Huguenot and Scottish parents in New York State, but the family moved to a large New Jersey estate, within sight of the ocean, when he was ten. He attended Princeton in the same class as James Madison and Hugh Henry Bracken-ridge, collaborating with the latter on their commencement poem, "The Rising Glory of America." After his graduation Freneau moved restlessly from job to job. He taught school, shipped out as a sailor, visited and dreamed in the West Indies, returned to enlist in the Revolutionary army, was captured and nearly died in a British prison ship, and served as a captain in the coastal trade. After entering politics on the side of the Jeffersonians he was appointed a government clerk of foreign languages, and eked out a precarious living as farmer, sea captain, and journalist. Though he was determined from the first to be a poet ("To write was my sad destiny / The worst of trades, we all agree") circumstances were on the whole against him. Much of his work was elicited by the Revolutionary War or by the political battles of the Federalist period, not the kind of poetry he was naturally drawn to or the kind he wrote best. A large part of his energy was consumed in newspaper work and by some six hundred essays on various topics published in journals. He also suffered from want of an audience to encourage him and to respond to his better verse.

Freneau's poetry, issued in collected editions in 1786, 1788, 1809, and 1815, falls into fairly clear divisions. His wartime verse reflects the heated passions of the times and his hatred of the British, whose treatment on the prison ship he neither forgot nor forgave. His political satires, modeled on the English tradition of Dryden and Churchill, and directed against the Federalists, were expert and effective, so much so that Washington himself called him "that rascal Freneau," and Jefferson affirmed that he "had saved our constitution, which was fast galloping into monarchy." An avowed radical, Freneau threw himself into a number of reform causes and wrote verses about them. His lyric verse, dealing with the themes of nature, transience, the past, and personal experience, shows him to have been a poet of genuine gifts and imagination. Though he echoed Collins, Gray, Akenside, and other English pre-Romantics, there is in his best lyric verse a freshness, originality, and haunting beauty unsurpassed in the poetry of the times. Late in life, Freneau also produced a small body of deist-Unitarian religious verse of excellent quality. Most of all, however, Freneau's importance as a poet lies in the fact that he alone, of his American generation, broke out of the constrictions of neoclassical imitation to look at life around him directly, read it imaginatively, and record it sensitively.

The text of all Freneau poems, unless otherwise noted, is that of Fred L. Pattee, *The Poems of Philip Freneau* (Princeton, 1902-7).

Further reading: *Poems of Freneau*, ed. H. H. Clark, 1929. Lewis Leary, *That Rascal Freneau*, 1941.

The Power of Fancy

Written while he was still a Princeton undergraduate, this poem reflects somewhat self-consciously Freneau's reading of Milton's "Il Penseroso" and of the fashionable English pre-Romantic poets, especially Joseph Warton, whose "Ode to Fancy" (1746) probably served as his model. A number of characteristics of pre-Romantic verse are implicit in the poem—the praise of the "fancy" as a transforming power; the use of the dream device; the interest in the melancholy, the exotic, and the distant; the classical and pastoral reference; and a vaguely deistic concept of the universe. Freneau's rimed tetrameter is a creative departure from the conventional couplet.

Wakeful, vagrant, restless thing,
Ever wandering on the wing,
Who thy wondrous source can find,
Fancy, regent of the mind;
A spark from Jove's resplendent throne, 5
But thy nature all unknown.
  This spark of bright, celestial flame,
From Jove's seraphic altar came,
And hence alone in man we trace,
Resemblance to the immortal race. 10
  Ah! what is all this mighty whole,
These suns and stars that round us roll!
What are they all, where'er they shine,
But Fancies of the Power Divine!
What is this globe, these lands, and seas, 15
And heat, and cold, and flowers, and trees,
And life, and death, and beast, and man,
And time—that with the sun began—
But thoughts on reason's scale combin'd,
Ideas of the Almighty mind! 20
  On the surface of the brain
Night after night she walks unseen,
Noble fabrics doth she raise
In the woods or on the seas,
On some high, steep, pointed rock, 25
Where the billows loudly knock
And the dreary tempests sweep
Clouds along the uncivil deep.
  Lo! she walks upon the moon,
Listens to the chimy tune 30
Of the bright, harmonious spheres,
And the song of angels hears;
Sees this earth a distant star,[1]
Pendant, floating in the air;
Leads me to some lonely dome, 35
Where Religion loves to come,
Where the bride of Jesus dwells,
And the deep ton'd organ swells
In notes with lofty anthems join'd,
Notes that half distract the mind. 40

Now like lightning she descends
To the prison of the fiends,
Hears the rattling of their chains,
Feels their never ceasing pains—
But, O never may she tell 45
Half the frightfulness of hell.
  Now she views Arcadian rocks,
Where the shepherds guard their flocks,
And, while yet her wings she spreads,
Sees chrystal streams and coral beds, 50
Wanders to some desert deep,
Or some dark, enchanted steep,
By the full moonlight doth shew
Forests of a dusky blue,
Where, upon some mossy bed, 55
Innocence reclines her head.
  Swift, she stretches o'er the seas
To the far off Hebrides,
Canvas on the lofty mast
Could not travel half so fast— 60
Swifter than the eagle's flight
Or instantaneous rays of light!
Lo! contemplative she stands
On Norwegia's rocky lands—
Fickle Goddess, set me down 65
Where the rugged winters frown
Upon Orca's[2] howling steep,
Nodding o'er the northern deep,
Where the winds tumultuous roar,
Vext that Ossian sings no more. 70
Fancy, to that land repair,
Sweetest Ossian slumbers there;
Waft me far to southern isles
Where the soften'd winter smiles,
To Bermuda's orange shades, 75
Or Demarara's[3] lovely glades;
Bear me o'er the sounding cape,
Painting death in every shape,
Where daring Anson[4] spread the sail
Shatter'd by the stormy gale— 80
Lo! she leads me wide and far,
Sense can never follow her—
Shape thy course o'er land and sea,
Help me to keep pace with thee,
Lead me to yon' chalky cliff, 85
Over rock and over reef,
Into Britain's fertile land,
Stretching far her proud command.
Look back and view, thro' many a year,
Caesar, Julius Caesar, there. 90
  Now to Tempe's verdant wood,
Over the mid-ocean flood
Lo! the islands of the sea—

The Power of Fancy. [1] Milton's Paradise Lost, B. ii, v. 1052. [Freneau's note.]

[2] Possibly the Orkney Islands, north of Scotland.
[3] British Guiana.
[4] Commander of a British expedition to the South Pacific, 1740–44.

Sappho, Lesbos mourns for thee:
Greece, arouse thy humbled head,   95
Where are all thy mighty dead
Who states to endless ruin hurl'd
And carried vengeance through the world?—
Troy, thy vanish'd pomp resume,
Or, weeping at thy Hector's tomb,   100
Yet those faded scenes renew,
Whose memory is to Homer due.
Fancy, lead me wandering still
Up to Ida's cloud-topt hill;
Not a laurel there doth grow   105
But in vision thou shalt show,—
Every sprig on Virgil's tomb
Shall in livelier colours bloom,
And every triumph Rome has seen
Flourish on the years between.   110
    Now she bears me far away
In the east to meet the day,
Leads me over Ganges' streams,
Mother of the morning beams—
O'er the ocean hath she ran,   115
Places me on Tinian;[5]
Farther, farther in the east,
Till it almost meets the west,
Let us wandering both be lost
On Taitis sea-beat coast,   120
Bear me from that distant strand,
Over ocean, over land,
To California's golden shore—
Fancy, stop, and rove no more.
    Now, tho' late, returning home,   125
Lead me to Belinda's[6] tomb;
Let me glide as well as you
Through the shroud and coffin too,
And behold, a moment, there,
All that once was good and fair—   130
Who doth here so soundly sleep?
Shall we break this prison deep?—
Thunders cannot wake the maid,
Lightnings cannot pierce the shade,
And tho' wintry tempests roar,   135
Tempests shall disturb no more.
    Yet must those eyes in darkness stay,
That once were rivals to the day?—
Like heaven's bright lamp beneath the main
They are but set to rise again.   140
    Fancy, thou the muses' pride,
In thy painted realms reside
Endless images of things,
Fluttering each on golden wings,
Ideal objects, such a store,   145
The universe could hold no more:
Fancy, to thy power I owe

[5] Island in the Marianas, in the South Pacific.
[6] A conventional name in 18th-century poetry for a lost sweetheart.

Half my happiness below;
By thee Elysian groves were made,
Thine were the notes that Orpheus play'd;   150
By thee was Pluto charm'd so well
While rapture seiz'd the sons of hell—
Come, O come—perceiv'd by none,
You and I will walk alone.

1770

FROM *The Beauties of Santa Cruz*[1]

Freneau spent the early years of the Revolution on the island of Santa Cruz (St. Croix) in the Danish West Indies, an experience to which he looked back "as Adam did after he was banished from the bowers of Eden." A long (111 stanzas), loosely organized poem, which ranges over a number of topics, it does succeed in conveying Freneau's fresh response to the color, loveliness, and luxury of Caribbean island life.

Sweet orange grove, the fairest of the isle,
  In thy soft shade luxuriously reclin'd,
Where, round my fragrant bed, the flowrets smile,
  In sweet delusions I deceive my mind.

But Melancholy's glooms assail my breast,
  For potent nature reigns despotic here;—
A nation ruin'd, and a world oppress'd,
  Might rob the boldest Stoic of a tear.

1

Sick of thy northern glooms, come, shepherd, seek
More equal climes, and a serener sky:
Why shouldst thou toil amid thy frozen ground,
Where half year's snows, a barren prospect lie,

2

When thou mayst go where never frost was seen,   5
Or north-west winds with cutting fury blow,
Where never ice congeal'd the limpid stream,
Where never mountain tipt its head with snow?

3

Twice seven days prosperous gales thy barque shall
    bear
To isles that flourish in perpetual green,   10
Where richest herbage glads each shady vale,
And ever verdant plants on every hill are seen.

The Beauties of Santa Cruz. [1] Or St. Croix, a Danish island (in the American Archipelago), commonly, tho' erroneously included in the cluster of the Virgin Islands; belonging to the crown of Denmark. [Freneau's note.]

4

Nor dread the dangers of the billowy deep,
Autumnal winds shall safely waft thee o'er;
Put off the timid heart, or, man unblest,   15
Ne'er shalt thou reach this gay enchanting shore.

5

Thus Judah's tribes beheld the promis'd land,
While Jordan's angry waters swell'd between;
Thus trembling on the brink I see them stand,
Heav'n's type in view, the Canaanitish green.   20

6

Thus, some mean souls, in spite of age and care,
Are so united to this globe below,
They never wish to cross death's dusky main,
That parting them and happiness doth flow.

7

Though reason's voice might whisper to the soul   25
That nobler climes for man the gods design—
Come, shepherd, haste—the northern breezes blow,
No more the slumbering winds thy barque confine.

8

From the vast caverns of old ocean's bed,
Fair Santa Cruz, arising, laves her waist,   30
The threat'ning waters roar on every side,
For every side by ocean is embrac'd.

9

Sharp, craggy rocks repel the surging brine,
Whose cavern'd sides by restless billows wore,
Resemblance claim to that remoter isle   35
Where once the winds' proud lord the sceptre bore.

10

Betwixt old Cancer and the mid-way line,
In happiest climate lies this envied isle,
Trees bloom throughout the year, streams ever flow,
And fragrant Flora wears a lasting smile.   40

11

Cool, woodland streams from shaded clifts descend,
The dripping rock no want of moisture knows,
Supply'd by springs that on the skies depend,
That fountain feeding as the current flows.

12

Such were the isles which happy Flaccus sung,   45
Where one tree blossoms while another bears,
Where spring forever gay and ever young,
Walks her gay round through her unwearied years.

13

Such were the climes which youthful Eden saw
Ere crossing fates destroy'd her golden reign—   50
Reflect upon thy loss, unhappy man,
And seek the vales of Paradise again.

* * * * *

43

Yon' cotton shrubs with bursting knobs behold,
Their snow white locks these humble groves array;
On slender trees the blushing coffee hangs   55
Like thy fair cherry, and would tempt thy stay.

44

Safe from the winds, in deep retreats, they rise;
Their utmost summit may thy arm attain;
Taste the moist fruit, and from thy closing eyes
Sleep shall retire, with all his drowsy train.   60

45

The spicy berry, they guava call,
Swells in the mountains on a stripling tree;
These some admire, and value more than all,
My humble verse, besides, unfolds to thee.

46

The smooth white cedar, here, delights the eye,   65
The bay-tree, with its aromatic green,
The sea-side grapes, sweet natives of the sand,
And pulse, of various kinds, on trees are seen.

47

Here mingled vines that downward shadows cast,
Here, cluster'd grapes from loaded boughs depend,
Their leaves no frosts, their fruits no cold winds
    blast,   71
But, rear'd by suns, to time alone they bend.

48

The plantane and banana flourish here,
Of hasty growth, and love to fix their root
Where some soft stream of ambling water flows,   75
To yield full moisture to their cluster'd fruit.

49

No other trees so vast a leaf can boast,
So broad, so long—through these refresh'd I stray,
And though the noon-sun all his radiance shed,
These friendly leaves shall shade me all the way,   80

50

And tempt the cooling breeze to hasten there,
With its sweet odorous breath to charm the grove;
High shades and verdant seats, while underneath
A little stream by mossy banks doth rove,

51

Where once the Indian dames slept with their
     swains,   85
Or fondly kiss'd the moon-light eves away;
The lovers fled, the tearful stream remains,
And only I console it with my lay.

52

Among the shades of yonder whispering grove
The green palmittoes mingle, tall and fair,   90
That ever murmur, and forever move,
Fanning with wavy bough the ambient air.

53

Pomegranates grace the wild, and sweet-sops there
Ready to fall, require thy helping hand,
Nor yet neglect the papaw or mamee   95
Whose slighted trees with fruits unheeded stand.

54

Those shaddocks juicy shall thy taste delight,
And yon' high fruits, the richest of the wood,
That cling in clusters to the mother tree,
The cocoa-nut; rich, milky, healthful food.   100

55

O grant me, gods, if yet condemn'd to stray,
At least to spend life's sober evening here,
To plant a grove where winds yon' shelter'd bay,
And pluck these fruits that frost nor winter fear.

1776

FROM *The British Prison Ship*

Freneau returned from the West Indies in 1778, served for a time in the New Jersey militia, and in 1780 joined the crew of the privateer *Aurora* as third mate. The *Aurora* was captured by the British *Iris*, its crew confined on the prison ship *Scorpion*, lying in New York Harbor, and later transferred to the hospital ship *Hunter*. Immediately on his release Freneau wrote this poem of three cantos, published in 1781, the first dealing with the capture, the second with his confinement aboard the *Scorpion*, and the last with conditions on the *Hunter*. He carried a lifelong hatred of the British for the sickness, brutality, and horror he saw and experienced during his imprisonment, quite evident in the bitterness of the poem.

Canto III.—The Hospital Prison Ship

Now tow'rd the *Hunter's* gloomy sides we came,
A slaughter-house, yet hospital in name;[1]
For none came there (to pass through all degrees)
'Till half consum'd, and dying with disease;—
But when too near with labouring oars we ply'd,   5
The Mate with curses drove us from the side;
That wretch who, banish'd from the navy crew,
Grown old in blood, did here his trade renew;
His serpent's tongue, when on his charge let loose,
Utter'd reproaches, scandal, and abuse,   10
Gave all to hell who dar'd his king disown,
And swore mankind were made for George alone:
Ten thousand times, to irritate our woe,
He wish'd us founder'd in the gulph below;
Ten thousand times he brandish'd high his stick,   15
And swore as often that we were not sick—
And yet so pale!—that we were thought by some
A freight of ghosts from Death's dominions come—
But calm'd at length—for who can always rage,
Or the fierce war of endless passion wage,   20
He pointed to the stairs that led below
To damps, disease, and varied shapes of woe—
Down to the gloom I took my pensive way,
Along the decks the dying captives lay;
Some struck with madness, some with scurvy
     pain'd,   25

The British Prison Ship. [1]"The *Hunter* had been very newly put to the use of a hospital-ship. She was miserably dirty and cluttered. Her decks leaked to such a degree that the sick were deluged with every shower of rain. Between decks they lay along struggling in the agonies of death; dying with putrid and bilious fevers; lamenting their hard fate to die at such a fatal distance from their friends; others totally insensible, and yielding their last breath in all the horrors of light-headed frenzy. . . . Our allowance in the *Hunter*, to those upon full diet, was one pound of bread and one pound of fresh beef per diem; to those upon half diet, one pound of bread and one-half pound of beef or mutton per diem. Every other day we had a cask of spruce beer sent on board. Our fresh meat was generally heads or shanks, and would just answer to make soup."—Freneau's Journal.

But still of putrid fevers most complain'd!
On the hard floors these wasted objects laid,
There toss'd and tumbled in the dismal shade,
There no soft voice their bitter fate bemoan'd,
And Death strode stately, while the victims
    groan'd;   30
Of leaky decks I heard them long complain,
Drown'd as they were in deluges of rain,
Deny'd the comforts of a dying bed,
And not a pillow to support the head—
How could they else but pine, and grieve, and sigh,
Detest a wretched life—and wish to die?   36

    Scarce had I mingled with this dismal band
When a thin spectre seiz'd me by the hand—
"And art thou come, (death heavy on his eyes)
And art thou come to these abodes," he cries;   40
"Why didst thou leave the *Scorpion's* dark retreat,
And hither haste a surer death to meet?
Why didst thou leave thy damp infected cell?
If that was purgatory, this is hell—
We, too, grown weary of that horrid shade,   45
Petitioned early for the doctor's aid;
His aid denied, more deadly symptoms came,
Weak, and yet weaker, glow'd the vital flame;
And when disease had worn us down so low
That few could tell if we were ghosts or no,   50
And all asserted, death would be our fate—
Then to the doctor we were sent—too late.
Here wastes away Autolycus the brave,
Here young Orestes finds a wat'ry grave,
Here gay Alcander,[2] gay, alas! no more,   55
Dies far sequester'd from his native shore;
He late, perhaps, too eager for the fray,
Chac'd the vile Briton o'er the wat'ry way
'Till fortune jealous, bade her clouds appear,   59
Turn'd hostile to his fame, and brought him here.

    "Thus do our warriors, thus our heroes fall,
Imprison'd here, base ruin meets them all,
Or, sent afar to Britain's barbarous shore,
There die neglected, and return no more:
Ah! rest in peace, poor, injur'd, parted shade,   65
By cruel hands in death's dark weeds array'd,
But happier climes, where suns unclouded shine,
Light undisturb'd, and endless peace are thine."—
    From Brookland groves a Hessian doctor[3] came,
Not great his skill, nor greater much his fame;   70
Fair Science never call'd the wretch her son,
And Art disdain'd the stupid man to own;—
Can you admire that Science was so coy,
Or Art refus'd his genius to employ!—
Do men with brutes an equal dullness share,   75

[2] Autolycus, son of Hermes; Orestes, son of Agamemnon;
and Alcander, a character in a famous French romance, were
all once held captive.
[3] The doctor came from the British hospital ship *Hunter*,
stationed near Brookland, Maryland.

Or cuts yon' grovelling mole the midway air?
In polar worlds can Eden's blossoms blow?
Do trees of God in barren desarts grow?
Are loaded vines to Etna's summit known,
Or swells the peach beneath the torrid zone?—   80
Yet still he doom'd his genius to the rack,
And, as you may suppose, was own'd a quack.
    He on his charge the healing work begun
With antimonial mixtures, by the tun,
Ten minutes was the time he deign'd to stay,   85
The time of grace allotted once a day—
He drencht us well with bitter draughts, 'tis true,
Nostrums from hell, and cortex from Peru—
Some with his pills he sent to Pluto's reign,
And some he blister'd with his flies of Spain;   90
His cream of Tartar walk'd its deadly round,[4]
Till the lean patient at the potion frown'd,
And swore that hemlock, death, or what you will,
Were nonsense to the drugs that stuff'd his bill.—
On those refusing he bestow'd a kick,   95
Or menac'd vengeance with his walking stick;
Here uncontroul'd he exercis'd his trade,
And grew experienced by the deaths he made;
By frequent blows we from his cane endur'd
He kill'd at least as many as he cur'd;   100
On our lost comrades built his future fame,
And scatter'd fate, where'er his footsteps came.
    Some did not seem obedient to his will,
And swore he mingled poison with his pill,
But I acquit him by a fair confession,   105
He was no Englishman—he was a Hessian[5]—
Although a dunce, he had some sense of sin,
Or else the Lord knows where we now had been;
Perhaps in that far country sent to range   109
Where never prisoner meets with an exchange—
Then had we all been banish'd out of time
Nor I return'd to plague the world with rhyme.
    Fool though he was, yet candour must confess
Not chief Physician was this dog of Hesse—
One master o'er the murdering tribe was plac'd,   115
By him the rest were honour'd or disgrac'd;—
Once, and but once, by some strange fortune led
He came to see the dying and the dead—

[4] Peruvian bark was a remedy for fevers; Spanish fly, a
blistering agent; cream of tartar, a cathartic.
[5] "A German doctor attended every morning at eight o'clock
and administered such remedies as were thought proper.
Thus things went on, two or three dying every day, who were
carried on shore and buried in the bank, till three of our
crew, who had got pretty hearty, stole the boat one night and
made their escape. This occasioned new trouble. The doctor
refused to come on board, and as he rowed past us next
morning to see somebody in the *Jersey*, which lay near us,
some of the sick calling to him for blisters, he told them to
put tar on their backs, which would serve as well as anything,
and so rowed away. However, after two or three days his
wrath was appeased, and he deigned to come on board
again."—Freneau's *Journal*.

He came—but anger so deform'd his eye,
And such a faulchion glitter'd on his thigh,   120
And such a gloom his visage darken'd o'er,
And two such pistols in his hands he bore!
That, by the gods!—with such a load of steel
He came, we thought, to murder, not to heal—
Hell in his heart, and mischief in his head,   125
He gloom'd destruction, and had smote us dead,
Had he so dar'd—but fate with-held his hand—
He came—blasphem'd—and turn'd again to land.
    From this poor vessel, and her sickly crew
An English ruffian all his titles drew,   130
Captain, esquire, commander, too, in chief,
And hence he gain'd his bread, and hence his beef,
But, sir, you might have search'd creation round
Ere such another miscreant could be found—
Though unprovok'd, an angry face he bore,   135
We stood astonish'd at the oaths he swore;
He swore, till every prisoner stood aghast,
And thought him Satan in a brimstone blast;
He wish'd us banish'd from the public light,
He wish'd us shrouded in perpetual night!   140
That were he king, no mercy would he show,
But drive all rebels to the world below;
That if we scoundrels did not scrub the decks
His staff should break our damn'd rebellious necks;
He swore, besides, that if the ship took fire   145
We too should in the pitchy flame expire;
And meant it so—this tyrant, I engage,
Had lost his breath to gratify his rage.—
    If where he walk'd a captive carcase lay,
Still dreadful was the language of the day—   150
He call'd us dogs, and would have us'd us so,
But vengeance check'd the meditated blow,
The vengeance from our injur'd nation due
To him, and all the base, unmanly crew.   154
    Such food they sent, to make complete our woes,
It look'd like carrion torn from hungry crows,
Such vermin vile on every joint were seen,
So black, corrupted, mortified, and lean
That once we try'd to move our flinty chief,
And thus address'd him, holding up the beef: 160
    "See, captain, see! what rotten bones we pick,
What kills the healthy cannot cure the sick:
Not dogs on such by Christian men are fed,
And see, good master, see, what lousy bread!"
    "Your meat or bread (this man of flint replied)
Is not my care to manage or provide—   166
But this, damn'd rebel dogs, I'd have you know,
That better than you merit we bestow;
Out of my sight!"——nor more he deign'd to say,
But whisk'd about, and frowning, strode away.   170
    Each day, at least three carcases we bore,
And scratch'd them graves along the sandy shore;
By feeble hands the shallow graves were made,
No stone memorial o'er the corpses laid;
In barren sands, and far from home, they lie,   175

No friend to shed a tear, when passing by;
O'er the mean tombs insulting Britons tread,
Spurn at the sand, and curse the rebel dead.
    When to your arms these fatal islands fall,
(For first or last they must be conquer'd all)   180
Americans! to rites sepulchral just,
With gentlest footstep press this kindred dust,
And o'er the tombs, if tombs can then be found,
Place the green turf, and plant the myrtle round.
    Americans! a just resentment shew,   185
And glut revenge on this detested foe;
While the warm blood exults the glowing vein
Still shall resentment in your bosoms reign,
Can you forget the greedy Briton's ire,
Your fields in ruin, and your domes on fire,   190
No age, no sex from lust and murder free,
And, black as night, the hell born refugee!
Must York[6] forever your best blood entomb,
And these gorg'd monsters triumph in their doom,
Who leave no art of cruelty untry'd;   195
Such heavy vengeance, and such hellish pride!
Death has no charms—his realms dejected lie
In the dull climate of a clouded sky;
Death has no charms, except in British eyes,
See, arm'd for death, the infernal miscreants rise;
See how they pant to stain the world with gore,   201
And millions murder'd, still would murder more;
This selfish race, from all the world disjoin'd,
Perpetual discord spread throughout mankind,
Aim to extend their empire o'er the ball,   205
Subject, destroy, absorb, and conquer all,
As if the power that form'd us did condemn
All other nations to be slaves to them—
Rouse from your sleep, and crush the thievish band,
Defeat, destroy, and sweep them from the land,   210
Ally'd like you, what madness to despair,
Attack the ruffians while they linger there;
There Tryon sits, a monster all complete,
See Clinton there with vile Knyphausen[7] meet,
And every wretch whom honour should detest   215
There finds a home—and Arnold[8] with the rest.
Ah! traitors, lost to every sense of shame,
Unjust supporters of a tyrant's claim;
Foes to the rights of freedom and of men,   219
Flush'd with the blood of thousands you have slain,
To the just doom the righteous skies decree
We leave you, toiling still in cruelty,
Or on dark plans in future herds to meet,
Plans form'd in hell, and projects half complete:
The years approach that shall to ruin bring   225
Your lords, your chiefs, your miscreant of a king,

[6] New York.
[7] William Tryon was governor of New York, 1771–78; General Henry Clinton succeeded Howe as commander of the British forces in 1778; General William von Knyphausen commanded the Hessian troops after 1777.
[8] Benedict Arnold.

Whose murderous acts shall stamp his name
    accurs'd,
And his last triumphs more than damn the first.
1781

The Vanity of Existence

To Thyrsis[1]

In youth, gay scenes attract our eyes,
    And not suspecting their decay
Life's flowery fields before us rise,
    Regardless of its winter day.

But vain pursuits and joys as vain,   5
    Convince us life is but a dream.
Death is to wake, to rise again
    To that true life you best esteem.

So nightly on some shallow tide,
    Oft have I seen a splendid show;   10
Reflected stars on either side,
    And glittering moons were seen below.

But when the tide had ebbed away,
    The scene fantastic with it fled,
A bank of mud around me lay,   15
    And sea-weed on the river's bed.
1781

To the Memory of the Brave Americans

Under General Greene, in South Carolina, who fell in the action of September 8, 1781 [1]

At Eutaw Springs the valiant died;
    Their limbs with dust are covered o'er—
Weep on, ye springs, your tearful tide;
    How many heroes are no more!

If in this wreck of ruin, they   5
    Can yet be thought to claim a tear,
O smite your gentle breast, and say
    The friends of freedom slumber here!

Thou, who shalt trace this bloody plain,
    If goodness rules thy generous breast,   10
Sigh for the wasted rural reign;
    Sigh for the shepherds, sunk to rest!

The Vanity of Existence. [1] A conventional dedication adopted from English pastoral poetry; Thyrsis was a shepherd mentioned by Theocritus.

To the Brave Americans. [1] General Nathanael Greene's troops engaged the British under Cornwallis at Eutaw Springs, South Carolina, with a loss of seven hundred men.

Stranger, their humble graves adorn;
    You too may fall, and ask a tear;
'Tis not the beauty of the morn   15
    That proves the evening shall be clear.—

They saw their injured country's woe;
    The flaming town, the wasted field;
Then rushed to meet the insulting foe;
    They took the spear—but left the shield.   20

Led by thy conquering genius, Greene,
    The Britons they compelled to fly;
None distant viewed the fatal plain,
    None grieved, in such a cause to die—

But, like the Parthian, famed of old,   25
    Who, flying, still their arrows threw,
These routed Britons, full as bold,
    Retreated, and retreating slew.[2]

Now rest in peace, our patriot band;
    Though far from nature's limits thrown,   30
We trust they find a happier land,
    A brighter sunshine of their own.
1781

The Wild Honey Suckle[1]

Fair flower, that dost so comely grow,
Hid in this silent, dull retreat,
Untouched thy honied blossoms blow,
Unseen thy little branches greet:
    No roving foot shall crush thee here,   5
    No busy hand provoke a tear.

By Nature's self in white arrayed,
She bade thee shun the vulgar eye,
And planted here the guardian shade,
And sent soft waters murmuring by;   10
    Thus quietly thy summer goes,
    Thy days declining to repose.

Smit with those charms, that must decay,
I grieve to see your future doom;
They died—nor were these flowers more gay,   15
The flowers that did in Eden bloom;
    Unpitying frosts, and Autumn's power
    Shall leave no vestige of this flower.

[2] After the first engagement the British fled in confusion. Greene, in his eagerness, pursued them too closely, and sheltered by the brick house, they inflicted upon the advancing Americans the greater part of the loss of life incurred during the battle. [Freneau's note.]

The Wild Honey Suckle. [1] The white swamp honeysuckle of the Carolinas.

From morning suns and evening dews
At first thy little being came: 20
If nothing once, you nothing lose,
For when you die you are the same;
    The space between, is but an hour,
    The frail duration of a flower.

1786

To an Author

Your leaves bound up compact and fair,
In neat array at length prepare,
To pass their hour on learning's stage,
To meet the surly critic's rage;
The statesman's slight, the smatterer's sneer—   5
Were these, indeed, your only fear,
You might be tranquil and resigned:
What most should touch your fluttering mind;
Is that, few critics will be found
To sift your works, and deal the wound.   10

Thus, when one fleeting year is past
On some bye-shelf your book is cast—
Another comes, with something new,
And drives you fairly out of view:
With some to praise, but more to blame,   15
The mind returns to—whence it came;
And some alive, who scarce could read
Will publish satires on the dead.

Thrice happy Dryden,[1] who could meet
Some rival bard in every street!   20
When all were bent on writing well
It was some credit to excel:—

Thrice happy Dryden, who could find
A Milbourne for his sport designed—
And Pope, who saw the harmless rage   25
Of Dennis bursting o'er his page
Might justly spurn the critic's aim,
Who only helped to swell his fame.

On these bleak climes by Fortune thrown,
Where rigid Reason reigns alone,   30
Where lovely Fancy has no sway,
Nor magic forms about us play—
Nor nature takes her summer hue
Tell me, what has the muse to do?—

An age employed in edging steel   35
Can no poetic raptures feel;
No solitude's attracting power,
No leisure of the noon day hour,

To an Author. [1] See Johnson's lives of the English Poets.
[Freneau's note.]

No shaded stream, no quiet grove
Can this fantastic century move;   40

The muse of love in no request—
Go—try your fortune with the rest,
One of the nine you should engage,
To meet the follies of the age:—

On one, we fear, your choice must fall—   45
The least engaging of them all—[2]
Her visage stern—an angry style—
A clouded brow—malicious smile—
A mind on murdered victims placed—
She, only she, can please the taste!   50

1778

The Indian Burying Ground

Freneau provided a note for this poem: "The North American Indians bury their dead in a sitting posture; decorating the corpse with wampum, the images of birds, quadrupeds, &c. And (if that of a warrior) with bows, arrows, tomahawks, and other military weapons."

In spite of all the learned have said,
  I still my old opinion keep;
The posture, that we give the dead,
  Points out the soul's eternal sleep.

Not so the ancients of these lands—   5
  The Indian, when from life released,
Again is seated with his friends,
  And shares again the joyous feast.

His imaged birds, and painted bowl,
  And venison, for a journey dressed,   10
Bespeak the nature of the soul,
  Activity, that knows no rest.

His bow, for action ready bent,
  And arrows, with a head of stone,
Can only mean that life is spent,   15
  And not the old ideas gone.

Thou, stranger, that shalt come this way,
  No fraud upon the dead commit—
Observe the swelling turf, and say
  They do not lie, but here they sit.   20

Here still a lofty rock remains,
  On which the curious eye may trace
(Now wasted, half, by wearing rains)
  The fancies of a ruder race.

[2] I.e., the muse of satire.

Here still an aged elm aspires,   25
    Beneath whose far-projecting shade
(And which the shepherd still admires)
    The children of the forest played!

There oft a restless Indian queen
    (Pale Shebah, with her braided hair)   30
And many a barbarous form is seen
    To chide the man that lingers there.

By midnight moons, o'er moistening dews;
    In habit for the chase arrayed,
The hunter still the deer pursues,   35
    The hunter and the deer, a shade!

And long shall timorous fancy see
    The painted chief, and pointed spear,
And Reason's self shall bow the knee
    To shadows and delusions here.   40

                       1788

To a Republican

With Mr. Paine's Rights of Man

Thus briefly sketch'd the sacred Rights of Man,
How inconsistent with the Royal Plan!
Which for itself exclusive honour craves,
Where some are masters born, and millions slaves.
With what contempt must every eye look down   5
On that base, childish bauble call'd a crown,
The gilded bait, that lures the crowd, to come,
Bow down their necks, and meet a slavish doom;
The source of half the miseries men endure,   9
The quack that kills them, while it seems to cure.
Rous'd by the Reason of his manly page,
Once more shall Paine a listening world engage:
From Reason's source, a bold reform he brings,
In raising up mankind, he pulls down kings,
Who, source of discord, patrons of all wrong,   15
On blood and murder have been fed too long:
Hid from the world, and tutor'd to be base,
The curse, the scourge, the ruin of our race,
Theirs was the task, a dull designing few,
To shackle beings that they scarcely knew,   20
Who made this globe the residence of slaves,
And built their thrones on systems form'd by
      knaves—
Advance, bright years, to work their final fall,
And haste the period that shall crush them all.   24
Who, that has read and scann'd the historic page
But glows, at every line, with kindling rage,
To see by them the rights of men aspers'd,
Freedom restrain'd, and Nature's law revers'd,
Men, rank'd with beasts, by monarchs will'd away,
And bound young fools, or madmen to obey: 30

Now driven to wars, and now oppress'd at home,
Compell'd in crowds o'er distant seas to roam,
From India's climes the plundered prize to bring
To glad the strumpet, or to glut the king.
    Columbia, hail! immortal be thy reign: 35
Without a king, we till the smiling plain;
Without a king, we trace the unbounded sea,
And traffic round the globe, through each degree;
Each foreign clime our honour'd flag reveres,
Which asks no monarch, to support the Stars: 40
Without a king, the Laws maintain their sway,
While honour bids each generous heart obey.
Be ours the task the ambitious to restrain,
And this great lesson teach—that kings are vain;
That warring realms to certain ruin haste,   45
That kings subsist by war, and wars are waste:
So shall our nation, form'd on Virtue's plan,
Remain the guardian of the Rights of Man,
A vast Republic, fam'd through every clime,
Without a king, to see the end of time.   50

                      1792, 1795

On the Uniformity and Perfection of Nature

This poem and the one that follows are direct statements of Freneau's deism, published after the movement had declined. Freneau presents a familiar set of concepts and attitudes: the First Cause, reason, nature, the Newtonian world machine, law and order, optimism ("all is right," "Heaven below"), a religion of truth and goodness and tolerance. Text: Harry Hayden Clark, *Poems of Freneau* (New York, 1929).

On one fix'd point all nature moves,
Nor deviates from the track she loves;
Her system, drawn from reason's source,
She scorns to change her wonted course.

Could she descend from that great plan   5
To work unusual things for man,
To suit the insect of an hour—
This would betray a want of power,

Unsettled in its first design
And erring, when it did combine   10
The parts that form the vast machine,
The figures sketch'd on nature's scene.

Perfections of the great first cause
Submit to no contracted laws,
But all-sufficient, all-supreme,   15
Include no trivial views in them.

Who looks through nature with an eye
That would the scheme of heaven descry,

Observes her constant, still the same,
In all her laws, through all her frame. 20

No imperfection can be found
In all that is, above, around,—
All, nature made, in reason's sight
Is order all and all is right.

1815

On the Religion of Nature

Text: H. H. Clark, *Poems of Freneau* (New York, 1929).

The power that gives with liberal hand
    The blessings man enjoys, while here,
And scatters through a smiling land
    The abundant products of the year;
        That power of nature, ever bless'd,   5
        Bestow'd religion with the rest.

Born with ourselves, her early sway
    Inclines the tender mind to take
The path of right, fair virtue's way
    Its own felicity to make.   10

This universally extends
And leads to no mysterious ends.

Religion, such as nature taught,
    With all divine perfection suits;
Had all mankind this system sought   15
    Sophists would cease their vain disputes,
        And from this source would nations know
        All that can make their heaven below.

This deals not curses on mankind,
    Or dooms them to perpetual grief,   20
If from its aid no joys they find,
    It damns them not for unbelief;
        Upon a more exalted plan
        Creatress nature dealt with man—

Joy to the day, when all agree   25
    On such grand systems to proceed,
From fraud, design, and error free,
    And which to truth and goodness lead:
        Then persecution will retreat
        And man's religion be complete.   30

1815

CHARLES BROCKDEN BROWN [1771–1810]

CHARLES BROCKDEN BROWN, born into a Philadelphia Quaker family, was educated as a lawyer, but at the age of nineteen he was so much attracted to literature that he soon gave up the law. Fascinated by poetry (he planned several long epics before he was sixteen), he surrendered verse for the essay and fiction after he moved to New York, where he met many of the literary men of the day, among them the poet Timothy Dwight, and William Dunlap, the producer-playwright who became Brown's first biographer. During his three years in New York he wrote *Alcuin* (1798), a defense of women's rights, and the six novels on which his reputation rests—*Wieland* (1798), *Edgar Huntly* (1799), *Ormond* (1799), *Arthur Mervyn* (1799–1800), *Clara Howard* (1801), and *Jane Talbot* (1801). He then returned to Philadelphia, edited periodicals, entered business, and contributed essays and critical pieces to the magazines, including his own *American Register, or General Repository of History, Politics, and Science*. Never in good health, he died of tuberculosis at thirty-nine.

Brown, who considered himself a "story-telling moralist," managed to weave sensation, mystery, sentiment, extravagant adventure, and native scenery into fiction that remains compelling despite his often turgid style and clumsy structure. He was strongly influenced, of course, by the popular eighteenth-century sentimental romances of such writers as Samuel Richardson, and by the Gothic novels of Mrs. Radcliffe and others. His novels evince his fascination with such devices as ventriloquism, sleepwalking, and hypnotism; his relish for Poesque ratiocination and horror; his use of realistic detail in the manner of

Defoe; and his liking for powerfully sensational and imaginative scenes. His novels were especially popular in England, where Keats, Shelley, William Godwin (one of Brown's own favorites) and William Hazlitt were among his readers.

Further reading: David Lee Clark, *Charles Brockden Brown: Pioneer Voice of America*, 1952. Donald A. Ringe, *Charles Brockden Brown*, 1966.

PREFACE TO *Edgar Huntly*

Caught up in the wave of literary patriotism of the Republican years, Brown believed that the novel ought to be domesticated and nationalized by the use of American themes and American materials. Certainly, he wrote in 1800, "the scene displayed by four millions of actors on the vast stage bounded by the Ocean, Florida, Mississippi, and St. Lawrence, for the three lustrums ensuing the revolution which made the Anglo-Belgico-Teutonico-North Americans a nation," called out for chroniclers. The country needed novelists who could properly use "the motleyness, the endless variety of habits, ranks and conditions in our country . . . , their domestic maxims and habits, their social principles and prejudices. . . ." In *Edgar Huntly* he practiced what he preached. He introduced a conflict which soon became a staple of the American novel—the frontier war between settler and Indian—and used his directly observed impressions of the Delaware River country to introduce the wilderness theme in American fiction. Text: *The Novels of Charles Brockden Brown*, 6 vols. (Philadelphia, 1887).

To the Public

The flattering reception that has been given, by the public, to Arthur Mervyn, has prompted the writer to solicit a continuance of the same favour, and to offer to the world a new performance.

America has opened new views to the naturalist and politician, but has seldom furnished themes to the moral painter. That new springs of action and new motives to curiosity should operate,—that the field of investigation, opened to us by our own country, should differ essentially from those which exist in Europe,—may be readily conceived. The sources of amusement to the fancy and instruction to the heart, that are peculiar to ourselves, are equally numerous and inexhaustible. It is the purpose of this work to profit by some of these sources; to exhibit a series of adventures, growing out of the condition of our country, and connected with one of the most common and most wonderful diseases or affections of the human frame.

One merit the writer may at least claim:—that of calling forth the passions and engaging the sympathy of the reader by means hitherto unemployed by preceding authors. Puerile superstition and exploded manners, Gothic castles and chimeras, are the materials usually employed for this end. The incidents of Indian hostility, and the perils of the Western wilderness, are far more suitable; and for a native of America to overlook these would admit of no apology. These, therefore, are, in part, the ingredients of this tale, and these he has been ambitious of depicting in vivid and faithful colours. The success of his efforts must be estimated by the liberal and candid reader.

1799

FROM *Ormond; or The Secret Witness*

The plot of this novel is built about the inexorable pursuit of Constantia Dudley by the strangely attractive, mysterious, and coldly intellectual Ormond. Ormond, when he meets Constantia, already has a beautiful and submissive mistress, Helena, who commits suicide when Ormond casts her off. After some extremely complicated maneuverings, Ormond, in a powerfully written scene, confronts Constantia at her dark, deserted country house. When he attempts rape, she kills him with her penknife, and horrified at her deed, is herself saved from suicide only by the fortunate arrival of a friend. Ormond, like his predecessor Carwin in *Wieland*, is one of Brown's Gothic hero-villains of tremendous will, great knowledge, and little conscience, while Constantia, a woman of strength, intelligence, and character, is his best-conceived heroine. Text: *The Novels of Charles Brockden Brown*, 6 vols. (Philadelphia, 1887).

Chapter XII

I know no task more arduous than a just delineation of the character of Ormond. To scrutinize and ascertain our own principles are abundantly difficult. To exhibit these principles to the world with absolute sincerity can scarcely be expected. We are prompted to conceal and to feign by a thousand motives; but truly to portray the motives and relate the actions of another appears utterly impossible. The attempt, however, if made with fidelity and diligence, is not without its use.

To comprehend the whole truth, with regard to the character and conduct of another, may be denied to any human being; but different observers will have, in their pictures, a greater or less portion of this truth. No representation will be wholly false; and some, though not perfectly, may yet be considerably, exempt from error.

Ormond was, of all mankind, the being most difficult and most deserving to be studied. A fortunate concurrence of incidents has unveiled his actions to me with more distinctness than to any other. My knowledge is far from being absolute; but I am conscious of a kind of duty, first to my friend, and secondly to mankind, to impart the knowledge I possess.

I shall omit to mention the means by which I became acquainted with his character, nor shall I enter, at this time, into every part of it. His political projects are likely to possess an extensive influence on the future condition of this Western World. I do not conceive myself authorized to communicate a knowledge of his schemes, which I gained in some sort surreptitiously, or, at least, by means of which he was not apprized. I shall merely explain the maxims by which he was accustomed to regulate his private deportment.

No one could entertain loftier conceptions of human capacity than Ormond, but he carefully distinguished between men in the abstract, and men as they are. The former were beings to be impelled, by the breath of accident, in a right or a wrong road; but, whatever direction they should receive, it was the property of their nature to persist in it. Now, this impulse had been given. No single being could rectify the error. It was the business of the wise man to form a just estimate of things, but not to attempt, by individual efforts, so chimerical an enterprise as that of promoting the happiness of mankind. Their condition was out of the reach of a member of a corrupt society to control. A mortal poison pervaded the whole system, by means of which every thing received was converted into bane and purulence. Efforts designed to ameliorate the condition of an individual were sure of answering a contrary purpose. The principles of the social machine must be rectified, before men can be beneficially active. Our motives may be neutral or beneficent, but our actions tend merely to the production of evil.

The idea of total forbearance was not less delusive. Man could not be otherwise than a cause of perpetual operation and efficacy. He was part of a machine, and as such had not power to withhold his agency. Contiguousness to other parts—that is, to other men—was all that was necessary to render him a powerful concurrent. What, then, was the conduct incumbent on him? Whether he went forward or stood still, whether his motives were malignant, or kind, or indifferent, the mass of evils was equally and necessarily augmented. It did not follow from these preliminaries that virtue and duty were terms without a meaning, but they require us to promote our own happiness, and not the happiness of others. Not because the former end is intrinsically preferable, not because the happiness of others is unworthy of primary consideration, but because it is not to be attained. Our power in the present state of things is subjected to certain limits. A man may reasonably hope to accomplish his end, when he proposes nothing but his own good. Any other point is inaccessible.

He must not part with benevolent desire: this is a constituent of happiness. He sees the value of general and particular felicity; he sometimes paints it to his fancy; but, if this be rarely done, it is in consequence of virtuous sensibility, which is afflicted on observing that his pictures are reversed in the real state of mankind. A wise man will relinquish the pursuit of general benefit, but not the desire of that benefit, or the perception of that in which this benefit consists, because these are among the ingredients of virtue and the sources of his happiness.

Principles, in the looser sense of that term, have little influence on practice. Ormond was, for the most part, governed, like others, by the influences of education and present circumstances. It required a vigilant discernment to distinguish whether the stream of his actions flowed from one or the other. His income was large, and he managed it nearly on the same principles as other men. He thought himself entitled to all the splendour and ease which it would purchase; but his taste was elaborate and correct. He gratified his love of the beautiful, because the sensations it afforded were pleasing, but made no sacrifices to the love of distinction. He gave no expensive entertainments for the sake of exciting the admiration of stupid gazers, or the flattery or envy of those who shared them. Pompous equipage and retinue were modes of appropriating the esteem of mankind which he held in profound contempt. The garb of his attendants was fashioned after the model suggested by his imagination, and not in compliance with the dictates of custom.

He treated with systematic negligence the etiquette that regulates the intercourse of persons of a certain class. He everywhere acted, in this respect, as if he were alone, or among familiar associates. The very appellations of Sir, and Madam, and Mister, were, in his apprehension, servile and ridiculous; and, as custom or law had annexed no penalty to the neglect of these, he conformed to his own opinions. It was easier for him to reduce his notions of equality to practice than for most others. To level himself with others was an act of condescension and not of arrogance. It was requisite to descend rather than to rise,—a task the most easy, if we regard the obstacles flowing from the prejudice of mankind, but far most difficult, if the motives of the agent be considered.

That in which he chiefly placed his boast was his sincerity. To this he refused no sacrifice. In consequence of this, his deportment was disgusting to weak minds, by a certain air of ferocity and haughty negligence. He was without the attractions of candour, because he regarded not the happiness of others but in subservience to his sincerity. Hence it was natural to suppose that the character of this man was easily understood. He affected to conceal nothing. No one appeared more exempt from the instigations of vanity. He set light by the good opinions of others, had no compassion for their prejudices, and hazarded assertions in their presence which he knew would be, in the highest degree, shocking to their previous notions. They might take it, he would say, as they list. Such were his conceptions, and the last thing he would give up was the use of his tongue. It was his way to give utterance to the suggestions of his understanding. If they were disadvantageous to him in the opinions of others, it was well. He did not wish to be regarded in any light but the true one. He was contented to be rated by the world at his just value. If they esteemed him for qualities he did not possess, was he wrong in rectifying their mistake? but, in reality, if they valued him for that to which he had no claim, and which he himself considered as contemptible, he must naturally desire to show them their error, and forfeit that praise which, in his own opinion, was a badge of infamy.

In listening to his discourse, no one's claim to sincerity appeared less questionable. A somewhat different conclusion would be suggested by a survey of his actions. In early youth he discovered in himself a remarkable facility in imitating the voice and gestures of others. His memory was eminently retentive, and these qualities would have rendered his career, in the theatrical profession, illustrious, had not his condition raised him above it. His talents were occasionally exerted for the entertainment of convivial parties and private circles, but he gradually withdrew from such scenes, as he advanced in age, and devoted his abilities to higher purposes.

His aversion to duplicity had flowed from experience of its evils. He had frequently been made its victim: in consequence of this his temper had become suspicious, and he was apt to impute deceit on occasions when others, of no inconsiderable sagacity, were abundantly disposed to confidence. One transaction had occurred in his life, in which the consequences of being misled by false appearances were of the utmost moment to his honour and safety. The usual mode of solving his doubts he deemed insufficient, and the eagerness of his curiosity tempted him, for the first time, to employ, for this end, his talents at imitation. He therefore assumed a borrowed character and guise, and performed his part with so much skill as fully to accomplish his design. He whose mask would have secured him from all other attempts was thus taken through an avenue which his caution had overlooked, and

the hypocrisy of his pretensions unquestionably ascertained.

Perhaps, in a comprehensive view, the success of this expedient was unfortunate. It served to recommend this method of encountering deceit, and informed him of the extent of those powers which are so liable to be abused. A subtlety much inferior to Ormond's would suffice to recommend this mode of action It was defensible on no other principle than necessity. The treachery of mankind compelled him to resort to it. If they should deal in a manner as upright and explicit as himself, it would be superfluous. But since they were in the perpetual use of stratagems and artifices, it was allowable, he thought, to wield the same arms.

It was easy to perceive, however, that this practice was recommended to him by other considerations. He was delighted with the power it conferred. It enabled him to gain access, as if by supernatural means, to the privacy of others, and baffle their profoundest contrivances to hide themselves from his view. It flattered him with the possession of something like omniscience. It was, besides, an art in which, as in others, every accession of skill was a source of new gratification. Compared with this, the performance of the actor is the sport of children. This profession he was accustomed to treat with merciless ridicule, and no doubt some of his contempt arose from a secret comparison between the theatrical species of imitation and his own. He blended in his own person the functions of poet and actor, and his dramas were not fictitious but real. The end that he proposed was not the amusement of a playhouse mob. His were scenes in which hope and fear exercised a genuine influence, and in which was maintained that resemblance to truth so audaciously and grossly violated on the stage.

It is obvious how many singular conjunctures must have grown out of this propensity. A mind of uncommon energy like Ormond's, which had occupied a wide sphere of action, and which could not fail of confederating its efforts with those of minds like itself, must have given birth to innumerable incidents, not unworthy to be exhibited by the most eloquent historian. It is not my business to relate any of these. The fate of Miss Dudley is intimately connected with his. What influence he obtained over her destiny, in consequence of this dexterity, will appear in the sequel.

It arose from these circumstances that no one was more impenetrable than Ormond, though no one's real character seemed more easily discerned. The projects that occupied his attention were diffused over an ample space; and his instruments and coadjutors were culled from a field whose bounds were those of the civilized world. To the vulgar eye, therefore, he appeared a man of speculation and seclusion, and was equally inscrutable in his real and assumed characters. In his real, his intents were too lofty and comprehensive, as well as too assiduously shrouded from profane inspection, for them to scan. In the latter, appearances were merely calculated to mislead and not to enlighten.

In his youth he had been guilty of the usual excesses incident to his age and character. These had disappeared and yielded place to a more regular and circumspect system of action. In the choice of his pleasures he still exposed himself to the censure of the world. Yet there was more of grossness and licentiousness in the expression of his tenets, than in the tenets themselves. So far as temperance regards the maintenance of health, no man adhered to its precepts with more fidelity; but he esteemed some species of connection with the other sex as venial, which mankind in general are vehement in condemning.

In his intercourse with women he deemed himself superior to the allurements of what is called love. His inferences were drawn from a consideration of the physical propensities of a human being. In his scale of enjoyments, the gratifications which belonged to these were placed at the bottom. Yet he did not entirely disdain them, and, when they could be purchased without the sacrifice of superior advantages, they were sufficiently acceptable.

His mistake on this head was the result of his ignorance. He had not hitherto met with a female worthy of his confidence. Their views were limited and superficial, or their understandings were betrayed by the tenderness of their hearts. He found in them no intellectual energy, no superiority to what he accounted vulgar prejudice, and no affinity with the sentiments which he cherished with most devotion. Their presence had been capable of exciting no emotion which he did not quickly discover to be vague and sensual; and the uniformity of his experience at length instilled into him a belief that the intellectual constitution of females was essentially defective. He denied the reality of that passion which claimed a similitude or sympathy of minds as one of its ingredients.

Chapter XIII

He resided in New York some time before he took up his abode in Philadelphia. He had some pecuniary concerns with a merchant of that place. He occasionally frequented his house, finding, in the society which it afforded him, scope for amusing speculation, and opportunities of gaining a species of knowledge of which at that time he stood in need. There was one daughter of the family who of course constituted a member of the domestic circle.

Helena Cleves was endowed with every feminine and fascinating quality. Her features were modified by the most transient sentiments, and were the seat of a softness at all times blushful and bewitching. All those graces of symmetry, smoothness, and lustre, which assemble in the imagination of the painter when he calls from the bosom of her natal deep the Paphian divinity, blended their perfections in the shade, complexion, and hair of this lady. Her voice was naturally thrilling and melodious, and her utterance clear and distinct. A musical education had added to all these advantages the improvements of art, and no one could swim in the dance with such airy and transporting elegance.

It is obvious to inquire whether her mental were, in any degree, on a level with her exterior accomplishments. Should you listen to her talk, you would be liable to be deceived in this respect. Her utterance was so just, her phrases so happy, and her language so copious and correct, that the hearer was apt to be impressed with an ardent veneration of her abilities; but the truth is, she was calculated to excite emotions more voluptuous than dignified. Her presence produced a trance of the senses rather than an illumination of the soul. It was a topic of wonder how she should have so carefully separated the husk from the kernel, and be so absolute a mistress of the vehicle of knowledge with so slender means of supplying it; yet it is difficult to judge but from comparison. To say that Helena Cleves was silly or ignorant would be hatefully unjust. Her understanding bore no disadvantageous comparison with that of the majority of her sex; but, when placed in competition with that of some eminent females or of Ormond, it was exposed to the risk of contempt.

This lady and Ormond were exposed to mutual examination. The latter was not unaffected by the radiance that environed this girl, but her true character was easily discovered, and he was accustomed to regard her merely as an object charming to the senses. His attention to her was dictated by this principle. When she sang or talked, it was not unworthy of the strongest mind to be captivated with her music and her elocution; but these were the limits which he set to his gratifications. That sensations of a different kind never ruffled his tranquillity must not be supposed, but he too accurately estimated their consequences to permit himself to indulge them.

Unhappily, the lady did not exercise equal fortitude. During a certain interval Ormond's visits were frequent, and she insensibly contracted for him somewhat more than reverence. The tenor of his discourse was little adapted to cherish her hopes. In the declaration of his opinions he was never withheld by scruples of decorum or a selfish regard to his own interest. His matrimonial tenets were harsh and repulsive. A woman of keener penetration would have predicted, from them, the disappointment of her wishes; but Helena's mind was uninured to the discussion of logical points and the tracing of remote consequences. His presence inspired feelings which would not permit her to bestow an impartial attention on his arguments. It is not enough to say that his reasonings failed to convince her: the combined influence of passion and an unenlightened understanding hindered her from fully comprehending them. All she gathered was a vague conception of something magnificent and vast in his character.

Helena was destined to experience the vicissitudes of fortune. Her father died suddenly and left her without provision. She was compelled to accept the invitations of a kinswoman, and live, in some sort, a life of dependence. She was not qualified to sustain this reverse of fortune in a graceful manner. She could not bear the diminution of her customary indulgences, and to these privations were added the inquietudes of a passion which now began to look with an aspect of hopelessness.

These events happened in the absence of Ormond. On his return he made himself acquainted with them. He saw the extent of this misfortune to a woman of Helena's character, but knew not in what manner it might be effectually obviated. He esteemed it incumbent on him to pay her a visit in her new abode. This token at least of respect or remembrance his duty appeared to prescribe.

This visit was unexpected by the lady. Surprise is the enemy of concealment. She was oppressed with a sense of her desolate situation. She was sitting in her own apartment in a museful posture. Her fancy was occupied with the image of Ormond, and her tears were flowing at the thought of their eternal separation, when he entered softly and unperceived by her. A tap upon the shoulder was the first signal of his presence. So critical an interview could not fail of unveiling the true state of the lady's heart. Ormond's suspicions were excited, and these suspicions speedily led to an explanation.

Ormond retired to ruminate on this discovery. I have already mentioned his sentiments respecting love. His feelings relative to Helena did not contradict his principles, yet the image which had formerly been exquisite in loveliness had now suddenly gained unspeakable attractions. This discovery had set the question in a new light. It was of sufficient importance to make him deliberate. He reasoned somewhat in the following manner:—

"Marriage is absurd. This flows from the general and incurable imperfection of the female character. No woman can possess that worth which would induce me to enter into this contract, and bind myself, without power of revoking the decree, to her so-

ciety. This opinion may possibly be erroneous; but it is undoubtedly true with respect to Helena, and the uncertainty of the position in general will increase the necessity of caution in the present case. That woman may exist whom I should not fear to espouse. This is not her. Some accident may cause our meeting. Shall I then disable myself, by an irrevocable obligation, from profiting by so auspicious an occurrence?"

This girl's society was to be enjoyed in one of two ways. Should he consult his inclination, there was little room for doubt. He had never met with one more highly qualified for that species of intercourse which he esteemed rational. No man more abhorred the votaries of licentiousness. Nothing was more detestable to him than a mercenary alliance. Personal fidelity, and the existence of that passion of which he had, in the present case, the good fortune to be the object, were indispensable in his scheme. The union was indebted for its value on the voluntariness with which it was formed, and the entire acquiescence of the judgment of both parties in its rectitude. Dissimulation and artifice were wholly foreign to the success of his project. If the lady thought proper to assent to his proposal it was well. She did so because assent was more eligible than refusal.

She would, no doubt, prefer marriage. She would deem it more conducive to happiness. This was an error. This was an opinion, his reasons for which he was at liberty to state to her; at least it was justifiable in refusing to subject himself to loathsome and impracticable obligations. Certain inconveniences attended women who set aside, on these occasions, the sanction of law; but these were imaginary. They owed their force to the errors of the sufferer. To annihilate them, it was only necessary to reason justly; but, allowing these inconveniences their full weight and an indestructible existence, it was but a choice of evils. Were they worse in this lady's apprehension than an eternal and hopeless separation? Perhaps they were. If so, she would make her election accordingly. He did nothing but lay the conditions before her. If his scheme should obtain the concurrence of her unbiassed judgment, he should rejoice. If not, her conduct should be uninfluenced by him. Whatever way she should decide, he would assist her in adhering to her decision, but would, meanwhile, furnish her with the materials of a right decision.

This determination was singular. Many will regard it as incredible. No man, it will be thought, can put this deception on himself, and imagine that there was genuine beneficence in a scheme like this. Would the lady more consult her happiness by adopting than by rejecting it? There can be but one answer. It cannot be supposed that Ormond, in stating this proposal, acted with all the impartiality that he pretended; that he did not employ fallacious exaggerations and ambiguous expedients; that he did not seize every opportunity of triumphing over her weakness, and building his success rather on the illusions of her heart than the convictions of her understanding. His conclusions were specious but delusive, and were not uninfluenced by improper biasses; but of this he himself was scarcely conscious, and it must be at least admitted that he acted with scrupulous sincerity.

An uncommon degree of skill was required to introduce this topic so as to avoid the imputation of an insult. This scheme was little in unison with all her preconceived notions. No doubt, the irksomeness of her present situation, the allurements of luxury and ease which Ormond had to bestow, and the revival of her ancient independence and security, had some share in dictating her assent.

Her concurrence was by no means cordial and unhesitating. Remorse and the sense of dishonour pursued her to her retreat, though chosen with a view of shunning their intrusions; and it was only when the reasonings and blandishments of her lover were exhibited, that she was lulled into temporary tranquillity.

She removed to Philadelphia. Here she enjoyed all the consolations of opulence. She was mistress of a small but elegant mansion. She possessed all the means of solitary amusement, and frequently enjoyed the company of Ormond. These, however, were insufficient to render her happy. Certain reflections might, for a time, be repressed or divested of their sting, but they insinuated themselves at every interval, and imparted to her mind a hue of dejection from which she could not entirely relieve herself.

She endeavoured to acquire a relish for the pursuits of literature, by which her lonely hours might be cheered; but of this, even in the blithesomeness and serenity of her former days, she was incapable,—much more so now when she was the prey of perpetual inquietude. Ormond perceived this change, not without uneasiness. All his efforts to reconcile her to her present situation were fruitless. They produced a momentary effect upon her. The softness of her temper and her attachment to him would, at his bidding, restore her to vivacity and ease, but the illumination seldom endured longer than his presence and the novelty of some amusement which he had furnished her.

At his next visit, perhaps, he would find that a new task awaited him. She indulged herself in no recriminations or invectives. She could not complain that her lover had deceived her. She had voluntarily and deliberately accepted the conditions prescribed. She regarded her own disposition to repine as a species of injustice. She laid no claim to an increase

of tenderness. She hinted not a wish for a change of situation; yet she was unhappy. Tears stole into her eyes, and her thoughts wandered into gloomy reverie, at moments when least aware of their approach, and least willing to indulge them.

Was a change to be desired? Yes; provided that change was equally agreeable to Ormond, and should be seriously proposed by him. Of this she had no hope. As long as his accents rung in her ears, she even doubted whether it were to be wished. At any rate, it was impossible to gain his approbation to it. Her destiny was fixed. It was better than the cessation of all intercourse, yet her heart was a stranger to all permanent tranquillity.

Her manners were artless and ingenuous. In company with Ormond her heart was perfectly unveiled. He was her divinity, to whom every sentiment was visible, and to whom she spontaneously uttered what she thought, because the employment was pleasing, because he listened with apparent satisfaction, and because, in fine, it was the same thing to speak and to think in his presence. There was no inducement to conceal from him the most evanescent and fugitive ideas.

Ormond was not an inattentive or indifferent spectator of those appearances. His friend was unhappy. She shrunk aghast from her own reproaches and the contumelies of the world. This morbid sensibility he had endeavoured to cure, but hitherto in vain. What was the amount of her unhappiness? Her spirits had formerly been gay; but her gayety was capable of yielding place to soul-ravishing and solemn tenderness. Her sedateness was, at those times, the offspring not of reflection but of passion. There still remained much of her former self. He was seldom permitted to witness more than the traces of sorrow. In answer to his inquiries, she, for the most part, described sensations that were gone, and which she flattered herself and him would never return; but this hope was always doomed to disappointment. Solitude infallibly conjured up the ghost which had been laid, and it was plain that argument was no adequate remedy for this disease.

How far would time alleviate its evils? When the novelty of her condition should disappear, would she not regard it with other eyes? By being familiar with contempt, it will lose its sting; but is that to be wished? Must not the character be thoroughly depraved before the scorn of our neighbours shall become indifferent? Indifference, flowing from a sense of justice, and a persuasion that our treatment is unmerited, is characteristic of the noblest minds; but indifference to obloquy, because we are habituated to it, is a token of peculiar baseness. This, therefore, was a remedy to be ardently deprecated.

He had egregiously overrated the influence of truth and his own influence. He had hoped that his victory was permanent. In order to the success of truth, he was apt to imagine that nothing was needful but opportunities for a complete exhibition of it. They that inquire and reason with sufficient deliberateness and caution must inevitably accomplish their end. These maxims were confuted in the present case. He had formed no advantageous conceptions of Helena's capacity. His aversion to matrimony arose from those conceptions; but experience had shown him that his conclusions, unfavourable as they were, had fallen short of the truth. Convictions which he had conceived her mind to be sufficiently strong to receive and retain were proved to have made no other than a momentary impression. Hence his objections to ally himself to a mind inferior to his own were strengthened rather than diminished. But he could not endure the thought of being instrumental to her misery.

Marriage was an efficacious remedy, but he could not as yet bring himself to regard the aptitude of this cure as a subject of doubt. The idea of separation sometimes occurred to him. He was not unapprehensive of the influence of time and absence in curing the most vehement passion, but to this expedient the lady could not be reconciled. He knew her too well to believe that she would willingly adopt it. But the only obstacle to this scheme did not flow from the lady's opposition. He would probably have found upon experiment as strong an aversion to adopt it in himself as in her.

It was easy to see the motives by which he would be likely to be swayed into a change of principles. If marriage were the only remedy, the frequent repetition of this truth must bring him insensibly to doubt the rectitude of his determinations against it. He deeply reflected on the consequences which marriage involves. He scrutinized with the utmost accuracy the character of his friend, and surveyed it in all its parts. Inclination could not fail of having some influence on his opinions. The charms of this favourite object tended to impair the clearness of his view and extenuate or conceal her defects. He entered on the enumeration of her errors with reluctance. Her happiness, had it been wholly disconnected with his own, might have had less weight in the balance; but now, every time the scales were suspended, this consideration acquired new weight.

Most men are influenced, in the formation of this contract, by regards purely physical. They are incapable of higher views. They regard with indifference every tie that binds them to their contemporaries or to posterity. Mind has no part in the motives that guide them. They choose a wife as they choose any household movable, and when the irritation of the senses has subsided, the attachment that remains is the offspring of habit.

Such were not Ormond's modes of thinking. His

creed was of too extraordinary a kind not to merit explication. The terms of this contract were, in his eyes, iniquitous and absurd. He could not think with patience of a promise which no time could annul, which pretended to ascertain contingencies and regulate the future. To forego the liberty of choosing his companion, and bind himself to associate with one whom he despised; to raise to his own level one whom nature had irretrievably degraded; to avow, and persist in his adherence to, a falsehood, palpable and loathsome to his understanding; to affirm that he was blind, when in full possession of his senses; to shut his eyes and grope in the dark, and call upon the compassion of mankind on his infirmity, when his organs were in no degree impaired, and the scene around him was luminous and beautiful,—was a height of infatuation that he could never attain. And why should he be thus self-degraded? Why should he take a laborious circuit to reach a point which, when attained, was trivial, and to which reason had pointed out a road short and direct?

A wife is generally nothing more than a household superintendent. This function could not be more wisely vested than it was at present. Every thing in his domestic system was fashioned on strict and inflexible principles. He wanted instruments and not partakers of his authority,—one whose mind was equal and not superior to the cogent apprehension and punctual performance of his will; one whose character was squared, with mathematical exactness, to his situation. Helena, with all her faults, did not merit to be regarded in this light. Her introduction would destroy the harmony of his scheme, and be, with respect to herself, a genuine debasement. A genuine evil would thus be substituted for one that was purely imaginary.

Helena's intellectual deficiencies could not be concealed. She was a proficient in the elements of no science. The doctrine of lines and surfaces was as disproportionate with her intellects as with those of the mock-bird. She had not reasoned on the principles of human action, nor examined the structure of society. She was ignorant of the past or present condition of mankind. History had not informed her of the one, nor the narratives of voyages nor the deductions of geography of the other. The heights of eloquence and poetry were shut out from her view. She could not commune, in their native dialect, with the sages of Rome and Athens. To her those perennial fountains of wisdom and refinement were sealed. The constitution of nature, the attributes of its Author, the arrangement of the parts of the external universe, and the substance, modes of operation, and ultimate destiny of human intelligence, were enigmas unsolved and insoluble by her.

But this was not all. The superstructure could for the present be spared. Nay, it was desirable that the province of rearing it should be reserved for him. All he wanted was a suitable foundation; but this Helena did not possess. He had not hitherto been able to create in her the inclination or the power. She had listened to his precepts with docility. She had diligently conned the lessons which he had prescribed, but the impressions were as fleeting as if they had been made on water. Nature seemed to have set impassable limits to her attainments.

This, indeed, was an unwelcome belief. He struggled to invalidate it. He reflected on the immaturity of her age. What but crude and hasty views was it reasonable to expect at so early a period? If her mind had not been awakened, it had proceeded, perhaps, from the injudiciousness of his plans, or merely from their not having been persisted in. What was wanting but the ornaments of mind to render this being all that poets have feigned of angelic nature? When he indulged himself in imaging the union of capacious understanding with her personal loveliness, his conceptions swelled to a pitch of enthusiasm, and it seemed as if no labour was too great to be employed in the production of such a creature. And yet, in the midst of his glowings, he would sink into sudden dejection at the recollection of that which passion had, for a time, excluded. To make her wise it would be requisite to change her sex. He had forgotten that his pupil was a female, and her capacity therefore limited by nature. This mortifying thought was outbalanced by another. Her attainments, indeed, were suitable to the imbecility of her sex; but did she not surpass, in those attainments, the ordinary rate of women? They must not be condemned because they are outshone by qualities that are necessarily male births.

Her accomplishments formed a much more attractive theme. He overlooked no article in the catalogue. He was confounded at one time, and encouraged at another, on remarking the contradictions that seemed to be included in her character. It was difficult to conceive the impossibility of passing that barrier which yet she was able to touch. She was no poet. She listened to the rehearsal without emotion, or was moved, not by the substance of the passage, by the dazzling image or the magic sympathy, but by something adscititious; yet usher her upon the stage, and no poet would wish for a more powerful organ of his conceptions. In assuming this office, she appeared to have drank in the very soul of the dramatist. What was wanting in judgment was supplied by memory, in the tenaciousness of which she has seldom been rivalled.

Her sentiments were trite and undigested, but were decorated with all the fluences and melodies of elocution. Her musical instructor had been a Sicilian, who had formed her style after the Italian model. This man had likewise taught her his own language. He had supplied her chiefly with Sicilian compositions, both in poetry and melody, and was content to be unclassical for the sake of the feminine and voluptuous graces of his native dialect.

Ormond was an accurate judge of the proficiency of Helena, and of the felicity with which these accomplishments were suited to her character. When his pupil personated the victims of anger and grief, and poured forth the fiery indignation of Calista, or the maternal despair of Constance, or the self-contentions of Ipsipile, he could not deny the homage which her talents might claim.

Her Sicilian tutor had found her no less tractable as a votary of painting. She needed only the education of Angelica to exercise as potent and prolific a pencil. This was incompatible with her condition, which limited her attainments to the elements of this art. It was otherwise with music. Here there was no obstacle to skill, and here the assiduities of many years, in addition to a prompt and ardent genius, set her beyond the hopes of rivalship.

Ormond had often amused his fancy with calling up images of excellence in this art. He saw no bounds to the influence of habit in augmenting the speed and multiplying the divisions of muscular motion. The fingers, by their form and size, were qualified to outrun and elude the most vigilant eye. The sensibility of keys and wires had limits; but these limits depended on the structure of the instrument, and the perfection of its structure was proportioned to the skill of the artist. On well-constructed keys and strings, was it possible to carry diversities of movement and pressure too far? How far they could be carried was mere theme of conjecture, until it was his fate to listen to the magical performances of Helena, whose volant finger seemed to be self-impelled. Her touches were creative of a thousand forms of *piano,* and of numberless transitions from grave to quick, perceptible only to ears like her own.

In the selection and arrangement of notes there are no limits to luxuriance and celerity. Helena had long relinquished the drudgery of imitation. She never played but when there were motives to fervour, and when she was likely to ascend without impediment, and to maintain for a suitable period her elevation, to the element of new ideas. The lyrics of Milton and of Metastasio she sung with accompaniments that never tired, because they were never repeated. Her harp and clavichord supplied her with endless combinations; and these, in the opinion of Ormond, were not inferior to the happiest exertions of Handel and Arne.

Chess was his favourite amusement. This was the only game which he allowed himself to play. He had studied it with so much zeal and success, that there were few with whom he deigned to contend. He was prone to consider it as a sort of criterion of human capacity. He who had acquired skill in this *science* could not be infirm in mind; and yet he found in Helena a competitor not unworthy of all his energies. Many hours were consumed in this employment, and here the lady was sedate, considerate, extensive in foresight, and fertile in expedients.

Her deportment was graceful, inasmuch as it flowed from a consciousness of her defects. She was devoid of arrogance and vanity, neither imagining herself better than she was, and setting light by those qualifications which she unquestionably possessed. Such was the mixed character of this woman.

Ormond was occupied with schemes of a rugged and arduous nature. His intimate associates and the partakers of his confidence were imbued with the same zeal and ardent in the same pursuits. Helena could lay no claim to be exalted to this rank. That one destitute of this claim should enjoy the privileges of his wife was still a supposition truly monstrous. Yet the image of Helena, fondly loving him, and a model, as he conceived, of tenderness and constancy, devoured by secret remorse, and pursued by the scorn of mankind,—a mark for slander to shoot at, and an outcast of society,—did not visit his meditations in vain. The rigour of his principles began now to relent.

He considered that various occupations are incident to every man. He cannot be invariably employed in the promotion of one purpose. He must occasionally unbend, if he desires that the springs of his mind should retain their due vigour. Suppose his life were divided between business and amusement: this was a necessary distribution, and sufficiently congenial with his temper. It became him to select with skill his sources of amusement. It is true that Helena was unable to participate in his graver occupations: what then? In whom were blended so many pleasurable attributes? In her were assembled an exquisite and delicious variety. As it was, he was daily in her company. He should scarcely be more so if marriage should take place. In that case, no change in their mode of life would be necessary. There was no need of dwelling under the same roof. His revenue was equal to the support of many household establishments. His personal independence would remain equally inviolable. No time, he thought, would diminish his influence over the mind of Helena, and it was not to be forgotten that the transition would to her be happy. It would reinstate her in the esteem of the world, and dispel those phantoms of remorse and shame by which she was at present persecuted.

These were plausible considerations. They tended at least to shake his resolutions. Time would probably have completed the conquest of his pride, had not a new incident set the question in a new light.

Chapter XXVIII

While occupied with these reflections, the light hastily disappeared, and darkness, rendered, by a cloudy atmosphere, uncommonly intense, succeeded. She had the means of lighting a lamp that hung against the wall, but had been too much immersed in thought to notice the deepening of the gloom. Recovering from her reverie, she looked around her with some degree of trepidation, and prepared to strike a spark that would enable her to light her lamp.

She had hitherto indulged an habitual indifference to danger. Now the presence of Ormond, the unknown purpose that led him hither, and the defencelessness of her condition, inspired her with apprehensions to which she had hitherto been a stranger. She had been accustomed to pass many nocturnal hours in this closet. Till now, nothing had occurred that made her enter it with circumspection or continue in it with reluctance.

Her sensations were no longer tranquil. Each minute that she spent in this recess appeared to multiply her hazards. To linger here appeared to her the height of culpable temerity. She hastily resolved to return to the farmer's dwelling, and, on the morrow, to repair to New York. For this end she was desirous to produce a light. The materials were at hand.

She lifted her hand to strike the flint, when her ear caught a sound which betokened the opening of the door that led into the next apartment. Her motion was suspended, and she listened as well as a throbbing heart would permit. That Ormond's was the hand that opened, was the first suggestion of her fears. The motives of this unseasonable entrance could not be reconciled with her safety. He had given no warning of his approach, and the door was opened with tardiness and seeming caution.

Sounds continued, of which no distinct conception could be obtained, or the cause that produced them assigned. The floors of every apartment being composed, like the walls and ceiling, of cement, footsteps were rendered almost undistinguishable. It was plain, however, that some one approached her own door.

The panic and confusion that now invaded her was owing to surprise, and to the singularity of her situation. The mansion was desolate and lonely. It was night. She was immersed in darkness. She had not the means, and was unaccustomed to the office, of repelling personal injuries. What injuries she had reason to dread, who was the agent, and what were his motives, were subjects of vague and incoherent meditation.

Meanwhile, low and imperfect sounds, that had in them more of inanimate than human, assailed her ear. Presently they ceased. An inexplicable fear deterred her from calling. Light would have exercised a friendly influence. This it was in her power to produce, but not without motion and noise; and these, by occasioning the discovery of her being in the closet, might possibly enhance her danger.

Conceptions like these were unworthy of the mind of Constantia. An interval of silence succeeded, interrupted only by the whistling of the blast without. It was sufficient for the restoration of her courage. She blushed at the cowardice which had trembled at a sound. She considered that Ormond might, indeed, be near, but that he was probably unconscious of her situation. His coming was not with the circumspection of an enemy. He might be acquainted with the place of her retreat, and had come to obtain an interview, with no clandestine or mysterious purposes. The noises she had heard had, doubtless, proceeded from the next apartment, but might be produced by some harmless or vagrant creature.

These considerations restored her tranquillity. They enabled her, deliberately, to create a light, but they did not dissuade her from leaving the house. Omens of evil seemed to be connected with this solitary and darksome abode. Besides, Ormond had unquestionably entered upon this scene. It could not be doubted that she was the object of his visit. The farm-house was a place of meeting more suitable and safe than any other. Thither, therefore, she determined immediately to return.

The closet had but one door, and this led into the chamber where the sounds had arisen. Through this chamber, therefore, she was obliged to pass, in order to reach the staircase, which terminated in the hall below.

Bearing the light in her left hand, she withdrew the bolt of the door and opened. In spite of courageous efforts, she opened with unwillingness, and shuddered to throw a glance forward or advance a step into the room. This was not needed, to reveal to her the cause of her late disturbance. Her eye instantly lighted on the body of a man, supine, motionless, stretched on the floor, close to the door through which she was about to pass.

A spectacle like this was qualified to startle her. She shrunk back, and fixed a more steadfast eye upon the prostrate person. There was no mark of blood or of wounds, but there was something in the attitude more significant of death than of sleep. His face rested on the floor, and his ragged locks concealed what part of his visage was not hidden by his posture. His garb was characterized by fashionable elegance, but was polluted with dust.

The image that first occurred to her was that of Ormond. This instantly gave place to another, which was familiar to her apprehension. It was at first too indistinctly seen to suggest a name. She continued to gaze and to be lost in fearful astonishment. Was this the person whose entrance had been overheard, and who had dragged himself hither to die at her door? Yet, in that case, would not groans and expiring efforts have testified his condition and invoked her succour? Was he not brought hither in the arms of his assassin? She mused upon the possible motives that induced some one thus to act, and upon the connection that might subsist between her destiny and that of the dead.

Her meditations, however fruitless in other respects, could not fail to show her the propriety of hastening from this spot. To scrutinize the form or face of the dead was a task to which her courage was unequal. Suitably accompanied and guarded, she would not scruple to return and ascertain, by the most sedulous examination, the cause of this ominous event.

She stepped over the breathless corpse, and hurried to the staircase. It became her to maintain the command of her muscles and joints, and to proceed without faltering or hesitation. Scarcely had she reached the entrance of the hall, when, casting anxious looks forward, she beheld a human figure. No scrutiny was requisite to inform her that this was Ormond.

She stopped. He approached her with looks and gestures placid but solemn. There was nothing in his countenance rugged or malignant. On the contrary, there were tokens of compassion.

"So," said he, "I expected to meet you. A light, gleaming from the window, marked you out. This and Laffert's directions have guided me."

"What," said Constantia, with discomposure in her accent, "was your motive for seeking me?"

"Have you forgotten," said Ormond, "what passed at our last interview? The evil that I then predicted is at hand. Perhaps you were incredulous; you accounted me a madman or deceiver; now I am come to witness the fulfilment of my words and the completion of your destiny. To rescue you I have not come: that is not within the compass of human powers.

"Poor Constantia," he continued, in tones that manifested genuine sympathy, "look upon thyself as lost. The toils that beset thee are inextricable. Summon up thy patience to endure the evil. Now will the last and heaviest trial betide thy fortitude. I could weep for thee, if my manly nature would permit. This is the scene of thy calamity, and this the hour."

These words were adapted to excite curiosity mingled with terror. Ormond's deportment was of an unexampled tenor, as well as that evil which he had so ambiguously predicted. He offered no protection from danger, and yet gave no proof of being himself an agent or auxiliary. After a minute's pause, Constantia, recovering a firm tone, said,—

"Mr. Ormond, your recent deportment but ill accords with your professions of sincerity and plain dealing. What your purpose is, or whether you have any purpose, I am at a loss to conjecture. Whether you most deserve censure or ridicule, is a point which you afford me not the means of deciding, and to which, unless on your own account, I am indifferent. If you are willing to be more explicit, or if there be any topic on which you wish further to converse, I will not refuse your company to Laffert's dwelling. Longer to remain here would be indiscreet and absurd."

So saying, she motioned towards the door. Ormond was passive, and seemed indisposed to prevent her departure, till she laid her hand upon the lock. He then, without moving from his place, exclaimed,—

"Stay! Must this meeting, which fate ordains to be the last, be so short? Must a time and place so suitable for what remains to be said and done be neglected or misused? No. You charge me with duplicity, and deem my conduct either ridiculous or criminal. I have stated my reasons for concealment, but these have failed to convince you. Well, here is now an end to doubt. All ambiguities are preparing to vanish."

When Ormond began to speak, Constantia paused to hearken to him. His vehemence was not of that nature which threatened to obstruct her passage. It was by entreaty that he apparently endeavoured to detain her steps, and not by violence. Hence arose her patience to listen. He continued:—

"Constantia! thy father is dead. Art thou not desirous of detecting the author of his fate? Will it afford thee no consolation to know that the deed is punished? Wilt thou suffer me to drag the murderer to thy feet? Thy justice will be gratified by this sacrifice. Somewhat will be due to him who avenged thy wrong in the blood of the perpetrator. What sayest thou? Grant me thy permission, and in a moment I will drag him hither."

These words called up the image of the person whose corpse she had lately seen. It was readily conceived that to him Ormond alluded; but this was the assassin of her father, and his crime had been detected and punished by Ormond! These images

had no other effect than to urge her departure: she again applied her hand to the lock, and said,—

"This scene must not be prolonged. My father's death I desire not to hear explained or to see revenged, but whatever information you are willing or able to communicate must be deferred."

"Nay," interrupted Ormond, with augmented vehemence, "art thou equally devoid of curiosity and justice? Thinkest thou that the enmity which bereft thy father of life will not seek thy own? There are evils which I cannot prevent thee from enduring, but there are, likewise, ills which my counsel will enable thee and thy friend to shun. Save me from witnessing thy death. Thy father's destiny is sealed; all that remained was to punish his assassin; but thou and thy Sophia still live. Why should ye perish by a like stroke?"

This intimation was sufficient to arrest the steps of Constantia. She withdrew her hand from the door, and fixed eyes of the deepest anxiety on Ormond:— "What mean you? How am I to understand——"

"Ah!" said Ormond, "I see thou wilt consent to stay. Thy detention shall not be long. Remain where thou art during one moment,—merely while I drag hither thy enemy and show thee a visage which thou wilt not be slow to recognise." Saying this, he hastily ascended the staircase, and quickly passed beyond her sight.

Deportment thus mysterious could not fail of bewildering her thoughts. There was somewhat in the looks and accents of Ormond, different from former appearances; tokens of a hidden purpose and a smothered meaning were perceptible,—a mixture of the inoffensive and the lawless, which, added to the loneliness and silence that encompassed her, produced a faltering emotion. Her curiosity was overpowered by her fear, and the resolution was suddenly conceived of seizing this opportunity to escape.

A third time she put her hand to the lock and attempted to open. The effort was ineffectual. The door that was accustomed to obey the gentlest touch was now immovable. She had lately unlocked and passed through it. Her eager inspection convinced her that the principal bolt was still withdrawn, but a small one was now perceived, of whose existence she had not been apprized, and over which her key had no power.

Now did she first harbour a fear that was intelligible in its dictates. Now did she first perceive herself sinking in the toils of some lurking enemy. Hope whispered that this foe was not Ormond. His conduct had bespoken no willingness to put constraint upon her steps. He talked not as if he was aware of this obstruction, and yet his seeming acquiescence might have flowed from a knowledge that she had no power to remove beyond his reach.

He warned her of danger to her life, of which he was her self-appointed rescuer. His counsel was to arm her with sufficient caution; the peril that awaited her was imminent; this was the time and place of its occurrence, and here she was compelled to remain, till the power that fastened would condescend to loose the door. There were other avenues to the hall. These were accustomed to be locked; but Ormond had found access, and, if all continued fast, it was incontestable that he was the author of this new impediment.

The other avenues were hastily examined. All were bolted and locked. The first impulse led her to call for help from without; but the mansion was distant from Laffert's habitation. This spot was wholly unfrequented. No passenger was likely to be stationed where her call could be heard. Besides, this forcible detention might operate for a short time, and be attended with no mischievous consequences. Whatever was to come, it was her duty to collect her courage and encounter it.

The steps of Ormond above now gave tokens of his approach. Vigilant observance of this man was all that her situation permitted. A vehement effort restored her to some degree of composure. Her stifled palpitations allowed her steadfastly to notice him as he now descended the stairs, bearing a lifeless body in his arms. "There!" said he, as he cast it at her feet; "whose countenance is that? Who would imagine that features like those belonged to an assassin and impostor?"

Closed eyelids and fallen muscles could not hide from her lineaments so often seen. She shrunk back and exclaimed, "Thomas Craig!"[1]

A pause succeeded, in which she alternately gazed at the countenance of this unfortunate wretch and at Ormond. At length, the latter exclaimed,—

"Well, my girl, hast thou examined him? Dost thou recognise a friend or an enemy?"

"I know him well: but how came this? What purpose brought him hither? Who was the author of his fate?"

"Have I not already told thee that Ormond was his own avenger and thine? To thee and to me he has been a robber. To him thy father is indebted for the loss not only of property but life. Did crimes like these merit a less punishment? And what recompense is due to him whose vigilance pursued him hither and made him pay for his offences with his blood? What benefit have I received at thy hand to authorize me, for thy sake, to take away his life?"

"No benefit received from me," said Constantia, "would justify such an act. I should have abhorred myself for annexing to my benefits so bloody a con-

dition. It calls for no gratitude or recompense. Its suitable attendant is remorse. That he is a thief, I know but too well; that my father died by his hand is incredible. No motives or means——"

"Why so?" interrupted Ormond. "Does not sleep seal up the senses? Cannot closets be unlocked at midnight? Cannot adjoining houses communicate by doors? Cannot these doors be hidden from suspicion by a sheet of canvas?"

These words were of startling and abundant import. They reminded her of circumstances in her father's chamber, which sufficiently explained the means by which his life was assailed. The closet, and its canvas-covered wall; the adjoining house untenanted and shut up—but this house, though unoccupied, belonged to Ormond. From the inferences which flowed hence, her attention was withdrawn by her companion, who continued:—

"Do these means imply the interposal of a miracle? His motives? What scruples can be expected from a man inured from infancy to cunning and pillage? Will he abstain from murder when urged by excruciating poverty, by menaces of persecution, by terror of expiring on the gallows?"

Tumultuous suspicions were now awakened in the mind of Constantia. Her faltering voice scarcely allowed her to ask, "How know *you* that Craig was thus guilty?—that these were his incitements and means?"

Ormond's solemnity now gave place to a tone of sarcasm and looks of exultation:—"Poor Constantia! Thou art still pestered with incredulity and doubts! My veracity is still in question! My knowledge, girl, is infallible. That these were his means of access I cannot be ignorant, for I pointed them out. He was urged by these motives, for they were stated and enforced by me. His was the deed, for I stood beside him when it was done."

These, indeed, were terms that stood in no need of further explanation. The veil that shrouded this formidable being was lifted high enough to make him be regarded with inexplicable horror. What his future acts should be, how his omens of ill were to be solved, were still involved in uncertainty.

In the midst of fears for her own safety, by which Constantia was now assailed, the image of her father was revived; keen regret and vehement upbraiding were conjured up.

"Craig, then, was the instrument, and yours the instigation, that destroyed my father! In what had he offended you? What cause had he given for resentment?"

"Cause!" replied he, with impetuous accents. "Resentment! None. My motive was benevolent; my deed conferred a benefit. I gave him sight and took away his life, from motives equally wise. Know you not that Ormond was fool enough to set value on

[1] Craig had embezzled the fortune of Stephen Dudley, Constantia's blind father, and murdered him—but, as she does not know, at Ormond's instigation.

the affections of a woman? These were sought with preposterous anxiety and endless labour. Among other facilitators of his purpose, he summoned gratitude to his aid. To snatch you from poverty, to restore his sight to your father, were expected to operate as incentives to love.

"But here I was the dupe of error. A thousand prejudices stood in my way. These, provided our intercourse were not obstructed, I hoped to subdue. The rage of innovation seized your father: this, blended with a mortal antipathy to me, made him labour to seduce you from the bosom of your peaceful country; to make you enter on a boisterous sea; to visit lands where all is havoc and hostility; to snatch you from the influence of my arguments.

"This new obstacle I was bound to remove. While revolving the means, chance and his evil destiny threw Craig in my way. I soon convinced him that his reputation and his life were in my hands. His retention of these depended upon my will, on the performance of conditions which I prescribed.

"My happiness and yours depended on your concurrence with my wishes. Your father's life was an obstacle to your concurrence. For killing him, therefore, I may claim your gratitude. His death was a due and disinterested offering at the altar of your felicity and mine.

"My deed was not injurious to him. At his age, death, whose coming at some period is inevitable, could not be distant. To make it unforeseen and brief, and void of pain,—to preclude the torments of a lingering malady, a slow and visible descent to the grave,—was the dictate of beneficence. But of what value was a continuance of his life? Either you would have gone with him to Europe or have stayed at home with me. In the first case, his life would have been rapidly consumed by perils and cares. In the second, separation from you, and union with me,—a being so detestable,—would equally have poisoned his existence.

"Craig's cowardice and crimes made him a pliant and commodious tool. I pointed out the way. The unsuspected door which led into the closet of your father's chamber was made, by my direction, during the life of Helena. By this avenue I was wont to post myself where all your conversations could be overheard. By this avenue an entrance and retreat were afforded to the agent of my newest purpose.

"Fool that I was! I solaced myself with the belief that all impediments were now smoothed, when a new enemy appeared. My folly lasted as long as my hope. I saw that to gain your affections, fortified by antiquated scruples and obsequious to the guidance of this new monitor, was impossible. It is not my way to toil after that which is beyond my reach. If the greater good be inaccessible, I learn to be contented with the less.

"I have served you with successless sedulity. I have set an engine in act to obliterate an obstacle to your felicity, and lay your father at rest. Under my guidance, this engine was productive only of good. Governed by itself or by another, it will only work you harm. I have, therefore, hastened to destroy it. Lo! it is now before you motionless and impotent.

"For this complexity of benefit I look for no reward. I am not tired of well-doing. Having ceased to labour for an unattainable good, I have come hither to possess myself of all that I now crave, and by the same deed to afford you an illustrious opportunity to signalize your wisdom and your fortitude."

During this speech, the mind of Constantia became more deeply pervaded with dread of some overhanging but incomprehensible evil. The strongest impulse was to gain a safe asylum, at a distance from this spot and from the presence of this extraordinary being. This impulse was followed by the recollection that her liberty was taken away, that egress from the hall was denied her, and that this restriction might be part of some conspiracy of Ormond against her life.

Security from danger like this would be, in the first place, sought, by one of Constantia's sex and opinions, in flight. This had been rendered, by some fatal chance or by the precautions of her foe, impracticable. Stratagem or force was all that remained to elude or disarm her adversary. For the contrivance and execution of fraud, all the habits of her life and all the maxims of her education had conspired to unfit her. Her force of muscles would avail her nothing against the superior energy of Ormond.

She remembered that to inflict death was no iniquitous exertion of self-defence, and that the penknife which she held in her hand was capable of this service. She had used it to remove any lurking obstruction in the wards of her key, supposing, for a time, this to be the cause of her failing to withdraw the bolt of the door. This resource was, indeed, scarcely less disastrous and deplorable than any fate from which it could rescue her. Some uncertainty still involved the intentions of Ormond. As soon as he paused, she spoke:—

"How am I to understand this prelude? Let me know the full extent of my danger,—why it is that I am hindered from leaving this house, and why this interview was sought."

"Ah, Constantia, this, indeed, is merely a prelude to a scene that is to terminate my influence over thy fate. When this is past I have sworn to part with thee forever. Art thou still dubious of my purpose? Art thou not a woman? And have I not entreated for thy love and been rejected?

"Canst thou imagine that I aim at thy life? My avowals of love were sincere; my passion was vehement and undisguised. It gave dignity and value to a gift in thy power, as a woman, to bestow. This has been denied. That gift has lost none of its value in my eyes. What thou refusest to bestow it is in my power to extort. I came for that end. When this end is accomplished, I will restore thee to liberty."

These words were accompanied by looks that rendered all explanation of their meaning useless. The evil reserved for her, hitherto obscured by half-disclosed and contradictory attributes, was now sufficiently apparent. The truth in this respect unveiled itself with the rapidity and brightness of an electrical flash.

She was silent. She cast her eyes at the windows and doors. Escape through them was hopeless. She looked at those lineaments of Ormond which evinced his disdain of supplication and inexorable passions. She felt that entreaty and argument would be vain; that all appeals to his compassion and benevolence would counteract her purpose, since, in the unexampled conformation of this man's mind, these principles were made subservient to his most flagitious designs. Considerations of justice and pity were made, by a fatal perverseness of reasoning, champions and bulwarks of his most atrocious mistakes.

The last extremes of opposition, the most violent expedients for defence, would be justified by being indispensable. To find safety for her honour, even in the blood of an assailant, was the prescription of duty. The equity of this species of defence was not, in the present confusion of her mind, a subject of momentary doubt.

To forewarn him of her desperate purpose would be to furnish him with means of counteraction. Her weapon would easily be wrested from her feeble hand. Ineffectual opposition would only precipitate her evil destiny. A rage, contented with nothing less than her life, might be awakened in his bosom. But was not this to be desired? Death, untimely and violent, was better than the loss of honour.

This thought led to a new series of reflections. She involuntarily shrunk from the act of killing: but would her efforts to destroy her adversary be effectual? Would not his strength and dexterity easily repel or elude them? Her power in this respect was questionable, but her power was undeniably sufficient to a different end. The instrument which could not rescue her from this injury by the destruction of another might save her from it by her own destruction.

These thoughts rapidly occurred; but the resolution to which they led was scarcely formed, when Ormond advanced towards her. She recoiled a few steps, and, showing the knife which she held, said,—

"Ormond! Beware! Know that my unalterable resolution is to die uninjured. I have the means in my power. Stop where you are; one step more, and I plunge this knife into my heart. I know that to contend with your strength or your reason would be vain. To turn this weapon against you I should not fear, if I were sure of success; but to that I will not trust. To save a greater good by the sacrifice of life is in my power, and that sacrifice shall be made."

"Poor Constantia!" replied Ormond, in a tone of contempt; "so thou preferrest thy imaginary honour to life! To escape this injury without a name or substance, without connection with the past or future, without contamination of thy purity or thraldom of thy will, thou wilt kill thyself; put an end to thy activity in virtue's cause; rob thy friend of her solace, the world of thy beneficence, thyself of being and pleasure?

"I shall be grieved for the fatal issue of my experiment; I shall mourn over thy martyrdom to the most opprobrious and contemptible of all errors: but that thou shouldst undergo the trial is decreed. There is still an interval of hope that thy cowardice is counterfeited, or that it will give place to wisdom and courage.

"Whatever thou intendest by way of prevention or cure, it behooves thee to employ with steadfastness. Die with the guilt of suicide and the brand of cowardice upon thy memory, or live with thy claims to felicity and approbation undiminished. Choose which thou wilt. Thy decision is of moment to thyself, but of none to me. Living or dead, the prize that I have in view shall be mine."

1799

WILLIAM ELLERY CHANNING [1780–1842]

THOUGH "infidelity" was fast declining by 1800, the decline did not mean that old-fashioned Calvinist orthodoxy had won the day, for "unitarian" doctrines were already well established in many Congregational and Presbyterian congregations. Kindred movements, both deism and Unitarianism professed to be rational and liberal, and they were at one in opposing Calvinism. Rejecting the doctrine of man's total depravity, they affirmed the exalted nature and unlimited possibilities of man. On the other hand, they differed in that deism was a "natural religion" (a religion based on nature in its scientific aspects) and Unitarianism essentially traditionally Christian in its principles. Numbers of younger ministers, especially in New England, increasingly dissatisfied with the rigors of orthodoxy, turned toward this liberalized theology. They shouted no dissent, but quietly made their churches Unitarian, one after another, without changing pastors or houses of worship, almost without disturbing their parishioners' minds.

The central figure in this development was a Boston minister, William Ellery Channing. Born in Rhode Island, he graduated from Harvard in 1798, tutored in a Virginia family, read the deists and political radicals, studied theology, and in 1803 was installed in Boston's Federal Street Church, where he remained the rest of his life. Though Channing never meant to lead any movement, the Unitarian liberals sought him out. The clarity and conviction of his sermons and essays soon made him a recognized leader of the liberal wing and projected him more and more into the controversy. His sermon on "Unitarian Christianity," preached at the ordination of the Reverend Jared Sparks at Baltimore in 1819, became a rallying point for theological liberals, and his essay-review in *The Christian Examiner* for 1820, "The Moral Argument Against Calvinism," which he characterized as "a false theology," attracted national attention. He opposed the orthodox variety of Calvinism, he once said, "inasmuch as it prostrates the independence of the mind, teaches men that they are naturally incapable of discerning religious truth, generates a timid, superstitious dependence on those who profess to have been brought from darkness into light, and so commonly infuses into its professors a censorious and uncharitable spirit." He later helped to organize a conference of liberal ministers, which in 1825 became the American Unitarian Association. As minister, editor, and lecturer, Channing's influence on his and the next generation was large indeed; his theological, social, and political views filtered through New England's intellectual life. Active in the antislavery, pacifist, and temperance movements, and a friend to reform in all fields, Channing said in the preface to his collected works that there were two master principles which governed him: respect for human nature and reverence for human liberty.

Further reading: Arthur W. Brown, *Always Young for Liberty*, 1956. Madeleine H. Rice, *The Life of W. E. Channing*, 1961. Robert L. Patterson, *The Philosophy of W. E. Channing*, 1952.

FROM *Remarks on National Literature*

Originally written as a review-article for *The Christian Examiner* in 1830; Channing revised and retitled it for inclusion in his collected works in 1841. Despite its title, Channing's use of the term "national" was neither narrow nor chauvinistic. Though he advises American authors to draw inspiration from the American experience and to use American themes, he never conceived of literature as something to be produced in cultural isolation, and was fully aware of the interconnections of all art in all times and places. What he proposes is an American literature that expresses the national character, but since literature reflects the moral qualities of the nation which produces it, America cannot expect to produce great national literature until the nation itself is great. A call for cultural independence that preceded Emerson's *American Scholar* by seven years, Channing's essay called for national self-cultivation and self-reliance. "A country," he wrote, "like an individual, has dignity and power only in proportion as it is self-founded. There is a great stir to secure to ourselves the manufacturing of our own clothing. We say, let others spin and weave for us, but let them not think for us." Text: *Works*, 1848 edition, Volume I.

° ° ° Do we possess, indeed, what may be called a national literature? Have we produced eminent writers in the various departments of intellectual effort? Are our chief resources of instruction and literary enjoyment furnished from ourselves? We regret that the reply to these questions is so obvious. The few standard works which we have produced, and which promise to live, can hardly, by any courtesy, be denominated a national literature. On this point, if marks and proofs of our real condition were needed, we should find them in the current apologies for our deficiencies. Our writers are accustomed to plead in our excuse, our youth, the necessities of a newly settled country, and the direction of our best talents to practical life. Be the pleas sufficient or not, one thing they prove, and that is, our consciousness of having failed to make important contributions to the interests of the intellect. We have few names to place by the side of the great names in science and literature on the other side of the ocean. We want those lights which make a country conspicuous at a distance. Let it not be said, that European envy denies our just claims. In an age like this, when the literary world forms a great family, and the products of mind are circulated more rapidly than those of machinery, it is a nation's own fault, if its name be not pronounced with honor beyond itself. We have ourselves heard, and delighted to hear, beyond the Alps, our country designated as the land of Franklin. This name had scaled that mighty barrier, and made us known where our institutions and modes of life were hardly better understood than those of the natives of our forests.

We are accustomed to console ourselves for the absence of a commanding literature, by urging our superiority to other nations in our institutions for the diffusion of elementary knowledge through all classes of the community. We have here just cause for boasting, though perhaps less than we imagine. That there are gross deficiencies in our common schools, and that the amount of knowledge which they communicate, when compared with the time spent in its acquisition, is lamentably small, the community begin to feel. There is a crying need for a higher and more quickening kind of instruction than the laboring part of society have yet received, and we rejoice that the cry begins to be heard. But, allowing our elementary institutions to be ever so perfect, we confess that they do not satisfy us. We want something more. A dead level of intellect, even if it should rise above what is common in other nations, would not answer our wishes and hopes for our country. We want great minds to be formed among us, minds which shall be felt afar, and through which we may act on the world. We want the human intellect to do its utmost here. We want this people to obtain a claim on the gratitude of the human race, by adding strength to the foundation, and fulness and splendor to the developement of moral and religious truth; by originality of thought, by discoveries of science, and by contributions to the refining pleasures of taste and imagination.

With these views we do and must lament, that, however we surpass other nations in providing for, and spreading elementary instruction, we fall behind many in provision for the liberal training of the intellect, for forming great scholars, for communicating that profound knowledge, and that thirst for higher truths, which can alone originate a commanding literature. The truth ought to be known. There is among us much superficial knowledge, but little severe, persevering research; little of that consuming passion for new truth, which makes outward things worthless; little resolute devotion to a high intellectual culture. There is nowhere a literary atmosphere, or such an accumulation of literary influence, as determines the whole strength of the mind to its own enlargement, and to the manifestation of itself in enduring forms. Few among us can be said to have followed out any great subject of thought patiently, laboriously, so as to know thoroughly what others have discovered and taught concerning it, and thus to occupy a ground from which new views may be gained. Of course, exceptions are to be found. This country has produced original and profound thinkers. We have named Franklin, and we may name Edwards, one of the greatest men of his age, though unhappily his mind was lost, in a great degree, to literature, and we fear to religion, by vassalage to a false theology. His work on the Will throws, indeed, no light on human nature, and, notwithstanding the nobleness of the subject, gives no great or elevated thoughts; but, as a specimen of logical acuteness and controversial power, it certainly ranks in the very highest class of metaphysical writings. We might also name living authors who do honor to their country. Still, we may say, we chiefly prize what has been done among us, as a promise of higher and more extensive effort. Patriotism, as well as virtue, forbids us to burn incense to national vanity. The truth should be seen and felt. In an age of great intellectual activity, we rely chiefly for intellectual excitement and enjoyment on foreign minds, nor is our own mind felt abroad. Whilst clamoring against dependence on European manufactures, we contentedly rely on Europe for the nobler and more important fabrics of the intellect. We boast of our political institutions, and receive our chief teachings, books, impressions, from the school of monarchy. True, we labor under disadvantages. But, if our liberty deserves the praise which it receives, it is more than a balance for these. We believe that it is. We believe that it does open to us an indefinite intellectual progress. Did we not so regard it, we should value it little. If hereditary governments minister most to the growth of the mind, it were better to restore them than to cling to a barren freedom. Let us not expose liberty to this reproach. Let us prove, by more generous provisions for the diffusion of elementary knowledge, for the training of great minds, and for the joint culture of the moral and intellectual powers, that we are more and more instructed, by freedom, in the worth and greatness of human nature, and in the obligation of contributing to its strength and glory.

We have spoken of the condition of our literature. We now proceed to the consideration of the causes which obstruct its advancement; and we are immediately struck by one so prevalent, as to deserve distinct notice. We refer to the common doctrine, that we need, in this country, useful knowledge, rather than profound, extensive, and elegant literature, and that this last, if we covet it, may be imported from abroad in such variety and abundance, as to save us the necessity of producing it among ourselves. How far are these opinions just? This question we purpose to answer.

That useful knowledge should receive our first and chief care, we mean not to dispute. ° ° °

We have said that we prize, as highly as any, useful knowledge. But by this we mean knowledge which answers and ministers to our complex and various nature; we mean that which is useful, not only to the animal man, but to the intellectual, moral, and religious man; useful to a being of spiritual faculties, whose happiness is to be found in their free and harmonious exercise. We grant, that there

is primary necessity for that information and skill by which subsistence is earned, and life is preserved; for it is plain that we must live, in order to act and improve. But life is the means; action and improvement the end; and who will deny that the noblest utility belongs to that knowledge, by which the chief purpose of our creation is accomplished? According to these views, a people should honor and cultivate, as unspeakably useful, that literature which corresponds to, and calls forth, the highest faculties; which expresses and communicates energy of thought, fruitfulness of invention, force of moral purpose, a thirst for the true, and a delight in the beautiful. According to these views, we attach special importance to those branches of literature which relate to human nature, and which give it a consciousness of its own powers. History has a noble use, for it shows us human beings in various and opposite conditions, in their strength and weakness, in their progress and relapses, and thus reveals the causes and means by which the happiness and virtue of the race may be enlarged. Poetry is useful, by touching deep springs in the human soul; by giving voice to its more delicate feelings; by breathing out, and making more intelligible, the sympathy which subsists between the mind and the outward universe; by creating beautiful forms of manifestations for great moral truths. Above all, that higher philosophy, which treats of the intellectual and moral constitution of man, of the foundation of knowledge, of duty, of perfection, of our relations to the spiritual world, and especially to God; this has a usefulness so peculiar as to throw other departments of knowledge into obscurity; and a people, among whom this does not find honor, has little ground to boast of its superiority to uncivilized tribes. It will be seen from these remarks, that utility, with us, has a broad meaning. In truth, we are slow to condemn as useless, any researches or discoveries of original and strong minds, even when we discern in them no bearing on any interests of mankind; for all truth is of a prolific nature, and has connexions not immediately perceived; and it may be, that what we call vain speculations, may, at no distant period, link themselves with some new facts or theories, and guide a profound thinker to the most important results. The ancient mathematician, when absorbed in solitary thought, little imagined that his theorems, after the lapse of ages, were to be applied by the mind of Newton to the solution of the mysteries of the universe, and not only to guide the astronomer through the heavens, but the navigator through the pathless ocean. For ourselves, we incline to hope much from truths, which are particularly decried as useless; for the noblest and most useful truth is of an abstract or universal nature; and yet the abstract, though susceptible of infinite application, is generally, as we know, opposed to the practical.

We maintain, that a people, which has any serious purpose of taking a place among improved communities, should studiously promote within itself every variety of intellectual exertion. It should resolve strenuously to be surpassed by none. It should feel that mind is the creative power, through which all the resources of nature are to be turned to account, and by which a people is to spread its influence, and establish the noblest form of empire. It should train within itself men able to understand and to use whatever is thought and discovered over the whole earth. The whole mass of human knowledge should exist among a people, not in neglected libraries, but in its higher minds. Among its most cherished institutions, should be those, which will ensure to it ripe scholars, explorers of ancient learning, profound historians and mathematicians, intellectual laborers devoted to physical and moral science, and to the creation of a refined and beautiful literature.

Let us not be misunderstood. We have no desire to rear in our country a race of pedants, of solemn triflers, of laborious commentators on the mysteries of a Greek accent or a rusty coin. We would have men explore antiquity, not to bury themselves in its dust, but to learn its spirit, and so to commune with its superior minds, as to accumulate on the present age, the influences of whatever was great and wise in former times. What we want is, that those among us, whom God has gifted to comprehend whatever is now known, and to rise to new truths, may find aids and institutions to fit them for their high calling, and may become at once springs of a higher intellectual life to their own country, and joint workers with the great of all nations and times in carrying forward their race.

We know that it will be said, that foreign scholars, bred under institutions which this country cannot support, may do our intellectual work, and send us books and learning to meet our wants. To this we have much to answer. In the first place, we reply, that, to avail ourselves of the higher literature of other nations, we must place ourselves on a level with them. The products of foreign machinery we can use, without any portion of the skill that produced them. But works of taste and genius, and profound investigations of philosophy, can only be estimated and enjoyed through a culture and power corresponding to that from which they sprung.

In the next place, we maintain, that it is an immense gain to a people, to have in its own bosom, among its own sons, men of distinguished intellect. Such men give a spring and life to a community by their presence, their society, their fame; and what deserves remark, such men are nowhere so felt as in a republic like our own; for here the different classes of society flow together and act powerfully on each other, and a free communication, elsewhere unknown, is established between the gifted few and the many. It is one of the many good fruits of liberty, that it increases the diffusiveness of intellect; and accordingly a free country is, above all others, false to itself, in withholding from its superior minds the means of enlargement.

We next observe, and we think the observation important, that the facility with which we receive the literature of foreign countries, instead of being a reason for neglecting our own, is a strong motive for its cultivation. We mean not to be paradoxical, but we believe that it would be better to admit no books from abroad, than to make them substitutes for our own intellectual activity. The more we receive from other countries, the greater the need of an original literature. A people, into whose minds the thoughts of foreigners are poured perpetually, needs an energy within itself to resist, to modify this mighty influence, and, without it, will inevitably sink under the worst bondage, will become intellectually tame and enslaved. We have certainly no desire to complete our restrictive system, by adding to it a literary non-intercourse law. We rejoice in the increasing intellectual connexion between this country and the old world. But sooner would we rupture it, than see our country sitting passively at the feet of foreign teachers. It were better to have no literature, than form ourselves unresistingly on a foreign one. The true sovereigns of a country are those who determine its mind, its modes of thinking, its tastes, its principles; and we cannot consent to lodge this sovereignty in the hands of strangers. A country, like an individual, has dignity and power only in proportion as it is self-formed. There is a great stir to secure to ourselves the manufacturing of our own clothing. We say, let others spin and weave for us, but let them not think for us. A people, whose government and laws are nothing but the embodying of public opinion, should jealously guard this opinion against foreign dictation. We need a literature to counteract, and to use wisely the literature which we import. We need an inward power proportionate to that which is exerted on us, as the means of self-subsistence. It is particularly true of a people, whose institutions demand for their support a free and bold spirit, that they should be able to subject to a manly and independent criticism, whatever comes from abroad. These views seem to us to deserve serious attention. We are more and more a reading people. Books are already among the most powerful influences here. The question is, shall Europe, through these, fashion us after its pleasure? Shall America be only an echo of what is thought and written under the aristocracies beyond the ocean?

Another view of the subject is this. A foreign literature will always, in a measure, be foreign. It has sprung from the soul of another people, which, however like, is still not our own soul. Every people has much in its own character and feelings, which can only be embodied by its own writers, and which, when transfused through literature, makes it touching and true, like the voice of our earliest friend.

We now proceed to an argument in favor of native literature, which, if less obvious, is, we believe, not less sound than those now already adduced. We have hitherto spoken of literature as the expression, the communication, of the higher minds in a community. We now add, that it does much more than is commonly supposed, to *form* such minds, so that, without it, a people wants one of the chief means of educating or perfecting talent and genius. One of the great laws of our nature, and a law singularly important to social beings, is, that the intellect enlarges and strengthens itself by expressing worthily its best views. In this, as in other respects, it is more blessed to give than to receive. Superior minds are formed, not merely by solitary thought, but almost as much by communication. Great thoughts are never fully possessed, till he who has conceived them has given them fit utterance. One of the noblest and most invigorating labors of genius is, to clothe its conceptions in clear and glorious forms, to give them existence in other souls. Thus literature creates, as well as manifests, intellectual power, and, without it, the highest minds will never be summoned to the most invigorating action. ° ° °

We come now to our last, and what we deem a weighty argument in favor of a native literature. We desire and would cherish it, because we hope from it important aids to the cause of truth and human nature. We believe, that a literature, springing up in this new soil, would bear new fruits, and, in some respects, more precious fruits, than are elsewhere produced. We know that our hopes may be set down to the account of that national vanity, which, with too much reason, is placed by foreigners among our besetting sins. But we speak from calm and deliberate conviction. We are inclined to believe, that, as a people, we occupy a position, from which the great subjects of literature may be viewed more justly than from those which most other nations hold. Undoubtedly we labor under disadvantages. We want the literary apparatus of Europe; her libraries, her universities, her learned institutions, her race of professed scholars, her spots consecrated by the memory of sages, and a thousand stirring associations which hover over ancient nurseries of learning. But the mind is not a local power. Its spring is within itself, and, under the inspiration of liberal and high feeling, it may attain and worthily

express nobler truth than outward helps could reveal.

The great distinction of our country is, that we enjoy some peculiar advantages for understanding our own nature. Man is the great subject of literature, and juster and profounder views of man may be expected here, than elsewhere. In Europe, political and artificial distinctions have, more or less, triumphed over and obscured our common nature. In Europe, we meet kings, nobles, priests, peasants. How much rarer is it to meet *men;* by which we mean, human beings conscious of their own nature, and conscious of the utter worthlessness of all outward distinctions, compared with what is treasured up in their own souls. Man does not value himself as man. It is for his blood, his rank, or some artificial distinction, and not for the attributes of humanity, that he holds himself in respect. The institutions of the old world all tend to throw obscurity over what we most need to know, and that is, the worth and claims of a human being. We know that great improvements in this respect are going on abroad. Still the many are too often postponed to the few. The mass of men are regarded as instruments to work with, as materials to be shaped for the use of their superiors. That consciousness of our own nature, which contains, as a germ, all nobler thoughts, which teaches us at once self-respect and respect for others, and which binds us to God by filial sentiment and hope, this has been repressed, kept down by establishments founded in force; and literature, in all its departments, bears, we think, the traces of this inward degradation. We conceive that our position favors a juster and profounder estimate of human nature. We mean not to boast, but there are fewer obstructions to that moral consciousness, that consciousness of humanity, of which we have spoken. Man is not hidden from us by so many disguises as in the old world. The essential equality of all human beings, founded on the possession of a spiritual, progressive, immortal nature, is, we hope, better understood; and nothing more than this single conviction is needed, to work the mightiest changes in every province of human life and of human thought.

We have stated what seems to us our most important distinction. But our position has other advantages. The mere circumstance of its being a new one, gives reason to hope for some new intellectual activity, some fresher views of nature and life. We are not borne down by the weight of antiquated institutions, time-hallowed abuses, and the remnants of feudal barbarism. The absence of a religious establishment is an immense gain, as far as originality of mind is in question; for an establishment, however advantageous in other respects, is, by its nature, hostile to discovery and progress. To keep the mind where it is, to fasten the notions of one age on all future time, is its aim and proper business; and if it happened, as has generally been the case, to grow up in an age of strife and passion, when, as history demonstrates, the church was overrun with error, it cannot but perpetuate darkness and mental bondage. Among us, intellect, though far from being free, has broken some of the chains of other countries, and is more likely, we conceive, to propose to itself its legitimate object, truth,—everlasting and universal truth.

We have no thought of speaking contemptuously of the literature of the old world. It is our daily nutriment. We feel our debt to be immense to the glorious company of pure and wise minds, which in foreign lands have bequeathed us in writing their choicest thoughts and holiest feelings. Still we feel, that all existing literature has been produced under influences, which have necessarily mixed with it much error and corruption; and that the whole of it ought to pass, and must pass, under rigorous review. For example, we think that the history of the human race is to be re-written. Men imbued with the prejudices which thrive under aristocracies and state religions, cannot understand it. Past ages, with their great events, and great men, are to undergo, we think, a new trial, and to yield new results. It is plain, that history is already viewed under new aspects, and we believe, that the true principles for studying and writing it are to be unfolded here, at least as rapidly as in other countries. It seems to us that in literature an immense work is yet to be done. The most interesting questions to mankind are yet in debate. Great principles are yet to be settled in criticism, in morals, in politics; and, above all, the true character of religion is to be rescued from the disguises and corruptions of ages. We want a reformation. We want a literature, in which genius will pay supreme, if not undivided homage, to truth and virtue; in which the childish admiration of what has been called greatness, will give place to a wise moral judgment; which will breathe reverence for the mind, and elevating thoughts of God. The part which this country is to bear in this great intellectual reform, we presume not to predict. We feel, however, that, if true to itself, it will have the glory and happiness of giving new impulses to the human mind. This is our cherished hope. We should have no heart to encourage native literature, did we not hope that it would become instinct with a new spirit. We cannot admit the thought, that this country is to be only a repetition of the old world. We delight to believe that God, in the fulness of time, has brought a new continent to light, in order that the human mind should move here with a new freedom, should frame new social institutions, should explore new paths, and reap new harvests. We are accustomed to estimate nations by their creative energies, and we shall blush for our country, if, in circumstances so peculiar, original, and creative, it shall satisfy itself with a passive reception and mechanical reiteration of the thoughts of strangers.

1830, 1841

FROM *Christianity a Rational Religion*

The development of Channing's theology followed a rather clearly defined course, once he determined its direction. He wanted, he said, to return "spirituality" to religion, and to do so meant that he must re-assess the Calvinism that had driven it out and explain the Unitarianism that would bring it back. His Baltimore sermon of 1819, titled "Unitarian Christianity," set the two opposing systems against each other—new liberalism against old orthodoxy—to assert the superiority of the one over the other. His essay "The Moral Argument Against Calvinism," the following year, showed the basic inconsistencies between the doctrines of Calvinism and the perfections of God; God could not be, Channing argued, what Calvinism had made Him. His sermon of 1826, awkwardly titled "Unitarianism Christianity Most Favorable to Piety," concluded that of the two theologies, Unitarian and orthodox, the former possessed "a superior tendency to form an elevated religious character."

Channing in a sense provided a bridge from the Enlightenment to the Transcendentalists. He believed in the essential goodness and rationality of human nature, the reasonableness of nature and religion, the unity of God, the sufficiency of the individual, the moral emphasis of theology, the need for a social, humanitarian Christianity. The epitaph on his tombstone summarized his faith best— "He breathed into theology a humane spirit." Yet Channing too was a child of romanticism. A friend of Coleridge and an admiring student of *Biographia Literaria* and *The Friend,* he also knew Wordsworth (who read to him from the manuscript of *The Prelude*), Carlyle, Kant, and Cousin, and he moved with the philosophical and psychological currents of the times. He saw religion and poetry as two edges of the same tool, which "pierces beneath the exterior of life to the depths of the soul, and which lays open its mysterious workings, borrowing from the whole outward creation fresh images and correspondences, with which to illuminate the secrets of the world within us." His essay on the uses of reason (in the Romantic sense) in religion provides a preview of a central principle of the Transcendentalist philosophy. Text: *Works,* 1848 edition, Volume IV.

Christianity is a Rational religion. Were it not so, I should be ashamed to profess it. I am aware that it is the fashion with some to decry reason, and to set up revelation as an opposite authority. This error though countenanced by good men, and honestly maintained for the defence of the Christian cause, ought to be earnestly withstood; for it virtually surrenders our religion into the hands of the unbeliever. It saps the foundation to strengthen the building. It places our religion in hostility to human nature, and gives to its adversaries the credit of vindicating the rights and noblest powers of the mind.

We must never forget that our rational nature is the greatest gift of God. For this we owe him our chief gratitude. It is a greater gift than any outward aid or benefaction, and no doctrine which degrades it can come from its Author. The developement of it is the end of our being. Revelation is but a means, and is designed to concur with nature, providence, and God's spirit, in carrying forward reason to its perfection. I glory in Christianity because it enlarges, invigorates, exalts my rational nature. If I could not be a Christian without ceasing to be rational, I should not hesitate as to my choice. I feel myself bound to sacrifice to Christianity property, reputation, life; but I ought not to sacrifice to any religion, that reason which lifts me above the brute and constitutes me a man. I can conceive no sacrilege greater than to prostrate or renounce the highest faculty which we have derived from God. In so doing we should offer violence to the divinity within us. Christianity wages no war with reason, but is one with it, and is given to be its helper and friend.

I wish, in the present discourse, to illustrate and confirm the views now given. My remarks will be arranged under two heads. I propose, first, to show that Christianity is founded on, and supposes, the authority of reason, and cannot therefore oppose it without subverting itself. My object in this part of the discourse will be to expose the error of those who hope to serve revelation by disparaging reason. ° ° ° —Before I begin, let me observe that this discussion, from the nature of the subject, must assume occasionally an abstract form, and will demand serious attention. I am to speak of Reason, the chief faculty of the mind; and no simplicity of language in treating such a topic can exempt the hearer from the necessity of patient effort of thought.

I am to begin with showing that the Christian revelation is founded on the authority of reason, and consequently cannot oppose it; and here it may be proper to settle the meaning of the word Reason. One of the most important steps towards the truth is to determine the import of terms. Very often fierce controversies have sprung from obscurity of language, and the parties, on explaining themselves, have discovered that they have been spending their strength in a war of words. What, then, is reason?

The term Reason is used with so much latitude, that to fix its precise limits is not an easy task. In this respect it agrees with the other words which express the intellectual faculties. One idea, however, is always attached to it. All men understand by reason the highest faculty or energy of the mind. Without laboring for a philosophical definition that will comprehend all its exercises, I shall satisfy myself with pointing out two of its principal characteristics or functions.

First, it belongs to reason to comprehend Universal truths. This is among its most important offices. There are particular and there are universal truths. The last are the noblest, and the capacity of perceiving them is the distinction of intelligent beings; and these belong to reason. Let me give my meaning by some illustrations. I see a stone falling to the ground. This is a particular truth; but I do not stop here. I believe that not only this particular stone falls towards the earth, but that every particle of matter, in whatever world, tends, or, as is sometimes said, is attracted towards all other matter. Here is a universal truth, a principle extending to the whole material creation, and essential to its existence. This truth belongs to reason.—Again, I see a man producing some effect, a manufacture, a house. Here is a particular truth. But I am not only capable of seeing particular causes and effects; I am sure that every thing which begins to exist, no matter when or where, must have a cause, that no change ever has taken place or ever will take place without a cause. Here is a universal truth, something true here and everywhere, true now and through eternity; and this truth belongs to reason.—Again, I see with my eyes, I traverse with my hands, a limited space; but this is not all. I am sure, that, beyond the limits which my limbs or senses reach, there is an unbounded space; that, go where I will, an infinity will spread around me. Here is another universal truth, and this belongs to reason. The idea of Infinity is indeed one of the noblest conceptions of this faculty.—Again, I see a man conferring a good on another. Here is a particular truth or perception. But my mind is not confined to this. I see and feel that it is right for all intelligent beings, exist when or where they may, to do good, and wrong for them to seek the misery of others. Here is a universal truth, a law extending from God to the lowest human being; and this belongs to reason. I trust I have conveyed to you my views in regard to the first characteristic of this highest power of the soul. Its office is to discern universal truths, great and eternal principles. But it does not stop here. Reason is also exercised in applying these universal truths to particular cases, beings, events. For example, reason teaches me, as we have seen, that all changes without exception require a cause; and in conformity to this principle, it prompts me to seek the particular causes of the endless changes and appearances which fall under my observation. Thus reason is perpetually at work on the ideas furnished us by the senses, by consciousness, by memory, associating them with its own great truths, or investing them with its own universality.

I now proceed to the second function of reason, which is indeed akin to the first. Reason is the power which tends, and is perpetually striving, to reduce our various thoughts to Unity or Consistency. Perhaps the most fundamental conviction of reason is, that all truths agree together; that inconsistency is the mark of error. Its intensest, most earnest effort is to bring concord into the intellect, to reconcile what seem to be clashing views. On the observation of a new fact, reason strives to incorporate it with former knowledge. It can allow nothing to stand separate in the mind. It labors to bring together scattered truths, and to give them the strength and beauty of a vital order. Its end and delight is harmony. It is shocked by an inconsistency in belief, just as a fine ear is wounded by a discord. It carries within itself an instinctive consciousness, that all things which exist are intimately bound together; and it cannot rest until it has connected whatever we witness with the infinite whole. Reason, according to this view, is the most glorious form or exercise of the intellectual nature. It corresponds to the unity of God and the universe, and seeks to make the soul the image and mirror of this sublime unity.

I have thus given my views of reason; but, to prevent all perversion, before I proceed to the main discussion, let me offer a word or two more of explanation. In this discourse, when I speak of the accordance of revelation with reason, I suppose this faculty to be used deliberately, conscientiously, and with the love of truth. Men often baptize with the name of reason their prejudices, unexamined notions, or opinions adopted through interest, pride, or other unworthy biasses. It is not uncommon to hear those who sacrifice the plainest dictates of the rational nature to impulse and passion, setting themselves up as oracles of reason. Now when I say revelation must accord with reason, I do not mean by the term the corrupt and superficial opinions of men who have betrayed and debased their rational powers. I mean reason, calmly, honestly exercised for the acquisition of truth and the invigoration of virtue.

After these explanations, I proceed to the discussion of the two leading principles to which this Discourse is devoted.

First, I am to show that revelation is founded on the authority of reason, and cannot therefore oppose or disparage it without subverting itself. Let me state a few of the considerations which convince me of the truth of this position. The first is, that reason alone makes us capable of receiving a revelation. It must previously exist and operate, or we should be wholly unprepared for the communications of Christ. Revelation, then, is built on reason. You will see the truth of these remarks if you will consider to whom revelation is sent. Why is it given to men rather than to brutes? Why have not God's messengers gone to the fields to proclaim his glad tidings to bird and beast? The answer is obvious. These want reason; and, wanting this, they have no capacity or preparation for revealed truth. And not only would revelation be lost on the brute; let it speak to the child, before his rational faculties have been awakened, and before some ideas of duty and his own nature have been developed, and it might as well speak to a stone. Reason is the preparation and ground of revelation.

This truth will be still more obvious, if we consider, not only to whom, but in what way, the Christian revelation is communicated. How is it conveyed? In words. Did it make these words? No. They were in use ages before its birth. Again I ask, Did it make the ideas or thoughts which these words express? No. If the hearers of Jesus had not previously attached ideas to the terms which he employed, they could not have received his meaning. He might as well have spoken to them in a foreign tongue. Thus the ideas which enter into Christianity subsisted before. They were ideas of reason; so that to this faculty revelation owes the materials of which it is composed.

Revelation, we must remember, is not our earliest teacher. Man is not born with the single power of reading God's word, and sent immediately to that guide. His eyes open first on another volume, that of the creation. Long before he can read the Bible, he looks round on the earth and sky. He reads the countenances of his friends, and hears and understands their voices. He looks, too, by degrees within himself, and acquires some ideas of his own soul. Thus his first school is that of nature and reason, and this is necessary to prepare him for a communication from Heaven. Revelation does not find the mind a blank, a void, prepared to receive unresistingly whatever may be offered; but finds it in possession of various knowledge from nature and experience, and, still more, in possession of great principles, fundamental truths, moral ideas, which are derived from itself, and which are the germs of all its future improvement. This last view is peculiarly important. The mind does not receive every thing from abroad. Its great ideas arise from itself, and by those native lights it reads and comprehends the volumes of nature and revelation. We speak, indeed, of nature and revelation as making known to us an intelligent First Cause; but the ideas of intelligence and causation we derive originally from our own nature. The elements of the idea of God we gather from ourselves. Power, wisdom, love, virtue, beauty, and happiness, words which contain all that is glorious in the universe and interesting in our existence, express attributes of the mind, and are understood by us only through consciousness. It is true, these ideas or principles of reason are often obscured by thick clouds, and mingled with many and deplorable errors. Still they are never lost. Christianity recognises them, is built on them, and needs them as its interpreters. If an illustration of these views be required, I would point you to what may be called the most fundamental idea of religion. I mean the idea of right, of duty. Do we derive this originally and wholly from sacred books? Has not every human being, whether born within or beyond the bounds of revelation, a sense of the distinction between right and wrong? Is there not an earlier voice than revelation, approving or rebuking men according to their deeds? In barbarous ages is not conscience heard? And does it not grow more articulate with the progress of society? Christianity does not create, but presupposes the idea of duty; and the same may be said of other great convictions. Revelation, then, does not stand alone, nor is it addressed to a blank and passive mind. It was meant to be a joint worker with other teachers, with nature, with Providence, with conscience, with our rational powers; and as these all are given us by God, they cannot differ from each other. God must agree with himself. He has but one voice. It is man who speaks with jarring tongues. Nothing but harmony can come from the Creator; and, accordingly, a religion claiming to be from God, can give no surer proof of falsehood than by contradicting those previous truths which God is teaching by our very nature. We have thus seen that reason prepares us for a divine communication, and that it furnishes the ideas or materials of which revelation consists. This is my first consideration.

I proceed to a second. I affirm, then, that revelation rests on the authority of reason, because to this faculty it submits the evidences of its truth, and nothing but the approving sentence of reason binds us to receive and obey it. This is a very weighty consideration. Christianity, in placing itself before the tribunal of reason and in resting its claims on the sanction of this faculty, is one of the chief witnesses to the authority and dignity of our rational nature. That I have ascribed to this faculty its true and proper office, may be easily made to appear. I take the New Testament in hand, and on what ground do I receive its truths as divine? I see nothing on its pages but the same letters in which other books are written. No miraculous voice from Heaven assures me that it is God's word, nor does any mysterious voice within my soul command me to believe the supernatural works of Christ. How, then, shall I

settle the question of the origin of this religion? I must examine it by the same rational faculties by which other subjects are tried. I must ask what are its evidences, and I must lay them before reason, the only power by which evidence can be weighed. I have not a distinct faculty given me for judging a revelation. I have not two understandings, one for inquiring into God's word and another into his works. As with the same bodily eye I now look on the earth, now on the heavens, so with the same power of reason I examine now nature, now revelation. Reason must collect and weigh the various proofs of Christianity. It must especially compare this system with those great moral convictions, which are written by the finger of God on the heart, and which make man a law to himself. A religion subverting these, it must not hesitate to reject, be its evidences what they may. A religion, for example, commanding us to hate and injure society, reason must instantly discard, without even waiting to examine its proofs. From these views we learn, not only that it is the province of reason to judge of the truth of Christianity, but, what is still more important, that the rules or tests by which it judges are of its own dictation. The laws which it applies in this case have their origin in itself. No one will pretend, that revelation can prescribe the principles by which the question of its own truth should be settled; for, until proved to be true, it has no authority. Reason must prescribe the tests or standards, to which a professed communication from God should be referred; and among these none are more important than that moral law, which belongs to the very essence, and is the deepest conviction, of the rational nature. Revelation, then, rests on reason, and in opposing it, would act for its own destruction.

I have given two views. I have shown that revelation draws its ideas or materials from reason, and that it appeals to this power as the judge of its truth. I now assert, thirdly, that it rests on the authority of reason, because it needs and expects this faculty to be its interpreter, and without this aid would be worse than useless. How is the right of interpretation, the real meaning, of Scriptures to be ascertained? I answer, By reason. I know of no process by which the true sense of the New Testament is to pass from the page into my mind without the use of my rational faculties. It will not be pretended that this book is so exceedingly plain, its words so easy, its sentences so short, its meaning so exposed on the surface, that the whole truth may be received in a moment and without any intellectual effort. There is no such miraculous simplicity in the Scriptures. In truth, no book can be written so simply as to need no exercise of reason. Almost every word has more than one meaning, and judgment is required to select the particular sense intended by the writer. Of all books, perhaps the Scriptures need most the use of reason for their just interpretation; and this, not from any imperfection, but from the strength, boldness, and figurative character of their style, and from the distance of the time when they were written. I open the New Testament and my eye lights on this passage; "If thy hand offend thee, cut it off and cast it from thee." Is this language to be interpreted in its plainest and most obvious sense? Then I must mutilate my body, and become a suicide. I look again, and I find Jesus using these words to the Jews; "Fill ye up the measure of your iniquities." Am I to interpret this according to the letter, or the first ideas which it suggests? Then Jesus commanded his hearers to steep themselves in crime, and was himself a minister of sin. It is only by a deliberate use of reason, that we can penetrate beneath the figurative, hyperbolical, and often obscure style of the New Testament, to the real meaning. Let me go to the Bible, dismissing my reason and taking the first impression which the words convey, and there is no absurdity, however gross, into which I shall not fall. I shall ascribe a limited body to God, and unbounded knowledge to man, for I read of God having limbs, and of man knowing all things. Nothing is plainer, than that I must compare passage with passage, and limit one by another, and especially limit all by those plain and universal principles of reason, which are called common sense, or I shall make revelation the patron of every folly and vice. So essential is reason to the interpretation of the Christian records. Revelation rests upon its authority. Can it then oppose it, or teach us to hold it in light esteem?

I have now furnished the proofs of my first position, that revelation is founded on reason; and in discussing this, I have wished not only to support the main doctrine, but to teach you to reverence, more perhaps than you have done, your rational nature. This has been decried by theologians, until men have ceased to feel its sacredness and dignity. It ought to be regarded as God's greatest gift. It is his image within us. To renounce it would be to offer a cruel violence to ourselves, to take our place among the brutes. ° ° °

FROM *The Character and Writings of Fenelon*

Channing did not consider himself to be either author or critic, but in the course of his work as editor, lecturer, and essayist he produced a substantial amount of literary criticism. A follower of Lord Kames, Blair, Alison, and the other eighteenth-century arbiters of taste who dominated American critical theory, he wrote essays on Milton, Shakespeare, Napoleon, Fénelon, and others that attracted attention at home and abroad. Channing's critical theories derived from his philosophical and theological position; they were, as William Hazlitt said, "pulpit criticisms," and as such were typical of the religious-centered literary ideas of his time and place. A moralistic critic, he conceived of great literature as an expression of "the best views of the best intellects," which helped men to interpret what they saw and experienced. Books, he wrote, "open and fix our eyes upon what passes without and within." The function of art, he said in his essay on Milton (1826), is "to awaken kindred virtue and greatness in other souls," and the duty of the artist "to stir up our own and others' breasts to an exhilarating pursuit of high and evergrowing attainments in intellect and virtues." That religion and literature, in his opinion, suffered divorcement in the intellectual and literary circles of his age, seemed to him a matter of urgent importance. Text: *Works*, 1848 edition, Volume I.

[Religion and Literature]

It is, we fear, an unquestionable fact, that religion, considered as an intellectual subject, is in a great measure left to a particular body of men, as a professional concern; and the fact is as much to be wondered at as deplored. It is wonderful that any mind, and especially a superior one, should not see in religion the highest object of thought. It is wonderful that the infinite God, the noblest theme of the universe, should be considered as a monopoly of professed theologians; that a subject so vast, awful, and exalting, as our relation to the Divinity, should be left to technical men, to be handled so much for sectarian purposes. Religion is the property and dearest interest of the human race. Every man has an equal concern in it. It should be approached with an independence on human authority. It should be rescued from all the factions, which have seized upon it as their particular possession. Men of the highest intellect should feel, that, if there be a God, then his character and our relation to him throw all other subjects into obscurity, and that the intellect, if not consecrated to him, can never attain its true use, its full dimensions, and its proper happiness. Religion, if it be true, is central truth, and all knowledge, which is not gathered round it, and quickened and illuminated by it, is hardly worthy the name. To this great theme we would summon all orders of mind, the scholar, the statesman, the student of nature, and the observer of life. It is a subject to which every faculty and every acquisition may pay tribute, which may receive aids and lights from the accuracy of the logician, from the penetrating spirit of philosophy, from the intuitions of genius, from the researches of history, from the science of the mind, from physical science, from every branch of criticism, and, though last not least, from the spontaneous suggestions and the moral aspirations of pure but unlettered men.

It is a fact which shocks us, and which shows the degraded state of religion, that not a few superior minds look down upon it as a subject beneath their investigation. Though allied with all knowledge, and especially with that of human nature and human duty, it is regarded as a separate and inferior study, particularly fitted to the gloom of a convent, and the seclusion of a minister. Religion is still confounded, in many and in gifted minds, with the jargon of monks, and the subtilties and strifes of theologians. It is thought a mystery, which, far from coalescing, wars with our other knowledge. It is never ranked with the sciences which expand and adorn the mind. It is regarded as a method of escaping future ruin, not as a vivifying truth through which the intellect and heart are alike to be invigorated and enlarged. Its bearing on the great objects of thought and the great interests of life is hardly suspected. This degradation of religion into a technical study, this disjunction of it from morals, from philosophy, from the various objects of liberal research, has done it infinite injury, has checked its progress, has perpetuated errors which gathered round it in times of barbarism and ignorance, has made it a mark for the sophistry and ridicule of the licentious, and has infused a lurking skepticism into many powerful understandings. Nor has religion suffered alone. The whole mind is darkened by the obscuration of this its central light. Its reasonings and judgments become unstable through want of this foundation to rest upon. Religion is to the whole sphere of truth, what God is to the universe, and in dethroning it, or confining it to a narrow range, we commit very much such an injury on the soul, as the universe would suffer, were the Infinite Being to abandon it, or to contract his energy to a small province of his creation.

The injury done to literature by divorcing it from religion is a topic worthy of separate discussion. Literature has thus lost power and permanent interest. It has become, in a great measure, superficial, an image of transient modes of thought and of arbitrary forms of life, not the organ and expression of immutable truth, and of deep workings of the soul. We beg not to be misunderstood. We have no desire that literature should confine itself wholly or chiefly to religious topics, and we hardly know a greater calamity which it could incur, than by degenerating into religious cant. Next to profaneness, we dread the affectation of piety and the mechanical repetition of sacred phraseology. We only lament, that literature has so generally been the product and utterance of minds, which have not lived, thought, and written, under the light of a rational and sublime faith. Severed from this, it wants the principle of immortality. We do not speak lightly when we say, that all works of the intellect, which have not in some measure been quickened by the spirit of religion, are doomed to perish or to lose their power; and that genius is preparing for itself a sepulchre, when it disjoins itself from the Universal Mind. Religion is not always to remain in its present dark, depressed condition. Already there are signs of a brighter day. It begins to be viewed more generously. It is gradually attracting to itself superior understandings. It is rising from the low rank of a professional, technical study, and asserting its supremacy among the objects of the mind. A new era, we trust, is opening upon the world, and all literature will feel its power. In proportion as the true and sublime conception of God shall unfold itself in the soul, and shall become there a central sun, shedding its beams on all objects of thought, there will be a want of sympathy with all works which have not been quickened by this heavenly influence. It will be felt that the poet has known little of nature, that he has seen it only under clouds, if he have not seen it under this celestial light. It will be felt, that man, the great subject of literature, when viewed in separation from his Maker and his end, can be as little understood and portrayed, as a plant torn from the soil in which it grew, and cut off from communication with the clouds and sun.

We are aware that objections will spring up to the doctrine, that all literature should be produced under the influence of religion. We shall be told, that in this way literature will lose all variety and spirit, that a monotonous and solemn hue will spread itself over writing, and that a library will have the air of a tomb. We do not wonder at this fear. Religion has certainly been accustomed to speak in sepulchral tones, and to wear any aspect but a bright and glowing one. It has lost its free and various movement. But let us not ascribe to its nature, what has befallen it from adverse circumstances. The truth is, that religion, justly viewed, surpasses all other principles, in giving a free and manifold action to the mind. It recognises in every faculty and sentiment the workmanship of God, and assigns a sphere of agency to each. It takes our whole nature under its guardianship, and with a parental love ministers to its inferior as well as higher gratifications. False religion mutilates the soul, sees evil in our innocent sensibilities, and rules with a tyrant's frown and rod. True religion is a mild and lawful sovereign, governing to protect, to give strength, to unfold all our inward resources. We believe, that, under its influence, literature is to pass its present limits, and to put itself forth in original forms of composition. Religion is of all principles most fruitful, multiform, and unconfined. It is sympathy with that Being, who seems to delight in diversifying the modes of his agency, and the products of his wisdom and power. It does not chain us to a few essential duties, or express itself in a few unchanging modes of writing. It has the liberality and munificence of nature, which not only produces the necessary root and grain, but pours forth fruits and flowers. It has the variety and bold contrasts of nature, which, at the foot of the awful mountain, scoops out the freshest, sweetest valleys, and embosoms, in the wild, troubled ocean, islands, whose vernal airs, and loveliness, and teeming fruitfulness, almost breathe the joys of Paradise. Religion will accomplish for literature what it most needs; that is, will give it depth, at the same time that it heightens its grace and beauty. The union of these attributes is most to be desired. Our literature is lamentably superficial, and to some the beautiful and the superficial even seem to be naturally conjoined. Let not beauty be so wronged. It resides chiefly in profound thoughts and feelings. It overflows chiefly in the writings of poets, gifted with a sublime and piercing vision. A beautiful literature springs from the depth and fulness of intellectual and moral life, from an energy of thought and feeling, to which nothing, as we believe, ministers so largely as enlightened religion.

So far from a monotonous solemnity overspreading literature in consequence of the all-pervading influence of religion, we believe, that the sportive and comic forms of composition, instead of being abandoned, will only be refined and improved. We know that these are supposed to be frowned upon by piety; but they have their root in the constitution which God has given us, and ought not therefore to be indiscriminately condemned. The propensity to wit and laughter does indeed, through excessive indulgence, often issue in a character of heartless levity, low mimicry, or unfeeling ridicule. It often seeks gratification in regions of impurity, throws a gayety round vice, and sometimes even pours contempt on virtue. But, though often and mournfully perverted, it is still a gift of God, and may and ought to minister, not only to innocent pleasure, but to the intellect and the heart. Man was made for relaxation as truly as for labor; and by a law of his nature, which has not received the attention it deserves, he finds perhaps no relaxation so restorative, as that in which he reverts to his childhood, seems to forget his wisdom, leaves the imagination to exhilarate itself by sportive inventions, talks of amusing incongruities in conduct and events, smiles at the innocent eccentricities and odd mistakes of those whom he most esteems, allows himself in arch allusions or kind-

hearted satire, and transports himself into a world of ludicrous combinations. We have said, that, on these occasions, the mind seems to put off its wisdom; but the truth is, that, in a pure mind, wisdom retreats, if we may so say, to its centre, and there, unseen, keeps guard over this transient folly, draws delicate lines which are never to be passed in the freest moments, and, like a judicious parent watching the sports of childhood, preserves a stainless innocence of soul in the very exuberance of gayety. This combination of moral power with wit and humor, with comic conceptions and irrepressible laughter, this union of mirth and virtue, belongs to an advanced stage of the character; and we believe, that, in proportion to the diffusion of an enlightened religion, this action of the mind will increase, and will overflow in compositions, which, joining innocence to sportiveness, will communicate unmixed delight. Religion is not at variance with occasional mirth. In the same character, the solemn thought and the sublime emotions of the improved Christian, may be joined with the unanxious freedom, buoyancy, and gayety of early years.

We will add but one more illustration of our views. We believe, that the union of religion with genius will favor that species of composition to which it may seem at first to be least propitious. We refer to that department of literature, which has for its object the delineation of the stronger and more terrible and guilty passions. Strange as it may appear, these gloomy and appalling features of our nature may be best comprehended and portrayed by the purest and noblest minds. The common idea is, that overwhelming emotions, the more they are experienced, can the more effectually be described. We have one strong presumption against this doctrine. Tradition leads us to believe, that Shakespeare, though he painted so faithfully and fearfully the storms of passion, was a calm and cheerful man. The passions are too engrossed by their objects to meditate on themselves; and none are more ignorant of their growth and subtile workings, than their own victims. Nothing reveals to us the secrets of our own souls like religion; and in disclosing to us, in ourselves, the tendency of passion to absorb every energy, and to spread its hues over every thought, it gives us a key to all souls; for, in all, human nature is essentially one, having the same spiritual elements, and the same grand features. ° ° °

1829

The Romantic Movement

YOUTH, SAID EMERSON, is romantic. It was a circumstance of far-reaching implications for American literature that when our writers were starting to create an independent literary culture, Europe was communicating romantic enthusiasms and America was full of youthful vigor. The first settlers had brought with them from the Old World a mature culture, and later colonials assimilated their American experiences within an intellectual and literary context that was primarily a European import. Now, with political independence won by revolution, and with national confidence and self-consciousness enhanced by the War of 1812, Americans were ready to shape and express a civilization that should be uniquely that of a new people on the face of the earth.

The American Scene

The environment of our writers from Irving to Whitman was a yeasty one. Physical America itself was growing at a spectacular rate. In 1820 the people of the United States numbered 9,638,000; in 1860 they had increased to 31,443,000, owing partly to immigration. Even more amazing was the expansion in territory. By 1821, as many as eleven states had been added to the original thirteen. From New England and the Upper South pioneers moved into the rich valley of the Ohio and Mississippi. Chicago, in 1833, had a population of only 350, but by 1870 about 300,000. When California was annexed from Mexico in 1848, wide open spaces beckoned all the way to the Pacific.

East and Middle West were linked by the Erie Canal, and then came the age of railroads—the Baltimore and Ohio, the Pennsylvania, and others, till by 1860 the iron rails covered 30,000 miles. The general aspect of the country was still agricultural; yet by 1860 the value of its manufactures equaled that of its crops. Sectional differences were so great that, as one historian has said, the civilizations of North and South were as wide apart as those of

Canada and Mexico today. The South was now the Cotton Kingdom, with white fields, black slaves, and an attachment to Sir Walter Scott, in whose novels, as S. E. Morison puts it, "the cotton lord and his lady found a romantic mirror of their life and ideals." But it was the democratic West—the land of the advancing frontier—that seemed the America of the future. "Europe," said Emerson, "stretches to the Alleghenies; America lies beyond." The winning of the West was in a sense a romanticism of action, reaching its climax in the discovery of gold in California, from which the fever of sudden riches spread rapidly to the East and even to Europe. The speed with which the West was effectively settled is a main feature of this period. In vain did John Quincy Adams, like Jefferson before him, wish to avoid the evils of a too rapid expansion by preserving the Western lands for a planned development over centuries.

And yet in a very real sense the America of the future was not the agricultural West, but the industrial East. Even before the Civil War, the pattern of a business civilization was well established. The Industrial Revolution arrived in a land as rich in resources as it was vast in extent, a land with a *laissez-faire* economy that made the competition for success and wealth unbridled. A succession of newly invented machines was the means to a tremendous increase in productivity and trade. By 1840 the United States had 1200 cotton textile factories, chiefly in New England, and the pig-iron industry, centered in eastern Pennsylvania, raised its production tenfold in the forty years preceding 1850. The crops of the Middle West were pouring east in ever-growing volume. Assuredly America was the land of opportunity.

Was it also, in Washington Irving's phrase, the "Land of the Almighty Dollar"? If so, it was hardly because Americans were peculiarly sinful in their love of riches, for better examples of unrestrained materialism and its attendant abuses could be found in industrial England. But there is no question that wealth seemed astonishingly easy to attain. "In the seething America of the 1830's and 1840's," says a prominent historian, "both immigrant and old American felt that, with just a little luck, fortune might be waiting for him around the corner. Hadn't Astor made $20,000,000, Girard left $6,000,000, while men in every community were evidently getting rich on a large if less spectacular scale?" There had always, of course, been a materialistic as well as an idealistic aspect to the American dream.

At any rate, Americans pursued business with abandon. A traveler described New York about 1840 as "the busiest community that any man could desire to live in. In the streets all is hurry and bustle; the very carts, instead of being drawn by horses at a walking pace, are often met at a gallop, and always in a brisk trot. The whole of the population seen in the streets seems to enjoy this bustle, and add to it by their own rapid pace." Travelers generally frowned upon this American speed, as in the eighteenth century they had deplored American indolence. Visitors from England, in the East, looked in vain for public parks, games and sports, or walking in the country. As work had been a virtue among the Puritans, so now the making of money was conceived as a patriotic duty, a contribution to the rapid development of the country. A leisure class seemed inappropriate when the man of inherited wealth, as an observer tells us, saw "nobody about him not engaged in business." Cultural activities were commonly disparaged because they reduced the speed of money-making; literature and music were more suitable for women. Everything seemed to conspire to encourage a type of businessman full of drive and zest in his vocation but otherwise empty. A crass plutocracy was taking the place of the old aristocracy.

And the prizes were open to all. The eighteenth century had stressed the "free" in the concept of "free and equal," especially the free, rational mind, and the Revolution brought political freedom. The early national period was zealous not only for the "free" but for the "equal." Equality was dramatized by the Jacksonian upheaval. From this time dates the custom of telling the American boy that someday he may be President of the United States. In many ways the middle-class leadership that took the place of the aristocracy flattered and served the common man, the laborer and farmer. It is significant that the Whig party in 1840 deemed it wise to ignore the patrician origin of William Henry Harrison and to picture him, in the campaign, as seated before a log cabin with a barrel of hard cider. State after state extended the ballot, and an effective public school system was undertaken in earnest. There were many workers for humanitarian reforms: pris-

on reform, temperance, the granting of women's rights, the abolition of slavery, the last of which increasingly cast the others in shadow. To the old conservative families of the East and South, it seemed that they were living out of context in this century of the common man, not to say of commonness. But there were also patricians like Ralph Waldo Emerson who accepted the changing world and welcomed "the near, the low, the common."

While the prosperous were growing in wealth and power and the common man was comfortable and could hope to be prosperous, Americans became brash and boastful. They scorned the Old World monarchies far overseas and feared no nation under the sun. Seeing the rapid progress of the country in material power, in science and technology, apparently in every department of life, they readily transformed the eighteenth-century idea of progress into a religion, and envisaged for their land a resplendent future. The only dark cloud in sight was slavery, but 99 per cent of Northern businessmen, it has been estimated, believed that if the North held its tongue and kept its fingers out, the problem would somehow solve itself without ruining business and breaking up the Union.

The spirit of nationalism throve along with this zest for business expansion and optimism over the future. In America as in Europe, the cosmopolitanism of the eighteenth century was followed by the nationalism of the nineteenth. It emerged symbolically during the War of 1812 in the guise of "Uncle Sam," and was expressed in the patriotic gaiety and bombastic oratory of Fourth of July celebrations. In a mood we would now call isolationist, America turned its back on the Atlantic and in the 1820's announced the Monroe Doctrine that the Americas were for Americans. By the middle of the century the slogan "Manifest Destiny" suggested rather that the Americas were for the Americans of the United States. In their patriotic zeal and their appetite for expansion, many people came to feel that the great American democracy should include territories that nature seemed to have intended for her: Canada, the Caribbean, Mexico, Central America, the islands of the Pacific.

Thus an expansive self-reliance showed itself on the national as on the individual level. It showed itself also, between these two extremes, on the level of the section and the state. A section of the United States, as the historian Turner put it, is a "potential nation," or "the faint image of a European nation." It is a part of our national domain conscious of its own tradition, material interests, social ideals, as different from those of other sections. Before the Civil War the country had four sections: East (the old North), South, Middle West, and Far West. The secession of the South was a violent assertion of its self-reliance. There was a similar sense of unity and pride within the individual state. It was not so much the South that seceded as one southern state after another. The great war that followed substantially settled the relation of states' rights, sectional interests, and the Union.

Despite young America's growing absorption in business and material progress, an adequate public for the new literary movement was prepared in a number of ways. The romantic impulse from Europe might well have proved fruitless if there had not been strong American roots favoring romanticism. Some of them have already been indicated. One was America's patriotic nationalism, crude but capable of idealistic refinement. Another was its democratic society, with far more liberty, equality, and fraternity than in the aristocratic eighteenth century. Another was the emphasis on the individual man, the self-reliant man, encouraged both by a *laissez-faire* economy and the individualism of the frontier. Another was the mood of optimism natural in a land of opportunity.

But the most vital preparation for such writers as Emerson, Thoreau, Hawthorne, Melville, and Whitman was a religious spirit that goes back to the men and women who settled America. Puritans, Quakers, Anglicans and others had left in the American mind an enduring reverence and a sensitive conscience. The worldliness and rationalism of the age of Franklin could bank the old religious fires, but not quench them. In the early nineteenth century, revivals flamed up afresh; more important perhaps was a piety expressed in day-by-day observances. As we read in an autobiography by S. G. Goodrich, "In most families the first exercise of the morning was reading the Bible, followed by prayer, at which all were assembled, including the servants and helpers of the kitchen and the farm." Calvinists were still far from extinct, especially in the country, while the Unitarians were well established among the upper classes in cities and town. If Unitarianism was related on one side to Locke and eighteenth-century rationalism, it was related on the other to Emerson and the Transcendentalist movement. Already in the words of William Ellery Channing, the great leader of the Unitarians, one can see the thoughts of Emerson and his contemporaries emerging. "We must start in religion," Channing had said, "from our own souls. In these is the fountain of all divine truth. . . . The soul is the spring of our knowledge of God."

Often closely connected with these various types of religious devotion was a hunger of the mind, shown by the Lyceum and other schemes for popular lectures, which spread over the country. In 1834, when this cultural movement was at its height, the local lyceums totaled about 3,000. A favorite speaker was Ralph Waldo Emerson, whose tours took him even beyond the Mississippi in midwinter. Meanwhile, in publications, literary taste had long been nourished, after a fashion, by sentimental and Gothic novels and dramas. Poor though they were in quality, they opened the way for something better by stirring sympathetic feelings and an appetite for the strange and mysterious.

To preserve what was strong in the spiritual and imaginative background, to deepen what was shallow, to refine and diversify what was crude and over-simple, to transform what was faintly felt into a whole new vision of life and art—this was to be the task of the literary artists of the Romantic Movement.

The Romantic Revolt

Since the closing years of the eighteenth century, the more sensitive minds in America as in Europe, had become increasingly less comfortable in the world of ideas established so long ago by Newton, Locke, and Pope. They were profoundly dissatisfied with a rationalism and neoclassicism daily more remote from their experience. In the political realm there was no real problem, since the democratic ideas of the eighteenth century were still held valid, needing only fuller expression in theory and practice. But in the vast realm of thought and feeling concerning the deity, and nature, and human nature and destiny, and an art suited to a new outlook on life—here a tremendous change seemed called for.

Romanticism provided a new and more relevant set of affirmations, which may be summarized as follows. Man is something more than a thinking machine in a machine universe. We cannot be content with ideas clear and consistent at the expense of truth; something is always left out. Reality is too large and diverse, too vital and fluid, to be compassed by cool reason. Nor is common sense sufficient; it may be the way to wealth and easy living, but not to high thinking or deep feeling. The world we live in is not a dead machine, but rather a living, breathing being. God is not outside the universe, forgetting and forgotten, but in it and in us, an immanent presence. Man does not come into the world as a blank page to be written on, but as a spirit trailing clouds of glory. What then is a poet? Not a polite tailor in words, dressing nature and human nature to advantage, not a wit writing an artificial language for town and court, but a man speaking to all men of our common humanity and the experiences of the heart. He is an inspired bard, a creative, original genius expressing his innermost self, which is always taking new forms, reshaping its world in new visions of truth and beauty. As Josiah Royce was later to sum up the German romantic school, it proclaimed:

> Trust your genius; follow your noble heart; change your doctrine whenever your heart changes, and change your heart often. Such is the practical creed of the romanticists. The world, you see, is after all the world of the inner life.... The world is essentially what men of genius make it. Let us be men of genius, and make what we choose.

The secret of life, in the new outlook, lay not in the head but in the heart. Reality was to be sought not through conscious thought but through immediate intuitive perception: the kingdom of God was within. The head brought only doubt and barrenness; man must trust the heart—feeling—desire—the yearning for fulfillment—the Faustian spirit of aspiration. The human spirit had to be emancipated, freed from the tyranny of everything exterior to itself, whether this was a Calvinistic dogma of depravity, or a cramping rationalism, or a common-sense obsession with the pots and pans of practical life. Freed from these it might regain the sense of wonder, the bloom of the world; might dwell upon the strange, the mysterious, the miraculous, might hope for a revelation here and now.

The inner life and its needs, in the romantic view, are not identical in all men. If men are born free and equal in worth as human beings, they are also born different, no two of them alike. Each should therefore be true to himself, express his uniquely valuable self. It is hardly mere accident that the new words compounded with *self* in the nineteenth century were not often like the old *self-conceit, self-esteem, self-denial*, which now seemed unpleasant, but rather *self-expression, self-realization self-culture, self-help, self-reliance*, which seemed attractive.

The Romantic Movement was strikingly international. In America, as in all the major countries of Europe, it had native roots but was fertilized and brought to fruition by foreign influences. Each country sought a national culture, an organic expression of its special "genius." As a result, differing interests and emphases characterize the romanticisms of England, Germany, France, Spain, Russia, the United States. But the resemblances are at least equally obvious. National self-reliance did not mean isolationism of the mind. The thinkers, artists, and critics who led the way used suggestions wherever they found them, not only in native experience but in any land where a renewal was in progress. In France they looked largely to England, in England to Germany, in Germany to England, for ideas and attitudes, for visions of the good life, for the inspiration of imaginative art. In the United States they looked to many European countries, above all England and Germany, where the movement flourished about two decades earlier than in the New World.

In Germany they saw philosophy given a new start by Immanuel Kant, whose critiques, as they understood, had demolished the Age of Reason at its very foundations and made possible the erection of a new structure in harmony with man's high aspirations. Starting from Kant, Fichte had declared his "world-positing ego"—an inner spiritual activity which enables each individual to build his own world. Then came the poetic philosopher Schelling, with his idea, dear to many romanticists, that spirit within man is the same as spirit within nature. Along with the philosophers were fascinating literary figures: not only the towering Goethe—one of Emerson's "Representative Men"—but a whole Romantic School, bold and brilliant (Tieck, Novalis, the Schlegels, and others). Here, then, was a dazzling array of systematic thinkers and creative writers who had broken with the eighteenth century and at length carried the movement, as Carlyle said, to completion. It is true that Americans often knew them only slightly and understood them ill—much as Marx and Freud fared in the twentieth century. Yet at least they were convinced, by Coleridge and Carlyle, that Germany had led in a direction they wanted to go in their own way.

In England too they saw the old thought and literary art dissolved, the new taking form. If many were convinced that the core of the movement was in Germany, all American writers were naturally drawn to England by habit, sentiment, and language: what they found could be readily assimilated. Wordsworth illustrated for them a poetic sensibility expressed in simple language, profound in feeling and imagination, in contact with the spiritual "Presences" of Nature (instead of the deistic "absentee" Creator) and with the lives of common folk glorified by human dignity. Coleridge, for the Transcendentalists at any rate, made his impression chiefly through his prose writings, in which the new German philosophy and the tradition of Platonism were combined with religious earnestness. He seemed to validate the intuitive and imaginative powers of man that rationalism had so long neglected. And then there was the young romantic Carlyle, escaping from both Scottish Calvinism and the Age of Reason with the aid of his beloved Germans, exemplifying a hatred of artificiality and sham, a love of sincerity and wonder, an awareness of the Infinite, that vast reservoir of power upon which great men draw so much and lesser men too little.

Although Carlyle's *Sartor Resartus* was first published in book form in America, with a preface by his friend Emerson, oddly enough Emerson failed to mention him when, in 1840, he sketched the course of the new movement. "This love of the Infinite," he wrote in *The Dial*, ". . . this new love of the vast, always native in Germany, was imported into France by De Staël, appeared in England in Coleridge, Wordsworth, Byron, Shelley, . . . and finds a most genial climate in the American mind." Many other traits of European romanticism were acclimatized by American writers looking for incitement, doctrine, example. Not content merely to look from afar, many of them made the Atlantic crossing, in days when it was slow and uncomfortable, to see the Old World intimately with their own eyes. Of our thirteen chief writers, Irving to Whitman, only three did not know Europe at first hand. Clearly, the War of Independence did not end, among American intellectuals, the sense of an Atlantic community.

Literary Centers of American Romanticism

"Who reads an American book?" Sydney Smith's question in the *Edinburgh Review* of 1820 was painfully galling to Americans. They were, as Irving said, "a young people, necessarily an imitative one," but they were also sensitive and ambitious. They knew only too well how little they had written to merit British approbation in the two hundred years since the Plymouth plantation, or in the thirty-seven years since the recognition of the American Republic. Yet in fact a national literature was beginning in the city of New York at this very time, as witness *The Sketch Book* by Irving in 1819-20 and *The Spy* by Cooper in 1821. Bryant was soon to join them.

These three early romantics, born in the eighteenth century, did most of their best work during the years 1810–35. The genial pen of Irving, schooled in neoclassic prose, made the picturesque past of Europe and America live. Cooper, while no stylist, could tell a story and describe graphically the forest frontier with its rather too noble Indians. Bryant, assimilating the English pre-romantics and Wordsworth, wrote, with poetic dignity and breadth, of nature and death. With these three "Knickerbocker" writers were associated others prominent in their day but now generally forgotten.

Most of the Knickerbocker writers were drawn to New York by advantages it offered the man of letters. Intent though the new metropolis was on commercial enterprise, its wealth made for cultural advance, for publishing houses, magazines, and newspapers (including the *Evening Post* long edited by Bryant). In 1820 the city's population was 123,000; by 1840 it was 312,000. Early in the century it had the air of a country town, with half-built streets—a "hobbledehoy metropolis" Cooper called it. As seen by Charles Dickens in 1842, it was still a straggling city, low and flat, without plumbing, its waterfront bristling with masts, its streets roamed by scavenger hogs; but it also had many stately residences richly furnished and adorned with silverware and oil portraits. Old families, Dutch and English, saw the cherished past fading as the *nouveau riche* took charge. The Hudson Valley market-town was becoming the urban symbol of a fast-moving young America devoted to commerce, industry, and finance.

It is a far cry from the solid materialism of New York to the airy idealism of Concord. The place was only a village, one of thousands in the nation, yet in it was a stir of mind and spirit that affected American life and letters for decades. Less than twenty miles from Boston, Concord was a community of 2,000 when Thoreau was born there—he was the only native in the literary group. The village was on a quietly gliding stream, bordered by dwarf willows and wild grape vines (whence the cultivated Concord grape). Meadows led to uplands and small lakes called ponds. Walden Pond, where Emerson owned woodland, was less than a two-mile walk from his house on the Lexington road at the edge of town. In another part of the rambling white village was the Old Manse, where Emerson and then Hawthorne lived for a time, close to the hallowed spot at the river where

> . . . once the embattled farmers stood
> And fired the shot heard round the world.

In this historic association Concord may symbolize the nationalistic impulse of American romanticism. But its roots go much deeper, to the time when Old Concord was the first inland plantation of the Massachusetts Colony and had as its first minister an ancestor of Emerson. To this pleasant little town, where plain living and high thinking had always seemed natural, Emerson came to reside in 1834, followed after some years by Bronson Alcott, Ellery Channing (poet nephew of the Unitarian leader), and Hawthorne. At times Margaret Fuller lived there, and at all times Concord-born Thoreau.

Before the Concord group began to form, Massachusetts had nothing comparable to the activity of the Connecticut Wits or the New York group of early romantics. In the whole state, Emerson remarked dryly in his journal, "from 1790 to 1820, there was not a book, a speech, a conversation, or a thought," and for the years after 1820 he could name only Channing, Webster, and Edward Everett. But the Transcendental movement, for which Concord was to be famous, was gathering, and by 1836 burst forth with vigor. In September 1836, Emerson, Alcott, George Ripley, F. H. Hedge and two others "chanced to confer together," as Hedge recalled, "on the state of current opinion in theology and philosophy, which we agreed in thinking very unsatisfactory . . . What we strongly felt was dissatisfaction with the reigning sensuous philosophy, dating from Locke, on which our Unitarian theology was based." Hedge went on to say that, thanks to the writings of Coleridge and Carlyle, "there was a promise in the air of a new era of intellectual life." Later meetings were attended at one time or another by Orestes Brownson, Margaret Fuller, Jones Very, Thoreau, and others of less interest today. These informal gatherings led to a quarterly magazine, *The Dial*, edited by Margaret Fuller and later Emerson, which ran for four years. They also helped to create an atmosphere that produced, in time, such social experiments as the "ideal" communities of Brook Farm and Fruitlands, as well as Thoreau's one-man experiment at Walden Pond.

What was this "Transcendentalism" that everyone was talking about in eastern Massachusetts and few professed to understand? Often described in a single phrase as "Romanticism on Puritan soil," the Transcendental movement was both a spiritual affirmation and an intellectual effort to restore—but in a vastly changed form—the high conception of the human soul and destiny in which Puritan New England had been schooled so long but which a rationalism based on the senses had overlaid with a burden become intolerable. It is a return to something like the flashes of divinity in the poems of Edward Taylor, or Jonathan Edwards' divine and supernatural light, or the Inner Light of the Quakers, or the exalted vision of Being in Plato and the Platonic tradition down to Coleridge. Vague and eclectic, Transcendentalism sought support not only in Kant and other Germans, but in Plato, Plotinus, the Hindu epics, and wherever the sages and the poets seemed to have touched a high reality. It differed from its New England background of Calvinism in celebrating not the omnipotence of God but the limitless possibilities of the self.

Two men of Concord perhaps offer the best way to grasp the significance of Transcendentalism, through their lives and their writings. Emerson was the leader of the movement, yet gathered no disciples. The only way to follow him was, paradoxically, to go one's own way, be wholly one's self and nowise an imitator. Emerson's own way led him to resign his ministry in the Unitarian church and to seek a strictly personal religion, together with a new vocation, that of writing and lecturing to further spiritual ends. In *Nature* he condensed with at least a show of system the doctrine and aspiration of the new movement. His address on the American Scholar was the definitive declaration of cultural independence. In a long stream of lectures and essays on well-nigh every aspect of life, he expressed the optimism, the confident self-reliance of the young Republic, preached the limitless capacities of man, of every man no matter how common. He encouraged the United States of that day to think out the implications of its democratic slogans, and to aim at an

achievement in the realm of the spirit equal to its achievement in material prosperity. In his desire to call forth the best that the self might exalt itself to, he magnified the spark of divinity that seems to touch man, till the self appeared to be God. It was only later, in essays not regarded as among the most "Emersonian," that he doubted this bold extension of romantic individualism, and limited it with a respect for actual experience and the concept of a Fate that reminds us that men are but human. On the other hand Emerson came to feel, through faith in progress, a new source of optimism. In general it may fairly be said of him, as James T. Adams has said, that "in no other author can we get so close to the whole of the American spirit."

An even more resolute man of Concord was Emerson's friend Thoreau. Austerely self-sufficient, nonconformist by principle and practice, he led his own life as completely as anyone could without wholly breaking away from society, as he demonstrated by his temporary hermitage at Walden Pond. He followed where the spirit led, had no other vocation, refused to let any deadening routine interfere with his effort to keep himself fresh and alert in his relation with himself and the world. What little he needed to sustain himself, unmarried, he easily earned by doing odd jobs. He loved nature without sentimentalism, sauntered to watch the seasons and entertain thoughts, often alone, often with a companion. In his best writing he described the life of nature sensitively, and examined the values of human existence with honesty and wit. "The transcendental philosophy," he said waggishly, "needs the leaven of humor to render it light and digestible." He inveighed against low aims, stupid conventions, and the meaningless pursuit of material prosperity. The scope of thought in which he lived is indicated well enough by an entry in his journal in 1851: "Perchance this window-seat in which we sit discoursing Transcendentalism, with only Germany and Greece stretching behind our minds, was made so deep because this was a few years ago a garrison-house," i.e., of the Puritans against the Indians. Germany and Greece represent Thoreau's concern with the European tradition, in what he considered its truest moments, from Homer down to his own contemporaries. At the same time he made the Puritan past of New England very real to himself, and persistently studied the Indians, since whatever was wild in nature or man had for him a fundamental value.

Viewed from the abodes of urbanity and scholarship in Boston and Cambridge, the Transcendentalists looked like eccentrics. Lowell pictured Thoreau as mainly an egotist with scant logic and no humor. And he found the group in general, at least its faddist fringe, simply comical:

Every form of intellectual and physical dyspepsia brought forth its gospel. . . . No brain but had its private maggot, which must have found pitiably short commons sometimes. Not a few impecunious zealots abjured the use of money (unless earned by other people), professing to live on the internal revenues of the spirit. Some had an assurance of instant millennium so soon as hooks and eyes should be substituted for buttons. . . . Many foreign revolutionists out of work added to the general misunderstanding their contribution of broken English in every most ingenious form of fracture.

Beside a passage like this we may extract a sentence from the privacy of Emerson's journal, where he speaks of Longfellow in his mansion at Cambridge. "If Socrates were here we could go and talk with him; but Longfellow we cannot go and talk with; there is a palace, and servants, and a row of bottles of different colored wines, and wine glasses, and fine coats." To Concord *that* was oddity; the appropriate thing was plain living. But in truth Longfellow had a gracious, simple nature and was no more spoiled by affluence than the great Virginian who had made this same "palace" his headquarters—George Washington.

Longfellow had probably a wider influence on his own generation than any other American writer save Emerson. He domesticated for the ordinary American the courtly muses of Europe. To a middle-class nation undernourished by Puritan moralism and Neoclassic rationalism, he brought in obvious and familiar rhythms the warmth, the color, the rich variety, the sentiment and magic, of the unfamiliar old cultures abroad, German, Spanish, Portuguese, Italian, Belgian, Scandinavian. He did this, to be sure, romantically, ignoring (as Irving had done) the living present of Europe, slighting the great illuminations of its past, and placing his emphasis rather on the picturesque, the "quaint," a realm of beauty and strangeness, a dream-world offering escape— life being "prosaic in this country to the last degree." From a prosaic present he turned not only to the European but also the American past. As he said, "The dreary old Puritanical times begin to look romantic in the distance." The moralistic twist which he gave his poems made them acceptable to a middle-class nation very definitely on the side of virtue. With that kept in view it was ready, at last, to enter the palace of art.

Longfellow, and Lowell after him, held the professorship of *belles-lettres* at Harvard. Oliver Wendell Holmes was professor of medicine and dean of the medical school. When Lowell entered Harvard as a student in 1834, there were only 220 undergraduates. According to Edward Everett Hale, "The whole drift of fashion, occupation, and habit among the undergraduates ran in lines suggested by literature." The books they bought or took from the library were works of literature—not theology, or politics, or science. "Some Philadelphia publisher had printed in one volume Coleridge's poems, Shelley's, and Keats' . . . you saw the book pretty much everywhere."

Aside from the three academic writers of Cambridge, Boston had literati of its own. Among them was Thomas W. Parsons, a native of the city, a dentist who wrote accomplished poetry and who loved Dante as Longfellow and Lowell did, translating admirably most of the *Divine Comedy*. There was Orestes Brownson, prominent as editor of the *Democratic Review* and other quarterlies, writer of numerous books including a novel, and successively a Presbyterian, a Universalist, an independent, a Unitarian minister, and finally a Roman Catholic of uncertain orthodoxy. There was Francis Parkman, born in Boston, still regarded today as the greatest of American historians, who applied to the epic struggle of France and England in America a combination of the scientific method of German scholarship and the literary approach of Walter Scott.

The Romantic View of Life

These, then, are the broad facts of American romanticism: its revolt—against the rationalism that dominated the eighteenth century and lingered among the Unitarians; its affirmation—the supremacy of the heart, the inner life of the self; its environment—expansive, optimistic young America from about 1820 to the Civil War; its radial center—Transcendental Concord.

If we have nowhere presented a set definition of romanticism, American or international, this is because its complexities have eluded all scholarly efforts to reduce it to an acceptable formula. The significance of the literature of the period will, however, be clearer if we make some attempt to explore and describe the romantic quest, if not to define it. As a starting point, the phrase "Individualism in feeling and imagination" may serve as a convenient label for the complex elements entering into romantic literature; but only an analysis will make such a label really useful.

The individualism demanded by the romantics was something other than the rational individualism of the age of Franklin and Jefferson. Jefferson had said: "Fix reason firmly in her seat, and call to her tribunal every fact, every opinion. . . . Neither believe nor reject anything because other persons . . . have rejected or believed it. Your own reason is the only oracle given you by heaven." The romantics shared this hostility to authority, but not the deference to reason. They boldly unfixed reason from her seat, and declared that the true oracle is intuition— something they knew without reasoning, something that satisfied the instincts of the heart. The individualism they proclaimed was that of the whole self, in which the affirmation of the feelings and imagination seemed to be central.

"Trust thyself: every heart vibrates to that iron string," said Emerson. He said: "If the single man plant himself indomitably on his instincts, and there abide, the huge world will come round to him." He said: "Whoso would be a man, must be a nonconformist." He said: "The root and seed of democracy is the doctrine, Judge for yourself. Reverence thyself."

Self-reliance has been justified in two opposite ways—because all men are different from each other, and because they are all alike. The view that they are different has been associated with romanticism ever since Rousseau began his *Confessions* by declaring that he was made unlike anybody he had ever seen; different, if not better. All men, it seems, are born free and different, and each should be himself and pursue happiness in his own way. "Is it not the chief disgrace in the world," asked Emerson, "not to yield that peculiar fruit which each man was created to bear?" The dignity of man requires that a man insist on himself and never imitate other men. In the same vein Walt Whitman speaks of the thought that comes to us, a thought calm "like the stars, shining eternal. This is the thought of identity—yours for you, as mine for me." A man, says Whitman, has his "own central idea and purpose," grows from it and to it. While he may gather and absorb influences from outside, he must never imperil "the precious idiocrasy and special nativity and intention that he is, the man's self." This idea of the uniqueness of every man runs, as an assumption if not an assertion, all through the Romantic Movement.

In direct contrast is the idea of the Neoclassic Age that all men are basically the same: not the uniqueness of men but the unity of man, not the particular man but the universal man. The two views do not, of course, exclude each other, but simply emphasize two aspects of humanity. Both views are common in this period, both the romantic sense of difference or novelty and the old classical sense—going back to Socrates and Plato—of sameness or universality. We have quoted Emerson's doctrine of uniqueness, but actually his prevailing emphasis was on unity, though in the end he gave unity itself a romantic twist. In a *Dial* paper he directly contrasted the two views, and left no doubt as to his choice of emphasis. There is, he said, a healthy subjectivism and an unhealthy subjectivism. The danger of subjectivism is shown when it is indulged by the narrow-minded and the selfish, in whom it is a form of personal vanity, or escape from inner sickness. This is the "abominable self." On the other hand, there is an impersonal subjectivism. "A

man may say I, and never refer to himself as an individual. . . . The great man, even whilst he relates a private fact personal to him, is really leading us away from him to an universal experience." The reason is, "that there is One Mind, and that all the powers and privileges which lie in any, lie in all." This last quotation, it will be observed, sums up the central drift of essay after essay in Emerson's best-known writings. Thus, in *Essays, First Series*, Emerson prefixed a motto in which he says (as he wants us to say):

> I am owner of the sphere,
> Of the seven stars and the solar year,
> Of Caesar's hand, and Plato's brain,
> Of Lord Christ's heart, and Shakespeare's strain.

Whitman later said much the same thing, beginning his "Song of Myself" with a line that looks purely personal till the second line makes it universal:

> I celebrate myself, and sing myself,
> And what I assume you shall assume.

Harmonious though this kind of thought is with the classical tradition, it takes on, we feel, a romantic cast. Perhaps it is the focus on the ego—the inflated ego—the very notion of a "Song of Myself" in place of, say, Pope's "Essay on Man." Or we may say it is the bold pride of the romantic instead of the ethical moderation inculcated by a classical author like Homer or Sophocles. Or we may say, rather, that a romantic optimism, a too ready slipping into illusion, causes a certain blindness to the facts of life. In sober truth, few individuals who plant themselves indomitably on their instincts will find the huge world coming round to them. Emerson, as usual, suggests his own corrective, remarking upon the "yawning difference" "between men as they ought to be and as they are." His doubts that men have it in their power to bring into being all that is latent but buried in them, begin early in his writings and multiply and deepen as he moves on to scan the meaning of Experience, of Illusions, of Fate. He had called genius "a larger imbibing of the common heart," or "a large infusion of Deity," but his efforts to encourage and confidently call forth in every man the vast riches of humanity—to democratize genius, so to speak—were typical only of Transcendentalism in its heyday.

It was the *feeling* individual, rather, with most romantics. Not developing their outlook, like Emerson, ministerially, they placed at the center of the self feeling and imagination. They sought every kind of experience and responded with sensuous warmth, trusting the heart wherever it led.

Feeling—love—the heart: these were bepraised in the Romantic period as reason had been in the Neoclassic. For a hundred years sentimentalism, reacting against the rule of reason, had proclaimed the goodness of human nature, the virtue of the man of feeling. In the romantic triumph this sentimentalism was changed into something rich and strange. Feeling became far more genuine, complicated, and interesting. It was still at war with the eighteenth-century kind of reason: "that false secondary power," Wordsworth called it, "by which we multiply distinctions," an analytic power by which we divide and divide vital reality till we "break down all grandeur." Feeling, a synthetic power, preserves vital reality, the meaning of things in their wholeness.

Romanticism restored to literature the emotional vitality of the Renaissance, interrupted by the long reign of neo- and pseudo-classicism. But now, in literature as in life, feeling was far more introverted and personal. It was individual joy, rapture, love, longing, regret, fear, hope, faith, enthusiasm, despair, an auto-registration of moods. These feelings were experienced with the keen sensibility and tumult of a youthful spirit—most romantics died early or became less romantic. The feeling perhaps most typical, internationally, was that of longing (in German, *Sehnsucht*), a vague longing for love, beauty, the infinite. The poetry of ancient classicism was the poetry of enjoyment, said A. W. Schlegel, and that of romanticism is the poetry of desire, a desire that can never be satisfied, an indefinite desire that must end in melancholy.

Is the romantic, then, like the sentimentalist, a man of feeling instead of a man of reason or of action? Basically, perhaps; and yet one must recognize a great difference. The feeling of the sentimentalist is weak and shallow; that of the romantic, stronger and deeper. The sentimentalist luxuriates in feeling for its own sake; the romantic, while he may often do this, is engaged in a quest of high truth through imagination. He believes in feeling as a value; he believes also that its value depends on an exertion of imagination. This is one of his key words, an old word which he used in a new way that has been common ever since. Before the romantic period, imagination had been synonymous with memory, a calling up of things past, or, by extension, a creation of something new by a recombination of things remembered. But now it transcended these old uses, came to be thought of as an instrument of insight into a truth above the field of the senses. Truth, it was held, lies in feeling, but it is the imagination that finds it. The really vital meanings of human life cannot be approached by the systematic and external operations of science, but only by an immediate emotional perception, warm flashes of intuition or imagination, a knowledge from within the human spirit.

The concept of imagination is so important that it will be worth while to review a famous statement of it. In his preface to *Lyrical Ballads* Wordsworth announced that the object of this new departure in poetry was to take situations from common life—in which "the essential passions of the heart" are clearest—and "to throw over them a certain coloring of imagination, whereby ordinary things should be presented to the mind in an unusual aspect." That is, the poetic mind does not see nature and life prosaically, as literal fact, but throws over them (as Coleridge put it in one of his poems),

A light, a glory, a fair luminous cloud
Enveloping the earth.

How does this happen? First, something that the poet sees or experiences stirs an emotion in him. Secondly, this emotion is recollected in the tranquillity of meditation, till the actual emotion has become a poetic emotion. Thirdly, this poetic emotion, now grown powerful, spontaneously overflows in expression. So far the poet. Other persons, reading the poem, have their feelings strengthened and purified. Most readers, belonging to "the poor loveless ever-anxious crowd," as Coleridge calls them, need to be awakened from "the lethargy of custom" and to see life freshly with eyes of wonder. As moonlight gives an ordinary and familiar scene or experience a new and richer meaning, so the romantic imagination, shedding the light of the human spirit, adds, says Wordsworth,

the gleam,
The light that never was, on sea or land,
The consecration and the poet's dream.

The views of the two poets are so close that we may speak of the Wordsworth-Coleridge concept of imagination. Again and again, from Bryant to Whitman, we are reminded of it in American criticism. Poe, for example, maintains that it is not the business of the poet to express passion—what we have called the "actual emotion"—but to "elevate the soul" by an image of Supernal Beauty. In an imaginative poem, he says, at every stroke of the lyre we hear a ghostly echo; in every glimpse of beauty "we catch, through long and wild vistas, dim bewildering visions of a far more ethereal beauty *beyond*." Poetry should have "the *vagueness* of exaltation," "a certain wild license and *indefiniteness*": "the atmosphere of the mystic," a "breath of faëry." Poe was obviously following, in his own way, the theory as well as the practice of Coleridge and Shelley.

The romantic imagination was not equally satisfactory to all the leaders of the American movement. Lowell, especially, became highly suspicious of "cloud-castles," and called for wisdom, judgment, reason to steady and guide the poet, as in the ethical imagination of the Greeks and Shakespeare and the spiritual imagination of his beloved Dante. While he complained that Wordsworth could not see "beyond the limits of his own consciousness and experience," he held that Dante, though himself the protagonist of the *Divine Comedy*, had for his theme not a man but man, whose highest end was to "climb through every phase of human experience to that transcendental and super-sensual region where the true, the good, and the beautiful blend in the white light of God." Deploring the irresponsibility to which the romantic imagination was inclined, Lowell also comdemned its frequent morbidity or "liver-complaint." So did Walt Whitman, and more significantly, because the ground of his criticism was an optimism just as characteristically romantic as the pessimism he brushed aside. Of the modern tendency "to turn everything to pathos, ennui, morbidity, dissatisfaction, death," Whitman remarked abruptly: "I call this thing in our modern literature delirium tremens." Its presence in the wholesome air of the New World he attributed to the influence of the decadent Old World. "Europe, with all its glories," is "a vast abnormal ward or hysterical sick-chamber."

Like the indefinite, the remote and strange attracted the romantic imagination. Perhaps no one has put so neatly as Emerson the contrast between things near seen with realistic eyes and things remote seen by the idealizing imagination: "Every ship is romantic, save that we are sailing in." But it was Poe who most deliberately cultivated the addition of strangeness to beauty, in prose as well as verse. Attracted, as Hawthorne was also, by the horrors and mysteries that the "Gothic" writers had exploited so crudely, he made them shapes of beauty, as in "The Fall of the House of Usher." To the humdrum actual world he opposed visions of Dream-Land, the Valley of Many-Colored Grass, or "ultimate dim Thule." Longfellow was to find inspiration in the Middle Ages; Irving's imagination was similarly captured by early Spain. To some of the Transcendentalists, Asia counted far more than did the European Middle Ages: Emerson found Asia rich in suggestions of a spiritual view of life, and Thoreau immersed himself as in bracing waters in the Bhagavad-Gita, the Vedas, the Vishnu Purana, the Institute of Menu. On one occasion, on meeting Walt Whitman, who struck him as "wonderfully like the Orientals," he asked whether he had read them. "No," replied Whitman, "tell me about them." And for Whitman too the "mystic Orient" became important.

Whatever inspiration American writers found in foreign lands, they derived most of their subject-matter from their native past. A nationalistic, self-reliant America must grow from roots in its own soil, even though that soil was poor when compared (as by Irving) with Europe's "storied and poetical asso-ciations." To Emerson at sea, homeward bound from the Old World, "America, my country" was a

> Land without history, . . .
> No castles, no cathedrals, and no kings;
> Land of the forest. . . .

Yet it was not therefore to be disowned, but rather prized for whatever it could offer. From Irving to Whitman, American writers explored their domestic heritage.

Irving pictured the Dutch of New Amsterdam in his rollicking *Knickerbocker's History* and the best of his short tales. The Puritan background became foreground in the fine art of Hawthorne's *The Scarlet Letter* and of short pieces like "The Maypole of Merry Mount" and "Young Goodman Brown." The Revolutionary period inspired a life of Washington by Irving and *The Spy* by Cooper. The Indians appear in the novels of Cooper and of William Gilmore Simms, in Longfellow's *Hiawatha*, in the historical writing of Parkman. Whitman gives numerous glimpses of the American past. These are only examples. Through the writers named, and others, one could adumbrate the first two centuries of the American experience.

While re-creating much of the older America, the writers of the romantic period correspondingly slighted contemporary themes, though there were important exceptions such as Lowell's *Biglow Papers* and Melville's *Moby-Dick*. They were even more aloof from the present when dealing with the European scene. Thus, Irving romantically closed his eyes to the England of the Industrial Revolution, with its factories, mines, and social problems, preferring Westminster Abbey, Stratford-on-Avon, and picturesque byways. Even Emerson, shifting his focus from America, found all of his "Representative Men" in the European past.

In one important romantic respect, however, Emerson's "land of the forest" was peerless: the opportunities it afforded for kinship and correspondence with nature. "Never need an American," said Irving, "look beyond his own country for the sublime and beautiful of natural scenery." To Irving nature was just scenery, but to the more typical romantics it was a spiritual resource valid when religion had faded, a living being (not Newton's machine) speaking to the soul in a language that feeling and imagination could understand. Nature, the near thing, was indubitably American, but the new attitude toward it came with the romantic impulse from abroad. Among the early European enthusiasts for wild nature had been Rousseau. To him nature was both a standard of simplicity and virtue and a refuge from harsh actuality. The introspective, complicated Germans went further, and fell into an ambiguity from which romanticism never quite extricated itself. On the one hand, it seemed to them, nature is a personality, a friend—even, perhaps, a divine friend—that sympathizes with man's sorrow, works upon his feelings, speaks to him of beauty, freedom, peace, happiness, touches him with intimations of high truth. On the other hand, when nature comes alive in this manner, it is really man—the poetically endowed man—who gives the life he seems to receive. Does man, as Wordsworth suggests, half create and half perceive?

However this mystery may be resolved, the essential fact, for romanticism, remains the kinship of man and nature. We strike it at once, in the opening lines of the first great poem in the American movement, Bryant's "Thanatopsis":

> To him who in the love of Nature holds
> Communion with her visible forms, she speaks
> A various language.

It was Emerson who formulated most carefully, in his book on *Nature*, the relation of the inner and outer worlds. "The lover of nature," he says, "is he whose inward and outward senses are still truly adjusted to each other." In the fields and woods he finds himself, with delight, "not alone and unacknowledged. They nod to me, and I to them." "It is certain that the power to produce this delight does not reside in nature, but in man, or in a harmony of both," though actually, as Emerson goes on, the human soul seems to be swallowing up nature, assimilating the Not Me to the Me. The harmony of the two, in his theory, depends on the relation of correspondence. "Every appearance in nature corresponds to some state of the mind." He gives familiar examples: an enraged man is a lion, a firm one is a rock, light and darkness are knowledge and ignorance. But "Every natural fact is a symbol of some spiritual fact." In *Nature* Emerson thought of all these symbols as fixed and permanent; later, as changing and transitory—so many brief illuminations. But the important thing is that correspondence meant for him what Providence had meant to his Puritan ancestors; that nature, to the sensitive human spirit, was a revelation taking the place of the Bible. Emerson might have made much of the one Puritan, Jonathan Edwards, who had glimpsed this possibility. Had he had access to Edwards' *Images or Shadows of Divine Things* (unpublished until 1947), he would surely have read with a shock of recognition:

> Why is it not rational to suppose that the corporeal and visible world should be designedly made and constituted in analogy to the more spiritual, noble, and real world? It is certainly agreeable to what is apparently the method of God's working.

To feel kinship with nature in her gentler aspects was not difficult. One could be at home where nature invited the domesticities of hedgerow, orchard, pasture, woodlot—a more or less humanized nature. But what of wild nature? This was America's original distinction. Stretching westward from the ocean, even beyond the Father of Waters, this "land of the forest" powerfully affected the imagination of many romantic writers. Even Irving, with his face toward the Old World, remembers America's "trackless forests, where vegetation puts forth all its magnificence." "The mighty forest" dominates Bryant's "Thanatopsis," "A Forest Hymn," and other poems. Cooper gave a full picture of it: the ancient woods with soaring trees, the black mystery at night, the lakes and mountains, here and there human figures swallowed up in the landscape. Hawthorne restored the old Puritan forest, as in a famous scene of *The Scarlet Letter*, or in the sinister adventures of Young Goodman Brown "in the heart of the dark wilderness." Emerson thought of calling his first collected essays *Forest Essays*, and worshipped the pine gods in "Wood Notes."

But it was Thoreau who best communicated the tonic freedom of the forest, its wildness and beauty in large and small. In *The Maine Woods* he described a nature "savage and awful, though beautiful." *Walden* bore as a subtitle *Life in the Woods*; the life was that of wild creatures and plants as well as his own among them. To get to the heart of reality, it seemed to Thoreau, he must enter deeply into the wild. True, the inner spiritual reality was for him as for Emerson final. Yet, by the doctrine of correspondence, the inner was closely bound up with the outer reality. When the mood of wildness was on, he could "eat the brown earth," or desire to seize and devour a woodchuck raw. He loved rainstorms, and enjoyed wading in cold, bracing swamps—"a sort of baptism." As he might have put it, the Wild made him wild. But such adventures in feeling were matched by an intellectual conviction: that all civilization refers back to primitive nature and from time to time must return to its source of vitality, or decay and die. This was symbolized for him in the old fable of Romulus and Remus. The children of the Roman Empire, not being suckled by wolves, had to yield place to the northern barbarians who were. The continent of America, he goes on to say, is the she-wolf of our time. Here the moribund civilization of Europe can be reinvigorated and found a new Rome. It is not surprising that Thoreau rejoiced when he read Whitman's "very brave and American" *Leaves of Grass*: "Though rude, and sometimes ineffectual, it is a great primitive poem,—an alarum or trumpet-note ringing through the American camp."

With Whitman we come to one more object of romantic enthusiasm: the common man. He is the natural, earthy man. Everything, says Whitman, "comes out of the dirt—everything: everything comes out of the people, the everyday people, the people as you find them and leave them: not university people, not F.F.V. people." The People, yes the People—this has been the cry of the modern world ever since the eighteenth century. Then, as Emerson noted, such poets as Goldsmith (*The Deserted Village*), Burns ("The Cotter's Saturday Night"), and Cowper (*The Task*) had begun to celebrate plain folk and wholesome rustic living. But it was Wordsworth who most memorably celebrated not only the natural world but the common man who lived in it, beginning with the "underprivileged" people of the *Lyrical Ballads* and rising to a climax in the shepherd poem "Michael."

In America, where the equalitarian spirit of the frontier was added to the democratic ideology inherited from the eighteenth century, writers like Bryant, Cooper, and Hawthorne were sympathetic toward the Jacksonian revolution, and Emerson (as Whitman recognized) formed a view of life basically democratic despite his patrician origin and training. No one placed a higher valuation than Emerson on the latent powers of every man: "Each man shall feel the world is his, and man shall treat with man as a sovereign state with a sovereign state." In the main he presented his thought abstractly, as the titles of his essays indicate, leaving to others a more concrete, flesh-and-blood representation. Thus, it was Whittier who gave the dignity of verse to farmers, lumbermen, and shoemakers, and who in *Snow-Bound* dwelt with loving memory upon what Emerson had called "the meaning of household life." It was Whittier also who most passionately espoused the cause of the common man made slave, though Emerson, Thoreau, Longfellow, and Lowell also took part, each in his own way.

But the cause of the common man belonged especially to Whitman. In him the currents of romantic individualism and humanitarian altruism ran strong and ran together, blending self-pride and universal sympathy. Son of a carpenter, brought up in the country and in the "village" of Brooklyn, Whitman lived his life outside the circles of gentility and learning. Common people were, for him, the "divine average," the promise of a future America leading the modern world. United in a "universal democratic comradeship," in "adhesiveness or love, that fuses, ties and aggregates, making the races comrades, and fraternizing all," they must equally possess self-pride, "a rich, luxuriant, varied personalism," "the pride and centripetal isolation of a human being in himself." With Emerson, he conceived that greatness was for each individual, waiting only to be

claimed. How far he was inclined to carry romantic egoism is indicated by a notebook entry: "If I walk with Jah in Heaven and he assume to be intrinsically greater than I it offends me, and I shall certainly withdraw from Heaven."

Here was a poet of the people, by the people, and for the people. Ironically, the people themselves preferred Longfellow.

Literary Art

"Trust your genius." The romantics trusted it in art, as in life. For them the essence of literary art, like the essence of living, was self-expression. This meant a pivotal change in the concept of literature. The new concept can be made clearer by glancing back at the old. Through the ages, from Plato and Aristotle down to Dr. Johnson, the classical mind had viewed literature as an imitation of life, a representation of the actions of men.

The romantics rejected this literary theory. The theory, and still more the practice, had been distorted and diminished during the long reign of neo- and pseudo-classicism by the development of conventions and rules. The time seemed ripe for a fresh start. For the old concept of literature as an *imitation* the romantics substituted the concept of literature as an *expression*. It might be the expression of a state of society, or of a national spirit, but characteristically it was assumed to be an expression of self, of the writer's own personality and experience in the world as he knew it or chose to make it. Literature became largely confessional—personal, autobiographic, lyrical. The traditional epic disappeared. The familiar essay became far more personal, as in Lamb. For the first time in the history of literature, the lyric became the typical kind of poetry. The romantic revival was indeed a period of great lyrical poetry, expressing keen and subtle sense impressions and an immense range of emotions—joy, ecstasy, love, yearning, regret—with a spontaneity and intensity reminiscent of the Renaissance. Small wonder that Emerson, while aware of the Puritan in himself, exclaimed approvingly, "This writing is blood-warm." What life might be is shown not by the practical and prudential crowd, whose existence is almost a death-in-life, but by the poet, who lives creatively and freely, building his inner world of beauty and high meaning, and externalizing it in words.

This closeness to personal experience is characteristic of the poetry of Bryant, Poe, Emerson, Longfellow, and many other American writers, but most notably of Walt Whitman. Glancing backward from old age, he himself described *Leaves of Grass* as "an attempt, from first to last, to put a *Person*, a human being (myself, in the latter half of the Nineteenth

Century, in America), freely, fully and truly on record." The book was a memorable contribution to that art of the self which is typical of the Romantic Movement. The German romantics were personal on principle: Novalis had declared, "The novel is a life in the form of a book." Whitman went one step further:

> Camerado, this is no book,
> Who touches this touches a man.

The idea that a work of literary art grows out of experience and expresses a life lived brings us to the doctrine of organic form. This favorite romantic doctrine was not new but renovated. It appears in Greek thought as early as Plato, who said that a work of art should be like a living creature. After the middle of the eighteenth century it was affirmed by Edward Young, in whose view a work of original genius "may be said to be of a vegetable nature; it grows, it is not made." Here was an idea highly appropriate to romanticism. As the universe is not a machine but a living entity, so a work of art is not a mechanical construction but an organic structure. Like A. W. Schlegel in Germany, Coleridge wrote: "The organic form is innate; it shapes, as it develops itself from within, and its fullness of development is one and the same with the perfection of its outward form. Such as the life is, such is the form." Mechanical form, on the other hand, is consciously imposed from the outside: "The form is mechanic when on any given material we impress a predetermined form, ... as when to a mass of wet clay we give whatever shape we wish it to retain when hardened."

Pursuing this biological analogy, romanticism conceives of any excellent work of art as a structure growing in an environment, developing from a living germ. Each part has its proper function, and all the parts work together as a unit. Among the parts that may enter into the complex unity and harmony of a particular work of art are diction, rhythm, image, symbol, ideas, attitude, tone, setting, character, incident, etc. Thus a successful poem, says Coleridge, offers "such delight from the *whole*, as is compatible with a distinct gratification from each component part." The parts "mutually support and explain each other." Successful poetry, in his view, cannot be written by deliberate effort; the organic principle applies to the poet as well as the poem—he is born and not made, though he can cultivate his gift.

Emerson conceives that the eternal power expresses itself in the poet's intuition, and the poet's intuition expresses itself in the words and music of the poem. Spirit gives the divine hint to the poet, and the poet passes it on to all men, in a form that is excellent in proportion as it is determined by the hint itself, not arbitrarily devised by the poet. "For it is not meters, but a meter-making argument that makes a poem—a thought so passionate and alive that like the spirit of a plant or an animal it has an architecture of its own, and adorns nature with a new thing." Like all beauty, it has "fitness," a perfect adaptation of means to end. Form is not "outside embellishment" as the eighteenth century seemed to think, but already dictated by content. "A verse is not a vehicle to carry a sentence as a jewel is carried in a case: the verse must be alive, and inseparable from its contents, as the soul of man inspires and directs the body." The superior poem cannot be analyzed; you cannot separate word and thought. But in the inferior poem they fall apart, and you can distinguish between the vague thought and the awkward or conventional expression. Strictly, in the ideal poem, "There is always a right word, and every other than that is wrong."

Evidently the organic principle could be used to explain any aspect of creation: the man of genius, the intuition that flashed upon his inward eye, the shaping spirit of his imagination, the expression of his vision in an aesthetic order governing even the word. Not only order but disorder, according to A. W. Schlegel. Classical art, he said, reflects "a world submitted to a beautiful order," but romantic art responds to "the secret attraction to a chaos which lies concealed in the very bosom of the ordered universe and is perpetually striving after new and marvellous births."

Yet the wish to escape restraints may explain the presence in romantic art of so much that is experimental, uneven, disproportionate, pretentious, inconsistent, fragmentary, or simply careless. We might attribute romantic disorder to the stress placed upon the values of living rather than the values of art, which made the search for beauty a quest of the poetic life rather than the patient and loving production of works of art. When they did concentrate upon an artifact, the romantics were inclined to value content more than form, despite the theory that the two are inseparable. The wonder is that they nevertheless produced so many shapes of beauty that are contemplated with pleasure today, notably, in our own literature, *Moby-Dick*, which confronts the chaos of life with a powerful aesthetic control, and *The Scarlet Letter*, in which the problem of evil is treated with the tight economy and perfect harmony of mature art.

Tight economy and perfect harmony were deliberately chosen as aesthetic goals in the conscious art of Poe. In this he was closer to the classicists than the romantics. Here was one theorist who, in contrast to Emerson and Whitman, had scant use for the organic view of art, that form grows naturally out of idea. In theory and practice alike, he believed that art should be rational. Yet he was not wholly a classicist. He himself reported, in romantic terms, "My life has been *whim*—impulse—passion—a longing for solitude—a scorn of all things present in an earnest desire for the future." If that was his life, his life and his art were anything but identical. To him the natural man was the rational man: "Man's chief idiosyncracy being reason, it follows that his savage condition—his condition of action *without* reason—is his *un*natural state." Writing a poem or story is a kind of action, requiring in high degree the powers of causality, i.e., a perception of the causes needed to produce a desired effect. Imagination is "never otherwise than analytic." Originality is not "a mere matter of impulse or inspiration" but rather a matter of purposeful construction: "To originate is carefully, patiently, and understandingly to combine." In Poe's view, art is almost a mathematical logic. In many of his tales he used mathematics or discussed its nature, and he was absorbed in problems and puzzles of all sorts, from cryptography to plagiarism, some of which he presented in a new art form, the detective story.

Though Poe was exceptional in displaying his thought concerning external form, we may infer that most romantic writers reflected upon technical problems far more than their published works show. For example, even if some of them had little to say about symbolism, they were generally agreed that it is an invaluable artistic method for expressing a complex and difficult kind of meaning.

Through the symbol, as they conceived, the indefinite could be suggested through a concrete representation, and the abstract thus made tangible. Instead of using familiar symbols such as the crown of monarchy and the cross of Christianity, a writer could devise fresh ones of his own choosing. Some might be made obvious to any reader; others might be left vague, stimulating the imagination to find the most fitting abstract equivalent. Symbolism is not the same as allegory. In an allegory there is a fixed and coherent system of signs, whereas a symbol can stand alone, serve a temporary purpose—a flash of illumination. It may appear once or repeatedly, and the same image may at various times represent quite different things. A good example of a symbol is the ethereal dream-maiden, in Rousseau, Novalis, Shelley, Poe, Melville.

A symbol dominates the masterpiece of Hawthorne, from title—*The Scarlet Letter*—to the very end. And as he showed in one short tale after another, his mind characteristically brooded upon or played with symbols, often with a tantalizing ambiguity. Reality, he felt, was something far too complex and uncertain to be set down in terms of reason and denotative statement. This is why Melville declared that in reading Hawthorne, "It is not the brain that can test such a man; it is only the heart."

Melville himself well exemplified his own belief that "You must have plenty of sea-room to tell the Truth in." There is plenty of sea-room in *Moby-Dick*, a work that owed something to Hawthorne's deep probings, Carlyle's flashes of insight, Shakespeare's grappling with the essence of things, but mainly grew out of his own experience and speculation. Symbols irradiate the whole fable, help to bind it together. Some are used only to enlighten details of the action. The same image may symbolize quite different things in different contexts. The sea can suggest mystery, the source of life, its end, an alien element, or a friendly one. And readers interpreting with both brain and heart are by no means always agreed as to what is symbolized. Like Hawthorne, unlike most romantics, Melville was obsessed with the problem of evil in the universe. To the ship's captain with the Old Testament name of Ahab, the monstrous White Whale symbolizes "that intangible malignity which has been from the beginning; to whose dominion even the modern Christians ascribe one-half of the worlds ... all the subtle demonisms of life and thought; all evil. . . ." Hating the inscrutable,—"be the white whale agent, or be the white whale ·principal,"—Ahab defies the universe. "I'd strike the sun if it insulted me. . . . Who's over me?"

Turning now to the question of style, in poetry and prose, we shall find relatively little on the subject in the writings of the two great innovators: Wordsworth in England and Whitman in America. Like romantic writers in general, they were more absorbed in "life values" than in "art values."

In the well-known preface to *Lyrical Ballads* poetic style is treated as mainly a matter of language and diction. As the term *ballad* implies, Wordsworth did not propose to abandon the long-established conventions of meter and rhyme. But he attacked with vigor the neoclassic convention of a "poetic diction" apart from the diction of prose and of actual speech. He pointed out that writers in early times, feeling powerfully, used a daring and figurative language, but that later writers (apparently in the eighteenth century) maintained this language without a correspondence of feeling. They used it mechanically, unconcerned about the contrast between the heightened language and their low-keyed feelings. Wordsworth gives an example from Gray:

> In vain to me the smiling mornings shine,
> And reddening Phoebus lifts his golden fire;
> The birds in vain their amorous descant join
> Or cheerful fields resume their green attire.

Such language he finds artificial and gaudy, without the urgency of genuine feeling. To restore vitality, to bring expression close to real life once more, Wordsworth proposes the experiment of employing "a selection of the real language of men in a state of vivid sensation." It is not to be the language of gentlemen or of the craft of poets, but a "plainer and more emphatic language" suited to "humble and rustic life." Incidentally, he will have scant use for the personifications (Hope, Peace, and the like, with capital letters) by means of which poets had sought an easy elevation. What he wishes to do, in short, is to write like "a man speaking to men."

By the time of Emerson and Longfellow this "blood-warm" manner of writing was common. Poetry was much closer to the currents of real life, its language more concrete, its verse freed from the stylized heroic couplet and diversified to serve many ends. Yet romanticism itself tended to form a poetic diction and style of its own, a vague and too readily flowing eloquence. We can see this style beginning in Wordsworth and Coleridge, established as a pattern by Byron and Shelley, followed in varying degrees by Bryant, Poe, Whittier, Longfellow, and Lowell.

To the bold, independent mind of Walt Whitman, this stylized romantic verse seemed anything but an inevitable expression of modern democratic America. Rhyme, for example—"venerable and heavenly forms of chiming versification"—he regarded as fitting for the feudal order, not for the democratic. Whitman felt, as he declared in his 1855 preface to *Leaves of Grass*, that the genius of the United States lay "most in the common people." The true meaning of simplicity, the "art of art," was perhaps suggested to him by the natural man, the "indescribable freshness and unconsciousness about an illiterate person." But simplicity was suggested even more, in his preface, by lower orders of life: "To speak in literature with the perfect rectitude and insouciance of the movements of animals and the unimpeachableness of the sentiment of trees in the woods and grass by the roadside is the flawless triumph of art." For such simple communication he will need "new free forms" of expression: "The cleanest expression is that which finds no sphere worthy of itself and makes one." In his own poems Whitman proceeded (with hints from various sources including Biblical verse) to create a new form, which came to be called free verse, avowedly if not always actually dispensing with poetic diction, personification, rhyme, stanza, and meter. He retained only the verse line, which, on the organic principle, should tally the substance expressed. The result might be called a free-and-easy, unadorned poetry, fitly illustrated by the daguerreotype used in the first edition—Walt in workingman's clothes, nonchalant and self-sufficient, "me imperturbe." Here was a poetry intended, more truly than in Wordsworth's theory, to be the natural speech of a man speaking to men, an exalted conversational medium. Similar experiments were later to be made by Robert Frost, Carl Sandburg, and T. S. Eliot.

The new view of life also brought a new way of writing prose. The prose desired by the Neoclassic Age had had the formal clarity and order of a Greek temple. Proper words were in proper places, and unity, proportion, and balance produced a design that appealed to the mind. In the Romantic Movement, on the other hand, prose had a more flowing contour, like that of romantic music, appealing to the senses and emotions. There is another significant contrast. Neoclassic prose was thought of as a *human* medium, essentially the same for all who wrote. (In practice, this implied writing with the easy dignity of eighteenth-century gentlemen.) But when emphasis was shifted from the samenesses of men to their differences, it was also shifted from social communication to self-expression. Style became, consciously or unconsciously, a more *personal* medium: the mirror of a man's peculiar individuality, the echo of his uniqueness, the flavor of his special sensibility.

A good American example of what style meant under romantic auspices is offered by Thoreau. Like Poe and Hawthorne, he wrote a prose blending the old virtues of rational design and the new virtues of emotional imagery and color expressed in terms of a distinct personality. Few writers give us so strong a sense of their own essence. Prominent in the author of *Walden* are his disciplined integrity, his play of mind, his love of beauty, features of his writing that also enter into his conscious reflections on style.

Often he speaks of style in organic terms, as when he says, "It is not in man to determine what his style shall be." But this means no resting on his oars. Only by sustained effort can a man learn to write well, for "Every sentence is the result of a long probation." Mind, body and senses, he says, must work together: "Expression is the act of a whole man." A writer needs intercourse with men and things, and especially labor with his hands, which is "the best method of removing palaver and sentimentality out of one's style." Calluses on the hands will have much to do with the writing of "tougher truth" and the firmness of his sentences. As Thoreau says finely, "A sentence should read as if its author, had he held a plow instead of a pen, could have drawn a furrow deep and straight to the end." He liked to speak with the homely reality of the farmer, being suspicious of genteel literary men and college professors, so often "weak and flimsy." With Puritan integrity and Yankee common sense he proclaims that "the one great rule of composition—and if I were a professor of rhetoric I should insist on this—is to *speak the truth*."

Nothing is harder than perfect truth, honesty, candor, but if a writer can achieve it, "the rest will follow." Of the rest he says little, but for him, judging from his writing, it included color and warmth, surprise of the mind, a loving precision in shaping the thought, and a "concentrated and nutty" quality—his own was somewhat acrid, like an acorn.

Surprise came from the use of paradox, conceits, puns, sundry kinds of wit and humor. Color and warmth came from keen senses and health, faithful observation, sensitive imagery, sympathetic response to the theme. With his reserved temperament, Thoreau generally avoided speaking directly of beauty, but it is prominent in one illuminating passage, which sums up his own notion of prose style:

> In writing, conversation should be folded many times thick. It is the height of art that, on the first perusal, plain common sense should appear; on the second, severe truth; and on a third, beauty; and, having these warrants for its depth and reality, we may then enjoy the beauty for evermore.

Both in life and in art, the extremes of romanticism were avoided in England and the United States. In these countries there was little of the extravagance, the chaos, the license of German romanticism. Though the English had largely started the movement, they were restrained, as in other periods, by their aversion to extremes and their respect for tradition. In America, the strongest restraint came from the old Puritan culture, its discipline still effective even when the sanctioning beliefs had evaporated, as one can readily see in Emerson and Hawthorne. At the same time, common sense—Anglo-Saxon and Yankee—had a sobering effect on men like Emerson, Thoreau, and Lowell. Furthermore, the romantic revolt was moderate because American rationalism and neoclassicism had been moderate, and because the way to a romantic outlook had been gradually prepared by the fluid frontier of a land of opportunity, and by the democratic revolution that preceded the French Revolution by about twenty years. The heady ideas of European romanticism in full tide came to a nation of free men accustomed to belief in human dignity and habituated to self-control no less than to self-assertion.

Earlier Romantics

WASHINGTON IRVING [1783–1859]

WASHINGTON IRVING was born into a wealthy New York City merchant family and educated privately for the law. However, since he preferred to write essays for two newspapers edited by his brother Peter, he soon decided to follow a literary career. In 1802–1803 he wrote a series of delightfully impudent satires on city society for his brother's papers under the pseudonym of "Jonathan Oldstyle, Gent.," and his career was launched. The Irving family sent young Washington to Europe for two years, 1804–1806, and although he was admitted to the bar on his return and taken into the family firm, he showed little interest in either law or business. Instead he joined with his brother William, James Kirke Paulding, and several other young men who called themselves "The Nine Worthies of Cockloft Hall" and lived the pleasant, carefree lives of men-about-town. In 1807 and 1808 they published the series of satiric essays called *Salmagundi*, which enjoyed a good deal of popularity and showed also a great deal of promise. In 1809 Irving's fiancée, Mathilda Hoffman, died, a tragic loss from which he never recovered. He threw himself into the completion of his *History of New York*, published that same year, which gave him an immediate reputation as a burlesque humorist and advanced his career another step.

In 1815, in the prime of life, Irving went to England on business, unaware that he was to make his literary reputation abroad and to remain there for seventeen years. The family firm failed not long after, and Irving for the first time in his life was thrown upon his own resources. His friendship with Sir Walter Scott, publisher John Murray and the London literati stood him in good stead as he resumed his writing (which he had allowed to lapse for ten years), for it resulted in Murray's publication of *The Sketch Book* (1819–20), which catapulted him into instant fame on both sides of the Atlantic. After *Bracebridge Hall* (1822), a continuation of the *Sketch Book* style, he lived in Germany for a year, published *Tales of a Traveller* (1824), spent some months in London and Paris, and went to Madrid to serve in the American Legation. The appeal of Spain to his imagination produced *The Life of Columbus* (1828) and *The Companions of Columbus* (1831); two historical studies, *The Conquest of Granada* (1829) and *The Conquest of Spain* (1835); and his last volume of tales, *The Alhambra* (1832). After *The Alhambra* Irving turned to history, biography, and travel; his work lost much of the imaginativeness and vitality that marked his Hudson Valley, German, English, and Spanish stories and sketches, though it may have gained in prestige.

Irving returned to the United States in 1832, to find its social, political, and economic complexion drastically changed. This was Jacksonian America, in the full flush of its ebullient and energetic nationalism and there seemed to be little place for an aristocratic Knickerbocker gentleman. However, Irving adjusted to the new society in time; he became interested in the frontier, took an extended tour into the prairies, and wrote three books about the new West—*Astoria* (1834), an account of John Jacob Astor's fur empire; *A Tour on the Prairies* (1835), an expansion of his travel journal; and *The Adventures of Captain Bonneville* (1837), a Rocky Mountain scout and explorer.

Irving's literary fame constantly elicited offers of various political sinecures and finally, in 1842, he accepted the post of Minister to Spain for three years, after which he returned to New York to settle at Sunnyside, his gracious country home at Tarrytown, near "Sleepy Hollow," where he completed his *Life of Mahomet* (1850) and his five-volume *Life of Washington* (1859). Although he wrote no fiction after 1832, Irving's contributions to the development of the American short tale were of great importance; he lent it style, skill, atmosphere, characterization, and respectability, and both Poe and Hawthorne, who perfected the form after him, owed much to Irving's beginnings. Nor should it be forgotten that Irving was America's first internationally-known man of letters, an intermediary between the literary Old and New Worlds who impressed his example on both his own and foreign culture.

Further reading: Edward Wagenknecht, *Washington Irving*, 1962. Van Wyck Brooks, *The World of Washington Irving*, 1944.

FROM *Salmagundi*

In 1807–1808 Washington Irving, his brother William, and James K. Paulding published in New York a series of periodical essays called *Salmagundi: or, The Whim Whams and Opinions of Launcelot Langstaff, Esq., and Others*, modeled on *The Spectator*. Twenty issues were published, with essays assigned to fictitious "critics, amateurs, dilettanti, and cognoscenti"—William Wizard handled general literary criticism, Pindar Cockloft wrote on poetry, Anthony Evergreen served as social commentator, while Launcelot Langstaff wrote on any topic he wished. Nine essays were ascribed to a Tripolitan sea-captain named Mustapha, held temporarily as a prisoner in New York (the United States had been at war with Tripoli from 1803 to 1805), who reported his observations on the American scene to his superiors at the Bashaw's court, a device borrowed from Oliver Goldsmith's popular *Citizen*

of the World essays of 1760–61. Text: *Works of Washington Irving*, Philadelphia, 1870–71, the Knickerbocker Edition. A *salmagundi* was a dish of mixed herrings and chopped meat, highly seasoned with oil, vinegar, pepper, and onions.

No. I

(Saturday, January 24, 1807)

As everybody knows, or ought to know, what a SALMAGUNDI is, we shall spare ourselves the trouble of an explanation; besides, we despise trouble as we do everything low and mean, and hold the man who would incur it unnecessarily as an object worthy our highest pity and contempt. Neither will we puzzle our heads to give an account of ourselves, for two reasons; first, because it is nobody's business; secondly, because if it were, we do not hold ourselves bound to attend to anybody's business but our own; and even *that* we take the liberty of neglecting when it suits our inclination. To these we might add a third, that very few men *can* give a tolerable account of themselves, let them try ever so hard; but this reason, we candidly avow, would not hold good with ourselves.

There are, however, two or three pieces of information which we bestow gratis on the public, chiefly because it suits our own pleasure and convenience that they should be known, and partly because we do not wish that there should be any ill will between us at the commencement of our acquaintance.

Our intention is simply to instruct the young, reform the old, correct the town, and castigate the age; this is an arduous task, and therefore we undertake it with confidence. We intend for this purpose to present a striking picture of the town; and as everybody is anxious to see his own phiz on canvas, however stupid or ugly it may be, we have no doubt but the whole town will flock to our exhibition. Our picture will necessarily include a vast variety of figures; and should any gentleman or lady be displeased with the inveterate truth of their likenesses, they may ease their spleen by laughing at those of their neighbors—this being what *we* understand by *poetical justice*.

Like all true and able editors, we consider ourselves infallible; and therefore, with the customary diffidence of our brethren of the quill, we shall take the liberty of interfering in all matters either of a public or private nature. We are critics, amateurs, dilettanti and cognoscenti; and as we know "by the pricking of our thumbs," that every opinion which we may advance in either of those characters will be correct, we are determined, though it may be questioned, contradicted, or even controverted, yet it shall never be revoked.

We beg the public particularly to understand that we solicit no patronage. We are determined, on the contrary, that the patronage shall be entirely on our side. We have nothing to do with the pecuniary concerns of the paper; its success will yield us neither pride nor profit—nor will its failure occasion to us either loss or mortification. We advise the public, therefore, to purchase our numbers merely for their own sakes; if they do not, let them settle the affair with their consciences and posterity.

To conclude, we invite all editors of newspapers and literary journals to praise us heartily in advance, as we assure them that we intend to deserve their praises. To our next-door neighbor, "Town," [1] we hold out a hand of amity, declaring to him that, after ours, his paper will stand the best chance for

[1] The title of a New York newspaper.

immortality. We proffer an exchange of civilities: he shall furnish us with notices of epic poems and tobacco; and we, in return, will enrich him with original speculations on all manner of subjects, together with "the rummaging of my grandfather's mahogany chest of drawers," "the life and amours of mine Uncle John," "anecdotes of the Cockloft family," and learned quotations from that unheard of writer of folios, *Linkum Fidelius*.

No. XIV

(Saturday, September 16, 1807)

LETTER FROM MUSTAPHA RUB-A-DUB KELI KHAN, TO ASEM HACCHEM, PRINCIPAL SLAVE-DRIVER TO HIS HIGHNESS THE BASHAW OF TRIPOLI

Health and joy to the friend of my heart! May the angel of peace ever watch over thy dwelling, and the star of prosperity shed its benignant lustre on all thy undertakings. Far other is the lot of thy captive friends: his brightest hopes extend but to a lengthened period of weary captivity, and memory only adds to the measure of his griefs, by holding up a mirror which reflects with redoubled charms the hours of past felicity. In midnight slumbers my soul holds sweet converse with the tender objects of its affections: it is then the exile is restored to his country; it is then the wide waste of waters that rolls between us disappears, and I clasp to my bosom the companion of my youth; I awake and find it but a vision of the night. The sigh will rise; the tear of dejection will steal adown my cheek; I fly to my pen, and strive to forget myself and my sorrows in conversing with my friend.

In such a situation, my good Asem, it cannot be expected that I should be able so wholly to abstract myself from my own feelings, as to give thee a full and systematic account of the singular people among whom my disastrous lot has been cast. I can only find leisure from my own individual sorrows to entertain thee occasionally with some of the most prominent features of their character; and now and then a solitary picture of their most preposterous eccentricities.

I have before observed that among the distinguishing characteristics of the people of this logocracy is their invincible love of talking, and that I could compare the nation to nothing but a mighty windmill. Thou art doubtless at a loss to conceive how this mill is supplied with grist; or, in other words, how it is possible to furnish subjects to supply the perpetual motion of so many tongues.

The genius of the nation appears in its highest lustre in this particular in the discovery, or rather the application, of a subject which seems to supply an inexhaustible mine of words. It is nothing more, my friend, than "politics"; a word which, I declare to thee, has perplexed me almost as much as the redoubtable one of economy. On consulting a dictionary of this language, I found it denoted the science of government; and the relations, situations, and dispositions of states and empires. Good! thought I; for a people who boast of governing themselves, there could not be a more important subject of investigation. I therefore listened attentively, expecting to hear from "the most enlightened people under the sun,"—for so they modestly term themselves,—sublime disputations on the science of legislation, and precepts of political wisdom that would not have disgraced our great prophet and legislator himself!—but, alas, Asem! how continually are my expectations disappointed! how dignified a meaning does this word bear in the dictionary; how despicable its common application; I find it extending to every contemptible discussion of local animosity, and every petty altercation of insignificant individuals. It embraces, alike, all manner of concerns; from the organization of a divan, the election of a bashaw, or the levying of an army, to the appointment of a constable, the personal disputes of two miserable slangwhangers, the cleaning of the streets, or the economy of a dirt cart. A couple of politicians will quarrel, with the most vociferous pertinacity, about the character of a bum-bailiff whom nobody cares for; or the deportment of a little great man whom nobody knows; and this is called talking politics; nay! it is but few days since that I was annoyed by a debate between two of my fellow-lodgers, who were magnanimously employed in condemning a luckless wight to infamy because he chose to wear a red coat, and to entertain certain erroneous opinions some thirty years ago. Shocked at their illiberal and vindictive spirit, I rebuked them for thus indulging in slander and uncharitableness, about the color of a coat, which had doubtless for many years been worn out; or the belief in errors, which in all probability had been long since atoned for and abandoned; but they justified themselves by alleging that they were only engaged in politics, and exerting that liberty of speech, and freedom of discussion, which was the glory and safeguard of their national independence. "O Mahomet!" thought I, "what a country must that be, which builds its political safety on ruined characters and the persecution of individuals!"

Into what transports of surprise and incredulity am I continually betrayed, as the character of this eccentric people gradually develops itself to my observations. Every new research increases the perplexities in which I am involved, and I am more than ever at a loss where to place them in the scale of my estimation. It is thus the philosopher, in pursuing truth through the labyrinth of doubt, error, and misrepresentation, frequently finds himself bewildered in the mazes of contradictory experience; and almost wishes he could quietly retrace his wandering steps, steal back into the path of honest ignorance, and jog on once more in contented indifference.

How fertile in these contradictions is this extensive logocracy! Men of different nations, manners, and languages, live in this country in the most perfect harmony; and nothing is more common than to see individuals whose respective governments are at variance taking each other by the hand and exchanging the offices of friendship. Nay, even on the subject of religion, which, as it affects our dearest interests, our earliest opinions and prejudices, some warmth and heartburnings might be excused, which, even in our enlightened country, is so fruitful in difference between man and man!—even religion occasions no dissension among these people; and it has even been discovered by one of their sages that believing in one god or twenty gods "neither breaks a man's leg nor picks his pocket."[1] The idolatrous Persian may here bow down before his everlasting fire, and prostrate himself toward the glowing east. The Chinese may adore his Fo, or his Josh; the Egyptian, his stork; and the Mussulman practise, unmolested, the divine precepts of our immortal prophet. Nay, even the forlorn, abandoned Atheist, who lies down at night without committing himself to the protection of Heaven, and rises in the morning without returning thanks for his safety! who hath no deity but his own will; whose soul, like the sandy desert, is barren of every flower of hope to throw a solitary bloom over the dead level of sterility and soften the wide extent of desolation; whose darkened views extend not beyond the horizon that bounds his cheerless existence; to whom no blissful perspective opens beyond the grave—even he is suffered to indulge in his desperate opinions without exciting one other emotion than pity or contempt. But this mild and tolerating spirit reaches not beyond the pale of religion: once differ in politics, in mere theories, visions, and chimeras, the growth of interest, of folly or madness, and deadly warfare ensues; every eye flashes fire, every tongue is loaded with reproach, and every heart is filled with gall and bitterness.

At this period several unjustifiable and serious injuries on the part of the barbarians of the British Islands have given a new impulse to the tongue and the pen, and occasioned a terrible wordy fever. Do not suppose, my friend, that I mean to condemn any

[1]Jefferson, in his *Notes on Virginia*, says, "The legislative powers of government extend to such acts only as are injurious to others. But it does me no injury for my neighbor to say there are twenty gods or no god. It neither picks my pocket nor breaks my leg." [Irving's note.]

proper and dignified expression of resentment for injuries. On the contrary I love to see a word before a blow; for, "in the fullness of the heart the tongue moveth." But my long experience has convinced me that people who talk the most about taking satisfaction for affronts generally content themselves with talking instead of revenging the insult; like the street women of this country, who after a prodigious scolding quietly sit down and fan themselves cool as fast as possible. But to return: the rage for talking has now, in consequence of the aggressions I alluded to, increased to a degree far beyond what I have observed heretofore. In the gardens of His Highness of Tripoli are fifteen thousand bee-hives, three hundred peacocks, and a prodigious number of parrots and baboons: and yet I declare to thee, Asem, that their buzzing, and squalling, and chattering is nothing compared to the wild uproar and war of words now raging within the bosom of this mighty and distracted logocracy. Politics pervade every city, every village, every temple, every porterhouse: the universal question is, "What is the news?" This is a kind of challenge to political debate; and as no two men think exactly alike, 't is ten to one that before they finish all the polite phrases in the language are exhausted by way of giving fire and energy to argument. What renders this talking fever more alarming is, that the people appear to be in the unhappy state of a patient whose palate loathes the medicine best calculated for the cure of his disease, and seem anxious to continue the full enjoyment of their chattering epidemic. They alarm each other by direful reports and fearful apprehensions; as I have seen a lot of old wives in this country entertain themselves with stories of ghosts and goblins until their imaginations were in a most agonizing panic. Every day begets some new tale big with agitation; and the busy goddess, Rumor, to speak in the poetic language of the Christians, is constantly in motion. She mounts her rattling stage-wagon and gallops about the country, freighted with a load of "hints," "informations," "extracts of letters from respectable gentlemen," "observations of respectable correspondents," and "unquestionable authorities";—which her high-priests, the slangwhangers, retail to their sapient followers, with all the solemnity and all the authenticity of oracles. True it is, the unfortunate slangwhangers are sometimes at a loss for food to supply this insatiable appetite for intelligence; and are, not unfrequently, reduced to the necessity of manufacturing dishes suited to the taste of the times, to be served up as morning and evening repasts to their disciples.

When the hungry politician is thus full charged with important information he sallies forth to give due exercise to his tongue; and tells all he knows, to everybody he meets. Now it is a thousand to one that every person he meets is just as wise as himself, charged with the same articles of information, and possessed of the same violent inclination to give it vent; for in this country every man adopts some particular slangwhanger as the standard of his judgment, and reads everything he writes if he reads nothing else; which is doubtless the reason why the people of this logocracy are so marvellously enlightened. So away they tilt at each other with their borrowed lances, advancing to the combat with the opinions and speculations of their respective slangwhangers, which, in all probability, are diametrically opposite. Here then arises as fair an opportunity for a battle of words as heart could wish; and thou mayst rely upon it, Asem, they do not let it pass unimproved. They sometimes begin with argument; but in process of time, as the tongue begins to wax wanton, other auxiliaries become necessary: recrimination commences; reproach follows close at its heels; from political abuse they proceed to personal, and thus often is a friendship of years trampled down by this contemptible enemy, this gigantic dwarf of POLITICS, the mongrel issue of grovelling ambition and aspiring ignorance!

There would be but little harm, indeed, in all this, if it ended merely in a broken head; for this might soon be healed and the scar, if any remained, might serve as a warning ever after against the indulgence of political intemperance; at the worst, the loss of such heads as these would be a gain to the nation. But the evil extends far deeper; it threatens to impair all social intercourse, and even to sever the sacred union of family and kindred. The convivial table is disturbed; the cheerful fireside is invaded; the smile of social hilarity is chased away; the bond of social love is broken by the everlasting intrusion of this fiend of contention who lurks in the sparkling bowl, crouches by the fireside, in the friendly circle, infests every avenue to pleasure; and, like the scowling incubus, sits on the bosom of society, pressing down and smothering every throb and pulsation of liberal philanthropy.

But thou wilt perhaps ask, "What can these people dispute about? One would suppose that, being all free and equal, they would harmonize as brothers; children of the same parent, and equal heirs of the same inheritance." This theory is most exquisite, my good friend, but in practice it turns out the very dream of a madman. Equality, Asem, is one of the most consummate scoundrels that ever crept from the brain of a political juggler—a fellow who thrusts his hand into the pocket of honest industry, or enterprising talent, and squanders their hard-earned profits on profligate idleness or indolent stupidity. There will always be an inequality among mankind so long as a portion of it is enlightened and industrious, and the rest idle and ignorant. The one will acquire a larger share of wealth, and its attendant comforts, refinements, and luxuries of life, and the influence and power which those will always possess who have the greatest ability of administering to the necessities of their fellow-creatures. These advantages will inevitably excite envy; and envy as inevitably begets ill-will—hence arises that eternal warfare which the lower orders of society are waging against those who have raised themselves by their own merits, or have been raised by the merits of their ancestors, above the common level. In a nation possessed of quick feelings and impetuous passions, the hostility might engender deadly broils and bloody commotions; but here it merely vents itself in high-sounding words, which lead to continual breaches of decorum, or in the insidious assassination of character and a restless propensity among the base to blacken every reputation which is fairer than their own.

I cannot help smiling, sometimes, to see the solicitude with which the people of America, so called from the country having been first discovered by Christopher Columbus, battle about them when any election takes place, as if they had the least concern in the matter, or were to be benefited by an exchange of bashaws; they really seem ignorant that none but the bashaws and their dependents are at all interested in the event, and that the people at large will not find their situation altered in the least. I formerly gave thee an account of an election which took place under my eye. The result has been that the people, as some of the slangwhangers say, have obtained a glorious triumph, which, however, is flatly denied by the opposite slangwhangers, who insist that their party is composed of the true sovereign people; and that the others are all Jacobins, Frenchmen, and Irish rebels. I ought to apprise thee that the last is a term of great reproach here; which, perhaps, thou wouldst not otherwise imagine, considering that it is not many years since this very people were engaged in a revolution, the failure of which would have subjected them to the same ignominious epithet, and a participation in which is now the highest recommendation to public confidence. By Mahomet, but it cannot be denied that the consistency of this people, like everything else appertaining to them, is on a prodigious great scale! To return, however, to the event of the election. The people triumphed; and much good has it done them. I, for my part, expected to see wonderful changes, and most magical metamorphoses. I expected to see the people all rich, that they would be all gentleman bashaws, riding in their coaches and faring sumptuously every day, emancipated from toil and revelling in luxurious ease. Wilt thou credit me, Asem, when I declare unto thee, that everything remains exactly in the same state it was before the last wordy campaign? Except a few noisy retainers who have crept into office, and a few noisy patriots, on the other side, who have been kicked out, there is not the least difference. The laborer toils for his daily support; the beggar still lives on the charity of those who have any charity to bestow; and the only solid satisfaction the multitude have reaped is, that they have got a new governor, or bashaw, whom they will praise, idolize, and exalt for awhile, and afterward, notwithstanding the sterling merits he really possesses, in compliance with immemorial custom, they will abuse, calumniate, and trample him under foot.

Such, my dear Asem, is the way in which the wise people of "the most enlightened country under the sun," are amused with straws, and puffed up with mighty conceits; like a certain fish I have seen here, which, having his belly tickled for a short time, will swell and puff himself up to twice his usual size, and become a mere bladder of wind and vanity.

The blessing of a true Mussulman light on thee, good Asem; ever while thou livest be true to thy prophet; and rejoice that, though the boasting political chatterers of this logocracy cast upon thy countrymen the ignominious epithet of slaves, thou livest in a country where the people, instead of being at the mercy of a tyrant with a million of heads, have nothing to do but submit to the will of a bashaw of only three tails.

Ever thine,

MUSTAPHA.

FROM *A History of New-York*

Irving in 1808 planned to collaborate with his brother Peter on a parody of a popular guidebook, Dr. Samuel Latham Mitchill's *Picture of New-York* (1807), which would be "written in a serio-comic vein, and treating local errors, follies, and abuses with good-humored satire." Peter, however, left for Europe, and Irving became so fascinated by his study of old Dutch New York that he decided to write a comic history of that period alone. Aside from its burlesque elements, the book contains a good deal of reasonably authentic historical material; it is also tremendously allusive, reflecting on almost every page Irving's readings in Cervantes, Homer, Fielding, Sterne, Swift, Malory, and dozens of other sources. He introduced his book to the public by an intricate literary hoax, first placing advertisements in the papers asking for information concerning "a small, elderly gentleman, dressed in an old black coat and cocked hat," named Diedrich Knickerbocker. Knickerbocker's appearance was reported in several places, until finally his landlord announced that he was selling a manuscript, found in the old man's hotel room, to defray his overdue bills. The *History* appeared shortly afterwards.

Irving's aim, he later wrote, "was to embody the traditions of the city in an amusing form; to illustrate its local humors, customs, and peculiarities; to clothe home scenes and places and familiar names with those imaginative and whimsical associations so seldom met with in our new country, but which live like charms and spells about the cities of the old world, binding the heart of the native inhabitant to his home." He created Diedrich Knicker-

bocker as a gentle burlesque of the old Dutch New York-
ers and their descendants, but the name was soon adopted
by the public at large to designate any New Yorker, and
Father Knickerbocker, this "very worthy good sort of old
gentleman, though a little queer in his ways," became the
city's patron saint. Text: *A History of New-York from the
Beginning of the World to the End of the Dutch Dynasty*
(New York, 1849). The title page of the original edition in
1809 added: "Containing among many Surprising and Curious Matters, the Unutterable Ponderings of Walter the
Doubter, the Disastrous Projects of William the Testy, and
the Chivalric Achievements of Peter the Headstrong, the
three Dutch Governors of New Amsterdam; being the
only Authentic History of the Times that ever hath been,
or ever will be Published. By Diedrich Knickerbocker."
The *History* was divided into seven books: Book I treats of
the history of the world to the Dutch settlement of New
Amsterdam; Book II records the founding of the province;
Book III covers the period of Wouter Van Twiller; Book
IV records the reign of William the Testy, a rather pointed
burlesque of Thomas Jefferson and his administration;
Books V, VI, and VII are devoted to the governorship of
Peter Stuyvesant.

Book III

In Which Is Recorded the Golden Reign of Wouter Van Twiller

CHAPTER I

OF THE RENOWNED WOUTER VAN TWILLER, HIS UN-
PARALLELED VIRTUES—AS LIKEWISE HIS UNUTTER-
ABLE WISDOM IN THE LAW CASE OF WANDLE
SCOONHOVEN AND BARENT BLEECKER—AND THE
GREAT ADMIRATION OF THE PUBLIC THEREAT.

Grievous and very much to be commiserated is the
task of the feeling historian, who writes the history
of his native land. If it fall to his lot to be the
recorder of calamity or crime, the mournful page is
watered with his tears—nor can he recall the most
prosperous and blissful era, without a melancholy
sigh at the reflection, that it has passed away for
ever! I know not whether it be owing to an immoderate love for the simplicity of former times, or
to that certain tenderness of heart incident to all
sentimental historians; but I candidly confess that I
cannot look back on the happier days of our city,
which I now describe, without great dejection of
spirits. With faltering hand do I withdraw the curtain of oblivion, that veils the modest merit of our
venerable ancestors, and as their figures rise to my
mental vision, humble myself before their mighty
shades.

Such are my feelings when I revisit the family
mansion of the Knickerbockers, and spend a lonely
hour in the chamber where hang the portraits of my
forefathers, shrouded in dust, like the forms they
represent. With pious reverence do I gaze on the
countenances of those renowned burghers, who
have preceded me in the steady march of existence—whose sober and temperate blood now
meanders through my veins, flowing slower and
slower in its feeble conduits, until its current shall
soon be stopped for ever!

These, I say to myself, are but frail memorials of
the mighty men who flourished in the days of the
patriarchs; but who, alas, have long since mouldered
in that tomb, towards which my steps are insensibly
and irresistibly hastening! As I pace the darkened
chamber and lose myself in melancholy musings, the
shadowy images around me almost seem to steal
once more into existence—their countenances to assume the animation of life—their eyes to pursue me
in every movement! Carried away by the delusions
of fancy, I almost imagine myself surrounded by the
shades of the departed, and holding sweet converse
with the worthies of antiquity! Ah, hapless Diedrich!
born in a degenerate age, abandoned to the buffet-
ings of fortune—a stranger and a weary pilgrim in
thy native land—blest with no weeping wife, nor
family of helpless children; but doomed to wander
neglected through those crowded streets, and el-
bowed by foreign upstarts from those fair abodes
where once thine ancestors held sovereign empire!

Let me not, however, lose the historian in the
man, nor suffer the doting recollections of age to
overcome me, while dwelling with fond garrulity on
the virtuous days of the patriarchs—on those sweet
days of simplicity and ease, which never more will
dawn on the lovely island of Manna-hata.

These melancholy reflections have been forced
from me by the growing wealth and importance of
New-Amsterdam, which, I plainly perceive, are to
involve it in all kinds of perils and disasters. Already,
as I observed at the close of my last book, they had
awakened the attention of the mother country. The
usual mark of protection shown by mother countries
to wealthy colonies was forthwith manifested; a governor being sent out to rule over the province and
squeeze out of it as much revenue as possible. The
arrival of a governor of course put an end to the
protectorate of Oloffe the Dreamer. He appears,
however, to have dreamt to some purpose during his
sway, as we find him afterwards living as a patroon
on a great landed estate on the banks of the Hudson; having virtually forfeited all right to his ancient
appellation of Kortlandt or Lackland.

It was in the year of our Lord 1629 that Mynheer
Wouter Van Twiller was appointed governor of the
province of Nieuw-Nederlandts, under the commission and control of their High Mightinesses the
Lords States General of the United Netherlands, and
the privileged West India Company.

This renowned old gentleman arrived at New-
Amsterdam in the merry month of June, the

sweetest month in all the year; when dan Apollo seems to dance up the transparent firmament—when the robin, the thrush, and a thousand other wanton songsters make the woods to resound with amorous ditties, and the luxurious little boblincon revels among the clover blossoms of the meadows—all which happy coincidence persuaded the old dames of New-Amsterdam, who were skilled in the art of foretelling events, that this was to be a happy and prosperous administration.

The renowned Wouter (or Walter) Van Twiller, was descended from a long line of Dutch burgomasters, who had successively dozed away their lives, and grown fat upon the bench of magistracy in Rotterdam; and who had comported themselves with such singular wisdom and propriety, that they were never either heard or talked of—which, next to being universally applauded, should be the object of ambition of all magistrates and rulers. There are two opposite ways by which some men make a figure in the world; one by talking faster than they think; and the other by holding their tongues and not thinking at all. By the first many a smatterer acquires the reputation of a man of quick parts; by the other many a dunderpate, like the owl, the stupidest of birds, comes to be considered the very type of wisdom. This, by the way, is a casual remark, which I would not for the universe have it thought I apply to Governor Van Twiller. It is true he was a man shut up within himself, like an oyster, and rarely spoke except in monosyllables; but then it was allowed he seldom said a foolish thing. So invincible was his gravity that he was never known to laugh or even to smile through the whole course of a long and prosperous life. Nay if a joke were uttered in his presence, that set light-minded hearers in a roar, it was observed to throw him into a state of perplexity. Sometimes he would deign to inquire into the matter, and when, after much explanation, the joke was made as plain as a pike-staff; he would continue to smoke his pipe in silence, and at length, knocking out the ashes would exclaim, "Well! I see nothing in all that to laugh about."

With all his reflective habits, he never made up his mind on a subject. His adherents accounted for this by the astonishing magnitude of his ideas. He conceived every subject on so grand a scale that he had not room in his head to turn it over and examine both sides of it. Certain it is that if any matter were propounded to him on which ordinary mortals would rashly determine at first glance, he would put on a vague, mysterious look; shake his capacious head; smoke some time in profound silence, and at length observe that "he had his doubts about the matter," which gained him the reputation of a man slow of belief, and not easily imposed upon. What is more, it gained him a lasting name: for to this habit of the mind has been attributed his surname of Twiller, which is said to be a corruption of the original Twijfler, or, in plain English, *Doubter*.

The person of this illustrious old gentleman was formed and proportioned, as though it had been moulded by the hands of some cunning Dutch statuary, as a model of majesty and lordly grandeur. He was exactly five feet six inches in height, and six feet five inches in circumference. His head was a perfect sphere, and of such stupendous dimensions, that dame Nature with all her sex's ingenuity, would have been puzzled to construct a neck capable of supporting it, wherefore she wisely declined the attempt, and settled it firmly on the top of his backbone, just between the shoulders. His body was oblong and particularly capacious at bottom; which was wisely ordered by Providence, seeing that he was a man of sedentary habits, and very averse to the idle labor of walking. His legs were short, but sturdy in proportion to the weight they had to sustain; so that when erect he had not a little the appearance of a beer barrel on skids. His face, that infallible index of the mind, presented a vast expanse, unfurrowed by any of those lines and angles which disfigure the human countenance with what is termed expression. Two small gray eyes twinkled feebly in the midst, like two stars of lesser magnitude in a hazy firmament; and his full-fed cheeks, which seemed to have taken toll of every thing that went into his mouth, were curiously mottled and streaked with dusky red, like a spitzenberg apple.

His habits were as regular as his person. He daily took his four stated meals, appropriating exactly an hour to each; he smoked and doubted eight hours, and he slept the remaining twelve of the four-and-twenty. Such was the renowned Wouter Van Twiller—a true philosopher, for his mind was either elevated above, or tranquilly settled below, the cares and perplexities of this world. He had lived in it for years, without feeling the least curiosity to know whether the sun revolved round it, or it round the sun; and he had watched, for at least half a century, the smoke curling from his pipe to the ceiling, without once troubling his head with any of those numerous theories, by which a philosopher would have perplexed his brain, in accounting for its rising above the surrounding atmosphere.

In his council he presided with great state and solemnity. He sat in a huge chair of solid oak, hewn in the celebrated forest of the Hague, fabricated by an experienced timmerman of Amsterdam, and curiously carved about the arms and feet, into exact imitations of gigantic eagle's claws. Instead of a sceptre he swayed a long Turkish pipe, wrought with jasmin and amber, which had been presented to a stadtholder of Holland, at the conclusion of a treaty with one of the petty Barbary powers. In this stately chair would he sit, and this magnificent pipe would he smoke, shaking his right knee with a constant motion, and fixing his eye for hours together upon a little print of Amsterdam, which hung in a black frame against the opposite wall of the council chamber. Nay, it has even been said, that when any deliberation of extraordinary length and intricacy was on the carpet, the renowned Wouter would shut his eyes for full two hours at a time, that he might not be disturbed by external objects—and at such times the internal commotion of his mind was evinced by certain regular guttural sounds, which his admirers declared were merely the noise of conflict, made by his contending doubts and opinions.

It is with infinite difficulty I have been enabled to collect these biographical anecdotes of the great man under consideration. The facts respecting him were so scattered and vague, and divers of them so questionable in point of authenticity, that I have had to give up the search after many, and decline the admission of still more, which would have tended to heighten the coloring of his portrait.

I have been the more anxious to delineate fully the person and habits of Wouter Van Twiller, from the consideration that he was not only the first, but also the best governor that ever presided over this ancient and respectable province; and so tranquil and benevolent was his reign, that I do not find throughout the whole of it, a single instance of any offender being brought to punishment—a most indubitable sign of a merciful governor, and a case unparalleled, excepting in the reign of the illustrious King Log, from whom, it is hinted, the renowned Van Twiller was a lineal descendant.

The very outset of the career of this excellent magistrate was distinguished by an example of legal acumen, that gave flattering presage of a wise and equitable administration. The morning after he had been installed in office, and at the moment that he was making his breakfast from a prodigious earthen dish, filled with milk and Indian pudding, he was interrupted by the appearance of Wandle Schoonhoven, a very important old burgher of New-Amsterdam, who complained bitterly of one Barent Bleecker, inasmuch as he refused to come to a settlement of accounts, seeing that there was a heavy balance in favor of the said Wandle. Governor Van Twiller, as I have already observed, was a man of few words; he was likewise a mortal enemy to multiplying writings—or being disturbed at his breakfast. Having listened attentively to the statement of Wandle Schoonhoven, giving an occasional grunt, as he shoveled a spoonful of Indian pudding into his mouth—either as a sign that he relished the dish, or comprehended the story—he called unto him his constable, and pulling out of his breeches pocket a huge jack-knife, dispatched it after the defendant as a summons, accompanied by his tobacco-box as a warrant.

This summary process was as effectual in those simple days as was the seal ring of the great Haroun Alraschid among the true believers. The two parties being confronted before him, each produced a book of accounts, written in a language and character that would have puzzled any but a High Dutch commentator, or a learned decipherer of Egyptian obelisks. The sage Wouter took them one after the other, and having poised them in his hands, and attentively counted over the number of leaves, fell straightway into a very great doubt, and smoked for half an hour without saying a word; at length, laying his finger beside his nose, and shutting his eyes for a moment, with the air of a man who has just caught a subtle idea by the tail, he slowly took his pipe from his mouth, puffed forth a column of tobacco smoke, and with marvellous gravity and solemnity pronounced—that having carefully counted over the leaves and weighed the books, it was found, that one was just as thick and as heavy as the other—therefore it was the final opinion of the court that the accounts were equally balanced—therefore Wandle should give Barent a receipt, and Barent should give Wandle a receipt—and the constable should pay the costs.

This decision being straightway made known, diffused general joy throughout New-Amsterdam, for the people immediately perceived, that they had a very wise and equitable magistrate to rule over them. But its happiest effect was, that not another lawsuit took place throughout the whole of his administration—and the office of constable fell into such decay, that there was not one of those losel scouts known in the province for many years. I am the more particular in dwelling on this transaction, not only because I deem it one of the most sage and righteous judgments on record, and well worthy the attention of modern magistrates; but because it was a miraculous event in the history of the renowned Wouter—being the only time he was ever known to come to a decision in the whole course of his life.

1809

FROM *The Sketch Book*

In 1820 the English critic Sydney Smith sneered "And who, the wide world over, reads an American book?" The answer was already forthcoming, for within a few weeks Irving's *Sketch Book*, published by the great London publisher John Murray with Sir Walter Scott's blessing, took the reading public of Great Britain and America by storm. The complete edition contained thirty-two selections, only three—"Rip Van Winkle," "The Spectre Bridegroom," and "The Legend of Sleepy Hollow"—classifiable as tales, all of them reworkings of German legendary stories, provided with American backgrounds. As its name suggested, the book was chiefly composed of sketches of English life ("A Sunday in London"), comments on English customs ("Rural Funerals"), observations on famous places ("Westminster Abbey"), literary musings, anecdotes, and even two essays on the American Indian. The three tales were Irving's first experiments in the literary form soon to become the short story, to whose development he made his own unique and decisive contributions. He wrote later:

"I consider a story merely as a frame on which to stretch my materials. It is the play of thought, and sentiment and language; the weaving in of characters, lightly yet expressively delineated; the familiar and faithful exhibition of scenes in common life; and the half concealed vein of humour that is often playing through the whole—these are among what I aim at, and upon which I felicitate myself in proportion as I think I succeed. . . .

"I have preferred adopting a mode of sketches & short tales rather than long works, because I chose to take a line of writing peculiar to myself; rather than fall into the manner or school of any other writer: and there is a constant activity of thought and nicety of execution required in writings of this kind, more than the world appears to imagine. . . . In these shorter writings every page must have its merit. The author must be continually piquant—woe to him if he makes an awkward sentence or writes a stupid page; the critics are sure to pounce upon it. Yet if he succeed: the very variety and piquancy of his writings; nay their very brevity; makes them frequently recurred to—and when the mere interest of the story is exhausted, he begins to get credit for his touches of pathos or humour; his points of wit or turns of language. . . ."

The text follows that of the Knickerbocker Edition of the *Works*, Philadelphia, 1870–71. The sketches and stories were published originally in seven installments in New York between May 1819 and September 1820, then collected and published in London.

The Author's Account of Himself [1]

"I am of this mind with Homer, that as the snaile that crept out of her shel was turned eftsoons into a toad, and thereby was forced to make a stoole to sit on; so the traveller that straggleth from his owne country is in a short time transformed into so monstrous a shape, that he is faine to alter his mansion with his manners, and to live where he can, not where he would."—Lyly's *Euphues*.

I was always fond of visiting new scenes, and observing strange characters and manners. Even when a mere child I began my travels, and made many tours of discovery into foreign parts and unknown regions of my native city, to the frequent alarm of my parents, and the emolument of the town-crier. As I grew into boyhood, I extended the range of my observations. My holiday afternoons were spent in rambles about the surrounding country. I made myself familiar with all its places famous in history or fable. I knew every spot where a murder or robbery had been committed, or a ghost

[1] Presumably "Geoffrey Crayon, Gent.," the character invented by Irving to serve as author of *The Sketch Book*.

seen. I visited the neighboring villages, and added greatly to my stock of knowledge by noting their habits and customs, and conversing with their sages and great men. I even journeyed one long summer's day to the summit of the most distant hill, whence I stretched my eye over many a mile of *terra incognita,* and was astonished to find how vast a globe I inhabited.

This rambling propensity strengthened with my years. Books of voyages and travels became my passion, and in devouring their contents, I neglected the regular exercises of the school. How wistfully would I wander about the pier-heads in fine weather, and watch the parting ships, bound to distant climes; with what longing eyes would I gaze after their lessening sails and waft myself in imagination to the ends of the earth!

Further reading and thinking, though they brought this vague inclination into more reasonable bounds, only served to make it more decided. I visited various parts of my own country; and had I been merely a lover of fine scenery, I should have felt little desire to seek elsewhere its gratification, for on no country have the charms of nature been more prodigally lavished. Her mighty lakes, like oceans of liquid silver; her mountains, with their bright aerial tints; her valleys, teeming with wild fertility; her tremendous cataracts, thundering in their solitudes; her boundless plains, waving with spontaneous verdure; her broad deep rivers, rolling in solemn silence to the ocean; her trackless forests, where vegetation puts forth all its magnificence; her skies, kindling with the magic of summer clouds and glorious sunshine;—no, never need an American look beyond his own country for the sublime and beautiful of natural scenery.

But Europe held forth the charms of storied and poetical association. There were to be seen the masterpieces of art, the refinements of highly cultivated society, the quaint peculiarities of ancient and local custom. My native country was full of youthful promise: Europe was rich in the accumulated treasures of age. Her very ruins told the history of times gone by, and every mouldering stone was a chronicle. I longed to wander over the scenes of renowned achievement,—to tread, as it were, in the footsteps of antiquity,—to loiter about the ruined castle,—to meditate on the falling tower,—to escape, in short, from the commonplace realities of the present, and lose myself among the shadowy grandeurs of the past.

I had, beside all this, an earnest desire to see the great men of the earth. We have, it is true, our great men in America: not a city but has an ample share of them. I have mingled among them in my time, and been almost withered by the shade into which they cast me; for there is nothing so baleful to a small man as the shade of a great one, particularly the great man of a city. But I was anxious to see the great men of Europe; for I had read in the works of various philosophers, that all animals degenerated in America, and man among the number.[2] A great man of Europe, thought I, must therefore be as superior to a great man of America, as a peak of the Alps to a highland of the Hudson; and in this idea I was confirmed, by observing the comparative importance and swelling magnitude of many English travellers among us, who, I was assured, were very little people in their own country. I will visit this land of wonders, thought I, and see the gigantic race from which I am degenerated.

It has been either my good or evil lot to have my roving passion gratified. I have wandered through different countries, and witnessed many of the shifting scenes of life. I cannot say that I have studied them with the eye of a philosopher, but rather with the sauntering gaze with which humble lovers of the picturesque stroll from the window of one print-shop to another, caught sometimes by the delineations of beauty, sometimes by the distortions of caricature, and sometimes by the loveliness of landscape. As it is the fashion for modern tourists to travel pencil in hand, and bring home their portfolios filled with sketches, I am disposed to get up a few for the entertainment of my friends. When, however, I look over the hints and memorandums I have taken down for the purpose, my heart almost fails me at finding how my idle humor has led me aside from the great objects studied by every regular traveller who would make a book. I fear I shall give equal disappointment with an unlucky landscape-painter, who had travelled on the continent, but, following the bent of his vagrant inclination, had sketched in nooks, and corners, and by-places. His sketchbook was accordingly crowded with cottages, and landscapes, and obscure ruins; but he had neglected to paint St. Peter's, or the Coliseum; the cascade of Terni, or the bay of Naples; and had not a single glacier or volcano in his whole collection.

Rip Van Winkle

A POSTHUMOUS WRITING OF
DIEDRICH KNICKERBOCKER.

By Woden, God of Saxons,
From whence comes Wensday, that is Wodensday,
Truth is a thing that ever I will keep
Unto thylke day in which I creep into
My sepulchre—
                                    —Cartwright.

[2]A theory expounded especially by the French philosopher the Comte de Buffon.

The following Tale was found among the papers of the late Diedrich Knickerbocker, an old gentleman of New York, who was very curious in the Dutch history of the province, and the manners of the descendants from its primitive settlers. His historical researches, however, did not lie so much among books as among men; for the former are lamentably scanty on his favorite topics; whereas he found the old burghers, and still more their wives, rich in that legendary lore so invaluable to true history. Whenever, therefore, he happened upon a genuine Dutch family, snugly shut up in its low-roofed farmhouse, under a spreading sycamore, he looked upon it as a little clasped volume of black-letter, and studied it with the zeal of a book-worm.

The result of all these researches was a history of the province during the reign of the Dutch governors, which he published some years since. There have been various opinions as to the literary character of his work, and, to tell the truth, it is not a whit better than it should be. Its chief merit is its scrupulous accuracy, which indeed was a little questioned on its first appearance, but has since been completely established; and it is now admitted into all historical collections as a book of unquestionable authority.

The old gentleman died shortly after the publication of his work; and now that he is dead and gone, it cannot do much harm to his memory to say that his time might have been much better employed in weightier labors. He, however, was apt to ride his hobby his own way; and though it did now and then kick up the dust a little in the eyes of his neighbors, and grieve the spirit of some friends, for whom he felt the truest deference and affection, yet his errors and follies are remembered "more in sorrow than in anger," and it begins to be suspected that he never intended to offend. But however his memory may be appreciated by critics, it is still held dear by many folk whose good opinion is well worth having; particularly by certain biscuit-makers, who have gone so far as to imprint his likeness on their New-Year cakes; and have thus given him a chance for immortality, almost equal to being stamped on a Waterloo Medal, or a Queen Anne's Farthing.[1]]

Whoever has made a voyage up the Hudson must remember the Kaatskill mountains. They are a dismembered branch of the great Appalachian family, and are seen away to the west of the river, swelling up to a noble height, and lording it over the surrounding country. Every change of season, every change of weather, indeed, every hour of the day, produces some change in the magical hues and shapes of these mountains, and they are regarded by all the good wives, far and near, as perfect barometers. When the weather is fair and settled, they are clothed in blue and purple, and print their bold outlines on the clear evening sky; but sometimes, when the rest of the landscape is cloudless, they will gather a hood of gray vapors about their summits,

[1]All British veterans of the Battle of Waterloo received a medal bearing the likeness of the Prince Regent; the copper farthing bore Queen Anne's.

which, in the last rays of the setting sun, will glow and light up like a crown of glory.

At the foot of these fairy mountains, the voyager may have descried the light smoke curling up from a village, whose shingle roofs gleam among the trees, just where the blue tints of the upland melt away into the fresh green of the nearer landscape. It is a little village, of great antiquity, having been founded by some of the Dutch colonists in the early times of the province, just about the beginning of the government of the good Peter Stuyvesant (may he rest in peace!), and there were some of the houses of the original settlers standing within a few years, built of small yellow bricks brought from Holland, having latticed windows and gable fronts, surmounted with weathercocks.

In that same village, and in one of these very houses (which, to tell the precise truth, was sadly time-worn and weather-beaten), there lived, many years since, while the country was yet a province of Great Britain, a simple, good-natured fellow, of the name of Rip Van Winkle. He was a descendant of the Van Winkles who figured so gallantly in the chivalrous days of Peter Stuyvesant, and accompanied him to the siege of Fort Christina. He inherited, however, but little of the martial character of his ancestors. I have observed that he was a simple, good-natured man; he was, moreover, a kind neighbor, and an obedient, hen-pecked husband. Indeed, to the latter circumstance might be owing that meekness of spirit which gained him such universal popularity; for those men are most apt to be obsequious and conciliating abroad, who are under the discipline of shrews at home. Their tempers, doubtless, are rendered pliant and malleable in the fiery furnace of domestic tribulation; and a curtain-lecture is worth all the sermons in the world for teaching the virtues of patience and long-suffering. A termagant wife may, therefore, in some respects, be considered a tolerable blessing; and if so, Rip Van Winkle was thrice blessed.

Certain it is, that he was a great favorite among all the good wives of the village, who, as usual with the amiable sex, took his part in all family squabbles; and never failed, whenever they talked those matters over in their evening gossipings, to lay all the blame on Dame Van Winkle. The children of the village, too, would shout with joy whenever he approached. He assisted at their sports, made their playthings, taught them to fly kites and shoot marbles, and told them long stories of ghosts, witches, and Indians. Whenever he went dodging about the village, he was surrounded by a troop of them, hanging on his skirts, clambering on his back, and playing a thousand tricks on him with impunity; and not a dog would bark at him throughout the neighborhood.

The great error in Rip's composition was an insuperable aversion to all kinds of profitable labor. It could not be from the want of assiduity or perseverance; for he would sit on a wet rock, with a rod as long and heavy as a Tartar's lance, and fish all day without a murmur, even though he should not be encouraged by a single nibble. He would carry a fowling-piece on his shoulder for hours together, trudging through woods and swamps, and up hill and down dale, to shoot a few squirrels or wild pigeons. He would never refuse to assist a neighbor even in the roughest toil, and was a foremost man at all country frolics for husking Indian corn, or building stone fences; the women of the village, too, used to employ him to run their errands, and to do such little odd jobs as their less obliging husbands would not do for them. In a word, Rip was ready to attend to anybody's business but his own; but as to doing family duty, and keeping his farm in order, he found it impossible.

In fact, he declared it was of no use to work on his farm; it was the most pestilent little piece of ground in the whole country; everything about it went wrong, and would go wrong, in spite of him. His fences were continually falling to pieces; his cow would either go astray, or get among the cabbages; weeds were sure to grow quicker in his fields than anywhere else; the rain always made a point of setting in just as he had some out-door work to do; so that though his patrimonial estate had dwindled away under his management, acre by acre, until there was little more left than a mere patch of Indian corn and potatoes, yet it was the worst conditioned farm in the neighborhood.

His children, too, were as ragged and wild as if they belonged to nobody. His son Rip, an urchin begotten in his own likeness, promised to inherit the habits, with the old clothes, of his father. He was generally seen trooping like a colt at his mother's heels, equipped in a pair of his father's cast-off galligaskins,[2] which he had much ado to hold up with one hand, as a fine lady does her train in bad weather.

Rip Van Winkle, however, was one of those happy mortals, of foolish, well-oiled dispositions, who take the world easy, eat white bread or brown, whichever can be got with least thought or trouble, and would rather starve on a penny than work for a pound. If left to himself, he would have whistled life away in perfect contentment; but his wife kept continually dinning in his ears about his idleness, his carelessness, and the ruin he was bringing on his family. Morning, noon, and night, her tongue was incessantly going, and everything he said or did was sure to produce a torrent of household eloquence.

[2] Trousers.

Rip had but one way of replying to all lectures of the kind, and that, by frequent use, had grown into a habit. He shrugged his shoulders, shook his head, cast up his eyes, but said nothing. This, however, always provoked a fresh volley from his wife; so that he was fain to draw off his forces, and take to the outside of the house—the only side which, in truth, belongs to a hen-pecked husband.

Rip's sole domestic adherent was his dog Wolf, who was as much hen-pecked as his master; for Dame Van Winkle regarded them as companions in idleness, and even looked upon Wolf with an evil eye, as the cause of his master's going so often astray. True it is, in all points of spirit befitting an honorable dog, he was as courageous an animal as ever scoured the woods; but what courage can withstand the ever-enduring and all-besetting terrors of a woman's tongue? The moment Wolf entered the house his crest fell, his tail drooped to the ground, or curled between his legs, he sneaked about with a gallows air, casting many a sidelong glance at Dame Van Winkle, and at the least flourish of a broomstick or ladle he would fly to the door with yelping precipitation.

Times grew worse and worse with Rip Van Winkle as years of matrimony rolled on; a tart temper never mellows with age, and a sharp tongue is the only edged tool that grows keener with constant use. For a long while he used to console himself, when driven from home, by frequenting a kind of perpetual club of the sages, philosophers, and other idle personages of the village, which held its sessions on a bench before a small inn, designated by a rubicund portrait of His Majesty George the Third. Here they used to sit in the shade through a long, lazy summer's day, talking listlessly over village gossip, or telling endless sleepy stories about nothing. But it would have been worth any statesman's money to have heard the profound discussions that sometimes took place, when by chance an old newspaper fell into their hands from some passing traveller. How solemnly they would listen to the contents, as drawled out by Derrick Van Bummel, the schoolmaster, a dapper learned little man, who was not to be daunted by the most gigantic word in the dictionary; and how sagely they would deliberate upon public events some months after they had taken place.

The opinions of this junto were completely controlled by Nicholas Vedder, patriarch of the village, and landlord of the inn, at the door of which he took his seat from morning till night, just moving sufficiently to avoid the sun and keep in the shade of a large tree; so that the neighbors could tell the hour by his movements as accurately as by a sundial. It is true he was rarely heard to speak, but smoked his pipe incessantly. His adherents, however (for every great man has his adherents), perfectly understood him, and knew how to gather his opinions. When anything that was read or related displeased him, he was observed to smoke his pipe vehemently, and to send forth short, frequent, and angry puffs; but when pleased, he would inhale the smoke slowly and tranquilly, and emit it in light and placid clouds; and sometimes, taking the pipe from his mouth, and letting the fragrant vapor curl about his nose, would gravely nod his head in token of perfect approbation.

From even this stronghold the unlucky Rip was at length routed by his termagant wife, who would suddenly break in upon the tranquillity of the assemblage and call the members all to naught; nor was that august personage, Nicholas Vedder himself, sacred from the daring tongue of this terrible virago, who charged him outright with encouraging her husband in habits of idleness.

Poor Rip was at last reduced almost to despair; and his only alternative, to escape from the labor of the farm and clamor of his wife, was to take gun in hand and stroll away into the woods. Here he would sometimes seat himself at the foot of a tree, and share the contents of his wallet with Wolf, with whom he sympathized as a fellow-sufferer in persecution. "Poor Wolf," he would say, "thy mistress leads thee a dog's life of it, but never mind, my lad, whilst I live thou shalt never want a friend to stand by thee!" Wolf would wag his tail, look wistfully in his master's face, and if dogs can feel pity, I verily believe he reciprocated the sentiment with all his heart.

In a long ramble of the kind on a fine autumnal day, Rip had unconsciously scrambled to one of the highest parts of the Kaatskill mountains. He was after his favorite sport of squirrel-shooting, and the still solitudes had echoed and re-echoed with the reports of his gun. Panting and fatigued, he threw himself, late in the afternoon, on a green knoll, covered with mountain herbage, that crowned the brow of a precipice. From an opening between the trees he could overlook all the lower country for many a mile of rich woodland. He saw at a distance the lordly Hudson, far, far below him, moving on its silent but majestic course, with the reflection of a purple cloud, or the sail of a lagging bark, here and there sleeping on its glassy bosom, and at last losing itself in the blue highlands.

On the other side he looked down into a deep mountain glen, wild, lonely, and shagged, the bottom filled with fragments from the impending cliffs, and scarcely lighted by the reflected rays of the setting sun. For some time Rip lay musing on this scene; evening was gradually advancing; the mountains began to throw their long blue shadows over the valleys; he saw that it would be dark long before he could reach the village, and he heaved a heavy sigh when he thought of encountering the terrors of Dame Van Winkle.

As he was about to descend, he heard a voice from a distance, hallooing, "Rip Van Winkle, Rip Van Winkle!" He looked round, but could see nothing but a crow winging its solitary flight across the mountain. He thought his fancy must have deceived him, and turned again to descend, when he heard the same cry ring through the still evening air: "Rip Van Winkle! Rip Van Winkle!"—at the same time Wolf bristled up his back, and giving a low growl, skulked to his master's side, looking fearfully down into the glen. Rip now felt a vague apprehension stealing over him; he looked anxiously in the same direction, and perceived a strange figure slowly toiling up the rocks, and bending under the weight of something he carried on his back. He was surprised to see any human being in this lonely and unfrequented place; but supposing it to be some one of the neighborhood in need of his assistance, he hastened down to yield it.

On nearer approach he was still more surprised at the singularity of the stranger's appearance. He was a short, square-built old fellow, with thick bushy hair, and a grizzled beard. His dress was of the antique Dutch fashion,—a cloth jerkin strapped around the waist—several pair of breeches, the outer one of ample volume, decorated with rows of buttons down the sides, and bunches at the knees. He bore on his shoulders a stout keg, that seemed full of liquor, and made signs for Rip to approach and assist him with the load. Though rather shy and distrustful of this new acquaintance, Rip complied with his usual alacrity; and mutually relieving one another, they clambered up a narrow gully, apparently the dry bed of a mountain torrent. As they ascended, Rip every now and then heard long, rolling peals, like distant thunder, that seemed to issue out of a deep ravine, or rather cleft, between lofty rocks, toward which their rugged path conducted. He paused for an instant, but supposing it to be the muttering of one of those transient thunder-showers which often take place in mountain heights, he proceeded. Passing through the ravine, they came to a hollow, like a small amphitheatre, surrounded by perpendicular precipices, over the brinks of which impending trees shot their branches, so that you only caught glimpses of the azure sky and the bright evening cloud. During the whole time Rip and his companion had labored on in silence; for though the former marvelled greatly what could be the object of carrying a keg of liquor up this wild mountain, yet there was something strange and incomprehensible about the unknown, that inspired awe and checked familiarity.

On entering the amphitheatre, new objects of wonder presented themselves. On a level spot in the centre was a company of odd-looking personages playing at ninepins. They were dressed in a quaint, outlandish fashion; some wore short doublets, others jerkins, with long knives in their belts, and most of them had enormous breeches, of similar style with that of the guide's. Their visages, too, were peculiar: one had a large beard, broad face, and small piggish eyes; the face of another seemed to consist entirely of nose, and was surmounted by a white sugar-loaf hat, set off with a little red cock's tail. They all had beards of various shapes and colors. There was one who seemed to be the commander. He was a stout old gentleman, with a weather-beaten countenance; he wore a laced doublet, broad belt and hanger, high crowned hat and feather, red stockings, and high-heeled shoes, with roses[3] in them. The whole group reminded Rip of the figures in an old Flemish painting, in the parlor of Dominie Van Shaick, the village parson, and which had been brought over from Holland at the time of the settlement.

What seemed particularly odd to Rip was, that, though these folks were evidently amusing themselves, yet they maintained the gravest faces, the most mysterious silence, and were, withal, the most melancholy party of pleasure he had ever witnessed. Nothing interrupted the stillness of the scene but the noise of the balls, which, whenever they rolled, echoed along the mountains like rumbling peals of thunder.

As Rip and his companion approached them, they suddenly desisted from their play, and stared at him with such fixed, statue-like gaze, and such strange, uncouth, lack-lustre countenances, that his heart turned within him, and his knees smote together. His companion now emptied the contents of the keg into large flagons, and made signs to him to wait upon the company. He obeyed with fear and trembling; they quaffed the liquor in profound silence, and then returned to their game.

By degrees Rip's awe and apprehension subsided. He even ventured, when no eye was fixed upon him, to taste the beverage, which he found had much of the flavor of excellent Hollands.[4] He was naturally a thirsty soul, and was soon tempted to repeat the draught. One taste provoked another; and he reiterated his visits to the flagon so often that at length his senses were overpowered, his eyes swam in his head, his head gradually declined, and he fell into a deep sleep.

On waking, he found himself on the green knoll whence he had first seen the old man of the glen. He rubbed his eyes—it was a bright sunny morning. The birds were hopping and twittering among the

[3] Rosettes.
[4] Gin.

bushes, and the eagle was wheeling aloft, and breasting the pure mountain breeze. "Surely," thought Rip, "I have not slept here all night." He recalled the occurrences before he fell asleep. The strange man with a keg of liquor—the mountain ravine—the wild retreat among the rocks—the woe-begone party at ninepins—the flagon—"Oh! that flagon! that wicked flagon!" thought Rip, "what excuse shall I make to Dame Van Winkle?"

He looked round for his gun, but in place of the clean, well-oiled fowling-piece, he found an old firelock lying by him, the barrel encrusted with rust, the lock falling off, and the stock worm-eaten. He now suspected that the grave roisters of the mountains had put a trick upon him, and, having dosed him with liquor, had robbed him of his gun. Wolf, too, had disappeared, but he might have strayed away after a squirrel or partridge. He whistled after him, and shouted his name, but all in vain; the echoes repeated his whistle and shout, but no dog was to be seen.

He determined to revisit the scene of the last evening's gambol, and if he met with any of the party, to demand his dog and gun. As he rose to walk, he found himself stiff in the joints, and wanting in his usual activity. "These mountain beds do not agree with me," thought Rip, "and if this frolic should lay me up with a fit of the rheumatism, I shall have a blessed time with Dame Van Winkle." With some difficulty he got down into the glen: he found the gully up which he and his companion had ascended the preceding evening; but to his astonishment a mountain stream was now foaming down it, leaping from rock to rock, and filling the glen with babbling murmurs. He, however, made shift to scramble up its sides, working his toilsome way through thickets of birch, sassafras, and witch-hazel, and sometimes tripped up or entangled by the wild grape-vines that twisted their coils or tendrils from tree to tree, and spread a kind of network in his path.

At length he reached to where the ravine had opened through the cliffs to the amphitheatre; but no traces of such opening remained. The rocks presented a high, impenetrable wall, over which the torrent came tumbling in a sheet of feathery foam, and fell into a broad deep basin, black from the shadows of the surrounding forest. Here, then, poor Rip was brought to a stand. He again called and whistled after his dog; he was only answered by the cawing of a flock of idle crows, sporting high in air about a dry tree that overhung a sunny precipice; and who, secure in their elevation, seemed to look down and scoff at the poor man's perplexities. What was to be done? the morning was passing away, and Rip felt famished for want of his breakfast. He grieved to give up his dog and gun; he dreaded to meet his wife; but it would not do to starve among the mountains. He shook his head, shouldered the rusty firelock, and, with a heart full of trouble and anxiety, turned his footsteps homeward.

As he approached the village he met a number of people, but none whom he knew, which somewhat surprised him, for he had thought himself acquainted with every one in the country round. Their dress, too, was of a different fashion from that to which he was accustomed. They all stared at him with equal marks of surprise, and whenever they cast their eyes upon him, invariably stroked their chins. The constant recurrence of this gesture induced Rip, involuntarily, to do the same, when, to his astonishment, he found his beard had grown a foot long!

He had now entered the skirts of the village. A troop of strange children ran at his heels, hooting after him, and pointing at his gray beard. The dogs, too, not one of which he recognized for an old acquaintance, barked at him as he passed. The very village was altered; it was larger and more populous. There were rows of houses which he had never seen before, and those which had been his familiar haunts had disappeared. Strange names were over the doors—strange faces at the windows—everything was strange. His mind now misgave him; he began to doubt whether both he and the world around him were not bewitched. Surely this was his native village, which he had left but the day before. There stood the Kaatskill mountains—there ran the silver Hudson at a distance—there was every hill and dale precisely as it had always been. Rip was sorely perplexed. "That flagon last night," thought he, "has addled my poor head sadly!"

It was with some difficulty that he found the way to his own house, which he approached with silent awe, expecting every moment to hear the shrill voice of Dame Van Winkle. He found the house gone to decay—the roof fallen in, the windows shattered, and the doors off the hinges. A half-starved dog that looked like Wolf was skulking about it. Rip called him by name, but the cur snarled, showed his teeth, and passed on. This was an unkind cut indeed. "My very dog," sighed poor Rip, "has forgotten me!"

He entered the house, which, to tell the truth, Dame Van Winkle had always kept in neat order. It was empty, forlorn, and apparently abandoned. This desolateness overcame all his connubial fears—he called loudly for his wife and children—the lonely chambers rang for a moment with his voice, and then all again was silence.

He now hurried forth, and hastened to his old resort, the village inn, but it too was gone. A large rickety wooden building stood in its place, with great gaping windows, some of them broken and mended with old hats and petticoats, and over the door was painted, "The Union Hotel, by Jonathan Doolittle." Instead of the great tree that used to shelter the quiet little Dutch inn of yore, there now was reared a tall naked pole, with something on the top that looked like a red night-cap,[5] and from it was fluttering a flag, on which was a singular assemblage of stars and stripes;—all this was strange and incomprehensible. He recognized on the sign, however, the ruby face of King George, under which he had smoked so many a peaceful pipe; but even this was singularly metamorphosed. The red coat was changed for one of blue and buff, a sword was held in the hand instead of a sceptre, the head was decorated with a cocked hat, and underneath was painted in large characters, GENERAL WASHINGTON.

There was, as usual, a crowd of folk about the door, but none that Rip recollected. The very character of the people seemed changed. There was a busy, bustling, disputatious tone about it, instead of the accustomed phlegm and drowsy tranquillity. He looked in vain for the sage Nicholas Vedder, with his broad face, double chin, and fair long pipe, uttering clouds of tobacco-smoke instead of idle speeches; or Van Bummel, the schoolmaster, doling forth the contents of an ancient newspaper. In place of these, a lean, bilious-looking fellow, with his pockets full of handbills, was haranguing vehemently about rights of citizens—elections—members of congress — liberty — Bunker's Hill — heroes of seventy-six—and other words, which were a perfect Babylonish jargon to the bewildered Van Winkle.

The appearance of Rip, with his long, grizzled beard, his rusty fowling-piece, his uncouth dress, and an army of women and children at his heels, soon attracted the attention of the tavern-politicians. They crowded round him, eying him from head to foot with great curiosity. The orator bustled up to him, and, drawing him partly aside, inquired "On which side he voted?" Rip stared in vacant stupidity. Another short but busy little fellow pulled him by the arm, and, rising on tiptoe, inquired in his ear, "Whether he was Federal or Democrat?" Rip was equally at a loss to comprehend the question; when a knowing, self-important old gentleman, in a sharp cocked hat, made his way through the crowd, putting them to the right and left with his elbows as he passed, and planting himself before Van Winkle, with one arm akimbo, the other resting on his cane, his keen eyes and sharp hat penetrating, as it were, into his very soul, demanded in an austere tone, "What brought him to the election with a gun on his shoulder, and a mob at his heels; and whether he meant to breed a riot in the village?"—"Alas! gentlemen," cried Rip, somewhat dismayed, "I am a poor quiet man, a native of the place, and a loyal subject of the King, God bless him!"

Here a general shout burst from the by-standers—"A tory! a tory! a spy! a refugee! hustle him! away with him!" It was with great difficulty that the self-important man in the cocked hat restored order; and, having assumed a tenfold austerity of brow, demanded again of the unknown culprit, what he came there for, and whom he was seeking? The poor man humbly assured him that he meant no harm, but merely came there in search of some of his neighbors, who used to keep about the tavern.

"Well—who are they?—name them."

Rip bethought himself a moment, and inquired, "Where's Nicholas Vedder?"

There was a silence for a little while, when an old man replied, in a thin piping voice, "Nicholas Vedder! why, he is dead and gone these eighteen years! There was a wooden tombstone in the churchyard that used to tell all about him, but that's rotten and gone too."

"Where's Brom Dutcher?"

"Oh, he went off to the army in the beginning of the war; some say he was killed at the storming of Stony Point—others say he was drowned in a squall at the foot of Antony's Nose.[6] I don't know—he never came back again."

"Where's Van Bummel, the schoolmaster?"

"He went off to the wars too, was a great militia general, and is now in congress."

Rip's heart died away at hearing of these sad changes in his home and friends, and finding himself thus alone in the world. Every answer puzzled him too, by treating of such enormous lapses of time, and of matters which he could not understand: war—congress—Stony Point—he had no courage to ask after any more friends, but cried out in despair, "Does nobody here know Rip Van Winkle?"

"Oh, Rip Van Winkle!" exclaimed two or three, "oh, to be sure! that's Rip Van Winkle yonder, leaning against the tree."

Rip looked, and he beheld a precise counterpart of himself, as he went up the mountain; apparently as lazy, and certainly as ragged. The poor fellow was now completely confounded. He doubted his own identity, and whether he was himself or another man. In the midst of his bewilderment, the man in the cocked hat demanded who he was, and what was his name.

"God knows," exclaimed he, at his wit's end; "I'm not myself—I'm somebody else—that's me yonder—no—that's somebody else got into my shoes—I was myself last night, but I fell asleep on the mountain, and they've changed my gun, and everything's

---

[5] A "liberty cap," symbol of the recent Revolution.

[6] A headland and mountain near West Point.

changed, and I'm changed, and I can't tell what's my name, or who I am!"

The by-standers began now to look at each other, nod, wink significantly, and tap their fingers against their foreheads. There was a whisper, also, about securing the gun, and keeping the old fellow from doing mischief, at the very suggestion of which the self-important man in the cocked hat retired with some precipitation. At this critical moment a fresh, comely woman pressed through the throng to get a peep at the gray-bearded man. She had a chubby child in her arms, which, frightened at his looks, began to cry. "Hush, Rip," cried she, "hush, you little fool; the old man won't hurt you." The name of the child, the air of the mother, the tone of her voice, all awakened a train of recollections in his mind. "What is your name, my good woman?" asked he.

"Judith Gardenier."

"And your father's name?"

"Ah, poor man, Rip Van Winkle was his name, but it's twenty years since he went away from home with his gun, and never has been heard of since,— his dog came home without him; but whether he shot himself, or was carried away by the Indians, nobody can tell. I was then but a little girl."

Rip had but one question more to ask; but he put it with a faltering voice:

"Where's your mother?"

"Oh, she too had died but a short time since; she broke a bloodvessel in a fit of passion at a New England pedler."

There was a drop of comfort, at least, in this intelligence. The honest man could contain himself no longer. He caught his daughter and her child in his arms. "I am your father!" cried he—"Young Rip Van Winkle once—old Rip Van Winkle now!—Does nobody know poor Rip Van Winkle?"

All stood amazed, until an old woman, tottering out from among the crowd, put her hand to her brow, and peering under it in his face for a moment, exclaimed, "Sure enough! it is Rip Van Winkle—it is himself! Welcome home again, old neighbor. Why, where have you been these twenty long years?"

Rip's story was soon told, for the whole twenty years had been to him but as one night. The neighbors stared when they heard it; some were seen to wink at each other, and put their tongues in their cheeks: and the self-important man in the cocked hat, who, when the alarm was over, had returned to the field, screwed down the corners of his mouth, and shook his head—upon which there was a general shaking of the head throughout the assemblage.

It was determined, however, to take the opinion of old Peter Vanderdonk, who was seen slowly advancing up the road. He was a descendant of the historian of that name, who wrote one of the earliest accounts of the province. Peter was the most ancient inhabitant of the village, and well versed in all the wonderful events and traditions of the neighborhood. He recollected Rip at once, and corroborated his story in the most satisfactory manner. He assured the company that it was a fact, handed down from his ancestor the historian, that the Kaatskill mountains had always been haunted by strange beings. That it was affirmed that the great Hendrick Hudson, the first discoverer of the river and country, kept a kind of vigil there every twenty years, with his crew of the *Half-moon*; being permitted in this way to revisit the scenes of his enterprise, and keep a guardian eye upon the river and the great city called by his name.[7] That his father had once seen them in their old Dutch dresses playing at ninepins in a hollow of the mountain; and that he himself had heard, one summer afternoon, the sound of their balls, like distant peals of thunder.

To make a long story short, the company broke up and returned to the more important concerns of the election. Rip's daughter took him home to live with her; she had a snug, well-furnished house, and a stout, cheery farmer for a husband, whom Rip recollected for one of the urchins that used to climb upon his back. As to Rip's son and heir, who was the ditto of himself, seen leaning against the tree, he was employed to work on the farm; but evinced an hereditary disposition to attend to anything else but his business.

Rip now resumed his old walks and habits; he soon found many of his former cronies, though all rather the worse for the wear and tear of time; and preferred making friends among the rising generation, with whom he soon grew into great favor.

Having nothing to do at home, and being arrived at that happy age when a man can be idle with impunity, he took his place once more on the bench at the inn-door, and was reverenced as one of the patriarchs of the village, and a chronicle of the old times "before the war." It was some time before he could get into the regular track of gossip, or could be made to comprehend the strange events that had taken place during his torpor. How that there had been a revolutionary war,—that the country had thrown off the yoke of old England,—and that, instead of being a subject of his Majesty George the Third, he was now a free citizen of the United States. Rip, in fact, was no politician; the changes of states and empires made but little impression on him; but there was one species of despotism under which he had long groaned, and that was—petticoat government. Happily that was at an end; he had got his neck out of the yoke of matrimony, and could go in and out whenever he pleased, without dreading

[7] Hudson, New York, was an important shipping center in Irving's time.

the tyranny of Dame Van Winkle. Whenever her name was mentioned, however, he shook his head, shrugged his shoulders, and cast up his eyes; which might pass either for an expression of resignation to his fate, or joy at his deliverance.

He used to tell his story to every stranger that arrived at Mr. Doolittle's hotel. He was observed, at first, to vary on some points every time he told it, which was, doubtless, owing to his having so recently awaked. It at last settled down precisely to the tale I have related, and not a man, woman, or child in the neighborhood but knew it by heart. Some always pretended to doubt the reality of it, and insisted that Rip had been out of his head, and that this was one point on which he always remained flighty. The old Dutch inhabitants, however, almost universally gave it full credit. Even to this day they never hear a thunderstorm of a summer afternoon about the Kaatskill, but they say Hendrick Hudson and his crew are at their game of ninepins; and it is a common wish of all hen-pecked husbands in the neighborhood, when life hangs heavy on their hands, that they might have a quieting draught out of Rip Van Winkle's flagon.

NOTE.

The foregoing Tale, one would suspect, had been suggested to Mr. Knickerbocker by a little German superstition about the Emperor Frederick *der Rothbart,* and the Kypphäuser mountain: the subjoined note, however, which he had appended to the tale, shows that it is an absolute fact, narrated with his usual fidelity.

"The story of Rip Van Winkle may seem incredible to many, but nevertheless I give it my full belief, for I know the vicinity of our old Dutch settlements to have been very subject to marvellous events and appearances. Indeed, I have heard many stranger stories than this, in the villages along the Hudson; all of which were too well authenticated to admit of a doubt. I have even talked with Rip Van Winkle myself, who, when last I saw him, was a very venerable old man, and so perfectly rational and consistent on every other point, that I think no conscientious person could refuse to take this into the bargain; nay, I have seen a certificate on the subject taken before a country justice and signed with a cross, in the justice's own handwriting. The story, therefore, is beyond the possibility of doubt.
"D. K."

POSTSCRIPT.

The following are travelling notes from a memorandum-book of Mr. Knickerbocker.

The Kaatsberg, or Catskill Mountains, have always been a region full of fable. The Indians considered them the abode of spirits, who influenced the weather, spreading sunshine or clouds over the landscape, and sending good or bad hunting-seasons. They were ruled by an old squaw spirit, said to be their mother. She dwelt on the highest peak of the Catskills, and had charge of the doors of day and night to open and shut them at the proper hour. She hung up the new moons in the skies, and cut up the old ones into stars. In times of drought, if properly propitiated, she would spin light summer clouds out of cobwebs and morning dew, and send them off from the crest of the mountain, flake after flake, like flakes of carded cotton, to float in the air; until, dissolved by the heat of the sun, they would fall in gentle showers, causing the grass to spring, the fruits to ripen, and the corn to grow an inch an hour. If displeased, however, she would brew up clouds black as ink, sitting in the midst of them like a bottle-bellied spider in the midst of its web; and when these clouds broke, woe betide the valleys!

In old times, say the Indian traditions, there was a kind of Manitou or Spirit, who kept about the wildest recesses of the Catskill Mountains, and took a mischievous pleasure in wreaking all kinds of evils and vexations upon the red men. Sometimes he would assume the form of a bear, a panther, or a deer, lead the bewildered hunter a weary chase through tangled forests and among ragged rocks; and then spring off with a loud ho! ho! leaving him aghast on the brink of a beetling precipice or raging torrent.

The favorite abode of this Manitou is still shown. It is a great rock or cliff on the loneliest part of the mountains, and, from the flowering vines which clamber about it, and the wild flowers which abound in its neighborhood, is known by the name of the Garden Rock. Near the foot of it is a small lake, the haunt of the solitary bittern, with water-snakes basking in the sun on the leaves of the pond-lilies which lie on the surface. This place was held in great awe by the Indians, insomuch that the boldest hunter would not pursue his game within its precincts. Once upon a time, however, a hunter who had lost his way, penetrated to the Garden Rock, where he beheld a number of gourds placed in the crotches of trees. One of these he seized and made off with it, but in the hurry of his retreat he let it fall among the rocks, when a great stream gushed forth, which washed him away and swept him down precipices, where he was dashed to pieces, and the stream made its way to the Hudson, and continues to flow to the present day; being the identical stream known by the name of the Kaaterskill.

The Legend of Sleepy Hollow

FOUND AMONG THE PAPERS OF
THE LATE DIEDRICH KNICKERBOCKER

A pleasing land of drowsy head it was,
    Of dreams that wave before the half-shut eye,
And of gay castles in the clouds that pass,
    For ever flushing round a summer sky.
            Castle of Indolence.

In the bosom of one of those spacious coves which indent the eastern shore of the Hudson, at that broad expansion of the river denominated by the ancient Dutch navigators the Tappan Zee, and where they always prudently shortened sail, and implored the protection of St. Nicholas when they crossed, there lies a small market-town or rural port, which by some is called Greensburgh, but which is more generally and properly known by the name of Tarry Town. This name was given, we are told, in former days, by the good housewives of the adjacent country, from the inveterate propensity of their husbands to linger about the village tavern on market-days. Be that as it may, I do not vouch for the fact, but merely advert to it for the sake of being precise and authentic. Not far from this village, perhaps about two miles, there is a little valley, or rather lap of land, among high hills, which is one of the quietest places in the whole world. A small brook glides through it, with just murmur enough to lull one to repose; and the occasional whistle of a quail, or tapping of a woodpecker, is almost the only sound that ever breaks in upon the uniform tranquillity.

I recollect that, when a stripling, my first exploit in squirrel-shooting was in a grove of tall walnut-trees that shades one side of the valley. I had wandered into it at noon-time, when all nature is particularly quiet, and was startled by the roar of my own gun, as it broke the Sabbath stillness around, and was prolonged and reverberated by the angry echoes. If ever I should wish for a retreat, whither I might steal from the world and its distractions, and dream quietly away the remnant of a troubled life, I know of none more promising than this little valley.

From the listless repose of the place, and the peculiar character of its inhabitants, who are descendants from the original Dutch settlers, this sequestered glen has long been known by the name of SLEEPY HOLLOW, and its rustic lads are called the Sleepy Hollow Boys throughout all the neighboring country. A drowsy, dreamy influence seems to hang over the land, and to pervade the very atmosphere. Some say that the place was bewitched by a high German doctor,[1] during the early days of the settlement; others, that an old Indian chief, the prophet or wizard of his tribe, held his pow-wows there before the country was discovered by Master Hendrick Hudson. Certain it is, the place still continues under the sway of some bewitching power, that holds a spell over the minds of the good people, causing them to walk in a continual reverie. They are given to all kinds of marvellous beliefs; are subject to trances and visions; and frequently see strange sights, and hear music and voices in the air. The whole neighborhood abounds with local tales, haunted spots, and twilight superstitions; stars shoot and meteors glare oftener across the valley than in any other part of the country, and the nightmare,[2] with her whole ninefold, seems to make it the favorite scene of her gambols.

The dominant spirit, however, that haunts this enchanted region, and seems to be commander-in-chief of all the powers of the air, is the apparition of a figure on horseback without a head. It is said by some to be the ghost of a Hessian trooper, whose head had been carried away by a cannon-ball, in some nameless battle during the Revolutionary War, and who is ever and anon seen by the country folk, hurrying along in the gloom of night, as if on the wings of the wind. His haunts are not confined to the valley, but extend at times to the adjacent roads, and especially to the vicinity of a church at no great distance. Indeed, certain of the most authentic historians of those parts, who have been careful in collecting and collating the floating facts concerning this spectre, allege that the body of the trooper, having been buried in the churchyard, the ghost rides forth to the scene of battle in nightly quest of his head; and that the rushing speed with which he sometimes passes along the Hollow, like a midnight blast, is owing to his being belated, and in a hurry to get back to the churchyard before daybreak.

Such is the general purport of this legendary superstition, which has furnished materials for many a wild story in that region of shadows; and the spectre is known, at all the country firesides, by the name of the Headless Horseman of Sleepy Hollow.

It is remarkable that the visionary propensity I have mentioned is not confined to the native inhabitants of the valley, but is unconsciously imbibed by every one who resides there for a time. However wide awake they may have been before they entered that sleepy region, they are sure, in a little time, to inhale the witching influence of the air, and begin to grow imaginative, to dream dreams, and see apparitions.

I mention this peaceful spot with all possible laud; for it is in such little retired Dutch valleys, found here and there embosomed in the great State of New York, that population, manners, and customs remain fixed; while the great torrent of migration and improvement, which is making such incessant changes in other parts of this restless country, sweeps by them unobserved. They are like those little nooks of still water which border a rapid stream; where we may see the straw and bubble riding quietly at anchor, or slowly revolving in their mimic harbor, undisturbed by the rush of the passing current. Though many years have elapsed since I trod the drowsy shades of Sleepy Hollow, yet I question whether I should not still find the same

---

[1] "High" or southern German.

[2] A particular kind of witch, accompanied by nine assistants.

trees and the same families vegetating in its sheltered bosom.

In this by-place of nature, there abode, in a remote period of American history, that is to say, some thirty years since, a worthy wight of the name of Ichabod Crane; who sojourned, or, as he expressed it, "tarried," in Sleepy Hollow, for the purpose of instructing the children of the vicinity. He was a native of Connecticut, a State which supplies the Union with pioneers for the mind as well as for the forest, and sends forth yearly its legions of frontier woodsmen and country schoolmasters. The cognomen of Crane was not inapplicable to his person. He was tall, but exceedingly lank, with narrow shoulders, long arms and legs, hands that dangled a mile out of his sleeves, feet that might have served for shovels, and his whole frame most loosely hung together. His head was small, and flat at top, with huge ears, large green glassy eyes, and a long snipe nose, so that it looked like a weathercock perched upon his spindle neck, to tell which way the wind blew. To see him striding along the profile of a hill on a windy day, with his clothes bagging and fluttering about him, one might have mistaken him for the genius of famine descending upon the earth, or some scarecrow eloped from a corn-field.

His school-house was a low building of one large room, rudely constructed of logs; the windows partly glazed, and partly patched with leaves of old copy-books. It was most ingeniously secured at vacant hours by a withe twisted in the handle of the door, and stakes set against the window-shutters; so that, though a thief might get in with perfect ease, he would find some embarrassment in getting out: an idea most probably borrowed by the architect, Yost Van Houten, from the mystery of an eel-pot. The school-house stood in a rather lonely but pleasant situation, just at the foot of a woody hill, with a brook running close by, and a formidable birch-tree growing at one end of it. From hence the low murmur of his pupils' voices, conning over their lessons, might be heard on a drowsy summer's day, like the hum of a bee-hive; interrupted now and then by the authoritative voice of the master, in the tone of menace or command; or, peradventure, by the appalling sound of the birch, as he urged some tardy loiterer along the flowery path of knowledge. Truth to say, he was a conscientious man, and ever bore in mind the golden maxim, "Spare the rod and spoil the child."—Ichabod Crane's scholars certainly were not spoiled.

I would not have it imagined, however, that he was one of those cruel potentates of the school, who joy in the smart of their subjects; on the contrary, he administered justice with discrimination rather than severity, taking the burden off the backs of the weak, and laying it on those of the strong. Your mere puny stripling, that winced at the least flourish of the rod, was passed by with indulgence; but the claims of justice were satisfied by inflicting a double portion on some little, tough, wrong-headed, broad-skirted Dutch urchin, who sulked and swelled and grew dogged and sullen beneath the birch. All this he called "doing his duty" by their parents; and he never inflicted a chastisement without following it by the assurance, so consolatory to the smarting urchin, that "he would remember it, and thank him for it the longest day he had to live."

When school-hours were over, he was even the companion and playmate of the larger boys; and on holiday afternoons would convoy some of the smaller ones home, who happened to have pretty sisters, or good housewives for mothers, noted for the comforts of the cupboard. Indeed it behooved him to keep on good terms with his pupils. The revenue arising from his school was small, and would have been scarcely sufficient to furnish him with daily bread, for he was a huge feeder, and, though lank, had the dilating powers of an anaconda; but to help out his maintenance, he was, according to country custom in those parts, boarded and lodged at the houses of the farmers, whose children he instructed. With these he lived successively a week at a time; thus going the rounds of the neighborhood, with all his worldly effects tied up in a cotton handkerchief.

That all this might not be too onerous on the purses of his rustic patrons, who are apt to consider the costs of schooling a grievous burden, and schoolmasters as mere drones, he had various ways of rendering himself both useful and agreeable. He assisted the farmers occasionally in the lighter labors of their farms; helped to make hay; mended the fences; took the horses to water; drove the cows from pasture; and cut wood for the winter fire. He laid aside, too, all the dominant dignity and absolute sway with which he lorded it in his little empire, the school, and became wonderfully gentle and ingratiating. He found favor in the eyes of the mothers, by petting the children, particularly the youngest; and like the lion bold, which whilom so magnanimously the lamb did hold, he would sit with a child on one knee, and rock a cradle with his foot for whole hours together.

In addition to his other vocations, he was the singing-master of the neighborhood, and picked up many bright shillings by instructing the young folks in psalmody. It was a matter of no little vanity to him, on Sundays, to take his station in front of the church-gallery, with a band of chosen singers; where, in his own mind, he completely carried away the palm from the parson. Certain it is, his voice resounded far above all the rest of the congregation;

and there are peculiar quavers still to be heard in that church, and which may even be heard half a mile off, quite to the opposite side of the mill-pond, on a still Sunday morning, which are said to be legitimately descended from the nose of Ichabod Crane. Thus, by divers little makeshifts in that ingenious way which is commonly denominated "by hook and by crook," the worthy pedagogue got on tolerably enough, and was thought, by all who understood nothing of the labor of headwork, to have a wonderfully easy life of it.

The schoolmaster is generally a man of some importance in the female circle of a rural neighborhood; being considered a kind of idle, gentleman-like personage, of vastly superior taste and accomplishments to the rough country swains, and, indeed, inferior in learning only to the parson. His appearance, therefore, is apt to occasion some little stir at the tea-table of a farm-house, and the addition of a supernumerary dish of cakes or sweet-meats, or, peradventure, the parade of a silver tea-pot. Our man of letters, therefore, was peculiarly happy in the smiles of all the country damsels. How he would figure among them in the churchyard, between services on Sundays! gathering grapes for them from the wild vines that overrun the surrounding trees; reciting for their amusement all the epitaphs on the tombstones; or sauntering, with a whole bevy of them, along the banks of the adjacent mill-pond; while the more bashful country bumpkins hung sheepishly back, envying his superior elegance and address.

From his half itinerant life, also, he was a kind of travelling gazette, carrying the whole budget of local gossip from house to house: so that his appearance was always greeted with satisfaction. He was, moreover, esteemed by the women as a man of great erudition, for he had read several books quite through, and was a perfect master of Cotton Mather's *History of New England Witchcraft*, in which, by the way, he most firmly and potently believed.

He was, in fact, an odd mixture of small shrewdness and simple credulity. His appetite for the marvellous, and his powers of digesting it, were equally extraordinary; and both had been increased by his residence in this spellbound region. No tale was too gross or monstrous for his capacious swallow. It was often his delight, after his school was dismissed in the afternoon, to stretch himself on the rich bed of clover bordering the little brook that whimpered by his school-house, and there con over old Mather's direful tales, until the gathering dusk of the evening made the printed page a mere mist before his eyes. Then, as he wended his way, by swamp and stream, and awful woodland, to the farm-house where he happened to be quartered, every sound of nature, at that witching hour, fluttered his excited imagination;

the moan of the whippoorwill[3] from the hill-side; the boding cry of the treetoad, that harbinger of storm; the dreary hooting of the screech-owl, or the sudden rustling in the thicket of birds frightened from their roost. The fire-flies, too, which sparkled most vividly in the darkest places, now and then startled him, as one of uncommon brightness would stream across his path; and if, by chance, a huge blockhead of a beetle came winging his blundering flight against him, the poor varlet was ready to give up the ghost, with the idea that he was struck with a witch's token. His only resource on such occasions, either to drown thought or drive away evil spirits, was to sing psalm-tunes; and the good people of Sleepy Hollow, as they sat by their doors of an evening, were often filled with awe, at hearing his nasal melody, "in linkèd sweetness long drawn out," floating from the distant hill, or along the dusky road.

Another of his sources of fearful pleasure was, to pass long winter evenings with the old Dutch wives, as they sat spinning by the fire, with a row of apples roasting and spluttering along the hearth, and listen to their marvellous tales of ghosts and goblins, and haunted fields, and haunted brooks, and haunted bridges, and haunted houses, and particularly of the headless horseman, or Galloping Hessian of the Hollow, as they sometimes called him. He would delight them equally by his anecdotes of witchcraft, and of the direful omens and portentous sights and sounds in the air, which prevailed in the earlier times of Connecticut; and would frighten them wofully with speculations upon comets and shooting-stars, and with the alarming fact that the world did absolutely turn round, and that they were half the time topsy-turvy!

But if there was a pleasure in all this, while snugly cuddling in the chimney-corner of a chamber that was all of a ruddy glow from the crackling wood-fire, and where, of course, no spectre dared to show his face, it was dearly purchased by the terrors of his subsequent walk homewards. What fearful shapes and shadows beset his path amidst the dim and ghastly glare of a snowy night!—With what wistful look did he eye every trembling ray of light streaming across the waste fields from some distant window!—How often was he appalled by some shrub covered with snow, which, like a sheeted spectre, beset his very path!—How often did he shrink with curdling awe at the sound of his own steps on a frosty crust beneath his feet; and dread to look over his shoulder, lest he should behold some uncouth being tramping close behind him!—and how often was he thrown into complete dismay by

[3] The whippoorwill is a bird which is only heard at night. It receives its name from its note, which is thought to resemble those words. [Irving's note.]

some rushing blast, howling among the trees, in the idea that it was the Galloping Hessian on one of his nightly scourings!

All these, however, were mere terrors of the night, phantoms of the mind that walk in darkness; and though he had seen many spectres in his time, and been more than once beset by Satan in divers shapes, in his lonely perambulations, yet daylight put an end to all these evils; and he would have passed a pleasant life of it, in despite of the devil and all his works, if his path had not been crossed by a being that causes more perplexity to mortal man than ghosts, goblins, and the whole race of witches put together, and that was—a woman.

Among the musical disciples who assembled, one evening in each week, to receive his instructions in psalmody, was Katrina Van Tassel, the daughter and only child of a substantial Dutch farmer. She was a blooming lass of fresh eighteen; plump as a partridge; ripe and melting and rosy-cheeked as one of her father's peaches, and universally famed, not merely for her beauty, but her vast expectations. She was withal a little of a coquette, as might be perceived even in her dress, which was a mixture of ancient and modern fashions, as most suited to set off her charms. She wore the ornaments of pure yellow gold, which her great-great-grandmother had brought over from Saardam; the tempting stomacher of the olden time; and withal a provokingly short petticoat, to display the prettiest foot and ankle in the country round.

Ichabod Crane had a soft and foolish heart towards the sex; and it is not to be wondered at that so tempting a morsel soon found favor in his eyes; more especially after he had visited her in her paternal mansion. Old Baltus Van Tassel was a perfect picture of a thriving, contented, liberal-hearted farmer. He seldom, it is true, sent either his eyes or his thoughts beyond the boundaries of his own farm; but within those everything was snug, happy, and well-conditioned. He was satisfied with his wealth, but not proud of it; and piqued himself upon the hearty abundance rather than the style in which he lived. His stronghold was situated on the banks of the Hudson, in one of those green, sheltered, fertile nooks in which the Dutch farmers are so fond of nestling. A great elm-tree spread its broad branches over it; at the foot of which bubbled up a spring of the softest and sweetest water, in a little well, formed of a barrel; and then stole sparkling away through the grass, to a neighboring brook, that bubbled along among alders and dwarf willows. Hard by the farm-house was a vast barn, that might have served for a church; every window and crevice of which seemed bursting forth with the treasures of the farm; the flail was busily resounding within it from morning till night; swallows and martins skimmed twittering about the eaves; and rows of pigeons, some with one eye turned up, as if watching the weather, some with their heads under their wings, or buried in their bosoms, and others swelling, and cooing, and bowing about their dames, were enjoying the sunshine on the roof. Sleek unwieldly porkers were grunting in the repose and abundance of their pens; whence sallied forth, now and then, troops of sucking pigs, as if to snuff the air. A stately squadron of snowy geese were riding in an adjoining pond, convoying whole fleets of ducks; regiments of turkeys were gobbling through the farm-yard, and guinea fowls fretting about it, like ill-tempered housewives, with their peevish discontented cry. Before the barn-door strutted the gallant cock, that pattern of a husband, a warrior, and a fine gentleman, clapping his burnished wings, and crowing in the pride and gladness of his heart— sometimes tearing up the earth with his feet, and then generously calling his ever-hungry family of wives and children to enjoy the rich morsel which he had discovered.

The pedagogue's mouth watered, as he looked upon this sumptuous promise of luxurious winter fare. In his devouring mind's eye he pictured to himself every roasting-pig running about with a pudding in his belly, and an apple in his mouth; the pigeons were snugly put to bed in a comfortable pie, and tucked in with a coverlet of crust; the geese were swimming in their own gravy; and the ducks pairing cosily in dishes, like snug married couples, with a decent competency of onion-sauce. In the porkers he saw carved out the future sleek side of bacon, and juicy relishing ham; not a turkey but he beheld daintily trussed up, with its gizzard under its wing, and, peradventure, a necklace of savory sausages; and even bright chanticleer himself lay sprawling on his back, in a side-dish, with uplifted claws, as if craving that quarter which his chivalrous spirit disdained to ask while living.

As the enraptured Ichabod fancied all this, and as he rolled his great green eyes over the fat meadowlands, the rich fields of wheat, of rye, of buckwheat, and Indian corn, and the orchard burdened with ruddy fruit, which surrounded the warm tenement of Van Tassel, his heart yearned after the damsel who was to inherit these domains, and his imagination expanded with the idea how they might be readily turned into cash, and the money invested in immense tracts of wild land, and shingle palaces in the wilderness. Nay, his busy fancy already realized his hopes, and presented to him the blooming Katrina, with a whole family of children, mounted on the top of a wagon loaded with household trumpery, with pots and kettles dangling beneath; and he beheld himself bestriding a pacing mare, with a colt at her heels, setting out for Kentucky, Tennessee, or the Lord knows where.

When he entered the house, the conquest of his heart was complete. It was one of those spacious farm-houses, with high-ridged, but lowly-sloping roofs, built in the style handed down from the first Dutch settlers; the low projecting eaves forming a piazza along the front, capable of being closed up in bad weather. Under this were hung flails, harness, various utensils of husbandry, and nets for fishing in the neighboring river. Benches were built along the sides for summer use; and a great spinning-wheel at one end, and a churn at the other, showed the various uses to which this important porch might be devoted. From this piazza the wandering Ichabod entered the hall, which formed the centre of the mansion and the place of usual residence. Here, rows of resplendent pewter, ranged on a long dresser, dazzled his eyes. In one corner stood a huge bag of wool ready to be spun; in another a quantity of linsey-woolsey just from the loom; ears of Indian corn, and strings of dried apples and peaches, hung in gay festoons along the walls, mingled with the gaud of red peppers; and a door left ajar gave him a peep into the best parlor, where the claw-footed chairs and dark mahogany tables shone like mirrors; and irons,[4] with their accompanying shovel and tongs, glistened from their covert of asparagus tops; mock-oranges and conch-shells decorated the mantel-piece; strings of various colored birds' eggs were suspended above it, a great ostrich egg was hung from the centre of the room, and a corner-cupboard, knowingly left open, displayed immense treasures of old silver and well-mended china.

From the moment Ichabod laid his eyes upon these regions of delight, the peace of his mind was at an end, and his only study was how to gain the affections of the peerless daughter of Van Tassel. In this enterprise, however, he had more real difficulties than generally fell to the lot of a knight-errant of yore, who seldom had anything but giants, enchanters, fiery dragons, and such like easily conquered adversaries, to contend with; and had to make his way merely through gates of iron and brass, and walls of adamant, to the castle-keep, where the lady of his heart was confined; all which he achieved as easily as a man would carve his way to the centre of a Christmas pie; and then the lady gave him her hand as a matter of course. Ichabod, on the contrary, had to win his way to the heart of a country coquette, beset with a labyrinth of whims and caprices, which were forever presenting new difficulties and impediments; and he had to encounter a host of fearful adversaries of real flesh and blood, the numerous rustic admirers, who beset

every portal to her heart; keeping a watchful and angry eye upon each other, but ready to fly out in the common cause against any new competitor.

Among these the most formidable was a burly, roaring, roistering blade, of the name of Abraham, or, according to the Dutch abbreviation, Brom Van Brunt, the hero of the country round, which rang with his feats of strength and hardihood. He was broad-shouldered and double-jointed, with short, curly black hair, and a bluff but not unpleasant countenance, having a mingled air of fun and arrogance. From his Herculean frame and great powers of limb, he had received the nickname of BROM BONES, by which he was universally known. He was famed for great knowledge and skill in horsemanship, being as dexterous on horseback as a Tartar. He was foremost at all races and cockfights; and, with the ascendency which bodily strength acquires in rustic life, was the umpire in all disputes, setting his hat on one side, and giving his decisions with an air and tone admitting of no gainsay or appeal. He was always ready for either a fight or a frolic; but had more mischief than ill-will in his composition; and, with all his overbearing roughness, there was a strong dash of waggish good-humor at the bottom. He had three or four boon companions, who regarded him as their model, and at the head of whom he scoured the country, attending every scene of feud or merriment for miles round. In cold weather he was distinguished by a fur cap, surmounted with a flaunting fox's tail; and when the folks at a country gathering descried this well-known crest at a distance, whisking about among a squad of hard riders, they always stood by for a squall. Sometimes his crew would be heard dashing along past the farm-houses at midnight, with whoop and halloo, like a troop of Don Cossacks; and the old dames, startled out of their sleep, would listen for a moment till the hurry-scurry had clattered by, and then exclaim, "Ay, there goes Brom Bones and his gang!" The neighbors looked upon him with a mixture of awe, admiration and good will; and when any madcap prank, or rustic brawl, occurred in the vicinity, always shook their heads, and warranted Brom Bones was at the bottom of it.

This rantipole[5] hero had for some time singled out the blooming Katrina for the object of his uncouth gallantries; and though his amorous toyings were something like the gentle caresses and endearments of a bear, yet it was whispered that she did not altogether discourage his hopes. Certain it is, his advances were signals for rival candidates to retire, who felt no inclination to cross a line in his amours; insomuch, that, when his horse was seen tied to Van Tassel's paling on a Sunday night, a sure sign that his

[4] Probably a misprint for *andirons*.

[5] Reckless.

master was courting, or, as it is termed, "sparking," within, all other suitors passed by in despair, and carried the war into other quarters.

Such was the formidable rival with whom Ichabod Crane had to contend, and, considering all things, a stouter man than he would have shrunk from the competition, and a wiser man would have despaired. He had, however, a happy mixture of pliability and perseverance in his nature; he was in form and spirit like a supple-jack[6]—yielding, but tough; though he bent, he never broke; and though he bowed beneath the slightest pressure yet, the moment it was away—jerk! he was as erect, and carried his head as high as ever.

To have taken the field openly against his rival would have been madness; for he was not a man to be thwarted in his amours, any more than that stormy lover, Achilles. Ichabod, therefore, made his advances in a quiet and gently insinuating manner. Under cover of his character of singing-master, he had made frequent visits at the farm-house; not that he had anything to apprehend from the meddlesome interference of parents, which is so often a stumbling-block in the path of lovers. Balt Van Tassel was an easy, indulgent soul; he loved his daughter better even than his pipe, and, like a reasonable man and an excellent father, let her have her way in everything. His notable little wife, too, had enough to do to attend to her housekeeping and manage her poultry; for, as she sagely observed, ducks and geese are foolish things, and must be looked after, but girls can take care of themselves. Thus while the busy dame bustled about the house, or plied her spinning-wheel at one end of the piazza, honest Balt would sit smoking his evening pipe at the other, watching the achievements of a little wooden warrior, who, armed with a sword in each hand, was most valiantly fighting the wind on the pinnacle of the barn. In the meantime, Ichabod would carry on his suit with the daughter by the side of the spring under the great elm, or sauntering along in the twilight,—that hour so favorable to the lover's eloquence.

I profess not to know how women's hearts are wooed and won. To me they have always been matters of riddle and admiration. Some seem to have but one vulnerable point or door of access, while others have a thousand avenues, and may be captured in a thousand different ways. It is a great triumph of skill to gain the former, but a still greater proof of generalship to maintain possession of the latter, for the man must battle for his fortress at every door and window. He who wins a thousand common hearts is therefore entitled to some renown; but he who keeps undisputed sway over the heart of a coquette, is indeed a hero. Certain it is, this was not the case with the redoubtable Brom

6 A kind of walking stick or cane.

Bones; and from the moment Ichabod Crane made his advances, the interests of the former evidently declined; his horse was no longer seen tied at the palings on Sunday nights, and a deadly feud gradually arose between him and the preceptor of Sleepy Hollow.

Brom, who had a degree of rough chivalry in his nature, would fain have carried matters to open warfare, and have settled their pretensions to the lady according to the mode of those most concise and simple reasoners, the knights-errant of yore—by single combat; but Ichabod was too conscious of the superior might of his adversary to enter the lists against him: he had overheard a boast of Bones, that he would "double the schoolmaster up, and lay him on a shelf of his own school-house;" and he was too wary to give him an opportunity. There was something extremely provoking in this obstinately pacific system; it left Brom no alternative but to draw upon the funds of rustic waggery in his disposition, and to play off boorish practical jokes upon his rival. Ichabod became the object of whimsical persecution to Bones and his gang of rough riders. They harried his hitherto peaceful domains smoked out his singing-school, by stopping up the chimney; broke into the school-house at night, in spite of its formidable fastenings of withe and window-stakes, and turned everything topsy-turvy: so that the poor schoolmaster began to think all the witches in the country held their meetings there. But what was still more annoying, Brom took opportunities of turning him into ridicule in presence of his mistress, and had a scoundrel dog whom he taught to whine in the most ludicrous manner, and introduced as a rival of Ichabod's to instruct her in psalmody.

In this way matters went on for some time, without producing any material effect on the relative situation of the contending powers. On a fine autumnal afternoon, Ichabod, in pensive mood, sat enthroned on the lofty stool whence he usually watched all the concerns of his little literary realm. In his hand he swayed a ferule, that sceptre of despotic power; the birch of justice reposed on three nails, behind the throne, a constant terror to evil-doers; while on the desk before him might be seen sundry contraband articles and prohibited weapons, detected upon the persons of idle urchins; such as half-munched apples, popguns, whirligigs, fly-cages, and whole legions of rampant little paper game-cocks. Apparently there had been some appalling act of justice recently inflicted, for his scholars were all busily intent upon their books, or slyly whispering behind them with one eye kept upon the master; and a kind of buzzing stillness reigned throughout the school-room. It was suddenly interrupted by the appearance of a negro, in tow-cloth jacket and trousers, a round-crowned fragment of a hat, like the cap of Mercury, and mounted on the back of a ragged, wild, half-broken colt, which he managed with a rope by way of halter. He came clattering up to the school-door with an invitation to Ichabod to attend a merry-making or "quilting frolic," to be held that evening at Mynheer Van Tassel's; and having delivered his message with that air of importance, and effort at fine language, which a negro is apt to display on petty embassies of the kind, he dashed over the brook, and was seen scampering away up the Hollow, full of the importance and hurry of his mission.

All was now bustle and hubbub in the late quiet school-room. The scholars were hurried through their lessons, without stopping at trifles; those who were nimble skipped over half with impunity, and those who were tardy had a smart application now and then in the rear, to quicken their speed, or help them over a tall word. Books were flung aside without being put away on the shelves, inkstands were overturned, benches thrown down, and the whole school was turned loose an hour before the usual time, bursting forth like a legion of young imps, yelping and racketing about the green, in joy at their early emancipation.

The gallant Ichabod now spent at least an extra half-hour at his toilet, brushing and furbishing up his best and indeed only suit of rusty black, and arranging his locks by a bit of broken looking-glass, that hung up in the school-house. That he might make his appearance before his mistress in the true style of a cavalier, he borrowed a horse from the farmer with whom he was domiciliated, a choleric old Dutchman, of the name of Hans Van Ripper, and, thus gallantly mounted, issued forth, like a knight-errant in quest of adventures. But it is meet I should, in the true spirit of romantic story, give some account of the looks and equipments of my hero and his steed. The animal he bestrode was a broken-down plough-horse, that had outlived almost everything but his viciousness. He was gaunt and shagged, with a ewe neck and a head like a hammer; his rusty mane and tail were tangled and knotted with burrs; one eye had lost its pupil, and was glaring and spectral; but the other had the gleam of a genuine devil in it. Still he must have had fire and mettle in his day, if we may judge from the name he bore of Gunpowder. He had, in fact, been a favorite steed of his master's, the choleric Van Ripper, who was a furious rider, and had infused, very probably, some of his own spirit into the animal; for, old and broken-down as he looked, there was more of the lurking devil in him than in any young filly in the country.

Ichabod was a suitable figure for such a steed. He rode with short stirrups, which brought his knees nearly up to the pommel of the saddle; his sharp elbows stuck out like grasshoppers'; he carried his whip perpendicularly in his hand, like a sceptre, and, as his horse jogged on, the motion of his arms was not unlike the flapping of a pair of wings. A small wool hat rested on the top of his nose, for so his scanty strip of forehead might be called; and the skirts of his black coat fluttered out almost to the horse's tail. Such was the appearance of Ichabod and his steed, as they shambled out of the gate of Hans Van Ripper, and it was altogether such an apparition as is seldom to be met with in broad daylight.

It was, as I have said, a fine autumnal day, the sky was clear and serene, and nature wore that rich and golden livery which we always associate with the idea of abundance. The forests had put on their sober brown and yellow, while some trees of the tenderer kind had been nipped by the frosts into brilliant dyes of orange, purple, and scarlet. Streaming files of wild ducks began to make their appearance high in the air; the bark of the squirrel might be heard from the groves of beech and hickory nuts, and the pensive whistle of the quail at intervals from the neighboring stubble-field.

The small birds were taking their farewell banquets. In the fulness of their revelry, they fluttered, chirping and frolicking, from bush to bush, and tree to tree, capricious from the very profusion and variety around them. There was the honest cockrobin, the favorite game of stripling sportsmen, with its loud querulous notes; and the twittering blackbirds flying in sable clouds; and the golden-winged woodpecker, with his crimson crest, his broad black gorget, and splendid plumage; and the cedarbird, with its red-tipt wings and yellow-tipt tail, and its little monteiro cap[7] of feathers; and the blue jay, that noisy coxcomb, in his gay light-blue coat and white under-clothes, screaming and chattering, nodding and bobbing and bowing, and pretending to be on good terms with every songster of the grove.

As Ichabod jogged slowly on his way, his eye, ever open to every symptom of culinary abundance, ranged with delight over the treasures of jolly autumn. On all sides he beheld vast store of apples; some hanging in oppressive opulence on the trees; some gathered into baskets and barrels for the market; others heaped up in rich piles for the cider-press. Farther on he beheld great fields of Indian corn, with its golden ears peeping from their leafy coverts, and holding out the promise of cakes and hasty-pudding; and the yellow pumpkins lying beneath them, turning up their fair round bellies to the sun, and giving ample prospects of the most luxurious of pies; and anon he passed the fragrant buck-

---

[7] A variety of hunting cap.

wheat fields, breathing the odor of the bee-hive, and as he beheld them, soft anticipations stole over his mind of dainty slapjacks, well buttered, and garnished with honey or treacle, by the delicate little dimpled hand of Katrina Van Tassel.

Thus feeding his mind with many sweet thoughts and "sugared suppositions," he journeyed along the sides of a range of hills which look out upon some of the goodliest scenes of the mighty Hudson. The sun gradually wheeled his broad disk down into the west. The wide bosom of the Tappan Zee lay motionless and glossy, excepting that here and there a gentle undulation waved and prolonged the blue shadow of the distant mountain. A few amber clouds floated in the sky, without a breath of air to move them. The horizon was of a fine golden tint, changing gradually into a pure apple-green, and from that into the deep blue of the mid-heaven. A slanting ray lingered on the woody crests of the precipices that overhung some parts of the river, giving greater depth to the dark-gray and purple of their rocky sides. A sloop was loitering in the distance, dropping slowly down with the tide, her sail hanging uselessly against the mast; and as the reflection of the sky gleamed along the still water, it seemed as if the vessel was suspended in the air.

It was toward evening that Ichabod arrived at the castle of the Heer Van Tassel, which he found thronged with the pride and flower of the adjacent country. Old farmers, a spare leathern-faced race, in homespun coats and breeches, blue stockings, huge shoes, and magnificent pewter buckles. Their brisk withered little dames, in close crimped caps, long-waisted shortgowns, homespun petticoats, with scissors and pincushions, and gay calico pockets hanging on the outside. Buxom lasses, almost as antiquated as their mothers, excepting where a straw hat, a fine ribbon, or perhaps a white frock, gave symptoms of city innovation. The sons, in short square-skirted coats with rows of stupendous brass buttons, and their hair generally queued in the fashion of the times, especially if they could procure an eel-skin for the purpose, it being esteemed, throughout the country, as a potent nourisher and strengthener of the hair.

Brom Bones, however, was the hero of the scene, having come to the gathering on his favorite steed, Daredevil, a creature, like himself, full of mettle and mischief, and which no one but himself could manage. He was, in fact, noted for preferring vicious animals, given to all kinds of tricks, which kept the rider in constant risk of his neck, for he held a tractable well-broken horse as unworthy of a lad of spirit.

Fain would I pause to dwell upon the world of charms that burst upon the enraptured gaze of my hero, as he entered the state parlor of Van Tassel's mansion. Not those of the bevy of buxom lasses, with their luxurious display of red and white; but the ample charms of a genuine Dutch country tea-table, in the sumptuous time of autumn. Such heaped-up platters of cakes of various and almost indescribable kinds, known only to experienced Dutch housewives! There was the doughty doughnut, the tenderer oly koek, and the crisp and crumbling cruller; sweet cakes and short cakes, ginger-cakes and honey-cakes, and the whole family of cakes. And then there were apple-pies and peach-pies and pumpkin-pies; besides slices of ham and smoked beef; and moreover delectable dishes of preserved plums, and peaches, and pears, and quinces; not to mention broiled shad and roasted chickens; together with bowls of milk and cream, all mingled higgledy-piggledy, pretty much as I have enumerated them, with the motherly tea-pot sending up its clouds of vapor from the midst—Heaven bless the mark! I want breath and time to discuss this banquet as it deserves, and am too eager to get on with my story. Happily, Ichabod Crane was not in so great a hurry as his historian, but did ample justice to every dainty.

He was a kind and thankful creature, whose heart dilated in proportion as his skin was filled with good cheer; and whose spirits rose with eating as some men's do with drink. He could not help, too, rolling his large eyes round him as he ate, and chuckling with the possibility that he might one day be lord of all this scene of almost unimaginable luxury and splendor. Then, he thought, how soon he'd turn his back upon the old school-house; snap his fingers in the face of Hans Van Ripper, and every other niggardly patron, and kick any itinerant pedagogue out-of-doors that should dare to call him comrade!

Old Baltus Van Tassel moved about among his guests with a face dilated with content and good-humor, round and jolly as the harvest-moon. His hospitable attentions were brief, but expressive, being confined to a shake of the hand, a slap on the shoulder, a loud laugh, and a pressing invitation to "fall to, and help themselves."

And now the sound of the music from the common room, or hall, summoned to the dance. The musician was an old gray-headed negro, who had been the itinerant orchestra of the neighborhood for more than half a century. His instrument was as old and battered as himself. The greater part of the time he scraped on two or three strings, accompanying every movement of the bow with a motion of the head; bowing almost to the ground, and stamping with his foot whenever a fresh couple were to start.

Ichabod prided himself upon his dancing as much as upon his vocal powers. Not a limb, not a fibre about him was idle; and to have seen his loosely hung frame in full motion, and clattering about the room, you would have thought Saint Vitus himself, that blessed patron of the dance, was figuring before you in person. He was the admiration of all the negroes; who, having gathered, of all ages and sizes, from the farm and the neighborhood, stood forming a pyramid of shining black faces at every door and window, gazing with delight at the scene, rolling their white eyeballs, and showing grinning rows of ivory from ear to ear. How could the flogger of urchins be otherwise than animated and joyous? the lady of his heart was his partner in the dance, and smiling graciously in reply to all his amorous oglings; while Brom Bones, sorely smitten with love and jealousy, sat brooding by himself in one corner.

When the dance was at an end, Ichabod was attracted to a knot of the sager folks, who, with old Van Tassel, sat smoking at one end of the piazza, gossiping over former times, and drawing out long stories about the war.

This neighborhood, at the time of which I am speaking, was one of those highly favored places which abound with chronicle and great men. The British and American line had run near it during the war; it had, therefore, been the scene of marauding, and infested with refugees, cow-boys,[8] and all kinds of border chivalry. Just sufficient time has elapsed to enable each story-teller to dress up his tale with a little becoming fiction, and, in the indistinctness of his recollection, to make himself the hero of every exploit.

There was the story of Doffue Martling, a large blue-bearded Dutchman, who had nearly taken a British frigate with an old iron nine-pounder from a mud breastwork, only that his gun burst at the sixth discharge. And there was an old gentleman who shall be nameless, being too rich a mynheer to be lightly mentioned, who, in the battle of White Plains, being an excellent master of defence, parried a musket-ball with a small sword, insomuch that he absolutely felt it whiz round the blade, and glance off at the hilt; in proof of which he was ready at any time to show the sword, with the hilt a little bent. There were several more that had been equally great in the field, not one of whom but was persuaded that he had a considerable hand in bringing the war to a happy termination.

But all these were nothing to the tales of ghosts and apparitions that succeeded. The neighborhood is rich in legendary treasures of the kind. Local tales and superstitions thrive best in these sheltered long-settled retreats; but are trampled underfoot by the shifting throng that forms the population of most of our country places. Besides, there is no encouragement for ghosts in most of our villages, for they have scarcely had time to finish their first nap, and turn themselves in their graves before their surviving

[8]Name given to guerrillas during the Revolution.

friends have travelled away from the neighborhood; so that when they turn out at night to walk their rounds, they have no acquaintance left to call upon. This is perhaps the reason why we so seldom hear of ghosts, except in our long-established Dutch communities.

The immediate cause, however, of the prevalence of supernatural stories in these parts was doubtless owing to the vicinity of Sleepy Hollow. There was a contagion in the very air that blew from that haunted region; it breathed forth an atmosphere of dreams and fancies infecting all the land. Several of the Sleepy Hollow people were present at Van Tassel's and, as usual, were doling out their wild and wonderful legends. Many dismal tales were told about funeral trains, and mourning cries and wailings heard and seen about the great tree where the unfortunate Major André was taken, and which stood in the neighborhood. Some mention was made also of the woman in white, that haunted the dark glen at Raven Rock, and was often heard to shriek on winter nights before a storm, having perished there in the snow. The chief part of the stories, however, turned upon the favorite spectre of Sleepy Hollow, the headless horseman, who had been heard several times of late, patrolling the country; and, it was said, tethered his horse nightly among the graves in the churchyard.

The sequestered situation of this church seems always to have made it a favorite haunt of troubled spirits. It stands on a knoll, surrounded by locust-trees and lofty elms, from among which its decent whitewashed walls shine modestly forth, like Christian purity beaming through the shades of retirement. A gentle slope descends from it to a silver sheet of water, bordered by high trees, between which, peeps may be caught at the blue hills of the Hudson. To look upon its grass-grown yard, where the sunbeams seem to sleep so quietly, one would think that there at least the dead might rest in peace. On one side of the church extends a wide woody dell, along which raves a large brook among broken rocks and trunks of fallen trees. Over a deep black part of the stream, not far from the church, was formerly thrown a wooden bridge; the road that led to it, and the bridge itself, were thickly shaded by overhanging trees, which cast a gloom about it, even in the daytime, but occasioned a fearful darkness at night. This was one of the favorite haunts of the headless horseman; and the place where he was most frequently encountered. The tale was told of old Brouwer, a most heretical disbeliever in ghosts, how he met the horseman returning from his foray into Sleepy Hollow, and was obliged to get up behind him; how they galloped over bush and brake, over hill and swamp, until they reached the bridge; when the horseman suddenly turned into a skeleton, threw old Brouwer into the brook, and sprang away over the tree-tops with a clap of thunder.

This story was immediately matched by a thrice marvellous adventure of Brom Bones, who made light of the galloping Hessian as an arrant jockey. He affirmed that, on returning one night from the neighboring village of Sing Sing, he had been overtaken by this midnight trooper; that he had offered to race with him for a bowl of punch, and should have won it too, for Daredevil beat the goblin horse all hollow, but, just as they came to the church bridge, the Hessian bolted, and vanished in a flash of fire.

All these tales, told in that drowsy undertone with which men talk in the dark, the countenances of the listeners only now and then receiving a casual gleam from the glare of a pipe, sank deep in the mind of Ichabod. He repaid them in kind with large extracts from his invaluable author, Cotton Mather, and added many marvellous events that had taken place in his native State of Connecticut, and fearful sights which he had seen in his nightly walks about the Sleepy Hollow.

The revel now gradually broke up. The old farmers gathered together their families in their wagons, and were heard for some time rattling along the hollow roads, and over the distant hills. Some of the damsels mounted on pillions behind their favorite swains, and their light-hearted laughter, mingling with the clatter of hoofs, echoed along the silent woodlands, sounding fainter and fainter until they gradually died away—and the late scene of noise and frolic was all silent and deserted. Ichabod only lingered behind, according to the custom of country lovers, to have a *tête-à-tête* with the heiress, fully convinced that he was now on the high road to success. What passed at this interview I will not pretend to say, for in fact I do not know. Something, however, I fear me, must have gone wrong, for he certainly sallied forth, after no very great interval, with an air quite desolate and chop-fallen.—Oh, these women! these women! Could that girl have been playing off any of her coquettish tricks?—Was her encouragement of the poor pedagogue all a mere sham to secure her conquest of his rival?—Heaven only knows, not I!—Let it suffice to say, Ichabod stole forth with the air of one who had been sacking a hen-roost, rather than a fair lady's heart. Without looking to the right or left to notice the scene of rural wealth on which he had so often gloated, he went straight to the stable, and with several hearty cuffs and kicks, roused his steed most uncourteously from the comfortable quarters in which he was soundly sleeping, dreaming of mountains of corn and oats, and whole valleys of timothy and clover.

It was the very witching time of night that Ichabod, heavy-hearted and crestfallen, pursued his travel homewards, along the sides of the lofty hills which rise above Tarry Town, and which he had traversed so cheerily in the afternoon. The hour was as dismal as himself. Far below him, the Tappan Zee spread its dusky and indistinct waste of waters, with here and there the tall mast of a sloop riding quietly at anchor under the land. In the dead hush of midnight he could even hear the barking of the watch-dog from the opposite shore of the Hudson; but it was so vague and faint as only to give an idea of his distance from this faithful companion of man. Now and then, too, the long-drawn crowing of a cock, accidentally awakened, would sound far, far off, from some farm-house away among the hills—but it was like a dreaming sound in his ear. No signs of life occurred near him, but occasionally the melancholy chirp of a cricket, or perhaps the gutteral twang of a bull-frog, from a neighboring marsh, as if sleeping uncomfortably, and turning suddenly in his bed.

All the stories of ghosts and goblins that he had heard in the afternoon, now came crowding upon his recollection. The night grew darker and darker; the stars seemed to sink deeper in the sky, and driving clouds occasionally hid them from his sight. He had never felt so lonely and dismal. He was, moreover, approaching the very place where many of the scenes of the ghost-stories had been laid. In the centre of the road stood an enormous tulip-tree, which towered like a giant above all the other trees of the neighborhood, and formed a kind of landmark. Its limbs were gnarled, and fantastic, large enough to form trunks for ordinary trees, twisting down almost to the earth, and rising again into the air. It was connected with the tragical story of the unfortunate André, who had been taken prisoner hard by; and was universally known by the name of Major André's tree. The common people regarded it with a mixture of respect and superstition, partly out of sympathy for the fate of its ill-starred namesake, and partly from the tales of strange sights and doleful lamentations told concerning it.

As Ichabod approached this fearful tree, he began to whistle: he thought his whistle was answered,—it was but a blast sweeping sharply through the dry branches. As he approached a little nearer, he thought he saw something white, hanging in the midst of the tree,—he paused and ceased whistling; but on looking more narrowly, perceived that it was a place where the tree had been scathed by lightning, and the white wood laid bare. Suddenly he heard a groan,—his teeth chattered and his knees smote against the saddle: it was but the rubbing of one huge bough upon another, as they were swayed about by the breeze. He passed the tree in safety; but new perils lay before him.

About two hundred yards from the tree a small

brook crossed the road, and ran into a marshy and thickly wooded glen, known by the name of Wiley's swamp. A few rough logs, laid side by side, served for a bridge over this stream. On that side of the road where the brook entered the wood, a group of oaks and chestnuts, matted thick with wild grape-vines, threw a cavernous gloom over it. To pass this bridge was the severest trial. It was at this identical spot that the unfortunate André was captured, and under the covert of those chestnuts and vines were the sturdy yeomen concealed who surprised him. This has ever since been considered a haunted stream, and fearful are the feelings of the school boy who has to pass it alone after dark.

As he approached the stream, his heart began to thump; he summoned up, however, all his resolu-tion, gave his horse half a score of kicks in the ribs, and attempted to dash briskly across the bridge; but instead of starting forward, the perverse old animal made a lateral movement, and ran broadside against the fence. Ichabod, whose fears increased with the delay, jerked the reins on the other side, and kicked lustily with the contrary foot: it was all in vain; his steed started, it is true, but it was only to plunge to the opposite side of the road into a thicket of brambles and alder bushes. The schoolmaster now bestowed both whip and heel upon the starveling ribs of old Gunpowder, who dashed forward, snuf-fling and snorting, but came to a stand just by the bridge, with a suddenness that had nearly sent his rider sprawling over his head. Just at this moment a plashy tramp by the side of the bridge caught the sensitive ear of Ichabod. In the dark shadow of the grove, on the margin of the brook, he beheld something huge, misshapen, black and towering. It stirred not, but seemed gathered up in the gloom, like some gigantic monster ready to spring upon the traveller.

The hair of the affrighted pedagogue rose upon his head with terror. What was to be done? To turn and fly was now too late; and besides, what chance was there of escaping ghost or goblin, if such it was, which could ride upon the wings of the wind? Sum-moning up, therefore, a show of courage, he de-manded in stammering accents—"Who are you?" He received no reply. He repeated his demand in a still more agitated voice. Still there was no answer. Once more he cudgelled the sides of the inflexible Gunpowder, and, shutting his eyes, broke forth with involuntary fervor into a psalm-tune. Just then the shadowy object of alarm put itself in motion, and, with a scramble and a bound, stood at once in the middle of the road. Though the night was dark and dismal, yet the form of the unknown might now in some degree be ascertained. He appeared to be a horseman of large dimensions, and mounted on a black horse of powerful frame. He made no offer of

molestation or sociability, but kept aloof on one side of the road, jogging along on the blind side of old Gunpowder, who had now got over his fright and waywardness.

Ichabod, who had no relish for this strange mid-night companion, and bethought himself of the ad-venture of Brom Bones with the Galloping Hessian, now quickened his steed, in hopes of leaving him behind. The stranger, however, quickened his horse to an equal pace. Ichabod pulled up, and fell into a walk, thinking to lag behind,—the other did the same. His heart began to sink within him; he endeav-ored to resume his psalm-tune, but his parched tongue clove to the roof of his mouth, and he could not utter a stave. There was something in the moody and dogged silence of this pertinacious companion, that was mysterious and appalling. It was soon fear-fully accounted for. On mounting a rising ground, which brought the figure of his fellow-traveller in relief against the sky, gigantic in height, and muffled in a cloak, Ichabod was horror-struck, on perceiving that he was headless!—but his horror was still more increased, on observing that the head, which should have rested on his shoulders, was carried before him on the pommel of the saddle: his terror rose to desperation; he rained a shower of kicks and blows upon Gunpowder, hoping, by a sudden movement, to give his companion the slip,—but the spectre started full jump with him. Away then they dashed, through thick and thin; stones flying, and sparks flashing at every bound. Ichabod's flimsy garments fluttered in the air, as he stretched his long lank body away over his horse's head, in the eagerness of his flight.

They had now reached the road which turns off to Sleepy Hollow; but Gunpowder, who seemed possessed with a demon, instead of keeping up it, made an opposite turn, and plunged headlong downhill to the left. This road leads through a sandy hollow, shaded by trees for about a quarter of a mile, where it crosses the bridge famous in goblin story, and just beyond swells the green knoll on which stands the whitewashed church.

As yet the panic of the steed had given his unskil-ful rider an apparent advantage in the chase; but just as he had got half-way through the hollow, the girths of the saddle gave way, and he felt it slipping from under him. He seized it by the pommel, and endeavored to hold it firm, but in vain; and had just time to save himself by clasping old Gunpowder round the neck, when the saddle fell to the earth, and he heard it trampled underfoot by his pursuer. For a moment, the terror of Hans Van Ripper's wrath passed across his mind—for it was his Sunday saddle; but this was no time for petty fears; the goblin was hard on his haunches; and (unskilful rider that he was!) he had much ado to maintain his seat;

sometimes slipping on one side, sometimes on another, and sometimes jolted on the high ridge of his horse's backbone, with a violence that he verily feared would cleave him asunder.

An opening in the trees now cheered him with the hopes that the church-bridge was at hand. The wavering reflection of a silver star in the bosom of the brook told him that he was not mistaken. He saw the walls of the church dimly glaring under the trees beyond. He recollected the place where Brom Bones' ghostly competitor had disappeared. "If I can but reach that bridge," thought Ichabod, "I am safe." Just then he heard the black steed panting and blowing close behind him; he even fancied that he felt his hot breath. Another convulsive kick in the ribs, and old Gunpowder sprang upon the bridge; he thundered over the resounding planks; he gained the opposite side; and now Ichabod cast a look behind to see if his pursuer should vanish, according to rule, in a flash of fire and brimstone. Just then he saw the goblin rising in his stirrups, and in the very act of hurling his head at him. Ichabod endeavored to dodge the horrible missile, but too late. It encountered his cranium with a tremendous crash,—he was tumbled headlong into the dust, and Gunpowder, the black steed, and the goblin rider, passed by like a whirlwind.

The next morning the old horse was found without his saddle, and with the bridle under his feet, soberly cropping the grass at his master's gate. Ichabod did not make his appearance at breakfast;—dinner-hour came, but no Ichabod. The boys assembled at the school-house, and strolled idly about the banks of the brook; but no schoolmaster. Hans Van Ripper now began to feel some uneasiness about the fate of poor Ichabod, and his saddle. An inquiry was set on foot, and after diligent investigation they came upon his traces. In one part of the road leading to the church was found the saddle trampled in the dirt; the tracks of horses' hoofs deeply dented in the road, and evidently at furious speed, were traced to the bridge, beyond which, on the bank of a broad part of the brook, where the water ran deep and black, was found the hat of the unfortunate Ichabod, and close beside it a shattered pumpkin.

The brook was searched, but the body of the schoolmaster was not to be discovered. Hans Van Ripper, as executor of his estate, examined the bundle which contained all his worldly effects. They consisted of two shirts and a half; two stocks for the neck; a pair or two of worsted stockings, an old pair of corduroy small-clothes; a rusty razor; a book of psalm-tunes, full of dogs' ears; and a broken pitch-pipe. As to the books and furniture of the school-house, they belonged to the community, excepting Cotton Mather's *History of Witchcraft*, a New Eng-

land *Almanac*, and a book of dreams and fortune-telling; in which last was a sheet of foolscap much scribbled and blotted in several fruitless attempts to make a copy of verses in honor of the heiress of Van Tassel. These magic books and the poetic scrawl were forthwith consigned to the flames by Hans Van Ripper, who from that time forward determined to send his children no more to school; observing, that he never knew any good come of this same reading and writing. Whatever money the schoolmaster possessed, and he had received his quarter's pay but a day or two before, he must have had about his person at the time of his disappearance.

The mysterious event caused much speculation at the church on the following Sunday. Knots of gazers and gossips were collected in the churchyard, at the bridge, and at the spot where the hat and pumpkin had been found. The stories of Brouwer, of Bones, and a whole budget of others, were called to mind; and when they had diligently considered them all, and compared them with the symptoms of the present case, they shook their heads, and came to the conclusion that Ichabod had been carried off by the Galloping Hessian. As he was a bachelor, and in nobody's debt, nobody troubled his head any more about him. The school was removed to a different quarter of the Hollow, and another pedagogue reigned in his stead.

It is true, an old farmer, who had been down to New York on a visit several years after, and from whom this account of the ghostly adventure was received, brought home the intelligence that Ichabod Crane was still alive; that he had left the neighborhood, partly through fear of the goblin and Hans Van Ripper, and partly in mortification at having been suddenly dismissed by the heiress; that he had changed his quarters to a distant part of the country; had kept school and studied law at the same time, had been admitted to the bar, turned politician, electioneered, written for the newspapers, and finally had been made a justice of the Ten Pound Court.[9] Brom Bones too, who shortly after his rival's disappearance conducted the blooming Katrina in triumph to the altar, was observed to look exceedingly knowing whenever the story of Ichabod was related, and always burst into a hearty laugh at the mention of the pumpkin; which led some to suspect that he knew more about the matter than he chose to tell.

The old country wives, however, who are the best judges of these matters, maintain to this day that Ichabod was spirited away by supernatural means; and it is a favorite story often told about the neighborhood round the winter evening fire. The bridge became more than ever an object of superstitious

[9] Small claims court, restricted to cases involving ten pounds in money value.

awe, and that may be the reason why the road has been altered of late years, so as to approach the church by the border of the millpond. The school-house, being deserted, soon fell to decay, and was reported to be haunted by the ghost of the unfortunate pedagogue; and the ploughboy, loitering homeward of a still summer evening, has often fancied his voice at a distance, chanting a melancholy psalm-tune, among the tranquil solitudes of Sleepy Hollow.

POSTSCRIPT, FOUND IN THE HANDWRITING OF MR. KNICKERBOCKER.

The preceding Tale is given, almost in the precise words in which I heard it related at a Corporation meeting of the ancient city of Manhattoes, at which were present many of its sagest and most illustrious burghers. The narrator was a pleasant, shabby, gentlemanly old fellow, in pepper-and-salt clothes, with a sadly humorous face; and one whom I strongly suspected of being poor,—he made such efforts to be entertaining. When his story was concluded, there was much laughter and approbation, particularly from two or three deputy aldermen, who had been asleep the greater part of the time. There was, however, one tall, dry-looking old gentleman, with beetling eyebrows, who maintained a grave and rather severe face throughout; now and then folding his arms, inclining his head, and looking down upon the floor, as if turning a doubt over in his mind. He was one of your wary men, who never laugh, but on good grounds—when they have reason and the law on their side. When the mirth of the rest of the company had subsided and silence was restored, he leaned one arm on the elbow of his chair, and sticking the other akimbo, demanded, with a slight but exceedingly sage motion of the head, and contraction of the brow, what was the moral of the story, and what it went to prove?

The story-teller, who was just putting a glass of wine to his lips, as a refreshment after his toils, paused for a moment, looked at his inquirer with an air of infinite deference, and, lowering the glass slowly to the table, observed, that the story was intended most logically to prove:

"There is no situation in life but has its advantages and pleasures—provided we will but take a joke as we find it;

"That, therefore, he that runs races with goblin troopers is likely to have rough riding of it.

"*Ergo*, for a country schoolmaster to be refused the hand of a Dutch heiress, is a certain step to high preferment in the state."

The cautious old gentleman knit his brows tenfold closer after this explanation, being sorely puzzled by ratiocination of the syllogism; while, methought, the one in pepper-and-salt eyed him with something of a triumphant leer. At length he observed, that all this was very well, but still he thought the story a little on the extravagant—there were one or two points on which he had his doubts.

"Faith, sir," replied the story-teller, "as to that matter, I don't believe one half of it myself."

D. K.

A Sunday in London

In a preceding paper I have spoken of an English Sunday in the country and its tranquillizing effect upon the landscape; but where is its sacred influence more strikingly apparent than in the very heart of that great Babel, London? On this sacred day the gigantic monster is charmed into repose. The intolerable din and struggle of the week are at an end. The shops are shut. The fires of forges and manufactories are extinguished, and the sun, no longer obscured by murky clouds of smoke, pours down a sober yellow radiance into the quiet streets. The few pedestrians we meet, instead of hurrying forward with anxious countenances, move leisurely along; their brows are smoothed from the wrinkles of business and care; they have put on their Sunday looks and Sunday manners with their Sunday clothes, and are cleansed in mind as well as in person.

And now the melodious clangor of bells from church-towers summons their several flocks to the fold. Forth issues from his mansion the family of the decent tradesman, the small children in the advance; then the citizen and his comely spouse, followed by the grown-up daughters, with small morocco-bound prayer-books laid in the folds of their pocket-handkerchiefs. The house-maid looks after them from the window, admiring the finery of the family, and receiving, perhaps, a nod and smile from her young mistresses, at whose toilet she has assisted.

Now rumbles along the carriage of some magnate of the city, peradventure an alderman or a sheriff; and now the patter of many feet announces a procession of charity scholars in uniforms of antique cut, and each with a prayer-book under his arm.

The ringing of bells is at an end; the rumbling of the carriages has ceased; the pattering of feet is heard no more; the flocks are folded in ancient churches, cramped up in by-lanes and corners of the crowded city, where the vigilant beadle keeps watch, like the shepherd's dog, round the threshold of the sanctuary. For a time everything is hushed, but soon is heard the deep, pervading sound of the organ, rolling and vibrating through the empty lanes and courts, and the sweet chanting of the choir, making them resound with melody and praise. Never have I been more sensible of the sanctifying effect of church music than when I have heard it thus poured forth, like a river of joy, through the inmost recesses of this great metropolis, elevating it, as it were, from all the sordid pollutions of the week, and bearing the poor world-worn soul on a tide of triumphant harmony to heaven.

The morning service is at an end. The streets are again alive with the congregations returning to their homes, but soon again relapse into silence. Now comes on the Sunday dinner, which to the city trades-man is a meal of some importance. There is more leisure for social enjoyment at the board. Members of the family can now gather together who are sepa-rated by the laborious occupations of the week. A school-boy may be permitted on that day to come to the paternal home; an old friend of the family takes his accustomed Sunday seat at the board, tells over his well-known stories, and rejoices young and old with his well-known jokes.

On Sunday afternoon the city pours forth its legions to breathe the fresh air and enjoy the sunshine of the parks and rural environs. Satirists may say what they please about the rural enjoyments of a London citizen on Sunday, but to me there is something delightful in beholding the poor prisoner of the crowded and dusty city enabled thus to come forth once a week and throw himself upon the green bosom of Nature. He is like a child restored to the mother's breast, and they who first spread out these noble parks and magnificent pleasure-grounds which surround this huge metropolis have done at least as much for its health and morality as if they had expend-ed the amount of cost in hospitals, prisons, and penitentiaries.

FROM *The Alhambra*

Irving spent the years 1826–32 in Spain as a member of the American Legation in Madrid. The materials and sur-roundings of Moorish Spain fired his imagination as had the legends of the Rhine and the folklore of Dutch New York and the Hudson Valley; he knew Spanish well, traveled widely through the country seeking out the best of its art and architecture, and explored most of its famous library and manuscript collections. For four months in 1829 he lived in the Alhambra, the splendid medieval palace built by the Moorish kings of Granada, writing of it, "How many legends and traditions, true and fabulous,—how many songs and ballads, Arabian and Spanish, of love and war and chivalry are associated with this pile!" His collec-tion of Moorish tales, named after the palace, derived from his Spanish experience. The text follows that of the Knickerbocker Edition of the *Works*, Philadelphia, 1870–71. First published in the collection of 1832, the tale was revised by Irving in 1851 in this version.

The Legend of the Moor's Legacy

Just within the fortress of the Alhambra, in front of the royal palace, is a broad open esplanade, called the place or square of the cisterns, (la plaza de los algibes,) so called from being undermined by reservoirs of water, hidden from sight, and which have existed from the time of the Moors. At one corner of this esplanade is a Moorish well, cut through the living rock to a great depth, the water of which is cold as ice and clear as crystal. The wells made by the Moors are always in repute, for it is well known what pains they took to penetrate to the purest and sweetest springs and fountains. The one of which we now speak is famous throughout Granada, insomuch that water-carriers, some bear-ing great water-jars on their shoulders, others driv-ing asses before them, laden with earthen vessels, are ascending and descending the steep woody ave-nues of the Alhambra from early dawn until a late hour of the night.

Fountains and wells, ever since the Scriptural days, have been noted gossiping places in hot cli-mates, and at the well in question there is a kind of perpetual club kept up during the livelong day, by the invalids, old women, and other curious, do-noth-ing folk of the fortress, who sit here on the stone benches under an awning spread over the well to shelter the toll-gatherer from the sun, and dawdle over the gossip of the fortress, and question every water-carrier that arrives about the news of the city, and make long comments on everything they hear and see. Not an hour of the day but loitering house-wives and idle maid-servants may be seen, lingering with pitcher on head or in hand, to hear the last of the endless tattle of these worthies.

Among the water-carriers who once resorted to this well there was a sturdy, strong-backed, bandy-legged little fellow, named Pedro Gil, but called Peregil for shortness. Being a water-carrier, he was a Gallego, or native of Gallicia, of course. Nature seems to have formed races of men as she has of animals for different kinds of drudgery. In France the shoe-blacks are all Savoyards, the porters of hotels all Swiss, and in the days of hoops and hair powder in England, no man could give the regular swing to a sedan chair, but a bog-trotting Irishman. So in Spain the carriers of water and bearers of burdens are all sturdy little natives of Gallicia. No man says, "Get me a porter," but, "Call a Gallego."

To return from this digression. Peregil the Gallego had begun business with merely a great earthen jar, which he carried upon his shoulder; by degrees he rose in the world, and was enabled to purchase an assistant of a correspondent class of animals, being a stout shaggy-haired donkey. On each side of this his long-eared aid-de-camp, in a kind of pannier, were slung his water-jars covered with fig leaves to pro-tect them from the sun. There was not a more in-dustrious water-carrier in all Granada, nor one more merry withal. The streets rang with his cheerful voice as he trudged after his donkey, singing forth the usual summer note that resounds through the Spanish towns: *"Quien quiere agua—agua mas fria que la nieve.—*Who wants water—water colder than snow—who wants water from the well of the Alhambra—cold as ice and clear as crystal?" When he served a customer with a sparkling glass, it was always with a pleasant word that caused a smile, and if, perchance, it was a comely dame, or dimpling damsel, it was always with a sly leer and a compliment to her beauty that was irresistible. Thus Peregil the Gallego was noted throughout all Granada for being one of the civilest, pleasantest, and happiest of mortals. Yet it is not he who sings loudest and jokes most that has the lightest heart. Under all this air of merriment, honest Peregil had his cares and troubles. He had a large family of ragged children to support, who were hungry and clamorous as a nest of young swallows, and beset him with their outcries for food whenever he came home of an evening. He had a helpmate, too, who was anything but a help to him. She had been a village beauty before marriage, noted for her skill at dancing the bolero and rattling the castañets, and she still retained her early propensities, spending the hard earnings of honest Peregil in frippery, and laying the very donkey under requisition for junketing parties into the country on Sundays, and saints' days, and those innumerable holidays which are rather more numerous in Spain than the days of the week. With all this she was a little of a slattern, something more of a lie-a-bed, and, above all, a gossip of the first water; neglecting house, household, and everything else, to loiter slipshod in the houses of her gossip neighbors.

He, however, who tempers the wind to the shorn lamb, accommodates the yoke of matrimony to the submissive neck. Peregil bore all the heavy dispensations of wife and children with as meek a spirit as his donkey bore the water-jars; and, however he might shake his ears in private, never ventured to question the household virtues of his slattern spouse.

He loved his children too, even as an owl loves its owlets, seeing in them his own image multiplied and perpetuated, for they were a sturdy, long-backed, bandy-legged little brood. The great pleasure of honest Peregil was, whenever he could afford himself a scanty holiday and had a handful of maravedis to spare, to take the whole litter forth with him, some in his arms, some tugging at his skirts, and some trudging at his heels, and to treat them to a gambol among the orchards of the Vega, while his wife was dancing with her holiday friends in the *angosturas* of the Darro.

It was a late hour one summer night, and most of the water-carriers had desisted from their toils. The day had been uncommonly sultry; the night was one of those delicious moonlights, which tempt the inhabitants of southern climes to indemnify themselves for the heat and inaction of the day, by lingering in the open air and enjoying its tempered sweetness until after midnight. Customers for water were therefore still abroad. Peregil, like a considerate, painstaking father, thought of his hungry children.

"One more journey to the well," said he to himself, "to earn a Sunday's *puchero*[1] for the little ones." So saying, he trudged manfully up the steep avenue of the Alhambra, singing as he went, and now and then bestowing a hearty thwack with a cudgel on the flanks of his donkey, either by way of cadence to the song, or refreshment to the animal: for dry blows serve in lieu of provender in Spain, for all beasts of burden.

When arrived at the well, he found it deserted by every one except a solitary stranger in Moorish garb, seated on a stone bench in the moonlight. Peregil paused at first, and regarded him with surprise, not unmixed with awe, but the Moor feebly beckoned him to approach.

"I am faint and ill," said he; "aid me to return to the city, and I will pay thee double what thou couldst gain by thy jars of water."

The honest heart of the little water-carrier was touched with compassion at the appeal of the stranger. "God forbid," said he, "that I should ask fee or reward for doing a common act of humanity."

He accordingly helped the Moor on his donkey, and set off slowly for Granada, the poor Moslem being so weak that it was necessary to hold him on the animal to keep him from falling to the earth.

When they entered the city, the water-carrier demanded whither he should conduct him. "Alas!" said the Moor, faintly, "I have neither home nor habitation. I am a stranger in the land. Suffer me to lay my head this night beneath thy roof, and thou shalt be amply repaid."

Honest Peregil thus saw himself unexpectedly saddled with an infidel guest, but he was too humane to refuse a night's shelter to a fellow-being in so forlorn a plight; so he conducted the Moor to his dwelling. The children, who had sallied forth, open-mouthed as usual, on hearing the tramp of the donkey, ran back with affright, when they beheld the turbaned stranger, and hid themselves behind their mother. The latter stepped forth intrepidly, like a ruffling hen before her brood, when a vagrant dog approaches.

"What infidel companion," cried she, "is this you have brought home at this late hour, to draw upon us the eyes of the Inquisition?"

"Be quiet, wife," replied the Gallego, "here is a poor sick stranger, without friend or home: wouldst thou turn him forth to perish in the streets?"

The wife would still have remonstrated, for, although she lived in a hovel, she was a furious stickler for the credit of her house; the little water-carrier, however, for once was stiff-necked, and refused to bend beneath the yoke. He assisted the poor Moslem to alight, and spread a mat and a sheepskin for

[1] Pottage.

him, on the ground, in the coolest part of the house; being the only kind of bed that his poverty afforded.

In a little while the Moor was seized with violent convulsions, which defied all the ministering skill of the simple water-carrier. The eye of the poor patient acknowledged his kindness. During an interval of his fits he called him to his side, and addressing him in a low voice; "My end," said he, "I fear is at hand. If I die I bequeath you this box as a reward for your charity." So saying, he opened his albornoz, or cloak, and showed a small box of sandal-wood, strapped round his body.

"God grant, my friend," replied the worthy little Gallego, "that you may live many years to enjoy your treasure, whatever it may be."

The Moor shook his head; he laid his hand upon the box, and would have said something more concerning it, but his convulsions returned with increased violence, and in a little while he expired.

The water-carrier's wife was now as one distracted. "This comes," said she, "of your foolish good-nature, always running into scrapes to oblige others. What will become of us when this corpse is found in our house? We shall be sent to prison as murderers; and if we escape with our lives, shall be ruined by notaries and alguazils."[2]

Poor Peregil was in equal tribulation, and almost repented himself of having done a good deed. At length a thought struck him. "It is not yet day," said he. "I can convey the dead body out of the city and bury it in the sands on the banks of the Xenil. No one saw the Moor enter our dwelling, and no one will know anything of his death." So said, so done. The wife aided him. They rolled the body of the unfortunate Moslem in the mat on which he had expired, laid it across the ass, and Peregil set out with it for the banks of the river.

As ill luck would have it, there lived opposite to the water-carrier a barber, named Pedrillo Pedrugo, one of the most prying, tattling, mischief-making, of his gossipy tribe. He was a weasel-faced, spider-legged varlet, supple and insinuating; the famous Barber of Seville[3] could not surpass him for his universal knowledge of the affairs of others, and he had no more power of retention than a sieve. It was said that he slept but with one eye at a time, and kept one ear uncovered, so that, even in his sleep, he might see and hear all that was going on. Certain it is, he was a sort of scandalous chronicle for the quidnuncs of Granada, and had more customers than all the rest of the fraternity.

This meddlesome barber heard Peregil arrive at an unusual hour at night, and the exclamations of his wife and children. His head was instantly popped

out of a little window which served him as a lookout, and he saw his neighbor assist a man in Moorish garb into his dwelling. This was so strange an occurrence that Pedrillo Pedrugo slept not a wink that night—every five minutes he was at his loophole, watching the lights that gleamed through the chinks of his neighbor's door, and before daylight he beheld Peregil sally forth with his donkey unusually laden.

The inquisitive barber was in a fidget; he slipped on his clothes, and, stealing forth silently, followed the water-carrier at a distance, until he saw him dig a hole in the sandy bank of the Xenil, and bury something that had the appearance of a dead body.

The barber hied him home and fidgeted about his shop, setting everything upside down, until sunrise. He then took a basin under his arm, and sallied forth to the house of his daily customer, the Alcalde.[4]

The Alcalde was just risen. Pedrillo Pedrugo seated him in a chair, threw a napkin round his neck, put a basin of hot water under his chin, and began to mollify his beard with his fingers.

"Strange doings," said Pedrugo, who played barber and newsmonger at the same time. "Strange doings! Robbery, and murder, and burial, all in one night!"

"Hey? how? What is that you say?" cried the Alcalde.

"I say," replied the barber, rubbing a piece of soap over the nose and mouth of the dignitary, for a Spanish barber disdains to employ a brush; "I say that Peregil the Gallego has robbed and murdered a Moorish Mussulman, and buried him this blessed night,—*maldita sea la noche*,—accursed be the night for the same!"

"But how do you know all this?" demanded the Alcalde.

"Be patient, Señor, and you shall hear all about it," replied Pedrillo, taking him by the nose and sliding a razor over his cheek. He then recounted all that he had seen, going through both operations at the same time, shaving his beard, washing his chin, and wiping him dry with a dirty napkin, while he was robbing, murdering, and burying the Moslem.

Now it so happened that this Alcalde was one of the most overbearing, and at the same time most griping and corrupt curmudgeons in all Granada. It could not be denied, however, that he set a high value upon justice, for he sold it at its weight in gold. He presumed the case in point to be one of murder and robbery; doubtless there must be rich spoil; how was it to be secured into the legitimate hands of the law? for as to merely entrapping the delinquent—that would be feeding the gallows: but entrapping the booty—that would be enriching the

[2]Constables.
[3]In Beaumarchais' *The Barber of Seville* (1775).
[4]Mayor.

judge; and such, according to his creed, was the great end of justice. So thinking, he summoned to his presence his trustiest alguazil; a gaunt, hungry-looking varlet, clad, according to the custom of his order, in the ancient Spanish garb—a broad black beaver, turned up at its sides; a quaint ruff, a small black cloak dangling from his shoulders; rusty black underclothes that set off his spare wiry frame; while in his hand he bore a slender white wand, the dreaded insignia of his office. Such was the legal bloodhound of the ancient Spanish breed, that he put upon the traces of the unlucky water-carrier; and such was his speed and certainty that he was upon the haunches of poor Peregil before he had returned to his dwelling, and brought both him and his donkey before the dispenser of justice.

The Alcalde bent upon him one of the most terrific frowns. "Hark ye, culprit," roared he in a voice that made the knees of the little Gallego smite together,—"Hark, ye culprit! there is no need of denying thy guilt: everything is known to me. A gallows is the proper reward for the crime thou hast committed, but I am merciful, and readily listen to reason. The man that has been murdered in thy house was a Moor, an infidel, the enemy of our faith. It was doubtless in a fit of religious zeal that thou hast slain him. I will be indulgent, therefore; render up the property of which thou hast robbed him, and we will hush the matter up."

The poor water-carrier called upon all the saints to witness his innocence; alas! not one of them appeared, and if they had, the Alcalde would have disbelieved the whole calendar. The water-carrier related the whole story of the dying Moor with the straightforward simplicity of truth, but it was all in vain: "Wilt thou persist in saying," demanded the judge, "that this Moslem had neither gold nor jewels, which were the object of thy cupidity?"

"As I hope to be saved, your worship," replied the water-carrier, "he had nothing but a small box of sandal-wood, which he bequeathed to me in reward for my services."

"A box of sandal-wood! a box of sandal-wood!" exclaimed the Alcalde, his eyes sparkling at the idea of precious jewels, "and where is this box? where have you concealed it?"

"An it please your grace," replied the water-carrier, "it is in one of the panniers of my mule, and heartily at the service of your worship."

He had hardly spoken the words when the keen alguazil darted off and reappeared in an instant with the mysterious box of sandal-wood. The Alcalde opened it with an eager and trembling hand; all pressed forward to gaze upon the treasure it was expected to contain; when, to their disappointment, nothing appeared within but a parchment scroll, covered with Arabic characters, and an end of a waxen taper!

When there is nothing to be gained by the conviction of a prisoner, justice, even in Spain, is apt to be impartial. The Alcalde, having recovered from his disappointment and found that there was really no booty in the case, now listened dispassionately to the explanation of the water-carrier, which was corroborated by the testimony of his wife. Being convinced, therefore, of his innocence, he discharged him from arrest; nay more, he permitted him to carry off the Moor's legacy, the box of sandal-wood and its contents, as the well-merited reward of his humanity; but he retained his donkey in payment of cost and charges.

Behold the unfortunate little Gallego reduced once more to the necessity of being his own water-carrier, and trudging up to the well of the Alhambra with a great earthen jar upon his shoulder. As he toiled up the hill in the heat of a summer noon his usual good-humor forsook him. "Dog of an Alcalde!" would he cry, "to rob a poor man of the means of his subsistence—of the best friend he had in the world!" And then, at the remembrance of the beloved companion of his labors, all the kindness of his nature would break forth. "Ah, donkey of my heart!" would he exclaim, resting his burden on a stone, and wiping the sweat from his brow. "Ah, donkey of my heart! I warrant thee thou thinkest of thy old master! I warrant me thou missest the water-jars—poor beast!"

To add to his afflictions his wife received him, on his return home, with whimperings and repinings; she had clearly the vantage-ground of him, having warned him not to commit the egregious act of hospitality which had brought on him all these misfortunes, and like a knowing woman, she took every occasion to throw her superior sagacity in his teeth. If her children lacked food, or needed a new garment, she could answer with a sneer, "Go to your father; he is heir to king Chico of the Alhambra. Ask him to help you out of the Moor's strong box."

Was ever poor mortal so soundly punished, for having done a good action! The unlucky Peregil was grieved in flesh and spirit, but still he bore meekly with the railings of his spouse. At length one evening, when, after a hot day's toil, she taunted him in the usual manner, he lost all patience. He did not venture to retort upon her, but his eye rested upon the box of sandal-wood, which lay on a shelf with lid half open, as if laughing in mockery at his vexation. Seizing it up he dashed it with indignation to the floor. "Unlucky was the day that I ever set eyes on thee," he cried, "or sheltered thy master beneath my roof."

As the box struck the floor the lid flew wide

open, and the parchment scroll rolled forth. Peregil sat regarding the scroll for some time in moody silence. At length rallying his ideas, "Who knows," thought he, "but this writing may be of some importance, as the Moor seems to have guarded it with such care." Picking it up, therefore, he put it in his bosom, and the next morning, as he was crying water through the streets, he stopped at the shop of a Moor, a native of Tangiers, who sold trinkets and perfumery in the Zacatin,[5] and asked him to explain the contents.

The Moor read the scroll attentively, then stroked his beard and smiled. "This manuscript," said he, "is a form of incantation for the recovery of hidden treasure, that is under the power of enchantment. It is said to have such virtue that the strongest bolts and bars, nay the adamantine rock itself will yield before it."

"Bah!" cried the little Gallego, "what is all that to me! I am no enchanter, and know nothing of buried treasure." So saying he shouldered his water-jar, left the scroll in the hands of the Moor, and trudged forward on his daily rounds.

That evening, however, as he rested himself about the twilight at the well of the Alhambra, he found a number of gossips assembled at the place, and their conversation, as is not unusual at that shadowy hour, turned upon old tales and traditions of a supernatural nature. Being all poor as rats, they dwelt with peculiar fondness upon the popular theme of enchanted riches left by the Moors in various parts of the Alhambra. Above all, they concurred in the belief that there were great treasures buried deep in the earth under the tower of the Seven Floors.

These stories made an unusual impression on the mind of the honest Peregil, and they sank deeper and deeper into his thoughts as he returned alone down the darkling avenues. "If, after all, there should be treasure hid beneath that tower—and if the scroll I left with the Moor should enable me to get at it!" In the sudden ecstasy of the thought he had well-nigh let fall his water-jar.

That night he tumbled and tossed, and could scarcely get a wink of sleep for the thoughts that were bewildering his brain. Bright and early, he repaired to the shop of the Moor, and told him all that was passing in his mind. "You can read Arabic," said he, "suppose we go together to the tower and try the effect of the charm; if it fails we are no worse off than before, but if it succeeds we will share equally all the treasure we may discover."

"Hold," replied the Moslem, "this writing is not sufficient of itself; it must be read at midnight, by the light of a taper singularly compounded and pre-

pared, the ingredients of which are not within my reach. Without such a taper the scroll is of no avail."

"Say no more!" cried the little Gallego. "I have such a taper at hand and will bring it here in a moment." So saying he hastened home, and soon returned with the end of yellow wax taper that he had found in the box of sandal-wood.

The Moor felt it, and smelt of it. "Here are rare and costly perfumes," said he, "combined with this yellow wax. This is the kind of taper specified in the scroll. While this burns, the strongest walls and most secret caverns will remain open; woe to him, however, who lingers within until it be extinguished. He will remain enchanted with the treasure."

It was now agreed between them to try the charm that very night. At a late hour, therefore, when nothing was stirring but bats and owls, they ascended the woody hill of the Alhambra, and approached that awful tower, shrouded by trees and rendered formidable by so many traditionary tales.

By the light of a lantern, they groped their way through bushes, and over fallen stones, to the door of a vault beneath the tower. With fear and trembling they descended a flight of steps cut into the rock. It led to an empty chamber, damp and drear, from which another flight of steps led to a deeper vault. In this way they descended four several flights, leading into as many vaults, one below the other, but the floor of the fourth was solid, and though, according to tradition, there remained three vaults still below, it was said to be impossible to penetrate farther, the residue being shut up by strong enchantment. The air of this vault was damp and chilly, and had an earthy smell, and the light scarce cast forth any rays. They paused here for a time in breathless suspense, until they faintly heard the clock of the watch-tower strike midnight; upon this they lit the waxen taper, which diffused an odor of myrrh, and frankincense, and storax.

The Moor began to read in a hurried voice. He had scarce finished, when there was a noise as of subterraneous thunder. The earth shook, and the floor yawning open disclosed a flight of steps. Trembling with awe they descended, and by the light of the lantern found themselves in another vault, covered with Arabic inscriptions. In the centre stood a great chest, secured with seven bands of steel, at each end of which sat an enchanted Moor in armor, but motionless as a statue, being controlled by the power of the incantation. Before the chest were several jars filled with gold and silver and precious stones. In the largest of these they thrust their arms up to the elbow, and at every dip hauled forth hands full of broad yellow pieces of Moorish gold, or bracelets and ornaments of the

[5]A market in Granada.

same precious metal, while occasionally a necklace of Oriental pearl would stick to their fingers. Still they trembled and breathed short while cramming their pockets with the spoils; and cast many a fearful glance at the two enchanted Moors, who sat grim and motionless, glaring upon them with unwinking eyes. At length, struck with sudden panic at some fancied noise, they both rushed up the staircase, tumbled over one another into the upper apartment, overturned and extinguished the waxen taper, and the pavement again closed with a thundering sound.

Filled with dismay, they did not pause until they had groped their way out of the tower, and beheld the stars shining through the trees. Then seating themselves upon the grass, they divided the spoil determining to content themselves for the present with this mere skimming of the jars, but to return on some future night and drain them to the bottom. To make sure of each other's good faith, also, they divided the talismans between them, one retaining the scroll and the other the taper; this done, they set off with light hearts and well-lined pockets for Granada.

As they wended their way down the hill, the shrewd Moor whispered a word of counsel in the ear of the simple little water-carrier.

"Friend Peregil," said he, "all this affair must be kept a profound secret until we have secured the treasure and conveyed it out of harm's way. If a whisper of it gets to the ear of the Alcalde we are undone!"

"Certainly!" replied the Gallego; "nothing can be more true."

"Friend Peregil," said the Moor, "you are a discreet man, and I make no doubt can keep a secret; but—you have a wife——"

"She shall not know a word of it!" replied the little water-carrier sturdily.

"Enough," said the Moor, "I depend upon thy discretion and thy promise."

Never was promise more positive and sincere; but alas! what man can keep a secret from his wife? Certainly not such a one as Peregil the water-carrier, who was one of the most loving and tractable of husbands. On his return home he found his wife moping in a corner.

"Mighty well!" cried she, as he entered; "you've come at last; after rambling about until this hour of the night. I wonder you have not brought home another Moor as a house-mate." Then bursting into tears she began to wring her hands and smite her breast. "Unhappy woman that I am!" exclaimed she, "what will become of me! My house stripped and plundered by lawyers and alguazils; my husband a do-no-good that no longer brings home bread to his family, but goes rambling about, day and night, with infidel Moors. Oh, my children! my children! what will become of us; we shall all have to beg in the streets!"

Honest Peregil was so moved by the distress of his spouse, that he could not help whimpering also. His heart was as full as his pocket, and not to be restrained. Thrusting his hand into the latter he hauled forth three or four broad gold pieces and slipped them into her bosom. The poor woman stared with astonishment, and could not understand the meaning of this golden shower. Before she could recover her surprise, the little Gallego drew forth a chain of gold and dangled it before her, capering with exultation, his mouth distended from ear to ear.

"Holy Virgin protect us!" exclaimed the wife. "What hast thou been doing, Peregil? Surely thou hast not been committing murder and robbery!"

The idea scarce entered the brain of the poor woman than it became a certainty with her. She saw a prison and a gallows in the distance, and a little bandy-legged Gallego hanging pendent from it; and, overcome by the horrors conjured up by her imagination, fell into violent hysterics.

What could the poor man do? He had no other means of pacifying his wife and dispelling the phantoms of her fancy, than by relating the whole story of his good fortune. This, however, he did not do until he had exacted from her the most solemn promise to keep it a profound secret from every living being.

To describe her joy would be impossible. She flung her arms round the neck of her husband, and almost strangled him with her caresses. "Now, wife!" exclaimed the little man with honest exultation, "what say you now to the Moor's legacy? Henceforth never abuse me for helping a fellow creature in distress."

The honest Gallego retired to his sheepskin mat, and slept soundly as if on a bed of down. Not so his wife.—She emptied the whole contents of his pockets upon the mat, and sat counting gold pieces of Arabic coin, trying on necklaces and ear-rings, and fancying the figure she would one day make when permitted to enjoy her riches.

On the following morning the honest Gallego took a broad golden coin, and repaired with it to a jeweller's shop in the Zacatin to offer it for sale; pretending to have found it among the ruins of the Alhambra. The jeweller saw that it had an Arabic inscription and was of the purest gold; he offered, however, but a third of its value, with which the water-carrier was perfectly content. Peregil now bought new clothes for his little flock, and all kinds of toys, together with ample provisions for a hearty meal, and returning to his dwelling set all his children dancing around him, while he capered in the midst, the happiest of fathers.

The wife of the water-carrier kept her promise of secrecy with surprising strictness. For a whole day and a half she went about with a look of mystery and a heart swelling almost to bursting, yet she held her peace, though surrounded by her gossips. It is true she could not help giving herself a few airs, apologized for her ragged dress, and talked of ordering a new basquiña[6] all trimmed with gold lace and bugles, and a new lace mantilla. She threw out hints of her husband's intention of leaving off his trade of water-carrying, as it did not altogether agree with his health. In fact she thought they should all retire to the country for the summer, that the children might have the benefit of the mountain air, for there was no living in the city in this sultry season.

The neighbors stared at each other, and thought the poor woman had lost her wits, and her airs and graces and elegant pretentions were the theme of universal scoffing and merriment among her friends, the moment her back was turned.

If she restrained herself abroad, however, she indemnified herself at home, and, putting a string of rich Oriental pearls round her neck, Moorish bracelets on her arms; an aigrette of diamonds on her head, sailed backwards and forwards in her slattern rags about the room, now and then stopping to admire herself in a broken mirror. Nay, in the impulse of her simple vanity, she could not resist on one occasion showing herself at the window, to enjoy the effect of her finery on the passers by.

As the fates would have it, Pedrillo Pedrugo, the meddlesome barber, was at this moment sitting idly in his shop on the opposite side of the street, when his ever watchful eye caught the sparkle of a diamond. In an instant he was at his loophole, reconnoitring the slattern spouse of the water-carrier, decorated with the splendor of an eastern bride. No sooner had he taken an accurate inventory of her ornaments than he posted off with all speed to the Alcalde. In a little while the hungry alguazil was again on the scent, and before the day was over, the unfortunate Peregil was once more dragged into the presence of the judge.

"How is this villain!" cried the Alcalde in a furious voice. "You told me that the infidel who died in your house left nothing behind but an empty coffer, and now I hear of your wife flaunting in her rags decked out with pearls and diamonds. Wretch, that thou art! prepare to render up the spoils of thy miserable victim, and to swing on the gallows that is already tired of waiting for thee."

The terrified water-carrier fell on his knees, and made a full relation of the marvellous manner in which he had gained his wealth. The Alcalde, the alguazil, and the inquisitive barber listened with

[6]A petticoat worn by Spanish women.

greedy ears to the Arabian tale of enchanted treasure. The alguazil was despatched to bring the Moor who had assisted in the incantation. The Moslem entered half frightened out of his wits at finding himself in the hands of the harpies of the law. When he beheld the water-carrier standing with sheepish look and downcast countenance, he comprehended the whole matter. "Miserable animal," said he, as he passed near him, "did I not warn thee against babbling to thy wife?"

The story of the Moor coincided exactly with that of his colleague; but the Alcalde affected to be slow of belief, and threw out menaces of imprisonment and rigorous investigation.

"Softly, good Señor Alcalde," said the Mussulman, who by this time had recovered his usual shrewdness and self-possession. "Let's not mar fortune's favors in the scramble for them. Nobody knows anything of this matter but ourselves; let us keep the secret. There is wealth enough in the cave to enrich us all. Promise a fair division, and all shall be produced; refuse, and the cave shall remain forever closed."

The Alcalde consulted apart with the alguazil. The latter was an old fox in his profession. "Promise anything," said he, "until you get possession of the treasure. You may then seize upon the whole, and if he or his accomplice dare to murmur, threaten them with the fagot and the stake as infidels and sorcerers."

The Alcalde relished the advice. Smoothing his brow and turning to the Moor,—"This is a strange story," said he, "and may be true, but I must have ocular proof of it. This very night you must repeat the incantation in my presence. If there really be such treasure, we shall share it amicably between us, and say nothing further of the matter; if ye have deceived me, expect no mercy at my hands. In the meantime you must remain in custody."

The Moor and the water-carrier cheerfully agreed to these conditions, satisfied that the event would prove the truth of their words.

Towards midnight the Alcalde sallied forth secretly, attended by the alguazil and the meddlesome barber, all strongly armed. They conducted the Moor and the water-carrier as prisoners, and were provided with the stout donkey of the latter, to bear off the expected treasure. They arrived at the tower without being observed, and tying the donkey to a fig-tree, descended into the fourth vault of the tower.

The scroll was produced, the yellow waxen taper lighted, and the Moor read the form of incantation. The earth trembled as before, and the pavement opened with a thundering sound, disclosing the narrow flight of steps. The Alcalde, the alguazil, and the barber were struck aghast, and could not summon courage to descend. The Moor and the water-carrier entered the lower vault and found the two Moors seated as before, silent and motionless. They removed two of the great jars filled with golden coin and precious stones. The water-carrier bore them up one by one upon his shoulders, but though a strong-back little man, and accustomed to carry burdens, he staggered beneath their weight, and found, when slung on each side of his donkey, they were as much as the animal could bear.

"Let us be content for the present," said the Moor; "here is as much treasure as we can carry off without being perceived, and enough to make us all wealthy to our heart's desire."

"Is there more treasure remaining behind?" demanded the Alcalde.

"The greatest prize of all," said the Moor; "a huge coffer, bound with bands of steel, and filled with pearls and precious stones."

"Let us have up the coffer by all means," cried the grasping Alcalde.

"I will descend for no more," said the Moor, doggedly. "Enough is enough for a reasonable man; more is superfluous."

"And I," said the water-carrier, "will bring up no further burden to break the back of my poor donkey."

Finding commands, threats, and entreaties equally vain, the Alcalde turned to his two adherents. "Aid me," said he, "to bring up the coffer, and its contents shall be divided between us." So saying he descended the steps, followed, with trembling reluctance, by the alguazil and the barber.

No sooner did the Moor behold them fairly earthed than he extinguished the yellow taper: the pavement closed with its usual crash, and the three worthies remained buried in its womb.

He then hastened up the different flights of steps, nor stopped until in the open air. The little water-carrier followed him as fast as his short legs would permit.

"What hast thou done?" cried Peregil, as soon as he could recover breath. "The Alcalde and the other two are shut up in the vault!"

"It is the will of Allah!" said the Moor, devoutly.

"And you will not release them?" demanded the Gallego.

"Allah forbid!" replied the Moor, smoothing his beard. "It is written in the book of fate that they shall remain enchanted until some future adventurer arrive to break the charm. The will of God be done!" So saying he hurled the end of the waxen taper far among the gloomy thickets of the glen.

There was now no remedy; so the Moor and the water-carrier proceeded with the richly-laden donkey towards the city: nor could honest Peregil refrain from hugging and kissing his long-eared fel-low-laborer, thus restored to him from the clutches of the law; and, in fact, it is doubtful which gave the simple-hearted little man most joy at the moment, the gaining of the treasure or the recovery of the donkey.

The two partners in good luck divided their spoil amicably and fairly, except that the Moor, who had a little taste for trinketry, made out to get into his heap the most of the pearls and precious stones, and other baubles, but then he always gave the water-carrier in lieu magnificent jewels of massy gold of five times the size, with which the latter was heartily content. They took care not to linger within reach of accidents, but made off to enjoy their wealth undisturbed in other countries. The Moor returned to Africa, to his native city of Tangiers, and the Gallego, with his wife, his children, and his donkey, made the best of his way to Portugal. Here, under the admonition and tuition of his wife, he became a personage of some consequence, for she made the worthy little man array his long body and short legs in doublet and hose, with a feather in his hat and a sword by his side; and, laying aside his familiar appellation of Peregil, assume the more sonorous title of Don Pedro Gil. His progeny grew up a thriving and merry-hearted, though short and bandy-legged generation; while Señora Gil, be-fringed, be-laced, and be-tasseled from her head to her heels, with glittering rings on every finger, became a model of slattern fashion and finery.

As to the Alcalde, and his adjuncts, they remained shut up under the great tower of the Seven Floors, and there they remain spellbound at the present day. Whenever there shall be a lack in Spain of pimping barbers, sharking alguazils, and corrupt Alcaldes, they may be sought after; but if they have to wait until such time for their deliverance, there is danger of their enchantment enduring until doomsday.

1832, 1851

FROM *A Tour on the Prairies*

Irving returned to the United States in 1832 after seventeen years abroad, intending to publish an American book. The accounts of the Western country intrigued him, and that same year he set out with H. L. Ellsworth, commissioner in charge of the removal of the Indians to the southwest, traveling down the Ohio and Mississippi to St. Louis, up the Missouri to Independence, on horseback across Indian country to Fort Gibson, Arkansas, and beyond into Pawnee country. He kept a rather scanty set of notes which he expanded into *A Tour on the Prairies,* published in 1835, his first book written about America since the *Knickerbocker History.* It is clear that Irving simply did not know what to do with such new experiences as buffalo, savages, frontiersmen, and this broad new country. A cultivated, urbanized man, he could not record his observations without romanticizing them so that the picture of the West which emerged was an idealized, Europeanized version of what wild nature should look like. Thus he reacts to what he sees in terms of what he knows—seeing an Indian on horseback as a museum object, a frontier scout and his Indian companion as "preux chevalier" and squire, and Gothic castles in the Arkansas forest. The text follows the London edition of 1835.

Chapter VII

In the morning early, (Oct. 12,) the two Creeks who had been sent express by the commander of Fort Gibson, to stop the company of rangers, arrived at our encampment on their return. They had left the company encamped about fifty miles distant, in a fine place on the Arkansas, abounding in game, where they intended to await our arrival. This news spread animation throughout our party, and we set out on our march, at sunrise, with renewed spirit.

In mounting our steeds, the young Osage attempted to throw a blanket upon his wild horse. The fine, sensitive animal took fright, reared and recoiled. The attitudes of the wild horse and the almost naked savage would have formed studies for a painter or a statuary.

I often pleased myself, in the course of our march, with noticing the appearance of the young Count and his newly enlisted follower, as they rode before me. Never was preux chevalier better suited with an esquire. The Count was well mounted, and, as I have before observed, was a bold and graceful rider. He was fond, too, of caracoling his horse, and dashing about in the buoyancy of youthful spirits. His dress was a gay Indian hunting-frock, of dressed deer-skin, setting well to the shape, dyed of a beautiful purple, and fancifully embroidered with silks of various colors; as if it had been the work of some Indian beauty, to decorate a favorite chief. With this he wore leathern pantaloons and moccasins, a foraging-cap, and a double-barrelled gun slung by a bandoleer athwart his back: so that he was quite a picturesque figure as he managed gracefully his spirited steed.

The young Osage would ride close behind him on his wild and beautifully mottled horse, which was decorated with crimson tufts of hair. He rode, with his finely shaped head and bust naked; his blanket being girt round his waist. He carried his rifle in one hand, and managed his horse with the other, and seemed ready to dash off at a moment's warning, with his youthful leader, on any madcap foray or scamper. The Count, with the sanguine anticipations of youth, promised himself many hardy adventures and exploits in company with his youthful "brave," when we should get among the buffaloes, in the Pawnee hunting-grounds.

After riding some distance, we crossed a narrow, deep stream, upon a solid bridge, the remains of an old beaver dam; the industrious community which had constructed it had all been destroyed. Above us, a streaming flight of wild geese, high in air, and making a vociferous noise, gave note of the waning year.

About half-past ten o'clock we made a halt in a forest, where there was abundance of pea-vine. Here we turned the horses loose to graze. A fire was made, water procured from an adjacent spring, and in a short time our little Frenchman, Tonish, had a pot of coffee prepared for our refreshment. While partaking of it, we were joined by an old Osage, one of a small hunting party who had recently passed this way. He was in search of his horse, which had wandered away, or been stolen. Our half-breed, Beatte, made a wry face on hearing of Osage hunters in this direction. "Until we pass those hunters," said he, "we shall see no buffaloes. They frighten away everything like a prairie on fire."

The morning repast being over, the party amused themselves in various ways. Some shot with their rifles at mark, others lay asleep half buried in the deep bed of foliage, with their heads resting on their saddles; others gossiped round the fire at the foot of a tree, which sent up wreaths of blue smoke among the branches. The horses banqueted luxuriously on the pea-vines, and some lay down and rolled amongst them.

We were overshadowed by lofty trees, with straight, smooth trunks, like stately columns; and as the glancing rays of the sun shone through the transparent leaves, tinted with the many-colored hues of autumn, I was reminded of the effect of sunshine among the stained windows and clustering columns of a Gothic cathedral. Indeed there is a grandeur and solemnity in our spacious forests of the West, that awaken in me the same feeling I have experienced in those vast and venerable piles, and the sound of the wind sweeping through them supplies occasionally the deep breathings of the organ.

About noon the bugle sounded to horse, and we were again on the march, hoping to arrive at the encampment of the rangers before night; as the old Osage had assured us it was not above ten or twelve miles distant. In our course through a forest, we passed by a lonely pool, covered with the most magnificent water-lilies I have ever beheld; among which swam several wood-ducks, one of the most beautiful of water-fowl, remarkable for the gracefulness and brilliancy of its plumage.

After proceeding some distance farther, we came down upon the banks of the Arkansas, at a place where tracks of numerous horses, all entering the water, showed where a party of Osage hunters had recently crossed the river on their way to the buffalo range. After letting our horses drink in the river, we continued along its bank for a space, and then across prairies, where we saw a distant smoke, which we hoped might proceed from the encampment of the rangers. Following what we supposed to be their trail, we came to a meadow in which were a number of horses grazing; they were not, however, the horses of the troop. A little farther on, we reached a straggling Osage village, on the banks of the Arkansas. Our arrival created quite a sensation. A number of old men came forward and shook hands with us all severally; while the women and children huddled together in groups, staring at us wildly, chattering and laughing among themselves. We found that all the young men of the village had departed on a hunting expedition, leaving the women and children and old men behind. Here the Commissioner made a speech from on horseback; informing his hearers of the purport of his mission, to promote a general peace among the tribes of the West, and urging them to lay aside all warlike and bloodthirsty notions, and not to make any wanton attacks upon the Pawnees. This speech being interpreted by Beatte, seemed to have a most pacifying effect upon the multitude, who promised faithfully that, as far as in them lay, the peace should not be disturbed; and indeed their age and sex gave some reason to trust that they would keep their word.

Still hoping to reach the camp of the rangers before nightfall, we pushed on until twilight, when we were obliged to halt on the borders of a ravine. The rangers bivouacked under trees, at the bottom of the dell, while we pitched our tent on a rocky knoll near a running stream. The night came on dark and overcast, with flying clouds, and much appearance of rain. The fires of the rangers burnt brightly in the dell, and threw strong masses of light upon the robber-looking groups that were cooking, eating, and drinking around them. To add to the wildness of the scene, several Osage Indians, visitors from the village we had passed, were mingled among the men. Three of them came and seated themselves by our fire. They watched everything that was going on round them in silence, and looked like figures of monumental bronze. We gave them food, and, what they most relished, coffee; for the Indians partake in the universal fondness for this beverage, which pervades the West. When they had made their supper, they stretched themselves side by side before the fire, and began a low nasal chant, drumming with their hands upon their breasts by way of accompaniment. Their chant seemed to consist of regular staves, every one terminating, not in a melodious cadence, but in the abrupt interjection huh! uttered almost like a hiccup. This chant, we were told by our interpreter, Beatte, related to ourselves, our ap-

pearance, our treatment of them, and all that they knew of our plans. In one part they spoke of the young Count, whose animated character and eagerness for Indian enterprise had struck their fancy, and they indulged in some waggery about him and the young Indian beauties, that produced great merriment among our half-breeds.

This mode of improvising is common throughout the savage tribes; and in this way, with a few simple inflections of the voice, they chant all their exploits in war and hunting, and occasionally indulge in a vein of comic humor and dry satire, to which the Indians appear to me much more prone than is generally imagined.

In fact, the Indians that I have had an opportunity of seeing in real life are quite different from those described in poetry. They are by no means the stoics that they are represented: taciturn, unbending, without a tear or a smile. Taciturn they are, it is true, when in company with white men, whose good-will they distrust, and whose language they do not understand; but the white man is equally taciturn under like circumstances. When the Indians are among themselves, however, there cannot be greater gossips. Half their time is taken up in talking over their adventures in war and hunting, and in telling whimsical stories. They are great mimics and buffoons, also, and entertain themselves excessively at the expense of the whites with whom they have associated, and who have supposed them impressed with profound respect for their grandeur and dignity. They are curious observers, noting everything in silence, but with a keen and watchful eye; occasionally exchanging a glance or a grunt with each other, when anything particularly strikes them; but reserving all comments until they are alone. Then it is that they give full scope to criticism, satire, mimicry, and mirth.

In the course of my journey along the frontier I have had repeated opportunities of noticing their excitability and boisterous merriment at their games; and have occasionally noticed a group of Osages sitting round a fire until a late hour at night, engaged in the most animated and lively conversation; and at times making the woods resound with peals of laughter. As to tears, they have them in abundance, both real and affected; at times they make a merit of them. No one weeps more bitterly or profusely at the death of a relative or friend; and they have stated times when they repair to howl and lament at their graves. I have heard doleful wailings at daybreak in the neighboring Indian villages, made by some of the inhabitants, who go out at that hour into the fields to mourn and weep for the dead; at such times, I am told, the tears will stream down their cheeks in torrents.

As far as I can judge, the Indian of poetical fiction is, like the shepherd of pastoral romance, a mere personification of imaginary attributes.

The nasal chant of our Osage guests gradually died away; they covered their heads with their blankets and fell fast asleep, and in a little while all was silent, excepting the pattering of scattered raindrops upon our tent.

In the morning our Indian visitors breakfasted with us, but the young Osage who was to act as esquire to the Count in his knight-errantry on the prairies, was nowhere to be found. His wild horse, too, was missing, and, after many conjectures, we came to the conclusion that he had taken "Indian leave" of us in the night. We afterwards ascertained that he had been persuaded so to do by the Osages we had recently met with; who had represented to him the perils that would attend him in an expedition to the Pawnee hunting-grounds, where he might fall into the hands of the implacable enemies of his tribe; and, what was scarcely less to be apprehended, the annoyances to which he would be sub-jected from the capricious and overbearing conduct of the white men; who, as I have witnessed in my own short experience, are prone to treat the poor Indians as little better than brute animals. Indeed, he had had a specimen of it himself in the narrow escape he made from the infliction of "Lynch's law," by the hard-winking worthy of the frontier, for the flagitious crime of finding a stray horse.

The disappearance of the youth was generally regretted by our party, for we had all taken a great fancy to him from his handsome, frank, and manly appearance, and the easy grace of his deportment. He was indeed a native-born gentleman. By none, however, was he so much lamented as by the young Count, who thus suddenly found himself deprived of his esquire. I regretted the departure of the Osage for his own sake, for we should have cherished him throughout the expedition, and I am convinced, from the munificent spirit of his patron, he would have returned to his tribe laden with wealth of beads and trinkets and Indian blankets.

1835

JAMES FENIMORE COOPER [1789–1851]

COOPER WAS BORN in New Jersey, but when he was only a little more than a year old he was taken to Cooperstown, New York, in territory only recently claimed from the forest and still surrounded by it. At Cooperstown his father, Judge William Cooper, held almost feudal control over the settlement and huge tracts of wilderness-land; young James (he added Fenimore, his mother's family name, to his own later) grew up as a young baronial aristocrat. He was privately educated by an English tutor at Albany, studied at Yale without much interest or distinction, was dismissed after a student prank, shipped out with the merchant marine, and later entered the United States Navy. After marrying Susan DeLancey, daughter of a wealthy and former Tory family, he resigned his midshipman's commission and assumed his inherited role as cultivated country gentleman on his estate in Westchester County, New York.

Cooper drifted into authorship by accident. To prove to his wife that he could write a better book than the sentimental English society novel she was reading, he wrote one of his own, published as *Precaution* (1820), which was good enough to prove his point, but not to satisfy his taste. Thus he began *The Spy* (1821), an absorbing story of the American Revolution, the best novel yet written in America and a highly popular one. Its chief figure, the shrewd, deceptive, furtive peddler, Harvey Birch, who plays the game of double agent to perfection, is one of the major character creations of early American fiction. Cooper moved his next novel to the life he knew as a boy in Cooperstown, and in 1823 published *The Pioneers,* the first of the famous Leatherstocking Tales, which eventually included *The Last of the Mohicans* (1826), *The Prairie* (1827), *The Pathfinder*

(1840), and *The Deerslayer* (1841). *The Pioneers* introduced Cooper's second and greatest character creation, Natty Bumppo the noble frontiersman (whose Indian friends Uncas, Chingachgook, and Hardheart were noble savages too), who in his simplicity and freedom embodied all the virtues of wilderness life. Immediately after *The Pioneers* came *The Pilot* (1824), the first of eleven sea novels and the one which introduced Cooper's third major character creation, Long Tom Coffin, the prototype of the tough, wise, salty Yankee sailor. Within three years, therefore, Cooper opened three great veins of native literary materials—the Revolutionary past, the sea, and the frontier—and American fiction was never the same again.

His literary reputation firmly established, Cooper moved to New York City. During the years 1826–33 he traveled extensively in Europe, and on his return became embroiled in a variety of political and literary controversies and an almost equal number of libel suits, most of which he won. A democrat by conviction and an aristocrat by nature and training, Cooper found much in Jackson's America to criticize. He continued to produce books in a steady stream (thirty-two novels alone during his lifetime) but broadened his range to include social criticism, manners, travel, history, biography, political and social commentaries, and satires and allegories, as well as novels of the sea, the frontier, and the American past. The "Littlepage" series, *Satanstoe* (1845), *The Chainbearer* (1846), and *The Redskins* (1846), for example, dealt with the clash between aristocrat and democrat in upstate New York during the Anti-Rent troubles of the eighteen-forties. *The Monikins* (1835), *The Crater* (1848), *Homeward Bound* and *Home as Found* (both 1848) were satires or allegories. *Notions of the Americans* (1828), *A Letter to his Countrymen* (1834), and *The American Democrat* (1838) were constructive critiques of the American system.

Cooper's fictional techniques, drawn from the historical and sentimental novel traditions of the eighteenth and early nineteenth century, were unfortunately already obsolescent before he finished his work, as compared to those developments in the American novel deriving from more sophisticated and expert practitioners such as Poe, Hawthorne, and Melville. His old-fashioned discursive style and his overly theatrical dramatics no longer attract the modern reader, who is often unwilling to accept the conventions of the older tradition within which Cooper wrote. However, within the limits of his artistic techniques and concepts, Cooper's work can still generate power, and his epic of the wilderness, The Leatherstocking Tales, is so much a part of the mainstream of the American mythos that no student of American literature can afford to lack acquaintance with it.

Further reading: Robert E. Spiller, *Fenimore Cooper: Critic of His Times*, 1931. Donald Ringe, *James Fenimore Cooper*, 1962. Henry Nash Smith, *Virgin Land* (especially chaps. 6 and 21), 1950.

FROM *Notions of the Americans*

Cooper, who resented the condescension and ignorance of many Europeans concerning American life and culture, set himself in this book to the task of informing and correcting them. Built about the device of letters presumably written home by an intelligent English traveler in the United States, it represents the earliest of Cooper's several attempts to explain the United States and to defend its character and institutions against foreign criticism. However, it was not especially well received in England, and detracted from his popularity abroad. Text: From the first edition of 1828, Philadelphia; subtitled "Picked Up by a Travelling Bachelor."

[Problems of a Native Literature]

The literature of the United States has, indeed, two powerful obstacles to conquer before (to use a mercantile expression) it can ever enter the markets of its own country on terms of perfect equality with that of England. Solitary and individual works of genius may, indeed, be occasionally brought to light, under the impulses of the high feeling which has conceived them; but, I fear, a good, wholesome, profitable and continued pecuniary support, is the applause that talent most craves. The fact, that an American publisher can get an English work without money, must, for a few years longer, (unless legislative protection shall be extended to their own authors,) have a tendency to repress a national literature. No man will pay a writer for an epic, a tragedy, a sonnet, a history, or a romance, when he can get a work of equal merit for nothing. I have conversed with those who are conversant on the subject, and, I confess, I have been astonished at the information they imparted.

A capital American publisher has assured me that there are not a dozen writers in this country, whose works he should feel confidence in publishing at all, while he reprints hundreds of English books without the least hesitation. This preference is by no means so much owing to any difference in merit, as to the fact that, when the price of the original author is to be added to the uniform hazard which accompanies all literary speculations, the risk becomes too great. The general taste of the reading world in this country is better than that of England.[1] The fact is both proved and explained by the circumstance that thousands of works that are printed and read in the mother country, are not printed and read here. The publisher on this side of the Atlantic has the advantage of seeing the reviews of every book he wishes to print, and, what is of far more importance, he knows, with the exception of books that he is sure of selling, by means of a name, the decision of the English critics before he makes his choice. Nine times in ten, popularity, which is all he looks for, is a sufficient test of general merit. Thus, while you find every English work of character, or notoriety, on the shelves of an American book-store, you may ask in vain for most of the trash that is so greedily devoured in the circulating libraries of the mother country, and which would be just as eagerly devoured here, had not a better taste been created by a compelled abstinence. That taste must now be overcome before such works could be sold at all.

When I say that books are not rejected here, from any want of talent in the writers, perhaps I ought to explain. I wish to express something a little different. Talent is sure of too many avenues to wealth and honours, in America, to seek, unnecessarily, an unknown and hazardous path. It is better paid in the ordinary pursuits of life, than it would be likely to be paid by an adventure in which an extraordinary and skilful, because practised, foreign competition is certain. Perhaps high talent does not often make the trial with the American bookseller; but it is precisely for the reason I have named.

The second obstacle against which American lit-

erature has to contend, is in the poverty of materials. There is scarcely an ore which contributes to the wealth of the author, that is found, here, in veins as rich as in Europe. There are no annals for the historian; no follies (beyond the most vulgar and commonplace) for the satirist; no manners for the dramatist; no obscure fictions for the writer of romance; no gross and hardy offences against decorum for the moralist; nor any of the rich artificial auxiliaries of poetry. The weakest hand can extract a spark from the flint, but it would baffle the strength of a giant to attempt kindling a flame with a pudding-stone. I very well know there are theorists who assume that the society and institutions of this country are or ought to be, particularly favourable to novelties and variety. But the experience of one month, in these States, is sufficient to show any observant man the falsity of their position. The effect of a promiscuous assemblage any where, is to create a standard of deportment; and great liberty permits every one to aim at its attainment. I have never seen a nation so much alike in my life, as the people of the United States, and what is more, they are not only like each other, but they are remarkably like that which common sense tells them they ought to resemble. No doubt, traits of character that are a little peculiar, without, however, being either very poetical, or very rich, are to be found in remote districts; but they are rare, and not always happy exceptions. In short, it is not possible to conceive a state of society in which more of the attributes of plain good sense, or fewer of the artificial absurdities of life, are to be found, than here. There is no costume for the peasant, (there is scarcely a peasant at all,) no wig for the judge, no baton for the general, no diadem for the chief magistrate. The darkest ages of their history are illuminated by the light of truth; the utmost efforts of their chivalry are limited by the laws of God; and even the deeds of their sages and heroes are to be sung in a language that would differ but little from a version of the ten commandments. However useful and respectable all this may be in actual life, it indicates but one direction to the man of genius.

1828

FROM *The American Democrat*

The American Democrat, a careful and incisive analysis of the social and political contexts of contemporary America, remains the clearest statement of Cooper's mature democratic beliefs. In it, he attempted to formulate and to justify his concept of an ideal society in terms of what he considered to be basic American principles. Though nominally a member of Jackson's Democratic party, he was not happy with what he felt were its dangerous "leveling" tendencies, or with the political factionalism and partisanship it seemed to engender. Cooper did not fear democ-

---

[1] The writer does not mean that the best taste of America is better than that of England; perhaps it is not quite so good; but, as a whole, the American reading world requires better books than the whole of the English reading world. [Cooper's note.]

racy, but rather its excesses and abuses, particularly the possibility that the rule of an intelligent majority might degenerate into a tyranny of the masses, and judiciously restrained freedom into unrestrained license. Text: H. L. Mencken, ed., *The American Democrat* (New York, 1931).

[Equality]

Equality, in a social sense, may be divided into that of condition, and that of rights. Equality of condition is incompatible with civilization, and is found only to exist in those communities that are but slightly removed from the savage state. In practice, it can only mean a common misery.

Equality of rights is a peculiar feature of democracies. These rights are properly divided into civil and political, though even these definitions are not to be taken as absolute, or as literally exact.

Under the monarchies of the old world, there exist privileged classes, possessed of exclusive rights. For a long period the nobles were exempted from taxes, and many other charges, advantages that are still enjoyed by them, in certain countries. In England, even, the nobles are entitled to hereditary advantages that are denied to those who are of inferior birth. All these distinctions are done away with in principle, in countries where there exists a professed equality of rights, though there is probably no community that does not make some distinctions between the political privileges of men. If this be true, there is strictly no equality of political rights, any where, although there may be, and is, a nearer approach to an equality of civil rights.

By political rights we understand, the suffrage, eligibility to office, and a condition of things that admits of no distinction between men, unless on principles that are common to all. Thus, though a man is not qualified to vote until he has reached the age of twenty-one, the regulation does not affect political equality, since all are equally subjected to the rule, and all become electors on attaining the same age.

With an equality of civil rights, all men are equal before the law; all classes of the community being liable equally to taxation, military service, jury duties, and to the other impositions attendant on civilization, and no one being exempted from its control, except on general rules, which are dependent on the good of all, instead of the exemption's belonging to the immunities of individuals, estates, or families. An equality of civil rights may be briefly defined to be an absence of privileges.

The distinction between the equality of civil and political rights is material, one implying merely equality before the administration of the law, the other, equality in the power to frame it.

An equality of civil rights is never absolute, but we are to understand by the term, such an equality only, as is compatible with general justice and the relations between the different members of families. Thus, women nowhere possess precisely the same rights as men, or men the same rights as women. The wife, usually, can neither sue nor be sued, while the husband, except in particular cases, is made liable to all legal claims on account of the wife. Minors are deprived of many of their civil rights, or, it would be better to say, do not attain them, until they reach a period of life that has been arbitrarily fixed, and which varies in different countries, according to their several policies.

Neither is equality of political rights ever absolute. In those countries where the suffrage is said to be universal, exceptions exist, that arise from the necessity of things, or from that controlling policy which can never be safely lost sight of in the management of human affairs. The interests of women being thought to be so identified with those of their male relatives as to become, in a great degree, inseparable, females are, almost generally, excluded from the possession of political rights. There can be no doubt that society is greatly the gainer, by thus excluding one half its members, and the half that is best adapted to give a tone to its domestic happiness, from the strife of parties, and the fierce struggles of political controversies. Men are also excluded from political rights previously to having attained the age prescribed by law. Paupers, those who have no fixed abodes, and aliens in law, though their lives may have been principally passed in the country, are also excluded from the enjoyment of political rights, every where. Thus birthright is almost universally made a source of advantage. These exceptions, however, do not very materially affect the principle of political equality, since the rules are general, and have been made solely with a reference to the good of society, or to render the laws less liable to abuses in practice.

It follows, that equality, whether considered in connection with our civil or political rights, must not be taken as a general and absolute condition of society, but as such an equality as depends on principles that are equitable, and which are suited to the actual wants of men.

[Aristocrat and Democrat]

We live in an age when the words aristocrat and democrat are much used, without regard to the real significations. An aristocrat is one of a few who possess the political power of a country; a democrat, one of the many. The words are also properly applied to those who entertain notions favorable to aristocratical or democratical forms of government. Such persons are not necessarily either aristocrats or democrats in fact, but merely so in opinion. Thus a member of a democratical government may have an aristocratical bias, and vice versa.

To call a man who has the habits and opinions of a gentleman, an aristocrat from that fact alone, is an abuse of terms and betrays ignorance of the true principles of government, as well as of the world. It must be an equivocal freedom under which every one is not the master of his own innocent acts and associations; and he is a sneaking democrat indeed who will submit to be dictated to, in those habits over which neither law nor morality assumes a right of control.

Some men fancy that a democrat can only be one who seeks the level, social, mental and moral, of the majority, a rule that would at once exclude all men of refinement, education, and taste from the class. These persons are enemies of democracy, as they at once render it impracticable. They are usually great sticklers for their own associations and habits, too, though unable to comprehend any of a nature that are superior. They are, in truth, aristocrats in principle, though assuming a contrary pretension, the groundwork of all their feelings and arguments being self. Such is not the intention of liberty, whose aim is to leave every man to be the master of his own acts; denying hereditary honors, it is true, as unjust and unnecessary, but not denying the inevitable consequences of civilization.

The law of God is the only rule of conduct in this, as in other matters. Each man should do as he would be done by. Were the question put to the greatest advocate of indiscriminate association, whether he would submit to have his company and habits dictated to him, he would be one of the first to resist the tyranny; for they who are the most rigid in maintaining their own claims in such matters, are usually the loudest in decrying those whom they fancy to be better off than themselves. Indeed, it may be taken as a rule in social intercourse, that he who is the most apt to question the pretensions of others is the most conscious of the doubtful position he himself occupies; thus establishing the very claims he affects to deny, by letting his jealousy of it be seen. Manners, education, and refinement, are positive things, and they bring with them innocent tastes which are productive of high enjoyments; and it is as unjust to deny their possessors their indulgence as it would be to insist on the less fortunate's passing the time they would rather devote to athletic amusements, in listening to operas for which they have no relish, sung in a language they do not understand.

All that democracy means, is as equal a participation in rights as is practicable; and to pretend that social equality is a condition of popular institutions is to assume that the latter are destructive of civilization, for, as nothing is more self-evident than the impossibility of raising all men to the highest standard of tastes and refinement, the alternative would be to reduce the entire community to the lowest. The whole embarrassment on this point exists in the difficulty of making men comprehend qualities they do not themselves possess. We can all perceive the difference between ourselves and our inferiors, but when it comes to a question of the difference between us and our superiors, we fail to appreciate merits of which we have no proper conceptions. In face of this obvious difficulty, there is the safe and just governing rule, already mentioned, or that of permitting every one to be the undisturbed judge of his own habits and associations, so long as they are innocent and do not impair the rights of others to be equally judges for themselves. It follows, that social intercourse must regulate itself, independently of institutions, with the exception that the latter, while they withhold no natural, bestow no factitious advantages beyond those which are inseparable from the rights of property, and general civilization.

In a democracy, men are just as free to aim at the highest attainable places in society, as to attain the largest fortunes; and it would be clearly unworthy of all noble sentiment to say that the grovelling competition for money shall alone be free, while that which enlists all the liberal acquirements and elevated sentiments of the race, is denied the democrat. Such an avowal would be at once a declaration of the inferiority of the system, since nothing but ignorance and vulgarity could be its fruits.

The democratic gentleman must differ in many essential particulars from the aristocratical gentleman, though in their ordinary habits and tastes they are virtually identical. Their principles vary; and, to a slight degree, their deportment accordingly. The democrat, recognizing the right of all to participate in power, will be more liberal in his general sentiments, a quality of superiority in itself; but in conceding this much to his fellow man, he will proudly maintain his own independence of vulgar domination as indispensable to his personal habits. The same principles and manliness that would induce him to depose a royal despot would induce him to resist a vulgar tyrant.

There is no more capital, though more common error, than to suppose him an aristocrat who maintains his independence of habits; for democracy asserts the control of the majority, only, in matters of law, and not in matters of custom. The very object of the institution is the utmost practicable personal liberty, and to affirm the contrary, would be sacrificing the end to the means.

An aristocrat, therefore is merely one who fortifies his exclusive privileges by positive institutions, and a democrat, one who is willing to admit of a free competition, in all things. To say, however, that the last supposes this competition will lead to nothing, is an assumption that means are employed without any reference to an end. He is the purest democrat who best maintains his rights, and no rights can be dearer to a man of cultivation, than exemptions from unseasonable invasions on his time, by the coarse-minded and ignorant.

[Liberty]

Liberty, like equality, is a word more used than understood. Perfect and absolute liberty is as incompatible with the existence of society, as equality of condition. It is impracticable in a state of nature even, since, without the protection of the law, the strong would oppress and enslave the weak. We are then to understand by liberty, merely such a state of the social compact as permits the members of a community to lay no more restraints on themselves, than are required by their real necessities, and obvious interests. To this definition may be added, that it is a requisite of liberty, that the body of a nation should retain the power to modify its institutions, as circumstances shall require.

The natural disposition of all men being to enjoy a perfect freedom of action, it is a common error to suppose that the nation which possesses the mildest laws, or laws that impose the least personal restraints, is the freest. This opinion is untenable, since the power that concedes this freedom of action, can recall it. Unless it is lodged in the body of the community itself, there is, therefore, no pledge for the continuance of such a liberty. A familiar, supposititious case will render this truth more obvious.

A slave holder in Virginia is the master of two slaves: to one he grants his liberty, with the means to go to a town in a free state. The other accompanies his old associate clandestinely. In this town, they engage their services voluntarily, to a common master, who assigns to them equal shares in the same labor, paying them the same wages. In time, the master learns their situation, but, being an indulgent man, he allows the slave to retain his present situation. In all material things, these brothers are equal; they labor together, receive the same wages, and eat of the same food. Yet one is bond, and the other free, since it is in the power of the master, or of his heir, or of his assignee, at any time, to reclaim the services of the one who was not legally manumitted, and reduce him again to the condition of slavery. One of these brothers is the master of his own acts, while the other, though temporarily enjoying the same privileges, holds them subject to the will of a superior.

This is an all important distinction in the consideration of political liberty, since the circumstances of no two countries are precisely the same, and all municipal regulations ought to have direct reference to the actual condition of a community. It follows, that no country can properly be deemed free, unless the body of the nation possess, in the last resort, the legal power to frame its laws according to its wants. This power must also abide in the nation, or it becomes merely an historical fact, for he that was once free is not necessarily free always, any more than he that was once happy, is to consider himself happy in perpetuity.

This definition of liberty is new to the world, for a government founded on such principles is a novelty. Hitherto, a nation has been deemed free, whose people were possessed of a certain amount of franchises, without any reference to the general repository of power. Such a nation may not be absolutely enslaved, but it can scarcely be considered in possession of an affirmative political liberty, since it is not the master of its own fortunes.

Having settled what is the foundation of liberty, it remains to be seen by what process a people can exercise this authority over themselves. The usual course is to refer all matters of choice to the decision of majorities. The common axiom of democracies, however, which says that "the majority must rule," is to be received with many limitations. Were the majority of a country to rule without restraint, it is probable as much injustice and oppression would follow, as are found under the dominion of one. It belongs to the nature of men to arrange themselves in parties, to lose sight of truth and justice in partizanship and prejudice, to mistake their own impulses for that which is proper, and to do wrong because they are indisposed to seek the right. Were it wise to trust power, unreservedly, to majorities, all fundamental and controlling laws would be unnecessary, since they might, as occasion required, emanate from the will of numbers. Constitutions would be useless.

The majority rules in prescribed cases, and in no other. It elects to office, it enacts ordinary laws, subject however to the restrictions of the constitution, and it decides most of the questions that arise in the primitive meetings of the people; questions that do not usually affect any of the principal interests of life.

The majority does not rule in settling fundamental laws, under the constitution; or when it does rule in such cases, it is with particular checks produced by time and new combinations; it does not pass judgment in trials at law, or under impeachment, and it is impotent in many matters touching vested rights. In the state of New York, the majority is impotent, in granting corporations, and in appropriating money for local purposes.

Though majorities often decide wrong, it is believed that they are less liable to do so than minorities. There can be no question that the educated and affluent classes of a country, are more capable of coming to wise and intelligent decisions in affairs of state, than the mass of a population. Their wealth and leisure afford them opportunities for observation and comparison, while their general information and greater knowledge of character, enable them to judge more accurately of men and measures. That these opportunities are not properly used, is owing to the unceasing desire of men to turn their advantages to their own particular benefit, and to their passions. All history proves, when power is the sole possession of a few, that it is perverted to their sole advantage, the public suffering in order that their rulers may prosper. The same nature which imposes the necessity of governments at all, seems to point out the expediency of confiding its control, in the last resort, to the body of the nation, as the only lasting protection against gross abuses.

We do not adopt the popular polity because it is perfect, but because it is less imperfect than any other. As man, by his nature, is liable to err, it is vain to expect an infallible whole that is composed of fallible parts. The government that emanates from a single will, supposing that will to be pure, enlightened, impartial, just and consistent, would be the best in the world, were it attainable for men. Such is the government of the universe, the result of which is perfect harmony. As no man is without spot in his justice, as no man has infinite wisdom, or infinite mercy, we are driven to take refuge in the opposite extreme, or in a government of many.

It is common for the advocates of monarchy and aristocracy to deride the opinions of the mass, as no more than the impulses of ignorance and prejudices. While experience unhappily shows that this charge has too much truth, it also shows that the educated and few form no exemption to the common rule of humanity. The most intelligent men of every country in which there is liberty of thought and action, yielding to their interests or their passions, are always found taking the opposite extremes of contested questions, thus triumphantly refuting an arrogant proposition, that of the exclusive fitness of the few to govern, by an unanswerable fact. The minority of a country is never known to agree, except in its efforts to reduce and oppress the majority. Were this not so, parties would be unknown in all countries but democracies, whereas the factions of aristocracies have been among the fiercest and least governable of any recorded in history.

Although real political liberty can have but one character, that of a popular base, the world contains many modifications of governments that are, more or less, worthy to be termed free. In most of these states, however, the liberties of the mass, are of the negative character of franchises, which franchises are not power of themselves, but merely an exemption from the abuses of power. Perhaps no state exists, in which the people, either by usage, or by direct concessions from the source of authority, do not possess some of these franchises; for, if there is no such thing, in practice, as perfect and absolute liberty, neither is there any such thing, in practice, as total and unmitigated slavery. In the one case, nature has rendered men incapable of enjoying freedom without restraint, and in the other, incapable of submitting, entirely without resistance, to oppression. The harshest despots are compelled to acknowledge the immutable principles of eternal justice, affecting necessity and the love of right, for their most ruthless deeds. ° ° °

It is usual to maintain, that in democracies the tyranny of majorities is a greater evil than the oppression of minorities in narrow systems. Although this evil is exaggerated, since the laws being equal in their action it is not easy to oppress the few without oppressing all, it undeniably is the weak side of a popular government. To guard against this, we have framed constitutions, which point out the cases in which the majority shall decide, limiting their power, and bringing that they do possess within the circle of certain general and just principles. It will be elsewhere shown that it is a great mistake for the American citizen to take sides with the public, in doubtful cases affecting the rights of individuals, as this is the precise form in which oppression is the most likely to exhibit itself in a popular government.

Although it is true, that no genuine liberty can exist without being based on popular authority in the last resort, it is equally true that it can not exist when thus based, without many restraints on the power of the mass. These restraints are necessarily various and numerous. A familiar example will show their action. The majority of the people of a state might be in debt to its minority. Were the power of the former unrestrained, circumstances might arise in which they would declare depreciated bank notes a legal tender, and thus clear themselves of their liabilities, at the expense of their creditors. To prevent this, the constitution orders that nothing shall be made a legal tender but the precious metals, thus limiting the power of majorities in a way that the government is not limited in absolute monarchies, in which paper is often made to possess the value of gold and silver.

Liberty therefore may be defined to be a controlling authority that resides in the body of a nation, but so restrained as only to be exercised on certain general principles that shall do as little violence to natural justice, as is compatible with the peace and security of society.

1838

PREFACE TO *The Leatherstocking Tales*

Cooper wrote this preface for a new edition of his novels to be published by Putnam's in New York. The novels known as "The Leatherstocking Tales" were not written in order of the development of their chief character, and the series did not begin to display its epic qualities until the third of the five appeared. *The Pioneers* (1823) introduced Leatherstocking, or Natty Bumppo, as an old man living in an upper New York State settlement in 1793, in conflict with the forces of civilization which had already replaced the frontier forest of his youth. In *The Last of the Mohicans* (1826) Cooper returned Natty, now named "Hawkeye," to the French and Indian Wars and Montcalm's siege of Fort Henry in 1757, while in *The Prairie* (1827), laid in the trans-Mississippi West about 1805, he chronicled the aged frontiersman's last days and death. However, in *The Pathfinder* (1840) Cooper returned once more to Natty's youth and the New York State frontier of the 1760's. In *The Deerslayer* (1841), laid there twenty years earlier, he introduced the boy to his first meaningful contact with the Indian and the wilderness, the contact that was to occupy the rest of his life. The text of this and subsequent selections from the novels is that of the Townsend edition of 1859–61, New York, the first definitive edition, also known as the "Darley" edition because of the illustrations by F. O. C. Darley.

This series of Stories, which has obtained the name of "The Leather-Stocking Tales," has been written in a very desultory and inartificial manner. The order in which the several books appeared was essentially different from that in which they would have been presented to the world, had the regular course of their incidents been consulted. In the Pioneers, the first of the series written, the Leather-Stocking is represented as already old, and driven from his early haunts in the forest, by the sound of the axe, and the smoke of the settler. "The Last of the Mohicans," the next book in the order of publication, carried the readers back to a much earlier period in the history of our hero, representing him as middle-aged, and in the fullest vigor of manhood. In the Prairie, his career terminates, and he is laid in his grave. There, it was originally the intention to leave him, in the expectation that, as in the case of the human mass, he would soon be forgotten. But a latent regard for this character induced the author to resuscitate him in "The Pathfinder," a book that was not long after succeeded by "The Deerslayer," thus completing the series as it now exists.

While the five books that have been written were originally published in the order just mentioned, that of the incidents, insomuch as they are connected with the career of their principal character, is, as has been stated, very different. Taking the life of the Leather-Stocking as a guide, "The Deerslayer" should have been the opening book, for in that work he is seen just emerging into manhood; to be succeeded by "The Last of the Mohicans," "The Pathfinder," "The Pioneers," and "The Prairie." This arrangement embraces the order of events, though far from being that in which the books at first appeared. "The Pioneers" was published in 1822; "The Deerslayer" in 1841; making the interval between them nineteen years. Whether these progressive years have had a tendency to lessen the value of the last-named book, by lessening the native fire of its author, or of adding somewhat in the way of improved taste and a more matured judgment, is for others to decide.

If anything from the pen of the writer of these romances is at all to outlive himself, it is, unquestionably, the series of "The Leather-Stocking Tales." To say this, is not to predict a very lasting reputation for the series itself, but simply to express the belief it will outlast any, or all, of the works from the same hand.

It is undeniable that the desultory manner in which "The Leather-Stocking Tales" were written, has, in a measure, impaired their harmony, and otherwise lessened their interest. This is proved by the fate of the two books last published, though probably the two most worthy an enlightened and cultivated reader's notice. If the facts could be ascertained, it is probable the result would show that of all those (in America, in particular) who have read the three first books of the series, not one in ten has a knowledge of the existence even of the two last. Several causes have tended to produce this result. The long interval of time between the appearance of "The Prairie" and that of "The Pathfinder," was itself a reason why the later books of the series should be overlooked. There was no longer novelty to attract attention, and the interest was materially impaired by the manner in which events were necessarily anticipated, in laying the last of the series first before the world. With the generation that is now coming on the stage this fault will be partially removed by the edition contained in the present work, in which the several tales will be arranged solely in reference to their connexion with each other.

The author has often been asked if he had any original in his mind, for the character of Leather-Stocking. In a physical sense, different individuals known to the writer in early life, certainly presented themselves as models, through his recollections; but in a moral sense this man of the forest is purely a creation. The idea of delineating a character that possessed little of civilization but its highest principles as they are exhibited in the uneducated, and all of savage life that is not incompatible with these great rules of conduct, is perhaps natural to the situation in which Natty was placed. He is too proud of his origin to sink into the condition of the wild Indian, and too much a man of the woods not to imbibe as much as was at all desirable, from his friends and companions. In a moral point of view it was the intention to illustrate the effect of seed scattered by the way side. To use his own language, his "gifts" were "white gifts," and he was not disposed to bring on them discredit. On the other hand, removed from nearly all the temptations of civilized life, placed in the best associations of that which is deemed savage, and favorably disposed by nature to improve such advantages, it appeared to the writer that his hero was a fit subject to represent the better qualities of both conditions, without pushing either to extremes.

There was no violent stretch of the imagination, perhaps, in supposing one of civilized associations in childhood, retaining many of his earliest lessons amid the scenes of the forest. Had these early impressions, however, not been sustained by continued, though casual connexion with men of his own color, if not of his own caste, all our information goes to show he would soon have lost every trace of his origin. It is believed that sufficient attention was paid to the particular circumstances in which this individual was placed, to justify the picture of his qualities that has been drawn. The Delawares early attracted the attention of the missionaries, and were a tribe unusually influenced by their precepts and example. In many instances they became Christians, and cases occurred in which their subsequent lives gave proof of the efficacy of the great moral changes that had taken place within them.

A leading character in a work of fiction has a fair right to the aid which can be obtained from a poetical view of the subject. It is in this view, rather than in one more strictly circumstantial, that Leather-Stocking has been drawn. The imagination has no great task in portraying to itself a being removed from the every-day inducements to err, which abound in civilized life, while he retains the best and simplest of his early impressions; who sees God in the forest; hears him in the winds; bows to him in the firmament that o'ercanopies all; submits to his sway in a humble belief of his justice and mercy; in a word, a being who finds the impress of the Deity in all the works of nature, without any of the blots produced by the expedients, and passion, and mistakes of man. This is the most that has been attempted in the character of Leather-Stocking. Had this been done without any of the drawbacks of humanity the picture would have been, in all probability, more pleasing than just. In order to preserve the *vrai-semblable*, therefore, traits derived from the prejudices, tastes, and even the weaknesses of his youth, have been mixed up with these higher qualities and longings, in a way, it is hoped, to represent a reasonable picture of human nature, without offering to the spectator a "monster of goodness."

It has been objected to these books that they give a more favorable picture of the red man than he deserves. The writer apprehends that much of this objection arises from the habits of those who have made it. One of his critics, on the appearance of the first work in which Indian character was portrayed, objected that its "characters were Indians of the school of Heckewelder, rather than of the school of nature."[1] These words quite probably contain the substance of the true answer to the objection. Heckewelder was an ardent, benevolent missionary, bent on the good of the red man, and seeing in him one who had the soul, reason, and characteristics of a fellow-being. The critic is understood to have been a very distinguished agent of the government, one very familiar with Indians, as they are seen at the councils to treat for the sale of their lands, where little or none of their domestic qualities come in play, and where, indeed, their evil passions are known to have the fullest scope. As just would it be to draw conclusions of the general state of American society from the scenes of the capital, as to suppose that the negotiating of one of these treaties is a fair picture of Indian life.

It is the privilege of all writers of fiction, more particularly when their works aspire to the elevation of romances, to present the *beau-idéal* of their characters to the reader. This it is which constitutes poetry, and to suppose that the red man is to be represented only in the squalid misery or in the degraded moral state that certainly more or less belongs to his condition, is, we apprehend, taking a very narrow view of an author's privileges. Such criticism would have deprived the world of even Homer.

1850

FROM *The Deerslayer*

Deerslayer's killing of his first Indian was a moment of crucial importance in his life, and Cooper prepared for and explored it carefully. There is a ritualistic flavor to the passage, an almost formal treatment of what was, for the boy Natty, his initiation into frontier manhood and the

[1] The book by the Moravian missionary, the Reverend John Heckewelder, *Account of the History, Manners, and Customs of the Indian Nations* . . . (1819), was an important source of information for Cooper.

irrevocable loss of his youthful innocence. Each of the antagonists acts out his part in the ceremony according to his nature, with grace, skill, and respect for the other's role. In this passage, as well, Cooper introduces the doctrine of "gifts," the idea that although all men are basically the same in nature, each man has certain "gifts" or propensities, imposed upon him by experience and environment. Thus the white man and the Indian are destined to play out different roles in the wilderness drama, each acting according to his "gifts." (I Corinthians xii.4–13 speaks of the "diversities of gifts . . . , but the same spirit" in all men.)

Chapter VII

"Clear, placid Leman! Thy contrasted lake
With the wild world I dwelt in, is a thing
Which warns me, with its stillness, to forsake
Earth's troubled waters for a purer spring.
This quiet sail is as a noiseless wing
To waft me from distraction: once I loved
Torn ocean's roar, but thy soft murmuring
Sounds sweet as if a sister's voice reproved,
That I with stern delights should e'er have been so moved."

—Byron.

Day had fairly dawned before the young man, whom we have left in the situation described in the last chapter, again opened his eyes. This was no sooner done, than he started up, and looked about him with the eagerness of one who suddenly felt the importance of accurately ascertaining his precise position. His rest had been deep and undisturbed; and when he awoke, it was with a clearness of intellect and a readiness of resources that were much needed at that particular moment. The sun had not risen, it is true, but the vault of heaven was rich with the winning softness that "brings and shuts the day," while the whole air was filled with the carols of birds, the hymns of the feathered tribe. These sounds first told Deerslayer the risks he ran. The air, for wind it could scarce be called, was still light, it is true, but it had increased a little in the course of the night, and as the canoes were mere feathers on the water, they had drifted twice the expected distance; and, what was still more dangerous, had approached so near the base of the mountain that here rose precipitously from the eastern shore, as to render the carols of the birds plainly audible. This was not the worst. The third canoe had taken the same direction, and was slowly drifting towards a point where it must inevitably touch, unless turned aside by a shift of wind, or human hands. In other respects, nothing presented itself to attract attention, or to awaken alarm. The castle stood on its shoal, nearly abreast of the canoes, for the drift had amounted to miles in the course of the night, and the ark lay fastened to its piles, as both had been left so many hours before.

As a matter of course, Deerslayer's attention was first given to the canoe ahead. It was already quite near the point, and a very few strokes of the paddle sufficed to tell him that it must touch before he could possibly overtake it. Just at this moment, too, the wind inopportunely freshened, rendering the drift of the light craft much more rapid and certain. Feeling the impossibility of preventing a contact with the land, the young man wisely determined not to heat himself with unnecessary exertions; but first looking to the priming of his piece, he proceeded slowly and warily towards the point, taking care to make a little circuit, that he might be exposed on only one side, as he approached.

The canoe adrift being directed by no such intelligence, pursued its proper way, and grounded on a small sunken rock, at the distance of three or four yards from the shore. Just at that moment, Deerslayer had got abreast of the point, and turned the bows of his own boat to the land; first casting loose his tow, that his movements might be unencumbered. The canoe hung an instant on the rock; then it rose a hair's-breadth on an almost imperceptible swell of the water, swung round, floated clear, and reached the strand. All this the young man noted, but it neither quickened his pulses nor hastened his hand. If any one had been lying in wait for the arrival of the waif, he must be seen, and the utmost caution in approaching the shore became indispensable; if no one was in ambush, hurry was unnecessary. The point being nearly diagonally opposite to the Indian encampment, he hoped the last, though the former was not only possible, but probable; for the savages were prompt in adopting all the expedients of their particular modes of warfare, and quite likely had many scouts searching the shores for craft to carry them off to the castle. As a glance at the lake from any height or projection would expose the smallest object on its surface, there was little hope that either of the canoes could pass unseen; and Indian sagacity needed no instruction to tell which way a boat or a log would drift, when the direction of the wind was known. As Deerslayer drew nearer and nearer to the land, the stroke of his paddle grew slower, his eye became more watchful, and his ears and nostrils almost dilated with the effort to detect any lurking danger. 'Twas a trying moment for a novice, nor was there the encouragement which even the timid sometimes feel, when conscious of being observed and commended. He was entirely alone, thrown on his own resources, and was cheered by no friendly eye, emboldened by no encouraging voice. Notwithstanding all these circumstances, the most experienced veteran in forest warfare could not have behaved better. Equally free from recklessness and hesitation, his advance was marked by a sort of philosophical prudence, that appeared to render him superior to all motives but those which were best calculated to effect his purpose. Such was the commencement of a career in forest exploits, that afterwards rendered this man, in his way, and under the limits of his habits and opportunities, as renowned as many a hero whose name has adorned the pages of works more celebrated than legends simple as ours can ever become.

When about a hundred yards from the shore, Deerslayer rose in the canoe, gave three or four vigorous strokes with the paddle, sufficient of themselves to impel the bark to land, and then quickly laying aside the instrument of labor, he seized that of war. He was in the very act of raising the rifle, when a sharp report was followed by the buzz of a bullet that passed so near his body, as to cause him involuntarily to start. The next instant Deerslayer staggered, and fell his whole length in the bottom of the canoe. A yell—it came from a single voice—followed, and an Indian leaped from the bushes upon the open area of the point, bounding towards the canoe. This was the moment the young man desired. He rose on the instant, and levelled his own rifle at his uncovered foe; but his finger hesitated about pulling the trigger on one whom he held at such a disadvantage. This little delay, probably, saved the life of the Indian, who bounded back into the cover as swiftly as he had broken out of it. In the meantime Deerslayer had been swiftly approaching the land, and his own canoe reached the point just as his enemy disappeared. As its movements had not been directed, it touched the shore a few yards from the other boat; and though the rifle of his foe had to be loaded, there was not time to secure his prize, and to carry it beyond danger, before he would be exposed to another shot. Under the circumstances, therefore, he did not pause an instant, but dashed into the woods and sought a cover.

On the immediate point there was a small open area, partly in native grass, and partly beach, but a dense fringe of bushes lined its upper side. This narrow belt of dwarf vegetation passed, one issued immediately into the high and gloomy vaults of the forest. The land was tolerably level for a few hundred feet, and then it rose precipitously in a mountain-side. The trees were tall, large, and so free from under-brush, that they resembled vast columns, irregularly scattered, upholding a dome of leaves. Although they stood tolerably close together, for their ages and size, the eye could penetrate to considerable distances; and bodies of men, even, might have engaged beneath their cover, with concert and intelligence.

Deerslayer knew that his adversary must be employed in re-loading, unless he had fled. The former proved to be the case, for the young man had no sooner placed himself behind a tree, than he caught a glimpse of the arm of the Indian, his body being concealed by an oak, in the very act of forcing the leathered bullet home. Nothing would have been easier than to spring forward, and decide the affair by a close assault on his unprepared foe; but every feeling of Deerslayer revolted at such a step, although his own life had just been attempted from a cover. He was yet unpractised in the ruthless expedients of savage warfare, of which he knew nothing except by tradition and theory, and it struck him as an unfair advantage to assail an unarmed foe. His color had heightened, his eye frowned, his lips were compressed, and all his energies were collected and ready; but, instead of advancing to fire, he dropped his rifle to the usual position of a sportsman in readiness to catch his aim, and muttered to himself, unconscious that he was speaking—

"No, no—that may be red-skin warfare, but it's not a Christian's gifts. Let the miscreant charge, and then we'll take it out like men; for the canoe he *must* not, and *shall* not have. No, no; let him have time to load, and God will take care of the right!"

All this time the Indian had been so intent on his own movements, that he was even ignorant that his enemy was in the wood. His only apprehension was, that the canoe would be recovered and carried away before he might be in readiness to prevent it. He had sought the cover from habit, but was within a few feet of the fringe of bushes, and could be at the margin of the forest in readiness to fire in a moment. The distance between him and his enemy was about fifty yards, and the trees were so arranged by nature that the line of sight was not interrupted, except by the particular trees behind which each party stood.

His rifle was no sooner loaded, than the savage glanced around him, and advanced incautiously as regarded the real, but stealthily as respected the fancied position of his enemy, until he was fairly exposed. Then Deerslayer stepped from behind his own cover, and hailed him.

"This-a-way, red-skin; this-a-way, if you're looking for me," he called out. "I'm young in war, but not so young as to stand on an open beach to be shot down like an owl, by daylight. It rests on yourself whether it's peace or war atween us; for my gifts are white gifts, and I'm not one of them that thinks it valiant to slay human mortals, singly, in the woods."

The savage was a good deal startled by this sudden discovery of the danger he ran. He had a little knowledge of English, however, and caught the drift of the other's meaning. He was also too well schooled to betray alarm, but, dropping the butt of his rifle to the earth, with an air of confidence, he made a gesture of lofty courtesy. All this was done with the ease and self-possession of one accustomed to consider no man his superior. In the midst of this consummate acting, however, the volcano that raged within caused his eyes to glare, and his nostrils to dilate, like those of some wild beast that is suddenly prevented from taking the fatal leap.

"Two canoe," he said, in the deep guttural tones of his race, holding up the number of fingers he mentioned, by way of preventing mistakes; "one for you—one for me."

"No, no, Mingo, that will never do. You own neither; and neither shall you have, as long as I can prevent it. I know it's war atween your people and mine, but that's no reason why human mortals should slay each other, like savage creatur's that meet in the woods; go your way, then, and leave me to go mine. The world is large enough for us both; and when we meet fairly in battle, why, the Lord will order the fate of each of us."

"Good!" exclaimed the Indian; "my brother missionary—great talk; all about Manitou."

"Not so—not so, warrior. I'm not good enough for the Moravians, and am too good for most of the other vagabonds that preach about in the woods. No, no, I'm only a hunter, as yet, though afore the peace is made, 'tis like enough there'll be occasion to strike a blow at some of your people. Still, I wish it to be done in fair fight, and not in a quarrel about the ownership of a miserable canoe."

"Good! My brother very young—but he very wise. Little warrior—great talker. Chief, sometimes, in council."

"I don't know this, nor do I say it, Injin," returned Deerslayer, coloring a little at the ill-concealed sarcasm of the other's manner; "I look forward to a life in the woods, and I only hope it may be a peaceable one. All young men must go on the war-path, when there's occasion, but war isn't needfully massacre. I've seen enough of the last, this very night, to know that Providence frowns on it; and I now invite you to go your own way, while I go mine; and hope that we may part fri'nds."

"Good! My brother has two scalp—grey hair under t'other. Old wisdom—young tongue."

Here the savage advanced with confidence, his hand extended, his face smiling, and his whole bearing denoting amity and respect. Deerslayer met his offered friendship in a proper spirit, and they shook hands cordially, each endeavoring to assure the other of his sincerity and desire to be at peace.

"All have his own," said the Indian; "my canoe, mine; your canoe, your'n. Go look; if your'n, you keep; if mine, I keep."

"That's just, red-skin; though you must be wrong in thinking the canoe your property. Howsever, seein' is believin', and we'll go down to the shore, where you may look with your own eyes; for it's likely you'll object to trustin' altogether to mine."

The Indian uttered his favorite exclamation of "good!" and then they walked, side by side, towards the shore. There was no apparent distrust in the manner of either, the Indian moving in advance, as if he wished to show his companion that he did not fear turning his back to him. As they reached the open ground, the former pointed towards Deerslayer's boat, and said emphatically—

"No mine—pale-face canoe. *This* red-man's. No want other man's canoe—want his own."

"You're wrong, red-skin, you're altogether wrong. This canoe was left in old Hutter's keeping, and is his'n according to all law, red or white, till its owner comes to claim it. Here's the seats and the stitching of the bark to speak for themselves. No man ever know'd an Injin to turn off such work."

"Good! My brother little ole—big wisdom. Injin no make him. White man's work."

"I'm glad you think so, for holding out to the contrary might have made ill blood atween us; every one having a right to take possession of his own. I'll just shove the canoe out of reach of dispute at once, as the quickest way of settling difficulties."

While Deerslayer was speaking, he put a foot against the end of the light boat, and giving a vigorous shove, he sent it out into the lake a hundred feet or more, where, taking the true current, it would necessarily float past the point, and be in no further danger of coming ashore. The savage started at this ready and decided expedient, and his companion saw that he cast a hurried and fierce glance at his own canoe, or that which contained the paddles. The change of manner, however, was but momentary, and then the Iroquois resumed his air of friendliness, and a smile of satisfaction.

"Good!" he repeated, with stronger emphasis than ever. "Young head, old mind. Know how to settle quarrel. Farewell, brother. He go to house in water—muskrat house—Injin go to camp; tell chiefs no find canoe."

Deerslayer was not sorry to hear this proposal, for he felt anxious to join the females, and he took the offered hand of the Indian very willingly. The parting words were friendly, and, while the red-man walked calmly towards the wood, with the rifle in the hollow of his arm, without once looking back in uneasiness or distrust, the white man moved towards the remaining canoe, carrying his piece in the same pacific manner, it is true, but keeping his eyes fastened on the movements of the other. This distrust, however, seemed to be altogether uncalled for, and, as if ashamed to have entertained it, the young man averted his look, and stepped carelessly up to his boat. Here he began to push the canoe from the shore, and to make his other preparations for departing. He might have been thus employed a minute, when, happening to turn his face towards the land, his quick and certain eye told him, at a glance, the imminent jeopardy in which his life was placed. The black, ferocious eyes of the savage were glancing on him, like those of the crouching tiger, through a small opening in the bushes, and the muzzle of his rifle seemed already to be opening in a line with his own body.

Then, indeed, the long practice of Deerslayer, as a hunter, did him good service. Accustomed to fire with the deer on the bound, and often when the precise position of the animal's body had in a manner to be guessed at, he used the same expedients here. To cock and poise his rifle were the acts of a single moment and a single motion; then, aiming almost without sighting, he fired into the bushes where he knew a body ought to be, in order to sustain the appalling countenance which alone was visible. There was not time to raise the piece any higher, or to take a more deliberate aim. So rapid were his movements, that both parties discharged their pieces at the same instant, the concussions mingling in one report. The mountains, indeed, gave back but a single echo. Deerslayer dropped his piece, and stood, with head erect, steady as one of the pines in the calm of a June morning, watching the result; while the savage gave the yell that has become historical for its appalling influence, leaped through the bushes and came bounding across the open ground, flourishing a tomahawk. Still Deerslayer moved not, but stood with his unloaded rifle fallen against his shoulders, while, with a hunter's habits, his hands were mechanically feeling for the powder-horn and charger. When about forty feet from his enemy, the savage hurled his keen weapon; but it was with an eye so vacant, and a hand so unsteady and feeble, that the young man caught it by the handle as it was flying past him. At that instant the Indian staggered and fell his whole length on the ground.

"I know'd it—I know'd it!" exclaimed Deerslayer, who was already preparing to force a fresh bullet into his rifle; "I know'd it must come to this, as soon as I had got the range from the creatur's eyes. A man sights suddenly, and fires quick, when his own life's in danger; yes, I know'd it would come to this. I was about the hundredth part of a second too quick for him, or it might have been bad for me! The riptyle's bullet has just grazed my side—but, say what you will for or ag'in 'em, a red-skin is by no means as sartain with powder and ball as a white man. Their gifts don't seem to lie that-a-way. Even Chingachgook, great as he is in other matters, isn't downright deadly with the rifle."

By this time the piece was reloaded, and Deerslayer, after tossing the tomahawk into the canoe, advanced to his victim, and stood over him, leaning on his rifle, in melancholy attention. It was the first instance in which he had seen a man fall in battle—it was the first fellow-creature against whom he had ever seriously raised his own hand. The sensations were novel; and regret with the freshness of our better feelings, mingled with his triumph. The Indian was not dead, though shot directly through the body. He lay on his back motionless, but his eyes, now full of consciousness, watched each action of his victor—as the fallen bird regards the fowler—jealous of every movement. The man probably expected the fatal blow which was to precede the loss of his scalp; or perhaps he anticipated that this latter act of cruelty would precede his death. Deerslayer read his thoughts; and he found a melancholy satisfaction in relieving the apprehensions of the helpless savage.

"No, no, red-skin," he said; "you've nothing more to fear from me. I am of a Christian stock, and scalping is not of my gifts. I'll just make sartain of your rifle, and then come back and do you what sarvice I can. Though here I can't stay much longer, as the crack of three rifles will be apt to bring some of your devils down upon me."

The close of this was said in a sort of a soliloquy, as the young man went in quest of the fallen rifle. The piece was found where its owner had dropped it, and was immediately put into the canoe. Laying his own rifle at its side, Deerslayer then returned and stood over the Indian again.

"All inmity atween you and me's at an ind, red-skin," he said; "and you may set your heart at rest on the score of the scalp, or any further injury. My gifts are white, as I've told you; and I hope my conduct will be white also!"

Could looks have conveyed all they meant, it is probable Deerslayer's innocent vanity on the subject of color would have been rebuked a little; but he comprehended the gratitude that was expressed in the eyes of the dying savage, without in the least detecting the bitter sarcasm that struggled with the better feeling.

"Water!" ejaculated the thirsty and unfortunate creature; "give poor Injin water."

"Aye, water you shall have, if you drink the lake dry. I'll just carry you down to it, that you may take your fill. This is the way, they tell me, with all wounded people—water is their greatest comfort and delight."

So saying, Deerslayer raised the Indian in his arms, and carried him to the lake. Here he first helped him to take an attitude in which he could appease his burning thirst; after which he seated himself on a stone, and took the head of his wounded adversary in his own lap, and endeavored to soothe his anguish in the best manner he could.

"It would be sinful in me to tell you your time hadn't come, warrior," he commenced, "and therefore I'll not say it. You've passed the middle age already, and, considerin' the sort of lives ye lead, your days have been pretty well filled. The principal thing now, is to look forward to what comes next. Neither red-skin nor pale-face, on the whole, calculates much on sleepin' for ever; but both expect to live in another world. Each has his gifts, and will be judged by 'em, and, I suppose, you've thought these matters over enough, not to stand in need of sarmons when the trial comes. You'll find your happy hunting-grounds, if you've been a just Injin; if an onjust, you'll meet your desarts in another way. I've my own ideas about these things; but you're too old and exper'enced to need any explanations from one as young as I."

"Good!" ejaculated the Indian, whose voice retained its depth even as life ebbed away; "young head—ole wisdom!"

"It's sometimes a consolation, when the ind comes, to know that them we've harmed, or *tried* to harm, forgive us. I suppose natur' seeks this relief, by way of getting a pardon on 'arth; as we never can know whether He pardons, who is all in all, till judgment itself comes. It's soothing to know that *any* pardon at such times; and that, I conclude, is the secret. Now, as for myself, I overlook altogether your designs ag'in my life; first, because no harm came of 'em; next, because it's your gifts, and natur', and trainin', and I ought not to have trusted you at all; and, finally and chiefly, because I can bear no ill-will to a dying man, whether heathen or Christian. So put your heart at ease, so far as I'm consarned; you know best what other matters ought to trouble you, or what ought to give you satisfaction in so trying a moment."

It is probable that the Indian had some of the fearful glimpses of the unknown state of being which God in mercy seems at times to afford to all the human race; but they were necessarily in conformity with his habits and prejudices. Like most of his people, and like too many of our own, he thought more of dying in a way to gain applause among those he left than to secure a better state of existence hereafter. While Deerslayer was speaking, his mind was a little bewildered, though he felt that the intention was good; and when he had done, a regret passed over his spirit that none of his own tribe were present to witness his stoicism, under extreme bodily suffering, and the firmness with which he met his end. With the high innate courtesy that so often distinguishes the Indian warrior before he becomes corrupted by too much intercourse with the worst class of the white men, he endeavored to express his thankfulness for the other's good intentions, and to let him understand that they were appreciated.

"Good!" he repeated, for this was an English word much used by the savages—"good—young head; young *heart*, too. *Old* heart tough; no shed tear. Hear Indian when he die, and no want to lie—what he call him?"

"Deerslayer is the name I bear now, though the Delawares have said that when I get back from this war-path, I shall have a more manly title, provided I can 'arn one."

"That good name for boy—poor name for warrior. He get better quick. No fear *there*"—the savage had strength sufficient, under the strong excitement he felt, to raise a hand and tap the young man on his breast—"eye sartain—finger lightning—aim, death—great warrior soon. No Deerslayer—Hawkeye—Hawkeye—Hawkeye. Shake hand."

Deerslayer—or Hawkeye, as the youth was then first named, for in after years he bore the appellation throughout all that region—Deerslayer took the hand of the savage, whose last breath was drawn in that attitude, gazing in admiration at the countenance of a stranger, who had shown so much readiness, skill, and firmness, in a scene that was equally trying and novel. When the reader remembers it is the highest gratification an Indian can receive to see his enemy betray weakness, he will be better able to appreciate the conduct which had extorted so great a concession at such a moment.

"His spirit has fled!" said Deerslayer, in a suppressed, melancholy voice. "Ah's me! Well, to this we must all come, sooner or later; and he is happiest, let his skin be of what color it may, who is best fitted to meet it. Here lies the body of no doubt a brave warrior, and the soul is already flying towards its heaven or hell, whether that be a happy hunting-ground, a place scant of game; regions of glory, according to Moravian doctrine, or flames of fire! So it happens, too, as regards other matters! Here have old Hutter and Hurry Harry got themselves into difficulty, if they hav'n't got themselves into torment and death, and all for a bounty that luck offers to me in what many would think a lawful and suitable manner. But not a farthing of such money shall cross my hand. White I was born, and white will I die; clinging to color to the last, even though the King's Majesty, his governors, and all his councils, both at home and in the Colonies, forget from what they come, and where they hope to go, and all for a little advantage in warfare. No, no—warrior, hand of mine shall never molest your scalp, and so your soul may rest in peace on the p'int of making a decent appearance, when the body comes to join it, in your own land of spirits."

Deerslayer arose as soon as he had spoken. Then he placed the body of the dead man in a sitting posture, with its back against the little rock, taking the necessary care to prevent it from falling or in any way settling into an attitude that might be thought unseemly by the sensitive, though wild notions of a savage. When this duty was performed, the young man stood gazing at the grim countenance of his fallen foe, in a sort of melancholy abstraction. As was his practice, however, a habit gained by living so much alone in the forest, he then began again to give utterance to his thoughts and feelings aloud.

"I didn't wish your life, red-skin," he said, "but you left me no choice atween killing or being killed. Each party acted according to his gifts, I suppose, and blame can light on neither. You were treacherous, according to your natur' in war, and I was a little oversightful, as I'm apt to be in trusting others. Well, this is my first battle with a human mortal, though it's not likely to be the last. I have fou't most of the creatur's of the forest, such as bears, wolves, painters, and catamounts, but this is the beginning with the red-skins. If I was Injin born, now, I might tell of this, or carry in the scalp, and boast of the expl'ite afore the whole tribe; or, if my inimy had only been even a bear, 'twould have been nat'ral and proper to let everybody know what had happened; but I don't well see how I'm to let even Chingachgook into this secret, so long as it can be done only by boasting with a white tongue. And why should I wish to boast of it a'ter all? It's slaying a human, although he was a savage; and how do I know that he was a just Injin; and that he has not been taken away suddenly to anything but happy hunting-grounds. When it's onsartain whether good or evil has been done, the wisest way is not to be boastful—still, I *should* like Chingachgook to know that I haven't discredited the Delawares or my training!"

Part of this was uttered aloud, while part was merely muttered between the speaker's teeth; his more confident opinions enjoying the first advantage, while his doubts were expressed in the latter mode. Soliloquy and reflection received a startling interruption, however, by the sudden appearance of a second Indian on the lake shore, a few hundred yards from the point. This man, evidently another scout, who had probably been drawn to the place by the reports of the rifles, broke out of the forest with so little caution that Deerslayer caught a view of his person before he was himself discovered. When the latter event did occur, as was the case a moment later, the savage gave a loud yell, which was answered by a dozen voices from different parts of the mountain-side. There was no longer any time for delay; in another minute the boat was quitting the shore under long and steady sweeps of the paddle.

As soon as Deerslayer believed himself to be at a safe distance, he ceased his efforts, permitting the little bark to drift, while he leisurely took a survey of the state of things. The canoe first sent adrift was floating before the air, quite a quarter of a mile above him, and a little nearer to the shore than he

wished, now that he knew more of the savages were so near at hand. The canoe shoved from the point was within a few yards of him, he having directed his own course towards it on quitting the land. The dead Indian lay in grim quiet where he had left him, the warrior who had shown himself from the forest had already vanished, and the woods themselves were as silent and seemingly deserted as the day they came fresh from the hands of their great Creator. This profound stillness, however, lasted but a moment. When time had been given to the scouts of the enemy to reconnoitre, they burst out of the thicket upon the naked point, filling the air with yells of fury at discovering the death of their companion. These cries were immediately succeeded by shouts of delight when they reached the body and clustered eagerly around it. Deerslayer was a sufficient adept in the usages of the natives to understand the reason of the change. The yell was the customary lamentation at the loss of a warrior, the shout a sign of rejoicing that the conqueror had not been able to secure the scalp; the trophy, without which a victory is never considered complete. The distance at which the canoes lay probably prevented any attempts to injure the conqueror, the American Indian, like the panther of his own woods, seldom making any effort against his foe unless tolerably certain it is under circumstances that may be expected to prove effective.

As the young man had no longer any motive to remain near the point, he prepared to collect his canoes, in order to tow them off to the castle. That nearest was soon in tow, when he proceeded in quest of the other, which was all this time floating up the lake. The eye of Deerslayer was no sooner fastened on this last boat, than it struck him that it was nearer to the shore than it would have been had it merely followed the course of the gentle current of air. He began to suspect the influence of some unseen current in the water, and he quickened his exertions, in order to regain possession of it before it could drift in to a dangerous proximity to the woods. On getting nearer, he thought that the canoe had a perceptible motion through the water, and, as it lay broadside to the air, that this motion was taking it towards the land. A few vigorous strokes of the paddle carried him still nearer, when the mystery was explained. Something was evidently in motion on the off-side of the canoe or that which was furthest from himself, and closer scrutiny showed that it was a naked human arm. An Indian was lying in the bottom of the canoe, and was propelling it slowly, but certainly, to the shore, using his hand as a paddle. Deerslayer understood the whole artifice at a glance. A savage had swum off to the boat while he was occupied with his enemy on the point, got possession, and was using these means to urge it to the shore.

Satisfied that the man in the canoe could have no arms, Deerslayer did not hesitate to dash close alongside of the retiring boat, without deeming it necessary to raise his own rifle. As soon as the wash of the water, which he made in approaching, became audible to the prostrate savage, the latter sprang to his feet, and uttered an exclamation that proved how completely he was taken by surprise.

"If you've enj'yed yourself enough in that canoe, red-skin," Deerslayer coolly observed, stopping his own career in sufficient time to prevent an absolute collision between the two boats—"if you've enj'yed yourself enough in that canoe, you'll do a prudent act by taking to the lake ag'in. I'm reasonable in these matters, and don't crave your blood, though there's them about that would look upon you more as a due-bill for the bounty than a human mortal. Take to the lake this minute, afore we get to hot words."

The savage was one of those who did not understand a word of English, and he was indebted to the gestures of Deerslayer, and to the expression of an eye that did not often deceive, for an imperfect comprehension of his meaning. Perhaps, too, the sight of the rifle that lay so near the hand of the white man quickened his decision. At all events, he crouched like a tiger about to take his leap, uttered a yell, and the next instant his naked body disappeared in the water. When he rose to take breath, it was at the distance of several yards from the canoe, and the hasty glance he threw behind him denoted how much he feared the arrival of a fatal messenger from the rifle of his foe. But the young man made no indication of any hostile intention. Deliberately securing the canoe to the others, he began to paddle from the shore; and by the time the Indian reached the land, and had shaken himself, like a spaniel on quitting the water, his dreaded enemy was already beyond rifle-shot on his way to the castle. As was so much his practice, Deerslayer did not fail to soliloquize on what had just occurred, while steadily pursuing his course towards the point of destination.

"Well, well"—he commenced—"'twould have been wrong to kill a human mortal without an object. Scalps are of no account with me, and life is sweet, and ought not to be taken marcilessly by them that have white gifts. The savage was a Mingo, it's true; and I make no doubt he is, and will be as long as he lives, a ra'al riptyle and vagabond; but that's no reason I should forget my gifts and color. No, no—let him go; if ever we meet ag'in, rifle in hand, why then 'twill be seen which has the stoutest heart and the quickest eye. Hawkeye! That's not a bad name for a warrior, sounding much more manful and valiant than Deerslayer! 'Twouldn't be a bad title to begin with, and it has been fairly 'arned. If 'twas Chingachgook, now, he might go home and boast of his deeds, and the chiefs would name him Hawkeye in a minute; but it don't become white blood to brag, and 'tisn't easy to see how the matter can be known unless I do. Well, well—everything is in the hands of Providence; this affair as well as another; I'll trust to that for getting my desarts in all things."

Having thus betrayed what might be termed his weak spot, the young man continued to paddle in silence, making his way diligently, and as fast as his tows would allow him, towards the castle. By this time the sun had not only risen, but it had appeared over the eastern mountains, and was shedding a flood of glorious light on this as yet unchristened sheet of water. The whole scene was radiant with beauty; and no one unaccustomed to the ordinary history of the woods would fancy it had so lately witnessed incidents so ruthless and barbarous. As he approached the building of old Hutter, Deerslayer thought, or rather *felt*, that its appearance was in singular harmony with all the rest of the scene. Although nothing had been consulted but strength and security, the rude, massive logs, covered with their rough bark, the projecting roof, and the form, would contribute to render the building picturesque in almost any situation, while its actual position added novelty and piquancy to its other points of interest.

When Deerslayer drew nearer to the castle, however, objects of interest presented themselves that at once eclipsed any beauties that might have distinguished the scenery of the lake, and the site of the singular edifice. Judith and Hetty stood on the platform before the door, Hurry's door-yard, awaiting his approach with manifest anxiety; the former, from time to time, taking a survey of his person and of the canoes through the old ship's spy-glass that has been already mentioned. Never probably did this girl seem more brilliantly beautiful than at that moment; the flush of anxiety and alarm increasing her color to its richest tints, while the softness of her eyes, a charm that even poor Hetty shared with her, was deepened by intense concern. Such, at least, without pausing or pretending to analyse motives, or to draw any other very nice distinctions between cause and effect, were the opinions of the young man, as his canoes reached the side of the ark, where he carefully fastened all three before he put his foot on the platform.

1841

FROM *Satanstoe*

Cooper, although best known as a writer of adventure tales of sea and forest in the Scott tradition, was also a novelist of manners, as befitted an admirer of Fanny Burney and Jane Austen. *Satanstoe,* according to its preface, was intended to be "a chronicle of manners," and George Sand thought it one of Cooper's best. The novel re-creates a superb picture of pre-Revolutionary Dutch New York, drawn with care, warmth, humor, and more than a trace of sentimental nostalgia for a time, place, and people a century gone.

The "Littlepage Novels" (*Satanstoe*, 1845; *The Chainbearer*, 1845; *The Redskins*, 1846) were based on the so-called "Anti-Rent War" in New York in 1839–46, a conflict between landowners and tenants which to Cooper symbolized a deeper conflict in Jacksonian society between democrats and aristocrats, haves and have-nots. However, the thesis of *Satanstoe*, while an important element of the novel, is never fully integrated into the narrative and never seriously interferes with the chronicle of Cornelius Littlepage and the provincial society he lives in.

Of combined English and Dutch heritage, Littlepage, owner of the estate "Satanstoe" near Mamaroneck, Westchester County, New York, and a staunch upholder of "the Protestant Succession, the House of Hanover, and King George II," represents the modest, responsible aristocracy of mid-eighteenth-century New York. Although the novel concerns Corny's romance with Anneke Mordaunt and his troubles with his tenants, it is dominated by the contrast Cooper sets up (as Irving had done) between the New England Yankee (Jason Newcome) and the New York Dutchman (Guert Van Eyck), which to Cooper represented a fundamental clash of temperaments and values. The Yankee is materialistic, narrow, hypocritical, shrewd, educated; the Dutchman is generous, impulsive, energetic, and essentially uneducated. As Cooper implies, the Yankee's code of behavior and action is likely to dominate American society in the end. Like Littlepage, Cooper admitted to a "neighborly antipathy" toward New England.

Chapter III

"Believe me, thou talkest of an admirable conceited fellow. Has he any unbraided wares?"
"Pr'ythee, bring him in; and let him approach singing."
Winter's Tale.

I have no intention of taking the reader with me through college, where I remained the usual term of four years. These four years were not idled away, as sometimes happens, but were fairly improved. I read all of the New Testament, in Greek; several of Cicero's Orations; every line of Horace, Satires and Odes; four books of the Iliad; Tully de Oratore, throughout; besides paying proper attention to geography, mathematics, and other of the usual branches. Moral philosophy, in particular, was closely attended to, senior year, as well as astronomy. We had a telescope that showed us all four of Jupiter's moons. In other respects, Nassau[1] might be called the seat of learning. One of our class purchased a second-hand copy of Euripides, in town, and we had it in college all of six months; though it was never my good fortune to see it, as the young man who owned it was not much disposed to let profane eyes view his treasure. Nevertheless, I am certain the copy of the work was in college; and we took good care to let the Yale men hear of it more than once. I do not believe *they* ever saw even the outside of a Euripides. As for the telescope, I can testify of my own knowledge; having seen the moons of Jupiter as often as ten times, with my own eyes, aided by its magnifiers. We had a tutor who was expert among the stars, and who, it was generally believed, would have been able to see the ring of Saturn, could he have found the planet; which, as it turned out, he was unable to do.

My four college years were very happy years. The vacations came often, and I went home invariably; passing a day or two with my aunt Legge, in going or coming. The acquisition of knowledge was always agreeable to me; and I may say it without vanity, I trust, at this time of life, I got the third honor of my class. We should have graduated four, but one of our class was compelled to quit us at the end of junior year, on account of his health. He was an unusually hard student, and it was generally admitted that he would have taken the first honor had he remained. We were thought to acquit ourselves with credit at the commencement; although I afterward heard my grandfather tell Mr. Worden,[2] that he was of opinion the addresses would have been more masculine and commendable, had less been said of the surprising growth, prosperity, and power of the colonies. He had no objection to the encouragement of a sound, healthful, patriotic feeling; but to him it appeared that something more novel might have better pleased the audience. This may have been true, as all three of us had something to say on the subject; and it is a proof how much we thought alike, that our language was almost as closely assimilated as our ideas.

As for the Powles' Hook Ferry, it was an unpleasant place I will allow; though by the time I was junior I thought nothing of it. My mother, however, was glad when it was passed for the last time. I remember the very first words that escaped her, after she had kissed me on my final return from college, were, "Well, Heaven be praised, Corny! you will never again have any occasion to cross that frightful ferry, now college is completely done with?" My poor mother little knew how much greater dangers I was subsequently called on to encounter, in another direction. Nor was she minutely accurate in her anticipations, since I have crossed the ferry in question, several times in later life; the

---

[1] Princeton was chartered in 1746 as the Presbyterian College of New Jersey, opened in Elizabethtown, moved to Newark, and finally settled at Princeton in 1756. Young Littlepage, on the advice of Col. Follock, was not sent to a New England college, where he would "I'arn how to bray and cheat."

[2] Rector of the parish, who had tutored Littlepage in Latin and Greek for the college entrance examinations.

distances not appearing to be as great, of late years, as they certainly seemed to be in my youth.

It was a feather in a young man's cap to have gone through college, in 1755, which was the year I graduated. It is true, the university men, who had been home for their learning, were more or less numerous; but they were of a class that held itself aloof from the smaller gentry, and most of them were soon placed in office, adding the dignity of public trusts to their acquisitions—the former in a manner overshadowing the latter. But I was nearer to the body of the community, and my position admitted more of comparative excellence, as it might be. No one thinks of certain habits, opinions, manners, and tastes, in the circle where they are expected to be found; but, it is a different thing where all, or any of these peculiarities form the exception. I am afraid more was anticipated from my college education than has ever been realized; but I will say this for my *Alma Mater,* that I am not conscious my acquisitions at college have ever been of any disadvantage to me; and I rather think they have, in some degree at least, contributed to the little success that has attended my humble career.

I kept up my intimacy with Dirck Follock, during the whole time I remained at college. He continued the classics with Mr. Worden, for two years after I left the school; but I could not discover that his progress amounted to any thing worth mentioning. The master used to tell the colonel that "Dirck's progress was slow and sure;" and this did not fail to satisfy a man who had a constitutional aversion to much of the head-over-heels rate of doing things among the English population. Colonel Follock, as we always called him, except when my father or grandfather asked him to drink a glass of wine, or drank his health in the first glass after the cloth was removed, when he was invariably styled Colonel Van Valkenburgh, at full length; but Colonel Follock was quite content that his son and heir should know no more than he knew himself, after making proper allowances for the difference in years and experience. By the time I returned home, however, a material change had been made in the school. Mr. Worden fell heir to a moderate competency at home, and he gave up teaching, a business he had never liked, accordingly. It was even thought he was a shade less zealous in his parochial duties, after the acquisition of this fifty pounds sterling a-year, than he had previously been; though I am far from insisting on the fact's being so. At any rate, it was not in the power of fifty pounds per annum to render Mr. Worden apathetic on the subject of the church; for he continued a most zealous churchman down to the hour of his death; and this was something, even admitting that he was not quite so zealous as a

Christian. The church being the repository of the faith, if not the faith itself, it follows that its friends are akin to religion, though not absolutely religious. I have always liked a man the better for being what I call a sound, warm-hearted churchman, though his habits may have been a little free.

It was necessary to supply the place left vacant by the emigration of Mr. Worden, or to abandon a school that had got to be the nucleus of knowledge in Westchester. There was a natural desire, at first, to obtain another scholar from home; but no such person offering, a Yale College graduate was accepted, though not without sundry rebellions, and plenty of distrust. The moment he appeared, Colonel Follock and Major Nicholas Oothout, another respectable Dutch neighbor, withdrew their sons; and from that hour Dirck never went to school again. It is true, Westchester was not properly a Dutch county, like Rockland, and Albany, and Orange, and several others along the river; but it had many respectable families in it, of that extraction, without alluding to such heavy people as the Van Cortlands, Felipses, Beekmans, and two or three others of that stamp. Most of our important county families had a different origin, as in the case of the Morrises, of Morrisania, and of the Manor of Fordham, the Pells, of Pelham, the Heathcotes, of Mamanneck, the branch of the De Lanceys at West Farms, the Jays, of Rye, etc., etc. All these came of the English or Huguenot stock. Among these last, more or less Dutch blood was to be found, however; though Dutch prejudices were a good deal weakened. Although few of these persons sent their boys to this school, they were consulted in the selection of a master; and I have always supposed that their indifference was the cause that the county finally obtained the services of a Yankee from Yale.

The name of the new pedagogue was Jason Newcome, or, as he pronounced the latter appellation himself, Noocome. As he affected a pedantic way of pronouncing the last syllable long, or as it was spelt, he rather called himself Noo-comb, instead of Newcum, as is the English mode, whence he soon got the nickname of Jason Old Comb among the boys; the lank, orderly arrangement of his jet-black, and somewhat greasy-looking locks, contributing their share toward procuring for him the *soubriquet,* as I believe the French call it. As this Mr. Newcome will have a material part to play in the succeeding portions of this narrative, it may be well to be a little more minute in his description.

I found Jason fully established in the school, on my return from college. I remember we met very much like two strange birds, that see each other for the first time on the same dunghill; or two quadrupeds, in their original interview in a common herd.

It was New Haven against Newark; though the institution, after making as many migrations as the House of Loretto, finally settled down at Princeton, a short time before I took my degree. I was consequently entitled to call myself a graduate of Newark—a sort of scholar that is quite as great a curiosity in the country as a Queen Anne's farthing, or a book printed in the fifteenth century. I remember the first evening we two spent in company, as well as if the meeting occurred only last night. It was at Satanstoe, and Mr. Worden was present. Jason had a liberal supply of Puritanical notions, which were bred in-and-in in his moral, and I had almost said, in his physical system; nevertheless, he could unbend; and I did not fail to observe that very evening, a gleam of covert enjoyment on his sombre countenance, as the hot-stuff, the cards, and the pipes were produced, an hour or two before supper—a meal we always had hot and comfortable. This covert satisfaction, however, was not exhibited without certain misgiving looks, as if the neophyte in these innocent enjoyments distrusted his right to possess his share. I remember in particular, when my mother laid two or three new, clean packs of cards on the table, that Jason cast a stealthy glance over his shoulder, as if to make certain that the act was not noted by the minister, or the "neighbors." The neighbors!—what a contemptible being a man becomes, who lives in constant dread of the comments and judgments of these social supervisors! and what a wretch, the habit of deferring to no principle better than their decision has made many a being, who has had originally the materials of something better in him, than has been developed by the *surveillance* of ignorance, envy, vulgarity, gossiping and lying! In those cases in which education, social position, opportunities, and experience have made any material difference between the parties, the man who yields to such a government, exhibits the picture of a giant held in bondage by a pigmy. I have always remarked, too, that they who are best qualified to sit in this neighborhood-tribunal, generally keep most aloof from it, as repugnant to their tastes and habits, thus leaving its decisions to the portions of the community least qualified to make such as are either just or enlightened.

I felt a disposition to laugh outright, at the manner in which Jason betrayed a sneaking consciousness of crime, as he saw my meek, innocent, simpleminded, just and warm-hearted mother lay the cards on the table that evening. His sense of guilt was purely conventional, while my mother's sense of innocence existed in the absence of false instruction, and in the purity of her intentions. One had been taught no exaggerated and false notion of sin—nay, a notion that is impious, as it is clearly impious in man to torture acts that are perfectly innocent *per se*, into formal transgressions of the law of God—while the other had been educated under the narrow and exaggerated notions of a provincial sect, and had obtained a species of conscience that was purely dependent on his miserable schooling. I heard my grandfather say that Jason actually showed the white of his eyes the first time he saw Mr. Worden begin to deal, and he still looked, the whole time we were at whist, as if he expected some one might enter, and tell of his delinquency. I soon discovered that Jason had a much greater dread of being told of, than of doing such things as taking a hand at whist, or drinking a glass of punch, from which I inferred his true conscience drew perceptible distinctions between the acts and the penalties he had been accustomed to see inflicted on them. He was much disposed to a certain sort of frailty; but it was a sneaking disposition to the last.

But the amusing part of the exhibition, that first evening of our acquaintance, was Mr. Worden showing off his successor's familiarity with the classics. Jason had not the smallest notion of quantity; and he pronounced the Latin very much as one would read Mohawk, from a vocabulary made out by a hunter, or a savant of the French academy. As I had received the benefit of Mr. Worden's own instruction, I could do better, and, generally, my knowledge of the classics went beyond that of Jason. The latter's English, too, was long a source of amusement with us all, though my grandfather often expressed strong disgust at it. Even Colonel Follock did not scruple to laugh at Newcome's English, which, as he frequently took occasion to say, "hat a ferry remarkable sount to it." As this peculiarity of Jason's extended a good way into the Anglo-Saxon race, in the part of the country in which he was born, it may be well to explain what I mean a little more at large.

Jason was the son of an ordinary Connecticut farmer, of the usual associations, and with no other pretension to education than such as was obtained in a common school, or any reading which did not include the Scriptures, some half a dozen volumes of sermons and polemical works, all the latter of which were vigorously as well as narrowly one-sided, and a few books that had been expressly written to praise New England, and to undervalue all the rest of the earth. As the family knew nothing of the world beyond the limits of its own township, and an occasional visit to Hartford, on what is called "election-day," Jason's early life was necessarily of the most contracted experience. His English, as a matter of course, was just that of his neighborhood and class of life; which was far from being either very elegant or very Doric. But on this rustic, provincial, or rather, hamlet foundation, Jason had reared a superstructure of New Haven finish and proportions. As he kept school before he went to college, while he was in college, and after he left college, the whole energies of his nature became strangely directed to just such reforms of language as would be apt to strike the imagination of a pedagogue of his calibre. In the first place, he had brought from home with him a great number of sounds that were decidedly vulgar and vicious, and with these in full existence in himself, he had commenced his system of reform on other people. As is common with all tyros, he fancied a very little knowledge sufficient authority for very great theories. His first step was to improve the language, by adapting sound in spelling, and he insisted on calling angel, *an*-gel, because a-n spelt an; chamber, *cham*-ber, for the same reason; and so on through a long catalogue of similarly constructed words. "English," he did not pronounce as "*Ing*-lish," but as "*English*," for instance; and "nothing" (Anglice *nuth*ing), as *noth*-ing; or, perhaps, it were better to say "*naw*-thin'." While Jason showed himself so much of a purist with these and many other words, he was guilty of some of the grossest possible mistakes, that were directly in opposition to his own theory. Thus, while he affectedly pronounced "none," (nun), as "known," he did not scruple to call "stone," "stun," and "home," "hum." The idea of pronouncing "clerk," as it should be, or "clark," greatly shocked him, as it did to call "hearth," "h'arth;" though he did not hesitate to call this good earth of ours, the " 'arth," "Been," he pronounced "ben," of course, and "roof," he called "ruff," in spite of all his purism.

From the foregoing specimens, half a dozen among a thousand, the reader will get an accurate notion of this weakness in Jason's character. It was heightened by the fact that the young man commenced his education, such as it was, late in life, and it is rare indeed that either knowledge or tastes thus acquired are entirely free from exaggeration. Though Jason was several years my senior, like myself he was a recent graduate, and it will be easy enough to imagine the numberless discussions that took place between us, on the subject of our respective acquisitions. I say "respective," instead of mutual acquisitions, because there was nothing mutual about it, or *them*. Neither our classics, our philosophy, nor our mathematics would seem to have been the same, but each man apparently had a science, or a language of his own, and which had been derived from the institution where he had been taught. In the classics I was much the strongest, particularly in the quantities, but Jason had the best of it in mathematics. In spite of his conceit, his vulgarity, his English, his provincialism, and the awkwardness with which he wore his tardily acquired information, this man had strong points about him, and a native shrewdness that would have told much more in his favor had it not been accompanied by a certain evasive manner, that caused one constantly to suspect his sincerity, and which often induced those who were accustomed to him, to imagine he had a sneaking propensity that rendered him habitually hypocritical. Jason held New York in great contempt, a feeling he was not always disposed to conceal, and of necessity his comparisons were usually made with the state of things in Connecticut, and much to the advantage of the latter. To one thing, however, he was much disposed to defer, and that was money. Connecticut had not then, nor has it now, a single individual who would be termed rich in New York; and Jason, spite of his provincial conceit, spite of his overweening notions of moral and intellectual superiority, could no more prevent this profound deference for wealth, than he could substitute for a childhood of vulgarity and neglect, the grace, refinement and knowledge which the boys of the more fortunate classes in life obtain as it might be without knowing it. Yes, Jason bowed down to the golden calf, in spite of his Puritanism, his love of liberty, his pretension to equality and the general strut of his disposition and manner.

Such is an outline of the character and qualifications of the man whom I found, on my return from college, at the head of Mr. Worden's school. We soon became acquainted, and I do not know which got the most ideas from the other, in course of the first fortnight. Our conversation and arguments were free, almost to rudeness, and little mercy was shown to our respective prejudices. Jason was ultra levelling in his notions of social intercourse, while I had the opinions of my own colony, in which the distinctions of classes are far more strongly marked than is usual in New England, out of Boston, and its immediate association. Still Jason deferred to names, as well as money, though it was in a way very different from my own. New England was, and is, loyal to the crown; but having the right to name many of its own governors, and possessing many other political privileges through the charters that were granted to her people, in order to induce them to settle that portion of the continent, they do not always manifest the feeling in a way to be agreeable to those who have a proper reverence for the crown. Among other points, growing out of this difference in training, Jason and I had sundry arguments on the subject of professions, trades and callings. It was evident he fancied the occupation of a schoolmaster next in honor to that of a clergyman. The clergy formed a species of aristocracy, according to his notions; but no man could commence life under more favorable auspices, than by taking a school.

The following dialogue occurred between us, on this subject; and I was so much struck with the novelty of my companion's notions, as to make a note of it, as soon as we parted.

"I wonder your folks don't think of giving you suthin' to do, Corny," commenced Jason, one day, after our acquaintance had ripened into a sort of belligerent intimacy. "You're near nineteen, now, and ought to begin to think of bringing suthin' in, to pay for all the outgoin's."

By "your folks," Jason meant the family of Littlepage; and the blood of that family quickened a little within me, at the idea of being profitably employed, in the manner intimated, because I had reached the mature and profitable age of nineteen.

"I do not understand you exactly, Mr. Newcome, by your bringing something in," answered I, with dignity enough to put a man of ordinary delicacy on his guard.

"Bringing suthin' in is good English, I hope, Mr. Littlepage. I mean that your edication has cost your folks enough to warrant them in calling on you for a little interest. How much do you suppose, now, has been spent on your edication, beginning at the time you first went to Mr. Worden, and leaving off the day you quitted Newark?"

"Really, I have not the smallest notion; the subject has never crossed my mind."

"Did the old folks never say any thing to you about it?—never foot up the total?"

"I am sure it is not easy to see how this could be done, for I could not help them in the least."

"But your father's books would tell that, as doubtless it all stands charged against you."

"Stands charged against me! How, sir! do you imagine my father makes a charge in a book against me, whenever he pays a few pounds for my education?"

"Certainly; how else could he tell how much you have had?—though, on reflection, as you are an only child, it does not make so much difference. You probably will get all, in the end."

"And had I a brother, or a sister, do you imagine, Mr. Newcome, each shilling we spent would be set down in a book, as charges against us?"

"How else, in natur', could it be known which had had the most, or any sort of justice be done between you?"

"Justice would be done, by our common father's giving to each just as much of his own money as he might see fit. What is it to me, if he chose to give my brother a few hundred pounds more than he chose to give me? The money is his, and he may do with it as he choose."

"An hundred pounds is an awful sight of money!" exclaimed Jason, betraying by his countenance how deeply he felt the truth of this. "If you have had

money in such large sums, so much the more reason why you should set about doing suthin' to repay the old gentleman. Why not set up a school!"

"Sir!"

"Why not set up a school, I say? You might have had this of mine, had you been a little older; but once in, fast in, with me. Still, schools are wanted, and you might get a tolerable good recommend. I dare say your tutor would furnish a certificate."

This word "recommend" was used by Jason for "recommendation;" the habit of putting verbs in the places of substantives, and vice versa, being much in vogue with him.

"And do you really think that one who is destined to inherit Satanstoe, would act advisedly to set up a school? Recollect, Mr. Newcome, that my father and grandfather have both borne the king's commission; and that the last bears it, at this very moment, through his representative, the governor."

"What of all that? What better business is there than keeping a good school? If you are high in your notions, get to be made a tutor in that New Jersey college. Recollect that a tutor in a college is somebody. I did hope for such a place, but having a governor's son against me, as a candidate, there was no chance."

"A governor's son a candidate for a tutorship in a college! You are pleased to trifle with me, Mr. Newcome."

"It's true as the gospel. You thought some smaller fish put me down, but he was the son of the governor. But, why do you give that vulgar name to your father's farm—Satanstoe is not decent; yet, Corny, I've heard you use it before your own mother!"

"That you may hear every day, and my mother use it too, before her own son. What fault do you find with the name of Satanstoe?"

"Fault!—In the first place it is irreligious and profane; then it is ungenteel and vulgar, and only fit to be used in low company. Moreover, it is opposed to history and revelation, the evil one having a huff, if you will, but no toes. Such a name couldn't stand a fortnight before public opinion in New England."

"Yes, that may be very true; but we do not care enough for his Satanic majesty in the colony of New York, to treat him with so much deference. As for the 'huffs,' as you call them——"

"Why, what do you call 'em, Mr. Littlepage?"

"Hoofs, Mr. Newcome; that is the New York pronunciation of the word."

"I care nothing for York pronunciation, which every body knows is Dutch and full of corruptions. You'll never do any thing worth speaking of in this colony, Corny, until you pay more attention to your schools."

"I do not know what you call attention, Mr. Jason, unless we have paid it already. Here, I have the caption, or rather preamble of a law, on that very subject, that I copied out of the statute-book on purpose to show you, and which I will now read in order to prove to you how things really stand in the colony."

"Read away," rejoined Jason, with an air of sufficient disdain.

Read I did, and in the following sententious and comprehensive language, viz.:—"Whereas the youth of this colony are found, by manifold experience, to be not inferior in their natural geniuses to the youth of any other country in the world, therefore be it enacted, etc."[3]

"There, sir," I said in exultation, "you have chapter and verse for the true character of the rising generation in the colony of New York."

"And what does that preamble lead to?" demanded Jason, a little staggered at finding the equality of our New York intellects established so clearly by legislative enactment.

"It is the preamble to an act establishing the free schools of New York, in which the learned languages have now been taught these twenty years; and you will please to remember that another law has not long been passed, establishing a college in town."

"Well, curious laws do sometimes get into the statute-books, and a body must take them as he finds them. I dare say Connecticut might have a word to say on the same subject, if you would give her a chance. Have you heard the wonderful news from Philadelphia, Corny, that has just come among us?"

"I have heard nothing of late; for you know I

have been over in Rockland, with Dirck Follock, for the last two weeks, and news never reaches that family, or indeed that county."

"No, that is true enough," answered Jason, dryly; "News and a Dutchman have no affinity, or attraction, as we would say in philosophy; though there is gravitation enough on one side, ha! boy?"

Here Jason laughed outright, for he was always delighted whenever he could get a side-hit at the children of Holland, whom he appeared to regard as a race occupying a position between the human family and the highest class of the unintellectual animals. But it is unnecessary to dwell longer on this dialogue, my object being merely to show the general character of Jason's train of thought, in order to be better understood when I come to connect his opinions with his acts.

Dirck and myself were much together after my return from college. I passed weeks at a time with him, and he returned my visits with the utmost freedom and good will. Each of us had now got his growth, and it would have done the heart of Frederick of Prussia good, to have seen my young friend after he had ended his nineteenth year. In stature he measured exactly six feet three, and he gave every promise of filling up in proportion. Dirck was none of your roundly-turned, Apollo-built fellows, but he had shoulders that his little, short, solid, but dumpy-looking mother, who was of the true stock, could scarcely span, when she pulled his head down to give him a kiss; which she did regularly, as Dirck told me himself, twice each year; that is to say, Christmas and New-Year. His complexion was fair, his limbs large and well proportioned, his hair light, his eyes blue, and his face would have been thought handsome by most persons. I will not deny, however, that there was a certain ponderosity, both of mind and body, about my friend, that did not very well accord with the general notion of grace and animation. Nevertheless, Dirck was a sterling fellow, as true as steel, as brave as a game-cock, and as honest as noonday light.

Jason was a very different sort of person, in many essentials. In figure, he was also tall, but he was angular, loose-jointed and swinging—slouching would be the better word, perhaps. Still, he was not without strength, having worked on a farm until he was near twenty; and he was as active as a cat; a result that took the stranger a little by surprise, when he regarded only his loose, quavering sort of build. In the way of thought, Jason would think two feet to Dirck's one; but I am far from certain that it was always in so correct a direction. Give the Dutchman time, he was very apt to come out right; whereas Jason, I soon discovered, was quite liable to come to wrong conclusions, and particularly so in all

[3] This quotation would seem to be accurate, and it is somewhat curious to trace the reason why a preamble so singular should have been prefixed to the law. Was it not owing to the oft-repeated and bold assertions of Europeans, that man deteriorated in this hemisphere? Any American who has been a near observer of European opinion even in our day, must have been frequently amused at the expression of surprise and doubt that so often escapes the residents of the old world, when they discover any thing that particularly denotes talent coming from the new. I make little question that this extraordinary preamble is a sort of indirect answer to an imputation that was known to be as general, in that age, as it was felt to be unjust. My own experience would lead me to think native capacity more abundant in America than in the midland countries of Europe, and quite as frequently met with as in Italy itself; and I have often heard teachers, both English and French, admit that their American and West India scholars were generally the readiest and cleverest in their schools. The great evil under which this country labors, in this respect, is the sway of numbers, which is constantly elevating mediocrity and spurious talent to high places. In America we have a *higher average* of intelligence, while we have far less of the *higher class;* and I attribute the latter fact to the control of those who have never enjoyed the means of appreciating excellence.—*Editor.* [Cooper's note.]

matters that were a little adverse, and which affected his own apparent interests. Dirck, moreover, was one of the best-natured fellows that breathed; it being almost impossible to excite him to anger; when it did come, however, the earthquake was scarcely more terrific. I have seen him enraged, and would as soon encounter a wild-boar in an open field, as run against his course, while in the fit.

Modesty will hardly permit me to say much of myself. I was well-grown, active, strong, for my years; and, I am inclined to think, reasonably well-looking; though I would prefer that this much should be said by any one but myself. Dirck and I often tried our manhood together, when youngsters, and I was the better chap until my friend reached his eighteenth year, when the heavy metal of the young Dutch giant told in our struggles. After that period was past, I found Dirck too much for me, in a close gripe, though my extraordinary activity rendered the inequality less apparent than it might

otherwise have proved. I ought not to apply the term of "extraordinary" to any thing about myself, but the word escaped me unconsciously, and I shall let it stand. One thing I will say, notwithstanding, let the reader think of it as he may: I was good-natured and well-disposed to my fellow-creatures, and had no greater love of money than was necessary to render me reasonably discreet.

Such is an outline of the characters and persons of three of the principal actors in the scenes I am about to relate; scenes that will possess some interest for those who love to read accounts of adventures in a new country, however much they may fail in interesting others, when I speak of the condition and events of the more civilized condition of society, that was enjoyed, even in my youth, in such old counties as Westchester, and such towns as York.

1845

WILLIAM CULLEN BRYANT [1794-1878]

IN AN AUTOBIOGRAPHICAL ACCOUNT of his early years Bryant tells of his birth at Cummington, in the Berkshire hills of Massachusetts; of his father, a poetry-loving physician, and of his mother, descended from John and Priscilla Alden; of his maternal grandfather, a devout Calvinist in whose home he spent much of his childhood; of his enthusiasm over Pope and the great neoclassic writers; and of his early determination to be a poet himself. Born into a conservative Federalist country family, far from Boston and urban sophistication, young Bryant was raised in an atmosphere of old-fashioned New England morality and seriousness. He began writing poems at the age of eight, and at fourteen published his first poem, a neoclassic satire against Jefferson called "The Embargo." After study at Williams College and his admission to the law, his horizons broadened, the range of his poetry widened, his skill at his craft advanced, and his own ideas were modified by his discovery of Wordsworthian romanticism and Jacksonian politics. After the publication of his first volume of *Poems* (1821), young Bryant was regarded, until the rise of Longfellow's popularity, as America's leading poet, and he continued to be second only to Longfellow in public esteem for the next two generations.

In 1825 Bryant moved to New York, entered journalism, and in 1829, after two years as its assistant editor, became editor of the powerful New York *Evening Post,* a position he held for the next forty-nine years. Under his editorship the *Post* became the leading liberal newspaper of the period; in its editorial columns Bryant supported free speech, trade unionism, collective bargaining, legal and penal reform, the abolition of slavery, and Democratic administrations from Jackson to Pierce. He joined the new Republican Party in 1855, supported Lincoln and the Civil War, and after it joined in the reform movements in politics which succeeded the Grant administration.

Bryant's career as a journalist reduced the amount of his poetic output, but never submerged it. He continued to write poetry, to lecture about it, and to edit his own and others' volumes. He also spent years on a translation of the *Iliad* and the *Odyssey*, which appeared in 1870 and 1872, and he never hesitated to lend his support to liberal causes. He died, in fact, after exposing himself to the elements in his eightieth year during an outdoor tribute to the Italian patriot Mazzini in Central Park.

Further reading: *William Cullen Bryant: Representative Selections*, ed. Tremaine McDowell, 1935. Howard H. Peckham, *Gotham Yankee: A Biography of William Cullen Bryant*, 1950.

Thanatopsis

Bryant apparently began this poem, the most famous he ever wrote and one of his most characteristic, when he was sixteen. In its original version it began with "Yet a few days . . ." (line 17) and ended with ". . . and make their bed with thee" (line 66), suggesting that it was a fragment, a fashionable device in contemporary poetry. In 1821 he added the present introduction and conclusion. The text of this and subsequent poems is that of Bryant's own edition of *Poems: Collected and Arranged by the Author* (New York, 1865). The Greek "thanatopsis" means "view of death."

    To him who in the love of Nature holds
Communion with her visible forms, she speaks
A various language; for his gayer hours
She has a voice of gladness, and a smile
And eloquence of beauty, and she glides   5
Into his darker musings, with a mild
And healing sympathy, that steals away
Their sharpness ere he is aware. When thoughts
Of the last bitter hour come like a blight
Over thy spirit, and sad images   10
Of the stern agony, and shroud, and pall,
And breathless darkness, and the narrow house,
Make thee to shudder, and grow sick at heart;—
Go forth, under the open sky, and list
To Nature's teachings, while from all around—   15
Earth and her waters, and the depths of air,—
Comes a still voice—Yet a few days, and thee
The all-beholding sun shall see no more
In all his course; nor yet in the cold ground,
Where thy pale form was laid, with many tears,   20
Nor in the embrace of ocean, shall exist
Thy image. Earth, that nourished thee, shall claim
Thy growth, to be resolved to earth again,
And, lost each human trace, surrendering up
Thine individual being, shalt thou go   25
To mix for ever with the elements,
To be a brother to the insensible rock
And to the sluggish clod, which the rude swain
Turns with his share, and treads upon. The oak
Shall send his roots abroad, and pierce thy mould.

Yet not to thine eternal resting-place   31
Shalt thou retire alone,—nor couldst thou wish
Couch more magnificent. Thou shalt lie down
With patriarchs of the infant world—with kings,
The powerful of the earth—the wise, the good,   35
Fair forms, and hoary seers of ages past,
All in one mighty sepulchre. The hills
Rock-ribbed and ancient as the sun; the vales
Stretching in pensive quietness between;
The venerable woods; rivers that move   40
In majesty, and the complaining brooks
That make the meadows green; and, poured round
    all,
Old ocean's gray and melancholy waste,—
Are but the solemn decorations all
Of the great tomb of man. The golden sun,   45
The planets, all the infinite host of heaven,
Are shining on the sad abodes of death,
Through the still lapse of ages. All that tread
The globe are but a handful to the tribes
That slumber in its bosom.—Take the wings   50
Of morning, traverse Barca's[1] desert sands,
Or lose thyself in the continuous woods
Where rolls the Oregan,[2] and hears no sound,
Save his own dashings—yet—the dead are there:
And millions in those solitudes, since first   55
The flight of years began, have laid them down
In their last sleep—the dead reign there alone.
So shalt thou rest, and what if thou withdraw
In silence from the living and no friend
Take note of thy departure? All that breathe   60
Will share thy destiny. The gay will laugh
When thou art gone, the solemn brood of care
Plod on, and each one as before will chase
His favourite phantom; yet all these shall leave
Their mirth and their employments, and shall
    come,   65
And make their bed with thee. As the long train
Of ages glide away, the sons of men,
The youth in life's green spring, and he who goes
In the full strength of years, matron, and maid,
And the sweet babe, and the gray-headed man,—

Thanatopsis. [1] Northern Africa.
[2] The Columbia River.

Shall one by one be gathered to thy side,   71
By those, who in their turn shall follow them.

So live, that when thy summons comes to join
The innumerable caravan, which moves
To that mysterious realm, where each shall take   75
His chamber in the silent halls of death,
Thou go not, like the quarry-slave at night,
Scourged to his dungeon, but, sustained and soothed
By an unfaltering trust, approach thy grave
Like one who wraps the drapery of his couch   80
About him, and lies down to pleasant dreams.

1811   1817, 1821

Inscription for the Entrance to a Wood

First published with "Thanatopsis" in the same issue of
the *North American Review* in September 1817, under the
title "A Fragment." In revising the poem in 1821 Bryant
added the closing lines, beginning with "The cool wind
...." The actual wood was a grove of trees in front of his
boyhood home in Cummington, Massachusetts.

Stranger, if thou hast learned a truth which needs
No school of long experience, that the world
Is full of guilt and misery, and hast seen
Enough of all its sorrows, crimes, and cares,
To tire thee of it, enter this wild wood   5
And view the haunts of Nature. The calm shade
Shall bring a kindred calm, and the sweet breeze
That makes the green leaves dance, shall waft a
        balm
To thy sick heart. Thou wilt find nothing here
Of all that pained thee in the haunts of men   10
And made thee loathe thy life. The primal curse
Fell, it is true, upon the unsinning earth,
But not in vengeance. God hath yoked to guilt
Her pale tormentor, misery. Hence these shades
Are still the abodes of gladness; the thick roof   15
Of green and stirring branches is alive
And musical with birds, that sing and sport
In wantonness of spirit; while below
The squirrel, with raised paws and form erect,
Chirps merrily. Throngs of insects in the shade   20
Try their thin wings and dance in the warm beam
That waked them into life. Even the green trees
Partake the deep contentment; as they bend
To the soft winds, the sun from the blue sky
Looks in and sheds a blessing on the scene.   25
Scarce less the cleft-born wild-flower seems to enjoy
Existence, than the wingèd plunderer
That sucks its sweets. The mossy rocks themselves,
And the old and ponderous trunks of prostrate trees
That lead from knoll to knoll a causey[1] rude,   30

Inscription. [1] Causeway.

Or bridge the sunken brook, and their dark roots,
With all their earth upon them, twisting high,
Breathe fixed tranquillity. The rivulet
Sends forth glad sounds, and tripping o'er its bed
Of pebbly sands, or leaping down the rocks,   35
Seems, with continuous laughter, to rejoice
In its own being. Softly tread the marge,
Lest from her midway perch thou scare the wren
That dips her bill in water. The cool wind,
That stirs the stream in play, shall come to thee,   40
Like one that loves thee nor will let thee pass
Ungreeted, and shall give its light embrace.

1815   1817, 1821

To a Waterfowl

In December 1815, Bryant walked from Cummington to
Plainfield, Massachusetts, to inquire into opportunities
there for beginning the practice of law. He wrote in a
letter "that he felt, as he walked up the hills, very forlorn
and desolate indeed, not knowing what was to become of
him in the big world. . . . The sun had already set, leaving
behind it one of those brilliant seas of chrysolite and opal
which often flood the New England skies; and while he
was looking upon the rosy splendor with rapt admiration,
a solitary bird made wing along the illuminated horizon.
He watched the lone wanderer until it was lost in the
distance, asking himself whither it had come and to what
home it was flying. When he went to the house where he
was to stop for the night, his mind was still full of what he
had seen and felt, and he wrote these lines." (Parke Godwin, *A Biography of William Cullen Bryant*, 1883)

Whither, midst falling dew,
While glow the heavens with the last steps of day,
Far, through their rosy depths, dost thou pursue
        Thy solitary way?

Vainly the fowler's eye   5
Might mark thy distant flight to do thee wrong,
As, darkly seen against the crimson sky,
        Thy figure floats along.

Seek'st thou the plashy brink
Of weedy lake, or marge of river wide,   10
Or where the rocking billows rise and sink
        On the chafed ocean side?

There is a Power whose care
Teaches thy way along that pathless coast,—
The desert and illimitable air,—   15
        Lone wandering, but not lost.

All day thy wings have fanned,
At that far height, the cold thin atmosphere,
Yet stoop not, weary, to the welcome land,
        Though the dark night is near.   20

And soon that toil shall end;
Soon shalt thou find a summer home and rest,
And scream among thy fellows; reeds shall bend,
    Soon, o'er thy sheltered nest.

Thou'rt gone, the abyss of heaven   25
Hath swallowed up thy form; yet, on my heart
Deeply hath sunk the lesson thou hast given,
    And shall not soon depart.

He who, from zone to zone,   29
Guides through the boundless sky thy certain flight,
In the long way that I must tread alone,
    Will lead my steps aright.

1815   1818

A Winter Piece

The time has been that these wild solitudes,
Yet beautiful as wild, were trod by me
Oftener than now; and when the ills of life
Had chafed my spirit—when the unsteady pulse
Beat with strange flutterings—I would wander
    forth   5
And seek the woods. The sunshine on my path
Was to me as a friend. The swelling hills,
The quiet dells retiring far between,
With gentle invitation to explore
Their windings, were a calm society   10
That talked with me and soothed me. Then the
    chant
Of birds, and chime of brooks, and soft caress
Of the fresh sylvan air, made me forget
The thoughts that broke my peace, and I began
To gather simples by the fountain's brink,   15
And lose myself in day-dreams. While I stood
In nature's loneliness, I was with one
With whom I early grew familiar, one
Who never had a frown for me, whose voice
Never rebuked me for the hours I stole   20
From cares I loved not, but of which the world
Deems highest, to converse with her. When
    shrieked
The bleak November winds, and smote the woods,
And the brown fields were herbless, and the shades,
That met above the merry rivulet,   25
Were spoiled, I sought, I loved them still; they
    seemed
Like old companions in adversity.
Still there was beauty in my walks; the brook,
Bordered with sparkling frost-work, was as gay
As with its fringe of summer flowers. Afar,   30
The village with its spires, the path of streams,
And dim receding valleys, hid before
By interposing trees, lay visible
Through the bare grove, and my familiar haunts

Seemed new to me. Nor was I slow to come   35
Among them, when the clouds, from their still skirts,
Had shaken down on earth the feathery snow,
And all was white. The pure keen air abroad,
Albeit it breathed no scent of herb, nor heard
Love-call of bird nor merry hum of bee,   40
Was not the air of death. Bright mosses crept
Over the spotted trunks, and the close buds,
That lay along the boughs, instinct with life,
Patient, and waiting the soft breath of Spring,
Feared not the piercing spirit of the North.   45
The snow-bird twittered on the beechen bough,
And 'neath the hemlock, whose thick branches bent
Beneath its bright cold burden, and kept dry
A circle, on the earth, of withered leaves,
The partridge found a shelter. Through the snow   50
The rabbit sprang away. The lighter track
Of fox, and the racoon's broad path were there,
Crossing each other. From his hollow tree,
The squirrel was abroad, gathering the nuts
Just fallen, that asked the winter cold and sway   55
Of winter blast, to shake them from their hold.

But winter has yet brighter scenes,—he boasts
Splendors beyond what gorgeous Summer knows;
Or Autumn with his many fruits, and woods   59
All flushed with many hues. Come when the rains
Have glazed the snow, and clothed the trees with
    ice;
While the slant sun of February pours
Into the bowers a flood of light. Approach!
The incrusted surface shall upbear thy steps,
And the broad arching portals of the grove   65
Welcome thy entering. Look! the massy trunks
Are cased in the pure crystal; each light spray,
Nodding and tinkling in the breath of heaven,
Is studded with its trembling water-drops,
That glimmer with an amethystine light.   70
But round the parent stem the long low boughs
Bend, in a glittering ring, and arbors hide
The glassy floor. Oh! you might deem the spot
The spacious cavern of some virgin mine,   74
Deep in the womb of earth—where the gems grow,
And diamonds put forth radiant rods and bud
With amethyst and topaz—and the place
Lit up, most royally, with the pure beam
That dwells in them. Or haply the vast hall
Of fairy palace, that outlasts the night,   80
And fades not in the glory of the sun;—
Where crystal columns send forth slender shafts
And crossing arches; and fantastic aisles
Wind from the sight in brightness, and are lost
Among the crowded pillars. Raise thine eye;   85
Thou seest no cavern roof, no palace vault;
There the blue sky and the white drifting cloud
Look in. Again the wildered fancy dreams
Of spouting fountains, frozen as they rose,

And fixed, with all their branching jets, in air,   90
And all their sluices sealed. All, all is light;
Light without shade. But all shall pass away
With the next sun. From numberless vast trunks,
Loosened, the crashing ice shall make a sound
Like the far roar of rivers, and the eve   95
Shall close o'er the brown woods as it was wont.

And it is pleasant, when the noisy streams
Are just set free, and milder suns melt off
The plashy snow, save only the firm drift
In the deep glen or the close shade of pines,—   100
'Tis pleasant to behold the wreaths of smoke
Roll up among the maples of the hill,
Where the shrill sound of youthful voices wakes
The shriller echo, as the clear pure lymph,   104
That from the wounded trees, in twinkling drops,
Falls, mid the golden brightness of the morn,
Is gathered in with brimming pails, and oft,
Wielded by sturdy hands, the stroke of axe
Makes the woods ring. Along the quiet air,
Come and float calmly off the soft light clouds,   110
Such as you see in summer, and the winds
Scarce stir the branches. Lodged in sunny cleft,
Where the cold breezes come not, blooms alone
The little wind-flower, whose just opened eye
Is blue as the spring heaven it gazes at—   115
Startling the loiterer in the naked groves
With unexpected beauty, for the time
Of blossoms and green leaves is yet afar.
And ere it comes, the encountering winds shall oft
Muster their wrath again, and rapid clouds   120
Shade heaven, and bounding on the frozen earth
Shall fall their volleyed stores, rounded like hail
And white like snow, and the loud North again
Shall buffet the vexed forest in his rage.
1820

To Cole, the Painter, Departing for Europe

Thomas Cole (1801–48), born in England, came to the United States in 1819 to become one of the most famous landscape painters of the "Hudson River" school. A close friend of Bryant's, he had similar tastes in art and much in common with his view of American nature.

Thine eyes shall see the light of distant skies:
    Yet, Cole! thy heart shall bear to Europe's strand
    A living image of our own bright land,
Such as upon thy glorious canvas lies;
Lone lakes—savannas where the bison roves—   5
    Rocks rich with summer garlands—solemn
        streams—
    Skies, where the desert eagle wheels and
        screams—

Spring bloom and autumn blaze of boundless groves.
Fair scenes shall greet thee where thou goest—fair,
    But different—every where the trace of men,   10
    Paths, homes, graves, ruins, from the lowest glen
To where life shrinks from the fierce Alpine air,
    Gaze on them, till the tears shall dim thy sight,
    But keep that earlier, wilder image bright.
1829

The Prairies

Two of Bryant's brothers settled in Illinois, where he visited them in 1832, his first contact with the frontier country. The poem which grew out of his experience combined his consciousness of the great new American West with conventional romantic themes of the transience of life and the ruins of ancient empires.

These are the gardens of the Desert,[1] these
The unshorn fields, boundless and beautiful,
For which the speech of England has no name—
The Prairies. I behold them for the first,
And my heart swells, while the dilated sight   5
Takes in the encircling vastness. Lo! they stretch
In airy undulations, far away,
As if the ocean, in his gentlest swell,
Stood still, with all his rounded billows fixed,
And motionless for ever.— Motionless?—   10
No—they are all unchained again. The clouds
Sweep over with their shadows, and, beneath,
The surface rolls and fluctuates to the eye;
Dark hollows seem to glide along and chase
The sunny ridges. Breezes of the South!   15
Who toss the golden and the flame-like flowers,
And pass the prairie-hawk that, poised on high,
Flaps his broad wings, yet moves not—ye have
        played
Among the palms of Mexico and vines
Of Texas, and have crisped the limpid brooks   20
That from the fountains of Sonora glide
Into the calm Pacific—have ye fanned
A nobler or a lovelier scene than this?
Man hath no part in all this glorious work:
The hand that built the firmament hath heaved   25
And soothed these verdant swells, and sown their
        slopes
With herbage, planted them with island groves,
And hedged them round with forests. Fitting floor
For this magnificent temple of the sky—
With flowers whose glory and whose multitude   30
Rival the constellations! The great heavens
Seem to stoop down upon the scene in love,—
A nearer vault, and of a tenderer blue,
Than that which bends above our eastern hills.

The Prairies. Bryant uses the word in its Biblical sense, meaning a vast, uninhabited region.

As o'er the verdant waste I guide my steed,   35
Among the high rank grass that sweeps his sides,
The hollow beating of his footstep seems
A sacrilegious sound. I think of those
Upon whose rest he tramples. Are they here—
The dead of other days?—and did the dust   40
Of these fair solitudes once stir with life
And burn with passion? Let the mighty mounds
That overlook the rivers, or that rise
In the dim forest crowded with old oaks,
Answer. A race, that long has passed away,   45
Built them;—a disciplined and populous race
Heaped, with long toil, the earth, while yet the
          Greek
Was hewing the Pentelicus² to forms
Of symmetry, and rearing on its rock
The glittering Parthenon. These ample fields   50
Nourished their harvests, here their herds were fed,
When haply by their stalls the bison lowed,
And bowed his maned shoulder to the yoke.
All day this desert murmured with their toils,
Till twilight blushed, and lovers walked, and wooed
In a forgotten language, and old tunes,   56
From instruments of unremembered form,
Gave the soft winds a voice. The red man came—
The roaming hunter tribes, warlike and fierce,
And the mound-builders vanished from the earth.
The solitude of centuries untold   61
Has settled where they dwelt. The prairie-wolf³
Hunts in their meadows, and his fresh-dug den
Yawns by my path. The gopher mines the ground
Where stood their swarming cities. All is gone;   65
All—save the piles of earth that hold their bones,
The platforms where they worshipped unknown
          gods,
The barriers which they builded from the soil
To keep the foe at bay—till o'er the walls
The wild beleaguerers broke, and, one by one   70
The strongholds of the plain were forced, and
          heaped
With corpses. The brown vultures of the wood
Flocked to those vast uncovered sepulchres,
And sat, unscared and silent, at their feast.
Haply some solitary fugitive,   75
Lurking in marsh and forest, till the sense
Of desolation and of fear became
Bitterer than death, yielded himself to die.
Man's better nature triumphed then. Kind words
Welcomed and soothed him; the rude con-
          querors   80
Seated the captive with their chiefs; he chose
A bride among their maidens, and at length
Seemed to forget—yet ne'er forgot—the wife
Of his first love, and her sweet little ones,
Butchered, amid their shrieks, with all his race.   85

² Mount Pentelicus, in Greece, was noted for its marble
quarries.
³ The coyote.

Thus change the forms of being. Thus arise
Races of living things, glorious in strength,
And perish, as the quickening breath of God
Fills them, or is withdrawn. The red man, too,
Has left the blooming wilds he ranged so long,   90
And, nearer to the Rocky Mountains, sought
A wider hunting-ground. The beaver builds
No longer by these streams, but far away,
On waters whose blue surface ne'er gave back
The white man's face—among Missouri's springs,   95
And pools whose issues swell the Oregan,
He rears his little Venice. In these plains
The bison feeds no more. Twice twenty leagues
Beyond remotest smoke of hunter's camp,
Roams the majestic brute, in herds that shake   100
The earth with thundering steps—yet here I meet
His ancient footprints stamped beside the pool.

Still this great solitude is quick with life.
Myriads of insects, gaudy as the flowers
They flutter over, gentle quadrupeds,   105
And birds, that scarce have learned the fear of man,
Are here, and sliding reptiles of the ground,
Startlingly beautiful. The graceful deer
Bounds to the wood at my approach. The bee,
A more adventurous colonist than man,   110
With whom he came across the eastern deep,
Fills the savannas⁴ with his murmurings,
And hides his sweets, as in the golden age,
Within the hollow oak. I listen long
To his domestic hum, and think I hear   115
The sound of that advancing multitude
Which soon shall fill these deserts. From the ground
Comes up the laugh of children, the soft voice
Of maidens, and the sweet and solemn hymn
Of Sabbath worshippers. The low of herds   120
Blends with the rustling of the heavy grain
Over the dark-brown furrows. All at once
A fresher wind sweeps by, and breaks my dream,
And I am in the wilderness alone.
1832   1833

FROM *Lectures on Poetry*

Bryant delivered four lectures to the Athenaeum Society
of New York in 1825 and 1826, collected and published in
1884 by his son-in-law, Parke Godwin. The text is that of
Godwin, *The Prose Writings of William Cullen Bryant*,
(New York, 1884).

Lecture I
On the Nature of Poetry

Of the nature of poetry different ideas have been
entertained. The ancient critics seemed to suppose
that they did something toward giving a tolerable

⁴ Treeless, rolling country.

notion of it by calling it a mimetic or imitative art, and classing it with sculpture and painting. Of its affinity with these arts there can be no doubt; but that affinity seems to me to consist almost wholly in the principles by which they all produce their effect, and not in the manner in which those principles are reduced to practice. There is no propriety in applying to poetry the term *imitative* in a literal and philosophical sense, as there is in applying it to painting and sculpture. The latter speak to the senses; poetry speaks directly to the mind. They reproduce sensible objects, and, by means of these, suggest the feeling or sentiment connected with them; poetry, by the symbols of words, suggests both the sensible object and the association. I should be glad to learn how a poem descriptive of a scene or an event is any more an imitation of that scene or that event than a prose description would be. A prose composition giving an account of the proportions and dimensions of a building, and the materials of which it is constructed, is certainly, so far as mere exactness is concerned, a better imitation of it than the finest poem that could be written about it. Yet who, after all, ever thought of giving such a composition the name of an imitation? The truth is, painting and sculpture are, literally, imitative arts, while poetry is only metaphorically so. The epithet as applied to poetry may be well enough, perhaps, as a figure of speech, but to make a metaphor the foundation of a philosophical classification is putting it to a service in which it is sure to confuse what it professes to make clear.

I would rather call poetry a suggestive art. Its power of affecting the mind by pure suggestion, and employing, instead of a visible or tangible imitation, arbitrary symbols, as unlike as possible to the things with which it deals, is what distinguishes this from its two sister arts. It is owing to its operation by means of suggestion that it affects different minds with such different degrees of force. In a picture or a statue the colors and forms employed by the artist impress the senses with the greatest distinctness. In painting, there is little—in sculpture, there is less— for the imagination to supply. It is true that different minds, according to their several degrees of cultivation, will receive different degrees of pleasure from the productions of these arts, and that the moral associations they suggest will be variously felt, and in some instances variously interpreted. Still, the impression made on the senses is in all cases the same; the same figures, the same lights and shades, are seen by all beholders alike. But the creations of Poetry have in themselves nothing of this precision and fixedness of form, and depend greatly for their vividness and clearness of impression upon the mind to which they are presented. Language, the great machine with which her miracles are wrought, is contrived to have an application to all possible things; and wonderful as this contrivance is, and numerous and varied as are its combinations, it is still limited and imperfect, and, in point of comprehensiveness, distinctness, and variety, falls infinitely short of the mighty and diversified world of matter and mind of which it professes to be the representative. It is, however, to the very limitation of this power of language, as it seems to me, that Poetry owes her magic. The most detailed of her descriptions, which, by the way, are not always the most striking, are composed of a few touches; they are glimpses of things thrown into the mind; here and there a trace of the outline; here a gleam of light, and there a dash of shade. But these very touches act like a spell upon the imagination and awaken it to greater activity, and fill it, perhaps, with greater delight than the best defined objects could do. The imagination is the most active and the least susceptible of fatigue of all the faculties of the human mind; its more intense exercise is tremendous, and sometimes unsettles the reason; its repose is only a gentle sort of activity; nor am I certain that it is ever quite unemployed, for even in our sleep it is still awake and busy, and amuses itself with fabricating our dreams. To this restless faculty—which is unsatisfied when the whole of its work is done to its hands, and which is ever wandering from the combination of ideas directly presented to it to other combinations of its own—it is the office of poetry to furnish the exercise in which it delights. Poetry is that art which selects and arranges the symbols of thought in such a manner as to excite it the most powerfully and delightfully. The imagination of the reader is guided, it is true, by the poet, and it is his business to guide it skilfully and agreeably; but the imagination in the mean time is by no means passive. It pursues the path which the poet only points out, and shapes its visions from the scenes and allusions which he gives. It fills up his sketches of beauty with what suits its own highest conceptions of the beautiful, and completes his outline of grandeur with the noblest images its own stores can furnish. It is obvious that the degree of perfection with which this is done must depend greatly upon the strength and cultivation of that faculty. For example, in the following passage, in which Milton describes the general mother passing to her daily task among the flowers:

> "With goddess-like demeanor forth she went
> Not unattended, for on her as queen
> A pomp of winning graces waited still."

The coldest imagination, on reading it, will figure to itself, in the person of Eve, the finest forms, attitudes, and movements of female loveliness and dignity, which, after all, are not described, but only hinted at by the poet. A warmer fancy, kindling at the delicate allusions in these lines, will not only bestow these attractions on the principal figure, but will fill the air around her with beauty, and people it with the airy forms of the graces; it will see the delicate proportions of their limbs, the lustre of their flowing hair, and the soft light of their eyes. Take, also, the following passage from the same poet, in which, speaking of Satan, he says:

> "His face
> Deep scars of thunder had entrenched, and care
> Sat on his faded cheek—but under brows
> Of dauntless courage and considerate pride
> Waiting revenge; cruel his eye but cast
> Signs of remorse and passion to behold
> The fellows of his crime, the followers rather,
> (Far other once beheld in bliss), condemned
> For evermore to have their lot in pain."

The imagination of the reader is stimulated by the hints in this powerful passage to form to itself an idea of the features in which reside this strong expression of malignity and dejection—the brow, the cheek, the eye of the fallen angel, bespeaking courage, pride, the settled purpose of revenge, anxiety, sorrow for the fate of his followers, and fearfully marked with the wrath of the Almighty. There can be no doubt that the picture which this passage calls up in the minds of different individuals will vary accordingly as the imagination is more or less vivid, or more or less excited in the perusal. It will vary, also, accordingly as the individual is more or less experienced in the visible expression of strong passion, and as he is in the habit of associating the idea of certain emotions with certain configurations of the countenance.

There is no question that one principal office of poetry is to excite the imagination, but this is not its sole, nor perhaps its chief, province; another of its ends is to touch the heart, and, as I expect to show in this lecture, it has something to do with the understanding. I know that some critics have made poetry to consist solely in the exercise of the imagination. They distinguish poetry from pathos. They talk of pure poetry, and by this phrase they mean passages of mere imagery, with the least possible infusion of human emotion. I do not know by what authority these gentlemen take the term poetry from the people, and thus limit its meaning.

In its ordinary acceptation, it has, in all ages and all countries, included something more. When we speak of a poem, we do not mean merely a tissue of striking images. The most beautiful poetry is that which takes the strongest hold of the feelings, and, if it is really the most beautiful, then it is poetry in the highest sense. Poetry is constantly resorting to the language of the passions to heighten the effect of her pictures; and, if this be not enough to entitle that language to the appellation of poetical, I am not aware of the meaning of the term. Is there no

poetry in the wrath of Achilles? Is there no poetry in the passage where Lear, in the tent of Cordelia, just recovered from his frenzy, his senses yet infirm and unassured, addresses his daughter as she kneels to ask his blessing?

> "Pray do not mock me;
> I am a very foolish, fond old man,
> Fourscore and upward:
> Not an hour more or less, and to deal plainly
> I fear I am not in my perfect mind."

Is there no poetry in the remorse of Othello, in the terrible consciousness of guilt which haunts Macbeth, or the lamentations of Antony over the body of his friend, the devoted love of Juliet, and the self-sacrificing affection of Cleopatra? In the immortal work of Milton, is there no poetry in the penitence of Adam, or in the sorrows of Eve at being excluded from Paradise? The truth is, that poetry which does not find its way to the heart is scarcely deserving of the name; it may be brilliant and ingenious, but it soon wearies the attention. The feelings and the imagination, when skilfully touched, act reciprocally on each other. For example, when the poet introduces Ophelia, young, beautiful, and unfortunate, the wildness of frenzy in her eye, dressed with fantastic garlands of wild flowers, and singing snatches of old tunes, there is a picture for the imagination, but it is one which affects the heart. But when, in the midst of her incoherent talk, she utters some simple allusion to her own sorrows, as when she says,

> "We know what we are, but know not what we
> may be,"

this touching sentence, addressed merely to our sympathy, strongly excites the imagination. It sets before us the days when she knew sorrow only by name, before her father was slain by the hand of her lover, and before her lover was estranged, and makes us feel the heaviness of that affliction which crushed a being so gentle and innocent and happy.

Those poems, however, as I have already hinted, which are apparently the most affluent of imagery, are not always those which most kindle the reader's imagination. It is because the ornaments with which they abound are not naturally suggested by the subject, not poured forth from a mind warmed and occupied by it; but a forced fruit of the fancy, produced by labor, without spontaneity or excitement.

The language of passion is naturally figurative, but its figures are only employed to heighten the intensity of the expression; they are never introduced for their own sake. Important, therefore, as may be the office of the imagination in poetry, the great spring of poetry is emotion. It is this power that holds the key of the storehouse where the mind has laid up its images, and that alone can open it without violence. All the forms of fancy stand ever in its sight, ready to execute its bidding. Indeed, I doubt not that most of the offences against good taste in this kind of composition are to be traced to the absence of emotion. A desire to treat agreeably or impressively a subject by which the writer is himself little moved, leads him into great mistakes about the means of effecting his purpose. This is the origin of cold conceits, of prosing reflections, of the minute painting of uninteresting circumstances, and of the opposite extremes of tameness and extravagance. On the other hand, strong feeling is always a sure guide. It rarely offends against good taste, because it instinctively chooses the most effectual means of communicating itself to others. It gives a variety to the composition it inspires, with which the severest taste is delighted. It may sometimes transgress arbitrary rules, or offend against local associations, but it speaks a language which reaches the heart in all countries and all times. Everywhere are the sentiments of fortitude and magnanimity uttered in strains that brace our own nerves, and the dead mourned in accents that draw our tears.

But poetry not only addresses the passions and the imagination; it appeals to the understanding also. So far as this position relates to the principles of taste which lie at the foundation of all poetry, and by which its merits are tried, I believe its truth will not be doubted. These principles have their origin in the reason of things, and are investigated and applied by the judgment. True it is that they may be observed by one who has never speculated about them, but it is no less true that their observance always gratifies the understanding with the fitness, the symmetry, and the congruity it produces. To write fine poetry requires intellectual faculties of the highest order, and among these, not the least important, is the faculty of reason. Poetry is the worst mask in the world behind which folly and stupidity could attempt to hide their features. Fitter, safer, and more congenial to them is the solemn discussion of unprofitable questions. Any obtuseness of apprehension or incapacity for drawing conclusions, which shows a deficiency or want of cultivation of the reasoning power, is sure to expose the unfortunate poet to contempt and ridicule.

But there is another point of view in which poetry may be said to address the understanding—I mean in the direct lessons of wisdom that it delivers. Remember that it does not concern itself with abstract reasonings, nor with any course of investigation that fatigues the mind. Nor is it merely didactic; but this does not prevent it from teaching truths which the mind instinctively acknowledges. The elements of moral truth are few and simple, but their combinations with human actions are as innumer-

able and diversified as the combinations of language. Thousands of inductions resulting from the application of great principles to human life and conduct lie, as it were, latent in our minds, which we have never drawn for ourselves, but which we admit the moment they are hinted at, and which, though not abstruse, are yet new. Nor are these of less value because they require no laborious research to discover them. The best riches of the earth are produced on its surface, and we need no reasoning to teach us the folly of a people who should leave its harvests ungathered to dig for its ores. The truths of which I have spoken, when possessing any peculiar force or beauty, are properly within the province of the art of which I am treating, and, when recommended by harmony of numbers, become poetry of the highest kind. Accordingly, they abound in the works of the most celebrated poets. When Shakespeare says of mercy,

> "it is twice blessed—
> It blesses him that gives and him that takes,"

does he not utter beautiful poetry as well as unquestionable truth? There are passages also in Milton of the same kind, which sink into the heart like the words of an oracle. For instance:

> "Evil into the mind of God or man
> May come and go so unapproved, and leave
> No spot or blame behind."

Take, also, the following example from Cowper, in which he bears witness against the guilt and folly of princes:

> "War is a game which, were their subjects wise,
> Kings should not play at. Nations would do well
> To extort their truncheons from the puny hands
> Of heroes whose infirm and baby minds
> Are gratified with mischief, and who spoil,
> Because men suffer it, their toy—the world."

I call these passages poetry, because the mind instantly acknowledges their truth and feels their force, and is moved and filled and elevated by them. Nor does poetry refuse to carry on a sort of process of reasoning by deducing one truth from another. Her demonstrations differ, however, from ordinary ones by requiring that each step should be in itself beautiful or striking, and that they all should carry the mind to the final conclusion without the consciousness of labor.

All the ways by which poetry affects the mind are open also to the prose-writer. All that kindles the imagination, all that excites emotion, all those moral truths that find an echo in our bosoms, are his property as well as that of the poet. It is true that in the ornaments of style the poet is allowed a greater license, but there are many excellent poems which are not distinguished by any liberal use of the figures of speech from prose writings composed with the same degree of excitement. What, then, is the ground of the distinction between prose and poetry? This is a question about which there has been much debate, but one which seems to me of easy solution to those who are not too ambitious of distinguishing themselves by profound researches into things already sufficiently clear. I suppose that poetry differs from prose, in the first place, by the employment of metrical harmony. It differs from it, in the next place, by excluding all that disgusts, all that tasks and fatigues the understanding, and all matters which are too trivial and common to excite any emotion whatever. Some of these, verse cannot raise into dignity; to others, verse is an encumbrance: they are, therefore, all unfit for poetry; put them into verse, and they are prose still.

A distinction has been attempted to be made between poetry and eloquence, and I acknowledge that there is one; but it seems to me that it consists solely in metrical arrangement. Eloquence is the poetry of prose; poetry is the eloquence of verse. The maxim that the poet is born and the orator made is a pretty antithesis, but a moment's reflection will convince us that one can become neither without natural gifts improved by cultivation. By eloquence I do not mean mere persuasiveness: there are many processes of argument that are not susceptible of eloquence, because they require close and painful attention. But by eloquence I understand those appeals to our moral perceptions that produce emotion as soon as they are uttered. It is in these that the orator is himself affected with the feelings he would communicate, that his eyes glisten, and his frame seems to dilate, and his voice acquires an unwonted melody, and his sentences arrange themselves into a sort of measure and harmony, and the listener is chained in involuntary and breathless attention. This is the very enthusiasm that is the parent of poetry. Let the same man go to his closet and clothe in numbers conceptions full of the same fire and spirit, and they will be poetry.

In conclusion, I will observe that the elements of poetry make a part of our natures, and that every individual is more or less a poet. In this "bank-note world," as it has been happily denominated, we sometimes meet with individuals who declare that they have no taste for poetry. But by their leave I will assert they are mistaken; they have it, although they may have never cultivated it. Is there any one among them who will confess himself insensible to the beauty of order or to the pleasure of variety— two principles, the happy mingling of which makes the perfection of poetic numbers? Is there any one whose eye is undelighted with beautiful forms and colors, whose ear is not charmed by sweet sounds, and who sees no loveliness in the returns of light and darkness, and the changes of the seasons? Is there any one for whom the works of Nature have no associations but such as relate to his animal wants? Is there any one to whom her great courses and operations show no majesty, to whom they impart no knowledge, and from whom they hide no secrets? Is there any one who is attached by no ties to his fellow-beings, who has no hopes for the future, and no memory of the past? Have they all forgotten the days and the friends of their childhood, and do they all shut their eyes to the advances of age? Have they nothing to desire and nothing to lament, and are their minds never darkened with the shadows of fear? Is it, in short, for these men that life has no pleasures and no pains, the grave no solemnity, and the world to come no mysteries? All these things are the sources of poetry, and they are not only part of ourselves, but of the universe, and will expire only with the last of the creatures of God.

1825   1884

FROM *American Society as a Field for Fiction*

Originally published as part of a review of Catherine Sedgwick's novel *Redwood* in the *North American Review*, April 1825, and republished in Parke Godwin's *Prose Writings* under the revised title. The text is Godwin's.

There is nothing paradoxical in the opinion which maintains that all civilized countries—we had almost said all countries whatever—furnish matter for copies of real life, embodied in works of fiction, which shall be of lasting and general interest. Wherever there are human nature and society there are subjects for the novelist. The passions and affections, virtue and vice, are of no country. Everywhere love comes to touch the hearts of the young, and everywhere scorn and jealousy, the obstacles of fortune and the prudence of the aged, are at hand to disturb the course of love. Everywhere there exists the greed of wealth, the lust of power, and the wish to be admired; courage braving real dangers, and cowardice shrinking from imaginary ones; friendship and hatred, and all the train of motives and impulses which affect the minds and influence the conduct of men. They not only exist everywhere, but they exist, infinitely diversified and compounded, in various degrees of suppression and restraint, or fostered into unnatural growth and activity, modified by political institutions and laws, by national religions and subdivisions of those religions, by different degrees of refinement and civilization, of poverty or of abundance, by arbitrary usages handed down from indefinite antiquity, and even by local situation and climate. Nor is there a single one of all these innumerable modifications of human character and human emotion which is not, in some degree, an object of curiosity and interest. Over all the world is human sagacity laying its plans, and chance and the malice of others are thwarting them, and fortune is raising up one man and throwing down another. In none of the places of human habitation are the accesses barred against joy or grief; the kindness of the good carries gladness into families, and the treachery of the false friend brings sorrow and ruin; in all countries are tears shed over the graves of the excellent, the brave, and the beautiful, and the oppressed breathe freer when the oppressor has gone to his account. Everywhere has Nature her features of grandeur and of beauty, and these features receive a moral expression from the remembrances of the past and the interests of the present. On her face, as on an immense theatre, the passions and pursuits of men are performing the great drama of human existence. At every moment, and in every corner of the world, these mighty and restless agents are perpetually busy, under an infinity of forms and disguises, and the great representation goes on with that majestic continuity and uninterrupted regularity which mark all the courses of nature. Who, then, will undertake to say that the hand of genius may not pencil off a few scenes acted in our vast country, and amid our large population, that shall interest and delight the world?

It is a native writer only that must and can do this. It is he that must show how the infinite diversities of human character are yet further varied by causes that exist in our own country, exhibit our peculiar modes of thinking and action and mark the effect of these upon individual fortunes and happiness. A foreigner is manifestly incompetent to the task; his observation would rest only upon the more general and obvious traits of our national character, a thousand delicate shades of manner would escape his notice, many interesting peculiarities would never come to his knowledge, and many more he would misapprehend. It is only on his native soil that the author of such works can feel himself on safe and firm ground, that he can move confidently and fearlessly, and put forth the whole strength of his powers without risk of failure. His delineations of character and action, if executed with ability, will have a raciness and freshness about them which will attest their fidelity, the secret charm which belongs to truth and nature, and without which even the finest genius cannot invest a system of adscititious and imaginary manners. It is this quality which recommends them powerfully to the sympathy and interest even of those who are unacquainted with the original from which they are drawn, and makes such pictures from such hands so delightful and captivating to the foreigner. By superadding to the novelty of the manners described the interest of a narrative, they create a sort of illusion which places him in the midst of the country where the action of the piece is going on. He beholds the scenery of a distant land, hears its inhabitants conversing about their own concerns in their own dialect, finds himself in the bosom of its families, is made the depositary of their secrets and the observer of their fortunes, and becomes an inmate of their firesides without stirring from his own. Thus it is that American novels are eagerly read in Great Britain, and novels descriptive of English and Scottish manners as eagerly read in America.

It has been objected that the habits of our countrymen are too active and practical; that they are too universally and continually engrossed by the cares and occupations of business to have leisure for that intrigue, those plottings and counter-plottings, which are necessary to give a sufficient degree of action and eventfulness to the novel of real life. It is said that we need for this purpose a class of men whose condition in life places them above the necessity of active exertion, and who are driven to the practice of intrigue because they have nothing else to do. It remains, however, to be proved that any considerable portion of this ingredient is necessary in the composition of a successful novel. To require that it should be made up of nothing better than the manoeuvres of those whose only employment is to glitter at places of public resort, to follow a perpetual round of amusements, and to form plans to outshine, thwart, and vex each other, is confining the writer to a narrow and most barren circle. It is requiring an undue proportion of heartlessness, selfishness, and vice in his pictures of society. It is compelling him to go out of the wholesome atmosphere of those classes, where the passions and affections have their most salutary and natural play, and employ his observations on that where they are the most perverted, sophisticated, and corrupt.

But will it be seriously contended that he can have no other resource than the rivalries and machinations of the idle, the frivolous, and the dissolute, to keep the reader from yawning over his pictures? Will it be urged that no striking and interesting incidents can come to pass without their miserable aid? If our country be not the country of intrigue, it is at least the country of enterprise; and nowhere are the great objects that worthily interest the passions and call forth the exertions of men pursued with more devotion and perseverance. The agency of chance, too, is not confined to the shores of Europe; our countrymen have not attained a sufficient degree of certainty in their calculations to exclude it from ours. It would really seem to us that these two sources, along with that blessed quality of intrigue which even the least favorable view of our society will allow us, are abundantly fertile in interesting occurrences for all the purposes of the novelist. Besides, it should be recollected that it is not in any case the dull diary of ordinary occupations or amusements that forms the groundwork of his plot. On the contrary, it is some event, or at least a series of events, of unusual importance, standing out in strong relief from the rest of the biography of his principal characters, and to which the daily habits of their lives, whatever may be their rank or condition, are only a kind of accompaniment.

But the truth is that the distinctions of rank and the amusements of elegant idleness are but the surface of society, and only so many splendid disguises put upon the reality of things. They are trappings which the writer of real genius, the anatomist of the human heart, strips away when he would exhibit his characters as they are, and engage our interest for them as beings of our own species. He reduces them to the same great level where distinctions of rank are nothing and difference of character everything. It is here that James I and Charles II and Louis IX and Rob Roy and Jeanie Deans and Meg Merrilies are, by the author of the "Waverley Novels," made to meet. The monarch must come down from the dim elevation of his throne; he must lay aside the assumed and conventional manners of his station, and unbend and unbosom himself with his confidants before that illustrious master will condescend to describe him. In the artificial sphere in which the great move, they are only puppets and pageants, but here they are men. A narrative the scene of which is laid at the magnificent levees of princes, in the drawing-rooms of nobles, and the bright assemblies of fashion, may be a very pretty, showy sort of thing, and so may a story of the glittering dances and pranks of fairies. But we soon grow weary of all this and ask for objects of sympathy and regard; for something the recollection of which shall dwell on the heart, and to which it will love to recur; for something, in short, which is natural, the unaffected traits of strength and weakness, of the tender and the comic, all which the pride of rank either removes from observation or obliterates.

If these things have any value, we hesitate not to say that they are to be found abundantly in the characters of our countrymen, formed as they are under the influences of our free institutions, and shooting into a large and vigorous, though sometimes irregular, luxuriance. They exist most abundantly in our more ancient settlements, and amid the more homogeneous races of our large populations, where the causes that produce them have operated longest and with most activity. It is there that the human mind has learned best to enjoy our fortunate and equal institutions, and to profit by them. In the

countries of Europe the laws chain men down to the condition in which they were born. This observation, of course, is not equally true of all those countries, but, when they are brought into comparison with ours, it is in some degree applicable to them all. Men spring up and vegetate and die without thinking of passing from the sphere in which they find themselves any more than the plants they cultivate think of removing from the places where they are rooted. It is the tendency of this rigid and melancholy destiny to contract and stint the intellectual faculties, to prevent the development of character and to make the subjects of it timid, irresolute, and imbecile. With us, on the contrary, where the proudest honors in the State and the highest deference in society are set equally before all our citizens, a wholesome and quickening impulse is communicated to all parts of the social system. All are possessed with a spirit of ambition and a love of adventure, an intense competition calls forth and exalts the passions and faculties of men, their characters become strongly defined, their minds acquire a hardihood and an activity which can be gained by no other discipline, and the community, throughout all its conditions, is full of bustle and change and action.

Whoever will take the pains to pursue this subject a little into its particulars will be surprised at the infinite variety of forms of character which spring up under the institutions of our country. Religion is admitted on all hands to be a mighty agent in moulding the human character; and, accordingly, with the perfect allowance and toleration of all religions, we see among us their innumerable and diverse influences upon the manners and temper of our people. Whatever may be his religious opinions, no one is restrained by fear of consequences from avowing them, but is left to nurse his peculiarities of doctrine into what importance he pleases. The Quaker is absolved from submission to the laws in those particulars which offend his conscience, the Moravian finds no barriers in the way of his work of proselytism and charity, the Roman Catholic is subjected to no penalty for pleasing himself with the magnificent ceremonial of his religion, and the Jew worships unmolested in his synagogue. In many parts of our country we see communities of that strange denomination, the Shakers, distinguished from their neighbors by a garb, a dialect, an architecture, a way of worship, of thinking, and of living, as different as if they were in fact of a different origin, instead of being collected from the families around them. In other parts we see small neighborhoods of the Seventh Day Baptists, retaining their simplicity of manners and quaintness of language delivered down from their fathers. Here we find the austerities of puritanism preserved to this day, there the rights and doctrines of the Church of

England are shown in their effect on the manners of the people, and yet in another part of the country springs up a new and numerous sect, who wash one another's feet and profess to revive the primitive habits of the apostolic times.

It is in our country also that these differences of character, which grow naturally out of geographical situation, are least tampered with and repressed by political regulations. The adventurous and roving natives of our sea-coasts and islands are a different race of men from those who till the interior, and the hardy dwellers of our mountainous districts are not like the inhabitants of the rich plains that skirt our mighty lakes and rivers. The manners of the Northern States are said to be characterized by the keenness and importunity of their climate, and those of the Southern to partake of the softness of theirs. In our cities you will see the polished manners of the European capitals, but pass into the more quiet and unvisited parts of the country, and you will find men whom you might take for the first planters of our colonies. The descendants of the Hollanders have not forgotten the traditions of their fathers, and the legends of Germany are still recited, and the ballads of Scotland still sung, in settlements whose inhabitants derive their origin from those countries. It is hardly possible that the rapid and continual growth and improvement of our country, a circumstance wonderfully exciting to the imagination and altogether unlike anything witnessed in other countries, should not have some influence in forming our national character. At all events, it is a most fertile source of incident. It does for us in a few short years what in Europe is a work of centuries. The hardy and sagacious native of the Eastern States settles himself in the wilderness by the side of the emigrant from the British Isles; the pestilence of the marshes is braved and overcome; the bear and wolf and catamount are chased from their haunts; and then you see cornfields and roads and towns springing up as if by enchantment. In the mean time pleasant Indian villages, situated on the skirts of their hunting-grounds, with their beautiful green plats for dancing and martial exercises, are taken into the bosom of our extending population, while new States are settled and cities founded far beyond them. Thus a great deal of history is crowded into a brief space. Each little hamlet in a few seasons has more events and changes to tell of than a European village can furnish in a course of ages.

But, if the writer of fictitious history does not find all the variety he wishes in the various kinds of our population, descended, in different parts of our country, from ancestors of different nations, and yet preserving innumerable and indubitable tokens of their origin, if the freedom with which every man is suffered to take his own way in all things not affecting the peace and good order of society does not furnish him with a sufficient diversity of characters, employments, and modes of life, he has got other resources. He may bring into his plots men whose characters and manners were formed by the institutions and modes of society in the nations beyond the Atlantic, and he may describe them faithfully as things which he has observed and studied. If he is not satisfied with indigenous virtue, he may take for the model of his characters men of whom the Old World is not worthy, and whom it has cast out from its bosom. If domestic villany be not dark enough for his pictures, here are fugitives from the justice of Europe come to prowl in America. If the coxcombs of our own country are not sufficiently exquisite, affected, and absurd, here are plenty of silken fops from the capitals of foreign kingdoms. If he finds himself in need of a class of men more stupid and degraded than are to be found among the natives of the United States, here are crowds of the wretched peasantry of Great Britain and Germany, flying for refuge from intolerable suffering, in every vessel that comes to our shores. Hither, also, resort numbers of that order of men who, in foreign countries, are called the middling class, the most valuable part of the communities they leave, to enjoy a moderate affluence, where the abuses and exactions of a distempered system of government cannot reach them to degrade them to the condition of the peasantry. Our country is the asylum of the persecuted preachers of new religions and the teachers of political doctrines which Europe will not endure; a sanctuary for dethroned princes and the consorts of slain emperors. When we consider all these innumerable differences of character, native and foreign, this infinite variety of pursuits and objects, this endless diversity and change of fortunes, and behold them gathered and grouped into one vast assemblage in our own country, we shall feel little pride in the sagacity or the skill of that native author who asks for a richer or a wider field of observation.

1825, 1884

EDGAR ALLAN POE [1809–1849]

"The saddest and the strangest figure in American literary history," Killis Campbell called him. "Few writers have lived a life so full of struggle and disappointment, and none have lived and died more completely out of sympathy with their times." Poe was, nevertheless, deeply indebted to the English romantic writers, and his neurotic personality reminds us of various wayward geniuses in European romanticism.

Edgar Poe was the child of itinerant actors. Within less than three years after his birth in Boston, his father deserted the family and his mother died in poverty at Richmond, Virginia. It may well be that the sight of his mother dying of tuberculosis made an impression that eventually transmuted itself into fictional forms (Berenice, Morella, Eleanora, Ligeia). The child Edgar was taken into the home of a Richmond merchant, Allan, whose name Poe later added to his own. He was never formally adopted, and his relations with his foster-parents were never happy. From 1815 to 1820 he studied at schools in England, and during the next five years in Richmond. In February 1826 he entered the University of Virginia. Apparently in an attempt to supplement an insufficient allowance from his foster-father, Poe resorted to gambling and ran up heavy debts. At this time, too, he acquired a reputation as a hard drinker. Allan refused to pay his debts and took him out of the University in December. They quarreled bitterly and decisively, and in 1827 Poe ran away and enlisted, in Boston, as a private in the U.S. Army under the name of Edgar A. Perry. In Boston, too, he brought out his first book, a thin volume called *Tamerlane and Other Poems. By a Bostonian.*

Within two years the young soldier had found time to produce another book of poems, *Al Aaraaf, Tamerlane, and Minor Poems,* and had risen to the rank of sergeant-major. With Allan's help, virtually the last he was to receive from that source, he secured an appointment to West Point, entering in July 1830. Less than eight months later, he deliberately got himself dismissed for neglect of duty. From this time on, Poe was dependent on his pen for a livelihood.

A volume of poems issued in 1831 showed a new sureness: here were "Israfel," "To Helen," "The City in the Sea." The next four years he spent mostly in Baltimore, boarding there with his aunt, Mrs. Clemm, and writing poems and stories. In 1833 the *Baltimore Saturday Visitor* awarded him a prize of $100 for the best short story submitted in its contest. It was one of his few financial successes. In 1835 he removed to Richmond and became editor of the *Southern Literary Messenger,* an able and successful editor noted for his caustic book reviews in a day when criticism was indulgent.

In 1836 he married his cousin Virginia Clemm, a girl of thirteen, with Mrs. Clemm joining the Poe household to give it some measure of stability throughout its various moves and misfortunes. Poe quit the *Messenger,* partly because he felt that his salary was less than he deserved; spent a year in New York; then settled in Philadelphia, and became editor of *Graham's Magazine.* His *Tales of the Grotesque and Arabesque* were published in 1840, and in 1843 "The Gold Bug" won him another $100 prize. But his wife was ill, he dreaded her death, he drank, he could not make a decent living. In 1844 he returned to New York to seek new opportunities.

The next year "The Raven" brought him fame and ten dollars. He was editor of the *Broadway Journal* for two years, till it failed. In 1847 he was working on his *Eureka: an*

Essay on the Material and Spiritual Universe, and his wife was dying. The rest of his story is one of poverty, intoxication, frequent illness, mistaken love affairs, and fine poems. In 1848 he attempted suicide with laudanum. In 1849 he visited Richmond for the last time, and became engaged to a sweetheart of his youth, now a wealthy widow. The remaining events are obscure. In Baltimore he was found unconscious at a ward polling place, and died four days later, at age 40.

Such are the chief external facts of his life. It is still difficult to say what sort of person the man himself was. Unfortunate throughout his life, Poe was also unfortunate in his literary executor, the Reverend Rufus W. Griswold, an editor and compiler who wrote a memoir in which, by a combination of truth, half-truth, and lies, he pictured Poe as an almost diabolic figure. Poe's defenders, in turn, tended to romanticize him as a persecuted genius. The sordid story and the romantic legend were equally unsatisfactory. Partisanship has often dogged even the efforts of careful scholars to give a convincing portrait.

Similarly, critical opinion of Poe's writings has veered between extremes of enthusiasm and distaste. The Irish poet Yeats judged Poe to be "always and for all lands a great lyric poet," and many French authors, such as Maupassant, Baudelaire, and Valéry, extolled him as an original artist of high distinction. In France, indeed, Poe has generally been hailed as the founder of modern poetry, especially Symbolist poetry. In the United States, on the other hand, he has been disparaged by writers in many camps. Emerson once summed him up as "the jingle man," and Henry James pronounced an enthusiasm for Poe's work as "the mark of a decidedly primitive stage of reflection." Still others have dismissed him as vague, disorderly, perverse, or simply monotonous.

Poe's range may be narrow, but within his own dimensions he is a fascinating, important, and at times even a brilliant writer. Edgar Poe was a writer who could not embrace America as Emerson or Whitman could. On the contrary, he rejected a great deal of the contemporary cultural scene: he disliked America's early subservience to British standards, the narrow provincialism that replaced it, and the general anti-poetic quality of American life. Along with the dominant culture, Poe repudiated the scientific spirit and the prevailing commercial values that, according to him, had taken over America. He looked elsewhere for significance and fulfillment. In his writing he explored the possibilities of experience beyond the factual, ordinary world. He sought a transcendent world of inviolate beauty; he explored the chaos and terror of psychological disintegration and madness; and he tried to transform the mundane world with the power of a brilliant critical and analytic mind.

Text: For the poetry reprinted here, the textual source is Floyd Stovall's edition of *The Poems of Edgar Allan Poe* (Charlottesville, 1965); for the criticism, *Selections from the Critical Writings of Edgar Allan Poe*, ed. F. C. Prescott (New York, 1909); for the tales, the Virginia Edition of *The Complete Works of Edgar Allan Poe*, ed. James A. Harrison (New York, 1902).

Further reading: A. H. Quinn, *Edgar Allan Poe: A Critical Biography*, 1941. Edward H. Davidson, *Poe: A Critical Study*, 1959; and *Selected Writings of Edgar Allan Poe*, 1956. Vincent Buranelli, *Edgar Allan Poe*, 1961. Edward Wagenknecht, *Edgar Allan Poe: The Man Behind the Legend*, 1963. *Poe: A Collection of Critical Essays*, ed. Robert Regan, 1967. Richard Wilbur, *Poe: Complete Poems*, 1959.

Dreams

Oh! that my young life were a lasting dream!
My spirit not awak'ning till the beam
Of an Eternity should bring the morrow.
Yes! tho' that long dream were of hopeless sorrow,
'Twere better than the cold reality   5
Of waking life, to him whose heart must be,
And hath been still, upon the lovely earth,
A chaos of deep passion, from his birth.
But should it be—that dream eternally
Continuing—as dreams have been to me   10

In my young boyhood—should it thus be giv'n,
'Twere folly still to hope for higher Heav'n.
For I have revell'd when the sun was bright
I' the summer sky, in dreams of living light
And loveliness,—have left my very heart   15
In climes of mine imagining—apart
From mine own home, with beings that have been
Of mine own thought—what more could I have
      seen?
'Twas once—and only once—and the wild hour   19
From my remembrance shall not pass—some pow'r
Or spell had bound me—'twas the chilly wind
Came o'er me in the night, and left behind
Its image on my spirit—or the moon
Shone on my slumbers in her lofty noon
Too coldly—or the stars—howe'er it was,   25
That dream was as that night-wind—let it pass.

I *have been* happy, tho' but in a dream.
I have been happy—and I love the theme:
Dreams! in their vivid colouring of life
As in that fleeting, shadowy, misty strife   30
Of semblance with reality which brings
To the delirious eye, more lovely things
Of Paradise and Love—and all our own!
Than young Hope in his sunniest hour hath known.

                                                      1827

The Happiest Day, The Happiest Hour

The happiest day—the happiest hour
  My sear'd and blighted heart hath known,
The highest hope of pride and power,
  I feel hath flown.

Of power! said I? yes! such I ween,   5
  But they have vanish'd long, alas!
The visions of my youth have been—
  But let them pass.

And, pride, what have I now with thee?
  Another brow may ev'n inherit   10
The venom thou hast pour'd on me—
  Be still, my spirit!

The happiest day—the happiest hour
  Mine eyes shall see—have ever seen—
The brightest glance of pride and power,   15
  I feel—have been:

But were that hope of pride and power
  Now offer'd, with the pain
Ev'n *then* I felt—that brightest hour
  I would not live again: 20

For on its wing was dark alloy,
  And as it flutter'd—fell
An essence—powerful to destroy
  A soul that knew it well.

                                                      1827

A Dream Within a Dream

Take this kiss upon the brow!
And, in parting from you now,
Thus much let me avow—
You are not wrong, who deem
That my days have been a dream;   5
Yet if Hope has flown away
In a night, or in a day,
In a vision, or in none,
Is it therefore the less *gone?*
All that we see or seem   10
Is but a dream within a dream.

I stand amid the roar
Of a surf-tormented shore,
And I hold within my hand
Grains of the golden sand—   15
How few! yet how they creep
Through my fingers to the deep,
While I weep—while I weep!
O God! can I not grasp
Them with a tighter clasp?   20
O God! can I not save
One from the pitiless wave?
Is *all* that we see or seem
But a dream within a dream?

                                          1827, 1829, 1849

Song from Al Aaraaf

Al Aaraaf, according to Poe, is "a medium between
Heaven and Hell where men suffer no punishment yet do
not attain that tranquil and even happiness which they
suppose to be characteristic of heavenly enjoyment." In
the song given below, Nesace, the presiding spirit of Al
Aaraaf, wakes the attendant spirits, one of whom is Ligeia.
The song illustrates Poe's early cultivation of verse as a
form of music. The sounds of the word combinations, the
bright rhythm of the two-accented lines, the slowing of
the tempo by the alternating rhymes—by such means
plainly does this passage "to melody run."

" 'Neath blue-bell or streamer—
  Or tufted wild spray
That keeps, from the dreamer,
  The moonbeam away—
Bright beings! that ponder,   5
  With half closing eyes,
On the stars which your wonder

Hath drawn from the skies,
Till they glance thro' the shade, and
  Come down to your brow   10
Like—eyes of the maiden
  Who calls on you now—
Arise! from your dreaming
  In violet bowers,
To duty beseeming   15
  These star-litten hours—
And shake from your tresses
  Encumber'd with dew
The breath of those kisses
  That cumber them too—   20
(O! how, without you, Love!
  Could angels be blest?)
Those kisses of true love
  That lull'd ye to rest!
Up!—shake from your wing   25
  Each hindering thing:
The dew of the night—
  It would weigh down your flight;
And true love caresses—
  O! leave them apart!   30
They are light on the tresses,
  But lead on the heart.

"Ligeia! Ligeia!
  My beautiful one!
Whose harshest idea   35
  Will to melody run,
O! is it thy will
  On the breezes to toss?
Or, capriciously still,
  Like the lone Albatross,[1]   40
Incumbent on night
  (As she on the air)
To keep watch with delight
  On the harmony there?

"Ligeia! wherever   45
  Thy image may be,
No magic shall sever
  Thy music from thee.
Thou hast bound many eyes
  In a dreamy sleep—   50
But the strains still arise
  Which *thy* vigilance keep—
The sound of the rain
  Which leaps down to the flower,
And dances again   55
  In the rhythm of the shower—
The murmur that springs
  From the growing of grass
Are the music of things—

But are modell'd, alas!—   60
Away, then, my dearest,
  O! hie thee away
To springs that lie clearest
  Beneath the moon-ray—
To lone lake that smiles,   65
  In its dream of deep rest,
At the many star-isles
  That enjewel its breast—
Where wild flowers, creeping,
  Have mingled their shade,   70
On its margin is sleeping
  Full many a maid—
Some have left the cool glade, and
  Have slept with the bee—[2]
Arouse them, my maiden,   75
  On moorland and lea—
Go! breathe on their slumber,
  All softly in ear,
The musical number
  They slumber'd to hear—   80
For what can awaken
  An angel so soon
Whose sleep hath been taken
  Beneath the cold moon,
As the spell which no slumber   85
  Of witchery may test,
The rhythmical number
  Which lull'd him to rest?"

                          1829

Romance

Poe chose this poem as the preface to a group of his poems published in 1829, and as the introduction to the entire volume of 1831.

Romance, who loves to nod and sing,
With drowsy head and folded wing,
Among the green leaves as they shake
Far down within some shadowy lake,
To me a painted paroquet   5
Hath been—a most familiar bird—
Taught me my alphabet to say—
To lisp my very earliest word
While in the wild wood I did lie,
A child—with a most knowing eye.   10

Of late, eternal Condor years
So shake the very Heaven on high
With tumult as they thunder by,
I have no time for idle cares
Through gazing on the unquiet sky.   15
And when an hour with calmer wings

Song from Al Aaraaf. [1] The albatross is said to sleep on the wing. [Poe's note.]

[2] The wild bee will not sleep in the shade if there be moonlight. [Poe's note.]

Its down upon my spirit flings—
That little time with lyre and rhyme
To while away—forbidden things!
My heart would feel to be a crime   20
Unless it trembled with the strings.

                              1829

Sonnet—To Science

The poem served as an introduction to Poe's long poem
"Al Aaraaf" (1829, 1845), which is, according to Edward
Davidson, "Poe's youthful, inconclusive version of the Fall
of Man."

Science! true daughter of Old Time thou art!
Who alterest all things with thy peering eyes.
Why preyest thou thus upon the poet's heart,
Vulture, whose wings are dull realities?   4
How should he love thee? or how deem thee wise,
Who wouldst not leave him in his wandering
To seek for treasure in the jewelled skies,
Albeit he soared with an undaunted wing?
Hast thou not dragged Diana from her car?
And driven the Hamadryad[1] from the wood   10
To seek a shelter in some happier star?
Hast thou not torn the Naiad from her flood,
The Elfin from the green grass, and from me
The summer dream beneath the tamarind tree?

                              1829

To Helen

"To Helen" may have been inspired by Mrs. Jane Stanard,
of Richmond, mother of a school friend. She died in 1824,
when Poe was fifteen. In letters, he later spoke of her as
"the first purely ideal love of my soul," and as "an angel
to my forlorn and darkened nature." But more important-
ly, Helen represents Poe's ideal of beauty. She appears
here as an idealized, classical, aesthetic figure (not a human or sexual one at all) who evokes the glory and grandeur of the past.

Helen, thy beauty is to me
    Like those Nicéan[1] barks of yore,
That gently, o'er a perfumed sea,
    The weary, way-worn wanderer bore
    To his own native shore.   5

On desperate seas long wont to roam,
    Thy hyacinth hair, thy classic face,
Thy Naiad airs have brought me home
    To the glory that was Greece
And the grandeur that was Rome.   10

To Science. [1] A figure in "Al Aaraaf."
To Helen. [1] Probably without specific reference—suggestive
and evocative, but nothing more.

Lo! in yon brilliant window-niche
    How statue-like I see thee stand,
    The agate lamp within thy hand!
Ah, Psyche, from the regions which
    Are Holy-Land!   15

                              1831, 1845

Israfel

Poe's note: "And the angel Israfel, whose heart-strings are
a lute, and who has the sweetest voice of all God's creatures.—KORAN." Apparently Poe quoted not the Koran
itself but George Sale's Discourse (1734) on the Koran,
inserting from Béranger the phrase about the heart-strings.

In Heaven a spirit doth dwell
    "Whose heart-strings are a lute;"
None sing so wildly well
As the angel Israfel,
And the giddy stars (so legends tell)   5
Ceasing their hymns, attend the spell
    Of his voice, all mute.

Tottering above
    In her highest noon,
    The enamoured moon   10
Blushes with love,
    While, to listen, the red levin
    (With the rapid Pleiads, even,
    Which were seven,)
    Pauses in Heaven.   15

And they say (the starry choir
    And the other listening things)
That Israfeli's fire
Is owing to that lyre
    By which he sits and sings—   20
The trembling living wire
Of those unusual strings.

But the skies that angel trod,
    Where deep thoughts are a duty—
Where Love's a grown-up God—   25
    Where the Houri glances are
Imbued with all the beauty
    Which we worship in a star.

Therefore, thou art not wrong,
    Israfeli, who despisest   30
An unimpassioned song;
To thee the laurels belong,
    Best bard, because the wisest!
Merrily live, and long!

The ecstasies above   35
    With thy burning measures suit—
Thy grief, thy joy, thy hate, thy love,

With the fervour of thy lute—
Well may the stars be mute!

Yes, Heaven is thine; but this   40
  Is a world of sweets and sours;
  Our flowers are merely—flowers,
And the shadow of thy perfect bliss
  Is the sunshine of ours.

If I could dwell   45
Where Israfel
  Hath dwelt, and he where I,
He might not sing so wildly well
  A mortal melody,
While a bolder note than this might swell   50
  From my lyre within the sky.

          1831

The Sleeper

At midnight, in the month of June,
I stand beneath the mystic moon.
An opiate vapor, dewy, dim,
Exhales from out her golden rim,
And, softly dripping, drop by drop,   5
Upon the quiet mountain top,
Steals drowsily and musically
Into the universal valley.
The rosemary nods upon the grave;
The lily lolls upon the wave;   10
Wrapping the fog about its breast,
The ruin moulders into rest;
Looking like Lethe, see! the lake
A conscious slumber seems to take,
And would not, for the world, awake.   15
All Beauty sleeps!—and lo! where lies
Irene, with her Destinies!

Oh, lady bright! can it be right—
This window open to the night?
The wanton airs, from the tree-top,   20
Laughingly through the lattice drop—
The bodiless airs, a wizard rout,
Flit through thy chamber in and out,
And wave the curtain canopy
So fitfully—so fearfully—   25
Above the closed and fringéd lid
'Neath which thy slumb'ring soul lies hid,
That, o'er the floor and down the wall,
Like ghosts the shadows rise and fall!
Oh, lady dear, hast thou no fear?   30
Why and what art thou dreaming here?
Sure thou art come o'er far-off seas,
A wonder to these garden trees!
Strange is thy pallor! strange thy dress!
Strange, above all, thy length of tress,   35
And this all solemn silentness!

The lady sleeps! Oh, may her sleep,
Which is enduring, so be deep!
Heaven have her in its sacred keep!
This chamber changed for one more holy,   40
This bed for one more melancholy,
I pray to God that she may lie
Forever with unopened eye,
While the pale sheeted ghosts go by!

My love, she sleeps! Oh, may her sleep,   45
As it is lasting, so be deep!
Soft may the worms about her creep!
Far in the forest, dim and old,
For her may some tall vault unfold—
Some vault that oft hath flung its black   50
And wingéd panels fluttering back,
Triumphant, o'er the crested palls,
Of her grand family funerals—
Some sepulchre, remote, alone,
Against whose portal she hath thrown,   55
In childhood, many an idle stone—
Some tomb from out whose sounding door
She ne'er shall force an echo more,
Thrilling to think, poor child of sin!
It was the dead who groaned within.   60

          1831, 1845

The City in the Sea

The earlier titles Poe used for this poem suggest its meaning: "The Doomed City," "The City of Sin," "The City in the Sea: a Prophecy." The prototype for the city is obviously Gomorrah. Poe's concern here is not with ideal beauty, but with the creation of a strange, mysterious, unreal world that suggests sin, decay, and death.

Lo! Death has reared himself a throne
In a strange city lying alone
Far down within the dim West,
Where the good and the bad and the worst and the
    best
Have gone to their eternal rest.   5
There shrines and palaces and towers
(Time-eaten towers that tremble not!)
Resemble nothing that is ours.
Around, by lifting winds forgot,
Resignedly beneath the sky   10
The melancholy waters lie.

No rays from the holy heaven come down
On the long night-time of that town;
But light from out the lurid sea
Streams up the turrets silently—   15
Gleams up the pinnacles far and free—
Up domes—up spires—up kingly halls—
Up fanes—up Babylon-like walls—
Up shadowy long-forgotten bowers

Of sculptured ivy and stone flowers—   20
Up many and many a marvelous shrine
Whose wreathèd friezes intertwine
The viol, the violet, and the vine.

Resignedly beneath the sky
The melancholy waters lie.   25
So blend the turrets and shadows there
That all seem pendulous in air,
While from a proud tower in the town
Death looks gigantically down.

There open fanes and gaping graves   30
Yawn level with the luminous waves;
But not the riches there that lie
In each idol's diamond eye—
Not the gaily-jewelled dead
Tempt the waters from their bed;   35
For no ripples curl, alas!
Along that wilderness of glass—
No swellings tell that winds may be
Upon some far-off happier sea—
No heavings hint that winds have been   40
On seas less hideously serene.

But lo, a stir is in the air!
The wave—there is a movement there!
As if the towers had thrust aside,
In slightly sinking, the dull tide—   45
As if their tops had feebly given
A void within the filmy Heaven.
The waves have now a redder glow—
The hours are breathing faint and low—
And when, amid no earthly moans,   50
Down, down that town shall settle hence,
Hell, rising from a thousand thrones,
Shall do it reverence.

                              1831, 1845

Lenore

The poem may refer to the marriage of a woman Poe
loved to an older man or to his grief at the death of his
foster-mother, but essentially it is a good example of Poe's
view that the death of a young and beautiful woman is a
peculiarly poetic theme. By combining melancholy with
beauty, the theme, supposedly, becomes one of the most
effective for realizing ideal beauty.

Ah, broken is the golden bowl![1]—the spirit flown
    forever!
Let the bell toll!—a saintly soul floats on the Stygian
    River:—
And, Guy De Vere, hast *thou* no tear?—weep now
    or never more!
See! on yon drear and rigid bier low lies thy love,
    Lenore!

Lenore. [1] See Ecclesiastes xii.6.

Come! let the burial rite be read—the funeral song
    be sung!—   5
An anthem for the queenliest dead that ever died so
    young—
A dirge for her the doubly dead in that she died so
    young.

"Wretches! ye loved her for her wealth and ye
    hated her for her pride;
And when she fell in feeble health, ye blessed her—
    that she died:
How *shall* the ritual, then, be read?—the requiem
    how be sung   10
By you—by yours, the evil eye—by yours, the slan-
    derous tongue
That did to death the innocence that died, and died
    so young?"

Peccavimus:—[2] yet rave not thus! but let a Sabbath
    song
Go up to God so solemnly the dead may feel no
    wrong!
The sweet Lenore hath gone before, with Hope that
    flew beside,   15
Leaving thee wild for the dear child that should
    have been thy bride—
For her, the fair and debonair, that now so lowly
    lies,
The life upon her yellow hair, but not within her
    eyes—
The life still there upon her hair, the death upon her
    eyes.

"Avaunt!—avaunt! to friends from fiends the indig-
    nant ghost is riven—   20
From Hell unto a high estate within the utmost
    Heaven—
From moan and groan to a golden throne beside the
    King of Heaven:—
Let *no* bell toll, then, lest her soul, amid its hal-
    lowed mirth,
Should catch the note as it doth float up from the
    damned Earth!
And I—to-night my heart is light:—no dirge will I
    upraise,   25
But waft the angel on her flight with a Paean of old
    days!"

                              1831, 1843, 1845

The Valley of Unrest

The poem was originally published as "The Valley of Nis"
(Sin).

Once it smiled a silent dell
Where the people did not dwell;

[2] "We have sinned."

They had gone unto the wars,
Trusting to the mild-eyed stars,
Nightly, from their azure towers,   5
To keep watch above the flowers,
In the midst of which all day
The red sun-light lazily lay.
Now each visitor shall confess
The sad valley's restlessness.   10
Nothing there is motionless—
Nothing save the airs that brood
Over the magic solitude.
Ah, by no wind are stirred those trees
That palpitate like the chill seas   15
Around the misty Hebrides!
Ah, by no wind those clouds are driven
That rustle through the unquiet Heaven
Uneasily, from morn till even,
Over the violets there that lie   20
In myriad types of the human eye—
Over the lilies there that wave
And weep above a nameless grave!
They wave:—from out their fragrant tops
Eternal dews come down in drops.   25
They weep:—from off their delicate stems
Perennial tears descend in gems.

                                        1831, 1845

The Coliseum

Poe chose the Coliseum as a symbol for the "grandeur, gloom, and glory"—the greatness—of a past civilization which still has a present magical, mysterious meaning.

Type of the antique Rome! Rich reliquary
Of lofty contemplation left to Time
By buried centuries of pomp and power!
At length—at length—after so many days
Of weary pilgrimage and burning thirst,   5
(Thirst for the springs of lore that in thee lie,)
I kneel, an altered and an humble man,
Amid thy shadows, and so drink within
My very soul thy grandeur, gloom, and glory!

Vastness! and Age! and Memories of Eld!   10
Silence! and Desolation! and dim Night!
I feel ye now—I feel ye in your strength—
O spells more sure than e'er Judaean king
Taught in the gardens of Gethsemane!
O charms more potent than the rapt Chaldee   15
Ever drew down from out the quiet stars!

Here, where a hero fell, a column falls!
Here, where the mimic eagle glared in gold,
A midnight vigil holds the swarthy bat!   19
Here, where the dames of Rome their gilded hair
Waved to the wind, now wave the reed and thistle!
Here, where on golden throne the monarch lolled,

Glides, spectre-like, unto his marble home,
Lit by the wan light of the horned moon,
The swift and silent lizard of the stones!   25

But stay! these walls—these ivy-clad arcades—
These mouldering plinths—these sad and blackened
        shafts—
These vague entablatures—this crumbling frieze—
These shattered cornices—this wreck—this ruin—
These stones—alas! these gray stones—are they
        all—   30
All of the famed, and the colossal left
By the corrosive Hours to Fate and me?

"Not all"—the Echoes answer me—"not all!
Prophetic sounds and loud, arise forever
From us, and from all Ruin, unto the wise,   35
As melody from Memnon[1] to the Sun.
We rule the hearts of mightiest men—we rule
With a despotic sway all giant minds.
We are not impotent—we pallid stones.
Not all our power is gone—not all our fame—   40
Not all the magic of our high renown—
Not all the wonder that encircles us—
Not all the mysteries that in us lie—
Not all the memories that hang upon
And cling around about us as a garment,   45
Clothing us in a robe of more than glory."

                                        1833, 1845

To One in Paradise

This poem first appeared in Poe's story "The Assignation."

Thou wast that all to me love,
    For which my soul did pine—
A green isle in the sea, love,
    A fountain and a shrine,
All wreathed with fairy fruits and flowers,   5
    And all the flowers were mine.

Ah, dream too bright to last!
    Ah, starry Hope! that didst arise
But to be overcast!
    A voice from out the Future cries,   10
"On! on!"—but o'er the Past
    (Dim gulf!) my spirit hovering lies
Mute, motionless, aghast!

For, alas! alas! with me
    The light of Life is o'er!   15
No more—no more—no more—
    (Such language holds the solemn sea
To the sands upon the shore)

The Coliseum. [1] A huge statue at Thebes that emitted music when touched by the sun.

Shall bloom the thunder-blasted tree,
Or the stricken eagle soar!   20

And all my days are trances,
  And all my nightly dreams
Are where thy grey eye glances,
  And where thy footstep gleams—
In what ethereal dances,   25
  By what eternal streams.

1834, 1845

Dream-Land

Lines 9-20 include particularly effective examples of Poe's imagery that negates or breaks down conventional time and space relationships. Poe approaches the "other world" by negating conventional reality or by placing it in a strange context. "Ultimate" is used in the sense of farthest, as in the Latin *ultima Thule*. Thule was the Greek and Latin name for the northernmost land, but came to be used for any very distant region—even, as here by Poe, a region outside space and time.

By a route obscure and lonely,
Haunted by ill angels only,
Where an Eidolon, named NIGHT,
On a black throne reigns upright,
I have reached these lands but newly   5
From an ultimate dim Thule—
From a wild weird clime that lieth, sublime,
  Out of SPACE—out of TIME.

Bottomless vales and boundless floods,
And chasms, and caves, and Titan woods,   10
With forms that no man can discover
For the tears that drip all over;
Mountains toppling evermore
Into seas without a shore;
Seas that restlessly aspire,   15
Surging, unto skies of fire;
Lakes that endlessly outspread
Their lone waters—lone and dead,—
Their still waters—still and chilly
With the snows of the lolling lily.   20

By the lakes that thus outspread
Their lone waters, lone and dead,—
Their sad waters, sad and chilly
With the snows of the lolling lily,—
By the mountains—near the river   25
Murmuring lowly, murmuring ever,—
By the grey woods,—by the swamp
Where the toad and the newt encamp,—
By the dismal tarns and pools
  Where dwell the Ghouls,—   30
By each spot the most unholy—
In each nook most melancholy,—

There the traveller meets, aghast,
Sheeted Memories of the Past—
Shrouded forms that start and sigh   35
As they pass the wanderer by—
White-robed forms of friends long given,
In agony, to the Earth—and Heaven.

For the heart whose woes are legion
'Tis a peaceful, soothing region—   40
For the spirit that walks in shadow
'Tis—oh 'tis an Eldorado!
But the traveller, travelling through it,
May not—dare not openly view it;
Never its mysteries are exposed   45
To the weak human eye unclosed;
So wills its King, who hath forbid
The uplifting of the fringéd lid;
And thus the sad Soul that here passes
Beholds it but through darkened glasses.   50

By a route obscure and lonely,
Haunted by ill angels only,
Where an Eidolon, named NIGHT,
On a black throne reigns upright,
I have wandered home but newly   55
From this ultimate dim Thule.

1844

The Raven

"The Raven" provides an obvious transition from the poems to the tales, for its themes are typical of the poems, yet its narrative structure and its narrator are characteristic of the tales. The poem traces the psychological disintegration of a sensitive and initially stable mind.

Poe did not discuss such matters in the essay, "The Philosophy of Composition," in which he presented an analysis of his composition of "The Raven." To what extent one may trust the accuracy of Poe's account of the making of the poem is uncertain. The essay, however, provides useful suggestions about the idea and structure of the poem.

Once upon a midnight dreary, while I pondered,
    weak and weary,
Over many a quaint and curious volume of forgotten
    lore—
While I nodded, nearly napping, suddenly there
    came a tapping,
As of some one gently rapping, rapping at my
    chamber door.
" 'Tis some visitor," I muttered, "tapping at my
    chamber door—   5
  Only this and nothing more."

Ah, distinctly I remember it was in the bleak
    December;
And each separate dying ember wrought its ghost
    upon the floor.

Eagerly I wished the morrow;—vainly I had sought
to borrow
From my books surcease of sorrow—sorrow for the
lost Lenore—   10
For the rare and radiant maiden whom the angels
name Lenore—
    Nameless *here* for evermore.

And the silken, sad, uncertain rustling of each
purple curtain
Thrilled me—filled me with fantastic terrors never
felt before;
So that now, to still the beating of my heart, I stood
repeating   15
" 'Tis some visitor entreating entrance at my
chamber door—
Some late visitor entreating entrance at my chamber
door;—
    This it is and nothing more."

Presently my soul grew stronger; hesitating then no
longer,
"Sir," said I, "or Madam, truly your forgiveness I
implore;   20
But the fact is I was napping, and so gently you
came rapping,
And so faintly you came tapping, tapping at my
chamber door,
That I scarce was sure I heard you"—here I opened
wide the door;—
    Darkness there and nothing more.

Deep into that darkness peering, long I stood there
wondering, fearing,   25
Doubting, dreaming dreams no mortal ever dared to
dream before;
But the silence was unbroken, and the stillness gave
no token,
And the only word there spoken was the whispered
word, "Lenore?"
This I whispered, and an echo murmured back the
word, "Lenore!"
    Merely this and nothing more.   30

Back into the chamber turning, all my soul within
me burning,
Soon again I heard a tapping somewhat louder than
before.
"Surely," said I, "surely that is something at my
window lattice;
Let me see, then, what thereat is, and this mystery
explore—
Let my heart be still a moment and this mystery
explore;—   35
    'Tis the wind and nothing more!"

Open here I flung the shutter, when, with many a
flirt and flutter,
In there stepped a stately Raven of the saintly days
of yore;
Not the least obeisance made he; not a minute
stopped or stayed he;
But, with mien of lord or lady, perched above my
chamber door—   40
Perched upon a bust of Pallas[1] just above my
chamber door—
    Perched, and sat, and nothing more.

Then this ebony bird beguiling my sad fancy into
smiling,
By the grave and stern decorum of the countenance
it wore,
"Though thy crest be shorn and shaven, thou," I
said, "art sure no craven,   45
Ghastly grim and ancient Raven wandering from the
Nightly shore—
Tell me what thy lordly name is on the Night's
Plutonian shore!"
    Quoth the Raven "Nevermore."

Much I marvelled this ungainly fowl to hear discourse so plainly,
Though its answer little meaning—little relevancy
bore;   50
For we cannot help agreeing that no living human
being
Ever yet was blessed with seeing bird above his
chamber door—
Bird or beast upon the sculptured bust above his
chamber door,
    With such name as "Nevermore."

But the Raven, sitting lonely on the placid bust,
spoke only   55
That one word, as if his soul in that one word he did
outpour.
Nothing farther then he uttered—not a feather then
he fluttered—
Till I scarcely more than muttered "Other friends
have flown before—
On the morrow *he* will leave me, as my hopes have
flown before."
    Then the bird said "Nevermore."   60

Startled at the stillness broken by reply so aptly
spoken,
"Doubtless," said I, "what it utters is its only stock
and store
Caught from some unhappy master whom unmerci-
ful Disaster

The Raven. [1] Pallas Athene, goddess of wisdom.

Followed fast and followed faster till his songs one
    burden bore—
Till the dirges of his Hope that melancholy burden
    bore   65
  Of 'Never—nevermore.' "

But the Raven still beguiling all my fancy into
    smiling,
Straight I wheeled a cushioned seat in front of bird,
    and bust and door;
Then, upon the velvet sinking, I betook myself to
    linking
Fancy unto fancy, thinking what this ominous bird
    of yore—   70
What this grim, ungainly, ghastly, gaunt, and omi-
    nous bird of yore
  Meant in croaking "Nevermore."

This I sat engaged in guessing, but no syllable
    expressing
To the fowl whose fiery eyes now burned into my
    bosom's core;
This and more I sat divining, with my head at ease
    reclining   75
On the cushion's velvet lining that the lamp-light
    gloated o'er,
But whose velvet-violet lining with the lamp-light
    gloating o'er,
  She shall press, ah, nevermore!

Then, methought, the air grew denser, perfumed
    from an unseen censer
Swung by Seraphim whose foot-falls tinkled on the
    tufted floor.   80
"Wretch," I cried, "thy God hath lent thee—by
    these angels he hath sent thee
Respite—respite and nepenthe from thy memories
    of Lenore;
Quaff, oh quaff this kind nepenthe and forget this
    lost Lenore!"
  Quoth the Raven "Nevermore."

"Prophet!" said I, "thing of evil!—prophet still, if
    bird or devil!—   85
Whether Tempter sent, or whether tempest tossed
    thee here ashore,
Desolate yet all undaunted, on this desert land en-
    chanted—
On this home by Horror haunted—tell me truly, I
    implore—
Is there—*is* there balm in Gilead?[2]—tell me—tell
    me, I implore!"
  Quoth the Raven "Nevermore."   90

"Prophet!" said I, "thing of evil!—prophet still, if
    bird or devil!
By that Heaven that bends above us—by that God
    we both adore—

[2] See Jeremiah viii.22; the reference is to a medicinal herb.

Tell this soul with sorrow laden if, within the distant
    Aidenn,[3]
It shall clasp a sainted maiden whom the angels
    name Lenore—
Clasp a rare and radiant maiden whom the angels
    name Lenore."   95
  Quoth the Raven "Nevermore."

"Be that word our sign of parting, bird or fiend!" I
    shrieked, upstarting—
"Get thee back into the tempest and the Night's
    Plutonian shore!
Leave no black plume as a token of that lie thy soul
    hath spoken!
Leave my loneliness unbroken!—quit the bust above
    my door!   100
Take thy beak from out my heart, and take thy form
    from off my door!"
  Quoth the Raven "Nevermore."

And the Raven, never flitting, still is sitting, *still* is
    sitting
On the pallid bust of Pallas just above my chamber
    door;
And his eyes have all the seeming of a demon's that
    is dreaming,   105
And the lamp-light o'er him streaming throws his
    shadow on the floor;
And my soul from out that shadow that lies floating
    on the floor
  Shall be lifted—nevermore!

                                                           1845

Ulalume

The poem, apparently, describes a region similar to the
one through which Poe often walked on his way to his
wife's grave in Mamaroneck. Weir refers to Robert Weir,
a well-known nineteenth-century "misty" landscape painter. Auber refers to a French composer, Daniel François
Auber, who wrote *La Lac des Fées*. Yaanek refers to a
then recently discovered volcano in Antarctica, Mt. Erebus.
The poem dramatizes the speaker's recognition that
he cannot accept human, sexual love and thus reject the
ideal love his dead wife represents.

The skies they were ashen and sober;
  The leaves they were crispèd and sere—
  The leaves they were withering and sere;
It was night in the lonesome October
  Of my most immemorial year: 5
It was hard by the dim lake of Auber,
  In the misty mid region of Weir:—
It was down by the dank tarn of Auber,
  In the ghoul-haunted woodland of Weir.

Here once, through an alley Titanic,   10
  Of cypress, I roamed with my Soul—

[3] The Moslem paradise.

Of cypress, with Psyche, my Soul.
These were days when my heart was volcanic
  As the scoriac rivers that roll—
  As the lavas that restlessly roll   15
Their sulphurous currents down Yaanek,
  In the ultimate climes of the pole—
That groan as they roll down Mount Yaanek,
  In the realms of the Boreal Pole.

Our talk had been serious and sober,   20
  But our thoughts they were palsied and sere—
  Our memories were treacherous and sere;
For we knew not the month was October,
  And we marked not the night of the year—
  (Ah, night of all nights in the year!)   25
We noted not the dim lake of Auber,
  (Though once we have journeyed down here)
Remembered not the dank tarn of Auber,
  Nor the ghoul-haunted woodland of Weir.

And now, as the night was senescent,   30
  And star-dials pointed to morn—
  As the star-dials hinted of morn—
At the end of our path a liquescent
  And nebulous lustre was born
Out of which a miraculous crescent   35
  Arose with a duplicate horn—
Astarte's bediamonded crescent,
  Distinct with its duplicate horn.

And I said—"She is warmer than Dian;
  She rolls through an ether of sighs—   40
  She revels in a region of sighs.
She has seen that the tears are not dry on
  These cheeks where the worm never dies,
And has come past the stars of the Lion,
  To point us the path to the skies—   45
  To the Lethean peace of the skies—
Come up, in despite of the Lion,
  To shine on us with her bright eyes—
Come up, through the lair of the Lion,
  With Love in her luminous eyes."   50

But Psyche, uplifting her finger,
  Said—"Sadly this star I mistrust—
  Her pallor I strangely mistrust—
Ah, hasten!—ah, let us not linger!
  Ah, fly!—let us fly!—for we must."   55
In terror she spoke; letting sink her
  Wings till they trailed in the dust—
In agony sobbed; letting sink her
  Plumes till they trailed in the dust—
  Till they sorrowfully trailed in the dust.   60

I replied—"This is nothing but dreaming.
  Let us on, by this tremulous light!
  Let us bathe in this crystalline light!
Its Sibyllic splendor is beaming

With Hope and in Beauty to-night—   65
See!—it flickers up the sky through the night!
Ah, we safely may trust to its gleaming
  And be sure it will lead us aright—
We safely may trust to a gleaming
  That cannot but guide us aright   70
  Since it flickers up to Heaven through the night."

Thus I pacified Psyche and kissed her,
  And tempted her out of her gloom—
  And conquered her scruples and gloom;
And we passed to the end of the vista—   75
  But were stopped by the door of a tomb—
  By the door of a legended tomb:—
And I said—"What is written, sweet sister,
  On the door of this legended tomb?"
She replied—"Ulalume—Ulalume!—   80
  'Tis the vault of thy lost Ulalume!"

Then my heart it grew ashen and sober
  As the leaves that were crispèd and sere—
  As the leaves that were withering and sere—
And I cried—"It was surely October,   85
  On *this* very night of last year,
  That I journeyed—I journeyed down here!—
  That I brought a dread burden down here—
  On this night of all nights in the year,
  Ah, what demon has tempted me here?   90
Well I know, now, this dim lake of Auber—
  This misty mid region of Weir:—
Well I know, now, this dank tarn of Auber—
  This ghoul-haunted woodland of Weir."

Said we, then—the two, then—"Ah, can it   95
  Have been that the woodlandish ghouls—
  The pitiful, the merciful ghouls,
To bar up our way and to ban it
  From the secret that lies in these wolds—   99
  From the thing that lies hidden in these wolds—
Have drawn up the spectre of a planet
  From the limbo of lunary souls—
This sinfully scintillant planet
  From the Hell of the planetary souls?"

1847

For Annie

For Mrs. Annie Richmond, of Lowell, Massachusetts, a
friend of Poe's.

Thank Heaven! the crisis—
  The danger is past,
And the lingering illness
  Is over at last—
And the fever called "Living"   5
  Is conquered at last.

Sadly, I know
   I am shorn of my strength,
And no muscle I move
   As I lie at full length—   10
But no matter!—I feel
   I am better at length.

And I rest so composedly
   Now, in my bed,
That any beholder   15
   Might fancy me dead—
Might start at beholding me,
   Thinking me dead.

The moaning and groaning,
   The sighing and sobbing,   20
Are quieted now,
   With that horrible throbbing
At heart:—ah, that horrible,
   Horrible throbbing!

The sickness—the nausea—   25
   The pitiless pain—
Have ceased, with the fever
   That maddened my brain—
With the fever called "Living"
   That burned in my brain.   30

And oh! of all tortures
   That torture the worst
Has abated—the terrible
   Torture of thirst
For the napthaline river   35
   Of Passion accurst:—
I have drank of a water
   That quenches all thirst:—

Of a water that flows,
   With a lullaby sound,   40
From a spring but a very few
   Feet under ground—
From a cavern not very far
   Down under ground.

And ah! let it never   45
   Be foolishly said
That my room it is gloomy
   And narrow my bed;
For a man never slept
   In a different bed—   50
And, to *sleep,* you must slumber
   In just such a bed.

My tantalized spirit
   Here blandly reposes,
Forgetting, or never   55
   Regretting, its roses—

Its old agitations
   Of myrtles and roses:

For now, while so quietly
   Lying, it fancies   60
A holier odor
   About it, of pansies—
A rosemary odor,
   Commingled with pansies—
With rue and the beautiful   65
   Puritan pansies.

And so it lies happily,
   Bathing in many
A dream of the truth
   And the beauty of Annie—   70
Drowned in a bath
   Of the tresses of Annie.

She tenderly kissed me,
   She fondly caressed,
And then I fell gently   75
   To sleep on her breast—
Deeply to sleep
   From the heaven of her breast.

When the light was extinguished,
   She covered me warm,   80
And she prayed to the angels
   To keep me from harm—
To the queen of the angels
   To shield me from harm.

And I lie so composedly,   85
   Now, in my bed,
(Knowing her love)
   That you fancy me dead—
And I rest so contentedly,
   Now, in my bed,   90
(With her love at my breast)
   That you fancy me dead—
That you shudder to look at me,
   Thinking me dead:—

But my heart it is brighter   95
   Than all of the many
Stars in the sky,
   For it sparkles with Annie—
It glows with the light
   Of the love of my Annie—   100
With the thought of the light
   Of the eyes of my Annie.

1849

Annabel Lee

Various suggestions have been made about the "real" woman. Davidson suggests that Mrs. Sarah Royster Shelton (Poe's youthful love) is the intended person. She and Poe were separated for a long time, in part because of interfering relatives. Poe was engaged to her during the last months of his life.

It was many and many a year ago,
  In a kingdom by the sea,
That a maiden there lived whom you may know
  By the name of Annabel Lee;
And this maiden she lived with no other thought   5
  Than to love and be loved by me.

She was a child and *I* was a child,
  In this kingdom by the sea,
But we loved with a love that was more than love—
  I and my Annabel Lee—   10
With a love that the wingèd seraphs of Heaven
  Coveted her and me.

And this was the reason that, long ago,
  In this kingdom by the sea,
A wind blew out of a cloud by night   15
  Chilling my Annabel Lee;
So that her high-born kinsmen came
  And bore her away from me,
To shut her up in a sepulchre
  In this kingdom by the sea.   20

The angels, not half so happy in Heaven,
  Went envying her and me:—
Yes! that was the reason (as all men know,
  In this kingdom by the sea)
That the wind came out of the cloud chilling   25
  And killing my Annabel Lee.

But our love it was stronger by far than the love
  Of those who were older than we—
  Of many far wiser than we—
And neither the angels in Heaven above   30
  Nor the demons down under the sea
Can ever dissever my soul from the soul
  Of the beautiful Annabel Lee:—

For the moon never beams without bringing me
    dreams
  Of the beautiful Annabel Lee;   35
And the stars never rise but I feel the bright eyes
  Of the beautiful Annabel Lee:
And so all the night-tide, I lie down by the side
Of my darling, my darling, my life and my bride
  In her sepulchre there by the sea—   40
  In her tomb by the side of the sea.
                                                    1849

Eldorado

The poem doubtless comments on the California gold rush, but its theme is quite typical of Poe's poetry: the contrast between an ideal, unreachable world and the fallen one in which men live.

Gaily bedight,
  A gallant knight,
In sunshine and in shadow,
  Had journeyed long,
  Singing a song,   5
In search of Eldorado.

But he grew old—
  This knight so bold—
And o'er his heart a shadow
  Fell as he found   10
  No spot of ground
That looked like Eldorado.

And, as his strength
  Failed him at length,
He met a pilgrim shadow—   15
  "Shadow," said he,
  "Where can it be—
This land of Eldorado?"

"Over the Mountains
  Of the Moon,   20
Down the Valley of the Shadow,
  Ride, boldly ride,"
  The shade replied,—
"If you seek for Eldorado!"
1849

The Poetic Principle

Originally a lecture written in 1848, "The Poetic Principle" was published in 1850, after Poe's death.

To Poe, the end of art is pleasure, not truth. So that pleasure may be intense, the work of art, whether poetry or prose, must have unity and brevity. In poetry, pleasure should be aroused by the creation of beauty—not a mere duplication of the concrete beauties of the world, but a suggestion of a higher order of beauty which may be called supernal. Since music brings us close to the supernal, the musical elements of verse—meter, rhythm, and rhyme—are essential.

In speaking of the Poetic Principle, I have no design to be either thorough or profound. While discussing, very much at random, the essentiality of what we call Poetry, my principal purpose will be to cite for consideration, some few of those minor English or American poems which best suit my own taste, or which, upon my own fancy, have left the most definite impression. By "minor poems" I mean, of course, poems of little length. And here, in the beginning, permit me to say a few words in regard to a somewhat peculiar principle, which, whether rightfully or wrongfully, has always had its influence in my own critical estimate of the poem. I hold that a long poem does not exist. I maintain that the

LENGTH

phrase, "a long poem," is simply a flat contradiction in terms.

ELEVATING EXCITEMENT

I need scarcely observe that a poem deserves its title only inasmuch as it excites, by elevating the soul. The value of the poem is in the ratio of this elevating excitement. But all excitements are, through a psychal necessity, transient. That degree of excitement which would entitle a poem to be so called at all, cannot be sustained throughout a composition of any great length. After the lapse of half an hour, at the very utmost, it flags—fails—a revulsion ensues—and then the poem is, in effect, and in fact, no longer such.

There are, no doubt, many who have found difficulty in reconciling the critical dictum that the "Paradise Lost" is to be devoutly admired throughout, with the absolute impossibility of maintaining for it, during perusal, the amount of enthusiasm which that critical dictum would demand. This great work, in fact, is to be regarded as poetical, only when, losing sight of that vital requisite in all works of Art, Unity, we view it merely as a series of minor poems. If, to preserve its Unity—its totality of effect or impression—we read it (as would be necessary) at a single sitting, the result is but a constant alternation of excitement and depression. After a passage of what we feel to be true poetry, there follows, inevitably, a passage of platitude which no critical pre-judgment can force us to admire; but if, upon completing the work, we read it again, omitting the first book—that is to say, commencing with the second—we shall be surprised at now finding that admirable which we before condemned—that damnable which we had previously so much admired. It follows from all this that the ultimate, aggregate, or absolute effect of even the best epic under the sun, is a nullity:—and this is precisely the fact.

In regard to the Iliad, we have, if not positive proof, at least very good reason for believing it intended as a series of lyrics; but, granting the epic intention, I can say only that the work is based in an imperfect sense of art. The modern epic is, of the suppositious ancient model, but an inconsiderate and blindfold imitation. But the day of these artistic anomalies is over. If, at any time, any very long poem *were* popular in reality, which I doubt, it is at least clear that no very long poem will ever be popular again.

That the extent of a poetical work is, *ceteris paribus*,[1] the measure of its merit, seems undoubtedly, when we thus state it, a proposition sufficiently absurd—yet we are indebted for it to the Quarterly Reviews. Surely there can be nothing in mere *size*, abstractly considered—there can be nothing in mere *bulk*, so far as a volume is concerned, which has so

[1] Other things being equal.

continuously elicited admiration from these saturnine pamphlets! A mountain, to be sure, by the mere sentiment of physical magnitude which it conveys, *does* impress us with a sense of the sublime—but no man is impressed after *this* fashion by the material grandeur of even "The Columbiad."[2] Even the Quarterlies have not instructed us to be so impressed by it. *As yet*, they have not *insisted* on our estimating Lamartine[3] by the cubic foot, or Pollok[4] by the pound—but what else are we to *infer* from their continual prating about "sustained effort"? If, by "sustained effort," any little gentleman has accomplished an epic, let us frankly commend him for the effort—if this indeed be a thing commendable—but let us forbear praising the epic on the effort's account. It is to be hoped that common sense, in the time to come, will prefer deciding upon a work of art, rather by the impression it makes, by the effect it produces, than by the time it took to impress the effect, or by the amount of "sustained effort" which has been found necessary in effecting the impression. The fact is, that perseverance is one thing, and genius quite another; nor can all the Quarterlies in Christendom confound them. By and by, this proposition, with many which I have just been urging, will be received as self-evident. In the mean time, by being generally condemned as falsities, they will not be essentially damaged as truths.

On the other hand, it is clear that a poem may be improperly brief. Undue brevity degenerates into mere epigrammatism. A *very* short poem, while now and then producing a brilliant or vivid, never produces a profound or enduring effect. There must be the steady pressing down of the stamp upon the wax. De Béranger[5] has wrought innumerable things, pungent and spirit-stirring; but, in general, they have been too imponderous to stamp themselves deeply into the public attention; and thus, as so many feathers of fancy, have been blown aloft only to be whistled down the wind.

A remarkable instance of the effect of undue brevity in depressing a poem—in keeping it out of the popular view—is afforded by the following exquisite little Serenade:

> I arise from dreams of thee
> In the first sweet sleep of night,
> When the winds are breathing low,
> And the stars are shining bright;
> I arise from dreams of thee,
> And a spirit in my feet
> Has led me—who knows how?—
> To thy chamber-window, sweet!

[2] Once called America's tin-plated epic; written by Joel Barlow, published in 1807.
[3] Alphonse de Lamartine (1790–1869), French poet.
[4] Robert Pollok (1798–1827), Scottish poet.
[5] Pierre Jean de Béranger (1780–1857), French lyric poet.

The wandering airs, they faint
    On the dark, the silent stream—
The Champak odors fail
    Like sweet thoughts in a dream;
The nightingale's complaint,
    It dies upon her heart,
As I must die on thine,
    O, beloved as thou art!

O, lift me from the grass!
    I die, I faint, I fail!
Let thy love in kisses rain
    On my lips and eyelids pale.
My cheek is cold and white, alas!
    My heart beats loud and fast:
Oh! press it close to thine again,
    Where it will break at last!

Very few, perhaps, are familiar with these lines—yet no less a poet than Shelley is their author. Their warm, yet delicate and ethereal imagination will be appreciated by all—but by none so thoroughly as by him who has himself arisen from sweet dreams of one beloved, to bathe in the aromatic air of a southern midsummer night.

One of the finest poems by Willis[6]—the very best, in my opinion, which he has ever written—has, no doubt, through this same defect of undue brevity, been kept back from its proper position, not less in the critical than in the popular view.

The shadows lay along Broadway,
    'Twas near the twilight tide—
And slowly there a lady fair
    Was walking in her pride.
Alone walked she; but, viewlessly,
    Walked spirits at her side.

Peace charmed the street beneath her feet,
    And Honour charmed the air;
And all astir looked kind on her,
    And called her good as fair—
For all God ever gave to her
    She kept with chary care.

She kept with care her beauties rare
    From lovers warm and true—
For her heart was cold to all but gold,
    And the rich came not to woo—
But honoured well are charms to sell
    If priests the selling do.

Now walking there was one more fair—
    A slight girl, lily pale;
And she had unseen company
    To make the spirit quail—
'Twixt Want and Scorn she walked forlorn,
    And nothing could avail.

No mercy now can clear her brow
    For this world's peace to pray;

For, as love's wild prayer dissolved in air,
    Her woman's heart gave way!—
But the sin forgiven by Christ in heaven
    By man is cursed alway!

In this composition we find it difficult to recognize the Willis who has written so many mere "verses of society." The lines are not only richly ideal, but full of energy while they breathe an earnestness—an evident sincerity of sentiment—for which we look in vain throughout all the other works of this author.

While the epic mania—while the idea that, to merit in poetry, prolixity is indispensable—has, for some years past, been gradually dying out of the public mind, by mere dint of its own absurdity—we find it succeeded by a heresy too palpably false to be long tolerated, but one which, in the brief period it has already endured, may be said to have accomplished more in the corruption of our Poetical Literature than all its other enemies combined. I allude to the heresy of *The Didactic*. It has been assumed, tacitly and avowedly, directly and indirectly, that the ultimate object of all Poetry is Truth. Every poem, it is said, should inculcate a moral; and by this moral is the poetical merit of the work to be adjudged. We Americans especially have patronized this happy idea; and we Bostonians, very especially, have developed it in full. We have taken it into our heads that to write a poem simply for the poem's sake, and to acknowledge such to have been our design, would be to confess ourselves radically wanting in the true Poetic dignity and force:—but the simple fact is, that, would we but permit ourselves to look into our own souls, we should immediately there discover that under the sun there neither exists nor *can* exist any work more thoroughly dignified—more supremely noble than this very poem—this poem *per se*—this poem which is a poem and nothing more—this poem written solely for the poem's sake.

With as deep a reverence for the True as ever inspired the bosom of man, I would, nevertheless, limit, in some measure, its modes of inculcation. I would limit to enforce them. I would not enfeeble them by dissipation. The demands of Truth are severe. She has no sympathy with the myrtles. All *that* which is so indispensable in Song is precisely all *that* with which *she* has nothing whatever to do. It is but making her a flaunting paradox, to wreathe her in gems and flowers. In enforcing a truth, we need severity rather than efflorescence of language. We must be simple, precise, terse. We must be cool, calm, unimpassioned. In a word, we must be in that mood which, as nearly as possible, is the exact converse of the poetical. *He* must be blind, indeed, who does not perceive the radical and chasmal differences between the truthful and the poetical modes

[6] N. P. Willis (1806–67), popular poet and contemporary of Poe's.

TRUTH-TELLING AS ANTI-POETICAL

of inculcation. He must be theory-mad beyond redemption who, in spite of these differences, shall still persist in attempting to reconcile the obstinate oils and waters of Poetry and Truth.

Dividing the world of mind into its three most immediately obvious distinctions, we have the Pure Intellect, Taste, and the Moral Sense. I place Taste in the middle, because it is just this position which, in the mind, it occupies. It holds intimate relations with either extreme; but from the Moral Sense is separated by so faint a difference that Aristotle has not hesitated to place some of its operations among the virtues themselves. Nevertheless, we find the *offices* of the trio marked with a sufficient distinction. Just as the Intellect concerns itself with Truth, so Taste informs us of the Beautiful while the Moral Sense is regardful of Duty. Of this latter, while Conscience teaches the obligation, and Reason the expediency, Taste contents herself with displaying the charms:—waging war upon Vice solely on the ground of her deformity—her disproportion—her animosity to the fitting, to the appropriate, to the harmonious—in a word, to Beauty.

An immortal instinct, deep within the spirit of man, is thus, plainly, a sense of the Beautiful. This it is which administers to his delight in the manifold forms, and sounds, and odors, and sentiments amid which he exists. And just as the lily is repeated in the lake, or the eyes of Amaryllis in the mirror, so is the mere oral or written repetition of these forms, and sounds, and colors, and odors, and sentiments, a duplicate source of delight. But this mere repetition is not poetry. He who shall simply sing, with however glowing enthusiasm, or with however vivid a truth of description, of the sights, and sounds, and odors, and colors, and sentiments, which greet *him* in the common with all mankind—he, I say, has yet failed to prove his divine title. There is still a something in the distance which he has been unable to attain. We have still a thirst unquenchable, to allay which he has not shown us the crystal springs. This thirst belongs to the immortality of Man. It is at once a consequence and an indication of his perennial existence. It is the desire of the moth for the star. It is no mere appreciation of the Beauty before us—but a wild effort to reach the Beauty above. Inspired by an ecstatic prescience of the glories beyond the grave, we struggle, by multiform combinations among the things and thoughts of Time, to attain a portion of that Loveliness whose very elements, perhaps, appertain to eternity alone. And thus when by Poetry—or when by Music, the most entrancing of the Poetic moods—we find ourselves melted into tears—we weep then—not as the Abbaté Gravina[7] supposes—through excess of pleasure, but through a certain, petulant, impatient sorrow at

[7]Giovanni Gravina (1664-1718), Italian critic.

our inability to grasp *now*, wholly, here on earth, at once and forever, those divine and rapturous joys, of which *through* the poem, or *through* the music, we attain to but brief and indeterminate glimpses.

The struggle to apprehend the supernal Loveliness—this struggle, on the part of souls fittingly constituted—has given to the world all *that* which it (the world) has ever been enabled at once to understand and to *feel* as poetic.

The Poetic Sentiment, of course, may develop itself in various modes—in Painting, in Sculpture, in Architecture, in the Dance—very especially in Music—and very peculiarly, and with a wide field, in the composition of the Landscape Garden. Our present theme, however, has regard only to its manifestation in words. And here let me speak briefly on the topic of rhythm. Contenting myself with the certainty that Music, in its various modes of meter, rhythm, and rhyme, is of so vast a moment in Poetry as never to be wisely rejected—is so vitally important an adjunct, that he is simply silly who declines its assistance, I will not now pause to maintain its absolute essentiality. It is in Music, perhaps, that the soul most nearly attains the great end for which, when inspired by the Poetic Sentiment, it struggles—the creation of supernal Beauty. It *may* be, indeed, that here this sublime end is, now and then, attained *in fact*. We are often made to feel, with a shivering delight, that from an earthly harp are stricken notes which *cannot* have been unfamiliar to the angels. And thus there can be little doubt that in the union of Poetry with Music in its popular sense, we shall find the widest field for the Poetic development. The old Bards and Minnesingers had advantages which we do not possess—and Thomas Moore, singing his own songs, was, in the most legitimate manner, perfecting them as poems.

To recapitulate, then:—I would define, in brief, the Poetry of words as *The Rhythmical Creation of Beauty*. Its sole arbiter is Taste. With the Intellect or with the Conscience, it has only collateral relations. Unless incidentally, it has no concern whatever either with Duty or with Truth.

A few words, however, in explanation. *That* pleasure which is at once the most pure, the most elevating, and the most intense, is derived, I maintain, from the contemplation of the Beautiful. In the contemplation of Beauty we alone find it possible to attain that pleasurable elevation, or excitement, *of the soul*, which we recognize as the Poetic Sentiment, and which is so easily distinguished from Truth, which is the satisfaction of the Reason, or from Passion, which is the excitement of the heart. I make Beauty, therefore—using the word as inclusive of the sublime—I make Beauty the province of the poem, simply because it is an obvious rule of Art that effects should be made to spring as directly as possible from their causes:—no one as yet having been weak enough to deny that the peculiar elevation in question is at least *most readily* attainable in the poem. It by no means follows, however, that the incitements of Passion, or the precepts of Duty, or even the lessons of Truth, may not be introduced into a poem, and with advantage; for they may subserve, incidentally, in various ways, the general purposes of the work:—but the true artist will always contrive to tone them down in proper subjection to that *Beauty* which is the atmosphere and the real essence of the poem.[8]

From Alfred Tennyson—although in perfect sincerity I regard him as the noblest poet that ever lived—I have left myself time to cite only a very brief specimen. I call him, and *think* him the noblest of poets—*not* because the impressions he produces are, at *all* times, the most profound—*not* because the poetical excitement which he induces is, at *all* times, the most intense—but because it *is*, at all times, the most ethereal—in other words, the most elevating and most pure. No poet is so little of the earth, earthy. What I am about to read is from his last long poem, "The Princess:"

> Tears, idle tears, I know not what they mean,
> Tears from the depth of some divine despair
> Rise in the heart, and gather to the eyes,
> In looking on the happy Autumn fields,
> And thinking of the days that are no more.

> Fresh as the first beam glittering on a sail
> That brings our friends up from the underworld,
> Sad as the last which reddens over one
> That sinks with all we love below the verge;
> So sad, so fresh, the days that are no more.

> Ah, sad and strange as in dark summer dawns
> The earliest pipe of half-awaken'd birds
> To dying ears, when unto dying eyes
> The casement slowly grows a glimmering square;
> So sad, so strange, the days that are no more.

> Dear as remember'd kisses after death,
> And sweet as those by hopeless fancy feign'd
> On lips that are for others; deep as love,
> Deep as first love, and wild with all regret;
> O Death in Life, the days that are no more.

Thus, although in a very cursory and imperfect manner, I have endeavored to convey to you my conception of the Poetic Principle. It has been my purpose to suggest that, while this Principle itself is, strictly and simply, the Human Aspiration for Supernal Beauty, the manifestation of the Principle is always found in *an elevating excitement of the Soul—* quite independent of that passion which is the intoxi-

[8] In a passage here omitted, Poe presented, and briefly commented on, poems by Longfellow, Bryant, Pinkney, Moore, Hood, Byron.

cation of the Heart—or of that Truth which is the satisfaction of the Reason. For in regard to Passion, alas! its tendency is to degrade, rather than to elevate the Soul. Love, on the contrary—Love—the true, the divine Eros—the Uranian, as distinguished from the Dionaean Venus—is unquestionably the purest and truest of all poetical themes. And in regard to Truth—if, to be sure, through the attainment of a truth, we are led to perceive a harmony where none was apparent before, we experience at once the true poetical effect—but this effect is referable to the harmony alone, and not in the least degree to the truth which merely served to render the harmony manifest.

We shall reach, however, more immediately a distinct conception of what the true Poetry is, by mere reference to a few of the simple elements which induce in the Poet himself the true poetical effect. He recognizes the ambrosia which nourishes his soul, in the bright orbs that shine in Heaven—in the volutes of the flower—in the clustering of low shrubberies—in the waving of the grain-fields—in the slanting of tall, Eastern trees—in the blue distance of mountains—in the grouping of clouds—in the twinkling of half-hidden brooks—in the gleaming of silver rivers—in the repose of sequestered lakes—in the star-mirroring depths of lonely wells. He perceives it in the songs of birds—in the harp of Aeolus—in the sighing of the night-wind—in the repining voice of the forest—in the surf that complains to the shore—in the fresh breath of the woods—in the scent of the violet—in the voluptuous perfume of the hyacinth—in the suggestive odor that comes to him, at eventide, from far-distant, undiscovered islands, over dim oceans, illimitable and unexplored. He owns it in all noble thoughts—in all unworldly motives—in all holy impulses—in all chivalrous, generous and self-sacrificing deeds. He feels it in the beauty of woman—in the grace of her step—in the lustre of her eye—in the melody of her voice—in her soft laughter—in her sigh—in the harmony of the rustling of her robes. He deeply feels it in her winning endearments—in her burning enthusiasms—in her gentle charities—in her meek and devotional endurances—but above all—ah, far above all—he kneels to it—he worships it in the faith, in the purity, in the strength, in the altogether divine majesty—of her *love*.

Let me conclude—by the recitation of yet another brief poem—one very different in character from any that I have before quoted. It is by Motherwell, and is called "The Song of the Cavalier." With our modern and altogether rational ideas of the absurdity and impiety of warfare, we are not precisely in that frame of mind best adapted to sympathize with the sentiments, and thus to appreciate the real excellence of the poem. To do this fully, we must identify ourselves, in fancy, with the soul of the old cavalier.

> Then mounte! then mounte, brave gallants, all,
>   And don your helmes amaine:
> Deathe's couriers, Fame and Honour, call
>   Us to the field againe.
> No shrewish teares shall fill our eye
>   When the sword-hilt's in our hand,—
> Heart-whole we'll part, and no whit sighe
>   For the fayrest of the land;
> Let piping swaine, and craven wight,
>   Thus weepe and puling crye,
> Our business is like men to fight,
>   And hero-like to die!

1848   1850

The Philosophy of Composition

First printed in *Graham's Magazine*, April, 1846. Though himself a romantic in the effects produced by his art, Poe rejected the extreme view (common among romantics) that literary works, especially poems, are written unconsciously in a state of inspiration ("ecstatic intuition"). In this essay he embraces the opposite extreme: that they are written with conscious deliberation. Taking "The Raven" as an example, he affirms that he constructed it "with the precision and rigid consequence of a mathematical problem." He presents an analysis of the artistic questions he faced and the arguments he used in answering them. His account of the writing of "The Raven" may exaggerate the calculation and consciousness involved, though he actually worked on the poem for four years. Nevertheless, the essay is valuable because it identifies important elements in the poem and because it develops important aspects of Poe's theory of poetry.

Charles Dickens, in a note now lying before me, alluding to an examination I once made of the mechanism of "Barnaby Rudge," says—"By the way, are you aware that Godwin wrote his "Caleb Williams" backwards? He first involved his hero in a web of difficulties, forming the second volume, and then, for the first, cast about him for some mode of accounting for what had been done."

I cannot think this the *precise* mode of procedure on the part of Godwin—and indeed what he himself acknowledges, is not altogether in accordance with Mr. Dickens' idea—but the author of "Caleb Williams" was too good an artist not to perceive the advantage derivable from at least a somewhat similar process. Nothing is more clear than that every plot, worth the name, must be elaborated to its *dénouement* before anything be attempted with the pen. It is only with the *dénouement* constantly in view that we can give a plot its indispensable air of consequence, or causation, by making the incidents, and especially the tone at all points, tend to the development of the intention.

There is a radical error, I think, in the usual mode of constructing a story. Either history affords a thesis—or one is suggested by an incident of the day—or, at best, the author sets himself to work in the combination of striking events to form merely the basis of his narrative—designing, generally, to fill in with description, dialogue, or autorial comment, whatever crevices of fact, or action, may, from page to page, render themselves apparent.

I prefer commencing with the consideration of an *effect*. Keeping originality *always* in view—for he is false to himself who ventures to dispense with so obvious and so easily attainable a source of interest—I say to myself, in the first place, "Of the innumerable effects, or impressions, of which the heart, the intellect, or (more generally) the soul is susceptible, what one shall I, on the present occasion, select?" Having chosen a novel, first, and secondly a vivid effect, I consider whether it can be best wrought by incident or tone—whether by ordinary incidents and peculiar tone, or the converse, or by peculiarity both of incident and tone—afterward looking about me (or rather within) for such combinations of event, or tone, as shall best aid me in the construction of the effect.

I have often thought how interesting a magazine paper might be written by any author who would—that is to say, who could—detail, step by step, the processes by which any one of his compositions attained its ultimate point of completion. Why such a paper has never been given to the world, I am much at a loss to say—but, perhaps, the autorial vanity has had more to do with the omission than any one other cause. Most writers—poets in especial—prefer having it understood that they compose by a species of fine frenzy—an ecstatic intuition—and would positively shudder at letting the public take a peep behind the scenes, at the elaborate and vacillating crudities of thought—at the true purposes seized only at the last moment—at the innumerable glimpses of idea that arrived not at the maturity of full view—at the fully matured fancies discarded in despair as unmanageable—at the cautious selections and rejections—at the painful erasures and interpolations—in a word, at the wheels and pinions—the tackle for scene-shifting—the step-ladders and demon-traps—the cock's feathers, the red paint and the black patches, which, in ninety-nine cases out of the hundred, constitute the properties of the literary *histrio*.

I am aware, on the other hand, that the case is by no means common, in which an author is at all in condition to retrace the steps by which his conclusions have been attained. In general, suggestions, having arisen pell-mell, are pursued and forgotten in a similar manner.

For my own part, I have neither sympathy with

the repugnance alluded to nor, at any time, the least difficulty in recalling to mind the progressive steps of any of my compositions; and, since the interest of an analysis, or reconstruction, such as I have considered a *desideratum*, is quite independent of any real or fancied interest in the thing analyzed, it will not be regarded as a breach of decorum on my part to show the *modus operandi* by which some one of my own works was put together. I select "The Raven," as the most generally known. It is my design to render it manifest that no one point in its composition is referable either to accident or intuition—that the work proceeded, step by step, to its completion with the precision and rigid consequence of a mathematical problem.

Let us dismiss, as irrelevant to the poem, *per se*, the circumstance—or say the necessity—which, in the first place, gave rise to the intention of composing *a* poem that should suit at once the popular and the critical taste.

We commence, then, with this intention.

The initial consideration was that of extent. If any literary work is too long to be read at one sitting, we must be content to dispense with the immensely important effect derivable from unity of impression—for, if two sittings be required, the affairs of the world interfere, and everything like totality is at once destroyed. But since, *ceteris paribus*, no poet can afford to dispense with *anything* that may advance his design, it but remains to be seen whether there is, in extent, any advantage to counterbalance the loss of unity which attends it. Here I say no, at once. What we term a long poem is, in fact, merely a succession of brief ones—that is to say, of brief poetical effects. It is needless to demonstrate that a poem is such, only inasmuch as it intensely excites, by elevating, the soul; and all intense excitements are, through a psychal necessity, brief. For this reason, at least one half of the "Paradise Lost" is essentially prose—a succession of poetical excitements interspersed, *inevitably*, with corresponding depressions—the whole being deprived, through the extremeness of its length, of the vastly important artistic element, totality, or unity, of effect.

It appears evident, then, that there is a distinct limit, as regards length, to all works of literary art—the limit of a single sitting—and that, although in certain classes of prose composition, such as "Robinson Crusoe" (demanding no unity), this limit may be advantageously overpassed, it can never properly be overpassed in a poem. Within this limit, the extent of a poem may be made to bear mathematical relation to its merit—in other words, to the excitement or elevation—again in other words, to the degree of true poetical effect which it is capable of inducing; for it is clear that the brevity must be in direct ratio of the intensity of the intended effect:—this, with

one proviso—that a certain degree of duration is absolutely requisite for the production of any effect at all.

Holding in view these considerations, as well as that degree of excitement which I deemed not above the popular, while not below the critical, taste, I reached at once what I conceived the proper *length* for my intended poem—a length of about one hundred lines. It is, in fact, a hundred and eight.

My next thought concerned the choice of an impression, or effect, to be conveyed: and here I may as well observe that, throughout the construction, I kept steadily in view the design of rendering the work *universally* appreciable. I should be carried too far out of my immediate topic were I to demonstrate a point upon which I have repeatedly insisted, and which, with the poetical, stands not in the slightest need of demonstration—the point, I mean, that Beauty is the sole legitimate province of the poem. A few words, however, in elucidation of my real meaning, which some of my friends have evinced a disposition to misrepresent. That pleasure which is at once the most intense, the most elevating, and the most pure, is, I believe, found in the contemplation of the beautiful. When, indeed, men speak of Beauty, they mean, precisely, not a quality, as is supposed, but an effect—they refer, in short, just to that intense and pure elevation of *soul*—*not* of intellect, or of heart—upon which I have commented, and which is experienced in consequence of contemplating "the beautiful." Now I designate Beauty as the province of the poem, merely because it is an obvious rule of Art that effects should be made to spring from direct causes—that objects should be attained through means best adapted for their attainment—no one as yet having been weak enough to deny that the peculiar elevation alluded to is *most readily* attained in the poem. Now the object Truth, or the satisfaction of the intellect, and the object Passion, or the excitement of the heart, are, although attainable, to a certain extent, in poetry, far more readily attainable in prose. Truth, in fact, demands a precision, and Passion, a *homeliness* (the truly passionate will comprehend me) which are absolutely antagonistic to that Beauty which, I maintain, is the excitement, or pleasurable elevation, of the soul. It by no means follows from anything here said, that passion, or even truth, may not be introduced, and even profitably introduced, into a poem—for they may serve in elucidation, or aid the general effect, as do discords in music, by contrast—but the true artist will always contrive, first, to tone them into proper subservience to the predominant aim, and, secondly, to enveil them, as far as possible, in that Beauty which is the atmosphere and the essence of the poem.

Regarding, then, Beauty as my province, my next

question referred to the *tone* of its highest manifestation—and all experience has shown that this tone is one of *sadness*. Beauty of whatever kind, in its supreme development, invariably excites the sensitive soul to tears. Melancholy is thus the most legitimate of all the poetical tones.

BEAUTY → MELANCHOLY

The length, the province, and the tone, being thus determined, I betook myself to ordinary induction, with the view of obtaining some artistic piquancy which might serve me as a key-note in the construction of the poem—some pivot upon which the whole structure might turn. In carefully thinking over all the usual artistic effects—or more properly *points*, in the theatrical sense—I did not fail to perceive immediately that no one had been so universally employed as that of the *refrain*. The universality of its employment sufficed to assure me of its intrinsic value, and spared me the necessity of submitting it to analysis. I considered it, however, with regard to its susceptibility of improvement, and soon saw it to be in a primitive condition. As commonly used, the *refrain*, or burden, not only is limited to lyric verse, but depends for its impression upon the force of monotone—both in sound and thought. The pleasure is deduced solely from the sense of identity—of repetition. I resolved to diversify, and so vastly heighten, the effect, by adhering, in general, to the monotone of sound, while I continually varied that of thought: that is to say, I determined to produce continuously novel effects, by the variation *of the application* of the *refrain*—the *refrain* itself remaining, for the most part, unvaried.

These points being settled, I next bethought me of the *nature* of my *refrain*. Since its application was to be repeatedly varied, it was clear that the *refrain* itself must be brief, for there would have been an insurmountable difficulty in frequent variations of application in any sentence of length. In proportion to the brevity of the sentence, would, of course, be the facility of the variation. This led me at once to a single word as the best *refrain*.

The question now arose as to the *character* of the word. Having made up my mind to a *refrain*, the division of the poem into stanzas was, of course, a corollary: the *refrain* forming the close to each stanza. That such a close, to have force, must be sonorous and susceptible of protracted emphasis, admitted no doubt: and these considerations inevitably led me to the long *o* as the most sonorous vowel, in connection with *r* as the producible consonant.

The sound of the *refrain* being thus determined, it became necessary to select a word embodying this sound, and at the same time in the fullest possible keeping with that melancholy which I had predetermined as the tone of the poem. In such a search it would have been absolutely impossible to overlook the word "Nevermore." In fact, it was the very first which presented itself.

The next *desideratum* was a pretext for the continuous use of the one word "nevermore." In observing the difficulty which I at once found in inventing a sufficiently plausible reason for its continuous repetition, I did not fail to perceive that this difficulty arose solely from the pre-assumption that the word was to be so continuously or monotonously spoken by a *human* being—I did not fail to perceive, in short, that the difficulty lay in the reconciliation of this monotony with the exercise of reason on the part of the creature repeating the word. Here, then, immediately arose the idea of a *non*-reasoning creature capable of speech; and, very naturally, a parrot, in the first instance, suggested itself, but was superseded forthwith by a Raven, as equally capable of speech, and infinitely more in keeping with the intended *tone*.

I had now gone so far as the conception of a Raven—the bird of ill omen—monotonously repeating the one word, "Nevermore," at the conclusion of each stanza, in a poem of melancholy tone, and in length about one hundred lines. Now, never losing sight of the object *supremeness*, or perfection, at all points, I asked myself—"Of all melancholy topics, what, according to the *universal* understanding of mankind, is the *most* melancholy?" Death—was the obvious reply. "And when," I said, "is this most melancholy of topics most poetical?" From what I have already explained at some length, the answer, here also, is obvious—"When it most closely allies itself to *Beauty*: the death, then, of a beautiful woman is, unquestionably, the most poetical topic in the world—and equally is it beyond doubt that the lips best suited for such topic are those of a bereaved lover."

I had now to combine the two ideas, of a lover lamenting his deceased mistress and a Raven continuously repeating the word "Nevermore"—I had to combine these, bearing in mind my design of varying, at every turn, the *application* of the word repeated; but the only intelligible mode of such combination is that of imagining the Raven employing the word in answer to the queries of the lover. And here it was that I saw at once the opportunity afforded for the effect on which I had been depending—that is to say, the effect of the *variation of application*. I saw that I could make the first query propounded by the lover—the first query to which the Raven should reply "Nevermore"—that I could make this first query a commonplace one—the second less so—the third still less, and so on—until at length the lover, startled from his original *nonchalance* by the melancholy character of the word itself—by its frequent repetition—and by a consideration of the ominous reputation of the fowl that uttered it—is at length excited to superstition, and wildly propounds queries of a far different character—queries whose solution he has passionately at heart—propounds them half in superstition and half in that species of despair which delights in self-torture—propounds them not altogether because he believes in the prophetic or demoniac character of the bird (which, reason assures him, is merely repeating a lesson learned by rote) but because he experiences a phrenzied pleasure in so modeling his questions as to receive from the *expected* "Nevermore" the most delicious because the most intolerable of sorrow. Perceiving the opportunity thus afforded me—or, more strictly, thus forced upon me in the progress of the construction—I first established in mind the climax, or concluding query—that query to which "Nevermore" should be in the last place an answer—that in reply to which this word "Nevermore" should involve the utmost conceivable amount of sorrow and despair.

Here then the poem may be said to have its beginning—at the end, where all works of art should begin—for it was here, at this point of my preconsiderations, that I first put pen to paper in the composition of the stanza:

"Prophet," said I, "thing of evil! prophet still if bird or devil!
By that heaven that bends above us—by that God we both adore,
Tell this soul with sorrow laden, if within the distant Aidenn,
It shall clasp a sainted maiden whom the angels name Lenore—
Clasp a rare and radiant maiden whom the angels name Lenore."
Quoth the raven "Nevermore."

I composed this stanza, at this point, first that, by establishing the climax, I might the better vary and graduate, as regards seriousness and importance, the preceding queries of the lover—and, secondly, that I might definitely settle the rhythm, the metre, and the length and general arrangement of the stanza—as well as graduate the stanzas which were to precede, so that none of them might surpass this in rhythmical effect. Had I been able, in the subsequent composition, to construct more vigorous stanzas, I should, without scruple, have purposely enfeebled them, so as not to interfere with the climacteric effect.

And here I may as well say a few words of the versification. My first object (as usual) was originality. The extent to which this has been neglected, in versification, is one of the most unaccountable things in the world. Admitting that there is little possibility of variety in mere *rhythm*, it is still clear that the possible varieties of metre and stanza are absolutely infinite—and yet, *for centuries, no man, in verse, has ever done, or ever seemed to think of doing, an original thing*. The fact is, originality (unless in minds of very unusual force) is by no means a matter, as some suppose, of impulse or intuition. In general, to be found, it must be elaborately sought, and although a positive merit of the highest class, demands in its attainment less of invention than negation.

Of course, I pretend to no originality in either the rhythm or metre of the "Raven." The former is trochaic—the latter is octameter acatalectic, alternating with heptameter catalectic repeated in the *refrain* of the fifth verse, and terminating with tetrameter catalectic. Less pedantically—the feet employed throughout (trochees) consist of a long syllable followed by a short: the first line of the stanza consists of eight of these feet—the second of seven and a half (in effect two-thirds)—the third of eight—the fourth of seven and a half—the fifth the same—the sixth three and a half. Now, each of these lines, taken individually, has been employed before, and what originality the "Raven" has, is in their *combination into stanza;* nothing even remotely approaching this combination has ever been attempted. The effect of this originality of combination is aided by other unusual, and some altogether novel effects, arising from an extension of the application of the principles of rhyme and alliteration.

The next point to be considered was the mode of bringing together the lover and the Raven—and the first branch of this consideration was the *locale*. For this the most natural suggestion might seem to be a forest, or the fields—but it has always appeared to me that a close *circumscription of space* is absolutely necessary to the effect of insulated incident:—it has the force of a frame to a picture. It has an indisputable moral power in keeping concentrated the attention, and, of course, must not be confounded with mere unity of place.

I determined, then, to place the lover in his chamber—in a chamber rendered sacred to him by memories of her who had frequented it. The room is represented as richly furnished—this is mere pursuance of the ideas I have already explained on the subject of Beauty, as the sole true poetical thesis.

The *locale* being thus determined, I had now to introduce the bird—and the thought of introducing him through the window, was inevitable. The idea of making the lover suppose, in the first instance, that the flapping of the wings of the bird against the shutter, is a "tapping" at the door, originated in a wish to increase, by prolonging, the reader's curiosity, and in a desire to admit the incidental effect arising from the lover's throwing open the door, finding all dark, and thence adopting the half-fancy that it was the spirit of his mistress that knocked.

I made the night tempestuous, first, to account for the Raven's seeking admission, and secondly, for the effect of contrast with the (physical) serenity within the chamber.

I made the bird alight on the bust of Pallas, also for the effect of contrast between the marble and the plumage—it being understood that the bust was absolutely *suggested* by the bird—the bust of *Pallas* being chosen, first, as most in keeping with the scholarship of the lover, and, secondly, for the sonorousness of the word, Pallas, itself.

About the middle of the poem, also, I have availed myself of the force of contrast, with a view of deepening the ultimate impression. For example, an air of the fantastic—approaching as nearly to the ludicrous as was admissible—is given to the Raven's entrance. He comes in "with many a flirt and flutter."

> Not the *least obeisance made he*—not a moment
>   stopped or stayed he,
> *But with mien of lord or lady*, perched above my
>   chamber door.

In the two stanzas which follow, the design is more obviously carried out:—

> Then this ebony bird beguiling my sad fancy into
>   smiling
> By the *grave and stern decorum of the countenance
>   it wore*,
> "Though thy *crest be shorn and shaven* thou," I
>   said, "art sure no craven,
> Ghastly grim and ancient Raven wandering from
>   the nightly shore—
> Tell me what thy lordly name is on the Night's
>   Plutonian shore!"
>   Quoth the Raven "Nevermore."

> Much I marvelled *this ungainly fowl* to hear
>   discourse so plainly,
> Though its answer little meaning—little relevancy
>   bore;
> For we cannot help agreeing that no living human
>   being
> *Ever yet was blessed with seeing bird above his
>   chamber door*—
> *Bird or beast upon the sculptured bust above his
>   chamber door,*
>   With such name as "Nevermore."

The effect of the *dénouement* being thus provided for, I immediately drop the fantastic for a tone of the most profound seriousness:—this tone commencing in the stanza directly following the one last quoted, with the line,

> But the Raven, sitting lonely on that placid bust,
>   spoke only, etc.

From this epoch the lover no longer jests—no longer sees anything even of the fantastic in the Raven's demeanor. He speaks of him as a "grim, ungainly, ghastly, gaunt, and ominous bird of yore," and feels the "fiery eyes" burning into his "bosom's core." This revolution of thought, or fancy, on the lover's part, is intended to induce a similar one on the part of the reader—to bring the mind into a proper frame for the *dénouement*—which is now brought about as rapidly and as *directly* as possible.

With the *dénouement* proper—with the Raven's reply, "Nevermore," to the lover's final demand if he shall meet his mistress in another world—the poem, in its obvious phase, that of a simple narrative, may be said to have its completion. So far, everything is within the limits of the accountable—of the real. A raven, having learned by rote the single word "Nevermore," and having escaped from the custody of its owner, is driven at midnight, through the violence of a storm, to seek admission at a window from which a light still gleams—the chamber-window of a student, occupied half in poring over a volume, half in dreaming of a beloved mistress deceased. The casement being thrown open at the fluttering of the bird's wings, the bird itself perches on the most convenient seat out of the immediate reach of the student, who, amused by the incident and the oddity of the visitor's demeanor, demands of it, in jest and without looking for a reply, its name. The raven addressed, answers with its customary word, "Nevermore"—a word which finds immediate echo in the melancholy heart of the student, who, giving utterance aloud to certain thoughts suggested by the occasion, is again startled by the fowl's repetition of "Nevermore." The student now guesses the state of the case, but is impelled, as I have before explained, by the human thirst for self-torture, and in part by superstition, to propound such queries to the bird as will bring him, the lover, the most of the luxury of sorrow, through the anticipated answer "Nevermore." With the indulgence, to the extreme, of this self-torture, the narration, in what I have termed its first or obvious phase, has a natural termination, and so far there has been no overstepping of the limits of the real.

But in subjects so handled, however skilfully, or with however vivid an array of incident, there is always a certain hardness or nakedness, which repels the artistical eye. Two things are invariably required—first, some amount of complexity, or more properly, adaptation; and, secondly, some amount of suggestiveness—some undercurrent, however indefinite, of meaning. It is this latter, in especial, which imparts to a work of art so much of that *richness* (to borrow from colloquy a forcible term) which we are too fond of confounding with *the ideal*. It is the *excess* of the suggested meaning—it is the rendering this the upper instead of the undercurrent of the theme—which turns into prose (and that of the very flattest kind) the so called poetry of the so called transcendentalists.

Holding these opinions, I added the two concluding stanzas of the poem—their suggestiveness being thus made to pervade all the narrative which has preceded them. The undercurrent of meaning is rendered first apparent in the lines—

> "Take thy beak from out my heart, and take thy
>   form from off my door!"
> Quoth the Raven "Nevermore!"

It will be observed that the words, "from out my heart," involve the first metaphorical expression in the poem. They, with the answer, "Nevermore," dispose the mind to seek a moral in all that has been previously narrated. The reader begins now to regard the Raven as emblematical—but it is not until the very last line of the very last stanza, that the intention of making him emblematical of *Mournful and Never-ending Remembrance* is permitted distinctly to be seen:

> And the Raven, never flitting, still is sitting, still is
>   sitting,
> On the pallid bust of Pallas, just above my chamber
>   door;
> And his eyes have all the seeming of a demon's that
>   is dreaming,
> And the lamplight o'er him streaming throws his
>   shadow on the floor;
> And my soul *from out that shadow* that lies floating
>   on the floor
>   Shall be lifted—nevermore.

1846

Hawthorne's Twice-Told Tales

The two major Poe essays included here are mainly theoretical. But he also wrote a great bulk of practical criticism, discussing particular authors and books, with a high degree of independence, honesty, and insight. The two kinds often overlap, as in his essay on Hawthorne, where he is reviewing the second edition of *Twice-Told Tales* and at the same time setting forth his theory of the short story. The essay may be read for the light it sheds on his own fiction, examples of which are printed directly after this selection.

We said a few hurried words about Mr. Hawthorne in our last number, with the design of speaking more fully in the present. We are still, however, pressed for room, and must necessarily discuss his volumes more briefly and more at random than their high merits deserve.

The book professes to be a collection of *tales*, yet is, in two respects, misnamed. These pieces are now in their third republication, and, of course, are thrice-told. Moreover, they are by no means *all* tales, either in the ordinary or in the legitimate understanding of the term. Many of them are pure essays; for example, "Sights from a Steeple," "Sunday at Home," "Little Annie's Ramble," "A Rill from the Town Pump," "The Toll-Gatherer's Day," "The Haunted Mind," "The Sister Years," "Snow-Flakes," "Night Sketches," and "Foot-Prints on the Sea-Shore." We mention these matters chiefly on account of their discrepancy with that marked precision and finish by which the body of the work is distinguished.

Of the Essays just named, we must be content to speak in brief. They are each and all beautiful, without being characterized by the polish and adaptation so visible in the tales proper. A painter would at once note their leading or predominant feature, and style it *repose*. There is no attempt at effect. All is quiet, thoughtful, subdued. Yet this repose may exist simultaneously with high originality of thought; and Mr. Hawthorne has demonstrated the fact. At every turn we meet with novel combinations; yet these combinations never surpass the limits of the quiet. We are soothed as we read; and withal is a calm astonishment that ideas so apparently obvious have never occurred or been presented to us before. Herein our author differs materially from Lamb or Hunt or Hazlitt—who, with vivid originality of manner and expression, have less of the true novelty of thought than is generally supposed, and whose originality, at best, has an uneasy and meretricious quaintness, replete with startling effects unfounded in nature, and inducing trains of reflection which lead to no satisfactory result. The Essays of Hawthorne have much of the character of Irving, with more of originality and less of finish; while, compared with the Spectator, they have a vast superiority at all points. The Spectator, Mr. Irving, and Mr. Hawthorne have in common that tranquil and subdued manner which we have chosen to denominate *repose*; but, in the case of the two former, this repose is attained rather by the absence of novel combination, or of originality, than otherwise, and consists chiefly in the calm, quiet, unostentatious expression of commonplace thoughts, in an unambitious, unadulterated Saxon. In them, by strong effort, we are made to conceive the absence of all. In the essays before us the absence of effort is too obvious to be mistaken, and a strong undercurrent of *suggestion* runs continuously beneath the upper stream of the tranquil thesis. In short, these effusions of Mr. Hawthorne are the product of a truly imaginative intellect, restrained, and in some measure repressed, by fastidiousness of taste, by constitutional melancholy and by indolence.

But it is of his tales that we desire principally to speak. The tale proper, in our opinion, affords unquestionably the fairest field for the exercise of the loftiest talent, which can be afforded by the wide domains of mere prose. Were we bidden to say how the highest genius could be most advantageously employed for the best display of its own powers, we should answer, without hesitation—in the composition of a rhymed poem, not to exceed in length what might be perused in an hour. Within this limit alone can the highest order of true poetry exist. We need only here say, upon this topic, that, in almost all classes of composition, the unity of effect or impression is a point of the greatest importance. It is clear, moreover, that this unity cannot be thoroughly preserved in productions whose perusal cannot be completed at one sitting. We may continue the reading of a prose composition, from the very nature of prose itself, much longer than we can persevere, to any good purpose, in the perusal of a poem. This latter, if truly fulfilling the demands of the poetic sentiment, induces an exaltation of the soul which cannot be long sustained. All high excitements are necessarily transient. Thus a long poem is a paradox. And, without unity of impression, the deepest effects cannot be brought about. Epics were the offspring of an imperfect sense of Art, and their reign is no more. A poem *too* brief may produce a vivid, but never an intense or enduring impression. Without a certain continuity of effort—without a certain duration or repetition of purpose—the soul is never deeply moved. There must be the dropping of the water upon the rock. De Béranger has wrought brilliant things—pungent and spirit-stirring—but, like all immassive bodies, they lack *momentum,* and thus fail to satisfy the Poetic Sentiment. They sparkle and excite, but, from want of continuity, fail deeply to impress. Extreme brevity will degenerate into epigrammatism; but the sin of extreme length is even more unpardonable. *In medio tutissimus ibis.*[1]

Were we called upon, however, to designate that class of composition which, next to such a poem as we have suggested, should best fulfil the demands of high genius—should offer it the most advantageous field of exertion—we should unhesitatingly speak of the prose tale, as Mr. Hawthorne has here exemplified it. We allude to the short prose narrative, requiring from a half-hour to one or two hours in its perusal. The ordinary novel is objectionable, from its length, for reasons already stated in substance. As it cannot be read at one sitting, it deprives itself, of course, of the immense force derivable from *totality.* Worldly interests intervening during the pauses of perusal, modify, annul, or counteract, in a greater or less degree, the impressions of the book. But

simple cessation in reading, would, of itself, be sufficient to destroy the true unity. In the brief tale, however, the author is enabled to carry out the fulness of his intention, be it what it may. During the hour of perusal the soul of the reader is at the writer's control. There are no external or extrinsic influences—resulting from weariness or interruption.

A skillful literary artist has constructed a tale. If wise, he has not fashioned his thoughts to accommodate his incidents; but having conceived, with deliberate care, a certain unique or single *effect* to be wrought out, he then invents such incidents—he then combines such events as may best aid him in establishing this preconceived effect. If his very initial sentence tend not to the outbringing of this effect, then he has failed in his first step. In the whole composition there should be no word written, of which the tendency, direct or indirect, is not to the one pre-established design. And by such means, with such care and skill, a picture is at length painted which leaves in the mind of him who contemplates it with a kindred art, a sense of the fullest satisfaction. The idea of the tale has been presented unblemished, because undisturbed; and this is an end unattainable by the novel. Undue brevity is just as exceptionable here as in the poem; but undue length is yet more to be avoided.

We have said that the tale has a point of superiority even over the poem. In fact, while the *rhythm* of this latter is an essential aid in the development of the poem's highest idea—the idea of the Beautiful—the artificialities of this rhythm are an inseparable bar to the development of all points of thought or expression which have their basis in *Truth.* But Truth is often, and in very great degree, the aim of the tale. Some of the finest tales are tales of ratiocination. Thus the field of this species of composition, if not in so elevated a region on the mountain of Mind, is a table-land of far vaster extent than the domain of the mere poem. Its products are never so rich, but infinitely more numerous, and more appreciable by the mass of mankind. The writer of the prose tale, in short, may bring to his theme a vast variety of modes or inflections of thought and expression—(the ratiocinative, for example, the sarcastic, or the humorous) which are not only antagonistical to the nature of the poem, but absolutely forbidden by one of its most peculiar and indispensable adjuncts; we allude, of course, to rhythm. It may be added here, *par parenthèse,* that the author who aims at the purely beautiful in a prose tale is laboring at a great disadvantage. For Beauty can be better treated in the poem. Not so with terror, or passion, or horror, or a multitude of such other points. And here it will be seen how full of prejudice are the usual animadversions against those *tales of effect,* many fine examples of which

---

[1] "You travel most safely the middle road."

were found in the earlier numbers of Blackwood.[2] The impressions produced were wrought in a legitimate sphere of action, and constituted a legitimate although sometimes an exaggerated interest. They were relished by every man of genius: although there were found many men of genius who condemned them without just ground. The true critic will but demand that the design intended be accomplished, to the fullest extent, by the means most advantageously applicable.

We have very few American tales of real merit—we may say, indeed, none with the exception of "The Tales of a Traveller" of Washington Irving, and these "Twice-Told Tales" of Mr. Hawthorne. Some of the pieces of Mr. John Neal[3] abound in vigor and originality; but, in general, his compositions of this class are excessively diffuse, extravagant, and indicative of an imperfect sentiment of Art. Articles at random are, now and then, met with in our periodicals which might be advantageously compared with the best effusions of the British Magazines; but, upon the whole, we are far behind our progenitors in this department of literature.

Of Mr. Hawthorne's Tales we should say, emphatically, that they belong to the highest region of Art—an Art subservient to genius of a very lofty order. We had supposed, with good reason for so supposing, that he had been thrust into his present position by one of the impudent *cliques* which beset our literature, and whose pretensions it is our full purpose to expose at the earliest opportunity; but we have been most agreeably mistaken. We know of few compositions which the critic can more honestly commend than these "Twice-Told Tales." As Americans, we feel proud of the book.

Mr. Hawthorne's distinctive trait is invention, creation, imagination, originality—a trait which, in the literature of fiction, is positively worth all the rest. But the nature of the originality, so far as regards its manifestation in letters, is but imperfectly understood. The inventive or original mind as frequently displays itself in novelty of *tone* as in novelty of matter. Mr. Hawthorne is original at *all* points.

It would be a matter of some difficulty to designate the best of these tales; we repeat that, without exception, they are beautiful. "Wakefield" is remarkable for the skill with which an old idea—a well-known incident—is worked up or discussed. A man of whims conceives the purpose of quitting his wife and residing *incognito*, for twenty years, in her immediate neighborhood. Something of this kind actually happened in London. The force of Mr. Hawthorne's tale lies in the analysis of the motives

which must or might have impelled the husband to such folly, in the first instance, with the possible causes of his perseverance. Upon this thesis a sketch of singular power has been constructed.

"The Wedding Knell" is full of the boldest imagination—an imagination fully controlled by taste. The most captious critic could find no flaw in this production.

"The Minister's Black Veil" is a masterly composition of which the sole defect is that to the rabble its exquisite skill will be *caviare*. The *obvious* meaning of this article will be found to smother its insinuated one. The *moral* put into the mouth of the dying minister will be supposed to convey the *true* import of the narrative; and that a crime of dark dye (having reference to the "young lady") has been committed, is a point which only minds congenial with that of the author will perceive.

"Mr. Higginbotham's Catastrophe" is vividly original and managed most dexterously.

"Dr. Heidegger's Experiment" is exceedingly well imagined, and executed with surpassing ability. The artist breathes in every line of it.

"The White Old Maid" is objectionable, even more than the "Minister's Black Veil," on the score of its mysticism. Even with the thoughtful and analytic, there will be much trouble in penetrating its entire import.

"The Hollow of the Three Hills" we would quote in full had we space;—not as evincing higher talent than any of the other pieces, but as affording an excellent example of the author's peculiar ability. The subject is commonplace. A witch subjects the Distant and the Past to the view of a mourner. It has been the fashion to describe, in such cases, a mirror in which the images of the absent appear; or a cloud of smoke is made to arise, and thence the figures are gradually unfolded. Mr. Hawthorne has wonderfully heightened his effect by making the ear, in place of the eye, the medium by which the fantasy is conveyed. The head of the mourner is enveloped in the cloak of the witch, and within its magic folds there arise sounds which have an all-sufficient intelligence. Throughout this article also, the artist is conspicuous—not more in positive than in negative merits. Not only is all done that should be done, but (what perhaps is an end with more difficulty attained) there is nothing done which should not be. Every word *tells*, and there is not a word which does *not* tell.

In "Howe's Masquerade" we observe something which resembles plagiarism[4]—but which *may be* a very flattering coincidence of thought. We quote the passage in question.

---

[2] An English periodical started in 1817.

[3] Neal (1793–1876) was an American writer who contributed to *Blackwood's* in the 1820's.

[4] Unlikely, since Hawthorne published his tale a year before Poe's.

With a dark flush of wrath upon his brow they saw the general *draw his sword* and *advance to meet* the figure *in the cloak* before the latter had stepped one pace upon the floor.

"Villain, *unmuffle yourself*," cried he, "you pass no farther!"

The figure, without blanching a hair's breadth from the sword which was pointed at his breast, made a solemn pause, and lowered the cape of the cloak from his face, yet not sufficiently for the spectators to catch a glimpse of it. But Sir William Howe had evidently seen enough. The sternness of his countenance gave place to a look of wild amazement, if not horror, while he recoiled several steps from the figure, *and let fall his sword* upon the floor.

The idea here is, that the figure in the cloak is the phantom or reduplication of Sir William Howe; but in an article called "William Wilson," one of the "Tales of the Grotesque and Arabesque," we have not only the same idea, but the same idea similarly presented in several respects. We quote two paragraphs, which our readers may compare with what has been already given. We have italicized, above, the immediate particulars of resemblance.

The brief moment in which I averted my eyes had been sufficient to produce, apparently, a material change in the arrangement at the upper or farther end of the room. A large mirror, it appeared to me, now stood where none had been perceptible before; and as I stepped up to it in extremity of terror, mine own image, but with features all pale and dabbled in blood, *advanced* with a feeble and tottering gait to meet me.

Thus it appeared I say, but was not. It was Wilson, who then stood before me in the agonies of dissolution. Not a line in all the marked and singular lineaments of that face which was not even identically mine own. *His mask and cloak lay where he had thrown them, upon the floor.*

Here it will be observed that, not only are the two general conceptions identical, but there are various *points* of similarity. In each case the figure seen is the wraith or duplication of the beholder. In each case the scene is a masquerade. In each case the figure is cloaked. In each, there is a quarrel—that is to say, angry words pass between the parties. In each the beholder is enraged. In each the cloak and sword fall upon the floor. The "villain, unmuffle yourself," of Mr. H. is precisely paralleled by a passage at page 56 of "William Wilson."

In the way of objection we have scarcely a word to say of these tales. There is, perhaps, a somewhat too general or prevalent *tone*—a tone of melancholy and mysticism. The subjects are insufficiently varied. There is not so much of *versatility* evinced as we might well be warranted in expecting from the high powers of Mr. Hawthorne. But beyond these trivial exceptions we have really none to make. The style is

purity itself. Force abounds. High imagination gleams from every page. Mr. Hawthorne is a man of the truest genius. We only regret that the limits of our Magazine will not permit us to pay him that full tribute of commendation, which, under other circumstances, we should be so eager to pay.

1842

Ligeia

The story contains a number of allusions which Poe hardly expected the reader to recognize. Many of them are little more than decorative and do not clarify or enrich the meaning. It may be worth noting, however, that in the paragraph beginning "For eyes we have no models" is a reference to a proverb that came from the Greek philosopher Democritus: "Truth lies at the bottom of a well." The source of the epigraph has never been identified; Poe may have invented it and attributed it to the English clergyman and philosopher Glanvill (1636–80) who wrote on the occult and supernatural.

And the will therein lieth, which dieth not. Who knoweth the mysteries of the will, with its vigor? For God is but a great will pervading all things by nature of its intentness. Man doth not yield himself to the angels, nor unto death utterly, save only through the weakness of his feeble will.—*Joseph Glanvill.*

I cannot, for my soul, remember how, when, or even precisely where, I first became acquainted with the lady Ligeia. Long years have since elapsed, and my memory is feeble through much suffering. Or, perhaps, I cannot *now* bring these points to mind, because, in truth, the character of my beloved, her rare learning, her singular yet placid cast of beauty, and the thrilling and enthralling eloquence of her low musical language, made their way into my heart by paces so steadily and stealthily progressive that they have been unnoticed and unknown. Yet I believe that I met her first and most frequently in some large, old, decaying city near the Rhine. Of her family—I have surely heard her speak. That it is of a remotely ancient date cannot be doubted. Ligeia! Ligeia! Buried in studies of a nature more than all else adapted to deaden impressions of the outward world, it is by that sweet word alone—by Ligeia—that I bring before mine eyes in fancy the image of her who is no more. And now, while I write, a recollection flashes upon me that I have *never known* the paternal name of her who was my friend and my betrothed, and who became the partner of my studies, and finally the wife of my bosom. Was it a playful charge on the part of my Ligeia? or was it a test of my strength of affection, that I should institute no inquiries upon this point? or was it rather a caprice of my own—a wildly

romantic offering on the shrine of the most passionate devotion? I but indistinctly recall the fact itself—what wonder that I have utterly forgotten the
circumstances which originated or attended it? And,
indeed, if ever that spirit which is entitled *Romance*—if ever she, the wan and the misty-winged
Ashtophet of idolatrous Egypt, presided, as they tell,
over marriages ill-omened, then most surely she presided over mine.

There is one dear topic, however, on which my
memory fails me not. It is the *person* of Ligeia. In
stature she was tall, somewhat slender, and, in her
latter days, even emaciated. I would in vain attempt
to portray the majesty, the quiet ease, of her demeanor, or the incomprehensible lightness and elasticity
of her footfall. She came and departed as a shadow.
I was never made aware of her entrance into my
closed study save by the dear music of her low
sweet voice, as she placed her marble hand upon
my shoulder. In beauty of face no maiden ever
equalled her. It was the radiance of an opium-
dream—an airy and spirit-lifting vision more wildly
divine than the phantasies which hovered about the
slumbering souls of the daughters of Delos. Yet her
features were not of that regular mould which we
have been falsely taught to worship in the classical
labors of the heathen. "There is no exquisite
beauty," says Bacon, Lord Verulam, speaking truly
of all the forms and *genera* of beauty, "without
some *strangeness* in the proportion." Yet, although I
saw that the features of Ligeia were not of a classic
regularity—although I perceived that her loveliness
was indeed "exquisite," and felt that there was
much of "strangeness" pervading it, yet I have tried
in vain to detect the irregularity and to trace home
my own perception of "the strange." I examined the
contour of the lofty and pale forehead—it was faultless—how cold indeed that word when applied to a
majesty so divine!—the skin rivalling the purest
ivory, the commanding extent and repose, the gentle
prominence of the regions above the temples; and
then the raven-black, the glossy, the luxuriant, and
naturally-curling tresses, setting forth the full force
of the Homeric epithet, "hyacinthine"! I looked at
the delicate outlines of the nose—and nowhere but
in the graceful medallions of the Hebrews had I
beheld a similar perfection. There were the same
luxurious smoothness of surface, the same scarcely
perceptible tendency to the aquiline, the same harmoniously curved nostrils speaking the free spirit. I
regarded the sweet mouth. Here was indeed the
triumph of all things heavenly—the magnificent turn
of the short upper lip—the soft, voluptuous slumber
of the under—the dimples which sported, and the
color which spoke—the teeth glancing back, with a
brilliancy almost startling, every ray of the holy light
which fell upon them in her serene and placid, yet

most exultingly radiant of all smiles. I scrutinized
the formation of the chin—and here, too, I found
the gentleness of breadth, the softness and the majesty, the fullness and the spirituality, of the Greek—
the contour which the god Apollo revealed but in a
dream, to Cleomenes, the son of the Athenian. And
then I peered into the large eyes of Ligeia.

For eyes we have no models in the remotely antique. It might have been, too, that in these eyes of
my beloved lay the secret to which Lord Verulam
alludes. They were, I must believe, far larger than
the ordinary eyes of our own race. They were even
fuller than the fullest of the gazelle eyes of the tribe
of the valley of Nourjahad. Yet it was only at intervals—in moments of intense excitement—that this
peculiarity became more than slightly noticeable in
Ligeia. And at such moments was her beauty—in
my heated fancy thus it appeared perhaps—the
beauty of beings either above or apart from the
earth—the beauty of the fabulous Houri of the
Turk. The hue of the orbs was the most brilliant of
black, and, far over them, hung jetty lashes of great
length. The brows, slightly irregular in outline, had
the same tint. The "strangeness," however, which I
found in the eyes, was of a nature distinct from the
formation, or the color, or the brilliancy of the features, and must, after all, be referred to the *expression*. Ah, word of no meaning! behind whose vast
latitude of mere sound we intrench our ignorance of
so much of the spiritual. The expression of the eyes
of Ligeia! How for long hours have I pondered upon
it! How have I, through the whole of a midsummer
night, struggled to fathom it! What was it—that
something more profound than the well of Democritus—which lay far within the pupils of my beloved?
What *was* it? I was possessed with a passion to
discover. Those eyes! those large, those shining,
those divine orbs! they became to me twin stars of
Leda, and I to them devoutest of astrologers.

There is no point, among the many incomprehensible anomalies of the science of mind, more thrillingly exciting than the fact—never, I believe, noticed
in the schools—that in our endeavors to recall to
memory something long forgotten, we often find
ourselves *upon the very verge* of remembrance,
without being able, in the end, to remember. And
thus how frequently, in my intense scrutiny of
Ligeia's eyes, have I felt approaching the full knowledge of their expression—felt it approaching—yet
not quite be mine—and so at length entirely depart!
And (strange, oh strangest mystery of all!) I found,
in the commonest objects of the universe, a circle of
analogies to that expression. I mean to say that,
subsequently to the period when Ligeia's beauty
passed into my spirit, there dwelling as in a shrine, I
derived, from many existences in the material world,
a sentiment such as I felt always aroused within me

by her large and luminous orbs. Yet not the more could I define that sentiment, or analyze, or even steadily view it. I recognized it, let me repeat, sometimes in the survey of a rapidly-growing vine—in the contemplation of a moth, a butterfly, a chrysalis, a stream of running water. I have felt it in the ocean; in the falling of a meteor. I have felt it in the glances of unusually aged people. And there are one or two stars in heaven—(one especially, a star of the sixth magnitude, double and changeable, to be found near the large star in Lyra)—in a telescopic scrutiny of which I have been made aware of the feeling. I have been filled with it by certain sounds from stringed instruments, and not unfrequently by passages from books. Among innumerable other instances, I well remember something in a volume of Joseph Glanvill, which (perhaps merely from its quaintness—who shall say?) never failed to inspire me with the sentiment:—"And the will therein lieth, which dieth not. Who knoweth the mysteries of the will, with its vigor? For God is but a great will pervading all things by nature of its intentness. Man doth not yield him to the angels, nor unto death utterly, save only through the weakness of his feeble will."

Length of years, and subsequent reflection, have enabled me to trace, indeed, some remote connection between this passage in the English moralist and a portion of the character of Ligeia. An *intensity* in thought, action, or speech, was possibly, in her, a result, or at least an index, of that gigantic volition which, during our long intercourse, failed to give other and more immediate evidence of its existence. Of all the women whom I have ever known, she, the outwardly calm, the ever-placid Ligeia, was the most violently a prey to the tumultuous vultures of stern passion. And of such passion I could form no estimate, save by the miraculous expansion of those eyes which at once so delighted and appalled me—by the almost magical melody, modulation, distinctness and placidity of her very low voice—and by the fierce energy (rendered doubly effective by contrast with her manner of utterance) of the wild words which she habitually uttered.

I have spoken of the learning of Ligeia: it was immense—such as I have never known in woman. In the classical tongues was she deeply proficient, and as far as my own acquaintance extended in regard to the modern dialects of Europe, I have never known her at fault. Indeed upon any theme of the most admired, because simply the most abstruse of the boasted erudition of the academy, have I *ever* found Ligeia at fault? How singularly—how thrillingly, this one point in the nature of my wife has forced itself, at this late period only, upon my attention! I said her knowledge was such as I have never known in woman—but where breathes the man who has traversed, and successfully, *all* the wide areas of moral, physical, and mathematical science? I saw not then what I now clearly perceive, that the acquisitions of Ligeia were gigantic, were astounding; yet I was sufficiently aware of her infinite supremacy to resign myself, with a child-like confidence, to her guidance through the chaotic world of metaphysical investigation at which I was most busily occupied during the earlier years of our marriage. With how vast a triumph—with how vivid a delight—with how much of all that is ethereal in hope—did I *feel*, as she bent over me in studies but little sought—but less known—that delicious vista by slow degrees expanding before me, down whose long, gorgeous, and all untrodden path, I might at length pass onward to the goal of a wisdom too divinely precious not to be forbidden!

How poignant, then, must have been the grief with which, after some years, I beheld my well-grounded expectations take wings to themselves and fly away! Without Ligeia I was but as a child groping benighted. Her presence, her readings alone, rendered vividly luminous the many mysteries of the transcendentalism in which we were immersed. Wanting the radiant lustre of her eyes, letters, lambent and golden, grew duller than Saturnian lead. And now those eyes shone less and less frequently upon the pages over which I pored. Ligeia grew ill. The wild eyes blazed with a too—too glorious effulgence; the pale fingers became of the transparent waxen hue of the grave, and the blue veins upon the lofty forehead swelled and sank impetuously with the tides of the most gentle emotion. I saw that she must die—and I struggled desperately in spirit with the grim Azrael. And the struggles of the passionate wife were, to my astonishment, even more energetic than my own. There had been much in her stern nature to impress me with the belief that, to her, death would have come without its terrors;—but not so. Words are impotent to convey any just idea of the fierceness of resistance with which she wrestled with the Shadow. I groaned in anguish at the pitiable spectacle. I would have soothed—I would have reasoned; but, in the intensity of her wild desire for life,—for life—*but* for life—solace and reason were alike the uttermost of folly. Yet not until the last instance, amid the most convulsive writhings of her fierce spirit, was shaken the external placidity of her demeanor. Her voice grew more gentle—grew more low—yet I would not wish to dwell upon the wild meaning of the quietly uttered words. My brain reeled as I hearkened entranced, to a melody more than mortal—to assumptions and aspirations which mortality had never before known.

That she loved me I should not have doubted;

and I might have been easily aware that, in a bosom such as hers, love would have reigned no ordinary passion. But in death only, was I fully impressed with the strength of her affection. For long hours, detaining my hand, would she pour out before me the overflowing of a heart whose more than passionate devotion amounted to idolatry. How had I deserved to be so blessed by such confessions?—how had I deserved to be so cursed with the removal of my beloved in the hour of her making them? But upon this subject I cannot bear to dilate. Let me say only, that in Ligeia's more than womanly abandonment to a love, alas! all unmerited, all unworthily bestowed, I at length recognized the principle of her longing with so wildly earnest a desire for the life which was now fleeing so rapidly away. It is this wild longing—it is this eager vehemence of desire for life—*but for life*—that I have no power to portray—no utterance capable of expressing.

At high noon of the night in which she departed, beckoning me, peremptorily, to her side, she bade me repeat certain verses composed by herself not many days before. I obeyed her. They were these:[1]

Lo! 'tis a gala night
    Within the lonesome latter years!
An angel throng, bewinged, bedight
    In veils, and drowned in tears,
Sit in a theatre, to see
    A play of hopes and fears,
While the orchestra breathes fitfully
    The music of the spheres.

Mimes, in the form of God on high,
    Mutter and mumble low,
And hither and thither fly—
    Mere puppets they, who come and go
At bidding of vast formless things
    That shift the scenery to and fro,
Flapping from out their Condor wings
    Invisible Wo!

That motley drama!—oh, be sure
    It shall not be forgot!
With its Phantom chased forever more,
    By a crowd that seize it not,
Through a circle that ever returneth in
    To the self-same spot,
And much of Madness, and more of Sin,
    And Horror the soul of the plot.

But see, amid the mimic rout
    A crawling shape intrude!
A blood-red thing that writhes from out
    The scenic solitude!
It writhes—it writhes!—with mortal pangs
    The mimes become its food,

[1] Poe added the poem to the story in 1845. "Ligeia" appeared originally in 1838, and the poem was published separately in 1843.

And seraphs sob at vermin fangs
    In human gore imbued.

Out—out are the lights—out all!
    And over each quivering form,
The curtain, a funeral pall,
    Comes down with the rush of a storm,
While the angels, all pallid and wan,
    Uprising, unveiling, affirm
That the play is the tragedy, "Man,"
    And its hero the Conqueror Worm.

"O God!" half shrieked Ligeia, leaping to her feet and extending her arms aloft with a spasmodic movement, as I made an end of these lines—"O God! O Divine Father!—shall these things be undeviatingly so?—shall this Conqueror be not once conquered? Are we not part and parcel in Thee? Who—who knoweth the mysteries of the will with its vigor? Man doth not yield him to the angels, *nor unto death utterly*, save only through the weakness of his feeble will."

And now, as if exhausted with emotion, she suffered her white arms to fall, and returned solemnly to her bed of death. And as she breathed her last sighs, there came mingled with them a low murmur from her lips. I bent to them my ear and distinguished, again the concluding words of the passage in Glanvill—"*Man doth not yield him to the angels, nor unto death utterly, save only through the weakness of his feeble will.*"

She died;—and I, crushed into the very dust with sorrow, could no longer endure the lonely desolation of my dwelling in the dim and decaying city by the Rhine. I had no lack of what the world calls wealth. Ligeia had brought me far more, very far more than ordinarily falls to the lot of mortals. After a few months, therefore, of weary and aimless wandering, I purchased, and put in some repair, an abbey, which I shall not name, in one of the wildest and least frequented portions of fair England. The gloomy and dreary grandeur of the building, the almost savage aspect of the domain, the many melancholy and time-honored memories connected with both, had much in unison with the feelings of utter abandonment which had driven me into that remote and unsocial region of the country. Yet although the external abbey, with its verdant decay hanging about it, suffered but little alteration, I gave way, with a child-like perversity, and perchance with a faint hope of alleviating my sorrows, to a display of more than regal magnificence within.—For such follies, even in childhood, I had imbibed a taste and now they came back to me as if in the dotage of grief. Alas I feel how much even of incipient madness might have been discovered in the gorgeous and fantastic draperies, in the solemn carvings of

Egypt, in the wild cornices and furniture, in the Bedlam patterns of the carpets of tufted gold! I had become a bounden slave in the trammels of opium, and my labors and my orders had taken a coloring from my dreams. But these absurdities I must not pause to detail. Let me speak only of that one chamber, ever accursed, whither, in a moment of mental alienation, I led from the altar as my bride—as the successor of the unforgotten Ligeia—the fair-haired and blue-eyed Lady Rowena Trevanion, of Tremaine.

There is no individual portion of the architecture and decoration of that bridal chamber which is not now visibly before me. Where were the souls of the haughty family of the bride, when, through thirst of gold, they permitted to pass the threshold of an apartment *so* bedecked, a maiden and a daughter so beloved? I have said that I minutely remember the details of the chamber—yet I am sadly forgetful on topics of deep moment—and here there was no system, no keeping, in the fantastic display, to take hold upon the memory. The room lay in a high turret of the castellated abbey, was pentagonal in shape, and of capacious size. Occupying the whole southern face of the pentagon was the sole window—an immense sheet of unbroken glass from Venice—a single pane, and tinted of a leaden hue, so that the rays of either the sun or moon, passing through it, fell with a ghastly lustre on the objects within. Over the upper portion of this huge window, extended the trellis-work of an aged vine, which clambered up the massy walls of the turret. The ceiling, of gloomy-looking oak, was excessively lofty, vaulted, and elaborately fretted with the wildest and most grotesque specimens of a semi-Gothic, semi-Druidical device. From out the most central recess of this melancholy vaulting, depended, by a single chain of gold with long links, a huge censer of the same metal, Saracenic in pattern, and with many perforations so contrived that there writhed in and out of them, as if endued with a serpent vitality, a continual succession of parti-colored fires.

Some few ottomans and golden candelabra, of Eastern figure, were in various stations about—and there was the couch, too—the bridal couch—of an Indian model, and low, and sculptured of solid ebony, with a pall-like canopy above. In each of the angles of the chamber stood on end a gigantic sarcophagus of black granite, from the tombs of the kings over against Luxor, with their aged lids full of immemorial sculpture. But in the draping of the apartment lay, alas! the chief phantasy of all. The lofty walls, gigantic in height—even unproportionably so—were hung from summit to foot, in vast folds, with a heavy and massive-looking tapestry—tapestry of a material which was found alike as a carpet on the floor, as a covering for the ottomans

and the ebony bed, as a canopy for the bed, and as the gorgeous volutes of the curtains which partially shaded the window. The material was the richest cloth of gold. It was spotted all over, at irregular intervals, with arabesque figures, about a foot in diameter, and wrought upon the cloth in patterns of the most jetty black. But these figures partook of the true character of the arabesque only when regarded from a single point of view. By a contrivance now common, and indeed traceable to a very remote period of antiquity, they were made changeable in aspect. To one entering the room, they bore the appearance of simple monstrosities; but upon a farther advance, this appearance gradually departed; and, step by step, as the visitor moved his station in the chamber, he saw himself surrounded by an endless succession of the ghastly forms which belong to the superstition of the Norman, or arise in the guilty slumbers of the monk. The phantasmagoric effect was vastly heightened by the artificial introduction of a strong continual current of wind behind the draperies—giving a hideous and uneasy animation to the whole.

In halls such as these—in a bridal chamber such as this—I passed, with the Lady of Tremaine, the unhallowed hours of the first month of our marriage—passed them with but little disquietude. That my wife dreaded the fierce moodiness of my temper—that she shunned me and loved me but little—I could not help perceiving; but it gave me rather pleasure than otherwise. I loathed her with a hatred belonging more to demon than to man. My memory flew back, (oh, with what intensity of regret!) to Ligeia, the beloved, the august, the beautiful, the entombed. I revelled in recollections of her purity, of her wisdom, of her lofty, her ethereal nature, of her passionate, her idolatrous love. Now, then, did my spirit fully and freely burn with more than all the fires of her own. In the excitement of my opium dreams (for I was habitually fettered in the shackles of the drug), I would call aloud upon her name, during the silence of the night, or among the sheltered recesses of the glens by day, as if, through the wild eagerness, the solemn passion, the consuming ardor of my longing for the departed, I could restore her to the pathway she had abandoned—ah, *could* it be forever?—upon the earth,

About the commencement of the second month of the marriage, the Lady Rowena was attacked with sudden illness, from which her recovery was slow. The fever which consumed her, rendered her nights uneasy; and in her perturbed state of half-slumber, she spoke of sounds, and of motions, in and about the chamber of the turret, which I concluded had no origin save in the distemper of her fancy, or perhaps in the phantasmagoric influences of the chamber itself. She became at length convalescent—finally well. Yet but a brief period elapsed, ere a second more violent disorder again threw her upon a bed of suffering; and from this attack her frame, at all times feeble, never altogether recovered. Her illnesses were, after this epoch, of alarming character, and of more alarming recurrence, defying alike the knowledge and the great exertions of her physicians. With the increase of the chronic disease, which had thus, apparently, taken too sure hold upon her constitution to be eradicated by human means, I could not fail to observe a similar increase in the nervous irritation of her temperament, and in her excitability by trivial causes of fear. She spoke again, and now more frequently and pertinaciously, of the sounds—of the slight sounds—and of the unusual motions among the tapestries, to which she had formerly alluded.

One night, near the closing in of September, she pressed this distressing subject with more than usual emphasis upon my attention. She had just awakened from an unquiet slumber, and I had been watching, with feelings half of anxiety, half of vague terror, the workings of her emaciated countenance. I sat by the side of her ebony bed, upon one of the ottomans of India. She partly arose, and spoke, in an earnest low whisper, of sounds which she *then* heard, but which I could not hear—of motions which she *then* saw, but which I could not perceive. The wind was rushing hurriedly behind the tapestries, and I wished to show her (what, let me confess it, I could not *all* believe) that those almost inarticulate breathings, and those very gentle variations of the figures upon the wall, were but the natural effects of that customary rushing of the wind. But a deadly pallor, overspreading her face, had proved to me that my exertions to reassure her would be fruitless. She appeared to be fainting, and no attendants were within call. I remembered where was deposited a decanter of light wine which had been ordered by her physicians, and hastened across the chamber to procure it. But, as I stepped beneath the light of the censer, two circumstances of a startling nature attracted my attention. I had felt that some palpable although invisible object had passed lightly by my person; and I saw that there lay upon the golden carpet, in the very middle of the rich lustre thrown from the censer, a shadow—a faint, indefinite shadow of angelic aspect—such as might be fancied for the shadow of a shade. But I was wild with the excitement of an immoderate dose of opium, and heeded these things but little, nor spoke of them to Rowena. Having found the wine, I recrossed the chamber, and poured out a gobletful, which I held to the lips of the fainting lady. She had now partially recovered, however, and took the vessel herself, while I sank upon an ottoman near me, with my eyes fastened upon her person. It was then that I became dis-

tinctly aware of a gentle foot-fall upon the carpet, and near the couch; and in a second thereafter, as Rowena was in the act of raising the wine to her lips, I saw, or may have dreamed that I saw, fall within the goblet, as if from some invisible spring in the atmosphere of the room, three or four large drops of a brilliant and ruby-colored fluid. If this I saw—not so Rowena. She swallowed the wine unhesitatingly, and I forbore to speak to her of a circumstance which must, after all, I considered, have been but the suggestion of a vivid imagination, rendered morbidly active by the terror of the lady, by the opium, and by the hour.

Yet I cannot conceal it from my own perception that, immediately subsequent to the fall of the ruby-drops, a rapid change for the worse took place in the disorder of my wife; so that, on the third subsequent night, the hands of her menials prepared her for the tomb, and on the fourth, I sat alone, with her shrouded body, in that fantastic chamber which had received her as my bride.—Wild visions, opium-engendered, flitted, shadow-like before me. I gazed with unquiet eye upon the sarcophagi in the angles of the room, upon the varying figures of the drapery, and upon the writhing of the particolored fires in the censer overhead. My eyes then fell, as I called to mind the circumstances of a former night, to the spot beneath the glare of the censer where I had seen the faint traces of the shadow. It was there, however, no longer; and breathing with greater freedom, I turned my glances to the pallid and rigid figure upon the bed. Then rushed upon me a thousand memories of Ligeia—and then came back upon my heart, with the turbulent violence of a flood, the whole of that unutterable wo with which I had regarded *her* thus enshrouded. The night waned; and still, with a bosom full of bitter thoughts of the one only and supremely beloved, I remained gazing upon the body of Rowena.

It might have been midnight, or perhaps earlier, or later, for I had taken no note of time, when a sob, low, gentle, but very distinct, startled me from my revery.—I *felt* that it came from the bed of ebony—the bed of death. I listened in an agony of superstitious terror—but there was no repetition of the sound. I strained my vision to detect any motion in the corpse—but there was not the slightest perceptible. Yet I could not have been deceived. I *had* heard the noise, however faint, and my soul was awakened within me. I resolutely and perseveringly kept my attention riveted upon the body. Many minutes elapsed before any circumstance occurred tending to throw light upon the mystery. At length it became evident that a slight, a very feeble, and barely noticeable tinge of color had flushed up within the cheeks, and along the sunken small veins of the eyelids. Through a species of unutterable horror and awe, for which the language of mortality has no sufficiently energetic expression, I felt my heart cease to beat, my limbs grow rigid where I sat. Yet a sense of duty finally operated to restore my self-possession. I could no longer doubt that we had been precipitate in our preparations—that Rowena still lived. It was necessary that some immediate exertion be made; yet the turret was altogether apart from the portion of the abbey tenanted by the servants—there were none within call—I had no means of summoning them to my aid without leaving the room for many minutes—and this I could not venture to do. I therefore struggled alone in my endeavors to call back the spirit still hovering. In a short period it was certain, however, that a relapse had taken place; the color disappeared from both eyelid and cheek, leaving a wanness even more than that of marble; the lips became doubly shrivelled and pinched up in the ghastly expression of death; a repulsive clamminess and coldness overspread rapidly the surface of the body; and all the usual rigorous stiffness immediately supervened. I fell back with a shudder upon the couch from which I had been so startlingly aroused, and again gave myself up to passionate waking visions of Ligeia.

An hour thus elapsed when (could it be possible?) I was a second time aware of some vague sound issuing from the region of the bed. I listened—in extremity of horror. The sound came again—it was a sigh. Rushing to the corpse, I saw—distinctly saw—a tremor upon the lips. In a minute afterwards they relaxed, disclosing a bright line of the pearly teeth. Amazement now struggled in my bosom with the profound awe which had hitherto reigned there alone. I felt that my vision grew dim, that my reason wandered; and it was only by a violent effort that I at length succeeded in nerving myself to the task which duty thus once more had pointed out. There was now a partial glow upon the forehead and upon the cheek and throat; a perceptible warmth pervaded the whole frame; there was even a slight pulsation at the heart. The lady *lived;* and with redoubled ardor I betook myself to the task of restoration. I chafed and bathed the temples and the hands, and used every exertion which experience, and no little medical reading, could suggest. But in vain. Suddenly, the color fled, the pulsation ceased, the lips resumed the expression of the dead, and, in an instant afterward, the whole body took upon itself the icy chilliness, the livid hue, the intense rigidity, the sunken outline, and all the loathsome peculiarities of that which has been, for many days, a tenant of the tomb.

And again I sunk into visions of Ligeia—and again, (what marvel that I shudder while I write?) *again* there reached my ears a low sob from the region of the ebony bed. But why shall I minutely detail the unspeakable horrors of that night? Why shall I pause to relate how, time after time, until near the period of the gray dawn, this hideous drama of revivification was repeated; how each terrific relapse was only into a sterner and apparently more irredeemable death; how each agony wore the aspect of a struggle with some invisible foe; and how each struggle was succeeded by I know not what of wild change in the personal appearance of the corpse? Let me hurry to a conclusion.

The greater part of the fearful night had worn away, and she who had been dead, once again stirred—and now more vigorously than hitherto, although arousing from a dissolution more appalling in its utter hopelessness than any. I had long ceased to struggle or to move, and remained sitting rigidly upon the ottoman, a helpless prey to a whirl of violent emotions, of which extreme awe was perhaps the least terrible, the least consuming. The corpse, I repeat, stirred, and now more vigorously than before. The hues of life flushed up with unwonted energy into the countenance—the limbs relaxed—and, save that the eyelids were yet pressed heavily together, and that the bandages and draperies of the grave still imparted their charnel character to the figure, I might have dreamed that Rowena had indeed shaken off, utterly, the fetters of Death. But if this idea was not, even then, altogether adopted, I could at least doubt no longer, when, arising from the bed, tottering, with feeble steps, with closed eyes, and with the manner of one bewildered in a dream, the thing that was enshrouded advanced bodily and palpably into the middle of the apartment.

I trembled not—I stirred not—for a crowd of unutterable fancies connected with the air, the stature, the demeanor of the figure, rushing hurriedly through my brain, had paralyzed—had chilled me into stone. I stirred not—but gazed upon the apparition. There was a mad disorder in my thoughts—a tumult unappeasable. Could it, indeed, be the *living* Rowena who confronted me? Could it indeed be Rowena *at all*—the fair-haired, the blue-eyed Lady Rowena Trevanion of Tremaine? Why, *why* should I doubt it? The bandage lay heavily about the mouth—but then might it not be the mouth of the breathing Lady of Tremaine? And the cheeks—there were the roses as in her noon of life—yes, these might indeed be the fair cheeks of the living Lady of Tremaine. And the chin, with its dimples, as in health, might it not be hers? but *had she then grown taller since her malady?* What inexpressible madness seized me with that thought? One bound, and I had reached her feet! Shrinking from my touch, she let fall from her head, unloosened, the ghastly cerements which had confined it, and there streamed forth, into the rushing atmosphere of the

WALKS

chamber, huge masses of long and dishevelled hair; *it was blacker than the raven wings of the midnight!* And now slowly opened *the eyes* of the figure which stood before me. "Here then, at least," I shrieked aloud, "can I never—can I never be mistaken—these are the full, and the black, and the wild eyes—of my lost love—of the lady—of the LADY LIGEIA."

1838

The Fall of the House of Usher

The epigraph may be translated: "His heart is a lute held up; as soon as it is touched it resounds." This we may remember when we come to the characterization of Usher, with his "morbid acuteness of the senses" and "excessive nervous agitation." Cf. "Israfel," line 2.

Son coeur est un luth suspendu;
Sitôt qu'on le touche il résonne.
—*De Béranger.*

During the whole of a dull, dark, and soundless day in the autumn of the year, when the clouds hung oppressively low in the heavens, I had been passing alone, on horseback, through a singularly dreary tract of country; and at length found myself, as the shades of the evening drew on, within view of the melancholy House of Usher. I know not how it was—but, with the first glimpse of the building, a sense of insufferable gloom pervaded my spirit. I say insufferable; for the feeling was unrelieved by any of that half-pleasurable, because poetic, sentiment, with which the mind usually receives even the sternest natural images of the desolate or terrible. I looked upon the scene before me—upon the mere house, and the simple landscape features of the domain—upon the bleak walls—upon the vacant eye-like windows—upon a few rank sedges—and upon a few white trunks of decayed trees—with an utter depression of soul which I can compare to no earthly sensation more properly than to the after-dream of the reveller upon opium—the bitter lapse into everyday life—the hideous dropping off of the veil. There was an iciness, a sinking, a sickening of the heart—an unredeemed dreariness of thought which no goading of the imagination could torture into aught of the sublime. What was it—I paused to think—what was it that so unnerved me in the contemplation of the House of Usher? It was a mystery all insoluble; nor could I grapple with the shadowy fancies that crowded upon me as I pondered. I was forced to fall back upon the unsatisfactory conclusion, that while, beyond doubt, there *are* combinations of very simple natural objects which have the power of thus affecting us, still the analysis of this

power lies among considerations beyond our depth. It was possible, I reflected, that a mere different arrangement of the particulars of the scene, of the details of the picture, would be sufficient to modify, or perhaps to annihilate its capacity for sorrowful impression; and acting upon this idea, I reined my horse to the precipitous brink of a black and lurid tarn that lay in unruffled lustre by the dwelling, and gazed down—but with a shudder even more thrilling than before—upon the remodelled and inverted images of the gray sedge, and the ghastly tree-stems, and the vacant and eye-like windows.

Nevertheless, in this mansion of gloom I now proposed to myself a sojourn of some weeks. Its proprietor, Roderick Usher, had been one of my boon companions in boyhood; but many years had elapsed since our last meeting. A letter, however, had lately reached me in a distant part of the country—a letter from him—which in its wildly importunate nature, had admitted of no other than a personal reply. The MS. gave evidence of nervous agitation. The writer spoke of acute bodily illness—of a mental disorder which oppressed him—and of an earnest desire to see me, as his best, and indeed his only personal friend, with a view of attempting, by the cheerfulness of my society, some alleviation of his malady. It was the manner in which all this, and much more, was said—it was the apparent *heart* that went with his request—which allowed me no room for hesitation; and I accordingly obeyed forthwith what I still considered a very singular summons.

Although, as boys, we had been even intimate associates, yet I really knew little of my friend. His reserve had been always excessive and habitual. I was aware, however, that his very ancient family had been noted, time out of mind, for a peculiar sensibility of temperament, displaying itself, through long ages, in many works of exalted art, and manifested, of late, in repeated deeds of munificent yet unobtrusive charity, as well as in a passionate devotion to the intricacies, perhaps even more than to the orthodox and easily recognizable beauties, of musical science. I had learned, too, the very remarkable fact, that the stem of the Usher race, all time-honored as it was, had put forth, at no period, any enduring branch; in other words, that the entire family lay in the direct line of descent, and had always, with very trifling and very temporary variation, so lain. It was this deficiency, I considered, while running over in thought the perfect keeping of the character of the premises with the accredited character of the people, and while speculating upon the possible influence which the one, in the long lapse of centuries, might have exercised upon the other—it was this deficiency, perhaps, of collateral issue, and the consequent undeviating transmission, from sire to son, of the patrimony with the name, which had, at length, so identified the two as to merge the original title of the estate in the quaint and equivocal appellation of the "House of Usher"—an appellation which seemed to include, in the minds of the peasantry who used it, both the family and the family mansion.

I have said that the sole effect of my somewhat childish experiment—that of looking down within the tarn—had been to deepen the first singular impression. There can be no doubt that the consciousness of the rapid increase of my superstition—for why should I not so term it?—served mainly to accelerate the increase itself. Such, I have long known, is the paradoxical law of all sentiments having terror as a basis. And it might have been for this reason only, that, when I again uplifted my eyes to the house itself, from its image in the pool, there grew in my mind a strange fancy—a fancy so ridiculous, indeed, that I but mention it to show the vivid force of the sensations which oppressed me. I had so worked upon my imagination as really to believe that about the whole mansion and domain there hung an atmosphere peculiar to themselves and their immediate vicinity—an atmosphere which had no affinity with the air of heaven, but which had reeked up from the decayed trees, and the gray wall, and the silent tarn—a pestilent and mystic vapour, dull, sluggish, faintly discernible, and leaden-hued.

Shaking off from my spirit what *must* have been a dream, I scanned more narrowly the real aspect of the building. Its principal feature seemed to be that of an excessive antiquity. The discoloration of ages had been great. Minute fungi overspread the whole exterior, hanging in a fine tangled web-work from the eaves. Yet all this was apart from any extraordinary dilapidation. No portion of the masonry had fallen; and there appeared to be a wild inconsistency between its still perfect adaptation of parts, and the crumbling condition of the individual stones. In this there was much that reminded me of the specious totality of old wood-work which has rotted for long years in some neglected vault, with no disturbance from the breath of the external air. Beyond this indication of extensive decay, however, the fabric gave little token of instability. Perhaps the eye of a scrutinising observer might have discovered a barely perceptible fissure, which, extending from the roof of the building in front, made its way down the wall in a zigzag direction, until it became lost in the sullen waters of the tarn.

Noticing these things, I rode over a short causeway to the house. A servant in waiting took my horse, and I entered the Gothic archway of the hall. A valet, of stealthy step, thence conducted me, in silence, through many dark and intricate passages in

my progress to the *studio* of his master. Much that I encountered on the way contributed, I know not how, to heighten the vague sentiments of which I have already spoken. While the objects around me—while the carvings of the ceilings, the sombre tapestries of the walls, the ebon blackness of the floors, and the phantasmagoric armorial trophies which rattled as I strode, were but matters to which, or to such as which, I had been accustomed from my infancy—while I hesitated not to acknowledge how familiar was all this—I still wondered to find how unfamiliar were the fancies which ordinary images were stirring up. On one of the staircases, I met the physician of the family. His countenance, I thought, wore a mingled expression of low cunning and perplexity. He accosted me with trepidation and passed on. The valet now threw open a door and ushered me into the presence of his master.

The room in which I found myself was very large and lofty. The windows were long, narrow, and pointed, and at so vast a distance from the black oaken floor as to be altogether inaccessible from within. Feeble gleams of encrimsoned light made their way through the trellised panes, and served to render sufficiently distinct the more prominent objects around; the eye, however, struggled in vain to reach the remoter angles of the chamber, or the recesses of the vaulted and fretted ceiling. Dark draperies hung upon the walls. The general furniture was profuse, comfortless, antique, and tattered. Many books and musical instruments lay scattered about, but failed to give any vitality to the scene. I felt that I breathed an atmosphere of sorrow. An air of stern, deep, and irredeemable gloom hung over and pervaded all.

Upon my entrance, Usher arose from a sofa on which he had been lying at full length, and greeted me with a vivacious warmth which had much in it, I at first thought, of an overdone cordiality—of the constrained effort of the *ennuyé* man of the world. A glance, however, at his countenance convinced me of his perfect sincerity. We sat down; and for some moments, while he spoke not, I gazed upon him with a feeling half of pity, half of awe. Surely, man had never before so terribly altered, in so brief a period, as had Roderick Usher! It was with difficulty that I could bring myself to admit the identity of the wan being before me with the companion of my early boyhood. Yet the character of his face had been at all times remarkable. A cadaverousness of complexion; an eye large, liquid, and luminous beyond comparison; lips somewhat thin and very pallid, but of a surpassingly beautiful curve; a nose of a delicate Hebrew model, but with a breadth of nostril unusual in similar formations; a finely moulded chin, speaking, in its want of prominence, of a want of moral energy; hair of a more than web-like softness and tenuity; these features, with an inordinate expansion above the regions of the temple, made up altogether a countenance not easily to be forgotten. And now in the mere exaggeration of the prevailing character of these features, and of the expression they were wont to convey, lay so much of change that I doubted to whom I spoke. The now ghastly pallor of the skin, and the now miraculous lustre of the eye, above all things startled and even awed me. The silken hair, too, had been suffered to grow all unheeded, and as, in its wild gossamer texture, it floated rather than fell about the face, I could not, even with effort, connect its arabesque expression with any idea of simple humanity.

In the manner of my friend I was at once struck with an incoherence—an inconsistency; and I soon found this to arise from a series of feeble and futile struggles to overcome an habitual trepidancy—an excessive nervous agitation. For something of this nature I had indeed been prepared, no less by his letter, than by reminiscences of certain boyish traits, and by conclusions deduced from his peculiar physical conformation and temperament. His action was alternately vivacious and sullen. His voice varied rapidly from a tremendous indecision (when the animal spirits seemed utterly in abeyance) to that species of energetic concision—that abrupt, weighty, unhurried, and hollow-sounding enunciation—that leaden, self-balanced and perfectly modulated guttural utterance, which may be observed in the lost drunkard, or the irreclaimable eater of opium, during the periods of his most intense excitement.

It was thus that he spoke of the object of my visit, of his earnest desire to see me, and of the solace he expected me to afford him. He entered, at some length, into what he conceived to be the nature of his malady. It was, he said, a constitutional and a family evil, and one for which he despaired to find a remedy—a mere nervous affection, he immediately added, which would undoubtedly soon pass off. It displayed itself in a host of unnatural sensations. Some of these, as he detailed them, interested and bewildered me; although, perhaps, the terms and the general manner of the narration had their weight. He suffered much from a morbid acuteness of the senses; the most insipid food was alone endurable; he could wear only garments of certain texture; the odours of all flowers were oppressive; his eyes were tortured by even a faint light; and there were but peculiar sounds, and these from stringed instruments, which did not inspire him with horror.

To an anomalous species of terror I found him a bounden slave. "I shall perish," said he, "I *must* perish in this deplorable folly. Thus, thus, and not otherwise, shall I be lost. I dread the events of the future, not in themselves, but in their results. I shudder at the thought of any, even the most trivial, incident, which may operate upon this intolerable agitation of soul. I have, indeed, no abhorrence of danger, except in its absolute effect—in terror. In this unnerved—in this pitiable condition, I feel that the period will sooner or later arrive when I must abandon life and reason together, in some struggle with the grim phantasm, FEAR."

I learned, moreover, at intervals, and through broken and equivocal hints, another singular feature of his mental condition. He was enchained by certain superstitious impressions in regard to the dwelling which he tenanted, and whence, for many years, he had never ventured forth—in regard to an influence whose supposititious force was conveyed in terms too shadowy here to be re-stated—an influence which some peculiarities in the mere form and substance of his family mansion, had, by dint of long sufferance, he said, obtained over his spirit—an effect which the *physique* of the gray walls and turrets, and of the dim tarn into which they all looked down, had, at length, brought about upon the *morale* of his existence.

He admitted, however, although with hesitation, that much of the peculiar gloom which thus afflicted him could be traced to a more natural and far more palpable origin—to the severe and long-continued illness—indeed to the evidently approaching dissolution—of a tenderly beloved sister—his sole companion for long years—his last and only relative on earth. "Her decease," he said, with a bitterness which I can never forget, "would leave him (him the hopeless and the frail) the last of the ancient race of the Ushers." While he spoke, the lady Madeline (for so was she called) passed slowly through a remote portion of the apartment, and, without having noticed my presence, disappeared. I regarded her with an utter astonishment not unmingled with dread—and yet I found it impossible to account for such feelings. A sensation of stupor oppressed me, as my eyes followed her retreating steps. When a door, at length, closed upon her, my glance sought instinctively and eagerly the countenance of the brother—but he had buried his face in his hands, and I could only perceive that a far more than ordinary wanness had overspread the emaciated fingers through which trickled many passionate tears.

The disease of the lady Madeline had long baffled the skill of her physicians. A settled apathy, a gradual wasting away of the person, and frequent although transient affections of a partially cataleptical character, were the unusual diagnosis. Hitherto she had steadily borne up against the pressure of her malady, and had not betaken herself finally to bed; but, on the closing in of the evening of my arrival at the house, she succumbed (as her brother told me at night with inexpressible agitation) to the prostrating power of the destroyer; and I learned that the glimpse I had obtained of her person would thus probably be the last I should obtain—that the lady, at least while living, would be seen by me no more.

For several days ensuing, her name was unmentioned by either Usher or myself: and during this period I was busied in earnest endeavours to alleviate the melancholy of my friend. We painted and read together; or I listened, as if in a dream, to the wild improvisations of his speaking guitar. And thus, as a closer and still closer intimacy admitted me more unreservedly into the recesses of his spirit, the more bitterly did I perceive the futility of all attempt at cheering a mind from which darkness, as if an inherent positive quality, poured forth upon all objects of the moral and physical universe, in one unceasing radiation of gloom.

I shall ever bear about me a memory of the many solemn hours I thus spent alone with the master of the House of Usher. Yet I should fail in any attempt to convey an idea of the exact character of the studies, or of the occupations, in which he involved me, or led me the way. An excited and highly distempered ideality threw a sulphureous lustre over all. His long improvised dirges will ring forever in my ears. Among other things, I hold painfully in mind a certain singular perversion and amplification of the wild air of the last waltz of Von Weber. From the paintings over which his elaborate fancy brooded, and which grew, touch by touch, into vaguenesses at which I shuddered the more thrillingly, because I shuddered knowing not why;—from these paintings (vivid as their images now are before me) I would in vain endeavour to educe more than a small portion which should lie within the compass of merely written words. By the utter simplicity, by the nakedness of his designs, he arrested and overawed attention. If ever mortal painted an idea, that mortal was Roderick Usher. For me at least—in the circumstances then surrounding me—there arose, out of the pure abstractions which the hypochondriac contrived to throw upon his canvas, an intensity of intolerable awe, no shadow of which felt I ever yet in the contemplation of the certainly glowing yet too concrete reveries of Fuseli.

One of the phantasmagoric conceptions of my friend, partaking not so rigidly of the spirit of abstraction, may be shadowed forth, although feebly, in words. A small picture presented the interior of an immensely long and rectangular vault or tunnel, with low walls, smooth, white, and without interruption or device. Certain accessory points of the design served well to convey the idea that this excavation lay at an exceeding depth below the surface of the earth. No outlet was observed in any portion of its vast extent, and no torch, or other artificial source of light was discernible; yet a flood of intense rays rolled throughout, and bathed the whole in a ghastly and inappropriate splendour.

I have just spoken of that morbid condition of the auditory nerve which rendered all music intolerable to the sufferer, with the exception of certain effects of stringed instruments. It was, perhaps, the narrow limits to which he thus confined himself upon the guitar, which gave birth, in great measure, to the fantastic character of his performances. But the fervid *facility* of his *impromptus* could not be so accounted for. They must have been, and were, in the notes, as well as in the words of his wild fantasias (for he not unfrequently accompanied himself with rhymed verbal improvisations), the result of that intense mental collectedness and concentration to which I have previously alluded as observable only in particular moments of the highest artificial excitement. The words of one of these rhapsodies I have easily remembered. I was, perhaps, the more forcibly impressed with it, as he gave it, because, in the under or mystic current of its meaning, I fancied that I perceived, and for the first time, a full consciousness on the part of Usher, of the tottering of his lofty reason upon her throne. The verses, which were entitled "The Haunted Palace,"[1] ran very nearly, if not accurately, thus:

I

In the greenest of our valleys,
  By good angels tenanted,
Once a fair and stately palace—
  Radiant palace—reared its head.
In the monarch Thought's dominion—
  It stood there!
Never seraph spread a pinion
  Over fabric half so fair!

II

Banners yellow, glorious, golden,
  On its roof did float and flow,
(This—all this—was in the olden
  Time long ago)
And every gentle air that dallied,
  In that sweet day,
Along the ramparts plumed and pallid,
  A wingèd odour went away.

III

Wanderers in that happy valley
  Through two luminous windows saw
Spirits moving musically
  To a lute's well-tunèd law,
Round about a throne, where sitting
  (Porphyrogene!)
In state his glory well befitting,
  The ruler of the realm was seen.

[1] The poem was first published, separately, in 1839, five months before Poe incorporated it into the story.

IV

And all with pearl and ruby glowing
  Was the fair palace door,
Through which came flowing, flowing, flowing
  And sparkling evermore,
A troop of Echoes, whose sweet duty
  Was but to sing,
In voices of surpassing beauty,
  The wit and wisdom of their king.

V

But evil things, in robes of sorrow,
  Assailed the monarch's high estate;
(Ah, let us mourn, for never morrow
  Shall dawn upon him, desolate!)
And round about his home, the glory
  That blushed and bloomed
Is but a dim-remembered story
  Of the old time entombed.

VI

And travellers now within that valley,
  Through the red-litten windows, see
Vast forms that move fantastically
  To a discordant melody;
While, like a ghastly rapid river,
  Through the pale door,
A hideous throng rush out forever,
  And laugh—but smile no more.

I well remember that suggestions arising from this ballad, led us into a train of thought, wherein there became manifest an opinion of Usher's which I mention not so much on account of its novelty, (for other men[2] have thought thus,) as on account of the pertinacity with which he maintained it. This opinion, in its general form, was that of the sentience of all vegetable things. But, in his disordered fancy, the idea had assumed a more daring character, and trespassed, under certain conditions, upon the kingdom of inorganization. I lack words to express the full extent, or the earnest *abandon* of his persuasion. The belief, however, was connected (as I have previously hinted) with the gray stones of the home of his forefathers. The conditions of the sentience had been here, he imagined, fulfilled in the method of collocation of these stones—in the order of their arrangement, as well as in that of the many *fungi* which overspread them, and of the decayed trees which stood around—above all, in the long undisturbed endurance of this arrangement, and in its reduplication in the still waters of the tarn. Its evidence—the evidence of the sentience—was to be seen, he said, (and I here started as he spoke,) in the gradual yet certain condensation of an atmosphere of their own about the waters and the walls. The

result was discoverable, he added, in that silent, yet importunate and terrible influence which for centuries had moulded the destinies of his family, and which made *him* what I now saw him—what he was. Such opinions need no comment, and I will make none.

Our books[3]—the books which, for years, had formed no small portion of the mental existence of the invalid—were, as might be supposed, in strict keeping with this character of phantasm. We pored together over such works as the *Ververt et Chartreuse* of Gresset; the *Belphegor* of Machiavelli; the *Heaven and Hell* of Swedenborg; the *Subterranean Voyage of Nicholas Klimm* by Holberg; the *Chiromancy* of Robert Flud, of Jean D'Indaginé, and of De la Chambre; the *Journey into the Blue Distance* of Tieck; and the *City of the Sun* of Campanella. One favorite volume was a small octavo edition of the *Directorium Inquisitorum*, by the Dominican Eymeric de Gironne; and there were passages in Pomponius Mela, about the old African Satyrs and Aegipans, over which Usher would sit dreaming for hours. His chief delight, however, was found in the perusal of an exceedingly rare and curious book in quarto Gothic—the manual of a forgotten church—the *Vigiliae Mortuorum secundum Chorum Ecclesiae Maguntinae.*[4]

I could not help thinking of the wild ritual of this work, and of its probable influence upon the hypochondriac, when one evening, having informed me abruptly that the lady Madeline was no more, he stated his intention of preserving her corpse for a fortnight, (previously to its final interment,) in one of the numerous vaults within the main walls of the building. The worldly reason, however, assigned for this singular proceeding, was one which I did not feel at liberty to dispute. The brother had been led to his resolution (so he told me) by consideration of the unusual character of the malady of the deceased, of certain obtrusive and eager inquiries on the part of her medical men, and of the remote and exposed situation of the burial-ground of the family. I will not deny that when I called to mind the sinister countenance of the person whom I met upon the staircase, on the day of my arrival at the house, I had no desire to oppose what I regarded as at best but a harmless, and by no means an unnatural, precaution.

At the request of Usher, I personally aided him in the arrangements for the temporary entombment.

---

[2] Watson, Dr. Percival, Spallanzani, and especially the Bishop of Llandaff.—See "Chemical Essays," vol. v. [Poe's note.]

[3] Davidson indicates that all the volumes in Usher's library are authentic except for the *Mad Trist*, mentioned later in the story. The works deal mainly with the occult and magical.

[4] Vigils for the Dead according to the Choir of the Church of Mayence.

The body having been encoffined, we two alone bore it to its rest. The vault in which we placed it (and which had been so long unopened that our torches, half smothered in its oppressive atmosphere, gave us little opportunity for investigation) was small, damp, and entirely without means of admission for light; lying, at great depth, immediately beneath that portion of the building in which was my own sleeping apartment. It had been used, apparently, in remote feudal times, for the worst purposes of a donjon-keep, and in later days as a place of deposit for powder, or some other highly combustible substance, as a portion of its floor, and the whole interior of a long archway through which we reached it, were carefully sheathed with copper. The door, of massive iron, had been, also, similarly protected. Its immense weight caused an unusually sharp grating sound, as it moved upon its hinges.

Having deposited our mournful burden upon tressels within this region of horror, we partially turned aside the yet unscrewed lid of the coffin, and looked upon the face of the tenant. A striking similitude between the brother and sister now first arrested my attention; and Usher, divining, perhaps, my thoughts, murmured out some few words from which I learned that the deceased and himself had been twins, and that sympathies of a scarcely intelligible nature had always existed between them. Our glances, however, rested not long upon the dead—for we could not regard her unawed. The disease which had thus entombed the lady in the maturity of youth, had left, as usual in all maladies of a strictly cataleptical character, the mockery of a faint blush upon the bosom and the face, and that suspiciously lingering smile upon the lip which is so terrible in death. We replaced and screwed down the lid, and, having secured the door of iron, made our way, with toil, into the scarcely less gloomy apartments of the upper portion of the house.

And now, some days of bitter grief having elapsed, an observable change came over the features of the mental disorder of my friend. His ordinary manner had vanished. His ordinary occupations were neglected or forgotten. He roamed from chamber to chamber with hurried, unequal, and objectless step. The pallor of his countenance had assumed, if possible, a more ghastly hue—but the luminousness of his eye had utterly gone out. The once occasional huskiness of his tone was heard no more; and a tremulous quaver, as if of extreme terror, habitually characterized his utterance. There were times, indeed, when I thought his unceasingly agitated mind was labouring with some oppressive secret, to divulge which he struggled for the necessary courage. At times, again, I was obliged to resolve all into the mere inexplicable vagaries of madness, for I beheld him gazing upon vacancy for long

hours, in an attitude of the profoundest attention, as if listening to some imaginary sound. It was no wonder that his condition terrified—that it infected me. I felt creeping upon me, by slow yet certain degrees, the wild influences of his own fantastic yet impressive superstitions.

It was, especially, upon retiring to bed late in the night of the seventh or eighth day after the placing of the lady Madeline within the donjon, that I experienced the full power of such feelings. Sleep came not near my couch,—while the hours waned and waned away. I struggled to reason off the nervousness which had dominion over me. I endeavoured to believe that much, if not all, of what I felt, was due to the bewildering influence of the gloomy furniture of the room—of the dark and tattered draperies, which, tortured into motion by the breath of a rising tempest, swayed fitfully to and fro upon the walls, and rustled uneasily about the decorations of the bed. But my efforts were fruitless. An irrepressible tremour gradually pervaded my frame; and, at length, there sat upon my very heart an incubus of utterly causeless alarm. Shaking this off with a gasp and a struggle, I uplifted myself upon the pillows, and, peering earnestly within the intense darkness of the chamber, hearkened—I know not why, except that an instinctive spirit prompted me—to certain low and indefinite sounds which came, through the pauses of the storm, at long intervals, I knew not whence. Overpowered by an intense sentiment of horror, unaccountable yet unendurable, I threw on my clothes with haste (for I felt that I should sleep no more during the night), and endeavoured to arouse myself from the pitiable condition into which I had fallen, by pacing rapidly to and fro through the apartment.

I had taken but few turns in this manner, when a light step on an adjoining staircase arrested my attention. I presently recognized it as that of Usher. In an instant afterward he rapped, with a gentle touch, at my door, and entered, bearing a lamp. His countenance was, as usual, cadaverously wan—but, moreover, there was a species of mad hilarity in his eyes—an evidently restrained *hysteria* in his whole demeanour. His air appalled me—but anything was preferable to the solitude which I had so long endured, and I even welcomed his presence as a relief.

"And you have not seen it?" he said abruptly, after having stared about him for some moments in silence—"you have not then seen it?—but, stay! you shall." Thus speaking, and having carefully shaded his lamp, he hurried to one of the casements, and threw it freely open to the storm.

The impetuous fury of the entering gust nearly lifted us from our feet. It was, indeed, a tempestuous yet sternly beautiful night, and one wildly singular in its terror and its beauty. A whirlwind had apparently collected its force in our vicinity; for there were frequent and violent alterations in the direction of the wind; and the exceeding density of the clouds (which hung so low as to press upon the turrets of the house) did not prevent our perceiving the life-like velocity with which they flew careering from all points against each other, without passing away into the distance. I say that even their exceeding density did not prevent our perceiving this—yet we had no glimpse of the moon or stars—nor was there any flashing forth of the lightning. But the under surfaces of the huge masses of agitated vapour, as well as all terrestrial objects immediately around us, were glowing in the unnatural light of a faintly luminous and distinctly visible gaseous exhalation which hung about and enshrouded the mansion.

"You must not—you shall not behold this!" said I, shudderingly, to Usher, as I led him, with a gentle violence, from the window to a seat. "These appearances, which bewilder you, are merely electrical phenomena not uncommon—or it may be that they have their ghastly origin in the rank miasma of the tarn. Let us close this casement;—the air is chilling and dangerous to your frame. Here is one of your favourite romances. I will read, and you shall listen;—and so we will pass away this terrible night together."

The antique volume which I had taken up was the *Mad Trist* of Sir Launcelot Canning; but I had called it a favourite of Usher's more in sad jest than in earnest; for, in truth, there is little in its uncouth and unimaginative prolixity which could have had interest for the lofty and spiritual ideality of my friend. It was, however, the only book immediately at hand; and I indulged a vague hope that the excitement which now agitated the hypochondriac, might find relief (for the history of mental disorder is full of similar anomalies) even in the extremeness of the folly which I should read. Could I have judged, indeed, by the wild overstrained air of vivacity with which he hearkened, or apparently hearkened, to the words of the tale, I might well have congratulated myself upon the success of my design.

I had arrived at that well-known portion of the story where Ethelred, the hero of the *Trist*, having sought in vain for peaceable admission into the dwelling of the hermit, proceeds to make good an entrance by force. Here, it will be remembered, the words of the narrative run thus:

"And Ethelred, who was by nature of a doughty heart, and who was now mighty withal, on account of the powerfulness of the wine which he had drunken, waited no longer to hold parley with the hermit, who, in sooth, was of an obstinate and maliceful turn, but, feeling the rain upon his shoulders, and fearing the rising of the tempest, uplifted his mace outright, and with blows, made quickly room in the plankings of the door for his gauntleted hand; and now pulling therewith sturdily, he so cracked, and ripped, and tore all asunder, that the noise of the dry and hollow-sounding wood alarumed and reverberated throughout the forest."

At the termination of this sentence I started, and for a moment, paused; for it appeared to me (although I at once concluded that my excited fancy had deceived me)—it appeared to me that, from some very remote portion of the mansion, there came, indistinctly, to my ears, what might have been, in its exact similarity of character, the echo (but a stifled and dull one certainly) of the very cracking and ripping sound which Sir Launcelot had so particularly described. It was, beyond doubt, the coincidence alone which had arrested my attention; for, amid the rattling of the sashes of the casements, and the ordinary commingled noises of the still increasing storm, the sound, in itself, had nothing, surely, which should have interested or disturbed me. I continued the story:

"But the good champion Ethelred, now entering within the door, was sore enraged and amazed to perceive no signal of the maliceful hermit; but, in the stead thereof, a dragon of a scaly and prodigious demeanour, and of a fiery tongue, which sate in guard before a palace of gold, with a floor of silver; and upon the wall there hung a shield of shining brass with this legend enwritten—

Who entereth herein, a conqueror hath bin;
Who slayeth the dragon, the shield he shall win.

And Ethelred uplifted his mace, and struck upon the head of the dragon, which fell before him, and gave up his pesty breath, with a shriek so horrid and harsh, and withal so piercing, that Ethelred had fain to close his ears with his hands against the dreadful noise of it, the like whereof was never before heard."

Here again I paused abruptly, and now with a feeling of wild amazement—for there could be no doubt whatever that, in this instance, I did actually hear (although from what direction it proceeded I found it impossible to say) a low and apparently distant, but harsh, protracted, and most unusual screaming or grating sound—the exact counterpart of what my fancy had already conjured up for the dragon's unnatural shriek as described by the romancer.

Oppressed, as I certainly was, upon the occurrence of this second and most extraordinary coincidence, by a thousand conflicting sensations, in which wonder and extreme terror were predominant, I still retained sufficient presence of mind to avoid exciting, by any observation, the sensitive nervousness of my companion. I was by no means certain that he had noticed the sounds in question; although, assuredly, a strange alteration had, during the last few minutes, taken place in his demeanour. From a position fronting my own, he had gradually brought round his chair, so as to sit with his face to the door of the chamber; and thus I could but partially perceive his features, although I saw that his lips trembled as if he were murmuring inaudibly. His head had dropped upon his breast—yet I knew that he was not asleep, from the wide and rigid opening of the eye as I caught a glance of it in profile. The motion of his body, too, was at variance with this idea—for he rocked from side to side with a gentle yet constant and uniform sway. Having rapidly taken notice of all this, I resumed the narrative of Sir Launcelot, which thus proceeded:

"And now, the champion, having escaped from the terrible fury of the dragon, bethinking himself of the brazen shield, and of the breaking up of the enchantment which was upon it, removed the carcass from out of the way before him, and approached valorously over the silver pavement of the castle to where the shield was upon the wall; which in sooth tarried not for his full coming, but fell down at his feet upon the silver floor, with a mighty great and terrible ringing sound."

No sooner had these syllables passed my lips, than—as if a shield of brass had indeed, at the moment, fallen heavily upon a floor of silver—I became aware of a distinct, hollow, metallic, and clangorous, yet apparently muffled reverberation. Completely unnerved, I leaped to my feet; but the measured rocking movement of Usher was undisturbed. I rushed to the chair in which he sat. His eyes were bent fixedly before him, and throughout his whole countenance there reigned a stony rigidity. But as I placed my hand upon his shoulder, there came a strong shudder over his whole person; a sickly smile quivered about his lips; and I saw that he spoke in a low, hurried, and gibbering murmur, as if unconscious of my presence. Bending closely over him, I at length drank in the hideous import of his words.

"Not hear it?—yes, I hear it, and *have* heard it. Long—long—long—many minutes, many hours, many days, have I heard it—yet I dared not—oh, pity me, miserable wretch that I am!—I dared not—I *dared* not speak! *We have put her living in the tomb!* Said I not that my senses were acute? I *now* tell you that I heard her first feeble movements in the hollow coffin. I heard them—many, many days ago—yet I dared not—*I dared not speak!* And now—to-night—Ethelred—ha! ha!—the breaking of the hermit's door, and the death-cry of the dragon, and the clangour of the shield!—say, rather, the rending of her coffin, and the grating of the iron hinges of her prison, and her struggles within the coppered archway of the vault! Oh whither shall I fly? Will she not be here anon? Is she not hurrying to upbraid me for my haste? Have I not heard her footstep on the stair? Do I not distinguish that heavy and horrible beating of her heart? MADMAN!"—here he sprang furiously to his feet, and shrieked out his syllables, as if in the effort he were giving up his soul—"MADMAN! I TELL YOU THAT SHE NOW STANDS WITHOUT THE DOOR!"

As if in the superhuman energy of his utterance there had been found the potency of a spell—the huge antique panels to which the speaker pointed, threw slowly back, upon the instant, their ponderous and ebony jaws. It was the work of the rushing gust—but then without those doors there DID stand the lofty and enshrouded figure of the lady Madeline of Usher. There was blood upon her white robes, and the evidence of some bitter struggle upon every portion of her emaciated frame. For a moment she remained trembling and reeling to and fro upon the threshold, then, with a low moaning cry, fell heavily inward upon the person of her brother, and, in her violent and now final death-agonies, bore him to the floor a corpse, and a victim to the terrors he had anticipated.

From that chamber, and from that mansion, I fled aghast. The storm was still abroad in all its wrath as I found myself crossing the old causeway. Suddenly there shot along the path a wild light, and I turned to see whence a gleam so unusual could have issued; for the vast house and its shadows were alone behind me. The radiance was that of the full, setting, and blood-red moon, which now shone vividly through that once barely-discernible fissure of which I have before spoken as extending from the roof of the building, in a zigzag direction, to the base. While I gazed, this fissure rapidly widened—there came a fierce breath of the whirlwind—the entire orb of the satellite burst at once upon my sight—my brain reeled as I saw the mighty walls rushing asunder—there was a long tumultuous shouting sound like the voice of a thousand waters—and the deep and dank tarn at my feet closed sullenly and silently over the fragments of the "HOUSE OF USHER."

1839

The Masque of the Red Death

The "Red Death" had long devastated the country. No pestilence had ever been so fatal, or so hideous. Blood was its Avatar and its seal—the redness and the horror of blood. There were sharp pains, and sudden dizziness, and then profuse bleeding at the pores, with dissolution. The scarlet stains upon the body, and especially upon the face of the victim, were the pest ban which shut him out from the aid and from the sympathy of his fellow-men. And the whole seizure, progress and termination of the disease, were the incidents of half an hour.

But the Prince Prospero was happy and dauntless and sagacious. When his dominions were half depopulated, he summoned to his presence a thousand hale and light-hearted friends from among the knights and dames of his court, and with these retired to the deep seclusion of one of his castellated abbeys. This was an extensive and magnificent structure, the creation of the prince's own eccentric yet august taste. A strong and lofty wall girdled it in. This wall had gates of iron. The courtiers, having entered, brought furnaces and massy hammers and welded the bolts. They resolved to leave means neither of ingress or egress to the sudden impulses of despair or of frenzy from within. The abbey was amply provisioned. With such precautions the courtiers might bid defiance to contagion. The external world could take care of itself. In the meantime it was folly to grieve, or to think. The prince had provided all the appliances of pleasure. There were buffoons, there were improvisatori, there were ballet-dancers, there were musicians, there was Beauty, there was wine. All these and security were within. Without was the "Red Death."

It was toward the close of the fifth or sixth month of his seclusion, and while the pestilence raged most furiously abroad, that the Prince Prospero entertained his thousand friends at a masked ball of the most unusual magnificence.

It was a voluptuous scene, that masquerade. But first let me tell of the rooms in which it was held. There were seven—an imperial suite. In many palaces, however, such suites form a long and straight vista, while the folding-doors slide back nearly to the walls on either hand, so that the view of the whole extent is scarcely impeded. Here the case was very different; as might have been expected from the duke's love of the *bizarre*. The apartments were so irregularly disposed that the vision embraced but little more than one at a time. There was a sharp turn at every twenty or thirty yards, and at each turn a novel effect. To the right and left, in the middle of each wall, a tall and narrow Gothic window looked out upon a closed corridor which pursued the windings of the suite. These windows were of stained glass whose color varied in accordance with the prevailing hue of the decorations of the chamber into which it opened. That at the eastern extremity was hung, for example, in blue—and vividly blue were its windows. The second chamber was purple in its ornaments and tapestries, and here the panes were purple. The third was green

throughout, and so were the casements. The fourth was furnished and lighted with orange—the fifth with white—the sixth with violet. The seventh apartment was closely shrouded in black velvet tapestries that hung all over the ceiling and down the walls, falling in heavy folds upon a carpet of the same material and hue. But in this chamber only, the color of the windows failed to correspond with the decorations. The panes here were scarlet—a deep blood color. Now in no one of the seven apartments was there any lamp or candelabrum, amid the profusion of golden ornaments that lay scattered to and fro or depended from the roof. There was no light of any kind emanating from lamp or candle within the suite of chambers. But in the corridors that followed the suite there stood, opposite to each window, a heavy tripod bearing a brazier of fire that projected its rays through the tinted glass and so glaringly illuminated the room. And thus were produced a multitude of gaudy and fantastic appearances. But in the western or black chamber the effect of the fire-light that streamed upon the dark hangings through the blood-tinted panes, was ghastly in the extreme, and produced so wild a look upon the countenances of those who entered, that there were few of the company bold enough to set foot within its precincts at all.

It was in this apartment, also, that there stood against the western wall a gigantic clock of ebony. Its pendulum swung to and fro with a dull, heavy, monotonous clang; and, when the minute-hand made the circuit of the face, and the hour was to be stricken, there came from the brazen lungs of the clock a sound which was clear and loud and deep and exceedingly musical, but of so peculiar a note and emphasis that, at each lapse of an hour, the musicians of the orchestra were constrained to pause, momentarily, in their performance, to hearken to the sound; and thus the waltzers perforce ceased their evolutions; and there was a brief disconcert of the whole gay company; and, while the chimes of the clock yet rang, it was observed that the giddiest grew pale, and the more aged and sedate passed their hands over their brows as if in confused reverie or meditation. But when the echoes had fully ceased, a light laughter at once pervaded the assembly; the musicians looked at each other and smiled as if at their own nervousness and folly, and made whispering vows, each to the other, that the next chiming of the clock should produce in them no similar emotion; and then, after the lapse of sixty minutes, (which embrace three thousand and six hundred seconds of the Time that flies,) there came yet another chiming of the clock, and then were the same disconcert and tremulousness and meditation as before.

But, in spite of these things, it was a gay and magnificent revel. The tastes of the duke were peculiar. He had a fine eye for colors and effects. He disregarded the *decora* of mere fashion. His plans were bold and fiery, and his conceptions glowed with barbaric lustre. There are some who would have thought him mad. His followers felt that he was not. It was necessary to hear and see and touch him to be *sure* that he was not.

He had directed, in great part, the moveable embellishments of the seven chambers, upon occasion of this great *fête;* and it was his own guiding taste which had given character to the masqueraders. Be sure they were grotesque. There were much glare and glitter and piquancy and phantasm—much of what has been since seen in "Hernani." [1] There were arabesque figures with unsuited limbs and appointments. There were delirious fancies such as the madman fashions. There was much of the beautiful, much of the wanton, much of the *bizarre*, something of the terrible, and not a little of that which might have excited disgust. To and fro in the seven chambers there stalked, in fact, a multitude of dreams. And these—the dreams—writhed in and about, taking hue from the rooms, and causing the wild music of the orchestra to seem as the echo of their steps. And, anon, there strikes the ebony clock which stands in the hall of the velvet. And then, for a moment, all is still, and all is silent save the voice of the clock. The dreams are stiff-frozen as they stand. But the echoes of the chime die away—they have endured but an instant—and a light, half-subdued laughter floats after them as they depart. And now again the music swells, and the dreams live, and writhe to and fro more merrily than ever, taking hue from the many tinted windows through which stream the rays from the tripods. But to the chamber which lies most westwardly of the seven, there are now none of the maskers who venture; for the night is waning away; and there flows a ruddier light through the blood-colored panes; and the blackness of the sable drapery appalls; and to him whose foot falls upon the sable carpet, there comes from the near clock of ebony a muffled peal more solemnly emphatic than any which reaches *their* ears who indulge in the more remote gaieties of the other apartments.

But these other apartments were densely crowded, and in them beat feverishly the heart of life. And the revel went whirlingly on, until at length there commenced the sounding of midnight upon the clock. And then the music ceased, as I have told; and the evolutions of the waltzers were

[1] A play by Victor Hugo, presented in 1830.

quieted; and there was an uneasy cessation of all things as before. But now there were twelve strokes to be sounded by the bell of the clock; and thus it happened, perhaps, that more of thought crept, with more of time, into the meditations of the thoughtful among those who revelled. And thus, too, it happened, perhaps, that before the last echoes of the last chime had utterly sunk into silence, there were many individuals in the crowd who had found leisure to become aware of the presence of a masked figure which had arrested the attention of no single individual before. And the rumor of this new presence having spread itself whisperingly around, there arose at length from the whole company a buzz, or murmur, expressive of disapprobation and surprise—then, finally, of terror, of horror, and of disgust.

In an assembly of phantasms such as I have painted, it may well be supposed that no ordinary appearance could have excited such sensation. In truth the masquerade license of the night was nearly unlimited; but the figure in question had out-Heroded Herod, and gone beyond the bounds of even the prince's indefinite decorum. There are chords in the hearts of the most reckless which cannot be touched without emotion. Even with the utterly lost, to whom life and death are equally jests, there are matters of which no jests can be made. The whole company, indeed, seemed now deeply to feel that in the costume and bearing of the stranger neither wit nor propriety existed. The figure was tall and gaunt, and shrouded from head to foot in the habiliments of the grave. The mask which concealed the visage was made so nearly to resemble the countenance of a stiffened corpse that the closest scrutiny must have had difficulty in detecting the cheat. And yet all this might have been endured, if not approved, by the mad revellers around. But the mummer had gone so far as to assume the type of the Red Death. His vesture was dabbled in *blood*—and his broad brow, with all the features of the face, was besprinkled with the scarlet horror.

When the eyes of Prince Prospero fell upon this spectral image (which with a slow and solemn movement, as if more fully to sustain its *rôle*, stalked to and fro among the waltzers) he was seen to be convulsed, in the first moment, with a strong shudder either of terror or distaste; but, in the next, his brow reddened with rage.

"Who dares?" he demanded hoarsely of the courtiers who stood near him—"who dares insult us with this blasphemous mockery? Seize him and unmask him—that we may know whom we have to hang at sunrise, from the battlements!"

It was in the eastern or blue chamber in which

stood the Prince Prospero as he uttered these words. They rang throughout the seven rooms loudly and clearly—for the prince was a bold and robust man, and the music had become hushed at the waving of his hand.

It was in the blue room where stood the prince, with a group of pale courtiers by his side. At first, as he spoke, there was a slight rushing movement of this group in the direction of the intruder, who at the moment was also near at hand, and now, with deliberate and stately step, made closer approach to the speaker. But from a certain nameless awe with which the mad assumption of the mummer had inspired the whole party, there were found none who put forth hand to seize him; so that, unimpeded, he passed within a yard of the prince's person; and, while the vast assembly, as if with one impulse, shrank from the centres of the rooms to the walls, he made his way uninterruptedly, but with the same solemn and measured step which had distinguished him from the first, through the blue chamber to the purple—through the purple to the green—through the green to the orange—through this again to the white—and even thence to the violet, ere a decided movement had been made to arrest him. It was then, however, that the Prince Prospero, maddening with rage and the shame of his own momentary cowardice, rushed hurriedly through the six chambers, while none followed him on account of a deadly terror that had seized upon all. He bore aloft a drawn dagger, and had approached, in rapid impetuosity, to within three or four feet of the retreating figure, when the latter, having attained the extremity of the velvet apartment, turned suddenly and confronted his pursuer. There was a sharp cry—and the dagger dropped gleaming upon the sable carpet, upon which, instantly afterwards, fell prostrate in death the Prince Prospero. Then, summoning the wild courage of despair, a throng of the revellers at once threw themselves into the black apartment, and, seizing the mummer, whose tall figure stood erect and motionless within the shadow of the ebony clock, gasped in unutterable horror at finding the grave-cerements and corpse-like mask, which they handled with so violent a rudeness, untenanted by any tangible form.

And now was acknowledged the presence of the Red Death. He had come like a thief in the night. And one by one dropped the revellers in the blood-bedewed halls of their revel, and died each in the despairing posture of his fall. And the life of the ebony clock went out with that of the last of the gay. And the flames of the tripods expired. And Darkness and Decay and the Red Death held illimitable dominion over all.

1842

The Purloined Letter

Very different from the tales of tone or atmosphere are the "tales of ratiocination," or detective stories. "The Purloined Letter" is one of a series concerning M. Dupin, the prototype of Conan Doyle's Sherlock Holmes. The epigraph: "Nothing is more odious to wisdom than too great cleverness." It has not been located in Seneca, however.

Nil sapientiae odiosius acumine nimio.
— Seneca.

At Paris, just after dark one gusty evening in the autumn of 18—, I was enjoying the twofold luxury of meditation and a meerschaum, in company with my friend C. Auguste Dupin, in his little back library, or book-closet, *au troisième, No. 33, Rue Dunôt, Faubourg St. Germain.* For one hour at least we had maintained a profound silence; while each, to any casual observer, might have seemed intently and exclusively occupied with the curling eddies of smoke that oppressed the atmosphere of the chamber. For myself, however, I was mentally discussing certain topics which had formed matter for conversation between us at an earlier period of the evening; I mean the affair of the Rue Morgue, and the mystery attending the murder of Marie Rogêt.[1] I looked upon it, therefore, as something of a coincidence, when the door of our apartment was thrown open and admitted our old acquaintance, Monsieur G—, the Prefect of the Parisian police.

We gave him a hearty welcome; for there was nearly half as much of the entertaining as of the contemptible about the man, and we had not seen him for several years. We had been sitting in the dark, and Dupin now arose for the purpose of lighting a lamp, but sat down again, without doing so, upon G.'s saying that he had called to consult us, or rather to ask the opinion of my friend, about some official business which had occasioned a great deal of trouble.

"If it is any point requiring reflection," observed Dupin, as he forebore to enkindle the wick, "we shall examine it to better purpose in the dark."

"That is another of your odd notions," said the Prefect, who had a fashion of calling every thing "odd" that was beyond his comprehension, and thus lived amid an absolute legion of "oddities."

"Very true," said Dupin, as he supplied his visitor with a pipe, and rolled towards him a comfortable chair.

"And what is the difficulty now?" I asked. "Nothing more in the assassination way, I hope?"

"Oh no; nothing of that nature. The fact is, the

[1] Cases solved in other Poe stories: "The Murders in the Rue Morgue" and "The Mystery of Marie Roget."

business is *very* simple indeed, and I make no doubt that we can manage it sufficiently well ourselves; but then I thought Dupin would like to hear the details of it, because it is so excessively *odd*."

"Simple and odd," said Dupin.

"Why, yes; and not exactly that, either. The fact is, we have all been a good deal puzzled because the affair *is* so simple, and yet baffles us altogether."

"Perhaps it is the very simplicity of the thing which puts you at fault," said my friend.

"What nonsense you *do* talk!" replied the Prefect, laughing heartily.

"Perhaps the mystery is a little *too* plain," said Dupin.

"Oh, good heavens! who ever heard of such an idea?"

"A little *too* self-evident."

"Ha! ha! ha!—ha! ha! ha!—ho! ho! ho!"—roared our visitor, profoundly amused, "oh, Dupin, you will be the death of me yet!"

"And what, after all, *is* the matter on hand?" I asked.

"Why, I will tell you," replied the Prefect, as he gave a long, steady, and contemplative puff, and settled himself in his chair. "I will tell you in a few words; but, before I begin, let me caution you that this is an affair demanding the greatest secrecy, and that I should most probably lose the position I now hold, were it known that I confided it to any one."

"Proceed," said I.

"Or not," said Dupin.

"Well, then; I have received personal information, from a very high quarter, that a certain document of the last importance has been purloined from the royal apartments. The individual who purloined it is known; this beyond a doubt; he was seen to take it. It is known, also, that it still remains in his possession."

"How is this known?" asked Dupin.

"It is clearly inferred," replied the Prefect, "from the nature of the document, and from the non-appearance of certain results which would at once arise from its passing *out* of the robber's possession;—that is to say, from his employing it as he must design in the end to employ it."

"Be a little more explicit," I said.

"Well, I may venture so far as to say that the paper gives its holder a certain power in a certain quarter where such power is immensely valuable." The Prefect was fond of the cant of diplomacy.

"Still I do not quite understand," said Dupin.

"No? Well; the disclosure of the document to a third person, who shall be nameless, would bring in question the honor of a personage of most exalted station; and this fact gives the holder of the document an ascendancy over the illustrious personage whose honor and peace are so jeopardized."

"But this ascendancy," I interposed, "would depend upon the robber's knowledge of the loser's knowledge of the robber. Who would dare—"

"The thief," said G—, "is the Minister D—, who dares all things, those unbecoming as well as those becoming a man. The method of the theft was not less ingenious than bold. The document in question—a letter, to be frank—had been received by the personage robbed while alone in the royal *boudoir*. During its perusal she was suddenly interrupted by the entrance of the other exalted personage from whom especially it was her wish to conceal it. After a hurried and vain endeavor to thrust it in a drawer, she was forced to place it, open as it was, upon a table. The address, however, was uppermost, and, the contents thus unexposed, the letter escaped notice. At this juncture enters the Minister D—. His lynx eye immediately perceives the paper, recognizes the handwriting of the address, observes the confusion of the personage addressed, and fathoms her secret. After some business transactions, hurried through in his ordinary manner, he produces a letter somewhat similar to the one in question, opens it, pretends to read it, and then places it in close juxtaposition to the other. Again he converses, for some fifteen minutes, upon the public affairs. At length, in taking leave, he takes also from the table the letter to which he had no claim. Its rightful owner saw, but, of course, dared not call attention to the act, in the presence of the third personage who stood at her elbow. The minister decamped; leaving his own letter—one of no importance—upon the table."

"Here, then," said Dupin to me, "you have precisely what you demand to make the ascendancy complete—the robber's knowledge of the loser's knowledge of the robber."

"Yes," replied the Prefect; "and the power thus attained has, for some months past, been wielded, for political purposes, to a very dangerous extent. The personage robbed is more thoroughly convinced, every day, of the necessity of reclaiming her letter. But this, of course, cannot be done openly. In fine, driven to despair, she has committed the matter to me."

"Than whom," said Dupin, amid a perfect whirlwind of smoke, "no more sagacious agent could, I suppose, be desired, or even imagined."

"You flatter me," replied the Prefect; "but it is possible that some such opinion may have been entertained."

"It is clear," said I, "as you observe, that the letter is still in possession of the minister; since it is this possession, and not any employment of the letter, which bestows the power. With the employment the power departs."

"True," said G.; "and upon this conviction I proceeded. My first care was to make thorough search of the minister's hotel; and here my chief embarrassment lay in the necessity of searching without his knowledge. Beyond all things, I have been warned of the danger which would result from giving him reason to suspect our design."

"But," said I, "you are quite *au fait* in these investigations. The Parisian police have done this thing often before."

"O yes; and for this reason I did not despair. The habits of the minister gave me, too, a great advantage. He is frequently absent from home all night. His servants are by no means numerous. They sleep at a distance from their master's apartment, and, being chiefly Neapolitans, are readily made drunk. I have keys, as you know, with which I can open any chamber or cabinet in Paris. For three months a night has not passed, during the greater part of which I have not been engaged, personally, in ransacking the D— Hôtel. My honor is interested, and, to mention a great secret, the reward is enormous. So I did not abandon the search until I had become fully satisfied that the thief is a more astute man than myself. I fancy that I have investigated every nook and corner of the premises in which it is possible that the paper can be concealed."

"But is it not possible," I suggested, "that although the letter may be in the possession of the minister, as it unquestionably is, he may have concealed it elsewhere than upon his own premises?"

"This is barely possible," said Dupin. "The present peculiar condition of affairs at court, and especially of those intrigues in which D— is known to be involved, would render the instant availability of the document—its susceptibility of being produced at a moment's notice—a point of nearly equal importance with its possession."

"Its susceptibility of being produced?" said I.

"That is to say, of being *destroyed*," said Dupin.

"True," I observed; "the paper is clearly then upon the premises. As for its being upon the person of the minister, we may consider that as out of the question."

"Entirely," said the Prefect. "He has been twice waylaid, as if by footpads, and his person rigorously searched under my own inspection."

"You might have spared yourself this trouble," said Dupin. "D—, I presume, is not altogether a fool, and, if not, must have anticipated these waylayings, as a matter of course."

"Not *altogether* a fool," said G., "but then he's a poet, which I take to be only one remove from a fool."

"True," said Dupin, after a long and thoughtful whiff from his meerschaum, "although I have been guilty of certain doggerel myself."

"Suppose you detail," said I, "the particulars of your search."

"Why the fact is, we took our time, and we searched *every where*. I have had long experience in these affairs. I took the entire building, room by room; devoting the nights of a whole week to each. We examined, first, the furniture of each apartment. We opened every possible drawer; and I presume you know that, to a properly trained police agent, such a thing as a *secret* drawer is impossible. Any man is a dolt who permits a 'secret' drawer to escape him in a search of this kind. The thing is *so* plain. There is a certain amount of bulk—of space— to be accounted for in every cabinet. Then we have accurate rules. The fiftieth part of a line could not escape us. After the cabinets we took the chairs. The cushions we probed with the fine long needles you have seen me employ. From the tables we removed the tops."

"Why so?"

"Sometimes the top of a table, or other similarly arranged piece of furniture, is removed by the person wishing to conceal an article; then the leg is excavated, the article deposited within the cavity, and the top replaced. The bottoms and tops of bedposts are employed in the same way."

"But could not the cavity be detected by sounding?" I asked.

"By no means, if, when the article is deposited, a sufficient wadding of cotton be placed around it. Besides, in our case, we were obliged to proceed without noise."

"But you could not have removed—you could not have taken to pieces *all* articles of furniture in which it would have been possible to make a deposit in the manner you mention. A letter may be compressed into a thin spiral roll, not differing much in shape or bulk from a large knitting-needle, and in this form it might be inserted into the rung of a chair, for example. You did not take to pieces all the chairs?"

"Certainly not; but we did better—we examined the rungs of every chair in the hotel, and, indeed, the jointings of every description of furniture, by the aid of a most powerful microscope. Had there been any traces of recent disturbance we should not have failed to detect it instantly. A single grain of gimlet-dust, for example, would have been as obvious as an apple. Any disorder in the glueing—any unusual gaping in the joints—would have sufficed to insure detection."

"I presume you looked to the mirrors, between the boards and the plates, and you probed the beds and the bed-clothes, as well as the curtains and carpets."

"That of course; and when we had absolutely completed every particle of the furniture in this way, then we examined the house itself. We divided its entire surface into compartments, which we numbered, so that none might be missed; then we scrutinized each individual square inch throughout the premises, including the two houses immediately adjoining, with the microscope, as before."

"The two houses adjoining!" I exclaimed; "you must have had a great deal of trouble."

"We had; but the reward offered is prodigious."

"You include the *grounds* about the houses?"

"All the grounds are paved with brick. They gave us comparatively little trouble. We examined the moss between the bricks, and found it undisturbed."

"You looked among D—'s papers, of course, and into the books of the library?"

"Certainly; we opened every package and parcel; we not only opened every book, but we turned over every leaf in each volume, not contenting ourselves with a mere shake, according to the fashion of some of our police officers. We also measured the thickness of every book-*cover*, with the most accurate admeasurement, and applied to each the most jealous scrutiny of the microscope. Had any of the bindings been recently meddled with, it would have been utterly impossible that the fact should have escaped observation. Some five or six volumes, just from the hands of the binder, we carefully probed, longitudinally, with the needles."

"You explored the floors beneath the carpets?"

"Beyond doubt. We removed every carpet, and examined the boards with the microscope."

"And the paper on the walls?"

"Yes."

"You looked into the cellars?"

"We did."

"Then," I said, "you have been making a miscalculation, and the letter is *not* upon the premises, as you suppose."

"I fear you are right there," said the Prefect. "And now, Dupin, what would you advise me to do?"

"To make a thorough re-search of the premises."

"That is absolutely needless," replied G—. "I am not more sure that I breathe than I am that the letter is not at the Hôtel."

"I have no better advice to give you," said Dupin. "You have, of course, an accurate description of the letter?"

"Oh yes!"—And here the Prefect, producing a memorandum-book, proceeded to read aloud a minute account of the internal, and especially of the external appearance of the missing document. Soon after finishing the perusal of this description, he took his departure, more entirely depressed in spirits than I had ever known the good gentleman before.

In about a month afterwards he paid us another visit, and found us occupied very nearly as before.

He took a pipe and a chair and entered into some ordinary conversation. At length I said,—

"Well, but G—, what of the purloined letter? I presume you have at last made up your mind that there is no such thing as overreaching the Minister?"

"Confound him, say I—yes; I made the re-examination, however, as Dupin suggested—but it was all labor lost, as I knew it would be."

"How much was the reward offered, did you say?" asked Dupin.

"Why, a very great deal—a *very* liberal reward—I don't like to say how much, precisely; but one thing I *will* say, that I wouldn't mind giving my individual check for fifty thousand francs to any one who could obtain me that letter. The fact is, it is becoming of more and more importance every day; and the reward has been lately doubled. If it were trebled, however, I could do no more than I have done."

"Why, yes," said Dupin, drawlingly, between the whiffs of his meerschaum, "I really—think, G—, you have not exerted yourself—to the utmost in this matter. You might—do a little more, I think, eh?"

"How?—in what way?"

"Why—puff, puff—you might—puff, puff—employ counsel in the matter, eh?—puff, puff, puff. Do you remember the story they tell of Abernethy?"

"No; hang Abernethy!"

"To be sure! hang him and welcome. But, once upon a time, a certain rich miser conceived the design of spunging upon this Abernethy for a medical opinion. Getting up, for this purpose, an ordinary conversation in a private company, he insinuated his case to the physician, as that of an imaginary individual.

" 'We will suppose,' said the miser, 'that his symptoms are such and such; now, doctor, what would *you* have directed him to take?' "

" 'Take!' said Abernethy, 'why, take *advice*, to be sure.' "

"But," said the Prefect, a little discomposed, "I am *perfectly* willing to take advice, and to pay for it. I would *really* give fifty thousand francs to any one who would aid me in the matter."

"In that case," replied Dupin, opening a drawer, and producing a check-book, "you may as well fill me up a check for the amount mentioned. When you have signed it, I will hand you the letter."

I was astounded. The Prefect appeared absolutely thunder-stricken. For some minutes he remained speechless and motionless, looking incredulously at my friend with open mouth, and eyes that seemed starting from their sockets; then, apparently recovering himself in some measure, he seized a pen, and after several pauses and vacant stares, finally filled up and signed a check for fifty thousand francs, and handed it across the table to Dupin. The latter examined it carefully and deposited it in his pocket-book; then, unlocking an *escritoire*, took thence a letter and gave it to the Prefect. This functionary grasped it in a perfect agony of joy, opened it with a trembling hand, cast a rapid glance at its contents, and then, scrambling and struggling to the door, rushed at length unceremoniously from the room and from the house, without having uttered a syllable since Dupin had requested him to fill up the check.

When he had gone, my friend entered into some explanations.

"The Parisian police," he said, "are exceedingly able in their way. They are persevering, ingenious, cunning, and thoroughly versed in the knowledge which their duties seem chiefly to demand. Thus, when G— detailed to us his mode of searching the premises at the Hôtel D—, I felt entire confidence in his having made a satisfactory investigation—so far as his labors extended."

"So far as his labors extended?" said I.

"Yes," said Dupin. "The measures adopted were not only the best of their kind, but carried out to absolute perfection. Had the letter been deposited within the range of their search, these fellows would, beyond a question, have found it."

I merely laughed—but he seemed quite serious in all that he said.

"The measures, then," he continued, "were good in their kind, and well executed; their defect lay in their being inapplicable to the case, and to the man. A certain set of highly ingenious resources are, with the Prefect, a sort of Procrustean bed, to which he forcibly adapts his designs. But he perpetually errs by being too deep or too shallow, for the matter in hand; and many a schoolboy is a better reasoner than he. I knew one about eight years of age, whose success at guessing in the game of 'even and odd' attracted universal admiration. This game is simple, and is played with marbles. One player holds in his hand a number of these toys, and demands of another whether that number is even or odd. If the guess is right, the guesser wins one; if wrong, he loses one. The boy to whom I allude won all the marbles of the school. Of course he had some principle of guessing; and this lay in mere observation and admeasurement of the astuteness of his opponents. For example, an arrant simpleton is his opponent, and, holding up his closed hand, asks, 'are they even or odd?' Our schoolboy replies, 'odd,' and loses; but upon the second trial he wins, for he then says to himself, 'the simpleton had them even upon the first trial, and his amount of cunning is just sufficient to make him have them odd upon the second; I will therefore guess odd';—he guesses odd, and wins. Now, with a simpleton a degree above the first, he would have reasoned thus: 'This

fellow finds that in the first instance I guessed odd, and, in the second, he will propose to himself upon the first impulse, a simple variation from even to odd, as did the first simpleton; but then a second thought will suggest that this is too simple a variation, and finally he will decide upon putting it even as before. I will therefore guess even';—he guesses even, and wins. Now this mode of reasoning in the schoolboy, whom his fellows termed 'lucky,'—what, in its last analysis, is it?"

"It is merely," I said, "an identification of the reasoner's intellect with that of his opponent."

"It is," said Dupin; "and, upon inquiring of the boy by what means he effected the *thorough* identification in which his success consisted, I received answer as follows: 'When I wish to find out how wise, or how stupid, or how good, or how wicked is any one, or what are his thoughts at the moment, I fashion the expression of my face, as accurately as possible, in accordance with the expression of his, and then wait to see what thoughts or sentiments arise in my mind or heart, as if to match or correspond with the expression.' This response of the schoolboy lies at the bottom of all the spurious profundity which has been attributed to Rochefoucauld, to La Bougive, to Machiavelli, and to Campanella."

"And the identification," I said, "of the reasoner's intellect with that of his opponent, depends, if I understand you aright, upon the accuracy with which the opponent's intellect is admeasured."

"For its practical value it depends upon this," replied Dupin; "and the Prefect and his cohort fail so frequently, first, by default of this identification, and, secondly, by ill-admeasurement, or rather through non-admeasurement of the intellect with which they are engaged. They consider only their *own* ideas of ingenuity; and, in searching for anything hidden, advert only to the modes in which *they* would have hidden it. They are right in this much—that their own ingenuity is a faithful representative of that of *the mass;* but when the cunning of the individual felon is diverse in character from their own, the felon foils them, of course. This always happens when it is above their own, and very usually when it is below. They have no variation of principle in their investigations; at best, when urged by some unusual emergency—by some extraordinary reward—they extend or exaggerate their old modes of *practice,* without touching their principles. What, for example, in this case of D—, has been done to vary the principle of action? What is all this boring, and probing, and sounding, and scrutinizing with the microscope, and dividing the surface of the building into registered square inches—what is it all but an exaggeration *of the application* of the one principle or set of principles of search, which are based upon the one set of notions regarding human ingenuity, to which the Prefect, in the long routine of his duty, has been accustomed? Do you not see he has taken it for granted that *all* men proceed to conceal a letter—not exactly in a gimlet-hole bored in a chair-leg—but, at least, in *some* out-of-the-way hole or corner suggested by the same tenor of thought which would urge a man to secrete a letter in a gimlet-hole bored in a chair-leg? And do you not see also, that such *recherchés* nooks for concealment are adapted only for ordinary occasions, and would be adopted only by ordinary intellects; for, in all cases of concealment, a disposal of the article concealed—a disposal of it in this *recherché* manner,—is, in the very first instance, presumable and presumed; and thus its discovery depends, not at all upon the acumen, but altogether upon the mere care, patience, and determination of the seekers; and where the case is of importance—or, what amounts to the same thing in the policial eyes, when the reward is of magnitude,—the qualities in question have *never* been known to fail. You will now understand what I meant in suggesting that, had the purloined letter been hidden any where within the limits of the Prefect's examination—in other words, had the principle of its concealment been comprehended within the principles of the Prefect—its discovery would have been a matter altogether beyond question. This functionary, however, has been thoroughly mystified; and the remote source of his defeat lies in the supposition that the Minister is a fool, because he has acquired renown as a poet. All fools are poets; this the Prefect *feels;* and he is merely guilty of a *non distributio medii*[2] in thence inferring that all poets are fools."

"But is this really the poet?" I asked. "There are two brothers, I know; and both have attained reputation in letters. The Minister I believe has written learnedly on the Differential Calculus. He is a mathematician, and no poet."

"You are mistaken; I know him well; he is both. As poet *and* mathematician, he would reason well; as mere mathematician, he could not have reasoned at all, and thus would have been at the mercy of the Prefect."

"You surprise me," I said, "by these opinions, which have been contradicted by the voice of the world. You do not mean to set at naught the well-digested idea of centuries. The mathematical reason has long been regarded as *the* reason *par excellence.*"

"'*Il y a à parier,*'" replied Dupin, quoting from Chamfort, "'*que toute idée publique, toute convention reçue, est une sottise, car elle a convenu au plus*

grand nombre.'[3] The mathematicians, I grant you, have done their best to promulgate the popular error to which you allude, and which is none the less an error for its promulgation as truth. With an art worthy a better cause, for example, they have insinuated the term 'analysis' into application to algebra. The French are the originators of this particular deception; but if a term is of any importance—if words derive any value from applicability—then 'analysis' conveys 'algebra' about as much as, in Latin, '*ambitus*' implies 'ambition,' '*religio*' 'religion,' or '*homines honesti*' a set of *honorable* men."

"You have a quarrel on hand, I see," said I, "with some of the algebraists of Paris; but proceed."

"I dispute the availability, and thus the value, of that reason which is cultivated in any especial form other than the abstractly logical. I dispute, in particular, the reason educed by mathematical study. The mathematics are the science of form and quantity; mathematical reasoning is merely logic applied to observation upon form and quantity. The great error lies in supposing that even the truths of what is called *pure* algebra, are abstract or general truths. And this error is so egregious that I am confounded at the universality with which it has been received. Mathematical axioms are *not* axioms of general truth. What is true of *relation*—of form and quantity—is often grossly false in regard to morals, for example. In this latter science it is very usually *un*true that the aggregated parts are equal to the whole. In chemistry also the axiom fails. In the consideration of motive it fails; for two motives, each of a given value, have not, necessarily, a value when united, equal to the sum of their values apart. There are numerous other mathematical truths which are only truths within the limits of *relation.* But the mathematician argues, from his *finite truths*, through habit, as if they were of an absolutely general applicability—as the world indeed imagines them to be. Bryant, in his very learned 'Mythology,' mentions an analogous source of error, when he says that 'although the Pagan fables are not believed, yet we forget ourselves continually, and make inferences from them as existing realities.' With the algebraists, however, who are Pagans themselves, the 'Pagan fables' *are* believed, and the inferences are made, not so much through lapse of memory, as through an unaccountable addling of the brains. In short, I never yet encountered the mere mathematician who could be trusted out of equal roots, or one who did not clandestinely hold it as a point of his faith that $x^2 + px$ was absolutely and unconditionally equal to q. Say to one of these gentlemen, by way of experiment, if you please, that you believe occasions may occur where $x^2 + px$ is *not* altogether equal to q,

[2] Undistributed middle.

[3] "I'll wager, that every idea which is generally held, every set convention, is a stupidity; for it has suited the majority."

and, having made him understand what you mean, get out of his reach as speedily as convenient, for, beyond doubt, he will endeavor to knock you down.

"I mean to say," continued Dupin, while I merely laughed at his last observations, "that if the Minister had been no more than a mathematician, the Prefect would have been under no necessity of giving me this check. I knew him, however, as both mathematician and poet, and my measures were adapted to his capacity, with reference to the circumstances by which he was surrounded. I knew him as a courtier, too, and as a bold *intriguant*. Such a man, I considered, could not fail to be aware of the ordinary policial modes of action. He could not have failed to anticipate—and events have proved that he did not fail to anticipate—the waylayings to which he was subjected. He must have foreseen, I reflected, the secret investigations of his premises. His frequent absences from home at night, which were hailed by the Prefect as certain aids to his success, I regarded only as *ruses,* to afford opportunity for thorough search to the police, and thus the sooner to impress them with the conviction to which G—, in fact, did finally arrive—the conviction that the letter was not upon the premises. I felt, also, that the whole train of thought, which I was at some pains in detailing to you just now, concerning the invariable principle of policial action in searches for articles concealed—I felt that this whole train of thought would necessarily pass through the mind of the Minister. It would imperatively lead him to despise all the ordinary *nooks* of concealment. *He* could not, I reflected, be so weak as not to see that the most intricate and remote recess of his hotel would be as open as his commonest closets to the eyes, to the probes, to the gimlets, and to the microscopes of the Prefect. I saw, in fine, that he would be driven, as a matter of course, to *simplicity,* if not deliberately induced to it as a matter of choice. You will remember, perhaps, how desperately the Prefect laughed when I suggested, upon our first interview, that it was just possible this mystery troubled him so much on account of its being *so very* self-evident."

"Yes," said I, "I remember his merriment well. I really thought he would have fallen into convulsions."

"The material world," continued Dupin, "abounds with the very strict analogies to the immaterial; and thus some color of truth has been given to the rhetorical dogma, that metaphor, or simile, may be made to strengthen an argument, as well as to embellish a description. The principle of the *vis inertiae*,[4] for example, seems to be identical in physics and metaphysics. It is not more true in the former, that a large body is with more difficulty set in

motion than a smaller one, and that its subsequent *momentum* is commensurate with this difficulty, than it is, in the latter, that intellects of the vaster capacity, while more forcible, more constant, and more eventful in their movements than those of inferior grade, are yet the less readily moved, and more embarrassed and full of hesitation in the first few steps of their progress. Again: have you ever noticed which of the street signs, over the shop doors, are the most attractive of attention?"

"I have never given the matter a thought," I said.

"There is a game of puzzles," he resumed, "which is played upon a map. One party playing requires another to find a given word—the name of town, river, state or empire—any word, in short, upon the motley and perplexed surface of the chart. A novice in the game generally seeks to embarrass his opponents by giving them the most minutely lettered names; but the adept selects such words as stretch, in large characters, from one end of the chart to the other. These, like the over-largely lettered signs and placards of the street, escape observation by dint of being excessively obvious; and here the physical oversight is precisely analogous with the moral inapprehension by which the intellect suffers to pass unnoticed those considerations which are too obtrusively and too palpably self-evident. But this is a point, it appears, somewhat above or beneath the understanding of the Prefect. He never once thought it probable, or possible, that the Minister had deposited the letter immediately beneath the nose of the whole world, by way of best preventing any portion of that world from perceiving it.

"But the more I reflected upon the daring, dashing, and discriminating ingenuity of D—; upon the fact that the document must always have been *at hand,* if he intended to use it to good purpose; and upon the decisive evidence, obtained by the Prefect, that it was not hidden within the limits of that dignitary's ordinary search—the more satisfied I became that, to conceal this letter, the Minister had resorted to the comprehensive and sagacious expedient of not attempting to conceal it at all.

"Full of these ideas, I prepared myself with a pair of green spectacles, and called one fine morning, quite by accident, at the Ministerial hotel. I found D— at home, yawning, lounging, and dawdling, as usual, and pretending to be in the last extremity of *ennui.* He is, perhaps, the most really energetic human being now alive—but that is only when nobody sees him.

"To be even with him, I complained of my weak eyes, and lamented the necessity of the spectacles, under cover of which I cautiously and thoroughly surveyed the apartment, while seemingly intent only upon the conversation of my host.

"I paid especial attention to a large writing-table

[4] Force of inertia.

near which he sat, and upon which lay confusedly, some miscellaneous letters and other papers, with one or two musical instruments and a few books. Here, however, after a long and very deliberate scrutiny, I saw nothing to excite particular suspicion.

"At length my eyes, in going the circuit of the room, fell upon a trumpery filigree card-rack of pasteboard, that hung dangling by a dirty blue ribbon, from a little brass knob just beneath the middle of the mantel-piece. In this rack, which had three or four compartments, were five or six visiting cards and a solitary letter. This last was much soiled and crumpled. It was torn nearly in two, across the middle—as if a design, in the first instance, to tear it entirely up as worthless, had been altered, or stayed, in the second. It had a large black seal, bearing the D— cipher *very* conspicuously, and was addressed, in a diminutive female hand, to D—, the minister, himself. It was thrust carelessly, and even, as it seemed, contemptuously, into one of the upper divisions of the rack.

"No sooner had I glanced at this letter, than I concluded it to be that of which I was in search. To be sure, it was, to all appearance, radically different from the one of which the Prefect had read us so minute a description. Here the seal was large and black, with the D— cipher; there it was small and red, with the ducal arms of the S— family. Here, the address, to the Minister, was diminutive and feminine; there the superscription, to a certain royal personage, was markedly bold and decided; the size alone formed a point of correspondence. But, then, the *radicalness* of these differences, which was excessive; the dirt; the soiled and torn condition of the paper, so inconsistent with the *true* methodical habits of D—, and so suggestive of a design to delude the beholder into an idea of the worthlessness of the document; these things, together with the hyperobtrusive situation of this document, full in the view of every visitor, and thus exactly in accordance with the conclusions to which I had previously arrived; these things, I say, were strongly corroborative of suspicion, in one who came with the intention to suspect.

"I protracted my visit as long as possible, and, while I maintained a most animated discussion with the Minister, on a topic which I knew well had never failed to interest and excite him, I kept my attention really riveted upon the letter. In this examination, I committed to memory its external appearance and arrangement in the rack; and also fell, at length, upon a discovery which set at rest whatever trivial doubt I might have entertained. In scrutinizing the edges of the paper, I observed them to be more *chafed* than seemed necessary. They presented the *broken* appearance which is manifested when a stiff paper, having been once folded and pressed with a folder, is refolded in a reversed direction, in the same creases or edges which had formed the original fold. This discovery was sufficient. It was clear to me that the letter had been turned, as a glove, inside out, re-directed, and resealed. I bade the Minister good morning, and took my departure at once, leaving a gold snuff-box upon the table.

"The next morning I called for the snuff-box, when we resumed, quite eagerly, the conversation of the preceding day. While thus engaged, however, a loud report, as if of a pistol, was heard immediately beneath the windows of the hotel, and was succeeded by a series of fearful screams, and the shoutings of a mob. D— rushed to a casement, threw it open, and looked out. In the meantime, I stepped to the card-rack, took the letter, put it in my pocket, and replaced it by a *fac-simile* (so far as regards externals,) which I had carefully prepared at my lodgings; imitating the D— cipher, very readily, by means of a seal formed of bread.

"The disturbance in the street had been occasioned by the frantic behavior of a man with a musket. He had fired it among a crowd of women and children. It proved, however, to have been without ball, and the fellow was suffered to go his way as a lunatic or a drunkard. When he had gone, D— came from the window, whither I had followed him immediately upon securing the object in view. Soon afterwards I bade him farewell. The pretended lunatic was a man in my own pay."

"But what purpose had you," I asked, "in replacing the letter by a *fac-simile?* Would it not have been better, at the first visit, to have seized it openly, and departed?"

"D—," replied Dupin, "is a desperate man, and a man of nerve. His hotel, too, is not without attendants devoted to his interests. Had I made the wild attempt you suggest, I might never have left the Ministerial presence alive. The good people of Paris might have heard of me no more. But I had an object apart from these considerations. You know my political prepossessions. In this matter, I act as a partisan of the lady concerned. For eighteen months the Minister has had her in his power. She has now him in hers—since, being unaware that the letter is not in his possession, he will proceed with his exactions as if it was. Thus will he inevitably commit himself, at once, to his political destruction. His downfall, too, will not be more precipitate than awkward. It is all very well to talk about the *facilis descensus Averni;*[5] but in all kinds of climbing, as Catalani said of singing, it is far more easy to get up than to come down. In the present instance I have no sympathy—at least no pity—for him who descends. He is that *monstrum horrendum,*[6] an unprincipled man of genius. I confess, however, that I

[5] Easy descent to Hades.
[6] Horrible monster.

should like very well to know the precise character of his thoughts, when, being defied by her whom the Prefect terms 'a certain personage,' he is reduced to opening the letter which I left for him in the card-rack."

"How? did you put any thing particular in it?"

"Why—it did not seem altogether right to leave the interior blank—that would have been insulting. D—, at Vienna once, did me an evil turn, which I told him, quite good-humoredly, that I should remember. So, as I knew he would feel some curiosity in regard to the identity of the person who had outwitted him, I thought it a pity not to give him a clue. He is well acquainted with my MS., and I just copied into the middle of the blank sheet the words—

> —*Un dessein si funeste,*
> *S'il n'est digne d'Atrée, est digne de Thyeste.*[7]

They are to be found in Crébillon's 'Atrée.'"

1845

The Cask of Amontillado

This story of revenge illustrates admirably Poe's doctrines of unity and economy. The theme is announced in the first sentence and sustained undeviatingly to the last ("May he rest in peace."). While the plot is very simple, some intellectual complexity is attained through irony: the meaning of an act or speech is often contrary to that seemingly indicated.

The thousand injuries of Fortunato I had borne as I best could, but when he ventured upon insult I vowed revenge. You, who so well know the nature of my soul, will not suppose, however, that I gave utterance to a threat. *At length* I would be avenged; this was a point definitely settled—but the very definitiveness with which it was resolved precluded the idea of risk. I must not only punish but punish with impunity. A wrong is unredressed when retribution overtakes its redresser. It is equally unredressed when the avenger fails to make himself felt as such to him who has done the wrong.

It must be understood that neither by word nor deed had I given Fortunato cause to doubt my good will. I continued, as was my wont, to smile in his face, and he did not perceive that my smile *now* was at the thought of his immolation.

He had a weak point—this Fortunato—although in other regards he was a man to be respected and even feared. He prided himself on his connoisseurship in wine. Few Italians have the true virtuoso spirit. For the most part their enthusiasm is adopted

to suit the time and opportunity, to practise imposture upon the British and Austrian *millionaires*. In painting and gemmary, Fortunato, like his countrymen, was a quack, but in the matter of old wines he was sincere. In this respect I did not differ from him materially;—I was skilful in the Italian vintages myself, and bought largely whenever I could.

It was about dusk, one evening during the supreme madness of the carnival season, that I encountered my friend. He accosted me with excessive warmth, for he had been drinking much. The man wore motley. He had on a tight-fitting parti-striped dress, and his head was surmounted by the conical cap and bells. I was so pleased to see him that I thought I should never have done wringing his hand.

I said to him—"My dear Fortunato, you are luckily met. How remarkably well you are looking to-day. But I have received a pipe of what passes for Amontillado, and I have my doubts."

"How?" said he. "Amontillado? A pipe? Impossible! And in the middle of the carnival!"

"I have my doubts," I replied; "and I was silly enough to pay the full Amontillado price without consulting you in the matter. You were not to be found, and I was fearful of losing a bargain."

"Amontillado!"

"I have my doubts."

"Amontillado!"

"And I must satisfy them."

"Amontillado!"

"As you are engaged, I am on my way to Luchresi. If any one has a critical turn it is he. He will tell me—"

"Luchresi cannot tell Amontillado from Sherry."

"And yet some fools will have it that his taste is a match for your own."

"Come, let us go."

"Whither?"

"To your vaults."

"My friend, no; I will not impose upon your good nature. I perceive you have an engagement. Luchresi—"

"I have no engagement;—come."

"My friend, no. It is not the engagement, but the severe cold with which I perceive you are afflicted. The vaults are insufferably damp. They are encrusted with nitre."

"Let us go, nevertheless. The cold is merely nothing. Amontillado! You have been imposed upon. And as for Luchresi, he cannot distinguish Sherry from Amontillado."

Thus speaking, Fortunato possessed himself of my arm; and putting on a mask of black silk and drawing a *roquelaire* closely about my person, I suffered him to hurry me to my palazzo.

There were no attendants at home; they had absconded to make merry in honour of the time. I had told them that I should not return until the morning,

---

[7] "So deadly a scheme, if it is not worthy of Atreus, is at least worthy of Thyestes." In Greek legend, Thyestes seduced the wife of his brother Atreus; and Atreus, in revenge, killed Thyestes' sons and served them to their father at a banquet.

and had given them explicit orders not to stir from the house. These orders were sufficient, I well knew, to insure their immediate disappearance, one and all, as soon as my back was turned.

I took from their sconces two flambeaux, and giving one to Fortunato, bowed him through several suites of rooms to the archway that led into the vaults. I passed down a long and winding staircase, requesting him to be cautious as he followed. We came at length to the foot of the descent, and stood together upon the damp ground of the catacombs of the Montresors.

The gait of my friend was unsteady, and the bells upon his cap jingled as he strode.

"The pipe," he said.

"It is farther on," said I; "but observe the white web-work which gleams from these cavern walls."

He turned towards me, and looked into my eyes with two filmy orbs that distilled the rheum of intoxication.

"Nitre?" he asked, at length.

"Nitre," I replied. "How long have you had that cough?"

"Ugh! ugh! ugh!—ugh! ugh! ugh!—ugh! ugh! ugh!—ugh! ugh! ugh!—ugh! ugh! ugh!"

My poor friend found it impossible to reply for many minutes.

"It is nothing," he said, at last.

"Come," I said, with decision, "we will go back; your health is precious. You are rich, respected, admired, beloved; you are happy, as once I was. You are a man to be missed. For me it is no matter. We will go back; you will be ill, and I cannot be responsible. Besides, there is Luchresi—"

"Enough," he said; "the cough is a mere nothing; it will not kill me. I shall not die of a cough."

"True—true," I replied; "and, indeed, I had no intention of alarming you unnecessarily—but you should use all proper caution. A draught of this Medoc will defend us from the damps."

Here I knocked off the neck of a bottle which I drew from a long row of its fellows that lay upon the mould.

"Drink," I said, presenting him the wine.

He raised it to his lips with a leer. He paused and nodded to me familiarly, while his bells jingled.

"I drink," he said, "to the buried that repose around us."

"And I to your long life."

He again took my arm, and we proceeded.

"These vaults," he said, "are extensive."

"The Montresors," I replied, "were a great and numerous family."

"I forget your arms."

"A huge human foot d'or, in a field azure; the foot crushes a serpent rampant whose fangs are imbedded in the heel."

"And the motto?"

"Nemo me impune lacessit."[1]

"Good!" he said.

The wine sparkled in his eyes and the bells jingled. My own fancy grew warm with the Medoc. We had passed through long walls of piled skeletons, with casks and puncheons intermingling, into the inmost recesses of the catacombs. I paused again, and this time I made bold to seize Fortunato by an arm above the elbow.

"The nitre!" I said; "see, it increases. It hangs like moss upon the vaults. We are below the river's bed. The drops of moisture trickle among the bones. Come, we will go back ere it is too late. Your cough—"

"It is nothing," he said; "let us go on. But first, another draught of the Medoc."

I broke and reached him a flagon of De Grâve. He emptied it at a breath. His eyes flashed with a fierce light. He laughed and threw the bottle upwards with a gesticulation I did not understand.

I looked at him in surprise. He repeated the movement—a grotesque one.

"You do not comprehend?" he said.

"Not I," I replied.

"Then you are not of the brotherhood."

"How?"

"You are not of the masons."

"Yes, yes," I said; "yes, yes."

"You? Impossible! A mason?"

"A mason," I replied.

"A sign," he said, "a sign."

"It is this," I answered, producing from beneath the folds of my *roquelaire* a trowel.

"You jest," he exclaimed, recoiling a few paces. "But let us proceed to the Amontillado."

"Be it so," I said, replacing the tool beneath the cloak and again offering him my arm. He leaned upon it heavily. We continued our route in search of the Amontillado. We passed through a range of low arches, descended, passed on, and descending again, arrived at a deep crypt, in which the foulness of the air caused our flambeaux rather to glow than flame.

At the most remote end of the crypt there appeared another less spacious. Its walls had been lined with human remains, piled to the vault overhead, in the fashion of the great catacombs of Paris. Three sides of this interior crypt were still ornamented in this manner. From the fourth side the bones had been thrown down, and lay promiscuously upon the earth, forming at one point a mound of some size. Within the wall thus exposed by the displacing of the bones, we perceived a still interior crypt or recess, in depth about four feet, in width three, in height six or seven. It seemed to have been constructed for no especial use within itself, but formed merely the interval between two of the

[1] "No one can harm me with impunity."

colossal supports of the roof of the catacombs, and was backed by one of their circumscribing walls of solid granite.

It was in vain that Fortunato, uplifting his dull torch, endeavoured to pry into the depth of the recess. Its termination the feeble light did not enable us to see.

"Proceed," I said; "herein is the Amontillado. As for Luchresi—"

"He is an ignoramus," interrupted my friend, as he stepped unsteadily forward, while I followed immediately at his heels. In an instant he had reached the extremity of the niche, and finding his progress arrested by the rock, stood stupidly bewildered. A moment more and I had fettered him to the granite. In its surface were two iron staples, distant from each other about two feet, horizontally. From one of these depended a short chain, from the other a padlock. Throwing the links about his waist, it was but the work of a few seconds to secure it. He was too much astounded to resist. Withdrawing the key I stepped back from the recess.

"Pass your hand," I said, "over the wall; you cannot help feeling the nitre. Indeed, it is *very* damp. Once more let me *implore* you to return. No? Then I must positively leave you. But I must first render you all the little attentions in my power."

"The Amontillado!" ejaculated my friend, not yet recovered from his astonishment.

"True," I replied; "the Amontillado."

As I said these words I busied myself among the pile of bones of which I have before spoken. Throwing them aside, I soon uncovered a quantity of building stone and mortar. With these materials and with the aid of my trowel, I began vigorously to wall up the entrance of the niche.

I had scarcely laid the first tier of the masonry when I discovered that the intoxication of Fortunato had in a great measure worn off. The earliest indication I had of this was a low moaning cry from the depth of the recess. It was *not* the cry of a drunken man. There was then a long and obstinate silence. I laid the second tier, and the third, and the fourth; and then I heard the furious vibrations of the chain. The noise lasted for several minutes, during which, that I might hearken to it with the more satisfaction, I ceased my labours and sat down upon the bones. When at last the clanking subsided, I resumed the trowel, and finished without interruption the fifth, the sixth, and the seventh tier. The wall was now nearly upon a level with my breast. I again paused, and holding the flambeaux over the mason-work, threw a few feeble rays upon the figure within.

A succession of loud and shrill screams, bursting suddenly from the throat of the chained form, seemed to thrust me violently back. For a brief moment I hesitated, I trembled. Unsheathing my rapier, I began to grope with it about the recess; but the thought of an instant reassured me. I placed my hand upon the solid fabric of the catacombs, and felt satisfied. I reapproached the wall; I replied to the yells of him who clamoured. I re-echoed, I aided, I surpassed them in volume and in strength. I did this, and the clamourer grew still.

It was now midnight, and my task was drawing to a close. I had completed the eighth, the ninth and the tenth tier. I had finished a portion of the last and the eleventh; there remained but a single stone to be fitted and plastered in. I struggled with its weight; I placed it partially in its destined position. But now there came from out the niche a low laugh that erected the hairs upon my head. It was succeeded by a sad voice, which I had difficulty in recognizing as that of the noble Fortunato. The voice said—

"Ha! ha! ha!—he! he! he!—a very good joke, indeed—an excellent jest. We will have many a rich laugh about it at the palazzo—he! he! he!—over our wine—he! he! he!"

"The Amontillado!" I said.

"He! he! he!—he! he! he!—yes, the Amontillado. But is it not getting late? Will not they be awaiting us at the palazzo, the Lady Fortunato and the rest? Let us be gone."

"Yes," I said, "let us be gone."

"*For the love of God, Montresor!*"

"Yes," I said, "for the love of God!"

But to these words I hearkened in vain for a reply. I grew impatient. I called aloud—

"Fortunato!"

No answer. I called again—

"Fortunato!"

No answer still. I thrust a torch through the remaining aperture and let it fall within. There came forth in return only a jingling of the bells. My heart grew sick; it was the dampness of the catacombs that made it so. I hastened to make an end of my labour. I forced the last stone into its position; I plastered it up. Against the new masonry I re-erected the old rampart of bones. For the half of a century no mortal has disturbed them. *In pace requiescat!*[2]

1846

---

[2] "May he rest in peace!"

Romanticism on Puritan Soil

RALPH WALDO EMERSON [1803-1882]

LIKE POE, Emerson was born in Boston. "His soul received its bent," said Charles Eliot Norton, "from the innocent America of before 1830," an America that had a "confident, sweet, morning spirit." (In the opinion of Norton, who was professor of the history of fine art at Harvard in Emerson's later years, the mood of young America limited his mind, encouraged him in an optimism that became a bigotry.)

Along with the buoyant optimism of the new nation, Emerson had the moral enthusiasm of his Puritan heritage. While Poe was the son of wandering actors, grew up in Virginia, and became an advocate of art for art's sake, Emerson was the son of a Unitarian minister, was shaped by his Massachusetts ancestry and environment, and believed in art for life's sake—or morals' sake. Behind him stretched impressively a long line of ministers of the Gospel. His own father, William Emerson, was minister of the First Church, Unitarian, in Boston. He died when the boy was not quite eight years old. Thereafter the widow and her four boys attended the church of William Ellery Channing. Mrs. Emerson was a highly competent mother. His Aunt Mary Moody Emerson was a pious and stimulating woman who held before him, as he put it later, an "immeasurably high standard." He was brought up in poverty; at times he and a brother had to share the use of a winter overcoat. Yet all four managed to go through Harvard. Emerson was messenger for the president, and waited on table; he graduated at the middle of his class. To help his brother William, he spent the next three years in teaching, shyly, in a school for young ladies.

He entered the Harvard divinity school in 1825, his studies handicapped by physical ailments, the care of a brother temporarily insane, and the need of more school teaching. His license to preach, given late in 1826, implied not so much a proof of capacity as a vote of confidence. At this juncture a new ailment, in the lungs, sent him to South Carolina and Florida for a long winter. In 1829 he became pastor of the Second Church, the church of the Mathers, now Unitarian, and in the same year married Ellen Tucker—"17 years old," he reported, "and very beautiful, by universal consent," but of delicate health. Within less than a year and a half her life was taken by tuberculosis. The white plague was almost a family institution: it brought death also to Emerson's two younger brothers, and dogged his own career for about six years, years in what he called the house of Pain.

He was also struggling in the house of doubt. First—as early as 1824—he had questioned whether the ministry, after all, was his true vocation. His love of eloquence boded well for his preaching, but was he not lacking in self-confidence among men, in warmth of heart, in moral worth? As time went on he questioned not so much his own fitness as the Christian ministry itself. Did not even the Unitarian church involve restraints upon the free spiritual life? And was it not a worship of dead forms rather than a vital faith? "The profession," he said, in his journal "is antiquated." In December 1832 he resigned his charge. Disagreement with his congregation over celebration of the Lord's Supper was only the immediate occasion. Bereaved, ill, and adrift in the world, he sailed for Europe on Christmas Day.

When he returned in the following September, he had regained his health and won a new assurance. In the course of his travels, from Italy to Scotland, he had seen his contemporary heroes—Landor, Coleridge, Carlyle, Wordsworth—and found them "all deficient, all these four . . . in insight into religious truth. They have no idea of that species of moral truth which I call the first philosophy." He must have meant that he had a better idea of it himself. In November he began giving lectures. In the next year he settled in Concord, thenceforth his home. In 1835 he married Lydia Jackson. In 1836 his son Waldo was born, and his book *Nature* was published.

With this book he launched what turned out to be a series of three great Transcendental challenges. In them we can see the interplay of many forces: the old Puritan spirit, the deistic tendency of Unitarianism, an optimistic nationalism, the doctrines of the Platonic tradition, the impulse of the Romantic Movement. In *Nature* the challenge lay mainly in the field of philosophy. In the address on the American Scholar it was mainly in literature—the fit education of the writer. In his Divinity School address it was in religion. Emerson's years of frustration and groping were at an end. In place of the "antiquated" faith of his fathers, he had achieved a new faith of his own, vital if unorthodox.

He had also achieved a new vocation—that of the lecturer. Two of the three challenges were lectures. His love of eloquence, frustrated when he resigned his pulpit, found expression on the public lecture platform. Why he became one of the most popular lecturers in America is suggested by Lowell's essay "Emerson the Lecturer." In this way he nearly doubled the income he received from the estate of his first wife. He gave hundreds upon hundreds of lectures, ranging repeatedly as far as the West, even beyond the Mississippi. Cheerfully he bore the hardships of travel in those days, and temperatures of 20 below zero. "This climate and people are a new test for the wares of a man of letters."

As a man of letters, he mostly arrived at his published results indirectly, writing in his private journal, writing lectures based largely on his journal, finally writing essays based on both journal and lectures and publishing them as books. His most famous books were the *Essays* of 1841 and a second series in 1844. Most of the essays dealt with abstractions, such as Self-Reliance, Compensation, Love, The Over-Soul, The Poet, Manners, Politics, and were suggestive and inspirational rather than closely reasoned. These two volumes came with the flood-tide of Transcendentalism, far more memorably registered in them than in the four years' run of *The Dial*, the periodical organ of the movement edited by Margaret Fuller and Emerson.

In many of the essays his faith in the religion of the self was at its height, but in a few, such as that on Experience, we begin to see the later Emerson, forced by growing experience to recognize that man is not always a god but a creature limited by heredity, temperament, circumstance, suffering. The later Emerson appears in some of the poems, in *Representative Men* (1850), in *English Traits* (1856), most notably in the essays of *The Conduct of Life* (1860). His old optimism still shone, but the bright light of his faith did not blind him to the dark realities of the human lot.

In his own day and long after, Emerson was regarded as a Yankee Plato, or, in the phrase of Oliver Wendell Holmes, as "a winged Franklin"—"a soaring nature, ballasted with sense." In the cynical period between two world wars, his wings were often clipped by those critics who complained, not without justification, of his bland optimism, or his insistent preaching, or his rhetorical eloquence, or his intangible pantheism and mysticism, or his indifference to reason. In the years that have followed, he has impressed scholars with his important place in the development of American civilization, and interested critics in his qualities of mind and personality, especially in his "psychological ambivalence," i.e. his effort to perceive sharply, and keep himself poised between, the conflicting elements of life, such as free will and fate.

Texts: *The Complete Works of Ralph Waldo Emerson*, Centenary Edition (Boston, 1903–4). *The Journals of Ralph Waldo Emerson*, edited by E. W. Emerson and W. E. Forbes (Boston, 1909–14).

Further reading: R. L. Rusk, *The Life of Ralph Waldo Emerson*, 1949. S. E. Whicher,

Freedom and Fate: an Inner Life of Ralph Waldo Emerson, 1953. V. C. Hopkins, *Spires of Form: a Study of Emerson's Aesthetic Theory,* 1951. Sherman Paul, *Emerson's Angle of Vision,* 1952. *Emerson: a Collection of Critical Essays,* ed. M. R. Konvitz and S. E. Whicher, 1962. Jonathan Bishop, *Emerson on the Soul,* 1964. Joel Porte, *Emerson and Thoreau: Transcendentalists in Conflict,* 1966.

FROM HIS *Journals*

Emerson began his journals in 1820, when he was a junior in college, and continued them for fifty-five years. When they were published (1909–14; edited by E. W. Emerson and W. E. Forbes) they made a set of ten substantial volumes, from which, in 1926, Bliss Perry extracted *The Heart of Emerson's Journals.* The Journals and Miscellaneous Notebooks are now being brought out in a definitive multi-volume scholarly edition by the Harvard University Press (1960–). The texts of the following selections are from the edition of Emerson and Forbes.

(age 21)

It is my own humor to despise pedigree. I was educated to prize it. The kind Aunt whose cares instructed my youth (and whom may God reward), told me oft the virtues of her and mine ancestors. They have been clergymen for many generations, and the piety of all and the eloquence of many is yet praised in the Churches. But the dead sleep in their moonless night; my business is with the living.

(age 28)

A sect or party is an elegant incognito devised to save a man from the vexation of thinking.

(age 29)

The hour of decision. It seems not worth while for them who charge others with exalting forms above the moon to fear forms themselves with extravagant dislike. ° ° ° I know very well that it is a bad sign in a man to be too conscientious, and stick at gnats. The most desperate scoundrels have been the over-refiners. Without accommodation society is impracticable. But this ordinance [the Lord's Supper] is esteemed the most sacred of religious institutions, and I cannot go habitually to an institution which they esteem holiest with indifference and dislike. [*White Mountains, July 15, 1832*]

Sailed from Boston for Malta, December 25, 1832, in Brig Jasper, Captain Ellis, 236 tons, laden with logwood, mahogany, tobacco, sugar, coffee, beeswax, cheese, etc.

The good Captain rejoices much in my ignorance. He confounded me the other day about the book in the Bible where God was not mentioned, and last night upon St. Paul's shipwreck. Yet I comforted myself at midnight with *Lycidas.* What marble beauty in that classic pastoral.

Perhaps it is a pernicious mistake, yet, rightly seen, I believe it is sound philosophy, that wherever we go, whatever we do, self is the sole subject we study and learn. Montaigne said, himself was all he knew. Myself is much more than I know, and yet I know nothing else. The chemist experiments upon his new salt by trying its affinity to all the various substances he can command, arbitrarily selected, and thereby discloses the most wonderful properties in his subject. And I bring myself to sea, to Malta, to Italy, to find new affinities between me and my fellow men, to observe narrowly the affections, weaknesses, surprises, hopes, doubts, which new sides of the panorama shall call forth in me. Mean, sneakingly mean, would be this philosophy, a reptile unworthy of the name, if *self* be used in the low sense, but as self means Devil, so it means God.

I have been to the Opera, and thought three *taris,* the price of a ticket, rather too much for the whistle. It is doubtless a vice to turn one's eyes inward too much, but I am my own comedy and tragedy. [*Sicily*]

Tonight I heard the *Miserere* sung in St. Peter's and with less effect than yesterday. But what a temple! When night was settling down upon it and a long religious procession moved through a part of the church, I got an idea of its immensity such as I had not before. You walk about on its ample, marble pavement as you would on a common, so free are you of your neighbors; and throngs of people are lost upon it. And what beautiful lights and shades on its mighty gilded arches and vaults and far windows and brave columns, and its rich-clad priests that look as if they were the pictures come down from the walls and walking. [*Rome*]

I ought not to forget the ballet between the acts. Goethe laughs at those who force every work of art into the narrow circle of their own prejudices and cannot admire a picture as a picture, and a tune as a tune. So I was willing to look at this as a ballet, and to see that it was admirable, but I could not help feeling the while that it were better for mankind if there were no such dancers. I have since learned God's decision on the same, in the fact that all the *ballerine* are nearly idiotic.

(age 30)

I collect nothing that can be touched or tasted or smelled, neither cameo, painting, nor medallion; nothing in my trunk but old clothes; but I value much the growing picture which the ages have painted and which I reverently survey.

Pray what brought you here, grave sir? the moving Boulevard seems to say. [*Paris*]

I went this evening into Frascati's, long the most noted of the gambling houses or hells of Paris.

Went into St. Paul's, where service was saying. Poor church. [*London*]

I thank the Great God who has led me through this European scene, this last schoolroom in which he has pleased to instruct me, from Malta's isle, through Sicily, through Italy, through Switzerland, through France, through England, through Scotland, in safety and pleasure, and has now brought me to the shore and the ship that steers westward. He has shown me the men I wished to see,—Landor, Coleridge, Carlyle, Wordsworth; he has thereby comforted and confirmed me in my convictions. Many things I owe to the sight of these men. I shall judge more justly, less timidly, of wise men forevermore. [*Liverpool*]

The men of Europe will say, Expound; let us hear. What is it that is to convince the faithful and at the same time the philosopher? Let us hear this new thing. It is very old. It is the old revelation, that perfect beauty is perfect goodness, it is the development of the wonderful congruities of the moral law of human nature. Let me enumerate a few of the remarkable properties of that nature. A man contains all that is needful to his government within himself. He is made a law unto himself. All real good or evil that can befall him must be from himself. He only can do himself any good or any harm. Nothing can be given to him or taken from him but always there is a compensation. There is a correspondence between the human soul and everything that exists in the world—more properly, everything that is known to man. Instead of studying things without the principles of them, all may be penetrated unto within him. Every act puts the agent in a

new condition. The purpose of life seems to be to acquaint a man with himself. He is not to live to the future as described to him, but to live to the real future by living to the real present. The highest revelation is that God is in every man.

(age 31)

Hail to the quiet fields of my fathers! Not wholly unattended by supernatural friendship and favor, let me come hither. Bless my purposes as they are simple and virtuous. Coleridge's fine letter (in London *Literary Gazette*, September 13, 1834) comes in aid of the very thoughts I was revolving. And be it so. Henceforth I design not to utter any speech, poem, or book that is not entirely and peculiarly my work. I will say at public lectures, and the like, those things which I have meditated for their own sake, and not for the first time with a view to that occasion. (*Concord, November 15, 1834.*)

(age 32)

You affirm that the moral development contains all the intellectual, and that Jesus was the perfect man. I bow in reverence unfeigned before that benign man. I know more, hope more, am more, because he has lived. But, if you tell me that in your opinion he has fulfilled all the conditions of man's existence, carried out to the utmost, at least by implication, all man's powers, I suspend my assent. I do not see in him cheerfulness: I do not see in him the love of natural science: I see in him no kindness for art; I see in him nothing of Socrates, of Laplace, of Shakespeare. The perfect man should remind us of all great men. Do you ask me if I would rather resemble Jesus than any other man? If I should say Yes, I should suspect myself of superstition.

I bought my house and two acres six rods of land of John T. Coolidge for 3,500 dollars.

I was married to Lydia Jackson.

(age 33)

Transcendentalism means, says our accomplished Mrs. B.,[1] with a wave of her hand, *a little beyond*.

The grey present, the white future.

Pleasant walk yesterday, the most pleasant of days. At Walden Pond I found a new musical instrument which I call the ice-harp. A thin coat of ice covered a part of the pond, but melted around the

[1] Probably Almira Penniman Barlow, a family friend (see the Harvard edition of the Journals).

edge of the shore. I threw a stone upon the ice which rebounded with a shrill sound, and falling again and again, repeated the note with pleasing modulation. I thought at first it was the "peep, peep" of a bird I had scared. I was so taken with the music that I threw down my stick and spent twenty minutes in throwing stones single or in handfuls on this crystal drum.

Margaret Fuller left us yesterday morning. Among other things that make her visit valuable and memorable, this is not the least, that she gave me five or six lessons in German pronunciation, never by my offer and rather against my will each time, so that now, spite of myself, I shall always have to thank her for a great convenience—which she foresaw.

(age 35)

The unbelief of the age is attested by the loud condemnation of trifles. Look at our silly religious papers. Let a minister wear a cane, or a white hat, go to a theatre, or avoid a Sunday School, let a school-book with a Calvinistic sentence or a Sunday School book without one be heard of, and instantly all the old grannies squeak and gibber and do what they call "sounding an alarm," from Bangor to Mobile. Alike nice and squeamish is its ear. You must on no account say "stink" or "Damn."

"Seek ye first the kingdom of God, and all these things shall be added unto you." What! Art? Hamlets? Ballads?

A *College.*—My College should have Allston, Greenough, Bryant, Irving, Webster, Alcott, summoned for its domestic professors. And if I must send abroad (and, if we send for dancers and singers and actors, why not at the same prices for scholars?), Carlyle, Hallam, Campbell, should come and read lectures on History, Poetry, Letters. I would bid my men come for the love of God and man, promising them an open field and a boundless opportunity, and they should make their own terms. Then I would open my lecture rooms to the wide nation; and they should pay, each man, a fee that should give my professor a remuneration fit and noble. Then I should see the lecture-room, the college, filled with life and hope. Students would come from afar; for who would not ride a hundred miles to hear some one of these men giving his selectest thoughts to those who received them with joy? I should see living learning; the Muse once more in the eye and cheek of the youth.

(age 36)

Nature will not have us fret or fume. When we come out of the Caucus or the Abolition Convention or the Temperance Meeting, she says to us, "So hot, my little Sir!" I fear the criticism of the sun and moon.

I know no means of calming the fret and perturbation into which too much sitting, too much talking, brings me, so perfect as labor. I have no animal spirits; therefore, when surprised by company and kept in a chair for many hours, my heart sinks, my brow is clouded and I think I will run for Acton woods, and live with the squirrels henceforward. But my garden is nearer, and my good hoe, as it bites the ground, revenges my wrongs, and I have less lust to bite my enemies. I confess I work at first with a little venom, lay to a little unnecessary strength. But by smoothing the rough hillocks, I smooth my temper; by extracting the long roots of the piper-grass, I draw out my own splinters; and in a short time I can hear the bobolink's song and see the blessed deluge of light and color that rolls around me.

What Possibilities!—In the country church, I see the cousins of Napoleon, of Wellington, of Wilberforce, of Bentham, of Humboldt. A little air and sunshine, an hour of need, a provoking society, would call out the right fire from these slumbering peasants.

On Sunday we heard sulphurous Calvinism. The preacher railed at Lord Byron. I thought Lord Byron's vice better than Rev. Mr. M.'s virtue.

When I was thirteen years old, my Uncle Samuel Ripley one day asked me, "How is it, Ralph, that all the boys dislike you and quarrel with you, whilst the grown people are fond of you?" Now am I thirty-six and the fact is reversed,—the old people suspect and dislike me, and the young love me.

(age 37)

Yesterday George and Sophia Ripley, Margaret Fuller and Alcott discussed here the Social Plans [Brook Farm]. I wished to be convinced, to be thawed, to be made nobly mad by the kindlings before my eye of a new dawn of human piety. But this scheme was arithmetic and comfort: this was a hint borrowed from the Tremont House and United States Hotel; a rage in our poverty and politics to live rich and gentlemanlike, an anchor to leeward against a change of weather; a prudent forecast on the probable issue of the great questions of Pauperism and Poverty. And not once could I be inflamed, but sat aloof and thoughtless; my voice faltered and fell. It was not the cave of persecution which is the palace of spiritual power, but only a room in the Astor House hired for the Transcendentalists. I do not wish to remove from my present prison to a prison a little larger. I wish to break all prisons. I have not yet conquered my own house. It irks and repents me. Shall I raise the siege of this hencoop, and march baffled away to a pretended siege of Babylon? It seems to me that so to do were to dodge the problem I am set to solve, and to hide my impotency in the thick of a crowd. I can see too, afar,—that I should not find myself more than now,—no, not so much, in that select, but not by me selected, fraternity. Moreover, to join this body would be to traverse all my long trumpeted theory, and the instinct which spoke from it, that one man is a counterpoise to a city,—that a man is stronger than a city, that his solitude is more prevalent and beneficent than the concert of crowds.

(age 38)

I remember, when a child, in the pew on Sundays amusing myself with saying over common words as "black," "white," "board," etc., twenty or thirty times, until the word lost all meaning and fixedness, and I began to doubt which was the right name for the thing, when I saw that neither had any natural relation, but all were arbitrary. It was a child's first lesson in Idealism.

At Cambridge, the last Wednesday, I met twenty members of my college class and spent the day with them. Governor Kent of Maine presided, Upham, Quincy, Lowell, Gardner, Loring, Gorham, Motte, Wood, Blood, Cheney, Withington, Bulfinch, Reed, Burton, Stetson, Lane, Angier, Hilliard, Farnsworth, Dexter, Emerson. It was strange how fast the company returned to their old relation, and the whole mass of college nonsense came back in a flood. They all associated perfectly, were an unit for the day—men who now never meet. Each resumed his old place. The change in them was really very little in twenty years, although every man present was married, and all but one fathers. I too resumed my old place and found myself as of old a spectator rather than a fellow. I drank a great deal of wine (for me) with the wish to raise my spirits to the pitch of good fellowship, but wine produced on me its old effect, and I grew graver with every glass. Indignation and eloquence will excite me, but wine does not.

I saw in Boston Fanny Elssler in the ballet of *Nathalie.* ° ° ° The chief beauty is in the extreme grace of her movement, the variety and nature of her attitude, the winning fun and spirit of all her little coquetries, the beautiful erectness of her body, and the freedom and determination which she can so easily assume, and, what struck me much, the air of perfect sympathy with the house. ° ° °

I should not think of danger to young women stepping with their father or brother out of happy and guarded parlors into this theatre to return in a few hours to the same; but I can easily suppose that it is not the safest resort for college boys who have left metaphysics, conic sections, or Tacitus to see these tripping satin slippers, and they may not forget this graceful, silvery swimmer when they have retreated again to their baccalaureate cells.

It is a great satisfaction to see the best in each kind, and as a good student of the world, I desire to let pass nothing that is excellent in its own kind unseen, unheard.

The *Dial*[2] is to be sustained or ended, and I must settle the question, it seems, of its life or death. I wish it to live, but do not wish to be its life. Neither do I like to put it in the hands of the Humanity and Reform Men, because they trample on letters and poetry; nor in the hands of the Scholars, for they are dead and dry.

Alcott sees the law of man truer and farther than any one ever did. Unhappily, his conversation never loses sight of his own personality. He never quotes; he never refers; his only illustration is his own biography. His topic yesterday is Alcott on the 17th October; today, Alcott on the 18th October; tomorrow, on the 19th. So will it be always. The poet, rapt into future times or into deeps of nature admired for themselves, lost in their law, cheers us with a lively charm; but this noble genius discredits genius to me. I do not want any more such persons to exist.

If I go into the churches in these days, I usually find the preacher in proportion to his intelligence to be cunning, so that the whole institution sounds hollow. X, the ablest of all the Unitarian clergy, spread popular traps all over the lecture which I heard in the Odeon. But in the days of the Pilgrims and the Puritans, the preachers were the victims of the same faith with which they whipped and persecuted other men, and their sermons are strong, imaginative, fervid, and every word a cube of stone.

[2] Published from July 1840–April 1844; a quarterly magazine of literature, philosophy and religion; published the work of the Transcendentalists.

(age 39)

I hear with pleasure that a young girl in the midst of rich, decorous Unitarian friends in Boston is well-nigh persuaded to join the Roman Catholic Church. Her friends, who are also my friends, lamented to me the growth of this inclination. But I told them that I think she is to be greatly congratulated on the event. She has lived in great poverty of events. In form and years a woman, she is still a child, having had no experiences, and although of a fine, liberal, susceptible, expanding nature, has never yet found any worthy object of attention; has not been in love, not been called out by any taste, except lately by music, and sadly wants adequate objects. In this church, perhaps, she shall find what she needs, in a power to call out the slumbering religious sentiment. It is unfortunate that the guide who has led her into this path is a young girl of a lively, forcible, but quite external character, who teaches her the historical argument for the Catholic faith. I told A. that I hoped she would not be misled by attaching any importance to that. If the offices of the church attracted her, if its beautiful forms and humane spirit draw her, if St. Augustine and St. Bernard, Jesus and Madonna, cathedral music and masses, then go, for thy dear heart's sake, but do not go out of this icehouse of Unitarianism, all external, into an icehouse again of external. At all events, I charged her to pay no regard to dissenters, but to suck that orange thoroughly.

It is greatest to believe and to hope well of the world, because he who does so, quits the world of experience, and makes the world he lives in.

(age 41)

Be an opener of doors for such as come after thee, and do not try to make the universe a blind alley.

There is not the slightest probability that the college will foster an eminent talent in any youth. If he refuses prayers and recitations, they will torment and traduce and expel him, though he were Newton or Dante.

Even for those whom I really love I have not animal spirits.

I like man, but not men.

(age 44)

Eager, solicitous, hungry, rabid, busy-bodied America attempting many things, vain, ambitious to feel thy own existence, and convince others of thy talent, by attempting and hastily accomplishing much; yes, catch thy breath and correct thyself, and failing here, prosper out there; speed and fever are never greatness; but reliance and serenity and waiting.

The Superstitions of our Age:
The fear of Catholicism;
The fear of pauperism;
The fear of immigration;
The fear of manufacturing interests;
The fear of radicalism or democracy;
And faith in the steam engine.

(age 46)

Love is temporary and ends with marriage. Marriage is the perfection which love aimed at, ignorant of what it sought. Marriage is a good known only to the parties,—a relation of perfect understanding, aid, contentment, possession of themselves and of the world,—which dwarfs love to green fruit.

(age 48)

This filthy enactment (The Fugitive Slave Law)[3] was made in the nineteenth century, by people who could read and write. I will not obey it, by God.

(age 52)

A *practical man* is the hobby of the age. Well, when I read German philosophy, or wrote verses, I was willing to concede there might be too much of these, and that the Western pioneer with axe on his shoulder, and still moving West as the settlements approached him, had his merits.

Whipple said of the author of "Leaves of Grass" that he had every leaf but the fig leaf.

(age 58)

Why has never the poorest country college offered me a professorship of rhetoric? I think I could have taught an orator, though I am none.

(age 59)

I like people who can do things. When Edward and I struggled in vain to drag our big calf into the barn, the Irish girl put her finger into the calf's mouth, and led her in directly.

[3] The 1850 law providing for the return of escaped Negro slaves to their owners.

(age 60)

I went to Dartmouth College, and found the same old Granny system which I met there twenty-five years ago. The President has an aversion to emulation, as injurious to the character of the pupils. He therefore forbids the election of members into the two literary societies by merit, but arranges that the first scholar alphabetically on the list shall be assigned to the Adelphi, and the second to the Mathesians, and the third to the Adelphi, and the fourth to the Mathesians; and so on. Every student belonging to the one or the other. "Well, but there is a first scholar in the class, is there not, and he has the first oration at Commencement?" "Oh, no, the parts are assigned by lot." The amiable student who explained it added that it tended to remove disagreeable excitement from the societies. I answered, "Certainly, and it would remove more if there were no college at all." I recommended morphine in liberal doses at the College Commons.

(age 65)

A man never gets acquainted with himself, but is always a surprise. We get daily news of the world within, as well as of the world outside, and not less of the central than of the surface facts. A new thought is awaiting him every morning.

(age 66)

Dr. Hedge tells us that the Indian asked John Eliot, "Why God did not kill the Devil?" One would like to know what was Eliot's answer.

(age 67)

In Yosemite, grandeur of these mountains perhaps unmatched in the globe; for here they strip themselves like athletes for exhibition, and stand perpendicular granite walls, showing their entire height, and wearing a liberty cap of snow on their head.

At the request of Galen Clark, our host at Mariposa, and who is, by State appointment, the protector of the trees, and who went with us to the Mammoth Groves, I selected a Sequoia Gigantea, near Galen's Hospice, in the presence of our party, and named it *Samoset*, in memory of the first Indian ally of the Plymouth Colony, and I gave Mr. Clark directions to procure a tin plate, and have the inscription painted thereon in the usual form of the named trees: and paid him its cost.

(age 59–69)

A man's style is his mind's voice. Wooden minds, wooden voices.

Fate.°°° Even the chickens running up and down, and pecking at each white spot and at each other as ridden by chicken nature, seem ever and anon to have a pause of consideration, then hurry on again to be chickens. Men have more pause.

(age 70)

Egypt. Mrs. Helen Bell, it seems, was asked, "What do you think the Sphinx said to Mr. Emerson?" "Why," replied Mrs. Bell, "the Sphinx probably said to him, 'You're another.'"

Thought

I am not poor, but I am proud,
  Of one inalienable right,
Above the envy of the crowd,—
  Thought's holy light.

Better it is than gems or gold, 5
  And oh! it cannot die,
But thought will glow when the sun grows cold,
  And mix with Deity.
1823

Grace

How much, preventing God, how much I owe
To the defences thou hast round me set;
Example, custom, fear, occasion slow,—
These scorned bondmen were my parapet.
I dare not peep over this parapet 5
To gauge with glance the roaring gulf below,
The depths of sin to which I had descended,
Had not these me against myself defended.
1833   1842

The Rhodora:

On Being Asked, Whence is the Flower?

Emerson chooses to write about a flower of the American forest rather than the rose or violet of English poetry. Later, in his little book on *Nature*, he formulated in philosophical terms the idea expressed here: that beauty needs no "excuse." When, as in the experience of this poem, he is in the presence of beauty, it seems supreme. But generally he speaks of other ultimate ends; it is equally true for him that goodness needs no excuse, that truth needs no excuse. Unlike Poe, he associates "an interchangeable Truth, Beauty, and Goodness, each wholly interfused in the other." "the eternal trinity of Truth, Goodness, and Beauty, each in its perfection including the three."

In May, when sea-winds pierced our solitudes,
I found the fresh Rhodora in the woods,
Spreading its leafless blooms in a damp nook,
To please the desert and the sluggish brook.
The purple petals, fallen in the pool,   5
Made the black water with their beauty gay;
Here might the redbird[1] come his plumes to cool,
And court the flower that cheapens his array.
Rhodora! if the sages ask thee why
This charm is wasted on the earth and sky,   10
Tell them, dear, that if eyes were made for seeing,
Then Beauty is its own excuse for being:[2]
Why thou wert there, O rival of the rose!
I never thought to ask, I never knew:
But, in my simple ignorance, suppose   15
The self-same Power that brought me there brought
          you.
1834

Each and All

The germ of the poem was probably an 1834 journal entry where Emerson had stated this abstraction in connection with a parable. "I remember when I was a boy going upon the beach and being charmed with the colors and forms of the shells. I picked up many and put them in my pocket. When I got home I could find nothing that I gathered—nothing but some dry, ugly mussel and snail shells. Thence I learned that Composition was more important than the beauty of individual forms to Effect. On the shore they lay wet and social, by the sea and under the sky."

Another journal passage, perhaps a memory of his European trip, gave him the beginning of his poem: "The shepherd or the beggar [the "clown," i.e. rustic, of the poem] in his red cloak little knows what a charm he gives to the wide landscape that charms you on the mountain-top and whereof he makes the most agreeable feature, and I [know] no more the part my individuality plays in the All."

The poem opens with this and three other separate situations, the meaning of which is crystallized in the statement of lines 11 and 12. Then come three experiences of enchantment and disillusion—the sparrow, the shells, the

The Rhodora. [1] Presumably the scarlet tanager.
[2] Cf. *Nature,* the concluding paragraph of Chapter II, "Beauty": "The world thus exists to the soul to satisfy the desire of beauty. This element I call an ultimate end. No reason can be asked or given why the soul seeks beauty. Beauty, in its largest and profoundest sense, is one expression for the universe. God is the all-fair. Truth, and goodness, and beauty, are but different faces of the same All. But beauty in nature is not ultimate. It is the herald of inward and eternal beauty, and is not alone a solid and satisfactory good. It must stand as a part, and not as yet the last or highest expression of the final cause of Nature."

maiden. Beauty seems a cheat of the immature; is not truth more to be desired? (Lines 37–39.) The answer, romantically conceived, is given in the rest of the poem. With Emerson, however, the answer represents a poetic mood rather than his prevailing outlook.

There are various awkwardnesses in images, movement of thought and feeling, pattern of meter and rhyme. Yet the lack of conventional design and finish is offset by an intriguing unexpectedness, growing out of free perception. Emerson's "rough" technique will prepare us for Whitman, Emily Dickinson, and many poets of the twentieth century.

Little thinks, in the field, yon red-cloaked clown
Of thee from the hill-top looking down;
The heifer that lows in the upland farm,
Far-heard, lows not thine ear to charm;
The sexton, tolling his bell at noon,   5
Deems not that great Napoleon
Stops his horse, and lists with delight,
Whilst his files sweep round yon Alpine height;
Nor knowest thou what argument
Thy life to thy neighbor's creed has lent.   10
All are needed by each one;
Nothing is fair or good alone.
I thought the sparrow's note from heaven,
Singing at dawn on the alder bough;
I brought him home, in his nest, at even;   15
He sings the song, but it cheers not now,
For I did not bring home the river and sky;—
He sang to my ear,—they sang to my eye.
The delicate shells lay on the shore;
The bubbles of the latest wave   20
Fresh pearls to their enamel gave,
And the bellowing of the savage sea
Greeted their safe escape to me.
I wiped away the weeds and foam,
I fetched my sea-born treasures home;   25
But the poor, unsightly, noisome things
Had left their beauty on the shore
With the sun and the sand and the wild uproar.
The lover watched his graceful maid,
As 'mid the virgin train she strayed,   30
Nor knew her beauty's best attire
Was woven still by the snow-white choir.
At last she came to his hermitage,
Like the bird from the woodlands to the cage;—
The gay enchantment was undone,   35
A gentle wife, but fairy none.
Then I said, "I covet truth;
Beauty is unripe childhood's cheat;
I leave it behind with the games of youth:"—
As I spoke, beneath my feet   40
The ground-pine curled its pretty wreath,
Running over the club-moss burrs;
I inhaled the violet's breath;
Around me stood the oaks and firs;
Pine-cones and acorns lay on the ground;   45

Over me soared the eternal sky,
Full of light and of deity;
Again I saw, again I heard,
The rolling river, the morning bird;—
Beauty through my senses stole; 50
I yielded myself to the perfect whole.
1834?

Concord Hymn

Sung at the Completion of the Battle Monument, July 4, 1837

By the rude bridge that arched the flood,
  Their flag to April's breeze unfurled,
Here once the embattled farmers stood
  And fired the shot heard round the world.

The foe long since in silence slept; 5
  Alike the conqueror silent sleeps;
And Time the ruined bridge has swept
  Down the dark stream which seaward creeps.

On this green bank, by this soft stream,
  We set to-day a votive stone; 10
That memory may their deed redeem,
  When, like our sires, our sons are gone.

Spirit, that made those heroes dare
  To die, and leave their children free,
Bid Time and Nature gently spare 15
  The shaft we raise to them and thee.
1837

The Problem

Seven years before, Emerson had made his decision to abandon the minister's vocation. But the problem he had faced continued to haunt him. It is stated clearly in the journal: "I dislike to be a clergyman and refuse to be one. Yet how rich a music would be to me a holy clergyman in my town. It seems to me he cannot be a man, quite and whole; yet how plain is the need of one, and how high, yes, highest is the function. Here is division of labor that I like not: a man must sacrifice his manhood for the social good. Something is wrong; I see not what."

I like a church; I like a cowl;
I love a prophet of the soul;
And on my heart monastic aisles
Fall like sweet strains, or pensive smiles;
Yet not for all his faith can see 5
Would I that cowlèd churchman be.

Why should the vest on him allure,
Which I could not on me endure?

Not from a vain or shallow thought
His awful Jove young Phidias brought; 10
Never from lips of cunning fell
The thrilling Delphic oracle;
Out from the heart of nature rolled
The burdens of the Bible old;
The litanies of nations came, 15
Like the volcano's tongue of flame,
Up from the burning core below,—
The canticles of love and woe:
The hand that rounded Peter's dome
And groined the aisles of Christian Rome 20
Wrought in a sad sincerity;
Himself from God he could not free;
He builded better than he knew;—
The conscious stone to beauty grew.

Know'st thou what wove yon woodbird's nest 25
Of leaves, and feathers from her breast?
Or how the fish outbuilt her shell,
Painting with morn her annual cell?
Or how the sacred pine-tree adds
To her old leaves new myriads? 30
Such and so grew these holy piles,
Whilst love and terror laid the tiles.
Earth proudly wears the Parthenon,
As the best gem upon her zone,
And Morning opes with haste her lids 35
To gaze upon the Pyramids;
O'er England's abbeys bends the sky,
As on its friends, with kindred eye;
For out of Thought's interior sphere
These wonders rose to upper air; 40
And Nature gladly gave them place,
Adopted them into her race,
And granted them an equal date
With Andes and with Ararat.

These temples grew as grows the grass; 45
Art might obey, but not surpass.
The passive Master lent his hand
To the vast soul that o'er him planned;
And the same power that reared the shrine
Bestrode the tribes that knelt within. 50
Ever the fiery Pentecost
Girds with one flame the countless host,
Trances the heart through chanting choirs,
And through the priest the mind inspires.
The word unto the prophet spoken 55
Was writ on tables yet unbroken;
The word by seers or sibyls told,
In groves of oak, or fanes of gold,
Still floats upon the morning wind,
Still whispers to the willing mind. 60
One accent of the Holy Ghost
The heedless world hath never lost.
I know what say the fathers wise,—

The Book itself before me lies,
Old *Chrysostom*,[1] best Augustine,   65
And he who blent both in his line,
The younger *Golden Lips* or mines,
Taylor,[2] the Shakespeare of divines.
His words are music in my ear,
I see this cowlèd portrait dear;   70
And yet, for all his faith could see,
I would not the good bishop be.
1839

Woodnotes, I

Emerson's journal at the time of this poem reflects a re-current romantic irresponsibility. "My life is a May game, I will live as I like. I defy your strait-laced, weary, social ways and modes. Blue is the sky, green the fields and groves, fresh the springs, glad the rivers. . . ." "I wish to write such rhymes as shall not suggest a restraint, but contrariwise the wildest freedom." In regard to nature lore, Emerson always deferred to his young friend Thoreau, who had reached manhood only a year or two before this poem was written. Thoreau is almost certainly the "forest seer" of the passage beginning at line 30.

1

When the pine tosses its cones
To the song of its waterfall tones,
Who speeds to the woodland walks?
To birds and trees who talks?
Caesar of his leafy Rome,   5
There the poet is at home.
He goes to the river-side,—
Not hook nor line hath he;
He stands in the meadows wide,—
Nor gun nor scythe to see.   10
Sure some god his eye enchants:
What he knows nobody wants.
In the wood he travels glad,
Without better fortune had,
Melancholy without bad.   15
Knowledge this man prizes best
Seems fantastic to the rest:
Pondering shadows, colors, clouds,
Grass-buds and caterpillar-shrouds,
Boughs on which the wild bees settle,   20
Tints that spot the violet's petal,
Why Nature loves the number five,
And why the star-form she repeats:
Lover of all things alive,
Wonderer at all he meets,   25
Wonderer chiefly at himself,
Who can tell him what he is?

Or how meet in human elf
Coming and past eternities?

2

And such I knew, a forest seer,   30
A minstrel of the natural year,
Foreteller of the vernal ides,
Wise harbinger of spheres and tides,
A lover true, who knew by heart
Each joy the mountain dales impart;   35
It seemed that Nature could not raise
A plant in any secret place,
In quaking bog, on snowy hill,
Beneath the grass that shades the rill,
Under the snow, between the rocks,   40
In damp fields known to bird and fox,
But he would come in the very hour
It opened in its virgin bower,
As if a sunbeam showed the place,
And tell its long-descended race.   45
It seemed as if the breezes brought him,
It seemed as if the sparrows taught him;
As if by secret sight he knew
Where, in far fields, the orchis grew.
Many haps fall in the field   50
Seldom seen by wishful eyes,
But all her shows did Nature yield,
To please and win this pilgrim wise.
He saw the partridge drum in the woods;
He heard the woodcock's evening hymn;   55
He found the tawny thrushes' broods;
And the shy hawk did wait for him;
What others did at distance hear,
And guessed within the thicket's gloom,
Was shown to this philosopher,   60
And at his bidding seemed to come.

3

In unploughed Maine he sought the lumberers' gang
Where from a hundred lakes young rivers sprang;
He trode the unplanted forest floor, whereon
The all-seeing sun for ages hath not shone;   65
Where feeds the moose, and walks the surly bear,
And up the tall mast runs the woodpecker.
He saw beneath dim aisles, in odorous beds,
The slight Linnaea hang its twin-born heads,   69
And blessed the monument of the man of flowers,
Which breathes his sweet fame through the north-
    ern bowers.
He heard, when in the grove, at intervals,
With sudden roar the aged pine-tree falls,—
One crash, the death-hymn of the perfect tree,
Declares the close of its green century.   75
Low lies the plant to whose creation went
Sweet influence from every element;
Whose living towers the years conspired to build,
Whose giddy top the morning loved to gild.

The Problem. [1] John of Antioch (345?–407), Greek church father, called "Golden Mouth" (Chrysostom) for his *Homilies.*
[2] Jeremy Taylor (1613–67), English theologian and author of *Holy Living* and *Holy Dying.*

Through these green tents, by eldest Nature
  dressed,   80
He roamed, content alike with man and beast.
Where darkness found him he lay glad at night;
There the red morning touched him with its light.
Three moons his great heart him a hermit made,
So long he roved at will the boundless shade.   85
The timid it concerns to ask their way,
And fear what foe in caves and swamps can stray,
To make no step until the event is known,
And ills to come as evils past bemoan.
Not so the wise; no coward watch he keeps   90
To spy what danger on his pathway creeps;
Go where he will, the wise man is at home,
His hearth the earth,—his hall the azure dome;
Where his clear spirit leads him, there's his road
By God's own light illumined and foreshowed.   95

4

'Twas one of the charmèd days
When the genius of God doth flow;
The wind may alter twenty ways,
A tempest cannot blow;
It may blow north, it still is warm;   100
Or south, it still is clear;
Or east, it smells like a clover-farm;
Or west, no thunder fear.
The musing peasant, lowly great,
Beside the forest water sate;   105
The rope-like pine-roots crosswise grown
Composed the network of his throne;
The wide lake, edged with sand and grass,
Was burnished to a floor of glass,
Painted with shadows green and proud   110
Of the tree and of the cloud.
He was the heart of all the scene;
On him the sun looked more serene;
To hill and cloud his face was known,—
It seemed the likeness of their own;   115
They knew by secret sympathy
The public child of earth and sky.
"You ask," he said, "what guide
Me through trackless thickets led,
Through thick-stemmed woodlands rough and wide
I found the water's bed.   121
The watercourses were my guide;
I travelled grateful by their side,
Or through their channel dry;
They led me through the thicket damp,   125
Through brake and fern, the beavers' camp,
Through beds of granite cut my road,
And their resistless friendship showed.
The falling waters led me,
The foodful waters fed me,   130
And brought me to the lowest land,
Unerring to the ocean sand.
The moss upon the forest bark

Was pole-star when the night was dark;
The purple berries in the wood   135
Supplied me necessary food;
For Nature ever faithful is
To such as trust her faithfulness.
When the forest shall mislead me,
When the night and morning lie,   140
When sea and land refuse to feed me,
'Twill be time enough to die;
Then will yet my mother yield
A pillow in her greenest field,
Nor the June flowers scorn to cover   145
The clay of their departed lover."

                                                            1840

The Sphinx

In 1859 Emerson wrote: "I have often been asked the meaning of "The Sphinx." It is this:—The perception of identity unites all things and explains one by another, and the most rare and strange is equally facile as the most common. But if the mind live only in particulars, and see only differences (wanting the power to see the whole—all in each), then the world addresses to this mind a question it cannot answer, and each new fact tears it to pieces, and it is vanquished by a distracting variety."

The Sphinx is drowsy,
  Her wings are furled:
Her ear is heavy,
  She broods on the world.
"Who'll tell me my secret   5
  The ages have kept?—
I awaited the seer
  While they slumbered and slept:—

"The fate of the man-child,
  The meaning of man;   10
Known fruit of the unknown;
  Daedalian plan;
Out of sleeping a waking,
  Out of waking a sleep;
Life death overtaking;   15
  Deep underneath deep?

"Erect as a sunbeam,
  Upspringeth the palm
The elephant browses,
  Undaunted and calm;   20
In beautiful motion
  The thrush plies his wings;
Kind leaves of his covert,
  Your silence he sings.

"The waves, unashamed,   25
  In difference sweet,

Play glad with the breezes,
  Old playfellows meet;
The journeying atoms,
  Primordial wholes,
Firmly draw, firmly drive,   30
  By their animate poles.

"Sea, earth, air, sound, silence,
  Plant, quadruped, bird,
By one music enchanted,
  One deity stirred,—   35
Each the other adorning,
  Accompany still;
Night veileth the morning,
  The vapor the hill.   40

"The babe by its mother
  Lies bathèd in joy;
Glide its hours uncounted,—
  The sun is its toy;
Shines the peace of all being,   45
  Without cloud, in its eyes;
And the sum of the world
  In soft miniature lies.

"But man crouches and blushes,
  Absconds and conceals;   50
He creepeth and peepeth,
  He palters and steals;
Infirm, melancholy,
  Jealous glancing around,
An oaf, an accomplice,   55
  He poisons the ground.

"Out spoke the great mother,
  Beholding his fear;—
At the sound of her accents
  Cold shuddered the sphere:—   60
'Who has drugged my boy's cup?
  Who has mixed my boy's bread?
Who, with sadness and madness,
  Has turned my child's head?'"

I heard a poet answer   65
  Aloud and cheerfully,
"Say on, sweet Sphinx! thy dirges
  Are pleasant songs to me.
Deep love lieth under
  These pictures of time;   70
They fade in the light of
  Their meaning sublime.

"The fiend that man harries
  Is love of the Best;
Yawns the pit of the Dragon,[1]   75
  Lit by rays from the Blest.

The Sphinx. [1] A reference to Satan.

The Lethe of Nature
  Can't trance him again,
Whose soul sees the perfect,
  Which his eyes seek in vain.   80

"To vision profounder,
  Man's spirit must dive;
His aye-rolling orb
  At no goal will arrive;
The heavens that now draw him   85
  With sweetness untold,
Once found,—for new heavens
  He spurneth the old.

"Pride ruined the angels,
  Their shame them restores;   90
Lurks the joy that is sweetest
  In stings of remorse.
Have I a lover
  Who is noble and free?—
I would he were nobler   95
  Than to love me.

"Eterne alternation
  Now follows, now flies;
And under pain, pleasure,—
  Under pleasure, pain lies.   100
Love works at the centre,
  Heart-heaving alway;
Forth speed the strong pulses
  To the borders of day.

"Dull Sphinx, Jove keep thy five wits;   105
  Thy sight is growing blear;
Rue, myrrh and cummin[2] for the Sphinx,
  Her muddy eyes to clear!"
The old Sphinx bit her thick lip,—
  Said, "Who taught thee me to name?   110
I am thy spirit, yoke-fellow;
  Of thine eye I am eyebeam.

"Thou art the unanswered question;
  Couldst see thy proper eye,
Alway it asketh, asketh;   115
  And each answer is a lie.
So take thy quest through nature,
  It through thousand natures ply;
Ask on, thou clothed eternity;
  Time is the false reply."   120

Uprose the merry Sphinx,
  And crouched no more in stone;
She melted into purple cloud,
  She silvered in the moon;
She spired into a yellow flame;   125
  She flowered in blossoms red;

[2] Presumably healing herbs.

She flowed into a foaming wave:
    She stood Monadnoc's head.

Thorough a thousand voices
    Spoke the universal dame;   130
"Who telleth one of my meanings
    Is master of all I am."

                  1841

The Snow-Storm

Announced by all the trumpets of the sky,
Arrives the snow, and, driving o'er the fields,
Seems nowhere to alight: the whited air
Hides hills and woods, the river, and the heaven,
And veils the farm-house at the garden's end.   5
The sled and traveller stopped, the courier's feet
Delayed, all friends shut out, the housemates sit
Around the radiant fireplace, enclosed
In a tumultuous privacy of storm.

    Come see the north wind's masonry.   10
Out of an unseen quarry evermore
Furnished with tile, the fierce artificer
Curves his white bastions with projected roof
Round every windward stake, or tree, or door.
Speeding the myriad-handed, his wild work   15
So fanciful, so savage, nought cares he
For number or proportion. Mockingly,
On coop or kennel he hangs Parian wreaths;
A swan-like form invests the hidden thorn;
Fills up the farmer's lane from wall to wall,   20
Maugre the farmer's sighs; and at the gate
A tapering turret overtops the work.
And when his hours are numbered, and the world
Is all his own, retiring, as he were not,
Leaves, when the sun appears, astonished Art   25
To mimic in slow structures, stone by stone,
Built in an age, the mad wind's night-work,
The frolic architecture of the snow.

                  1841

Ode

Inscribed to W. H. Channing

William Henry Channing, a nephew of the Unitarian
leader, William Ellery Channing, was a vigorous political
activist, as well as an active Transcendentalist, who had
probably urged Emerson to participate in the Abolitionist
cause. Emerson's poem not only answers Channing's immediate challenge; it defends, as well, Emerson's whole
individualistic position.

Though loath to grieve
The evil time's sole patriot,
I cannot leave

My honeyed thought
For the priest's cant,   5
Or the statesman's rant.

If I refuse
My study for their politique,
Which at the best is trick,
The angry Muse   10
Puts confusion in my brain.

But who is he that prates
Of the culture of mankind,
Of better arts and life?
Go, blindworm, go,   15
Behold the famous States
Harrying Mexico
With rifle and with knife!

Or who, with accent bolder,
Dare praise the freedom-loving mountaineer?   20
I found by thee, O rushing Contoocook!
And in thy valleys, Agiochook!
The jackals of the negro-holder.

The God who made New Hampshire
Taunted the lofty land   25
With little men;—
Small bat and wren
House in the oak:—
If earth-fire cleave
The upheaved land, and bury the folk,   30
The southern crocodile would grieve.
Virtue palters; Right is hence;
Freedom praised, but hid;
Funeral eloquence
Rattles the coffin-lid.   35

What boots thy zeal,
O glowing friend,
That would indignant rend
The northland from the south?
Wherefore? to what good end?   40
Boston Bay and Bunker Hill
Would serve things still;—
Things are of the snake.

The horseman serves the horse,
The neatherd serves the neat,   45
The merchant serves the purse,
The eater serves his meat;
'Tis the day of the chattel,
Web to weave, and corn to grind;
Things are in the saddle,   50
And ride mankind.

There are two laws discrete,
Not reconciled,—

Law for man, and law for thing;
The last builds town and fleet,   55
But it runs wild,
And doth the man unking.

'Tis fit the forest fall,
The steep be graded,
The mountain tunnelled,   60
The sand shaded,
The orchard planted,
The glebe tilled,
The prairie granted,
The steamer built.   65

Let man serve law for man;
Live for friendship, live for love,
For truth's and harmony's behoof;
The state may follow how it can,
As Olympus follows Jove.   70

Yet do not I implore
The wrinkled shopman to my sounding woods,
Nor bid the unwilling senator
Ask votes of thrushes in the solitudes.
Every one to his chosen work;—   75
Foolish hands may mix and mar;
Wise and sure the issues are.
Round they roll till dark is light,
Sex to sex, and even to odd;—
The over-god   80
Who marries Right to Might,
Who peoples, unpeoples,—
He who exterminates
Races by stronger races,
Black by white faces,—   85
Knows to bring honey
Out of the lion;
Grafts gentlest scion
On pirate and Turk.

The Cossack eats Poland,   90
Like stolen fruit;
Her last noble is ruined,
Her last poet mute:
Straight, into double band
The victors divide;   95
Half for freedom strike and stand;—
The astonished Muse finds thousands at her side.

    1846

Merlin

In medieval romance Merlin was a legendary Welsh bard, as well as counselor of King Arthur. Emerson has the bardic tradition in mind more than the Arthurian. He used the name, with some of its romantic connotations, to represent himself, as poet, ideally.

1

Thy trivial harp will never please
Or fill my craving ear;
Its chords should ring as blows the breeze,
Free, peremptory, clear.
No jingling serenader's art,   5
Nor tinkle of piano strings,
Can make the wild blood start
In its mystic springs.
The kingly bard
Must smite the chords rudely and hard,   10
As with hammer or with mace;
That they may render back
Artful thunder, which conveys
Secrets of the solar track,
Sparks of the supersolar blaze.   15
Merlin's blows are strokes of fate,
Chiming with the forest tone,
When boughs buffet boughs in the wood;
Chiming with the gasp and moan
Of the ice-imprisoned flood;   20
With the pulse of manly hearts;
With the voice of orators;
With the din of city arts;
With the cannonades of wars;
With the marches of the brave;   25
And prayers of might from martyrs' cave.

Great is the art,
Great be the manners, of the bard.
He shall not his brain encumber
With the coil of rhythm and number;   30
But, leaving rule and pale forethought,
He shall aye climb
For his rhyme.
"Pass in, pass in," the angels say,
"In to the upper doors,   35
Nor count compartments of the floors,
But mount to paradise
By the stairway of surprise."

Blameless master of the games,
King of sport that never shames,   40
He shall daily joy dispense
Hid in song's sweet influence.
Forms more cheerly live and go,
What time the subtle mind
Sings aloud the tune whereto   45
Their pulses beat,
And march their feet,
And their members are combined.

By Sybarites beguiled,
He shall no task decline;   50
Merlin's mighty line

Extremes of nature reconciled,—
Bereaved a tyrant of his will,
And made the lion mild.
Songs can the tempest still,   55
Scattered on the stormy air,
Mould the year to fair increase,
And bring in poetic peace.

He shall not seek to weave,
In weak, unhappy times,   60
Efficacious rhymes;
Wait his returning strength.
Bird that from the nadir's floor
To the zenith's top can soar,—
The soaring orbit of the muse exceeds that journey's
      length.   65
Nor profane affect to hit
Or compass that, by meddling wit,
Which only the propitious mind
Publishes when 'tis inclined.
There are open hours   70
When the God's will sallies free,
And the dull idiot might see
The flowing fortunes of a thousand years;—
Sudden, at unawares,
Self-moved, fly-to the doors,   75
Nor sword of angels could reveal
What they conceal.

2

The rhyme of the poet
Modulates the king's affairs;
Balance-loving Nature   80
Made all things in pairs.
To every foot its antipode;
Each color with its counter glowed;
To every tone beat answering tones,
Higher or graver;   85
Flavor gladly blends with flavor;
Leaf answers leaf upon the bough;
And match the paired cotyledons.
Hands to hands, and feet to feet,
In one body grooms and brides;   90
Eldest rite, two married sides
In every mortal meet.
Light's far furnace shines,
Smelting balls and bars,
Forging double stars,   95
Glittering twins and trines.
The animals are sick with love,
Lovesick with rhyme;
Each with all propitious Time
Into chorus wove.   100

Like the dancers' ordered band,
Thoughts come also hand in hand;

In equal couples mated,
Or else alternated;
Adding by their mutual gage,   105
One to other, health and age.
Solitary fancies go
Short-lived wandering to and fro,
Most like to bachelors,
Or an ungiven maid,   110
Not ancestors,
With no posterity to make the lie afraid,
Or keep truth undecayed.
Perfect-paired as eagle's wings,
Justice is the rhyme of things;   115
Trade and counting use
The self-same tuneful muse;
And Nemesis,
Who with even matches odd.
Who athwart space redresses   120
The partial wrong,
Fills the just period,
And finishes the song.

Subtle rhymes, with ruin rife,
Murmur in the house of life,   125
Sung by the Sisters as they spin;
In perfect time and measure they
Build and unbuild our echoing clay.
As the two twilights of the day
Fold us music-drunken in.   130

1846

Bacchus

In "Bacchus" the "wine which never grew" becomes the symbol for poetic inspiration—for an ideal vision. This poem and "Merlin" provide important Emersonian statements about poetry. They can be usefully compared to Poe's "Israfel."

Bring me wine, but wine which never grew
In the belly of the grape,
Or grew on vine whose tap-roots, reaching through
Under the Andes to the Cape,
Suffered no savor of the earth to scape.   5

Let its grapes the morn salute
From a nocturnal root,
Which feels the acrid juice
Of Styx and Erebus;
And turns the woe of Night,   10
By its own craft, to a more rich delight,

We buy ashes for bread;
We buy diluted wine;
Give me of the true,—
Whose ample leaves and tendrils curled   15

Among the silver hills of heaven
Draw everlasting dew;
Wine of wine,
Blood of the world,
Form of forms, and mould of statures,   20
That I intoxicated,
And by the draught assimilated,
May float at pleasure through all natures;
The bird-language rightly spell,
And that which roses say so well.   25

Wine that is shed
Like the torrents of the sun
Up the horizon walls,
Or like the Atlantic streams, which run
When the South Sea calls.   30

Water and bread,
Food which needs no transmuting,
Rainbow-flowering, wisdom-fruiting,
Wine which is already man,
Food which teach and reason can.   35

Wine which Music is,—
Music and wine are one,—
That I, drinking this,
Shall hear far Chaos talk with me;
Kings unborn shall walk with me;   40
And the poor grass shall plot and plan
What it will do when it is man.
Quickened so, will I unlock
Every crypt of every rock.

I thank the joyful juice   45
For all I know;—
Winds of remembering
Of the ancient being blow,
And seeming-solid walls of use
Open and flow.   50

Pour, Bacchus! the remembering wine;
Retrieve the loss of me and mine!
Vine for vine be antidote,
And the grape requite the lote!
Haste to cure the old despair,—   55
Reason in Nature's lotus drenched,
The memory of ages quenched;
Give them again to shine;
Let wine repair what this undid;
And where the infection slid,   60
A dazzling memory revive;
Refresh the faded tints,
Recut the aged prints,
And write my old adventures with the pen
Which on the first day drew,   65

Upon the tablets blue,
The dancing Pleiads and eternal men.
1846

Compensation

The Centenary Edition of the poems prints these lines as a
single poem; but the Essays show that each group of lines
is a separate motto and separate poem.

The wings of Time are black and white,
Pied with morning and with night,
Mountain tall and ocean deep
Trembling balance duly keep.
In changing moon and tidal wave   5
Glows the feud of Want and Have.
Gauge of more and less through space,
Electric star or pencil plays,
The lonely Earth amid the balls
That hurry through the eternal halls,   10
A makeweight flying to the void,
Supplemental asteroid,
Or compensatory spark,
Shoots across the neutral Dark.

Man's the elm, and Wealth the vine;   15
Stanch and strong the tendrils twine:
Though the frail ringlets thee deceive,
None from its stock that vine can reave.
Fear not, then, thou child infirm,
There's no god dare wrong a worm;   20
Laurel crowns cleave to deserts,
And power to him who power exerts.
Hast not thy share? On winged feet,
Lo! it rushes thee to meet;
And all that Nature made thy own,   25
Floating in air or pent in stone,
Will rive the hills and swim the sea,
And, like thy shadow, follow thee.
                                                  1847

Give All to Love

Emerson's belief in "compensation" and his belief in a
spiritual reality enable him to urge the detachment of the
last two stanzas.

Give all to love;
Obey thy heart;
Friends, kindred, days,
Estate, good-fame,
Plans, credit and the Muse,—   5
Nothing refuse.

'Tis a brave master;
Let it have scope:

Follow it utterly,
Hope beyond hope: 10
High and more high
It dives into noon,
With wing unspent,
Untold intent;
But it is a god, 15
Knows its own path
And the outlets of the sky.

It was never for the mean;
It requireth courage stout.
Souls above doubt, 20
Valor unbending,
It will reward,—
They shall return
More than they were,
And ever ascending. 25

Leave all for love;
Yet, hear me, yet,
One word more thy heart behoved,
One pulse more of firm endeavor,—
Keep thee to-day, 30
To-morrow, forever,
Free as an Arab
Of thy beloved.

Cling with life to the maid;
But when the surprise, 35
First vague shadow of surmise
Flits across her bosom young,
Of a joy apart from thee,
Free be she, fancy-free;
Nor thou detain her vesture's hem, 40
Nor the palest rose she flung
From her summer diadem.

Though thou loved her as thyself,
As a self of purer clay,
Though her parting dims the day, 45
Stealing grace from all alive;
Heartily know,
When half-gods go,
The gods arrive.

1847

Ode to Beauty

Who gave thee, O Beauty,
The keys of this breast,—
Too credulous lover
Of blest and unblest?
Say, when in lapsed ages 5
Thee knew I of old?
Or what was the service

For which I was sold?
When first my eyes saw thee,
I found me thy thrall, 10
By magical drawings,
Sweet tyrant of all!
I drank at thy fountain
False waters of thirst;
Thou intimate stranger, 15
Thou latest and first!
Thy dangerous glances
Make women of men;
New-born, we are melting
Into nature again. 20

Lavish, lavish promiser,
Nigh persuading gods to err!
Guest of million painted forms,
Which in turn thy glory warms!
The frailest leaf, the mossy bark, 25
The acorn's cup, the raindrop's arc,
The swinging spider's silver line,
The ruby of the drop of wine,
The shining pebble of the pond,
Thou inscribest with a bond, 30
In thy momentary play,
Would bankrupt nature to repay.

Ah, what avails it
To hide or to shun
Whom the Infinite One 35
Hath granted his throne?
The heaven high over
Is the deep's lover;
The sun and sea,
Informed by thee, 40
Before me run
And draw me on,
Yet fly me still,
As Fate refuses
To me the heart Fate for me chooses. 45
Is it that my opulent soul
Was mingled from the generous whole;
Sea-valleys and the deep of skies
Furnished several supplies;
And the sands whereof I'm made 50
Draw me to them, self-betrayed?

I turn the proud portfolio
Which holds the grand designs
Of Salvator, of Guercino,
And Piranesi's lines.[1] 55
I hear the lofty paeans

Ode to Beauty. [1]According to Edward Emerson, Margaret
Fuller sent the portfolio. Salvator Rosa, Guercino, and Piranesi were Italian painters of the 17th and 18th centuries.

Of the masters of the shell,[2]
Who heard the starry music
And recount the numbers well;
Olympian bards who sung   60
Divine Ideas below,
Which always find us young
And always keep us so.[3]
Oft, in streets or humblest places,
I detect far-wandered graces,   65
Which, from Eden wide astray,
In lowly homes have lost their way.

Thee gliding through the sea of form,
Like the lightning through the storm,
Somewhat not to be possessed,   70
Somewhat not to be caressed,
No feet so fleet could ever find,
No perfect form could ever bind.
Thou eternal fugitive,
Hovering over all that live,   75
Quick and skilful to inspire
Sweet, extravagant desire,
Starry space and lily-bell
Filling with thy roseate smell,
Wilt not give the lips to taste   80
Of the nectar which thou hast.

All that's good and great with thee
Works in close conspiracy;
Thou hast bribed the dark and lonely
To report thy features only,   85
And the cold and purple morning
Itself with thoughts of thee adorning;
The leafy dell, the city mart,
Equal trophies of thine art;
E'en the flowing azure air   90
Thou hast touched for my despair;
And, if I languish into dreams,
Again I meet the ardent beams.
Queen of things! I dare not die
In Being's deeps past ear and eye;   95
Lest there I find the same deceiver
And be the sport of Fate forever.
Dread Power, but dear! if God thou be,
Unmake me quite, or give thyself to me!

                                        1847

Hamatreya

Emerson here adapted to his own poetical use a passage
from the Hindu *Vishnu Purana* which he had copied into
his journal: "These, and other kings who with perishable
frames have possessed this ever-enduring world, and who,

[2]Apollo formed the lyre, the instrument of music and
poetry, from a shell.
[3]These four lines served as the motto for "The Poet."

blinded with deceptive notions of individual occupation,
have indulged the feeling that suggests 'This earth is
mine,—it is my son's,—it belongs to my dynasty,'—have
all passed away. So, many who reigned before them, many
who succeeded them, and many who are yet to come,
have ceased or will cease to be. Earth laughs, as if smiling
with autumnal flowers to behold her kings unable to effect
the subjugation of themselves. I will repeat to you, Mai-
treya [Emerson's Hamatreya], the stanzas that were
chanted by Earth."

The names in the first line of the poem are those of the
first settlers of Concord.

Bulkeley, Hunt, Willard, Hosmer, Meriam, Flint,
Possessed the land which rendered to their toil
Hay, corn, roots, hemp, flax, apples, wool and wood.
Each of these landlords walked amidst his farm,
Saying, " 'Tis mine, my children's and my name's.   5
How sweet the west wind sounds in my own trees!
How graceful climb those shadows on my hill!
I fancy these pure waters and the flags
Know me, as does my dog: we sympathize;
And, I affirm, my actions smack of the soil."   10

Where are these men? Asleep beneath their
     grounds:
And strangers, fond as they, their furrows plough.
Earth laughs in flowers, to see her boastful boys
Earth-proud, proud of the earth which is not theirs;
Who steer the plough, but cannot steer their feet   15
Clear of the grave.
They added ridge to valley, brook to pond,
And sighed for all that bounded their domain;
"This suits me for a pasture; that's my park;
We must have clay, lime, gravel, granite-ledge,   20
And misty lowland, where to go for peat.
The land is well,—lies fairly to the south.
'Tis good, when you have crossed the sea and back,
To find the sitfast acres where you left them."
Ah! the hot owner sees not Death, who adds   25
Him to his land, a lump of mould the more.
Hear what the Earth says:—

EARTH-SONG

"Mine and yours;
Mine, not yours.
Earth endures;   30
Stars abide—
Shine down in the old sea;
Old are the shores;
But where are old men?
I who have seen much,   35
Such have I never seen.

"The lawyer's deed
Ran sure,

In tail,
To them, and to their heirs   40
Who shall succeed,
Without fail,
Forevermore.

"Here is the land,
Shaggy with wood,   45
With its old valley,
Mound and flood.
But the heritors?—
Fled like the flood's foam.
The lawyer, and the laws,   50
And the kingdom,
Clean swept herefrom.

"They called me theirs,
Who so controlled me;
Yet every one   55
Wished to stay, and is gone,
How am I theirs,
If they cannot hold me,
But I hold them?"

When I heard the Earth-song   60
I was no longer brave;
My avarice cooled
Like lust in the chill of the grave.
                                      1847

The Apology

Think me not unkind and rude
    That I walk alone in grove and glen;
I go to the god of the wood
    To fetch his word to men.

Tax not my sloth that I   5
    Fold my arms beside the brook;
Each cloud that floated in the sky
    Writes a letter in my book.

Chide me not, laborious band,
    For the idle flowers I brought;   10
Every aster in my hand
    Goes home loaded with a thought.

There was never mystery
    But 'tis figured in the flowers;
Was never secret history   15
    But birds tell it in the bowers.

One harvest from thy field
    Homeward brought the oxen strong;

A second crop thine acres yield,
    Which I gather in a song.   20
                                      1846

Fable

The mountain and the squirrel
Had a quarrel,
And the former called the latter "Little Prig;"
Bun replied,
"You are doubtless very big;   5
But all sorts of things and weather
Must be taken in together,
To make up a year
And a sphere.
And I think it no disgrace   10
To occupy my place.
If I'm not so large as you,
You are not so small as I,
And not half so spry.
I'll not deny you make   15
A very pretty squirrel track;
Talents differ; all is well and wisely put;
If I cannot carry forests on my back,
Neither can you crack a nut."
                                      1845

Days

Eleven years earlier, he had written to Margaret Fuller: "Heaven walks among us ordinarily muffled in such triple or tenfold disguises that the wisest are deceived and no one suspects the days to be gods." In 1847, on the eve of his birthday, he wrote in his journal: "The days come and go like muffled and veiled figures sent from a distant friendly party, but they say nothing, and if we do not use the gifts they bring, they carry them as silently away."

Daughters of Time, the hypocritic Days,
Muffled and dumb like barefoot dervishes,
And marching single in an endless file,
Bring diadems and fagots in their hands.
To each they offer gifts after his will,   5
Bread, kingdoms, stars, and sky that holds them all.
I, in my pleachèd garden, watched the pomp,
Forgot my morning wishes, hastily
Took a few herbs and apples, and the Day
Turned and departed silent. I, too late,   10
Under her solemn fillet saw the scorn.
1851

Two Rivers

By the doctrine of correspondence, the river flowing through the meadows is a symbol of the unbounded Spirit that flows through all things: through the river itself, all of nature, and man, and time.

Thy summer voice, Musketaquit,[1]
Repeats the music of the rain;
But sweeter rivers pulsing flit
Through thee, as thou through Concord Plain.

Thou in thy narrow banks art pent: 5
The stream I love unbounded goes
Through flood and sea and firmament;
Through light, through life, it forward flows.

I see the inundation sweet,
I hear the spending of the stream   10
Through years, through men, through Nature fleet,
Through love and thought, through power and
    dream.

Musketaquit, a goblin strong,
Of shard and flint makes jewels gay;
They lose their grief who hear his song,   15
And where he winds is the day of day.

So forth and brighter fares my stream,—
Who drink it shall not thirst again;
No darkness stains its equal gleam,
And ages drop in it like rain.   20
1856

Brahma

Why Emerson was attracted to Oriental thought, as well
as to Plato and Neo-Platonism, may be seen in his essay on
Plato. "In all nations there are minds which incline to
dwell in the conception of the fundamental Unity.... This
tendency finds its highest expression in the religious writings of the East, and chiefly in the Indian Scriptures."
  In its day "Brahma" was ridiculed as incomprehensible.
But its difficulties would have vanished, as Emerson remarked, if readers had mentally altered Brahma to
Jehovah.

If the red slayer think he slays,
  Or if the slain think he is slain,
They know not well the subtle ways
  I keep, and pass, and turn again.

Far or forgot to me is near;   5
  Shadow and sunlight are the same;
The vanished gods to me appear;
  And one to me are shame and fame.

They reckon ill who leave me out;
  When me they fly, I am the wings;   10
I am the doubter and the doubt,
  And I the hymn the Brahmin sings.

Two Rivers. [1] The Concord River.

The strong gods pine for my abode,
  And pine in vain the sacred Seven;[1]
But thou, meek lover of the good!   15
  Find me, and turn thy back on heaven.
1856

Water

Unpublished in Emerson's lifetime, these lines and the
following quatrain, "Nahant," were first printed in an Ap-
pendix to the Riverside Edition of the Poems (1883) in a
group of "Fragments on Nature and Life." Hyatt H. Waggoner, in *American Poets from the Puritans to the Present*
(1968) treats both fragments as a single poem in two parts,
finding the first suggestive of Robert Frost's "Sand
Dunes," the second of T. S. Eliot's "The Dry Salvages."

The water understands
Civilization well;
It wets my foot, but prettily,
It chills my life, but wittily,
It is not disconcerted,   5
It is not broken-hearted:
Well used, it decketh joy,
Adorneth, doubleth joy:
Ill used, it will destroy,
In perfect time and measure   10
With a face of golden pleasure
Elegantly destroy.

                   1883

Nahant

A journal entry of 1853 reads: "At Nahant the eternal play
of the sea seems the anti-clock, or destroyer of the memory of time." The quatrain is untitled in the Riverside
Edition.

All day the waves assailed the rock,
  I heard no church-bell chime,
The sea-beat scorns the minster clock
  And breaks the glass of Time.

                   1883

Terminus

It is time to be old
To take in sail:—
The god of bounds,
Came to me in his fatal rounds,
And said: "No more!   5
No farther shoot
Thy broad ambitious branches, and thy root.

Brahma. [1] The highest saints in the Hindu faith.

[handwritten margin note: INSIGHT & REVELATION, NOT TRADITION]

Fancy departs: no more invent;
Contract thy firmament
To compass of a tent.   10
There's not enough for this and that,
Make thy option which of two;
Economize the failing river,
Not the less revere the Giver;
Leave the many and hold the few.   15
Timely wise, accept the terms,
Soften the fall with wary foot;
A little while
Still plan and smile,
And,—fault of novel germs,—   20
Mature the unfallen fruit.
Curse, if thou wilt, thy sires,
Bad husbands of their fires,
Who, when they gave thee breath,
Failed to bequeath   25
The needful sinew stark as once,
The Baresark marrow to thy bones,
But left a legacy of ebbing veins,
Inconstant heat and nerveless reins,—
Amid the Muses, left thee deaf and dumb,   30
Amid the gladiators, halt and numb."

As the bird trims her to the gale,
I trim myself to the storm of time;
I man the rudder, reef the sail,
Obey the voice at eve obeyed at prime: 35
"Lowly faithful, banish fear,
Right onward drive unharmed;
The port, well worth the cruise, is near,
And every wave is charmed."
1860

Nature

Emerson first published *Nature* in September 1836. It was in effect the manifesto of the Transcendental movement. It was also the summation of Emerson's previous thinking, and a ground-plan for his future work. It stated the case for a philosophy of idealism suggested to Emerson by the romantic Coleridge and, behind him, by the new German philosophers. It was reprinted in 1849.

The book is not easy reading. Despite a show of method, it is the work of a mind impatient of close logical thinking. Emerson does not attempt, in the manner of philosophers, carefully to build a demonstration. He throws out affirmations supported by images rather than arguments, and appeals for an instinctive response rather than rational assent. It is, actually, a meditative prose poem. Only the Introduction and first chapter are included here.

Introduction

Our age is retrospective. It builds the sepulchres of the fathers. It writes biographies, histories, and criticism. The foregoing generations beheld God and

nature face to face; we, through their eyes. Why should not we also enjoy an original relation to the universe? Why should not we have a poetry and philosophy of insight and not of tradition, and a religion by revelation to us, and not the history of theirs? Embosomed for a season in nature, whose floods of life stream around and through us, and invite us, by the powers they supply, to action proportioned to nature, why should we grope among the dry bones of the past, or put the living generation into masquerade out of its faded wardrobe? The sun shines to-day also. There is more wool and flax in the fields. There are new lands, new men, new thoughts. Let us demand our own works and laws and worship.

[handwritten margin note: ALL QUESTIONS ANSWERABLE → OF ANSWERABLE MIND IN FINITE? SENSING]

Undoubtedly we have no questions to ask which are unanswerable. We must trust the perfection of the creation so far as to believe that whatever curiosity the order of things has awakened in our minds, the order of things can satisfy. Every man's condition is a solution in hieroglyphic to those inquiries he would put. He acts it as life, before he apprehends it as truth. In like manner, nature is already, in its forms and tendencies, describing its own design. Let us interrogate the great apparition that shines so peacefully around us. Let us inquire, to what end is nature?

All science has one aim, namely, to find a theory of nature. We have theories of races and of functions, but scarcely yet a remote approach to an idea of creation. We are now so far from the road to truth, that religious teachers dispute and hate each other, and speculative men are esteemed unsound and frivolous. But to a sound judgment, the most abstract truth is the most practical. Whenever a true theory appears, it will be its own evidence. Its test is, that it will explain all phenomena. Now many are thought not only unexplained but inexplicable; as language, sleep, madness, dreams, beasts, sex.

[handwritten margin note: DEFINITIONS OF NATURE —]

Philosophically considered, the universe is composed of Nature and the Soul. Strictly speaking, therefore, all that is separate from us, all which Philosophy distinguishes as the NOT ME, that is, both nature and art, all other men and my own body, must be ranked under this name, NATURE. In enumerating the values of nature and casting up their sum, I shall use the word in both senses;—in its common and in its philosophical import. In inquiries so general as our present one, the inaccuracy is not material; no confusion of thought will occur. *Nature,* in the common sense, refers to essences unchanged by man; space, the air, the river, the leaf. *Art* is applied to the mixture of his will with the same things, as in a house, a canal, a statue, a picture. But his operations taken together are so insignificant, a little chipping, baking, patching, and washing, that in an impression so grand as that of the world on the human mind, they do not vary the result.

I. Nature

To go into solitude, a man needs to retire as much from his chamber as from society. I am not solitary whilst I read and write, though nobody is with me. But if a man would be alone, let him look at the stars. The rays that come from those heavenly worlds will separate between him and what he touches. One might think the atmosphere was made transparent with this design, to give man, in the heavenly bodies, the perpetual presence of the sublime. Seen in the streets of cities, how great they are! If the stars should appear one night in a thousand years, how would men believe and adore; and preserve for many generations the remembrance of the city of God which had been shown! But every night come out these envoys of beauty, and light the universe with their admonishing smile.

The stars awaken a certain reverence, because though always present, they are inaccessible; but all natural objects make a kindred impression, when the mind is open to their influence. Nature never wears a mean appearance. Neither does the wisest man extort her secret, and lose his curiosity by finding out all her perfection. Nature never became a toy to a wise spirit. The flowers, the animals, the mountains, reflected the wisdom of his best hour, as much as they had delighted the simplicity of his childhood.

When we speak of nature in this manner, we have a distinct but most poetical sense in the mind. We mean the integrity of impression made by manifold natural objects. It is this which distinguishes the stick of timber of the wood-cutter from the tree of the poet. The charming landscape which I saw this morning is indubitably made up of some twenty or thirty farms. Miller owns this field, Locke that, and Manning the woodland beyond. But none of them owns the landscape. There is a property in the horizon which no man has but he whose eye can integrate all the parts, that is, the poet. This is the best part of these men's farms, yet to this their warranty-deeds give no title.

To speak truly, few adult persons can see nature. Most persons do not see the sun. At least they have a very superficial seeing. The sun illuminates only the eye of the man, but shines into the eye and heart of the child. The lover of nature is he whose inward and outward senses are still truly adjusted to each other; who has retained the spirit of infancy even into the era of manhood. His intercourse with heaven and earth becomes part of his daily food. In the presence of nature a wild delight runs through the man, in spite of real sorrows. Nature says,—he is my creature, and maugre all his impertinent griefs, he shall be glad with me. Not the sun or the summer alone, but every hour and season yields its tribute of delight; for every hour and change corresponds to and authorizes a different state of the mind, from breathless noon to grimmest midnight. Nature is a setting that fits equally well a comic or a mourning piece. In good health, the air is a cordial of incredible virtue. Crossing a bare common, in snow puddles, at twilight, under a clouded sky, without having in my thoughts any occurrence of special good fortune, I have enjoyed a perfect exhilaration. I am glad to the brink of fear. In the woods, too, a man casts off his years, as the snake his slough, and at what period soever of life is always a child. In the woods is perpetual youth. Within these plantations of God, a decorum and sanctity reign, a perennial festival is dressed, and the guest sees not how he should tire of them in a thousand years. In the woods, we return to reason and faith. There I feel that nothing can befall me in life,—no disgrace, no calamity (leaving me my eyes), which nature cannot repair. Standing on the bare ground,—my head bathed by the blithe air, and uplifted into infinite space,—all mean egotism vanishes. I become a transparent eyeball; I am nothing; I see all; the currents of the Universal Being circulate through me. I am part or parcel of God. The name of the nearest friend sounds then foreign and accidental: to be brothers, to be acquaintances, master or servant, is then a trifle and a disturbance. I am the lover of uncontained and immortal beauty. In the wilderness, I find something more dear and connate than in streets or villages. In the tranquil landscape, and especially in the distant line of the horizon, man beholds somewhat as beautiful as his own nature.

The greatest delight which the fields and woods minister is the suggestion of an occult relation between man and the vegetable. I am not alone and unacknowledged. They nod to me, and I to them. The waving of the boughs in the storm is new to me and old. It takes me by surprise, and yet is not unknown. Its effect is like that of a higher thought or a better emotion coming over me, when I deemed I was thinking justly or doing right.

Yet it is certain that the power to produce this delight does not reside in nature, but in man, or in a harmony of both. It is necessary to use these pleasures with great temperance. For nature is not always tricked in holiday attire, but the same scene which yesterday breathed perfume and glittered as for the frolic of the nymphs is overspread with melancholy to-day. Nature always wears the colors of the spirit. To a man laboring under calamity, the heat of his own fire hath sadness in it. Then there is a kind of contempt of the landscape felt by him who has just lost by death a dear friend. The sky is less grand as it shuts down over less worth in the population.]

1836

The American Scholar

(Phi Beta Kappa Address at Harvard, 1837)

Scarcely a year after *Nature* came another challenge, this time concerning "the study of letters." Emerson attacked the conventional scholar-specialist, not "Man Thinking"— the "decent, indolent, complaisant" man, not the "free and brave" one. This was an awkward criticism to present on so decorous an occasion. But Emerson spoke out. He spoke to the hearts of the young, reaching depths they had not been aware of. Oliver Wendell Holmes called the Address "our intellectual Declaration of Independence."

Earlier announcements of American cultural self-reliance had been premature or superficial; Emerson's was timely and profound. It was profound because the independent mind, as he conceived, rested upon principles not simply national but universal, valid for all men. And it was timely because the hope which romanticism had encouraged in the few could be offered to the educated public at a moment when its wise and courageous leadership was badly needed. "The present generation," Emerson had written in his journal, "is bankrupt of principles and hope, as of property." It was the time of the panic of 1837, the most severe business panic the country had yet known. It was a time of economic fear that accented the timidity and conformity in all realms of thought, political, moral, religious, educational. Far from leading the way with courage and wisdom, the scholar class, as Emerson described it, had itself succumbed to timidity and conformity. He felt obliged to state the case for self-reliance strongly, even exaggeratedly, in order to awaken a response.

I greet you on the recommencement of our literary year. Our anniversary is one of hope, and, perhaps, not enough of labor. We do not meet for games of strength or skill, for the recitation of histories, tragedies, and odes, like the ancient Greeks; for parliaments of love and poesy, like the Troubadours; nor for the advancement of science, like our contemporaries in the British and European capitals. Thus far, our holiday has been simply a friendly sign of the survival of the love of letters amongst a people too busy to give to letters any more. As such it is precious as the sign of an indestructible instinct. Perhaps the time is already come when it ought to be, and will be, something else; when the sluggard intellect of this continent will look from under its iron lids and fill the postponed expectation of the world with something better than the exertions of mechanical skill. Our day of dependence, our long apprenticeship to the learning of other lands, draws to a close. The millions that around us are rushing into life, cannot always be fed on the sere remains of foreign harvests. Events, actions arise, that must be sung, that will sing themselves. Who can doubt that poetry will revive and lead in a new age, as the star in the constellation Harp, which now flames in our zenith, astronomers announce, shall one day be the pole-star for a thousand years?

In this hope I accept the topic which not only usage but the nature of our association seem to prescribe to this day,—the American Scholar. Year by year we come up hither to read one more chapter of his biography. Let us inquire what light new days and events have thrown on his character and his hopes.

It is one of those fables which out of an unknown antiquity convey an unlooked-for wisdom, that the gods, in the beginning, divided Man into men, that he might be more helpful to himself; just as the hand was divided into fingers, the better to answer its end.

The old fable[1] covers a doctrine ever new and sublime; that there is One Man,—present to all particular men only partially, or through one faculty; and that you must take the whole society to find the whole man. Man is not a farmer, or a professor, or an engineer, but he is all. Man is priest, and scholar, and statesman, and producer, and soldier. In the *divided* or social state these functions are parcelled out to individuals, each of whom aims to do his stint of the joint work, whilst each other performs his. The fable implies that the individual, to possess himself, must sometimes return from his own labor to embrace all the other laborers. But, unfortunately, this original unit, this fountain of power, has been so distributed to multitudes, has been so minutely subdivided and peddled out, that it is spilled into drops, and cannot be gathered. The state of society is one in which the members have suffered amputation from the trunk, and strut about so many walking monsters,—a good finger, a neck, a stomach, an elbow, but never a man.

Man is thus metamorphosed into a thing, into many things. The planter, who is Man sent out into the field to gather food, is seldom cheered by an idea of the true dignity of his ministry. He sees his bushel and his cart, and nothing beyond, and sinks into the farmer, instead of Man on the farm. The tradesman scarcely ever gives an ideal worth to his work, but is ridden by the routine of his craft, and the soul is subject to dollars. The priest becomes a form; the attorney a statute-book; the mechanic a machine; the sailor a rope of the ship.

[1] It is told in Plato's *Symposium* and mentioned in "Of Brotherly Love" in Plutarch's *Morals*.

In this distribution of functions the scholar is the delegated intellect. In the right state he is *Man Thinking*. In the degenerate state, when the victim of society, he tends to become a mere thinker, or still worse, the parrot of other men's thinking.

In this view of him, as Man Thinking, the theory of his office is contained. Him Nature solicits with all her placid, all her monitory pictures; him the past instructs; him the future invites. Is not indeed every man a student, and do not all things exist for the student's behoof? And, finally is not the true scholar the only true master? But the old oracle said, "All things have two handles: beware of the wrong one." In life, too often, the scholar errs with mankind and forfeits his privilege. Let us see him in his school, and consider him in reference to the main influences he receives.

I. The first in time and the first in importance of the influences upon the mind is that of nature. Every day, the sun; and, after sunset, Night and her stars. Ever the winds blow; ever the grass grows. Every day, men and women, conversing—beholding and beholden. The scholar is he of all men whom this spectacle most engages. He must settle its value in his mind. What is nature to him? There is never a beginning, there is never an end, to the inexplicable continuity of this web of God, but always circular power returning into itself. Therein it resembles his own spirit, whose beginning, whose ending, he never can find,—so entire, so boundless. Far too as her splendors shine, system on system shooting like rays, upward, downward, without center, without circumference,—in the mass and in the particle, Nature hastens to render account of herself to the mind. Classification begins. To the young mind every thing is individual, stands by itself. By and by, it finds how to join two things and see in them one nature; then three, then three thousand; and so, tyrannized over by its own unifying instinct, it goes on tying things together, diminishing anomalies, discovering roots running under ground whereby contrary and remote things cohere and flower out from one stem. It presently learns that since the dawn of history there has been a constant accumulation and classifying of facts. But what is classification but the perceiving that these objects are not chaotic, and are not foreign, but have a law which is also a law of the human mind? The astronomer discovers that geometry, a pure abstraction of the human mind, is the measure of planetary motion. The chemist finds proportions and intelligible method throughout matter; and science is nothing but the finding of analogy, identity, in the most remote parts. The ambitious soul sits down before each refractory fact; one after another reduces all strange constitutions, all

new powers, to their class and their law, and goes on forever to animate the last fibre of organization, the outskirts of nature, by insight.

Thus to him, to this schoolboy under the bending dome of day, is suggested that he and it proceed from one root; one is leaf and one is flower; relation, sympathy, stirring in every vein. And what is that root? Is not that the soul of his soul? A thought too bold; a dream too wild. Yet when this spiritual light shall have revealed the law of more earthly natures,—when he has learned to worship the soul, and to see that the natural philosophy that now is, is only the first gropings of its gigantic hand, he shall look forward to an ever expanding knowledge as to a becoming creator. He shall see that nature is the opposite of the soul, answering to it part for part. One is seal and one is print. Its beauty is the beauty of his own mind. Its laws are the laws of his own mind. Nature then becomes to him the measure of his attainments. So much of nature as he is ignorant of, so much of his own mind does he not yet possess. And, in fine, the ancient precept, "Know thyself," and the modern precept, "Study nature," become at last one maxim.

II. The next great influence into the spirit of the scholar is the mind of the Past,—in whatever form, whether of literature, of art, of institutions, that mind is inscribed. Books are the best type of the influence of the past, and perhaps we shall get at the truth,—learn the amount of this influence more conveniently,—by considering their value alone.

The theory of books is noble. The scholar of the first age received into him the world around; brooded thereon; gave it the new arrangement of his own mind, and uttered it again. It came into him life; it went out from him truth. It came to him short-lived actions; it went out from him immortal thoughts. It came to him business; it went from him poetry. It was a dead fact; now, it is quick thought. It can stand, and it can go. It now endures, it now flies, it now inspires. Precisely in proportion to the depth of mind from which it issued, so high does it soar, so long does it sing.

Or, I might say, it depends on how far the process had gone, of transmuting life into truth. In proportion to the completeness of the distillation, so will the purity and imperishableness of the product be. But none is quite perfect. As no air-pump can by any means make a perfect vacuum, so neither can any artist entirely exclude the conventional, the local, the perishable from his book, or write a book of pure thought, that shall be as efficient, in all respects, to a remote posterity, as to contemporaries, or rather to the second age. Each age, it is found, must write its own books; or rather, each generation for the next succeeding. The books of an older period will not fit this.

Yet hence arises a grave mischief. The sacredness which attaches to the act of creation, the act of thought, is transferred to the record. The poet chanting was felt to be a divine man: henceforth the chant is divine also. The writer was a just and wise spirit: henceforward it is settled the book is perfect; as love of the hero corrupts into worship of his statue. Instantly the book becomes noxious: the guide is a tyrant. The sluggish and perverted mind of the multitude, slow to open to the incursions of Reason, having once so opened, having once received this book, stands upon it, and makes an outcry if it is disparaged. Colleges are built on it. Books are written on it by thinkers, not by Man Thinking; by men of talent, that is, who start wrong, who set out from accepted dogmas, not from their own sight of principles. Meek young men grow up in libraries, believing it their duty to accept the views which Cicero, which Locke, which Bacon, have given; forgetful that Cicero, Locke, and Bacon were only young men in libraries when they wrote these books.

Hence, instead of Man Thinking, we have the bookworm. Hence the book-learned class, who value books, as such; not as related to nature and the human constitution, but as making a sort of Third Estate with the world and the soul. Hence the restorers of readings, the emendators, the bibliomaniacs of all degrees.

Books are the best of things, well used; abused, among the worst. What is the right use? What is the one end which all means go to effect? They are for nothing but to inspire. I had better never see a book than to be warped by its attraction clean out of my own orbit, and made a satellite instead of a system. The one thing in the world, of value, is the active soul. This every man is entitled to; this every man contains within him, although in almost all men obstructed and as yet unborn. The soul active sees absolute truth and utters truth, or creates. In this action it is genius; not the privilege of here and there a favorite, but the sound estate of every man. In its essence it is progressive. The book, the college, the school of art, the institution of any kind, stop with some past utterance of genius. This is good, say they,—let us hold by this. They pin me down. They look backward and not forward. But genius looks foward: the eyes of man are set in his forehead, not in his hindhead: man hopes: genius creates. Whatever talents may be, if the man create not, the pure efflux of the Deity is not his;—cinders and smoke there may be, but not yet flame. There are creative manners, there are creative actions, and creative words; manners, actions, words, that is, in-dicative of no custom or authority, but springing spontaneous from the mind's own sense of good and fair.

On the other part, instead of being its own seer, let it receive from another mind its truth, though it were in torrents of light, without periods of solitude, inquest, and self-recovery, and a fatal disservice is done. Genius is always sufficiently the enemy of genius by over-influence. The literature of every nation bears me witness. The English dramatic poets have Shakespearized now for two hundred years.

Undoubtedly there is a right way of reading, so it be sternly subordinated. Man Thinking must not be subdued by his instruments. Books are for the scholar's idle times. When he can read God directly, the hour is too precious to be wasted in other men's transcripts of their readings. But when the intervals of darkness come, as come they must,—when the sun is hid and the stars withdraw their shining,—we repair to the lamps which were kindled by their ray, to guide our steps to the East again, where the dawn is. We hear, that we may speak. The Arabian proverb says, "A fig tree, looking on a fig tree, becometh fruitful."

It is remarkable, the character of the pleasure we derive from the best books. They impress us with the conviction that one nature wrote and the same reads. We read the verses of one of the great English poets, of Chaucer, of Marvell, of Dryden, with the most modern joy,—with a pleasure, I mean, which is in great part caused by the abstraction of all *time* from their verses. There is some awe mixed with the joy of our surprise, when this poet, who lived in some past world, two or three hundred years ago, says that which lies close to my own soul, that which I also had well-nigh thought and said. But for the evidence thence afforded to the philosophical doctrine of the identity of all minds, we should suppose some preëstablished harmony, some foresight of souls that were to be, and some preparation of stores for their future wants, like the fact observed in insects, who lay up food before death for the young grub they shall never see.

I would not be hurried by any love of system, by any exaggeration of instincts, to underrate the Book. We all know, that as the human body can be nourished on any food, though it were boiled grass and the broth of shoes, so the human mind can be fed by any knowledge. And great and heroic men have existed who had almost no other information than by the printed page. I only would say that it needs a strong head to bear that diet. One must be an inventor to read well. As the proverb says, "He that would bring home the wealth of the Indies, must carry out the wealth of the Indies." There is then creative reading as well as creative writing.

When the mind is braced by labor and invention, the page of whatever book we read becomes luminous with manifold allusion. Every sentence is doubly significant, and the sense of our author is as broad as the world. We then see, what is always true, that as the seer's hour of vision is short and rare among heavy days and months, so is its record, perchance the least part of his volume. The discerning will read, in his Plato or Shakespeare, only that least part,—only the authentic utterances of the oracle;—all the rest he rejects, were it never so many times Plato's and Shakespeare's.

Of course there is a portion of reading quite indispensable to a wise man. History and exact science he must learn by laborious reading. Colleges, in like manner, have their indispensable office,—to teach elements. But they can only highly serve us when they aim not to drill, but to create; when they gather from far every ray of various genius to their hospitable halls, and by the concentrated fires, set the hearts of their youth on flame. Thought and knowledge are natures in which apparatus and pretension avail nothing. Gowns and pecuniary foundations, though of towns of gold, can never countervail the least sentence or syllable of wit.[2] Forget this, and our American colleges will recede in their public importance, whilst they grow richer every year.

III. There goes in the world a notion that the scholar should be a recluse, a valetudinarian,—as unfit for any handiwork or public labor as a penknife for an axe. The so-called "practical men" sneer at speculative men, as if, because they speculate or *see*, they could do nothing. I have heard it said that the clergy,—who are always, more universally than any other class, the scholars of their day,—are addressed as women; that the rough, spontaneous conversation of men they do not hear, but only a mincing and diluted speech. They are often virtually disfranchised; and indeed there are advocates for their celibacy. As far as this is true of the studious classes, it is not just and wise. Action is with the scholar subordinate, but it is essential. Without it he is not yet man. Without it thought can never ripen into truth. Whilst the world hangs before the eye as a cloud of beauty, we cannot even see its beauty. Inaction is cowardice, but there can be no scholar without the heroic mind. The preamble of thought, the transition through which it passes from the unconscious to the conscious, is action. Only so much do I know, as I have lived. Instantly we know whose words are loaded with life, and whose not.

The world,—this shadow of the soul, or *other me*,—lies wide around. Its attractions are the keys which unlock my thoughts and make me acquainted

[2] I.e., intellect or reason.

with myself. I run eagerly into this resounding tumult. I grasp the hands of those next to me, and take my place in the ring to suffer and to work, taught by an instinct that so shall the dumb abyss be vocal with speech. I pierce its order; I dissipate its fear; I dispose of it within the circuit of my expanding life. So much only of life as I know by experience, so much of the wilderness have I vanquished and planted, or so far have I extended my being, my dominion. I do not see how any man can afford, for the sake of his nerves and his nap, to spare any action in which he can partake. It is pearls and rubies to his discourse. Drudgery, calamity, exasperation, want, are instructors in eloquence and wisdom. The true scholar grudges every opportunity of action past by, as a loss of power. It is the raw material out of which the intellect moulds her splendid products. A strange process too, this by which experience is converted into thought, as a mulberry leaf is converted into satin. The manufacture goes forward at all hours.

The actions and events of our childhood and youth are now matters of calmest observation. They lie like fair pictures in the air. No so with our recent actions,—with the business which we now have in hand. On this we are quite unable to speculate. Our affections as yet circulate through it. We no more feel or know it than we feel the feet, or the hand, or the brain of our body. The new deed is yet a part of life,—remains for a time immersed in our unconscious life. In some contemplative hour it detaches itself from the life like a ripe fruit, to become a thought of the mind. Instantly it is raised, transfigured; the corruptible has put on incorruption. Henceforth it is an object of beauty, however base its origin and neighborhood. Observe too the impossibility of antedating this act. In its grub state, it cannot fly, it cannot shine, it is a dull grub. But suddenly, without observation, the selfsame thing unfurls beautiful wings, and is an angel of wisdom. So is there no fact, no event, in our private history, which shall not, sooner or later, lose its adhesive, inert form, and astonish us by soaring from our body into the empyrean. Cradle and infancy, school and playground, the fear of boys, and dogs, and ferules, the love of little maids and berries, and many another fact that once filled the whole sky, are gone already; friend and relative, profession and party, town and country, nation and world, must also soar and sing.

Of course, he who has put forth his total strength in fit actions has the richest return of wisdom. I will not shut myself out of this globe of action, and transplant an oak into a flowerpot, there to hunger and pine; nor trust the revenue of some single faculty, and exhaust one vein of thought, much like those Savoyards, who, getting their livelihood by carving shepherds, shepherdesses, and smoking Dutchmen, for all Europe, went out one day to the mountain to find stock, and discovered that they had whittled up the last of their pine trees. Authors we have, in numbers, who have written out their vein, and who, moved by a commendable prudence, sail for Greece or Palestine, follow the trapper into the prairie, or ramble round Algiers, to replenish their merchantable stock.

If it were only for a vocabulary, the scholar would be covetous of action. Life is our dictionary. Years are well spent in country labors; in town; in the insight into trades and manufactures; in frank intercourse with many men and women; in science; in art; to the one end of mastering in all their facts a language by which to illustrate and embody our perceptions. I learn immediately from any speaker how much he has already lived, through the poverty or the splendor of his speech. Life lies behind us as the quarry from whence we get tiles and copestones for the masonry of to-day. This is the way to learn grammar. Colleges and books only copy the language which the field and the work-yard made.

But the final value of action, like that of books, and better than books, is that it is a resource. The great principle of Undulation in nature, that shows itself in the inspiring and expiring of the breath; in desire and satiety; in the ebb and flow of the sea; in day and night; in heat and cold; and, as yet more deeply ingrained in every atom and every fluid, is known to us under the name of Polarity,—these "fits of easy transmission and reflection," as Newton called them, are the law of nature because they are the law of spirit.

The mind now thinks, now acts, and each fit reproduces the other. When the artist has exhausted his materials, when the fancy no longer paints, when thoughts are no longer apprehended and books are a weariness,—he has always the resource *to live*. Character is higher than intellect. Thinking is the function. Living is the functionary. The stream retreats to its source. A great soul will be strong to live, as well as strong to think. Does he lack organ or medium to impart his truths? He can still fall back on this elemental force of living them. This is a total act. Thinking is a partial act. Let the grandeur of justice shine in his affairs. Let the beauty of affection cheer his lowly roof. Those "far from fame," who dwell and act with him, will feel the force of his constitution in the doings and passages of the day better than it can be measured by any public and designed display. Time shall teach him that the scholar loses no hour which the man lives. Herein he unfolds the sacred germ of his instinct, screened from influence. What is lost in seemliness is gained in strength. Not out of those on whom systems of education have exhausted their culture, comes the helpful giant to destroy the old or to build the new, but out of unhandselled[3] savage nature; out of terrible Druids and Berserkers come at last Alfred and Shakespeare.

I hear therefore with joy whatever is beginning to be said of the dignity and necessity of labor to every citizen. There is virtue yet in the hoe and the spade, for learned as well as for unlearned hands. And labor is everywhere welcome; always we are invited to work; only be this limitation observed, that a man shall not for the sake of wider activity sacrifice any opinion to the popular judgments and modes of action.

I have now spoken of the education of the scholar by nature, by books, and by action. It remains to say somewhat of his duties.

They are such as become Man Thinking. They may all be comprised in self-trust. The office of the scholar is to cheer, to raise, and to guide men by showing them facts amidst appearances. He plies the slow, unhonored, and unpaid task of observation. Flamsteed[4] and Herschel,[5] in their glazed observatories, may catalogue the stars with the praise of all men, and the results being splendid and useful, honor is sure. But he, in his private observatory, cataloguing obscure and nebulous stars of the human mind, which as yet no man has thought of as such,—watching days and months sometimes for a few facts; correcting still his old records;—must relinquish display and immediate fame. In the long period of his preparation he must betray often an ignorance and shiftlessness in popular arts, incurring the disdain of the able who shoulder him aside. Long he must stammer in his speech; often forego the living for the dead. Worse yet, he must accept—how often!—poverty and solitude. For the ease and pleasure of treading the old road, accepting the fashions, the education, the religion of society, he takes the cross of making his own, and, of course, the self-accusation, the faint heart, the frequent uncertainty and loss of time, which are the nettles and tangling vines in the way of the self-relying and self-directed; and the state of virtual hostility in which he seems to stand to society and especially to educated society. For all this loss and scorn, what offset? He is to find consolation in exercising the highest functions of human nature. He is one who raises himself from private considerations and breathes and lives on public and illustrious thoughts. He is the world's eye. He is the world's heart. He is to resist the vulgar prosperity that retrogrades ever

[3] Primitive, untouched, unused, or unknown.
[4] John Flamsteed (1646–1719), a British astronomer.
[5] William Herschel (1738–1822), an English astronomer whose son, John Frederick William (1792–1871), was an astronomer and chemist active during Emerson's life.

428 The Romantic Movement

to barbarism, by preserving and communicating heroic sentiments, noble biographies, melodious verse, and the conclusions of history. Whatsoever oracles the human heart, in all emergencies, in all solemn hours, has uttered as its commentary on the world of actions,—these he shall receive and impart. And whatsoever new verdict Reason from her inviolable seat pronounces on the passing men and events of to-day,—this he shall hear and promulgate.

These being his functions, it becomes him to feel all confidence in himself, and to defer never to the popular cry. He and he only knows the world. The world of any moment is the merest appearance. Some great decorum, some fetish of a government, some ephemeral trade, or war, or man, is cried up by half mankind and cried down by the other half, as if all depended on this particular up or down. The odds are that the whole question is not worth the poorest thought which the scholar has lost in listening to the controversy. Let him not quit his belief that a popgun is a popgun, though the ancient and honorable of the earth affirm it to be the crack of doom. In silence, in steadiness, in severe abstraction, let him hold by himself; add observation to observation, patient of neglect, patient of reproach, and bide his own time,—happy enough if he can satisfy himself alone that this day he has seen something truly. Success treads on every right step. For the instinct is sure, that prompts him to tell his brother what he thinks. He then learns that in going down into the secrets of his own mind he has descended into the secrets of all minds. He learns that he who has mastered any law in his private thoughts, is master to that extent of all men whose language he speaks, and of all into whose language his own can be translated. The poet, in utter solitude remembering his spontaneous thoughts and recording them, is found to have recorded that which men in crowded cities find true for them also. The orator distrusts at first the fitness of his frank confessions, his want of knowledge of the persons he addresses, until he finds that he is the complement of his hearers;—that they drink his words because he fulfils for them their own nature; the deeper he dives into his privatest, secretest presentiment, to his wonder he finds this is the most acceptable, most public, and universally true. The people delight in it; the better part of every man feels, This is my music; this myself.

In self-trust all the virtues are comprehended. Free should the scholar be,—free and brave. Free even to the definition of freedom, "without any hindrance that does not arise out of his own constitution." Brave; for fear is a thing which a scholar by his very function puts behind him. Fear always springs from ignorance. It is a shame to him if his tranquility, amid dangerous times, arise from the presumption that like children and women his is a protected class; or if he seek a temporary peace by the diversion of his thoughts from politics or vexed questions, hiding his head like an ostrich in the flowering bushes, peeping into microscopes, and turning rhymes, as a boy whistles to keep his courage up. So is the danger a danger still; so is the fear worse. Manlike let him turn and face it. Let him look into its eye and search its nature, inspect its origin,—see the whelping of this lion,—which lies no great way back; he will then find in himself a perfect comprehension of its nature and extent; he will have made his hands meet on the other side, and can henceforth defy it and pass on superior. The world is his who can see through its pretension. What deafness, what stone-blind custom, what overgrown error you behold is there only by sufferance,—by your sufferance. See it to be a lie, and you have already dealt it its mortal blow.

Yes, we are the cowed,—we the trustless. It is a mischievous notion that we are come late into nature; that the world was finished a long time ago. As the world was plastic and fluid in the hands of God, so it is ever to so much of his attributes as we bring to it. To ignorance and sin, it is flint. They adapt themselves to it as they may; but in proportion as a man has any thing in him divine, the firmament flows before him and takes his signet and form. Not he is great who can alter matter, but he who can alter my state of mind. They are the kings of the world who give the color of their present thought to all nature and all art, and persuade men by the cheerful serenity of their carrying the matter, that this thing which they do is the apple which the ages have desired to pluck, now at last ripe, and inviting nations to the harvest. The great man makes the great thing. Wherever Macdonald sits, there is the head of the table.[6] Linnaeus makes botany the most alluring of studies, and wins it from the farmer and the herb-woman; Davy, chemistry; and Cuvier, fossils. The day is always his who works in it with serenity and great aims. The unstable estimates of men crowd to him whose mind is filled with a truth, as the heaped waves of the Atlantic follow the moon.

For this self-trust, the reason is deeper than can be fathomed,—darker than can be enlightened. I might not carry with me the feeling of my audience in stating my own belief. But I have already shown the ground of my hope, in adverting to the doctrine that man is one. I believe man has been wronged; he has wronged himself. He has almost lost the light that can lead him back to his prerogatives. Men are become of no account. Men in history, men in the

---

[6] A proverbial saying.

world of to-day, are bugs, are spawn, and are called "the mass" and "the herd." In a century, in a millennium, one or two men; that is to say, one or two approximations to the right state of every man. All the rest behold in the hero or the poet their own green and crude being,—ripened; yes, and are content to be less, so *that* may attain to its full stature. What a testimony, full of grandeur, full of pity, is borne to the demands of his own nature, by the poor clansman, the poor partisan, who rejoices in the glory of his chief. The poor and the low find some amends to their immense moral capacity, for their acquiescence in a political and social inferiority. They are content to be brushed like flies from the path of a great person, so that justice shall be done by him to that common nature which it is the dearest desire of all to see enlarged and glorified. They sun themselves in the great man's light, and feel it to be their own element. They cast the dignity of man from their downtrod selves upon the shoulders of a hero, and will perish to add one drop of blood to make that great heart beat, those giant sinews combat and conquer. He lives for us, and we live in him.

Men, such as they are, very naturally seek money or power; and power because it is as good as money,—the "spoils," so called, "of office." And why not? for they aspire to the highest, and this, in their sleep-walking, they dream is highest. Wake them and they shall quit the false good and leap to the true, and leave governments to clerks and desks. This revolution is to be wrought by the gradual domestication of the idea of Culture. The main enterprise of the world for splendor, for extent, is the upbuilding of a man. Here are the materials strewn along the ground. The private life of one man shall be a more illustrious monarchy, more formidable to its enemy, more sweet and serene in its influence to its friend, than any kingdom in history. For a man, rightly viewed, comprehendeth the particular natures of all men. Each philosopher, each bard, each actor has only done for me, as by a delegate, what one day I can do for myself. The books which once we valued more than the apple of the eye, we have quite exhausted. What is that but saying that we have come up with the point of view which the universal mind took through the eyes of one scribe; we have been that man, and have passed on. First, one, then another, we drain all cisterns, and waxing greater by all these supplies, we crave a better and more abundant food. The man has never lived that can feed us ever. The human mind cannot be enshrined in a person who shall set a barrier on any one side to this unbounded, unboundable empire. It is one central fire, which, flaming now out of the lips of Etna, lightens the capes of Sicily, and now

out of the throat of Vesuvius, illuminates the towers and vineyards of Naples. It is one light which beams out of a thousand stars. It is one soul which animates all men.

But I have dwelt perhaps tediously upon this abstraction of the Scholar. I ought not to delay longer to add what I have to say of nearer reference to the time and to this country.

Historically, there is thought to be a difference in the ideas which predominate over successive epochs, and there are data for marking the genius of the Classic, of the Romantic, and now of the Reflective or Philosophical age. With the views I have intimated of the oneness or the identity of the mind through all individuals, I do not much dwell on these differences. In fact, I believe each individual passes through all three. The boy is a Greek; the youth, romantic; the adult, reflective. I deny not, however, that a revolution in the leading idea may be distinctly enough traced.

Our age is bewailed as the age of Introversion. Must that needs be evil? We, it seems, are critical; we are embarrassed with second thoughts; we cannot enjoy any thing for hankering to know whereof the pleasure consists; we are lined with eyes; we see with our feet; the time is infected with Hamlet's unhappiness,

Sicklied o'er with the pale cast of thought.

It is so bad then? Sight is the last thing to be pitied. Would we be blind? Do we fear lest we should outsee nature and God, and drink truth dry? I look upon the discontent of the literary class as a mere announcement of the fact that they find themselves not in the state of mind of their fathers, and regret the coming state as untried; as a boy dreads the water before he has learned that he can swim. If there is any period one would desire to be born in, is it not the age of Revolution; when the old and the new stand side by side and admit of being compared; when the energies of all men are searched by fear and by hope; when the historic glories of the old can be compensated by the rich possibilities of the new era? This time, like all times, is a very good one, if we but know what to do with it.

I read with some joy of the auspicious signs of the coming days, as they glimmer already through poetry and art, through philosophy and science, through church and state.

One of these signs is the fact that the same movement which effected the elevation of what was called the lowest class in the state, assumed in literature a very marked and as benign an aspect. Instead of the sublime and beautiful, the near, the low, the common, was explored and poetized. That which had been negligently trodden under foot by those who were harnessing and provisioning themselves for long journeys into far countries, is suddenly found to be richer than all foreign parts. The literature of the poor, the feelings of the child, the philosophy of the street, the meaning of household life, are the topics of the time. It is a great stride. It is a sign—is it not?—of new vigor when the extremities are made active, when currents of warm life run into the hands and the feet. I ask not for the great, the remote, the romantic; what is doing in Italy or Arabia; what is Greek art, or Provençal minstrelsy; I embrace the common, I explore and sit at the feet of the familiar, the low. Give me insight into to-day, and you may have the antique and future worlds. What would we really know the meaning of? The meal in the firkin; the milk in the pan; the ballad in the street; the news of the boat; the glance of the eye; the form and the gait of the body;—show me the ultimate reason of these matters; show me the sublime presence of the highest spiritual cause lurking, as always it does lurk, in these suburbs and extremities of nature; let me see every trifle bristling with the polarity that ranges it instantly on an eternal law; and the shop, the plough, and the ledger referred to the like cause by which light undulates and poets sing;—and the world lies no longer a dull miscellany and lumber-room, but has form and order; there is no trifle, there is no puzzle, but one design unites and animates the farthest pinnacle and the lowest trench.

This idea has inspired the genius of Goldsmith, Burns, Cowper, and, in a newer time, of Goethe, Wordsworth, and Carlyle. This idea they have differently followed and with various success. In contrast with their writing, the style of Pope, of Johnson, of Gibbon, looks cold and pedantic. This writing is blood-warm. Man is surprised to find that things near are not less beautiful and wondrous than things remote. The near explains the far. The drop is a small ocean. A man is related to all nature. This perception of the worth of the vulgar is fruitful in discoveries. Goethe, in this very thing the most modern of the moderns, has shown us as none ever did, the genius of the ancients.

There is one man of genius who has done much for this philosophy of life, whose literary value has never yet been rightly estimated;—I mean Emanuel Swedenborg. The most imaginative of men, yet writing with the precision of a mathematician, he endeavored to engraft a purely philosophical Ethics on the popular Christianity of his time. Such an attempt of course must have difficulty which no genius could surmount. But he saw and showed the connection between nature and the affections of the soul. He pierced the emblematic or spiritual character of the visible, audible, tangible world. Especially did his shade-loving muse hover over and interpret the lower parts of nature; he showed the mysterious bond that allies moral evil to the foul material forms, and has given in epical parables a theory of insanity, of beasts, of unclean and fearful things.

Another sign of our times, also marked by an analogous political movement, is the new importance given to the single person. Every thing that tends to insulate the individual,—to surround him with barriers of natural respect, so that each man shall feel the world is his, and man shall treat with man as a sovereign state with a sovereign state,—tends to true union as well as greatness. "I learned," said the melancholy Pestalozzi, "that no man in God's wide earth is either willing or able to help any other man." Help must come from the bosom alone. The scholar is that man who must take up into himself all the ability of the time, all the contributions of the past, all the hopes of the future. He must be an university of knowledges. If there be one lesson more than another which should pierce his ear, it is, The world is nothing, the man is all; in yourself is the law of all nature, and you know not yet how a globule of sap ascends; in yourself slumbers the whole of Reason; it is for you to know all; it is for you to dare all. Mr. President and Gentlemen, this confidence in the unsearched might of man belongs, by all motives, by all prophecy, by all preparation, to the American Scholar. We have listened too long to the courtly muses of Europe. The spirit of the American freeman is already suspected to be timid, imitative, tame. Public and private avarice make the air we breathe thick and fat. The scholar is decent, indolent, complaisant. See already the tragic consequence. The mind of this country, taught to aim at low objects, eats upon itself. There is no work for any but the decorous and the complaisant. Young men of the fairest promise, who begin life upon our shores, inflated by the mountain winds, shined upon by all the stars of God, find the earth below not in unison with these, but are hindered from action by the disgust which the principles on which business is managed inspire, and turn drudges, or die of disgust, some of them suicides. What is the remedy? They did not yet see, and thousands of young men as hopeful now crowding to the barriers for the career do not yet see, that if the single man plant himself indomitably on his instincts, and there abide, the huge world will come round to him. Patience,—patience; with the shades of all the good and great for company; and for solace the perspective of your own infinite life; and for work the study and the communication of principles, the making those instincts prevalent, the conversion of the world. Is it not the chief disgrace in the world, not to be an unit;—not to be reckoned one character;—not to yield that peculiar fruit which each man was created to bear, but to be reckoned in the gross, in the hundred, or the thousand, of the party, the section, to which we belong; and our opinion predicted geographically, as the north, or the south? Not so, brothers and friends,— please God, ours shall not be so. We will walk on our own feet; we will work with our own hands; we will speak our own minds. The study of letters shall be no longer a name for pity, for doubt, and for sensual indulgence. The dread of man and the love of man shall be a wall of defence and a wreath of joy around all. A nation of men will for the first time exist, because each believes himself inspired by the Divine Soul which also inspires all men.

1837

Divinity School Address

Emerson gave this address at Cambridge one year after "The American Scholar." Its presentation caused a good deal of controversy. In it Emerson expresses his wonder at the potential beauty of man and the world and his reverence for the spirit that informs the world. He refers to that spirit variously as Deity, Virtue, and moral sentiment. The address contains Emerson's famous—and doubtless exaggerated and simplistic—pronouncement concerning evil: "Good is positive. Evil is merely privative, not absolute: it is like cold, which is the privation of heat." Although Emerson may think that man and his world are basically healthy or good because of the universal law which pervades existence, he nevertheless recognized in his life and elsewhere in his writing that evil and suffering are significant aspects of the world as-it-is. The address also includes a bold criticism of historical or institutional Christianity, so it served for religion a function similar to the one "The American Scholar" served for scholarship.

In this refulgent summer, it has been a luxury to draw the breath of life. The grass grows, the buds burst, the meadow is spotted with fire and gold in the tint of flowers. The air is full of birds, and sweet with the breath of the pine, the balm-of-Gilead, and the new hay. Night brings no gloom to the heart with its welcome shade. Through the transparent darkness the stars pour their almost spiritual rays. Man under them seems a young child, and his huge globe a toy. The cool night bathes the world as with a river, and prepares his eyes again for the crimson dawn. The mystery of nature was never displayed more happily. The corn and the wine have been freely dealt to all creatures, and the never-broken silence with which the old bounty goes forward has not yielded yet one word of explanation. One is constrained to respect the perfection of this world in which our senses converse. How wide; how rich; what invitation from every property it gives to every faculty of man! In its fruitful soils; in its navigable sea; in its mountains of metal and stone; in its forests of all woods; in its animals; in its chemical ingredients; in the powers and path of light, heat, attraction and life, it is well worth the pith and heart of great men to subdue and enjoy it. The planters, the mechanics, the inventors, the astronomers, the builders of cities, and the captains, history delights to honor.

But when the mind opens and reveals the laws which traverse the universe and make things what they are, then shrinks the great world at once into a mere illustration and fable of this mind. What am I? and What is? asks the human spirit with a curiosity new-kindled, but never to be quenched. Behold these outrunning laws, which our imperfect apprehension can see tend this way and that, but not come full circle. Behold these infinite relations, so like, so unlike; many, yet one. I would study, I would know, I would admire forever. These works of thought have been the entertainments of the human spirit in all ages.

A more secret, sweet, and overpowering beauty appears to man when his heart and mind open to the sentiment of virtue. Then he is instructed in what is above him. He learns that his being is without bound; that to the good, to the perfect, he is born, low as he now lies in evil and weakness. That which he venerates is still his own, though he has not realized it yet. *He ought.* He knows the sense of that grand word, though his analysis fails to render account of it. When in innocency or when by intellectual perception he attains to say,—"I love the Right; Truth is beautiful within and without for evermore. Virtue, I am thine; save me; use me; thee will I serve, day and night, in great, in small, that I may be not virtuous, but virtue;"—then is the end of the creation answered, and God is well pleased.

The sentiment of virtue is a reverence and delight in the presence of certain divine laws. It perceives that this homely game of life we play, covers, under what seem foolish details, principles that astonish. The child amidst his baubles is learning the action of light, motion, gravity, muscular force; and in the game of human life, love, fear, justice, appetite, man, and God, interact. These laws refuse to be adequately stated. They will not be written out on paper, or spoken by the tongue. They elude our persevering thought; yet we read them hourly in each other's faces, in each other's actions, in our own remorse. The moral traits which are all globed into every virtuous act and thought,—in speech we must sever, and describe or suggest by painful enumeration of many particulars. Yet, as this sentiment is the essence of all religion, let me guide your eye to the precise objects of the sentiment, by an enumeration of some of those classes of facts in which this element is conspicuous.

The intuition of the moral sentiment is an insight

of the perfection of the laws of the soul. These laws execute themselves. They are out of time, out of space, and not subject to circumstance. Thus in the soul of man there is a justice whose retributions are instant and entire. He who does a good deed is instantly ennobled. He who does a mean deed is by the action itself contracted. He who puts off impurity, thereby puts on purity. If a man is at heart just, then in so far is he God; the safety of God, the immortality of God, the majesty of God do enter into that man with justice. If a man dissemble, deceive, he deceives himself, and goes out of acquaintance with his own being. A man in the view of absolute goodness, adores, with total humility. Every step so downward, is a step upward. The man who renounces himself, comes to himself.

See how this rapid intrinsic energy worketh everywhere, righting wrongs, correcting appearances, and bringing up facts to a harmony with thoughts. Its operation in life, though slow to the senses, is at last as sure as in the soul. By it a man is made the Providence to himself, dispensing good to his goodness, and evil to his sin. Character is always known. Thefts never enrich; alms never impoverish; murder will speak out of stone walls. The least admixture of a lie,—for example, the taint of vanity, any attempt to make a good impression, a favorable appearance,—will instantly vitiate the effect. But speak the truth, and all nature and all spirits help you with unexpected furtherance. Speak the truth, and all things alive or brute are vouchers, and the very roots of the grass underground there do seem to stir and move to bear you witness. See again the perfection of the Law as it applies itself to the affections, and becomes the law of society. As we are, so we associate. The good, by affinity, seek the good; the vile, by affinity, the vile. Thus of their own volition, souls proceed into heaven, into hell.

These facts have always suggested to man the sublime creed that the world is not the product of manifold power, but of one will, of one mind; and that one mind is everywhere active, in each ray of the star, in each wavelet of the pool; and whatever opposes that will is everywhere balked and baffled, because things are made so, and not otherwise. Good is positive. Evil is merely privative, not absolute: it is like cold, which is the privation of heat. All evil is so much death or nonentity. Benevolence is absolute and real. So much benevolence as a man hath, so much life hath he. For all things proceed out of this same spirit, which is differently named love, justice, temperance, in its different applications, just as the ocean receives different names on the several shores which it washes. All things proceed out of the same spirit, and all things conspire with it. Whilst a man seeks good ends, he is strong by the whole strength of nature. In so far as he roves from these ends, he bereaves himself of

EVIL NOT REAL

power, or auxiliaries; his being shrinks out of all remote channels, he becomes less and less, a mote, a point, until absolute badness is absolute death.

The perception of this law of laws awakens in the mind a sentiment which we call the religious sentiment, and which makes our highest happiness. Wonderful is its power to charm and to command. It is a mountain air. It is the embalmer of the world. It is myrrh and storax, and chlorine and rosemary. It makes the sky and the hills sublime, and the silent song of the stars is it. By it is the universe made safe and habitable, not by science or power. Thought may work cold and intransitive in things, and find no end or unity; but the dawn of the sentiment of virtue on the heart, gives and is the assurance that Law is sovereign over all natures; and the worlds, time, space, eternity, do seem to break out into joy.

This sentiment is divine and deifying. It is the beatitude of man. It makes him illimitable. Through it, the soul first knows itself. It corrects the capital mistake of the infant man, who seeks to be great by following the great, and hopes to derive advantages *from another*,—by showing the fountain of all good to be in himself, and that he, equally with every man, is an inlet into the deeps of Reason. When he says, "I ought;" when love warms him; when he chooses, warned from on high, the good and great deed; then, deep melodies wander through his soul from Supreme Wisdom.—Then he can worship, and be enlarged by this worship; for he can never go behind this sentiment. In the sublimest flights of the soul, rectitude is never surmounted, love is never outgrown.

This sentiment lies at the foundation of society, and successively creates all forms of worship. The principle of veneration never dies out. Man fallen into superstition, into sensuality, is never quite without the visions of the moral sentiment. In like manner, all the expressions of this sentiment are sacred and permanent in proportion to their purity. The expressions of this sentiment affect us more than all other compositions. The sentences of the oldest time, which ejaculate this piety, are still fresh and fragrant. This thought dwelled always deepest in the minds of men in the devout and contemplative East; not alone in Palestine, where it reached its purest expression, but in Egypt, in Persia, in India, in China. Europe has always owed to oriental genius its divine impulses. What these holy bards said, all sane men found agreeable and true. And the unique impression of Jesus upon mankind, whose name is not so much written as ploughed into the history of this world, is proof of the subtle virtue of this infusion.

Meantime, whilst the doors of the temple stand open, night and day, before every man, and the oracles of this truth cease never, it is guarded by one stern condition; this, namely: it is an intuition. It cannot be received at second hand. Truly speaking, it is not instruction, but provocation, that I can receive from another soul. What he announces, I must find true in me, or reject; and on his word, or as his second, be he who he may, I can accept nothing. On the contrary, the absence of this primary faith is the presence of degradation. As is the flood, so is the ebb. Let this faith depart, and the very words it spake and the things it made become false and hurtful. Then falls the church, the state, art, letters, life. The doctrine of the divine nature being forgotten, a sickness infects and dwarfs the constitution. Once man was all; now he is an appendage, a nuisance. And because the indwelling Supreme Spirit cannot wholly be got rid of, the doctrine of it suffers this perversion, that the divine nature is attributed to one or two persons, and denied to all the rest, and denied with fury. The doctrine of inspiration is lost; the base doctrine of the majority of voices usurps the place of the doctrine of the soul. Miracles, prophecy, poetry, the ideal life, the holy life, exist as ancient history merely; they are not in the belief, nor in the aspiration of society; but, when suggested, seem ridiculous. Life is comic or pitiful as soon as the high ends of being fade out of sight, and man becomes near-sighted, and can only attend to what addresses the senses.

These general views, which, whilst they are general, none will contest, find abundant illustration in the history of religion, and especially in the history of the Christian church. In that, all of us have had our birth and nurture. The truth contained in that, you, my young friends, are now setting forth to teach. As the Cultus, or established worship of the civilized world, it has great historical interest for us. Of its blessed words, which have been the consolation of humanity, you need not that I should speak. I shall endeavor to discharge my duty to you on this occasion, by pointing out two errors in its administration, which daily appear more gross from the point of view we have just now taken.

Jesus Christ belonged to the true race of prophets. He saw with open eye the mystery of the soul. Drawn by its severe harmony, ravished with its beauty, he lived in it, and had his being there. Alone in all history he estimated the greatness of man. One man was true to what is in you and me. He saw that God incarnates himself in man, and evermore goes forth anew to take possession of his World. He said, in this jubilee of sublime emotion, "I am divine. Through me, God acts; through me, speaks. Would you see God, see me; or see thee, when thou also thinkest as I now think." But what a distortion did his doctrine and memory suffer in the same, in the next, and the following ages! There is no doctrine of the Reason which will bear to be taught by the Understanding. The understanding caught this high chant from the poet's lips, and said, in the next age,

."This was Jehovah come down out of heaven. I will kill you, if you say he was a man." The idioms of his language and the figures of his rhetoric have usurped the place of his truth; and churches are not built on his principles, but on his tropes. Christianity became a Mythus, as the poetic teaching of Greece and of Egypt, before. He spoke of miracles; for he felt that man's life was a miracle, and all that man doth, and he knew that this daily miracle shines as the character ascends. But the word Miracle, as pronounced by Christian churches, gives a false impression; it is Monster. It is not one with the blowing clover and the falling rain.

He felt respect for Moses and the prophets, but no unfit tenderness at postponing their initial revelations to the hour and the man that now is; to the eternal revelation in the heart. Thus was he a true man. Having seen that the law in us is commanding, he would not suffer it to be commanded. Boldly, with hand, and heart, and life, he declared it was God. Thus is he, as I think, the only soul in history who has appreciated the worth of man.

1. In this point of view we become sensible of the first defect of historical Christianity. Historical Christianity has fallen into the error that corrupts all attempts to communicate religion. As it appears to us, and as it has appeared for ages, it is not the doctrine of the soul, but an exaggeration of the personal, the positive, the ritual. It has dwelt, it dwells, with noxious exaggeration about the *person* of Jesus. The soul knows no persons. It invites every man to expand to the full circle of the universe, and will have no preferences but those of spontaneous love. But by this eastern monarchy of a Christianity, which indolence and fear have built, the friend of man is made the injurer of man. The manner in which his name is surrounded with expressions which were once sallies of admiration and love, but are now petrified into official titles, kills all generous sympathy and liking. All who hear me, feel that the language that describes Christ to Europe and America is not the style of friendship and enthusiasm to a good and noble heart, but is appropriated and formal,—paints a demigod, as the Orientals or the Greeks would describe Osiris or Apollo. Accept the injurious impositions of our early catechetical instruction, and even honesty and self-denial were but splendid sins, if they did not wear the Christian name. One would rather be

"A pagan, suckled in a creed outworn," [1]

than to be defrauded of his manly right in coming into nature and finding not names and places, not land and professions, but even virtue and truth foreclosed and monopolized. You shall not be a man

[1] Wordsworth's sonnet, "The world is too much with us," line 10.

even. You shall not own the world; you shall not dare and live after the infinite Law that is in you, and in company with the infinite Beauty which heaven and earth reflect to you in all lovely forms; but you must subordinate your nature to Christ's nature; you must accept our interpretations, and take his portrait as the vulgar draw it.

That is always best which gives me to myself. The sublime is excited in me by the great stoical doctrine, Obey thyself. That which shows God in me, fortifies me. That which shows God out of me, makes me a wart and a wen. There is no longer a necessary reason for my being. Already the long shadows of untimely oblivion creep over me, and I shall decease forever.

The divine bards are the friends of my virtue, of my intellect, of my strength. They admonish me that the gleams which flash across my mind are not mine, but God's; that they had the like, and were not disobedient to the heavenly vision. So I love them. Noble provocations go out from them, inviting me to resist evil; to subdue the world; and to Be. And thus, by his holy thoughts, Jesus serves us, and thus only. To aim to convert a man by miracles is a profanation of the soul. A true conversion, a true Christ, is now, as always, to be made by the reception of beautiful sentiments. It is true that a great and rich soul, like his, falling among the simple, does so preponderate, that, as his did, it names the world. The world seems to them to exist for him, and they have not yet drunk so deeply of his sense as to see that only by coming again to themselves, or to God in themselves, can they grow forevermore. It is a low benefit to give me something; it is a high benefit to enable me to do somewhat of myself. The time is coming when all men will see that the gift of God to the soul is not a vaunting, overpowering, excluding sanctity, but a sweet, natural goodness, a goodness like thine and mine, and that so invites thine and mine to be and to grow.

The injustice of the vulgar tone of preaching is not less flagrant to Jesus than to the souls which it profanes. The preachers do not see that they make his gospel not glad, and shear him of the locks of beauty and the attributes of heaven. When I see a majestic Epaminondas, or Washington; when I see among my contemporaries a true orator, an upright judge, a dear friend; when I vibrate to the melody and fancy of a poem; I see beauty that is to be desired. And so lovely, and with yet more entire consent of my human being, sounds in my ear the severe music of the bards that have sung of the true God in all ages. Now do not degrade the life and dialogues of Christ out of the circle of this charm, by insulation and peculiarity. Let them lie as they befell, alive and warm, part of human life and of the landscape and of the cheerful day.

2. The second defect of the traditionary and limited way of using the mind of Christ is a consequence of the first; this, namely; that the Moral Nature, that Law of laws whose revelations introduce greatness—yea, God himself—into the open soul, is not explored as the fountain of the established teaching in society. Men have come to speak of the revelation as somewhat long ago given and done, as if God were dead. The injury to faith throttles the preacher; and the goodliest of institutions becomes an uncertain and inarticulate voice.

It is very certain that it is the effect of conversation with the beauty of the soul, to beget a desire and need to impart to others the same knowledge and love. If utterance is denied, the thought lies like a burden on the man. Always the seer is a sayer. Somehow his dream is told; somehow he publishes it with solemn joy: sometimes with pencil on canvas, sometimes with chisel on stone, sometimes in towers and aisles of granite, his soul's worship is builded; sometimes in anthems of indefinite music; but clearest and most permanent, in words.

The man enamored of this excellency becomes its priest or poet. The office is coeval with the world. But observe the condition, the spiritual limitation of the office. The spirit only can teach. Not any profane man, not any sensual, not any liar, not any slave can teach, but only he can give, who has; he only can create, who is. The man on whom the soul descends, through whom the soul speaks, alone can teach. Courage, piety, love, wisdom, can teach; and every man can open his door to these angels, and they shall bring him the gift of tongues. But the man who aims to speak as books enable, as synods use, as the fashion guides, and as interest commands, babbles. Let him hush.

To this holy office you propose to devote yourselves. I wish you may feel your call in throbs of desire and hope. The office is the first in the world. It is of that reality that it cannot suffer the deduction of any falsehood. And it is my duty to say to you that the need was never greater of new revelation than now. From the views I have already expressed, you will infer the sad conviction, which I share, I believe, with numbers, of the universal decay and now almost death of faith in society. The soul is not preached. The Church seems to totter to its fall, almost all life extinct. On this occasion, any complaisance would be criminal which told you, whose hope and commission it is to preach the faith of Christ, that the faith of Christ is preached.

It is time that this ill-suppressed murmur of all thoughtful men against the famine of our churches;—this moaning of the heart because it is bereaved of the consolation, the hope, the grandeur that come alone out of the culture of the moral nature,— should be heard through the sleep of indolence, and over the din of routine. This great and perpetual office of the preacher is not discharged. Preaching is the expression of the moral sentiment in application to the duties of life. In how many churches, by how many prophets, tell me, is man made sensible that he is an infinite Soul; that the earth and heavens are passing into his mind; that he is drinking forever the soul of God? Where now sounds the persuasion, that by its very melody imparadises my heart, and so affirms its own origin in heaven? Where shall I hear words such as in elder ages drew men to leave all and follow,—father and mother, house and land, wife and child? Where shall I hear these august laws of moral being so pronounced as to fill my ear, and I feel ennobled by the offer of my uttermost action and passion? The test of the true faith, certainly, should be its power to charm and command the soul, as the laws of nature control the activity of the hands,—so commanding that we find pleasure and honor in obeying. The faith should blend with the light of rising and of setting suns, with the flying cloud, the singing bird, and the breath of flowers. But now the priest's Sabbath has lost the splendor of nature; it is unlovely; we are glad when it is done; we can make, we do make, even sitting in our pews, a far better, holier, sweeter, for ourselves.

Whenever the pulpit is usurped by a formalist, then is the worshipper defrauded and disconsolate. We shrink as soon as the prayers begin, which do not uplift, but smite and offend us. We are fain to wrap our cloaks about us, and secure, as best we can, a solitude that hears not. I once heard a preacher who sorely tempted me to say I would go to church no more. Men go, thought I, where they are wont to go, else had no soul entered the temple in the afternoon. A snow-storm was falling around us. The snow-storm was real, the preacher merely spectral, and the eye felt the sad contrast in looking at him, and then out of the window behind him into the beautiful meteor of the snow. He had lived in vain. He had no one word intimating that he had laughed or wept, was married or in love, had been commended, or cheated, or chagrined. If he had ever lived and acted, we were none the wiser for it. The capital secret of his profession, namely, to convert life into truth, he had not learned. Not one fact in all his experience had he yet imported into his doctrine. This man had ploughed and planted and talked and bought and sold; he had read books; he had eaten and drunken; his head aches, his heart throbs; he smiles and suffers; yet was there not a surmise, a hint, in all the discourse, that he had ever lived at all. Not a line did he draw out of real history. The true preacher can be known by this, that he deals out to the people his life,—life passed through the fire of thought. But of the bad preacher,

it could not be told from his sermon what age of the world he fell in; whether he had a father or a child; whether he was a freeholder or a pauper; whether he was a citizen or a countryman; or any other fact of his biography. It seemed strange that the people should come to church. It seemed as if their houses were very unentertaining, that they should prefer this thoughtless clamor. It shows that there is a commanding attraction in the moral sentiment, that can lend a faint tint of light to dulness and ignorance coming in its name and place. The good hearer is sure he has been touched sometimes; is sure there is somewhat to be reached, and some word that can reach it. When he listens to these vain words, he comforts himself by their relation to his remembrance of better hours, and so they clatter and echo unchallenged.

I am not ignorant that when we preach unworthily, it is not always quite in vain. There is a good ear, in some men, that draws supplies to virtue out of very indifferent nutriment. There is poetic truth concealed in all the commonplaces of prayer and of sermons, and though foolishly spoken, they may be wisely heard; for each is some select expression that broke out in a moment of piety from some stricken or jubilant soul, and its excellency made it remembered. The prayers and even the dogmas of our church are like the zodiac of Denderah and the astronomical monuments of the Hindoos, wholly insulated from anything now extant in the life and business of the people. They mark the height to which the waters once rose. But this docility is a check upon the mischief from the good and devout. In a large portion of the community, the religious service gives rise to quite other thoughts and emotions. We need not chide the negligent servant. We are struck with pity, rather, at the swift retribution of his sloth. Alas for the unhappy man that is called to stand in the pulpit, and *not* give bread of life. Everything that befalls, accuses him. Would he ask contributions for the missions, foreign or domestic? Instantly his face is suffused with shame, to propose to his parish that they should send money a hundred or a thousand miles, to furnish such poor fare as they have at home and would do well to go the hundred or the thousand miles to escape. Would he urge people to a godly way of living;—and can he ask a fellow-creature to come to Sabbath meetings, when he and they all know what is the poor uttermost they can hope for therein? Will he invite them privately to the Lord's Supper? He dares not. If no heart warm this rite, the hollow, dry, creaking formality is too plain, than that he can face a man of wit and energy and put the invitation without terror. In the street, what has he to say to the bold village blasphemer? The village blasphemer sees fear in the face, form, and gait of the minister.

Let me not taint the sincerity of this plea by any oversight of the claims of good men. I know and honor the purity and strict conscience of numbers of the clergy. What life the public worship retains, it owes to the scattered company of pious men, who minister here and there in the churches, and who, sometimes accepting with too great tenderness the tenet of the elders, have not accepted from others, but from their own heart, the genuine impulses of virtue, and so still command our love and awe, to the sanctity of character. Moreover, the exceptions are not so much to be found in a few eminent preachers, as in the better hours, the truer inspirations of all,—nay, in the sincere moments of every man. But, with whatever exception, it is still true that tradition characterizes the preaching of this country; that it comes out of the memory, and not out of the soul; that it aims at what is usual, and not at what is necessary and eternal; that thus historical Christianity destroys the power of preaching, by withdrawing it from the exploration of the moral nature of man; where the sublime is, where are the resources of astonishment and power. What a cruel injustice it is to that Law, the joy of the whole earth, which alone can make thought dear and rich; that Law whose fatal sureness the astronomical orbits poorly emulate;—that it is travestied and depreciated, that it is behooted and behowled, and not a trait, not a word of it articulated. The pulpit in losing sight of this Law, loses its reason, and gropes after it knows not what. And for want of this culture the soul of the community is sick and faithless. It wants nothing so much as a stern, high, stoical, Christian discipline, to make it know itself and the divinity that speaks through it. Now man is ashamed of himself; he skulks and sneaks through the world, to be tolerated, to be pitied, and scarcely in a thousand years does any man dare to be wise and good, and so draw after him the tears and blessings of his kind.

Certainly there have been periods when, from the inactivity of the intellect on certain truths, a greater faith was possible in names and persons. The Puritans in England and America found in the Christ of the Catholic Church and in the dogmas inherited from Rome, scope for their austere piety and their longings for civil freedom. But their creed is passing away, and none arises in its room. I think no man can go with his thoughts about him into one of our churches, without feeling that what hold the public worship had on men is gone, or going. It has lost its grasp on the affection of the good and the fear of the bad. In the country, neighborhoods, half parishes are *signing off*, to use the local term. It is already beginning to indicate character and religion to withdraw from the religious meetings. I have heard a devout person, who prized the Sabbath, say

in bitterness of heart, "On Sundays, it seems wicked to go to church." And the motive that holds the best there is now only a hope and a waiting. What was once a mere circumstance, that the best and the worst men in the parish, the poor and the rich, the learned and the ignorant, young and old, should meet one day as fellows in one house, in sign of an equal right in the soul, has come to be a paramount motive for going thither.

My friends, in these two errors, I think, I find the causes of a decaying church and a wasting unbelief. And what greater calamity can fall upon a nation than the loss of worship? Then all things go to decay. Genius leaves the temple to haunt the senate or the market. Literature becomes frivolous. Science is cold. The eye of youth is not lighted by the hope of other worlds, and age is without honor. Society lives to trifles, and when men die we do not mention them.

And now, my brothers, you will ask, What in these desponding days can be done by us? The remedy is already declared in the ground of our complaint of the Church. We have contrasted the Church with the Soul. In the soul then let the redemption be sought. Wherever a man comes, there comes revolution. The old is for slaves. When a man comes, all books are legible, all things transparent, all religions are forms. He is religious. Man is the wonderworker. He is seen amid miracles. All men bless and curse. He saith yea and nay, only. The stationariness of religion; the assumption that the age of inspiration is past, that the Bible is closed; the fear of degrading the character of Jesus by representing him as a man;—indicate with sufficient clearness the falsehood of our theology. It is the office of a true teacher to show us that God is, not was; that He speaketh, not spake. The true Christianity,—a faith like Christ's in the infinitude of man,—is lost. None believeth in the soul of man, but only in some man or person old and departed. Ah me! no man goeth alone. All men go in flocks to this saint or that poet, avoiding the God who seeth in secret. They cannot see in secret; they love to be blind in public. They think society wiser than their soul, and know not that one soul, and their soul, is wiser than the whole world. See how nations and races flit by on the sea of time and leave no ripple to tell where they floated or sunk, and one good soul shall make the name of Moses, or of Zeno, or of Zoroaster, reverend forever. None assayeth the stern ambition to be the Self of the nation and of nature, but each would be an easy secondary to some Christian scheme, or sectarian connection, or some eminent man. Once leave your own knowledge of God, your own sentiment, and take secondary knowledge, as St. Paul's, or George Fox's, or Swedenborg's, and you get wide from God with every year this secondary form lasts, and if, as now, for centuries,—the chasm yawns to that breadth, that men can scarcely be convinced there is in them anything divine.

Let me admonish you, first of all, to go alone; to refuse the good models, even those which are sacred in the imagination of men, and dare to love God without mediator or veil. Friends enough you shall find who will hold up to your emulation Wesleys and Oberlins. Saints and Prophets. Thank God for these good men, but say, "I also am a man." Imitation cannot go above its model. The imitator dooms himself to hopeless mediocrity. The inventor did it because it was natural to him, and so in him it has a charm. In the imitator something else is natural, and he bereaves himself of his own beauty, to come short of another man's.

Yourself a newborn bard of the Holy Ghost, cast behind you all conformity, and acquaint men at first hand with Deity. Look to it first and only, that fashion, custom, authority, pleasure, and money, are nothing to you,—are not bandages over your eyes, that you cannot see,—but live with the privilege of the immeasurable mind. Not too anxious to visit periodically all families and each family in your parish connection,—when you meet one of these men or women, be to them a divine man; be to them thought and virtue; let their timid aspirations find in you a friend; let their trampled instincts be genially tempted out in your atmosphere; let their doubts know that you have doubted, and their wonder feel that you have wondered. By trusting your own heart, you shall gain more confidence in other men. For all our penny-wisdom, for all our soul-destroying slavery to habit, it is not to be doubted that all men have sublime thoughts; that all men value the few real hours of life; they love to be heard; they love to be caught up into the vision of principles. We mark with light in the memory the few interviews we have had, in the dreary years of routine and of sin, with souls that made our souls wiser; that spoke what we thought; that told us what we knew; that gave us leave to be what we inly were. Discharge to men the priestly office, and, present or absent, you shall be followed with their love as by an angel.

And, to this end, let us not aim at common degrees of merit. Can we not leave, to such as love it, the virtue that glitters for the commendation of society, and ourselves pierce the deep solitudes of absolute ability and worth? We easily come up to the standard of goodness in society. Society's praise can be cheaply secured, and almost all men are content with those easy merits; but the instant effect of conversing with God will be to put them away. There are persons who are not actors, not speakers, but influences; persons too great for fame, for display; who disdain eloquence; to whom all we call art and artist, seems too nearly allied to show and by-ends, to the exaggeration of the finite and selfish, and loss of the universal. The orators, the poets, the commanders encroach on us only as fair women do, by our allowance and homage. Slight them by preoccupation of mind, slight them, as you can well afford to do, by high and universal aims, and they instantly feel that you have right, and that it is in lower places that they must shine. They also feel your right; for they with you are open to the influx of the all-knowing Spirit, which annihilates before its broad noon the little shades and gradations of intelligence in the compositions we call wiser and wisest.

In such high communion let us study the grand strokes of rectitude: a bold benevolence, an independence of friends, so that not the unjust wishes of those who love us shall impair our freedom, but we shall resist for truth's sake the freest flow of kindness, and appeal to sympathies far in advance; and,—what is the highest form in which we know this beautiful element,—a certain solidity of merit, that has nothing to do with opinion, and which is so essentially and manifestly virtue, that it is taken for granted that the right, the brave, the generous step will be taken by it, and nobody thinks of commending it. You would compliment a coxcomb doing a good act, but you would not praise an angel. The silence that accepts merit as the most natural thing in the world, is the highest applause. Such souls, when they appear, are the Imperial Guard of Virtue, the perpetual reserve, the dictators of fortune. One needs not praise their courage,—they are the heart and soul of nature. O my friends, there are resources in us on which we have not drawn. There are men who rise refreshed on hearing a threat; men to whom a crisis which intimidates and paralyzes the majority,—demanding not the faculties of prudence and thrift, but comprehension, immovableness, the readiness of sacrifice,—comes graceful and beloved as a bride. Napoleon said of Massena, that he was not himself until the battle began to go against him; then, when the dead began to fall in ranks around him, awoke his powers of combination, and he put on terror and victory as a robe. So it is in rugged crises, in unweariable endurance, and in aims which put sympathy out of question, that the angel is shown. But these are heights that we can scarce remember and look up to without contrition and shame. Let us thank God that such things exist.

And now let us do what we can to rekindle the smouldering, nigh quenched fire on the altar. The evils of the church that now is are manifest. The question returns, What shall we do? I confess, all attempts to project and establish a Cultus with new rites and forms, seem to me vain. Faith makes us, and not we it, and faith makes its own forms. All attempts to contrive a system are as cold as the new worship introduced by the French to the goddess of Reason,—to-day, pasteboard and filigree, and ending to-morrow in madness and murder. Rather let the breath of new life be breathed by you through the forms already existing. For if once you are alive, you shall find they shall become plastic and new. The remedy to their deformity is first, soul, and second, soul, and evermore, soul. A whole popedom of forms one pulsation of virtue can uplift and vivify. Two inestimable advantages Christianity has given us; first the Sabbath, the jubilee of the whole world, whose light dawns welcome alike into the closet of the philosopher, into the garret of toil, and into prison-cells, and everywhere suggests, even to the vile, the dignity of spiritual being. Let it stand forevermore, a temple, which new love, new faith, new sight shall restore to more than its first splendor to mankind. And secondly, the institution of preaching,—the speech of man to men,—essentially the most flexible of all organs, of all forms. What hinders that now, everywhere, in pulpits, in lecture-rooms, in houses, in fields, wherever the invitation of men or your own occasions lead you, you speak the very truth, as your life and conscience teach it, and cheer the waiting, fainting hearts of men with new hope and new revelation?

I look for the hour when that supreme Beauty which ravished the souls of those Eastern men, and chiefly of those Hebrews, and through their lips spoke oracles to all time, shall speak in the West also. The Hebrew and Greek Scriptures contain immortal sentences, that have been bread of life to millions. But they have no epical integrity; are fragmentary; are not shown in their order to the intellect. I look for the new Teacher that shall follow so far those shining laws that he shall see them come full circle; shall see their rounding complete grace; shall see the world to be the mirror of the soul; shall see the identity of the law of gravitation with purity of heart; and shall show that the Ought, that Duty, is one thing with Science, with Beauty, and with Joy.

1838

Self-Reliance

In this essay, Emerson asserts that a good society is a society of good individuals, and the only fundamental reform is the reform of one's self. The aims and effects of those known as reformers and humanitarians are superficial, and social progress is an illusion. Conformity, the virtue most widely valued, is the means by which free men are intimidated into slavery to society.

In affirming self-reliance vs. conformity, independence vs. subjection, the individual vs. society, Emerson had behind him an immense amount of American experience, including the settlement of New England by nonconformists, the stand of Roger Williams in favor of the individual conscience, the Inner Light of the Quakers, the passion of Jefferson for all freedoms, the Jacksonian assertion of the common man. Emerson's was a democratic individualism, but at the same time it was a spiritual individualism deeply related to European traditions reaching far back to early Christianity and the philosophy of Plato.

In "The American Scholar" and the "Divinity School Address" Emerson's art was that of the orator adapting his speech to a dignified occasion. Now he is an informal essayist. He is still, in a sense, addressing an audience ("you"), and he is still in a sense ministerial, seeking to stir unused depths in the listener's experience. Full of his subject and purpose, he sustains them through a lengthy discourse, repeating his main point—"trust thyself"—in many statements and over-statements, testing it by many applications to situations in life, alerting the reader by changes in tone and attitude. The essay is studded with pithy, quotable epigrams and with telling metaphors. And the diction, as Lowell said, is at once rich and homely, "like home-spun cloth-of-gold."

I read the other day some verses written by an eminent painter which were original and not conventional. The soul always hears an admonition in such lines, let the subject be what it may. The sentiment they instil is of more value than any thought they may contain. To believe your own thought, to believe that what is true for you in your private heart is true for all men,—that is genius. Speak your latent conviction, and it shall be the universal sense; for the inmost in due time becomes the outmost, and our first thought is rendered back to us by the trumpets of the Last Judgment. Familiar as the voice of the mind is to each, the highest merit we ascribe to Moses, Plato, and Milton is that they set at naught books and tradition, and spoke not what men, but what *they* thought. A man should learn to detect and watch that gleam of light which flashes across his mind from within, more than the lustre of the firmament of bards and sages. Yet he dismisses without notice his thought, because it is his. In every work of genius we recognize our own rejected thoughts; they come back to us with a certain alienated majesty. Great works of art have no more affecting lesson for us than this. They teach us to abide by our spontaneous impression with good-humored inflexibility then most when the whole cry of voices is on the other side. Else to-morrow a stranger will say with masterly good sense precisely what we have thought and felt all the time, and we shall be forced to take with shame our own opinion from another. There is a time in every man's education when he arrives at the conviction that envy is ignorance; that imitation is suicide; that he must take himself for better for worse as his portion; that though the wide universe is full of good, no kernel of nourishing corn can come to him but through his toil bestowed on that plot of ground which is given to him to till. The power which resides in him is new in nature, and none but he knows what that is which he can do, nor does he know until he has tried. Not for nothing one face, one character, one fact, makes much impression on him and another none. This sculpture in the memory is not without preëstablished harmony. The eye was placed where one ray should fall, that it might testify of that particular ray. We but half express ourselves, and are ashamed of that divine idea which each of us represents. It may be safely trusted as proportionate and of good issues, so it be faithfully imparted, but God will not have his work made manifest by cowards. A man is relieved and gay when he has put his heart into his work and done his best; but what he has said or done otherwise shall give him no peace. It is a deliverance which does not deliver. In the attempt his genius deserts him; no muse befriends; no invention, no hope.

Trust thyself: every heart vibrates to that iron string. Accept the place the divine providence has found for you, the society of your contemporaries, the connection of events. Great men have always done so, and confided themselves childlike to the genius of their age, betraying their perception that the absolutely trustworthy was seated at their heart, working through their hands, predominating in all their being. And we are now men, and must accept in the highest mind the same transcendent destiny; and not minors and invalids in a protected corner, not cowards fleeing before a revolution, but guides, redeemers, and benefactors, obeying the Almighty effort and advancing on Chaos and the Dark.

What pretty oracles nature yields us on this text in the face and behavior of children, babes, and even brutes! That divided and rebel mind, that distrust of a sentiment because our arithmetic has computed the strength and means opposed to our purpose, these have not. Their mind being whole, their eye is as yet unconquered, and when we look in their faces we are disconcerted. Infancy conforms to nobody; all conform to it; so that one babe commonly makes four or five out of the adults who prattle and play to it. So God has armed youth and puberty and manhood no less with its own piquancy and charm, and made it enviable and gracious and its claims not to be put by, if it will stand by itself. Do not think the youth has no force, because he cannot speak to you and me. Hark! in the next room his voice is sufficiently clear and emphatic. It seems he knows how to speak to his contemporaries. Bashful or bold then, he will know how to make us seniors very unnecessary.

The nonchalance of boys who are sure of a dinner, and would disdain as much as a lord to do or say aught to conciliate one, is the healthy attitude of human nature. A boy is in the parlor what the pit is

in the playhouse; independent, irresponsible, looking out from his corner on such people and facts as pass by, he tries and sentences them on their merits, in the swift, summary way of boys, as good, bad, interesting, silly, eloquent, troublesome. He cumbers himself never about consequences, about interests; he gives an independent, genuine verdict. You must court him; he does not court you. But the man is as it were clapped into jail by his consciousness. As soon as he has once acted or spoken with *éclat* he is a committed person, watched by the sympathy or the hatred of hundreds whose affections must now enter into his account. There is no Lethe for this. Ah, that he could pass again into his neutrality! Who can thus avoid all pledges and, having observed, observe again from the same unaffected, unbiased, unbribable, unaffrighted innocence,—must always be formidable. He would utter opinions on all passing affairs, which being seen to be not private but necessary, would sink like darts into the ear of men and put them in fear.

These are the voices which we hear in solitude, but they grow faint and inaudible as we enter into the world. Society everywhere is in conspiracy against the manhood of every one of its members. Society is a joint-stock company, in which the members agree, for the better securing of his bread to each shareholder, to surrender the liberty and culture of the eater. The virtue in most request is conformity. Self-reliance is its aversion. It loves not realities and creators, but names and customs.

Whoso would be a man, must be a nonconformist. He who would gather immortal palms must not be hindered by the name of goodness, but must explore if it be goodness. Nothing is at last sacred but the integrity of your own mind. Absolve you to yourself, and you shall have the suffrage of the world. I remember an answer which when quite young I was prompted to make to a valued adviser who was wont to importune me with the dear old doctrines of the church. On my saying, "What have I to do with the sacredness of traditions, if I live wholly from within?" my friend suggested,—"But these impulses may be from below, not from above." I replied, "They do not seem to me to be such; but if I am the Devil's child, I will live then from the Devil." No law can be sacred to me but that of my nature. Good and bad are but names very readily transferable to that or this; the only right is what is after my constitution; the only wrong what is against it. A man is to carry himself in the presence of all opposition as if everything were titular and ephemeral but he. I am ashamed to think how easily we capitulate to badges and names, to large societies and dead institutions. Every decent and well-spoken individual affects and sways me more than is right. I ought to go upright and vital, and speak the rude truth in all ways. If malice and vanity wear the coat of philanthropy, shall that pass? If an angry bigot assumes this bountiful cause of Abolition, and comes to me with his last news from Barbadoes,[1] why should I not say to him, "Go love thy infant; love thy woodchopper; be good-natured and modest; have that grace; and never varnish your hard, uncharitable ambition with this incredible tenderness for black folk a thousand miles off. Thy love afar is spite at home." Rough and graceless would be such greeting, but truth is handsomer than the affectation of love. Your goodness must have some edge to it,—else it is none. The doctrine of hatred must be preached, as the counteraction of the doctrine of love, when that pules and whines. I shun father and mother and wife and brother when my genius calls me. I would write on the lintels of the door-post, *Whim*. I hope it is somewhat better than whim at last, but we cannot spend the day in explanation. Expect me not to show cause why I seek or why I exclude company. Then again, do not tell me, as a good man did to-day, of my obligation to put all poor men in good situations. Are they *my* poor? I tell thee, thou foolish philanthropist, that I grudge the dollar, the dime, the cent I give to such men as do not belong to me and to whom I do not belong. There is a class of persons to whom by all spiritual affinity I am bought and sold; for them I will go to prison if need be; but your miscellaneous popular charities; the education at college of fools; the building of meeting-houses to the vain end to which many now stand; alms to sots, and the thousand-fold Relief Societies;—though I confess with shame I sometimes succumb and give the dollar, it is a wicked dollar, which by and by I shall have the manhood to withhold.

Virtues are, in the popular estimate, rather the exception than the rule. There is the man *and* his virtues. Men do what is called a good action, as some piece of courage or charity, much as they would pay a fine in expiation of daily non-appearance on parade. Their works are done as an apology or extenuation of their living in the world,—as invalids and the insane pay a high board. Their virtues are penances. I do not wish to expiate, but to live. My life is for itself and not for a spectacle. I much prefer that it should be of a lower strain, so it be genuine and equal, than that it should be glittering and unsteady. I wish it to be sound and sweet, and not to need diet and bleeding. I ask primary evidence that you are a man and refuse this appeal from the man to his actions. I know that for myself it makes no difference whether I do or forbear those actions which are reckoned excellent. I cannot consent to pay for a privilege where I have intrinsic

---

[1] Probably refers to the abolition of slavery there in 1833.

right. Few and mean as my gifts may be, I actually am, and do not need for my own assurance or the assurance of my fellows any secondary testimony.

What I must do is all that concerns me, not what the people think. This rule, equally arduous in actual and in intellectual life, may serve for the whole distinction between greatness and meanness. It is the harder because you will always find those who think they know what is your duty better than you know it. It is easy in the world to live after the world's opinion; it is easy in solitude to live after our own; but the great man is he who in the midst of the crowd keeps with perfect sweetness the independence of solitude.

The objection to conforming to usages that have become dead to you is that it scatters your force. It loses your time and blurs the impression of your character. If you maintain a dead church, contribute to a dead Bible-society, vote with a great party either for the government or against it, spread your table like base housekeepers,—under all these screens I have difficulty to detect the precise man you are: and of course so much force is withdrawn from all your proper life. But do your work, and I shall know you. Do your work, and you shall reinforce yourself. A man must consider what a blind-man's-buff is this game of conformity. If I know your sect I anticipate your argument. I hear a preacher announce for his text and topic the expediency of one of the institutions of his church. Do I not know beforehand that not possibly can he say a new and spontaneous word? Do I not know that with all this ostentation of examining the grounds of the institution he will do no such thing? Do I not know that he is pledged to himself not to look but at one side, the permitted side, not as a man, but as a parish minister? He is a retained attorney, and these airs of the bench are the emptiest affectation. Well, most men have bound their eyes with one or another handkerchief, and attached themselves to some one of these communities of opinion. This conformity makes them not false in a few particulars, authors of a few lies, but false in all particulars. Their every truth is not quite true. Their two is not the real two, their four not the real four; so that every word they say chagrins us and we know not where to begin to set them right. Meantime nature is not slow to equip us in the prison-uniform of the party to which we adhere. We come to wear one cut of face and figure, and acquire by degrees the gentlest asinine expression. There is a mortifying experience in particular, which does not fail to wreak itself also in the general history; I mean the "foolish face of praise," the forced smile which we put on in company where we do not feel at ease, in answer to conversation which does not interest us. The muscles, not spontaneously moved but moved by a low usurping wilfulness, grow tight about the outline of the face, with the most disagreeable sensation.

For nonconformity the world whips you with its displeasure. And therefore a man must know how to estimate a sour face. The by-standers look askance on him in the public street or in the friend's parlor. If this aversion had its origin in contempt and resistance like his own he might well go home with a sad countenance; but the sour faces of the multitude, like their sweet faces, have no deep cause, but are put on and off as the wind blows and a newspaper directs. Yet is the discontent of the multitude more formidable than that of the senate and the college. It is easy enough for a firm man who knows the world to brook the rage of the cultivated classes. Their rage is decorous and prudent, for they are timid, as being very vulnerable themselves. But when to their feminine rage the indignation of the people is added, when the ignorant and the poor are aroused, when the unintelligent brute force that lies at the bottom of society is made to growl and mow, it needs the habit of magnanimity and religion to treat it godlike as a trifle of no concernment.

The other terror that scares us from self-trust is our consistency; a reverence for our past act or word because the eyes of others have no other data for computing our orbit than our past acts, and we are loth to disappoint them.

But why should you keep your head over your shoulder? Why drag about this corpse of your memory, lest you contradict somewhat you have stated in this or that public place? Suppose you should contradict yourself; what then? It seems to be a rule of wisdom never to rely on your memory alone, scarcely even in acts of pure memory, but to bring the past for judgment into the thousand-eyed present, and live ever in a new day. In your metaphysics you have denied personality to the Deity, yet when the devout motions of the soul come, yield to them heart and life, though they should clothe God with shape and color. Leave your theory, as Joseph his coat in the hand of the harlot, and flee.

A foolish consistency is the hobgoblin of little minds, adored by little statesmen and philosophers and divines. With consistency a great soul has simply nothing to do. He may as well concern himself with his shadow on the wall. Speak what you think now in hard words and to-morrow speak what to-morrow thinks in hard words again, though it contradict everything you said to-day.—"Ah, so you shall be sure to be misunderstood."—Is it so bad then to be misunderstood? Pythagoras was misunderstood, and Socrates, and Jesus, and Luther, and Copernicus, and Galileo, and Newton, and every pure and wise spirit that ever took flesh. To be great is to be misunderstood.

I suppose no man can violate his nature. All the

AN ASSUMPTION

sallies of his will are rounded in by the law of his being, as the inequalities of Andes and Himmaleh are insignificant in the curve of the sphere. Nor does it matter how you gauge and try him. A character is like an acrostic or Alexandrian stanza;—read it forward, backward, or across, it still spells the same thing. In this pleasing contrite woodlife which God allows me, let me record day by day my honest thought without prospect or retrospect, and I cannot doubt, it will be found symmetrical, though I mean it not and see it not. My book should smell of pines and resound with the hum of insects. The swallow over my window should interweave that thread or straw he carries in his bill into my web also. We pass for what we are. Character teaches above our wills. Men imagine that they communicate their virtue or vice only by overt actions, and do not see that virtue or vice emit a breath every moment.

There will be an agreement in whatever variety of actions, so they be each honest and natural in their hour. For of one will, the actions will be harmonious, however unlike they seem. These varieties are lost sight of at a little distance, at a little height of thought. One tendency unites them all. The voyage of the best ship is a zigzag line of a hundred tacks. See the line from a sufficient distance, and it straightens itself to the average tendency. Your genuine action will explain itself and will explain your other genuine actions. Your conformity explains nothing. Act singly, and what you have already done singly will justify you now. Greatness appeals to the future. If I can be firm enough to-day to do right and scorn eyes, I must have done so much right before as to defend me now. Be it how it will, do right now. Always scorn appearances and you always may. The force of character is cumulative. All the foregone days of virtue work their health into this. What makes the majesty of the heroes of the senate and the field, which so fills the imagination? The consciousness of a train of great days and victories behind. They shed a united light on the advancing actor. He is attended as by a visible escort of angels. That is it which throws thunder into Chatham's voice, and dignity into Washington's port, and America into Adams's eye. Honor is venerable to us because it is no ephemera. It is always ancient virtue. We worship it to-day because it is not of to-day. We love it and pay it homage because it is not a trap for our love and homage, but is self-dependent, self-derived, and therefore of an old immaculate pedigree, even if shown in a young person.

I hope in these days we have heard the last of conformity and consistency. Let the words be gazetted and ridiculous henceforward. Instead of the gong for dinner, let us hear a whistle from the Spartan fife. Let us never bow and apologize more.

VIRTUE NOT MERELY IN OVERT ACTIONS, BUT EVERY ACTIONS.

ZIG-ZAG CONSISTENCY

A THEORY

A great man is coming to eat at my house. I do not wish to please him; I wish that he should wish to please me. I will stand here for humanity, and though I would make it kind, I would make it true. Let us affront and reprimand the smooth mediocrity and squalid contentment of the times, and hurl in the face of custom and trade and office, the fact which is the upshot of all history, that there is a great responsible Thinker and Actor working wherever a man works; that a true man belongs to no other time or place, but is the center of things. Where he is there is nature. He measures you and all men and all events. Ordinarily, everybody in society reminds us of somewhat else, or of some other person. Character, reality, reminds you of nothing else; it takes place of the whole creation. The man must be so much that he must make all circumstances indifferent. Every true man is a cause, a country, and an age; requires infinite spaces and numbers and time fully to accomplish his design;— and posterity seem to follow his steps as a train of clients. A man Caesar is born, and for ages after we have a Roman Empire. Christ is born, and millions of minds so grow and cleave to his genius that he is confounded with virtue and the possible of man. An institution is the lengthened shadow of one man; as, Monachism, of the Hermit Antony; the Reformation, of Luther; Quakerism, of Fox; Methodism, of Wesley; Abolition, of Clarkson.[2] Scipio, Milton called "the height of Rome"; and all history resolves itself very easily into the biography of a few stout and earnest persons.

Let a man then know his worth, and keep things under his feet. Let him not peep or steal, or skulk up and down with the air of a charity-boy, a bastard, or an interloper in the world which exists for him. But the man in the street, finding no worth in himself which corresponds to the force which built a tower or sculptured a marble god, feels poor when he looks on these. To him a palace, a statue, or a costly book have an alien and forbidding air, much like a gay equipage, and seem to say like that, "Who are you, Sir?" Yet they are all his, suitors for his notice, petitioners to his faculties that they will come out and take possession. The picture waits for my verdict; it is not to command me, but I am to settle its claims to praise. That popular fable of the sot who was picked up dead-drunk in the street, carried to the duke's house, washed and dressed and laid in the duke's bed, and, on his waking, treated with all obsequious ceremony like the duke, and assured that he had been insane, owes its popularity to the fact that it symbolizes so well the state of man, who is in the world a sort of sot, but now and then wakes up, exercises his reason and finds himself a true prince.

[2] Thomas Clarkson (1760-1846), a British abolitionist.

Our reading is mendicant and sycophantic. In history our imagination plays us false. Kingdom and lordship, power and estate, are a gaudier vocabulary than private John and Edward in a small house and common day's work; but the things of life are the same to both; the sum total of both is the same. Why all this deference to Alfred and Scanderbeg and Gustavus?[3] Suppose they were virtuous; did they wear out virtue? As great a stake depends on your private act to-day as followed their public and renowned steps. When private men shall act with original views, the lustre will be transferred from the actions of kings to those of gentlemen.

The world has been instructed by its kings, who have so magnetized the eyes of nations. It has been taught by this colossal symbol the mutual reverence that is due from man to man. The joyful loyalty with which men have everywhere suffered the king, the noble, or the great proprietor to walk among them by a law of his own, make his own scale of men and things and reverse theirs, pay for benefits not with money but with honor, and represent the law in his person, was the hieroglyphic by which they obscurely signified their consciousness of their own right and comeliness, the right of every man.

The magnetism which all original action exerts is explained when we inquire the reason of self-trust. Who is the Trustee? What is the aboriginal Self, on which a universal reliance may be grounded? What is the nature and power of that science-baffling star, without parallax, without calculable elements, which shoots a ray of beauty even into trivial and impure actions, if the least mark of independence appear? The inquiry leads us to that source, at once the essence of genius, of virtue, and of life, which we call Spontaneity or Instinct. We denote this primary wisdom as Intuition, whilst all later teachings are tuitions. In that deep force, the last fact behind which analysis cannot go, all things find their common origin. For the sense of being which in calm hours rises, we know not how, in the soul, is not diverse from things, from space, from light, from time, from man, but one with them and proceeds obviously from the same source whence their life and being also proceed. We first share the life by which things exist and afterwards see them as appearances in nature and forget that we have shared their cause. Here is the fountain of action and of thought. Here are the lungs of that inspiration which giveth man wisdom and which cannot be denied without impiety and atheism. We lie in the lap of immense intelligence, which makes us receivers of its truth and organs of its activity. When we discern justice, when we discern truth, we do nothing of

[3] Alfred the Great (849–899), king of England and national hero; Scanderbeg (1403?–1468), Albanian leader and national hero; Gustavus, Swedish king and hero.

ourselves, but allow a passage to its beams. If we ask whence this comes, if we seek to pry into the soul that causes, all philosophy is at fault. Its presence or its absence is all we can affirm. Every man discriminates between the voluntary acts of his mind and his involuntary perceptions, and knows that to his involuntary perceptions a perfect faith is due. He may err in the expression of them, but he knows that these things are so, like day and night, not to be disputed. My wilful actions and acquisitions are but roving;—the idlest reverie, the faintest native emotion, command my curiosity and respect. Thoughtless people contradict as readily the statement of perceptions as of opinions, or rather much more readily; for they do not distinguish between perception and notion. They fancy that I choose to see this or that thing. But perception is not whimsical, but fatal. If I see a trait, my children will see it after me, and in course of time all mankind,—although it may chance that no one has seen it before me. For my perception of it is as much a fact as the sun.

The relations of the soul to the divine spirit are so pure that it is profane to seek to interpose helps. It must be that when God speaketh he should communicate, not one thing, but all things; should fill the world with his voice; should scatter forth light, nature, time, souls, from the center of the present thought; and new date and new create the whole. Whenever a mind is simple and receives a divine wisdom, old things pass away,—means, teachers, texts, temples fall; it lives now, and absorbs past and future into the present hour. All things are made sacred by relation to it,—one as much as another. All things are dissolved to their center by their cause, and in the universal miracle petty and particular miracles disappear. If therefore a man claims to know and speak of God and carries you backward to the phraseology of some old mouldered nation in another country, in another world, believe him not. Is the acorn better than the oak which is its fulness and completion? Is the parent better than the child into whom he has cast his ripened being? Whence then this worship of the past? The centuries are conspirators against the sanity and authority of the soul. Time and space are but physiological colors which the eye makes, but the soul is light: where it is, is day; where it was, is night; and history is an impertinence and an injury if it be anything more than a cheerful apologue or parable of my being and becoming.

Man is timid and apologetic; he is no longer upright; he dares not say "I think," "I am," but quotes some saint or sage. He is ashamed before the blade of grass or the blowing rose. These roses under my window make no reference to former roses or to better ones; they are for what they are; they exist with God to-day. There is no time for them.

There is simply the rose; it is perfect in every moment of its existence. Before a leaf-bud has burst, its whole life acts; in the full-blown flower there is no more; in the leafless root there is no less. Its nature is satisfied and it satisfies nature in all moments alike. But man postpones or remembers; he does not live in the present, but with reverted eye laments the past, or, heedless of the riches that surround him, stands on tiptoe to foresee the future. He cannot be happy and strong until he too lives with nature in the present, above time.

This should be plain enough. Yet see what strong intellects dare not yet hear God himself unless he speak the phraseology of I know not what David, or Jeremiah, or Paul. We shall not always set so great a price on a few texts, on a few lives. We are like children who repeat by rote the sentences of grandames and tutors, and, as they grow older, of the men of talents and character they chance to see,—painfully recollecting the exact words they spoke; afterwards, when they come into the point of view which those had who uttered these sayings, they understand them and are willing to let the words go; for at any time they can use words as good when occasion comes. If we live truly, we shall see truly. It is as easy for the strong man to be strong, as it is for the weak to be weak. When we have new perception we shall gladly disburden the memory of its hoarded treasures as old rubbish. When a man lives with God, his voice shall be as sweet as the murmur of the brook and the rustle of the corn.

And now at last the highest truth on this subject remains unsaid; probably cannot be said: for all that we say is the far-off remembering of the intuition. That thought by what I can now nearest approach to say it, is this. When good is near you, when you have life in yourself, it is not by any known or accustomed way; you shall not discern the footprints of any other; you shall not see face of man; you shall not hear any name;—the way, the thought, the good, shall be wholly strange and new. It shall exclude example and experience. You take the way from man, not to man. All persons that ever existed are its forgotten ministers. Fear and hope are alike beneath it. There is somewhat low even in hope. In the hour of vision there is nothing that can be called gratitude, nor properly joy. The soul raised over passion beholds identity and eternal causation, perceives the self-existence of Truth and Right, and calms itself with knowing that all things go well. Vast spaces of nature, the Atlantic Ocean, the South Sea; long intervals of time, years, centuries, are of no account. This which I think and feel underlay every former state of life and circumstances, as it does underlie my present, and what is called life and what is called death.

Life only avails, not the having lived. Power

ceases in the instant of repose; it resides in the moment of transition from a past to a new state, in the shooting of the gulf, in the darting to an aim. This one fact the world hates; that the soul *becomes;* for that forever degrades the past, turns all riches to poverty, all reputation to a shame, confounds the saint with the rogue, shoves Jesus and Judas equally aside. Why then do we prate of self-reliance? Inasmuch as the soul is present there will be power not confident but agent. To talk of reliance is a poor external way of speaking. Speak rather of that which relies because it works and is. Who has more obedience than I masters me, though he should not raise his finger. Round him I must revolve by the gravitation of spirits. We fancy it rhetoric when we speak of eminent virtue. We do not yet see that virtue is Height, and that a man or a company of men, plastic and permeable to principles, by the law of nature must overpower and ride all cities, nations, kings, rich men, poets, who are not.

This is the ultimate fact which we so quickly reach on this, as on every topic, the resolution of all into the ever-blessed ONE. Self-existence is the attribute of the Supreme Cause, and it constitutes the measure of good by the degree in which it enters into all lower forms. All things real are so by so much virtue as they contain. Commerce, husbandry, hunting, whaling, war, eloquence, personal weight, are somewhat, and engage my respect as examples of its presence and impure action. I see the same law working in nature for conservation and growth. Power is, in nature, the essential measure of right. Nature suffers nothing to remain in her kingdoms which cannot help itself. The genesis and maturation of a planet, its poise and orbit, the bended tree recovering itself from the strong wind, the vital resources of every animal and vegetable, are demonstrations of the self-sufficing and therefore self-relying soul.

Thus all concentrates: let us not rove; let us sit at home with the cause. Let us stun and astonish the intruding rabble of men and books and institutions by a simple declaration of the divine fact. Bid the invaders take the shoes from off their feet, for God is here within. Let our simplicity judge them, and our docility to our own law demonstrate the poverty of nature and fortune beside our native riches.

But now we are a mob. Man does not stand in awe of man, nor is his genius admonished to stay at home, to put itself in communication with the internal ocean, but it goes abroad to beg a cup of water of the urns of other men. We must go alone. I like the silent church before the service begins, better than any preaching. How far off, how cool, how chaste the persons look, begirt each one with a precinct or sanctuary! So let us always sit. Why should we assume the faults of our friend, or wife, or father, or child, because they sit around our hearth,

or are said to have the same blood? All men have my blood and I all men's. Not for that will I adopt their petulance or folly, even to the extent of being ashamed of it. But your isolation must not be mechanical, but spiritual, that is, must be elevation. At times the whole world seems to be in conspiracy to importune you with emphatic trifles. Friend, climate, child, sickness, fear, want, charity, all knock at once at thy closet door and say,—"Come out unto us." But keep thy state; come not into their confusion. The power men possess to annoy me I give them by a weak curiosity. No man can come near me but through my act. "What we love that we have, but by desire we bereave ourselves of the love."

If we cannot at once rise to the sanctities of obedience and faith, let us at least resist our temptations; let us enter into the state of war and wake Thor and Woden, courage and constancy, in our Saxon breasts. This is to be done in our smooth times by speaking the truth. Check this lying hospitality and lying affection. Live no longer to the expectation of these deceived and deceiving people with whom we converse. Say to them, "O father, O mother, O wife, O brother, O friend, I have lived with you after appearances hitherto. Henceforward I am the truth's. Be it known unto you that henceforward I obey no law less than the eternal law. I will have no covenants but proximities. I shall endeavor to nourish my parents, to support my family, to be the chaste husband of one wife,—but these relations I must fill after a new and unprecedented way. I appeal from your customs. I must be myself. I cannot break myself any longer for you, or you. If you can love me for what I am, we shall be the happier. If you cannot, I will still seek to deserve that you should. I will not hide my tastes or aversions. I will so trust that what is deep is holy, that I will do strongly before the sun and moon whatever inly rejoices me and the heart appoints. If you are noble, I will love you; if you are not, I will not hurt you and myself by hypocritical attentions. If you are true, but not in the same truth with me, cleave to your companions; I will seek my own. I do this not selfishly but humbly and truly. It is alike your interest, and mine, and all men's, however long we have dwelt in lies, to live in truth. Does this sound harsh to-day? You will soon love what is dictated by your nature as well as mine, and if we follow the truth it will bring us out safe at last."—But so may you give these friends pain. Yes, but I cannot sell my liberty and my power, to save their sensibility. Besides, all persons have their moments of reason, when they look out into the region of absolute truth; then will they justify me and do the same thing.

The populace think that your rejection of popular standards is a rejection of all standard, and mere antinomianism; and the bold sensualist will use the name of philosophy to gild his crimes. But the law of consciousness abides. There are two confessionals, in one or the other of which we must be shriven. You may fulfil your round of duties by clearing yourself in the *direct*, or in the *reflex* way. Consider whether you have satisfied your relations to father, mother, cousin, neighbor, town, cat and dog— whether any of these can upbraid you. But I may also neglect this reflex standard and absolve me to myself. I have my own stern claims and perfect circle. It denies the name of duty to many offices that are called duties. But if I can discharge its debts it enables me to dispense with the popular code. If any one imagines that this law is lax, let him keep its commandment one day.

And truly it demands something godlike in him who has cast off the common motives of humanity and has ventured to trust himself for a taskmaster. High be his heart, faithful his will, clear his sight, that he may in good earnest be doctrine, society, law, to himself, that a simple purpose may be to him as strong as iron necessity is to others!

If any man consider the present aspects of what is called by distinction *society*, he will see the need of these ethics. The sinew and heart of man seem to be drawn out, and we are become timorous, desponding whimperers. We are afraid of truth, afraid of fortune, afraid of death, and afraid of each other. Our age yields no great and perfect persons. We want men and women who shall renovate life and our social state, but we see that most natures are insolvent, cannot satisfy their own wants, have an ambition out of all proportion to their practical force and do lean and beg day and night continually. Our housekeeping is mendicant, our arts, our occupations, our marriages, our religion we have not chosen, but society has chosen for us. We are parlor soldiers. We shun the rugged battle of fate, where strength is born.

If our young men miscarry in their first enterprises they lose all heart. If the young merchant fails, men say he is *ruined*. If the finest genius studies at one of our colleges and is not installed in an office within one year afterwards in the cities or suburbs of Boston or New York, it seems to his friends and to himself that he is right in being disheartened and in complaining the rest of his life. A sturdy lad from New Hampshire or Vermont, who in turn tries all the professions, who *teams it, farms it, peddles*, keeps a school, preaches, edits a newspaper, goes to Congress, buys a township, and so forth, in successive years, and always like a cat falls on his feet, is worth a hundred of these city dolls. He walks abreast with his days and feels no shame in not "studying a profession," for he does not postpone his life, but lives already. He has not one chance, but a hundred chances. Let a Stoic open the resources of man and tell men they are not leaning willows, but can and must detach themselves; that with the exercise of self-trust, new powers shall appear; that a man is the word made flesh, born to shed healing to the nations; that he should be ashamed of our compassion, and that the moment he acts from himself, tossing the laws, the books, idolatries and customs out of the window, we pity him no more but thank and revere him;—and that teacher shall restore the life of man to splendor and make his name dear to all history.

It is easy to see that a greater self-reliance must work a revolution in all the offices and relations of men; in their religion; in their education; in their pursuits; their modes of living; their association; in their property; in their speculative views.

1. In what prayers do men allow themselves! That which they call a holy office is not so much as brave and manly. Prayer looks abroad and asks for some foreign addition to come through some foreign virtue, and loses itself in endless mazes of natural and supernatural, and mediatorial and miraculous. Prayer that craves a particular commodity, anything less than all good, is vicious. Prayer is the contemplation of the facts of life from the highest point of view. It is the soliloquy of a beholding and jubilant soul. It is the spirit of God pronouncing his works good. But prayer as a means to effect a private end is meanness and theft. It supposes dualism and not unity in nature and consciousness. As soon as the man is at one with God, he will not beg. He will then see prayer in all action. The prayer of the farmer kneeling in his field to weed it, the prayer of the rower kneeling with the stroke of his oar, are true prayers heard throughout nature, though for cheap ends. Caratach, in Fletcher's *Bonduca*, when admonished to inquire the mind of the god Audate, replies,—

> His hidden meaning lies in our endeavors;
> Our valors are our best gods.

Another sort of false prayers are our regrets. Discontent is the want of self-reliance: it is infirmity of will. Regret calamities if you can thereby help the sufferer; if not attend your own work and already the evil begins to be repaired. Our sympathy is just as base. We come to them who weep foolishly and sit down and cry for company, instead of imparting to them truth and health in rough electric shocks, putting them once more in communication with their own reason. The secret of fortune is joy in our hands. Welcome evermore to gods and men is the self-helping man. For him all doors are flung wide; him all tongues greet, all honors crown, all eyes follow with desire. Our love goes out to him and embraces him because he did not need it. We solicitously and apologetically caress and celebrate him because he held on his way and scorned our disapprobation. The gods love him because men hated him. "To the persevering mortal," said Zoroaster, "the blessed Immortals are swift."

As men's prayers are a disease of the will, so are their creeds a disease of the intellect. They say with those foolish Israelites, "Let not God speak to us, lest we die. Speak thou, speak any man with us, and we will obey." Everywhere I am hindered of meeting God in my brother, because he has shut his own temple doors and recites fables merely of his brother's, or his brother's brother's God. Every new mind is a new classification. If it prove a mind of uncommon activity and power, a Locke, a Lavoisier, a Hutton,[4] a Bentham, a Fourier, it imposes its classification on other men, and lo! a new system. In proportion to the depth of the thought, and so to the number of the objects it touches and brings within reach of the pupil, is his complacency. But chiefly is this apparent in creeds and churches, which are also classifications of some powerful mind acting on the elemental thought of duty and man's relation to the Highest. Such is Calvinism, Quakerism, Swedenborgism. The pupil takes the same delight in subordinating everything to the new terminology as a girl who has just learned botany in seeing a new earth and new seasons thereby. It will happen for a time that the pupil will find his intellectual power has grown by the study of his master's mind. But in all unbalanced minds the classification is idolized, passes for the end and not for a speedily exhaustible means, so that the walls of the system blend to their eye in the remote horizon with the walls of the universe; the luminaries of heaven seem to them hung on the arch their master built. They cannot imagine how you aliens have any right to see,—how you can see; "It must be somehow that you stole the light from us." They do not yet perceive that light, unsystematic, indomitable, will break into any cabin, even into theirs. Let them chirp awhile and call it their own. If they are honest and do well, presently their neat new pinfold will be too strait and low, will crack, will lean, will rot and vanish, and the immortal light, all young and joyful, million-orbed, million-colored, will beam over the universe as on the first morning.

2. It is for want of self-culture that the superstition of Travelling, whose idols are Italy, England, Egypt, retains its fascination for all educated Americans. They who made England, Italy, or Greece venerable in the imagination, did so by sticking fast where they were, like an axis of the earth. In manly hours we feel that duty is our place. The soul is no traveller; the wise man stays at home, and when his necessities, his duties, on any occasion call him from his house, or into foreign lands, he is at home still and shall make men sensible by the expression of his countenance that he goes, the missionary of wisdom

and virtue, and visits cities and men like a sovereign and not like an interloper or a valet.

I have no churlish objection to the circumnavigation of the globe for the purposes of art, of study, and benevolence, so that the man is first domesticated, or does not go abroad with the hope of finding somewhat greater than he knows. He who travels to be amused, or to get somewhat which he does not carry, travels away from himself, and grows old even in youth among old things. In Thebes, in Palmyra, his will and mind have become old and dilapidated as they. He carries ruins to ruins.

Travelling is a fool's paradise. Our first journeys discover to us the indifference of places. At home I dream that at Naples, at Rome, I can be intoxicated with beauty and lose my sadness. I pack my trunk, embrace my friends, embark on the sea and at last wake up in Naples, and there beside me is the stern fact, the sad self, unrelenting, identical, that I fled from. I seek the Vatican and the palaces. I affect to be intoxicated with sights and suggestions, but I am not intoxicated. My giant goes with me wherever I go.

3. But the rage of travelling is a symptom of a deeper unsoundness affecting the whole intellectual action. The intellect is vagabond, and our system of education fosters restlessness. Our minds travel when our bodies are forced to stay at home. We imitate; and what is imitation but the travelling of the mind? Our houses are built with foreign taste; our shelves are garnished with foreign ornaments; our opinions, our tastes, our faculties, lean, and follow the Past and the Distant. The soul created the arts wherever they have flourished. It was in his own mind that the artist sought his model. It was an application of his own thought to the thing to be done and the conditions to be observed. And why need we copy the Doric or the Gothic model? Beauty, convenience, grandeur of thought and quaint expression are as near to us as to any, and if the American artist will study with hope and love the precise thing to be done by him, considering the climate, the soil, the length of the day, the wants of the people, the habit and form of the government, he will create a house in which all these will find themselves fitted, and taste and sentiment will be satisfied also.

Insist on yourself; never imitate. Your own gift you can present every moment with the cumulative force of a whole life's cultivation; but of the adopted talent of another you have only an extemporaneous half possession. That which each can do best, none but his Maker can teach him. No man yet knows what it is, nor can, till that person has exhibited it. Where is the master who could have taught Shakspeare? Where is the master who could have instructed Franklin, or Washington, or Bacon, or Newton? Every great man is a unique. The Scipion-

[4]James Hutton (1726–97), a Scottish geologist.

ism of Scipio is precisely that part he could not borrow. Shakspeare will never be made by the study of Shakspeare. Do that which is assigned you, and you cannot hope too much or dare too much. There is at this moment for you an utterance brave and grand as that of the colossal chisel of Phidias, or trowel of the Egyptians, or the pen of Moses or Dante, but different from all these. Not possibly will the soul, all rich, all eloquent, with thousand-cloven tongue, deign to repeat itself; but if you can hear what these patriarchs say, surely you can reply to them in the same pitch of voice; for the ear and the tongue are two organs of one nature. Abide in the simple and noble regions of thy life, obey thy heart, and thou shall reproduce the Foreworld again.

4. As our Religion, our Education, our Art look abroad, so does our spirit of society. All men plume themselves on the improvement of society, and no man improves.

Society never advances. It recedes as fast on one side as it gains on the other. It undergoes continual changes; it is barbarous, it is civilized, it is christianized, it is rich, it is scientific; but this change is not amelioration. For everything that is given something is taken. Society acquires new arts and loses old instincts. What a contrast between the well-clad, reading, writing, thinking American, with a watch, a pencil, and a bill of exchange in his pocket, and the naked New Zealander, whose property is a club, a spear, a mat and an undivided twentieth of a shed to sleep under! But compare the health of the two men and you shall see that the white man has lost his aboriginal strength. If the traveller tell us truly, strike the savage with a broad-axe and in a day or two the flesh shall unite and heal as if you struck the blow into soft pitch, and the same blow shall send the white to his grave.

The civilized man has built a coach, but has lost the use of his feet. He is supported on crutches, but lacks so much support of muscle. He has a fine Geneva watch, but he fails of the skill to tell the hour by the sun. A Greenwich nautical almanac he has, and so being sure of the information when he wants it, the man in the street does not know a star in the sky. The solstice he does not observe; the equinox he knows as little; and the whole bright calendar of the year is without a dial in his mind. His notebooks impair his memory; his libraries overload his wit; the insurance-office increases the number of accidents; and it may be a question whether machinery does not encumber; whether we have not lost by refinement some energy, by a Christianity, entrenched in establishments and forms, some vigor of wild virtue. For every Stoic was a Stoic; but in Christendom where is the Christian?

There is no more deviation in the moral standard than in the standard of height or bulk. No greater

men are now than ever were. A singular equality may be observed between the great men of the first and of the last ages; nor can all the science, art, religion, and philosophy of the nineteenth century avail to educate greater men than Plutarch's heroes, three or four and twenty centuries ago. Not in time is the race progressive. Phocion, Socrates, Anaxagoras, Diogenes, are great men, but they leave no class. He who is really of their class will not be called by their name, but will be his own man, and in his turn the founder of a sect. The arts and inventions of each period are only its costume and do not invigorate men. The harm of the improved machinery may compensate its good. Hudson and Behring accomplished so much in their fishing-boats as to astonish Parry and Franklin, whose equipment exhausted the resources of science and art. Galileo, with an opera-glass, discovered a more splendid series of celestial phenomena than any one since. Columbus found the New World in an undecked boat. It is curious to see the periodical disuse and perishing of means and machinery which were introduced with loud laudation a few years or centuries before. The great genius returns to essential man. We reckoned the improvements of the art of war among the triumphs of science, and yet Napoleon conquered Europe by the bivouac, which consisted of falling back on naked valor and disencumbering it of all aids. The Emperor held it impossible to make a perfect army, says Las Cases,[5] "without abolishing our arms, magazines, commissaries, and carriages, until, in imitation of the Roman custom, the soldier should receive his supply of corn, grind it in his handmill and bake his bread himself."

Society is a wave. The wave moves onward, but the water of which it is composed does not. The same particle does not rise from the valley to the ridge. Its unity is only phenomenal. The persons who make up a nation to-day, next year die, and their experience dies with them.

And so the reliance on Property, including the reliance on governments which protect it, is the want of self-reliance. Men have looked away from themselves and at things so long that they have come to esteem the religious, learned and civil institutions as guards of property, and they deprecate assaults on these, because they feel them to be assaults on property. They measure their esteem of each other by what each has, and not by what each is. But a cultivated man becomes ashamed of his property, out of new respect for his nature. Especially he hates what he has if he see that it is accidental,—came to him by inheritance, or gift, or crime; then he feels that it is not having; it does not belong to him, has no root in him and merely lies

[5] Bartolomé de las Casas (1474–1566), Bishop of Chiapas, Guatemala; known as the "Apostle of the Indies."

there because no revolution or no robber takes it away. But that which a man is, does always by necessity acquire; and what the man acquires, is living property, which does not wait the beck of rulers, or mobs, or revolutions, or fire, or storm, or bankruptcies, but perpetually renews itself wherever the man breathes. "Thy lot or portion of life,"[6] said the Caliph Ali, "is seeking after thee; therefore be at rest from seeking after it." Our dependence on these foreign goods leads us to our slavish respect for numbers. The political parties meet in numerous conventions; the greater the concourse and with each new uproar of announcement, The delegation from Essex! The Democrats from New Hampshire! The Whigs of Maine! the young patriot feels himself stronger than before by a new thousand of eyes and arms. In like manner the reformers summon conventions and vote and resolve in multitude. Not so, O friends! will the God deign to enter and inhabit you, but by a method precisely the reverse. It is only as a man puts off all foreign support and stands alone that I see him to be strong and to prevail. He is weaker by every recruit to his banner. Is not a man better than a town? Ask nothing of men, and, in the endless mutation, thou only firm column must presently appear the upholder of all that surrounds thee. He who knows that power is inborn, that he is weak because he has looked for good out of him and elsewhere, and, so perceiving, throws himself unhesitatingly on his thought, instantly rights himself, stands in the erect position, commands his limbs, works miracles; just as a man who stands on his feet is stronger than a man who stands on his head.

So use all that is called Fortune. Most men gamble with her, and gain all, and lose all, as her wheel rolls. But do thou leave as unlawful these winnings, and deal with Cause and Effect, the chancellors of God. In the Will work and acquire, and thou hast chained the wheel of Chance, and shall sit hereafter out of fear from her rotations. A political victory, a rise of rents, the recovery of your sick or the return of your absent friend, or some other favorable event raises your spirits, and you think good days are preparing for you. Do not believe it. Nothing can bring you peace but yourself. Nothing can bring you peace but the triumph of principles.

1841

The Poet

Emerson gave a lecture titled "The Poet" in 1841; after that he went on to develop his ideas into this second and almost entirely different statement. This essay, written at the height of Emerson's powers, explains his conception of

[6] Fourth caliph of the Muslim Arab empire, and cousin and son-in-law of Mohammed.

the new poet who would emerge in America. Although Emerson rejects the conventional poetry based on the past and looks to America for the ideal poet, many of his ideas are consistent with the romantic tradition and, in some respects, with modern poetic theory. Emerson's faith in the poet as seer and sayer, his belief that the poet through language and symbol could bring man and nature together, his concern with organic form, and his certainty that the great poet would liberate men are some of the major convictions that become part of his theory. However, these convictions, and indeed the entire essay, must be understood in the context of Emerson's idealism. "The Poet," Poe's "The Poetic Principle," and Whitman's "1855 Preface" are the most important critical statements about poetry written by American Romantics.

Those who are esteemed umpires of taste are often persons who have acquired some knowledge of admired pictures or sculptures, and have an inclination for whatever is elegant; but if you inquire whether they are beautiful souls, and whether their own acts are like fair pictures, you learn that they are selfish and sensual. Their cultivation is local, as if you should rub a log of dry wood in one spot to produce fire, all the rest remaining cold. Their knowledge of the fine arts is some study of rules and particulars, or some limited judgment of color or form, which is exercised for amusement or for show. It is a proof of the shallowness of the doctrine of beauty as it lies in the minds of our amateurs, that men seem to have lost the perception of the instant dependence of form upon soul. There is no doctrine of forms in our philosophy. We were put into our bodies, as fire is put into a pan to be carried about; but there is no accurate adjustment between the spirit and the organ, much less is the latter the germination of the former. So in regard to other forms, the intellectual men do not believe in any essential dependence of the material world on thought and volition. Theologians think it a pretty air-castle to talk of the spiritual meaning of a ship or a cloud, of a city or a contract, but they prefer to come again to the solid ground of historical evidence; and even the poets are contented with a civil and conformed manner of living, and to write poems from the fancy, at a safe distance from their own experience. But the highest minds of the world have never ceased to explore the double meaning, or shall I say, the quadruple or the centuple or much more manifold meaning, of every sensuous fact; Orpheus, Empedocles, Heraclitus, Plato, Plutarch, Dante, Swedenborg, and the masters of sculpture, picture and poetry. For we are not pans and barrows, nor even porters of the fire and torch-bearers, but children of the fire, made of it, and only the same divinity transmuted and at two or three removes, when we know least about it. And this hidden truth, that the fountains whence all this river of Time, and its creatures, floweth are intrinsically ideal and beautiful, draws us to the consideration of the nature and functions of the Poet, or the man of Beauty; to the means and materials he uses, and to the general aspect of the art in the present time.

The breadth of the problem is great, for the poet is representative. He stands among partial men for the complete man, and apprises us not of his wealth, but of the common wealth. The young man reveres men of genius, because, to speak truly, they are more himself than he is. They receive of the soul as he also receives, but they more. Nature enhances her beauty, to the eye of loving men, from their belief that the poet is beholding her shows at the same time. He is isolated among his contemporaries, by truth and by his art, but with this consolation in his pursuits, that they will draw all men sooner or later. For all men live by truth and stand in need of expression. In love, in art, in avarice, in politics, in labor, in games, we study to utter our painful secret. The man is only half himself, the other half is his expression.

Notwithstanding this necessity to be published, adequate expression is rare. I know not how it is that we need an interpreter, but the great majority of men seem to be minors, who have not yet come into possession of their own, or mutes, who cannot report the conversation they have had with nature. There is no man who does not anticipate a supersensual utility in the sun and stars, earth and water. These stand and wait to render him a peculiar service. But there is some obstruction or some excess of phlegm in our constitution, which does not suffer them to yield the due effect. Too feeble fall the impressions of nature on us to make us artists. Every touch should thrill. Every man should be so much an artist that he could report in conversation what had befallen him. Yet, in our experience, the rays or appulses have sufficient force to arrive at the senses, but not enough to reach the quick and compel the reproduction of themselves in speech. The poet is the person in whom these powers are in balance, the man without impediment, who sees and handles that which others dream of, traverses the whole scale of experience, and is representative of man, in virtue of being the largest power to receive and to impart.

For the Universe has three children, born at one time, which reappear under different names, in every system of thought, whether they be called cause, operation and effect; or, more poetically, Jove, Pluto, Neptune; or, theologically, the Father, the Spirit and the Son; but which we will call here the Knower, the Doer and the Sayer. These stand respectively for the love of truth, for the love of good, and for the love of beauty. These three are equal. Each is that which he is, essentially, so that he cannot be surmounted or analyzed, and each of these three has the power of the others latent in him and his own, patent.

The poet is the sayer, the namer, and represents beauty. He is a sovereign, and stands on the center. For the world is not painted or adorned, but is from the beginning beautiful; and God has not made some beautiful things, but Beauty is the creator of the universe. Therefore the poet is not any permissive potentate, but is emperor in his own right. Criticism is infested with a cant of materialism, which assumes that manual skill and activity is the first merit of all men, and disparages such as say and do not, overlooking the fact, that some men, namely poets, are natural sayers, sent into the world to the end of expression, and confounds them with those whose province is action but who quit it to imitate the sayers. But Homer's words are as costly and admirable to Homer as Agamemnon's victories are to Agamemnon. The poet does not wait for the hero or the sage, but, as they act and think primarily, so he writes primarily what will and must be spoken, reckoning the others, though primaries also, yet, in respect to him, secondaries and servants; as sitters or models in the studio of a painter, or as assistants who bring building-materials to an architect.

For poetry was all written before time was, and whenever we are so finely organized that we can penetrate into that region where the air is music, we hear those primal warblings and attempt to write them down, but we lose ever and anon a word or a verse and substitute something of our own, and thus miswrite the poem. The men of more delicate ear write down these cadences more faithfully, and these transcripts, though imperfect, become the songs of the nations. For nature is as truly beautiful as it is good, or as it is reasonable, and must as much appear as it must be done, or be known. Words and deeds are quite indifferent modes of the divine energy. Words are also actions, and actions are a kind of words.

The sign and credentials of the poet are that he announces that which no man foretold. He is the true and only doctor;[1] he knows and tells; he is the only teller of news, for he was present and privy to the appearance which he describes. He is a beholder of ideas and an utterer of the necessary and causal. For we do not speak now of men of poetical talents, or of industry and skill in metre, but of the true poet. I took part in a conversation the other day concerning a recent writer of lyrics, a man of subtle mind, whose head appeared to be a music-box of delicate tunes and rhythms, and whose skill and command of language we could not sufficiently praise. But when the question arose whether he was

[1] In the sense of teacher.

not only a lyrist but a poet, we were obliged to confess that he is plainly a contemporary, not an eternal man. He does not stand out of our low limitations, like a Chimborazo under the line, running up from a torrid base through all the climates of the globe, with belts of the herbage of every latitude on its high and mottled sides; but this genius is the landscape-garden of a modern house, adorned with fountains and statues, with well-bred men and women standing and sitting in the walks and terraces. We hear, through all the varied music, the ground-tone of conventional life. Our poets are men of talents who sing, and not the children of music. The argument is secondary, the finish of the verses is primary.

For it is not metres, but a metre-making argument that makes a poem,—a thought so passionate and alive that like the spirit of a plant or an animal it has an architecture of its own, and adorns nature with a new thing. The thought and the form are equal in the order of time, but in the order of genesis the thought is prior to the form. The poet has a new thought; he has a whole new experience to unfold; he will tell us how it was with him, and all men will be the richer in his fortune. For the experience of each new age requires a new confession, and the world seems always waiting for its poet. I remember when I was young how much I was moved one morning by tidings that genius had appeared in a youth who sat near me at table. He had left his work and gone rambling none knew whither, and had written hundreds of lines, but could not tell whether that which was in him was therein told; he could tell nothing but that all was changed,—man, beast, heaven, earth and sea. How gladly we listened! how credulous! Society seemed to be compromised. We sat in the aurora of a sunrise which was to put out all the stars. Boston seemed to be at twice the distance it had the night before, or was much farther than that. Rome,—what was Rome? Plutarch and Shakspeare were in the yellow leaf, and Homer no more should be heard of. It is much to know that poetry has been written this very day, under this very roof, by your side. What! that wonderful spirit has not expired! these stony moments are still sparkling and animated! I had fancied that the oracles were all silent, and nature had spent her fires; and behold! all night, from every pore, these fine auroras have been streaming. Every one has some interest in the advent of the poet, and no one knows how much it may concern him. We know that the secret of the world is profound, but who or what shall be our interpreter, we know not. A mountain ramble, a new style of face, a new person, may put the key into our hands. Of course the value of genius to us is in the veracity of its report. Talent may frolic and juggle; genius realizes and adds.

Mankind in good earnest have availed so far in understanding themselves and their work, that the foremost watchman on the peak announces his news. It is the truest word ever spoken, and the phrase will be the fittest, most musical, and the unerring voice of the world for that time.

All that we call sacred history attests that the birth of a poet is the principal event in chronology. Man, never so often deceived, still watches for the arrival of a brother who can hold him steady to a truth until he has made it his own. With what joy I begin to read a poem which I confide in as an inspiration! And now my chains are to be broken; I shall mount above these clouds and opaque airs in which I live,—opaque, though they seem transparent,—and from the heaven of truth I shall see and comprehend my relations. That will reconcile me to life and renovate nature, to see trifles animated by a tendency, and to know what I am doing. Life will no more be a noise; now I shall see men and women, and know the signs by which they may be discerned from fools and satans. This day shall be better than my birthday: then I became an animal; now I am invited into the science of the real. Such is the hope, but the fruition is postponed. Oftener it falls that this winged man, who will carry me into the heaven, whirls me into mists, then leaps and frisks about with me as it were from cloud to cloud, still affirming that he is bound heavenward; and I, being myself a novice, am slow in perceiving that he does not know the way into the heavens, and is merely bent that I should admire his skill to rise like a fowl or a flying fish, a little way from the ground or the water; but the all-piercing, all-feeding and ocular air of heaven that man shall never inhabit. I tumble down again soon into my old nooks, and lead the life of exaggerations as before, and have lost my faith in the possibility of any guide who can lead me thither where I would be.

But, leaving these victims of vanity, let us, with new hope, observe how nature, by worthier impulses, has insured the poet's fidelity to his office of announcement and affirming, namely by the beauty of things, which becomes a new and higher beauty when expressed. Nature offers all her creatures to him as a picture-language. Being used as a type, a second wonderful value appears in the object, far better than its old value, as the carpenter's stretched cord, if you hold your ear close enough, is musical in the breeze. "Things more excellent than every image," says Jamblichus, "are expressed through images." Things admit of being used as symbols because nature is a symbol, in the whole, and in every part. Every line we can draw in the sand has expression; and there is no body without its spirit or genius. All form is an effect of character; all condition, of the quality of the life; all harmony, of health; and for this reason a perception of beauty should be sympathetic, or proper only to the good. The beautiful rests on the foundations of the necessary. The soul makes the body, as the wise Spenser teaches:—

> So every spirit, as it is more pure,
> And hath in it the more of heavenly light,
> So it the fairer body doth procure
> To habit in, and it more fairly dight,
> With cheerful grace and amiable sight.
> For, of the soul, the body form doth take,
> For soul is form, and doth the body make.

Here we find ourselves suddenly not in a critical speculation but in a holy place, and should go very warily and reverently. We stand before the secret of the world, there where Being passes into Appearance and Unity into Variety.

The Universe is the externization of the soul. Wherever the life is, that bursts into appearance around it. Our science is sensual,[2] and therefore superficial. The earth and the heavenly bodies, physics and chemistry, we sensually treat, as if they were self-existent; but these are the retinue of that Being we have. "The mighty heaven," said Proclus,[3] "exhibits, in its transfigurations, clear images of the splendor of intellectual perceptions; being moved in conjunction with the unapparent periods of intellectual natures." Therefore science always goes abreast with the just elevation of the man, keeping step with religion and metaphysics; or the state of science is an index of our self-knowledge. Since everything in nature answers to a moral power, if any phenomenon remains brute and dark it is because the corresponding faculty in the observer is not yet active.

No wonder then, if these waters be so deep, that we hover over them with a religious regard. The beauty of the fable proves the importance of the sense; to the poet, and to all others; or, if you please, every man is so far a poet as to be susceptible of these enchantments of nature; for all men have the thoughts whereof the universe is the celebration. I find that the fascination resides in the symbol. Who loves nature? Who does not? Is it only poets, and men of leisure and cultivation, who live with her? No; but also hunters, farmers, grooms and butchers, though they express their affection in their choice of life and not in their choice of words. The writer wonders what the coachman or the hunter values in riding, in horses and dogs. It is not superficial qualities. When you talk with him he holds these at as slight a rate as you. His worship is sympathetic; he has no definitions, but he is commanded in nature by the living power which he feels to be

there present. No imitation or playing of these things would content him; he loves the earnest of the north wind, of rain, of stone and wood and iron. A beauty not explicable is dearer than a beauty which we can see to the end of. It is nature the symbol, nature certifying the supernatural, body overflowed by life which he worships with coarse, but sincere rites.

The inwardness and mystery of this attachment drives men of every class to the use of emblems. The schools of poets and philosophers are not more intoxicated with their symbols than the populace with theirs. In our political parties, compute the power of badges and emblems. See the great ball which they roll from Baltimore to Bunker Hill![4] In the political processions, Lowell goes in a loom, and Lynn in a shoe, and Salem in a ship. Witness the cider-barrel, the log-cabin, the hickory-stick, the palmetto, and all the cognizances of party. See the power of national emblems. Some stars, lilies, leopards, a crescent, a lion, an eagle, or other figure which came into credit God knows how, on an old rag of bunting, blowing in the wind on a fort at the ends of the earth, shall make the blood tingle under the rudest or the most conventional exterior. The people fancy they hate poetry, and they are all poets and mystics!

Beyond this universality of the symbolic language, we are apprised of the divineness of this superior use of things, whereby the world is a temple whose walls are covered with emblems, pictures and commandments of the Deity,—in this, that there is no fact in nature which does not carry the whole sense of nature; and the distinctions which we make in events and in affairs, of low and high, honest and base, disappear when nature is used as a symbol. Thought makes everything fit for use. The vocabulary of an omniscient man would embrace words and images excluded from polite conversation. What would be base, or even obscene, to the obscene, becomes illustrious, spoken in a new connection of thought. The piety of the Hebrew prophets purges their grossness. The circumcision is an example of the power of poetry to raise the low and offensive. Small and mean things serve as well as great symbols. The meaner the type by which a law is expressed, the more pungent it is, and the more lasting in the memories of men; just as we choose the smallest box or case in which any needful utensil can be carried. Bare lists of words are found suggestive to an imaginative and excited mind; as it is related of Lord Chatham that he was accustomed to read in Bailey's Dictionary when he was preparing to speak in Parliament. The poorest experience is rich enough for all the purposes of expressing thought. Why covet a knowledge of new facts? Day and night,

[2] Having to do with the senses generally; the word does not carry the modern connotation of sexuality.

[3] A Greek philosopher, a Neo-Platonist and follower of Plotinus.

[4] A political publicity stunt performed by the Whigs in 1840 to represent their steadily growing majority.

house and garden, a few books, a few actions, serve us as well as would all trades and all spectacles. We are far from having exhausted the significance of the few symbols we use. We can come to use them yet with a terrible simplicity. It does not need that a poem should be long. Every word was once a poem. Every new relation is a new word. Also we use defects and deformities to a sacred purpose, so expressing our sense that the evils of the world are such only to the evil eye. In the old mythology, mythologists observe, defects are ascribed to divine natures, as lameness to Vulcan, blindness to Cupid, and the like,—to signify exuberances.

For, as it is dislocation and detachment from the life of God that makes things ugly, the poet, who re-attaches things to nature and the Whole,—re-attaching even artificial things and violations of nature, to nature, by a deeper insight,—disposes very easily of the most disagreeable facts. Readers of poetry see the factory-village and the railway, and fancy that the poetry of the landscape is broken up by these; for these works of art are not yet consecrated in their reading; but the poet sees them fall within the great Order not less than the beehive or the spider's geometrical web. Nature adopts them very fast into her vital circles, and the gliding train of cars she loves like her own. Besides, in a centered mind, it signifies nothing how many mechanical inventions you exhibit. Though you add millions, and never so surprising, the fact of mechanics has not gained a grain's weight. The spiritual fact remains unalterable, by many or by few particulars; as no mountain is of any appreciable height to break the curve of the sphere. A shrewd country-boy goes to the city for the first time, and the complacent citizen is not satisfied with his little wonder. It is not that he does not see all the fine houses and know that he never saw such before, but he disposes of them as easily as the poet finds place for the railway. The chief value of the new fact is to enhance the great and constant fact of Life, which can dwarf any and every circumstance, and to which the belt of wampum and the commerce of America, are alike.

The world being thus put under the mind for verb and noun, the poet is he who can articulate it. For though life is great, and fascinates and absorbs; and though all men are intelligent of the symbols through which it is named; yet they cannot originally use them. We are symbols and inhabit symbols; workmen, work, and tools, words and things, birth and death, all are emblems; but we sympathize with the symbols, and, being infatuated with the economical uses of things, we do not know that they are thoughts. The poet, by an ulterior intellectual perception, gives them a power which makes their old use forgotten, and puts eyes, and a tongue, into every dumb and inanimate object. He perceives the independence of the thought on the symbol, the stability of the thought, the accidency and fugacity of the symbol. As the eyes of Lyncaeus were said to see through the earth, so the poet turns the world to glass, and shows us all things in their right series and procession. For through that better perception he stands one step nearer to things, and sees the flowing or metamorphosis; perceives that thought is multiform; that within the form of every creature is a force impelling it to ascend into a higher form; and following with his eyes the life, uses the forms which express that life, and so his speech flows with the flowing of nature. All the facts of the animal economy, sex, nutriment, gestation, birth, growth, are symbols of the passage of the world into the soul of man, to suffer there a change and reappear a new and higher fact. He uses forms according to the life, and not according to the form. This is true science. The poet alone knows astronomy, chemistry, vegetation and animation, for he does not stop at these facts, but employs them as signs. He knows why the plain or meadow of space was strown with these flowers we call suns and moons and stars; why the great deep is adorned with animals, with men, and gods; for, in every word he speaks he rides on them as the horses of thought.

By virtue of this science the poet is the Namer or Language-maker, naming things sometimes after their appearance, sometimes after their essence, and giving to every one its own name and not another's, thereby rejoicing the intellect, which delights in detachment or boundary. The poets made all the words, and therefore language is the archives of history, and, if we must say it, a sort of tomb of the muses. For though the origin of most of our words is forgotten, each word was at first a stroke of genius, and obtained currency because for the moment it symbolized the world to the first speaker and to the hearer. The etymologist finds the deadest word to have been once a brilliant picture. Language is fossil poetry. As the limestone of the continent consists of infinite masses of the shells of animalcules, so language is made up of images or tropes, which now, in their secondary use, have long ceased to remind us of their poetic origin. But the poet names the thing because he sees it, or comes one step nearer to it than any other. This expression or naming is not art, but a second nature, grown out of the first, as a leaf out of a tree. What we call nature is a certain self-regulated motion or change; and nature does all things by her own hands, and does not leave another to baptize her but baptizes herself; and this through the metamorphosis again. I remember that a certain poet[5] described it to me thus:—

Genius is the activity which repairs the decays of

[5] Emerson himself is that poet; he is working here with Platonic ideas.

things, whether wholly or partly of a material and finite kind. Nature, through all her kingdoms, insures herself. Nobody cares for planting the poor fungus; so she shakes down from the gills of one agaric countless spores, any one of which, being preserved, transmits new billions of spores tomorrow or next day. The new agaric of this hour has a chance which the old one had not. This atom of seed is thrown into a new place, not subject to the accidents which destroyed its parent two rods off. She makes a man; and having brought him to ripe age, she will no longer run the risk of losing this wonder at a blow, but she detaches from him a new self, that the kind may be safe from accidents to which the individual is exposed. So when the soul of the poet has come to ripeness of thought, she detaches and sends away from it its poems or songs,— a fearless, sleepless, deathless progeny, which is not exposed to the accidents of the weary kingdom of time; a fearless, vivacious offspring, clad with wings (such was the virtue of the soul out of which they came) which carry them fast and far, and infix them irrecoverably into the hearts of men. These wings are the beauty of the poet's soul. The songs, thus flying immortal from their mortal parent, are pursued by clamorous flights of censures, which swarm in far greater numbers and threaten to devour them; but these last are not winged. At the end of a very short leap they fall plump down and rot, having received from the souls out of which they came no beautiful wings. But the melodies of the poet ascend and leap and pierce into the deeps of infinite time.

So far the bard taught me, using his freer speech. But nature has a higher end, in the production of new individuals, than security, namely *ascension*, or the passage of the soul into higher forms. I knew in my younger days the sculptor who made the statue of the youth which stands in the public garden. He was, as I remember, unable to tell directly what made him happy or unhappy, but by wonderful indirections he could tell. He rose one day, according to his habit, before the dawn, and saw the morning break, grand as the eternity out of which it came, and, for many days after, he strove to express this tranquillity, and lo! his chisel had fashioned out of marble the form of a beautiful youth, Phosphorus, whose aspect is such that it is said all persons who look on it become silent. The poet also resigns himself to his mood, and that thought which agitated him is expressed, but *alter idem*,[6] in a manner totally new. The expression is organic, or the new type which things themselves take when liberated. As, in the sun, objects paint their images on the retina of the eye, so they, sharing the aspiration of the whole

universe, tend to paint a far more delicate copy of their essence in his mind. Like the metamorphosis of things into higher organic forms is their change into melodies. Over everything stands its daemon or soul, and, as the form of the thing is reflected by the eye, so the soul of the thing is reflected by a melody. The sea, the mountain-ridge, Niagara, and every flower-bed, pre-exist, or super-exist, in pre-cantations, which sail like odors in the air, and when any man goes by with an ear sufficiently fine, he overhears them and endeavors to write down the notes without diluting or depraving them. And herein is the legtimation of criticism, in the mind's faith that the poems are a corrupt version of some text in nature with which they ought to be made to tally. A rhyme in one of our sonnets should not be less pleasing than the iterated nodes of a seashell, or the resembing difference of a group of flowers. The pairing of the birds is an idyl, not tedious as our idyls are; a tempest is a rough ode, without falsehood or rant; a summer, with its harvest sown, reaped and stored, is an epic song, subordinating how many admirably executed parts. Why should not the symmetry and truth that modulate these, glide into our spirits, and we participate the invention of nature?

This insight, which expresses itself by what is called Imagination, is a very high sort of seeing, which does not come by study, but by the intellect being where and what it sees, by sharing the path or circuit of things through forms, and so making them translucid to others. The path of things is silent. Will they suffer a speaker to go with them? A spy they will not suffer; a lover, a poet, is the transcendency of their own nature,—him they will suffer. The condition of true naming, on the poet's part, is his resigning himself to the divine *aura* which breathes through forms, and accompanying that.

It is a secret which every intellectual man quickly learns, that, beyond the energy of his possessed and conscious intellect he is capable of a new energy (as of an intellect doubled on itself), by abandonment to the nature of things; that beside his privacy of power as an individual man, there is a great public power on which he can draw, by unlocking, at all risks, his human doors, and suffering the ethereal tides to roll and circulate through him: then he is caught up into the life of the Universe, his speech is thunder, his thought is law, and his words are universally intelligible as the plants and animals. The poet knows that he speaks adequately then only when he speaks somewhat wildly, or "with the flower of the mind"; not with the intellect used as an organ but with the intellect released from all service and suffered to take its direction from its celestial life; or as the ancients were wont to express themselves, not with intellect alone but with the

[6] The same, yet different.

intellect inebriated by nectar. As the traveller who has lost his way throws his reins on his horse's neck and trusts to the instinct of the animal to find his road, so must we do with the divine animal who carries us through this world. For if in any manner we can stimulate this instinct, new passages are opened for us into nature; the mind flows into and through things hardest and highest, and the metamorphosis is possible.

This is the reason why bards love wine, mead, narcotics, coffee, tea, opium, the fumes of sandalwood and tobacco, or whatever other procurers of animal exhilaration. All men avail themselves of such means as they can, to add this extraordinary power to their normal powers; and to this end they prize conversation, music, pictures, sculpture, dancing, theatres, travelling, war, mobs, fires, gaming, politics, or love, or science, or animal intoxication,— which are several coarser or finer *quasi*-mechanical substitutes for the true nectar, which is the ravishment of the intellect by coming nearer to the fact. These are auxiliaries to the centrifugal tendency of a man, to his passage out into free space, and they help him to escape the custody of that body in which he is pent up, and of that jail-yard of individual relations in which he is enclosed. Hence a great number of such as were professionally expressers of Beauty, as painters, poets, musicians and actors, have been more than others wont to lead a life of pleasure and indulgence; all but the few who received the true nectar; and, as it was a spurious mode of attaining freedom, as it was an emancipation not into the heavens but into the freedom of baser places, they were punished for that advantage they won, by a dissipation and deterioration. But never can any advantage be taken of nature by a trick. The spirit of the world, the great calm presence of the Creator, comes not forth to the sorceries of opium or of wine. The sublime vision comes to the pure and simple soul in a clean and chaste body. That is not an inspiration which we owe to narcotics, but some counterfeit excitement and fury. Milton says that the lyric poet may drink wine and live generously, but the epic poet, he who shall sing of the gods and their descent unto men, must drink water out of a wooden bowl. For poetry is not "Devil's wine," but God's wine. It is with this as it is with toys. We fill the hands and nurseries of our children with all manner of dolls, drums and horses; withdrawing their eyes from the plain face and sufficing objects of nature, the sun and the moon, the animals, the water and stones, which should be their toys. So the poet's habit of living should be set on a key so low that the common influences should delight him. His cheerfulness should be the gift of the sunlight; the air should suffice for his inspiration, and he should be tipsy with water. That spirit which suffices quiet hearts, which seems to come forth to such from every dry knoll of sere grass, from every pine-stump and half-imbedded stone on which the dull March sun shines, comes forth to the poor and hungry, and such as are of simple taste. If thou fill thy brain with Boston and New York, with fashion and covetousness, and wilt stimulate thy jaded senses with wine and French coffee, thou shalt find no radiance of wisdom in the lonely waste of the pinewoods.

If the imagination intoxicates the poet, it is not inactive in other men. The metamorphosis excites in the beholder an emotion of joy. The use of symbols has a certain power of emancipation and exhilaration for all men. We seem to be touched by a wand which makes us dance and run about happily, like children. We are like persons who come out of a cave or cellar into the open air. This is the effect on us of tropes, fables, oracles and all poetic forms. Poets are thus liberating gods. Men have really got a new sense, and found within their world another world, or nest of worlds; for, the metamorphosis once seen, we divine that it does not stop. I will not now consider how much this makes the charm of algebra and the mathematics, which also have their tropes, but it is felt in every definition; as, when Aristotle defines *space* to be an immovable vessel in which things are contained;—or when Plato defines a *line* to be a flowing point; or *figure* to be a bound of solid; and many the like. What a joyful sense of freedom we have when Vitruvius announces the old opinion of artists that no architect can build any house well who does not know something of anatomy. When Socrates, in Charmides, tells us that the soul is cured of its maladies by certain incantations, and that these incantations are beautiful reasons, from which temperance is generated in souls; when Plato[7] calls the world an animal, and Timaeus affirms that plants also are animals; or affirms a man to be a heavenly tree, growing with his root, which is his head, upward; and, as George Chapman, following him, writes,—

> So in our tree of man, whose nervie root
> Springs in his top;—

when Orpheus speaks of hoariness as "that white flower which marks extreme old age"; when Proclus calls the universe the statue of the intellect; when Chaucer, in his praise of "Gentilesse," compares good blood in mean condition to fire, which, though carried to the darkest house betwixt this and the mount of Caucasus, will yet hold its natural office and burn as bright as if twenty thousand men did it

---

[7] Both *Charmides* and *Timaeus* were written by Plato.

behold; when John saw, in the Apocalypse, the ruin of the world through evil, and the stars fall from heaven as the fig tree casteth her untimely fruit; when Aesop reports the whole catalogue of common daily relations through the masquerade of birds and beasts;—we take the cheerful hint of the immortality of our essence and its versatile habit and escapes, as when the gypsies say of themselves, "it is in vain to hang them, they cannot die."

The poets are thus liberating gods. The ancient British bards had for the title of their order, "Those who are free throughout the world." They are free, and they make free. An imaginative book renders us much more service at first, by stimulating us through its tropes, than afterward when we arrive at the precise sense of the author. I think nothing is of any value in books excepting the transcendental and extraordinary. If a man is inflamed and carried away by his thought, to that degree that he forgets the authors and the public and heeds only this one dream which holds him like an insanity, let me read his paper, and you may have all the arguments and histories and criticism. All the value which attaches to Pythagoras, Paracelsus, Cornelius Agrippa,[8] Cardan,[9] Kepler, Swedenborg, Schelling, Oken,[10] or any other who introduces questionable facts into his cosmogony, as angels, devils, magic, astrology, palmistry, mesmerism, and so on, is the certificate we have of departure from routine, and that here is a new witness. That also is the best success in conversation, the magic of liberty, which puts the world like a ball in our hands. How cheap even the liberty then seems; how mean to study, when an emotion communicates to the intellect the power to sap and upheave nature; how great the perspective! nations, times, systems, enter and disappear like threads in tapestry of large figure and many colors; dream delivers us to dream, and while the drunkenness lasts we will sell our bed, our philosophy, our religion, in our opulence.

There is good reason why we should prize this liberation. The fate of the poor shepherd, who, blinded and lost in the snowstorm, perishes in a drift within a few feet of his cottage door, is an emblem of the state of man. On the brink of the waters of life and truth, we are miserably dying. The inaccessibleness of every thought but that we are in, is wonderful. What if you come near to it; you are as remote when you are nearest as when you are far-

thest. Every thought is also a prison; every heaven is also a prison. Therefore we love the poet, the inventor, who in any form, whether in an ode or in an action or in looks and behavior, has yielded us a new thought. He unlocks our chains and admits us to a new scene.

This emancipation is dear to all men, and the power to impart it, as it must come from greater depth and scope of thought, is a measure of intellect. Therefore all books of the imagination endure, all which ascend to that truth that the writer sees nature beneath him, and uses it as his exponent. Every verse or sentence possessing this virtue will take care of its own immortality. The religions of the world are the ejaculations of a few imaginative men.

But the quality of the imagination is to flow, and not to freeze. The poet did not stop at the color or the form, but read their meaning; neither may he rest in this meaning, but he makes the same objects exponents of his new thought. Here is the difference betwixt the poet and the mystic, that the last nails a symbol to one sense, which was a true sense for a moment, but soon becomes old and false. For all symbols are fluxional; all language is vehicular and transitive, and is good, as ferries and horses are, for conveyance, not as farms and houses are, for homestead. Mysticism consists in the mistake of an accidental and individual symbol for an universal one. The morning-redness happens to be the favorite meteor to the eyes of Jacob Behmen,[11] and comes to stand to him for truth and faith; and, he believes, should stand for the same realities to every reader. But the first reader prefers as naturally the symbol of a mother and child, or a gardener and his bulb, or a jeweller polishing a gem. Either of these, or of a myriad more, are equally good to the person to whom they are significant. Only they must be held lightly, and be very willingly translated into the equivalent terms which others use. And the mystic must be steadily told,—All that you say is just as true without the tedious use of that symbol as with it. Let us have a little algebra, instead of this trite rhetoric,—universal signs, instead of these village symbols,—and we shall both be gainers. The history of hierarchies seems to show that all religious error consisted in making the symbol too stark and solid, and was at last nothing but an excess of the organ of language.

Swedenborg, of all men in the recent ages, stands eminently for the translator of nature into thought. I do not know the man in history to whom things stood so uniformly for words. Before him the metamorphosis continually plays. Every thing on which his eye rests, obeys the impulses of moral nature.

[8]Cornelius Agrippa (1486–1535), scholar and writer on occult sciences.
[9]Jerome Cardan (1501–76), Italian mathematician and writer on medicine and occult sciences.
[10]Lorenz Oken (1779–1851), German naturalist and participant in the Naturphilosophie movement.
[11]Jacob Boehme (1575–1624), a German mystic philosopher.

The figs become grapes whilst he eats them. When some of his angels affirmed a truth, the laurel twig which they held blossomed in their hands. The noise which at a distance appeared like gnashing and thumping, on coming nearer was found to be the voice of disputants. The men in one of his visions, seen in heavenly light, appeared like dragons, and seemed in darkness; but to each other they appeared as men, and when the light from heaven shone into their cabin, they complained of the darkness, and were compelled to shut the window that they might see.

There was this perception in him which makes the poet or seer an object of awe and terror, namely that the same man or society of men may wear one aspect to themselves and their companions, and a different aspect to higher intelligences. Certain priests, whom he describes as conversing very learnedly together, appeared to the children who were at some distance, like dead horses; and many the like misappearances. And instantly the mind inquires whether these fishes under the bridge, yonder oxen in the pasture, those dogs in the yard, are immutably fishes, oxen and dogs, or only so appear to me, and perchance to themselves appear upright men; and whether I appear as a man to all eyes. The Brahmins and Pythagoras propounded the same question, and if any poet has witnessed the transformation he doubtless found it in harmony with various experiences. We have all seen changes as considerable in wheat and caterpillars. He is the poet and shall draw us with love and terror, who sees through the flowing vest the firm nature, and can declare it.

I look in vain for the poet whom I describe. We do not with sufficient plainness or sufficient profoundness address ourselves to life, nor dare we chaunt our own times and social circumstance. If we filled the day with bravery, we should not shrink from celebrating it. Time and nature yield us many gifts, but not yet the timely man, the new religion, the reconciler, whom all things await. Dante's praise is that he dared to write his autobiography in colossal cipher, or into universality. We have yet had no genius in America, with tyrannous eye, which knew the value of our incomparable materials, and saw, in the barbarism and materialism of the times, another carnival of the same gods whose picture he so much admires in Homer; then in the Middle Ages; then in Calvinism. Banks and tariffs, the newspaper and caucus, Methodism and Unitarianism, are flat and dull to dull people, but rest on the same foundations of wonder as the town of Troy and the temple of Delphi, and are as swiftly passing away. Our log-rolling, our stumps and their politics, our fisheries, our Negroes and Indians, our boats and our repudiations, the wrath of rogues and the pusillanimity of honest men, the northern trade, the southern

planting, the western clearing, Oregon and Texas, are yet unsung. Yet America is a poem in our eyes; its ample geography dazzles the imagination, and it will not wait long for metres. If I have not found that excellent combination of gifts in my countrymen which I seek, neither could I aid myself to fix the idea of the poet by reading now and then in Chalmers's collection of five centuries of English poets. These are wits more than poets, though there have been poets among them. But when we adhere to the ideal of the poet, we have our difficulties even with Milton and Homer. Milton is too literary, and Homer too literal and historical.

But I am not wise enough for a national criticism, and must use the old largeness a little longer, to discharge my errand from the muse to the poet concerning his art.

Art is the path of the creator to his work. The paths or methods are ideal and eternal, though few men ever see them; not the artist himself for years, or for a lifetime, unless he come into the conditions. The painter, the sculptor, the composer, the epic rhapsodist, the orator, all partake one desire, namely to express themselves symmetrically and abundantly, not dwarfishly and fragmentarily. They found or put themselves in certain conditions, as, the painter and sculptor before some impressive human figures; the orator into the assembly of the people; and the others in such scenes as each has found exciting to his intellect; and each presently feels the new desire. He hears a voice, he sees a beckoning. Then he is apprised, with wonder, what herds of daemons hem him in. He can no more rest; he says, with the old painter, "By God it is in me and must go forth of me." He pursues a beauty, half seen, which flies before him. The poet pours out verses in every solitude. Most of the things he says are conventional, no doubt; but by and by he says something which is original and beautiful. That charms him. He would say nothing else but such things. In our way of talking we say, "That is yours, this is mine;" but the poet knows well that it is not his; that it is as strange and beautiful to him as to you; he would fain hear the like eloquence at length. Once having tasted this immortal ichor, he cannot have enough of it, and as an admirable creative power exists in these intellections, it is of the last importance that these things get spoken. What a little of all we know is said! What drops of all the sea of our science are baled up! and by what accident it is that these are exposed, when so many secrets sleep in nature! Hence the necessity of speech and song; hence these throbs and heart-beatings in the orator, at the door of the assembly, to the end namely that thought may be ejaculated as Logos, or Word.

Doubt not, O poet, but persist. Say "It is in me, and shall out." Stand there, balked and dumb, stuttering and stammering, hissed and hooted, stand and strive, until at last rage draw out of thee that *dream-power* which every night shows thee is thine own; a power transcending all limit and privacy, and by virtue of which a man is the conductor of the whole river of electricity. Nothing walks, or creeps, or grows, or exists, which must not in turn arise and walk before him as exponent of his meaning. Comes he to that power, his genius is no longer exhaustible. All the creatures by pairs and by tribes pour into his mind as into a Noah's ark, to come forth again to people a new world. This is like the stock of air for our respiration or for the combustion of our fireplace; not a measure of gallons, but the entire atmosphere if wanted. And therefore the rich poets, as Homer, Chaucer, Shakspeare, and Raphael, have obviously no limits to their works except the limits of their lifetime, and resemble a mirror carried through the street, ready to render an image of every created thing.

O poet! a new nobility is conferred in groves and pastures, and not in castles or by the sword-blade any longer. The conditions are hard, but equal. Thou shalt leave the world, and know the muse only. Thou shalt not know any longer the times, customs, graces, politics, or opinions of men, but shalt take all from the muse. For the time of towns is tolled from the world by funereal chimes, but in nature the universal hours are counted by succeeding tribes of animals and plants, and by growth of joy on joy. God wills also that thou abdicate a manifold and duplex life, and that thou be content that others speak for thee. Others shall be thy gentlemen and shall represent all courtesy and worldly life for thee; others shall do the great and resounding actions also. Thou shalt lie close hid with nature, and canst not be afforded to the Capitol or the Exchange. The world is full of renunciations and apprenticeships, and this is thine; thou must pass for a fool and a churl for a long season. This is the screen and sheath in which Pan has protected his well-beloved flower, and thou shalt be known only to thine own, and they shall console thee with tenderest love. And thou shalt not be able to rehearse the names of thy friends in thy verse, for an old shame before the holy ideal. And this is the reward: that the ideal shall be real to thee, and the impressions of the actual world shall fall like summer rain, copious, but not troublesome to thy invulnerable essence. Thou shalt have the whole land for thy park and manor, the sea for thy bath and navigation, without tax and without envy; the woods and the rivers thou shalt own, and thou shalt possess that wherein others are only tenants and boarders. Thou true land-lord! sea-lord! air-lord! Wherever snow falls or water flows or birds fly, wherever day and night meet in twilight, wherever the blue heaven is hung by clouds or sown with stars, wherever are forms with transparent boundaries, wherever are outlets into celestial space, wherever is danger, and awe, and love,—there is Beauty, plenteous as rain, shed for thee, and though thou shouldst walk the world over, thou shalt not be able to find a condition inopportune or ignoble.

1844

Experience

"Experience" presents a sharp contrast to Emerson's earlier work ("Nature" and "Self-Reliance," e.g.), for he speaks here from the point of view of a skeptic. Emerson is deeply aware of the paradox man lives—he lives in time, yet he conceives of a world beyond—and of the great limiting forces over which man has no control. The essay conveys Emerson's overwhelming sense of being trapped within experience and of being isolated from the ideal or spirit—the thought world, as Emerson refers to it. Nevertheless, Emerson expresses a continued faith in the thought world, even though he knows that it cannot immediately, if ever, be realized. The essay does not express Emerson's final view of experience, but it does show how seriously he grappled with contradiction, limitation, illusion, and change.

Where do we find ourselves? In a series of which we do not know the extremes, and believe that it has none. We wake and find ourselves on a stair; there are stairs below us, which we seem to have ascended; there are stairs above us, many a one, which go upward and out of sight. But the Genius which according to the old belief stands at the door by which we enter, and gives us the lethe to drink, that we may tell no tales, mixed the cup too strongly, and we cannot shake off the lethargy now at noonday. Sleep lingers all our lifetime about our eyes, as night hovers all day in the boughs of the fir-tree. All things swim and glitter. Our life is not so much threatened as our perception. Ghostlike we glide through nature, and should not know our place again. Did our birth fall in some fit of indigence and frugality in nature, that she was so sparing of her fire and so liberal of her earth that it appears to us that we lack the affirmative principle, and though we have health and reason, yet we have no superfluity of spirit for new creation? We have enough to live and bring the year about, but not an ounce to impart or to invest. Ah that our Genius were a little more of a genius! We are like millers on the lower levels of a stream, when the factories above them have exhausted the water. We too fancy that the upper people must have raised their dams.

If any of us knew what we were doing, or where we are going, then when we think we best know! We do not know to-day whether we are busy or idle. In times when we thought ourselves indolent, we have afterwards discovered that much was accomplished and much was begun in us. All our days are so unprofitable while they pass, that 't is wonderful where or when we ever got anything of this which we call wisdom, poetry, virtue. We never got it on any dated calendar day. Some heavenly days must have been intercalated somewhere, like those that Hermes won with dice of the Moon, that Osiris might be born.[1] It is said all martyrdoms looked mean when they were suffered. Every ship is a romantic object, except that we sail in. Embark, and the romance quits our vessel and hangs on every other sail in the horizon. Our life looks trivial, and we shun to record it. Men seem to have learned of the horizon the art of perpetual retreating and reference. "Yonder uplands are rich pasturage, and my neighbor has fertile meadow, but my field," says the querulous farmer, "only holds the world together." I quote another man's saying; unluckily that other withdraws himself in the same way, and quotes me. 'T is the trick of nature thus to degrade to-day; a good deal of buzz, and somewhere a result slipped magically in. Every roof is agreeable to the eye until it is lifted; then we find tragedy and moaning women and hard-eyed husbands and deluges of lethe, and the men ask, "What's the news?" as if the old were so bad. How many individuals can we count in society? how many actions? how many opinions? So much of our time is preparation, so much is routine, and so much retrospect, that the pith of each man's genius contracts itself to a very few hours. The history of literature—take the net result of Tiraboschi, Warton, or Schlegel[2]—is a sum of very few ideas and of very few original tales; all the rest being variation of these. So in this great society wide lying around us, a critical analysis would find very few spontaneous actions. It is almost all custom and gross sense. There are even few opinions, and these seem organic in the speakers, and do not disturb the universal necessity.

What opium is instilled into all disaster! It shows formidable as we approach it, but there is at last no rough rasping friction, but the most slippery sliding surfaces; we fall soft on a thought; *Ate Dea* is gentle,—

> "Over men's heads walking aloft,
> With tender feet treading so soft."

People grieve and bemoan themselves, but it is not half so bad with them as they say. There are moods in which we court suffering, in the hope that here at least we shall find reality, sharp peaks and edges of truth. But it turns out to be scene-painting and counterfeit. The only thing grief has taught me is to know how shallow it is. That, like all the rest, plays about the surface, and never introduces me into the reality, for contact with which we would even pay the costly price of sons and lovers. Was it Boscovich[3] who found out that bodies never come in contact? Well, souls never touch their objects. An innavigable sea washes with silent waves between us and the things we aim at and converse with. Grief too will make us idealists. In the death of my son, now more than two years ago, I seem to have lost a beautiful estate,—no more.[4] I cannot get it nearer to me. If to-morrow I should be informed of the bankruptcy of my principal debtors, the loss of my property would be a great inconvenience to me, perhaps, for many years; but it would leave me as it found me,—neither better nor worse. So is it with this calamity; it does not touch me; something which I fancied was a part of me, which could not be torn away without tearing me nor enlarged without enriching me, falls off from me and leaves no scar. It was caducous. I grieve that grief can teach me nothing, nor carry me one step into real nature. The Indian[5] who was laid under a curse that the wind should not blow on him, nor water flow to him, nor fire burn him, is a type of us all. The dearest events are summer-rain, and we the Para coats that shed every drop. Nothing is left us now but death. We look to that with a grim satisfaction, saying, There at least is reality that will not dodge us.

I take this evanescence and lubricity of all objects, which lets them slip through our fingers then when we clutch hardest, to be the most unhandsome part of our condition. Nature does not like to be observed, and likes that we should be her fools and playmates. We may have the sphere for our cricket-ball, but not a berry for our philosophy. Direct strokes she never gave us power to make; all our blows glance, all our hits are accidents. Our relations to each other are oblique and casual.

Dream delivers us to dream, and there is no end to illusion. Life is a train of moods like a string of beads, and as we pass through them they prove to be many-colored lenses which paint the world their own hue, and each shows only what lies in its focus.

---

[1] A legend recounted in Plutarch's *Morals,* "Of Isis and Osiris." Hermes won the extra days so that his child by Rhea could be born. The Sun (Rhea's husband) had forbade the child to be born on any day.

[2] Tiraboschi (1731–94), Italian literary historian. Thomas Warton (1728–90), author of *History of English Poetry.* Schlegel: August (1767–1845), who translated Shakespeare into German, or Friedrich (1772–1829) who wrote on German literature and Hindu poetry.

[3] Guiseppe Boscovich (1711–87), Serbo-Croatian astronomer and mathematician; one of the first to adopt Newton's gravitational theory.

[4] Waldo Emerson, his father's first child, died in 1842 at the age of five.

[5] In Robert Southey's *The Curse of Kehama.*

From the mountain you see the mountain. We animate what we can, and we see only what we animate. Nature and books belong to the eyes that see them. It depends on the mood of the man whether he shall see the sunset or the fine poem. There are always sunsets, and there is always genius; but only a few hours so serene that we can relish nature or criticism. The more or less depends on structure or temperament. Temperament is the iron wire on which the beads are strung. Of what use is fortune or talent to a cold and defective nature? Who cares what sensibility or discrimination a man has at some time shown, if he falls asleep in his chair? or if he laugh and giggle? or if he apologize? or is infected with egotism? or thinks of his dollar? or cannot go by food? or has gotten a child in his boyhood? Of what use is genius, if the organ is too convex or too concave and cannot find a focal distance within the actual horizon of human life? Of what use, if the brain is too cold or too hot, and the man does not care enough for results to stimulate him to experiment, and hold him up in it? or if the web is too finely woven, too irritable by pleasure and pain, so that life stagnates from too much reception without due outlet? Of what use to make heroic vows of amendment, if the same old law-breaker is to keep them? What cheer can the religious sentiment yield, when that is suspected to be secretly dependent on the seasons of the year and the state of the blood? I knew a witty physician who found the creed in the biliary duct, and used to affirm that if there was disease in the liver, the man became a Calvinist, and if that organ was sound, he became a Unitarian. Very mortifying is the reluctant experience that some unfriendly excess or imbecility neutralizes the promise of genius. We see young men who owe us a new world, so readily and lavishly they promise, but they never acquit the debt; they die young and dodge the account; or if they live they lose themselves in the crowd.

Temperament also enters fully into the system of illusions and shuts us in a prison of glass which we cannot see. There is an optical illusion about every person we meet. In truth they are all creatures of given temperament, which will appear in a given character, whose boundaries they will never pass; but we look at them, they seem alive, and we presume there is impulse in them. In the moment it seems impulse; in the year, in the lifetime, it turns out to be a certain uniform tune which the revolving barrel of the music-box must play. Men resist the conclusion in the morning, but adopt it as the evening wears on, that temper prevails over everything of time, place and condition, and is inconsumable in the flames of religion. Some modifications the moral sentiment avails to impose, but the individual texture holds its dominion, if not to bias the moral

judgments, yet to fix the measure of activity and of enjoyment.

I thus express the law as it is read from the platform of ordinary life, but must not leave it without noticing the capital exception. For temperament is a power which no man willingly hears any one praise but himself. On the platform of physics we cannot resist the contracting influences of so-called science. Temperament puts all divinity to rout. I know the mental proclivity of physicians. I hear the chuckle of the phrenologists. Theoretic kidnappers and slave-drivers, they esteem each man the victim of another, who winds him round his finger by knowing the law of his being; and, by such cheap signboards as the color of his beard or the slope of his occiput, reads the inventory of his fortunes and character. The grossest ignorance does not disgust like this impudent knowingness. The physicians say they are not materialists; but they are:—Spirit is matter reduced to an extreme thinness: O *so* thin!—But the definition of *spiritual* should be, *that which is its own evidence*. What notions do they attach to love! what to religion! One would not willingly pronounce these words in their hearing, and give them the occasion to profane them. I saw a gracious gentleman who adapts his conversation to the form of the head of the man he talks with! I had fancied that the value of life lay in its inscrutable possibilities; in the fact that I never know, in addressing myself to a new individual, what may befall me. I carry the keys of my castle in my hand, ready to throw them at the feet of my lord, whenever and in what disguise soever he shall appear. I know he is in the neighborhood, hidden among vagabonds. Shall I preclude my future by taking a high seat and kindly adapting my conversation to the shape of heads? When I come to that, the doctors shall buy me for a cent.— "But, sir, medical history; the report to the Institute; the proven facts!"—I distrust the facts and the inferences. Temperament is the veto or limitation-power in the constitution, very justly applied to restrain an opposite excess in the constitution, but absurdly offered as a bar to original equity. When virtue is in presence, all subordinate powers sleep. On its own level, or in view of nature, temperament is final. I see not, if one be once caught in this trap of so-called sciences, any escape for the man from the links of the chain of physical necessity. Given such an embryo, such a history must follow. On this platform one lives in a sty of sensualism, and would soon come to suicide. But it is impossible that the creative power should exclude itself. Into every intelligence there is a door which is never closed, through which the creator passes. The intellect, seeker of absolute truth, or the heart, lover of absolute good, intervenes for our succor, and at one whisper of these high powers we awake from ineffectual struggles with this nightmare. We hurl it into its own hell, and cannot again contract ourselves to so base a state.

The secret of the illusoriness is in the necessity of a succession of moods or objects. Gladly we would anchor, but the anchorage is quicksand. This onward trick of nature is too strong for us: *Pero si muove.*[6] When at night I look at the moon and stars, I seem stationary, and they to hurry. Our love of the real draws us to permanence, but health of body consists in circulation, and sanity of mind in variety or facility of association. We need change of objects. Dedication to one thought is quickly odious. We house with the insane, and must humor them; then conversation dies out. Once I took such delight in Montaigne that I thought I should not need any other book; before that, in Shakspeare; then in Plutarch; then in Plotinus; at one time in Bacon; afterwards in Goethe; even in Bettine; but now I turn the pages of either of them languidly, whilst I still cherish their genius. So with pictures; each will bear an emphasis of attention once, which it cannot retain, though we fain would continue to be pleased in that manner. How strongly I have felt of pictures that when you have seen one well, you must take your leave of it; you shall never see it again. I have had good lessons from pictures which I have since seen without emotion or remark. A deduction must be made from the opinion which even the wise express on a new book or occurrence. Their opinion gives me tidings of their mood, and some vague guess at the new fact, but is nowise to be trusted as the lasting relation between that intellect and that thing. The child asks, "Mamma, why don't I like the story as well as when you told it me yesterday?" Alas! child, it is even so with the oldest cherubim of knowledge. But will it answer thy question to say, Because thou wert born to a whole and this story is a particular? The reason of the pain this discovery causes us (and we make it late in respect to works of art and intellect) is the plaint of tragedy which murmurs from it in regard to persons, to friendship and love.

That immobility and absence of elasticity which we find in the arts, we find with more pain in the artist. There is no power of expansion in men. Our friends early appear to us as representatives of certain ideas which they never pass or exceed. They stand on the brink of the ocean of thought and power, but they never take the single step that would bring them there. A man is like a bit of Labrador spar, which has no lustre as you turn it in your hand until you come to a particular angle; then it shows deep and beautiful colors. There is no adaptation or universal applicability in men, but

[6] "Still, it moves."

each has his special talent, and the mastery of successful men consists in adroitly keeping themselves where and when that turn shall be oftenest to be practised. We do what we must, and call it by the best names we can, and would fain have the praise of having intended the result which ensues. I cannot recall any form of man who is not superfluous sometimes. But is not this pitiful? Life is not worth the taking, to do tricks in.

Of course it needs the whole society to give the symmetry we seek. The party-colored wheel must revolve very fast to appear white. Something is earned too by conversing with so much folly and defect. In fine, whoever loses, we are always of the gaining party. Divinity is behind our failures and follies also. The plays of children are nonsense, but very educative nonsense. So it is with the largest and solemnest things, with commerce, government, church, marriage, and so with the history of every man's bread, and the ways by which he is to come by it. Like a bird which alights nowhere, but hops perpetually from bough to bough, is the Power which abides in no man and in no woman, but for a moment speaks from this one, and for another moment from that one.

But what help from these fineries or pedantries? What help from thought? Life is not dialectics. We, I think, in these times, have had lessons enough of the futility of criticism. Our young people have thought and written much on labor and reform, and for all that they have written, neither the world nor themselves have got on a step. Intellectual tasting of life will not supersede muscular activity. If a man should consider the nicety of the passage of a piece of bread down his throat, he would starve. At Education Farm[7] the noblest theory of life sat on the noblest figures of young men and maidens, quite powerless and melancholy. It would not rake or pitch a ton of hay; it would not rub down a horse; and the men and maidens it left pale and hungry. A political orator wittily compared our party promises to western roads, which opened stately enough, with planted trees on either side to tempt the traveller, but soon became narrow and narrower and ended in a squirrel-track and ran up a tree. So does culture with us; it ends in headache. Unspeakably sad and barren does life look to those who a few months ago were dazzled with the splendor of the promise of the times. "There is now no longer any right course of action nor any self-devotion left among the Iranis."[8] Objections and criticism we have had our fill

[7] Brook Farm (1841–47), a communal-living experiment with which Emerson sympathized during its early years.
[8] Quoted from the *Desatir*, presumably a collection of the writings of ancient Persian prophets, including Zoroaster (Whicher, *Selections*, n. 492).

of. There are objections to every course of life and action, and the practical wisdom infers an indifferency, from the omnipresence of objection. The whole frame of things preaches indifferency. Do not craze yourself with thinking, but go about your business anywhere. Life is not intellectual or critical, but sturdy. Its chief good is for well-mixed people who can enjoy what they find, without question. Nature hates peeping, our mothers speak her very sense when they say, "Children, eat your victuals, and say no more of it." To fill the hour,—that is happiness; to fill the hour and leave no crevice for a repentance or an approval. We live amid surfaces, and the true art of life is to skate well on them. Under the oldest mouldiest conventions a man of native force prospers just as well as in the newest world, and that by skill of handling and treatment. He can take hold anywhere. Life itself is a mixture of power and form, and will not bear the least excess of either. To finish the moment, to find the journey's end in every step of the road, to live the greatest number of good hours, is wisdom. It is not the part of men, but of fanatics, or of mathematicians if you will, to say that, the shortness of life considered, it is not worth caring whether for so short a duration we were sprawling in want or sitting high. Since our office is with moments, let us husband them. Five minutes of to-day are worth as much to me as five minutes in the next millennium. Let us be poised, and wise, and our own, to-day. Let us treat the men and women well; treat them as if they were real; perhaps they are. Men live in their fancy, like drunkards whose hands are too soft and tremulous for successful labor. It is a tempest of fancies, and the only ballast I know is a respect to the present hour. Without any shadow of doubt, amidst this vertigo of shows and politics, I settle myself ever the firmer in the creed that we should not postpone and refer and wish, but do broad justice where we are, by whomsoever we deal with, accepting our actual companions and circumstances, however humble or odious, as the mystic officials to whom the universe has delegated its whole pleasure for us. If these are mean and malignant, their contentment, which is the last victory of justice, is a more satisfying echo to the heart than the voice of poets and the casual sympathy of admirable persons. I think that however a thoughtful man may suffer from the defects and absurdities of his company, he cannot without affectation deny to any set of men and women a sensibility to extraordinary merit. The coarse and frivolous have an instinct of superiority, if they have not a sympathy, and honor it in their blind capricious way with sincere homage.

The fine young people despise life, but in me, and in such as with me are free from dyspepsia, and to whom a day is a sound and solid good, it is a great excess of politeness to look scornful and to cry for company. I am grown by sympathy a little eager and sentimental, but leave me alone and I should relish every hour and what it brought me, the potluck of the day as heartily as the oldest gossip in the barroom. I am thankful for small mercies. I compared notes with one of my friends who expects everything of the universe and is disappointed when anything is less than the best, and I found that I begin at the other extreme, expecting nothing, and am always full of thanks for moderate goods. I accept the clangor and jangle of contrary tendencies. I find my account in sots and bores also. They give a reality to the circumjacent picture which such a vanishing meteorous appearance can ill spare. In the morning I awake and find the old world, wife, babes and mother, Concord and Boston, the dear old spiritual world and even the dear old devil not far off. If we will take the good we will find, asking no questions, we shall have heaping measures. The great gifts are not got by analysis. Everything good is on the highway. The middle region of our being is the temperate zone. We may climb into the thin and cold realm of pure geometry and lifeless science, or sink into that of sensation. Between these extremes is the equator of life, of thought, of spirit, of poetry,—a narrow belt. Moreover in popular experience everything good is on the highway. A collector peeps into all the picture-shops of Europe for a landscape of Poussin,[9] a crayon-sketch of Salvator;[10] but the Transfiguration, the Last Judgment, the Communion of Saint Jerome, and what are as transcendent as these, are on the walls of the Vatican, the Uffizi or the Louvre, where every footman may see them; to say nothing of Nature's pictures in every street, of sunsets and sunrises every day, and the sculpture of the human body never absent. A collector recently bought at public auction, in London, for one hundred and fifty-seven guineas, an autograph of Shakspeare; but for nothing a schoolboy can read Hamlet and can detect secrets of highest concernment yet unpublished therein. I think I will never read any but the commonest books,—the Bible, Homer Dante, Shakspeare and Milton. Then we are impatient of so public a life and plane, and run hither and thither for nooks and secrets. The imagination delights in the woodcraft of Indians, trappers and bee-hunters. We fancy that we are strangers, and not so intimately domesticated in the planet as the wild man and the wild beast and

---

[9] (1593/94–1665), great French painter of the 17th century; exponent of pictorial classicism
[10] Salvator Rosa (1615–73), Italian painter known for his wild landscapes and battle scenes.

bird. But the exclusion reaches them also; reaches the climbing, flying, gliding, feathered and four-footed man. Fox and woodchuck, hawk and snipe and bittern, when nearly seen, have no more root in the deep world than man, and are just such superficial tenants of the globe. Then the new molecular philosophy shows astronomical interspaces betwixt atom and atom, shows that the world is all outside; it has no inside.

The mid-world is best. Nature, as we know her, is no saint. The lights of the church, the ascetics, Gentoos and corn-eaters, she does not distinguish by any favor. She comes eating and drinking and sinning. Her darlings, the great, the strong, the beautiful, are not children of our law; do not come out of the Sunday School, nor weigh their food, nor punctually keep the commandments. If we will be strong with her strength we must not harbor such disconsolate consciences, borrowed too from the consciences of other nations. We must set up the strong present tense against all the rumors of wrath, past or to come. So many things are unsettled which it is of the first importance to settle;—and, pending their settlement, we will do as we do. Whilst the debate goes forward on the equity of commerce, and will not be closed for a century or two, New and Old England may keep shop. Law of copyright and international copyright is to be discussed, and in the interim we will sell our books for the most we can. Expediency of literature, reason of literature, lawfulness of writing down a thought, is questioned; much is to say on both sides, and, while the fight waxes hot, thou, dearest scholar, stick to thy foolish task, add a line every hour, and between whiles add a line. Right to hold land, right of property, is disputed, and the conventions convene, and before the vote is taken, dig away in your garden, and spend your earnings as a waif or godsend to all serene and beautiful purposes. Life itself is a bubble and a scepticism, and a sleep within a sleep. Grant it, and as much more as they will,—but thou, God's darling! heed thy private dream; thou wilt not be missed in the scorning and scepticism; there are enough of them; stay there in thy closet and toil until the rest are agreed what to do about it. Thy sickness, they say, and thy puny habit require that thou do this or avoid that, but know that thy life is a flitting state, a tent for a night, and do thou, sick or well, finish that stint. Thou art sick, but shalt not be worse, and the universe, which holds thee dear, shall be the better.

Human life is made up of the two elements, power and form, and the proportion must be invariably kept if we would have it sweet and sound. Each of these elements in excess makes a mischief as hurtful as its defect. Everything runs to excess; every good quality is noxious if unmixed, and, to carry the danger to the edge of ruin, nature causes each man's peculiarity to superabound. Here, among the farms, we adduce the scholars as examples of this treachery. They are nature's victims of expression. You who see the artist, the orator, the poet, too near, and find their life no more excellent than that of mechanics or farmers, and themselves victims of partiality, very hollow and haggard, and pronounce them failures, not heroes, but quacks,—conclude very reasonably that these arts are not for man, but are disease. Yet nature will not bear you out. Irresistible nature made men such, and makes legions more of such, every day. You love the boy reading in a book, gazing at a drawing or a cast; yet what are those millions who read and behold, but incipient writers and sculptors? Add a little more of that quality which now reads and sees, and they will seize the pen and chisel. And if one remembers how innocently he began to be an artist, he perceives that nature joined with his enemy. A man is a golden impossibility. The line he must walk is a hair's breadth. The wise through excess of wisdom is made a fool.

How easily, if fate would suffer it, we might keep forever these beautiful limits, and adjust ourselves, once for all, to the perfect calculation of the kingdom of known cause and effect. In the street and in the newspapers, life appears so plain a business that manly resolution and adherence to the multiplication-table through all weathers will insure success. But ah! presently comes a day, or is it only a half-hour, with its angel-whispering,—which discomfits the conclusions of nations and of years! To-morrow again every thing looks real and angular, the habitual standards are reinstated, common-sense is as rare as genius,—is the basis of genius, and experience is hands and feet to every enterprise;—and yet, he who should do his business on this understanding would be quickly bankrupt. Power keeps quite another road than the turnpikes of choice and will; namely the subterranean and invisible tunnels and channels of life. It is ridiculous that we are diplomatists, and doctors, and considerate people; there are no dupes like these. Life is a series of surprises, and would not be worth taking or keeping if it were not. God delights to isolate us every day, and hide from us the past and the future. We would look about us, but with grand politeness he draws down before us an impenetrable screen of purest sky, and another behind us of purest sky. "You will not remember," he seems to say, "and you will not expect." All good conversation, manners and action come from a spontaneity which forgets usages and makes the moment great. Nature hates calculators; her methods are saltatory and impulsive. Man lives by pulses; our organic movements are such; and the chemical and ethereal agents are undulatory and alternate; and the mind goes antagonizing on, and never prospers but by fits. We thrive by casualties. Our chief experiences have been casual. The most attractive class of people are those who are powerful obliquely and not by the direct stroke; men of genius, but not yet accredited; one gets the cheer of their light without paying too great a tax. Theirs is the beauty of the bird or the morning light, and not of art. In the thought of genius there is always a surprise; and the moral sentiment is well called "the newness," for it is never other; as new to the oldest intelligence as to the young child;—"the kingdom that cometh without observation."[11] In like manner, for practical success, there must not be too much design. A man will not be observed in doing that which he can do best. There is a certain magic about his properest action which stupefies your powers of observation, so that though it is done before you, you wist not of it. The art of life has a pudency, and will not be exposed. Every man is an impossibility until he is born; every thing impossible until we see a success. The ardors of piety agree at last with the coldest scepticism,—that nothing is of us or our works,—that all is of God. Nature will not spare us the smallest leaf of laurel. All writing comes by the grace of God, and all doing and having. I would gladly be moral and keep due metes and bounds, which I dearly love, and allow the most to the will of man; but I have set my heart on honesty in this chapter, and I can see nothing at last, in success or failure, than more or less of vital force supplied from the Eternal. The results of life are uncalculated and uncalculable. The years teach much which the days never know. The persons who compose our company converse, and come and go, and design and execute many things, and somewhat comes of it all, but an unlooked-for result. The individual is always mistaken. He designed many things, and drew in other persons as coadjutors, quarrelled with some or all, blundered much, and something is done; all are a little advanced, but the individual is always mistaken. It turns out somewhat new and very unlike what he promised himself.

The ancients, struck with this irreducibleness of the elements of human life to calculation, exalted Chance into a divinity; but that is to stay too long at the spark, which glitters truly at one point, but the universe is warm with the latency of the same fire. The miracle of life which will not be expounded but will remain a miracle, introduces a new element. In the growth of the embryo, Sir Everard Home[12] I

think noticed that the evolution was not from one central point, but coactive from three or more points. Life has no memory. That which proceeds in succession might be remembered, but that which is coexistent, or ejaculated from a deeper cause, as yet far from being conscious, knows not its own tendency. So is it with us, now sceptical or without unity, because immersed in forms and effects all seeming to be of equal yet hostile value, and now religious, whilst in the reception of spiritual law. Bear with these distractions, with this coetaneous growth of the parts; they will one day be *members*, and obey one will. On that one will, on that secret cause, they nail our attention and hope. Life is hereby melted into an expectation or a religion. Underneath the inharmonious and trivial particulars, is a musical perfection; the Ideal journeying always with us, the heaven without rent or seam. Do but observe the mode of our illumination. When I converse with a profound mind, or if at any time being alone I have good thoughts, I do not at once arrive at satisfactions, as when, being thirsty, I drink water; or go to the fire, being cold; no! but I am at first apprised of my vicinity to a new and excellent region of life. By persisting to read or to think, this region gives further sign of itself, as it were in flashes of light, in sudden discoveries of its profound beauty and repose, as if the clouds that covered it parted at intervals and showed the approaching traveller the inland mountains, with the tranquil eternal meadows spread at their base, whereon flocks graze and shepherds pipe and dance. But every insight from this realm of thought is felt as initial, and promises a sequel. I do not make it; I arrive there, and behold what was there already. I make! O no! I clap my hands in infantine joy and amazement before the first opening to me of this august magnificence, old with the love and homage of innumerable ages, young with the life of life, the sunbright Mecca of the desert. And what a future it opens! I feel a new heart beating with the love of the new beauty. I am ready to die out of nature and be born again into this new yet unapproachable America I have found in the West:—

"Since neither now nor yesterday began
  These thoughts, which have been ever, nor yet
    can
    A man be found who their first entrance knew."[13]

If I have described life as a flux of moods, I must now add that there is that in us which changes not and which ranks all sensations and states of mind. The consciousness in each man is a sliding scale, which identifies him now with the First Cause, and

---

[11] See Luke xvii.20.
[12] A Scottish surgeon (1756–1832).

[13] From Sophocles' *Antigone*.

now with the flesh of his body; life above life, in infinite degrees. The sentiment from which it sprung determines the dignity of any deed, and the question ever is, not what you have done or forborne, but at whose command you have done or forborne it.

Fortune, Minerva, Muse, Holy Ghost,—these are quaint names, too narrow to cover this unbounded substance. The baffled intellect must still kneel before this cause, which refuses to be named,—ineffable cause, which every fine genius has essayed to represent by some emphatic symbol, as, Thales by water, Anaximenes by air, Anaxagoras by (Noûs) thought, Zoroaster by fire, Jesus and the moderns by love; and the metaphor of each has become a national religion. The Chinese Mencius has not been the least successful in his generalization. "I fully understand language," he said, "and nourish well my vast-flowing vigor."—"I beg to ask what you call vast-flowing vigor?" said his companion. "The explanation," replied Mencius, "is difficult. This vigor is supremely great, and in the highest degree unbending. Nourish it correctly and do it no injury, and it will fill up the vacancy between heaven and earth. This vigor accords with and assists justice and reason, and leaves no hunger."—In our more correct writing we give to this generalization the name of Being, and thereby confess that we have arrived as far as we can go. Suffice it for the joy of the universe that we have not arrived at a wall, but at interminable oceans. Our life seems not present so much as prospective; not for the affairs on which it is wasted, but as a hint of this vast-flowing vigor. Most of life seems to be mere advertisement of faculty; information is given us not to sell ourselves cheap; that we are very great. So, in particulars, our greatness is always in a tendency or direction, not in an action. It is for us to believe in the rule, not in the exception. The noble are thus known from the ignoble. So in accepting the leading of the sentiments, it is not what we believe concerning the immortality of the soul or the like, but *the universal impulse to believe,* that is the material circumstance and is the principal fact in the history of the globe. Shall we describe this cause as that which works directly? The spirit is not helpless or needful of mediate organs. It has plentiful powers and direct effects. I am explained without explaining, I am felt without acting, and where I am not. Therefore all just persons are satisfied with their own praise. They refuse to explain themselves, and are content that new actions should do them that office. They believe that we communicate without speech and above speech, and that no right action of ours is quite unaffecting to our friends, at whatever distance; for the influence of action is not to be measured by miles. Why should I fret myself because a circumstance has occurred which hinders my presence where I was expected? If I am not at the meeting, my presence where I am should be as useful to the commonwealth of friendship and wisdom, as would be my presence in that place. I exert the same quality of power in all places. Thus journeys the mighty Ideal before us; it never was known to fall into the rear. No man ever came to an experience which was satiating, but his good is tidings of a better. Onward and onward! In liberated moments we know that a new picture of life and duty is already possible; the elements already exist in many minds around you of a doctrine of life which shall transcend any written record we have. The new statement will comprise the scepticisms as well as the faiths of society, and out of unbeliefs a creed shall be formed. For scepticisms are not gratuitous or lawless, but are limitations of the affirmative statement, and the new philosophy must take them in and make affirmations outside of them, just as much as it must include the oldest beliefs.

It is very unhappy, but too late to be helped, the discovery we have made that we exist. That discovery is called the Fall of Man. Ever afterwards we suspect our instruments. We have learned that we do not see directly, but mediately, and that we have no means of correcting these colored and distorting lenses which we are, or of computing the amount of their errors. Perhaps these subject-lenses have a creative power; perhaps there are no objects. Once we lived in what we saw; now, the rapaciousness of this new power, which threatens to absorb all things, engages us. Nature, art, persons, letters, religions, objects, successively tumble in, and God is but one of its ideas. Nature and literature are subjective phenomena; every evil and every good thing is a shadow which we cast. The street is full of humiliations to the proud. As the fop contrived to dress his bailiffs in his livery and make them wait on his guests at table, so the chagrins which the bad heart gives off as bubbles, at once take form as ladies and gentlemen in the street, shopmen or barkeepers in hotels, and threaten or insult whatever is threatenable and insultable in us. 'Tis the same with our idolatries. People forget that it is the eye which makes the horizon, and the rounding mind's eye which makes this or that man a type or representative of humanity, with the name of hero or saint. Jesus, the "providential man," is a good man on whom many people are agreed that these optical laws shall take effect. By love on one part and by forbearance to press objection on the other part, it is for a time settled that we will look at him in the centre of the horizon, and ascribe to him the properties that will attach to any man so seen. But the longest love or aversion has a speedy term. The great and crescive self, rooted in absolute nature, supplants all relative existence and ruins the kingdom of mortal friendship and love. Marriage (in what is called the spiritual world) is impossible, because of the inequality between every subject and every object. The subject is the receiver of Godhead, and at every comparison must feel his being enhanced by that cryptic might. Though not in energy, yet by presence, this magazine of substance cannot be otherwise than felt; nor can any force of intellect attribute to the object the proper deity which sleeps or wakes forever in every subject. Never can love make consciousness and ascription equal in force. There will be the same gulf between every me and thee as between the original and the picture. The universe is the bride of the soul. All private sympathy is partial. Two human beings are like globes, which can touch only in a point, and whilst they remain in contact all other points of each of the spheres are inert; their turn must also come, and the longer a particular union lasts the more energy of appetency the parts not in union acquire.

Life will be imaged, but cannot be divided nor doubled. Any invasion of its unity would be chaos. The soul is not twin-born but the only begotten, and though revealing itself as child in time, child in appearance, is of a fatal and universal power, admitting no co-life. Every day, every act betrays the ill-concealed deity. We believe in ourselves as we do not believe in others. We permit all things to ourselves, and that which we call sin in others is experiment for us. It is an instance of our faith in ourselves that men never speak of crime as lightly as they think; or every man thinks a latitude safe for himself which is nowise to be indulged to another. The act looks very differently on the inside and on the outside; in its quality and in its consequences. Murder in the murderer is no such ruinous thought as poets and romancers will have it; it does not unsettle him or fright him from his ordinary notice of trifles; it is an act quite easy to be contemplated; but in its sequel it turns out to be a horrible jangle and confounding of all relations. Especially the crimes that spring from love seem right and fair from the actor's point of view, but when acted are found destructive of society. No man at last believes that he can be lost, or that the crime in him is as black as in the felon. Because the intellect qualifies in our own case the moral judgments. For there is no crime to the intellect. That is antinomian or hypernomian, and judges law as well as fact. "It is worse than a crime, it is a blunder," said Napoleon, speaking the language of the intellect. To it, the world is a problem in mathematics or the science of quantity, and it leaves out praise and blame and all weak emotions. All stealing is comparative. If you come to absolutes, pray who does not steal? Saints are sad, because

they behold sin (even when they speculate) from the point of view of the conscience, and not of the intellect; a confusion of thought. Sin, seen from the thought, is a diminution, or *less;* seen from the conscience or will, it is pravity or *bad.* The intellect names it shade, absence of light, and no essence. The conscience must feel it as essence, essential evil. This it is not; it has an objective existence, but no subjective.

Thus inevitably does the universe wear our color, and every object fall successively into the subject itself. The subject exists, the subject enlarges; all things sooner or later fall into place. As I am, so I see; use what language we will, we can never say anything but what we are; Hermes, Cadmus, Columbus, Newton, Bonaparte, are the mind's ministers. Instead of feeling a poverty when we encounter a great man, let us treat the new-comer like a travelling geologist who passes through our estate and shows us good slate, or limestone, or anthracite, in our brush pasture. The partial action of each strong mind in one direction is a telescope for the objects on which it is pointed. But every other part of knowledge is to be pushed to the same extravagance, ere the soul attains her due sphericity. Do you see that kitten chasing so prettily her own tail? If you could look with her eyes you might see her surrounded with hundreds of figures performing complex dramas, with tragic and comic issues, long conversations, many characters, many ups and downs of fate,—and meantime it is only puss and her tail. How long before our masquerade will end its noise of tambourines, laughter and shouting, and we shall find it was a solitary performance? A subject and an object,—it takes so much to make the galvanic circuit complete, but magnitude adds nothing. What imports it whether it is Kepler and the sphere, Columbus and America, a reader and his book, or puss with her tail?

It is true that all the muses and love and religion hate these developments, and will find a way to punish the chemist who publishes in the parlor the secrets of the laboratory. And we cannot say too little of our constitutional necessity of seeing things under private aspects, or saturated with our humors. And yet is the God the native of these bleak rocks. That need makes in morals the capital virtue of self-trust. We must hold hard to this poverty, however scandalous, and by more vigorous self-recoveries, after the sallies of action, possess our axis more firmly. The life of truth is cold and so far mournful; but it is not the slave of tears, contritions and perturbations. It does not attempt another's work, nor adopt another's facts. It is a main lesson of wisdom to know your own from another's. I have learned that I cannot dispose of other people's facts; but I possess such a key to my own as persuades me, against all their denials, that they also have a key to theirs. A sympathetic person is placed in the dilemma of a swimmer among drowning men, who all catch at him, and if he give so much as a leg or finger they will drown him. They wish to be saved from the mischiefs of their vices, but not from their vices. Charity would be wasted on this poor waiting on the symptoms. A wise and hardy physician will say, *Come out of that*, as the first condition of advice.

In this our talking America we are ruined by our good nature and listening on all sides. This compliance takes away the power of being greatly useful. A man should not be able to look other than directly and forthright. A preoccupied attention is the only answer to the importunate frivolity of other people; an attention, and to an aim which makes their wants frivolous. This is a divine answer, and leaves no appeal and no hard thoughts. In Flaxman's[14] drawing of the Eumenides of Aeschylus, Orestes supplicates Apollo, whilst the Furies sleep on the threshold. The face of the god expresses a shade of regret and compassion, but is calm with the conviction of the irreconcilableness of the two spheres. He is born into other politics, into the eternal and beautiful. The man at his feet asks for his interest in turmoils of the earth, into which his nature cannot enter. And the Eumenides there lying express pictorially this disparity. The god is surcharged with his divine destiny.

Illusion, Temperament, Succession, Surface, Surprise, Reality, Subjectiveness—these are threads on the loom of time, these are the lords of life. I dare not assume to give their order, but I name them as I find them in my way. I know better than to claim any completeness for my picture. I am a fragment, and this is a fragment of me. I can very confidently announce one or another law, which throws itself into relief and form, but I am too young yet by some ages to compile a code. I gossip for my hour concerning the eternal politics. I have seen many fair pictures not in vain. A wonderful time I have lived in. I am not the novice I was fourteen, nor yet seven years ago. Let who will ask, Where is the fruit? I find a private fruit sufficient. This is a fruit,—that I should not ask for a rash effect from meditations, counsels and the hiving of truths. I should feel it pitiful to demand a result on this town and county, an overt effect on the instant month and year. The effect is deep and secular as the cause. It works on periods in which mortal lifetime is lost. All I know is reception; I am and I have: but I do not get, and when I have fancied I had gotten anything, I found I did not. I worship with wonder the great Fortune.

My reception has been so large, that I am not annoyed by receiving this or that superabundantly. I say to the Genius, if he will pardon the proverb, *In for a mill, in for a million.* When I receive a new gift, I do not macerate my body to make the account square, for if I should die I could not make the account square. The benefit overran the merit the first day, and has overrun the merit ever since. The merit itself, so-called, I reckon part of the receiving.

Also that hankering after an overt or practical effect seems to me an apostasy. In good earnest I am willing to spare this most unnecessary deal of doing. Life wears to me a visionary face. Hardest roughest action is visionary also. It is but a choice between soft and turbulent dreams. People disparage knowing and the intellectual life, and urge doing. I am very content with knowing, if only I could know. That is an august entertainment, and would suffice me a great while. To know a little would be worth the expense of this world. I hear always the law of Adrastia,[15] "that every soul which had acquired any truth, should be safe from harm until another period."

I know that the world I converse with in the city and in the farms, is not the world I *think*. I observe that difference, and shall observe it. One day I shall know the value and law of this discrepance. But I have not found that much was gained by manipular attempts to realize the world of thought. Many eager persons successively make an experiment in this way, and make themselves ridiculous. They acquire democratic manners, they foam at the mouth, they hate and deny. Worse, I observe that in the history of mankind there is never a solitary example of success,—taking their own tests of success. I say this polemically, or in reply to the inquiry, Why not realize your world? But far be from me the despair which prejudges the law by a paltry empiricism;— since there never was a right endeavor but it succeeded. Patience and patience, we shall win at the last. We must be very suspicious of the deceptions of the element of time. It takes a good deal of time to eat or to sleep, or to earn a hundred dollars, and a very little time to entertain a hope and an insight which becomes the light of our life. We dress our garden, eat our dinners, discuss the household with our wives, and these things make no impression, are forgotten next week; but, in the solitude to which every man is always returning, he has a sanity and revelations which in his passage into new worlds he will carry with him. Never mind the ridicule, never mind the defeat; up again, old heart!—it seems to

[14] John Flaxman (1775–1826), English sculptor and draftsman.

[15] Nemesis or Destiny: Greek goddess of retributive justice. The law of Destiny saves only those described in the quote. Emerson paraphrased Plato's *Phaedrus* (Centenary Edition, III, p. 309).

say,—there is victory yet for all justice; and the true romance which the world exists to realize will be the transformation of genius into practical power.

1844

Thoreau

"It was a pleasure and a privilege to walk with him," said Emerson of his Concord friend, fourteen years his junior. The rest of the Emerson family enjoyed him when, at times, he lived in the household, and he enjoyed them. As we have noted, Thoreau was almost certainly the "forest seer" of the poem "Woodnotes." Soon after his death, he was the subject of this engaging prose portrait, one of the best essays ever written on Thoreau.

Henry David Thoreau was the last male descendant of a French ancestor who came to this country from the Isle of Guernsey. His character exhibited occasional traits drawn from this blood, in singular combination with a very strong Saxon genius.

He was born in Concord, Massachusetts, on the 12th of July, 1817. He was graduated at Harvard College in 1837, but without any literary distinction. An iconoclast in literature, he seldom thanked colleges for their service to him, holding them in small esteem, whilst yet his debt to them was important. After leaving the University, he joined his brother in teaching a private school, which he soon renounced. His father was a manufacturer of lead-pencils, and Henry applied himself for a time to this craft, believing he could make a better pencil than was then in use. After completing his experiments, he exhibited his work to chemists and artists in Boston, and having obtained their certificates to its excellence and to its equality with the best London manufacture, he returned home contented. His friends congratulated him that he had now opened his way to fortune. But he replied that he should never make another pencil. "Why should I? I would not do again what I have done once." He resumed his endless walks and miscellaneous studies, making every day some new acquaintance with Nature, though as yet never speaking of zoölogy or botany, since, though very studious of natural facts, he was incurious of technical and textual science.

At this time, a strong, healthy youth, fresh from college, whilst all his companions were choosing their profession, or eager to begin some lucrative employment, it was inevitable that his thoughts should be exercised on the same question, and it required rare decision to refuse all the accustomed paths and keep his solitary freedom at the cost of disappointing the natural expectations of his family and friends: all the more difficult that he had a perfect probity, was exact in securing his own independence, and in holding every man to the like duty. But Thoreau never faltered. He was a born protestant. He declined to give up his large ambition of knowledge and action for any narrow craft or profession, aiming at a much more comprehensive calling, the art of living well. If he slighted and defied the opinions of others, it was only that he was more intent to reconcile his practice with his own belief. Never idle or self-indulgent, he preferred, when he wanted money, earning it by some piece of manual labor agreeable to him, as building a boat or a fence, planting, grafting, surveying, or other short work, to any long engagements. With his hardy habits and few wants, his skill in wood-craft, and his powerful arithmetic, he was very competent to live in any part of the world. It would cost him less time to supply his wants than another. He was therefore secure of his leisure.

A natural skill for mensuration, growing out of his mathematical knowledge and his habit of ascertaining the measures and distances of objects which interested him, the size of trees, the depth and extent of ponds and rivers, the height of mountains, and the air-line distance of his favorite summits,—this, and his intimate knowledge of the territory about Concord, made him drift into the profession of land-surveyor. It had the advantage for him that it led him continually into new and secluded grounds, and helped his studies of Nature. His accuracy and skill in this work were readily appreciated, and he found all the employment he wanted.

He could easily solve the problems of the surveyor, but he was daily beset with graver questions, which he manfully confronted. He interrogated every custom, and wished to settle all his practice on an ideal foundation. He was a protestant à outrance,[1] and few lives contain so many renunciations. He was bred to no profession; he never married; he lived alone; he never went to church; he never voted; he refused to pay a tax to the State; he ate no flesh, he drank no wine, he never knew the use of tobacco; and, though a naturalist, he used neither trap nor gun. He chose, wisely no doubt for himself, to be the bachelor of thought and Nature. He had no talent for wealth, and knew how to be poor without the least hint of squalor or inelegance. Perhaps he fell into his way of living without forecasting it much, but approved it with later wisdom. "I am often reminded," he wrote in his journal, "that if I had bestowed on me the wealth of Croesus, my aims must be still the same, and my means essentially the same." He had no temptations to fight against,—no appetites, no passions, no taste for elegant trifles. A fine house, dress, the manners and talk of highly cultivated people, were all thrown away on him. He much preferred a good Indian, and con-

[1] To the limit

sidered these refinements as impediments to conversation, wishing to meet his companion on the simplest terms. He declined invitations to dinner-parties, because there each was in every one's way, and he could not meet the individuals to any purpose. "They make their pride," he said, "in making their dinner cost much; I make my pride in making my dinner cost little." When asked at table what dish he preferred, he answered, "The nearest." He did not like the taste of wine, and never had a vice in his life. He said, "I have a faint recollection of pleasure derived from smoking dried lily-stems, before I was a man. I had commonly a supply of these. I have never smoked anything more noxious."

He chose to be rich by making his wants few, and supplying them himself. In his travels, he used the railroad only to get over so much country as was unimportant to the present purpose, walking hundreds of miles, avoiding taverns, buying a lodging in farmers' and fishermen's houses, as cheaper, and more agreeable to him, and because there he could better find the men and the information he wanted.

There was somewhat military in his nature, not to be subdued, always manly and able, but rarely tender, as if he did not feel himself except in opposition. He wanted a fallacy to oppose, a blunder to pillory, I may say required a little sense of victory, a roll of the drum, to call his powers into full exercise. It cost him nothing to say No; indeed he found it much easier than to say Yes. It seemed as if his first instinct on hearing a proposition was to controvert it, so impatient was he of the limitations of our daily thought. This habit, of course, is a little chilling to the social affections; and though the companion would in the end acquit him of any malice or untruth, yet it mars conversation. Hence, no equal companion stood in affectionate relations with one so pure and guileless. "I love Henry," said one of his friends, "but I cannot like him; and as for taking his arm, I should as soon think of taking the arm of an elm-tree."[2]

Yet, hermit and stoic as he was, he was really fond of sympathy, and threw himself heartily and childlike into the company of young people whom he loved, and whom he delighted to entertain, as he only could, with the varied and endless anecdotes of his experiences by field and river; and he was always ready to lead a huckleberry-party or a search for chestnuts or grapes. Talking, one day, of a public discourse, Henry remarked that whatever succeeded with the audience was bad. I said, "Who would not like to write something which all can read, like *Robinson Crusoe?* and who does not see with regret that his page is not solid with a right materialistic treatment, which delights everybody?" Henry ob-

jected, of course, and vaunted the better lectures which reached only a few persons. But, at supper, a young girl, understanding that he was to lecture at the Lyceum, sharply asked him "whether his lecture would be a nice, interesting story, such as she wished to hear, or whether it was one of those old philosophical things that she did not care about." Henry turned to her, and bethought himself, and, I saw, was trying to believe that he had matter that might fit her and her brother, who were to sit up and go to the lecture, if it was a good one for them.

He was a speaker and actor of the truth, born such, and was ever running into dramatic situations from this cause. In any circumstance it interested all bystanders to know what part Henry would take, and what he would say; and he did not disappoint expectation, but used an original judgment on each emergency. In 1845 he built himself a small framed house on the shores of Walden Pond, and lived there two years alone, a life of labor and study. This action was quite native and fit for him. No one who knew him would tax him with affectation. He was more unlike his neighbors in his thought than in his action. As soon as he had exhausted the advantages of that solitude, he abandoned it. In 1847, not approving some uses to which the public expenditure was applied, he refused to pay his town tax, and was put in jail.[3] A friend paid the tax for him, and he was released. The like annoyance was threatened the next year. But as his friends paid the tax, notwithstanding his protest, I believe he ceased to resist. No opposition or ridicule had any weight with him. He coldly and fully stated his opinion without affecting to believe that it was the opinion of the company. It was of no consequence if every one present held the opposite opinion. On one occasion he went to the University Library to procure some books. The librarian refused to lend them. Mr. Thoreau repaired to the President, who stated to him the rules and usages, which permitted the loan of books to resident graduates, to clergymen who were alumni, and to some others resident within a circle of ten miles' radius from the College. Mr. Thoreau explained to the President that the railroad had destroyed the old scale of distance,—that the library was useless, yes, and President and College useless, on the terms of his rules,—that the one benefit he owed to the College was its library,—that, at this moment, not only his want of books was imperative but he wanted a large number of books, and assured him that he, Thoreau, and not the librarian, was the proper custodian of these. In short, the President found the petitioner so formidable, and the rules getting to look so ridiculous,

---

[2] Emerson's own remark.

[3] Thoreau opposed the Government on the Mexican War issue.

that he ended by giving him a privilege which in his hands proved unlimited thereafter.

No truer American existed than Thoreau. His preference of his country and condition was genuine, and his aversation from English and European manners and tastes almost reached contempt. He listened impatiently to news or *bon-mots* gleaned from London circles; and though he tried to be civil, these anecdotes fatigued him. The men were all imitating each other, and on a small mould. Why can they not live as far apart as possible, and each be a man by himself? What he sought was the most energetic nature; and he wished to go to Oregon, not to London. "In every part of Great Britain," he wrote in his diary, "are discovered traces of the Romans, their funereal urns, their camps, their dwellings. But New England, at least, is not based on any Roman ruins. We have not to lay the foundations of our houses on the ashes of a former civilization."

But idealist as he was, standing for abolition of slavery, abolition of tariffs, almost for abolition of government, it is needless to say he found himself not only unrepresented in actual politics, but almost equally opposed to every class of reformers. Yet he paid the tribute of his uniform respect to the Anti-Slavery party. One man, whose personal acquaintance he had formed, he honored with exceptional regard. Before the first friendly word had been spoken for Captain John Brown, he sent notices to most houses in Concord that he would speak in a public hall on the condition and character of John Brown, on Sunday evening, and invited all people to come. The Republican Committee, the Abolitionist Committee, sent him word that it was premature and not advisable. He replied,—"I did not send to you for advice, but to announce that I am to speak." The hall was filled at an early hour by people of all parties, and his earnest eulogy of the hero was heard by all respectfully, by many with a sympathy that surprised themselves.[4]

It was said of Plotinus that he was ashamed of his body, and 'tis very likely he had good reason for it,—that his body was a bad servant, and he had not skill in dealing with the material world, as happens often to men of abstract intellect. But Mr. Thoreau was equipped with a most adapted and serviceable body. He was of short stature, firmly built, of light complexion, with strong, serious blue eyes, and a grave aspect,—his face covered in the late years with a becoming beard. His senses were acute, his frame well-knit and hardy, his hands strong and skillful in the use of tools. And there was a wonderful fitness of body and mind. He could pace sixteen rods more accurately than another man could measure them with rod and chain. He could find his path in the woods at night, he said, better by his feet than his eyes. He could estimate the measure of a tree very well by his eye; he could estimate the weight of a calf or a pig like a dealer. From a box containing a bushel or more of loose pencils, he could take up with his hands fast enough just a dozen pencils at every grasp. He was a good swimmer, runner, skater, boatman, and would probably outwalk most countrymen in a day's journey. And the relation of body to mind was still finer than we have indicated. He said he wanted every stride his legs made. The length of his walk uniformly made the length of his writing. If shut up in the house he did not write at all.

He had a strong common sense, like that which Rose Flammock the weaver's daughter in Scott's romance,[5] commends in her father, as resembling a yardstick, which, whilst it measures dowlas and diaper, can equally well measure tapestry and cloth of gold. He had always a new resource. When I was planting forest trees, and had procured half a peck of acorns, he said that only a small portion of them would be sound, and proceeded to examine them and select the sound ones. But finding this took time, he said, "I think if you put them all into water the good ones will sink"; which experiment we tried with success. He could plan a garden or a house or a barn; would have been competent to lead a "Pacific Exploring Expedition"; could give judicious counsel in the gravest private or public affairs.

He lived for the day, not cumbered and mortified by his memory. If he brought you yesterday a new proposition, he would bring you to-day another not less revolutionary. A very industrious man, and setting, like all highly organized men, a high value on his time, he seemed the only man of leisure in town, always ready for any excursion that promised well, or for conversation prolonged into late hours. His trenchant sense was never stopped by his rules of daily prudence, but was always up to the new occasion. He liked and used the simplest food, yet, when some one urged a vegetable diet, Thoreau thought all diets a very small matter, saying that "the man who shoots the buffalo lives better than the man who boards at the Graham House." He said, "You can sleep near the railroad and never be disturbed: Nature knows very well what sounds are worth attending to, and has made up her mind not to hear the railroad-whistle. But things respect the devout mind, and a mental ecstasy was never interrupted." He noted what repeatedly befell him, that, after receiving from a distance a rare plant, he would presently find the same in his own haunts. And those pieces of luck which happen only to good players

[4] Thoreau presented his defense, after the Harpers Ferry raid, on October 30, 1859.

[5] *The Betrothed* (1825).

happened to him. One day, walking with a stranger, who inquired where Indian arrow-heads could be found, he replied, "Everywhere," and, stooping forward, picked one on the instant from the ground. At Mount Washington, in Tuckerman's Ravine, Thoreau had a bad fall, and sprained his foot. As he was in the act of getting up from his fall, he saw for the first time the leaves of the *Arnica mollis*.[6]

His robust common sense, armed with stout hands, keen perceptions, and strong will, cannot yet account for the superiority which shone in his simple and hidden life. I must add the cardinal fact, that there was excellent wisdom in him, proper to a rare class of men, which showed him the material world as a means and symbol. This discovery, which sometimes yields to poets a certain casual and interrupted light, serving for the ornament of their writing, was in him an unsleeping insight; and whatever faults or obstructions of temperament might cloud it, he was not disobedient to the heavenly vision. In his youth, he said, one day, "The other world is all my art; my pencils will draw no other; my jack-knife will cut nothing else; I do not use it as a means." This was the muse and genius that ruled his opinions, conversation, studies, work and course of life. This made him a searching judge of men. At first glance he measured his companion, and, though insensible to some fine traits of culture, could very well report his weight and caliber. And this made the impression of genius which his conversation sometimes gave.

He understood the matter in hand at a glance, and saw the limitations and poverty of those he talked with, so that nothing seemed concealed from such terrible eyes. I have repeatedly known young men of sensibility converted in a moment to the belief that this was the man they were in search of, the man of men, who could tell them all they should do. His own dealing with them was never affectionate, but superior, didactic, scorning their petty ways,—very slowly conceding, or not conceding at all, the promise of his society at their houses, or even at his own. "Would he not walk with them?" "He did not know. There was nothing so important to him as his walk; he had no walks to throw away on company." Visits were offered him from respectful parties, but he declined them. Admiring friends offered to carry him at their own cost to the Yellowstone River,—to the West Indies,—to South America. But though nothing could be more grave or considered than his refusals, they remind one, in quite new relations, of that fop Brummell's reply to the gentleman who offered him his carriage in a shower, "But where will *you* ride, then?"—and

what accusing silences, and what searching and irresistible speeches, battering down all defenses, his companions can remember!

Mr. Thoreau dedicated his genius with such entire love to the fields, hills and waters of his native town, that he made them known and interesting to all reading Americans, and to people over the sea. The river[7] on whose banks he was born and died he knew from its springs to its confluence with the Merrimack. He had made summer and winter observations on it for many years, and at every hour of the day and night. The result of the recent survey of the Water Commissioners appointed by the State of Massachusetts he had reached by his private experiments, several years earlier. Every fact which occurs in the bed, on the banks, or in the air over it; the fishes, and their spawning and nests, their manners, their food; the shad-flies which fill the air on a certain evening once a year, and which are snapped at by the fishes so ravenously that many of these die of repletion; the conical heaps of small stones on the river-shallows, the huge nests of small fishes, one of which will sometimes overfill a cart; the birds which frequent the stream, heron, duck, sheldrake, loon, osprey; the snake, muskrat, otter, woodchuck and fox, on the banks; the turtle, frog, hyla and cricket, which made the banks vocal,—were all known to him, and, as it were, townsmen and fellow-creatures; so that he felt an absurdity or violence in any narrative of one of these by itself apart, and still more of its dimensions on an inch-rule, or in the exhibition of its skeleton, or the specimen of a squirrel or a bird in brandy. He liked to speak of the manners of the river, as itself a lawful creature, yet with exactness, and always to an observed fact. As he knew the river, so the ponds in this region.

One of the weapons he used, more important to him than microscope or alcohol-receiver to other investigators, was a whim which grew on him by indulgence, yet appeared in gravest statement, namely, of extolling his own town and neighborhood as the most favored center for natural observation. He remarked that the Flora of Massachusetts embraced almost all the important plants of America,—most of the oaks, most of the willows, the best pines, the ash, the maple, the beech, the nuts. He returned Kane's[8] "Arctic Voyage" to a friend of whom he had borrowed it, with the remark, that "Most of the phenomena noted might be observed in Concord." He seemed a little envious of the Pole, for the coincident sunrise and sunset, or five minutes' day after six months: a splendid fact which Annursnuc had

---

[6] A medicinal plant.

[7] The Concord River.

[8] Elisha Kent Kane, a celebrated Arctic explorer of the time, whose books Thoreau knew.

never afforded him. He found red snow in one of his walks, and told me that he expected to find yet the *Victoria regia*[9] in Concord. He was the attorney of the indigenous plants, and owned to a preference of the weeds to the imported plants, as of the Indian to the civilized man, and noticed, with pleasure, that the willow bean-poles of his neighbor had grown more than his beans. "See these weeds," he said, "which have been hoed at by a million farmers all spring and summer, and yet have prevailed, and just now come out triumphant over all lanes, pastures, fields and gardens, such is their vigor. We have insulted them with low names, too,—as Pigweed, Wormwood, Chickweed, Shad-blossom." He says, "They have brave names, too,—Ambrosia, Stellaria, Amelanchier, Amaranth, etc."

I think his fancy for referring everything to the meridian of Concord did not grow out of any ignorance or depreciation of other longitudes or latitudes, but was rather a playful expression of his conviction of the indifferency of all places, and that the best place for each is where he stands. He expressed it once in this wise: "I think nothing is to be hoped from you, if this bit of mould under your feet is not sweeter to you to eat than any other in this world, or in any world."

The other weapon with which he conquered all obstacles in science was patience. He knew how to sit immovable, a part of the rock he rested on, until the bird, the reptile, the fish, which had retired from him, should come back and resume its habits, nay, moved by curiosity, should come to him and watch him.

It was a pleasure and a privilege to walk with him. He knew the country like a fox or a bird, and passed through it as freely by paths of his own. He knew every track in the snow or on the ground, and what creature had taken this path before him. One must submit abjectly to such a guide, and the reward was great. Under his arm he carried an old music-book to press plants; in his pocket, his diary and pencil, a spy-glass for birds, microscope, jack-knife, and twine. He wore a straw hat, stout shoes, strong gray trousers, to brave scrub-oaks and smilax, and to climb a tree for a hawk's or a squirrel's nest. He waded into the pool for the water-plants, and his strong legs were no insignificant part of his armor. On the day I speak of he looked for the Menyanthes, detected it across the wide pool, and, on examination of the florets, decided that it had been in flower five days. He drew out of his breast-pocket his diary, and read the names of all the plants that should bloom on this day, whereof he kept account as a banker when his notes fall due. The Cypripedium not due till to-morrow. He

thought that, if waked up from a trance, in this swamp, he could tell by the plants what time of the year it was within two days. The redstart was flying about, and presently the fine grosbeaks, whose brilliant scarlet "makes the rash gazer wipe his eye," and whose fine clear note Thoreau compared to that of a tanager which has got rid of its hoarseness. Presently he heard a note which he called that of the night-warbler, a bird he had never identified, had been in search of twelve years, which always, when he saw it, was in the act of diving down into a tree or bush, and which it was in vain to seek; the only bird which sings indifferently by night and by day. I told him he must beware of finding and booking it, lest life should have nothing more to show him. He said, "What you seek in vain for, half your life, one day you come full upon, all the family at dinner. You seek it like a dream, and as soon as you find it you become its prey."

His interest in the flower or the bird lay very deep in his mind, was connected with Nature,—and the meaning of Nature was never attempted to be defined by him. He would not offer a memoir of his observations to the Natural History Society. "Why should I? To detach the description from its connections in my mind would make it no longer true or valuable to me: and they do not wish what belongs to it." His power of observation seemed to indicate additional senses. He saw as with microscope, heard as with ear-trumpet, and his memory was a photographic register of all he saw and heard. And yet none knew better than he that it is not the fact that imports, but the impression or effect of the fact on your mind. Every fact lay in glory in his mind, a type of the order and beauty of the whole.

His determination on Natural History was organic. He confessed that he sometimes felt like a hound or a panther, and, if born among Indians, would have been a fell hunter. But, restrained by his Massachusetts culture, he played out the game in this mild form of botany and ichthyology. His intimacy with animals suggested what Thomas Fuller records of Butler the apiologist, that "either he had told the bees things or the bees had told him." Snakes coiled round his legs; the fishes swam into his hand, and he took them out of the water; he pulled the woodchuck out of its hole by the tail and took the foxes under his protection from the hunters. Our naturalist had perfect magnanimity; he had no secrets; he would carry you to the heron's haunt, or even to his most prized botanical swamp,—possibly knowing that you could never find it again, yet willing to take his risks.

No college ever offered him a diploma, or a professor's chair; no academy made him its corresponding secretary, its discoverer, or even its member. Perhaps these learned bodies feared the satire of his

[9] A South American water lily.

presence. Yet so much knowledge of Nature's secret and genius few others possessed; none in a more large and religious synthesis. For not a particle of respect had he to the opinions of any man or body of men, but homage solely to the truth itself; and as he discovered everywhere among doctors some leaning of courtesy, it discredited them. He grew to be revered and admired by his townsmen, who had at first known him only as an oddity. The farmers who employed him as a surveyor soon discovered his rare accuracy and skill, his knowledge of their lands, of trees, of birds, of Indian remains and the like, which enabled him to tell every farmer more than he knew before of his own farm; so that he began to feel a little as if Mr. Thoreau had better rights in his land than he. They felt, too, the superiority of character which addressed all men with a native authority.

Indian relics abound in Concord,—arrow-heads, stone chisels, pestles, and fragments of pottery; and on the riverbank, large heaps of clam-shells and ashes mark spots which the savages frequented. These, and every circumstance touching the Indian, were important in his eyes. His visits to Maine were chiefly for love of the Indian. He had the satisfaction of seeing the manufacture of the bark-canoe, as well as of trying his hand in its management on the rapids. He was inquisitive about the making of the stone arrow-head, and in his last days charged a youth setting out for the Rocky Mountains to find an Indian who could tell him that: "It was well worth a visit to California to learn it." Occasionally, a small party of Penobscot Indians would visit Concord, and pitch their tents for a few weeks in summer on the river-bank. He failed not to make acquaintance with the best of them; though he well knew that asking questions of Indians is like catechizing beavers and rabbits. In his last visit to Maine he had great satisfaction from Joseph Polis, an intelligent Indian of Oldtown, who was his guide for some weeks.

He was equally interested in every natural fact. The depth of his perception found likeness of law throughout Nature, and I know not any genius who so swiftly inferred universal law from the single fact. He was no pedant of a department. His eye was open to beauty, and his ear to music. He found these, not in rare conditions, but wheresoever he went. He thought the best of music was in single strains; and he found poetic suggestion in the humming of the telegraph-wire.

His poetry might be bad or good; he no doubt wanted a lyric facility and technical skill, but he had the source of poetry in his spiritual perception. He was a good reader and critic, and his judgment on poetry was to the ground of it. He could not be deceived as to the presence or absence of the poetic element in any composition, and his thirst for this made him negligent and perhaps scornful of superficial graces. He would pass by many delicate rhythms, but he would have detected every live stanza or line in a volume, and knew very well where to find an equal poetic charm in prose. He was so enamoured of the spiritual beauty that he held all actual written poems in very light esteem in the comparison. He admired Aeschylus and Pindar; but, when some one was commending them, he said that Aeschylus and the Greeks, in describing Apollo and Orpheus, had given no song, or no good one. "They ought not to have moved trees, but to have chanted to the gods such a hymn as would have sung all their old ideas out of their heads, and new ones in." His own verses are often rude and defective. The gold does not yet run pure, is drossy and crude. The thyme and marjoram are not yet honey. But if he want lyric fineness and technical merits, if he have not the poetic temperament, he never lacks the causal thought, showing that his genius was better than his talent. He knew the worth of the Imagination for the uplifting and consolation of human life, and liked to throw every thought into a symbol. The fact you tell is of no value, but only the impression. For this reason his presence was poetic, always piqued the curiosity to know more deeply the secrets of his mind. He had many reserves, an unwillingness to exhibit to profane eyes what was still sacred in his own, and knew well how to throw a poetic veil over his experience. All readers of Walden will remember his mythical record of his disappointments:—

"I long ago lost a hound, a bay horse and a turtle-dove, and am still on their trail. Many are the travellers I have spoken concerning them, describing their tracks, and what calls they answered to. I have met one or two who have heard the hound, and the tramp of the horse, and even seen the dove disappear behind a cloud; and they seemed as anxious to recover them as if they had lost them themselves."

His riddles were worth the reading, and I confide that if at any time I do not understand the expression, it is yet just. Such was the wealth of his truth that it was not worth his while to use words in vain. His poem entitled "Sympathy" reveals the tenderness under that triple steel of stoicism, and the intellectual subtility it could animate. His classic poem on "Smoke" suggests Simonides, but is better than any poem of Simonides. His biography is in his verses. His habitual thought makes all his poetry a hymn to the Cause of causes, the Spirit which vivifies and controls his own:—

> I hearing get, who had but ears,
> And sight, who had but eyes before;
> I moments live, who lived but years,
> And truth discern, who knew but learning's lore.

And still more in these religious lines:

> Now chiefly is my natal hour,
> And only now my prime of life;
> I will not doubt the love untold,
> Which not my worth nor want have bought,
> Which wooed me young, and wooes me old,
> And to this evening hath me brought.[10]

Whilst he used in his writings a certain petulance of remark in reference to churches or churchmen, he was a person of a rare, tender and absolute religion, a person incapable of any profanation, by act or by thought. Of course, the same isolation which belonged to his original thinking and living detached him from the social religious forms. This is neither to be censured nor regretted. Aristotle long ago explained it, when he said, "One who surpasses his fellow-citizens in virtue is no longer a part of the city. Their law is not for him, since he is a law to himself."

Thoreau was sincerity itself, and might fortify the convictions of prophets in the ethical laws by his holy living. It was an affirmative experience which refused to be set aside. A truth-speaker he, capable of the most deep and strict conversation; a physician to the wounds of any soul; a friend, knowing not only the secret of friendship, but almost worshipped by those few persons who resorted to him as their confessor and prophet, and knew the deep value of his mind and great heart. He thought that without religion or devotion of some kind nothing great was ever accomplished: and he thought that the bigoted sectarian had better bear this in mind.

His virtues, of course, sometimes ran into extremes. It was easy to trace to the inexorable demand on all for exact truth that austerity which made this willing hermit more solitary even than he wished. Himself of a perfect probity, he required not less of others. He had a disgust at crime, and no worldly success would cover it. He detected paltering as readily in dignified and prosperous persons as in beggars, and with equal scorn. Such dangerous frankness was in his dealing that his admirers called him "that terrible Thoreau," as if he spoke when silent, and was still present when he had departed. I think the severity of his ideal interfered to deprive him of a healthy sufficiency of human society.

The habit of a realist to find things the reverse of their appearance inclined him to put every statement in a paradox. A certain habit of antagonism defaced his earlier writings,—a trick of rhetoric not quite outgrown in his later, of substituting for the obvious word and thought its diametrical opposite. He praised wild mountains and winter forests for their domestic air, in snow and ice he would find sultriness, and commended the wilderness for resembling Rome and Paris. "It was so dry, that you might call it wet."

The tendency to magnify the moment, to read all the laws of Nature in the one object or one combination under your eye, is of course comic to those who do not share the philosopher's perception of identity. To him there was no such thing as size. The pond was a small ocean; the Atlantic, a large Walden Pond. He referred every minute fact to cosmical laws. Though he meant to be just, he seemed haunted by a certain chronic assumption that the science of the day pretended completeness, and he had just found out that the savans[11] had neglected to discriminate a particular botanical variety, had failed to describe the seeds or count the sepals. "That is to say," we replied, "the blockheads were not born in Concord; but who said they were? It was their unspeakable misfortune to be born in London, or Paris, or Rome; but poor fellows, they did what they could, considering that they never saw Bateman's Pond, or Nine-Acre Corner, or Becky Stow's Swamp; besides, what were you sent into the world for, but to add this observation?"

Had his genius been only contemplative, he had been fitted to his life, but with his energy and practical ability he seemed born for great enterprise and for command; and I so much regret the loss of his rare powers of action, that I cannot help counting it a fault in him that he had no ambition. Wanting this, instead of engineering for all America, he was the captain of a huckleberry-party. Pounding beans is good to the end of pounding empires one of these days; but if, at the end of years, it is still only beans!

But these foibles, real or apparent, were fast vanishing in the incessant growth of a spirit so robust and wise, and which effaced its defeats with new triumphs. His study of Nature was a perpetual ornament to him, and inspired his friends with curiosity to see the world through his eyes, and to hear his adventures. They possessed every kind of interest.

He had many elegancies of his own, whilst he scoffed at conventional elegance. Thus, he could not bear to hear the sound of his own steps, the grit of gravel; and therefore never willingly walked in the road, but in the grass, on mountains and in woods. His senses were acute, and he remarked that by night every dwelling-house gives out bad air, like a slaughter-house. He liked the pure fragrance of melilot.[12] He honored certain plants with special regard, and, over all, the pond-lily,—then, the gentian, and the *Mikania scandens*,[13] and "life-everlasting," and a bass-tree which he visited every year when it bloomed in the middle of July, He thought the

---

[10] The lines are from Thoreau's "Inspiration."

[11] Savants; men of learning.

[12] Sweet clover.

[13] Climbing hempweed.

scent a more oracular inquisition than the sight,—more oracular and trustworthy. The scent, of course, reveals what is concealed from the other senses. By it he detected earthiness. He delighted in echoes, and said they were almost the only kind of kindred voices that he heard. He loved Nature so well, was so happy in her solitude, that he became very jealous of cities and the sad work which their refinements and artifices made with man and his dwelling. The axe was always destroying his forest. "Thank God," he said, "they cannot cut down the clouds!" "All kinds of figures are drawn on the blue ground with this fibrous white paint."

I subjoin a few sentences taken from his unpublished manuscripts, not only as records of his thought and feeling, but for their power of description and literary excellence:—

"Some circumstantial evidence is very strong, as when you find a trout in the milk."

"The chub is a soft fish, and tastes like boiled brown paper salted."

"The youth gets together his materials to build a bridge to the moon, or, perchance, a palace or temple on the earth, and, at length the middle-aged man concludes to build a woodshed with them."

"The locust z-ing."

"Devil's-needles zigzagging along the Nut-Meadow brook."

"Sugar is not so sweet to the palate as sound to the healthy ear."

"I put on some hemlock-boughs, and the rich salt crackling of their leaves was like mustard to the ear, the crackling of uncountable regiments. Dead trees love the fire."

"The bluebird carries the sky on his back."

"The tanager flies through the green foliage as if it would ignite the leaves."

"If I wish for a horse-hair for my compass-sight I must go to the stable; but the hair-bird, with her sharp eyes, goes to the road."

"Immortal water, alive even to the superficies."

"Fire is the most tolerable third party."

"Nature made ferns for pure leaves, to show what she could do in that line."

"No tree has so fair a bole and so handsome an instep as the beech."

"How did these beautiful rainbow-tints get into the shell of the fresh-water clam, buried in the mud at the bottom of our dark river?"

"Hard are the times when the infant's shoes are second-foot."

"We are strictly confined to our men to whom we give liberty."

"Nothing is so much to be feared as fear. Atheism may comparatively be popular with God himself."

"Of what significance the things you can forget? A little thought is sexton to all the world."

"How can we expect a harvest of thought who have not had a seed-time of character?"

"Only he can be trusted with gifts who can present a face of bronze to expectations."

"I ask to be melted. You can only ask of the metals that they be tender to the fire that melts them. To nought else can they be tender."

There is a flower known to botanists, one of the same genus with our summer plant called "Life-Everlasting," a *Gnaphalium* like that, which grows on the most inaccessible cliffs of the Tyrolese mountains, where the chamois dare hardly venture, and which the hunter, tempted by its beauty, and by his love (for it is immensely valued by the Swiss maidens), climbs the cliffs to gather, and is sometimes found dead at the foot, with the flower in his hand. It is called by botanists the *Gnaphalium leontopodium*, but by the Swiss *Edelweisse*, which signifies *Noble Purity*. Thoreau seemed to me living in the hope to gather this plant, which belonged to him of right. The scale on which his studies proceeded was so large as to require longevity, and we were the less prepared for his sudden disappearance. The country knows not yet, or in the least part, how great a son it has lost. It seems an injury that he should leave in the midst his broken task which none else can finish, a kind of indignity to so noble a soul that he should depart out of Nature before yet he has been really shown to his peers for what he is. But he, at least, is content. His soul was made for the noblest society; he had in a short life exhausted the capabilities of this world; wherever there is knowledge, wherever there is virtue, wherever there is beauty, he will find a home.

1862

HENRY DAVID THOREAU [1817–1862]

To EMERSON'S ACCOUNT of Thoreau it may be worth while to add this factual summary of his life: Born in Concord, Massachusetts, son of John Thoreau, pencil maker, and Cynthia Dunbar; attended the village academy; at Harvard, mastered Greek and read widely on his own account in English literature; graduated in 1837, the year of "The American Scholar," and thereafter was associated with Emerson; did some teaching, and began giving lectures; contributed to *The Dial*, both verse and prose; tutored William Emerson's children on Staten Island; lived for a time at Walden Pond; published in 1849 the first of his two books, *A Week on the Concord and Merrimack Rivers;* five years later published *Walden;* published essays gathered into books after his death (*The Maine Woods, A Yankee in Canada,* and *Cape Cod);* journeyed to Minnesota in search of health; died of tuberculosis in Concord the next year, age forty-four; between his return from college and his death had been away from Concord less than a year in all.

To outward seeming, it was an uneventful life, disappointing to his family, who had invested in his college education at some sacrifice, and to his friends, who saw it as a negation, a refusal or failure to utilize his talents. And yet, as later generations have more fully recognized, it was a life fraught with inward drama; and if the vocation he pursued was not what society expected of a Harvard graduate, it nevertheless lay at the heart of the Transcendental philosophy: self-realization, through a life lived organically in communion with nature, disciplined by the seasons, by the economy of self-support, and by the tension between the civilized and the primitive. *Walden,* as the distillation of his experience, is Thoreau's great achievement.

Text: *The Writings of Henry David Thoreau,* Walden Edition (Boston, 1906).

Further reading: *The Variorum Walden,* ed. Walter Harding, 1962. *A Week on the Concord and Merrimack Rivers. The Collected Poems of Henry Thoreau,* ed. Carl Bode. Sherman Paul, *The Shores of America: Thoreau's Inward Exploration,* 1958. Walter Harding, *A Thoreau Handbook,* 1959. John H. Hicks, ed., *Thoreau in Our Season,* 1966. Charles R. Anderson, *The Magic Circle of Walden,* 1968.

Letters to Emerson

When Emerson made his second trip to Europe, he left in his household Henry Thoreau, as man of all work and guardian for Lidian and the children. Thoreau's reports, below, reveal a genial human quality that alleviates the austere tendency of his published writings.

Concord, November 14, 1847

DEAR FRIEND,—I am but a poor neighbor to you here,—a very poor companion am I. I understand that very well, but that need not prevent my *writing* to you now. I have almost never written letters in my life, yet I think I can write as good ones as I frequently see, so I shall not hesitate to write this, such as it may be, knowing that you will welcome anything that reminds you of Concord.

I have banked up the young trees against the winter and the mice, and I will look out, in my careless way, to see when a pale is loose or a nail drops out of its place. The broad gaps, at least, I will occupy. I heartily wish I could be of good service to this household. But I, who have only used these ten digits so long to solve the problem of a living, how can I? The world is a cow that is hard to milk,—life does not come so easy,—and oh, how thinly it is watered ere we get it! But the young bunting calf, he will get at it. There is no way so direct. This is to earn one's living by the sweat of his brow. It is a little like joining a community, this life, to such a hermit as I am; and as I don't keep the accounts, I don't know whether the experiment will succeed or fail finally. At any rate, it is good for society, so I do not regret my transient nor my permanent share in it.

Lidian [Mrs. Emerson] and I make very good housekeepers. She is a very dear sister to me. Ellen and Edith and Eddy and Aunty Brown keep up the tragedy and comedy and tragic-comedy of life as usual. The two former have not forgotten their old acquaintance; even Edith carries a young memory in her head, I find. Eddy can teach us all how to pronounce. If you should discover any rare hoard of wooden or pewter horses, I have no doubt he will know how to appreciate it. He occasionally surveys mankind from my shoulders as wisely as ever Johnson did. I respect him not a little, though it is I that lift him up so unceremoniously. And sometimes I have to set him down again in a hurry, according to his "mere will and good pleasure." He very seriously asked me, the other day, "Mr. Thoreau, will you be my father?" I am occasionally Mr. Rough-and-tumble with him that I may not miss *him*, and lest he should miss *you* too much. So you must come back soon, or you will be superseded.

Alcott[1] has heard that I laughed, and so set the people laughing, at his arbor, though I never laughed louder than when I was on the ridge-pole. But now I have not laughed for a long time, it is so serious. He is very grave to look at. But, not knowing all this, I strove innocently enough, the other day, to engage his attention to my mathematics. "Did you ever study geometry, the relation of straight lines to curves, the transition from the finite to the infinite? Fine things about it in Newton and Leibnitz." But he would hear none of it,—men of taste preferred the natural curve. Ah, he is a crooked stick himself. He is getting on now so many *knots* an hour. There is one knot at present occupying the point of highest elevation,—the present highest point; and as many knots as are not handsome, I presume, are thrown down and cast into the pines. Pray show him this if you meet him anywhere in London, for I cannot make him hear much plainer words here. He forgets that I am neither old nor young, nor anything in particular, and behaves as if I had still some of the animal heat in me. As for the building, I feel a little oppressed when I come near it. It has no great disposition to be beautiful; it is certainly a wonderful structure, on the whole, and the fame of the architect will endure as long as it shall stand. I should not show you this side alone, if I did not suspect that Lidian had done complete justice to the other.

[1] Bronson Alcott spent the summer of 1847 building a summer house for Emerson. Built of gnarled and knotted wood, it apparently "was too fantastic to ever prove useful."—Harding and Bode, *The Correspondence of Thoreau*.

Mr. [Edmund] Hosmer has been working at a tannery in Stow for a fortnight, though he has just now come home sick. It seems that he was a tanner in his youth, and so he has made up his mind a little at last. This comes of reading the New Testament. Wasn't one of the Apostles a tanner? Mrs. Hosmer remains here, and John looks stout enough to fill his own shoes and his father's too.

Mr. Blood and his company have at length seen the stars through the great telescope, and he told me that he thought it was worth the while. Mr. Peirce made him wait till the crowd had dispersed (it was a Saturday evening), and then was quite polite,—conversed with him, and showed him the micrometer, etc.; and he said Mr. Blood's glass was large enough for all ordinary astronomical work. [Rev.] Mr. [Brazillai] Frost and Dr. [Josiah] Bartlett seemed disappointed that there was no greater difference between the Cambridge glass and the Concord one. They used only a power of 400. Mr. Blood tells me that he is too old to study the calculus or higher mathematics. At Cambridge they think that they have discovered traces of another satellite to Neptune. They have been obliged to exclude the public altogether, at last. The very dust which they raised, "which is filled with minute crystals," etc., as professors declare, having to be wiped off the glasses, would ere long wear them away. It is true enough, Cambridge college [Harvard] is really beginning to wake up and redeem its character and overtake the age. I see by the catalogue that they are about establishing a scientific school in connection with the university, at which any one above eighteen, on paying one hundred dollars annually (Mr. [Abbott] Lawrence's fifty thousand dollars will probably diminish this sum), may be instructed in the highest branches of science,—in astronomy, "theoretical and practical, with the use of the instruments" (so the great Yankee astronomer may be born without delay), in mechanics and engineering to the last degree. Agassiz will ere long commence his lectures in the zoölogical department. A chemistry class has already been formed under the direction of Professor [Eben N.] Horsford. A new and adequate building for the purpose is already being erected. They have been foolish enough to put at the end of all this earnest the old joke of a diploma. Let every sheep keep but his own skin, I say.

I have had a tragic correspondence, for the most part all on one side, with Miss——.[2] She did really wish to—I hesitate to write—marry me. That is the way they spell it. Of course I did not write a deliberate answer. How could I deliberate upon it? I sent

[2] Identified in *The Correspondence* as Sophia Foord, age 45 at the time of the letter. She lived at the Emersons' in late 1846 and early 1847.

back as distinct a *no* as I have learned to pronounce after considerable practice, and I trust that this *no* has succeeded. Indeed, I wished that it might burst, like hollow shot, after it had struck and buried itself and made itself felt there. *There was no other way.* I really had anticipated no such foe as this in my career.

I suppose you will like to hear of my book, though I have nothing worth writing about it. Indeed, for the last month or two I have forgotten it, but shall certainly remember it again. Wiley & Putnam, Munroe, the Harpers, and Crosby & Nichols have all declined printing it with the least risk to themselves; but Wiley & Putnam will print it in their series, and any of them anywhere, at *my* risk. If I liked the book well enough, I should not delay; but for the present I am indifferent. I believe this is, after all, the course you advised,—to let it lie.

I do not know what to say of myself. I sit before my green desk, in the chamber at the head of the stairs, and attend to my thinking, sometimes more, sometimes less distinctly. I am not unwilling to think great thoughts if there are any in the wind, but what they are I am not sure. They suffice to keep me awake while the day lasts, at any rate. Perhaps they will redeem some portion of the night ere long.

I can imagine you astonishing, bewildering, confounding, and sometimes delighting John Bull with your Yankee notions, and that he begins to take a pride in the relationship at last; introduced to all the stars of England in succession, after the lecture, until you pine to thrust your head once more into a genuine and unquestionable nebula, if there be any left. I trust a common man will be the most uncommon to you before you return to these parts. I have thought there was some advantage even in death, by which we "mingle with the herd of common men."

Hugh [the gardener][3] still has his eye on the Walden *agellum*, and orchards are waving there in the windy future for him. That's the where-I'll-go-next, thinks he; but no important steps are yet taken. He reminds me occasionally of this open secret of his, with which the very season seems to labor, and affirms seriously that as to his wants—wood, stone, or timber—I know better than he. That is a clincher which I shall have to avoid to some extent; but I fear that it is a wrought nail and will not break. Unfortunately, the day after cattle-show—the day after small beer—he was among the missing, but not long this time. The Ethiopian cannot change his skin nor the leopard his spots, nor indeed Hugh—his Hugh.

As I walked over Conantum, the other afternoon, I saw a fair column of smoke rising from the woods directly over my house that was (as I judged), and

[3] After Thoreau left the cabin at Walden Pond, he sold it to Hugh Whelan, Emerson's gardener.

already began to conjecture if my deed of sale would not be made invalid by this. But it turned out to be John Richardson's young wood, on the southeast of your field. It was burnt nearly all over, and up to the rails and the road. It was set on fire, no doubt, by the same Lucifer that lighted Brook's lot before.[4] So you see that your small lot is comparatively safe for this season, the back fire having been already set for you.

They have been choosing between John Keyes and Sam Staples, if the world wants to know it, as representative of this town, and Staples[5] is chosen. The candidates for governor—think of my writing this to you!—were Governor [George N.] Briggs and General [Caleb] Cushing, and Briggs is elected, though the Democrats have gained. Ain't I a brave boy to know so much of politics for the nonce? But I shouldn't have known it if Coombs hadn't told me. They have had a peace meeting here,—I shouldn't think of telling you if I didn't know anything would do for the English market,—and some men, Deacon Brown at the head, have signed a long pledge, swearing that they will "treat all mankind as brothers henceforth." I think I shall wait and see how they treat me first. I think that Nature meant kindly when she made our brothers few. However, my voice is still for peace. So good-by, and a truce to all joking, my dear friend, from

H. D. T.

Concord, February 23, 1848

DEAR WALDO,—For I think I have heard that that is your name,—my letter which was put last into the leathern bag arrived first. Whatever I may *call* you, I know you better than I know your name, and what becomes of the fittest name if in any sense you are here with him who *calls*, and not there simply to be called?

I believe I never thanked you for your lectures, one and all, which I heard formerly read here in Concord. I *know* I never have. There was some excellent reason each time why I did not; but it will never be too late. I have that advantage, at least, over you in my education.

Lidian is too unwell to write to you; so I must tell you what I can about the children and herself. I am afraid she has not told you how unwell she is,—or to-day perhaps we may say has been. She has been confined to her chamber four or five weeks, and three or four weeks, at least, to her bed, with the jaundice. The doctor, who comes once a day, does not let her read (nor can she now) nor *hear* much

[4] Lucifer is the railroad train that often set fire to the woods.

[5] The constable who arrested Thoreau in 1846 when he refused to pay taxes.

reading. She has written her letters to you, till recently, sitting up in bed, but he said he would not come again if she did so. She has Abby and Almira to take care of her, and Mrs. Brown to read to her; and I also, occasionally, have something to read or to say. The doctor says she must not expect to "take any comfort of her life" for a week or two yet. She wishes me to say that she has written two long and full letters to you about the household economies, etc., which she hopes have not been delayed. The children are quite well and full of spirits, and are going through a regular course of picture-seeing, with commentary by me, every evening, for Eddy's behoof. All the Annuals and "Diadems" are in requisition, and Eddy is forward to exclaim, when the hour arrives, "Now for the demdems!" I overheard this dialogue when Frank [Brown] came down to breakfast the other morning.

Eddy. "Why, Frank, I am astonished that you should leave your boots in the dining-room."

Frank. "I guess you mean *surprised*, don't you?"

Eddy. "No, boots!"

"If Waldo were here," said he, the other night, at bedtime, "we'd be four going upstairs." Would he like to tell papa anything? No, not anything; but finally, yes, he would,—that one of the white horses in his new barouche is broken! Ellen and Edith will perhaps speak for themselves, as I hear something about letters to be written by them.

Mr. Alcott seems to be reading well this winter: Plato, Montaigne, Ben Jonson, Beaumont and Fletcher, Sir Thomas Browne, etc., etc., "I believe I have read them all now, or nearly all,"—those English authors. He is rallying for another foray with his pen, in his latter years, not discouraged by the past, into that crowd of unexpressed ideas of his, that undisciplined Parthian army, which, as soon as a Roman soldier would face, retreats on all hands, occasionally firing backwards; easily routed, not easily subdued, hovering on the skirts of society. Another summer shall not be devoted to the raising of vegetables (Arbors?) which rot in the cellar for want of consumers; but perchance to the arrangement of the material, the brain-crop which the winter has furnished. I have good talks with him. His respect for Carlyle has been steadily increasing for some time. He has read him with new sympathy and appreciation.

I see Channing often. He also goes often to Alcott's, and confesses that he has made a discovery in him, and gives vent to his admiration or his confusion in characteristic exaggeration; but between this extreme and that you may get a fair report, and draw an inference if you can. Sometimes he will ride a broomstick still, though there is nothing to keep him, or it, up but a certain centrifugal force of whim, which is soon spent, and there lies your stick, not worth picking up to sweep an oven with now. His accustomed path is strewn with them. But then again, and perhaps for the most part, he sits on the Cliffs amid the lichens, or flits past on noiseless pinion, like the barred owl in the daytime, as wise and unobserved. He brought me a poem the other day, for me, on Walden Hermitage: not remarkable.

Lectures begin to multiply on my desk. I have one on Friendship which is new, and the materials of some others. I read one last week to the Lyceum, on The Rights and Duties of the Individual in Relation to Government,[6]—much to Mr. Alcott's satisfaction.

Joel Britton has failed and gone into chancery, but the woods continue to fall before the axes of other men. Neighbor Coombs was lately found dead in the woods near Goose Pond, with his half-empty jug, after he had been rioting a week. Hugh, by the last accounts, was still in Worcester County. Mr. Hosmer, who is himself again, and living in Concord, has just hauled the rest of your wood, amounting to about ten and a half cords.

The newspapers say that they have printed a pirated edition of your Essays in England. Is it as bad as they say, and undisguised and unmitigated piracy? I thought that the printed scrap would entertain Carlyle, notwithstanding its history. If this generation will see out of its hind-head, why then you may turn your back on its forehead. Will you forward it to him for me?

This stands written in your day-book: "September 3d. Received of Boston Savings Bank, on account of Charles Lane, his deposit with interest, $131.33. 16th. Received of Joseph Palmer, on account of Charles Lane, three hundred twenty-three 36/100 dollars, being the balance of a note on demand for four hundred dollars, with interest, $323.36."

If you have any directions to give about the trees, you must not forget that spring will soon be upon us.

Farewell. From your friend,

HENRY THOREAU

Sic Vita

I am a parcel of vain strivings tied
  By a chance bond together,
Dangling this way and that, their links
  Were made so loose and wide,
        Methinks,   5
  For milder weather.

[6]According to Alcott, read on January 26, 1848. Later printed as "Civil Disobedience."

A bunch of violets without their roots,
  And sorrel intermixed,[1]
Encircled by a wisp of straw
  Once coiled about their shoots, 10
    The law
  By which I'm fixed.

A nosegay which Time clutched from out
  Those fair Elysian fields,
With weeds and broken stems, in haste, 15
  Doth make the rabble rout
    That waste
  The day he yields.

And here I bloom for a short hour unseen,
  Drinking my juices up, 20
With no root in the land
  To keep my branches green,
    But stand
  In a bare cup.

Some tender buds were left upon my stem 25
  In mimicry of life,
But ah! the children will not know,
  Till time has withered them,
    The woe
  With which they're rife. 30

But now I see I was not plucked for naught,
  And after in life's vase
Of glass set while I might survive,
  But by a kind hand brought
    Alive 35
  To a strange place.

That stock thus thinned will soon redeem its hours,
  And by another year,
Such as God knows, with freer air,
  More fruits and fairer flowers 40
    Will bear,
  While I droop here.

                        1841

Winter Memories

Within the circuit of this plodding life
There enter moments of an azure hue,
Untarnished fair as is the violet
Or anemone, when the spring strews them
By some meandering rivulet, which make 5

Sic Vita. [1]At the time Thoreau wrote the poem (1837) flower symbolism was very popular. How much further meaning he intended is unknown, but violets surely stood for modesty, and sorrel for "wit ill-timed." (See Bode, *Collected Poems*, p. 351.)

The best philosophy untrue that aims
But to console man for his grievances.
I have remembered when the winter came,
High in my chamber in the frosty nights,
When in the still light of the cheerful moon, 10
On every twig and rail and jutting spout,
The icy spears were adding to their length
Against the arrows of the coming sun,
How in the shimmering noon of summer past
Some unrecorded beam slanted across 15
The upland pastures where the Johnswort grew;
Or heard, amid the verdure of my mind,
The bee's long smothered hum, on the blue flag
Loitering amidst the mead; or busy rill,
Which now through all its course stands still and
    dumb 20
Its own memorial,—purling at its play
Along the slopes, and through the meadows next,
Until its youthful sound was hushed at last
In the staid current of the lowland stream;
Or seen the furrows shine but late upturned, 25
And where the fieldfare[1] followed in the rear,
When all the fields around lay bound and hoar
Beneath a thick integument of snow.
So by God's cheap economy made rich
To go upon my winter's task again. 30

                        1842

The Inward Morning

Packed in my mind lie all the clothes
  Which outward nature wears,
And in its fashion's hourly change
  It all things else repairs

In vain I look for change abroad, 5
  And can no difference find,
Till some new ray of peace uncalled
  Illumes my inmost mind.

What is it gilds the trees and clouds,
  And paints the heavens so gay, 10
But yonder fast-abiding light
  With its unchanging ray?

Lo, when the sun streams through the wood,
  Upon a winter's morn,
Where'er his silent beams intrude 15
  The murky night is gone.

How could the patient pine have known
  The morning breeze would come,

Winter Memories. [1]A medium-sized European thrush.

Or humble flowers anticipate
    The insect's noonday hum,— 20

Till the new light with morning cheer
    From far streamed through the aisles,
And nimbly told the forest trees
    For many stretching miles?

I've heard within my inmost soul 25
    Such cheerful morning news,
In the horizon of my mind
    Have seen such orient hues,

As in the twilight of the dawn,
    When the first birds awake, 30
Are heard within some silent wood,
    Where they the small twigs break,

Or in the eastern skies are seen,
    Before the sun appears,
The harbingers of summer heats 35
    Which from afar he bears.
                                1842

Mist

Low-anchored cloud,
Newfoundland air,
Fountain-head and source of rivers,
Dew-cloth, dream drapery,
And napkin spread by fays; 5
Drifting meadow of the air,
Where bloom the daisied banks and violets,
And in whose fenny labyrinth
The bittern booms and heron wades;
Spirit of lakes and seas and rivers, 10
Bear only perfumes and the scent
Of healing herbs to just men's fields!
1842?

Smoke

Published in the *Dial*, April 1843, and republished in *Walden*, in which it is introduced as follows: "When the villagers were lighting their fires beyond the horizon, I too gave notice to the various wild inhabitants of Walden vale, by a smoky streamer from my chimney, that I was awake."

Light-winged smoke, Icarian bird,
Melting thy pinions in thy upward flight,
Lark without song, and messenger of dawn,
Circling above the hamlets as thy nest;
Or else, departing dream, and shadowy form 5
Of midnight vision, gathering up thy skirts;
By night star-veiling, and by day
Darkening the light and blotting out the sun;

Go thou my incense upward from this hearth,
And ask the Gods to pardon this clear flame. 10
                                1843

Inspiration

Whate'er we leave to God, God does,
    And blesses us;
The work we choose should be our own,
    God lets alone.

If with light head erect I sing, 5
    Though all the muses lend their force,
From my poor love of anything,
    The verse is weak and shallow as its source.

But if with bended neck I grope,
    Listening behind me for my wit, 10
With faith superior to hope,
    More anxious to keep back than forward it,

Making my soul accomplice there
    Unto the flame my heart hath lit,
Then will the verse forever wear,— 15
    Time cannot bend the line which God hath writ.

Always the general show of things
    Floats in review before my mind,
And such true love and reverence brings,
    That sometimes I forget that I am blind. 20

But now there comes unsought, unseen,
    Some clear, divine electuary,
And I who had but sensual been,
    Grow sensible, and as God is, am wary.

I hearing get who had but ears, 25
    And sight, who had but eyes before,
I moments live who lived but years,
    And truth discern who knew but learning's lore.

I hear beyond the range of sound,
    I see beyond the range of sight, 30
New earths and skies and seas around,
    And in my day the sun doth pale his light.

A clear and ancient harmony
    Pierces my soul through all its din,
As through its utmost melody,— 35
    Farther behind than they—farther within.

More swift its bolt than lightning is,
    Its voice than thunder is more loud,
It doth expand my privacies
    To all, and leave me single in the crowd. 40

It speaks with such authority,
    With so serene and lofty tone,
That idle Time runs gadding by,
    And leaves me with Eternity alone.

Then chiefly is my natal hour,   45
    And only then my prime of life,
Of manhood's strength it is the flower,
    'Tis peace's end and war's beginning strife.

'T hath come in summer's broadest noon,
    By a grey wall or some chance place,   50
Unseasoned time, insulted June,
    And vexed the day with its presuming face.

Such fragrance round my couch it makes,
    More rich than are Arabian drugs,
That my soul scents its life and wakes   55
    The body up beneath its perfumed rugs.

Such is the Muse—the heavenly maid,
    The star that guides our mortal course,
Which shows where life's true kernel's laid,
    Its wheat's fine flower, and its undying force.   60

She with one breath attunes the spheres,
    And also my poor human heart,
With one impulse propels the years
    Around, and gives my throbbing pulse its start.

I will not doubt forever more,   65
    Nor falter from a steadfast faith,
For though the system be turned o'er,
    God takes not back the word which once he saith.

I will then trust the love untold
    Which not my worth nor want has bought,   70
Which wooed me young and woos me old,
    And to this evening hath me brought.

My memory I'll educate
    To know the one historic truth,
Remembering to the latest date   75
    The only true and sole immortal youth.

Be but thy inspiration given,
    No matter through what danger sought,
I'll fathom hell or climb to heaven,
    And yet esteem that cheap which love has
        bought.   80

        Fame cannot tempt the bard
            Who's famous with his God,
        Nor laurel him reward
            Who hath his Maker's nod.

1848   1863

FROM HIS *Journal*

A large proportion of Thoreau's journal is little more than a record of observations of nature, of interest to him but of scant scientific or literary interest to the reader. One example: (August 1, 1854, the year of *Walden*) "Meadow-haying begun for a week. Erechthites, begun for four or five days in Moore's Swamp. Two turtle doves in the stubble beyond. *Hieracium Canadense*, apparently a day or two. Do not see stamens or thyme-leaved pinweed, but *perhaps* petals. Ground-nut well out." However, the journal also contains much that could be used, and often was used, as material for lectures and books. Entries of this eminently readable sort follow.

(1851)

It is the fault of some excellent writers—De Quincey's first impressions on seeing London suggest it to me—that they express themselves with too great fullness and detail. They give the most faithful, natural, and lifelike account of their sensations, mental and physical, but they lack moderation and sententiousness. They do not affect us by an ineffectual earnestness and a reserve of meaning, like a stutterer; they say all they mean. Their sentences are not concentrated and nutty. Sentences which suggest far more than they say, which have an atmosphere about them, which do not merely report an old, but make a new, impression; sentences which suggest as many things and are as durable as a Roman aqueduct; to frame these, that is the *art* of writing. Sentences which are expensive, towards which so many volumes, so much life, went; which lie like boulders on the page, up and down or across; which contain the seed of other sentences, not mere repetition, but creation; which a man might sell his grounds and castles to build. If De Quincey had suggested each of his pages in a sentence and passed on, it would have been far more excellent writing. His style is nowhere kinked and knotted up into something hard and significant, which you could swallow like a diamond, without digesting.

The glorious sandy banks far and near, caving and sliding,—far sandy slopes, the forts of the land,—where you see the naked flesh of New England, her garment being blown aside like that of the priests (of the Levites?) when they ascend to the altar. Seen through this November sky, these sands are dear to me, worth all the gold of California, suggesting Pactolus, while the Saxonville factory-bell sounds o'er the woods. That sound perchance it is that whets my vision. The shore suggests the seashore, and two objects at a distance near the shore look like seals on a sand-bar. Dear to me to lie in, this sand; fit to preserve the bones of a race for thousands of years to come. And this is my home, my native soil; and I am a New-Englander. Of thee, O earth, are my bone and sinew made; to thee, O sun, am I brother. It must be the largest lake in Middlesex. To this dust my body will gladly return as to its origin. Here have I my habitat. I am of thee.

(1852)

As I turned round the corner of Hubbard's Grove, saw a woodchuck, the first of the season, in the middle of the field, six or seven rods from the fence which bounds the wood, and twenty rods distant. I ran along the fence and cut him off, or rather overtook him, though he started at the same time. When I was only a rod and a half off, he stopped, and I did the same; then he ran again, and I ran up within three feet of him, when he stopped again, the fence being between us. I squatted down and surveyed him at my leisure. His eyes were dull black and rather inobvious, with a faint chestnut (?) iris, with but little expression and that more of resignation than of anger. The general aspect was a coarse grayish brown, a sort of grisel (?). A lighter brown next the skin, then black or very dark brown and tipped with whitish rather loosely. The head between a squirrel and a bear, flat on the top and dark brown, and darker still or black on the tip of the nose. The whiskers black, two inches long. The ears very small and roundish, set far back and nearly buried in the fur. Black feet, with long and slender claws for digging. It appeared to tremble, or perchance shivered with cold. When I moved, it gritted its teeth quite loud, sometimes striking the under jaw against the other chatteringly, sometimes grinding one jaw on the other, yet as if more from instinct than anger. Whichever way I turned, that way it headed. I took a twig a foot long and touched its snout, at which it started forward and bit the stick, lessening the distance between us to two feet, and still it held all the ground it gained. I played with it tenderly a while with the stick, trying to open its gritting jaws. Ever its long incisors, two above and two below, were presented. But I thought it would go to sleep if I stayed long enough. It did not sit upright as sometimes, but *standing* on its fore feet with its head down, *i.e.* half sitting, half standing. We sat looking at one another about half an hour, till we began to feel mesmeric influences. When I was tired, I moved away, wishing to see him run, but I could not start him. He would not stir as long as I was looking at him or could see him. I walked round him; he turned as fast and fronted me still. I sat down by his side within a foot. I talked to him *quasi* forest lingo, baby-talk, at any rate in a conciliatory tone, and thought that I had some influence on him. He gritted his teeth less. I chewed

checkerberry leaves and presented them to his nose at last without a grit; though I saw that by so much gritting of the teeth he had worn them rapidly and they were covered with a fine white powder, which, if you measured it thus, would have made his anger terrible. He did not mind any noise I might make. With a little stick I lifted one of his paws to examine it, and held it up at pleasure. I turned him over to see what color he was beneath (darker or more purely brown), though he turned himself back again sooner than I could have wished. His tail was also all brown, though not very dark, rat-tail like, with loose hairs standing out on all sides like a caterpillar brush. He had a rather mild look. I spoke kindly to him. I reached checkerberry leaves to his mouth. I stretched my hands over him, though he turned up his head and still gritted a little. I laid my hand on him, but immediately took it off again, instinct not being wholly overcome. If I had had a few fresh bean leaves, thus in advance of the season, I am sure I should have tamed him completely. It was a frizzly tail. His is a humble, terrestrial color like the partridge's, well concealed where dead wiry grass rises above darker brown or chestnut dead leaves,—a modest color. If I had had some food, I should have ended with stroking him at my leisure. Could easily have wrapped him in my handkerchief. He was not fat nor particularly lean. I finally had to leave him without seeing him move from the place. A large, clumsy, burrowing squirrel. *Arctomys,* bearmouse. I respect him as one of the natives. He lies there, by his color and habits so naturalized amid the dry leaves, the withered grass, and the bushes. A sound nap, too, he has enjoyed in his native fields, the past winter. I think I might learn some wisdom of him. His ancestors have lived here longer than mine. He is more thoroughly acclimated and naturalized than I. Bean leaves the red man raised for him, but he can do without them.

(1854)

There is no such thing as pure *objective* observation. Your observation, to be interesting, *i.e.* to be significant, must be *subjective*. The sum of what the writer of whatever class has to report is simply some human experience, whether he be poet or philosopher or man of science. The man of most science is the man most alive, whose life is the greatest event. Senses that take cognizance of outward things merely are of no avail. It matters not where or how far you travel,—the farther commonly the worse,— but how much alive you are. If it is possible to conceive of an event outside to humanity, it is not of the slightest significance, though it were the explosion of a planet. Every important worker will report what life there is in him. It makes no odds into what seeming deserts the poet is born. Though all his neighbors pronounce it a Sahara, it will be a paradise to him; for the desert which we see is the result of the barrenness of our experience. No mere willful activity whatever, whether in writing verses or collecting statistics, will produce true poetry or science. If you are really a sick man, it is indeed to be regretted, for you cannot accomplish so much as if you were well. All that a man has to say or do that can possibly concern mankind, is in some shape or other to tell the story of his love,—to sing, and if he is fortunate and keeps alive, he will be forever in love. This alone is to be alive to the extremities. It is a pity that this divine creature should ever suffer from cold feet; a still greater pity that the coldness so often reaches to his heart. I look over the report of the doings of a scientific association and am surprised that there is so little life to be reported; I am put off with a parcel of dry technical terms. Anything living is easily and naturally expressed in popular language. I cannot help suspecting that the life of these learned professors has been almost as inhuman and wooden as a rain-gauge or self-registering magnetic machine. They communicate no fact which rises to the temperature of blood-heat. It doesn't all amount to one rhyme.

This earth which is spread out like a map around me is but the lining of my inmost soul exposed.

I have brought home a half-bushel of grapes to scent my chamber with. It is impossible to get them home in a basket with all their rich bloom on them, which, no less than the form of the clusters, makes their beauty. As I paddled home with my basket of grapes in the bow, every now and then their perfume was wafted to me in the stern, and I thought that I was passing a richly laden vine on shore. Some goldfinches twitter over, while I am pulling down the vines from the birch-tops. The ripest rattle off and strew the ground before I reach the clusters, or, while I am standing on tiptoe and endeavoring gently to break the tough peduncle, the petiole of a leaf gets entangled in the bunch and I am compelled to strip them all off loosely.

(1855)

What a strong and hearty but reckless, hit-or-miss style had some of the early writers of New England, like Josselyn[1] and William Wood[2] and others elsewhere in those days; as if they spoke with a relish,

[1] John Josselyn (fl. 1638–75), an English scientific writer who visited Boston and Maine in 1638–39 and made a second trip in 1663–71. He published two books about his travels.

[2] William Wood (fl. 1629–35), an English colonist in Massachusetts who wrote an early description, New England's Prospect (1634).

smacking their lips like a coachwhip, caring more to speak heartily than scientifically true. They are not to be caught napping by the wonders of Nature in a new country, and perhaps are often more ready to appreciate them than she is to exhibit them. They give you one piece of nature, at any rate, and that is themselves. (Cotton Mather, too, has a rich phrase.) They use a strong, coarse, homely speech which cannot always be found in the dictionary, nor sometimes be heard in polite society, but which brings you very near to the thing itself described. The strong new soil speaks through them. I have just been reading some in Wood's "New England's Prospect." He speaks a good word for New England, indeed will come very near lying for her, and when he doubts the justness of his praise, he brings it out not the less roundly; as who cares if it is not so? we love her not the less for all that. Certainly that generation stood nearer to nature, nearer to the facts, than this, and hence their books have more life in them.

(1856)

When it was proposed to me to go abroad, rub off some rust, and *better my condition* in a worldly sense, I fear lest my life will lose some of its homeliness. If these fields and streams and woods, the phenomena of nature here, and the simple occupations of the inhabitants should cease to interest and inspire me, no culture or wealth would atone for the loss. I fear the dissipation that travelling, going into society, even the best, the enjoyment of intellectual luxuries, imply. If Paris is much in your mind, if it is more and more to you, Concord is less and less, and yet it would be a wretched bargain to accept the proudest Paris in exchange for my native village. At best, Paris could only be a school in which to learn to live here, a stepping-stone to Concord, a school in which to fit for this university. I wish so to live ever as to derive my satisfactions and inspirations from the commonest events, every-day phenomena, so that what my senses hourly perceive, my daily walk, the conversation of my neighbors, may inspire me, and I may dream of no heaven but that which lies about me. A man may acquire a taste for wine or brandy, and so lose his love for water, but should we not pity him?

I see the old pale-faced farmer out again on his sled now for the five-thousandth time,—Cyrus Hubbard, a man of a certain New England probity and worth, immortal and natural, like a natural product, like the sweetness of a nut, like the toughness of hickory. He, too, is a redeemer for me. How superior actually to the faith he professes! He is not an office-seeker. What an institution, what a revelation is a man! We are wont foolishly to think that the creed which a man professes is more significant than the fact he is. It matters not how hard the conditions seemed, how mean the world, for a man is a prevalent force and a new law himself. He is a system whose law is to be observed. The old farmer condescends to countenance still this nature and order of things. It is a great encouragement that an honest man makes this world his abode.

(1857)

These regular phenomena of the seasons get at last to be—they were *at first,* of course—simply and plainly phenomena or phases of my life. The seasons and all their changes are in me. I see not a dead eel or floating snake, or a gull, but it rounds my life and is like a line or accent in its poem. Almost I believe the Concord would not rise and overflow its banks again, were I not here. After a while I learn what my moods and seasons are. I would have nothing subtracted. I can imagine nothing added. My moods are thus periodical, not two days in my year alike. The perfect correspondence of Nature to man, so that he is at home in her!

(1859)

Time will soon destroy the works of famous painters and sculptors, but the Indian arrowhead will balk his efforts and Eternity will have to come to his aid. They are not fossil bones, but, as it were, fossil thoughts, forever reminding me of the mind that shaped them. I would fain know that I am treading in the tracks of human game,—that I am on the trail of mind,—and these little reminders never fail to set me right. When I see these signs I know that the subtle spirits that made them are not far off, into whatever form transmuted. What if you do plow and hoe amid them, and swear that not one stone shall be left upon another? They are only the less like to break in that case. When you turn up one layer you bury another so much the more securely. They are at peace with rust. This arrow-headed character promises to outlast all others. The larger pestles and axes may, perchance, grow scarce and be broken, but the arrowhead shall, perhaps, never cease to wing its way through the ages to eternity. It was originally winged for but a short flight, but it still, to my mind's eye, wings its way through the ages, bearing a message from the hand that shot it. Myriads of arrowpoints lie sleeping in the skin of the revolving earth, while meteors revolve in space. The footprint, the mind-print of the oldest men. When some Vandal chieftain has razed to the earth the British Museum, and, perchance, the winged bulls from Ninevah shall have lost most if not all of their

features, the arrowheads which the museum contains will, perhaps, find themselves at home again in familiar dust, and resume their shining in new springs upon the bared surface of the earth then, to be picked up for the thousandth time by the shepherd or savage that may be wandering there, and once more suggest their story to him.

There was a remarkable sunset, I think the 25th of October. The sunset sky reached quite from west to east, and it was the most varied in its forms and colors of any that I remember to have seen. At one time the clouds were most softly and delicately rippled, like the ripple-marks on sand. But it was hard for me to see its beauty then, when my mind was filled with Captain Brown.[3] So great a wrong as his fate implied overshadowed all beauty in the world.

Civil Disobedience

Thoreau, individualist and lover of beauty, could not ignore the great public problem of slavery. His house in Concord was a station on the underground railroad. He knew and admired Captain John Brown, and spoke for him even though public opinion was virtually solid against Brown. This was in 1859. More than a decade earlier, during the Mexican war, he had written "Resistance to Civil Government," later entitled "Civil Disobedience." It was a protest against slavery: "I cannot for an instant recognize that political organization as *my* government which is the *slave's* government also." At the same time it was a general protest against any form of political injustice and an affirmation of the obligation of passive resistance.

I heartily accept the motto, "That government is best which governs least;"[1] and I should like to see it acted up to more rapidly and systematically. Carried out, it finally amounts to this, which also I believe,—"That government is best which governs not at all;" and when men are prepared for it, that will be the kind of government which they will have. Government is at best but an expedient; but most governments are usually, and all governments are sometimes, inexpedient. The objections which have been brought against a standing army, and they are many and weighty, and deserve to prevail, may also at last be brought against a standing government. The standing army is only an arm of the standing government. The government itself, which is only the mode which the people have chosen to execute their will, is equally liable to be abused and

[3] John Brown raided Harpers Ferry in October 1859, where he was wounded and captured. Later, December 2, 1859, he was hanged. Thoreau wrote the passage on November 12.
Civil Disobedience. [1]Although the motto suggests Jefferson, it actually is from the masthead of the *Democratic Review,* a periodical for which Thoreau occasionally wrote. (Harding)

perverted before the people can act through it. Witness the present Mexican war, the work of comparatively a few individuals using the standing government as their tool; for, in the outset, the people would not have consented to this measure.

This American government,—what is it but a tradition, though a recent one, endeavoring to transmit itself unimpaired to posterity, but each instant losing some of its integrity? It has not the vitality and force of a single living man; for a single man can bend it to his will. It is a sort of wooden gun to the people themselves. But it is not the less necessary for this; for the people must have some complicated machinery or other, and hear its din, to satisfy that idea of government which they have. Governments show thus how successfully men can be imposed on, even impose on themselves, for their own advantage. It is excellent, we must all allow. Yet this government never of itself furthered any enterprise, but by the alacrity with which it got out of its way. *It* does not keep the country free. *It* does not settle the West. *It* does not educate. The character inherent in the American people has done all that has been accomplished; and it would have done somewhat more, if the government had not sometimes got in its way. For government is an expedient by which men would fain succeed in letting one another alone; and, as has been said, when it is most expedient, the governed are most let alone by it. Trade and commerce, if they were not made of india-rubber, would never manage to bounce over the obstacles which legislators are continually putting in their way; and, if one were to judge these men wholly by the effects of their actions and not partly by their intentions, they would deserve to be classed and punished with those mischievous persons who put obstructions on the railroads.

But, to speak practically and as a citizen, unlike those who call themselves no-government men, I ask for, not at once no government, but *at once* a better government. Let every man make known what kind of government would command his respect, and that will be one step toward obtaining it.

After all, the practical reason why, when the power is once in the hands of the people, a majority are permitted, and for a long period continue, to rule is not because they are most likely to be in the right, nor because this seems fairest to the minority, but because they are physically the strongest. But a government in which the majority rule in all cases cannot be based on justice, even as far as men understand it. Can there not be a government in which majorities do not virtually decide right and wrong, but conscience?—in which majorities decide only those questions to which the rule of expediency is applicable? Must the citizen ever for a moment, or in the least degree, resign his conscience to the legislator? Why has every man a conscience, then? I think that we should be men first, and subjects afterward. It is not desirable to cultivate a respect for the law, so much as for the right. The only obligation which I have a right to assume is to do at any time what I think right. It is truly enough said that a corporation has no conscience; but a corporation of conscientious men is a corporation *with* a conscience. Law never made men a whit more just; and, by means of their respect for it, even the well-disposed are daily made the agents of injustice. A common and natural result of an undue respect for law is, that you may see a file of soldiers, colonel, captain, corporal, privates, powder-monkeys, and all, marching in admirable order over hill and dale to the wars, against their wills, ay, against their common sense and consciences, which makes it very steep marching indeed, and produces a palpitation of the heart. They have no doubt that it is a damnable business in which they are concerned; they are all peaceably inclined. Now, what are they? Men at all? or small movable forts and magazines, at the service of some unscrupulous man in power? Visit the Navy-Yard, and behold a marine, such a man as an American government can make, or such as it can make a man with its black arts,—a mere shadow and reminiscence of humanity, a man laid out alive and standing, and already, as one may say, buried under arms with funeral accompaniments, though it may be,—

> "Not a drum was heard, not a funeral note,
>   As his corse to the rampart we hurried;
> Not a soldier discharged his farewell shot
>   O'er the grave where our hero we buried."[2]

The mass of men serve the state thus, not as men mainly, but as machines, with their bodies. They are the standing army, and the militia, jailers, constables, *posse comitatus*, etc. In most cases there is no free exercise whatever of the judgment or of the moral sense; but they put themselves on a level with wood and earth and stones; and wooden men can perhaps be manufactured that will serve the purpose as well. Such command no more respect than men of straw or a lump of dirt. They have the same sort of worth only as horses and dogs. Yet such as these even are commonly esteemed good citizens. Others—as most legislators, politicians, lawyers, ministers, and office-holders—serve the state chiefly with their heads; and, as they rarely make any moral distinctions, they are as likely to serve the devil, without *intending* it, as God. A very few—as heroes, patriots, martyrs, reformers in the great sense, and *men*—serve the state with their consciences also, and so necessarily resist it for the most part; and they are commonly

[2]Charles Wolfe (1791-1823), "Burial of Sir John Moore at Corunna."

treated as enemies by it. A wise man will only be useful as a man, and will not submit to be "clay," and "stop a hole to keep the wind away,"[3] but leave that office to his dust at least:—

> "I am too high-born to be propertied,
> To be a secondary at control,
> Or useful serving-man and instrument
> To any sovereign state throughout the world."[4]

He who gives himself entirely to his fellow-men appears to them useless and selfish; but he who gives himself partially to them is pronounced a benefactor and philanthropist.

How does it become a man to behave toward this American government to-day? I answer, that he cannot without disgrace be associated with it. I cannot for an instant recognize that political organization as *my* government which is the *slave's* government also.

All men recognize the right of revolution; that is, the right to refuse allegiance to, and to resist, the government, when its tyranny or its inefficiency are great and unendurable. But almost all say that such is not the case now. But such was the case, they think, in the Revolution of '75. If one were to tell me that this was a bad government because it taxed certain foreign commodities brought to its ports, it is most probable that I should not make an ado about it, for I can do without them. All machines have their friction; and possibly this does enough good to counterbalance the evil. At any rate, it is a great evil to make a stir about it. But when the friction comes to have its machine, and oppression and robbery are organized, I say, let us not have such a machine any longer. In other words, when a sixth of the population of a nation which has undertaken to be the refuge of liberty are slaves, and a whole country is unjustly overrun and conquered by a foreign army, and subjected to military law, I think that it is not too soon for honest men to rebel and revolutionize. What makes this duty the more urgent is the fact that the country so overrun is not our own, but ours is the invading army.

Paley,[5] a common authority with many on moral questions, in his chapter on the "Duty of Submission to Civil Government," resolves all civil obligation into expediency; and he proceeds to say that "so long as the interest of the whole society requires it, that is, so long as the established government cannot be resisted or changed without public inconveniency, it is the will of God . . . that the established government be obeyed,—and no longer. This principle being admitted, the justice of every particular case of resistance is reduced to a computation of the quantity of the danger and grievance on the one side, and of the probability and expense of redressing it on the other." Of this, he says, every man shall judge for himself. But Paley appears never to have contemplated those cases to which the rule of expediency does not apply, in which a people, as well as an individual, must do justice, cost what it may. If I have unjustly wrested a plank from a drowning man, I must restore it to him though I drown myself. This, according to Paley, would be inconvenient. But he that would save his life, in such a case, shall lose it. This people must cease to hold slaves, and to make war on Mexico, though it cost them their existence as a people.

In their practice, nations agree with Paley; but does any one think that Massachusetts does exactly what is right at the present crisis?

> "A drab of state, a cloth-o'-silver slut,
> To have her train borne up, and her soul trail in the dirt."[6]

Practically speaking, the opponents to a reform in Massachusetts are not a hundred thousand politicians at the South, but a hundred thousand merchants and farmers here,[7] who are more interested in commerce and agriculture than they are in humanity, and are not prepared to do justice to the slave and to Mexico, *cost what it may.* I quarrel not with far-off foes, but with those who, near at home, coöperate with, and do the bidding of, those far away, and without whom the latter would be harmless. We are accustomed to say, that the mass of men are unprepared; but improvement is slow, because the few are not materially wiser or better than the many. It is not so important that many should be as good as you, as that there be some absolute goodness somewhere; for that will leaven the whole lump. There are thousands who are *in opinion* opposed to slavery and to the war, who yet in effect do nothing to put an end to them; who, esteeming themselves children of Washington and Franklin, sit down with their hands in their pockets, and say that they know not what to do, and do nothing; who even postpone the question of freedom to the question of free trade, and quietly read the prices-current along with the latest advices from Mexico, after dinner, and, it may be, fall asleep over them both. What is the price-current of an honest man and patriot to-day? They hesitate, and they regret, and sometimes they petition; but they do nothing in earnest and with effect. They will wait, well disposed, for others to remedy the evil, that they may no longer have it to regret. At most, they give only a cheap vote, and a feeble countenance and God-

---

[3] "Imperious Caesar, dead and turn'd to clay,/Might stop a hole to keep the wind away." Shakespeare, *Hamlet* V.i. 236–37.

[4] Shakespeare, *King John* V.ii. 79–82.

[5] William Paley (1743–1805), from *Moral and Political Philosophy.*

[6] Cyril Tourneur, *The Revenger's Tragedy* IV.iv.

[7] Many Northerners resisted abolition because they feared it would damage the economy.

speed, to the right, as it goes by them. There are nine hundred and ninety-nine patrons of virtue to one virtuous man. But it is easier to deal with the real possessor of a thing than with the temporary guardian of it.

All voting is a sort of gaming, like checkers or backgammon, with a slight moral tinge to it, a playing with right and wrong, with moral questions; and betting naturally accompanies it. The character of the voters is not staked. I cast my vote, perchance, as I think right; but I am not vitally concerned that that right should prevail. I am willing to leave it to the majority. Its obligation, therefore, never exceeds that of expediency. Even voting *for the right* is *doing* nothing for it. It is only expressing to men feebly your desire that it should prevail. A wise man will not leave the right to the mercy of chance, nor wish it to prevail through the power of the majority. There is but little virtue in the action of masses of men. When the majority shall at length vote for the abolition of slavery, it will be because they are indifferent to slavery, or because there is but little slavery left to be abolished by their vote. *They* will then be the only slaves. Only *his* vote can hasten the abolition of slavery who asserts his own freedom by his vote.

I hear of a convention to be held at Baltimore,[8] or elsewhere, for the selection of a candidate for the Presidency, made up chiefly of editors, and men who are politicians by profession; but I think, what is it to any independent, intelligent, and respectable man what decision they may come to? Shall we not have the advantage of his wisdom and honesty, nevertheless? Can we not count upon some independent votes? Are there not many individuals in the country who do not attend conventions? But no: I find that the respectable man, so called, has immediately drifted from his position, and despairs of his country, when his country has more reason to despair of him. He forthwith adopts one of the candidates thus selected as the only *available* one, thus proving that he is himself *available* for any purposes of the demagogue. His vote is of no more worth than that of any unprincipled foreigner or hireling native, who may have been bought. O for a man who is a *man*, and, as my neighbor says, has a bone in his back which you cannot pass your hand through! Our statistics are at fault: the population has been returned too large. How many *men* are there to a square thousand miles in this country? Hardly one. Does not America offer any inducement for men to settle here? The American has dwindled into an Odd Fellow,[9]—one who may be known by the development of his organ of gregariousness, and

a manifest lack of intellect and cheerful self-reliance; whose first and chief concern, on coming into the world, is to see that the almshouses are in good repair; and, before yet he has lawfully donned the virile garb, to collect a fund for the support of the widows and orphans that may be; who, in short, ventures to live only by the aid of the Mutual Insurance company, which has promised to bury him decently.

It is not a man's duty, as a matter of course, to devote himself to the eradication of any, even the most enormous, wrong; he may still properly have other concerns to engage him; but it is his duty, at least, to wash his hands of it, and, if he gives it no thought longer, not to give it practically his support. If I devote myself to other pursuits and contemplations, I must first see, at least, that I do not pursue them sitting upon another man's shoulders. I must get off him first, that he may pursue his contemplations too. See what gross inconsistency is tolerated. I have heard some of my townsmen say, "I should like to have them order me out to help put down an insurrection of the slaves, or to march to Mexico;—see if I would go;" and yet these very men have each, directly by their allegiance, and so indirectly, at least, by their money, furnished a substitute. The soldier is applauded who refuses to serve in an unjust war by those who do not refuse to sustain the unjust government which makes the war; is applauded by those whose own act and authority he disregards and sets at naught; as if the state were penitent to that degree that it hired one to scourge it while it sinned, but not to that degree that it left off sinning for a moment. Thus, under the name of Order and Civil Government, we are all made at last to pay homage to and support our own meanness. After the first blush of sin comes its indifference; and from immoral it becomes, as it were, *unmoral*, and not quite unnecessary to that life which we have made.

The broadest and most prevalent error requires the most disinterested virtue to sustain it. The slight reproach to which the virtue of patriotism is commonly liable, the noble are most likely to incur. Those who, while they disapprove of the character and measures of a government, yield to it their allegiance and support are undoubtedly its most conscientious supporters, and so frequently the most serious obstacles to reform. Some[10] are petitioning the State to dissolve the Union, to disregard the requisitions of the President. Why do they not dissolve it themselves,—the union between themselves and the State,—and refuse to pay their quota into its treasury? Do not they stand in the same relation to the State that the State does to the Union? And have not the same reasons prevented the State from resist-

[8] The Democratic Party convention of 1848; it evaded the whole issue of slavery.

[9] The Independent Order of Odd Fellows, a fraternal society that still exists.

[10] Some radical abolitionists urged the Northern states to withdraw from the Union. (Harding)

ing the Union which have prevented them from resisting the State?

How can a man be satisfied to entertain an opinion merely, and enjoy *it?* Is there any enjoyment in it, if his opinion is that he is aggrieved? If you are cheated out of a single dollar by your neighbor, you do not rest satisfied with knowing that you are cheated, or with saying that you are cheated, or even with petitioning him to pay you your due; but you take effectual steps at once to obtain the full amount, and see that you are never cheated again. Action from principle, the perception and the performance of right, changes things and relations; it is essentially revolutionary, and does not consist wholly with anything which was. It not only divides States and churches, it divides families; ay, it divides the *individual,* separating the diabolical in him from the divine.

Unjust laws exist: shall we be content to obey them, or shall we endeavor to amend them, and obey them until we have succeeded, or shall we transgress them at once? Men generally, under such a government as this, think that they ought to wait until they have persuaded the majority to alter them. They think that, if they should resist, the remedy would be worse than the evil. But it is the fault of the government itself that the remedy *is* worse than the evil. *It* makes it worse. Why is it not more apt to anticipate and provide for reform? Why does it not cherish its wise minority? Why does it cry and resist before it is hurt? Why does it not encourage its citizens to be on the alert to point out its faults, and *do* better than it would have them? Why does it always crucify Christ, and excommunicate Copernicus[11] and Luther,[12] and pronounce Washington and Franklin rebels?

One would think, that a deliberate and practical denial of its authority was the only offence never contemplated by government; else, why has it not assigned its definite, its suitable and proportionate, penalty? If a man who has no property refuses but once to earn nine shillings for the State, he is put in prison for a period unlimited by any law that I know, and determined only by the discretion of those who placed him there; but if he should steal ninety times nine shillings from the State, he is soon permitted to go at large again.

If the injustice is part of the necessary friction of the machine of government, let it go, let it go: perchance it will wear smooth,—certainly the machine will wear out. If the injustice has a spring, or a pulley, or a rope, or a crank, exclusively for itself, then perhaps you may consider whether the remedy will not be worse than the evil; but if it is of such a

nature that it requires you to be the agent of injustice to another, then, I say, break the law. Let your life be a counter-friction to stop the machine. What I have to do is see, at any rate, that I do not lend myself to the wrong which I condemn.

As for adopting the ways which the State has provided for remedying the evil, I know not of such ways. They take too much time, and a man's life will be gone. I have other affairs to attend to. I came into this world, not chiefly to make this a good place to live in, but to live in it, be it good or bad. A man has not everything to do, but something; and because he cannot do *everything,* it is not necessary that he should do *something* wrong. It is not my business to be petitioning the Governor or the Legislature any more than it is theirs to petition me; and if they should not hear my petition, what should I do then? But in this case the State has provided no way: its very Constitution is the evil. This may seem to be harsh and stubborn and unconciliatory; but it is to treat with the utmost kindness and consideration the only spirit that can appreciate or deserves it. So is all change for the better, like birth and death, which convulse the body.

I do not hesitate to say, that those who call themselves Abolitionists should at once effectually withdraw their support, both in person and property, from the government of Massachusetts, and not wait till they constitute a majority of one, before they suffer the right to prevail through them. I think that it is enough if they have God on their side, without waiting for that other one. Moreover, any man more right than his neighbors constitutes a majority of one already.

I meet this American government, or its representative, the State government, directly, and face to face, once a year—no more—in the person of its tax-gatherer; this is the only mode in which a man situated as I am necessarily meets it; and it then says distinctly, Recognize me; and the simplest, the most effectual, and, in the present posture of affairs, the indispensablest mode of treating with it on this head, of expressing your little satisfaction with and love for it, is to deny it then. My civil neighbor, the tax-gatherer, is the very man I have to deal with,—for it is, after all, with men and not with parchment that I quarrel,—and he has voluntarily chosen to be an agent of the government. How shall he ever know well what he is and does as an officer of the government, or as a man, until he is obliged to consider whether he shall treat me, his neighbor, for whom he has respect, as a neighbor and well-disposed man, or as a maniac and disturber of the peace, and see if he can get over this obstruction to his neighborliness without a ruder and more impetuous thought or speech corresponding with his action. I know this well, that if one thousand, if one

---

[11]Copernicus (1473–1543) escaped excommunication because he was dying when his theory was published.

[12]Martin Luther (1483–1546) was excommunicated in 1520.

hundred, if ten men whom I could name,—if ten *honest* men only,—ay, if *one* HONEST man, in this State of Massachusetts, *ceasing to hold slaves*, were actually to withdraw from this copartnership, and be locked up in the county jail therefor, it would be the abolition of slavery in America. For it matters not how small the beginning may seem to be: what is once well done is done forever. But we love better to talk about it: that we say is our mission. Reform keeps many scores of newspapers in its service, but not one man. If my esteemed neighbor,[13] the State's ambassador, who will devote his days to the settlement of the question of human rights in the Council Chamber, instead of being threatened with the prisons of Carolina, were to sit down the prisoner of Massachusetts, that State which is so anxious to foist the sin of slavery upon her sister,—though at present she can discover only an act of inhospitality to be the ground of a quarrel with her,—the Legislature would not wholly waive the subject the following winter.

Under a government which imprisons any unjustly, the true place for a just man is also a prison. The proper place to-day, the only place which Massachusetts has provided for her freer and less desponding spirits, is in her prisons, to be put out and locked out of the State by her own act, as they have already put themselves out by their principles. It is there that the fugitive slave, and the Mexican prisoner on parole, and the Indian come to plead the wrongs of his race should find them; on that separate, but more free and honorable, ground, where the State places those who are not *with* her, but *against* her,—the only house in a slave State in which a free man can abide with honor. If any think that their influence would be lost there, and their voices no longer afflict the ear of the State, that they would not be as an enemy within its walls, they do not know by how much truth is stronger than error, nor how much more eloquently and effectively he can combat injustice who has experienced a little in his own person. Cast your whole vote, not a strip of paper merely, but your whole influence. A minority is powerless while it conforms to the majority; it is not even a minority then; but it is irresistible when it clogs by its whole weight. If the alternative is to keep all just men in prison, or give up war and slavery, the State will not hesitate which to choose. If a thousand men were not to pay their tax-bills this year, that would not be a violent and bloody measure, as it would be to pay them, and enable the State to commit violence and shed innocent blood. This is, in fact, the definition of a peaceable revolution, if any such is possible. If the tax-gatherer, or any other public officer, asks me, as one has done, "But what shall I do?" my answer is, "If you really wish to do anything, resign your office." When the subject has refused allegiance, and the officer has resigned his office, then the revolution is accomplished. But even suppose blood should flow. Is there not a sort of blood shed when the conscience is wounded? Through this wound a man's real manhood and immortality flow out, and he bleeds to an everlasting death. I see this blood flowing now.

I have contemplated the imprisonment of the offender, rather than the seizure of his goods,—though both will serve the same purpose,—because they who assert the purest right, and consequently are most dangerous to a corrupt State, commonly have not spent much time in accumulating property. To such the State renders comparatively small service, and a slight tax is wont to appear exorbitant, particularly if they are obliged to earn it by special labor with their hands. If there were one who lived wholly without the use of money, the State itself would hesitate to demand it of him. But the rich man—not to make any invidious comparison—is always sold to the institution which makes him rich. Absolutely speaking, the more money, the less virtue; for money comes between a man and his objects, and obtains them for him; and it was certainly no great virtue to obtain it. It puts to rest many questions which he would otherwise be taxed to answer; while the only new question which it puts is the hard but superfluous one, how to spend it. Thus his moral ground is taken from under his feet. The opportunities of living are diminished in proportion as what are called the "means" are increased. The best thing a man can do for his culture when he is rich is to endeavor to carry out those schemes which he entertained when he was poor. Christ answered the Herodians according to their condition. "Show me the tribute-money," said he;—and one took a penny out of his pocket;—if you use money which has the image of Caesar on it, and which he has made current and valuable, that is, *if you are men of the State*, and gladly enjoy the advantages of Caesar's government, then pay him back some of his own when he demands it. "Render therefore to Caesar that which is Caesar's, and to God those things which are God's,"[14]—leaving them no wiser than before as to which was which; for they did not wish to know.

When I converse with the freest of my neighbors, I perceive that, whatever they may say about the magnitude and seriousness of the question, and their regard for the public tranquillity, the long and the

[13] Samuel Hoar (1778-1856) was sent to South Carolina by Massachusetts in 1844 to protest the arrest of black seamen on Massachusetts ships in South Carolina waters. He was evicted from the state by legislative action. (Harding)

[14] Matthew xxii.19-21.

short of the matter is, that they cannot spare the protection of the existing government, and they dread the consequences to their property and families of disobedience to it. For my own part, I should not like to think that I ever rely on the protection of the State. But, if I deny the authority of the State when it presents its tax-bill, it will soon take and waste all my property, and so harass me and my children without end. This is hard. This makes it impossible for a man to live honestly, and at the same time comfortably, in outward respects. It will not be worth the while to accumulate property; that would be sure to go again. You must hire or squat somewhere, and raise but a small crop, and eat that soon. You must live within yourself, and depend upon yourself always tucked up and ready for a start, and not have many affairs. A man may grow rich in Turkey even, if he will be in all respects a good subject of the Turkish government. Confucius said: "If a state is governed by the principles of reason, poverty and misery are subjects of shame; if a state is not governed by the principles of reason, riches and honors are the subjects of shame."[15] No: until I want the protection of Massachusetts to be extended to me in some distant Southern port, where my liberty is endangered, or until I am bent solely on building up an estate at home by peaceful enterprise, I can afford to refuse allegiance to Massachusetts, and her right to my property and life. It costs me less in every sense to incur the penalty of disobedience to the State than it would to obey. I should feel as if I were worth less in that case.

Some years ago, the State met me in behalf of the Church,[16] and commanded me to pay a certain sum toward the support of a clergyman whose preaching my father attended, but never I myself. "Pay," it said, "or be locked up in the jail." I declined to pay. But, unfortunately, another man saw fit to pay it. I did not see why the schoolmaster should be taxed to support the priest, and not the priest the schoolmaster; for I was not the State's schoolmaster, but I supported myself by voluntary subscription. I did not see why the lyceum should not present its tax-bill, and have the State to back its demand, as well as the Church. However, at the request of the selectmen, I condescended to make some such statement as this in writing:—"Know all men by these presents, that I, Henry Thoreau, do not wish to be regarded as a member of any incorporated society which I have not joined." This I gave to the town

clerk; and he has it. The State, having thus learned that I did not wish to be regarded as a member of that church, has never made a like demand on me since; though it said that it must adhere to its original presumption that time. If I had known how to name them, I should then have signed off in detail from all the societies which I never signed on to; but I did not know where to find a complete list.

I have paid no poll-tax for six years. I was put into a jail once on this account, for one night;[17] and, as I stood considering the walls of solid stone, two or three feet thick, the door of wood and iron, a foot thick, and the iron grating which strained the light, I could not help being struck with the foolishness of that institution which treated me as if I were mere flesh and blood and bones, to be locked up. I wondered that it should have concluded at length that this was the best use it could put me to, and had never thought to avail itself of my services in some way. I saw that, if there was a wall of stone between me and my townsmen, there was a still more difficult one to climb or break through before they could get to be as free as I was. I did not for a moment feel confined, and the walls seemed a great waste of stone and mortar. I felt as if I alone of all my townsmen had paid my tax. They plainly did not know how to treat me, but behaved like persons who are underbred. In every threat and in every compliment there was a blunder; for they thought that my chief desire was to stand the other side of that stone wall. I could not but smile to see how industriously they locked the door on my meditations, which followed them out again without let or hindrance, and *they* were really all that was dangerous. As they could not reach me, they had resolved to punish my body; just as boys, if they cannot come at some person against whom they have a spite, will abuse his dog. I saw that the State was half-witted, that it was timid as a lone woman with her silver spoons, and that it did not know its friends from its foes, and I lost all my remaining respect for it, and pitied it.

Thus the State never intentionally confronts a man's sense, intellectual or moral, but only his body, his senses. It is not armed with superior wit or honesty, but with superior physical strength. I was not born to be forced. I will breathe after my own fashion. Let us see who is the strongest. What force has a multitude? They only can force me who obey a higher law than I. They force me to become like themselves. I do not hear of *men* being *forced* to live this way or that by masses of men. What sort of life were that to live? When I meet a government which says to me, "Your money or your life," why should I be in haste to give it my money? It may be in a great strait, and not know what to do: I cannot help

[15] Confucius, *Analects*.

[16] Churches then taxed their congregations. The taxes were billed and collected by town officials. The church (First Parish Church of Concord), which had assumed Thoreau wished to be a member, because his parents were, never billed him again. (Harding)

[17] July 23 or 24, 1846.

that. It must help itself; do as I do. It is not worth the while to snivel about it. I am not responsible for the successful working of the machinery of society. I am not the son of the engineer. I perceive that, when an acorn and a chestnut fall side by side, the one does not remain inert to make way for the other, but both obey their own laws, and spring and grow and flourish as best they can, till one, perchance, overshadows and destroys the other. If a plant cannot live according to its nature, it dies; and so a man.

The night in prison was novel and interesting enough. The prisoners in their shirt-sleeves were enjoying a chat and the evening air in the doorway, when I entered. But the jailer[18] said, "Come, boys, it is time to lock up;" and so they dispersed, and I heard the sound of their steps returning into the hollow apartments. My roommate was introduced to me by the jailer as "a first-rate fellow and a clever man." When the door was locked, he showed me where to hang my hat, and how he managed matters there. The rooms were whitewashed once a month; and this one, at least, was the whitest, most simply furnished, and probably the neatest apartment in the town. He naturally wanted to know where I came from, and what brought me there; and, when I had told him, I asked him in my turn how he came there, presuming him to be an honest man, of course; and, as the world goes, I believe he was. "Why," said he, "they accuse me of burning a barn; but I never did it." As near as I could discover, he had probably gone to bed in a barn when drunk, and smoked his pipe there; and so a barn was burnt. He had the reputation of being a clever man, had been there some three months waiting for his trial to come on, and would have to wait as much longer; but he was quite domesticated and contented, since he got his board for nothing, and thought that he was well treated.

He occupied one window, and I the other; and I saw that if one stayed there long, his principal business would be to look out the window. I had soon read all the tracts that were left there, and examined where former prisoners had broken out, and where a grate had been sawed off, and heard the history of the various occupants of that room; for I found that even here there was a history and a gossip which never circulated beyond the walls of the jail. Probably this is the only house in the town where verses are composed, which are afterward printed in a circular form, but not published. I was shown quite a long list of verses which were composed by some young men who had been detected in an attempt to escape, who avenged themselves by singing them.

[18] Sam Staples—jailer, constable, and tax collector—was a personal friend of Thoreau's.

I pumped my fellow-prisoner as dry as I could, for fear I should never see him again; but at length he showed me which was my bed, and left me to blow out the lamp.

It was like traveling into a far country, such as I had never expected to behold, to lie there for one night. It seemed to me that I never had heard the town clock strike before, nor the evening sounds of the village; for we slept with the windows open, which were inside the grating. It was to see my native village in the light of the Middle Ages, and our Concord was turned into a Rhine stream, and visions of knights and castles passed before me. They were the voices of old burghers that I heard in the streets. I was an involuntary spectator and auditor of whatever was done and said in the kitchen of the adjacent village inn,—a wholly new and rare experience to me. It was a closer view of my native town. I was fairly inside of it. I never had seen its institutions before. This is one of its peculiar institutions; for it is a shire town. I began to comprehend what its inhabitants were about.

In the morning, our breakfasts were put through the hole in the door, in small oblong-square tin pans, made to fit, and holding a pint of chocolate, with brown bread, and an iron spoon. When they called for the vessels again, I was green enough to return what bread I had left; but my comrade seized it, and said that I should lay that up for lunch or dinner. Soon after he was let out to work at haying in a neighboring field, whither he went every day, and would not be back till noon; so he bade me good-day, saying that he doubted if he should see me again.

When I came out of prison,—for some one[19] interfered, and paid that tax,—I did not perceive that great changes had taken place on the common, such as he observed who went in a youth and emerged a tottering and gray-headed man; and yet a change had to my eyes come over the scene,—the town, and State, and country,—greater than any that mere time could effect. I saw yet more distinctly the State in which I lived. I saw to what extent the people among whom I lived could be trusted as good neighbors and friends; that their friendship was for summer weather only; that they did not greatly propose to do right; that they were a distinct race from me by their prejudices and superstitions, as the Chinamen and Malays are; that in their sacrifices to humanity they ran no risks, not even to their property; that after all they were not so noble but they treated the thief as he had treated them, and hoped, by a certain outward observance and a few prayers, and by walking in a particular straight though useless path from time to time, to save their souls. This

[19] Probably his Aunt Maria Thoreau.

may be to judge my neighbors harshly; for I believe that many of them are not aware that they have such an institution as the jail in their village.

It was formerly the custom in our village, when a poor debtor came out of jail, for his acquaintances to salute him, looking through their fingers, which were crossed to represent the grating of a jail window, "How do ye do?" My neighbors did not thus salute me, but first looked at me, and then at one another, as if I had returned from a long journey. I was put into jail as I was going to the shoemaker's to get a shoe which was mended. When I was let out the next morning, I proceeded to finish my errand, and, having put on my mended shoe, joined a huckleberry party, who were impatient to put themselves under my conduct; and in half an hour,—for the horse was soon tackled,—was in the midst of a huckleberry field, on one of our highest hills, two miles off, and then the State was nowhere to be seen.

This is the whole history of "My Prisons." [20]

I have never declined paying the highway tax, because I am as desirous of being a good neighbor as I am of being a bad subject; and as for supporting schools, I am doing my part to educate my fellow-countrymen now. It is for no particular item in the tax-bill that I refuse to pay it. I simply wish to refuse allegiance to the State, to withdraw and stand aloof from it effectually. I do not care to trace the course of my dollar, if I could, till it buys a man or a musket to shoot one with,—the dollar is innocent,—but I am concerned to trace the effects of my allegiance. In fact, I quietly declare war with the State, after my fashion, though I will still make what use and get what advantage of her I can, as is usual in such cases.

If others pay the tax which is demanded of me, from a sympathy with the State, they do but what they have already done in their own case, or rather they abet injustice to a greater extent than the State requires. If they pay the tax from a mistaken interest in the individual taxed, to save his property, or prevent his going to jail, it is because they have not considered wisely how far they let their private feelings interfere with the public good.

This, then, is my position at present. But one cannot be too much on his guard in such a case, lest his action be biased by obstinacy or an undue regard for the opinions of men. Let him see that he does only what belongs to himself and to the hour.

I think sometimes, Why, this people mean well, they are only ignorant; they would do better if they knew how: why give your neighbors this pain to treat you as they are not inclined to? But I think

again, This is no reason why I should do as they do, or permit others to suffer much greater pain of a different kind. Again, I sometimes say to myself, When many millions of men, without heat, without ill will, without personal feeling of any kind, demand of you a few shillings only, without the possibility, such is their constitution, of retracting or altering their present demand, and without the possibility, on your side, of appeal to any other millions, why expose yourself to this overwhelming brute force? You do not resist cold and hunger, the winds and the waves, thus obstinately; you quietly submit to a thousand similar necessities. You do not put your head into the fire. But just in proportion as I regard this as not wholly a brute force, but partly a human force, and consider that I have relations to those millions as to so many millions of men, and not of mere brute or inanimate things, I see that appeal is possible, first and instantaneously, from them to the Maker of them, and, secondly, from them to themselves. But if I put my head deliberately into the fire, there is no appeal to fire or to the Maker of fire, and I have only myself to blame. If I could convince myself that I have any right to be satisfied with men as they are, and to treat them accordingly, and not according, in some respects, to my requisitions and expectations of what they and I ought to be, then, like a good Mussulman and fatalist, I should endeavor to be satisfied with things as they are, and say it is the will of God. And, above all, there is this difference between resisting this and a purely brute or natural force, that I can resist this with some effect; but I cannot expect, like Orpheus,[21] to change the nature of the rocks and trees and beasts.

I do not wish to quarrel with any man or nation. I do not wish to split hairs, to make fine distinctions, or set myself up as better than my neighbors. I seek rather, I may say, even an excuse for conforming to the laws of the land. I am but too ready to conform to them. Indeed, I have reason to suspect myself on this head; and each year, as the tax-gatherer comes round, I find myself disposed to review the acts and position of the general and State governments, and the spirit of the people, to discover a pretext for conformity.

> "We must affect our country as our parents,
> And if at any time we alienate
> Our love or industry from doing it honor,
> We must respect effects and teach the soul
> Matter of conscience and religion,
> And not desire of rule or benefit." [22]

[20] Reference to a popular book of that title by Silvio Pellico (1789–1854), an Italian revolutionary.

[21] In Greek mythology, Orpheus played his lyre so well that it affected "rocks and trees and beasts."

[22] From *The Battle of Alcazar* by George Peele (1558?–1597?). Thoreau reworded the passage and changed its meaning by removing it from context.

I believe that the State will soon be able to take all my work of this sort out of my hands, and then I shall be no better a patriot than my fellow-countrymen. Seen from a lower point of view, the Constitution, with all its faults, is very good; the law and the courts are very respectable; even this State and this American government are, in many respects, very admirable, and rare things, to be thankful for, such as a great many have described them; but seen from a point of view a little higher, they are what I have described them; seen from a higher still, and the highest, who shall say what they are, or that they are worth looking at or thinking of at all?

However, the government does not concern me much, and I shall bestow the fewest possible thoughts on it. It is not many moments that I live under a government, even in this world. If a man is thought-free, fancy-free, imagination-free, that which *is not* never for a long time appearing *to be* to him, unwise rulers or reformers cannot fatally interrupt him.

I know that most men think differently from myself; but those whose lives are by profession devoted to the study of these or kindred subjects content me as little as any. Statesmen and legislators, standing so completely within the institution, never distinctly and nakedly behold it. They speak of moving society, but have no resting-place without it. They may be men of a certain experience and discrimination, and have no doubt invented ingenious and even useful systems, for which we sincerely thank them; but all their wit and usefulness lie within certain not very wide limits. They are wont to forget that the world is not governed by policy and expediency. Webster[23] never goes behind government, and so cannot speak with authority about it. His words are wisdom to those legislators who contemplate no essential reform in the existing government; but for thinkers, and those who legislate for all time, he never once glances at the subject. I know of those whose serene and wise speculations on this theme would soon reveal the limits of his mind's range and hospitality. Yet, compared with the cheap professions of most reformers, and the still cheaper wisdom and eloquence of politicians in general, his are almost the only sensible and valuable words, and we thank Heaven for him. Comparatively, he is always strong, original, and, above all, practical. Still, his quality is not wisdom, but prudence. The lawyer's truth is not Truth, but consistency or a consistent expediency. Truth is always in harmony with herself, and is not concerned chiefly to reveal the justice that may consist with wrong-doing. He well deserves to be called, as he has been called, the Defender of the Constitution. There are really no blows to be given by him but defensive ones. He is not a leader, but a follower. His leaders are the men of '87.[24] "I have never made an effort," he says, "and never propose to make an effort; I have never countenanced an effort, and never mean to countenance an effort, to disturb the arrangement as originally made, by which the various States came into the Union."[25] Still thinking of the sanction which the Constitution gives to slavery, he says, "Because it was a part of the original compact,—let it stand." Notwithstanding his special acuteness and ability, he is unable to take a fact out of its merely political relations, and behold it as it lies absolutely to be disposed of by the intellect,—what, for instance, it behooves a man to do here in America to-day with regard to slavery,—but ventures, or is driven, to make some such desperate answer as the following, while professing to speak absolutely, and as a private man,—from which what new and singular code of social duties might be inferred? "The manner," says he, "in which the governments of those States where slavery exists are to regulate it is for their own consideration, under their responsibility to their constituents, to the general laws of propriety, humanity, and justice, and to God. Associations formed elsewhere, springing from a feeling of humanity, or any other cause, have nothing whatever to do with it. They have never received any encouragement from me, and they never will."[26]

They who know of no purer sources of truth, who have traced up its stream no higher, stand, and wisely stand, by the Bible and the Constitution, and drink at it there with reverence and humility; but they who behold where it comes trickling into this lake or that pool, gird up their loins once more, and continue their pilgrimage toward its fountain-head.

No man with a genius for legislation has appeared in America. They are rare in the history of the world. There are orators, politicians, and eloquent men, by the thousand; but the speaker has not yet opened his mouth to speak who is capable of settling the much vexed questions of the day. We love eloquence for its own sake, and not for any truth which it may utter, or any heroism it may inspire. Our legislators have not yet learned the comparative value of free trade and of freedom, of union, and of rectitude, to a nation. They have no genius or talent for comparatively humble questions of taxation and finance, commerce and manufactures and agriculture. If we were left solely to the wordy wit of legislators in Congress for our guidance, uncorrected by the seasonable experience and the effectual complaints of the people, America would not long retain her rank among the nations. For eighteen hundred years, though perchance I have no right to say it, the New Testament has been written; yet

[23] Daniel Webster (1782–1852).
[24] Those who framed the Constitution.
[25] From an 1845 speech by Webster.
[26] Speech, 1848.

where is the legislator who has wisdom and practical talent enough to avail himself of the light which it sheds on the science of legislation?

The authority of government, even such as I am willing to submit to,—for I will cheerfully obey those who know and can do better than I, and in many things even those who neither know nor can do so well,—is still an impure one: to be strictly just, it must have the sanction and consent of the governed. It can have no pure right over my person and property but what I concede to it. The progress from an absolute to a limited monarchy, from a limited monarchy to a democracy, is a progress toward a true respect for the individual. Even the Chinese philosopher was wise enough to regard the individual as the basis of the empire. Is a democracy, such as we know it, the last improvement possible in government? Is it not possible to take a step further towards recognizing and organizing the rights of man? There will never be a really free and enlightened State until the State comes to recognize the individual as a higher and independent power, from which all its own power and authority are derived, and treats him accordingly. I please myself with imagining a State at last which can afford to be just to all men, and to treat the individual with respect as a neighbor; which even would not think it inconsistent with its own repose if a few were to live aloof from it, not meddling with it, nor embraced by it, who fulfilled all the duties of neighbors and fellow-men. A State which bore this kind of fruit, and suffered it to drop off as fast as it ripened, would prepare the way for a still more perfect and glorious State, which also I have imagined, but not yet anywhere seen.

1847

FROM *Walden*

The reputation of Thoreau's masterpiece has grown apace in the twentieth century. The first edition—2,000 copies, published in 1854—probably more than sufficed till the death of Thoreau eight years later. Misrepresentation of his motives and actions by James Russell Lowell and Robert Louis Stevenson, who considered him a morbid solitary, hindered the growth of his fame for decades. But during the literary revival that set in about 1912, he became a major American author, and *Walden* an American classic.

Walden has four main aspects, is almost four simultaneous books. First, it is an account of an actual experience by a remarkable personality. A young man, not yet twenty-eight, undertakes in March 1845 an experiment in living, with a view to discovering what is really important to him and what is not. This aspect is indicated by the subtitle *Life in the Woods.*

The book is also a study of nature: of the lake known as Walden Pond, in summer and in winter; of animals and birds, frogs and turtles, ants and wasps, pickerel and perch; of the ground-nut and the pine tree; of rainstorms and snowstorms and the whole moving picture of the seasons. Close observation in the spirit of science is united with a living literary language.

At the same time, *Walden* is a view of modern society as seen by a critical and radical individualist: men, no longer free and creative, have been enslaved by labor and the division of labor; the Industrial Revolution has tended to produce a mechanized, standardized and conformist society destructive of simplicity, naturalness, integrity, depth, and contentment. Thoreau does not claim universal validity for his way of life, but urges the reader to "find and pursue *his own way,*" not some way derived from ancestors or contemporaries.

Finally, the book is a work of art, a group of substantially unified essays in which the personal experience, the study of nature, and the study of society are closely interrelated. The actual time-span of the Walden experiment was two years, two months, and two days; but, the two years being "similar," they are represented in the book with the unity of a single year, from spring to spring. Yet "Time is but the stream I go a-fishing in. . . . Its thin current slides away, but eternity remains." The tone is set by the sense of eternity, that which does not slide away but remains, that which is timeless, universal, absolute.

Of the eighteen chapters, or essays, six are given here, all except the long first chapter complete.

I. Economy

When I wrote the following pages, or rather the bulk of them, I lived alone, in the woods, a mile from any neighbor, in a house which I had built myself, on the shore of Walden Pond, in Concord, Massachusetts, and earned my living by the labor of my hands only. I lived there two years and two months. At present I am a sojourner in civilized life again.

I should not obtrude my affairs so much on the notice of my readers if very particular inquiries had not been made by my townsmen concerning my mode of life, which some would call impertinent, though they do not appear to me at all impertinent, but, considering the circumstances, very natural and pertinent. Some have asked what I got to eat; if I did not feel lonesome; if I was not afraid; and the like. Others have been curious to learn what portion of my income I devoted to charitable purposes; and some, who have large families, how many poor children I maintained. I will therefore ask those of my readers who feel no particular interest in me to pardon me if I undertake to answer some of these questions in this book. In most books, the I, or first person, is omitted; in this it will be retained; that, in respect to egotism, is the main difference. We commonly do not remember that it is, after all, always the first person that is speaking. I should not talk so much about myself if there were anybody else whom I knew as well. Unfortunately, I am confined to this theme by the narrowness of my experience. Moreover, I, on my side, require of every writer, first or last, a simple and sincere account of his own life, and not merely what he has heard of other men's lives; some such account as he would send to his kindred from a distant land; for if he has lived sincerely, it must have been in a distant land to me. Perhaps these pages are more particularly addressed to poor students. As for the rest of my readers, they will accept such portions as apply to them. I trust that none will stretch the seams in putting on the coat, for it may do good service to him whom it fits.

I would fain say something, not so much concerning the Chinese and Sandwich Islanders as you who read these pages; who are said to live in New England; something about your condition, especially your outward condition or circumstances in this world, in this town, what it is, whether it is necessary that it be as bad as it is, whether it cannot be improved as well as not. I have travelled a good deal in Concord; and everywhere, in shops, and offices, and fields, the inhabitants have appeared to me to be doing penance in a thousand remarkable ways. What I have heard of Bramins[1] sitting exposed to four fires and looking in the face of the sun; or hanging suspended, with their heads downward, over flames; or looking at the heavens over their shoulders "until it becomes impossible for them to resume their natural position, while from the twist of the neck nothing but liquids can pass into the stomach;" or dwelling, chained for life, at the foot of a tree; or measuring with their bodies, like caterpillars, the breadth of vast empires; or standing on one leg on the tops of pillars,—even these forms of conscious penance are hardly more incredible and astonishing than the scenes which I daily witness. The twelve labors of Hercules were trifling in comparison with those which my neighbors have undertaken; for they were only twelve, and had an end; but I could never see that these men slew or captured any monster or finished any labor. They have no friend Iolaus[2] to burn with a hot iron the root of the hydra's head, but as soon as one head is crushed, two spring up.

I see young men, my townsmen, whose misfortune it is to have inherited farms, houses, barns, cattle, and farming tools; for these are more easily acquired than got rid of. Better if they had been born in the open pasture and suckled by a wolf, that

they might have seen with clearer eyes what field they were called to labor in. Who made them serfs of the soil? Why should they eat their sixty acres, when man is condemned to eat only his peck of dirt? Why should they begin digging their graves as soon as they are born? They have got to live a man's life, pushing all these things before them, and get on as well as they can. How many a poor immortal soul have I met well-nigh crushed and smothered under its load, creeping down the road of life, pushing before it a barn seventy-five feet by forty, its Augean stables never cleansed, and one hundred acres of land, tillage, mowing, pasture, and wood-lot! The portionless, who struggle with no such unnecessary inherited encumbrances, find it labor enough to subdue and cultivate a few cubic feet of flesh. ° ° °

Near the end of March, 1845, I borrowed an axe and went down to the woods by Walden Pond, nearest to where I intended to build my house, and began to cut down some tall, arrowy white pines, still in their youth, for timber. It is difficult to begin without borrowing, but perhaps it is the most generous course thus to permit your fellow-men to have an interest in your enterprise. The owner of the axe, as he released his hold on it, said that it was the apple of his eye; but I returned it sharper than I received it. It was a pleasant hillside where I worked, covered with pine woods, through which I looked out on the pond, and a small open field in the woods where pines and hickories were springing up. The ice in the pond was not yet dissolved, though there were some open spaces, and it was all dark-colored and saturated with water. There were some slight flurries of snow during the days that I worked there; but for the most part when I came out on to the railroad, on my way home, its yellow sand-heap stretched away gleaming in the hazy atmosphere, and the rails shone in the spring sun, and I heard the lark and pewee and other birds already come to commence another year with us. They were pleasant spring days, in which the winter of man's discontent[3] was thawing as well as the earth, and the life that had lain torpid began to stretch itself. One day, when my axe had come off and I had cut a green hickory for a wedge, driving it with a stone, and had placed the whole to soak in a pond-hole in order to swell the wood, I saw a striped snake run into the water, and he lay on the bottom, apparently without inconvenience, as long as I stayed there, or more than a quarter of an hour; perhaps because he had not yet fairly come out of the torpid state. It appeared to me that for a like reason men remain in

[1] The highest Hindu caste, which often subjected themselves to penance as an act of devotion. The quotation that follows has not been identified.

[2] Hercules' servant, who aided him in defeating the Hydra (one of the twelve labors) by burning away the heads and burying the ninth immortal one.

[3] Cf. Shakespeare, *Richard III* I.i. 1–2: "Now is the winter of our discontent/Made glorious summer by this sun of York."

their present low and primitive condition; but if they should feel the influence of the spring of springs arousing them, they would of necessity rise to a higher and more ethereal life. I had previously seen the snakes in frosty mornings in my path with portions of their bodies still numb and inflexible, waiting for the sun to thaw them. On the 1st of April it rained and melted the ice, and in the early part of the day, which was very foggy, I heard a stray goose groping about over the pond and cackling as if lost, or like the spirit of the fog.

So I went on for some days cutting and hewing timber, and also studs and rafters, all with my narrow axe, not having many communicable or scholar-like thoughts, singing to myself,—

> Men say they know many things;
> But lo! they have taken wings,—
> The arts and sciences,
> And a thousand appliances:
> The wind that blows
> Is all that anybody knows.[4]

I hewed the main timbers six inches square, most of the studs on two sides only, and the rafters and floor timbers on one side, leaving the rest of the bark on, so that they were just as straight and much stronger than sawed ones. Each stick was carefully mortised or tenoned by its stump, for I had borrowed other tools by this time. My days in the woods were not very long ones; yet I usually carried my dinner of bread and butter, and read the newspaper in which it was wrapped, at noon, sitting amid the green pine boughs which I had cut off, and to my bread was imparted some of their fragrance, for my hands were covered with a thick coat of pitch. Before I had done I was more the friend than the foe of the pine tree, though I had cut down some of them, having become better acquainted with it. Sometimes a rambler in the wood was attracted by the sound of my axe, and we chatted pleasantly over the chips which I had made.

By the middle of April, for I made no haste in my work, but rather made the most of it, my house was framed and ready for the raising. I had already bought the shanty of James Collins, an Irishman who worked on the Fitchburg Railroad, for boards. James Collins' shanty was considered an uncommonly fine one. When I called to see it he was not at home. I walked about the outside, at first unobserved from within, the window was so deep and high. It was of small dimensions, with a peaked cottage roof, and not much else to be seen, the dirt being raised five feet all around as if it were a compost heap. The roof was the soundest part, though a good deal warped and made brittle by the

sun. Doorsill there was none, but a perennial passage for the hens under the door-board. Mrs. C. came to the door and asked me to view it from the inside. The hens were driven in by my approach. It was dark, and had a dirt floor for the most part, dank, clammy, and aguish, only here a board and there a board which would not bear removal. She lighted a lamp to show me the inside of the roof and the walls, and also that the board floor extended under the bed, warning me not to step into the cellar, a sort of dust hole two feet deep. In her own words, they were "good boards overhead, good boards all around, and a good window,"—of two whole squares originally, only the cat had passed out that way lately. There was a stove, a bed, and a place to sit, an infant in the house where it was born, a silk parasol, gilt-framed looking-glass, and a patent new coffee-mill nailed to an oak sapling, all told. The bargain was soon concluded, for James had in the meanwhile returned. I to pay four dollars and twenty-five cents to-night, he to vacate at five to-morrow morning, selling to nobody else meanwhile: I to take possession at six. It were well, he said, to be there early, and anticipate certain indistinct but wholly unjust claims on the score of ground rent and fuel. This he assured me was the only encumbrance. At six I passed him and his family on the road. One large bundle held their all,— bed, coffee-mill, looking-glass, hens,—all but the cat; she took to the woods and became a wild cat, and, as I learned afterward, trod in a trap set for woodchucks, and so became a dead cat at last.

I took down this dwelling the same morning, drawing the nails, and removed it to the pond-side by small cartloads, spreading the boards on the grass there to bleach and warp back again in the sun. One early thrush gave me a note or two as I drove along the woodland path. I was informed treacherously by a young Patrick that neighbor Seeley, an Irishman, in the intervals of the carting, transferred the still tolerable, straight, and drivable nails, staples, and spikes to his pocket, and then stood when I came back to pass the time of day, and look freshly up, unconcerned, with spring thoughts, at the devastation; there being a dearth of work, as he said. He was there to represent spectatordom, and help make this seemingly insignificant event one with the removal of the gods of Troy.[5]

I dug my cellar in the side of a hill sloping to the south, where a woodchuck had formerly dug his burrow, down through sumach and blackberry roots, and the lowest stain of vegetation, six feet square by seven deep, to a fine sand where potatoes would not freeze in any winter. The sides were left

[4] Thoreau's own lines.

[5] Upon the fall of Troy the Greeks removed the images of the gods from the city.

shelving, and not stoned; but the sun having never shone on them, the sand still keeps its place. It was but two hours' work. I took particular pleasure in this breaking of ground, for in almost all latitudes men dig into the earth for an equable temperature. Under the most splendid house in the city is still to be found the cellar where they store their roots as of old, and long after the superstructure has disappeared posterity remark its dent in the earth. The house is still but a sort of porch at the entrance of a burrow.

At length, in the beginning of May, with the help of some of my acquaintances,[6] rather to improve so good an occasion for neighborliness than from any necessity, I set up the frame of my house. No man was ever more honored in the character of his raisers than I. They are destined, I trust, to assist at the raising of loftier structures one day. I began to occupy my house on the 4th of July, as soon as it was boarded and roofed, for the boards were carefully feather-edged and lapped, so that it was perfectly impervious to rain, but before boarding I laid the foundation of a chimney at one end, bringing two cartloads of stones up the hill from the pond in my arms. I built the chimney after my hoeing in the fall, before a fire became necessary for warmth, doing my cooking in the meanwhile out of doors on the ground, early in the morning: which mode I still think is in some respects more convenient and agreeable than the usual one. When it stormed before my bread was baked, I fixed a few boards over the fire, and sat under them to watch my loaf, and passed some pleasant hours in that way. In those days, when my hands were much employed, I read but little, but the least scraps of paper which lay on the ground, my holder, or tablecloth, afforded me as much entertainment, in fact answered the same purpose as the Iliad. ° ° °

Before winter I built a chimney, and shingled the sides of my house, which were already impervious to rain, with imperfect and sappy shingles made of the first slice of the log, whose edges I was obliged to straighten with a plane.

I have thus a tight shingled and plastered house, ten feet wide by fifteen long, and eight-feet posts, with a garret and a closet, a large window on each side, two trap-doors, one door at the end, and a brick fireplace opposite. The exact cost of my house, paying the usual price for such materials as I used, but not counting the work, all of which was done by myself, was as follows; and I give the details because very few are able to tell exactly what their houses cost, and fewer still, if any, the separate cost of the various materials which compose them:—

Boards	$ 8 03½,	mostly shanty boards.
Refuse shingles for roof and sides . . .	4 00	
Laths	1 25	
Two second-hand windows with glass	2 43	
One thousand old brick.	4 00	
Two casks of lime . .	2 40	That was high.
Hair	0 31	More than I needed.
Mantle-tree iron. . . .	0 15	
Nails	3 90	
Hinges and screws . .	0 14	
Latch.	0 10	
Chalk.	0 01	
Transportation.	1 40	{ I carried a good part on my back.
In all	$28 12½	

These are all the materials, excepting the timber, stones, and sand, which I claimed by squatter's right. I have also a small woodshed adjoining, made chiefly of the stuff which was left after building the house.

I intend to build me a house which will surpass any on the main street in Concord in grandeur and luxury, as soon as it pleases me as much and will cost me no more than my present one.

I thus found that the student who wishes for a shelter can obtain one for a lifetime at an expense not greater than the rent which he now pays annually. If I seem to boast more than is becoming, my excuse is that I brag for humanity rather than for myself; and my shortcomings and inconsistencies do not affect the truth of my statement. Notwithstanding much cant and hypocrisy,—chaff which I find it difficult to separate from my wheat, but for which I am as sorry as any man,—I will breathe freely and stretch myself in this respect, it is such a relief to both the moral and physical system; and I am resolved that I will not through humility become the devil's attorney. I will endeavor to speak a good word for the truth. At Cambridge College[7] the mere rent of a student's room, which is only a little larger than my own, is thirty dollars each year, though the corporation had the advantage of building thirty-two side by side and under one roof, and the occupant suffers the inconvenience of many and noisy neighbors, and perhaps a residence in the fourth story.[8] I cannot but think that if we had more true wisdom in these respects, not only less education would be

[6]Among them: Emerson, Bronson Alcott, and W. E. Channing.

[7] Harvard College; Thoreau graduated from there in 1837.
[8] He presumably had a fourth-floor room in Hollis Hall.

needed, because, forsooth, more would already have been acquired, but the pecuniary expense of getting an education would in a great measure vanish. Those conveniences which the student requires at Cambridge or elsewhere cost him or somebody else ten times as great a sacrifice of life as they would with proper management on both sides. Those things for which the most money is demanded are never the things which the student most wants. Tuition, for instance, is an important item in the term bill, while for the far more valuable education which he gets by associating with the most cultivated of his contemporaries no charge is made. The mode of founding a college is, commonly, to get up a subscription of dollars and cents, and then, following blindly the principles of a division of labor to its extreme,—a principle which should never be followed but with circumspection,—to call in a contractor who makes this a subject of speculation, and he employs Irishmen or other operatives actually to lay the foundations, while the students that are to be are said to be fitting themselves for it; and for these oversights successive generations have to pay. I think that it would be *better than this*, for the students, or those who desire to be benefited by it, even to lay the foundation themselves. The student who secures his coveted leisure and retirement by systematically shirking any labor necessary to man obtains but an ignoble and unprofitable leisure, defrauding himself of the experience which alone can make leisure fruitful. "But," says one, "you do not mean that the students should go to work with their hands instead of their heads?" I do not mean that exactly, but I mean something which he might think a good deal like that; I mean that they should not *play* life, or *study* it merely, while the community supports them at this expensive game, but earnestly *live* it from beginning to end. How could youths better learn to live than by at once trying the experiment of living? Methinks this would exercise their minds as much as mathematics. If I wished a boy to know something about the arts and sciences, for instance, I would not pursue the common course, which is merely to send him into the neighborhood of some professor, where anything is professed and practised but the art of life;—to survey the world through a telescope or a microscope, and never with his natural eye; to study chemistry, and not learn how his bread is made, or mechanics, and not learn how it is earned; to discover new satellites to Neptune, and not detect the motes in his eyes, or to what vagabond he is a satellite himself; or to be devoured by the monsters that swarm all around him, while contemplating the monsters in a drop of vinegar. Which would have advanced the most at the end of a month,—the boy who had made his

own jackknife from the ore which he had dug and smelted, reading as much as would be necessary for this—or the boy who had attended the lectures on metallurgy at the Institute in the meanwhile, and had received a Rodgers penknife[9] from his father? Which would be most likely to cut his fingers? . . . To my astonishment I was informed on leaving college that I had studied navigation!—why, if I had taken one turn down the harbor I should have known more about it. Even the *poor* student studies and is taught only *political* economy, while that economy of living which is synonymous with philosophy is not even sincerely professed in our colleges. The consequence is, that while he is reading Adam Smith, Ricardo, and Say,[10] he runs his father in debt irretrievably. ° ° °

Before I finished my house, wishing to earn ten or twelve dollars by some honest and agreeable method, in order to meet my unusual expenses, I planted about two acres and a half of light and sandy soil near it chiefly with beans, but also a small part with potatoes, corn, peas, and turnips. The whole lot[11] contains eleven acres, mostly growing up to pines and hickories, and was sold the preceding season for eight dollars and eight cents an acre. One farmer said that it was "good for nothing but to raise cheeping squirrels on." I put no manure whatever on this land, not being the owner, but merely a squatter, and not expecting to cultivate so much again, and I did not quite hoe it all once. I got out several cords of stumps in plowing, which supplied me with fuel for a long time, and left small circles of virgin mould, easily distinguishable through the summer by the greater luxuriance of the beans there. The dead and for the most part unmerchantable wood behind my house, and the driftwood from the pond, have supplied the remainder of my fuel. I was obliged to hire a team and a man for the plowing, though I held the plow myself. My farm outgoes for the first season were, for implements, seed, work, etc., $14.72 1/2. The seed corn was given me. This never costs anything to speak of, unless you plant more than enough. I got twelve bushels of beans, and eighteen bushels of potatoes, beside some peas and sweet corn. The yellow corn and turnips were too late to come to anything. My whole income from the farm was

[9] Manufactured by Joseph Rodgers and Sons, Sheffield, England.

[10] Smith (1723-90), author of *The Wealth of Nations;* David Ricardo (1772-1823), English economist; Jean Baptiste Say (1767-1832), French economist.

[11] The land belonged to Emerson; he bought it in 1844. (Harding, *Variorum Walden,* p. 278)

Deducting the outgoes . . . . $23 44 / 14 72½

There are left . . . . $ 8 71½,

beside produce consumed and on hand at the time this estimate was made of the value of $4.50,—the amount on hand much more than balancing a little grass which I did not raise. All things considered, that is, considering the importance of a man's soul and of to-day, notwithstanding the short time occupied by my experiment, nay, partly even because of its transient character, I believe that that was doing better than any farmer in Concord did that year.

The next year I did better still, for I spaded up all the land which I required, about a third of an acre, and I learned from the experience of both years, not being in the least awed by many celebrated works on husbandry, Arthur Young[12] among the rest, that if one would live simply and eat only the crop which he raised, and raise no more than he ate, and not exchange it for an insufficient quantity of more luxurious and expensive things, he would need to cultivate only a few rods of ground, and that it would be cheaper to spade up that than to use oxen to plow it, and to select a fresh spot from time to time than to manure the old, and he could do all his necessary farm work as it were with his left hand at odd hours in the summer; and thus he would not be tied to an ox, or horse, or cow, or pig, as at present. I desire to speak impartially on this point, and as one not interested in the success or failure of the present economical and social arrangements. I was more independent than any farmer in Concord, for I was not anchored to a house or farm, but could follow the bent of my genius, which is a very crooked one, every moment. Beside being better off than they already, if my house had been burned or my crops had failed, I should have been nearly as well off as before. ° ° °

By surveying, carpentry, and day-labor of various other kinds in the village in the meanwhile, for I have as many trades as fingers, I had earned $13.34. The expense of food for eight months, namely, from July 4th to March 1st, the time when these estimates were made, though I lived there more than two years,—not counting potatoes, a little green corn, and some peas, which I had raised, nor considering the value of what was on hand at the last date,—was

[12]Author of many volumes on agriculture, e.g. *Rural Oeconomy, or Essays on the Practical Parts of Husbandry* (London, 1773).

Rice	$1 73½	
Molasses	1 73	Cheapest form of the saccharine.
Rye meal	1 04¾	
Indian meal	0 99¾	Cheaper than rye.
Pork	0 22	
Flour	0 88	Costs more than Indian meal, both money and trouble.
Sugar	0 80	
Lard	0 65	
Apples	0 25	
Dried apple	0 22	
Sweet potatoes . . .	0 10	
One pumpkin	0 6	
One watermelon . .	0 2	
Salt	0 3	

All experiments which failed.

Yes, I did eat $8.74, all told; but I should not thus unblushingly publish my guilt, if I did not know that most of my readers were equally guilty with myself, and that their deeds would look no better in print. The next year I sometimes caught a mess of fish for my dinner, and once I went so far as to slaughter a woodchuck which ravaged my bean-field,—effect his transmigration, as a Tartar would say,—and devour him, partly for experiment's sake; but though it afforded me a momentary enjoyment, notwithstanding a musky flavor, I saw that the longest use would not make that a good practice, however it might seem to have your woodchucks ready dressed by the village butcher.

Clothing and some incidental expenses within the same dates, though little can be inferred from this item, amounted to

$8 40¾

Oil and some household utensils 2 00

So that all the pecuniary outgoes, excepting for washing and mending, which for the most part were done out of the house, and their bills have not yet been received,—and these are all and more than all the ways by which money necessarily goes out in this part of the world,—were

House	$28 12½
Farm one year	14 72½
Food eight months	8 74
Clothing, etc., eight months .	8 40¾
Oil, etc., eight months	2 00
In all	$61 99¾

I address myself now to those of my readers who have a living to get. And to meet this I have for farm produce sold

Earned by day-labor $23 44
                           13 34

In all $36 78,

which subtracted from the sum of the outgoes leaves a balance of $25.21 3/4 on the one side,—this being very nearly the means with which I started, and the measure of expenses to be incurred,—and on the other, beside the leisure and independence and health thus secured, a comfortable house for me as long as I choose to occupy it.

These statistics, however accidental and therefore uninstructive they may appear, as they have a certain completeness, have a certain value also. Nothing was given me of which I have not rendered some account. It appears from the above estimate, that my food alone cost me in money about twenty-seven cents a week. It was, for nearly two years after this, rye and Indian meal without yeast, potatoes, rice, a very little salt pork, molasses, and salt; and my drink, water. It was fit that I should live on rice, mainly, who loved so well the philosophy of India. To meet the objections of some inveterate cavillers, I may as well state, that if I dined out occasionally,[13] as I always had done, and I trust shall have opportunities to do again, it was frequently to the detriment of my domestic arrangements. But the dining out, being, as I have stated, a constant element, does not in the least affect a comparative statement like this.

I learned from my two years' experience that it would cost incredibly little trouble to obtain one's necessary food, even in this latitude; that a man may use as simple a diet as the animals, and yet retain health and strength. I have made a satisfactory dinner, satisfactory on several accounts, simply off a dish of purslane (*Portulaca oleracea*) which I gathered in my cornfield, boiled and salted. I give the Latin on account of the savoriness of the trivial name. And pray what more can a reasonable man desire, in peaceful times, in ordinary noons, than a sufficient number of ears of green sweet corn boiled, with the addition of salt? Even the little variety which I used was a yielding to the demands of appetite, and not of health. Yet men have come to such a pass that they frequently starve, not for want of necessaries, but for want of luxuries; and I know a good woman who thinks that her son lost his life because he took to drinking water only. ° ° °

One young man of my acquaintance, who has inherited some acres, told me that he thought he should live as I did, *if he had the means.* I would not have any one adopt *my* mode of living on any

account; for, beside that before he has fairly learned it I may have found out another for myself, I desire that there may be as many different persons in the world as possible; but I would have each one be very careful to find out and pursue *his own* way, and not his father's or his mother's or his neighbor's instead. The youth may build or plant or sail, only let him not be hindered from doing that which he tells me he would like to do. It is by a mathematical point only that we are wise, as the sailor or the fugitive slave keeps the polestar in his eye; but that is sufficient guidance for all our life. We may not arrive at our port within a calculable period, but we would preserve the true course.

Undoubtedly, in this case, what is true for one is truer still for a thousand, as a large house is not proportionally more expensive than a small one, since one roof may cover, one cellar underlie, and one wall separate several apartments. But for my part, I preferred the solitary dwelling. Moreover, it will commonly be cheaper to build the whole yourself than to convince another of the advantage of the common wall; and when you have done this, the common partition, to be much cheaper, must be a thin one, and that other may prove a bad neighbor, and also not keep his side in repair. The only coöperation which is commonly possible is exceedingly partial and superficial; and what little true coöperation there is, is as if it were not, being a harmony inaudible to men. If a man has faith, he will coöperate with equal faith everywhere; if he has not faith, he will continue to live like the rest of the world, whatever company he is joined to. To coöperate in the highest as well as the lowest sense, means *to get our living together.* I heard it proposed lately that two young men should travel together over the world, the one without money, earning his means as he went, before the mast and behind the plow, the other carrying a bill of exchange in his pocket. It was easy to see that they could not long be companions or coöperate, since one would not *operate* at all. They would part at the first interesting crisis in their adventures. Above all, as I have implied, the man who goes alone can start to-day; but he who travels with another must wait till that other is ready, and it may be a long time before they get off.

But all this is very selfish, I have heard some of my townsmen say. I confess that I have hitherto indulged very little in philanthropic enterprises.[14] I have made some sacrifices to a sense of duty, and among others have sacrificed this pleasure also. There are those who have used all their arts to

---

[13] He occasionally dined at the Emersons'.

[14] Walter Harding points out, however, that Thoreau did a great deal for the Irish laborers in Concord.

[margin note, left: SIMPLICITY IN FOOD]

[margin note, right: FIND YOUR OWN WAY]

[margin note, right: COOPERATION]

persuade me to undertake the support of some poor family in the town; and if I had nothing to do—for the devil finds employment for the idle—I might try my hand at some such pastime as that. However, when I have thought to indulge myself in this respect, and lay their Heaven under an obligation by maintaining certain poor persons in all respects as comfortably as I maintain myself, and have even ventured so far as to make them the offer, they have one and all unhesitatingly preferred to remain poor. While my townsmen and women are devoted in so many ways to the good of their fellows, I trust that one at least may be spared to other and less humane pursuits. You must have a genius for charity as well as for anything else. As for Doing-good, that is one of the professions which are full. Moreover, I have tried it fairly, and, strange as it may seem, am satisfied that it does not agree with my constitution. Probably I should not consciously and deliberately forsake my particular calling to do the good which society demands of me, to save the universe from annihilation; and I believe that a like but infinitely greater steadfastness elsewhere is all that now preserves it. But I would not stand between any man and his genius; and to him who does this work, which I decline, with his whole heart and soul and life, I would say, Persevere, even if the world call it doing evil, as it is most likely they will.

I am far from supposing that my case is a peculiar one; no doubt many of my readers would make a similar defence. At doing something,—I will not engage that my neighbors shall pronounce it good,—I do not hesitate to say that I should be a capital fellow to hire; but what that is, it is for my employer to find out. What *good* I do, in the common sense of that word, must be aside from my main path, and for the most part wholly unintended. Men say, practically, Begin where you are and such as you are, without aiming mainly to become of more worth, and with kindness aforethought go about doing good. If I were to preach at all in this strain, I should say rather, Set about being good. As if the sun should stop when he had kindled his fires up to the splendor of a moon or a star of the sixth magnitude, and go about like a Robin Goodfellow,[15] peeping in at every cottage window, inspiring lunatics, and tainting meats, and making darkness visible, instead of steadily increasing his genial heat and beneficence till he is of such brightness that no mortal can look him in the face, and then, and in the meanwhile too, going about the world in his own orbit, doing it good, or rather, as a truer philosophy has discovered, the world going about him getting good. When Phaëton,[16] wishing to prove his heavenly birth by his beneficence, had the sun's chariot

[15] Known also as Puck.
[16] The son of Helios, the sun, in Greek mythology.

but one day, and drove out of the beaten track, he burned several blocks of houses in the lower streets of heaven, and scorched the surface of the earth, and dried up every spring, and made the great desert of Sahara, till at length Jupiter hurled him headlong to the earth with a thunderbolt, and the sun, through grief at his death, did not shine for a year.

There is no odor so bad as that which arises from goodness tainted. It is human, it is divine, carrion. If I knew for a certainty that a man was coming to my house with the conscious design of doing me good, I should run for my life, as from that dry and parching wind of the African deserts called the simoom, which fills the mouth and nose and ears and eyes with dust till you are suffocated, for fear that I should get some of his good done to me,—some of its virus mingled with my blood. No,—in this case I would rather suffer evil the natural way. A man is not a good *man* to me because he will feed me if I should be starving, or warm me if I should be freezing, or pull me out of a ditch if I should ever fall into one. I can find you a Newfoundland dog that will do as much. Philanthropy is not love for one's fellow-man in the broadest sense. Howard[17] was no doubt an exceedingly kind and worthy man in his way, and has his reward; but, comparatively speaking, what are a hundred Howards to *us*, if their philanthropy do not help *us* in our best estate, when we are most worthy to be helped? I never heard of a philanthropic meeting in which it was sincerely proposed to do any good to me, or the like of me.

The Jesuits were quite balked by those Indians who, being burned at the stake, suggested new modes of torture to their tormentors. Being superior to physical suffering, it sometimes chanced that they were superior to any consolation which the missionaries could offer; and the law to do as you would be done by fell with less persuasiveness on the ears of those who, for their part, did not care how they were done by, who loved their enemies after a new fashion, and came very near freely forgiving them all they did.

Be sure that you give the poor the aid they most need, though it be your example which leaves them far behind. If you give money, spend yourself with it, and do not merely abandon it to them. We make curious mistakes sometimes. Often the poor man is not so cold and hungry as he is dirty and ragged and gross. It is partly his taste, and not merely his misfortune. If you give him money, he will perhaps buy more rags with it. I was wont to pity the clumsy Irish laborers who cut ice on the pond, in such mean and ragged clothes, while I shivered in my more tidy and somewhat more fashionable garments, till, one bitter cold day, one who had slipped into

[17] John Howard (1726–90), English prison reformer.

the water came to my house to warm him, and I saw him strip off three pairs of pants and two pairs of stockings ere he got down to the skin, though they were dirty and ragged enough, it is true, and that he could afford to refuse the *extra* garments which I offered him, he had so many *intra* ones. This ducking was the very thing he needed. Then I began to pity myself, and I saw that it would be a greater charity to bestow on me a flannel shirt than a whole slop-shop on him. There are a thousand hacking at the branches of evil to one who is striking at the root, and it may be that he who bestows the largest amount of time and money on the needy is doing the most by his mode of life to produce that misery which he strives in vain to relieve. It is the pious slave-breeder devoting the proceeds of every tenth slave to buy a Sunday's liberty for the rest. Some show their kindness to the poor by employing them in their kitchens. Would they not be kinder if they employed themselves there? You boast of spending a tenth part of your income in charity; maybe you should spend the nine tenths so, and done with it. Society recovers only a tenth part of the property then. Is this owing to the generosity of him in whose possession it is found, or to the remissness of the officers of justice?

Philanthropy is almost the only virtue which is sufficiently appreciated by mankind. Nay, it is greatly overrated; and it is our selfishness which overrates it. A robust poor man, one sunny day here in Concord, praised a fellow-townsman to me, because, as he said, he was kind to the poor; meaning himself. The kind uncles and aunts of the race are more esteemed than its true spiritual fathers and mothers. I once heard a reverend lecturer on England, a man of learning and intelligence, after enumerating her scientific, literary, and political worthies, Shakespeare, Bacon, Cromwell, Milton, Newton, and others, speak next of her Christian heroes, whom, as if his profession required it of him, he elevated to a place far above all the rest, as the greatest of the great. They were Penn,[18] Howard, and Mrs. Fry.[19] Every one must feel the falsehood and cant of this. The last were not England's best men and women; only, perhaps, her best philanthropists.

I would not subtract anything from the praise that is due to philanthropy, but merely demand justice for all who by their lives and works are a blessing to mankind. I do not value chiefly a man's uprightness and benevolence, which are, as it were, his stem and leaves. Those plants of whose greenness withered we make herb tea for the sick serve but a humble

use, and are most employed by quacks. I want the flower and fruit of a man; that some fragrance be wafted over from him to me, and some ripeness flavor our intercourse. His goodness must not be a partial and transitory act, but a constant superfluity, which costs him nothing and of which he is unconscious. This is a charity that hides a multitude of sins. The philanthropist too often surrounds mankind with the remembrance of his own cast-off griefs as an atmosphere, and calls it sympathy. We should impart our courage, and not our despair, our health and ease, and not our disease, and take care that this does not spread by contagion. From what southern plains comes up the voice of wailing? Under what latitudes reside the heathen to whom we would send light? Who is that intemperate and brutal man whom we would redeem? If anything ail a man, so that he does not perform his functions, if he have a pain in his bowels even,—for that is the seat of sympathy,—he forthwith sets about reforming—the world. Being a microcosm himself, he discovers—and it is a true discovery, and he is the man to make it—that the world has been eating green apples; to his eyes, in fact, the globe itself is a great green apple, which there is danger awful to think of that the children of men will nibble before it is ripe; and straightway his drastic philanthropy seeks out the Esquimau and the Patagonian, and embraces the populous Indian and Chinese villages; and thus, by a few years of philanthropic activity, the powers in the meanwhile using him for their own ends, no doubt, he cures himself of his dyspepsia, the globe acquires a faint blush on one or both of its cheeks, as if it were beginning to be ripe, and life loses its crudity and is once more sweet and wholesome to live. I never dreamed of any enormity greater than I have committed. I never knew, and never shall know, a worse man than myself.

I believe that what so saddens the reformer is not his sympathy with his fellows in distress, but, though he be the holiest son of God, is his private ail. Let this be righted, let the spring come to him, the morning rise over his couch, and he will forsake his generous companions without apology. My excuse for not lecturing against the use of tobacco is, that I never chewed it, that is a penalty which reformed tobacco-chewers have to pay; though there are things enough I have chewed which I could lecture against. If you should ever be betrayed into any of these philanthropies, do not let your left hand know what your right hand does, for it is not worth knowing. Rescue the drowning and tie your shoestrings. Take your time, and set about some free labor.

Our manners have been corrupted by communication with the saints. Our hymn-books resound with a melodious cursing of God and enduring Him

---

[18] William Penn (1644–1718), founder of Pennsylvania and Quaker reformer.
[19] Elizabeth Fry (1780–1845), Quaker prison reformer.

forever. One would say that even the prophets and redeemers had rather consoled the fears than confirmed the hopes of man. There is nowhere recorded a simple and irrepressible satisfaction with the gift of life, any memorable praise of God. All health and success does me good, however far off and withdrawn it may appear; all disease and failure helps to make me sad and does me evil, however much sympathy it may have with me or I with it. If, then, we would indeed restore mankind by truly Indian, botanic, magnetic,[20] or natural means, let us first be as simple and well as Nature ourselves, dispel the clouds which hang over our own brows, and take up a little life into our pores. Do not stay to be an overseer of the poor, but endeavor to become one of the worthies of the world.

I read in the Gulistan, or Flower Garden, of Sheik Sadi of Shiraz,[21] that "they asked a wise man, saying: Of the many celebrated trees which the Most High God has created lofty and umbrageous, they call none azad, or free, excepting the cypress, which bears no fruit; what mystery is there in this? He replied: Each has its appropriate produce, and appointed season, during the continuance of which it is fresh and blooming, and during their absence dry and withered; to neither of which states is the cypress exposed, being always flourishing; and of this nature are the azads, or religious independents.—Fix not thy heart on that which is transitory; for the Dijlah, or Tigris, will continue to flow through Bagdad after the race of caliphs is extinct: if thy hand has plenty, be liberal as the date tree; but if it affords nothing to give away, be an azad, or free man, like the cypress."

II. Where I Lived, and What I Lived For

At a certain season of our life we are accustomed to consider every spot as the possible site of a house. I have thus surveyed the country on every side within a dozen miles of where I live. In imagination I have bought all the farms in succession, for all were to be bought, and I knew their price. I walked over each farmer's premises, tasted his wild apples, discoursed on husbandry with him, took his farm at his price, at any price, mortgaging it to him in my mind; even put a higher price on it,—took everything but a deed of it,—took his word for his deed, for I dearly love to talk,—cultivated it, and him too to some extent, I trust, and withdrew when I had enjoyed it long enough, leaving him to carry it on. This experience entitles me to be regarded as a sort of

real-estate broker by my friends. Wherever I sat, there I might live, and the landscape radiated from me accordingly. What is a house but a *sedes*, a seat?—better if a country seat. I discovered many a site for a house not likely to be soon improved, which some might have thought too far from the village, but to my eyes the village was too far from it. Well, there I might live, I said; and there I did live, for an hour, a summer and a winter life; saw how I could let the years run off, buffet the winter through, and see the spring come in. The future inhabitants of this region, wherever they may place their houses, may be sure that they have been anticipated. An afternoon sufficed to lay out the land into orchard, wood-lot, and pasture, and to decide what fine oaks or pines should be left to stand before the door, and whence each blasted tree could be seen to the best advantage; and then I let it lie, fallow perchance, for a man is rich in proportion to the number of things which he can afford to let alone.

My imagination carried me so far that I even had the refusal of several farms,—the refusal was all I wanted,—but I never got my fingers burned by actual possession. The nearest that I came to actual possession was when I bought the Hollowell place,[1] and had begun to sort my seeds, and collected materials with which to make a wheelbarrow to carry it on or off with; but before the owner gave me a deed of it, his wife—every man has such a wife—changed her mind and wished to keep it, and he offered me ten dollars to release him. Now, to speak the truth, I had but ten cents in the world, and it surpassed my arithmetic to tell, if I was that man who had ten cents, or who had a farm, or ten dollars, or all together. However, I let him keep the ten dollars and the farm too, for I had carried it far enough; or rather, to be generous, I sold him the farm for just what I gave for it, and, as he was not a rich man, made him a present of ten dollars, and still had my ten cents, and seeds, and materials for a wheelbarrow left. I found thus that I had been a rich man without any damage to my poverty. But I retained the landscape, and I have since annually carried off what it yielded without a wheelbarrow. With respect to landscapes,—

"I am monarch of all I *survey*,
My right there is none to dispute."[2]

I have frequently seen a poet withdraw, having enjoyed the most valuable part of a farm, while the crusty farmer supposed that he had got a few wild apples only. Why, the owner does not know it for

---

[20]Animal magnetism, a mode of healing then in vogue.
[21]Musee-Huddeen, Sheik Saadi, famous 13th-century Persian poet who wrote *The Gulistan or Rose Garden*.

[1]A farm on the Sudbury River near Concord.
[2]By William Cowper (1731-1800), from "Verses Supposed to be Written by Alexander Selkirk."

many years when a poet has put his farm in rhyme, the most admirable kind of invisible fence, has fairly impounded it, milked it, skimmed it, and got all the cream, and left the farmer only the skimmed milk.

The real attractions of the Hollowell farm, to me, were: its complete retirement, being about two miles from the village, half a mile from the nearest neighbor, and separated from the highway by a broad field; its bounding on the river, which the owner said protected it by its fogs from frosts in the spring, though that was nothing to me; the gray color and ruinous state of the house and barn, and the dilapidated fences, which put such an interval between me and the last occupant; the hollow and lichen-covered apple trees, gnawed by rabbits, showing what kind of neighbors I should have; but above all, the recollection I had of it from my earliest voyages up the river, when the house was concealed behind a dense grove of red maples, through which I heard the house-dog bark. I was in haste to buy it, before the proprietor finished getting out some rocks, cutting down the hollow apple trees, and grubbing up some young birches which had sprung up in the pasture, or, in short, had made any more of his improvements. To enjoy these advantages I was ready to carry it on; like Atlas, to take the world on my shoulders,—I never heard what compensation he received for that,—and do all those things which had no other motive or excuse but that I might pay for it and be unmolested in my possession of it; for I knew all the while that it would yield the most abundant crop of the kind I wanted, if I could only afford to let it alone. But it turned out as I have said.

All that I could say, then, with respect to farming on a large scale—I have always cultivated a garden—was, that I had had my seeds ready. Many think that seeds improve with age. I have no doubt that time discriminates between the good and the bad; and when at last I shall plant, I shall be less likely to be disappointed. But I would say to my fellows, once for all, As long as possible live free and uncommitted. It makes but little difference whether you are committed to a farm or the county jail.

Old Cato, whose "De Re Rusticâ" is my "Cultivator,"[3] says,—and the only translation I have seen makes sheer nonsense of the passage,—"When you think of getting a farm turn it thus in your mind, not to buy greedily; nor spare your pains to look at it, and do not think it enough to go round it once. The oftener you go there the more it will please you, if it is good." I think I shall not buy greedily, but go round and round it as long as I live, and be buried in it first, that it may please me the more at last.

The present was my next experiment of this kind, which I purpose to describe more at length, for convenience putting the experience of two years into one. As I have said, I do not propose to write an ode to dejection,[4] but to brag as lustily as chanticleer in the morning, standing on his roost, if only to wake my neighbors up.

When first I took up my abode in the woods, that is, began to spend my nights as well as days there, which, by accident, was on Independence Day, or the Fourth of July, 1845, my house was not finished for winter, but was merely a defence against the rain, without plastering or chimney, the walls being of rough, weather-stained boards, with wide chinks, which made it cool at night. The upright white hewn studs and freshly planed door and window casings gave it a clean and airy look, especially in the morning, when its timbers were saturated with dew, so that I fancied that by noon some sweet gum would exude from them. To my imagination it retained throughout the day more or less of this auroral character, reminding me of a certain house on a mountain which I had visited a year before. This was an airy and unplastered cabin, fit to entertain a travelling god, and where a goddess might trail her garments. The winds which passed over my dwelling were such as sweep over the ridges of mountains, bearing the broken strains, or celestial parts only, of terrestrial music. The morning wind forever blows, the poem of creation is uninterrupted; but few are the ears that hear it. Olympus is but the outside of the earth everywhere.

The only house I had been the owner of before, if I except a boat, was a tent, which I used occasionally when making excursions in the summer, and this is still rolled up in my garret; but the boat, after passing from hand to hand, has gone down the stream of time. With this more substantial shelter about me, I had made some progress toward settling in the world. This frame, so slightly clad, was a sort of crystallization around me, and reacted on the builder. It was suggestive somewhat as a picture in outlines. I did not need to go outdoors to take the air, for the atmosphere within had lost none of its freshness. It was not so much within-doors as behind a door where I sat, even in the rainiest weather. The Harivansa says, "An abode without birds is like a meat without seasoning." Such was not my abode,

[3] Probably refers to either *The Boston Cultivator* or *The New England Cultivator,* both published in Thoreau's lifetime. (Harding)

[4] The epigraph to *Walden* reads, "I do not propose to write an ode to dejection, but to brag as lustily as Chanticleer in the morning, standing on his roost, if only to wake my neighbors up." "Ode to dejection" refers to a poem of that title by Samuel Taylor Coleridge.

for I found myself suddenly neighbor to the birds; not by having imprisoned one, but having caged myself near them. I was not only nearer to some of those which commonly frequent the garden and the orchard, but to those wilder and more thrilling songsters of the forest which never, or rarely, serenade a villager,—the wood thrush, the veery, the scarlet tanager, the field sparrow, the whip-poor-will, and many others.

I was seated by the shore of a small pond, about a mile and a half south of the village of Concord and somewhat higher than it, in the midst of an extensive wood between that town and Lincoln, and about two miles south of that our only field known to fame, Concord Battle Ground;[5] but I was so low in the woods that the opposite shore, half a mile off, like the rest, covered with wood, was my most distant horizon. For the first week, whenever I looked out on the pond it impressed me like a tarn high up on the side of a mountain, its bottom far above the surface of other lakes, and, as the sun arose, I saw it throwing off its nightly clothing of mist, and here and there, by degrees, its soft ripples or its smooth reflecting surface was revealed, while the mists, like ghosts, were stealthily withdrawing in every direction into the woods, as at the breaking up of some nocturnal conventicle. The very dew seemed to hang upon the trees later into the day than usual, as on the sides of mountains.

This small lake was of most value as a neighbor in the intervals of a gentle rain-storm in August, when, both air and water being perfectly still, but the sky overcast, mid-afternoon had all the serenity of evening, and the wood thrush sang around, and was heard from shore to shore. A lake like this is never smoother than at such a time; and the clear portion of the air above it being shallow and darkened by clouds, the water, full of light and reflections, becomes a lower heaven itself so much the more important. From a hill-top near by, where the wood had been recently cut off, there was a pleasing vista southward across the pond, through a wide indentation in the hills which form the shore there, where their opposite sides sloping toward each other suggested a stream flowing out in that direction through a wooded valley, but stream there was none. That way I looked between and over the near green hills to some distant and higher ones in the horizon, tinged with blue. Indeed, by standing on tiptoe I could catch a glimpse of some of the peaks of the still bluer and more distant mountain ranges in the northwest, those true-blue coins from heaven's own mint, and also of some portion of the village. But in other directions, even from this point, I could not

see over or beyond the woods which surrounded me. It is well to have some water in your neighborhood, to give buoyancy to and float the earth. One value even of the smallest well is, that when you look into it you see that earth is not continent but insular. This is as important as that it keeps butter cool. When I looked across the pond from this peak toward the Sudbury meadows, which in time of flood I distinguished elevated perhaps by a mirage in their seething valley, like a coin in a basin, all the earth beyond the pond appeared like a thin crust insulated and floated even by this small sheet of intervening water, and I was reminded that this on which I dwelt was but *dry land.*

Though the view from my door was still more contracted, I did not feel crowded or confined in the least. There was pasture enough for my imagination. The low shrub oak plateau to which the opposite shore arose stretched away toward the prairies of the West and the steppes of Tartary, affording ample room for all the roving families of men. "There are none happy in the world but beings who enjoy freely a vast horizon,"—said Damodara,[6] when his herds required new and larger pastures.

Both place and time were changed, and I dwelt nearer to those parts of the universe and to those eras in history which had most attracted me. Where I lived was as far off as many a region viewed nightly by astronomers. We are wont to imagine rare and delectable places in some remote and more celestial corner of the system, behind the constellation of Cassiopeia's Chair, far from noise and disturbance. I discovered that my house actually had its site in such a withdrawn, but forever new and unprofaned, part of the universe. If it were worth the while to settle in those parts near to the Pleiades or the Hyades, to Aldebaran or Altair,[7] then I was really there, or at an equal remoteness from the life which I had left behind, dwindled and twinkling with as fine a ray to my nearest neighbor, and to be seen only in moonless nights by him. Such was that part of creation where I had squatted;—

> "There was a shepherd that did live,
> And held his thoughts as high
> As were the mounts whereon his flocks
> Did hourly feed him by."[8]

What should we think of the shepherd's life if his flocks always wandered to higher pastures than his thoughts?

Every morning was a cheerful invitation to make my life of equal simplicity, and I may say innocence, with Nature herself. I have been as sincere a wor-

[5] Where the first battle of the American Revolution occurred, April 19, 1775.

[6] Another name for Krishna.

[7] Constellations and stars.

[8] Lines from an anonymous poem set to music by Robert Jones in 1611.

shipper of Aurora as the Greeks. I got up early and bathed in the pond; that was a religious exercise, and one of the best things which I did. They say that characters were engraven on the bathing tub of King Tching-thang to this effect: "Renew thyself completely each day; do it again, and again, and forever again."[9] I can understand that. Morning brings back the heroic ages. I was as much affected by the faint hum of a mosquito making its invisible and unimaginable tour through my apartment at earliest dawn, when I was sitting with door and windows open, as I could be by any trumpet that ever sang of fame. It was Homer's requiem; itself an Iliad and Odyssey in the air, singing its own wrath and wanderings. There was something cosmical about it; a standing advertisement, till forbidden, of the everlasting vigor and fertility of the world. The morning, which is the most memorable season of the day, is the awakening hour. Then there is least somnolence in us; and for an hour, at least, some part of us awakes which slumbers all the rest of the day and night. Little is to be expected of that day, if it can be called a day, to which we are not awakened by our Genius, but by the mechanical nudgings of some servitor, are not awakened by our own newly acquired force and aspirations from within, accompanied by the undulations of celestial music, instead of factory bells, and a fragrance filling the air—to a higher life than we fell asleep from; and thus the darkness bear its fruit, and prove itself to be good, no less than the light. That man who does not believe that each day contains an earlier, more sacred, and auroral hour than he has yet profaned, has despaired of life, and is pursuing a descending and darkening way. After a partial cessation of his sensuous life, the soul of man, or its organs rather, are reinvigorated each day, and his Genius tries again what noble life it can make. All memorable events, I should say, transpire in morning time and in a morning atmosphere. The Vedas say, "All intelligences awake with the morning." Poetry and art, and the fairest and most memorable of the actions of men, date from such an hour. All poets and heroes, like Memnon, are the children of Aurora, and emit their music at sunrise. To him whose elastic and vigorous thought keeps pace with the sun, the day is a perpetual morning. It matters not what the clocks say or the attitudes and labors of men. Morning is when I am awake and there is a dawn in me. Moral reform is the effort to throw off sleep. Why is it that men give so poor an account of their day if they have not been slumbering? They are not such poor calculators. If they had not been overcome with drowsiness, they would have performed something. The millions are awake enough for physical labor; but

only one in a million is awake enough for effective intellectual exertion, only one in a hundred millions to a poetic or divine life. To be awake is to be alive. I have never yet met a man who was quite awake. How could I have looked him in the face?

We must learn to reawaken and keep ourselves awake, not by mechanical aids, but by an infinite expectation of the dawn, which does not forsake us in our soundest sleep. I know of no more encouraging fact than the unquestionable ability of man to elevate his life by a conscious endeavor. It is something to be able to paint a particular picture, or to carve a statue, and so to make a few objects beautiful; but it is far more glorious to carve and paint the very atmosphere and medium through which we look, which morally we can do. To affect the quality of the day, that is the highest of arts. Every man is tasked to make his life, even in its details, worthy of the contemplation of his most elevated and critical hour. If we refused, or rather used up, such paltry information as we get, the oracles would distinctly inform us how this might be done.

I went to the woods because I wished to live deliberately, to front only the essential facts of life, and see if I could not learn what it had to teach, and not, when I came to die, discover that I had not lived. I did not wish to live what was not life, living is so dear; nor did I wish to practise resignation, unless it was quite necessary. I wanted to live deep and suck out all the marrow of life, to live so sturdily and Spartan-like as to put to rout all that was not life, to cut a broad swath and shave close, to drive life into a corner, and reduce it to its lowest terms, and, if it proved to be mean, why then to get the whole and genuine meanness of it, and publish its meanness to the world; or if it were sublime, to know it by experience, and be able to give a true account of it in my next excursion. For most men, it appears to me, are in a strange uncertainty about it, whether it is of the devil or of God, and have *somewhat hastily* concluded that it is the chief end of man here to "glorify God and enjoy him forever."[10]

Still we live meanly, like ants; though the fable[11] tells us that we were long ago changed into men; like pygmies[12] we fight with cranes; it is error upon error, and clout upon clout, and our best virtue has for its occasion a superfluous and evitable wretchedness. Our life is frittered away by detail. An honest man has hardly need to count more than his ten fingers, or in extreme cases he may add his ten toes,

[9] Confucius, *The Great Learning.*

[10] From the "Shorter Catechism" in *The New England Primer.* Thoreau does not think much of that kind of devotion.

[11] In Greek mythology Aeacus, son of Jupiter and king of Oenopia, asked Jupiter to repeople his kingdom (decimated by pestilence) by changing ants into men. (Harding)

[12] Cf. *Iliad* III, the opening lines.

and lump the rest. Simplicity, simplicity, simplicity! I say, let your affairs be as two or three, and not a hundred or a thousand; instead of a million count half a dozen, and keep your accounts on your thumb-nail. In the midst of this chopping sea of civilized life, such are the clouds and storms and quicksands and thousand-and-one items to be allowed for, that a man has to live, if he would not founder and go to the bottom and not make his port at all, by dead reckoning, and he must be a great calculator indeed who succeeds. Simplify, simplify. Instead of three meals a day, if it be necessary eat but one; instead of a hundred dishes, five; and reduce other things in proportion. Our life is like a German Confederacy,[13] made up of petty states, with its boundary forever fluctuating, so that even a German cannot tell you how it is bounded at any moment. The nation itself, with all its so-called internal improvements, which, by the way are all external and superficial, is just such an unwieldy and overgrown establishment, cluttered with furniture and tripped up by its own traps, ruined by luxury and heedless expense, by want of calculation and a worthy aim, as the million households in the land; and the only cure for it, as for them, is in a rigid economy, a stern and more than Spartan simplicity of life and elevation of purpose. It lives too fast. Men think that it is essential that the *Nation* have commerce, and export ice, and talk through a telegraph, and ride thirty miles an hour, without a doubt, whether *they* do or not; but whether we should live like baboons or like men, is a little uncertain. If we do not get out sleepers,[14] and forge rails, and devote days and nights to the work, but go to tinkering upon our *lives* to improve *them*, who will build railroads? And if railroads are not built, how shall we get to heaven in season? But if we stay at home and mind our business, who will want railroads? We do not ride on the railroad; it rides upon us. Did you ever think what those sleepers are that underlie the railroad? Each one is a man, an Irishman, or a Yankee man. The rails are laid on them, and they are covered with sand, and the cars run smoothly over them. They are sound sleepers, I assure you. And every few years a new lot is laid down and run over; so that, if some have the pleasure of riding on a rail, others have the misfortune to be ridden upon. And when they run over a man that is walking in his sleep, a supernumerary sleeper in the wrong position, and wake him up, they suddenly stop the cars, and make a hue and cry about it, as if this were an exception. I am glad to know that it takes a gang of men for every five miles to keep the sleepers down and level in their beds as it

is, for this is a sign that they may sometime get up again.

Why should we live with such hurry and waste of life? We are determined to be starved before we are hungry. Men say that a stitch in time saves nine, and so they take a thousand stitches to-day to save nine to-morrow. As for *work*, we haven't any of any consequence. We have the Saint Vitus' dance, and cannot possibly keep our heads still. If I should only give a few pulls at the parish bell-rope, as for a fire, that is, without setting the bell, there is hardly a man on his farm in the outskirts of Concord, notwithstanding that press of engagements which was his excuse so many times this morning, nor a boy, nor a woman, I might almost say, but would forsake all and follow that sound, not mainly to save property from the flames, but, if we will confess the truth, much more to see it burn, since burn it must, and we, be it known, did not set it on fire,—or to see it put out, and have a hand in it, if that is done as handsomely; yes, even if it were the parish church itself. Hardly a man takes a half-hour's nap after dinner, but when he wakes he holds up his head and asks, "What's the news?" as if the rest of mankind had stood his sentinels. Some give directions to be waked every half-hour, doubtless for no other purpose; and then, to pay for it, they tell what they have dreamed. After a night's sleep the news is as indispensable as the breakfast. "Pray tell me anything new that has happened to a man anywhere on this globe,"—and he reads it over his coffee and rolls, that a man has had his eyes gouged out this morning on the Wachito River;[15] never dreaming the while that he lives in the dark unfathomed mammoth cave of this world, and has but the rudiment of an eye himself.

For my part, I could easily do without the post-office. I think that there are very few important communications made through it. To speak critically, I never received more than one or two letters in my life—I wrote this some years ago—that were worth the postage. The penny-post is, commonly, an institution through which you seriously offer a man that penny for his thoughts which is so often safely offered in jest. And I am sure that I never read any memorable news in a newspaper. If we read of one man robbed, or murdered, or killed by accident, or one house burned, or one vessel wrecked, or one steamboat blown up, or one cow run over on the Western Railroad,[16] or one mad dog killed, or one lot of grasshoppers in the winter,—we never need read of another. One is enough. If you are ac-

[13] The separate states were not really unified until 1871.
[14] Railroad ties; a pun, too.

[15] The Washita or Ouachita River flows from Arkansas into Louisiana.
[16] Connected Worcester, Massachusetts, and Albany, New York.

quainted with the principle, what do you care for a myriad instances and applications? To a philosopher all *news,* as it is called, is gossip, and they who edit and read it are old women over their tea. Yet not a few are greedy after this gossip. There was such a rush, as I hear, the other day at one of the offices to learn the foreign news by the last arrival, that several large squares of plate glass belonging to the establishment were broken by the pressure,—news which I seriously think a ready wit might write a twelvemonth, or twelve years, beforehand with sufficient accuracy. As for Spain, for instance, if you know how to throw in Don Carlos and the Infanta, and Don Pedro and Seville and Granada,[17] from time to time in the right proportions,—they may have changed the names a little since I saw the papers,—and serve up a bull-fight when other entertainments fail, it will be true to the letter, and give us as good an idea of the exact state or ruin of things in Spain as the most succinct and lucid reports under this head in the newspapers: and as for England, almost the last significant scrap of news from that quarter was the revolution of 1649;[18] and if you have learned the history of her crops for an average year, you never need attend to that thing again, unless your speculations are of a merely pecuniary character. If one may judge who rarely looks into the newspapers, nothing new does ever happen in foreign parts, a French revolution not excepted.

What news! how much more important to know what that is which was never old! "Kieou-he-yu (great dignitary of the state of Wei) sent a man to Khoung-tseu to know his news. Khoung-tseu caused the messenger to be seated near him, and questioned him in these terms: What is your master doing? The messenger answered with respect: My master desires to diminish the number of his faults, but he cannot come to the end of them. The messenger being gone, the philosopher remarked: What a worthy messenger! What a worthy messenger!"[19] The preacher, instead of vexing the ears of drowsy farmers on their day of rest at the end of the week,—for Sunday is the fit conclusion of an ill-spent week, and not the fresh and brave beginning of a new one,—with this one other draggle-tail of a sermon, should shout with thundering voice, "Pause! Avast! Why so seeming fast, but deadly slow?"

Shams and delusions are esteemed for soundest truths, while reality is fabulous. If men would steadily observe realities only, and not allow themselves to be deluded, life, to compare it with such things as we know, would be like a fairy tale and the Arabian Nights' Entertainments. If we respected only what is inevitable and has a right to be, music and poetry would resound along the streets. When we are unhurried and wise, we perceive that only great and worthy things have any permanent and absolute existence, that petty fears and petty pleasures are but the shadow of the reality. This is always exhilarating and sublime. By closing the eyes and slumbering, and consenting to be deceived by shows, men establish and confirm their daily life of routine and habit everywhere, which still is built on purely illusory foundations. Children, who play life, discern its true law and relations more clearly than men, who fail to live it worthily, but who think that they are wiser by experience, that is, by failure. I have read in a Hindoo book, that "there was a king's son, who, being expelled in infancy from his native city, was brought up by a forester, and, growing up to maturity in that state, imagined himself to belong to the barbarous race with which he lived. One of his father's ministers having discovered him, revealed to him what he was, and the misconception of his character was removed, and he knew himself to be a prince. So soul," continues the Hindoo philosopher, "from the circumstances in which it is placed, mistakes its own character, until the truth is revealed to it by some holy teacher, and then it knows itself to be *Brahme.*" I perceive that we inhabitants of New England live this mean life that we do because our vision does not penetrate the surface of things. We think that that *is* which *appears* to be. If a man should walk through this town and see only the reality, where, think you, would the "Mill-dam" go to? If he should give us an account of the realities he beheld there, we should not recognize the place in his description. Look at a meeting-house, or a court-house, or a jail, or a shop, or a dwelling-house, and say what that thing really is before a true gaze, and they would all go to pieces in your account of them. Men esteem truth remote, in the outskirts of the system, behind the farthest star, before Adam and after the last man. In eternity there is indeed something true and sublime. But all these times and places and occasions are now and here. God himself culminates in the present moment, and will never be more divine in the lapse of all the ages. And we are enabled to apprehend at all what is sublime and noble only by the perpetual instilling and drenching of the reality that surrounds us. The universe constantly and obediently answers to our conceptions; whether we travel fast or slow, the track is laid for us. Let us spend our lives in conceiving then. The poet or the artist never yet had so fair and noble a design but some of his posterity at least could accomplish it.

Let us spend one day as deliberately as Nature, and not be thrown off the track by every nutshell

IN THE PRESENT MOMENT

---

[17] Names in the news during the thirties and forties. Pedro and Carlos competed for Ferdinand's crown after he died in 1839. The Infanta became Queen Isabella in 1843.

[18] The year Cromwell abolished the monarchy.

[19] Confucius, *Analects.*

and mosquito's wing that falls on the rails. Let us rise early and fast, or break fast, gently and without perturbation; let company come and let company go, let the bells ring and the children cry,—determined to make a day of it. Why should we knock under and go with the stream? Let us not be upset and overwhelmed in that terrible rapid and whirlpool called a dinner, situated in the meridian shallows. Weather this danger and you are safe, for the rest of the way is down hill. With unrelaxed nerves, with morning vigor, sail by it, looking another way, tied to the mast like Ulysses.[20] If the engine whistles, let it whistle till it is hoarse for its pains. If the bell rings, why should we run? We will consider what kind of music they are like. Let us settle ourselves, and work and wedge our feet downward through the mud and slush of opinion, and prejudice, and tradition, and delusion, and appearance, that alluvion which covers the globe, through Paris and London, through New York and Boston and Concord, through Church and State, through poetry and philosophy and religion, till we come to a hard bottom and rocks in place, which we can call *reality*, and say, This is, and no mistake; and then begin, having a *point d'appui*, below freshet and frost and fire, a place where you might found a wall or a state, or set a lamp-post safely, or perhaps a gauge, not a Nilometer,[21] but a Realometer, that future ages might know how deep a freshet of shams and appearances had gathered from time to time. If you stand right fronting and face to face to a fact, you will see the sun glimmer on both its surfaces, as if it were a cimeter, and feel its sweet edge dividing you through the heart and marrow, and so you will happily conclude your mortal career. Be it life or death, we crave only reality. If we are really dying, let us hear the rattle in our throats and feel cold in the extremities; if we are alive, let us go about our business.

Time is but the stream I go a-fishing in. I drink at it; but while I drink I see the sandy bottom and detect how shallow it is. Its thin current slides away, but eternity remains. I would drink deeper; fish in the sky, whose bottom is pebbly with stars. I cannot count one. I know not the first letter of the alphabet. I have always been regretting that I was not as wise as the day I was born. The intellect is a cleaver; it discerns and rifts its way into the secret of things. I do not wish to be any more busy with my hands than is necessary. My head is hands and feet. I feel all my best faculties concentrated in it. My instinct tells me that my head is an organ for burrowing, as some creatures use their snout and

fore paws, and with it I would mine and burrow my way through these hills. I think that the richest vein is somewhere hereabouts, so by the divining-rod and thin rising vapors I judge; and here I will begin to mine.

IV. Sounds

But while we are confined to books, though the most select and classic, and read only particular written languages, which are themselves but dialects and provincial, we are in danger of forgetting the language which all things and events speak without metaphor, which alone is copious and standard. Much is published, but little printed. The rays which stream through the shutter will be no longer remembered when the shutter is wholly removed. No method nor discipline can supersede the necessity of being forever on the alert. What is a course of history or philosophy, or poetry, no matter how well selected, or the best society, or the most admirable routine of life, compared with the discipline of looking always at what is to be seen? Will you be a reader, a student merely, or a seer? Read your fate, see what is before you, and walk on into futurity.

I did not read books the first summer; I hoed beans. Nay, I often did better than this. There were times when I could not afford to sacrifice the bloom of the present moment to any work, whether of the head or hands. I love a broad margin to my life. Sometimes, in a summer morning, having taken my accustomed bath, I sat in my sunny doorway from sunrise till noon, rapt in a revery, amidst the pines and hickories and sumachs, in undisturbed solitude and stillness, while the birds sang around or flitted noiseless through the house, until by the sun falling in at my west window, or the noise of some traveller's wagon on the distant highway, I was reminded of the lapse of time. I grew in those seasons like corn in the night, and they were far better than any work of the hands would have been. They were not time subtracted from my life, but so much over and above my usual allowance. I realized what the Orientals mean by contemplation and the forsaking of works. For the most part, I minded not how the hours went. The day advanced as if to light some work of mine; it was morning, and lo, now it is evening, and nothing memorable is accomplished. Instead of singing like the birds, I silently smiled at my incessant good fortune. As the sparrow had its trill, sitting on the hickory before my door, so had I my chuckle or suppressed warble which he might hear out of my nest. My days were not days of the week, bearing the stamp of any heathen deity, nor were they minced into hours and fretted by the

---

[20]Ulysses had himself tied to his ship's mast so he could hear the Sirens' song but not be tempted to go to them.

[21]An ancient instrument that recorded the rise and fall of the Nile.

SOLITARY, IDLE IN A REVERY

ticking of a clock; for I lived like the Puri Indians, of whom it is said that "for yesterday, to-day, and to-morrow they have only one word, and they express the variety of meaning by pointing backward for yesterday, forward for to-morrow, and overhead for the passing day." [1] This was sheer idleness to my fellow-townsmen, no doubt; but if the birds and flowers had tried me by their standard, I should not have been found wanting. A man must find his occasions in himself, it is true. The natural day is very calm, and will hardly reprove his indolence.

I had this advantage, at least, in my mode of life, over those who were obliged to look abroad for amusement, to society and the theatre, that my life itself was become my amusement and never ceased to be novel. It was a drama of many scenes and without an end. If we were always, indeed, getting our living, and regulating our lives according to the last and best mode we had learned, we should never be troubled with ennui. Follow your genius closely enough, and it will not fail to show you a fresh prospect every hour. Housework was a pleasant pastime. When my floor was dirty I rose early, and, setting all my furniture out of doors on the grass, bed and bedstead making but one budget, dashed water on the floor, and sprinkled white sand from the pond on it, and then with a broom scrubbed it clean and white; and by the time the villagers had broken their fast the morning sun had dried my house sufficiently to allow me to move in again, and my meditations were almost uninterrupted. It was pleasant to see my whole household effects out on the grass, making a little pile like a gypsy's pack, and my three-legged table, from which I did not remove the books and pen and ink, standing amid the pines and hickories. They seemed glad to get out themselves, and as if unwilling to be brought in. I was sometimes tempted to stretch an awning over them and take my seat there. It was worth the while to see the sun shine on these things, and hear the free wind blow on them; so much more interesting most familiar objects look out of doors than in the house. A bird sits on the next bough, life-everlasting grows under the table, and blackberry vines run round its legs; pine cones, chestnut burs, and strawberry leaves are strewn about. It looked as if this was the way these forms came to be transferred to our furniture, to tables, chairs, and bedsteads,—because they once stood in their midst.

My house was on the side of a hill, immediately on the edge of the larger wood, in the midst of a young forest of pitch pines and hickories, and half a dozen rods from the pond, to which a narrow foot-path led down the hill. In my front yard grew the strawberry, blackberry, and life-everlasting, johns-wort and goldenrod, shrub oaks and sand cherry, blueberry and groundnut. Near the end of May, the sand cherry (*Cerasus pumila*) adorned the sides of the path with its delicate flowers arranged in umbels cylindrically about its short stems, which last, in the fall, weighed down with good-sized and handsome cherries, fell over in wreaths like rays on every side. I tasted them out of compliment to Nature, though they were scarcely palatable. The sumach (*Rhus glabra*) grew luxuriantly about the house, pushing up through the embankment which I had made, and growing five or six feet the first season. Its broad pinnate tropical leaf was pleasant though strange to look on. The large buds, suddenly pushing out late in the spring from dry sticks which had seemed to be dead, developed themselves as by magic into graceful green and tender boughs, an inch in diameter; and sometimes, as I sat at my window, so heedlessly did they grow and tax their weak joints, I heard a fresh and tender bough suddenly fall like a fan to the ground, when there was not a breath of air stirring, broken off by its own weight. In August, the large masses of berries, which, when in flower, had attracted many wild bees, gradually assumed their bright velvety crimson hue, and by their weight again bent down and broke the tender limbs.

As I sit at my window this summer afternoon, hawks are circling about my clearing; the tantivy of wild pigeons, flying by twos and threes athwart my view, or perching restless on the white pine boughs behind my house, gives a voice to the air; a fish hawk dimples the glassy surface of the pond and brings up a fish; a mink steals out of the marsh before my door and seizes a frog by the shore; the sedge is bending under the weight of the reed-birds flitting hither and thither; and for the last half-hour I have heard the rattle of railroad cars, now dying away and then reviving like the beat of a partridge, conveying travellers from Boston to the country. For I did not live so out of the world as that boy who, as I hear, was put out to a farmer in the east part of the town, but ere long ran away and came home again, quite down at the heel and homesick. He had never seen such a dull and out-of-the-way place; the folks were all gone off; why, you couldn't even hear the whistle! I doubt if there is such a place in Massachusetts now:—

"In truth, our village has become a butt
For one of those fleet railroad shafts, and o'er
Our peaceful plain its soothing sound is—Concord." [2]

The Fitchburg Railroad[3] touches the pond about a

---

[1] The Puri Indians are Brazilian. The quotation is from *A Lady's Voyage Round the World* by Ida Pfeiffer. (Harding)

[2] From W. E. Channing's "Walden Spring."
[3] Built in the 1840's, it connected Boston and Fitchburg.

hundred rods south of where I dwell. I usually go to the village along its causeway, and am, as it were, related to society by this link. The men on the freight trains, who go over the whole length of the road, bow to me as to an old acquaintance, they pass me so often, and apparently they take me for an employee; and so I am. I too would fain be a track-repairer somewhere in the orbit of the earth.

The whistle of the locomotive penetrates my woods summer and winter, sounding like the scream of a hawk sailing over some farmer's yard, informing me that many restless city merchants are arriving within the circle of the town, or adventurous country traders from the other side. As they come under one horizon, they shout their warning to get off the track to the other, heard sometimes through the circles of two towns. Here come your groceries, country; your rations, countrymen! Nor is there any man so independent on his farm that he can say them nay. And here's your pay for them! screams the countryman's whistle; timber like long battering-rams going twenty miles an hour against the city's walls, and chairs enough to seat all the weary and heavy-laden that dwell within them. With such huge and lumbering civility the country hands a chair to the city. All the Indian huckleberry hills are stripped, all the cranberry meadows are raked into the city. Up comes the cotton, down goes the woven cloth; up comes the silk, down goes the woollen; up come the books, but down goes the wit that writes them.

When I meet the engine with its train of cars moving off with planetary motion,—or, rather, like a comet, for the beholder knows not if with that velocity and with that direction it will ever revisit this system, since its orbit does not look like a returning curve,—with its steam cloud like a banner streaming behind in golden and silver wreaths, like many a downy cloud which I have seen, high in the heavens, unfolding its masses to the light,—as if this travelling demigod, this cloud-compeller, would ere long take the sunset sky for the livery of his train; when I hear the iron horse make the hills echo with his snort like thunder, shaking the earth with his feet, and breathing fire and smoke from his nostrils (what kind of winged horse or fiery dragon they will put into the new Mythology I don't know), it seems as if the earth had got a race now worthy to inhabit it. If all were as it seems, and men made the elements their servants for noble ends! If the cloud that hangs over the engine were the perspiration of heroic deeds, or as beneficent as that which floats over the farmer's fields, then the elements and Nature herself would cheerfully accompany men on their errands and be their escort.

I watch the passage of the morning cars with the same feeling that I do the rising of the sun, which is hardly more regular. Their train of clouds stretching far behind and rising higher and higher, going to heaven while the cars are going to Boston, conceals the sun for a minute and casts my distant field into the shade, a celestial train[4] beside which the petty train of cars which hugs the earth is but the barb of the spear. The stabler of the iron horse was up early this winter morning by the light of the stars amid the mountains, to fodder and harness his steed. Fire, too, was awakened thus early to put the vital heat in him and get him off. If the enterprise were as innocent as it is early! If the snow lies deep, they strap on his snowshoes, and, with the giant plow, plow a furrow from the mountains to the seaboard, in which the cars, like a following drill-barrow, sprinkle all the restless men and floating merchandise in the country for seed. All day the fire-steed flies over the country, stopping only that his master may rest, and I am awakened by his tramp and defiant snort at midnight, when in some remote glen in the woods he fronts the elements incased in ice and snow; and he will reach his stall only with the morning star, to start once more on his travels without rest or slumber. Or perchance, at evening, I hear him in his stable blowing off the superfluous energy of the day, that he may calm his nerves and cool his liver and brain for a few hours of iron slumber. If the enterprise were as heroic and commanding as it is protracted and unwearied!

Far through unfrequented woods on the confines of towns, where once only the hunter penetrated by day, in the darkest night dart these bright saloons without the knowledge of their inhabitants; this moment stopping at some brilliant station-house in town or city, where a social crowd is gathered, the next in the Dismal Swamp, scaring the owl and fox. The startings and arrivals of the cars are now the epochs in the village day. They go and come with such regularity and precision, and their whistle can be heard so far, that the farmers set their clocks by them, and thus one well-conducted institution regulates a whole country. Have not men improved somewhat in punctuality since the railroad was invented? Do they not talk and think faster in the depot than they did in the stage-office? There is something electrifying in the atmosphere of the former place. I have been astonished at the miracles it has wrought; that some of my neighbors, who, I should have prophesied, once for all, would never get to Boston by so prompt a conveyance, are on hand when the bell rings. To do things "railroad fashion" is now the byword; and it is worth the while to be warned so often and so sincerely by any

[4] Refers to Hawthorne's "The Celestial Railroad."

power to get off its track. There is no stopping to read the riot act, no firing over the heads of the mob, in this case. We have constructed a fate, an *Atropos,* that never turns aside. (Let that be the name of your engine.) Men are advertised that at a certain hour and minute these bolts will be shot toward particular points of the compass; yet it interferes with no man's business, and the children go to school on the other track. We live the steadier for it. We are all educated thus to be sons of Tell. The air is full of invisible bolts. Every path but your own is the path of fate. Keep on your own track, then.

What recommends commerce to me is its enterprise and bravery. It does not clasp its hands and pray to Jupiter. I see these men every day go about their business with more or less courage and content, doing more even than they suspect, and perchance better employed than they could have consciously devised. I am less affected by their heroism who stood up for half an hour in the front line of Buena Vista,[5] than by the steady and cheerful valor of the men who inhabit the snow-plow for their winter quarters; who have not merely the three-o'-clock-in-the-morning courage, which Bonaparte thought was the rarest, but whose courage does not go to rest so early, who go to sleep only when the storm sleeps or the sinews of their iron steed are frozen. On this morning of the Great Snow, perchance, which is still raging and chilling men's blood, I hear the muffled tone of their engine bell from out the fog bank of their chilled breath, which announces that the cars *are coming,* without long delay, notwithstanding the veto of a New England northeast snow-storm, and I behold the plowmen covered with snow and rime, their heads peering above the mould-board which is turning down other than daisies and the nests of field mice, like bowlders of the Sierra Nevada, that occupy an outside place in the universe.

Commerce is unexpectedly confident and serene, alert, adventurous, and unwearied. It is very natural in its methods withal, far more so than many fantastic enterprises and sentimental experiments, and hence its singular success. I am refreshed and expanded when the freight train rattles past me, and I smell the stores which go dispensing their odors all the way from Long Wharf[6] to Lake Champlain, reminding me of foreign parts, of coral reefs, and Indian oceans, and tropical climes, and the extent of the globe. I feel more like a citizen of the world at the sight of the palm-leaf[7] which will cover so many

flaxen New England heads the next summer, the Manilla hemp and cocoanut husks, the old junk, gunny bags, scrap iron, and rusty nails. This carload of torn sails is more legible and interesting now than if they should be wrought into paper and printed books. Who can write so graphically the history of the storms they have weathered as these rents have done? They are proof-sheets which need no correction. Here goes lumber from the Maine woods, which did not go out to sea in the last freshet, risen four dollars on the thousand because of what did go out or was split up; pine, spruce, cedar,—first, second, third, and fourth qualities, so lately all of one quality, to wave over the bear, and moose, and caribou. Next rolls Thomaston[8] lime, a prime lot, which will get far among the hills before it gets slacked. These rags in bales, of all hues and qualities, the lowest condition to which cotton and linen descend, the final result of dress,—of patterns which are now no longer cried up, unless it be in Milwaukee, as those splendid articles, English, French, or American prints, ginghams, muslins, etc., gathered from all quarters both of fashion and poverty, going to become paper of one color or a few shades only, on which, forsooth, will be written tales of real life, high and low, and founded on fact! This closed car smells of salt fish, the strong New England and commercial scent, reminding me of the Grand Banks[9] and the fisheries. Who has not seen a salt fish, thoroughly cured for this world, so that nothing can spoil it, and putting the perseverance of the saints to the blush? with which you may sweep or pave the streets, and split your kindlings, and the teamster shelter himself and his lading against sun, wind, and rain behind it,—and the trader, as a Concord trader once did, hang it up by his door for a sign when he commences business, until at last his oldest customer cannot tell surely whether it be animal, vegetable, or mineral, and yet it shall be as pure as a snowflake, and if it be put into a pot and boiled, will come out an excellent dunfish for a Saturday's dinner. Next Spanish hides, with the tails still preserving their twist and the angle of elevation they had when the oxen that wore them were careering over the pampas of the Spanish Main,—a type of all obstinacy, and evincing how almost hopeless and incurable are all constitutional vices. I confess, that practically speaking, when I have learned a man's real disposition, I have no hopes of changing it for the better or worse in this state of existence. As the Orientals say, "A cur's tail may be warmed, and pressed, and bound round with ligatures, and after a twelve years' labor bestowed upon it, still it will retain its natural form." The only effectual cure for

[5]A battle (1847) in the Mexican War.
[6]A major wharf in Boston harbor; some of the goods received there could have been carried by rail to Lake Champlain.
[7]A summer hat.

[8]In Maine.
[9]A major fishing ground off Newfoundland.

such inveteracies as these tails exhibit is to make glue of them, which I believe is what is usually done with them, and then they will stay put and stick. Here is a hogshead of molasses or of brandy directed to John Smith, Cuttingsville, Vermont, some trader among the Green Mountains, who imports for the farmers near his clearing, and now perchance stands over his bulkhead and thinks of the last arrivals on the coast, how they may affect the price for him, telling his customers this moment, as he has told them twenty times before this morning, that he expects some by the next train of prime quality. It is advertised in the Cuttingsville Times.

While these things go up other things come down. Warned by the whizzing sound, I look up from my book and see some tall pine, hewn on far northern hills, which has winged its way over the Green Mountains and the Connecticut, shot like an arrow through the township within ten minutes, and scarce another eye beholds it; going

> "to be the mast
> Of some great ammiral." [10]

And hark! here comes the cattle-train bearing the cattle of a thousand hills, sheepcots, stables, and cow-yards in the air, drovers with their sticks, and shepherd boys in the midst of their flocks, all but the mountain pastures, whirled along like leaves blown from the mountains by the September gales. The air is filled with the bleating of calves and sheep, and the hustling of oxen, as if a pastoral valley were going by. When the old bell-wether at the head rattles his bell, the mountains do indeed skip like rams and the little hills like lambs. A carload of drovers, too, in the midst, on a level with their droves now, their vocation gone, but still clinging to their useless sticks as their badge of office. But their dogs, where are they? It is a stampede to them; they are quite thrown out; they have lost the scent. Methinks I hear them barking behind the Peterboro' Hills, or panting up the western slope of the Green Mountains. They will not be in at the death. Their vocation, too, is gone. Their fidelity and sagacity are below par now. They will slink back to their kennels in disgrace, or perchance run wild and strike a league with the wolf and the fox. So is your pastoral life whirled past and away. But the bell rings, and I must get off the track and let the cars go by; —

> What's the railroad to me?
> I never go to see
> Where it ends.
> It fills a few hollows,
> And makes banks for the swallows,

[10] Milton, *Paradise Lost* I.293-94.

> It sets the sand a-blowing,
> And the blackberries a-growing, [11]

but I cross it like a cart-path in the woods. I will not have my eyes put out and my ears spoiled by its smoke and steam and hissing.

Now that the cars are gone by and all the restless world with them, and the fishes in the pond no longer feel their rumbling, I am more alone than ever. For the rest of the long afternoon, perhaps, my meditations are interrupted only by the faint rattle of a carriage or team along the distant highway.

Sometimes, on Sundays, I heard the bells, the Lincoln, Acton, Bedford, [12] or Concord bell, when the wind was favorable, a faint, sweet, and, as it were, natural melody, worth importing into the wilderness. At a sufficient distance over the woods this sound acquires a certain vibratory hum, as if the pine needles in the horizon were the strings of a harp which it swept. All sound heard at the greatest possible distance produces one and the same effect, a vibration of the universal lyre, just as the intervening atmosphere makes a distant ridge of earth interesting to our eyes by the azure tint it imparts to it. There came to me in this case a melody which the air had strained, and which had conversed with every leaf and needle of the wood, that portion of the sound which the elements had taken up and modulated and echoed from vale to vale. The echo is, to some extent, an original sound, and therein is the magic and charm of it. It is not merely a repetition of what was worth repeating in the bell, but partly the voice of the wood; the same trivial words and notes sung by a wood-nymph.

At evening, the distant lowing of some cow in the horizon beyond the woods sounded sweet and melodious, and at first I would mistake it for the voices of certain minstrels by whom I was sometimes serenaded, who might be straying over hill and dale; but soon I was not unpleasantly disappointed when it was prolonged into the cheap and natural music of the cow. I do not mean to be satirical, but to express my appreciation of those youths' singing, when I state that I perceived clearly that it was akin to the music of the cow, and they were at length one articulation of Nature.

Regularly at half-past seven, in one part of the summer, after the evening train had gone by, the whip-poor-wills chanted their vespers for half an hour, sitting on a stump by my door, or upon the ridge-pole of the house. They would begin to sing almost with as much precision as a clock, within five minutes of a particular time, referred to the setting

[11] Thoreau.
[12] Towns near Concord.

of the sun, every evening. I had a rare opportunity to become acquainted with their habits. Sometimes I heard four or five at once in different parts of the wood, by accident one a bar behind another, and so near me that I distinguished not only the cluck after each note, but often that singular buzzing sound like a fly in a spider's web, only proportionally louder. Sometimes one would circle round and round me in the woods a few feet distant as if tethered by a string, when probably I was near its eggs. They sang at intervals throughout the night, and were again as musical as ever just before and about dawn.

When other birds are still, the screech owls take up the strain, like mourning women their ancient u-lu-lu. Their dismal scream is truly Ben Jonsonian. Wise midnight hags! It is no honest and blunt tu-whit tu-who of the poets, but, without jesting, a most solemn graveyard ditty, the mutual consolations of suicide lovers remembering the pangs and the delights of supernal love in the infernal groves. Yet I love to hear their wailing, their doleful responses, trilled along the woodside; reminding me sometimes of music and singing birds; as if it were the dark and tearful side of music, the regrets and sighs that would fain be sung. They are the spirits, the low spirits and melancholy forebodings, of fallen souls that once in human shape night-walked the earth and did the deeds of darkness, now expiating their sins with their wailing hymns or threnodies in the scenery of their transgressions. They give me a new sense of the variety and capacity of that nature which is our common dwelling. *Oh-o-o-o-o that I never had been bor-r-r-n!* sighs one on this side of the pond, and circles with the restlessness of despair to some new perch on the gray oaks. Then—*that I never had been bor-r-r-n!* echoes another on the farther side with tremulous sincerity, and—*bor-r-r-n!* comes faintly from far in the Lincoln woods.

I was also serenaded by a hooting owl. Near at hand you could fancy it the most melancholy sound in Nature, as if she meant by this to stereotype and make permanent in her choir the dying moans of a human being,—some poor weak relic of mortality who has left hope behind, and howls like an animal, yet with human sobs, on entering the dark valley, made more awful by a certain gurgling melodiousness,—I find myself beginning with the letters *gl* when I try to imitate it,—expressive of a mind which has reached the gelatinous, mildewy stage in the mortification of all healthy and courageous thought. It reminded me of ghouls and idiots and insane howlings. But now one answers from far woods in a strain made really melodious by distance,—*Hoo hoo hoo, hoorer hoo;* and indeed for the most part it suggested only pleasing associations, whether heard by day or night, summer or winter.

I rejoice that there are owls. Let them do the idiotic and maniacal hooting for men. It is a sound admirably suited to swamps and twilight woods which no day illustrates, suggesting a vast and undeveloped nature which men have not recognized. They represent the stark twilight and unsatisfied thoughts which all have. All day the sun has shone on the surface of some savage swamp, where the single spruce stands hung with usnea lichens, and small hawks circulate above, and the chickadee lisps amid the evergreens, and the partridge and rabbit skulk beneath; but now a more dismal and fitting day dawns, and a different race of creatures awakes to express the meaning of Nature there.

Late in the evening I heard the distant rumbling of wagons over bridges,—a sound heard farther than almost any other at night,—the baying of dogs, and sometimes again the lowing of some disconsolate cow in a distant barn-yard. In the meanwhile all the shore rang with the trump of bullfrogs, the sturdy spirits of ancient wine-bibbers and wassailers, still unrepentant, trying to sing a catch in their Stygian lake,—if the Walden nymphs will pardon the comparison, for though there are almost no weeds, there are frogs there,—who would fain keep up the hilarious rules of their old festal tables, though their voices have waxed hoarse and solemnly grave, mocking at mirth, and the wine has lost its flavor, and become only liquor to distend their paunches, and sweet intoxication never comes to drown the memory of the past, but mere saturation and water-loggedness and distention. The most aldermanic, with his chin upon a heart-leaf, which serves for a napkin to his drooling chaps, under this northern shore quaffs a deep draught of the once scorned water, and passes round the cup with the ejaculation *tr-r-r-oonk, tr-r-r-oonk, tr-r-r-oonk!* and straightway comes over the water from some distant cove the same password repeated, where the next in seniority and girth has gulped down to his mark; and when this observance has made the circuit of the shores, then ejaculates the master of ceremonies, with satisfaction, *tr-r-r-oonk!* and each in his turn repeats the same down to the least distended, leakiest, and flabbiest paunched, that there be no mistake; and then the bowl goes round again and again, until the sun disperses the morning mist, and only the patriarch is not under the pond, but vainly bellowing *troonk* from time to time, and pausing for a reply.

I am not sure that I ever heard the sound of cock-crowing from my clearing, and I thought that it might be worth the while to keep a cockerel for his music merely, as a singing bird. The note of this once wild Indian pheasant is certainly the most remarkable of any bird's, and if they could be naturalized without being domesticated, it would soon become the most famous sound in our woods, surpassing the clangor of the goose and the hooting of the owl; and then imagine the cackling of the hens to fill the pauses when their lords' clarions rested! No wonder that man added this bird to his tame stock,—to say nothing of the eggs and drumsticks. To walk in a winter morning in a wood where these birds abounded, their native woods, and hear the wild cockerels crow on the trees, clear and shrill for miles over the resounding earth, drowning the feebler notes of other birds,—think of it! It would put nations on the alert. Who would not be early to rise, and rise earlier and earlier every successive day of his life, till he became unspeakably healthy, wealthy, and wise? This foreign bird's note is celebrated by the poets of all countries along with the notes of their native songsters. All climates agree with brave Chanticleer. He is more indigenous even than the natives. His health is ever good, his lungs are sound, his spirits never flag. Even the sailor on the Atlantic and Pacific is awakened by his voice; but its shrill sound never roused me from my slumbers. I kept neither dog, cat, cow, pig, nor hens, so that you would have said there was a deficiency of domestic sounds; neither the churn, nor the spinning-wheel, nor even the singing of the kettle, nor the hissing of the urn, nor children crying, to comfort one. An old-fashioned man would have lost his senses or died of ennui before this. Not even rats in the wall, for they were starved out, or rather were never baited in,—only squirrels on the roof and under the floor, a whip-poor-will on the ridge-pole, a blue jay screaming beneath the window, a hare or woodchuck under the house, a screech owl or a cat owl behind it, a flock of wild geese or a laughing loon on the pond, and a fox to bark in the night. Not even a lark or an oriole, those mild plantation birds, ever visited my clearing. No cockerels to crow nor hens to cackle in the yard. No yard! but unfenced nature reaching up to your very sills. A young forest growing up under your windows, and wild sumachs and blackberry vines breaking through into your cellar; sturdy pitch pines rubbing and creaking against the shingles for want of room, their roots reaching quite under the house. Instead of a scuttle or a blind blown off in the gale,—a pine tree snapped off or torn up by the roots behind your house for fuel. Instead of no path to the front-yard gate in the Great Snow,—no gate—no front-yard,—and no path to the civilized world.

XI. Higher Laws

As I came home through the woods with my string of fish, trailing my pole, it being now quite dark, I caught a glimpse of a woodchuck stealing across my path, and felt a strange thrill of savage delight, and was strongly tempted to seize and de-

vour him raw; not that I was hungry then, except for that wildness which he represented. Once or twice, however, while I lived at the pond, I found myself ranging the woods, like a half-starved hound, with a strange abandonment, seeking some kind of venison which I might devour, and no morsel could have been too savage for me. The wildest scenes had become unaccountably familiar. I found in myself, and still find, an instinct toward a higher, or, as it is named, spiritual life, as do most men, and another toward a primitive rank and savage one, and I reverence them both. I love the wild not less than the good. The wildness and adventure that are in fishing still recommended it to me. I like sometimes to take rank hold on life and spend my day more as the animals do. Perhaps I have owed to this employment and to hunting, when quite young, my closest acquaintance with Nature. They early introduce us to and detain us in scenery with which otherwise, at that age, we should have little acquaintance. Fishermen, hunters, woodchoppers, and others, spending their lives in the fields and woods, in a peculiar sense a part of Nature themselves, are often in a more favorable mood for observing her, in the intervals of their pursuits, than philosophers or poets even, who approach her with expectation. She is not afraid to exhibit herself to them. The traveller on the prairie is naturally a hunter, on the head waters of the Missouri and Columbia a trapper, and at the Falls of St. Mary[1] a fisherman. He who is only a traveller learns things at second-hand and by the halves, and is poor authority. We are most interested when science reports what those men already know practically or instinctively, for that alone is a true *humanity*, or account of human experience.

They mistake who assert that the Yankee has few amusements, because he has not so many public holidays, and men and boys do not play so many games as they do in England, for here the most primitive but solitary amusements of hunting, fishing, and the like have not yet given place to the former. Almost every New England boy among my contemporaries shouldered a fowling-piece between the ages of ten and fourteen; and his hunting and fishing grounds were not limited, like the preserves of an English nobleman, but were more boundless even than those of a savage. No wonder, then, that he did not oftener stay to play on the common. But already a change is taking place, owing, not to an increased humanity, but to an increased scarcity of game, for perhaps the hunter is the greatest friend of the animals hunted, not excepting the Humane Society.

Moreover, when at the pond, I wished sometimes to add fish to my fare for variety. I have actually

---

[1] In southeastern British Columbia. (Harding)

fished from the same kind of necessity that the first fishers did. Whatever humanity I might conjure up against it was all factitious, and concerned my philosophy more than my feelings. I speak of fishing only now, for I had long felt differently about fowling, and sold my gun before I went to the woods. Not that I am less humane than others, but I did not perceive that my feelings were much affected. I did not pity the fishes nor the worms. This was habit. As for fowling, during the last years that I carried a gun my excuse was that I was studying ornithology, and sought only new or rare birds. But I confess that I am now inclined to think that there is a finer way of studying ornithology than this. It requires so much closer attention to the habits of the birds, that, if for that reason only, I have been willing to omit the gun. Yet notwithstanding the objection on the score of humanity, I am compelled to doubt if equally valuable sports are ever substituted for these; and when some of my friends have asked me anxiously about their boys, whether they should let them hunt, I have answered, yes,—remembering that it was one of the best parts of my education,—*make* them hunters, though sportsmen only at first, if possible, mighty hunters at last, so that they shall not find game large enough for them in this or any vegetable wilderness,—hunters as well as fishers of men. Thus far I am of the opinion of Chaucer's nun, who

> "yave not of the text a pulled hen
> That saith that hunters ben not holy men."[2]

There is a period in the history of the individual, as of the race, when the hunters are the "best men," as the Algonquins called them. We cannot but pity the boy who has never fired a gun; he is no more humane, while his education has been sadly neglected. This was my answer with respect to those youths who were bent on this pursuit, trusting that they would soon outgrow it. No humane being, past the thoughtless age of boyhood, will wantonly murder any creature which holds its life by the same tenure that he does. The hare in its extremity cries like a child. I warn you, mothers, that my sympathies do not always make the usual phi-*anthropic* distinctions.

Such is oftenest the young man's introduction to the forest, and the most original part of himself. He goes thither at first as a hunter and fisher, until at last, if he has the seeds of a better life in him, he distinguishes his proper objects, as a poet or naturalist it may be, and leaves the gun and fish-pole behind. The mass of men are still and always young in this respect. In some countries a hunting parson is

[2]Prologue, *Canterbury Tales;* said about the monk, however.

no uncommon sight. Such a one might make a good shepherd's dog, but is far from being the Good Shepherd. I have been surprised to consider that the only obvious employment, except wood-chopping, ice-cutting, or the like business, which ever to my knowledge detained at Walden Pond for a whole half-day any of my fellow-citizens, whether fathers or children of the town, with just one exception, was fishing. Commonly they did not think that they were lucky, or well paid for their time, unless they got a long string of fish, though they had the opportunity of seeing the pond all the while. They might go there a thousand times before the sediment of fishing would sink to the bottom and leave their purpose pure; but no doubt such a clarifying process would be going on all the while. The Governor and his Council faintly remember the pond, for they went a-fishing there when they were boys; but now they are too old and dignified to go a-fishing, and so they know it no more forever. Yet even they expect to go to heaven at last. If the legislature regards it, it is chiefly to regulate the number of hooks to be used there; but they know nothing about the hook of hooks with which to angle for the pond itself, impaling the legislature for a bait. Thus, even in civilized communities, the embryo man passes through the hunter stage of development.

I have found repeatedly, of late years, that I cannot fish without falling a little in self-respect. I have tried it again and again. I have skill at it, and, like many of my fellows, a certain instinct for it, which revives from time to time, but always when I have done I feel that it would have been better if I had not fished. I think that I do not mistake. It is a faint intimation, yet so are the first streaks of morning. There is unquestionably this instinct in me which belongs to the lower orders of creation; yet with every year I am less a fisherman, though without more humanity or even wisdom; at present I am no fisherman at all. But I see that if I were to live in a wilderness I should again be tempted to become a fisher and hunter in earnest. Beside, there is something essentially unclean about this diet and all flesh, and I began to see where housework commences, and whence the endeavor, which costs so much, to wear a tidy and respectable appearance each day, to keep the house sweet and free from all ill odors and sights. Having been my own butcher and scullion and cook, as well as the gentleman for whom the dishes were served up, I can speak from an unusually complete experience. The practical objection to animal food in my case was its uncleanness; and besides, when I had caught and cleaned and cooked and eaten my fish, they seemed not to have fed me essentially. It was insignificant and unnecessary, and cost more than it came to. A little bread or a few potatoes would have done as well, with less trouble and filth. Like many of my contemporaries, I had rarely for many years used animal food, or tea, or coffee, etc.; not so much because of any ill effects which I had traced to them, as because they were not agreeable to my imagination. The repugnance to animal food is not the effect of experience, but is an instinct. It appeared more beautiful to live low and fare hard in many respects; and though I never did so, I went far enough to please my imagination. I believe that every man who has ever been earnest to preserve his higher or poetic faculties in the best condition has been particularly inclined to abstain from animal food, and from much food of any kind. It is a significant fact, stated by entomologists,—I find it in Kirby and Spence,—that "some insects in their perfect state, though furnished with organs of feeding, make no use of them;" and they lay it down as "a general rule, that almost all insects in this state eat much less than in that of larvae. The voracious caterpillar when transformed into a butterfly . . . and the gluttonous maggot when become a fly" content themselves with a drop or two of honey or some other sweet liquid. The abdomen under the wings of the butterfly still represents the larva. This is the tidbit which tempts his insectivorous fate. The gross feeder is a man in the larva state; and there are whole nations in that condition, nations without fancy or imagination, whose vast abdomens betray them.

It is hard to provide and cook so simple and clean a diet as will not offend the imagination; but this, I think, is to be fed when we feed the body; they should both sit down at the same table. Yet perhaps this may be done. The fruits eaten temperately need not make us ashamed of our appetites, nor interrupt the worthiest pursuits. But put an extra condiment into your dish, and it will poison you. It is not worth the while to live by rich cookery. Most men would feel shame if caught preparing with their own hands precisely such a dinner, whether of animal or vegetable food, as is every day prepared for them by others. Yet till this is otherwise we are not civilized, and, if gentlemen and ladies, are not true men and women. This certainly suggests what change is to be made. It may be vain to ask why the imagination will not be reconciled to flesh and fat. I am satisfied that it is not. Is it not a reproach that man is a carnivorous animal? True, he can and does live, in a great measure, by preying on other animals; but this is a miserable way,—as any one who will go to snaring rabbits, or slaughtering lambs, may learn,— and he will be regarded as a benefactor of his race who shall teach man to confine himself to a more innocent and wholesome diet. Whatever my own practice may be, I have no doubt that it is a part of the destiny of the human race, in its gradual improvement, to leave off eating animals, as surely as the savage tribes have left off eating each other when they came in contact with the more civilized.

If one listens to the faintest but constant suggestions of his genius, which are certainly true, he sees not to what extremes, or even insanity, it may lead him; and yet that way, as he grows more resolute and faithful, his road lies. The faintest assured objection which one healthy man feels will at length prevail over the arguments and customs of mankind. No man ever followed his genius till it misled him. Though the result were bodily weakness, yet perhaps no one can say that the consequences were to be regretted, for these were a life in conformity to higher principles. If the day and the night are such that you greet them with joy, and life emits a fragrance like flowers and sweet-scented herbs, is more elastic, more starry, more immortal,—that is your success. All nature is your congratulation, and you have cause momentarily to bless yourself. The greatest gains and values are farthest from being appreciated. We easily come to doubt if they exist. We soon forget them. They are the highest reality. Perhaps the facts most astounding and most real are never communicated by man to man. The true harvest of my daily life is somewhat as intangible and indescribable as the tints of morning or evening. It is a little star-dust caught, a segment of the rainbow which I have clutched.

Yet, for my part, I was never unusually squeamish; I could sometimes eat a fried rat with a good relish, if it were necessary. I am glad to have drunk water so long, for the same reason that I prefer the natural sky to an opium-eater's heaven. I would fain keep sober always; and there are infinite degrees of drunkenness. I believe that water is the only drink for a wise man: wine is not so noble a liquor; and think of dashing the hopes of a morning with a cup of warm coffee, or of an evening with a dish of tea! Ah, how low I fall when I am tempted by them! Even music may be intoxicating. Such apparently slight causes destroyed Greece and Rome, and will destroy England and America. Of all ebriosity, who does not prefer to be intoxicated by the air he breathes? I have found it to be the most serious objection to coarse labors long continued, that they compelled me to eat and drink coarsely also. But to tell the truth, I find myself at present somewhat less particular in these respects. I carry less religion to the table, ask no blessing; not because I am wiser than I was, but, I am obliged to confess, because, however much it is to be regretted, with years I have grown more coarse and indifferent. Perhaps these questions are entertained only in youth, as most believe of poetry. My practice is "nowhere," my opinion is here. Nevertheless I am far from regarding myself as one of those privileged ones to whom the Ved refers when it says, that "he who has true faith in the Omnipresent Supreme Being may eat all that exists," that is, is not bound to inquire what is his food, or who prepares it; and even in their case it is to be observed, as a Hindoo commentator has remarked, that the Vedant limits this privilege to "the time of distress."

Who has not sometimes derived an inexpressible satisfaction from his food in which appetite had no share? I have been thrilled to think that I owed a mental perception to the commonly gross sense of taste, that I have been inspired through the palate, that some berries which I had eaten on a hillside had fed my genius. "The soul not being mistress of herself," says Thseng-tseu, "one looks, and one does not see; one listens, and one does not hear; one eats, and one does not know the savor of food."[3] He who distinguishes the true savor of his food can never be a glutton; he who does not cannot be otherwise. A puritan may go to his brown-bread crust with as gross an appetite as ever an alderman to his turtle. Not that food which entereth into the mouth defileth a man, but the appetite with which it is eaten. It is neither the quality nor the quantity, but the devotion to sensual savors; when that which is eaten is not a viand to sustain our animal, or inspire our spiritual life, but food for the worms that possess us. If the hunter has a taste for mud-turtles, muskrats, and other such savage tidbits, the fine lady indulges a taste for jelly made of a calf's foot, or for sardines from over the sea, and they are even. He goes to the mill-pond, she to her preserve-pot. The wonder is how they, how you and I, can live this slimy, beastly life, eating and drinking.

Our whole life is startlingly moral. There is never an instant's truce between virtue and vice. Goodness is the only investment that never fails. In the music of the harp which trembles round the world it is the insisting on this which thrills us. The harp is the travelling patterer for the Universe's Insurance Company, recommending its laws, and our little goodness is all the assessment that we pay. Though the youth at last grows indifferent, the laws of the universe are not indifferent, but are forever on the side of the most sensitive. Listen to every zephyr for some reproof, for it is surely there, and he is unfortunate who does not hear it. We cannot touch a string or move a stop but the charming moral transfixes us. Many an irksome noise, go a long way off, is heard as music, a proud, sweet satire on the meanness of our lives.

We are conscious of an animal in us, which awakens in proportion as our higher nature slumbers. It is reptile and sensual, and perhaps cannot be wholly expelled; like the worms which, even in life and health, occupy our bodies. Possibly we may withdraw from it, but never change its nature. I fear that it may enjoy a certain health of its own; that we may be well, yet not pure. The other day I picked up the lower jaw of a hog, with white and sound teeth and tusks, which suggested that there was an animal health and vigor distinct from the spiritual. This creature succeeded by other means than temperance and purity. "That in which men differ from brute beasts," says Mencius, "is a thing very inconsiderable; the common herd lose it very soon; superior men preserve it carefully."[4] Who knows what sort of life would result if we had attained to purity? If I knew so wise a man as could teach me purity I would go to seek him forthwith. "A command over our passions, and over the external senses of the body, and good acts, are declared by the Ved to be indispensable in the mind's approximation to God." Yet the spirit can for the time pervade and control every member and function of the body, and transmute what in form is the grossest sensuality into purity and devotion. The generative energy, which, when we are loose, dissipates and makes us unclean, when we are continent invigorates and inspires us. Chastity is the flowering of man; and what are called Genius, Heroism, Holiness, and the like, are but various fruits which succeed it. Man flows at once to God when the channel of purity is open. By turns our purity inspires and our impurity casts us down. He is blessed who is assured that the animal is dying out in him day by day, and the divine being established. Perhaps there is none but has cause for shame on account of the inferior and brutish nature to which he is allied. I fear that we are such gods or demigods only as fauns and satyrs, the divine allied to beasts, the creatures of appetite, and that, to some extent, our very life is our disgrace.—

"How happy's he who hath due place assigned
To his beasts and disafforested his mind!

. . . .

Can use his horse, goat, wolf, and ev'ry beast,
And is not ass himself to all the rest!
Else man not only is the herd of swine,
But he's those devils too which did incline
Them to a headlong rage, and made them worse."[5]

All sensuality is one, though it takes many forms; all purity is one. It is the same whether a man eat, or drink, or cohabit, or sleep sensually. They are but one appetite, and we only need to see a person do any one of these things to know how great a sensualist he is. The impure can neither stand nor sit with purity. When the reptile is attacked at one mouth of his burrow, he shows himself at another. If you

---

[3] Confucius, *The Great Learning.*

[4] Meng-tse (372?–289? B.C.), Chinese philosopher and teacher of Confucianism.

[5] John Donne (1573–1631), "To Sir Edward Herbert at Julyers."

would be chaste, you must be temperate. What is chastity? How shall a man know if he is chaste? He shall not know it. We have heard of this virtue, but we know not what it is. We speak conformably to the rumor which we have heard. From exertion come wisdom and purity; from sloth ignorance and sensuality. In the student sensuality is a sluggish habit of mind. An unclean person is universally a slothful one, one who sits by a stove, whom the sun shines on prostrate, who reposes without being fatigued. If you would avoid uncleanness, and all the sins, work earnestly, though it be at cleaning a stable. Nature is hard to be overcome, but she must be overcome. What avails it that you are Christian, if you are not purer than the heathen, if you deny yourself no more, if you are not more religious? I know of many systems of religion esteemed heathenish whose precepts fill the reader with shame, and provoke him to new endeavors, though it be to the performance of rites merely.

I hesitate to say these things, but it is not because of the subject,—I care not how obscene my *words* are,—but because I cannot speak of them without betraying my impurity. We discourse freely without shame of one form of sensuality, and are silent about another. We are so degraded that we cannot speak simply of the necessary functions of human nature. In earlier ages, in some countries, every function was reverently spoken of and regulated by law. Nothing was too trivial for the Hindoo lawgiver, however offensive it may be to modern taste. He teaches how to eat, drink, cohabit, void excrement and urine, and the like, elevating what is mean, and does not falsely excuse himself by calling these things trifles.

Every man is the builder of a temple, called his body, to the god he worships, after a style purely his own, nor can he get off by hammering marble instead. We are all sculptors and painters, and our material is our own flesh and blood and bones. Any nobleness begins at once to refine a man's features, any meanness or sensuality to imbrute them.

John Farmer sat at his door one September evening, after a hard day's work, his mind still running on his labor more or less. Having bathed, he sat down to re-create his intellectual man. It was a rather cool evening, and some of his neighbors were apprehending a frost. He had not attended to the train of his thoughts long when he heard some one playing on a flute, and that sound harmonized with his mood. Still he thought of his work; but the burden of his thought was, that though this kept running in his head, and he found himself planning and contriving it against his will, yet it concerned him very little. It was no more than the scurf of his skin, which was constantly shuffled off. But the notes of the flute came home to his ears out of a different

sphere from that he worked in, and suggested work for certain faculties which slumbered in him. They gently did away with the street, and the village, and the state in which he lived. A voice said to him,— Why do you stay here and live this mean moiling life, when a glorious existence is possible for you? Those same stars twinkle over other fields than these.—But how to come out of this condition and actually migrate thither? All that he could think of was to practise some new austerity, to let his mind descend into his body and redeem it, and treat himself with ever increasing respect.

XII. Brute Neighbors

Sometimes I had a companion[1] in my fishing, who came through the village to my house from the other side of the town, and the catching of the dinner was as much a social exercise as the eating of it.

Hermit. I wonder what the world is doing now. I have not heard so much as a locust over the sweet-fern these three hours. The pigeons are all asleep upon their roosts,—no flutter from them. Was that a farmer's noon horn which sounded from beyond the woods just now? The hands are coming in to boiled salt beef and cider and Indian bread. Why will men worry themselves so? He that does not eat need not work. I wonder how much they have reaped. Who would live there where a body can never think for the barking of Bose?[2] And oh, the housekeeping! to keep bright the devil's door-knobs, and scour his tubs this bright day! Better not keep a house. Say, some hollow tree; and then for morning calls and dinner-parties! Only a woodpecker tapping. Oh, they swarm; the sun is too warm there; they are born too far into life for me. I have water from the spring, and a loaf of brown bread on the shelf.— Hark! I hear a rustling of the leaves. Is it some ill-fed village hound yielding to the instinct of the chase? or the lost pig which is said to be in these woods, whose tracks I saw after the rain? It comes on apace; my sumachs and sweetbriers tremble.— Eh, Mr. Poet, is it you? How do you like the world to-day?

Poet. See those clouds; how they hang! That's the greatest thing I have seen to-day. There's nothing like it in old paintings, nothing like it in foreign lands,—unless when we were off the coast of Spain. That's a true Mediterranean sky. I thought, as I have my living to get, and have not eaten to-day, that I might go a-fishing. That's the true industry for poets.

[1] William Ellery Channing the younger. He is the poet in the dialogue.
[2] Dog.

It is the only trade I have learned. Come, let's along.

Hermit. I cannot resist. My brown bread will soon be gone. I will go with you gladly soon, but I am just concluding a serious meditation. I think that I am near the end of it. Leave me alone, then, for a while. But that we may not be delayed, you shall be digging the bait meanwhile. Angleworms are rarely to be met with in these parts, where the soil was never fattened with manure; the race is nearly extinct. The sport of digging the bait is nearly equal to that of catching the fish, when one's appetite is not too keen; and this you may have all to yourself today. I would advise you to set in the spade down yonder among the ground-nuts, where you see the johnswort waving. I think that I may warrant you one worm to every three sods you turn up, if you look well in among the roots of the grass, as if you were weeding. Or, if you choose to go farther, it will not be unwise, for I have found the increase of fair bait to be very nearly as the squares of the distances.

Hermit alone. Let me see; where was I? Methinks I was nearly in this frame of mind; the world lay about at this angle. Shall I go to heaven or a-fishing? If I should soon bring this meditation to an end, would another so sweet occasion be likely to offer? I was as near being resolved into the essence of things as ever I was in my life. I fear my thoughts will not come back to me. If it would do any good, I would whistle for them. When they make us an offer, is it wise to say, We will think of it? My thoughts have left no track, and I cannot find the path again. What was it that I was thinking of? It was a very hazy day. I will just try these three sentences of Confut-see; they may fetch that state about again. I know not whether it was the dumps or a budding ecstasy. Mem. There never is but one opportunity of a kind.

Poet. How now, Hermit, is it too soon? I have got just thirteen whole ones, beside several which are imperfect or undersized; but they will do for the smaller fry; they do not cover up the hook so much. Those village worms are quite too large; a shiner may make a meal off one without finding the skewer.

Hermit. Well, then, let's be off. Shall we to the Concord? There's good sport there if the water be not too high.

Why do precisely these objects which we behold make a world? Why has man just these species of animals for his neighbors; as if nothing but a mouse could have filled this crevice? I suspect that Pilpay & Co.[3] have put animals to their best use, for they are all beasts of burden, in a sense, made to carry some portion of our thoughts.

The mice which haunted my house were not the common ones, which are said to have been introduced into the country, but a wild native kind not found in the village. I sent one to a distinguished naturalist,[4] and it interested him much. When I was building, one of these had its nest underneath the house, and before I had laid the second floor, and swept out the shavings, would come out regularly at lunch time and pick up the crumbs at my feet. It probably had never seen a man before; and it soon became quite familiar, and would run over my shoes and up my clothes. It could readily ascend the sides of the room by short impulses, like a squirrel, which it resembled in its motions. At length, as I leaned with my elbow on the bench one day, it ran up my clothes, and along my sleeve, and round and round the paper which held my dinner, while I kept the latter close, and dodged and played at bopeep with it; and when at last I held still a piece of cheese between my thumb and finger, it came and nibbled it, sitting in my hand, and afterward cleaned its face and paws, like a fly, and walked away.

A phoebe soon built in my shed, and a robin for protection in a pine which grew against the house. In June the partridge (*Tetrao umbellus*), which is so shy a bird, led her brood past my windows, from the woods in the rear to the front of my house, clucking and calling to them like a hen, and in all her behavior proving herself the hen of the woods. The young suddenly disperse on your approach, at a signal from the mother, as if a whirlwind had swept them away, and they so exactly resemble the dried leaves and twigs that many a traveller has placed his foot in the midst of a brood, and heard the whir of the old bird as she flew off, and her anxious calls and mewing, or seen her trail her wings to attract his attention, without suspecting their neighborhood. The parent will sometimes roll and spin round before you in such a dishabille, that you cannot, for a few moments, detect what kind of creature it is. The young squat still and flat, often running their heads under a leaf, and mind only their mother's directions given from a distance, nor will your approach make them run again and betray themselves. You may even tread on them, or have your eyes on them for a minute without discovering them. I have held them in my open hand at such a time, and still their only care, obedient to their mother and their instinct, was to squat there without fear or trembling. So perfect is this instinct, that once, when I had laid them on the leaves again, and one accidentally fell on its side, it was found with the rest in exactly the same position ten minutes afterward.

[3] Pilpay, or Bidpai, author of a collection of East Indian fables.

[4] Louis Agassiz, at Harvard in the late 1840's.

They are not callow like the young of most birds, but more perfectly developed and precocious even than chickens. The remarkably adult yet innocent expression of their open and serene eyes is very memorable. All intelligence seems reflected in them. They suggest not merely the purity of infancy, but a wisdom clarified by experience. Such an eye was not born when the bird was, but is coeval with the sky it reflects. The woods do not yield another such a gem. The traveller does not often look into such a limpid well. The ignorant or reckless sportsman often shoots the parent at such a time, and leaves these innocents to fall a prey to some prowling beast or bird, or gradually mingle with the decaying leaves which they so much resemble. It is said that when hatched by a hen they will directly disperse on some alarm, and so are lost, for they never hear the mother's call which gathers them again. These were my hens and chickens.

It is remarkable how many creatures live wild and free though secret in the woods, and still sustain themselves in the neighborhood of towns, suspected by hunters only. How retired the otter manages to live here! He grows to be four feet long, as big as a small boy, perhaps without any human being getting a glimpse of him. I formerly saw the raccoon in the woods behind where my house is built, and probably still heard their whinnering at night. Commonly I rested an hour or two in the shade at noon, after planting, and ate my lunch, and read a little by a spring which was the source of a swamp and of a brook, oozing from under Brister's Hill, half a mile from my field. The approach to this was through a succession of descending grassy hollows, full of young pitch pines, into a larger wood about the swamp. There, in a very secluded and shaded spot, under a spreading white pine, there was yet a clean, firm sward to sit on. I had dug out the spring and made a well of clear gray water, where I could dip up a pailful without roiling it, and thither I went for this purpose almost every day in midsummer, when the pond was warmest. Thither, too, the woodcock led her brood, to probe the mud for worms, flying but a foot above them down the bank, while they ran in a troop beneath; but a last, spying me, she would leave her young and circle round and round me, nearer and nearer till within four or five feet, pretending broken wings and legs, to attract my attention, and get off her young, who would already have taken up their march, with faint, wiry peep, single file through the swamp, as she directed. Or I heard the peep of the young when I could not see the parent bird. There too the turtle doves sat over the spring, or fluttered from bough to bough of the soft white pines over my head; or the red squirrel, coursing down the nearest bough, was particularly familiar and inquisitive. You only need sit still long enough in some attractive spot in the woods that all its inhabitants may exhibit themselves to you by turns.

I was witness to events of a less peaceful character. One day when I went out to my wood-pile, or rather my pile of stumps, I observed two large ants, the one red, the other much larger, nearly half an inch long, and black, fiercely contending with one another. Having once got hold they never let go, but struggled and wrestled and rolled on the chips incessantly. Looking farther, I was surprised to find that the chips were covered with such combatants, that it was not a *duellum*, but a *bellum*, a war between two races of ants, the red always pitted against the black, and frequently two red ones to one black. The legions of these Myrmidons[5] covered all the hills and vales in my wood-yard, and the ground was already strewn with the dead and dying, both red and black. It was the only battle which I have ever witnessed, the only battle-field I ever trod while the battle was raging; internecine war; the red republicans on the one hand, and the black imperialists on the other. On every side they were engaged in deadly combat, yet without any noise that I could hear, and human soldiers never fought so resolutely. I watched a couple that were fast locked in each other's embraces, in a little sunny valley amid the chips, now at noonday prepared to fight till the sun went down, or life went out. The smaller red champion had fastened himself like a vice to his adversary's front, and through all the tumblings on that field never for an instant ceased to gnaw at one of his feelers near the root, having already caused the other to go by the board; while the stronger black one dashed him from side to side, and, as I saw on looking nearer, had already divested him of several of his members. They fought with more pertinacity than bull-dogs. Neither manifested the least disposition to retreat. It was evident that their battle-cry was "Conquer or die." In the meanwhile there came along a single red ant on the hillside of this valley, evidently full of excitement, who either had despatched his foe, or had not yet taken part in the battle; probably the latter, for he had lost none of his limbs; whose mother had charged him to return with his shield or upon it. Or perchance he was some Achilles,[6] who had nourished his wrath apart, and had now come to avenge or rescue his Patroclus. He saw this unequal combat from afar,—for the blacks were nearly twice the size of the red,—he drew near with rapid pace till he stood on his guard within half an inch of the combatants; then, watching his opportunity, he sprang upon the black war-

[5] Soldiers from Thessaly who fought under Achilles in the Trojan War. Myrmes means ant in Greek.

[6] Did not participate in the Trojan War until his friend Patroclus was killed.

rior, and commenced his operations near the root of his right fore leg, leaving the foe to select among his own members; and so there were three united for life, as if a new kind of attraction had been invented which put all other locks and cements to shame. I should not have wondered by this time to find that they had their respective musical bands stationed on some eminent chip, and playing their national airs the while, to excite the slow and cheer the dying combatants. I was myself excited somewhat even as if they had been men. The more you think of it, the less the difference. And certainly there is not the fight recorded in Concord history, at least, if in the history of America, that will bear a moment's comparison with this, whether for the numbers engaged in it, or for the patriotism and heroism displayed. For numbers and for carnage it was an Austerlitz or Dresden.[7] Concord Fight![8] Two killed on the patriots' side, and Luther Blanchard wounded! Why here every ant was a Buttrick,—"Fire! for God's sake fire!"—and thousands shared the fate of Davis and Hosmer. There was not one hireling there. I have no doubt that it was a principle they fought for, as much as our ancestors, and not to avoid a three-penny tax on their tea; and the results of this battle will be as important and memorable to those whom it concerns as those of the battle of Bunker Hill, at least.

I took up the chip on which the three I have particularly described were struggling, carried it into my house, and placed it under a tumbler on my window-sill, in order to see the issue. Holding a microscope to the first-mentioned red ant, I saw that, though he was assiduously gnawing at the near fore leg of his enemy, having severed his remaining feeler, his own breast was all torn away, exposing what vitals he had there to the jaws of the black warrior, whose breastplate was apparently too thick for him to pierce; and the dark carbuncles of the sufferer's eyes shone with ferocity such as war only could excite. They struggled half an hour longer under the tumbler, and when I looked again the black soldier had severed the heads of his foes from their bodies, and the still living heads were hanging on either side of him like ghastly trophies at his saddle-bow, still apparently as firmly fastened as ever, and he was endeavoring with feeble struggles, being without feelers and with only the remnant of a leg, and I know not how many other wounds, to divest himself of them; which at length, after half an hour more, he accomplished. I raised the glass, and he went off over the window-sill in that crippled state. Whether he finally survived that combat, and spent the remainder of his days in some Hôtel des Invalides,[9] I do not know; but I thought that his industry would not be worth much thereafter. I never learned which party was victorious, nor the cause of the war; but I felt for the rest of that day as if I had had my feelings excited and harrowed by witnessing the struggle, the ferocity and carnage, of a human battle before my door.

Kirby and Spence[10] tell us that the battles of ants have long been celebrated and the date of them recorded, though they say that Huber[11] is the only modern author who appears to have witnessed them. "Aeneas Sylvius," say they, "after giving a very circumstantial account of one contested with great obstinacy by a great and small species on the trunk of a pear tree," adds that "'this action was fought in the pontificate of Eugenius the Fourth, in the presence of Nicholas Pistoriensis, an eminent lawyer, who related the whole history of the battle with the greatest fidelity.' A similar engagement between great and small ants is recorded by Olaus Magnus, in which the small ones, being victorious, are said to have buried the bodies of their own soldiers, but left those of their giant enemies a prey to the birds. This event happened previous to the expulsion of the tyrant Christiern the Second from Sweden."[12] The battle which I witnessed took place in the Presidency of Polk, five years before the passage of Webster's Fugitive-Slave Bill.

Many a village Bose, fit only to course a mud-turtle in a victualling cellar, sported his heavy quarters in the woods, without the knowledge of his master, and ineffectually smelled at old fox burrows and woodchucks' holes; led perchance by some slight cur which nimbly threaded the wood, and might still inspire a natural terror in its denizens;— now far behind his guide, barking like a canine bull toward some small squirrel which had treed itself for scrutiny, then, cantering off, bending the bushes with his weight, imagining that he is on the track of some stray member of the jerbilla family. Once I was surprised to see a cat walking along the stony shore of the pond, for they rarely wander so far from home. The surprise was mutual. Nevertheless the most domestic cat, which has lain on a rug all her days, appears quite at home in the woods, and, by her sly and stealthy behavior, proves herself more native there than the regular inhabitants. Once, when berrying, I met with a cat with young kittens in the woods, quite wild, and they all, like

[7] Sites of Napoleonic battles.

[8] The following names are associated with the battle of Concord.

[9] A hospital in Paris.

[10] William Kirby and William Spence, authors of *An Introduction to Entomology* (1846).

[11] François Huber (1750–1831), a Swiss entomologist.

[12] Aeneas Sylvius (1405–64) was Pope Pius II; Eugenius IV was pope from 1431 to 1447; Magnus (1490–1558) was archbishop of Uppsala; Christiern II was a 16th-century ruler of Denmark and Sweden. (Harding)

their mother, had their backs up and were fiercely spitting at me. A few years before I lived in the woods there was what was called a "winged cat" in one of the farmhouses in Lincoln nearest the pond, Mr. Gilian Baker's. When I called to see her in June, 1842, she was gone a-hunting in the woods, as was her wont (I am not sure whether it was a male or female, and so use the more common pronoun), but her mistress told me that she came into the neighborhood a little more than a year before, in April, and was finally taken into their house; that she was of a dark brownish-gray color, with a white spot on her throat, and white feet, and had a large bushy tail like a fox; that in the winter the fur grew thick and flatted out along her sides, forming strips ten or twelve inches long by two and a half wide, and under her chin like a muff, the upper side loose, the under matted like felt, and in the spring these appendages dropped off. They gave me a pair of her "wings," which I keep still. There is no appearance of a membrane about them. Some thought it was part flying squirrel or some other wild animal, which is not impossible, for, according to naturalists, prolific hybrids have been produced by the union of the marten and domestic cat. This would have been the right kind of cat for me to keep, if I had kept any; for why should not a poet's cat be winged as well as his horse?

In the fall the loon (Colymbus glacialis) came, as usual, to moult and bathe in the pond, making the woods ring with his wild laughter before I had risen. At rumor of his arrival all the Mill-dam sportsmen are on the alert, in gigs and on foot, two by two and three by three, with patent rifles and conical balls and spy-glasses. They come rustling through the woods like autumn leaves, at least ten men to one loon. Some station themselves on this side of the pond, some on that, for the poor bird cannot be omnipresent; if he dive here he must come up there. But now the kind October wind rises, rustling the leaves and rippling the surface of the water, so that no loon can be heard or seen, though his foes sweep the pond with spy-glasses, and make the woods resound with their discharges. The waves generously rise and dash angrily, taking sides with all water-fowl, and our sportsmen must beat a retreat to town and shop and unfinished jobs. But they were too often successful. When I went to get a pail of water early in the morning I frequently saw this stately bird sailing out of my cove within a few rods. If I endeavored to overtake him in a boat, in order to see how he would manoeuvre, he would dive and be completely lost, so that I did not discover him again, sometimes, till the latter part of the day. But I was more than a match for him on the surface. He commonly went off in a rain.

As I was paddling along the north shore one very

calm October afternoon, for such days especially they settle on to the lakes, like the milkweed down, having looked in vain over the pond for a loon, suddenly one, sailing out from the shore toward the middle a few rods in front of me, set up his wild laugh and betrayed himself. I pursued with a paddle and he dived, but when he came up I was nearer than before. He dived again, but I miscalculated the direction he would take, and we were fifty rods apart when he came to the surface this time, for I had helped to widen the interval; and again he laughed long and loud, and with more reason than before. He manoeuvred so cunningly that I could not get within half a dozen rods of him. Each time, when he came to the surface, turning his head this way and that, he coolly surveyed the water and the land, and apparently chose his course so that he might come up where there was the widest expanse of water and at the greatest distance from the boat. It was surprising how quickly he made up his mind and put his resolve into execution. He led me at once to the widest part of the pond, and could not be driven from it. While he was thinking one thing in his brain, I was endeavoring to divine his thought in mine. It was a pretty game, played on the smooth surface of the pond, a man against a loon. Suddenly your adversary's checker disappears beneath the board, and the problem is to place yours nearest to where his will appear again. Sometimes he would come up unexpectedly on the opposite side of me, having apparently passed directly under the boat. So long-winded was he and so unweariable, that when he had swum farthest he would immediately plunge again, nevertheless; and then no wit could divine where in the deep pond, beneath the smooth surface, he might be speeding his way like a fish, for he had time and ability to visit the bottom of the pond in its deepest part. It is said that loons have been caught in the New York lakes eighty feet beneath the surface, with hooks set for trout,—though Walden is deeper than that. How surprised must the fishes be to see this ungainly visitor from another sphere speeding his way amid their schools! Yet he appeared to know his course as surely under water as on the surface, and swam much faster there. Once or twice I saw a ripple where he approached the surface, just put his head out to reconnoitre, and instantly dived again. I found that it was as well for me to rest on my oars and wait his reappearing as to endeavor to calculate where he would rise; for again and again, when I was straining my eyes over the surface one way, I would suddenly be startled by his unearthly laugh behind me. But why, after displaying so much cunning, did he invariably betray himself the moment he came up by that loud laugh? Did not his white breast enough betray him? He was indeed a silly loon, I thought. I could commonly hear the plash of the water when he came up, and so also detected him. But after an hour he seemed as fresh as ever, dived as willingly, and swam yet farther than at first. It was surprising to see how serenely he sailed off with unruffled breast when he came to the surface, doing all the work with his webbed feet beneath. His usual note was this demoniac laughter, yet somewhat like that of a water-fowl; but occasionally, when he had balked me most successfully and come up a long way off, he uttered a long-drawn unearthly howl, probably more like that of a wolf than any bird; as when a beast puts his muzzle to the ground and deliberately howls. This was his looning,—perhaps the wildest sound that is ever heard here, making the woods ring far and wide. I concluded that he laughed in derision of my efforts, confident of his own resources. Though the sky was by this time overcast, the pond was so smooth that I could see where he broke the surface when I did not hear him. His white breast, the stillness of the air, and the smoothness of the water were all against him. At length, having come up fifty rods off, he uttered one of those prolonged howls, as if calling on the god of loons to aid him, and immediately there came a wind from the east and rippled the surface, and filled the whole air with misty rain, and I was impressed as if it were the prayer of the loon answered, and his god was angry with me; and so I left him disappearing far away on the tumultuous surface.

For hours, in fall days, I watched the ducks cunningly tack and veer and hold the middle of the pond, far from the sportsman; tricks which they will have less need to practise in Louisiana bayous. When compelled to rise they would sometimes circle round and round and over the pond at a considerable height, from which they could easily see to other ponds and the river, like black motes in the sky; and, when I thought they had gone off thither long since, they would settle down by a slanting flight of a quarter of a mile on to a distant part which was left free; but what beside safety they got by sailing in the middle of Walden I do not know, unless they love its water for the same reason that I do.

XVIII. Conclusion

To the sick the doctors wisely recommend a change of air and scenery. Thank Heaven, here is not all the world. The buckeye does not grow in New England, and the mockingbird is rarely heard here. The wild goose is more of a cosmopolite than we; he breaks his fast in Canada, takes a luncheon in the Ohio, and plumes himself for the night in a southern bayou. Even the bison, to some extent, keeps pace with the seasons, cropping the pastures of the Colorado only till a greener and sweeter grass awaits him by the Yellowstone. Yet we think that if rail fences are pulled down, and stone walls piled up on our farms, bounds are henceforth set to our lives and our fates decided. If you are chosen town clerk, forsooth, you cannot go to Tierra del Fuego this summer: but you may go to the land of infernal fire nevertheless. The universe is wider than our views of it.

Yet we should oftener look over the tafferel of our craft, like curious passengers, and not make the voyage like stupid sailors picking oakum. The other side of the globe is but the home of our correspondent. Our voyaging is only great-circle sailing, and the doctors prescribe for diseases of the skin merely. One hastens to southern Africa to chase the giraffe; but surely that is not the game he would be after. How long, pray, would a man hunt giraffes if he could? Snipes and woodcocks also may afford rare sport; but I trust it would be nobler game to shoot one's self.—

> "Direct your eye right inward, and you'll find
> A thousand regions in your mind
> Yet undiscovered. Travel them, and be
> Expert in home-cosmography."[1]

What does Africa,—what does the West stand for? Is not our own interior white on the chart? black though it may prove, like the coast, when discovered. Is it the source of the Nile, or the Niger, or the Mississippi, or a Northwest Passage around this continent, that we would find? Are these the problems which most concern mankind? Is Franklin[2] the only man who is lost, that his wife should be so earnest to find him? Does Mr. Grinnell[3] know where he himself is? Be rather the Mungo Park, the Lewis and Clark and Frobisher,[4] of your own streams and oceans; explore your own higher latitudes,—with shiploads of preserved meats to support you, if they be necessary; and pile the empty cans sky-high for a sign. Were preserved meats invented to preserve meat merely? Nay, be a Columbus to whole new continents and worlds within you, opening new channels, not of trade, but of thought. Every man is the lord of a realm beside which the earthly empire of the Czar is but a petty state, a hummock left by the ice. Yet some can be patriotic who have no *self*-respect, and sacrifice the greater to the less. They love the soil which makes their graves, but have no sympathy with the spirit which may still animate

[1] William Habington (1605-64), "To My Honoured Friend Sir Ed. P. Knight."
[2] Sir John Franklin (1786-1847), a British explorer who was lost in the Arctic.
[3] Henry Grinnell (1799-1874) of New York organized one of the expeditions that searched for Franklin.
[4] All famous explorers.

their clay. Patriotism is a maggot in their heads. What was the meaning of that South-Sea Exploring Expedition,[5] with all its parade and expense, but an indirect recognition of the fact that there are continents and seas in the moral world to which every man is an isthmus or an inlet, yet unexplored by him, but that it is easier to sail many thousand miles through cold and storm and cannibals, in a government ship, with five hundred men and boys to assist one, than it is to explore the private sea, the Atlantic and Pacific Ocean of one's being alone.—

> "Erret, et extremos alter scrutetur Iberos.
> Plus habet hic vitae, plus habet ille viae."
>
> Let them wander and scrutinize the outlandish
>   Australians.
> I have more of God, they more of the road.[6]

It is not worth the while to go round the world to count the cats in Zanzibar. Yet do this even till you can do better, and you may perhaps find some "Symmes' Hole"[7] by which to get at the inside at last. England and France, Spain and Portugal, Gold Coast and Slave Coast, all front on this private sea; but no bark from them has ventured out of sight of land, though it is without doubt the direct way to India. If you would learn to speak all tongues and conform to the customs of all nations, if you would travel farther than all travellers, be naturalized in all climes, and cause the Sphinx to dash her head against a stone, even obey the precept of the old philosopher, and Explore thyself. Herein are demanded the eye and the nerve. Only the defeated and deserters go to the wars, cowards that run away and enlist. Start now on that farthest western way, which does not pause at the Mississippi or the Pacific, nor conduct toward a worn-out China or Japan, but leads on direct, a tangent to this sphere, summer and winter, day and night, sun down, moon down, and at last earth down too.

It is said that Mirabeau[8] took to highway robbery "to ascertain what degree of resolution was necessary in order to place one's self in formal opposition to the most sacred laws of society." He declared that "a soldier who fights in the ranks does not require half so much courage as a foot-pad,"—"that honor and religion have never stood in the way of a well-considered and a firm resolve." This was manly, as the world goes; and yet it was idle, if not desperate. A saner man would have found himself often enough "in formal opposition" to what are deemed "the most sacred laws of society," through

obedience to yet more sacred laws, and so have tested his resolution without going out of his way. It is not for a man to put himself in such an attitude to society, but to maintain himself in whatever attitude he find himself through obedience to the laws of his being, which will never be one of opposition to a just government, if he should chance to meet with such.

I left the woods for as good a reason as I went there. Perhaps it seemed to me that I had several more lives to live, and could not spare any more time for that one. It is remarkable how easily and insensibly we fall into a particular route, and make a beaten track for ourselves. I had not lived there a week before my feet wore a path from my door to the pond-side; and though it is five or six years since I trod it, it is still quite distinct. It is true, I fear, that others may have fallen into it, and so helped to keep it open. The surface of the earth is soft and impressible by the feet of men; and so with the paths which the mind travels. How worn and dusty, then, must be the highways of the world, how deep the ruts of tradition and conformity! I did not wish to take a cabin passage, but rather to go before the mast and on the deck of the world, for there I could best see the moonlight amid the mountains. I do not wish to go below now.

I learned this, at least, by my experiment: that if one advances confidently in the direction of his dreams, and endeavors to live the life which he has imagined, he will meet with a success unexpected in common hours. He will put some things behind, will pass an invisible boundary; new, universal, and more liberal laws will begin to establish themselves around and within him; or the old laws be expanded, and interpreted in his favor in a more liberal sense, and he will live with the license of a higher order of beings. In proportion as he simplifies his life, the laws of the universe will appear less complex, and solitude will not be solitude, nor poverty poverty, nor weakness weakness. If you have built castles in the air, your work need not be lost; that is where they should be. Now put the foundations under them.

It is a ridiculous demand which England and America make, that you shall speak so that they can understand you. Neither men nor toadstools grow so. As if that were important, and there were not enough to understand you without them. As if Nature could support but one order of understandings, could not sustain birds as well as quadrupeds, flying as well as creeping things, and hish and whoa, which Bright[9] can understand, were the best English. As if there were safety in stupidity alone. I fear chiefly lest my expression may not be extra-vagant

---

[5] To the antarctic islands of the Pacific, 1838–42.

[6] From Claudian (fl. 395–404), "The Old Man of Verona." Note Thoreau's change of "Iberos" to "Australians."

[7] A bizarre theory of Captain John Cleves, advanced in 1818, that the earth was hollow and open at both poles.

[8] Count de Mirabeau (1749–91), statesman of the French Revolution.

[9] Oxen. The terms were used in driving oxen.

enough, may not wander far enough beyond the narrow limits of my daily experience, so as to be adequate to the truth of which I have been convinced. *Extra vagance!* it depends on how you are yarded. The migrating buffalo, which seeks new pastures in another latitude, is not extravagant like the cow which kicks over the pail, leaps the cowyard fence, and runs after her calf, in milking time. I desire to speak somewhere *without* bounds; like a man in a waking moment, to men in their waking moments; for I am convinced that I cannot exaggerate enough even to lay the foundation of a true expression. Who that has heard a strain of music feared then lest he should speak extravagantly any more forever? In view of the future or possible, we should live quite laxly and undefined in front, our outlines dim and misty on that side; as our shadows reveal an insensible perspiration toward the sun. The volatile truth of our words should continually betray the inadequacy of the residual statement. Their truth is instantly *translated;* its literal monument alone remains. The words which express our faith and piety are not definite; yet they are significant and fragrant like frankincense to superior natures.

Why level downward to our dullest perception always, and praise that as common sense? The commonest sense is the sense of men asleep, which they express by snoring. Sometimes we are inclined to class those who are once-and-a-half-witted with the half-witted, because we appreciate only a third part of their wit. Some would find fault with the morning red, if they ever got up early enough. "They pretend," as I hear, "that the verses of Kabir have four different senses; illusion, spirit, intellect, and the exoteric doctrine of the Vedas;" [10] but in this part of the world it is considered a ground for complaint if a man's writings admit of more than one interpretation. While England endeavors to cure the potato-rot, will not any endeavor to cure the brain-rot, which prevails so much more widely and fatally?

I do not suppose that I have attained to obscurity, but I should be proud if no more fatal fault were found with my pages on this score than was found with the Walden ice. Southern customers objected to its blue color, which is the evidence of its purity, as if it were muddy, and preferred the Cambridge ice, which is white, but tastes of weeds. The purity men love is like the mists which envelop the earth, and not like the azure ether beyond.

Some are dinning in our ears that we Americans, and moderns generally, are intellectual dwarfs compared with the ancients, or even the Elizabethan men. But what is that to the purpose? A living dog is better than a dead lion. Shall a man go and hang himself because he belongs to the race of pygmies, and not be the biggest pygmy that he can? Let every one mind his own business, and endeavor to be what he was made.

Why should we be in such desperate haste to succeed and in such desperate enterprises? If a man does not keep pace with his companions, perhaps it is because he hears a different drummer. Let him step to the music which he hears, however measured or far away. It is not important that he should mature as soon as an apple tree or an oak. Shall he turn his spring into summer? If the condition of things which we were made for is not yet, what were any reality which we can substitute? We will not be shipwrecked on a vain reality. Shall we with pains erect a heaven of blue glass over ourselves, though when it is done we shall be sure to gaze still at the true ethereal heaven far above, as if the former were not?

There was an artist in the city of Kouroo[11] who was disposed to strive after perfection. One day it came into his mind to make a staff. Having considered that in an imperfect work time is an ingredient, but into a perfect work time does not enter, he said to himself, It shall be perfect in all respects, though I should do nothing else in my life. He proceeded instantly to the forest for wood, being resolved that it should not be made of unsuitable material; and as he searched for and rejected stick after stick, his friends gradually deserted him, for they grew old in their works and died, but he grew not older by a moment. His singleness of purpose and resolution, and his elevated piety, endowed him, without his knowledge, with perennial youth. As he made no compromise with Time, Time kept out of his way, and only sighed at a distance because he could not overcome him. Before he had found a stock in all respects suitable the city of Kouroo was a hoary ruin, and he sat on one of its mounds to peel the stick. Before he had given it the proper shape the dynasty of the Candahars was at an end, and with the point of the stick he wrote the name of the last of that race in the sand, and then resumed his work. By the time he had smoothed and polished the staff Kalpa was no longer the pole-star; and ere he had put on the ferule and the head adorned with precious stones, Brahma had awoke and slumbered many times. But why do I stay to mention these things? When the finishing stroke was put to his work, it suddenly expanded before the eyes of the astonished artist into the fairest of all the creations of Brahma. He had made a new system in making a staff, a world with full and fair proportions; in which, though the old cities and dynasties had passed away, fairer and more glorious ones had

---

[10] From Garcin de Tassy, *Histoire de la Littérature Hindoui* (1839).

[11] A legend probably invented by Thoreau.

taken their places. And now he saw by the heap of shavings still fresh at his feet, that, for him and his work, the former lapse of time had been an illusion, and that no more time had elapsed than is required for a single scintillation from the brain of Brahma to fall on and inflame the tinder of a mortal brain. The material was pure, and his art was pure; how could the result be other than wonderful?

No face which we can give to a matter will stead us so well at last as the truth. This alone wears well. For the most part, we are not where we are, but in a false position. Through an infirmity of our natures, we suppose a case, and put ourselves into it, and hence are in two cases at the same time, and it is doubly difficult to get out. In sane moments we regard only the facts, the case that is. Say what you have to say, not what you ought. Any truth is better than make-believe. Tom Hyde, the tinker, standing on the gallows, was asked if he had anything to say. "Tell the tailors," said he, "to remember to make a knot in their thread before they take the first stitch." His companion's prayer is forgotten.

However mean your life is, meet it and live it; do not shun it and call it hard names. It is not so bad as you are. It looks poorest when you are richest. The faultfinder will find faults even in paradise. Love your life, poor as it is. You may perhaps have some pleasant, thrilling, glorious hours, even in a poor-house. The setting sun is reflected from the windows of the almshouse as brightly as from the rich man's abode; the snow melts before its door as early in the spring. I do not see but a quiet mind may live as contentedly there, and have as cheering thoughts, as in a palace. The town's poor seem to me often to live the most independent lives of any. Maybe they are simply great enough to receive without misgiving. Most think that they are above being supported by the town; but it oftener happens that they are not above supporting themselves by dishonest means, which should be more disreputable. Cultivate poverty like a garden herb, like sage. Do not trouble yourself much to get new things, whether clothes or friends. Turn the old; return to them. Things do not change; we change. Sell your clothes and keep your thoughts. God will see that you do not want society. If I were confined to a corner of a garret all my days, like a spider, the world would be just as large to me while I had my thoughts about me. The philosopher said: "From an army of three divisions one can take away its general, and put it in disorder; from the man the most abject and vulgar one cannot take away his thought." [12] Do not seek so anxiously to be developed, to subject yourself to many influences to be played on; it is all dissipation. Humility like darkness reveals the heavenly lights.

[12] Confucius, *Analects*.

The shadows of poverty and meanness gather around us, "and lo! creation widens to our view." [13] We are often reminded that if there were bestowed on us the wealth of Croesus, our aims must still be the same, and our means essentially the same. Moreover, if you are restricted in your range by poverty, if you cannot buy books and newspapers, for instance, you are but confined to the most significant and vital experiences; you are compelled to deal with the material which yields the most sugar and the most starch. It is life near the bone where it is sweetest. You are defended from being a trifler. No man loses ever on a lower level by magnanimity on a higher. Superfluous wealth can buy superfluities only. Money is not required to buy one necessary of the soul.

I live in the angle of a leaden wall, into whose composition was poured a little alloy of bell-metal. Often, in the repose of my mid-day, there reaches my ears a confused *tintinnabulum* from without. It is the noise of my contemporaries. My neighbors tell me of their adventures with famous gentlemen and ladies, what notabilities they met at the dinner-table; but I am no more interested in such things than in the contents of the Daily Times. The interest and the conversation are about costume and manners chiefly; but a goose is a goose still, dress it as you will. They tell me of California and Texas, of England and the Indies, of the Hon. Mr. —— of Georgia or of Massachusetts, all transient and fleeting phenomena, till I am ready to leap from their court-yard like the Mameluke bey. [14] I delight to come to my bearings,—not walk in procession with pomp and parade, in a conspicuous place, but to walk even with the Builder of the universe, if I may,—not to live in this restless, nervous, bustling, trivial Nineteenth Century, but stand or sit thoughtfully while it goes by. What are men celebrating? They are all on a committee of arrangements, and hourly expect a speech from somebody. God is only the president of the day, and Webster [15] is his orator. I love to weigh, to settle, to gravitate toward that which most strongly and rightfully attracts me;—not hang by the beam of the scale and try to weigh less,—not suppose a case, but take the case that is; to travel the only path I can, and that on which no power can resist me. It affords me no satisfaction to commence to spring an arch before I have got a solid foundation. Let us not play at kittly-benders. [16] There is a solid bottom everywhere. We read that the traveller

[13] Joseph Blanco White (1775-1841), English poet, "To Night." "Widened" in the poem.
[14] One man escaped a massacre of the Mamelukes ordered in 1811 by the Pasha of Egypt.
[15] Daniel Webster (1782-1852).
[16] A child's game: running out on thin ice and trying to not break through.

asked the boy if the swamp before him had a hard bottom. The boy replied that it had. But presently the traveller's horse sank in up to the girths, and he observed to the boy, "I thought you said that this bog had a hard bottom." "So it has," answered the latter, "but you have not got half way to it yet." So it is with the bogs and quicksands of society; but he is an old boy that knows it. Only what is thought, said, or done at a certain rare coincidence is good. I would not be one of those who will foolishly drive a nail into mere lath and plastering; such a deed would keep me awake nights. Give me a hammer, and let me feel for the furring. Do not depend on the putty. Drive a nail home and clinch it so faithfully that you can wake up in the night and think of your work with satisfaction,—a work at which you would not be ashamed to invoke the Muse. So will help you God, and so only. Every nail driven should be as another rivet in the machine of the universe, you carrying on the work.

Rather than love, than money, than fame, give me truth. I sat at a table where were rich food and wine in abundance, and obsequious attendance, but sincerity and truth were not; and I went away hungry from the inhospitable board. The hospitality was as cold as the ices. I thought that there was no need of ice to freeze them. They talked to me of the age of the wine and the fame of the vintage; but I thought of an older, a newer, and purer wine, of a more glorious vintage, which they had not got, and could not buy. The style, the house and grounds and "entertainment" pass for nothing with me. I called on the king, but he made me wait in his hall, and conducted like a man incapacitated for hospitality. There was a man in my neighborhood who lived in a hollow tree. His manners were truly regal. I should have done better had I called on him.

How long shall we sit in our porticoes practising idle and musty virtues, which any work would make impertinent? As if one were to begin the day with long-suffering, and hire a man to hoe his potatoes; and in the afternoon go forth to practise Christian meekness and charity with goodness aforethought! Consider the China pride and stagnant self-complacency of mankind. This generation inclines a little to congratulate itself on being the last of an illustrious line; and in Boston and London and Paris and Rome, thinking of its long descent, it speaks of its progress in art and science and literature with satisfaction. There are the Records of the Philosophical Societies, and the public Eulogies of *Great Men!* It is the good Adam contemplating his own virtue. "Yes, we have done great deeds, and sung divine songs, which shall never die,"—that is, as long as *we* can remember them. The learned societies and great men of Assyria,—where are they? What youthful philosophers and experimentalists we are! There is

not one of my readers who has yet lived a whole human life. These may be but the spring months in the life of the race. If we have had the seven-years' itch, we have not seen the seventeen-year locust yet in Concord. We are acquainted with a mere pellicle of the globe on which we live. Most have not delved six feet beneath the surface, nor leaped as many above it. We know not where we are. Beside, we are sound asleep nearly half our time. Yet we esteem ourselves wise, and have an established order on the surface. Truly, we are deep thinkers, we are ambitious spirits! As I stand over the insect crawling amid the pine needles on the forest floor, and endeavoring to conceal itself from my sight, and ask myself why it will cherish those humble thoughts, and hide its head from me who might, perhaps, be its benefactor, and impart to its race some cheering information, I am reminded of the greater Benefactor and Intelligence that stands over me the human insect.

There is an incessant influx of novelty into the world, and yet we tolerate incredible dulness. I need only suggest what kind of sermons are still listened to in the most enlightened countries. There are such words as joy and sorrow, but they are only the burden of a psalm, sung with a nasal twang, while we believe in the ordinary and mean. We think that we can change our clothes only. It is said that the British Empire is very large and respectable, and that the United States are a first-rate power. We do not believe that a tide rises and falls behind every man which can float the British Empire like a chip, if he should ever harbor it in his mind. Who knows what sort of seventeen-year locust will next come out of the ground? The government of the world I live in was not framed, like that of Britain, in after-dinner conversations over the wine.

The life in us is like the water in the river. It may rise this year higher than man has ever known it, and flood the parched uplands; even this may be the eventful year, which will drown out all our muskrats. It was not always dry land where we dwell. I see far inland the banks which the stream anciently washed, before science began to record its freshets. Every one has heard the story which has gone the rounds of New England, of a strong and beautiful bug which came out of the dry leaf of an old table of apple-tree wood, which had stood in a farmer's kitchen for sixty years, first in Connecticut, and afterward in Massachusetts,—from an egg deposited in the living tree many years earlier still, as appeared by counting the annual layers beyond it; which was heard gnawing out for several weeks, hatched perchance by the heat of an urn. Who does not feel his faith in a resurrection and immortality strengthened by hearing of this? Who knows what beautiful and winged life, whose egg has been buried for ages under many concentric layers of woodenness in the dead dry life of society, deposited at first in the alburnum of the green and living tree, which has been gradually converted into the semblance of its well-seasoned tomb,—heard perchance gnawing out now for years by the astonished family of man, as they sat round the festive board,—may unexpectedly come forth from amidst society's most trivial and handselled furniture, to enjoy its perfect summer life at last!

I do not say that John or Jonathan[17] will realize all this; but such is the character of that morrow which mere lapse of time can never make to dawn. The light which puts out our eyes is darkness to us. Only that day dawns to which we are awake. There is more day to dawn. The sun is but a morning star.

Life Without Principle

This essay was posthumously published in *The Atlantic Monthly* in October 1863. It was given as a lecture as early as 1854, entitled "Getting a Living" or "What Shall It Profit a Man if He Gain the Whole World but Lose His Own Soul." The essay restates and confirms many of the observations and opinions Thoreau expressed in *Walden*.

At a lyceum, not long since, I felt that the lecturer had chosen a theme too foreign to himself, and so failed to interest me as much as he might have done. He described things not in or near to his heart, but toward his extremities and superficies. There was, in this sense, no truly central or centralizing thought in the lecture. I would have had him deal with his privatest experience, as the poet does. The greatest compliment that was ever paid me was when one asked me what I *thought*, and attended to my answer. I am surprised, as well as delighted, when this happens, it is such a rare use he would make of me, as if he were acquainted with the tool. Commonly, if men want anything of me, it is only to know how many acres I make of their land,—since I am a surveyor,[1]—or, at most, what trivial news I have burdened myself with. They never will go to law for my meat; they prefer the shell. A man once came a considerable distance to ask me to lecture on Slavery; but on conversing with him, I found that he and his clique expected seven eighths of the lecture to be theirs, and only one eighth mine; so I declined. I take it for granted, when I am invited to lecture anywhere,—for I have had a little ex-

perience in that business,—that there is a desire to hear what *I think* on some subject, though I may be the greatest fool in the country,—and not that I should say pleasant things merely, or such as the audience will assent to; and I resolve, accordingly, that I will give them a strong dose of myself. They have sent for me, and engaged to pay for me, and I am determined that they shall have me, though I bore them beyond all precedent.

So now I would say something similar to you, my readers. Since *you* are my readers, and I have not been much of a traveler, I will not talk about people a thousand miles off, but come as near home as I can. As the time is short, I will leave out all the flattery, and retain all the criticism.

Let us consider the way in which we spend our lives.

This world is a place of business. What an infinite bustle! I am awaked almost every night by the panting of the locomotive. It interrupts my dreams. There is no sabbath. It would be glorious to see mankind at leisure for once. It is nothing but work, work, work. I cannot easily buy a blank-book to write thoughts in; they are commonly ruled for dollars and cents. An Irishman, seeing me making a minute in the fields, took it for granted that I was calculating my wages. If a man was tossed out of a window when an infant, and so made a cripple for life, or scared out of his wits by the Indians, it is regretted chiefly because he was thus incapacitated for—business! I think that there is nothing, not even crime, more opposed to poetry, to philosophy, ay, to life itself, than this incessant business.

There is a coarse and boisterous money-making fellow in the outskirts of our town, who is going to build a bank-wall under the hill along the edge of his meadow. The powers have put this into his head to keep him out of mischief, and he wishes me to spend three weeks digging there with him. The result will be that he will perhaps get some more money to hoard, and leave for his heirs to spend foolishly. If I do this, most will commend me as an industrious and hard-working man; but if I choose to devote myself to certain labors which yield more real profit, though but little money, they may be inclined to look on me as an idler. Nevertheless, as I do not need the police of meaningless labor to regulate me, and do not see anything absolutely praiseworthy in this fellow's undertaking any more than in many an enterprise of our own or foreign governments, however amusing it may be to him or them, I prefer to finish my education at a different school.

If a man walk in the woods for love of them half of each day, he is in danger of being regarded as a loafer; but if he spends his whole day as a speculator, shearing off those woods and making earth bald before her time, he is esteemed an industrious and

---

[17] Slang for an Englishman (John Bull) and an American (Brother Jonathan).

[1] From about 1845 on, Thoreau received a fairly regular income as a surveyor. Although he complained that the work used only his lowest talents, he enjoyed it because it not only paid; it kept him outdoors as well.

enterprising citizen. As if a town had no interest in its forests but to cut them down!

Most men would feel insulted if it were proposed to employ them in throwing stones over a wall, and then in throwing them back, merely that they might earn their wages. But many are no more worthily employed now. For instance: just after sunrise, one summer morning, I noticed one of my neighbors walking beside his team, which was slowly drawing a heavy hewn stone swung under the axle, surrounded by an atmosphere of industry,—his day's work begun,—his brow commenced to sweat,—a reproach to all sluggards and idlers,—pausing abreast the shoulders of his oxen, and half turning round with a flourish of his merciful whip, while they gained their length on him. And I thought, Such is the labor which the American Congress exists to protect,—honest, manly toil,—honest as the day is long,—that makes his bread taste sweet, and keeps society sweet,—which all men respect and have consecrated; one of the sacred band, doing the needful but irksome drudgery. Indeed, I felt a slight reproach, because I observed this from a window, and was not abroad and stirring about a similar business. The day went by, and at evening I passed the yard of another neighbor, who keeps many servants, and spends much money foolishly, while he adds nothing to the common stock, and there I saw the stone of the morning lying beside a whimsical structure intended to adorn this Lord Timothy Dexter's premises,[2] and the dignity forthwith departed from the teamster's labor, in my eyes. In my opinion, the sun was made to light worthier toil than this. I may add that his employer has since run off, in debt to a good part of the town, and, after passing through Chancery, has settled somewhere else, there to become once more a patron of the arts.

The ways by which you may get money almost without exception lead downward. To have done anything by which you earned money *merely* is to have been truly idle or worse. If the laborer gets no more than the wages which his employer pays him, he is cheated, he cheats himself. If you would get money as a writer or lecturer, you must be popular, which to go down perpendicularly. Those services which the community will most readily pay for, it is most disagreeable to render. You are paid for being something less than a man. The state does not commonly reward a genius any more wisely. Even the poet laureate would rather not have to celebrate the accidents of royalty. He must be bribed with a pipe of wine; and perhaps another poet is called away

from his muse to gauge that very pipe. As for my own business, even that kind of surveying which I could do with most satisfaction my employers do not want. They would prefer that I should do my work coarsely and not too well, ay, not well enough. When I observe that there are different ways of surveying, my employer commonly asks which will give him the most land, not which is most correct. I once invented a rule for measuring cord-wood, and tried to introduce it in Boston; but the measurer there told me that the sellers did not wish to have their wood measured correctly,—that he was already too accurate for them, and therefore they commonly got their wood measured in Charlestown before crossing the bridge.

The aim of the laborer should be, not to get his living, to get "a good job," but to perform well a certain work; and, even in a pecuniary sense, it would be economy for a town to pay its laborers so well that they would not feel that they were working for low ends, as for a livelihood merely, but for scientific, or even moral ends. Do not hire a man who does your work for money, but him who does it for love of it.

It is remarkable that there are few men so well employed, so much to their minds, but that a little money or fame would commonly buy them off from their present pursuit. I see advertisements for *active* young men, as if activity were the whole of a young man's capital. Yet I have been surprised when one has with confidence proposed to me, a grown man, to embark in some enterprise of his, as if I had absolutely nothing to do, my life having been a complete failure hitherto. What a doubtful compliment this to pay me! As if he had met me half-way across the ocean beating up against the wind, but bound nowhere, and proposed to me to go along with him! If I did, what do you think the underwriters would say? No, no! I am not without employment at this stage of the voyage. To tell the truth, I saw an advertisement for able-bodied seamen, when I was a boy, sauntering in my native port, and as soon as I came of age I embarked.

The community has no bribe that will tempt a wise man. You may raise money enough to tunnel a mountain, but you cannot raise money enough to hire a man who is minding *his own* business. An efficient and valuable man does what he can, whether the community pay him for it or not. The inefficient offer their inefficiency to the highest bidder, and are forever expecting to be put into office. One would suppose that they were rarely disappointed.

Perhaps I am more than usually jealous with respect to my freedom. I feel that my connection with and obligation to society are still very slight and

---

[2] "Lord" Timothy Dexter was a wealthy eccentric of Newburyport, Mass., who decorated the grounds of his mansion with life-sized wooden figures of mythological and historical characters.

transient. Those slight labors which afford me a livelihood, and by which it is allowed that I am to some extent serviceable to my contemporaries, are as yet commonly a pleasure to me, and I am not often reminded that they are a necessity. So far I am successful. But I foresee that if my wants should be much increased, the labor required to supply them would become a drudgery. If I should sell both my forenoons and afternoons to society, as most appear to do, I am sure that for me there would be nothing left worth living for. I trust that I shall never thus sell my birthright for a mess of pottage. I wish to suggest that a man may be very industrious, and yet not spend his time well. There is no more fatal blunderer than he who consumes the greater part of his life getting his living. All great enterprises are self-supporting. The poet, for instance, must sustain his body by his poetry, as a steam planing-mill feeds its boilers with the shavings it makes. You must get your living by loving. But as it is said of the merchants that ninety-seven in a hundred fail, so the life of men generally, tried by this standard, is a failure, and bankruptcy may be surely prophesied.

Merely to come into the world the heir of a fortune is not to be born, but to be still-born, rather. To be supported by the charity of friends, or a government pension,—provided you continue to breathe,—by whatever fine synonyms you describe these relations, is to go into the almshouse. On Sundays the poor debtor goes to church to take an account of stock, and finds, of course, that his outgoes have been greater than his income. In the Catholic Church, especially, they go into chancery, make a clean confession, give up all, and think to start again. Thus men will lie on their backs, talking about the fall of man, and never make an effort to get up.

As for the comparative demand which men make on life, it is an important difference between two, that the one is satisfied with a level success, that his marks can all be hit by point-blank shots, but the other, however low and unsuccessful his life may be, constantly elevates his aim, though at a very slight angle to the horizon. I should much rather be the last man,—though, as the Orientals say, "Greatness doth not approach him who is forever looking down; and all those who are looking high are growing poor."

It is remarkable that there is little or nothing to be remembered written on the subject of getting a living; how to make getting a living not merely honest and honorable, but altogether inviting and glorious; for if *getting* a living is not so, then living is not. One would think, from looking at literature, that this question had never disturbed a solitary individual's musings. Is it that men are too much dis-

gusted with their experience to speak of it? The lesson of value which money teaches, which the Author of the Universe has taken so much pains to teach us, we are inclined to skip altogether. As for the means of living, it is wonderful how indifferent men of all classes are about it, even reformers, so called,—whether they inherit, or earn, or steal it. I think that Society has done nothing for us in this respect, or at least has undone what she has done. Cold and hunger seem more friendly to my nature than those methods which men have adopted and advise to ward them off.

The title *wise* is, for the most part, falsely applied. How can one be a wise man, if he does not know any better how to live than other men?—if he is only more cunning and intellectually subtle? Does Wisdom work in a tread-mill? or does she teach how to succeed *by her example?* Is there any such thing as wisdom not applied to life? Is she merely the miller who grinds the finest logic? It is pertinent to ask if Plato got his *living* in a better way or more successfully than his contemporaries,—or did he succumb to the difficulties of life like other men? Did he seem to prevail over some of them merely by indifference, or by assuming grand airs? or find it easier to live, because his aunt remembered him in her will? The ways in which most men get their living, that is, live, are mere makeshifts, and a shirking of the real business of life,—chiefly because they do not know, but partly because they do not mean, any better.

The rush to California,[3] for instance, and the attitude, not merely of merchants, but of philosophers and prophets, so called, in relation to it, reflect the greatest disgrace on mankind. That so many are ready to live by luck, and so get the means of commanding the labor of others less lucky, without contributing any value to society! And that is called enterprise! I know of no more startling development of the immorality of trade, and all the common modes of getting a living. The philosophy and poetry and religion of such a mankind are not worth the dust of a puffball. The hog that gets his living by rooting, stirring up the soil so, would be ashamed of such company. If I could command the wealth of all the worlds by lifting my finger, I would not pay *such* a price for it. Even Mahomet[4] knew that God did not make this world in jest. It makes God to be a moneyed gentleman who scatters a handful of pennies in order to see mankind scramble for them. The world's raffle! A subsistence in the domains of Nature a thing to be raffled for! What a comment, what a satire, on our institutions! The conclusion

[3] Refers to the California Gold Rush that reached a peak in 1849–50.
[4] Mohammed (c. 570–632), founder of Islam.

will be, that mankind will hang itself upon a tree. And have all the precepts in all the Bibles taught men only this? and is the last and most admirable invention of the human race only an improved muck-rake? Is this the ground on which Orientals and Occidentals meet? Did God direct us so to get our living, digging where we never planted,—and He would, perchance, reward us with lumps of gold?

God gave the righteous man a certificate entitling him to food and raiment, but the unrighteous man found a facsimile of the same in God's coffers, and appropriated it, and obtained food and raiment like the former. It is one of the most extensive systems of counterfeiting that the world has seen. I did not know that mankind was suffering for want of gold. I have seen a little of it. I know that it is very malleable, but not so malleable as wit. A grain of gold will gild a great surface, but not so much as a grain of wisdom.

The gold-digger in the ravines of the mountains is as much a gambler as his fellow in the saloons of San Francisco. What difference does it make whether you shake dirt or shake dice? If you win, society is the loser. The gold-digger is the enemy of the honest laborer, whatever checks and compensations there may be. It is not enough to tell me that you worked hard to get your gold. So does the Devil work hard. The way of transgressors may be hard in many respects. The humblest observer who goes to the mines sees and says that gold-digging is of the character of a lottery; the gold thus obtained is not the same thing with the wages of honest toil. But, practically, he forgets what he has seen, for he has seen only the fact, not the principle, and goes into trade there, that is, buys a ticket in what commonly proves another lottery, where the fact is not so obvious.

After reading Howitt's[5] account of the Australian gold-diggings one evening, I had in my mind's eye, all night, the numerous valleys, with their streams, all cut up with foul pits, from ten to one hundred feet deep, and half a dozen feet across, as close as they can be dug, and partly filled with water,—the locality to which men furiously rush to probe for their fortunes,—uncertain where they shall break ground,—not knowing but the gold is under their camp itself,—sometimes digging one hundred and sixty feet before they strike the vein, or then missing it by a foot,—turned into demons, and regardless of each others' rights, in their thirst for riches,—whole valleys, for thirty miles, suddenly honeycombed by the pits of the miners, so that even hundreds are drowned in them,—standing in water, and covered with mud and clay, they work night and day, dying

[5] William Howitt (1792–1879), author of *Land, Labor, and Gold; or Two Years in Victoria* (1855).

of exposure and disease. Having read this, and partly forgotten it, I was thinking, accidentally, of my own unsatisfactory life, doing as others do; and with that vision of the diggings still before me, I asked myself why I might not be washing some gold daily, though it were only the finest particles,—why I might not sink a shaft down to the gold within me, and work that mine. *There* is a Ballarat, a Bendigo[6] for you,— what though it were a sulky-gully? At any rate, I might pursue some path, however solitary and narrow and crooked, in which I could walk with love and reverence. Wherever a man separates from the multitude, and goes his own way in this mood, there indeed is a fork in the road, though ordinary travelers may see only a gap in the paling. His solitary path across lots will turn out the *higher way* of the two.

Men rush to California and Australia as if the true gold were to be found in that direction; but that is to go to the very opposite extreme to where it lies. They go prospecting farther and farther away from the true lead, and are most unfortunate when they think themselves most successful. Is not our *native* soil auriferous? Does not a stream from the golden mountains flow through our native valley? and has not this for more than geologic ages been bringing down the shining particles and forming the nuggets for us? Yet, strange to tell, if a digger steal away, prospecting for this true gold, into the unexplored solitudes around us, there is no danger that any will dog his steps, and endeavor to supplant him. He may claim and undermine the whole valley even, both the cultivated and the uncultivated portions, his whole life long in peace, for no one will ever dispute his claim. They will not mind his cradles or his toms. He is not confined to a claim twelve feet square, as at Ballarat, but may mine anywhere, and wash the whole wide world in his tom.

Howitt says of the man who found the great nugget which weighed twenty-eight pounds, at the Bendigo diggings in Australia: "He soon began to drink; got a horse, and rode all about, generally at full gallop, and, when he met people, called out to inquire if they knew who he was, and then kindly informed them that he was 'the bloody wretch that had found the nugget.' At last he rode full speed against a tree, and nearly knocked his brains out." I think, however, there was no danger of that, for he had already knocked his brains out against the nugget. Howitt adds, "He is a hopelessly ruined man." But he is a type of the class. They are all fast men. Hear some of the names of the places where they dig: "Jackass Flat,"—"Sheep's-Head Gully,"— "Murderer's Bar," etc. Is there no satire in these

[6] In 1851 great quantities of gold were discovered in Australia. Ballarat and Bendigo are two places where it was found in amazing richness.

names? Let them carry their ill-gotten wealth where they will, I am thinking it will still be "Jackass Flat," if not "Murderer's Bar," where they live.

The last resource of our energy has been the robbing of graveyards on the Isthmus of Darien,[7] an enterprise which appears to be but in its infancy; for, according to late accounts, an act has passed its second reading in the legislature of New Granada,[8] regulating this kind of mining; and a correspondent of the "Tribune" writes: "In the dry season, when the weather will permit of the country being properly prospected, no doubt other rich *guacas* [that is, graveyards] will be found." To emigrants he says: "Do not come before December; take the Isthmus route in preference to the Boca del Toro one; bring no useless baggage, and do not cumber yourself with a tent; but a good pair of blankets will be necessary; a pick, shovel, and axe of good material will be almost all that is required:" advice which might have been taken from the "Burker's Guide." And he concludes with this line in Italics and small capitals: "*If you are doing well at home,* STAY THERE," which may fairly be interpreted to mean, "If you are getting a good living by robbing graveyards at home, stay there."

But why go to California for a text? She is the child of New England, bred at her own school and church.

It is remarkable that among all the preachers there are so few moral teachers. The prophets are employed in excusing the ways of men. Most reverend seniors, the *illuminati* of the age, tell me, with a gracious, reminiscent smile, betwixt an aspiration and a shudder, not to be too tender about these things,—to lump all that, that is, make a lump of gold of it. The highest advice I have heard on these subjects was groveling. The burden of it was,—It is not worth your while to undertake to reform the world in this particular. Do not ask how your bread is buttered; it will make you sick, if you do,—and the like. A man had better starve at once than lose his innocence in the process of getting his bread. If within the sophisticated man there is not an unsophisticated one, then he is but one of the devil's angels. As we grow old, we live more coarsely, we relax a little in our disciplines, and, to some extent, cease to obey our finest instincts. But we should be fastidious to the extreme of sanity, disregarding the gibes of those who are more unfortunate than ourselves.

In our science and philosophy, even, there is commonly no true and absolute account of things. The spirit of sect and bigotry has planted its hoof amid the stars. You have only to discuss the problem, whether the stars are inhabited or not, in order to discover it. Why must we daub the heavens as well as the earth? It was an unfortunate discovery that Dr. Kane[9] was a Mason, and that Sir John Franklin[10] was another. But it was a more cruel suggestion that possibly that was the reason why the former went in search of the latter. There is not a popular magazine in this country that would dare to print a child's thought on important subjects without comment. It must be submitted to the D.D.'s.[11] I would it were the chickadee-dees.

You come from attending the funeral of mankind to attend to a natural phenomenon. A little thought is sexton to all the world.

I hardly know an *intellectual* man, even, who is so broad and truly liberal that you can think aloud in his society. Most with whom you endeavor to talk soon come to a stand against some institution in which they appear to hold stock,—that is, some particular, not universal, way of viewing things. They will continually thrust their own low roof, with its narrow skylight, between you and the sky, when it is the unobstructed heavens you would view. Get out of the way with your cobwebs; wash your windows, I say! In some lyceums they tell me that they have voted to exclude the subject of religion. But how do I know what their religion is, and when I am near to or far from it? I have walked into such an arena and done my best to make a clean breast of what religion I have experienced, and the audience never suspected what I was about. The lecture was as harmless as moonshine to them. Whereas, if I had read to them the biography of the greatest scamps in history, they might have thought that I had written the lives of the deacons of their church. Ordinarily, the inquiry is, Where did you come from? or, Where are you going? That was a more pertinent question which I overheard one of my auditors put to another once,—"What does he lecture for?" It made me quake in my shoes.

To speak impartially, the best men that I know are not serene, a world in themselves. For the most part, they dwell in forms, and flatter and study effect only more finely than the rest. We select granite for the underpinning of our houses and barns; we build fences of stone; but we do not ourselves rest on an underpinning of granitic truth, the lowest primitive rock. Our sills are rotten. What stuff is the man made of who is not coexistent in our thought with the purest and subtilest truth? I often accuse my finest acquaintances of an immense frivol-

[7] Panama.

[8] Panama and Colombia when owned by Spain.

[9] Elisha Kent Kane (1820-57), arctic explorer who searched in 1853 for the remains of the Franklin expedition.

[10] Sir John Franklin (1786-1847), arctic explorer and author of narratives about polar voyages; lost at sea during a polar expedition.

[11] Doctors of Divinity.

ity; for, while there are manners and compliments we do not meet, we do not teach one another the lessons of honesty and sincerity that the brutes do, or of steadiness and solidity that the rocks do. The fault is commonly mutual, however; for we do not habitually demand any more of each other.

That excitement about Kossuth, consider how characteristic, but superficial, it was!—only another kind of politics or dancing. Men were making speeches to him all over the country, but each expressed only the thought, or the want of thought, of the multitude. No man stood on truth. They were merely banded together, as usual one leaning on another, and all together on nothing; as the Hindoos made the world rest on an elephant, the elephant on a tortoise, and the tortoise on a serpent, and had nothing to put under the serpent. For all fruit of that stir we have the Kossuth hat.

Just so hollow and ineffectual, for the most part, is our ordinary conversation. Surface meets surface. When our life ceases to be inward and private, conversation degenerates into mere gossip. We rarely meet a man who can tell us any news which he has not read in a newspaper, or been told by his neighbor; and, for the most part, the only difference between us and our fellow is that he has seen the newspaper, or been out to tea, and we have not. In proportion as our inward life fails, we go more constantly and desperately to the post-office. You may depend on it, that the poor fellow who walks away with the greatest number of letters, proud of his extensive correspondence, has not heard from himself this long while.

I do not know but it is too much to read one newspaper a week. I have tried it recently, and for so long it seems to me that I have not dwelt in my native region. The sun, the clouds, the snow, the trees say not so much to me. You cannot serve two masters. It requires more than a day's devotion to know and to possess the wealth of a day.

We may well be ashamed to tell what things we have read or heard in our day. I do not know why my news should be so trivial,—considering what one's dreams and expectations are, why the developments should be so paltry. The news we hear, for the most part, is not news to our genius. It is the stalest repetition. You are often tempted to ask why such stress is laid on a particular experience which you have had,—that, after twenty-five years, you should meet Hobbins, Registrar of Deeds, again on the sidewalk. Have you not budged an inch, then? Such is the daily news. Its facts appear to float in the atmosphere, insignificant as the sporules of fungi, and impinge on some neglected *thallus,* or surface of our minds, which affords a basis for them, and hence a parasitic growth. We should wash ourselves clean of such news. Of what consequence, though our planet explode, if there is no character involved in the explosion? In health we have not the least curiosity about such events. We do not live for idle amusement. I would not run round a corner to see the world blow up.

All summer, and far into the autumn, perchance, you unconsciously went by the newspapers and the news, and now you find it was because the morning and the evening were full of news to you. Your walks were full of incidents. You attended, not to the affairs of Europe, but to your own affairs in Massachusetts fields. If you chance to live and move and have your being in that thin stratum in which the events that make the news transpire,—thinner than the paper on which it is printed,—then these things will fill the world for you; but if you soar above or dive below that plane, you cannot remember nor be reminded of them. Really to see the sun rise or go down every day, so to relate ourselves to a universal fact, would preserve us sane forever. Nations! What are nations? Tartars, and Huns, and Chinamen! Like insects, they swarm. The historian strives in vain to make them memorable. It is for want of a man that there are so many men. It is individuals that populate the world. Any man thinking may say with the Spirit of Lodin,—

> "I look down from my height on nations,
> And they become ashes before me;—
> Calm is my dwelling in the clouds;
> Pleasant are the great fields of my rest."

Pray, let us live without being drawn by dogs, Esquimaux-fashion, tearing over hill and dale, and biting each other's ears.

Not without a slight shudder at the danger, I often perceive how near I had come to admitting into my mind the details of some trivial affair,—the news of the street; and I am astonished to observe how willing men are to lumber their minds with such rubbish,—to permit idle rumors and incidents of the most insignificant kind to intrude on ground which should be sacred to thought. Shall the mind be a public arena, where the affairs of the street and the gossip of the tea-table chiefly are discussed? Or shall it be a quarter of heaven itself,—an hypaethral temple, consecrated to the service of the gods? I find it so difficult to dispose of the few facts which to me are significant, that I hesitate to burden my attention with those which are insignificant, which only a divine mind could illustrate. Such is, for the most part, the news in newspapers and conversation. It is important to preserve the mind's chastity in this respect. Think of admitting the details of a single case of the criminal court into our thoughts, to stalk profanely through their very *sanctum sanctorum* for an hour, ay, for many hours! to make a very barroom of the mind's inmost apartment, as if for so long the dust of the street had occupied us,—the very street itself, with all its travel, its bustle, and filth, had passed through our thoughts' shrine! Would it not be an intellectual and moral suicide? When I have been compelled to sit spectator and auditor in a court-room for some hours, and have seen my neighbors, who were not compelled, stealing in from time to time, and tiptoeing about with washed hands and faces, it has appeared to my mind's eye, that, when they took off their hats, their ears suddenly expanded into vast hoppers for sound, between which even their narrow heads were crowded. Like the vanes of windmills, they caught the broad but shallow stream of sound, which, after a few titillating gyrations in their coggy brains, passed out the other side. I wondered if, when they got home, they were as careful to wash their ears as before their hands and faces. It has seemed to me, at such a time, that the auditors and the witnesses, the jury and the counsel, the judge and the criminal at the bar,—if I may presume him guilty before he is convicted,—were all equally criminal, and a thunderbolt might be expected to descend and consume them all together.

By all kinds of traps and signboards, threatening the extreme penalty of the divine law, exclude such trespassers from the only ground which can be sacred to you. It is so hard to forget what it is worse than useless to remember! If I am to be a thoroughfare, I prefer that it be of the mountain brooks, the Parnassian streams, and not the town sewers. There is inspiration, that gossip which comes to the ear of the attentive mind from the courts of heaven. There is the profane and stale revelation of the barroom and the police court. The same ear is fitted to receive both communications. Only the character of the hearer determines to which it shall be open, and to which closed. I believe that the mind can be permanently profaned by the habit of attending to trivial things, so that all our thoughts shall be tinged with triviality. Our very intellect shall be macadamized, as it were,—its foundation broken into fragments for the wheels of travel to roll over; and if you would know what will make the most durable pavement, surpassing rolled stones, spruce blocks, and asphaltum, you have only to look into some of our minds which have been subjected to this treatment so long.

If we have thus desecrated ourselves,—as who has not?—the remedy will be by wariness and devotion to reconsecrate ourselves, and make once more a fane of the mind. We should treat our minds, that is, ourselves, as innocent and ingenuous children, whose guardians we are, and be careful what objects and what subjects we thrust on their attention. Read not the Times. Read the Eternities. Conventionalities are at length as bad as impurities. Even the facts of science may dust the mind by their dryness, unless they are in a sense effaced each morning, or rather rendered fertile by the dews of fresh and

living truth. Knowledge does not come to us by details, but in flashes of light from heaven. Yes, every thought that passes through the mind helps to wear and tear it, and to deepen the ruts, which, as in the streets of Pompeii, evince how much it has been used. How many things there are concerning which we might well deliberate whether we had better know them,—had better let their peddling-carts be driven, even at the slowest trot or walk, over that bridge of glorious span by which we trust to pass at last from the farthest brink of time to the nearest shore of eternity! Have we no culture, no refinement,—but skill only to live coarsely and serve the Devil?—to acquire a little worldly wealth, or fame, or liberty, and make a false show with it, as if we were all husk and shell, with no tender and living kernel to us? Shall our institutions be like those chestnut burs which contain abortive nuts, perfect only to prick the fingers?

America is said to be the arena on which the battle of freedom is to be fought; but surely it cannot be freedom in a merely political sense that is meant. Even if we grant that the American has freed himself from a political tyrant, he is still the slave of an economical and moral tyrant. Now that the republic—the res-publica—has been settled, it is time to look after the res-privata,—the private state,—to see, as the Roman senate charged its consuls, "ne quid res-PRIVATA detrimenti caperet," that the private state receive no detriment.

Do we call this the land of the free? What is it to be free from King George and continue the slaves of King Prejudice? What is it to be born free and not to live free? What is the value of any political freedom, but as a means to moral freedom? Is it a freedom to be slaves, or a freedom to be free, of which we boast? We are a nation of politicians, concerned about the outmost defenses only of freedom. It is our children's children who may perchance be really free. We tax ourselves unjustly. There is a part of us which is not represented. It is taxation without representation. We quarter troops, we quarter fools and cattle of all sorts upon ourselves. We quarter our gross bodies on our poor souls, till the former eat up all the latter's substance.

With respect to a true culture and manhood, we are essentially provincial still, not metropolitan,—mere Jonathans.[12] We are provincial, because we do not find at home our standards; because we do not worship truth, but the reflection of truth; because we are warped and narrowed by an exclusive devotion to trade and commerce and manufactures and agriculture and the like, which are but means, and not the end.

So is the English Parliament provincial. Mere country bumpkins, they betray themselves, when

[12]Americans were typically called Jonathans to suggest roughness and provinciality.

any more important question arises for them to settle, the Irish question, for instance,—the English question why did I not say? Their natures are subdued to what they work in. Their "good breeding" respects only secondary objects. The finest manners in the world are awkwardness and fatuity when contrasted with a finer intelligence. They appear but as the fashions of past days,—mere courtliness, knee-buckles and small-clothes, out of date. It is the vice, but not the excellence of manners, that they are continually being deserted by the character; they are cast-off clothes or shells, claiming the respect which belonged to the living creature. You are presented with the shells instead of the meat, and it is no excuse generally, that, in the case of some fishes, the shells are of more worth than the meat. The man who thrusts his manners upon me does as if he were to insist on introducing me to his cabinet of curiosities, when I wished to see himself. It was not in this sense that the poet Decker called Christ "the first true gentleman that ever breathed." I repeat that in this sense the most splendid court in Christendom is provincial, having authority to consult about Transalpine interests only, and not the affairs of Rome. A praetor or proconsul would suffice to settle the questions which absorb the attention of the English Parliament and the American Congress.[13]

Government and legislation! these I thought were respectable professions. We have heard of heaven-born Numas, Lycurguses, and Solons,[14] in the history of the world, whose *names* at least may stand for ideal legislators; but think of legislating to *regulate* the breeding of slaves, or the exportation of tobacco! What have divine legislators to do with the exportation or the importation of tobacco? what humane ones with the breeding of slaves? Suppose you were to submit the question to any son of God,—and has He no children in the Nineteenth Century? is it a family which is extinct?—in what condition would you get it again? What shall a State like Virginia say for itself at the last day, in which these have been the principal, the staple productions? What ground is there for patriotism in such a State? I derive my facts from statistical tables which the States themselves have published.

A commerce that whitens every sea in quest of nuts and raisins, and makes slaves of its sailors for this purpose! I saw, the other day, a vessel which had been wrecked, and many lives lost, and her cargo of rags, juniper berries, and bitter almonds were strewn along the shore. It seemed hardly worth the while to tempt the dangers of the sea between Leghorn and New York for the sake of a cargo of juniper berries and bitter almonds. America sending to the Old World for her bitters! Is not the sea-brine, is not shipwreck, bitter enough to make the cup of life go down here? Yet such, to a great extent, is our boasted commerce; and there are those who style themselves statesmen and philosophers who are so blind as to think that progress and civilization depend on precisely this kind of interchange and activity,—the activity of flies about a molasses-hogshead. Very well, observes one, if men were oysters. And very well, answer I, if men were mosquitoes.

Lieutenant Herndon,[15] whom our government sent to explore the Amazon, and, it is said, to extend the area of slavery, observed that there was wanting there "an industrious and active population, who know what the comforts of life are, and who have artificial wants to draw out the great resources of the country." But what are the "artificial wants" to be encouraged? Not the love of luxuries, like the tobacco and slaves of, I believe, his native Virginia, nor the ice and granite and other material wealth of our native New England; nor are "the great resources of a country" that fertility or barrenness of soil which produces these. The chief want, in every State that I have been into, was a high and earnest purpose in its inhabitants. This alone draws out "the great resources" of Nature, and at last taxes her beyond her resources; for man naturally dies out of her. When we want culture more than potatoes, and illumination more than sugar-plums, then the great resources of a world are taxed and drawn out, and the result, or staple production, is, not slaves, nor operatives, but men,—those rare fruits called heroes, saints, poets, philosophers, and redeemers.

In short, as a snow-drift is formed where there is a lull in the wind, so, one would say, where there is a lull of truth, an institution springs up. But the truth blows right on over it, nevertheless, and at length blows it down.

What is called politics is comparatively something so superficial and inhuman, that practically I have never fairly recognized that it concerns me at all. The newspapers, I perceive, devote some of their columns specially to politics or government without charge; and this, one would say, is all that saves it; but as I love literature and to some extent the truth also, I never read those columns at any rate. I do not wish to blunt my sense of right so much. I have not got to answer for having read a single President's Message. A strange age of the world this, when empires, kingdoms, and republics come a-beg-

---

[13] "Transalpine interests" refers to matters far removed from the important affairs of Rome. Praetors and proconsuls were provincial officers in the Roman system of government. Thoreau's point: Congress wastes its time.

[14] Numa, legendary second king of Rome, founded the Roman religious system. Lycurgus, 9th century B.C., Spartan lawgiver. Solon (638–559 B.C.), Athenian statesman and lawgiver.

[15] W. L. Herndon led a U.S. Army expedition in 1851–52.

ging to a private man's door, and utter their complaints at his elbow! I cannot take up a newspaper but I find that some wretched government or other, hard pushed and on its last legs, is interceding with me, the reader, to vote for it,—more importunate than an Italian beggar; and if I have a mind to look at its certificate, made, perchance, by some benevolent merchant's clerk, or the skipper that brought it over, for it cannot speak a word of English itself, I shall probably read of the eruption of some Vesuvius, or the overflowing of some Po, true or forged, which brought it into this condition. I do not hesitate, in such a case, to suggest work, or the almshouse; or why not keep its castle in silence, as I do commonly? The poor President, what with preserving his popularity and doing his duty, is completely bewildered. The newspapers are the ruling power. Any other government is reduced to a few marines at Fort Independence. If a man neglects to read the Daily Times, government will go down on its knees to him, for this is the only treason in these days.

Those things which now most engage the attention of men, as politics and the daily routine, are, it is true, vital functions of human society, but should be unconsciously performed, like the corresponding functions of the physical body. They are *infra*-human, a kind of vegetation. I sometimes awake to a half-consciousness of them going on about me, as a man may become conscious of some of the processes of digestion in a morbid state, and so have the dyspepsia, as it is called. It is as if a thinker submitted himself to be rasped by the great gizzard of creation. Politics is, as it were, the gizzard of society, full of grit and gravel, and the two political parties are its two opposite halves,—sometimes split into quarters, it may be, which grind on each other. Not only individuals, but states, have thus a confirmed dyspepsia, which expresses itself, you can imagine by what sort of eloquence. Thus our life is not altogether a forgetting, but also, alas! to a great extent, a remembering, of that which we should never have been conscious of, certainly not in our waking hours. Why should we not meet, not always as dyspeptics, to tell our bad dreams, but sometimes as *eu*peptics, to congratulate each other on the ever-glorious morning? I do not make an exorbitant demand, surely.

1863

NATHANIEL HAWTHORNE [1804–1864]

OF HIS PURITAN ANCESTORS Hawthorne said, "Strong traits of their nature have intertwined themselves with mine." In the beginning the Hathornes (as they spelled the name) were a prominent family of the seaport town of Salem. The first settler, William Hathorne—"grave, bearded, sable-cloaked and steeple-crowned," as Hawthorne pictured him—was a magistrate who took part in the persecution of the Quakers. His son John was a judge conspicuous in the Salem witch trials. In the eighteenth century the Hathornes were sea-captains—including Nathaniel's father, who died in Dutch Guiana when the boy was four years old.

The widow, at age twenty-eight, shut herself into her own room in a solitude that lasted most of the rest of her life, and the boy, like his two sisters, also fell into solitary ways. When the family went to live for some years at Lake Sebago in Maine, they took their old habits from the city to the wilderness. Nathaniel was normal enough, to be sure, while a student at Bowdoin College, Brunswick, Maine, where he established lifelong friendships with Longfellow, Horatio Bridge, and Franklin Pierce, the future President of the United States. But, returned from college, he drifted into a seclusion that lasted twelve years. Near the end of this period he wrote to Longfellow: "I have secluded myself from society; and yet I never meant any such thing, nor dreamed what sort of life I was going to lead. I have made a captive of myself and put me into a dungeon; and now I cannot find the key to let myself out—and if the door were open, I should be almost afraid to come out." Actually, he did come out, in a raiding sort of fashion: by means of free passes on his uncle's stagecoach line he made a number of summer trips in New England, experiencing, he said, "as much of life as other people do in the whole year's round." But the bulk of his time he spent in dreaming and reflecting, in reading and writing. Under various assumed names, he published an undistinguished novel (*Fanshawe*) and sketches and stories partially collected, in 1837, in the first group of *Twice-Told Tales*. They did not describe what a later American writer called "the rich thicket of reality." As he said to Longfellow, with some overstatement, "I have seen so little of the world that I have nothing but thin air to concoct my stories of." But that little he commanded with an imaginative insight denied to most writers who have thrown themselves into the tumult of life.

Hawthorne's return to the "living world" (as he had called it in *Fanshawe*) came after he had met and fallen in love with Sophia Peabody. In 1838 he became engaged to her. In 1839–40 he served as weigher and gauger in the Boston Custom House, a position secured for him by his Democratic friends and lost through a change of political parties. Then, oddly enough, he became a member of the Brook Farm community. In 1842 he married and went to Concord, where, in the Old Manse, he spent four happy years. This was the period of the second collection of *Twice-Told Tales* and of *Mosses from an Old Manse*. Again he held a custom house position, this time in Salem, and again lost it through a change in administration. By this time he had the experience of fatherhood—a daughter Una, a son Julian. The family left Salem for good, removed to Lenox, to West Newton, to Concord.

Up to this time he had been a writer of sketches and short tales; now he took up the novel, or "romance": *The Scarlet Letter*, 1850; *The House of the Seven Gables*, 1851; *The Blithedale Romance*, 1853. At this juncture, too late for a full effect, he spent seven years in Europe. His friend Pierce, becoming President, nominated him consul at Liverpool. Resigning after three years, he toured the Continent, wrote *The Marble Faun* while living in Italy and in England, and returned to settle in The Wayside in Concord. Four years later, on a tour with Pierce, he died in New Hampshire.

Hawthorne felt strongly the impulse of the Romantic Movement: he shared its feeling for the strange and mysterious, its symbolical imagination and sportive fancy, and he turned to a regional past for much of his material. Yet he could not accept Transcendental optimism, nor did he celebrate nature, or the natural man, or the supremacy of beauty. Far deeper than his interest in the romanticism of his age was his feeling for the Christianity of New England in an earlier age. While he was skeptical of the Puritan theology and found the old intolerance repugnant, he agreed with his ancestors in focusing attention upon the problem of evil, the nature of sin, the contrast of pride and humility. Perversion, mystery, horror, and the like are never with him, as they were with Poe, merely materials for aesthetic use. On the other hand, he is not the moralist intent upon edification. Rather, he is a psychological type of literary artist, analyzing the inner life, the workings of the human heart and will, in a day when this could still be done as by Dante and Shakespeare (or Spenser and Bunyan, two of his favorites), without the help or the hindrance of the psychological science of the age of Freud. The best example is his own great book, his tragedy in the form of a novel, *The Scarlet Letter*.

Hawthorne's art is above all an art of symbols. Whether his story be a novel or a short tale, he works outward from some inner fact, some truth of the mind or soul, toward the concrete world, using a symbol, oftener a cluster of symbols, to link inner and outer and give body to his spiritual meaning. It may even seem, as W. C. Brownell said, that "everything means something else," or might mean various things. Are we to agree with Brownell and other able critics that this ambiguity is a defect in Hawthorne's art, a sign of weakness and confusion, or with R. H. Fogle and other recent able critics, that it is a source of strength, an enrichment of meaning and effect?

Further reading: *The Scarlet Letter. The House of the Seven Gables.* Randall Stewart, *Nathaniel Hawthorne* (biography), 1948. R. H. Fogle, *Hawthorne's Fiction*, 1952. Roy R. Male, *Hawthorne's Tragic Vision*, 1957. Hubert H. Hoeltje, *Inward Sky: The Mind and*

Heart of Nathaniel Hawthorne, 1962. H. H. Waggoner, *Hawthorne: A Critical Study,* 1963. Roy H. Pearce, ed., *Hawthorne Centenary Essays,* 1964. Frederick C. Crews, *The Sins of the Fathers,* 1966. A. N. Kaul, *Hawthorne: A Collection of Critical Essays,* 1966.

FROM HIS *Notebooks*

Text: *Passages from the American Note-Books,* ed. Sophia Hawthorne (Boston, 1868); *The American Notebooks,* ed. Randall Stewart (New Haven, 1932); *The English Notebooks,* ed. Randall Stewart (New York, 1941).

[Brook Farm]

The experimental community, Brook Farm, nine miles from Boston, lasted from 1841 to 1847. George Ripley was its leading spirit. He and others desired a way of life not complex, conventional, and selfishly acquisitive, but simple, natural, and cooperative. Emerson—who never joined—described its ideal, "to combine cultivation of mind and heart with a reasonable amount of daily labor," but was inclined to sum up the reality as "a perpetual picnic." Hawthorne gave a fictional account of Brook Farm in *The Blithedale Romance,* as well as a notebook record of his actual experience there.

Brook Farm, Oak Hill, April 13th, 1841.— . . . Here I am in a polar Paradise! I know not how to interpret this aspect of nature,—whether it be of good or evil omen to our enterprise. But I reflect that the Plymouth pilgrims arrived in the midst of storm, and stepped ashore upon mountain snowdrifts; and, nevertheless, they prospered, and became a great people,—and doubtless it will be the same with us. . . .

I have not yet taken my first lesson in agriculture, except that I went to see our cows foddered, yesterday afternoon. We have eight of our own; and the number is now increased by a transcendental heifer belonging to Miss Margaret Fuller. She is very fractious, I believe, and apt to kick over the milk-pail . . . . I intend to convert myself into a milkmaid this evening, but I pray Heaven that Mr. Ripley may be moved to assign me the kindliest cow in the herd, otherwise I shall perform my duty with fear and trembling. . . .

I like my brethren in affliction very well; and, could you see us sitting round our table at mealtimes, before the great kitchen fire, you would call it a cheerful sight. Mrs. B——is a most comfortable woman to behold. She looks as if her ample person were stuffed full of tenderness,—indeed, as if she were all one great, kind heart. . . .

April 14th, 10 a. m.— . . . I did not milk the cows last night, because Mr. Ripley was afraid to trust them to my hands, or me to their horns, I know not which. But this morning I have done wonders. Before breakfast, I went out to the barn and began to chop hay for the cattle, and with such "righteous vehemence," as Mr. Ripley says, did I labor, that in the space of ten minutes I broke the machine. Then I brought wood and replenished the fires; and finally went down to breakfast, and ate up a huge mound of buckwheat cakes. After breakfast, Mr. Ripley put a four-pronged instrument into my hands, which he gave me to understand was called a pitchfork; and he and Mr. Farley being armed with similar weapons, we all three commenced a gallant attack upon a heap of manure. This office being concluded, and I having purified myself, I sit down to finish this letter. . . .

Miss Fuller's cow hooks the other cows, and has made herself ruler of the herd, and behaves in a very tyrannical manner. . . I shall make an excellent husbandman,—I feel the original Adam reviving within me.

August 12th.— . . . I am very well, and not at all weary, for yesterday's rain gave us a holiday; and, moreover, the labors of the farm are not so pressing as they have been. And, joyful thought! in a little more than a fortnight I shall be free from my bondage,— . . . free to enjoy Nature,—free to think and feel! . . . Even my Custom House experience was not such a thraldom and weariness; my mind and heart were free. Oh, labor is the curse of the world, and nobody can meddle with it without becoming proportionably brutified! Is it a praiseworthy matter that I have spent five golden months in providing food for cows and horses? It is not so.

[Concord Friends]

After leaving the book at Mr. Emerson's, I returned through the woods, and entering Sleepy Hollow, I perceived a lady reclining near the path which bends along its verge. It was Margaret herself. She had been there the whole afternoon, meditating or reading; for she had a book in her hand, with some strange title, which I did not understand and have forgotten. She said that nobody had broken her solitude, and was just giving utterance to a theory that no inhabitant of Concord ever visited Sleepy Hollow, when we saw a whole group of people entering the sacred precincts. Most of them followed a path which led them remote from us; but an old man passed near us, and smiled to see Margaret lying on the ground, and me sitting by her side. He made some remark about the beauty of the afternoon, and withdrew himself into the shadow of the wood. Then we talked about Autumn—and about the pleasures of getting lost in the woods— and about the crows, whose voices Margaret had heard—and about the experiences of early child-hood, whose influence remains upon the character after the recollection of them has passed away—and about the sight of mountains from a distance, and the view from their summits—and about other matters of high and low philosophy. In the midst of our talk, we heard footsteps above us, on the high bank; and while the intruder was still hidden among the trees, he called to Margaret, of whom he had gotten a glimpse. Then he emerged from the green shade; and, behold, it was Mr. Emerson, who, in spite of his clerical consecration, had found no better way of spending the Sabbath than to ramble among the woods. He appeared to have had a pleasant time; for he said that there were Muses in the woods to-day, and whispers to be heard in the breezes. It being now nearly six o'clock, we separated, Mr. Emerson and Margaret towards his home, and I towards mine, where my little wife was very busy getting tea.

Last evening there was the most beautiful moon-light that ever hallowed this earthly world; and when I went to bathe in the river, which was as calm as death, it seemed like plunging down into the sky. But I had rather be on earth than even in the seventh heaven, just now.

Thursday, September 1st.—Mr. Thoreau dined with us yesterday. . . .

After dinner (at which we cut the first watermelon and musk melon that our garden has ripened), Mr. Thoreau and I walked up the bank of the river; and at a certain point, he shouted for his boat. Forthwith, a young man paddled it across the river, and Mr. Thoreau and I voyaged further up the stream, which soon became more beautiful than any picture, with its dark and quiet sheet of water, half shaded, half sunny, between high and wooded banks. The late rains have swollen the stream so much, that many trees are standing up to their knees, as it were, in the water; and boughs, which lately swung high in air, now dip and drink deep of the passing wave. As to the poor cardinals, which glowed upon the bank a few days since, I could see only a few of their scarlet caps, peeping above the tide. Mr. Thoreau managed the boat so perfectly, either with two paddles or with one, that it seemed instinct with his own will, and to require no physical effort to guide it. He said that, when some Indians visited Concord a few years since, he found that he had acquired, without a teacher, their precise method of propelling and steering a canoe. Nevertheless, being in want of money, he was desirous of selling the boat, of which he was so fit a pilot, and

which was built by his own hands; so I agreed to give him his price (only seven dollars) and according-ly became possessor of the Musketaquid. I wish I could acquire the aquatic skill of the original owner at as reasonable a rate.

Saturday, April 8th.—After journalizing yesterday afternoon, I went out and sawed and split wood till supper-time, then studied German (translating "Le-nore"), with an occasional glance at a beautiful sunset, which I could not enjoy sufficiently, by my-self, to induce me to lay aside the book. After lamp-light, finished "Lenore," and drowsed over Vol-taire's "Candide," occasionally refreshing myself with a tune from Mr. Thoreau's musical-box, which he had left in my keeping.

[Herman Melville]

Hawthorne and Melville had been neighbors in the Berk-shire Hills of Massachusetts. In 1856, the time of this record, they met in England.

We took a pretty long walk together, and sat down in a hollow among the sand hills (sheltering our-selves from the high, cool wind) and smoked a cigar. Melville, as he always does, began to reason of Provi-dence and futurity, and of everything that lies beyond human ken, and informed me that he had "pretty much made up his mind to be annihilated"; but still he does not seem to rest in that anticipation; and, I think, will never rest until he gets hold of a definite belief. It is strange how he persists—and has persisted ever since I knew him, and probably long before—in wandering to-and-fro over these deserts, as dismal and monotonous as the sand hills amid which we were sitting. He can neither believe, nor be comfortable in his unbelief; and he is too honest and courageous not to try to do one or the other . . . he has a very high and noble nature.

[Hints for Stories]

A change from a gay young girl to an old woman; the melancholy events, the effects of which have clustered around her character, and gradually imbued it with their influence, till she becomes a lover of sick-chambers, taking pleasure in receiving dying breaths and in laying out the dead; also having her mind full of funeral reminiscences, and possess-ing more acquaintances beneath the burial turf than above it.

The scene of a story or sketch to be laid within the light of a street-lantern; the time, when the lamp is near going out; and the catastrophe to be simulta-neous with the last flickering gleam.

In an old house, a mysterious knocking might be

heard on the wall, where had formerly been a doorway, now bricked up.

A snake, taken into a man's stomach and nourished there from fifteen years to thirty-five, tormenting him most horribly. A type of envy or some other evil passion.

A Fancy Ball, in which the prominent American writers should appear, dressed in character.

An idle man's pleasures and occupations and thoughts during a day spent by the sea-shore; among them, that of sitting on the top of a cliff, and throwing stones at his own shadow, far below.

Meditations about the main gaspipe of a great city—if the supply were to be stopped, what would happen? How many different scenes it sheds light on? It might be made emblematical of something.

To poison a person or a party of persons with the sacramental wine.

The semblance of a human face to be formed on the side of a mountain, or in the fracture of a small stone, by a *lusus naturae*. The face is an object of curiosity for years or centuries, and by and by a boy is born, whose features gradually assume the aspect of that portrait. At some critical juncture, the resemblance is found to be perfect. A prophecy may be connected.

My Kinsman, Major Molineux

The historical background of the story is important. It enables Hawthorne to write a complex tale that deals with an actual political and social situation (and thus with American history) as well as with a typical introduction of a young man to the city and with a symbolic journey into the underground. Text: From the first American edition of *The Snow-Image and Other Twice-Told Tales* (Boston, 1852).

After the kings of Great Britain had assumed the right of appointing the colonial governors, the measures of the latter seldom met with the ready and general approbation which had been paid to those of their predecessors, under the original charters. The people looked with most jealous scrutiny to the exercise of power which did not emanate from themselves, and they usually rewarded their rulers with slender gratitude for the compliances by which, in softening their instructions from beyond the sea, they had incurred the reprehension of those who gave them. The annals of Massachusetts Bay will inform us, that of six governors in the space of about forty years from the surrender of the old charter, under James II, two were imprisoned by a popular insurrection; a third, as Hutchinson[1] inclines to

believe, was driven from the province by the whizzing of a musket-ball; a fourth, in the opinion of the same historian, was hastened to his grave by continual bickerings with the House of Representatives; and the remaining two, as well as their successors, till the Revolution, were favored with few and brief intervals of peaceful sway. The inferior members of the court party, in times of high political excitement, led scarcely a more desirable life. These remarks may serve as a preface to the following adventures, which chanced upon a summer night, not far from a hundred years ago. The reader, in order to avoid a long and dry detail of colonial affairs, is requested to dispense with an account of the train of circumstances that had caused much temporary inflammation of the popular mind.

It was near nine o'clock of a moonlight evening, when a boat crossed the ferry with a single passenger, who had obtained his conveyance at that unusual hour by the promise of an extra fare. While he stood on the landing-place, searching in either pocket for the means of fulfilling his agreement, the ferryman lifted a lantern, by the aid of which, and the newly risen moon, he took a very accurate survey of the stranger's figure. He was a youth of barely eighteen years, evidently country-bred, and now, as it should seem, upon his first visit to town. He was clad in a coarse gray coat, well worn, but in excellent repair; his under garments were durably constructed of leather, and fitted tight to a pair of serviceable and well-shaped limbs; his stockings of blue yarn were the incontrovertible work of a mother or a sister; and on his head was a three-cornered hat, which in its better days had perhaps sheltered the graver brow of the lad's father. Under his left arm was a heavy cudgel, formed of an oak sapling and retaining a part of the hardened root; and his equipment was completed by a wallet, not so abundantly stocked as to incommode the vigorous shoulders on which it hung. Brown, curly hair, well-shaped features, and bright, cheerful eyes were nature's gifts, and worth all that art could have done for his adornment.

The youth, one of whose names was Robin, finally drew from his pocket the half of a little province bill of five shillings, which, in the depreciation in that sort of currency, did but satisfy the ferryman's demand, with the surplus of a sexangular piece of parchment, valued at three pence. He then walked forward into the town, with as light a step as if his day's journey had not already exceeded thirty miles, and with as eager an eye as if he were entering London city, instead of the little metropolis of a New England colony. Before Robin had proceeded far, however, it occurred to him that he knew not whither to direct his steps; so he paused, and looked up and down the narrow street, scrutinizing the

[1] Thomas Hutchinson (1711-80), royal governor of Massachusetts, 1769-74, and author of *The History of the Colony of Massachusetts-Bay* (1765).

small and mean wooden buildings that were scattered on either side.

"This low hovel cannot be my kinsman's dwelling," thought he, "nor yonder old house, where the moonlight enters at the broken casement; and truly I see none hereabouts that might be worthy of him. It would have been wise to inquire my way of the ferryman, and doubtless he would have gone with me, and earned a shilling from the Major for his pains. But the next man I meet will do as well."

He resumed his walk, and was glad to perceive that the street now became wider, and the houses more respectable in their appearance. He soon discerned a figure moving on moderately in advance, and hastened his steps to overtake it. As Robin drew nigh, he saw that the passenger was a man in years, with a full periwig of gray hair, a wide-skirted coat of dark cloth, and silk stockings rolled above his knees. He carried a long and polished cane, which he struck down perpendicularly before him, at every step; and at regular intervals he uttered two successive hems, of a peculiarly solemn and sepulchral intonation. Having made these observations, Robin laid hold of the skirt of the old man's coat, just when the light from the open door and windows of a barber's shop fell upon both their figures.

"Good evening to you, honored sir," said he, making a low bow, and still retaining his hold of the skirt. "I pray you tell me whereabouts is the dwelling of my kinsman, Major Molineux."

The youth's question was uttered very loudly; and one of the barbers, whose razor was descending on a well-soaped chin, and another who was dressing a Ramillies wig, left their occupations, and came to the door. The citizen, in the mean time, turned a long-favored countenance upon Robin, and answered him in a tone of excessive anger and annoyance. His two sepulchral hems, however, broke into the very center of his rebuke, with most singular effect, like a thought of the cold grave obtruding among wrathful passions.

"Let go my garment, fellow! I tell you, I know not the man you speak of. What! I have authority, I have—hem, hem—authority; and if this be the respect you show for your betters, your feet shall be brought acquainted with the stocks by daylight, tomorrow morning!"

Robin released the old man's skirt, and hastened away, pursued by an ill-mannered roar of laughter from the barber's shop. He was at first considerably surprised by the result of his question, but, being a shrewd youth, soon thought himself able to account for the mystery.

"This is some country representative," was his conclusion, "who has never seen the inside of my kinsman's door, and lacks the breeding to answer a stranger civilly. The man is old, or verily—I might be tempted to turn back and smite him on the nose. Ah, Robin, Robin! even the barber's boys laugh at you for choosing such a guide! You will be wiser in time, friend Robin."

He now became entangled in a succession of crooked and narrow streets, which crossed each other, and meandered at no great distance from the water-side. The smell of tar was obvious to his nostrils, the masts of vessels pierced the moonlight above the tops of the buildings, and the numerous signs, which Robin paused to read, informed him that he was near the center of business. But the streets were empty, the shops were closed, and lights were visible only in the second stories of a few dwelling-houses. At length, on the corner of a narrow lane, through which he was passing, he beheld the broad countenance of a British hero swinging before the door of an inn, whence proceeded the voices of many guests. The casement of one of the lower windows was thrown back, and a very thin curtain permitted Robin to distinguish a party at supper, round a well-furnished table. The fragrance of the good cheer steamed forth into the outer air, and the youth could not fail to recollect that the last remnant of his travelling stock of provision had yielded to his morning appetite, and that noon had found and left him dinnerless.

"O, that a parchment three-penny might give me a right to sit down at yonder table!" said Robin, with a sigh. "But the Major will make me welcome to the best of his victuals; so I will even step boldly in, and inquire my way to his dwelling."

He entered the tavern, and was guided by the murmur of voices and the fumes of tobacco, to the public room. It was a long and low apartment, with oaken walls, grown dark in the continual smoke, and a floor, which was thickly sanded, but of no immaculate purity. A number of persons—the larger part of whom appeared to be mariners, or in some way connected with the sea—occupied the wooden benches, or leather-bottomed chairs, conversing on various matters, and occasionally lending their attention to some topic of general interest. Three or four little groups were draining as many bowls of punch, which the West India trade had long since made a familiar drink in the colony. Others, who had the appearance of men who lived by regular and laborious handicraft, preferred the insulated bliss of an unshared potation, and became more taciturn under its influence. Nearly all, in short, evinced a predilection for the Good Creature in some of its various shapes, for this is a vice to which, as Fast Day sermons of a hundred years ago will testify, we have a long hereditary claim. The only guests to whom Robin's sympathies inclined him were two or three sheepish countrymen, who were using the inn somewhat after the fashion of a Turkish caravansary;

they had gotten themselves into the darkest corner of the room, and heedless of the Nicotian[2] atmosphere, were supping on the bread of their own ovens, and the bacon cured in their own chimney-smoke. But though Robin felt a sort of brotherhood with these strangers, his eyes were attracted from them to a person who stood near the door, holding whispered conversation with a group of ill-dressed associates. His features were separately striking almost to grotesqueness, and the whole face left a deep impression on the memory. The forehead bulged out into a double prominence, with a vale between; the nose came boldly forth in an irregular curve, and its bridge was of more than a finger's breadth; the eyebrows were deep and shaggy, and the eyes glowed beneath them like fire in a cave.

While Robin deliberated of whom to inquire respecting his kinsman's dwelling, he was accosted by the innkeeper, a little man in a stained white apron, who had come to pay his professional welcome to the stranger. Being in the second generation from a French Protestant, he seemed to have inherited the courtesy of his parent nation; but no variety of circumstances was ever known to change his voice from the one shrill note in which he now addressed Robin.

"From the country, I presume, sir?" said he, with a profound bow. "Beg leave to congratulate you on your arrival, and trust you intend a long stay with us. Fine town here, sir, beautiful buildings, and much that may interest a stranger. May I hope for the honor of your commands in respect to supper?"

"The man sees a family likeness! the rogue has guessed that I am related to the Major!" thought Robin, who had hitherto experienced little superfluous civility.

All eyes were now turned on the country lad, standing at the door, in his worn three-cornered hat, gray coat, leather breeches, and blue yarn stockings, leaning on an oaken cudgel, and bearing a wallet on his back.

Robin replied to the courteous innkeeper, with such an assumption of confidence as befitted the Major's relative. "My honest friend," he said, "I shall make it a point to patronize your house on some occasion, when"—here he could not help lowering his voice—"when I may have more than a parchment three-pence in my pocket. My present business," continued he, speaking with lofty confidence, "is merely to inquire my way to the dwelling of my kinsman, Major Molineux."

There was a sudden and general movement in the room, which Robin interpreted as expressing the eagerness of each individual to become his guide. But the innkeeper turned his eyes to a written paper

[2] The room was smoke-filled: probably a reference to Jacques Nicot, who introduced tobacco into France.

on the wall, which he read, or seemed to read, with occasional recurrences to the young man's figure.

"What have we here?" said he, breaking his speech into little dry fragments. "'Left the house of the subscriber, bounden servant, Hezekiah Mudge,—had on, when he went away, gray coat, leather breeches, master's third-best hat. One pound currency reward to whosoever shall lodge him in any jail of the providence.' Better trudge, boy; better trudge!"

Robin had begun to draw his hand towards the lighter end of the oak cudgel, but a strange hostility in every countenance induced him to relinquish his purpose of breaking the courteous innkeeper's head. As he turned to leave the room, he encountered a sneering glance from the bold-featured personage whom he had before noticed; and no sooner was he beyond the door, than he heard a general laugh, in which the innkeeper's voice might be distinguished, like the dropping of small stones into a kettle.

"Now, is it not strange," thought Robin, with his usual shrewdness, "is it not strange that the confession of an empty pocket should outweigh the name of my kinsman, Major Molineux? O, if I had one of those grinning rascals in the woods, where I and my oak sapling grew up together, I would teach him that my arm is heavy, though my purse be light!"

On turning the corner of the narrow lane, Robin found himself in a spacious street, with an unbroken line of lofty houses on each side, and a steepled building at the upper end, whence the ringing of a bell announced the hour of nine. The light of the moon, and the lamps from the numerous shop windows, discovered people promenading on the pavement, and amongst them Robin had hoped to recognize his hitherto inscrutable relative. The result of his former inquiries made him unwilling to hazard another, in a scene of such publicity, and he determined to walk slowly and silently up the street, thrusting his face close to that of every elderly gentleman, in search of the Major's lineaments. In his progress, Robin encountered many gay and gallant figures. Embroidered garments of showy colors, enormous periwigs, gold-laced hats, and silver-hilted swords glided past him, and dazzled his optics. Travelled youths, imitators of the European fine gentlemen of the period, trod jauntily along, half dancing to the fashionable tunes which they hummed, and making poor Robin ashamed of his quiet and natural gait. At length, after many pauses to examine the gorgeous display of goods in the shop-windows, and after suffering some rebukes for the impertinence of his scrutiny into people's faces, the Major's kinsman found himself near the steepled building, still unsuccessful in his search. As yet, however, he had seen only one side of the thronged street; so Robin crossed, and continued the same sort of inquisition down the opposite pavement, with stronger hopes than the philosopher seeking an honest man, but with no better fortune. He had arrived about midway towards the lower end, from which his course began, when he overheard the approach of some one, who struck down a cane on the flag-stones at every step, uttering at regular intervals, two sepulchral hems.

"Mercy on us!" quoth Robin, recognizing the sound.

Turning a corner, which chanced to be close at his right hand, he hastened to pursue his researches in some other part of the town. His patience now was wearing low, and he seemed to feel more fatigue from his rambles since he crossed the ferry, than from his journey of several days on the other side. Hunger also pleaded loudly within him, and Robin began to balance the propriety of demanding, violently, and with lifted cudgel, the necessary guidance from the first solitary passenger whom he should meet. While a resolution to this effect was gaining strength, he entered a street of mean appearance, on either side of which a row of ill-built houses was straggling towards the harbor. The moonlight fell upon no passenger along the whole extent, but in the third domicile which Robin passed there was a half-opened door, and his keen glance detected a woman's garment within.

"My luck may be better here," said he to himself.

Accordingly, he approached the door, and beheld it shut closer as he did so; yet an open space remained, sufficing for the fair occupant to observe the stranger, without a corresponding display on her part. All that Robin could discern was a strip of scarlet petticoat, and the occasional sparkle of an eye, as if the moonbeams were trembling on some bright thing.

"Pretty mistress," for I may call her so with a good conscience, thought the shrewd youth, since I know nothing to the contrary,—"my sweet pretty mistress, will you be kind enough to tell me whereabouts I must seek the dwelling of my kinsman, Major Molineux?"

Robin's voice was plaintive and winning, and the female, seeing nothing to be shunned in the handsome country youth, thrust open the door, and came forth into the moonlight. She was a dainty little figure, with a white neck, round arms, and a slender waist, at the extremity of which her scarlet petticoat jutted out over a hoop, as if she were standing in a balloon. Moreover, her face was oval and pretty, her hair dark beneath the little cap, and her bright eyes possessed a sly freedom, which triumphed over those of Robin.

"Major Molineux dwells here," said this fair woman.

Now, her voice was the sweetest Robin had heard that night, the airy counterpart of a stream of melted silver; yet he could not help doubting whether that sweet voice spoke Gospel truth. He looked up and down the mean street, and then surveyed the house before which they stood. It was a small, dark edifice of two stories, the second of which projected over the lower floor; and the front apartment had the aspect of a shop for petty commodities.

"Now truly I am in luck," replied Robin, cunningly, "and so indeed is my kinsman, the Major, in having so pretty a housekeeper. But I prithee trouble him to step to the door; I will deliver him a message from his friends in the country, and then go back to my lodgings at the inn."

"Nay, the Major has been a-bed this hour or more," said the lady of the scarlet petticoat; "and it would be to little purpose to disturb him to-night, seeing his evening draught was of the strongest. But he is a kind-hearted man, and it would be as much as my life's worth to let a kinsman of his turn away from the door. You are the good old gentleman's very picture, and I could swear that was his rainy-weather hat. Also he has garments very much resembling those leather small-clothes. But come in, I pray, for I bid you hearty welcome in his name."

So saying, the fair and hospitable dame took our hero by the hand; and the touch was light, and the force was gentleness, and though Robin read in her eyes what he did not hear in her words, yet the slender-waisted woman in the scarlet petticoat proved stronger than the athletic country youth. She had drawn his half-willing footsteps nearly to the threshold, when the opening of a door in the neighborhood startled the Major's housekeeper, and, leaving the Major's kinsman, she vanished speedily into her own domicile. A heavy yawn preceded the appearance of a man, who, like the Moonshine of Pyramus and Thisbe,[3] carried a lantern, needlessly aiding his sister luminary in the heavens. As he walked sleepily up the street, he turned his broad, dull face on Robin, and displayed a long staff, spiked at the end.

"Home, vagabond, home!" said the watchman, in accents that seemed to fall asleep as soon as they were uttered. "Home, or we'll set you in the stocks, by peep of day!"

"This is the second hint of the kind," thought Robin. "I wish they would end my difficulties, by setting me there to-night."

Nevertheless, the youth felt an instinctive antipathy towards the guardian of midnight order, which at first prevented him from asking his usual question. But just when the man was about to vanish

[3] Cf. Shakespeare, *A Midsummer Night's Dream* III. i.

behind the corner, Robin resolved not to lose the opportunity, and shouted lustily after him,—

"I say, friend! will you guide me to the house of my kinsman, Major Molineux?"

The watchman made no reply, but turned the corner and was gone; yet Robin seemed to hear the sound of drowsy laughter stealing along the solitary street. At that moment, also, a pleasant titter saluted him from the open window above his head; he looked up, and caught the sparkle of a saucy eye; a round arm beckoned to him, and next he heard light footsteps descending the staircase within. But Robin, being of the household of a New England clergyman, was a good youth, as well as a shrewd one; so he resisted temptation, and fled away.

He now roamed desperately, and at random, through the town, almost ready to believe that a spell was on him, like that by which a wizard of his country had once kept three pursuers wandering, a whole winter night, within twenty paces of the cottage which they sought. The streets lay before him, strange and desolate, and the lights were extinguished in almost every house. Twice, however, little parties of men, among whom Robin distinguished individuals in outlandish attire, came hurrying along; but though on both occasions they paused to address him, such intercourse did not at all enlighten his perplexity. They did but utter a few words in some language of which Robin knew nothing, and perceiving his inability to answer, bestowed a curse upon him in plain English, and hastened away. Finally, the lad determined to knock at the door of every mansion that might appear worthy to be occupied by his kinsman, trusting that perseverance would overcome the fatality that had hitherto thwarted him. Firm in this resolve, he was passing beneath the walls of a church, which formed the corner of two streets, when, as he turned into the shade of its steeple, he encountered a bulky stranger, muffled in a cloak. The man was proceeding with the speed of earnest business, but Robin planted himself full before him, holding the oak cudgel with both hands across his body, as a bar to further passage.

"Halt, honest man, and answer me a question," said he, very resolutely. "Tell me, this instant, whereabouts is the dwelling of my kinsman, Major Molineux!"

"Keep your tongue between your teeth, fool, and let me pass!" said a deep, gruff voice, which Robin partly remembered. "Let me pass, I say, or I'll strike you to the earth!"

"No, no, neighbor!" cried Robin, flourishing his cudgel, and then thrusting its larger end close to the man's muffled face. "No, no, I'm not the fool you take me for, nor do you pass till I have an answer to my question. Whereabouts is the dwelling of my kinsman, Major Molineux?"

The stranger, instead of attempting to force his passage stepped back into the moonlight, unmuffled his face, and stared full into that of Robin.

"Watch here an hour, and Major Molineux will pass by," said he.

Robin gazed with dismay and astonishment on the unprecedented physiognomy of the speaker. The forehead with its double prominence, the broad hooked nose, the shaggy eyebrows, and fiery eyes, were those which he had noticed at the inn, but the man's complexion had undergone a singular, or, more properly, a two-fold change. One side of the face blazed an intense red, while the other was black as midnight, the division line being in the broad bridge of the nose; and a mouth which seemed to extend from ear to ear was black or red, in contrast to the color of the cheek. The effect was as if two individual devils, a fiend of fire and a fiend of darkness had united themselves to form this infernal visage. The stranger grinned in Robin's face, muffled his parti-colored features, and was out of sight in a moment.

"Strange things we travellers see!" ejaculated Robin.

He seated himself, however, upon the steps of the church-door, resolving to wait the appointed time for his kinsman. A few moments were consumed in philosophical speculations upon the species of man who had just left him; but having settled this point shrewdly, rationally, and satisfactorily, he was compelled to look elsewhere for his amusement. And first he threw his eyes along the street. It was of more respectable appearance than most of those into which he had wandered; and the moon, creating, like the imaginative power, a beautiful strangeness in familiar objects, gave something of romance to a scene that might not have possessed it in the light of day. The irregular and often quaint architecture of the houses, some of whose roofs were broken into numerous little peaks, while others ascended, steep and narrow, into a single point, and others again were square; the pure snow-white of some of their complexions, the aged darkness of others, and the thousand sparklings, reflected from bright substances in the walls of many; these matters engaged Robin's attention for a while, and then began to grow wearisome. Next he endeavored to define the forms of distant objects, starting away, with almost ghostly indistinctness, just as his eye appeared to grasp them; and finally he took a minute survey of an edifice which stood on the opposite side of the street, directly in front of the church-door, where he was stationed. It was a large, square mansion, distinguished from its neighbors by a balcony, which rested on tall pillars, and by an elaborate Gothic window, communicating therewith.

"Perhaps this is the very house I have been seeking," thought Robin.

Then he strove to speed away the time, by listening to a murmur which swept continually along the street, yet was scarcely audible, except to an unaccustomed ear like his; it was a low, dull, dreamy sound, compounded of many noises, each of which was at too great a distance to be separately heard. Robin marvelled at this snore of a sleeping town, and marvelled more whenever its continuity was broken by now and then a distant shout, apparently loud where it originated. But altogether it was a sleep-inspiring sound, and, to shake off its drowsy influence, Robin arose, and climbed a window-frame, that he might view the interior of the church. There the moonbeams came trembling in, and fell down upon the deserted pews, and extended along the quiet aisles. A fainter yet more awful radiance was hovering around the pulpit, and one solitary ray had dared to rest upon the unopened page of the great Bible. Had nature, in that deep hour, become a worshipper in the house which man had builded? Or was that heavenly light the visible sanctity of the place,—visible because no earthly and impure feet were within the walls? The scene made Robin's heart shiver with a sensation of loneliness stronger than he had ever felt in the remotest depths of his native woods; so he turned away, and sat down again before the door. There were graves around the church, and now an uneasy thought obtruded into Robin's breast. What if the object of his search, which had been so often and so strangely thwarted, were all the time mouldering in his shroud? What if his kinsman should glide through yonder gate, and nod and smile to him in dimly passing by?

"O that any breathing thing were here with me!" said Robin.

Recalling his thoughts from this uncomfortable track, he sent them over forest, hill, and stream, and attempted to imagine how that evening of ambiguity and weariness had been spent by his father's household. He pictured them assembled at the door, beneath the tree, the great old tree, which had been spared for its huge twisted trunk, and venerable shade, when a thousand leafy brethren fell. There, at the going down of the summer sun, it was his father's custom to perform domestic worship, that the neighbors might come and join with him like brothers of the family, and that the wayfaring man might pause to drink at that fountain, and keep his heart pure by freshening the memory of home. Robin distinguished the seat of every individual of the little audience; he saw the good man in the midst, holding the Scriptures in the golden light that fell from the western clouds; he beheld him close

the book and all rise up to pray. He heard the old thanksgivings for daily mercies, the old supplications for their continuance, to which he had so often listened in weariness, but which were now among his dear remembrances. He perceived the slight inequality of his father's voice when he came to speak of the absent one; he noted how his mother turned her face to the broad and knotted trunk; how his elder brother scorned, because the beard was rough upon his upper lip, to permit his features to be moved; how the younger sister drew down a low hanging branch before her eyes; and how the little one of all, whose sports had hitherto broken the decorum of the scene, understood the prayer for her playmate, and burst into clamorous grief. Then he saw them go in at the door; and when Robin would have entered also, the latch tinkled into its place, and he was excluded from his home.

"Am I here, or there?" cried Robin, starting; for all at once, when his thoughts had become visible and audible in a dream, the long, wide, solitary street shone out before him.

He aroused himself, and endeavored to fix his attention steadily upon the large edifice which he had surveyed before. But still his mind kept vibrating between fancy and reality; by turns, the pillars of the balcony lengthened into the tall, bare stems of pines, dwindled down to human figures, settled again into their true shape and size, and then commenced a new succession of changes. For a single moment, when he deemed himself awake, he could have sworn that a visage—one which he seemed to remember, yet could not absolutely name as his kinsman's—was looking towards him from the Gothic window. A deeper sleep wrestled with and nearly overcame him, but fled at the sound of footsteps along the opposite pavement. Robin rubbed his eyes, discerned a man passing at the foot of the balcony, and addressed him in a loud, peevish, and lamentable cry.

"Hallo, friend! must I wait here all night for my kinsman, Major Molineux?"

The sleeping echoes awoke, and answered the voice; and the passenger, barely able to discern a figure sitting in the oblique shade of the steeple, traversed the street to obtain a nearer view. He was himself a gentleman in his prime, of open, intelligent, cheerful, and altogether prepossessing countenance. Perceiving a country youth, apparently homeless and without friends, he accosted him in a tone of real kindness, which had become strange to Robin's ears.

"Well, my good lad, why are you sitting here?" inquired he. "Can I be of service to you in any way?"

"I am afraid not, sir," replied Robin, despondingly; "yet I shall take it kindly, if you'll answer me a single question. I've been searching, half the night, for one Major Molineux; now, sir, is there really such a person in these parts, or am I dreaming?"

"Major Molineux! The name is not altogether strange to me," said the gentleman, smiling. "Have you any objection to telling me the nature of your business with him?"

Then Robin briefly related that his father was a clergyman, settled on a small salary, at a long distance back in the country, and that he and Major Molineux were brothers' children. The Major, having inherited riches, and acquired civil and military rank, had visited his cousin, in great pomp, a year or two before; had manifested much interest in Robin and an elder brother, and, being childless himself, had thrown out hints respecting the future establishment of one of them in life. The elder brother was destined to succeed to the farm which his father cultivated in the interval of sacred duties; it was therefore determined that Robin should profit by his kinsman's generous intentions, especially as he seemed to be rather the favorite, and was thought to possess other necessary endowments.

"For I have the name of being a shrewd youth," observed Robin, in this part of his story.

"I doubt not you deserve it," replied his new friend, good-naturedly; "but pray proceed."

"Well, sir, being nearly eighteen years old, and well-grown, as you see," continued Robin, drawing himself up to his full height, "I thought it high time to begin in the world. So my mother and sister put me in handsome trim, and my father gave me half the remnant of his last year's salary, and five days ago I started for this place, to pay the Major a visit. But, would you believe it, sir! I crossed the ferry a little after dark, and have yet found nobody that would show me the way to his dwelling;—only, an hour or two since, I was told to wait here, and Major Molineux would pass by."

"Can you describe the man who told you this?" inquired the gentleman.

"O, he was a very ill-favored fellow, sir," replied Robin, "with two great bumps on his forehead, a hook nose, fiery eyes,—and, what struck me as the strangest, his face was of two different colors. Do you happen to know such a man, sir?"

"Not intimately," answered the stranger, "but I chanced to meet him a little time previous to your stopping me. I believe you may trust his word, and that the Major will very shortly pass through this street. In the mean time, as I have a singular curiosity to witness your meeting, I will sit down here upon the steps, and bear you company."

He seated himself accordingly, and soon engaged his companion in animated discourse. It was but of brief continuance, however, for a noise of shouting, which had long been remotely audible, drew so much nearer that Robin inquired its cause.

"What may be the meaning of this uproar?" asked he. "Truly, if your town be always as noisy, I shall find little sleep, while I am an inhabitant."

"Why, indeed, friend Robin, there do appear to be three or four riotous fellows abroad to-night," replied the gentleman. "You must not expect all the stillness of your native woods, here in our streets. But the watch will shortly be at the heels of these lads, and"—

"Ay, and set them in the stocks by peep of day," interrupted Robin, recollecting his own encounter with the drowsy lantern-bearer. "But, dear sir, if I may trust my ears, an army of watchmen would never make head against such a multitude of rioters. There were at least a thousand voices went up to make that one shout."

"May not a man have several voices, Robin, as well as two complexions?" said his friend.

"Perhaps a man may but Heaven forbid that a woman should!" responded the shrewd youth, thinking of the seductive tones of the Major's housekeeper.

The sounds of a trumpet in some neighboring street now became so evident and continual, that Robin's curiosity was strongly excited. In addition to the shouts, he heard frequent bursts from many instruments of discord, and a wild and confused laughter filled up the intervals. Robin rose from the steps, and looked wistfully towards a point whither people seemed to be hastening.

"Surely some prodigious merry-making is going on," exclaimed he. "I have laughed very little since I left home, sir, and should be sorry to lose an opportunity. Shall we step round the corner by that darkish house, and take our share of the fun?"

"Sit down again, sit down, good Robin," replied the gentleman, laying his hand on the skirt of the gray coat. "You forget that we must wait here for your kinsman; and there is reason to believe that he will pass by, in the course of a very few moments."

The near approach of the uproar had now disturbed the neighborhood; windows flew open on all sides; and many heads, in the attire of the pillow, and confused by sleep suddenly broken, were protruded to the gaze of whoever had leisure to observe them. Eager voices hailed each other from house to house, all demanding the explanation, which not a soul could give. Half-dressed men hurried towards the unknown commotion, stumbling as they went over the stone steps that thrust themselves into the narrow foot-walk. The shouts, the laughter, and the tuneless bray, the antipodes of music, came onwards with increasing din, till scattered individuals, and then denser bodies, began to appear round a corner at the distance of a hundred yards.

"Will you recognize your kinsman, if he passes in this crowd?" inquired the gentleman.

"Indeed, I can't warrant it, sir; but I'll take my stand here, and keep a bright lookout," answered Robin, descending to the outer edge of the pavement.

A mighty stream of people now emptied into the street, and came rolling slowly towards the church. A single horseman wheeled the corner in the midst of them, and close behind him came a band of fearful wind-instruments, sending forth a fresher discord, now that no intervening buildings kept it from the ear. Then a redder light disturbed the moonbeams, and a dense multitude of torches shone along the street, concealing, by their glare, whatever object they illuminated. The single horseman, clad in a military dress, and bearing a drawn sword, rode onward as the leader, and, by his fierce and variegated countenance, appeared like war personified: the red of one cheek was an emblem of fire and sword; the blackness of the other betokened the mourning that attends them. In his train were wild figures in the Indian dress, and many fantastic shapes without a model, giving the whole march a visionary air, as if a dream had broken forth from some feverish brain, and were sweeping visibly through the midnight streets. A mass of people, inactive, except as applauding spectators, hemmed the procession in; and several women ran along the sidewalk, piercing the confusion of heavier sounds with their shrill voices of mirth or terror.

"The double-faced fellow has his eye upon me," muttered Robin, with an indefinite but an uncomfortable idea that he was himself to bear a part in the pageantry.

The leader turned himself in the saddle, and fixed his glance full upon the country youth, as the steed went slowly by. When Robin had freed his eyes from those fiery ones, the musicians were passing before him, and the torches were close at hand; but the unsteady brightness of the latter formed a veil which he could not penetrate. The rattling of wheels over the stones sometimes found its way to his ear, and confused traces of a human form appeared at intervals, and then melted into the vivid light. A moment more, and the leader thundered a command to halt: the trumpets vomited a horrid breath, and then held their peace; the shouts and laughter of the people died away, and there remained only a universal hum, allied to silence. Right before Robin's eyes was an uncovered cart. There the torches blazed the brightest, there the moon shone out like day, and there, in tar-and-feathery dignity, sat his kinsman, Major Molineux!

He was an elderly man, of large and majestic person, and strong, square features, betokening a steady soul; but steady as it was, his enemies had found means to shake it. His face was pale as death, and far more ghastly; the broad forehead was contracted in his agony, so that his eyebrows formed one grizzled line; his eyes were red and wild, and the foam hung white upon his quivering lip. His whole frame was agitated by a quick and continual tremor, which his pride strove to quell, even in those circumstances of overwhelming humiliation. But perhaps the bitterest pang of all was when his eyes met those of Robin; for he evidently knew him on the instant, as the youth stood witnessing the foul disgrace of a head grown gray in honor. They stared at each other in silence, and Robin's knees shook, and his hair bristled, with a mixture of pity and terror. Soon, however, a bewildering excitement began to seize upon his mind; the preceding adventures of the night, the unexpected appearance of the crowd, the torches, the confused din and the hush that followed, the spectre of his kinsman reviled by that great multitude,—all this, and, more than all, a perception of tremendous ridicule in the whole scene, affected him with a sort of mental inebriety. At that moment a voice of sluggish merriment saluted Robin's ears; he turned instinctively, and just behind the corner of the church stood the lantern-bearer, rubbing his eyes, and drowsily enjoying the lad's amazement. Then he heard a peal of laughter like the ringing of silvery bells; a woman twitched his arm, a saucy eye met his, and he saw the lady of the scarlet petticoat. A sharp, dry cachinnation appealed to his memory, and standing on tiptoe in the crowd, with his white apron over his head, he beheld the courteous little innkeeper. And lastly, there sailed over the heads of the multitude a great, broad laugh, broken in the midst by two sepulchral hems; thus, "Haw, haw, haw,—hem, hem,—haw, haw, haw, haw!"

The sound proceeded from the balcony of the opposite edifice, and thither Robin turned his eyes. In front of the Gothic window stood the old citizen, wrapped in a wide gown, his gray periwig exchanged for a night-cap, which was thrust back from his forehead, and his silk stockings hanging about his legs. He supported himself on his polished cane in a fit of convulsive merriment, which manifested itself on his solemn old features like a funny inscription on a tombstone. Then Robin seemed to hear the voices of the barbers, of the guests of the inn, and of all who had made sport of him that night. The contagion was spreading among the multitude, when, all at once, it seized upon Robin, and he sent forth a shout of laughter that echoed through the street,— every man shook his sides, every man emptied his lungs, but Robin's shout was the loudest there. The cloud-spirits peeped from their silvery islands, as the congregated mirth went roaring up the sky! The Man in the Moon heard the far bellow; "Oho," quoth he, "the old earth is frolicsome tonight!"

When there was a momentary calm in that tempestuous sea of sound, the leader gave the sign, the procession resumed its march. On they went, like fiends that throng in mockery around some dead potentate, mighty no more, but majestic still in his agony. On they went, in counterfeited pomp, in senseless uproar, in frenzied merriment, trampling all on an old man's heart. On swept the tumult, and left a silent street behind.

"Well, Robin, are you dreaming?" inquired the gentleman, laying his hand on the youth's shoulder.

Robin started, and withdrew his arm from the stone post to which he had instinctively clung, as the living stream rolled by him. His cheek was somewhat pale, and his eye not quite as lively as in the earlier part of the evening.

"Will you be kind enough to show me the way to the ferry?" said he, after a moment's pause.

"You have, then, adopted a new subject of inquiry?" observed his companion, with a smile.

"Why, yes, sir," replied Robin, rather dryly. "Thanks to you, and to my other friends, I have at last met my kinsman, and he will scarce desire to see my face again. I begin to grow weary of a town life, sir. Will you show me the way to the ferry?"

"No, my good friend Robin,—not to-night, at least," said the gentleman. "Some few days hence, if you wish it, I will speed you on your journey. Or, if you prefer to remain with us, perhaps, as you are a shrewd youth, you may rise in the world without the help of your kinsman, Major Molineux."

1832

Roger Malvin's Burial

Hawthorne makes use of history in this tale to provide a stage whereon the psychological and moral drama of guilt and choice can unfold. The place (the frontier in 1725) and the choice (between the self and an obligation to another) give the story an important political and social meaning; beyond that, Hawthorne is clearly concerned with the psychology of guilt and with a sin-sacrifice-redemption pattern. Text: From the author's revised edition of *Mosses from an Old Manse* (Boston, 1854).

One of the few incidents of Indian warfare naturally susceptible of the moonlight of romance was that expedition undertaken for the defence of the frontiers in the year 1725, which resulted in the well-remembered "Lovell's Fight."[1] Imagination, by casting certain circumstances judicially into the shade, may see much to admire in the heroism of a little band who gave battle to twice their number in the heart of the enemy's country. The open bravery displayed by both parties was in accordance with civilized ideas of valor; and chivalry itself might not blush to record the deeds of one or two individuals. The battle, though so fatal to those who fought, was not unfortunate in its consequences to the country; for it broke the strength of a tribe and conduced to the peace which subsisted during several ensuing years. History and tradition are unusually minute in their memorials of this affair; and the captain of a scouting party of frontier men has acquired as actual a military renown as many a victorious leader of thousands. Some of the incidents contained in the following pages will be recognized, notwithstanding the substitution of fictitious names, by such as have heard, from old men's lips, the fate of the few combatants who were in a condition to retreat after "Lovell's Fight."

The early sunbeams hovered cheerfully upon the tree-tops, beneath which two weary and wounded men had stretched their limbs the night before. Their bed of withered oak leaves was strewn upon the small level space, at the foot of a rock, situated near the summit of one of the gentle swells by which the face of the country is there diversified. The mass of granite, rearing its smooth, flat surface fifteen or twenty feet above their heads, was not unlike a gigantic gravestone, upon which the veins seemed to form an inscription in forgotten characters. On a tract of several acres around this rock, oaks and other hard-wood trees had supplied the place of the pines, which were the usual growth of the land; and a young and vigorous sapling stood close beside the travellers.

The severe wound of the elder man had probably deprived him of sleep; for, so soon as the first ray of sunshine rested on the top of the highest tree, he reared himself painfully from his recumbent posture and sat erect. The deep lines of his countenance and the scattered gray of his hair marked him as past the middle age; but his muscular frame would, but for the effects of his wound, have been as capable of sustaining fatigue as in the early vigor of life. Languor and exhaustion now sat upon his haggard features; and the despairing glance which he sent forward through the depths of the forest proved his own conviction that his pilgrimage was at an end. He next turned his eyes to the companion who reclined by his side. The youth—for he had scarcely attained the years of manhood—lay, with his head upon his arm, in the embrace of an unquiet sleep, which a thrill of pain from his wounds seemed each moment on the point of breaking. His right hand grasped a musket; and, to judge from the violent action of his features, his slumbers were bringing

[1] With the Penobscot Indians.

back a vision of the conflict of which he was one of the few survivors. A shout—deep and loud in his dreaming fancy—found its way in an imperfect murmur to his lips; and, starting even at the slight sound of his own voice, he suddenly awoke. The first act of reviving recollection was to make anxious inquiries respecting the condition of his wounded fellow-traveller. The latter shook his head.

"Reuben, my boy," he said, "this rock beneath which we sit will serve for an old hunter's gravestone. There is many and many a long mile of howling wilderness before us yet; nor would it avail me anything if the smoke of my own chimney were but on the other side of that swell of land. The Indian bullet was deadlier than I thought."

"You are weary with our three days' travel," replied the youth, "and a little longer rest will recruit you. Sit you here while I search the woods for the herbs and roots that must be our sustenance; and, having eaten, you shall lean on me, and we will turn our faces homeward. I doubt not that, with my help, you can attain to some one of the frontier garrisons."

"There is not two days' life in me, Reuben," said the other, calmly, "and I will no longer burden you with my useless body, when you can scarcely support your own. Your wounds are deep and your strength is failing fast; yet, if you hasten onward alone, you may be preserved. For me there is no hope, and I will await death here."

"If it must be so, I will remain and watch by you," said Reuben, resolutely.

"No, my son, no," rejoined his companion. "Let the wish of a dying man have weight with you; give me one grasp of your hand, and get you hence. Think you that my last moments will be eased by the thought that I leave you to die a more lingering death? I have loved you like a father, Reuben; and at a time like this I should have something of a father's authority. I charge you to be gone, that I may die in peace."

"And because you have been a father to me, should I therefore leave you to perish and to lie unburied in the wilderness?" exclaimed the youth. "No; if your end be in truth approaching, I will watch by you and receive your parting words. I will dig a grave here by the rock, in which, if my weakness overcome me, we will rest together; or, if Heaven gives me strength, I will seek my way home."

"In the cities and wherever men dwell," replied the other, "they bury their dead in the earth; they hide them from the sight of the living; but here, where no step may pass perhaps for a hundred years, wherefore should I not rest beneath the open sky, covered only by the oak leaves when the autumn winds shall strew them? And for a monument, here is this gray rock, on which my dying hand shall carve the name of Roger Malvin; and the traveller in days to come will know that here sleeps a hunter and a warrior. Tarry not, then, for a folly like this, but hasten away, if not for your own sake, for hers who will else be desolate."

Malvin spoke the last few words in a faltering voice, and their effect upon his companion was strongly visible. They reminded him that there were other and less questionable duties than that of sharing the fate of a man whom his death could not benefit. Nor can it be affirmed that no selfish feeling strove to enter Reuben's heart, though the consciousness made him more earnestly resist his companion's entreaties.

"How terrible to wait the slow approach of death in this solitude!" exclaimed he. "A brave man does not shrink in the battle; and, when friends stand round the bed, even women may die composedly; but here—"

"I shall not shrink even here, Reuben Bourne," interrupted Malvin. "I am a man of no weak heart; and, if I were, there is a surer support than that of earthly friends. You are young, and life is dear to you. Your last moments will need comfort far more than mine; and when you have laid me in the earth, and are alone, and night is settling on the forest, you will feel all the bitterness of the death that may now be escaped. But I will urge no selfish motive to your generous nature. Leave me for my sake, that, having said a prayer for your safety, I may have space to settle my account undisturbed by worldly sorrows."

"And your daughter,—how shall I dare to meet her eye?" exclaimed Reuben. "She will ask the fate of her father, whose life I vowed to defend with my own. Must I tell her that he travelled three days' march with me from the field of battle, and that then I left him to perish in the wilderness? Were it not better to lie down and die by your side than to return safe and say this to Dorcas?"

"Tell my daughter," said Roger Malvin, "that, though yourself sore wounded, and weak, and weary, you led my tottering footsteps many a mile, and left me only at my earnest entreaty, because I would not have your blood upon my soul. Tell her that through pain and danger you were faithful, and that, if your lifeblood could have saved me, it would have flowed to its last drop; and tell her that you will be something dearer than a father, and that my blessing is with you both, and that my dying eyes can see a long and pleasant path in which you will journey together."

As Malvin spoke he almost raised himself from the ground, and the energy of his concluding words seemed to fill the wild and lonely forest with a vision of happiness; but, when he sank exhausted upon his bed of oak leaves, the light which had kindled in Reuben's eye was quenched. He felt as if it were both sin and folly to think of happiness at such a moment. His companion watched his changing countenance, and sought with generous art to wile him to his own good.

"Perhaps I deceive myself in regard to the time I have to live," he resumed. "It may be that, with speedy assistance, I might recover of my wound. The foremost fugitives must, ere this, have carried tidings of our fatal battle to the frontiers, and parties will be out to succor those in like condition with ourselves. Should you meet one of these and guide them hither, who can tell but that I may sit by my own fireside again?"

A mournful smile strayed across the features of the dying man as he insinuated that unfounded hope; which, however, was not without its effect on Reuben. No merely selfish motive, nor even the desolate condition of Dorcas, could have induced him to desert his companion at such a moment—but his wishes seized on the thought that Malvin's life might be preserved, and his sanguine nature heightened almost to certainty the remote possibility of procuring human aid.

"Surely there is reason, weighty reason, to hope that friends are not far distant," he said, half aloud. "There fled one coward, unwounded, in the beginning of the fight, and most probably he made good speed. Every true man on the frontier would shoulder his musket at the news; and, though no party may range so far into the woods as this, I shall perhaps encounter them in one day's march. Counsel me faithfully," he added, turning to Malvin, in distrust of his own motives. "Were your situation mine, would you desert me while life remained?"

"It is now twenty years," replied Roger Malvin, sighing, however, as he secretly acknowledged the wide dissimilarity between the two cases,—"it is now twenty years since I escaped with one dear friend from Indian captivity near Montreal. We journeyed many days through the woods, till at length, overcome with hunger and weariness, my friend lay down and besought me to leave him; for he knew that, if I remained, we both must perish; and, with but little hope of obtaining succor, I heaped a pillow of dry leaves beneath his head and hastened on."

"And did you return in time to save him?" asked Reuben hanging on Malvin's words as if they were to be prophetic of his own success.

"I did," answered the other. "I came upon the camp of a hunting party before sunset of the same day. I guided them to the spot where my comrade was expecting death; and he is now a hale and hearty man upon his own farm, far within the frontiers, while I lie wounded here in the depths of the wilderness."

This example, powerful in effecting Reuben's de-

cision, was aided, unconsciously to himself, by the hidden strength of many another motive. Roger Malvin perceived that the victory was nearly won.

"Now, go, my son, and Heaven prosper you!" he said. "Turn not back with your friends when you meet them, lest your wounds and weariness overcome you; but send hitherward two or three, that may be spared, to search for me; and believe me, Reuben, my heart will be lighter with every step you take towards home." Yet there was, perhaps, a change both in his countenance and voice as he spoke thus; for, after all, it was a ghastly fate to be left expiring in the wilderness.

Reuben Bourne, but half convinced that he was acting rightly, at length raised himself from the ground and prepared himself for his departure. And first, though contrary to Malvin's wishes, he collected a stock of roots and herbs, which had been their only food during the last two days. This useless supply he placed within reach of the dying man, for whom, also, he swept together a bed of dry oak leaves. Then climbing to the summit of the rock, which on one side was rough and broken, he bent the oak sapling downward, and bound his handkerchief to the topmost branch. This precaution was not unnecessary to direct any who might come in search of Malvin; for every part of the rock, except its broad, smooth front, was concealed at a little distance by the dense undergrowth of the forest. The handkerchief had been the bandage of a wound upon Reuben's arm; and, as he bound it to the tree, he vowed by the blood that stained it that he would return, either to save his companion's life or to lay his body in the grave. He then descended, and stood, with downcast eyes, to receive Roger Malvin's parting words.

The experience of the latter suggested much and minute advice respecting the youth's journey through the trackless forest. Upon this subject he spoke with calm earnestness, as if he were sending Reuben to the battle or the chase while he himself remained secure at home, and not as if the human countenance that was about to leave him were the last he would ever behold. But his firmness was shaken before he concluded.

"Carry my blessing to Dorcas, and say that my last prayer shall be for her and you. Bid her to have no hard thoughts because you left me here,"—Reuben's heart smote him,—"for that your life would not have weighed with you if its sacrifice could have done me good. She will marry you after she has mourned a little while for her father; and Heaven grant you long and happy days, and may your children's children stand round your death bed! And, Reuben," added he, as the weakness of mortality made its way at last, "return, when your wounds are healed and your weariness refreshed,—return to this wild rock, and lay my bones in the grave, and say a prayer over them."

An almost superstitious regard, arising perhaps from the customs of the Indians, whose war was with the dead as well as the living, was paid by the frontier inhabitants to the rites of sepulture; and there are many instances of the sacrifice of life in the attempt to bury those who had fallen by the "sword of the wilderness." Reuben, therefore, felt the full importance of the promise which he most solemnly made to return and perform Roger Malvin's obsequies. It was remarkable that the latter, speaking his whole heart in his parting words, no longer endeavored to persuade the youth that even the speediest succor might avail to the preservation of his life. Reuben was internally convinced that he should see Malvin's living face no more. His generous nature would fain have delayed him, at whatever risk, till the dying scene were past; but the desire of existence and the hope of happiness had strengthened in his heart, and he was unable to resist them.

"It is enough," said Roger Malvin, having listened to Reuben's promise. "Go, and God speed you!"

The youth pressed his hand in silence, turned and was departing. His slow and faltering steps, however, had borne him but a little way before Malvin's voice recalled him.

"Reuben, Reuben," said he, faintly; and Reuben returned and knelt down by the dying man.

"Raise me, and let me lean against the rock," was his last request. "My face will be turned towards home, and I shall see you a moment longer as you pass among the trees."

Reuben, having made the desired alteration in his companion's posture, again began his solitary pilgrimage. He walked more hastily at first than was consistent with his strength; for a sort of guilty feeling, which sometimes torments men in their most justifiable acts, caused him to seek concealment from Malvin's eyes; but after he had trodden far upon the rustling leaves he crept back, impelled by a wild and painful curiosity, and, sheltered by the earthly roots of an uptorn tree, gazed earnestly at the desolate man. The morning sun was unclouded, and the trees and shrubs imbibed the sweet air of the month of May; yet there seemed a gloom on Nature's face, as if she sympathized with mortal pain and sorrow. Roger Malvin's hands were uplifted in a fervent prayer, some of the words of which stole through the stillness of the woods and entered Reuben's heart, torturing it with an unutterable pang. They were the broken accents of a petition for his own happiness and that of Dorcas; and, as the youth listened, conscience, or something in its similitude, pleaded strongly with him to return and lie down again by the rock. He felt how hard was the doom of the kind and generous being whom he had de-

serted in his extremity. Death would come like the slow approach of a corpse, stealing gradually towards him through the forest, and showing its ghastly and motionless features from behind a nearer and yet a nearer tree. But such must have been Reuben's own fate had he tarried another sunset; and who shall impute blame to him if he shrink from so useless a sacrifice? As he gave a parting look, a breeze waved the little banner upon the sapling oak and reminded Reuben of his vow.

Many circumstances combined to retard the wounded traveller in his way to the frontiers. On the second day the clouds, gathering densely over the sky, precluded the possibility of regulating his course by the position of the sun; and he knew not but that every effort of his almost exhausted strength was removing him farther from the home he sought. His scanty sustenance was supplied by the berries and other spontaneous products of the forest. Herds of deer, it is true, sometimes bounded past him, and partridges frequently whirred up before his footsteps; but his ammunition had been expended in the fight, and he had no means of slaying them. His wounds, irritated by the constant exertion in which lay the only hope of life, wore away his strength and at intervals confused his reason. But, even in the wanderings of intellect, Reuben's young heart clung strongly to existence; and it was only through absolute incapacity of motion that he at last sank down beneath a tree, compelled there to await death.

In this situation he was discovered by a party who, upon the first intelligence of the fight, had been despatched to the relief of the survivors. They conveyed him to the nearest settlement, which chanced to be that of his own residence.

Dorcas, in the simplicity of the olden time, watched by the bedside of her wounded lover and administered all those comforts that are in the sole gift of woman's heart and hand. During several days Reuben's recollection strayed drowsily among the perils and hardships through which he had passed, and he was incapable of returning definite answers to the inquiries with which many were eager to harass him. No authentic particulars of the battle had yet been circulated; nor could mothers, wives, and children tell whether their loved ones were detained by captivity or by the stronger chain of death. Dorcas nourished her apprehensions in silence till one afternoon when Reuben awoke from an unquiet sleep, and seemed to recognize her more perfectly than at any previous time. She saw that his intellect had become composed, and she could no longer restrain her filial anxiety.

"My father, Reuben?" she began; but the change in her lover's countenance made her pause.

The youth shrank as if with a bitter pain, and the

blood gushed vividly into his wan and hollow cheeks. His first impulse was to cover his face; but, apparently with a desperate effort, he half raised himself and spoke vehemently, defending himself against an imaginary accusation.

"Your father was sore wounded in the battle, Dorcas; and he bade me not burden myself with him, but only to lead him to the lakeside, that he might quench his thirst and die. But I would not desert the old man in his extremity, and, though bleeding myself, I supported him; I gave him half my strength, and led him away with me. For three days we journeyed on together, and your father was sustained beyond my hopes; but, awaking at sunrise on the fourth day, I found him faint and exhausted; he was unable to proceed; his life had ebbed away fast; and—"

"He died!" exclaimed Dorcas, faintly.

Reuben felt it impossible to acknowledge that his selfish love of life had hurried him away before her father's fate was decided. He spoke not; he only bowed his head; and, between shame and exhaustion, sank back and hid his face in the pillow. Dorcas wept when her fears were thus confirmed; but the shock, as it had been long anticipated, was on that account the less violent.

"You dug a grave for my poor father in the wilderness, Reuben?" was the question by which her filial piety manifested itself.

"My hands were weak; but I did what I could," replied the youth in a smothered tone. "There stands a noble tombstone above his head; and I would to Heaven I slept as soundly as he!"

Dorcas, perceiving the wildness of his latter words, inquired no further at the time; but her heart found ease in the thought that Roger Malvin had not lacked such funeral rites as it was possible to bestow. The tale of Reuben's courage and fidelity lost nothing when she communicated it to her friends; and the poor youth, tottering from his sick chamber to breathe the sunny air, experienced from every tongue the miserable and humiliating torture of unmerited praise. All acknowledged that he might worthily demand the hand of the fair maiden to whose father he had been "faithful unto death;" and, as my tale is not of love, it shall suffice to say that in the space of a few months Reuben became the husband of Dorcas Malvin. During the marriage ceremony the bride was covered with blushes; but the bridegroom's face was pale.

There was now in the breast of Reuben Bourne an incommunicable thought—something which he was to conceal most heedfully from her whom he most loved and trusted. He regretted, deeply and bitterly, the moral cowardice that had restrained his words when he was about to disclose the truth to Dorcas; but pride, the fear of losing her affection, the dread of universal scorn forbade him to rectify this falsehood. He felt that for leaving Roger Malvin he deserved no censure. His presence, the gratuitous sacrifice of his own life, would have added only another and a needless agony to the last moments of the dying man; but concealment had imparted to a justifiable act much of the secret effect of guilt; and Reuben, while reason told him that he had done right, experienced in no small degree the mental horrors which punish the perpetrator of undiscovered crime. By a certain association of ideas, he at times almost imagined himself a murderer. For years, also, a thought would occasionally recur, which, though he perceived all its folly and extravagance, he had not power to banish from his mind. It was a haunting and torturing fancy that his father-in-law was yet sitting at the foot of the rock, on the withered forest leaves, alive, and awaiting his pledged assistance. These mental deceptions, however, came and went, nor did he ever mistake them for realities; but in the calmest and clearest moods of his mind he was conscious that he had a deep vow unredeemed, and that an unburied corpse was calling to him out of the wilderness. Yet such was the consequence of his prevarication that he could not obey the call. It was now too late to require the assistance of Roger Malvin's friends in performing his long-deferred sepulture; and superstitious fears, of which none were more susceptible than the people of the outward settlements, forbade Reuben to go alone. Neither did he know where in the pathless and illimitable forest to seek that smooth and lettered rock at the base of which the body lay: his remembrance of every portion of his travel thence was indistinct, and the latter part had left no impression upon his mind. There was, however, a continual impulse, a voice audible only to himself, commanding him to go forth and redeem his vow; and he had a strange impression that, were he to make the trial, he would be led straight to Malvin's bones. But year after year that summons, unheard but felt, was disobeyed. His one secret thought became like a chain binding down his spirit and like a serpent gnawing into his heart; and he was transformed into a sad and downcast yet irritable man.

In the course of a few years after their marriage changes began to be visible in the external prosperity of Reuben and Dorcas. The only riches of the former had been his stout heart and strong arm; but the latter, her father's sole heiress, had made her husband master of a farm, under older cultivation, larger, and better stocked than most of the frontier establishments. Reuben Bourne, however, was a neglectful husbandman; and, while the lands of the other settlers became annually more fruitful, his deteriorated in the same proportion. The discouragements to agriculture were greatly lessened by the cessation of Indian war, during which men held the plough in one hand and the musket in the other, and were fortunate if the products of their dangerous labor were not destroyed, either in the field or in the barn, by the savage enemy. But Reuben did not profit by the altered condition of the country; nor can it be denied that his intervals of industrious attention to his affairs were but scantily rewarded with success. The irritability by which he had recently become distinguished, was another cause of his declining prosperity, as it occasioned frequent quarrels in his unavoidable intercourse with the neighboring settlers. The results of these were innumerable lawsuits; for the people of New England, in the earliest stages and wildest circumstances of the country, adopted, whenever attainable, the legal mode of deciding their differences. To be brief, the world did not go well with Reuben Bourne; and, though not till many years after his marriage, he was finally a ruined man, with but one remaining expedient against the evil fate that had pursued him. He was to throw sunlight into some deep recess of the forest, and seek subsistence from the virgin bosom of the wilderness.

The only child of Reuben and Dorcas was a son, now arrived at the age of fifteen years, beautiful in youth, and giving promise of a glorious manhood. He was peculiarly qualified for, and already began to excel in, the wild accomplishments of frontier life. His foot was fleet, his aim true, his apprehension quick, his heart glad and high; and all who anticipated the return of Indian war spoke of Cyrus Bourne as a future leader in the land. The boy was loved by his father with a deep and silent strength, as if whatever was good and happy in his own nature had been transferred to his child, carrying his affections with it. Even Dorcas, though loving and beloved, was far less dear to him; for Reuben's secret thoughts and insulated emotions had gradually made him a selfish man, and he could no longer love deeply except where he saw or imagined some reflection or likeness of his own mind. In Cyrus he recognized what he had himself been in other days; and at intervals he seemed to partake of the boy's spirit and to be revived with a fresh and happy life. Reuben was accompanied by his son in the expedition, for the purpose of selecting a tract of land and felling and burning the timber, which necessarily preceded the removal of the household gods. Two months of autumn were thus occupied after which Reuben Bourne and his young hunter returned to spend their last winter in the settlements.

It was early in the month of May that the little family snapped asunder whatever tendrils of affections had clung to inanimate objects, and bade farewell to the few who, in the blight of fortune, called themselves their friends. The sadness of the parting moment had, to each of the pilgrims, its peculiar alleviations. Reuben, a moody man, and misanthrop-

ic because unhappy, strode onward with his usual stern brow and downcast eye, feeling few regrets and disdaining to acknowledge any. Dorcas, while she wept abundantly over the broken ties by which her simple and affectionate nature had bound itself to every thing, felt that the inhabitants of her inmost heart moved on with her, and that all else would be supplied wherever she might go. And the boy dashed one teardrop from his eye, and thought of the adventurous pleasures of the untrodden forest.

O, who, in the enthusiasm of a daydream, has not wished that he were a wanderer in a world of summer wilderness, with one fair and gentle being hanging lightly on his arm? In youth his free and exulting step would know no barrier but the rolling ocean or the snow-topped mountains; a calmer manhood would choose a home where Nature had strewn a double wealth in the vale of some transparent stream; and when hoary age, after long, long years of that pure life, stole on and found him there, it would find him the father of a race, the patriarch of a people, the founder of a mighty nation yet to be. When death, like the sweet sleep which we welcome after a day of happiness, came over him, his far descendants would mourn over the venerated dust. Enveloped by tradition in mysterious attributes, the men of future generations would call him god-like; and remote posterity would see him standing, dimly glorious, far up the valley of a hundred centuries.

The tangled and gloomy forest through which the personages of my tale were wandering differed widely from the dreamer's land of fantasy; yet there was something in their way of life that Nature asserted as her own, and the gnawing cares which went with them from the world were all that now obstructed their happiness. One stout and shaggy steed, the bearer of all their wealth, did not shrink from the added weight of Dorcas; although her hardy breeding sustained her, during the latter part of each day's journey, by her husband's side. Reuben and his son, their muskets on their shoulders and their axes slung behind them, kept an unwearied pace, each watching with a hunter's eye for the game that supplied their food. When hunger bade, they halted and prepared their meal on the bank of some unpolluted forest brook, which, as they knelt down with thirsty lips to drink, murmured a sweet unwillingness, like a maiden at love's first kiss. They slept beneath a hut of branches, and awoke at peep of light refreshed for the toils of another day. Dorcas and the boy went on joyously, and even Reuben's spirit shone at intervals with an outward gladness; but inwardly there was a cold, cold sorrow, which he compared to the snow-drifts lying deep in the glens and hollows of the rivulets while the leaves were brightly green above.

Cyrus Bourne was sufficiently skilled in the travel

of the woods to observe that his father did not adhere to the course they had pursued in their expedition of the preceding autumn. They were now keeping farther to the north, striking out more directly from the settlements, and into a region of which savage beasts and savage men were as yet the sole possessors. The boy sometimes hinted his opinions upon the subject, and Reuben listened attentively, and once or twice altered the direction of their march in accordance with his son's counsel; but, having so done, he seemed ill at ease. His quick and wandering glances were sent forward, apparently in search of enemies lurking behind the tree trunks; and, seeing nothing there, he would cast his eyes backwards as if in fear of some pursuer. Cyrus, perceiving that his father gradually resumed the old direction, forbore to interfere; nor, though something began to weigh upon his heart, did his adventurous nature permit him to regret the increased length and the mystery of their way.

On the afternoon of the fifth day they halted, and made their simple encampment nearly an hour before sunset. The face of the country, for the last few miles, had been diversified by swells of land resembling huge waves of a petrified sea; and in one of the corresponding hollows, a wild and romantic spot, had the family reared their hut and kindled their fire. There is something chilling, and yet heartwarming, in the thought of these three, united by strong bands of love and insulated from all that breathe beside. The dark and gloomy pines looked down upon them, and, as the wind swept through their tops, a pitying sound was heard in the forest; or did those old trees groan in fear that men were come to lay the axe to their roots at last? Reuben and his son, while Dorcas made ready their meal, proposed to wander out in search of game, of which that day's march had afforded no supply. The boy, promising not to quit the vicinity of the encampment, bounded off with a step as light and elastic as that of the deer he hoped to slay; while his father, feeling a transient happiness as he gazed after him, was about to pursue an opposite direction. Dorcas, in the meanwhile, had seated herself near their fire of fallen branches, upon the mossgrown and mouldering trunk of a tree uprooted years before. Her employment, diversified by an occasional glance at the pot, now beginning to simmer over the blaze, was the perusal of the current year's Massachusetts Almanac, which, with the exception of an old blackletter Bible, comprised all the literary wealth of the family. None pay a greater regard to arbitrary divisions of time than those who are excluded from society; and Dorcas mentioned, as if the information were of importance, that it was now the twelfth of May. Her husband started.

"The twelfth of May! I should remember it well," muttered he, while many thoughts occasioned a momentary confusion in his mind. "Where am I? Whither am I wandering? Where did I leave him?"

Dorcas, too well accustomed to her husband's wayward moods to note any peculiarity of demeanor, now laid aside the almanac and addressed him in that mournful tone which the tender hearted appropriate to griefs long cold and dead.

"It was near this time of the month, eighteen years ago, that my poor father left this world for a better. He had a kind arm to hold his head and a kind voice to cheer him. Reuben, in his last moments; and the thought of the faithful care you took of him has comforted me many a time since. O, death would have been awful to a solitary man in a wild place like this!"

"Pray Heaven, Dorcas," said Reuben, in a broken voice,—"pray Heaven that neither of us three dies solitary and lies unburied in this howling wilderness!" And he hastened away, leaving her to watch the fire beneath the gloomy pines.

Reuben Bourne's rapid pace gradually slackened as the pang, unintentionally inflicted by the words of Dorcas, became less acute. Many strange reflections, however, thronged upon him; and, straying onward rather like a sleep walker than a hunter, it was attributable to no care of his own that his devious course kept him in the vicinity of the encampment. His steps were imperceptibly led almost in a circle; nor did he observe that he was on the verge of a tract of land heavily timbered, but not with pine trees. The place of the latter was here supplied by oaks and other of the harder woods; and around their roots clustered a dense and bushy undergrowth, leaving, however, barren spaces between the trees, thick strewn with withered leaves. Whenever the rustling of the branches or the creaking of the trunks made a sound, as if the forest were waking from slumber, Reuben instinctively raised the musket that rested on his arm, and cast a quick, sharp glance on every side; but, convinced by a partial observation that no animal was near, he would again give himself up to his thoughts. He was musing on the strange influence that had led him away from his premeditated course and so far into the depths of the wilderness. Unable to penetrate to the secret place of his soul where his motives lay hidden, he believed that a supernatural voice had called him onward and that a supernatural power had obstructed his retreat. He trusted that it was Heaven's intent to afford him an opportunity of expiating his sin; he hoped that he might find the bones so long unburied; and that, having laid the earth over them, peace would throw its sunlight into the sepulchre of his heart. From these thoughts he was aroused by a rustling in the forest at some distance from the spot to which he had wandered. Perceiving the motion of some object behind a thick veil of undergrowth, he fired, with the instinct of a hunter and the aim of a practiced marksman. A low moan, which told his success, and by which even animals can express their dying agony, was unheeded by Reuben Bourne. What were the recollections now breaking upon him?

The thicket into which Reuben had fired was near the summit of a swell of land, and was clustered around the base of a rock, which, in the shape and smoothness of one of its surfaces, was not unlike a gigantic gravestone. As if reflected in a mirror, its likeness was in Reuben's memory. He even recognized the veins which seemed to form an inscription in forgotten characters; everything remained the same, except that a thick covert of bushes shrouded the lower part of the rock, and would have hidden Roger Malvin had he still been sitting there. Yet in the next moment Reuben's eye was caught by another change that time had effected since he last stood where he was now standing again behind the earthy roots of the uptorn tree. The sapling to which he had bound the blood-stained symbol of his vow had increased and strengthened into an oak, far indeed from its maturity, but with no mean spread of shadowy branches. There was one singularity observable in this tree which made Reuben tremble. The middle and lower branches were in luxuriant life, and an excess of vegetation had fringed the trunk almost to the ground; but a blight had apparently stricken the upper part of the oak, and the very topmost bough was withered, sapless, and utterly dead. Reuben remembered how the little banner had fluttered on that topmost bough, when it was green and lovely, eighteen years before. Whose guilt had blasted it?

Dorcas, after the departure of the two hunters, continued her preparations for their evening repast. Her sylvan table was the moss-covered trunk of a large fallen tree, on the broadest part of which she had spread a snow-white cloth and arranged what were left of the bright pewter vessels that had been her pride in the settlements. It had a strange aspect, that one little spot of homely comfort in the desolate heart of Nature. The sunshine yet lingered upon the higher branches of the trees that grew on rising ground; but the shadows of evening had deepened into the hollow where the encampment was made, and the firelight began to redden as it gleamed up the tall trunks of the pines or hovered on the dense and obscure mass of foliage that circled round the spot. The heart of Dorcas was not sad; for she felt that it was better to journey in the wilderness with two whom she loved than to be a lonely woman in a crowd that cared not for her. As she busied herself in arranging seats of mouldering wood, covered with leaves, for Reuben and her son, her voice danced through the gloomy forest in the measure of a song that she had learned in youth. The rude melody, the

production of a bard who won no name, was descriptive of a winter evening in a frontier cottage, when, secured from savage inroad by the high-piled snow-drifts, the family rejoiced by their own fireside. The whole song possessed the nameless charm peculiar to unborrowed thought; but four continually-recurring lines shone out from the rest like the blaze of the hearth whose joys they celebrated. Into them, working magic with a few simple words, the poet had instilled the very essence of domestic love and household happiness, and they were poetry and picture joined in one. As Dorcas sang, the walls of her forsaken home seemed to encircle her; she no longer saw the gloomy pines, nor heard the wind which still, as she began each verse, sent a heavy breath through the branches, and died away in a hollow moan from the burden of the song. She was aroused by the report of a gun in the vicinity of the encampment; and either the sudden sound or her loneliness by the glowing fire caused her to tremble violently. The next moment she laughed in the pride of a mother's heart.

"My beautiful young hunter! My boy has slain a deer!" she exclaimed, recollecting that in the direction whence the shot proceeded Cyrus had gone to the chase.

She waited a reasonable time to hear her son's light step bounding over the rustling leaves to tell of his success. But he did not immediately appear; and she sent her cheerful voice among the trees in search of him.

"Cyrus! Cyrus!"

His coming was still delayed; and she determined, as the report had apparently been very near, to seek for him in person. Her assistance, also, might be necessary in bringing home the venison which she flattered herself he had obtained. She therefore set forward, directing her steps by the long-past sound, and singing as she went, in order that the boy might be aware of her approach and run to meet her. From behind the trunk of every tree, and from every hiding-place in the thick foliage of the undergrowth she hoped to discover the countenance of her son, laughing with the sportive mischief that is born of affection. The sun was now beneath the horizon, and the light that came down among the leaves was sufficiently dim to create many illusions in her expecting fancy. Several times she seemed indistinctly to see his face gazing out from among the leaves; and once she imagined that he stood beckoning to her at the base of a craggy rock. Keeping her eyes on this object, however, it proved to be no more than the trunk of an oak, fringed to the very ground with little branches, one of which, thrust out farther than the rest, was shaken by the breeze. Making her way round the foot of the rock, she suddenly found herself close to her husband, who had approached in another direction. Leaning

THE TREE

upon the butt of his gun, the muzzle of which rested upon the withered leaves, he was apparently absorbed in the contemplation of some object at his feet.

"How is this, Reuben? Have you slain the deer and fallen asleep over him?" exclaimed Dorcas, laughing cheerfully, on her first slight observation of his posture and appearance.

He stirred not, neither did he turn his eyes towards her; and a cold, shuddering fear, indefinite in its source and object, began to creep into her blood. She now perceived that her husband's face was ghastly pale, and his features were rigid, as if incapable of assuming any other expression than the strong despair which had hardened upon them. He gave not the slightest evidence that he was aware of her approach.

"For the love of Heaven, Reuben, speak to me!" cried Dorcas; and the strange sound of her own voice affrighted her even more than the dead silence.

Her husband started, stared into her face, drew her to the front of the rock, and pointed with his finger.

O, there lay the boy, asleep, but dreamless, upon the fallen forest leaves! His cheek rested upon his arm—his curled locks were thrown back from his brow—his limbs were slightly relaxed. Had a sudden weariness overcome the youthful hunter? Would his mother's voice arouse him? She knew that it was death.

"This broad rock is the gravestone of your near kindred, Dorcas," said her husband. "Your tears will fall at once over your father and your son."

She heard him not. With one wild shriek, that seemed to force its way from the sufferer's inmost soul, she sank insensible by the side of her dead boy. At that moment the withered topmost bough of the oak loosened itself in the stilly air, and fell in soft, light fragments upon the leaves, upon Reuben, upon his wife and child, and upon Roger Malvin's bones. Then Reuben's heart was stricken, and the tears gushed out like water from a rock. The vow that the wounded youth had made the blighted man had come to redeem. His sin was expiated—the curse was gone from him; and in the hour when he had shed blood dearer to him than his own, a prayer, the first for years, went up to Heaven from the lips of Reuben Bourne.

1832

The May-pole of Merry Mount

Hawthorne here uses the Puritan past to dramatize and interpret a conflict between "Jollity" and "Gloom." With freedom, saturnalian indulgence, pleasure, growth, and fertility on the one side, and with restraint, order, stability, self-denial, and morality on the other, the conflict may seem simplistic. Hawthorne, however, has written a tale about a complex psychological and moral opposition. As in all his historical tales, his use of the past is essentially an attempt to understand the present through it. His interpretation of Merry Mount should be compared with the account William Bradford gives in his history of Plymouth Plantation. Text: From the author's revised edition of *Twice-Told Tales* (Boston, 1851).

Bright were the days at Merry Mount, when the May-pole was the banner-staff of that gay colony! They who reared it, should their banner be triumphant, were to pour sunshine over New England's rugged hills, and scatter flower-seeds throughout the soil. Jollity and gloom were contending for an empire. Midsummer eve had come, bringing deep verdure to the forest, and roses in her lap, of a more vivid hue than the tender buds of Spring. But May, or her mirthful spirit, dwelt all the year round at Merry Mount, sporting with the Summer months, and revelling with Autumn, and basking in the glow of Winter's fireside. Through a world of toil and care she flitted with a dreamlike smile, and came hither to find a home among the lightsome hearts of Merry Mount.

Never had the May-pole been so gayly decked as at sunset on midsummer eve. This venerated emblem was a pine-tree, which had preserved the slender grace of youth, while it equalled the loftiest height of the old wood monarchs. From its top streamed a silken banner, colored like the rainbow. Down nearly to the ground, the pole was dressed with birchen boughs, and others of the liveliest green, and some with silvery leaves, fastened by ribbons that fluttered in fantastic knots of twenty different colors, but no sad ones. Garden flowers, and blossoms of the wilderness, laughed gladly forth amid the verdure, so fresh and dewy that they must have grown by magic on that happy pine tree. Where this green and flowery splendor terminated, the shaft of the May-pole was stained with the seven brilliant hues of the banner at its top. On the lowest green bough hung an abundant wreath of roses, some that had been gathered in the sunniest spots of the forest, and others, of still richer blush, which the colonists had reared from English seed. O, people of the Golden Age, the chief of your husbandry was to raise flowers!

But what was the wild throng that stood hand in hand about the May-pole? It could not be, that the fauns and nymphs, when driven from their classic groves and homes of ancient fable, had sought refuge, as all the persecuted did, in the fresh woods of the West. These were the Gothic monsters, though perhaps of Grecian ancestry. On the shoulders of a comely youth, uprose the head and branching antlers of a stag; a second, human in all other points, had the grim visage of a wolf; a third, still with the trunk and limbs of a mortal man, showed the beard and horns of a venerable he-goat. There was the likeness of a bear erect, brute in all but his hind legs, which were adorned with pink silk stockings. And here again, almost as wondrous, stood a real bear of the dark forest, lending each of his fore paws to the grasp of a human hand, and as ready for the dance as any in that circle. His inferior nature rose half way, to meet his companions as they stooped. Other faces wore the similitude of man or woman, but distorted or extravagant, with red noses pendulous before their mouths, which seemed of awful depth, and stretched from ear to ear in an eternal fit of laughter. Here might be seen the Salvage Man, well known in heraldry, hairy as a baboon, and girdled with green leaves. By his side, a nobler figure, but still a counterfeit, appeared an Indian hunter, with feathery crest and wampum belt. Many of this strange company wore fools-caps, and had little bells appended to their garments, tinkling with a silvery sound, responsive to the inaudible music of their gleesome spirits. Some youths and maidens were of soberer garb, yet well maintained their places in the irregular throng, by the expression of wild revelry upon their features. Such were the colonists of Merry Mount, as they stood in the broad smile of sunset, round their venerated May-pole.

Had a wanderer, bewildered in the melancholy forest, heard their mirth, and stolen a half-affrighted glance, he might have fancied them the crew of Comus, some already transformed to brutes, some midway between man and beast, and the others rioting in the flow of tipsy jollity that foreran the change. But a band of Puritans, who watched the scene, invisible themselves, compared the masques to those devils and ruined souls with whom their superstition peopled the black wilderness.

Within the ring of monsters, appeared the two airiest forms, that had ever trodden on any more solid footing than a purple and golden cloud. One was a youth in glistening apparel, with a scarf of the rainbow pattern crosswise on his breast. His right hand held a gilded staff, the ensign of high dignity among the revellers, and his left grasped the slender fingers of a fair maiden, not less gayly decorated than himself. Bright roses glowed in contrast with the dark and glossy curls of each, and were scattered round their feet, or had sprung up spontaneously there. Behind this lightsome couple, so close to the May-pole that its boughs shaded his jovial face, stood the figure of an English priest, canonically dressed, yet decked with flowers, in heathen fashion, and wearing a chaplet of the native vine leaves. By the riot of his rolling eye, and the pagan decorations of his holy garb, he seemed the wildest monster there, and the very Comus of the crew.

"Votaries of the May-pole," cried the flower-decked priest, "merrily, all day long, have the woods echoed to your mirth. But be this your merriest hour, my hearts! Lo, here stand the Lord and Lady of the May, whom I, a clerk of Oxford, and high priest of Merry Mount, am presently to join in holy matrimony. Up with your nimble spirits, ye morris-dancers, green men, and glee maidens, bears and wolves, and horned gentlemen! Come; a chorus now, rich with the old mirth of Merry England, and the wilder glee of this fresh forest; and then a dance, to show the youthful pair what life is made of, and how airily they should go through it! All ye that love the May-pole, lend your voices to the nuptial song of the Lord and Lady of the May!"

This wedlock was more serious than most affairs of Merry Mount, where jest and delusion, trick and fantasy, kept up a continual carnival. The Lord and Lady of the May, though their titles must be laid down at sunset, were really and truly to be partners for the dance of life, beginning the measure that same bright eve. The wreath of roses, that hung from the lowest green bough of the May-pole, had been twined for them, and would be thrown over both their heads, in symbol of their flowery union. When the priest had spoken, therefore, a riotous uproar burst from the rout of monstrous figures.

"Begin you the stave, reverend Sir," cried they all; "and never did the woods ring to such a merry peal as we of the May-pole shall send up!"

Immediately a prelude of pipe, cithern, and viol, touched with practised minstrelsy, began to play from a neighboring thicket, in such a mirthful cadence, that the boughs of the May-pole quivered to the sound. But the May Lord, he of the gilded staff, chancing to look into his Lady's eyes, was wonder-struck at the almost pensive glance that met his own.

"Edith, sweet Lady of the May," whispered he, reproachfully, "is yon wreath of roses a garland to hang above our graves, that you look so sad? O, Edith, this is our golden time! Tarnish it not by any pensive shadow of the mind; for it may be, that nothing of futurity will be brighter than the mere remembrance of what is now passing."

"That was the very thought that saddened me! How came it in your mind too?" said Edith, in a still lower tone than he; for it was high treason to be sad at Merry Mount. "Therefore do I sigh amid this festive music. And besides, dear Edgar, I struggle as with a dream, and fancy that these shapes of our jovial friends are visionary, and their mirth unreal, and that we are no true Lord and Lady of the May. What is the mystery in my heart?"

Just then, as if a spell had loosened them, down came a little shower of withering rose leaves from the May-pole. Alas, for the young lovers! No sooner had their hearts glowed with real passion than they were sensible of something vague and unsubstantial in their former pleasures, and felt a dreary presentiment of inevitable change. From the moment that they truly loved, they had subjected themselves to earth's doom of care and sorrow, and troubled joy, and had no more a home at Merry Mount. That was Edith's mystery. Now leave we the priest to marry them, and the masquers to sport round the Maypole, till the last sunbeam be withdrawn from its summit, and the shadows of the forest mingle gloomily in the dance. Meanwhile, we may discover who these gay people were.

Two hundred years ago, and more, the old world and its inhabitants became mutually weary of each other. Men voyaged by thousands to the West; some to barter glass beads, and such like jewels, for the furs of the Indian hunter; some to conquer virgin empires; and one stern band to pray. But none of these motives had much weight with the colonists of Merry Mount. Their leaders were men who had sported so long with life, that when Thought and Wisdom came, even these unwelcome guests were led astray by the crowd of vanities which they should have put to flight. Erring Thought and perverted Wisdom were made to put on masques, and play the fool. The men of whom we speak, after losing the heart's fresh gayety, imagined a wild philosophy of pleasure, and came hither to act out their latest day-dream. They gathered followers from all that giddy tribe, whose whole life is like the festal days of soberer men. In their train were minstrels, not unknown in London streets; wandering players, whose theatres had been the halls of noblemen; mummers, rope-dancers, and mountebanks, who would long be missed at wakes, church ales, and fairs; in a word, mirth makers of every sort, such as abounded in that age, but now began to be discountenanced by the rapid growth of Puritanism. Light had their footsteps been on land, and as lightly they came across the sea. Many had been maddened by their previous troubles into a gay despair; others were as madly gay in the flush of youth, like the May Lord and his Lady; but whatever might be the quality of their mirth, old and young were gay at Merry Mount. The young deemed themselves happy. The elder spirits, if they knew that mirth was but the counterfeit of happiness, yet followed the false shadow wilfully, because at least her garments glittered brightest. Sworn triflers of a lifetime, they would not venture among the sober truths of life, not even to be truly blest.

All the hereditary pastimes of Old England were transplanted hither. The King of Christmas was duly crowned, and the Lord of Misrule bore potent sway. On the Eve of St. John, they felled whole acres of the forest to make bonfires, and danced by the blaze all night, crowned with garlands, and throwing flowers into the flame. At harvest time, though their crop was of the smallest, they made an image with the sheaves of Indian corn, and wreathed it with autumnal garlands, and bore it home triumphantly. But what chiefly characterized the colonists of Merry Mount, was their veneration for the Maypole. It has made their true history a poet's tale. Spring decked the hallowed emblem with young blossoms and fresh green boughs; Summer brought roses of the deepest blush, and the perfected foliage of the forest; Autumn enriched it with that red and yellow gorgeousness, which converts each wildwood leaf into a painted flower; and Winter silvered it with sleet, and hung it round with icicles, till it flashed in the cold sunshine, itself a frozen sunbeam. Thus each alternate season did homage to the Maypole, and paid it a tribute of its own richest splendor. Its votaries danced round it, once, at least, in every month; sometimes they called it their religion, or their altar; but always it was the banner-staff of Merry Mount.

Unfortunately, there were men in the new world, of a sterner faith than these May-pole worshippers. Not far from Merry Mount was a settlement of Puritans, most dismal wretches, who said their prayers before daylight, and then wrought in the forest or the cornfield, till evening made it prayer time again. Their weapons were always at hand, to shoot down the straggling savage. When they met in conclave, it was never to keep up the old English mirth, but to hear sermons three hours long, or to proclaim bounties on the heads of wolves and the scalps of Indians. Their festivals were fast days, and their chief pastime the singing of psalms. Woe to the youth or maiden, who did but dream of a dance! The selectman nodded to the constable; and there sat the light-heeled reprobate in the stocks; or if he danced, it was round the whipping-post, which might be termed the Puritan May-pole.

A party of these grim Puritans, toiling through the difficult woods, each with a horseload of iron armor to burden his footsteps, would sometimes draw near the sunny precincts of Merry Mount. There were the silken colonists, sporting round their May-pole; perhaps teaching a bear to dance, or striving to communicate their mirth to the grave Indian; or masquerading in the skins of deer and wolves, which they had hunted for that especial purpose. Often, the whole colony were playing at blindman's buff, magistrates and all, with their eyes bandaged, except a single scape-goat, whom the blinded sinners pursued by the tinkling of the bells at his garments. Once, it is said, they were seen following a flower-decked corpse, with merriment and festive music, to his grave. But did the dead man laugh? In their quietest times, they sang ballads and told tales, for the edification of their pious visitors; or perplexed them with juggling tricks; or grinned at them through horse-collars; and when sport itself grew wearisome, they made game of their own stupidity, and began a yawning match. At the very least of these enormities, the men of iron shook their heads and frowned so darkly, that the revellers looked up, imagining that a momentary cloud had overcast the sunshine, which was to be perpetual there. On the other hand, the Puritans affirmed, that, when a psalm was pealing from their place of worship, the echo which the forest sent them back, seemed often like the chorus of a jolly catch, closing with a roar of laughter. Who but the fiend, and his bond-slaves, the crew of Merry Mount, had thus disturbed them? In due time, a feud arose, stern and bitter on one side, and as serious on the other as anything could be among such light spirits as had sworn allegiance to the May-pole. The future complexion of New England was involved in this important quarrel. Should the grizzly saints establish their jurisdiction over the gay sinners, then would their spirits darken all the clime, and make it a land of clouded visages, of hard toil, of sermon and psalm forever. But should the banner-staff of Merry Mount be fortunate, sunshine would break upon the hills, and flowers would beautify the forest and late posterity do homage to the May-pole.

After these authentic passages from history, we return to the nuptials of the Lord and Lady of the May. Alas! we have delayed too long, and must darken our tale too suddenly. As we glance again at the May-pole, a solitary sunbeam is fading from the summit, and leaves only a faint, golden tinge, blended with the hues of the rainbow banner. Even that dim light is now withdrawn, relinquishing the whole domain of Merry Mount to the evening gloom, which has rushed so instantaneously from the black surrounding woods. But some of these black shadows have rushed forth in human shape.

Yes, with the setting sun, the last day of mirth had passed from Merry Mount. The ring of gay masquers was disordered and broken; the stag lowered his antlers in dismay; the wolf grew weaker than a lamb; the bells of the morris dancers tinkled with tremulous affright. The Puritans had played a characteristic part in the May-pole mummeries. Their darksome figures were intermixed with the wild shapes of their foes, and made the scene a picture of the moment, when waking thoughts start up amid the scattered fantasies of a dream. The leader of the hostile party stood in the center of the circle, while the route of monsters cowered around him, like evil spirits in the presence of a dread magician. No fantastic foolery could look him in the face. So stern was the energy of his aspect, that the whole man, visage, frame and soul, seemed wrought of iron, gifted with life and thought, yet all of one substance with his headpiece and breastplate. It was the Puritan of Puritans; it was Endicott himself!

"Stand off, priest of Baal!" said he, with a grim frown, and laying no reverent hand upon the surplice. "I know thee, Blackstone![1] Thou art the man, who couldst not abide the rule even of thine own corrupted church, and hast come hither to preach iniquity, and to give example of it in thy life. But now shall it be seen that the Lord hath sanctified this wilderness for his peculiar people. Woe unto them that would defile it! And first, for this flower-decked abomination, the altar of thy worship!"

And with his keen sword, Endicott assaulted the hallowed May-pole. Nor long did it resist his arm. It groaned with a dismal sound; it showered leaves and rosebuds upon the remorseless enthusiast; and finally, with all its green boughs, and ribands, and flowers, symbolic of departed pleasures, down fell the banner-staff of Merry Mount. As it sank, tradition says, the evening sky grew darker, and the woods threw forth a more sombre shadow.

"There," cried Endicott, looking triumphantly on his work, "there lies the only May-pole in New England! The thought is strong within me, that, by its fall, is shadowed forth the fate of light and idle mirth makers, amongst us and our posterity. Amen, saith John Endicott."

"Amen!" echoed his followers.

But the votaries of the May-pole gave one groan for their idol. At the sound, the Puritan leader glanced at the crew of Comus, each a figure of broad mirth, yet, at this moment, strangely expressive of sorrow and dismay.

"Valiant captain," quoth Peter Palfrey, the Ancient of the band, "what order shall be taken with the prisoners?"

"I thought not to repent me of cutting down a May-pole," replied Endicott, "yet now I could find in my heart to plant it again, and give each of these bestial pagans one other dance round their idol. It would have served rarely for a whipping-post!"

"But there are pine-trees enow," suggested the lieutenant.

"True, good Ancient," said the leader. "Wherefore, bind the heathen crew, and bestow on them a small matter of stripes apiece, as earnest of our future justice. Set some of the rogues in the stocks to rest themselves, so soon as Providence shall bring us to one of our own well-ordered settlements, where

---

[1] Did Governor Endicott speak less positively, we should suspect a mistake here. The Rev. Mr. Blackstone, though an eccentric, is not known to have been an immoral man. We rather doubt his identity with the priest of Merry Mount. [Hawthorne's note.]

such accommodations may be found. Further penalties, such as branding and cropping of ears, shall be thought of hereafter."

"How many stripes for the priest?" inquired Ancient Palfrey.

"None as yet," answered Endicott, bending his iron frown upon the culprit. "It must be for the Great and General Court to determine, whether stripes and long imprisonment, and other grievous penalty, may atone for his transgressions. Let him look to himself! For such as violate our civil order, it may be permitted us to show mercy. But woe to the wretch that troubleth our religion!"

"And this dancing bear," resumed the officer. "Must he share the stripes of his fellows?"

"Shoot him through the head!" said the energetic Puritan. "I suspect witchcraft in the beast."

"Here be a couple of shining ones," continued Peter Palfrey, pointing his weapon at the Lord and Lady of the May. "They seem to be of high station among these misdoers. Methinks their dignity will not be fitted with less than a double share of stripes."

Endicott rested on his sword, and closely surveyed the dress and aspect of the hapless pair. There they stood, pale, downcast, and apprehensive. Yet there was an air of mutual support, and of pure affection, seeking aid and giving it, that showed them to be man and wife, with the sanction of a priest upon their love. The youth, in the peril of the moment, had dropped his gilded staff, and thrown his arm about the Lady of the May, who leaned against his breast, too lightly to burden him, but with weight enough to express that their destinies were linked together, for good or evil. They looked first at each other, and then into the grim captain's face. There they stood, in the first hour of wedlock, while the idle pleasures of which their companions were the emblems, had given place to the sternest cares of life, personified by the dark Puritans. But never had their youthful beauty seemed so pure and high, as when its glow was chastened by adversity.

"Youth," said Endicott, "ye stand in an evil case, thou and thy maiden wife. Make ready presently; for I am minded that ye shall both have a token to remember your wedding day!"

"Stern man," cried the May Lord, "how can I move thee? Were the means at hand, I would resist to the death. Being powerless, I entreat! Do with me as thou wilt, but let Edith go untouched!"

"Not so," replied the immitigable zealot. "We are not wont to show an idle courtesy to that sex, which requireth the stricter discipline. What sayest thou, maid? Shall thy silken bridegroom suffer thy share of the penalty, besides his own?"

"Be it death," said Edith, "and lay it all on me!"

Truly, as Endicott had said, the poor lovers stood in a woful case. Their foes were triumphant, their friends captive and abased, their home desolate, the benighted wilderness around them, and a rigorous destiny, in the shape of the Puritan leader, their only guide. Yet the deepening twilight could not altogether conceal that the iron man was softened; he smiled at the fair spectacle of early love; he almost sighed for the inevitable blight of early hopes.

"The troubles of life have come hastily on this young couple," observed Endicott, "We will see how they comport themselves under their present trials, ere we burden them with greater. If, among the spoil, there be any garments of a more decent fashion, let them be put upon the May Lord and his Lady, instead of their glistening vanities. Look to it, some of you."

"And shall not the youth's hair be cut?" asked Peter Palfrey, looking with abhorrence at the lovelock and long glossy curls of the young man.

"Crop it forthwith, and that in the true pumpkin shell fashion," answered the captain. "Then bring them along with us, but more gently than their fellows. There be qualities in the youth, which may make him valiant to fight, and sober to toil, and pious to pray; and in the maiden, that may fit her to become a mother in our Israel, bringing up babes in better nurture than her own hath been. Nor think ye, young ones, that they are the happiest, even in our lifetime of a moment, who misspend it in dancing round a May-pole!"

And Endicott, the severest Puritan of all who laid the rock foundation of New England, lifted the wreath of roses from the ruin of the May-pole, and threw it, with his own gauntleted hand, over the heads of the Lord and Lady of the May. It was a deed of prophecy. As the moral gloom of the world overpowers all systematic gayety, even so was their home of wild mirth made desolate amid the sad forest. They returned to it no more. But as their flowery garland was wreathed of the brightest roses that had grown there, so, in the tie that united them, were intertwined all the purest and best of their early joys. They went heavenward, supporting each other along the difficult path which it was their lot to tread, and never wasted one regretful thought on the vanities of Merry Mount.

1835

The Ambitious Guest

In this story Hawthorne dramatizes his interest in the cruel ironies of life over which men have no control. Security, happiness, and the promise of life simply mask the precarious condition in which all men live. Text: From the author's revised edition of *Twice-Told Tales* (Boston, 1851).

One September night, a family had gathered round their hearth, and piled it high with the driftwood of mountain streams, the dry cones of the pine, and the splintered ruins of great trees, that had come crashing down the precipice. Up the chimney roared the fire, and brightened the room with its broad blaze. The faces of the father and mother had a sober gladness; the children laughed; the eldest daughter was the image of Happiness at seventeen; and the aged grandmother, who sat knitting in the warmest place, was the image of Happiness grown old. They had found the "herb, heart's ease," in the bleakest spot of all New England. This family were situated in the Notch of the White Hills, where the wind was sharp throughout the year, and pitilessly cold in the winter—giving their cottage all its fresh inclemency, before it descended on the valley of the Saco. They dwelt in a cold spot and a dangerous one; for a mountain towered above their heads, so steep, that the stones would often rumble down its sides, and startle them at midnight.

The daughter had just uttered some simple jest, that filled them all with mirth, when the wind came through the Notch and seemed to pause before their cottage—rattling the door, with a sound of wailing and lamentation, before it passed into the valley. For a moment, it saddened them, though there was nothing unusual in the tones. But the family were glad again, when they perceived that the latch was lifted by some traveller, whose footsteps had been unheard amid the dreary blast, which heralded his approach, and wailed as he was entering, and went moaning away from the door.

Though they dwelt in such a solitude, these people held daily converse with the world. The romantic pass of the Notch is a great artery, through which the lifeblood of internal commerce is continually throbbing, between Maine, on one side, and the Green Mountains and the shores of the St. Lawrence on the other. The stage-coach always drew up before the door of the cottage. The wayfarer, with no companion but his staff, paused here to exchange a word, that the sense of loneliness might not utterly overcome him, ere he could pass through the cleft of the mountain, or reach the first house in the valley. And here the teamster, on his way to Portland market, would put up for the night; and, if a bachelor, might sit an hour beyond the usual bedtime, and steal a kiss from the mountain maid, at parting. It was one of those primitive taverns, where the traveller pays only for food and lodging, but meets with a homely kindness, beyond all price. When the footsteps were heard, therefore, between the outer door and the inner one, the whole family rose up, grandmother, children, and all, as if about to welcome some one who belonged to them, and whose fate was linked with theirs.

The door was opened by a young man. His face at first wore the melancholy expression, almost despondency, of one who travels a wild and bleak road, at nightfall and alone, but soon brightened up, when he saw the kindly warmth of his reception. He felt his heart spring forward to meet them all, from the old woman, who wiped a chair with her apron, to the little child that held out its arms to him. One glance and smile placed the stranger on a footing of innocent familiarity with the eldest daughter.

"Ah, this fire is the right thing!" cried he; "especially when there is such a pleasant circle round it. I am quite benumbed; for the Notch is just like the pipe of a great pair of bellows; it has blown a terrible blast in my face, all the way from Bartlett."

"Then you are going towards Vermont?" said the master of the house, as he helped to take a light knapsack off the young man's shoulders.

"Yes; to Burlington, and far enough beyond," replied he. "I meant to have been at Ethan Crawford's tonight; but a pedestrian lingers along such a road as this. It is no matter; for, when I saw this good fire, and all your cheerful faces, I felt as if you had kindled it on purpose for me, and were waiting my arrival. So I shall sit down among you, and make myself at home."

The frank-hearted stranger had just drawn his chair to the fire, when something like a heavy footstep was heard without, rushing down the steep side of the mountain, as with long and rapid strides, and taking such a leap, in passing the cottage, as to strike the opposite precipice. The family held their breath, because they knew the sound, and their guest held his, by instinct.

"The old mountain has thrown a stone at us, for fear we should forget him," said the landlord, recovering himself. "He sometimes nods his head, and threatens to come down; but we are old neighbors, and agree together pretty well, upon the whole. Besides, we have a sure place of refuge, hard by, if he should be coming in good earnest."

Let us now suppose the stranger to have finished his supper of bear's meat; and, by his natural felicity of manner, to have placed himself on a footing of kindness with the whole family, so that they talked as freely together, as if he belonged to their mountain brood. He was of a proud, yet gentle spirit—haughty and reserved among the rich and great; but ever ready to stoop his head to the lowly cottage door, and be like a brother or a son at the poor man's fireside. In the household of the Notch, he found warmth and simplicity of feeling, the pervading intelligence of New England, and a poetry of native growth, which they had gathered, when they little thought of it, from the mountain peaks and chasms, and at the very threshold of their romantic and dangerous abode. He had travelled far and alone; his whole life, indeed, had been a solitary path; for, with the lofty caution of his nature, he had kept himself apart from those who might otherwise have been his companions. The family, too, though so kind and hospitable, had that consciousness of unity among themselves, and separation from the world at large, which, in every domestic circle, should still keep a holy place, where no stranger may intrude. But, this evening, a prophetic sympathy impelled the refined and educated youth to pour out his heart before the simple mountaineers, and constrained them to answer him with the same free confidence. And thus it should have been. Is not the kindred of a common fate a closer tie than that of birth?

The secret of the young man's character was, a high and abstracted ambition. He could have borne to live an undistinguished life, but not to be forgotten in the grave. Yearning desire had been transformed to hope; and hope, long cherished, had become like certainty, that, obscurely as he journeyed now, a glory was to beam on all his pathway—though not, perhaps, while he was treading it. But, when posterity should gaze back into the gloom of what was now the present, they would trace the brightness of his footsteps, brightening as meaner glories faded, and confess, that a gifted one had passed from his cradle to his tomb, with none to recognise him.

"As yet," cried the stranger—his cheek glowing and his eye flashing with enthusiasm—"as yet, I have done nothing. Were I to vanish from the earth to-morrow, none would know so much of me as you; that a nameless youth came up, at nightfall, from the valley of the Saco, and opened his heart to you in the evening, and passed through the Notch, by sunrise, and was seen no more. Not a soul would ask—'Who was he?—Whither did the wanderer go?' But, I cannot die till I have achieved my destiny. Then, let Death come! I shall have built my monument!"

There was a continual flow of natural emotion, gushing forth amid abstracted reverie, which enabled the family to understand this young man's sentiments, though so foreign from their own. With quick sensibility of the ludicrous, he blushed at the ardor into which he had been betrayed.

"You laugh at me," said he, taking the eldest daughter's hand, and laughing himself. "You think my ambition as nonsensical as if I were to freeze myself to death on the top of Mount Washington,

only that people might spy at me from the country round about. And truly, that would be a noble pedestal for a man's statue!"

"It is better to sit here by this fire," answered the girl, blushing, "and be comfortable and contented, though nobody thinks about us."

"I suppose," said her father, after a fit of musing, "there is something natural in what the young man says; and if my mind had been turned that way, I might have felt just the same. It is strange, wife, how his talk has set my head running on things, that are pretty certain never to come to pass."

"Perhaps they may," observed the wife. "Is the man thinking what he will do when he is a widower?"

"No, no!" cried he, repelling the idea with reproachful kindness. "When I think of your death, Esther, I think of mine, too. But I was wishing we had a good farm, in Bartlett, or Bethlehem, or Littleton, or some other township round the White Mountains; but not where they could tumble on our heads. I should want to stand well with my neighbors, and be called 'Squire, and sent to General Court, for a term or two; for a plain, honest man may do as much good there as a lawyer. And when I should be grown quite an old man, and you an old woman, so as not to be long apart, I might die happy enough in my bed, and leave you all crying around me. A slate gravestone would suit me as well as a marble one—with just my name and age, and a verse of a hymn, and something to let people know, that I lived an honest man and died a Christian."

"There now!" exclaimed the stranger; "it is our nature to desire a monument, be it slate, or marble, or a pillar of granite, or a glorious memory in the universal heart of man."

"We're in a strange way, to-night," said the wife, with tears in her eyes. "They say it's a sign of something, when folks' minds go a wandering so. Hark to the children!"

They listened accordingly. The younger children had been put to bed in another room, but with an open door between, so that they could be heard talking busily among themselves. One and all seemed to have caught the infection from the fireside circle, and were outvying each other, in wild wishes, and childish projects of what they would do, when they came to be men and women. At length, a little boy, instead of addressing his brothers and sisters, called out to his mother.

"I'll tell you what I wish, mother," cried he. "I want you and father and grandma'm, and all of us, and the stranger too, to start right away, and go and take a drink out of the basin of the Flume!"

Nobody could help laughing at the child's notion of leaving a warm bed, and dragging them from a cheerful fire, to visit the basin of the Flume—a brook, which tumbles over the precipice, deep within the Notch. The boy had hardly spoken, when a wagon rattled along the road, and stopped a moment before the door. It appeared to contain two or three men, who were cheering their hearts with the rough chorus of a song, which resounded, in broken notes, between the cliffs, while the singers hesitated whether to continue their journey, or put up here for the night.

"Father," said the girl, "they are calling you by name."

But the good man doubted whether they had really called him, and was unwilling to show himself too solicitous of gain, by inviting people to patronize his house. He therefore did not hurry to the door; and the lash being soon applied, the travellers plunged into the Notch, still singing and laughing, though their music and mirth came back drearily from the heart of the mountain.

"There, mother!" cried the boy, again. "They'd have given us a ride to the Flume."

Again they laughed at the child's pertinacious fancy for a night ramble. But it happened, that a light cloud passed over the daughter's spirit; she looked gravely into the fire, and drew a breath that was almost a sigh. It forced its way, in spite of a little struggle to repress it. Then starting and blushing, she looked quickly round the circle, as if they had caught a glimpse into her bosom. The stranger asked what she had been thinking of.

"Nothing," answered she, with a downcast smile. "Only I felt lonesome just then."

"Oh, I have always had a gift of feeling what is in other people's hearts," said he, half seriously. "Shall I tell the secrets of yours? For I know what to think, when a young girl shivers by a warm hearth, and complains of lonesomeness at her mother's side. Shall I put these feelings into words?"

"They would not be a girl's feelings any longer, if they could be put into words," replied the mountain nymph, laughing, but avoiding his eye.

All this was said apart. Perhaps a germ of love was springing in their hearts, so pure that it might blossom in Paradise, since it could not be matured on earth; for women worship such gentle dignity as his; and the proud, contemplative, yet kindly soul is oftenest captivated by simplicity like hers. But, while they spoke softly, and he was watching the happy sadness, the lightsome shadows, the shy yearnings of a maiden's nature, the wind, through the Notch, took a deeper and drearier sound. It seemed, as the fanciful stranger said, like the choral strain of the spirits of the blast, who, in old Indian times, had their dwelling among these mountains, and made their heights and recesses a sacred region. There was a wail, along the road, as if a funeral were passing. To chase away the gloom, the family threw pine branches on their fire, till the dry leaves crackled and the flame arose, discovering once again a scene of peace and humble happiness. The light hovered about them fondly, and caressed them all. There were the little faces of the children, peeping from their bed apart, and here the father's frame of strength, the mother's subdued and careful mien, the high-browed youth, the budding girl, and the good old grandam, still knitting in the warmest place. The aged woman looked up from her task, and, with fingers ever busy, was the next to speak.

"Old folks have their notions," said she, "as well as young ones. You've been wishing and planning; and letting your heads run on one thing and another, till you've set my mind a wandering too. Now what should an old woman wish for, when she can go but a step or two before she comes to her grave? Children, it will haunt me night and day, till I tell you."

"What is it, mother?" cried the husband and wife, at once.

Then the old woman, with an air of mystery, which drew the circle closer round the fire, informed them that she had provided her grave-clothes some years before—a nice linen shroud, a cap with a muslin ruff, and every thing of a finer sort than she had worn since her wedding-day. But, this evening, an old superstition had strangely recurred to her. It used to be said, in her younger days, that, if any thing were amiss with a corpse, if only the ruff were not smooth, or the cap did not set right, the corpse, in the coffin and beneath the clods, would strive to put up its cold hands and arrange it. The bare thought made her nervous.

"Don't talk so, grandmother!" said the girl, shuddering.

"Now,"—continued the old woman, with singular earnestness, yet smiling strangely at her own folly,—"I want one of you, my children—when your mother is drest, and in the coffin—I want one of you to hold a looking-glass over my face. Who knows but I may take a glimpse at myself, and see whether all's right?"

"Old and young, we dream of graves and monuments," murmured the stranger youth. "I wonder how mariners feel, when the ship is sinking, and they, unknown and undistinguished, are to be buried together in the ocean—that wide and nameless sepulchre!"

For a moment, the old woman's ghastly conception so engrossed the minds of her hearers, that a sound, abroad in the night, rising like the roar of a blast, had grown broad, deep, and terrible, before the fated group were conscious of it. The house, and all within it, trembled; the foundations of the earth seemed to be shaken, as if this awful sound were the peal of the last trump. Young and old exchanged one wild glance, and remained an instant, pale, affrighted, without utterance, or power to move. Then the same shriek burst simultaneously from all their lips.

"The Slide! The Slide!"

The simplest words must intimate, but not portray, the unutterable horror of the catastrophe. The victims rushed from their cottage, and sought refuge in what they deemed a safer spot—where, in contemplation of such an emergency, a sort of barrier had been reared. Alas! they had quitted their security, and fled right into the pathway of destruction. Down came the whole side of the mountain, in a cataract of ruin. Just before it reached the house, the stream broke into two branches—shivered not a window there, but overwhelmed the whole vicinity, blocked up the road, and annihilated every thing in its dreadful course. Long ere the thunder of that great Slide had ceased to roar among the mountains, the mortal agony had been endured, and the victims were at peace. Their bodies were never found.

The next morning, the light smoke was seen stealing from the cottage chimney, up the mountainside. Within, the fire was yet smouldering on the hearth, and the chairs in a circle round it, as if the inhabitants had but gone forth to view the devastation of the Slide, and would shortly return, to thank Heaven for their miraculous escape. All had left separate tokens, by which those, who had known the family, were made to shed a tear for each. Who has not heard their name? The story had been told far and wide, and will for ever be a legend of these mountains. Poets have sung their fate.

There were circumstances, which led some to suppose that a stranger had been received into the cottage on this awful night, and had shared the catastrophe of all its inmates. Others denied that there were sufficient grounds for such a conjecture. Woe, for the high-souled youth, with his dream of Earthly Immortality! His name and person utterly unknown; his history, his way of life, his plans, a mystery never to be solved; his death and his existence, equally a doubt! Whose was the agony of that death-moment?

1835

Young Goodman Brown

Among the persons sentenced to death by Judge Hathorne in the Salem witch trials of 1692 were Goody Cloyse and Goody Cory, who figure in this story. To many contemporaries of Hawthorne's ancestor, witchcraft was a terrible menace. To Hawthorne himself, it was local history and a theme for the art of fiction—an opportunity to image forth the fraternity of Evil.

Like Robin, in "My Kinsman, Major Molineux," Young Goodman Brown makes a night journey; and darkness, for him also, provides "light" or knowledge. He discovers the

capacity for evil in all men—"the communion of [his] race." Brown, however, fails to realize that man may "have several voices . . . as well as two complexions." His inability to accept ambiguity and man's complexity separates him from others, and he thereafter leads a life of unforgiving loneliness.

Hawthorne found his material mainly in a work published in the year after the trials, Cotton Mather's *Wonders of the Invisible World: Being an Account of the Trials of Several Witches, Lately Executed in New-England*. He found his technique in the conventions of Gothic romance, which he refined and psychologized, focusing on interior experience.

Text: From the author's revised edition of *Mosses from an Old Manse* (Boston, 1854).

Young Goodman Brown came forth at sunset into the street of Salem village; but put his head back, after crossing the threshold, to exchange a parting kiss with his young wife. And Faith, as the wife was aptly named, thrust her own pretty head into the street, letting the wind play with the pink ribbons of her cap while she called to Goodman Brown.

"Dearest heart," whispered she, softly and rather sadly, when her lips were close to his ear, "prithee put off your journey until sunrise and sleep in your own bed to-night. A lone woman is troubled with such dreams and such thoughts that she's afeard of herself sometimes. Pray tarry with me this night, dear husband, of all nights in the year."

"My love and my Faith," replied young Goodman Brown, "of all nights in the year, this one night must I tarry away from thee. My journey, as thou callest it, forth and back again, must needs be done 'twixt now and sunrise. What, my sweet, pretty wife, dost thou doubt me already, and we but three months married?"

"Then God bless you!" said Faith, with the pink ribbons; "and may you find all well when you come back."

"Amen!" cried Goodman Brown. "Say thy prayers, dear Faith, and go to bed at dusk, and no harm will come to thee."

So they parted; and the young man pursued his way until, being about to turn the corner by the meeting house, he looked back and saw the head of Faith still peeping after him with a melancholy air, in spite of her pink ribbons.

"Poor little Faith!" thought he, for his heart smote him. "What a wretch am I to leave her on such an errand! She talks of dreams, too. Methought as she spoke there was trouble in her face, as if a dream had warned her what work is to be done to-night. But, no, no; 'twould kill her to think it. Well, she's a blessed angel on earth; and after this one night I'll cling to her skirts and follow her to heaven."

With this excellent resolve for the future, Goodman Brown felt himself justified in making more haste on his present evil purpose. He had taken a dreary road, darkened by all the gloomiest trees of the forest, which barely stood aside to let the narrow path creep through, and closed immediately behind. It was all as lonely as could be; and there is this peculiarity in such a solitude, that the traveller knows not who may be concealed by the innumerable trunks and the thick boughs overhead; so that with lonely footsteps he may yet be passing through an unseen multitude.

"There may be a devilish Indian behind every tree," said Goodman Brown to himself; and he glanced fearfully behind him as he added, "What if the devil himself should be at my very elbow!"

His head being turned back, he passed a crook of the road, and, looking forward again, beheld the figure of a man, in grave and decent attire, seated at the foot of an old tree. He arose at Goodman Brown's approach and walked onward side by side with him.

"You are late, Goodman Brown," said he. "The clock of the Old South was striking as I came through Boston; and that is full fifteen minutes agone."

"Faith kept me back a while," replied the young man, with a tremor in his voice, caused by the sudden appearance of his companion, though not wholly unexpected.

It was now deep dusk in the forest, and deepest in that part of it where these two were journeying. As nearly as could be discerned, the second traveller was about fifty years old, apparently in the same rank of life as Goodman Brown, and bearing a considerable resemblance to him, though perhaps more in expression than features. Still they might have been taken for father and son. And yet, though the elder person was as simply clad as the younger, and as simple in manner too, he had an indescribable air of one who knew the world, and who would not have felt abashed at the governor's dinner table or in King William's court,[1] were it possible that his affairs should call him thither. But the only thing about him that could be fixed upon as remarkable was his staff, which bore the likeness of a great black snake, so curiously wrought that it might almost be seen to twist and wriggle itself like a living serpent. This, of course, must have been an ocular deception, assisted by the uncertain light.

"Come, Goodman Brown," cried his fellow-traveller, "this is a dull pace for the beginning of a journey. Take my staff, if you are so soon weary."

"Friend," said the other, exchanging his slow pace for a full stop, "having kept covenant by meeting thee here, it is my purpose now to return whence I came. I have scruples touching the matter thou wot'st of."

"Sayest thou so?" replied he of the serpent, smiling apart. "Let us walk on, nevertheless, reasoning as we go; and if I convince thee not thou shalt turn back. We are but a little way in the forest yet."

"Too far! too far!" exclaimed the goodman, unconsciously resuming his walk. "My father never went into the woods on such an errand, nor his father before him. We have been a race of honest men and good Christians since the days of the martyrs; and shall I be the first of the name of Brown that ever took this path and kept"—

"Such company, thou wouldst say," observed the elder person, interpreting his pause. "Well said, Goodman Brown! I have been as well acquainted with your family as with ever a one among the Puritans; and that's no trifle to say. I helped your grandfather, the constable, when he lashed the Quaker woman so smartly through the streets of Salem; and it was I that brought your father a pitch-pine knot, kindled at my own hearth, to set fire to an Indian village, in King Philip's war.[2] They were my good friends, both; and many a pleasant walk have we had along this path, and returned merrily after midnight. I would fain be friends with you for their sake."

"If it be as thou sayest," replied Goodman Brown, "I marvel they never spoke of these matters; or, verily, I marvel not, seeing that the least rumor of the sort would have driven them from New England. We are a people of prayer, and good works to boot, and abide no such wickedness."

"Wickedness or not," said the traveller with the twisted staff, "I have a very general acquaintance here in New England. The deacons of many a church have drunk the communion wine with me; the selectmen of divers towns make me their chairman; and a majority of the Great and General Court are firm supporters of my interest. The governor and I, too—But these are state secrets."

"Can this be so?" cried Goodman Brown, with a stare of amazement at his undisturbed companion. "Howbeit, I have nothing to do with the governor and council; they have their own ways, and are no rule for a simple husbandman like me. But, were I to go on with thee, how should I meet the eye of that good old man, our minister, at Salem village? O, his voice would make me tremble both Sabbath day and lecture day."

Thus far the elder traveller had listened with due gravity; but now burst into a fit of irrepressible mirth, shaking himself so violently that his snakelike staff actually seemed to wriggle in sympathy.

"Ha! ha! ha!" shouted he again and again; then composing himself. "Well, go on, Goodman Brown, go on; but, prithee, don't kill me with laughing."

"Well, then, to end the matter at once," said Goodman Brown, considerably nettled, "there is my

---

[1] William III, king of England, 1689–1702.

[2] A war (1675–76) between New England colonists and a confederation of Indians led by King Philip or Metacomet.

wife, Faith. It would break her dear little heart; and I'd rather break my own."

"Nay, if that be the case," answered the other, "e'en go thy ways, Goodman Brown. I would not for twenty old women like the one hobbling before us that Faith should come to any harm."

As he spoke he pointed his staff at a female figure on the path, in whom Goodman Brown recognized a very pious and exemplary dame, who had taught him his catechism in youth, and was still his moral and spiritual adviser, jointly with the minister and Deacon Gookin.

"A marvel, truly, that Goody Cloyse[3] should be so far in the wilderness at nightfall," said he. "But with your leave, friend, I shall take a cut through the woods until we have left this Christian woman behind. Being a stranger to you, she might ask whom I was consorting with and whither I was going."

"Be it so," said his fellow-traveller. "Betake you to the woods, and let me keep the path."

Accordingly the young man turned aside, but took care to watch his companion, who advanced softly along the road until he had come within a staff's length of the old dame. She, meanwhile, was making the best of her way, with singular speed for so aged a woman, and mumbling some indistinct words—a prayer, doubtless—as she went. The traveller put forth his staff and touched her withered neck with what seemed the serpent's tail.

"The devil!" screamed the pious old lady.

"Then Goody Cloyse knows her old friend?" observed the traveller, confronting her and leaning on his writhing stick.

"Ah, forsooth, and is it your worship indeed?" cried the good dame. "Yea, truly is it, and in the very image of my old gossip, Goodman Brown, the grandfather of the silly fellow that now is. But—would your worship believe it?—my broomstick hath strangely disappeared, stolen, as I suspect, by that unhanged witch, Goody Cory, and that, too, when I was all anointed with the juice of smallage, and cinquefoil, and wolf's bane—"

"Mingled with fine wheat and the fat of a new-born babe," said the shape of old Goodman Brown.

"Ah, your worship knows the recipe," cried the old lady, cackling aloud. "So, as I was saying, being all ready for the meeting, and no horse to ride on, I made up my mind to foot it; for they tell me there is a nice young man to be taken into communion to-night. But now your good worship will lend me your arm, and we shall be there in a twinkling."

"That can hardly be," answered her friend. "I may not spare you my arm, Goody Cloyse; but here is my staff, if you will."

So saying, he threw it down at her feet, where,

[3]Goody, short for Goodwife, a standard term of address, similar to Goodman. Goody Cloyse, Goody Cory, and Martha Carrier were sentenced as "witches" in Salem in 1692.

perhaps, it assumed life, being one of the rods which its owner had formerly lent to the Egyptian magi. Of this fact, however, Goodman Brown could not take cognizance. He had cast up his eyes in astonishment, and, looking down again, beheld neither Goody Cloyse nor the serpentine staff, but his fellow-traveller alone, who waited for him as calmly as if nothing had happened

"That old woman taught me my catechism," said the young man; and there was a world of meaning in this simple comment.

They continued to walk onward, while the elder traveller exhorted his companion to make good speed and persevere in the path, discoursing so aptly that his arguments seemed rather to spring up in the bosom of his auditor than to be suggested by himself. As they went, he plucked a branch of maple to serve for a walking stick, and began to strip it of the twigs and little boughs, which were wet with evening dew. The moment his fingers touched them they became strangely withered and dried up as with a week's sunshine. Thus the pair proceeded, at a good free pace, until suddenly, in a gloomy hollow of the road, Goodman Brown sat himself down on the stump of a tree and refused to go any farther.

"Friend," said he, stubbornly, "my mind is made up. Not another step will I budge on this errand. What if a wretched old woman do choose to go to the devil when I thought she was going to heaven: is that any reason why I should quit my dear Faith and go after her?"

"You will think better of this by and by," said his acquaintance, composedly. "Sit here and rest yourself a while; and when you feel like moving again, there is my staff to help you along."

Without more words, he threw his companion the maple stick, and was as speedily out of sight as if he had vanished into the deepening gloom. The young man sat a few moments by the roadside, applauding himself greatly, and thinking with how clear a conscience he should meet the minister in his morning walk, nor shrink from the eye of good old Deacon Gookin. And what calm sleep would be his that very night, which was to have been spent so wickedly, but so purely and sweetly now, in the arms of Faith! Amidst these pleasant and praiseworthy meditations, Goodman Brown heard the tramp of horses along the road, and deemed it advisable to conceal himself within the verge of the forest, conscious of the guilty purpose that had brought him thither, though now so happily turned from it.

On came the hoof tramps and the voices of the riders, two grave old voices, conversing soberly as they drew near. These mingled sounds appeared to pass along the road, within a few yards of the young man's hiding-place; but, owing doubtless to the depth of the gloom at that particular spot, neither the travellers nor their steeds were visible. Though their figures brushed the small boughs by the wayside, it could not be seen that they intercepted, even for a moment, the faint gleam from the strip of bright sky athwart which they must have passed. Goodman Brown alternately crouched and stood on tiptoe, pulling aside the branches and thrusting forth his head as far as he durst without discerning so much as a shadow. It vexed him the more, because he could have sworn, were such a thing possible, that he recognized the voices of the minister and Deacon Gookin, jogging along quietly, as they were wont to do, when bound to some ordination or ecclesiastical council. While yet within hearing, one of the riders stopped to pluck a switch.

"Of the two, reverend sir," said the voice like the deacon's, "I had rather miss an ordination dinner than to-night's meeting. They tell me that some of our community are to be here from Falmouth and beyond, and others from Connecticut and Rhode Island, besides several of the Indian powwows, who, after their fashion, know almost as much deviltry as the best of us. Moreover, there is a goodly young woman to be taken into communion."

"Mighty well, Deacon Gookin!" replied the solemn old tones of the minister. "Spur up, or we shall be late. Nothing can be done, you know, until I get on the ground."

The hoofs clattered again; and the voices, talking so strangely in the empty air, passed on through the forest, where no church had ever been gathered or solitary Christian prayed. Whither, then, could these holy men be journeying so deep into the heathen wilderness? Young Goodman Brown caught hold of a tree for support, being ready to sink down on the ground, faint and overburdened with the heavy sickness of his heart. He looked up to the sky, doubting whether there really was a heaven above him. Yet there was the blue arch, and the stars brightening in it.

"With heaven above and Faith below, I will yet stand firm against the devil!" cried Goodman Brown.

While he still gazed upward into the deep arch of the firmament and had lifted his hands to pray, a cloud, though no wind was stirring, hurried across the zenith and hid the brightening stars. The blue sky was still visible, except directly overhead, where this black mass of cloud was sweeping swiftly northward. Aloft in the air, as if from the depths of the cloud, came a confused and doubtful sound of voices. Once the listener fancied that he could distinguish the accents of townspeople of his own, men and women, both pious and ungodly, many of whom he had met at the communion table, and had seen others rioting at the tavern. The next moment, so indistinct were the sounds, he doubted whether he had heard aught but the murmur of the old forest, whispering without a wind. Then came a stronger swell of those familiar tones, heard daily in the sunshine at Salem village, but never until now from a cloud of night. There was one voice, of a young woman, uttering lamentations, yet with an uncertain sorrow, and entreating for some favor, which, perhaps, it would grieve her to obtain; and all the unseen multitude, both saints and sinners, seemed to encourage her onward.

"Faith!" shouted Goodman Brown, in a voice of agony and desperation; and the echoes of the forest mocked him, crying, "Faith! Faith!" as if bewildered wretches were seeking her all through the wilderness.

The cry of grief, rage, and terror was yet piercing the night, when the unhappy husband held his breath for a response. There was a scream, drowned immediately in a louder murmur of voices, fading into far-off laughter, as the dark cloud swept away, leaving the clear and silent sky above Goodman Brown. But something fluttered lightly down through the air and caught on the branch of a tree. The young man seized it, and beheld a pink ribbon.

"My Faith is gone!" cried he, after one stupefied moment. "There is no good on earth; and sin is but a name. Come, devil; for to thee is this world given."

And, maddened with despair, so that he laughed loud and long, did Goodman Brown grasp his staff and set forth again, at such a rate that he seemed to fly along the forest path rather than to walk or run. The road grew wilder and drearier and more faintly traced, and vanished at length, leaving him in the heart of the dark wilderness, still rushing onward with the instinct that guides mortal man to evil. The whole forest was peopled with frightful sounds—the creaking of the trees, the howling of wild beasts, and the yell of Indians; while sometimes the wind tolled like a distant church bell, and sometimes gave a broad roar around the traveller, as if all Nature were laughing him to scorn. But he was himself the chief horror of the scene, and shrank not from its other horrors.

"Ha! ha! ha!" roared Goodman Brown when the wind laughed at him. "Let us hear which will laugh loudest. Think not to frighten me with your deviltry. Come witch, come wizard, come Indian powwow, come devil himself, and here comes Goodman Brown. You may as well fear him as he fear you."

In truth, all through the haunted forest there could be nothing more frightful than the figure of Goodman Brown. On he flew among the black pines, brandishing his staff with frenzied gestures, now giving vent to an inspiration of horrid blasphemy, and now shouting forth such laughter as set all the echoes of the forest laughing like demons around him. The fiend in his own shape is less hideous than when he rages in the breast of man. Thus sped the demoniac on his course, until, quivering among the trees, he saw a red light before him, as when the felled trunks and branches of a clearing have been set on fire, and throw up their lurid blaze against the sky, at the hour of midnight. He paused, in a lull of the tempest that had driven him onward, and heard the swell of what seemed a hymn, rolling solemnly from a distance with the weight of many voices. He knew the tune; it was a familiar one in the choir of the village meeting house. The verse died heavily away, and was lengthened by a chorus, not of human voices, but of all the sounds of the benighted wilderness pealing in awful harmony together. Goodman Brown cried out; and his cry was lost to his own ear by its unison with the cry of the desert.

In the interval of silence he stole forward until the light glared full upon his eyes. At one extremity of an open space, hemmed in by the dark wall of the forest, arose a rock, bearing some rude, natural resemblance either to an altar or a pulpit, and surrounded by four blazing pines, their tops aflame, their stems untouched, like candles at an evening meeting. The mass of foliage that had overgrown the summit of the rock was all on fire, blazing high into the night and fitfully illuminating the whole field. Each pendent twig and leafy festoon was in a blaze. As the red light arose and fell, a numerous congregation alternately shone forth, then disappeared in shadow, and again grew, as it were, out of the darkness, peopling the heart of the solitary woods at once.

"A grave and dark-clad company," quoth Goodman Brown.

In truth they were such. Among them, quivering to and fro between gloom and splendor, appeared faces that would be seen next day at the council board of the province, and others which, Sabbath after Sabbath, looked devoutly heavenward, and benignantly over the crowded pews, from the holiest pulpits in the land. Some affirm that the lady of the governor was there. At least there were high dames well known to her, and wives of honored husbands, and widows, a great multitude, and ancient maidens, all of excellent repute, and fair young girls, who trembled lest their mothers should espy them. Either the sudden gleams of light flashing over the obscure field bedazzled Goodman Brown, or he recognized a score of the church members of Salem village famous for their especial sanctity. Good old Deacon Gookin had arrived, and waited at the skirts of that venerable saint, his revered pastor. But, irreverently consorting with these grave, reputable, and pious people, these elders of the church, these chaste dames and dewy virgins, there were men of dissolute lives and women of spotted fame, wretches

given over to all mean and filthy vice, and suspected even of horrid crimes. It was strange to see that the good shrank not from the wicked, nor were the sinners abashed by the saints. Scattered also among their palefaced enemies were the Indian priests, or powwows, who had often scared their native forest with more hideous incantations than any known to English witchcraft.

"But where is Faith?" thought Goodman Brown; and, as hope came into his heart, he trembled.

Another verse of the hymn arose, a slow and mournful strain, such as the pious love, but joined to words which expressed all that our nature can conceive of sin, and darkly hinted at far more. Unfathomable to mere mortals is the lore of fiends. Verse after verse was sung; and still the chorus of the desert swelled between like the deepest tone of a mighty organ; and with the final peal of that dreadful anthem there came a sound, as if the roaring wind, the rushing streams, the howling beasts, and every other voice of the unconverted wilderness were mingling and according with the voice of guilty man in homage to the prince of all. The four blazing pines threw up a loftier flame, and obscurely discovered shapes and visages of horror on the smoke wreaths above the impious assembly. At the same moment the fire on the rock shot redly forth and formed a glowing arch above its base, where now appeared a figure. With reverence be it spoken, the figure bore no slight similitude, both in garb and manner, to some grave divine of the New England churches.

"Bring forth the converts!" cried a voice that echoed through the field and rolled into the forest.

At the word, Goodman Brown stepped forth from the shadow of the trees and approached the congregation, with whom he felt a loathful brotherhood by the sympathy of all that was wicked in his heart. He could have well nigh sworn that the shape of his own dead father beckoned him to advance, looking downward from a smoke wreath, while a woman, with dim features of despair, threw out her hand to warn him back. Was it his mother? But he had no power to retreat one step, nor to resist, even in thought, when the minister and good old Deacon Gookin seized his arms and led him to the blazing rock. Thither came also the slender form of a veiled female, led between Goody Cloyse, that pious teacher of the catechism, and Martha Carrier, who had received the devil's promise to be queen of hell. A rampant hag was she. And there stood the proselytes beneath the canopy of fire

"Welcome, my children," said the dark figure, "to the communion of your race. Ye have found thus young your nature and your destiny. My children, look behind you!"

They turned; and flashing forth, as it were, in a

sheet of flame, the fiend worshippers were seen; the smile of welcome gleamed darkly on every visage.

"There," resumed the sable form, "are all whom ye have reverenced from youth. Ye deemed them holier than yourselves, and shrank from your own sin, contrasting it with their lives of righteousness and prayerful aspirations heavenward. Yet here are they all in my worshipping assembly. This night it shall be granted you to know their secret deeds; how hoary-bearded elders of the church have whispered wanton words to the young maids of their households; how many a woman, eager for widow's weeds, has given her husband a drink at bedtime and let him sleep his last sleep in her bosom; how beardless youths have made haste to inherit their father's wealth; and how fair damsels—blush not, sweet ones—have dug little graves in the garden, and bidden me, the sole guest, to an infant's funeral. By the sympathy of your human hearts for sin ye shall scent out all the places—whether in church, bed-chamber, street, field, or forest—where crime has been committed, and shall exult to behold the whole earth one stain of guilt, one mighty blood spot. Far more than this. It shall be yours to penetrate, in every bosom, the deep mystery of sin, the fountain of all wicked arts, and which inexhaustibly supplies more evil impulses than human power—than my power at its utmost—can make manifest in deeds. And now, my children, look upon each other."

They did so; and, by the blaze of the hell-kindled torches, the wretched man beheld his Faith, and the wife her husband, trembling before that unhallowed altar.

"Lo, there ye stand, my children," said the figure, in a deep and solemn tone, almost sad with its despairing awfulness, as if his once angelic nature could yet mourn for our miserable race. "Depending upon one another's hearts, ye had still hoped that virtue were not all a dream. Now are ye undeceived. Evil is the nature of mankind. Evil must be your only happiness. Welcome again, my children, to the communion of your race."

"Welcome," repeated the fiend worshippers, in one cry of despair and triumph.

And there they stood, the only pair, as it seemed, who were yet hesitating on the verge of wickedness in this dark world. A basin was hollowed, naturally, in the rock. Did it contain water, reddened by the lurid light? or was it blood? or, perchance, a liquid flame? Herein did the shape of evil dip his hand and prepare to lay the mark of baptism upon their foreheads, that they might be partakers of the mystery of sin, more conscious of the secret guilt of others, both in deed and thought, than they could now be of their own. The husband cast one look at his pale wife, and Faith at him. What polluted wretches would the next glance show them to each other, shuddering alike at what they disclosed and what they saw!

"Faith! Faith!" cried the husband, "look up to heaven, and resist the wicked one."

Whether Faith obeyed, he knew not. Hardly had he spoken when he found himself amid calm night and solitude, listening to a roar of the wind which died heavily away through the forest. He staggered against the rock, and felt it chill and damp; while a hanging twig, that had been all on fire, besprinkled his cheek with the coldest dew.

The next morning young Goodman Brown came slowly into the street of Salem village, staring around him like a bewildered man. The good old minister was taking a walk along the graveyard to get an appetite for breakfast and meditate his sermon, and bestowed a blessing, as he passed, on Goodman Brown. He shrank from the venerable saint as if to avoid an anathema. Old Deacon Gookin was at domestic worship, and the holy words of his prayer were heard through the open window. "What God doth the wizard pray to?" quoth Goodman Brown. Goody Cloyse, that excellent old Christian, stood in the early sunshine at her own lattice, catechizing a little girl who had brought her a pint of morning's milk. Goodman Brown snatched away the child as from the grasp of the fiend himself. Turning the corner by the meeting-house, he spied the head of Faith, with the pink ribbons, gazing anxiously forth, and bursting into such joy at the sight of him that she skipped along the street and almost kissed her husband before the whole village. But Goodman Brown looked sternly and sadly into her face, and passed on without a greeting.

Had Goodman Brown fallen asleep in the forest and only dreamed a wild dream of a witch meeting?

Be it so, if you will; but, alas! it was a dream of evil omen for young Goodman Brown. A stern, a sad, a darkly meditative, a distrustful, if not a desperate, man did he become from the night of that fearful dream. On the Sabbath day, when the congregation were singing a holy psalm, he could not listen because an anthem of sin rushed loudly upon his ear and drowned all the blessed strain. When the minister spoke from the pulpit, with power and fervid eloquence and with his hand on the open Bible, of the sacred truths of our religion, and of saintlike lives and triumphant deaths, and of future bliss or misery unutterable, then did Goodman Brown turn pale, dreading lest the roof should thunder down upon the gray blasphemer and his hearers. Often, awaking suddenly at midnight, he shrank from the bosom of Faith; and at morning or eventide, when the family knelt down at prayer, he scowled, and muttered to himself, and gazed sternly at his wife, and turned away. And when he had lived long, and was borne to his grave, a hoary corpse, followed by Faith, an aged woman, and children and grandchildren, a goodly procession, besides neighbors not a few, they carved no hopeful verse upon his tombstone; for his dying hour was gloom.

1835

The Minister's Black Veil

A Parable[1]

Although Hawthorne gives the story a specific setting, he is interested primarily in the symbolic meaning of the Reverend Mr. Hooper's story—a parable, as the subtitle indicates. Mr. Hooper has discovered the inner darkness—the "secret sin"—which every man possesses. For him, however, that reality becomes definitive of life. The resulting loneliness and fear hopelessly separate him from his love and from all others. Like Goodman Brown's fate, Hooper's discovery and his inability to accept it and love, as well, imprison him, as Hawthorne says, "in that saddest of all prisons, his own heart." Text: From the author's revised edition of *Twice-Told Tales* (Boston, 1851).

The sexton stood in the porch of Milford meeting-house, pulling lustily at the bell-rope. The old people of the village came stooping along the street. Children with bright faces, tript merrily beside their parents, or mimicked a graver gait, in the conscious dignity of their Sunday clothes. Spruce bachelors looked sidelong at the pretty maidens, and fancied that the Sabbath sunshine made them prettier than on week-days. When the throng had mostly streamed into the porch, the sexton began to toll the bell, keeping his eye on the Reverend Mr. Hooper's door. The first glimpse of the clergyman's figure, was the signal for the bell to cease its summons.

"But what has good Parson Hooper got upon his face?" cried the sexton in astonishment.

All within hearing immediately turned about, and beheld the semblance of Mr. Hooper, pacing slowly his meditative way towards the meeting-house. With one accord they started, expressing more wonder than if some strange minister were coming to dust the cushions of Mr. Hooper's pulpit.

"Are you sure it is our parson?" inquired Goodman Gray of the sexton.

"Of a certainty it is good Mr. Hooper," replied the sexton. "He was to have exchanged pulpits with Parson Shute, of Westbury; but Parson Shute sent to

[1] Another clergyman in New England, Mr. Joseph Moody, of York, Maine, who died about eighty years since, made himself remarkable by the same eccentricity that is here related of the Reverend Mr. Hooper. In his case, however, the symbol had a different import. In early life he had accidentally killed a beloved friend; and from that day till the hour of his own death, he hid his face from men. [Hawthorne's note.]

excuse himself yesterday, being to preach a funeral sermon."

The cause of so much amazement may appear sufficiently slight. Mr. Hooper, a gentlemanly person, of about thirty, though still a bachelor, was dressed with due clerical neatness, as if a careful wife had starched his band, and brushed the weekly dust from his Sunday's garb. There was but one thing remarkable in his appearance. Swathed about his forehead, and hanging down over his face, so low as to be shaken by his breath, Mr. Hooper had on a black veil. On a nearer view, it seemed to consist of two folds of crape, which entirely concealed his features, except the mouth and chin, but probably did not intercept his sight, farther than to give a darkened aspect to all living and inanimate things. With this gloomy shade before him, good Mr. Hooper walked onward, at a slow and quiet pace, stooping somewhat and looking on the ground, as is customary with abstracted men, yet nodding kindly to those of his parishioners who still waited on the meeting-house steps. But so wonder-struck were they, that his greeting hardly met with a return.

"I can't really feel as if good Mr. Hooper's face was behind that piece of crape," said the sexton.

"I don't like it," muttered an old woman, as she hobbled into the meeting-house. "He has changed himself into something awful, only by hiding his face."

"Our parson has gone mad!" cried Goodman Gray, following him across the threshold.

A rumor of some unaccountable phenomenon had preceded Mr. Hooper into the meeting-house, and set all the congregation astir. Few could refrain from twisting their heads towards the door; many stood upright, and turned directly about; while several little boys clambered upon the seats, and came down again with a terrible racket. There was a general bustle, a rustling of the women's gowns and shuffling of the men's feet, greatly at variance with that hushed repose which should attend the entrance of the minister. But Mr. Hooper appeared not to notice the perturbation of his people. He entered with an almost noiseless step, bent his head mildly to the pews on each side, and bowed as he passed his oldest parishioner, a white-haired great-grandsire, who occupied an arm-chair in the centre of the aisle. It was strange to observe, how slowly this venerable man became conscious of something singular in the appearance of his pastor. He seemed not fully to partake of the prevailing wonder, till Mr. Hooper had ascended the stairs, and showed himself in the pulpit, face to face with his congregation, except for the black veil. That mysterious emblem was never once withdrawn. It shook with his measured breath as he gave out the psalm; it threw its obscurity between him and the holy page, as he read the Scriptures; and while he prayed, the veil lay heavily on his uplifted countenance. Did he seek to hide it from the dread Being whom he was addressing?

Such was the effect of this simple piece of crape, that more than one woman of delicate nerves was forced to leave the meeting-house. Yet perhaps the pale-faced congregation was almost as fearful a sight to the minister, as his black veil to them.

Mr. Hooper had the reputation of a good preacher, but not an energetic one: he strove to win his people heavenward, by mild, persuasive influences, rather than to drive them thither by the thunders of the Word. The sermon which he now delivered, was marked by the same characteristics of style and manner, as the general series of his pulpit oratory. But there was something, either in the sentiment of the discourse itself, or in the imagination of the auditors, which made it greatly the most powerful effort that they had ever heard from their pastor's lips. It was tinged, rather more darkly than usual, with the gentle gloom of Mr. Hooper's temperament. The subject had reference to secret sin, and those sad mysteries which we hide from our nearest and dearest, and would fain conceal from our own consciousness, even forgetting that the Omniscient can detect them. A subtle power was breathed into his words. Each member of the congregation, the most innocent girl, and the man of hardened breast, felt as if the preacher had crept upon them, behind his awful veil, and discovered their hoarded iniquity of deed or thought. Many spread their clasped hands on their bosoms. There was nothing terrible in what Mr. Hooper said; at least, no violence; and yet, with every tremor of his melancholy voice, the hearers quaked. An unsought pathos came hand in hand with awe. So sensible were the audience of some unwonted attribute in their minister, that they longed for a breath of wind to blow aside the veil, almost believing that a stranger's visage would be discovered, though the form, gesture, and voice were those of Mr. Hooper.

At the close of the services, the people hurried out with indecorous confusion, eager to communicate their pent-up amazement, and conscious of lighter spirits, the moment they lost sight of the black veil. Some gathered in little circles, huddled closely together, with their mouths all whispering in the centre; some went homeward alone, wrapt in silent meditation; some talked loudly, and profaned the Sabbath-day with ostentatious laughter. A few shook their sagacious heads, intimating that they could penetrate the mystery; while one or two affirmed that there was no mystery at all, but only that Mr. Hooper's eyes were so weakened by the midnight lamp, as to require a shade. After a brief interval, forth came good Mr. Hooper also, in the

rear of his flock. Turning his veiled face from one group to another, he paid due reverence to the hoary heads, saluted the middle-aged with kind dignity, as their friend and spiritual guide, greeted the young with mingled authority and love, and laid his hands on the little children's heads to bless them. Such was always his custom on the Sabbath-day. Strange and bewildered looks repaid him for his courtesy. None, as on former occasions, aspired to the honor of walking by their pastor's side. Old Squire Saunders, doubtless by an accidental lapse of memory, neglected to invite Mr. Hooper to his table, where the good clergyman had been wont to bless the food, almost every Sunday since his settlement. He returned, therefore, to the parsonage, and, at the moment of closing the door, was observed to look back upon the people, all of whom had their eyes fixed upon the minister. A sad smile gleamed faintly from beneath the black veil, and flickered about his mouth, glimmering as he disappeared.

"How strange," said a lady, "that a simple black veil, such as any woman might wear on her bonnet, should become such a terrible thing on Mr. Hooper's face!"

"Something must surely be amiss with Mr. Hooper's intellects," observed her husband, the physician of the village. "But the strangest part of the affair is the effect of this vagary, even on a sober-minded man like myself. The black veil, though it covers only our pastor's face, throws its influence over his whole person, and makes him ghostlike from head to foot. Do you not feel it so?"

"Truly do I," replied the lady; "and I would not be alone with him for the world. I wonder he is not afraid to be alone with himself!"

"Men sometimes are so," said her husband.

The afternoon service was attended with similar circumstances. At its conclusion, the bell tolled for the funeral of a young lady. The relatives and friends were assembled in the house, and the more distant acquaintances stood about the door, speaking of the good qualities of the deceased, when their talk was interrupted by the appearance of Mr. Hooper, still covered with his black veil. It was now an appropriate emblem. The clergyman stepped into the room where the corpse was laid, and bent over the coffin, to take a last farewell of his deceased parishioner. As he stooped, the veil hung straight down from his forehead, so that, if her eyelids had not been closed for ever, the dead maiden might have seen his face. Could Mr. Hooper be fearful of her glance, that he so hastily caught back the black veil? A person, who watched the interview between the dead and living, scrupled not to affirm, that, at the instant when the clergyman's features were disclosed, the corpse had slightly shuddered, rustling the shroud and muslin cap, though the countenance retained the composure of death. A superstitious old woman was the only witness of this prodigy. From the coffin, Mr. Hooper passed into the chamber of the mourners, and thence to the head of the staircase, to make the funeral prayer. It was a tender and heart-dissolving prayer, full of sorrow, yet so imbued with celestial hopes, that the music of a heavenly harp, swept by the fingers of the dead, seemed faintly to be heard among the saddest accents of the minister. The people trembled, though they but darkly understood him when he prayed that they, and himself, and all of mortal race, might be ready, as he trusted this young maiden had been, for the dreadful hour that should snatch the veil from their faces. The bearers went heavily forth, and the mourners followed, saddening all the street, with the dead before them, and Mr. Hooper in his black veil behind.

"Why do you look back?" said one in the procession to his partner.

"I had a fancy," replied she, "that the minister and the maiden's spirit were walking hand in hand."

"And so had I, at the same moment," said the other.

That night, the handsomest couple of Milford village were to be joined in wedlock. Though reckoned a melancholy man, Mr. Hooper had a placid cheerfulness for such occasions, which often excited a sympathetic smile, where livelier merriment would have been thrown away. There was no quality of his disposition which made him more beloved than this. The company at the wedding awaited his arrival with impatience, trusting that the strange awe, which had gathered over him throughout the day, would now be dispelled. But such was not the result. When Mr. Hooper came, the first thing that their eyes rested on was the same horrible black veil, which had added deeper gloom to the funeral, and could portend nothing but evil to the wedding. Such was its immediate effect on the guests, that a cloud seemed to have rolled duskily from beneath the black crape, and dimmed the light of the candles. The bridal pair stood up before the minister. But the bride's cold fingers quivered in the tremulous hand of the bridegroom, and her deathlike paleness caused a whisper, that the maiden who had been buried a few hours before, was come from her grave to be married. If ever another wedding were so dismal, it was that famous one, where they tolled the wedding knell. After performing the ceremony, Mr. Hooper raised a glass of wine to his lips, wishing happiness to the new married couple, in a strain of mild pleasantry that ought to have brightened the features of the guests, like a cheerful gleam from the hearth. At that instant, catching a glimpse of his figure in the looking-glass, the black veil involved his own spirit in the horror with which it overwhelmed all others. His frame shuddered—his lips grew white—he spilt the untasted wine upon the carpet—and rushed forth into the darkness. For the Earth, too, had on her Black Veil.

The next day, the whole village of Milford talked of little else than Parson Hooper's black veil. That, and the mystery concealed behind it, supplied a topic for discussion between acquaintances meeting in the street, and good women gossiping at their open windows. It was the first item of news that the tavern-keeper told to his guests. The children babbled of it on their way to school. One imitative little imp covered his face with an old black handkerchief, thereby so affrighting his playmates, that the panic seized himself, and he well nigh lost his wits by his own waggery.

It was remarkable that, of all the busybodies and impertinent people in the parish, not one ventured to put the plain question to Mr. Hooper, wherefore he did this thing. Hitherto, whenever there appeared the slightest call for such interference, he had never lacked advisers, nor shown himself averse to be guided by their judgment. If he erred at all, it was by so painful a degree of self-distrust, that even the mildest censure would lead him to consider an indifferent action as a crime. Yet, though so well acquainted with this amiable weakness, no individual among his parishioners chose to make the black veil a subject of friendly remonstrance. There was a feeling of dread, neither plainly confessed nor carefully concealed, which caused each to shift the responsibility upon another, till at length it was found expedient to send a deputation of the church, in order to deal with Mr. Hooper about the mystery, before it should grow into a scandal. Never did an embassy so ill discharge its duties. The minister received them with friendly courtesy, but became silent, after they were seated, leaving to his visitors the whole burthen of introducing their important business. The topic, it might be supposed, was obvious enough. There was the black veil, swathed round Mr. Hooper's forehead, and concealing every feature above his placid mouth, on which, at times, they could perceive the glimmering of a melancholy smile. But that piece of crape, to their imagination, seemed to hang down before his heart, the symbol of a fearful secret between him and them. Were the veil but cast aside, they might speak freely of it, but not till then. Thus they sat a considerable time, speechless, confused, and shrinking uneasily from Mr. Hooper's eye, which they felt to be fixed upon them with an invisible glance. Finally, the deputies returned abashed to their constituents, pronouncing the matter too weighty to be handled, except by a council of the churches, if, indeed, it might not require a general synod.

But there was one person in the village, unappalled by the awe with which the black veil had impressed all beside herself. When the deputies returned without an explanation, or even venturing to demand one, she, with the calm energy of her character, determined to chase away the strange cloud that appeared to be settling round Mr. Hooper, every moment more darkly than before. As his plighted wife, it should be her privilege to know what the black veil concealed. At the minister's first visit, therefore, she entered upon the subject, with a direct simplicity, which made the task easier both for him and her. After he had seated himself, she fixed her eyes steadfastly upon the veil, but could discern nothing of the dreadful gloom that had so overawed the multitude: it was but a double fold of crape, hanging down from his forehead to his mouth, and slightly stirring with his breath.

"No," said she aloud, and smiling, "there is nothing terrible in this piece of crape, except that it hides a face which I am always glad to look upon. Come, good sir, let the sun shine from behind the cloud. First lay aside your black veil: then tell me why you put it on."

Mr. Hooper's smile glimmered faintly.

"There is an hour to come," said he, "when all of us shall cast aside our veils. Take it not amiss, beloved friend, if I wear this piece of crape till then."

"Your words are a mystery too," returned the young lady. "Take away the veil from them, at least."

"Elizabeth, I will," said he, "so far as my vow may suffer me. Know, then, this veil is a type and a symbol, and I am bound to wear it ever, both in light and darkness, in solitude and before the gaze of multitudes, and as with strangers, so with my familiar friends. No mortal eye will see it withdrawn. This dismal shade must separate me from the world: even you, Elizabeth, can never come behind it!"

"What grievous affliction hath befallen you," she earnestly inquired, "that you should thus darken your eyes for ever?"

"If it be a sign of mourning," replied Mr. Hooper, "I, perhaps, like most other mortals, have sorrows dark enough to be typified by a black veil."

"But what if the world will not believe that it is the type of an innocent sorrow?" urged Elizabeth. "Beloved and respected as you are, there may be whispers, that you hide your face under the consciousness of secret sin. For the sake of your holy office, do away this scandal!"

The color rose into her cheeks, as she intimated the nature of the rumors that were already abroad in the village. But Mr. Hooper's mildness did not forsake him. He even smiled again—that same sad smile, which always appeared like a faint glimmer-

ing of light, proceeding from the obscurity beneath the veil.

"If I hide my face for sorrow, there is cause enough," he merely replied; "and if I cover it for secret sin, what mortal might not do the same?"

And with this gentle, but unconquerable obstinacy did he resist all her entreaties. At length Elizabeth sat silent. For a few moments she appeared lost in thought, considering, probably, what new methods might be tried, to withdraw her lover from so dark a fantasy, which, if it had no other meaning, was perhaps a symptom of mental disease. Though of a firmer character than his own, the tears rolled down her cheeks. But, in an instant, as it were, a new feeling took the place of sorrow: her eyes were fixed insensibly on the black veil, when, like a sudden twilight in the air, its terrors fell around her. She arose, and stood trembling before him.

"And do you feel it then at last?" said he mournfully.

She made no reply, but covered her eyes with her hand, and turned to leave the room. He rushed forward and caught her arm.

"Have patience with me, Elizabeth!" cried he passionately. "Do not desert me, though this veil must be between us here on earth. Be mine, and hereafter there shall be no veil over my face, no darkness between our souls! It is but a mortal veil—it is not for eternity! Oh! you know not how lonely I am, and how frightened, to be alone behind my black veil. Do not leave me in this miserable obscurity for ever!"

"Lift the veil but once, and look me in the face," said she.

"Never! It cannot be!" replied Mr. Hooper.

"Then, farewell!" said Elizabeth.

She withdrew her arm from his grasp, and slowly departed, pausing at the door, to give one long, shuddering gaze, that seemed almost to penetrate the mystery of the black veil. But, even amid his grief, Mr. Hooper smiled to think that only a material emblem had separated him from happiness, though the horrors, which it shadowed forth, must be drawn darkly between the fondest of lovers.

From that time no attempts were made to remove Mr. Hooper's black veil, or, by a direct appeal, to discover the secret which it was supposed to hide. By persons who claimed a superiority to popular prejudice, it was reckoned merely an eccentric whim, such as often mingles with the sober actions of men otherwise rational, and tinges them all with its own semblance of insanity. But with the multitude, good Mr. Hooper was irreparably a bugbear. He could not walk the street with any peace of mind, so conscious was he that the gentle and timid would turn aside to avoid him, and that others would make it a point of hardihood to throw themselves in his way. The impertinence of the latter class compelled him to give up his customary walk, at sunset, to the burial-ground; for when he leaned pensively over the gate, there would always be faces behind the grave-stones, peeping at his black veil. A fable went the rounds, that the stare of the dead people drove him thence. It grieved him, to the very depth of his kind heart, to observe how the children fled from his approach, breaking up their merriest sports, while his melancholy figure was yet afar off. Their instinctive dread caused him to feel, more strongly than aught else, that a preternatural horror was interwoven with the threads of the black crape. In truth, his own antipathy to the veil was known to be so great, that he never willingly passed before a mirror, nor stooped to drink at a still fountain, lest, in its peaceful bosom, he should be affrighted by himself. This was what gave plausibility to the whispers, that Mr. Hooper's conscience tortured him for some great crime too horrible to be entirely concealed, or otherwise than so obscurely intimated. Thus, from beneath the black veil, there rolled a cloud into the sunshine, an ambiguity of sin or sorrow, which enveloped the poor minister, so that love or sympathy could never reach him. It was said, that ghost and fiend consorted with him there. With self-shudderings and outward terrors, he walked continually in its shadow, groping darkly within his own soul, or gazing through a medium that saddened the whole world. Even the lawless wind, it was believed, respected his dreadful secret, and never blew aside the veil. But still good Mr. Hooper sadly smiled at the pale visages of the worldly throng as he passed by.

Among all its bad influences, the black veil had the one desirable effect, of making its wearer a very efficient clergyman. By the aid of his mysterious emblem—for there was no other apparent cause—he became a man of awful power, over souls that were in agony for sin. His converts always regarded him with a dread peculiar to themselves, affirming, though but figuratively, that, before he brought them to celestial light, they had been with him behind the black veil. Its gloom, indeed, enabled him to sympathize with all dark affections. Dying sinners cried aloud for Mr. Hooper, and would not yield their breath till he appeared; though ever, as he stooped to whisper consolation, they shuddered at the veiled face so near their own. Such were the terrors of the black veil, even when Death had bared his visage! Strangers came long distances to attend service at his church, with the mere idle purpose of gazing at his figure, because it was forbidden them to behold his face. But many were made to quake ere they departed! Once, during Governor Belcher's administration, Mr. Hooper was appointed to preach the election sermon. Covered with his black veil, he stood before the chief magistrate, the council, and the representatives, and wrought so deep an impression, that the legislative measures of that year were characterized by all the gloom and piety of our earliest ancestral sway.

In this manner Mr. Hooper spent a long life, irreproachable in outward act, yet shrouded in dismal suspicions; kind and loving, though unloved, and dimly feared; a man apart from men, shunned in their health and joy, but ever summoned to their aid in mortal anguish. As years wore on, shedding their snows above his sable veil, he acquired a name throughout the New England churches, and they called him Father Hooper. Nearly all his parishioners, who were of mature age when he was settled, had been borne away by many a funeral: he had one congregation in the church, and a more crowded one in the church-yard; and having wrought so late into the evening, and done his work so well, it was now good Father Hooper's turn to rest.

Several persons were visible by the shaded candle-light, in the death-chamber of the old clergyman. Natural connections he had none. But there was the decorously grave, though unmoved physician, seeking only to mitigate the last pangs of the patient whom he could not save. There were the deacons, and other eminently pious members of his church. There, also, was the Reverend Mr. Clark, of Westbury, a young and zealous divine, who had ridden in haste to pray by the bedside of the expiring minister. There was the nurse, no hired handmaiden of death, but one whose calm affection had endured thus long in secrecy, in solitude, amid the chill of age, and would not perish, even at the dying hour. Who, but Elizabeth! And there lay the hoary head of good Father Hooper upon the death-pillow, with the black veil still swathed about his brow and reaching down over his face, so that each more difficult gasp of his faint breath caused it to stir. All through life that piece of crape had hung between him and the world: it had separated him from cheerful brotherhood and woman's love, and kept him in that saddest of all prisons, his own heart; and still it lay upon his face, as if to deepen the gloom of his darksome chamber, and shade him from the sunshine of eternity.

For some time previous, his mind had been confused, wavering doubtfully between the past and the present, and hovering forward, as it were, at intervals, into the indistinctness of the world to come. There had been feverish turns, which tossed him from side to side, and wore away what little strength he had. But in his most convulsive struggles, and in the wildest vagaries of his intellect, when no other thought retained its sober influence, he still showed an awful solicitude lest the black veil should slip aside. Even if his bewildered soul could have forgotten, there was a faithful woman at his pillow, who, with averted eyes, would have covered that aged face, which she had last beheld in the comeliness of manhood. At length the death-stricken old man lay quietly in the torpor of mental and bodily exhaustion, with an imperceptible pulse, and breath that grew fainter and fainter, except when a long, deep, and irregular inspiration seemed to prelude the flight of his spirit.

The minister of Westbury approached the bedside.

"Venerable Father Hooper," said he, "the moment of your release is at hand. Are you ready for the lifting of the veil, that shuts in time from eternity?"

Father Hooper at first replied merely by a feeble motion of his head; then, apprehensive, perhaps, that his meaning might be doubtful, he exerted himself to speak.

"Yea," said he, in faint accents, "my soul hath a patient weariness until that veil be lifted."

"And is it fitting," resumed the Reverend Mr. Clark, "that a man so given to prayer, of such a blameless example, holy in deed and thought, so far as mortal judgment may pronounce; is it fitting that a father in the church should leave a shadow on his memory, that may seem to blacken a life so pure? I pray you, my venerable brother, let not this thing be! Suffer us to be gladdened by your triumphant aspect, as you go to your reward. Before the veil of eternity be lifted, let me cast aside this black veil from your face!"

And thus speaking, the Reverend Mr. Clark bent forward to reveal the mystery of so many years. But, exerting a sudden energy, that made all the beholders stand aghast, Father Hooper snatched both his hands from beneath the bed-clothes, and pressed them strongly on the black veil, resolute to struggle, if the minister of Westbury would contend with a dying man.

"Never!" cried the veiled clergyman. "On earth, never!"

"Dark old man!" exclaimed the affrighted minister, "with what horrible crime upon your soul are you now passing to the judgment?"

Father Hooper's breath heaved; it rattled in his throat; but, with a mighty effort, grasping forward with his hands, he caught hold of life, and held it back till he should speak. He even raised himself in bed; and there he sat, shivering with the arms of death around him, while the black veil hung down, awful, at that last moment, in the gathered terrors of a lifetime. And yet the faint, sad smile, so often there, now seemed to glimmer from its obscurity, and linger on Father Hooper's lips.

"Why do you tremble at me alone?" cried he, turning his veiled face round the circle of pale spectators. "Tremble also at each other! Have men avoided me, and women shown no pity, and children screamed and fled, only for my black veil? What, but the mystery which it obscurely typifies, has made this piece of crape so awful? When the friend shows his inmost heart to his friend; the lover to his best beloved; when man does not vainly shrink from the eye of his Creator, loathsomely treasuring up the secret of his sin; then deem me a monster, for the symbol beneath which I have lived, and die! I look around me, and, lo! on every visage a Black Veil!"

While his auditors shrank from one another, in mutual affright, Father Hooper fell back upon his pillow, a veiled corpse, with a faint smile lingering on the lips. Still veiled, they laid him in his coffin, and a veiled corpse they bore him to the grave. The grass of many years has sprung up and withered on that grave, the burial-stone is moss-grown, and good Mr. Hooper's face is dust; but awful is still the thought, that it mouldered beneath the Black Veil!

1836

The Celestial Railroad

Hawthorne's narrative ridicules the easy way of life recommended, as it seemed to him, by the Transcendentalists and especially the liberal Unitarians—the modernists of that day. Hawthorne far preferred the hard way proposed by the Puritans two centuries before. In his scheme of values to be served, he was less at home in his own world than in that of Cotton Mather's *Magnalia*, Milton's *Paradise Lost*, and Bunyan's *The Pilgrim's Progress*.

In *The Pilgrim's Progress*, a vivid allegorical tale, John Bunyan had described life as a hard journey. With his load of sins on his back and his Bible as a chart, Christian sets out on foot, fleeing from the City of Destruction, seeking the Celestial City. On the way are the Slough of Despond, the Wicket-Gate, the Hill Difficulty, the fiend Apollyon in the Valley of Humiliation, the Valley of the Shadow of Death, Vanity Fair, the Delectable Mountains, the River of Death.

What would a new *Pilgrim's Progress* be like—a modern journey of a pilgrim toward the Celestial City? Hawthorne sketched a satirical answer, followed the old pattern of incidents and places but suggested their equivalents in terms of mid-nineteenth-century life and attitudes.

Text: From the author's revised edition of *Mosses from an Old Manse* (Boston, 1854).

Not a great while ago, passing through the gate of dreams, I visited that region of the earth in which lies the famous City of Destruction. It interested me much to learn that by the public spirit of some of the inhabitants a railroad has recently been established between this populous and flourishing town and the Celestial City. Having a little time upon my hands, I resolved to gratify a liberal curiosity by making a trip thither. Accordingly, one fine morning after paying my bill at the hotel and directing the porter to stow my luggage behind a coach, I took my seat in the vehicle and set out for the station house. It was my good fortune to enjoy the company of a gentleman—one Mr. Smooth-it-away—who, though he had never actually visited the Celestial City, yet seemed as well acquainted with its laws, customs, policy, and statistics as with those of the City of Destruction, of which he was a native townsman. Being moreover a director of the railroad corporation and one of its largest stockholders, he had it in his power to give me all desirable information respecting that praiseworthy enterprise.

Our coach rattled out of the city, and at a short distance from its outskirts passed over a bridge of elegant construction, but somewhat too slight, as I imagined, to sustain any considerable weight. On both sides lay an extensive quagmire, which could not have been more disagreeable, either to sight or smell, had all the kennels of the earth emptied their pollution there.

"This," remarked Mr. Smooth-it-away, "is the famous Slough of Despond—a disgrace to all the neighborhood; and the greater, that it might so easily be converted into firm ground."

"I have understood," said I, "that efforts have been made for that purpose from time immemorial. Bunyan mentions that above twenty thousand cartloads of wholesome instructions had been thrown in here without effect."

"Very probably! And what effect could be anticipated from such unsubstantial stuff?" cried Mr. Smooth-it-away. "You observe this convenient bridge. We obtained a sufficient foundation for it by throwing into the slough some editions of books of morality; volumes of French philosophy and German rationalism; tracts, sermons, and essays of modern clergymen; extracts from Plato, Confucius, and various Hindoo sages, together with a few ingenious commentaries upon texts of Scripture,—all of which, by some scientific process, have been converted into a mass like granite. The whole bog might be filled up with similar matter."

It really seemed to me, however, that the bridge vibrated and heaved up and down in a very formidable manner; and, in spite of Mr. Smooth-it-away's testimony to the solidity of its foundation, I should be loath to cross it in a crowded omnibus, especially if each passenger were encumbered with as heavy luggage as that gentleman and myself. Nevertheless we got over without accident, and soon found ourselves at the station house. This very neat and spacious edifice is erected on the site of the little wicket gate, which formerly, as all old pilgrims will recollect, stood directly across the highway, and, by its inconvenient narrowness, was a great obstruction to the traveller of liberal mind and expansive stomach. The reader of John Bunyan will be glad to know that Christian's old friend Evangelist, who was accustomed to supply each pilgrim with a mystic roll, now presides at the ticket office. Some malicious persons it is true deny the identity of this reputable character with the Evangelist of old times, and even pretend to bring competent evidence of an imposture. Without involving myself in a dispute I shall merely observe that, so far as my experience goes, the square pieces of pasteboard now delivered to passengers are much more convenient and useful along the road than the antique roll of parchment. Whether they will be as readily received at the gate of the Celestial City I decline giving an opinion.

A large number of passengers were already at the station house awaiting the departure of the cars. By the aspect and demeanor of these persons it was easy to judge that the feelings of the community had undergone a very favorable change in reference to the celestial pilgrimage. It would have done Bunyan's heart good to see it. Instead of a lonely and ragged man, with a huge burden on his back, plodding along sorrowfully on foot while the whole city hooted after him, here were parties of the first gentry and most respectable people in the neighborhood setting forth towards the Celestial City as cheerfully as if the pilgrimage were merely a summer tour. Among the gentlemen were characters of deserved eminence—magistrates, politicians, and men of wealth, by whose example religion could not but be greatly recommended to their meaner brethren. In the ladies' apartment, too, I rejoiced to distinguish some of those flowers of fashionable society who are so well fitted to adorn the most elevated circles of the Celestial City. There was much pleasant conversation about the news of the day, topics of business, and politics, or the lighter matters of amusement; while religion, though indubitably the main thing at heart, was thrown tastefully into the background. Even an infidel would have heard little or nothing to shock his sensibility.

One great convenience of the new method of going on pilgrimage I must not forget to mention. Our enormous burdens, instead of being carried on our shoulders as had been the custom of old, were all snugly deposited in the baggage car, and, as I was assured, would be delivered to their respective owners at the journey's end. Another thing, likewise, the benevolent reader will be delighted to understand. It may be remembered that there was an ancient feud between Prince Beelzebub and the keeper of the wicket gate, and that the adherents of the former distinguished personage were accustomed to shoot deadly arrows at honest pilgrims while knocking at the door. This dispute, much to the credit as well of the illustrious potentate above mentioned as of the worthy and enlightened directors of the railroad, has been pacifically arranged on the principle of mutual compromise. The prince's subjects are now pretty numerously employed about the station house, some in taking care of the baggage, others in collecting fuel, feeding the engines, and such congenial occupations; and I can conscientiously affirm that persons more attentive to their business, more willing to accommodate, or more generally agreeable to the passengers, are not to be found on any railroad. Every good heart must surely exult at so satisfactory an arrangement of an immemorial difficulty.

"Where is Mr. Greatheart?" inquired I. "Beyond a doubt the directors have engaged that famous old champion to be chief conductor on the railroad?"

"Why, no," said Mr. Smooth-it-away, with a dry cough. "He was offered the situation of brakeman; but, to tell you the truth, our friend Greatheart has grown preposterously stiff and narrow in his old age. He has so often guided pilgrims over the road on foot that he considers it a sin to travel in any other fashion. Besides, the old fellow had entered so heartily into the ancient feud with Prince Beelzebub that he would have been perpetually at blows or ill language with some of the prince's subjects, and thus have embroiled us anew. So, on the whole, we were not sorry when honest Greatheart went off to the Celestial City in a huff and left us at liberty to choose a more suitable and accommodating man. Yonder comes the engineer of the train. You will probably recognize him at once."

The engine at this moment took its station in advance of the cars, looking, I must confess, much more like a sort of mechanical demon that would hurry us to the infernal regions than a laudable contrivance for smoothing our way to the Celestial City. On its top sat a personage almost enveloped in smoke and flame, which, not to startle the reader, appeared to gush from his own mouth and stomach as well as from the engine's brazen abdomen.

"Do my eyes deceive me?" cried I. "What on earth is this! A living creature? If so, he is own brother to the engine he rides upon!"

"Poh, poh, you are obtuse!" said Mr. Smooth-it-away, with a hearty laugh. "Don't you know Apollyon, Christian's old enemy, with whom he fought so fierce a battle in the Valley of Humiliation? He was the very fellow to manage the engine; and so we have reconciled him to the custom of going on pilgrimage, and engaged him as chief engineer."

"Bravo, bravo!" exclaimed I, with irrepressible enthusiasm; "this shows the liberality of the age; this proves, if anything can, that all musty prejudices are in a fair way to be obliterated. And how will Christian rejoice to hear of this happy transformation of his old antagonist! I promise myself great pleasure in informing him of it when we reach the Celestial City."

The passengers being all comfortably seated, we now rattled away merrily, accomplishing a greater distance in ten minutes than Christian probably trudged over in a day. It was laughable, while we glanced along, as it were, at the tail of a thunderbolt, to observe two dusty foot travelers in the old pilgrim guise, with cockle shell and staff, their mystic rolls of parchment in their hands and their intolerable burdens on their backs. The preposterous obstinacy of these honest people in persisting to groan and stumble along the difficult pathway rather than take advantage of modern improvements, excited great mirth among our wiser brotherhood. We greeted the two pilgrims with many pleasant gibes and a roar of laughter; whereupon they gazed at us with such woful and absurdly compassionate visages that our merriment grew tenfold more obstreperous. Apollyon also entered heartily into the fun, and contrived to flirt the smoke and flame of the engine, or of his own breath, into their faces, and envelop them in an atmosphere of scalding steam. These little practical jokes amused us mightily, and doubtless afforded the pilgrims the gratification of considering themselves martyrs.

At some distance from the railroad Mr. Smooth-it-away pointed to a large, antique edifice, which, he observed, was a tavern of long standing, and had formerly been a noted stopping-place for pilgrims. In Bunyan's road book it is mentioned as the Interpreter's House.

"I have long had a curiosity to visit that old mansion," remarked I.

"It is not one of our stations, as you perceive," said my companion. "The keeper was violently opposed to the railroad; and well he might be, as the track left his house of entertainment on one side, and thus was pretty certain to deprive him of all his reputable customers. But the footpath still passes his door; and the old gentleman now and then receives a call from some simple traveller, and entertains him with fare as old-fashioned as himself."

Before our talk on this subject came to a conclusion we were rushing by the place where Christian's burden fell from his shoulders at the sight of the Cross. This served as a theme for Mr. Smooth-it-away, Mr. Live-for-the-world, Mr. Hide-sin-in-the-heart, Mr. Scaly-conscience, and a knot of gentlemen from the town of Shun-repentance, to descant upon the inestimable advantages resulting from the safety of our baggage. Myself, and all the passengers indeed, joined with great unanimity in this view of the matter; for our burdens were rich in many things esteemed precious throughout the world; and, especially, we each of us possessed a great variety of favorite Habits, which we trusted would not be out of fashion even in the polite circles of the Celestial City. It would have been a sad spectacle to see such an assortment of valuable articles tumbling into the sepulchre. Thus pleasantly conversing on the favorable circumstances of our position as compared with those of past pilgrims and of narrow-minded ones at the present day, we soon found ourselves at the foot of the Hill Difficulty. Through the very heart of this rocky mountain a tunnel has been constructed of most admirable architecture, with a lofty arch and a spacious double track; so that, unless the earth and rocks should chance to crumble down, it will remain an eternal monument of the builder's skill and enterprise. It is a great though incidental advantage that the materials from the heart of the Hill Difficulty have been employed in filling up the Valley of Humiliation, thus obviating the necessity of descending into that disagreeable and unwholesome hollow.

"This is a wonderful improvement, indeed," said I. "Yet I should have been glad of an opportunity to visit the Palace Beautiful and be introduced to the charming young ladies—Miss Prudence, Miss Piety, Miss Charity, and the rest—who have the kindness to entertain pilgrims there."

"Young ladies!" cried Mr. Smooth-it-away, as soon as he could speak for laughing. "And charming young ladies! Why, my dear fellow, they are old maids, every soul of them—prim, starched, dry, and angular; and not one of them, I will venture to say, has altered so much as the fashion of her gown since the days of Christian's pilgrimage."

"Ah, well," said I, much comforted, "then I can very readily dispense with their acquaintance."

The respectable Apollyon was now putting on the steam at a prodigious rate, anxious, perhaps, to get rid of the unpleasant reminiscences connected with the spot where he had so disastrously encountered Christian. Consulting Mr. Bunyan's road-book, I perceived that we must now be within a few miles of the Valley of the Shadow of Death, into which doleful region, at our present speed, we should plunge much sooner than seemed at all desirable. In truth, I expected nothing better than to find myself in the ditch on one side or the quag on the other; but on communicating my apprehensions to Mr. Smooth-it-away, he assured me that the difficulties of this passage, even in its worst condition, had been vastly exaggerated, and that, in its present state of improvement, I might consider myself as safe as on any railroad in Christendom.

Even while we were speaking the train shot into the entrance of this dreaded Valley. Though I plead guilty to some foolish palpitations of the heart during our headlong rush over the causeway here con-structed, yet it were unjust to withhold the highest encomiums on the boldness of its original conception and the ingenuity of those who executed it. It was gratifying, likewise, to observe how much care had been taken to dispel the everlasting gloom and supply the defect of cheerful sunshine, not a ray of which has ever penetrated among these awful shadows. For this purpose, the inflammable gas which exudes plentifully from the soil is collected by means of pipes, and thence communicated to a quadruple row of lamps along the whole extent of the passage. Thus a radiance has been created even out of the fiery and sulphurous curse that rests forever upon the valley—a radiance hurtful, however, to the eyes, and somewhat bewildering, as I discovered by the changes which it wrought in the visages of my companions. In this respect, as compared with natural daylight, there is the same difference as between truth and falsehood; but if the reader have ever travelled through the dark Valley, he will have learned to be thankful for any light that he could get—if not from the sky above, then from the blasted soil beneath. Such was the red brilliancy of these lamps that they appeared to build walls of fire on both sides of the track, between which we held our course at lightning speed, while a reverberating thunder filled the Valley with its echoes. Had the engine run off the track—a catastrophe, it is whispered, by no means unprecedented,—the bottomless pit, if there be any such place, would undoubtedly have received us. Just as some dismal fooleries of this nature had made my heart quake there came a tremendous shriek, careering along the valley as if a thousand devils had burst their lungs to utter it, but which proved to be merely the whistle of the engine on arriving at a stopping-place.

The spot where we had now paused is the same that our friend Bunyan—a truthful man, but infected with many fantastic notions—has designated, in terms plainer than I like to repeat, as the mouth of the infernal region. This, however, must be a mistake, inasmuch as Mr. Smooth-it-away, while we remained in the smoky and lurid cavern, took occasion to prove that Tophet has not even a metaphorical existence. The place, he assured us, is no other than the crater of a half-extinct volcano, in which the directors had caused forges to be set up for the manufacture of railroad iron. Hence, also, is obtained a plentiful supply of fuel for the use of the engines. Whoever had gazed into the dismal obscurity of the broad cavern mouth, whence ever and anon darted huge tongues of dusky flame, and had seen the strange, half-shaped monsters, and visions of faces horribly grotesque, into which the smoke seemed to wreathe itself, and had heard the awful murmurs, and shrieks, and deep, shuddering whispers of the blast, sometimes forming themselves into words almost articulate, would have seized upon Mr. Smooth-it-away's comfortable explanation as greedily as we did. The inhabitants of the cavern, moreover, were unlovely personages, dark, smoke-begrimed, generally deformed, with misshapen feet, and a glow of dusky redness in their eyes as if their hearts had caught fire and were blazing out of the upper windows. It struck me as a peculiarity that the laborers at the forge and those who brought fuel to the engine, when they began to draw short breath, positively emitted smoke from their mouth and nostrils.

Among the idlers about the train, most of whom were puffing cigars which they had lighted at the flame of the crater, I was perplexed to notice several who, to my certain knowledge, had heretofore set forth by railroad for the Celestial City. They looked dark, wild, and smoky, with a singular resemblance, indeed, to the native inhabitants, like whom, also, they had a disagreeable propensity to ill-natured gibes and sneers, the habit of which had wrought a settled contortion of their visages. Having been on speaking terms with one of these persons,—an indolent, good-for-nothing fellow, who went by the name of Take-it-easy,—I called him, and inquired what was his business there.

"Did you not start," said I, "for the Celestial City?"

"That's a fact," said Mr. Take-it-easy, carelessly puffing some smoke into my eyes. "But I heard such bad accounts that I never took pains to climb the hill on which the city stands. No business doing, no fun going on, nothing to drink, and no smoking allowed, and a thrumming of church music from morning till night. I would not stay in such a place if they offered me house room and living free."

"But, my good Mr. Take-it-easy," cried I, "why take up your residence here, of all places in the world?"

"O," said the loafer, with a grin, "it is very warm hereabouts, and I meet with plenty of old acquaintances, and altogether the place suits me. I hope to see you back again some day soon. A pleasant journey to you."

While he was speaking the bell of the engine rang, and we dashed away, after dropping a few passengers, but receiving no new ones. Rattling onward through the Valley, we were dazzled with the fiercely gleaming gas lamps, as before. But sometimes, in the dark of intense brightness, grim faces, that bore the aspect and expression of individual sins, or evil passions, seemed to thrust themselves through the veil of light, glaring upon us, and stretching forth a great, dusky hand, as if to impede our progress. I almost thought that they were my own sins that appalled me there. These were freaks

of imagination—nothing more, certainly—mere delusions, which I ought to be heartily ashamed of; but all through the Dark Valley I was tormented, and pestered, and dolefully bewildered with the same kind of waking dreams. The mephitic gases of that region intoxicate the brain. As the light of natural day, however, began to struggle with the glow of the lanterns, these vain imaginations lost their vividness, and finally vanished with the first ray of sunshine that greeted our escape from the Valley of the Shadow of Death. Ere we had gone a mile beyond it I could well nigh have taken my oath that this whole gloomy passage was a dream.

At the end of the valley, as John Bunyan mentions, is a cavern, where, in his days, dwelt two cruel giants, Pope and Pagan, who had strown the ground about their residence with the bones of slaughtered pilgrims. These vile old troglodytes are no longer there; but into their deserted cave another terrible giant has thrust himself, and makes it his business to seize upon honest travellers and fatten them for his table with plentiful meals of smoke, mist, moonshine, raw potatoes, and sawdust. He is a German by birth, and is called Giant Transcendentalist; but as to his form, his features, his substance, and his nature generally, it is the chief peculiarity of this huge miscreant that neither he for himself, nor anybody for him, has ever been able to describe them. As we rushed by the cavern's mouth we caught a hasty glimpse of him, looking somewhat like an ill-proportioned figure, but considerably more like a heap of fog and duskiness. He shouted after us, but in so strange a phraseology that we knew not what he meant, nor whether to be encouraged or affrighted.

It was late in the day when the train thundered into the ancient city of Vanity, where Vanity Fair is still at the height of prosperity, and exhibits an epitome of whatever is brilliant, gay, and fascinating beneath the sun. As I purposed to make a considerable stay here, it gratified me to learn that there is no longer the want of harmony between the town's people and pilgrims, which impelled the former to such lamentably mistaken measures as the persecution of Christian and the fiery martyrdom of Faithful. On the contrary, as the new railroad brings with it great trade and a constant influx of strangers, the lord of Vanity Fair is its chief patron, and the capitalists of the city are among the largest stockholders. Many passengers stop to take their pleasure or make their profit in the Fair, instead of going onward to the Celestial City. Indeed, such are the charms of the place that people often affirm it to be the true and only heaven; stoutly contending that there is no other, that those who seek further are mere dreamers, and that, if the fabled brightness of the Celestial City lay but a bare mile beyond the gates of Vanity, they would not be fools enough to go thither. Without subscribing to these perhaps exaggerated encomiums, I can truly say that my abode in the city was mainly agreeable, and my intercourse with the inhabitants productive of much amusement and instruction.

Being naturally of a serious turn, my attention was directed to the solid advantages derivable from a residence here, rather than to the effervescent pleasures which are the grand object with too many visitants. The Christian reader, if he have had no accounts of the city later than Bunyan's time, will be surprised to hear that almost every street has its church, and that the reverend clergy are nowhere held in higher respect than at Vanity Fair. And well do they deserve such honorable estimation; for the maxims of wisdom and virtue which fall from their lips come from as deep a spiritual source, and tend to as lofty a religious aim, as those of the sagest philosophers of old. In justification of this high praise I need only mention the names of the Rev. Mr. Shallow-deep, the Rev. Mr. Stumble-at-truth, that fine old clerical character the Rev. Mr. This-to-day, who expects shortly to resign his pulpit to the Rev. Mr. That-tomorrow; together with the Rev. Mr. Bewilderment, the Rev. Mr. Clog-the-spirit, and, last and greatest, the Rev. Dr. Wind-of-doctrine. The labors of these eminent divines are aided by those of innumerable lecturers, who diffuse such a various profundity, in all subjects of human or celestial science, that any man may acquire an omnigenous erudition without the trouble of even learning to read. Thus literature is etherealized by assuming for its medium the human voice; and knowledge, depositing all its heavier particles, except, doubtless, its gold, becomes exhaled into a sound, which forthwith steals into the ever-open ear of the community. These ingenious methods constitute a sort of machinery, by which thought and study are done to every person's hand without his putting himself to the slightest inconvenience in the matter. There is another species of machine for the whole-sale manufacture of individual morality. This excellent result is effected by societies for all manner of virtuous purposes, with which a man has merely to connect himself, throwing, as it were, his quota of virtue into the common stock, and the president and directors will take care that the aggregate amount be well applied. All these, and other wonderful improvements in ethics, religion, and literature, being made plain to my comprehension by the ingenious Mr. Smooth-it-away, inspired me with a vast admiration of Vanity Fair.

It would fill a volume, in an age of pamphlets, were I to record all my observations in this great capital of human business and pleasure. There was an unlimited range of society—the powerful, the wise, the witty, and the famous in every walk of life; princes, presidents, poets, generals, artists, actors, and philanthropists,—all making their own market at the fair, and deeming no price too exorbitant for such commodities as hit their fancy. It was well worth one's while, even if he had no idea of buying or selling, to loiter through the bazaars and observe the various sorts of traffic that were going forward.

Some of the purchasers, I thought, made very foolish bargains. For instance, a young man having inherited a splendid fortune, laid out a considerable portion of it in the purchase of diseases, and finally spent all the rest for a heavy lot of repentance and a suit of rags. A very pretty girl bartered a heart as clear as crystal, and which seemed her most valuable possession, for another jewel of the same kind, but so worn and defaced as to be utterly worthless. In one shop there were a great many crowns of laurel and myrtle, which soldiers, authors, statesmen, and various other people pressed eagerly to buy; some purchased these paltry wreaths with their lives, others by a toilsome servitude of years, and many sacrificed whatever was most valuable, yet finally slunk away without the crown. There was a sort of stock or scrip, called Conscience, which seemed to be in great demand, and would purchase almost anything. Indeed, few rich commodities were to be obtained without paying a heavy sum in this particular stock, and a man's business was seldom very lucrative unless he knew precisely when and how to throw his hoard of conscience into the market. Yet as this stock was the only thing of permanent value, whoever parted with it was sure to find himself a loser in the long run. Several of the speculations were of a questionable character. Occasionally a member of Congress recruited his pocket by the sale of his constituents; and I was assured that public officers have often sold their country at very moderate prices. Thousands sold their happiness for a whim. Gilded chains were in great demand, and purchased with almost any sacrifice. In truth, those who desired, according to the old adage, to sell anything valuable for a song, might find customers all over the Fair; and there were innumerable messes of pottage, piping hot, for such as chose to buy them with their birthrights. A few articles, however, could not be found genuine at Vanity Fair. If a customer wished to renew his stock of youth the dealers offered him a set of false teeth and an auburn wig; if he demanded peace of mind, they recommended opium or a brandy bottle.

Tracts of land and golden mansions, situate in the Celestial City, were often exchanged, at very disadvantageous rates, for a few years' lease of small, dismal, inconvenient tenements in Vanity Fair. Prince Beelzebub himself took great interest in this sort of traffic, and sometimes condescended to meddle with smaller matters. I once had the pleasure to see him bargaining with a miser for his soul, which, after much ingenious skirmishing on both sides, his highness succeeded in obtaining at about the value of sixpence. The prince remarked, with a smile, that he was a loser by the transaction.

Day after day, as I walked the streets of Vanity, my manners and deportment became more and more like those of the inhabitants. The place began to seem like home; the idea of pursuing my travels to the Celestial City was almost obliterated from my mind. I was reminded of it, however, by the sight of the same pair of simple pilgrims at whom we had laughed so heartily when Apollyon puffed smoke and steam into their faces at the commencement of our journey. There they stood amidst the densest bustle of Vanity; the dealers offering them their purple and fine linen and jewels, the men of wit and humor gibing at them, a pair of buxom ladies ogling them askance, while the benevolent Mr. Smooth-it-away whispered some of his wisdom at their elbows, and pointed to a newly-erected temple; but there were these worthy simpletons, making the scene look wild and monstrous, merely by their sturdy repudiation of all part in its business or pleasures.

One of them—his name was Stick-to-the-right—perceived in my face, I suppose, a species of sympathy and almost admiration, which, to my own great surprise, I could not help feeling for this pragmatic couple. It prompted him to address me.

"Sir," inquired he, with a sad, yet mild and kindly voice, "do you call yourself a pilgrim?"

"Yes," I replied, "my right to that appellation is indubitable. I am merely a sojourner here in Vanity Fair, being bound to the Celestial City by the new railroad."

"Alas, friend," rejoined Mr. Stick-to-the-right, "I do assure you, and beseech you to receive the truth of my words, that that whole concern is a bubble. You may travel on it all your lifetime, were you to live thousands of years, and yet never get beyond the limits of Vanity Fair. Yea, though you should deem yourself entering the gates of the blessed city, it will be nothing but a miserable delusion."

"The Lord of the Celestial City," began the other pilgrim, whose name was Mr. Foot-it-to-heaven, "has refused, and will ever refuse, to grant an act of incorporation for this railroad; and, unless that be obtained, no passenger can ever hope to enter his dominions. Wherefore every man who buys a ticket must lay his account with losing the purchase money, which is the value of his own soul."

"Poh, nonsense!" said Mr. Smooth-it-away, taking my arm and leading me off, "these fellows ought to be indicted for a libel. If the law stood as it once did in Vanity Fair we should see them grinning through the iron bars of the prison window."

This incident made a considerable impression on my mind, and contributed with other circumstances to indispose me to a permanent residence in the city of Vanity; although, of course, I was not simple enough to give up my original plan of gliding along easily and commodiously by railroad. Still, I grew anxious to be gone. There was one strange thing that troubled me. Amid the occupations or amusements of the Fair, nothing was more common than for a person—whether at feast, theatre, or church, or trafficking for wealth and honors, or whatever he might be doing, and however unseasonable the interruption—suddenly to vanish like a soap bubble, and be never more seen of his fellows; and so accustomed were the latter to such little accidents that they went on with their business as quietly as if nothing had happened. But it was otherwise with me.

Finally, after a pretty long residence at the Fair, I resumed my journey towards the Celestial City, still with Mr. Smooth-it-away at my side. At a short distance beyond the suburbs of Vanity we passed the ancient silver mine, of which Demas was the first discoverer, and which is now wrought to great advantage, supplying nearly all the coined currency of the world. A little further onward was the spot where Lot's wife had stood forever under the semblance of a pillar of salt. Curious travellers have long since carried it away piecemeal. Had all regrets been punished as rigorously as this poor dame's were, my yearning for the relinquished delights of Vanity Fair might have produced a similar change in my own corporeal substance, and left me a warning to future pilgrims.

The next remarkable object was a large edifice, constructed of moss-grown stone, but in a modern and airy style of architecture. The engine came to a pause in its vicinity, with the usual tremendous shriek.

"This was formerly the castle of the redoubted giant Despair," observed Mr. Smooth-it-away; "but since his death Mr. Flimsy-faith has repaired it, and keeps an excellent house of entertainment here. It is one of our stopping-places."

"It seems but slightly put together," remarked I, looking at the frail yet ponderous walls. "I do not envy Mr. Flimsy-faith his habitation. Some day it will thunder down upon the heads of the occupants."

"We shall escape, at all events," said Mr. Smooth-it-away, "for Apollyon is putting on the steam again."

The road now plunged into a gorge of the Delectable Mountains, and traversed the field where in former ages the blind men wandered and stumbled among the tombs. One of these ancient tombstones had been thrust across the track by some malicious person, and gave the train of cars a terrible jolt. Far up the rugged side of a mountain I perceived a rusty iron door, half overgrown with bushes and creeping plants, but with smoke issuing from its crevices.

"Is that," inquired I, "the very door in the hillside which the shepherds assured Christian was a byway to hell?"

"That was a joke on the part of the shepherds," said Mr. Smooth-it-away, with a smile. "It is neither more nor less than the door of a cavern which they use as a smoke house for the preparation of mutton hams."

My recollections of the journey are now, for a little space, dim and confused, inasmuch as a singular drowsiness here overcame me, owing to the fact that we were passing over the enchanted ground, the air of which encourages a disposition to sleep. I awoke, however, as soon as we crossed the borders of the pleasant land of Beulah. All the passengers were rubbing their eyes, comparing watches, and congratulating one another on the prospect of arriving so seasonably at the journey's end. The sweet breezes of this happy clime came refreshingly to our nostrils; we beheld the glimmering gush of silver fountains, overhung by trees of beautiful foliage and delicious fruit, which were propagated by grafts from the celestial gardens. Once, as we dashed onward like a hurricane, there was a flutter of wings and the bright appearance of an angel in the air, speeding forth on some heavenly mission. The engine now announced the close vicinity of the final station house by one last and horrible scream, in which there seemed to be distinguishable every kind of wailing and woe, and bitter fierceness of wrath, all mixed up with the wild laughter of a devil or a madman. Throughout our journey, at every stopping-place, Apollyon had exercised his ingenuity in screwing the most abominable sounds out of the whistle of the steam engine; but in this closing effort he outdid himself, and created an infernal uproar, which, besides disturbing the peaceful inhabitants of Beulah, must have sent its discord even through the celestial gates.

While the horrid clamor was still ringing in our ears, we heard an exulting strain, as if a thousand instruments of music, with height, and depth, and sweetness in their tones, at once tender and triumphant, were struck in unison, to greet the approach of some illustrious hero, who had fought the good fight and won a glorious victory, and was come to lay aside his battered arms forever. Looking to ascertain what might be the occasion of this glad harmony, I perceived, on alighting from the cars, that a multitude of shining ones had assembled on the other side of the river, to welcome two poor pilgrims, who were just emerging from its depths. They were the same whom Apollyon and ourselves had persecuted with taunts, and gibes, and scalding steam, at the commencement of our journey—the same whose unworldly aspect and impressive words

had stirred my conscience amid the wild revellers of Vanity Fair.

"How amazingly well those men have got on," cried I to Mr. Smooth-it-away. "I wish we were secure of as good a reception."

"Never fear, never fear!" answered my friend. "Come, make haste; the ferry boat will be off directly, and in three minutes you will be on the other side of the river. No doubt you will find coaches to carry you up to the city gates."

A steam ferry boat, the last improvement on this important route, lay at the river side, puffing, snorting, and emitting all those other disagreeable utterances which betoken the departure to be immediate. I hurried on board with the rest of the passengers, most of whom were in great perturbation; some bawling out for their baggage; some tearing their hair and exclaiming that the boat would explode or sink; some already pale with the heaving of the stream; some gazing affrighted at the ugly aspect of the steersman; and some still dizzy with the slumberous influences of the Enchanted Ground. Looking back to the shore, I was amazed to discern Mr. Smooth-it-away waving his hand in token of farewell.

"Don't you go over to the Celestial City?" exclaimed I.

"O, no!" answered he with a queer smile, and that same disagreeable contortion of visage which I had remarked in the inhabitants of the Dark Valley. "O, no! I have come thus far only for the sake of your pleasant company. Good-by! We shall meet again."

And then did my excellent friend Mr. Smooth-it-away laugh outright, in the midst of which cachinnation a smoke-wreath issued from his mouth and nostrils, while a twinkle of lurid flame darted out of either eye, proving indubitably that his heart was all of a red blaze. The impudent fiend! To deny the existence of Tophet, when he felt its fiery tortures raging within his breast. I rushed to the side of the boat, intending to fling myself on shore; but the wheels, as they began their revolutions, threw a dash of spray over me so cold—so deadly cold, with the chill that will never leave those waters until Death be drowned in his own river—that, with a shiver and a heartquake I awoke. Thank heaven it was a Dream

1843

The Artist of the Beautiful

In this story Hawthorne deals with the common romantic theme of the sensitive, idealistic artist in a practical and materialistic society. Note how he works out the contrast through characters that embody it and through incidents that give it dramatic poignancy.

In European life and literature many romantic poets

and artists, feeling misunderstood and isolated like Hawthorne's hero, contemplated or committed self-destruction. But Owen Warland, possessing "force of character" along with "delicacy," learns to recognize that "the reward of all high performance must be sought within itself." Self-reliant, "he must stand up against mankind and be his own sole disciple, both as respects his genius and the objects to which it is directed." What is truly valuable to an artist is not a material symbol but his inner vision of beauty.

Text: From the author's revised edition of *Mosses from an Old Manse* (Boston, 1854).

An elderly man, with his pretty daughter on his arm, was passing along the street, and emerged from the gloom of the cloudy evening into the light that fell across the pavement from the window of a small shop. It was a projecting window; and on the inside were suspended a variety of watches, pinchbeck, silver, and one or two of gold, all with their faces turned from the street, as if churlishly disinclined to inform the wayfarers what o'clock it was. Seated within the shop, sidelong to the window, with his pale face bent earnestly over some delicate piece of mechanism on which was thrown the concentrated lustre of a shade lamp, appeared a young man.

"What can Owen Warland be about?" muttered old Peter Hovenden, himself a retired watchmaker and the former master of this same young man whose occupation he was now wondering at. "What can the fellow be about? These six months past I have never come by his shop without seeing him just as steadily at work as now. It would be a flight beyond his usual foolery to seek for the perpetual motion; and yet I know enough of my old business to be certain that what he is now so busy with is no part of the machinery of a watch."

"Perhaps, father," said Annie, without showing much interest in the question, "Owen is inventing a new kind of timekeeper. I am sure he has ingenuity enough."

"Poh, child! He has not the sort of ingenuity to invent anything better than a Dutch toy," answered her father, who had formerly been put to much vexation by Owen Warland's irregular genius. "A plague on such ingenuity! All the effect that ever I knew of it was, to spoil the accuracy of some of the best watches in my shop. He would turn the sun out of its orbit and derange the whole course of time, if, as I said before, his ingenuity could grasp anything bigger than a child's toy!"

"Hush, father! He hears you!" whispered Annie, pressing the old man's arm. "His ears are as delicate as his feelings; and you know how easily disturbed they are. Do let us move on."

So Peter Hovenden and his daughter Annie plodded on without further conversation, until in a by-street of the town they found themselves passing the open door of a blacksmith's shop. Within was seen the forge, now blazing up and illuminating the high and dusky roof, and now confining its lustre to a narrow precinct of the coal-strewn floor, according as the breath of the bellows was puffed forth or again inhaled into its vast leathern lungs. In the intervals of brightness it was easy to distinguish objects in remote corners of the shop and the horseshoes that hung upon the wall; in the momentary gloom the fire seemed to be glimmering amidst the vagueness of unenclosed space. Moving about in this red glare and alternate dusk was the figure of the blacksmith, well worthy to be viewed in so picturesque an aspect of light and shade, where the bright blaze struggled with the black night, as if each would have snatched his comely strength from the other. Anon he drew a whitehot bar of iron from the coals, laid it on the anvil, uplifted his arm of might, and was soon enveloped in the myriads of sparks which the strokes of his hammer scattered into the surrounding gloom.

"Now, that is a pleasant sight," said the old watch-maker. "I know what it is to work in gold; but give me the worker in iron after all is said and done. He spends his labor upon a reality. What say you, daughter Annie?"

"Pray don't speak so loud, father," whispered Annie. "Robert Danforth will hear you."

"And what if he should hear me?" said Peter Hovenden. "I say again, it is a good and a wholesome thing to depend upon main strength and reality, and to earn one's bread with the bare and brawny arm of a blacksmith. A watchmaker gets his brain puzzled by his wheels within a wheel, or loses his health or the nicety of his eyesight, as was my case, and finds himself at middle age, or a little after, past labor at his own trade and fit for nothing else, yet too poor to live at his ease. So I say once again, give me main strength for my money. And then, how it takes the nonsense out of a man! Did you ever hear of a blacksmith being such a fool as Owen Warland yonder?"

"Well said, uncle Hovenden!" shouted Robert Danforth from the forge, in a full, deep, merry voice, that made the roof re-echo. "And what says Miss Annie to that doctrine? She, I suppose, will think it a genteeler business to tinker up a lady's watch than to forge a horseshoe or make a gridiron."

Annie drew her father onward without giving him time for reply.

But we must return to Owen Warland's shop, and spend more meditation upon his history and character than either Peter Hovenden, or probably his daughter Annie, or Owen's old schoolfellow, Robert Danforth, would have thought due to so slight a subject. From the time that his little fingers could grasp a penknife, Owen had been remarkable for a delicate ingenuity, which sometimes produced

IMPRACTICAL FROM CHILDHOOD

pretty shapes in wood, principally figures of flowers and birds, and sometimes seemed to aim at the hidden mysteries of mechanism. But it was always for purposes of grace, and never with any mockery of the useful. He did not, like the crowd of schoolboy artisans, construct little windmills on the angle of a barn or watermills across the neighboring brook. Those who discovered such peculiarity in the boy as to think it worth their while to observe him closely, sometimes saw reason to suppose that he was attempting to imitate the beautiful movements of Nature as exemplified in the flight of birds or the activity of little animals. It seemed, in fact, a new development of the love of the beautiful, such as might have made him a poet, a painter, or a sculptor, and which was as completely refined from all utilitarian coarseness as it could have been in either of the fine arts. He looked with singular distaste at the stiff and regular processes of ordinary machinery. Being once carried to see a steam engine, in the expectation that his intuitive comprehension of mechanical principles would be gratified, he turned pale and grew sick, as if something monstrous and unnatural had been presented to him. This horror was partly owing to the size and terrible energy of the iron laborer; for the character of Owen's mind was microscopic, and tended naturally to the minute, in accordance with his diminutive frame and the marvellous smallness and delicate power of his fingers. Not that his sense of beauty was thereby diminished into a sense of prettiness. The beautiful idea has no relation to size, and may be as perfectly developed in a space too minute for any but microscopic investigation as within the ample verge that is measured by the arc of the rainbow. But, at all events, this characteristic minuteness in his objects and accomplishments made the world even more incapable than it might otherwise have been of appreciating Owen Warland's genius. The boy's relatives saw nothing better to be done—as perhaps there was not—than to bind him apprentice to a watchmaker, hoping that his strange ingenuity might thus be regulated and put to utilitarian purposes.

LARGE, POWERFUL MACHINERY

OPINION H.

Peter Hovenden's opinion of his apprentice has already been expressed. He could make nothing of the lad. Owen's apprehension of the professional mysteries, it is true, was inconceivably quick; but he altogether forgot or despised the grand object of a watchmaker's business, and cared no more for the measurement of time than if it had been merged into eternity. So long, however, as he remained under his old master's care, Owen's lack of sturdiness made it possible, by strict injunctions and sharp oversight, to restrain his creative eccentricity within bounds; but when his apprenticeship was served out, and he had taken the little shop which Peter Hovenden's failing eyesight compelled him to relinquish, then did people recognize how unfit a person

was Owen Warland to lead old blind Father Time along his daily course. One of his most rational projects was to connect a musical operation with the machinery of his watches, so that all the harsh dissonances of life might be rendered tuneful, and each flitting moment fall into the abyss of the past in golden drops of harmony. If a family clock was intrusted to him for repair,—one of those tall, ancient clocks that have grown nearly allied to human nature by measuring out the lifetime of many generations,—he would take upon himself to arrange a dance or funeral procession of figures across its venerable face, representing twelve mirthful or melancholy hours. Several freaks of this kind quite destroyed the young watchmaker's credit with that steady and matter-of-fact class of people who hold the opinion that time is not to be trifled with, whether considered as the medium of advancement and prosperity in this world or preparation for the next. His custom rapidly diminished—a misfortune, however, that was probably reckoned among his better accidents by Owen Warland, who was becoming more and more absorbed in a secret occupation which drew all his science and manual dexterity into itself, and likewise gave full employment to the characteristic tendencies of his genius. This pursuit had already consumed many months.

TOYS WITH TIME

After the old watchmaker and his pretty daughter had gazed at him out of the obscurity of the street, Owen Warland was seized with a fluttering of the nerves, which made his hand tremble too violently to proceed with such delicate labor as he was now engaged upon.

FLUTTERY NERVES

"It was Annie herself!" murmured he. "I should have known it, by this throbbing of my heart, before I heard her father's voice Ah, how it throbs! I shall scarcely be able to work again on this exquisite mechanism to-night. Annie! dearest Annie! thou shouldst give firmness to my heart and hand, and not shake them thus; for, if I strive to put the very spirit of beauty into form and give it motion, it is for thy sake alone. O throbbing heart, be quiet! If my labor be thus thwarted, there will come vague and unsatisfied dreams, which will leave me spiritless to-morrow."

As he was endeavoring to settle himself again to his task, the shop door opened and gave admittance to no other than the stalwart figure which Peter Hovenden had paused to admire, as seen amid the light and shadow of the blacksmith's shop. Robert Danforth had brought a little anvil of his own manufacture, and peculiarly constructed, which the young artist had recently bespoken. Owen examined the article, and pronounced it fashioned according to his wish.

"Why, yes," said Robert Danforth, his strong voice filling the shop as with the sound of a bass viol, "I consider myself equal to anything in the way of my own trade; though I should have made but a poor figure at yours with such a fist as this," added he, laughing, as he laid his vast hand beside the delicate one of Owen. "But what then? I put more main strength into one blow of my sledge hammer than all that you have expended since you were a 'prentice. Is not that the truth?"

BRUTE STRENGTH VS. SPIRIT

"Very probably," answered the low and slender voice of Owen. "Strength is an earthly monster. I make no pretensions to it. My force, whatever there may be of it, is altogether spiritual."

"Well, but, Owen, what are you about?" asked his old school-fellow, still in such a hearty volume of tone that it made the artist shrink, especially as the question related to a subject so sacred as the absorbing dream of his imagination. "Folks do say that you are trying to discover the perpetual motion."

PERPETUAL MOTION MACHINE?

"The perpetual motion? Nonsense!" replied Owen Warland, with a movement of disgust; for he was full of little petulances. "It can never be discovered. It is a dream that may delude men whose brains are mystified with matter, but not me. Besides, if such a discovery were possible, it would not be worth my while to make it only to have the secret turned to such purposes as are now effected by steam and water power. I am not ambitious to be honored with the paternity of a new kind of cotton machine."

"That would be droll enough!" cried the blacksmith, breaking out into such an uproar of laughter that Owen himself and the bell glasses on his workboard quivered in unison. "No, no, Owen! No child of yours will have iron joints and sinews. Well, I won't hinder you any more. Good night, Owen, and success; and if you need any assistance, so far as a downright blow of hammer upon anvil will answer the purpose, I'm your man."

And with another laugh the man of main strength left the shop.

"How strange it is," whispered Owen Warland to himself, leaning his head upon his hand, "that all my musings, my purposes, my passion for the beautiful, my consciousness of power to create it—a finer, more ethereal power, of which this earthly giant can have no conception,—all, all, look so vain and idle whenever my path is crossed by Robert Danforth! He would drive me mad were I to meet him often. His hard, brute force darkens and confuses the spiritual element within me; but I, too, will be strong in my own way. I will not yield to him."

OWEN SHAKEN BY DANFORTH'S VERY PRESENCE

He took from beneath a glass a piece of minute machinery, which he set in the condensed light of his lamp, and, looking intently at it through a magnifying glass, proceeded to operate with a delicate instrument of steel. In an instant, however, he fell back in his chair and clasped his hands, with a look of horror on his face that made its small features as impressive as those of a giant would have been.

BURSTS IT!

"Heaven! What have I done?" exclaimed he. "The vapor, the influence of that brute force,—it has bewildered me and obscured my perception. I have made the very stroke—the fatal stroke—that I have dreaded from the first. It is all over—the toil of months, the object of my life. I am ruined!"

And there he sat, in strange despair, until his lamp flickered in the socket and left the Artist of the Beautiful in darkness.

Thus it is that ideas, which grow up within the imagination and appear so lovely to it and of a value beyond whatever men call valuable, are exposed to be shattered and annihilated by contact with the practical. It is requisite for the ideal artist to possess a force of character that seems hardly compatible with its delicacy; he must keep his faith in himself while the incredulous world assails him with its utter disbelief; he must stand up against mankind and be his own sole disciple, both as respects his genius and the objects to which it is directed.

CONFLICT

For a time Owen Warland succumbed to this severe but inevitable test. He spent a few sluggish weeks with his head so continually resting in his hands that the townspeople had scarcely an opportunity to see his countenance. When at last it was again uplifted to the light of day, a cold, dull, nameless change was perceptible upon it. In the opinion of Peter Hovenden, however, and that order of sagacious understandings who think that life should be regulated, like clockwork, with leaden weights, the alteration was entirely for the better. Owen now, indeed, applied himself to business with dogged industry. It was marvellous to witness the obtuse gravity with which he would inspect the wheels of a great, old silver watch; thereby delighting the owner, in whose fob it had been worn till he deemed it a portion of his own life, and was accordingly jealous of its treatment. In consequence of the good report thus acquired, Owen Warland was invited by the proper authorities to regulate the clock in the church steeple. He succeeded so admirably in this matter of public interest that the merchants gruffly acknowledged his merits on 'Change; the nurse whispered his praises as she gave the potion in the sick chamber; the lover blessed him at the hour of appointed interview; and the town in general thanked Owen for the punctuality of dinner time. In a word, the heavy weight upon his spirits kept everything in order, not merely within his own system, but wheresoever the iron accents of the church clock were audible. It was a circumstance, though minute yet characteristic of his present state, that, when employed to engrave names or initials on silver spoons, he now wrote the requisite letters in the plainest possible style, omitting a variety of fanciful flourishes that had heretofore distinguished his work in this kind.

FUNCTION IN AN ACCEPTABLE WAY—

↓ LOVE!

One day, during the era of this happy transformation, old Peter Hovenden came to visit his former apprentice.

"Well, Owen," said he, "I am glad to hear such good accounts of you from all quarters, and especially from the town clock yonder, which speaks in your commendation every hour of the twenty-four. Only get rid altogether of your nonsensical trash about the beautiful, which I nor nobody else, nor yourself to boot, could ever understand,—only free yourself of that, and your success in life is as sure as daylight. Why, if you go on in this way, I should even venture to let you doctor this precious old watch of mine; though, except my daughter Annie, I have nothing else so valuable in the world."

"I should hardly dare touch it, sir," replied Owen, in a depressed tone; for he was weighed down by his old master's presence.

"In time," said the latter,—"in time, you will be capable of it."

The old watchmaker, with the freedom naturally consequent on his former authority, went on inspecting the work which Owen had in hand at the moment, together with other matters that were in progress. The artist, meanwhile, could scarcely lift his head. There was nothing so antipodal to his nature as this man's cold, unimaginative sagacity, by contact with which everything was converted into a dream except the densest matter of the physical world. Owen groaned in spirit and prayed fervently to be delivered from him.

"But what is this?" cried Peter Hovenden abruptly, taking up a dusty bell glass, beneath which appeared a mechanical something, as delicate and minute as the system of a butterfly's anatomy. "What have we here? Owen! Owen! there is witchcraft in these little chains, and wheels, and paddles. See! with one pinch of my finger and thumb I am going to deliver you from all future peril."

"For Heaven's sake," screamed Owen Warland, springing up with wonderful energy, "as you would not drive me mad, do not touch it! The slightest pressure of your finger would ruin me forever."

"Aha, young man! And is it so?" said the old watchmaker, looking at him with just enough of penetration to torture Owen's soul with the bitterness of worldly criticism. "Well, take your own course; but I warn you again that in this small piece of mechanism lives your evil spirit. Shall I exorcise him?"

"You are my evil spirit," answered Owen, much excited,—"you and the hard, coarse world! The leaden thoughts and the despondency that you fling upon me are my clogs, else I should long ago have achieved the task that I was created for."

Peter Hovenden shook his head, with the mixture of contempt and indignation which mankind, of whom he was partly a representative, deem themselves entitled to feel towards all simpletons who seek other prizes than the dusty one along the highway. He then took his leave, with an uplifted finger and a sneer upon his face that haunted the artist's dreams for many a night afterwards. At the time of his old master's visit, Owen was probably on the point of taking up the relinquished task; but, by this sinister event, he was thrown back into the state whence he had been slowly emerging.

But the innate tendency of his soul had only been accumulating fresh vigor during its apparent sluggishness. As the summer advanced he almost totally relinquished his business, and permitted Father Time, so far as the old gentleman was represented by the clocks and watches under his control, to stray at random through human life, making infinite confusion among the train of bewildered hours. He wasted the sunshine, as people said, in wandering through the woods and fields and along the banks of streams. There, like a child, he found amusement in chasing butterflies or watching the motions of water insects. There was something truly mysterious in the intentness with which he contemplated these living playthings as they sported on the breeze or examined the structure of an imperial insect whom he had imprisoned. The chase of butterflies was an apt emblem of the ideal pursuit in which he had spent so many golden hours; but would the beautiful idea ever be yielded to his hand like the butterfly that symbolized it? Sweet, doubtless, were these days, and congenial to the artist's soul. They were full of bright conceptions, which gleamed through his intellectual world as the butterflies gleamed through the outward atmosphere, and were real to him, for the instant, without the toil, and perplexity, and many disappointments of attempting to make them visible to the sensual eye. Alas that the artist, whether in poetry, or whatever other material, may not content himself with the inward enjoyment of the beautiful, but must chase the flitting mystery beyond the verge of his ethereal domain, and crush its frail being in seizing it with a material grasp. Owen Warland felt the impulse to give external reality to his ideas as irresistibly as any of the poets or painters who have arrayed the world in a dimmer and fainter beauty, imperfectly copied from the richness of their visions.

The night was now his time for the slow progress of re-creating the one idea to which all his intellectual activity referred itself. Always at the approach of dusk he stole into the town, locked himself within his shop, and wrought with patient delicacy of touch for many hours. Sometimes he was startled by the rap of the watchman, who, when all the world should be asleep, had caught the gleam of lamplight through the crevices of Owen Warland's shutters. Daylight, to the morbid sensibility of his mind, seemed to have an intrusiveness that interfered with his pursuits. On cloudy and inclement days, therefore, he sat with his head upon his hands, muffling, as it were, his sensitive brain in a mist of indefinite musings; for it was a relief to escape from the sharp distinctness with which he was compelled to shape out his thoughts during his nightly toil.

From one of these fits of torpor he was aroused by the entrance of Annie Hovenden, who came into the shop with the freedom of a customer, and also with something of the familiarity of a childish friend. She had worn a hole through her silver thimble, and wanted Owen to repair it.

"But I don't know whether you will condescend to such a task," said she, laughing, "now that you are so taken up with the notion of putting spirit into machinery."

"Where did you get that idea, Annie?" said Owen, starting in surprise.

"O, out of my own head," answered she, "and from something that I heard you say, long ago, when you were but a boy and I a little child. But come; will you mend this poor thimble of mine?"

"Anything for your sake, Annie," said Owen Warland,—"anything, even were it to work at Robert Danforth's forge."

"And that would be a pretty sight!" retorted Annie, glancing with imperceptible slightness at the artist's small and slender frame. "Well; here is the thimble."

"But that is a strange idea of yours," said Owen, "about the spiritualization of matter."

And then the thought stole into his mind that this young girl possessed the gift to comprehend him better than all the world besides. And what a help and strength would it be to him in his lonely toil if he could gain the sympathy of the only being whom he loved! To persons whose pursuits are insulated from the common business of life—who are either in advance of mankind or apart from it—there often comes a sensation of moral cold that makes the spirit shiver as if it had reached the frozen solitudes around the pole. What the prophet, the poet, the reformer, the criminal, or any other man with human yearnings, but separated from the multitude by a peculiar lot, might feel, poor Owen felt.

"Annie," cried he, growing pale as death at the thought, "how gladly would I tell you the secret of my pursuit! You, methinks, would estimate it rightly. You, I know, would hear it with a reverence that I must not expect from the harsh, material world."

"Would I not? to be sure I would!" replied Annie Hovenden, lightly laughing. "Come; explain to me quickly what is the meaning of this little whirligig, so delicately wrought that it might be a plaything for Queen Mab. See! I will put it in motion."

"Hold!" exclaimed Owen, "hold!"

Annie had but given the slightest possible touch, with the point of a needle, to the same minute portion of complicated machinery which has been more than once mentioned, when the artist seized her by the wrist with a force that made her scream aloud. She was affrighted at the convulsion of intense rage and anguish that writhed across his features. The next instant he let his head sink upon his hands.

"Go, Annie," murmured he; "I have deceived myself, and must suffer for it. I yearned for sympathy and thought, and fancied, and dreamed that you might give it me; but you lack the talisman, Annie, that should admit you into my secrets. That touch has undone the toils of months and the thought of a lifetime! It was not your fault, Annie; but you have ruined me!"

Poor Owen Warland! He had indeed erred, yet pardonably; for if any human spirit could have sufficiently reverenced the process so sacred in his eyes, it must have been a woman's. Even Annie Hovenden, possibly, might not have disappointed him had she been enlightened by the deep intelligence of love.

The artist spent the ensuing winter in a way that satisfied any persons who had hitherto retained a hopeful opinion of him that he was, in truth, irrevocably doomed to inutility as regarded the world, and to an evil destiny on his own part. The decease of a relative had put him in possession of a small inheritance. Thus freed from the necessity of toil, and having lost the steadfast influence of a great purpose,—great, at least, to him,—he abandoned himself to habits from which it might have been supposed the mere delicacy of his organization would have availed to secure him. But, when the ethereal portion of a man of genius is obscured, the earthly part assumes an influence the more uncontrollable, because the character is now thrown off the balance to which Providence had so nicely adjusted it, and which, in coarser natures, is adjusted by some other method. Owen Warland made proof of whatever show of bliss may be found in riot. He looked at the world through the golden medium of wine, and contemplated the visions that bubble up so gaily around the brim of the glass, and that people the air with shapes of pleasant madness, which so soon grow ghostly and forlorn. Even when this dismal and inevitable change had taken place, the young man might still have continued to quaff the cup of enchantments, though its vapor did but shroud life in gloom and fill the gloom with spectres that mocked at him. There was a certain irksomeness of spirit, which, being real, and the deepest sensation of which the artist was now conscious, was more intolerable than any fantastic miseries and horrors that the abuse of wine could summon up. In the latter case he could remember, even out of the midst of his trouble, that all was but a delusion; in the former, the heavy anguish was his actual life.

From this perilous state he was redeemed by an

incident which more than one person witnessed, but of which the shrewdest could not explain or conjecture the operation on Owen Warland's mind. It was very simple. On a warm afternoon of spring, as the artist sat among his riotous companions with a glass of wine before him, a splendid butterfly flew in at the open window and fluttered about his head.

"Ah," exclaimed Owen, who had drank freely, "are you alive again, child of the sun and playmate of the summer breeze, after your dismal winter's nap? Then it is time for me to be at work!"

And, leaving his unemptied glass upon the table, he departed and was never known to sip another drop of wine.

And now, again, he resumed his wanderings in the woods and fields. It might be fancied that the bright butterfly, which had come so spirit-like into the window as Owen sat with the rude revellers, was indeed a spirit commissioned to recall him to the pure, ideal life that had so etherealized him among men. It might be fancied that he went forth to seek this spirit in its sunny haunts; for still, as in the summer time gone by, he was seen to steal gently up wherever a butterfly had alighted, and lose himself in contemplation of it. When it took flight his eyes followed the winged vision, as if its airy track would show the path to heaven. But what could be the purpose of the unseasonable toil, which was again resumed, as the watchman knew by the lines of lamplight through the crevices of Owen Warland's shutters? The townspeople had one comprehensive explanation of all these singularities. Owen Warland had gone mad! How universally efficacious—how satisfactory, too, and soothing to the injured sensibility of narrowness and dulness—is this easy method of accounting for whatever lies beyond the world's most ordinary scope! From St. Paul's days down to our poor little Artist of the Beautiful, the same talisman had been applied to the elucidation of all mysteries in the words or deeds of men who spoke or acted too wisely or too well. In Owen Warland's case the judgment of his townspeople may have been correct. Perhaps he was mad. The lack of sympathy—that contrast between himself and his neighbors which took away the restraint of example—was enough to make him so. Or possibly he had caught just so much of the ethereal radiance as served to bewilder him, in an earthly sense, by its intermixture with the common daylight.

One evening, when the artist had returned from a customary ramble and had just thrown the lustre of his lamp on the delicate piece of work so often interrupted, but still taken up again, as if his fate were embodied in its mechanism, he was surprised by the entrance of old Peter Hovenden. Owen never met this man without a shrinking of the heart. Of all the world he was most terrible, by reason of a keen understanding which saw so distinctly what it did see, and disbelieved so uncompromisingly in what it could not see. On this occasion the old watchmaker had merely a gracious word or two to say.

"Owen, my lad," said he, "we must see you at my house to-morrow night."

The artist began to mutter some excuse.

"O, but it must be so," quoth Peter Hovenden, "for the sake of the days when you were one of the household. What, my boy! don't you know that my daughter Annie is engaged to Robert Danforth? We are making an entertainment, in our humble way, to celebrate the event."

"Ah!" said Owen.

That little monosyllable was all he uttered; its tone seemed cold and unconcerned to an ear like Peter Hovenden's; and yet there was in it the stifled outcry of the poor artist's heart, which he compressed within him like a man holding down an evil spirit. One slight outbreak, however, imperceptible to the old watchmaker, he allowed himself. Raising the instrument with which he was about to begin his work, he let it fall upon the little system of machinery that had, anew, cost him months of thought and toil. It was shattered by the stroke!

Owen Warland's story would have been no tolerable representation of the troubled life of those who strive to create the beautiful, if, amid all other thwarting influences, love had not interposed to steal the cunning from his hand. Outwardly he had been no ardent or enterprising lover; the career of his passion had confined its tumults and vicissitudes so entirely within the artist's imagination that Annie herself had scarcely more than a woman's intuitive perception of it; but, in Owen's view, it covered the whole field of his life. Forgetful of the time when she had shown herself incapable of any deep response, he had persisted in connecting all his dreams of artistical success with Annie's image; she was the visible shape in which the spiritual power that he worshipped, and on whose altar he hoped to lay a not unworthy offering, was made manifest to him. Of course he had deceived himself; there were no such attributes in Annie Hovenden as his imagination had endowed her with. She, in the aspect which she wore to his inward vision, was as much a creature of his own as the mysterious piece of mechanism would be were it ever realized. Had he become convinced of his mistake through the medium of successful love,—had he won Annie to his bosom, and there beheld her fade from angel into ordinary woman,—the disappointment might have driven him back, with concentrated energy, upon his sole remaining object. On the other hand, had he found Annie what he fancied, his lot would have been so rich in beauty that out of its mere redundancy he might have wrought the beautiful into many a worthier type than he had toiled for; but the guise in which his sorrow came to him, the sense that the angel of his life had been snatched away and given to a rude man of earth and iron, who could neither need nor appreciate her ministrations,—this was the very perversity of fate that makes human existence appear too absurd and contradictory to be the scene of one other hope or one other fear. There was nothing left for Owen Warland but to sit down like a man that had been stunned.

He went through a fit of illness. After his recovery his small slender frame assumed an obtuser garniture of flesh than it had ever before worn. His thin cheeks became round; his delicate little hand, so spiritually fashioned to achieve fairy taskwork, grew plumper than the hand of a thriving infant. His aspect had a childishness such as might have induced a stranger to pat him on the head—pausing, however, in the act, to wonder what manner of child was here. It was as if the spirit had gone out of him, leaving the body to flourish in a sort of vegetable existence. Not that Owen Warland was idiotic. He could talk, and not irrationally. Somewhat of a babbler, indeed, did people begin to think him; for he was apt to discourse at wearisome length of marvels of mechanism that he had read about in books, but which he had learned to consider as absolutely fabulous. Among them he enumerated the Man of Brass, constructed by Albertus Magnus, and the Brazen Head of Friar Bacon; and, coming down to later times, the automata of a little coach and horses, which it was pretended had been manufactured for the Dauphin of France; together with an insect that buzzed about the ear like a living fly, and yet was but a contrivance of minute steel springs. There was a story, too, of a duck that waddled, and quacked, and ate; though, had any honest citizen purchased it for dinner, he would have found himself cheated with the mere mechanical apparition of a duck.

"But all these accounts," said Owen Warland, "I am now satisfied are mere impositions."

Then, in a mysterious way, he would confess that he once thought differently. In his idle and dreamy days he had considered it possible, in a certain sense, to spiritualize machinery, and to combine with the new species of life and motion thus produced a beauty that should attain to the ideal which Nature has proposed to herself in all her creatures, but has never taken pains to realize. He seemed, however, to retain no very distinct perception either of the process of achieving this object or of the design itself.

"I have thrown it all aside now," he would say. "It was a dream such as young men are always mystifying themselves with. Now that I have acquired a little common sense, it makes me laugh to think of it."

Poor, poor and fallen Owen Warland! These were

the symptoms that he had ceased to be an inhabitant of the better sphere that lies unseen around us. He had lost his faith in the invisible, and now prided himself, as such unfortunates invariably do, in the wisdom which rejected much that even his eye could see, and trusted confidently in nothing but what his hand could touch. This is the calamity of men whose spiritual part dies out of them and leaves the grosser understanding to assimilate them more and more to the things of which alone it can take cognizance; but in Owen Warland the spirit was not dead nor passed away; it only slept.

How it awoke again is not recorded. Perhaps the torpid slumber was broken by a convulsive pain. Perhaps, as in a former instance, the butterfly came and hovered about his head and reinspired him,—as indeed this creature of the sunshine had always a mysterious mission for the artist,—reinspired him with the former purpose of his life. Whether it were pain or happiness that thrilled through his veins, his first impulse was to thank Heaven for rendering him again the being of thought, imagination, and keenest sensibility that he had long ceased to be.

"Now for my task," said he. "Never did I feel such strength for it as now."

Yet, strong as he felt himself, he was incited to toil the more diligently by an anxiety lest death should surprise him in the midst of his labors. This anxiety, perhaps, is common to all men who set their hearts upon anything so high, in their own view of it, that life becomes of importance only as conditional to its accomplishment. So long as we love life for itself, we seldom dread the losing it. When we desire life for the attainment of an object, we recognize the frailty of its texture. But, side by side with this sense of insecurity, there is a vital faith in our invulnerability to the shaft of death while engaged in any task that seems assigned by Providence as our proper thing to do, and which the world would have cause to mourn for should we leave it unaccomplished. Can the philosopher, big with the inspiration of an idea that is to reform mankind, believe that he is to be beckoned from this sensible existence at the very instant when he is mustering his breath to speak the word of light? Should he perish so, the weary ages may pass away—the world's, whose life sand may fall, drop by drop—before another intellect is prepared to develop the truth that might have been uttered then. But history affords many an example where the most precious spirit, at any particular epoch manifested in human shape, has gone hence untimely, without space allowed him, so far as mortal judgment could discern, to perform his mission on the earth. The prophet dies, and the man of torpid heart and sluggish brain lives on. The poet leaves his song half sung, or finishes it, beyond the scope of mortal ears, in a celestial choir.

[margin note: LINE ABOUT ART]

The painter—as Allston[1] did—leaves half his conception on the canvas to sadden us with its imperfect beauty, and goes to picture forth the whole, if it be no irreverence to say so, in the hues of heaven. But rather such incomplete designs of this life will be perfected nowhere. This so frequent abortion of man's dearest projects must be taken as a proof that the deeds of earth, however etherealized by piety or genius, are without value, except as exercises and manifestations of the spirit. In heaven, all ordinary thought is higher and more melodious than Milton's song. Then, would he add another verse to any strain that he had left unfinished here?

But to return to Owen Warland. It was his fortune, good or ill, to achieve the purpose of his life. Pass we over a long space of intense thought, yearning effort, minute toil, and wasting anxiety, succeeded by an instant of solitary triumph: let all this be imagined; and then behold the artist, on a winter evening, seeking admittance to Robert Danforth's fireside circle. There he found the man of iron, with his massive substance thoroughly warmed and attempered by domestic influences. And there was Annie, too, now transformed into a matron, with much of her husband's plain and sturdy nature, but imbued, as Owen Warland still believed, with a finer grace, that might enable her to be the interpreter between strength and beauty. It happened, likewise, that old Peter Hovenden was a guest this evening at his daughter's fireside, and it was his well-remembered expression of keen, cold criticism that first encountered the artist's glance.

"My old friend Owen!" cried Robert Danforth, starting up, and compressing the artist's delicate fingers within a hand that was accustomed to gripe bars of iron. "This is kind and neighborly to come to us at last. I was afraid your perpetual motion had bewitched you out of the remembrance of old times."

"We are glad to see you," said Annie, while a blush reddened her matronly cheek. "It was not like a friend to stay from us so long."

"Well, Owen," inquired the old watchmaker, as his first greeting, "how comes on the beautiful? Have you created it at last?"

The artist did not immediately reply, being startled by the apparition of a young child of strength that was tumbling about on the carpet,—a little personage who had come mysteriously out of the infinite, but with something so sturdy and real in his composition that he seemed moulded out of the densest substance which earth could supply. This hopeful infant crawled towards the newcomer, and setting himself on end, as Robert Danforth expressed the posture, stared at Owen with a look of

[margin note: CHILD]

[1] Washington Allston (1778–1843), an American painter.

such sagacious observation that the mother could not help exchanging a proud glance with her husband. But the artist was disturbed by the child's look, as imagining a resemblance between it and Peter Hovenden's habitual expression. He could have fancied that the old watchmaker was compressed into this baby shape, and looking out of those baby eyes, and repeating, as he now did, the malicious question:—

[margin note: LIKE GRANDPA?]

"The beautiful, Owen! How comes on the beautiful? Have you succeeded in creating the beautiful?"

"I have succeeded," replied the artist, with a momentary light of triumph in his eyes and a smile of sunshine, yet steeped in such depth of thought that it was almost sadness. "Yes, my friends, it is the truth. I have succeeded."

"Indeed!" cried Annie, a look of maiden mirthfulness peeping out of her face again. "And is it lawful, now, to inquire what the secret is?"

"Surely; it is to disclose it that I have come," answered Owen Warland. "You shall know, and see, and touch, and possess the secret! For, Annie,—if by that name I may still address the friend of my boyish years,—Annie, it is for your bridal gift that I have wrought this spiritualized mechanism, this harmony of motion, this mystery of beauty. It comes late indeed; but it is as we go onward in life, when objects begin to lose their freshness of hue and our souls their delicacy of perception, that the spirit of beauty is most needed. If,—forgive me, Annie,—if you know how to value this gift, it can never come too late."

He produced, as he spoke, what seemed a jewel box. It was carved richly out of ebony by his own hand, and inlaid with a fanciful tracery of pearl, representing a boy in pursuit of a butterfly, which, elsewhere, had become a winged spirit, and was flying heavenward; while the boy, or youth, had found such efficacy in his strong desire that he ascended from earth to cloud, and from cloud to celestial atmosphere, to win the beautiful. This case of ebony the artist opened, and bade Annie place her finger on its edge. She did so, but almost screamed as a butterfly fluttered forth, and, alighting on her finger's tip, sat waving the ample magnificence of its purple and gold-speckled wings, as if in prelude to a flight. It is impossible to express by words the glory, the splendor, the delicate gorgeousness which were softened into the beauty of this object. Nature's ideal butterfly was here realized in all its perfection; not in the pattern of such faded insects as flit among earthly flowers, but of those which hover across the meads of paradise for child-angels and the spirits of departed infants to disport themselves with. The rich down was visible upon its wings; the lustre of its eyes seemed instinct with spirit. The firelight glimmered around this wonder—the candles gleamed upon it; but it glistened apparently by its own radiance, and illuminated the finger and outstretched hand on which it rested with a white gleam like that of precious stones. In its perfect beauty, the consideration of size was entirely lost. Had its wings overreached the firmament, the mind could not have been more filled or satisfied.

"Beautiful! beautiful!" exclaimed Annie. "Is it alive? Is it alive?"

"Alive? To be sure it is," answered her husband. "Do you suppose any mortal has skill enough to make a butterfly, or would put himself to the trouble of making one, when any child may catch a score of them in a summer's afternoon? Alive? Certainly! But this pretty box is undoubtedly of our friend Owen's manufacture; and really it does him credit."

At this moment the butterfly waved its wings anew, with a motion so absolutely lifelike that Annie was startled, and even awestricken; for, in spite of her husband's opinion, she could not satisfy herself whether it was indeed a living creature or a piece of wondrous mechanism.

"Is it alive?" she repeated, more earnestly than before.

"Judge for yourself," said Owen Warland, who stood gazing in her face with fixed attention.

The butterfly now flung itself upon the air, fluttered around Annie's head, and soared into a distant region of the parlor, still making itself perceptible to sight by the starry gleam in which the motion of its wings enveloped it. The infant on the floor followed its course with his sagacious little eyes. After flying about the room, it returned in a spiral curve and settled again on Annie's finger.

"But is it alive?" exclaimed she again; and the finger on which the gorgeous mystery had alighted was so tremulous that the butterfly was forced to balance himself with his wings. "Tell me if it be alive, or whether you created it."

"Wherefore ask who created it, so it be beautiful?" replied Owen Warland. "Alive? Yes, Annie; it may well be said to possess life, for it has absorbed my own being into itself; and in the secret of that butterfly, and in its beauty,—which is not merely outward, but deep as its whole system,—is represented the intellect, the imagination, the sensibility, the soul of an Artist of the Beautiful! Yes; I created it. But"—and here his countenance somewhat changed—"this butterfly is not now to me what it was when I beheld it afar off in the daydreams of my youth."

"Be it what it may, it is a pretty plaything," said the blacksmith, grinning with childlike delight. "I wonder whether it would condescend to alight on such a great clumsy finger as mine? Hold it hither, Annie."

By the artist's direction, Annie touched her finger's tip to that of her husband; and, after a momentary delay, the butterfly fluttered from one to the other. It preluded a second flight by a similar, yet not precisely the same, waving of wings as in the first experiment; then, ascending from the blacksmith's stalwart finger, it rose in a gradually enlarging curve to the ceiling, made one wide sweep around the room, and returned with an undulating movement to the point whence it had started.

"Well, that does beat all nature!" cried Robert Danforth, bestowing the heartiest praise that he could find expression for; and, indeed, had he paused there, a man of finer words and nicer perception could not easily have said more. "That goes beyond me, I confess. But what then? There is more real use in one downright blow of my sledge hammer than in the whole five years' labor that our friend Owen has wasted on this butterfly."

Here the child clapped his hands and made a great babble of indistinct utterance, apparently demanding that the butterfly should be given him for a plaything.

Owen Warland, meanwhile, glanced sidelong at Annie, to discover whether she sympathized in her husband's estimate of the comparative value of the beautiful and the practical. There was, amid all her kindness towards himself, amid all the wonder and admiration with which she contemplated the marvelous work of his hands and incarnation of his idea, a secret scorn—too secret, perhaps, for her own consciousness, and perceptible only to such intuitive discernment as that of the artist. But Owen, in the latter stages of his pursuit, had risen out of the region in which such a discovery might have been torture. He knew that the world, and Annie as the representative of the world, whatever praise might be bestowed, could never say the fitting word nor feel the fitting sentiment which should be the perfect recompense of an artist who, symbolizing a lofty moral by a material trifle,—converting what was earthly to spiritual gold,—had won the beautiful into his handiwork. Not at this latest moment was he to learn that the reward of all high performance must be sought within itself, or sought in vain. There was, however, a view of the matter which Annie and her husband, and even Peter Hovenden, might fully have understood, and which would have satisfied them that the toil of years had here been worthily bestowed. Owen Warland might have told them that this butterfly, this plaything, this bridal gift of a poor watchmaker to a blacksmith's wife, was, in truth, a gem of art that a monarch would have purchased with honors and abundant wealth, and have treasured it among the jewels of his kingdom as the most unique and wondrous of them all. But the artist smiled and kept the secret to himself.

"Father," said Annie, thinking that a word of praise from the old watchmaker might gratify his former apprentice, "do come and admire this pretty butterfly."

"Let us see," said Peter Hovenden, rising from his chair, with a sneer upon his face that always made people doubt, as he himself did, in everything but a material existence. "Here is my finger for it to alight upon. I shall understand it better when once I have touched it."

But, to the increased astonishment of Annie, when the tip of her father's finger was pressed against that of her husband, on which the butterfly still rested, the insect drooped its wings and seemed on the point of falling to the floor. Even the bright spots of gold upon its wings and body, unless her eyes deceived her, grew dim, and the glowing purple took a dusky hue, and the starry lustre that gleamed around the blacksmith's hand became faint and vanished.

"It is dying! it is dying!" cried Annie, in alarm.

"It has been delicately wrought," said the artist, calmly. "As I told you, it has imbibed a spiritual essence—call it magnetism, or what you will. In an atmosphere of doubt and mockery its exquisite susceptibility suffers torture, as does the soul of him who instilled his own life into it. It has already lost its beauty; in a few moments more its mechanism would be irreparably injured."

"Take away your hand, father!" entreated Annie, turning pale. "Here is my child; let it rest on his innocent hand. There, perhaps, its life will revive and its colors grow brighter than ever."

Her father, with an acrid smile, withdrew his finger. The butterfly then appeared to recover the power of voluntary motion, while its hues assumed much of their original lustre, and the gleam of starlight, which was its most ethereal attribute, again formed a halo round about it. At first, when transferred from Robert Danforth's hand to the small finger of the child, this radiance grew so powerful that it positively threw the little fellow's shadow back against the wall. He, meanwhile, extended his plump hand as he had seen his father and mother do, and watched the waving of the insect's wings with infantine delight. Nevertheless, there was a certain odd expression of sagacity that made Owen Warland feel as if here were old Peter Hovenden, partially, and but partially, redeemed from his hard scepticism into childish faith.

"How wise the little monkey looks!" whispered Robert Danforth to his wife.

"I never saw such a look on a child's face," answered Annie, admiring her own infant, and with good reason, far more than the artistic butterfly. "The darling knows more of the mystery than we do."

As if the butterfly, like the artist, were conscious of something not entirely congenial in the child's nature, it alternately sparkled and grew dim. At length it arose from the small hand of the infant with an airy motion that seemed to bear it upward without an effort, as if the ethereal instincts with which its master's spirit had endowed it impelled this fair vision involuntarily to a higher sphere. Had there been no obstruction, it might have soared into the sky and grown immortal. But its lustre gleamed upon the ceiling; the exquisite texture of its wings brushed against that earthly medium; and a sparkle or two, as of stardust, floated downward and lay glimmering on the carpet. Then the butterfly came fluttering down, and, instead of returning to the infant, was apparently attracted towards the artist's hand.

"Not so! not so!" murmured Owen Warland, as if his handiwork could have understood him. "Thou hast gone forth out of thy master's heart. There is no return for thee."

With a wavering movement, and emitting a tremulous radiance, the butterfly struggled, as it were, towards the infant, and was about to alight upon his finger; but while it still hovered in the air, the little child of strength, with his grandsire's sharp and shrewd expression in his face, made a snatch at the marvellous insect and compressed it in his hand. Annie screamed. Old Peter Hovenden burst into a cold and scornful laugh. The blacksmith, by main force, unclosed the infant's hand, and found within the palm a small heap of glittering fragments, whence the mystery of beauty had fled forever. And as for Owen Warland, he looked placidly at what seemed the ruin of his life's labor, and which was yet no ruin. He had caught a far other butterfly than this. When the artist rose high enough to achieve the beautiful, the symbol by which he made it perceptible to mortal senses became of little value in his eyes while his spirit possessed itself in the enjoyment of the reality.

1844

Rappaccini's Daughter

Hawthorne's setting for this story is foreign and its source legendary. As his notebooks show, he had been reading in Sir Thomas Browne: "A story there passeth of an Indian king that sent unto Alexander a fair woman fed with aconites and other poisons, with this intent, either by converse or copulation complexionally to destroy him." Nevertheless, like his tales of the American past, "Rappaccini's Daughter" dramatizes the difficulties of perception, the ambiguity of action, and the complexity of character and motive. As the story unfolds, the complex, contradictory nature of each character becomes clearer, and by the end the characters have, in some sense, undergone a reversal of roles. At the beginning, for example, Beatrice seems to be both beautiful and inexpressibly terrible—the evil temptress inviting Giovanni to his doom. But the reader later discovers that Beatrice is the one victimized. Her father manipulates and destroys individuals for knowledge and power; Baglioni, whose antidote is a poison, turns out to be selfish, envious, and vengeful; and Giovanni destroys her love and her desire to live by his selfish, bitter attack. But the situation is not even so simple as that. In this story Hawthorne explores the possibilities of ambiguity, not to confuse, but to dramatize his sense of the tangled, complex web of human experience. Text: From the author's revised edition of *Mosses from an Old Manse* (Boston, 1854).

A young man, named Giovanni Guasconti, came, very long ago, from the more southern region of Italy, to pursue his studies at the University of Padua. Giovanni, who had but a scanty supply of gold ducats in his pocket, took lodgings in a high and gloomy chamber of an old edifice which looked not unworthy to have been the palace of a Paduan noble, and which, in fact, exhibited over its entrance the armorial bearings of a family long since extinct. The young stranger, who was not unstudied in the great poem of his country, recollected that one of the ancestors of this family, and perhaps an occupant of this very mansion, had been pictured by Dante as a partaker of the immortal agonies of his Inferno. These reminiscences and associations, together with the tendency to heartbreak natural to a young man for the first time out of his native sphere, caused Giovanni to sigh heavily as he looked around the desolate and ill-furnished apartment.

"Holy Virgin, signor!" cried old Dame Lisabetta, who, won by the youth's remarkable beauty of person, was kindly endeavoring to give the chamber a habitable air, "what a sigh was that to come out of a young man's heart! Do you find this old mansion gloomy? For the love of Heaven, then, put your head out of the window, and you will see as bright sunshine as you have left in Naples."

Guasconti mechanically did as the old woman advised, but could not quite agree with her that the Paduan sunshine was as cheerful as that of southern Italy. Such as it was, however, it fell upon a garden beneath the window and expended its fostering influences on a variety of plants, which seemed to have been cultivated with exceeding care.

"Does this garden belong to the house?" asked Giovanni.

"Heaven forbid, signor, unless it were fruitful of better pot herbs than any that grow there now," answered old Lisabetta. "No; that garden is cultivated by the own hands of Signor Giacomo Rappaccini, the famous doctor, who, I warrant him, has been heard of as far as Naples. It is said that he distils these plants into medicines that are as potent as a charm. Oftentimes you may see the signor doctor at work, and perchance the signora, his daughter, too, gathering the strange flowers that grow in the garden."

The old woman had now done what she could for the aspect of the chamber; and, commending the young man to the protection of the saints, took her departure.

Giovanni still found no better occupation than to look down into the garden beneath his window. From its appearance, he judged it to be one of those botanic gardens which were of earlier date in Padua than elsewhere in Italy or in the world. Or, not improbably, it might once have been the pleasure-place of an opulent family; for there was the ruin of a marble fountain in the center, sculptured with rare art, but so wofully shattered that it was impossible to trace the original design from the chaos of remaining fragments. The water, however, continued to gush and sparkle into the sunbeams as cheerfully as ever. A little gurgling sound ascended to the young man's window and made him feel as if the fountain were an immortal spirit, that sung its song unceasingly and without heeding the vicissitudes around it, while one century embodied it in marble and another scattered the perishable garniture on the soil. All about the pool into which the water subsided grew various plants, that seemed to require a plentiful supply of moisture for the nourishment of gigantic leaves, and, in some instances, flowers gorgeously magnificent. There was one shrub in particular, set in a marble vase in the midst of the pool, that bore a profusion of purple blossoms, each of which had the lustre and richness of a gem; and the whole together made a show so resplendent that it seemed enough to illuminate the garden, even had there been no sunshine. Every portion of the soil was peopled with plants and herbs, which, if less beautiful, still bore tokens of assiduous care, as if all had their individual virtues, known to the scientific mind that fostered them. Some were placed in urns, rich with old carving, and others in common garden pots; some crept serpent-like along the ground or climbed on high, using whatever means of ascent was offered them. One plant had wreathed itself round a statue of Vertumnus, which was thus quite veiled and shrouded in a drapery of hanging foliage, so happily arranged that it might have served a sculptor for a study.

While Giovanni stood at the window he heard a rustling behind a screen of leaves, and became aware that a person was at work in the garden. His figure soon emerged into view, and showed itself to be that of no common laborer, but a tall, emaciated, sallow, and sickly-looking man, dressed in a scholar's garb of black. He was beyond the middle term of life, with gray hair, a thin, gray beard, and a face singularly marked with intellect and cultivation, but which could never, even in his more youthful days, have expressed much warmth of heart.

Nothing could exceed the intentness with which this scientific gardener examined every shrub which grew in his path: it seemed as if he was looking into their inmost nature, making observations in regard to their creative essence, and discovering why one leaf grew in this shape and another in that, and wherefore such and such flowers differed among themselves in hue and perfume. Nevertheless, in spite of this deep intelligence on his part, there was no approach to intimacy between himself and these vegetable existences. On the contrary, he avoided their actual touch or the direct inhaling of their odors with a caution that impressed Giovanni most disagreeably; for the man's demeanor was that of one walking among malignant influences, such as savage beasts, or deadly snakes, or evil spirits, which, should he allow them one moment of license, would wreak upon him some terrible fatality. It was strangely frightful to the young man's imagination to see this air of insecurity in a person cultivating a garden, that most simple and innocent of human toils, and which had been alike the joy and labor of the unfallen parents of the race. Was this garden, then, the Eden of the present world? And this man, with such perception of harm in what his own hands caused to grow,—was he the Adam?

The distrustful gardener, while plucking away the dead leaves or pruning the too luxuriant growth of the shrubs, defended his hands with a pair of thick gloves. Nor were these his only armor. When, in his walk through the garden, he came to the magnificent plant that hung its purple gems beside the marble fountain, he placed a kind of mask over his mouth and nostrils, as if all this beauty did but conceal a deadlier malice; but, finding his task still too dangerous, he drew back, removed the mask, and called loudly, but in the infirm voice of a person affected with inward disease,—

"Beatrice! Beatrice!"

"Here am I, my father. What would you?" cried a rich and youthful voice from the window of the opposite house—a voice as rich as a tropical sunset, and which made Giovanni, though he knew not why, think of deep hues of purple or crimson and of perfumes heavily delectable, "Are you in the garden?"

"Yes, Beatrice," answered the gardener, "and I need your help."

Soon there emerged from under a sculptured portal the figure of a young girl, arrayed with as much richness of taste as the most splendid of the flowers, beautiful as the day, and with a bloom so deep and vivid that one shade more would have been too much. She looked redundant with life, health, and energy; all of which attributes were bound down and compressed, as it were, and girdled tensely, in their luxuriance, by her virgin zone.[1] Yet Giovanni's fancy must have grown morbid while he looked down into the garden; for the impression which the fair stranger made upon him was as if here were

another flower, the human sister of those vegetable ones, as beautiful as they, more beautiful than the richest of them, but still to be touched only with a glove, nor to be approached without a mask. As Beatrice came down the garden path, it was observable that she handled and inhaled the odor of several of the plants which her father had most sedulously avoided.

"Here, Beatrice," said the latter, "see how many needful offices require to be done to our chief treasure. Yet, shattered as I am, my life might pay the penalty of approaching it so closely as circumstances demand. Henceforth, I fear, this plant must be consigned to your sole charge."

"And gladly will I undertake it," cried again the rich tones of the young lady, as she bent towards the magnificent plant and opened her arms as if to embrace it. "Yes, my sister, my splendor, it shall be Beatrice's task to nurse and serve thee; and thou shalt reward her with thy kisses and perfumed breath, which to her is as the breath of life."

Then, with all the tenderness in her manner that was so strikingly expressed in her words, she busied herself with such attentions as the plant seemed to require; and Giovanni, at his lofty window, rubbed his eyes, and almost doubted whether it were a girl tending her favorite flower, or one sister performing the duties of affection to another. The scene soon terminated. Whether Dr. Rappaccini had finished his labors in the garden, or that his watchful eye had caught the stranger's face, he now took his daughter's arm and retired. Night was already closing in; oppressive exhalations seemed to proceed from the plants and steal upward past the open window; and Giovanni, closing the lattice, went to his couch and dreamed of a rich flower and beautiful girl. Flower and maiden were different, and yet the same, and fraught with some strange peril in either shape.

But there is an influence in the light of morning that tends to rectify whatever errors of fancy, or even of judgment, we may have incurred during the sun's decline, or among the shadows of the night, or in the less wholesome glow of moonshine. Giovanni's first movement, on starting from sleep, was to throw open the window and gaze down into the garden which his dreams had made so fertile of mysteries. He was surprised, and a little ashamed, to find how real and matter-of-fact an affair it proved to be, in the first rays of the sun which gilded the dewdrops that hung upon leaf and blossom, and, while giving a brighter beauty to each rare flower, brought everything within the limits of ordinary experience. The young man rejoiced that, in the heart of the barren city, he had the privilege of overlooking this spot of lovely and luxuriant vegetation. It would serve, he said to himself, as a symbolic language to keep him in communion with Nature. Neither the sickly and thoughtworn Dr. Giacomo

[1] A belt or girdle worn by unmarried women.

Rappaccini, it is true, nor his brilliant daughter, were now visible; so that Giovanni could not determine how much of the singularity which he attributed to both was due to their own qualities and how much to his wonder-working fancy; but he was inclined to take a most rational view of the whole matter.

In the course of the day he paid his respects to Signor Pietro Baglioni, professor of medicine in the university, a physician of eminent repute, to whom Giovanni had brought a letter of introduction. The professor was an elderly personage, apparently of genial nature and habits that might almost be called jovial. He kept the young man to dinner, and made himself very agreeable by the freedom and liveliness of his conversation, especially when warmed by a flask or two of Tuscan wine. Giovanni, conceiving that men of science, inhabitants of the same city, must needs be on familiar terms with one another, took an opportunity to mention the name of Dr. Rappaccini. But the professor did not respond with so much cordiality as he had anticipated.

"Ill would it become a teacher of the divine art of medicine," said Professor Pietro Baglioni, in answer to a question of Giovanni, "to withhold due and well-considered praise of a physician so eminently skilled as Rappaccini; but, on the other hand, I should answer it but scantily to my conscience were I to permit a worthy youth like yourself, Signor Giovanni, the son of an ancient friend, to imbibe erroneous ideas respecting a man who might hereafter chance to hold your life and death in his hands. The truth is, our worshipful Dr. Rappaccini has as much science as any member of the faculty—with perhaps one single exception—in Padua, or all Italy; but there are certain grave objections to his professional character."

"And what are they?" asked the young man.

"Has my friend Giovanni any disease of body or heart, that he is so inquisitive about physicians?" said the professor, with a smile. "But as for Rappaccini, it is said of him—and I, who know the man well, can answer for its truth—that he cares infinitely more for science than for mankind. His patients are interesting to him only as subjects for some new experiment. He would sacrifice human life, his own among the rest, or whatever else was dearest to him, for the sake of adding so much as a grain of mustard seed to the great heap of his accumulated knowledge."

"Methinks he is an awful man indeed," remarked Guasconti, mentally recalling the cold and purely intellectual aspect of Rappaccini. "And yet, worshipful professor, is it not a noble spirit? Are there many men capable of so spiritual a love of science?"

"God forbid," answered the professor, somewhat testily; "at least, unless they take sounder views of the healing art than those adopted by Rappaccini. It is his theory that all medicinal virtues are comprised within those substances which we term vegetable poisons. These he cultivates with his own hands, and is said even to have produced new varieties of poison, more horribly deleterious than Nature, without the assistance of this learned person, would ever have plagued the world withal. That the signor doctor does less mischief than might be expected with such dangerous substances is undeniable. Now and then, it must be owned, he has effected, or seemed to effect, a marvellous cure; but, to tell you my private mind, Signor Giovanni, he should receive little credit for such instances of success,—they being probably the work of chance,—but should be held strictly accountable for his failures, which may justly be considered his own work."

The youth might have taken Baglioni's opinions with many grains of allowance had he known that there was a professional warfare of long continuance between him and Dr. Rappaccini, in which the latter was generally thought to have gained the advantage. If the reader be inclined to judge for himself, we refer him to certain black-letter tracts on both sides, preserved in the medical department of the University of Padua.

"I know not, most learned professor," returned Giovanni, after musing on what had been said of Rappaccini's exclusive zeal for science,—"I know not how dearly this physician may love his art; but surely there is one object more dear to him. He has a daughter."

"Aha!" cried the professor, with a laugh. "So now our friend Giovanni's secret is out. You have heard of this daughter, whom all the young men in Padua are wild about, though not half a dozen have ever had the good hap to see her face. I know little of the Signora Beatrice save that Rappaccini is said to have instructed her deeply in his science, and that, young and beautiful as fame reports her, she is already qualified to fill a professor's chair. Perchance her father destines her for mine! Other absurd rumors there be, not worth talking about or listening to. So now, Signor Giovanni, drink off your glass of lachryma." [2]

Guasconti returned to his lodgings somewhat heated with the wine he had quaffed, and which caused his brain to swim with strange fantasies in reference to Dr. Rappaccini and the beautiful Beatrice. On his way, happening to pass by a florist's, he bought a fresh bouquet of flowers.

Ascending to his chamber, he seated himself near the window, but within the shadow thrown by the depth of the wall, so that he could look down into the garden with little risk of being discovered. All

[2] Lachryma Christi, a rich Neapolitan wine.

beneath his eye was a solitude. The strange plants were basking in the sunshine, and now and then nodding gently to one another, as if in acknowledgment of sympathy and kindred. In the midst, by the shattered fountain, grew the magnificent shrub, with its purple gems clustering all over it; they glowed in the air, and gleamed back again out of the depths of the pool, which thus seemed to overflow with colored radiance from the rich reflection that was steeped in it. At first, as we have said, the garden was a solitude. Soon, however,—as Giovanni had half hoped, half feared, would be the case,—a figure appeared beneath the antique sculptured portal, and came down between the rows of plants, inhaling their various perfumes as if she were one of those beings of old classic fable that lived upon sweet odors. On again beholding Beatrice, the young man was even startled to perceive how much her beauty exceeded his recollection of it; so brilliant, so vivid, was its character, that she glowed amid the sunlight, and, as Giovanni whispered to himself, positively illuminated the more shadowy intervals of the garden path. Her face being now more revealed than on the former occasion, he was struck by its expression of simplicity and sweetness—qualities that had not entered into his idea of her character, and which made him ask anew what manner of mortal she might be. Nor did he fail again to observe, or imagine, an analogy between the beautiful girl and the gorgeous shrub that hung its gemlike flowers over the fountain—a resemblance which Beatrice seemed to have indulged a fantastic humor in heightening, both by the arrangement of her dress and the selection of its hues.

Approaching the shrub, she threw open her arms, as with a passionate ardor, and drew its branches into an intimate embrace—so intimate that her features were hidden in its leafy bosom and her glistening ringlets all intermingled with the flowers.

"Give me thy breath, my sister," exclaimed Beatrice; "for I am faint with common air. And give me this flower of thine, which I separate with gentlest fingers from the stem and place it close beside my heart."

With these words the beautiful daughter of Rappaccini plucked one of the richest blossoms of the shrub, and was about to fasten it in her bosom. But now, unless Giovanni's draughts of wine had bewildered his senses, a singular incident occurred. A small orange-colored reptile, of the lizard or chameleon species, chanced to be creeping along the path, just at the feet of Beatrice. It appeared to Giovanni,—but, at the distance from which he gazed, he could scarcely have seen anything so minute,—it appeared to him, however, that a drop or two of moisture from the broken stem of the flower descended upon the lizard's head. For an instant the reptile con-

torted itself violently, and then lay motionless in the sunshine. Beatrice observed this remarkable phenomenon, and crossed herself, sadly, but without surprise; nor did she therefore hesitate to arrange the fatal flower in her bosom. There it blushed, and almost glimmered with the dazzling effect of a precious stone, adding to her dress and aspect the one appropriate charm which nothing else in the world could have supplied. But Giovanni, out of the shadow of his window, bent forward and shrank back, and murmured and trembled.

"Am I awake? Have I my senses?" said he to himself. "What is this being? Beautiful shall I call her, or inexpressibly terrible?"

Beatrice now strayed carelessly through the garden, approaching closer beneath Giovanni's window, so that he was compelled to thrust his head quite out of its concealment in order to gratify the intense and painful curiosity which she excited. At this moment there came a beautiful insect over the garden wall: it had, perhaps, wandered through the city, and found no flowers or verdure among those antique haunts of men until the heavy perfumes of Dr. Rappaccini's shrubs had lured it from afar. Without alighting on the flowers, this winged brightness seemed to be attracted by Beatrice, and lingered in the air and fluttered about her head. Now, here it could not be but that Giovanni Guasconti's eyes deceived him. Be that as it might, he fancied that, while Beatrice was gazing at the insect with childish delight, it grew faint and fell at her feet; its bright wings shivered; it was dead—from no cause that he could discern, unless it were the atmosphere of her breath. Again Beatrice crossed herself and sighed heavily as she bent over the dead insect.

An impulsive movement of Giovanni drew her eyes to the window. There she beheld the beautiful head of the young man—rather a Grecian than an Italian head, with fair, regular features, and a glistening of gold among his ringlets—gazing down upon her like a being that hovered in mid air. Scarcely knowing what he did, Giovanni threw down the bouquet which he had hitherto held in his hand.

"Signora," said he, "there are pure and healthful flowers. Wear them for the sake of Giovanni Guasconti."

"Thanks, signor," replied Beatrice, with her rich voice, that came forth as it were like a gush of music, and with a mirthful expression half childish and half womanlike. "I accept your gift, and would fain recompense it with this precious purple flower; but, if I toss it into the air, it will not reach you. So Signor Guasconti must even content himself with my thanks."

She lifted the bouquet from the ground, and then, as if inwardly ashamed at having stepped aside from her maidenly reserve to respond to a stranger's greeting, passed swiftly homeward through the garden. But few as the moments were, it seemed to Giovanni, when she was on the point of vanishing beneath the sculptured portal, that his beautiful bouquet was already beginning to wither in her grasp. It was an idle thought; there could be no possibility of distinguishing a faded flower from a fresh one at so great a distance.

For many days after this incident the young man avoided the window that looked into Dr. Rappaccini's garden, as if something ugly and monstrous would have blasted his eyesight had he been betrayed into a glance. He felt conscious of having put himself, to a certain extent, within the influence of an unintelligible power by the communication which he had opened with Beatrice. The wisest course would have been, if his heart were in any real danger, to quit his lodgings and Padua itself at once; the next wiser, to have accustomed himself, as far as possible, to the familiar and daylight view of Beatrice—thus bringing her rigidly and systematically within the limits of ordinary experience. Least of all, while avoiding her sight, ought Giovanni to have remained so near this extraordinary being that the proximity and possibility even of intercourse should give a kind of substance and reality to the wild vagaries which his imagination ran riot continually in producing. Guasconti had not a deep heart—or, at all events, its depths were not sounded now; but he had a quick fancy, and an ardent southern temperament, which rose every instant to a higher fever pitch. Whether or no Beatrice possessed those terrible attributes, that fatal breath, the affinity with those so beautiful and deadly flowers which were indicated by what Giovanni had witnessed, she had at least instilled a fierce and subtle poison into his system. It was not love, although her rich beauty was a madness to him; nor horror, even while he fancied her spirit to be imbued with the same baneful essence that seemed to pervade her physical frame; but a wild offspring of both love and horror that had each parent in it, and burned like one and shivered like the other. Giovanni knew not what to dread; still less did he know what to hope; yet hope and dread kept a continual warfare in his breast, alternately vanquishing one another and starting up afresh to renew the contest. Blessed are all simple emotions, be they dark or bright! It is the lurid intermixture of the two that produces the illuminating blaze of the infernal regions.

Sometimes he endeavored to assuage the fever of his spirit by a rapid walk through the streets of Padua or beyond its gates: his footsteps kept time with the throbbings of his brain, so that the walk was apt to accelerate itself to a race. One day he found himself arrested; his arm was seized by a portly personage, who had turned back on recogniz-ing the young man and expended much breath in overtaking him.

"Signor Giovanni! Stay, my young friend!" cried he. "Have you forgotten me? That might well be the case if I were as much altered as yourself."

It was Baglioni, whom Giovanni had avoided ever since their first meeting, from a doubt that the professor's sagacity would look too deeply into his secrets. Endeavoring to recover himself, he started forth wildly from his inner world into the outer one and spoke like a man in a dream.

"Yes; I am Giovanni Guasconti. You are Professor Pietro Baglioni. Now let me pass!"

"Not yet, not yet, Signor Giovanni Guasconti," said the professor, smiling, but at the same time scrutinizing the youth with an earnest glance. "What! did I grow up side by side with your father? and shall his son pass me like a stranger in these old streets of Padua? Stand still, Signor Giovanni; for we must have a word or two before we part."

"Speedily, then, most worshipful professor, speedily," said Giovanni, with feverish impatience. "Does not your worship see that I am in haste?"

Now, while he was speaking there came a man in black along the street, stooping and moving feebly like a person in inferior health. His face was all overspread with a most sickly and sallow hue, but yet so pervaded with an expression of piercing and active intellect that an observer might easily have overlooked the merely physical attributes and have seen only this wonderful energy. As he passed, this person exchanged a cold and distant salutation with Baglioni, but fixed his eyes upon Giovanni with an intentness that seemed to bring out whatever was within him worthy of notice. Nevertheless, there was a peculiar quietness in the look, as if taking merely a speculative, not human, interest in the young man.

"It is Dr. Rappaccini!" whispered the professor when the stranger had passed. "Has he ever seen your face before?"

"Not that I know," answered Giovanni, starting at the name.

"He *has* seen you! he must have seen you!" said Baglioni, hastily. "For some purpose or other, this man of science is making a study of you. I know that look of his! It is the same that coldly illuminates his face as he bends over a bird, a mouse, or a butterfly, which, in pursuance of some experiment, he has killed by the perfume of a flower; a look as deep as Nature itself, but without Nature's warmth of love. Signor Giovanni, I will stake my life upon it, you are the subject of one of Rappaccini's experiments!"

"Will you make a fool of me?" cried Giovanni, passionately. "*That*, signor professor, were an untoward experiment."

"Patience! patience!" replied the imperturbable

professor. "I tell thee, my poor Giovanni, that Rappaccini has a scientific interest in thee. Thou hast fallen into fearful hands! And the Signora Beatrice,—what part does she act in this mystery?"

But Guasconti, finding Baglioni's pertinacity intolerable, here broke away, and was gone before the professor could again seize his arm. He looked after the young man intently and shook his head.

"This must not be," said Baglioni to himself. "The youth is the son of my old friend, and shall not come to any harm from which the arcana of medical science can preserve him. Besides, it is too insufferable an impertinence in Rappaccini thus to snatch the lad out of my own hands, as I may say, and make use of him for his infernal experiments. This daughter of his! It shall be looked to. Perchance, most learned Rappaccini, I may foil you where you little dream of it!"

Meanwhile Giovanni had pursued a circuitous route, and at length found himself at the door of his lodgings. As he crossed the threshold he was met by old Lisabetta, who smirked and smiled, and was evidently desirous to attract his attention; vainly, however, as the ebullition of his feelings had momentarily subsided into a cold and dull vacuity. He turned his eyes full upon the withered face that was puckering itself into a smile, but seemed to behold it not. The old dame, therefore, laid her grasp upon his cloak.

"Signor! signor!" whispered she, still with a smile over the whole breadth of her visage, so that it looked not unlike a grotesque carving in wood, darkened by centuries. "Listen, signor! There is a private entrance into the garden!"

"What do you say?" exclaimed Giovanni, turning quickly about, as if an inanimate thing should start into feverish life. "A private entrance into Dr. Rappaccini's garden?"

"Hush! hush! not so loud!" whispered Lisabetta, putting her hand over his mouth. "Yes, into the worshipful doctor's garden, where you may see all his fine shrubbery. Many a young man in Padua would give gold to be admitted among those flowers."

Giovanni put a piece of gold into her hand.

"Show me the way," said he.

A surmise, probably excited by his conversation with Baglioni, crossed his mind, that this interposition of old Lisabetta might perchance be connected with the intrigue, whatever were its nature, in which the professor seemed to suppose that Dr. Rappaccini was involving him. But such a suspicion, though it disturbed Giovanni, was inadequate to restrain him. The instant that he was aware of the possibility of approaching Beatrice, it seemed an absolute necessity of his existence to do so. It mattered not whether she were angel or demon; he was irrevocably within her sphere, and must obey the law that whirled him onward, in ever-lessening circles, towards a result which he did not attempt to foreshadow; and yet, strange to say, there came across him a sudden doubt whether this intense interest on his part were not delusory; whether it were really of so deep and positive a nature as to justify him in now thrusting himself into an incalculable position; whether it were not merely the fantasy of a young man's brain, only slightly or not at all connected with his heart.

He paused, hesitated, turned half about, but again went on. His withered guide led him along several obscure passages, and finally undid a door, through which, as it was opened, there came the sight and sound of rustling leaves, with the broken sunshine glimmering among them. Giovanni stepped forth, and, forcing himself through the entanglement of a shrub that wreathed its tendrils over the hidden entrance, stood beneath his own window in the open area of Dr. Rappaccini's garden.

How often is it the case that, when impossibilities have come to pass and dreams have condensed their misty substance into tangible realities, we find ourselves calm, and even coldly self-possessed, amid circumstances which it would have been a delirium of joy or agony to anticipate! Fate delights to thwart us thus. Passion will choose his own time to rush upon the scene, and lingers sluggishly behind when an appropriate adjustment of events would seem to summon his appearance. So was it now with Giovanni. Day after day his pulses had throbbed with feverish blood at the improbable idea of an interview with Beatrice, and of standing with her, face to face, in this very garden, basking in the Oriental sunshine of her beauty, and snatching from her full gaze the mystery which he deemed the riddle of his own existence. But now there was a singular and untimely equanimity within his breast. He threw a glance around the garden to discover if Beatrice or her father were present, and, perceiving that he was alone, began a critical observation of the plants.

The aspect of one and all of them dissatisfied him; their gorgeousness seemed fierce, passionate, and even unnatural. There was hardly an individual shrub which a wanderer, straying by himself through a forest, would not have been startled to find growing wild, as if an unearthly face had glared at him out of the thicket. Several also would have shocked a delicate instinct by an appearance of artificialness indicating that there had been such commixture, and, as it were, adultery, of various vegetable species, that the production was no longer of God's making, but the monstrous offspring of man's depraved fancy, glowing with only an evil mockery of beauty. They were probably the result of experiment which in one or two cases had succeeded in mingling plants individually lovely into a compound possessing the questionable and ominous character that distinguished the whole growth of the garden. In fine, Giovanni recognized but two or three plants in the collection, and those of a kind that he well knew to be poisonous. While busy with these contemplations he heard the rustling of a silken garment, and, turning, beheld Beatrice emerging from beneath the sculptured portal.

Giovanni had not considered with himself what should be his deportment; whether he should apologize for his intrusion into the garden, or assume that he was there with the privity at least, if not by the desire, of Dr. Rappaccini or his daughter; but Beatrice's manner placed him at his ease, though leaving him still in doubt by what agency he had gained admittance. She came lightly along the path and met him near the broken fountain. There was surprise in her face, but brightened by a simple and kind expression of pleasure.

"You are a connoisseur in flowers, signor," said Beatrice, with a smile, alluding to the bouquet which he had flung her from the window. "It is no marvel, therefore, if the sight of my father's rare collection has tempted you to take a nearer view. If he were here, he could tell you many strange and interesting facts as to the nature and habits of these shrubs; for he has spent a lifetime in such studies, and this garden is his world."

"And yourself, lady," observed Giovanni, "if fame says true,—you likewise are deeply skilled in the virtues indicated by these rich blossoms and these spicy perfumes. Would you deign to be my instructress, I should prove an apter scholar than if taught by Signor Rappaccini himself."

"Are there such idle rumors?" asked Beatrice, with the music of a pleasant laugh. "Do people say that I am skilled in my father's science of plants? What a jest is there! No; though I have grown up among these flowers, I know no more of them than their hues and perfume; and sometimes methinks I would fain rid myself of even that small knowledge. There are many flowers here, and those not the least brilliant, that shock and offend me when they meet my eye. But pray, signor, do not believe these stories about my science. Believe nothing of me save what you see with your own eyes."

"And must I believe all that I have seen with my own eyes?" asked Giovanni, pointedly, while the recollection of former scenes made him shrink. "No, signora; you demand too little of me. Bid me believe nothing save what comes from your own lips."

It would appear that Beatrice understood him. There came a deep flush to her cheek; but she looked full into Giovanni's eyes, and responded to his gaze of uneasy suspicion with a queenlike haughtiness.

"I do so bid you, signor," she replied. "Forget whatever you may have fancied in regard to me. If true to the outward senses, still it may be false in its essence; but the words of Beatrice Rappaccini's lips are true from the depths of the heart outward. Those you may believe."

A fervor glowed in her whole aspect and beamed upon Giovanni's consciousness like the light of truth itself; but while she spoke there was a fragrance in the atmosphere around her, rich and delightful, though evanescent, yet which the young man, from an indefinable reluctance, scarcely dared to draw into his lungs. It might be the odor of the flowers. Could it be Beatrice's breath which thus embalmed her words with a strange richness, as if by steeping them in her heart? A faintness passed like a shadow over Giovanni and flitted away; he seemed to gaze through the beautiful girl's eyes into her transparent soul, and felt no more doubt or fear.

The tinge of passion that had colored Beatrice's manner vanished; she became gay, and appeared to derive a pure delight from her communion with the youth not unlike what the maiden of a lonely island might have felt conversing with a voyager from the civilized world. Evidently her experience of life had been confined within the limits of that garden. She talked now about matters as simple as the daylight or summer clouds, and now asked questions in reference to the city, or Giovanni's distant home, his friends, his mother, and his sisters—questions indicating such seclusion, and such lack of familiarity with modes and forms, that Giovanni responded as if to an infant. Her spirit gushed out before him like a fresh rill that was just catching its first glimpse of the sunlight and wondering at the reflections of earth and sky which were flung into its bosom. There came thoughts, too, from a deep source, and fantasies of a gemlike brilliancy, as if diamonds and rubies sparkled upward among the bubbles of the fountain. Ever and anon there gleamed across the young man's mind a sense of wonder that he should be walking side by side with the being who had so wrought upon his imagination, whom he had idealized in such hues of terror, in whom he had positively witnessed such manifestations of dreadful attributes—that he should be conversing with Beatrice like a brother, and should find her so human and so maidenlike. But such reflections were only momentary; the effect of her character was too real not to make itself familiar at once.

In this free intercourse they had strayed through the garden, and now, after many turns among its avenues, were come to the shattered fountain, beside which grew the magnificent shrub, with its treasury of glowing blossoms. A fragrance was diffused from it which Giovanni recognized as identical with that which he had attributed to Beatrice's breath, but incomparably more powerful. As her eyes fell upon it, Giovanni beheld her press her hand to her bosom as if her heart were throbbing suddenly and painfully.

"For the first time in my life," murmured she, addressing the shrub, "I had forgotten thee."

"I remember, signora," said Giovanni, "that you once promised to reward me with one of these living gems for the bouquet which I had the happy boldness to fling to your feet. Permit me now to pluck it as a memorial of this interview."

He made a step towards the shrub with extended hand; but Beatrice darted forward, uttering a shriek that went through his heart like a dagger. She caught his hand and drew it back with the whole force of her slender figure. Giovanni felt her touch thrilling through his fibres.

"Touch it not!" exclaimed she, in a voice of agony. "Not for thy life! It is fatal!"

Then, hiding her face, she fled from him and vanished beneath the sculptured portal. As Giovanni followed her with his eyes, he beheld the emaciated figure and pale intelligence of Dr. Rappaccini, who had been watching the scene, he knew not how long, within the shadow of the entrance.

No sooner was Guasconti alone in his chamber than the image of Beatrice came back to his passionate musings, invested with all the witchery that had been gathering around it ever since his first glimpse of her, and now likewise imbued with a tender warmth of girlish womanhood. She was human; her nature was endowed with all gentle and feminine qualities; she was worthiest to be worshipped; she was capable, surely, on her part, of the height and heroism of love. Those tokens which he had hitherto considered as proofs of a frightful peculiarity in her physical and moral system were now either forgotten or by the subtle sophistry of passion transmitted into a golden crown of enchantment, rendering Beatrice the more admirable by so much as she was the more unique. Whatever had looked ugly was now beautiful; or, if incapable of such a change, it stole away and hid itself among those shapeless half ideas which throng the dim region beyond the daylight of our perfect consciousness. Thus did he spend the night, nor fell asleep until the dawn had begun to awake the slumbering flowers in Dr. Rappaccini's garden, whither Giovanni's dreams doubtless led him. Up rose the sun in his due season, and, flinging his beams upon the young man's eyelids, awoke him to a sense of pain. When thoroughly aroused, he became sensible of a burning and tingling agony in his hand—in his right hand—the very hand which Beatrice had grasped in her own when he was on the point of plucking one of the gemlike flowers. On the back of that hand there was now a purple print like that of four small fingers, and the likeness of a slender thumb upon his wrist.

O, how stubbornly does love,—or even that cunning semblance of love which flourishes in the imagination, but strikes no depth of root into the heart,—how stubbornly does it hold its faith until the moment comes when it is doomed to vanish into thin mist! Giovanni wrapped a handkerchief about his hand and wondered what evil thing had stung him, and soon forgot his pain in a reverie of Beatrice.

After the first interview, a second was in the inevitable course of what we call fate. A third; a fourth; and a meeting with Beatrice in the garden was no longer an incident in Giovanni's daily life, but the whole space in which he might be said to live; for the anticipation and memory of that ecstatic hour made up the remainder. Nor was it otherwise with the daughter of Rappaccini. She watched for the youth's appearance and flew to his side with confidence as unreserved as if they had been playmates from early infancy—as if they were such playmates still. If, by any unwonted chance, he failed to come at the appointed moment, she stood beneath the window and sent up the rich sweetness of her tones to float around him in his chamber and echo and reverberate throughout his heart: "Giovanni! Giovanni! Why tarriest thou? Come down!" And down he hastened into that Eden of poisonous flowers.

But, with all this intimate familiarity, there was still a reserve in Beatrice's demeanor, so rigidly and invariably sustained that the idea of infringing it scarcely occurred to his imagination. By all appreciable signs, they loved; they had looked love with eyes that conveyed the holy secret from the depths of one soul into the depths of the other, as if it were too sacred to be whispered by the way; they had even spoken love in those gushes of passion when their spirits darted forth in articulated breath like tongues of long hidden flame; and yet there had been no seal of lips, no clasp of hands, nor any slightest caress such as love claims and hallows. He had never touched one of the gleaming ringlets of her hair; her garment—so marked was the physical barrier between them—had never been waved against him by a breeze. On the few occasions when Giovanni had seemed tempted to overstep the limit, Beatrice grew so sad, so stern, and withal wore such a look of desolate separation, shuddering at itself, that not a spoken word was requisite to repel him. At such times he was startled at the horrible suspicions that rose, monster-like, out of the caverns of his heart and stared him in the face; his love grew thin and faint as the morning mist; his doubts alone had substance. But, when Beatrice's face brightened again after the momentary shadow, she was transformed at once from the mysterious, questionable being whom he had watched with so much awe and horror; she was now the beautiful and unsophisticated girl whom he felt that his spirit knew with a certainty beyond all other knowledge.

A considerable time had now passed since Giovanni's last meeting with Baglioni. One morning, however, he was disagreeably surprised by a visit from the professor, whom he had scarcely thought of for whole weeks, and would willingly have forgotten still longer. Given up as he had long been to a pervading excitement, he could tolerate no companions except upon condition of their perfect sympathy with his present state of feeling. Such sympathy was not to be expected from Professor Baglioni.

The visitor chatted carelessly for a few moments about the gossip of the city and the university, and then took up another topic.

"I have been reading an old classic author lately," said he, "and met with a story that strangely interested me. Possibly you may remember it. It is of an Indian prince, who sent a beautiful woman as a present to Alexander the Great. She was as lovely as the dawn and gorgeous as the sunset; but what especially distinguished her was a certain rich perfume in her breath—richer than a garden of Persian roses. Alexander, as was natural to a youthful conqueror, fell in love at first sight with this magnificent stranger; but a certain sage physician, happening to be present, discovered a terrible secret in regard to her."

"And what was that?" asked Giovanni, turning his eyes downward to avoid those of the professor.

"That this lovely woman," continued Baglioni, with emphasis, "had been nourished with poisons from her birth upward, until her whole nature was so imbued with them that she herself had become the deadliest poison in existence. Poison was her element of life. With that rich perfume of her breath she blasted the very air. Her love would have been poison—her embrace death. Is not this a marvellous tale?"

"A childish fable," answered Giovanni, nervously starting from his chair. "I marvel how your worship finds time to read such nonsense among your graver studies."

"By the by," said the professor, looking uneasily about him, "what singular fragrance is this in your apartment? Is it the perfume of your gloves? It is faint, but delicious; and yet, after all, by no means agreeable. Were I to breathe it long, methinks it would make me ill. It is like the breath of a flower; but I see no flowers in the chamber."

"Nor are there any," replied Giovanni, who had turned pale as the professor spoke; "nor, I think, is there any fragrance except in your worship's imagination. Odors, being a sort of element combined of the sensual and the spiritual, are apt to deceive us in this manner. The recollection of a perfume, the bare idea of it, may easily be mistaken for a present reality."

"Ay; but my sober imagination does not often play such tricks," said Baglioni; "and, were I to fancy any kind of odor, it would be that of some vile apothecary drug, wherewith my fingers are likely enough to be imbued. Our worshipful friend Rappaccini, as I have heard, tinctures his medicaments with odors richer than those of Araby. Doubtless, likewise, the fair and learned Signora Beatrice would minister to her patients with draughts as sweet as a maiden's breath; but woe to him that sips them!"

Giovanni's face evinced many contending emotions. The tone in which the professor alluded to the pure and lovely daughter of Rappaccini was a torture to his soul; and yet the intimation of a view of her character, opposite to his own, gave instantaneous distinctness to a thousand dim suspicions, which now grinned at him like so many demons. But he strove hard to quell them and to respond to Baglioni with a true lover's perfect faith.

"Signor professor," said he, "you were my father's friend; perchance, too, it is your purpose to act a friendly part towards his son. I would fain feel nothing towards you save respect and deference; but I pray you to observe, signor, that there is one subject on which we must not speak. You know not the Signora Beatrice. You cannot, therefore, estimate the wrong—the blasphemy, I may even say—that is offered to her character by a light or injurious word."

"Giovanni! my poor Giovanni!" answered the professor, with a calm expression of pity, "I know this wretched girl far better than yourself. You shall hear the truth in respect to the poisoner Rappaccini and his poisonous daughter; yes, poisonous as she is beautiful. Listen; for, even should you do violence to my gray hairs, it shall not silence me. That old fable of the Indian woman has become a truth by the deep and deadly science of Rappaccini and in the person of the lovely Beatrice."

Giovanni groaned and hid his face.

"Her father," continued Baglioni, "was not restrained by natural affection from offering up his child in this horrible manner as the victim of his insane zeal for science; for, let us do him justice, he is as true a man of science as ever distilled his own heart in an alembic. What, then, will be your fate? Beyond a doubt you are selected as the material of some new experiment. Perhaps the result is to be death; perhaps a fate more awful still. Rappaccini, with what he calls the interest of science before his eyes, will hesitate at nothing."

"It is a dream," muttered Giovanni to himself; "surely it is a dream."

"But," resumed the professor, "be of good cheer, son of my friend. It is not yet too late for the rescue. Possibly we may even succeed in bringing back this miserable child within the limits of ordinary nature, from which her father's madness has estranged her. Behold this little silver vase! It was wrought by the hands of the renowned Benvenuto Cellini, and is well worthy to be a love gift to the fairest dame in Italy. But its contents are invaluable. One little sip of this antidote would have rendered the most virulent poisons of the Borgias innocuous. Doubt not that it will be as efficacious against those of Rappaccini. Bestow the vase, and the precious liquid within it, on your Beatrice, and hopefully await the result."

Baglioni laid a small, exquisitely wrought silver vial on the table and withdrew, leaving what he had said to produce its effects upon the young man's mind.

"We will thwart Rappaccini yet," thought he, chuckling to himself, as he descended the stairs; "but, let us confess the truth of him, he is a wonderful man—a wonderful man indeed; a vile empiric, however, in his practice, and therefore not to be tolerated by those who respect the good old rules of the medical profession."

Throughout Giovanni's whole acquaintance with Beatrice, he had occasionally, as we have said, been haunted by dark surmises as to her character; yet so thoroughly had she made herself felt by him as a simple, natural, most affectionate, and guileless creature, that the image now held up by Professor Baglioni looked as strange and incredible as if it were not in accordance with his own original conception. True, there were ugly recollections connected with his first glimpses of the beautiful girl; he could not quite forget the bouquet that withered in her grasp, and the insect that perished amid the sunny air, by no ostensible agency save the fragrance of her breath. These incidents, however, dissolving in the pure light of her character, had no longer the efficacy of facts, but were acknowledged as mistaken fantasies, by whatever testimony of the senses they might appear to be substantiated. There is something truer and more real than what we can see with the eyes and touch with the finger. On such better evidence had Giovanni founded his confidence in Beatrice, though rather by the necessary force of her high attributes than by any deep and generous faith on his part. But now his spirit was incapable of sustaining itself at the height to which the early enthusiasm of passion had exalted it; he fell down, grovelling among earthly doubts, and defiled therewith the pure whiteness of Beatrice's image. Not that he gave her up; he did but distrust. He resolved to institute some decisive test that should satisfy him, once for all, whether there were those dreadful peculiarities in her physical nature which could not be supposed to exist without some corresponding monstrosity of soul. His eyes, gazing down afar, might have deceived him as to the lizard, the insect, and the flowers; but if he could witness, at the distance of a few paces, the sudden blight of one fresh and healthful flower in Beatrice's hand, there

would be room for no further question. With this idea he hastened to the florist's and purchased a bouquet that was still gemmed with the morning dewdrops.

It was now the customary hour of his daily interview with Beatrice. Before descending into the garden, Giovanni failed not to look at his figure in the mirror—a vanity to be expected in a beautiful young man, yet, as displaying itself at that troubled and feverish moment, the token of a certain shallowness of feeling and insincerity of character. He did gaze, however, and said to himself that his features had never before possessed so rich a grace, nor his eyes such vivacity, nor his cheeks so warm a hue of superabundant life.

"At least," thought he, "her poison has not yet insinuated itself into my system. I am no flower to perish in her grasp."

With that thought he turned his eyes on the bouquet, which he had never once laid aside from his hand. A thrill of indefinable horror shot through his frame on perceiving that those dewy flowers were already beginning to droop; they wore the aspect of things that had been fresh and lovely yesterday. Giovanni grew white as marble, and stood motionless before the mirror, staring at his own reflection there as at the likeness of something frightful. He remembered Baglioni's remark about the fragrance that seemed to pervade the chamber. It must have been the poison in his breath! Then he shuddered—shuddered at himself. Recovering from his stupor, he began to watch with curious eye a spider that was busily at work hanging its web from the antique cornice of the apartment, crossing and recrossing the artful system of interwoven lines—as vigorous and active a spider as ever dangled from an old ceiling. Giovanni bent towards the insect, and emitted a deep, long breath. The spider suddenly ceased its toil; the web vibrated with a tremor originating in the body of the small artisan. Again Giovanni sent forth a breath, deeper, longer, and imbued with a venomous feeling out of his heart: he knew not whether he were wicked, or only desperate. The spider made a convulsive gripe with his limbs and hung dead across the window.

"Accursed! accursed!" muttered Giovanni, addressing himself. "Hast thou grown so poisonous that this deadly insect perishes by thy breath?"

At that moment a rich, sweet voice came floating up from the garden.

"Giovanni! Giovanni! It is past the hour! Why tarriest thou? Come down!"

"Yes," muttered Giovanni again. "She is the only being whom my breath may not slay! Would that it might!"

He rushed down, and in an instant was standing before the bright and loving eyes of Beatrice. A moment ago his wrath and despair had been so fierce that he could have desired nothing so much as to wither her by a glance; but with her actual presence there came influences which had too real an existence to be at once shaken off; recollections of the delicate and benign power of her feminine nature, which had so often enveloped him in a religious calm; recollections of many a holy and passionate outgush of her heart, when the pure fountain had been unsealed from its depths and made visible in its transparency to his mental eye; recollections which, had Giovanni known how to estimate them, would have assured him that all this ugly mystery was but an earthly illusion, and that, whatever mist of evil might seem to have gathered over her, the real Beatrice was a heavenly angel. Incapable as he was of such high faith, still her presence had not utterly lost its magic. Giovanni's rage was quelled into an aspect of sullen insensibility. Beatrice, with a quick spiritual sense, immediately felt that there was a gulf of blackness between them which neither he nor she could pass. They walked on together, sad and silent, and came thus to the marble fountain and to its pool of water on the ground, in the midst of which grew the shrub that bore gemlike blossoms. Giovanni was affrighted at the eager enjoyment—the appetite, as it were—with which he found himself inhaling the fragrance of the flowers.

"Beatrice," asked he, abruptly, "whence came this shrub?"

"My father created it," answered she, with simplicity.

"Created it! created it!" repeated Giovanni. "What mean you, Beatrice?"

"He is a man fearfully acquainted with the secrets of Nature," replied Beatrice; "and at the hour when I first drew breath, this plant sprang from the soil, the offspring of his science, of his intellect, while I was but his earthly child. Approach it not!" continued she, observing with terror that Giovanni was drawing nearer to the shrub. "It has qualities that you little dream of. But I, dearest Giovanni,—I grew up and blossomed with the plant and was nourished with its breath. It was my sister, and I loved it with a human affection; for, alas!—hast thou not suspected it?—there was an awful doom."

Here Giovanni frowned so darkly upon her that Beatrice paused and trembled. But her faith in his tenderness reassured her, and made her blush that she had doubted for an instant.

"There was an awful doom," she continued, "the effect of my father's fatal love of science, which estranged me from all society of my kind. Until Heaven sent thee, dearest Giovanni, O, how lonely was thy poor Beatrice!"

"Was it a hard doom?" asked Giovanni fixing his eyes upon her.

"Only of late have I known how hard it was," answered she, tenderly. "O, yes; but my heart was torpid, and therefore quiet."

Giovanni's rage broke forth from his sullen gloom like a lightning flash out of a dark cloud.

"Accursed one!" cried he, with venomous scorn and anger. "And, finding thy solitude wearisome, thou has severed me likewise from all the warmth of life and enticed me into thy region of unspeakable horror!"

"Giovanni!" exclaimed Beatrice, turning her large bright eyes upon his face. The force of his words had not found its way into her mind; she was merely thunderstruck.

"Yes, poisonous thing!" repeated Giovanni, beside himself with passion. "Thou hast done it! Thou hast blasted me! Thou hast filled my veins with poison! Thou hast made me as hateful, as ugly, as loathsome and deadly a creature as thyself—a world's wonder of hideous monstrosity! Now, if our breath be happily as fatal to ourselves as to all others, let us join our lips in one kiss of unutterable hatred, and so die!"

"What has befallen me?" murmured Beatrice, with a low moan out of her heart. "Holy Virgin, pity me, a poor heart-broken child!"

"Thou,—dost thou pray?" cried Giovanni, still with the same fiendish scorn. "Thy very prayers, as they come from thy lips, taint the atmosphere with death. Yes, yes; let us pray! Let us to church and dip our fingers in the holy water at the portal! They that come after us will perish as by a pestilence! Let us sign crosses in the air! It will be scattering curses abroad in the likeness of holy symbols!"

"Giovanni," said Beatrice, calmly, for her grief was beyond passion, "why dost thou join thyself with me thus in those terrible words? I, it is true, am the horrible thing thou namest me. But thou,—what hast thou to do, save with one other shudder at my hideous misery to go forth out of the garden and mingle with thy race, and forget that there ever crawled on earth such a monster as poor Beatrice?"

"Dost thou pretend ignorance?" asked Giovanni, scowling upon her. "Behold! this power have I gained from the pure daughter of Rappaccini."

There was a swarm of summer insects flitting through the air in search of the food promised by the flower odors of the fatal garden. They circled round Giovanni's head, and were evidently attracted towards him by the same influence which had drawn them for an instant within the sphere of several of the shrubs. He sent forth a breath among them, and smiled bitterly at Beatrice as at least a score of the insects fell dead upon the ground.

"I see it! I see it!" shrieked Beatrice. "It is my father's fatal science! No, no, Giovanni; it was not I! Never! never! I dreamed only to love thee and be with thee a little time, and so to let thee pass away, leaving but thine image in mine heart; for, Giovanni, believe it, though my body be nourished with poison, my spirit is God's creature, and craves love as its daily food. But my father,—he has united us in this fearful sympathy. Yes; spurn me, tread upon me, kill me! O, what is death after such words as thine? But it was not I. Not for a world of bliss would I have done it."

Giovanni's passion had exhausted itself in its outburst from his lips. There now came across him a sense, mournful, and not without tenderness, of the intimate and peculiar relationship between Beatrice and himself. They stood, as it were, in an utter solitude, which would be made none the less solitary by the densest throng of human life. Ought not, then, the desert of humanity around them to press this insulated pair closer together? If they should be cruel to one another, who was there to be kind to them? Besides, thought Giovanni, might there not still be a hope of his returning within the limits of ordinary nature, and leading Beatrice, the redeemed Beatrice, by the hand? O, weak, and selfish, and unworthy spirit, that could dream of an earthly union and earthly happiness as possible, after such deep love had been so bitterly wronged as was Beatrice's love by Giovanni's blighting words! No, no; there could be no such hope. She must pass heavily, with that broken heart, across the borders of Time—she must bathe her hurts in some fount of paradise, and forget her grief in the light of immortality, and *there* be well.

But Giovanni did not know it.

"Dear Beatrice," said he approaching her, while she shrank as always at his approach, but now with a different impulse, "dearest Beatrice, our fate is not yet so desperate. Behold! there is a medicine, potent as a wise physician has assured me, and almost divine in its efficacy. It is composed of ingredients the most opposite to those by which thy awful father has brought this calamity upon thee and me. It is distilled of blessed herbs. Shall we not quaff it together, and thus be purified from evil?"

"Give it me!" said Beatrice, extending her hand to receive the little silver vial which Giovanni took from his bosom. She added, with a peculiar emphasis, "I will drink; but do thou await the result."

She put Baglioni's antidote to her lips; and, at the same moment, the figure of Rappaccini emerged from the portal and came slowly towards the marble fountain. As he drew near, the pale man of science seemed to gaze with a triumphant expression at the beautiful youth and maiden, as might an artist who should spend his life in achieving a picture or a group of statuary and finally be satisfied with his success. He paused; his bent form grew erect with conscious power; he spread out his hands over them in the attitude of a father imploring a blessing upon his children; but those were the same hands that had thrown poison into the stream of their lives.

Giovanni trembled. Beatrice shuddered nervously, and pressed her hand upon her heart.

"My daughter," said Rappaccini, "thou art no longer lonely in the world. Pluck one of those precious gems from thy sister shrub and bid thy bridegroom wear it in his bosom. It will not harm him now. My science and the sympathy between thee and him have so wrought within his system that he now stands apart from common men, as thou dost, daughter of my pride and triumph, from ordinary women. Pass on, then, through the world, most dear to one another and dreadful to all besides!"

"My father," said Beatrice, feebly,—and still as she spoke she kept her hand upon her heart,—"wherefore didst thou inflict this miserable doom upon thy child?"

"Miserable!" exclaimed Rappaccini. "What mean you, foolish girl? Dost thou deem it misery to be endowed with marvelous gifts against which no power nor strength could avail an enemy—misery, to be able to quell the mightiest with a breath—misery, to be as terrible as thou art beautiful? Wouldst thou, then, have preferred the condition of a weak woman, exposed to all evil and capable of none?"

"I would fain have been loved, not feared," murmured Beatrice, sinking down upon the ground. "But now it matters not. I am going, father, where the evil which thou hast striven to mingle with my being will pass away like a dream—like the fragrance of these poisonous flowers, which will no longer taint my breath among the flowers of Eden. Farewell, Giovanni. Thy words of hatred are like lead within my heart; but they, too, will fall away as I ascend. O, was there not, from the first, more poison in thy nature than in mine?"

To Beatrice,—so radically had her earthly part been wrought upon by Rappaccini's skill,—as poison had been life, so the powerful antidote was death; and thus the poor victim of man's ingenuity and of thwarted nature, and of the fatality that attends all such efforts of perverted wisdom, perished there, at the feet of her father and Giovanni. Just at that moment Professor Pietro Baglioni looked forth from the window, and called loudly, in a tone of triumph mixed with horror, to the thunderstricken man of science,—

"Rappaccini! Rappaccini! and is *this* the upshot of your experiment!"

1844

Ethan Brand

A Chapter from an Abortive Romance

The idea of an Unpardonable Sin, the theme of this story, goes back to the New Testament: "He that shall blaspheme against the Holy Ghost hath never forgiveness, but is in danger of eternal damnation." (Mark iii. 28–29.)

The immediate germ of Hawthorne's story may be found in his notebooks, 1844: "The Unpardonable Sin might consist in a want of love and reverence for the Human Soul; in consequence of which the investigator pried into its dark depths, not with a hope or purpose of making it better, but from a cold philosophical curiosity— content that it should be wicked in whatever kind or degree, and only desiring to study it out. Would not this, in other words, be a separation of the intellect from the heart?" Another notebook entry reads: "The search of an investigator for the Unpardonable Sin—he at last finds it in his own heart and practice."

As Hawthorne conceives of human nature, a man should, ideally, maintain a balance between intellect and feeling. Ethan Brand (like Dr. Rappaccini) has long since lost this balance. His mind has been developed to the highest point; his heart has contracted, hardened, turned to stone. Intellectual pride and loss of human feeling have brought him to a bleak and terrible solitude, to alienation alike from his fellow human beings, Mother Earth, and God—a solitude signed and sealed in his final dramatic act.

Text: From the first American edition of *The Snow-Image and Other Twice-Told Tales* (Boston, 1852).

Bartram the lime-burner, a rough, heavy-looking man, begrimed with charcoal, sat watching his kiln, at nightfall, while his little son played at building houses with the scattered fragments of marble, when, on the hill-side below them, they heard a roar of laughter, not mirthful, but slow, and even solemn, like a wind shaking the boughs of the forest.

"Father, what is that?" asked the little boy, leaving his play, and pressing betwixt his father's knees.

"O, some drunken man, I suppose," answered the lime-burner; "some merry fellow from the bar-room in the village, who dared not laugh loud enough within doors, lest he should blow the roof of the house off. So here he is, shaking his jolly sides at the foot of Graylock."[1]

"But, father," said the child, more sensitive than the obtuse, middle-aged clown, "he does not laugh like a man that is glad. So the noise frightens me!"

"Don't be a fool, child!" cried his father, gruffly. "You will never make a man, I do believe; there is too much of your mother in you. I have known the rustling of a leaf startle you. Hark! Here comes the merry fellow, now. You shall see that there is no harm in him."

Bartram and his little son, while they were talking thus, sat watching the same lime-kiln that had been the scene of Ethan Brand's solitary and meditative life, before he began his search for the Unpardonable Sin. Many years, as we have seen, had now elapsed, since that portentous night when the IDEA was first developed. The kiln, however, on the mountain-side, stood unimpaired, and was in nothing changed since he had thrown his dark thoughts into

the intense glow of its furnace, and melted them, as it were, into the one thought that took possession of his life. It was a rude, round, tower-like structure, about twenty feet high, heavily built of rough stones, and with a hillock of earth heaped about the larger part of its circumference; so that the blocks and fragments of marble might be drawn by cart-loads, and thrown in at the top. There was an opening at the bottom of the tower, like an oven-mouth, but large enough to admit a man in a stooping posture, and provided with a massive iron door. With the smoke and jets of flame issuing from the chinks and crevices of this door, which seemed to give admittance into the hill-side, it resembled nothing so much as the private entrance to the infernal regions, which the shepherds of the Delectable Mountains[2] were accustomed to show to pilgrims.

There are many such lime-kilns in that tract of country, for the purpose of burning the white marble which composes a large part of the substance of the hills. Some of them, built years ago, and long deserted, with weeds growing in the vacant round of the interior, which is open to the sky, and grass and wild-flowers rooting themselves in the chinks of the stones, look already like relics of antiquity, and may yet be overspread with the lichens of centuries to come. Others, where the lime-burner still feeds his daily and night-long fire, afford points of interest to the wanderer among the hills, who seats himself on a log of wood or a fragment of marble, to hold a chat with the solitary man. It is a lonesome, and, when the character is inclined to thought, may be an intensely thoughtful occupation; as it proved in the case of Ethan Brand, who had mused to such strange purpose, in days gone by, while the fire in this very kiln was burning.

The man who now watched the fire was of a different order, and troubled himself with no thoughts save the very few that were requisite to his business. At frequent intervals, he flung back the clashing weight of the iron door, and, turning his face from the insufferable glare, thrust in huge logs of oak, or stirred the immense brands with a long pole. Within the furnace were seen the curling and riotous flames, and the burning marble, almost molten with the intensity of heat; while without, the reflection of the fire quivered on the dark intricacy of the surrounding forest, and showed in the foreground a bright and ruddy little picture of the hut, the spring beside its door, the athletic and coal-begrimed figure of the lime-burner, and the half-frightened child, shrinking into the protection of his father's shadow. And when again the iron door was closed, then reappeared the tender light of the half-full moon, which vainly strove to trace out the indistinct shapes of the neighboring mountains; and, in

---

[1] Mt. Greylock in the Berkshires; the highest point in Massachusetts.

[2] An allusion to the Delectable Mountains of John Bunyan's *The Pilgrim's Progress*.

the upper sky, there was a flitting congregation of clouds, still faintly tinged with the rosy sunset, though thus far down into the valley the sunshine had vanished long and long ago.

The little boy now crept still closer to his father, as footsteps were heard ascending the hill-side, and a human form thrust aside the bushes that clustered beneath the trees.

"Halloo! who is it?" cried the lime-burner, vexed at his son's timidity, yet half infected by it. "Come forward, and show yourself, like a man, or I'll fling this chunk of marble at your head!"

"You offer me a rough welcome," said a gloomy voice, as the unknown man drew nigh. "Yet I neither claim nor desire a kinder one, even at my own fireside."

To obtain a distincter view, Bartram threw open the iron door of the kiln, whence immediately issued a gush of fierce light, that smote full upon the stranger's face and figure. To a careless eye there appeared nothing very remarkable in his aspect, which was that of a man in a coarse, brown, country-made suit of clothes, tall and thin, with the staff and heavy shoes of a wayfarer. As he advanced, he fixed his eyes—which were very bright—intently upon the brightness of the furnace, as if he beheld, or expected to behold, some object worthy of note within it.

"Good evening, stranger," said the lime-burner; "whence come you, so late in the day?"

"I come from my search," answered the wayfarer; "for, at last, it is finished."

"Drunk!—or crazy!" muttered Bartram to himself. "I shall have trouble with the fellow. The sooner I drive him away, the better."

The little boy, all in a tremble, whispered to his father, and begged him to shut the door of the kiln, so that there might not be so much light; for that there was something in the man's face which he was afraid to look at, yet could not look away from. And, indeed, even the lime-burner's dull and torpid sense began to be impressed by an indescribable something in that thin, rugged, thoughtful visage, with the grizzled hair hanging wildly about it, and those deeply-sunken eyes, which gleamed like fires within the entrance of a mysterious cavern. But, as he closed the door, the stranger turned towards him, and spoke in a quiet, familiar way, that made Bartram feel as if he were a sane and sensible man, after all.

"Your task draws to an end, I see," said he. "This marble has already been burning three days. A few hours more will convert the stone to lime."

"Why, who are you?" exclaimed the lime-burner. "You seem as well acquainted with my business as I am myself."

"And well I may be," said the stranger; "for I followed the same craft many a long year, and here, too, on this very spot. But you are a newcomer in these parts. Did you never hear of Ethan Brand?"

"The man that went in search of the Unpardonable Sin?" asked Bartram, with a laugh.

"The same," answered the stranger. "He has found what he sought, and therefore he comes back again."

"What! then you are Ethan Brand himself?" cried the lime-burner, in amazement. "I am a newcomer here, as you say, and they call it eighteen years since you left the foot of Graylock. But, I can tell you, the good folks still talk about Ethan Brand, in the village yonder, and what a strange errand took him away from his lime-kiln. Well, and so you have found the Unpardonable Sin?"

"Even so!" said the stranger, calmly.

"If the question is a fair one," proceeded Bartram, "where might it be?"

Ethan Brand laid his finger on his own heart.

"Here!" replied he.

And then, without mirth in his countenance, but as if moved by an involuntary recognition of the infinite absurdity of seeking throughout the world for what was the closest of all things to himself, and looking into every heart, save his own, for what was hidden in no other breast, he broke into a laugh of scorn. It was the same slow, heavy laugh, that had almost appalled the lime-burner when it heralded the wayfarer's approach.

The solitary mountain-side was made dismal by it. Laughter, when out of place, mistimed, or bursting forth from a disordered state of feeling, may be the most terrible modulation of the human voice. The laughter of one asleep, even if it be a little child,—the madman's laugh,—the wild, screaming laugh of a born idiot,—are sounds that we sometimes tremble to hear, and would always willingly forget. Poets have imagined no utterance of fiends or hobgoblins so fearfully appropriate as a laugh. And even the obtuse lime-burner felt his nerves shaken, as this strange man looked inward at his own heart, and burst into laughter that rolled away into the night, and was indistinctly reverberated among the hills.

"Joe," said he to his little son, "scamper down to the tavern in the village, and tell the jolly fellows there that Ethan Brand has come back, and that he has found the Unpardonable Sin!"

The boy darted away on his errand, to which Ethan Brand made no objection, nor seemed hardly to notice it. He sat on a log of wood, looking steadfastly at the iron door of the kiln. When the child was out of sight, and his swift and light footsteps ceased to be heard treading first on the fallen leaves and then on the rocky mountain-path, the lime-burner began to regret his departure. He felt that the little fellow's presence had been a barrier between his guest and himself, and that he must now deal, heart to heart, with a man who, on his own confession, had committed the one only crime for which Heaven could afford no mercy. That crime, in its indistinct blackness, seemed to overshadow him. The lime-burner's own sins rose up within him, and made his memory riotous with a throng of evil shapes that asserted their kindred with the Master Sin, whatever it might be, which it was within the scope of man's corrupted nature to conceive and cherish. They were all of one family; they went to and fro between his breast and Ethan Brand's, and carried dark greetings from one to the other.

Then Bartram remembered the stories which had grown traditionary in reference to this strange man, who had come upon him like a shadow of the night, and was making himself at home in his old place, after so long absence that the dead people, dead and buried for years, would have had more right to be at home, in any familiar spot, than he. Ethan Brand, it was said, had conversed with Satan himself in the lurid blaze of this very kiln. The legend had been matter of mirth heretofore, but looked grisly now. According to this tale, before Ethan Brand departed on his search, he had been accustomed to evoke a fiend from the hot furnace of the lime-kiln, night after night, in order to confer with him about the Unpardonable Sin; the man and the fiend each laboring to frame the image of some mode of guilt which could neither be atoned for nor forgiven. And, with the first gleam of light upon the mountain-top, the fiend crept in at the iron door, there to abide the intensest element of fire, until again summoned forth to share in the dreadful task of extending man's possible guilt beyond the scope of Heaven's else infinite mercy.

While the lime-burner was struggling with the horror of these thoughts, Ethan Brand rose from the log, and flung open the door of the kiln. The action was in such accordance with the idea in Bartram's mind, that he almost expected to see the Evil One issue forth, red-hot, from the raging furnace.

"Hold! hold!" cried he, with a tremulous attempt to laugh; for he was ashamed of his fears, although they overmastered him. "Don't, for mercy's sake, bring out your devil now!"

"Man!" sternly replied Ethan Brand, "what need have I of the devil? I have left him behind me, on my track. It is with such half-way sinners as you that he busies himself. Fear not, because I open the door. I do but act by old custom, and am going to trim your fire, like a lime-burner, as I was once."

He stirred the vast coals, thrust in more wood, and bent forward to gaze into the hollow prison-house of the fire, regardless of the fierce glow that reddened upon his face. The lime-burner sat watching him, and half suspected his strange guest of a purpose, if not to evoke a fiend, at least to plunge bodily into the flames, and thus vanish from the

sight of man. Ethan Brand, however, drew quietly back, and closed the door of the kiln.

"I have looked," said he, "into many a human heart that was seven times hotter with sinful passions than yonder furnace is with fire. But I found not there what I sought. No, not the Unpardonable Sin!"

"What is the Unpardonable Sin?" asked the lime-burner; and then he shrank farther from his companion, trembling lest his question should be answered.

"It is a sin that grew within my own breast," replied Ethan Brand, standing erect, with a pride that distinguishes all enthusiasts of his stamp. "A sin that grew nowhere else! The sin of an intellect that triumphed over the sense of brotherhood with man and reverence for God, and sacrificed everything to its own mighty claims! The only sin that deserves a recompense of immortal agony! Freely, were it to do again, would I incur the guilt. Unshrinkingly I accept the retribution!"

"The man's head is turned," muttered the lime-burner to himself. "He may be a sinner, like the rest of us,—nothing more likely,—but, I'll be sworn, he is a madman too."

Nevertheless he felt uncomfortable at his situation, alone with Ethan Brand on the wild mountain-side, and was right glad to hear the rough murmur of tongues, and the footsteps of what seemed a pretty numerous party, stumbling over the stones and rustling through the underbrush. Soon appeared the whole lazy regiment that was wont to infest the village tavern, comprehending three or four individuals who had drunk flip beside the bar-room fire through all the winters, and smoked their pipes beneath the stoop through all the summers, since Ethan Brand's departure. Laughing boisterously, and mingling all their voices together in unceremonious talk, they now burst into the moonshine and narrow streaks of fire-light that illuminated the open space before the lime-kiln. Bartram set the door ajar again, flooding the spot with light, that the whole company might get a fair view of Ethan Brand, and he of them.

There, among other old acquaintances, was a once ubiquitous man, now almost extinct, but whom we were formerly sure to encounter at the hotel of every thriving village throughout the country. It was the stage-agent. The present specimen of the genus was a wilted and smoke-dried man, wrinkled and red-nosed, in a smartly-cut, brown, bob-tailed coat, with brass buttons, who, for a length of time unknown, had kept his desk and corner in the bar-room, and was still puffing what seemed to be the same cigar that he had lighted twenty years before. He had great fame as a dry joker, though, perhaps, less on account of any intrinsic humor than from a certain flavor of brandy-toddy and tobacco-smoke, which impregnated all his ideas and expressions, as well as his person. Another well-remembered though strangely-altered face was that of Lawyer Giles, as people still called him in courtesy; an elderly ragamuffin, in his soiled shirt-sleeves and tow-cloth trousers. This poor fellow had been an attorney, in what he called his better days, a sharp practitioner, and in great vogue among the village litigants; but flip, and sling, and toddy, and cocktails, imbibed at all hours, morning, noon, and night, had caused him to slide from intellectual to various kinds and degrees of bodily labor, till at last, to adopt his own phrase, he slid into a soap-vat. In other words, Giles was now a soap-boiler, in a small way. He had come to be but the fragment of a human being, a part of one foot having been chopped off by an axe, and an entire hand torn away by the devilish grip of a steam-engine. Yet, though the corporeal hand was gone, a spiritual member remained; for, stretching forth the stump, Giles steadfastly averred that he felt an invisible thumb and fingers with as vivid a sensation as before the real ones were amputated. A maimed and miserable wretch he was; but one, nevertheless, whom the world could not trample on, and had no right to scorn, either in this or any previous stage of his misfortunes, since he had still kept up the courage and spirit of a man, asked nothing in charity, and with his one hand—and that the left one—fought a stern battle against want and hostile circumstances.

Among the throng, too, came another personage, who, with certain points of similarity to Lawyer Giles, had many more of difference. It was the village doctor; a man of some fifty years, whom, at an earlier period of his life, we introduced as paying a professional visit to Ethan Brand during the latter's supposed insanity. He was now a purple-visaged, rude, and brutal, yet half-gentlemanly figure, with something wild, ruined, and desperate in his talk, and in all the details of his gesture and manners. Brandy possessed this man like an evil spirit, and made him as surly and savage as a wild beast, and as miserable as a lost soul; but there was supposed to be in him such wonderful skill, such native gifts of healing, beyond any which medical science could impart, that society caught hold of him, and would not let him sink out of its reach. So, swaying to and fro upon his horse, and grumbling thick accents at the bedside, he visited all the sick-chambers for miles about among the mountain towns, and sometimes raised a dying man, as it were, by miracle, or quite as often, no doubt, sent his patient to a grave that was dug many a year too soon. The doctor had an everlasting pipe in his mouth, and, as somebody said, in allusion to his habit of swearing, it was always alight with hell-fire.

These three worthies pressed forward, and greeted Ethan Brand each after his own fashion, earnestly inviting him to partake of the contents of a certain black bottle, in which, as they averred, he would find something far better worth seeking for than the Unpardonable Sin. No mind, which has wrought itself by intense and solitary meditation into a high state of enthusiasm, can endure the kind of contact with low and vulgar modes of thought and feeling to which Ethan Brand was now subjected. It made him doubt—and, strange to say, it was a painful doubt—whether he had indeed found the Unpardonable Sin, and found it within himself. The whole question on which he had exhausted life, and more than life, looked like a delusion.

"Leave me," he said bitterly, "ye brute beasts, that have made yourselves so, shrivelling up your souls with fiery liquors! I have done with you. Years and years ago, I groped into your hearts, and found nothing there for my purpose. Get ye gone!"

"Why, you uncivil scoundrel," cried the fierce doctor, "is that the way you respond to the kindness of your best friends? Then let me tell you the truth. You have no more found the Unpardonable Sin than yonder boy Joe has. You are but a crazy fellow,—I told you so twenty years ago,—neither better nor worse than a crazy fellow, and the fit companion of old Humphrey, here!"

He pointed to an old man, shabbily dressed, with long white hair, thin visage, and unsteady eyes. For some years past this aged person had been wandering about among the hills, inquiring of all travelers whom he met for his daughter. The girl, it seemed, had gone off with a company of circus-performers; and occasionally tidings of her came to the village, and fine stories were told of her glittering appearance as she rode on horseback in the ring, or performed marvelous feats on the tight-rope.

The white-haired father now approached Ethan Brand, and gazed unsteadily into his face.

"They tell me you have been all over the earth," said he, wringing his hands with earnestness. "You must have seen my daughter, for she makes a grand figure in the world, and everybody goes to see her. Did she send any word to her old father, or say when she was coming back?"

Ethan Brand's eye quailed beneath the old man's. That daughter, from whom he so earnestly desired a word of greeting, was the Esther of our tale, the very girl whom, with such cold and remorseless purpose, Ethan Brand had made the subject of a psychological experiment, and wasted, absorbed, and perhaps annihilated her soul, in the process.

"Yes," murmured he, turning away from the hoary wanderer; "it is no delusion. There is an Unpardonable Sin!"

While these things were passing, a merry scene

was going forward in the area of cheerful light, beside the spring and before the door of the hut. A number of the youth of the village, young men and girls, had hurried up the hill-side, impelled by curiosity to see Ethan Brand, the hero of so many a legend familiar to their childhood. Finding nothing, however, very remarkable in his aspect,—nothing but a sunburnt wayfarer, in plain garb and dusty shoes, who sat looking into the fire, as if he fancied pictures among the coals,—these young people speedily grew tired of observing him. As it happened, there was other amusement at hand. An old German Jew, traveling with a diorama on his back, was passing down the mountain-road towards the village just as the party turned aside from it, and, in hopes of eking out the profits of the day, the showman had kept them company to the lime-kiln.

"Come, old Dutchman," cried one of the young men, "let us see your pictures, if you can swear they are worth looking at!"

"O, yes, Captain," answered the Jew,—whether as a matter of courtesy or craft, he styled everybody Captain,—"I shall show you, indeed, some very superb pictures!"

So, placing his box in a proper position, he invited the young men and girls to look through the glass orifices of the machine, and proceeded to exhibit a series of the most outrageous scratchings and daubings, as specimens of the fine arts, that ever an itinerant showman had the face to impose upon his circle of spectators. The pictures were worn out, moreover, tattered, full of cracks and wrinkles, dingy with tobacco-smoke, and otherwise in a most pitiable condition. Some purported to be cities, public edifices, and ruined castles in Europe; other represented Napoleon's battles and Nelson's sea-fights; and in the midst of these would be seen a gigantic, brown, hairy hand,—which might have been mistaken for the Hand of Destiny, though, in truth, it was only the showman's,—pointing its forefinger to various scenes of the conflict, while its owner gave historical illustrations. When, with much merriment at its abominable deficiency of merit, the exhibition was concluded, the German bade little Joe put his head into the box. Viewed through the magnifying-glasses, the boy's round, rosy visage assumed the strangest imaginable aspect of an immense Titanic child, the mouth grinning broadly, and the eyes and every other feature overflowing with fun at the joke. Suddenly, however, that merry face turned pale, and its expression changed to horror, for this easily impressed and excitable child had become sensible that the eye of Ethan Brand was fixed upon him through the glass.

"You make the little man to be afraid, Captain," said the German Jew, turning up the dark and strong outline of his visage, from his stooping pos-

ture. "But look again, and, by chance, I shall cause you to see somewhat that is very fine, upon my word!"

Ethan Brand gazed into the box for an instant, and then starting back, looked fixedly at the German. What had he seen? Nothing, apparently; for a curious youth, who had peeped in almost at the same moment, beheld only a vacant space of canvas.

"I remember you now," muttered Ethan Brand to the showman.

"Ah, Captain," whispered the Jew of Nuremberg, with a dark smile, "I find it to be a heavy matter in my show-box,—this Unpardonable Sin! By my faith, Captain, it has wearied my shoulders, this long day, to carry it over the mountain."

"Peace," answered Ethan Brand, sternly, "or get thee into the furnace yonder!"

The Jew's exhibition had scarcely concluded, when a great, elderly dog—who seemed to be his own master, as no person in the company laid claim to him—saw fit to render himself the object of public notice. Hitherto, he had shown himself a very quiet, well-disposed old dog, going round from one to another, and, by way of being sociable, offering his rough head to be patted by any kindly hand that would take so much trouble. But now, all of a sudden, this grave and venerable quadruped, of his own mere motion, and without the slightest suggestion from anybody else, began to run round after his tail, which, to heighten the absurdity of the proceeding, was a great deal shorter than it should have been. Never was seen such headlong eagerness in pursuit of an object that could not possibly be attained; never was heard such a tremendous outbreak of growling, snarling, barking, and snapping,—as if one end of the ridiculous brute's body were at deadly and most unforgivable enmity with the other. Faster and faster, round about went the cur; and faster and still faster fled the unapproachable brevity of his tail; and louder and fiercer grew his yells of rage and animosity; until, utterly exhausted, and as far from the goal as ever, the foolish old dog ceased his performance as suddenly as he had begun it. The next moment he was as mild, quiet, sensible, and respectable in his deportment, as when he first scraped acquaintance with the company.

As may be supposed, the exhibition was greeted with universal laughter, clapping of hands, and shouts of encore, to which the canine performer responded by wagging all that there was to wag of his tail, but appeared totally unable to repeat his very successful effort to amuse the spectators.

Meanwhile, Ethan Brand had resumed his seat upon the log, and moved, it might be, by a perception of some remote analogy between his own case and that of this self-pursuing cur, he broke into the awful laugh, which, more than any other token, expressed the condition of his inward being. From that moment, the merriment of the party was at an end; they stood aghast, dreading lest the inauspicious sound should be reverberated around the horizon, and that mountain would thunder it to mountain, and so the horror be prolonged upon their ears. Then, whispering one to another that it was late,— that the moon was almost down,—that the August night was growing chill,—they hurried homewards, leaving the lime-burner and little Joe to deal as they might with their unwelcome guest. Save for these three human beings, the open space on the hillside was a solitude, set in a vast gloom of forest. Beyond that darksome verge, the firelight glimmered on the stately trunks and almost black foliage of pines, intermixed with the lighter verdure of sapling oaks, maples, and poplars, while here and there lay the gigantic corpses of dead trees, decaying on the leaf-strewn soil. And it seemed to little Joe—a timorous and imaginative child—that the silent forest was holding its breath, until some fearful thing should happen.

Ethan Brand thrust more wood into the fire, and closed the door of the kiln; then looking over his shoulder at the lime-burner and his son, he bade, rather than advised, them to retire to rest.

"For myself, I cannot sleep," said he. "I have matters that it concerns me to meditate upon. I will watch the fire, as I used to do in the old time."

"And call the devil out of the furnace to keep you company, I suppose," muttered Bartram, who had been making intimate acquaintance with the black bottle above-mentioned. "But watch, if you like, and call as many devils as you like! For my part, I shall be all the better for a snooze. Come, Joe!"

As the boy followed his father into the hut, he looked back at the wayfarer, and the tears came into his eyes, for his tender spirit had an intuition of the bleak and terrible loneliness in which this man had enveloped himself.

When they had gone, Ethan Brand sat listening to the crackling of the kindled wood, and looking at the little spirts of fire that issued through the chinks of the door. These trifles, however, once so familiar, had but the slightest hold of his attention, while deep within his mind he was reviewing the gradual but marvelous change that had been wrought upon him by the search to which he had devoted himself. He remembered how the night dew had fallen upon him,—how the dark forest had whispered to him,—how the stars had gleamed upon him,—a simple and loving man, watching his fire in the years gone by, and ever musing as it burned. He remembered with what tenderness, with what love and sympathy for mankind, and what pity for human guilt and woe, he had first begun to contemplate those ideas which afterwards became the inspiration of his life; with

what reverence he had then looked into the heart of man, viewing it as a temple originally divine, and, however desecrated, still to be held sacred by a brother; with what awful fear he had deprecated the success of his pursuit, and prayed that the Unpardonable Sin might never be revealed to him. Then ensued that vast intellectual development, which, in its progress, disturbed the counterpoise between his mind and heart. The Idea that possessed his life had operated as a means of education; it had gone on cultivating his powers to the highest point of which they were susceptible; it had raised him from the level of an unlettered laborer to stand on a star-lit eminence, whither the philosophers of the earth, laden with the lore of universities, might vainly strive to clamber after him. So much for the intellect! But where was the heart? That, indeed, had withered—had contracted—had hardened—had perished! It had ceased to partake of the universal throb. He had lost his hold of the magnetic chain of humanity. He was no longer a brother-man, opening the chambers or the dungeons of our common nature by the key of holy sympathy, which gave him a right to share in all its secrets; he was now a cold observer, looking on mankind as the subject of his experiment, and, at length, converting man and woman to be his puppets, and pulling the wires that moved them to such degrees of crime as were demanded for his study.

Thus Ethan Brand became a fiend. He began to be so from the moment that his moral nature had ceased to keep the pace of improvement with his intellect. And now, as his highest effort and inevitable development,—as the bright and gorgeous flower, and rich, delicious fruit of his life's labor,— he had produced the Unpardonable Sin!

"What more have I to seek? What more to achieve?" said Ethan Brand to himself. "My task is done, and well done!"

Starting from the log with a certain alacrity in his gait, and ascending the hillock of earth that was raised against the stone circumference of the lime-kiln, he thus reached the top of the structure. It was a space of perhaps ten feet across, from edge to edge, presenting a view of the upper surface of the immense mass of broken marble with which the kiln was heaped. All these innumerable blocks and fragments of marble were red-hot and vividly on fire, sending up great spouts of blue flame, which quivered aloft and danced madly, as within a magic circle, and sank and rose again, with continual and multitudinous activity. As the lonely man bent forward over this terrible body of fire, the blasting heat smote up against his person with a breath that, it might be supposed, would have scorched and shrivelled him up in a moment.

Ethan Brand stood erect, and raised his arms on

high. The blue flames played upon his face, and imparted the wild and ghastly light which alone could have suited its expression; it was that of a fiend on the verge of plunging into his gulf of intensest torment.

"O Mother Earth," cried he, "who art no more my Mother, and into whose bosom this frame shall never be resolved! O mankind, whose brotherhood I have cast off, and trampled thy great heart beneath my feet! O stars of heaven, that shone on me of old, as if to light me onward and upward!—farewell all, and forever. Come, deadly element of Fire,—henceforth my familiar friend! Embrace me, as I do thee!"

That night the sound of a fearful peal of laughter rolled heavily through the sleep of the lime-burner and his little son; dim shapes of horror and anguish haunted their dreams, and seemed still present in the rude hovel, when they opened their eyes to the daylight.

"Up, boy, up!" cried the lime-burner, staring about him. "Thank Heaven, the night is gone, at last; and rather than pass such another, I would watch my lime-kiln, wide awake, for a twelvemonth. This Ethan Brand, with his humbug of an Unpardonable Sin, has done me no such mighty favor, in taking my place!"

He issued from the hut, followed by little Joe, who kept fast hold of his father's hand. The early sunshine was already pouring its gold upon the mountain-tops; and though the valleys were still in shadow, they smiled cheerfully in the promise of the bright day that was hastening onward. The village, completely shut in by hills, which swelled away gently about it, looked as if it had rested peacefully in the hollow of the great hand of Providence. Every dwelling was distinctly visible; the little spires of the two churches pointed upwards, and caught a fore-glimmering of brightness from the sun-gilt skies upon their gilded weather-cocks. The tavern was astir, and the figure of the old, smoke-dried stage-agent, cigar in mouth, was seen beneath the stoop. Old Graylock was glorified with a golden cloud upon his head. Scattered likewise over the breasts of the surrounding mountains, there were heaps of hoary mist, in fantastic shapes, some of them far down into the valley, others high up towards the summits, and still others, of the same family of mist or cloud,

hovering in the gold radiance of the upper atmosphere. Stepping from one to another of the clouds that rested on the hills, and thence to the loftier brotherhood that sailed in air, it seemed almost as if a mortal man might thus ascend into the heavenly regions. Earth was so mingled with sky that it was a day-dream to look at it.

To supply that charm of the familiar and homely, which Nature so readily adopts into a scene like this, the stage-coach was rattling down the mountain-road, and the driver sounded his horn, while echo caught up the notes, and intertwined them into a rich and varied and elaborate harmony, of which the original performer could lay claim to little share. The great hills played a concert among themselves, each contributing a strain of airy sweetness.

Little Joe's face brightened at once.

"Dear father," cried he, skipping cheerily to and fro, "that strange man is gone, and the sky and the mountains all seem glad of it!"

"Yes," growled the lime-burner, with an oath, "but he has let the fire go down, and no thanks to him if five hundred bushels of lime are not spoiled. If I catch the fellow hereabouts again, I shall feel like tossing him into the furnace!"

With his long pole in his hand, he ascended to the top of the kiln. After a moment's pause, he called to his son.

"Come up here, Joe!" said he.

So little Joe ran up the hillock, and stood by his father's side. The marble was all burnt into perfect, snow-white lime. But on its surface, in the midst of the circle,—snow-white too, and thoroughly converted into lime,—lay a human skeleton, in the attitude of a person who, after long toil, lies down to long repose. Within the ribs—strange to say—was the shape of a human heart.

"Was the fellow's heart made of marble?" cried Bartram, in some perplexity at this phenomenon. "At any rate, it is burnt into what looks like special good lime; and, taking all the bones together, my kiln is half a bushel the richer for him."

So saying, the rude lime-burner lifted his pole, and, letting it fall upon the skeleton, the relics of Ethan Brand were crumbled into fragments.

1850

HERMAN MELVILLE [1819–1891]

HAWTHORNE HAD SHOWN that great fiction could come out of long seclusion; Melville showed that it could come out of intense adventurous experience.

When Melville was born, his father, Allan Melville, of distinguished New England Scottish ancestry, was a cultivated gentleman-merchant in New York, dealing in French fabrics, hose, perfumes, and the like. During a business depression he became bankrupt, and in 1830 tried to rehabilitate himself in Albany. There, two years later, he died, leaving Herman (a boy of thirteen) and seven other children. The widow, who had been Maria Gansevoort, of a notable New Netherland family, managed the domestic economy with skill. From parents in the Dutch Reformed Church she had acquired a piety that she sought to pass on to her children. In later years Melville retained a close knowledge of the Bible and a speculative awareness of the essential problems of religion. His formal schooling ended when he was only fifteen—after that he was educated by varied experience and wide reading.

He worked in a bank, he worked in a store, he worked on a farm, he did some teaching. Then, at age twenty, he had his first taste of sea life shipping as a cabin-boy on a freighter, and, though he did not know it, beginning to gather the primary subject-matter of his fiction. On this voyage he sampled the hard life of the seaman, and saw, not the famed charms of the Old World, but the waterfront slums of vice-ridden Liverpool. After his return he taught school off and on, then submitted again to what he later called "the everlasting itch for things remote."

After a trip to Illinois in 1840, he shipped, early the next year, on the whaler *Acushnet* ("my Yale College and Harvard") bound for the South Seas, and, as it turned out, was away nearly four years. After eighteen months on the ship he deserted, and with a companion lived in the society of cannibals, the Typees of the Marquesas Islands. Escaping on an Australian whaler to Tahiti, he shipped on another whaler that sailed in Japanese waters and eventually brought him to Honolulu. He joined the American navy, at length returned home on the frigate *United States,* and was discharged in Boston.

Graduated from the school of the sea, Melville entered the vocation of writing. He turned his wanderings into fiction, drawing into the net what he could find in books (such as Stewart's *A Visit to the South Seas* and Ames's *A Mariner's Sketches*). The result was a series of romances, varying in autobiographic content, all published within five years: *Typee* (1846), his life among the cannibals; *Omoo,* adventures in the South Seas; *Redburn,* the voyage to Liverpool; *Mardi,* the South Seas again, in an allegorical and satirical mode; *White-Jacket,* service in the navy; and *Moby-Dick* (1851), life on a whaling ship.

In 1847, the year of the second of these books, he married Elizabeth Shaw, daughter of the chief justice of Massachusetts. For nearly three years he lived and wrote in New York (visiting London and Paris in winter 1849–50). Then he settled with his wife and first child—he was soon to be father to two sons and two daughters—at Pittsfield, Massachusetts. While Hawthorne, a few miles away at Lenox, was writing *The House of the Seven Gables,* Melville was deep in *Moby-Dick, or The Whale,* a book "broiled," he told Hawthorne, "in hell-fire." In this book Melville did for the South Seas and the whalers what Cooper had done for the frontier and Mark Twain was to do for the great age of the Mississippi steamboats. More important, he created a fine story, an unforgettable character, an impressive wrestling with the problem of evil, and a rich, symphonic style.

Melville had poured his best into *Moby-Dick,* and felt that he had written himself out, though forty years of his life were still before him. For reasons not very clear, his art fell into a long decline. In 1852 he published *Pierre, or The Ambiguities,* a darkly symbolical study of good and evil, and then his last novels, *Israel Potter* and *The Confidence Man.* He tried shorter fiction in *The Piazza Tales,* showing great technical command in "Benito Cereno." He tried poetry: *Battle-Pieces and Aspects of the War* and *Clarel.* Then, surprisingly enough, late in life he achieved one more triumph—*Billy Budd,* a short novel left among his manuscripts and unpublished till 1924. Unlike Ahab and Pierre, his earlier heroes, Billy Budd, in tragic defeat, accepts the inscrutable law of life.

Once his writing career had turned awry, Melville could not expect to support his sizeable family by his pen. He received help from relatives, he tried lecturing, and in 1866 was appointed inspector of customs in New York, a post which he held for nearly twenty years. He died obscure.

Further reading: *Moby-Dick. Selected Poems,* ed. Hennig Cohen, 1964. Leon Howard, *Herman Melville: A Biography,* 1951. F. O. Matthiessen, *American Renaissance* (Book 3), 1941. Newton Arvin, *Herman Melville,* 1950. Edward Rosenberry, *Melville and the Comic Spirit,* 1955. Merlin Bowen, *The Long Encounter,* 1960. Warner Berthoff, *The Example of Melville,* 1963. Richard Chase, ed., *Melville: A Collection of Critical Essays,* 1962.

FROM *Hawthorne and His Mosses*

In July 1850 Melville came upon Hawthorne's *Mosses from an Old Manse.* In excited admiration he wrote a long review-article, concealed his authorship by signing it as "By a Virginian," and had it printed in the *Literary World* in the issues of August 17 and 24. Meanwhile—on August 5—Melville met Hawthorne for the first time, and they soon became friends.

The following paragraphs from the article are interesting not only for what they say about Hawthorne, but also for what they reveal about Melville himself, especially his passionate desire to probe to "the very axis of reality." It happens that at this time he was writing his own great novel, *Moby-Dick,* himself wrestling with "black" Truth. In his enthusiasm over the example of Hawthorne, he declares: "Hawthorne has dropped germinous seeds into my soul. He expands and deepens down, the more I contemplate him; and further and further shoots his strong New England roots in the hot soil of my Southern soul." When *Moby-Dick* was published it was dedicated to Nathaniel Hawthorne.

Text: *The Literary World,* August 17, 1850.

It is the least part of genius that attracts admiration. Where Hawthorne is known, he seems to be deemed a pleasant writer, with a pleasant style,—a sequestered, harmless man, from whom any deep and weighty thing would hardly be anticipated—a man who means no meanings. But there is no man, in whom humor and love, like mountain peaks, soar to such a rapt height as to receive the irradiations of the upper skies;—there is no man in whom humor and love are developed in that high form called genius; no such man can exist without also possessing, as the indispensable complement of these, a great, deep intellect, which drops down into the universe like a plummet. Or, love and humor are only the eyes through which such an intellect views

this world. The great beauty in such a mind is but the product of its strength. ° ° °

Spite of all the Indian-summer sunlight on the hither side of Hawthorne's soul, the other side—like the dark half of the physical sphere—is shrouded in a blackness, ten times black. But this darkness but gives more effect to the ever-moving dawn, that for ever advances through it, and circumnavigates his world. Whether Hawthorne has simply availed himself of this mystical blackness as a means to the wondrous effects he makes it to produce in his lights and shades; or whether there really lurks in him, perhaps unknown to himself, a touch of Puritanic gloom,—this, I cannot altogether tell. Certain it is, however, that this great power of blackness in him derives its force from its appeals to that Calvinistic sense of Innate Depravity and Original Sin, from whose visitations, in some shape or other, no deeply thinking mind is always and wholly free. For, in certain moods, no man can weigh this world without throwing in something, somehow like Original Sin, to strike the uneven balance. At all events, perhaps no writer has ever wielded this terrific thought with greater terror than this same harmless Hawthorne. Still more: this black conceit pervades him through and through. You may be witched by his sunlight,—transported by the bright gildings in the skies he builds over you; but there is the blackness of darkness beyond; and even his bright gildings but fringe and play upon the edges of thunder-clouds. In one word, the world is mistaken in this Nathaniel Hawthorne. He himself must often have smiled at its absurd misconception of him. He is immeasurably deeper than the plummet of the mere critic. For it is not the brain that can test such a man; it is only the heart. You cannot come to know greatness by inspecting it; there is no glimpse to be caught of it, except by intuition; you need not ring it, you but touch it, and you find it is gold.

Now, it is that blackness in Hawthorne, of which I have spoken, that so fixes and fascinates me. It may be, nevertheless, that it is too largely developed in him. Perhaps he does not give us a ray of his light for every shade of his dark. But however this may be, this blackness it is that furnishes the infinite obscure of his back-ground,—that back-ground, against which Shakspeare plays his grandest conceits, the things that have made for Shakspeare his loftiest but most circumscribed renown, as the profoundest of thinkers. For by philosophers Shakspeare is not adored as the great man of tragedy and comedy.—"Off with his head; so much for Buckingham!" This sort of rant, interlined by another hand, brings down the house,—those mistaken souls, who dream of Shakspeare as a mere man of Richard-the-Third humps and Macbeth daggers. But it is those deep far-away things in him; those occasional flashings-forth of the intuitive Truth in him; those short, quick probings at the very axis of reality;—these are the things that make Shakspeare, Shakspeare. Through the mouths of the dark characters of Hamlet, Timon, Lear, and Iago, he craftily says, or sometimes insinuates the things which we feel to be so terrifically true, that it were all but madness for any good man, in his own proper character, to utter, or even hint of them. Tormented into desperation, Lear, the frantic king, tears off the mask, and speaks the same madness of vital truth. But, as I before said, it is the least part of genius that attracts admiration. And so, much of the blind, unbridled admiration that has been heaped upon Shakspeare, has been lavished upon the least part of him. And few of his endless commentators and critics seem to have remembered, or even perceived, that the immediate products of a great mind are not so great as that undeveloped and sometimes undevelopable yet dimly-discernible greatness, to which those immediate products are but the infallible indices. In Shakspeare's tomb lies infinitely more than Shakspeare ever wrote. And if I magnify Shakspeare, it is not so much for what he did do as for what he did not do, or refrained from doing. For in this world of lies, Truth is forced to fly like a scared white doe in the woodlands; and only by cunning glimpses will she reveal herself, as in Shakspeare and other masters of the great Art of Telling the Truth,—even though it be covertly and by snatches.

But if this view of the all-popular Shakspeare be seldom taken by his readers, and if very few who extol him have ever read him deeply, or perhaps, only have seen him on the tricky stage (which alone made, and is still making him his mere mob renown)—if few men have time, or patience, or palate, for the spiritual truth as it is in that great

genius;—it is then no matter of surprise, that in a contemporaneous age, Nathaniel Hawthorne is a man as yet almost utterly mistaken among men. Here and there, in some quiet arm-chair in the noisy town, or some deep nook among the noiseless mountains, he may be appreciated for something of what he is. But unlike Shakspeare, who was forced to the contrary course by circumstances, Hawthorne (either from simple disinclination, or else from inaptitude) refrains from all the popularizing noise and show of broad farce and blood-besmeared tragedy; content with the still, rich utterance of a great intellect in repose, and which sends few thoughts into circulation, except they be arterialized at his large warm lungs, and expanded in his honest heart.

1850

Bartleby

The main protagonist of "Bartleby" is not the title character, but the lawyer-narrator. Bartleby's loneliness, despair, and terror disrupt the stable, prudent, affluent world in which the attorney has been so comfortably living and throw him into a state of serious psychological conflict. He is torn between the intolerance and incomprehension manifested by his colleagues and assistants, and his own sympathy for and understanding of the scrivener. The dramatic focus of the story is the manner in which the lawyer handles Bartleby's challenge.

"Bartleby" was Melville's first published short story, appearing anonymously in *Putnam's Monthly Magazine* in 1853. Melville included it in his collection of short pieces, *The Piazza Tales*, 1856. The text reprinted here is from Egbert S. Oliver's edition of *The Piazza Tales* (New York, 1948).

I am a rather elderly man. The nature of my avocations, for the last thirty years, has brought me into more than ordinary contact with what would seem an interesting and somewhat singular set of men, of whom, as yet, nothing, that I know of, has ever been written—I mean, the law-copyists, or scriveners. I have known very many of them, professionally and privately, and, if I pleased, could relate divers histories, at which good-natured gentlemen might smile, and sentimental souls might weep. But I waive the biographies of all other scriveners, for a few passages in the life of Bartleby, who was a scrivener, the strangest I ever saw, or heard of. While, of other law-copyists, I might write the complete life, of Bartleby nothing of that sort can be done. I believe that no materials exist, for a full and satisfactory biography of this man. It is an irreparable loss to literature. Bartleby was one of those beings of whom nothing is ascertainable, except from the original sources, and, in his case, those are very small. What my own astonished eyes saw of

Bartleby, *that* is all I know of him, except, indeed, one vague report, which will appear in the sequel. Ere introducing the scrivener, as he first appeared to me, it is fit I make some mention of myself, my *employés*, my business, my chambers, and general surroundings; because some such description is indispensable to an adequate understanding of the chief character about to be presented. Imprimis: I am a man who, from his youth upwards, has been filled with a profound conviction that the easiest way of life is the best. Hence, though I belong to a profession proverbially energetic and nervous, even to turbulence, at times, yet nothing of that sort have I ever suffered to invade my peace. I am one of those unambitious lawyers who never addresses a jury, or in any way draws down public applause; but, in the cool tranquillity of a snug retreat, do a snug business among rich men's bonds, and mortgages, and title-deeds. All who know me, consider me an eminently *safe* man. The late John Jacob Astor,[1] a personage little given to poetic enthusiasm, had no hesitation in pronouncing my first grand point to be prudence; my next, method. I do not speak it in vanity, but simply record the fact, that I was not unemployed in my profession by the late John Jacob Astor; a name which, I admit, I love to repeat; for it hath a rounded and orbicular sound to it, and rings like unto bullion. I will freely add, that I was not insensible to the late John Jacob Astor's good opinion.

Some time prior to the period at which this little history begins, my avocations had been largely increased. The good old office, now extinct in the State of New York, of a Master in Chancery,[2] had been conferred upon me. It was not a very arduous office, but very pleasantly remunerative. I seldom lose my temper; much more seldom indulge in dangerous indignation at wrongs and outrages; but, I must be permitted to be rash here, and declare, that I consider the sudden and violent abrogation of the office of Master in Chancery, by the new Constitution, as a —— premature act; inasmuch as I had counted upon a life-lease of the profits, whereas I only received those of a few short years. But this is by the way.

My chambers were up stairs, at No. — Wall Street. At one end, they looked upon the white wall of the interior of a spacious sky-light shaft, penetrating the building from top to bottom.

This view might have been considered rather tame than otherwise, deficient in what landscape painters call "life". But, if so, the view from the other end of my chambers offered, at least, a contrast, if nothing more. In that direction, my windows commanded an unobstructed view of a lofty brick wall, black by age and everlasting shade; which wall required no spy-glass to bring out its lurking beauties, but, for the benefit of all near-sighted spectators, was pushed up to within ten feet of my window panes. Owing to the great height of the surrounding buildings, and my chambers being on the second floor, the interval between this wall and mine not a little resembled a huge square cistern.

At the period just preceding the advent of Bartleby, I had two persons as copyists in my employment, and a promising lad as an office-boy. First, Turkey; second, Nippers; third, Ginger Nut. These may seem names, the like of which are not usually found in the Directory. In truth, they were nicknames, mutually conferred upon each other by my three clerks, and were deemed expressive of their respective persons or characters. Turkey was a short, pursy Englishman, of about my own age—that is, somewhere not far from sixty. In the morning, one might say, his face was of a fine florid hue, but after twelve o'clock, meridian—his dinner hour—it blazed like a grate full of Christmas coals; and continued blazing—but, as it were, with a gradual wane—till six o'clock, P.M., or thereabouts; after which, I saw no more of the proprietor of the face, which, gaining its meridian with the sun, seemed to set with it, to rise, culminate, and decline the following day, with the like regularity and undiminished glory. There are many singular coincidences I have known in the course of my life, not the least among which was the fact, that, exactly when Turkey displayed his fullest beams from his red and radiant countenance, just then, too, at that critical moment, began the daily period when I considered his business capacities as seriously disturbed for the remainder of the twenty-four hours. Not that he was absolutely idle, or averse to business, then; far from it. The difficulty was, he was apt to be altogether too energetic. There was a strange, inflamed, flurried, flighty recklessness of activity about him. He would be incautious in dipping his pen into his inkstand. All his blots upon my documents were dropped there after twelve o'clock, meridian. Indeed, not only would he be reckless, and sadly given to making blots in the afternoon, but, some days, he went further, and was rather noisy. At such times, too, his face flamed with augmented blazonry, as if cannel coal had been heaped on anthracite. He made an unpleasant racket with his chair; spilled his sandbox; in mending his pens, impatiently split them all to pieces, and threw them on the floor in a sudden passion; stood up, and leaned over his table, boxing his papers about in a most indecorous manner, very sad to behold in an elderly man like him. Neverthe-

---

[1]John Jacob Astor (1763–1848), financier; a symbol of wealth and achievement. The reference helps characterize the narrator's values.

[2]A sinecure that enabled the Master to collect fees regardless of the court decision.

less, as he was in many ways a most valuable person to me, and all the time before twelve o'clock, meridian, was the quickest, steadiest creature, too, accomplishing a great deal of work in a style not easily to be matched—for these reasons, I was willing to overlook his eccentricities, though, indeed, occasionally, I remonstrated with him. I did this very gently, however, because, though the civilest, nay, the blandest and most reverential of men in the morning, yet, in the afternoon, he was disposed, upon provocation, to be slightly rash with his tongue—in fact, insolent. Now, valuing his morning services as I did, and resolved not to lose them—yet, at the same time, made uncomfortable by his inflamed ways after twelve o'clock—and being a man of peace, unwilling by my admonitions to call forth unseemly retorts from him, I took upon me, one Saturday noon (he was always worse on Saturdays) to hint to him, very kindly, that, perhaps, now that he was growing old, it might be well to abridge his labors; in short, he need not come to my chambers after twelve o'clock, but, dinner over, had best go home to his lodgings, and rest himself till tea-time. But no; he insisted upon his afternoon devotions. His countenance became intolerably fervid, as he oratorically assured me—gesticulating with a long ruler at the other end of the room—that if his services in the morning were useful, how indispensable, then, in the afternoon?

"With submission, sir," said Turkey, on this occasion, "I consider myself your right-hand man. In the morning I but marshal and deploy my columns; but in the afternoon I put myself at their head, and gallantly charge the foe, thus"—and he made a violent thrust with the ruler.

"But the blots, Turkey," intimated I.

"True; but, with submission, sir, behold these hairs! I am getting old. Surely, sir, a blot or two of a warm afternoon is not to be severely urged against gray hairs. Old age—even if it blot the page—is honorable. With submission, sir, we *both* are getting old."

This appeal to my fellow-feeling was hardly to be resisted. At all events, I saw that go he would not. So, I made up my mind to let him stay, resolving, nevertheless, to see to it that, during the afternoon, he had to do with my less important papers.

Nippers, the second on my list, was a whiskered, sallow, and, upon the whole, rather piratical-looking young man, of about five and twenty. I always deemed him the victim of two evil powers—ambition and indigestion. The ambition was evinced by a certain impatience of the duties of a mere copyist, an unwarrantable usurpation of strictly professional affairs, such as the original drawing up of legal documents. The indigestion seemed betokened in an occasional nervous testiness and grinning irritability,

causing the teeth to audibly grind together over mistakes committed in copying; unnecessary maledictions, hissed, rather than spoken, in the heat of business; and especially by a continual discontent with the height of the table where he worked. Though of a very ingenious mechanical turn, Nippers could never get this table to suit him. He put chips under it, blocks of various sorts, bits of pasteboard, and at last went so far as to attempt an exquisite adjustment, by final pieces of folded blotting-paper. But no invention would answer. If, for the sake of easing his back, he brought the table lid at a sharp angle well up towards his chin, and wrote there like a man using the steep roof of a Dutch house for his desk, then he declared that it stopped the circulation in his arms. If now he lowered the table to his waistbands, and stooped over it in writing, then there was a sore aching in his back. In short, the truth of the matter was, Nippers knew not what he wanted. Or, if he wanted anything, it was to be rid of a scrivener's table altogether. Among the manifestations of his diseased ambition was a fondness he had for receiving visits from certain ambiguous-looking fellows in seedy coats, whom he called his clients. Indeed, I was aware that not only was he, at times, considerable of a ward-politician, but he occasionally did a little business at the Justices' courts, and was not unknown on the steps of the Tombs.[3] I have good reason to believe, however, that one individual who called upon him at my chambers, and who, with a grand air, he insisted was his client, was no other than a dun, and the alleged title-deed, a bill. But, with all his failings and the annoyances he caused me, Nippers, like his compatriot Turkey, was a very useful man to me; wrote a neat, swift hand; and, when he chose, was not deficient in a gentlemanly sort of deportment. Added to this, he always dressed in a gentlemanly sort of way; and so, incidentally, reflected credit upon my chambers. Whereas, with respect to Turkey, I had much ado to keep him from being a reproach to me. His clothes were apt to look oily, and smell of eating-houses. He wore his pantaloons very loose and baggy in summer. His coats were execrable; his hat not to be handled. But while the hat was a thing of indifference to me, inasmuch as his natural civility and deference, as a dependent Englishman, always led him to doff it the moment he entered the room, yet his coat was another matter. Concerning his coats, I reasoned with him; but with no effect. The truth was, I suppose, that a man with so small an income could not afford to sport such a lustrous face and a lustrous coat at one and the same time. As Nippers once observed, Turkey's money went chiefly for red ink. One winter day, I presented Turkey with a

[3]A large prison in New York City.

highly respectable-looking coat of my own—a padded gray coat, of a most comfortable warmth, and which buttoned straight up from the knee to the neck. I thought Turkey would appreciate the favor, and abate his rashness and obstreperousness of afternoons. But no; I verily believe that buttoning himself up in so downy and blanket-like a coat had a pernicious effect upon him—upon the same principle that too much oats are bad for horses. In fact, precisely as a rash, restive horse is said to feel his oats, so Turkey felt his coat. It made him insolent. He was a man whom prosperity harmed.

Though, concerning the self-indulgent habits of Turkey, I had my own private surmises, yet, touching Nippers, I was well persuaded that, whatever might be his faults in other respects, he was, at least, a temperate young man. But, indeed, nature herself seemed to have been his vintner, and, at his birth, charged him so thoroughly with an irritable, brandy-like disposition, that all subsequent potations were needless. When I consider how, amid the stillness of my chambers, Nippers would sometimes impatiently rise from his seat, and stooping over his table, spread his arms wide apart, seize the whole desk, and move it, and jerk it, with a grim, grinding motion on the floor, as if the table were a perverse voluntary agent, intent on thwarting and vexing him, I plainly perceive that, for Nippers, brandy-and-water were altogether superfluous.

It was fortunate for me that, owing to its peculiar cause—indigestion—the irritability and consequent nervousness of Nippers were mainly observable in the morning, while in the afternoon he was comparatively mild. So that, Turkey's paroxysms only coming on about twelve o'clock, I never had to do with their eccentricities at one time. Their fits relieved each other, like guards. When Nippers's was on, Turkey's was off; and *vice versa*. This was a good natural arrangement, under the circumstances.

Ginger Nut, the third on my list, was a lad, some twelve years old. His father was a car-man, ambitious of seeing his son on the bench instead of a cart, before he died. So he sent him to my office, as student at law, errand-boy, cleaner and sweeper, at the rate of one dollar a week. He had a little desk to himself, but he did not use it much. Upon inspection, the drawer exhibited a great array of the shells of various sorts of nuts. Indeed, to this quick-witted youth, the whole noble science of the law was contained in a nutshell. Not the least among the employments of Ginger Nut, as well as one which he discharged with the most alacrity, was his duty as cake and apple purveyor for Turkey and Nippers. Copying law-papers being proverbially a dry, husky sort of business, my two scriveners were fain to moisten their mouths very often with Spitzenbergs,

to be had at the numerous stalls nigh the Custom House and Post Office. Also, they sent Ginger Nut very frequently for that peculiar cake—small, flat, round, and very spicy—after which he had been named by them. Of a cold morning, when business was' but dull, Turkey would gobble up scores of these cakes, as if they were mere wafers—indeed, they sell them at the rate of six or eight for a penny—the scrape of his pen blending with the crunching of the crisp particles in his mouth. Of all the fiery afternoon blunders and flurried rashnesses of Turkey, was his once moistening a ginger-cake between his lips, and clapping it on to a mortgage, for a seal. I came within an ace of dismissing him then. But he mollified me by making an oriental bow, and saying—

"With submission, sir, it was generous of me to find you in stationery on my own account."

Now my original business—that of a conveyancer and title hunter, and drawer-up of recondite documents of all sorts—was considerably increased by receiving the master's office. There was now great work for scriveners. Not only must I push the clerks already with me, but I must have additional help.

In answer to my advertisement, a motionless young man one morning stood upon my office threshold, the door being open, for it was summer. I can see that figure now—pallidly neat, pitiably respectable, incurably forlorn! It was Bartleby.

After a few words touching his qualifications, I engaged him, glad to have among my corps of copyists a man of so singularly sedate an aspect, which I thought might operate beneficially upon the flighty temper of Turkey, and the fiery one of Nippers.

I should have stated before that ground glass folding-doors divided my premises into two parts, one of which was occupied by my scriveners, the other by myself. According to my humor, I threw open these doors, or closed them. I resolved to assign Bartleby a corner by the folding-doors, but on my side of them, so as to have this quiet man within easy call, in case any trifling thing was to be done. I placed his desk close up to a small side-window in that part of the room, a window which originally had afforded a lateral view of certain grimy back-yards and bricks, but which, owing to subsequent erections, commanded at present no view at all, though it gave some light. Within three feet of the panes was a wall, and the light came down from far above, between two lofty buildings, as from a very small opening in a dome. Still further to a satisfactory arrangement, I procured a high green folding screen, which might entirely isolate Bartleby from my sight, though not remove him from my voice. And thus, in a manner, privacy and society were conjoined.

At first, Bartleby did an extraordinary quantity of writing. As if long famishing for something to copy, he seemed to gorge himself on my documents. There was no pause for digestion. He ran a day and night line, copying by sun-light and by candle-light. I should have been quite delighted with his application, had he been cheerfully industrious. But he wrote on silently, palely, mechanically.

It is, of course, an indispensable part of a scrivener's business to verify the accuracy of his copy, word by word. Where there are two or more scriveners in an office, they assist each other in this examination, one reading from the copy, the other holding the original. It is a very dull, wearisome, and lethargic affair. I can readily imagine that, to some sanguine temperaments, it would be altogether intolerable. For example, I cannot credit that the mettlesome poet, Byron, would have contentedly sat down with Bartleby to examine a law document of, say five hundred pages, closely written in a crimpy hand.

Now and then, in the haste of business, it had been my habit to assist in comparing some brief document myself, calling Turkey or Nippers for this purpose. One object I had, in placing Bartleby so handy to me behind the screen, was, to avail myself of his services on such trivial occasions. It was on the third day, I think, of his being with me, and before any necessity had arisen for having his own writing examined, that, being much hurried to complete a small affair I had in hand, I abruptly called to Bartleby. In my haste and natural expectancy of instant compliance, I sat with my head bent over the original on my desk, and my right hand sideways, and somewhat nervously extended with the copy, so that, immediately upon emerging from his retreat, Bartleby might snatch it and proceed to business without the least delay.

In this very attitude did I sit when I called him, rapidly stating what it was I wanted him to do—namely, to examine a small paper with me. Imagine my surprise, nay, my consternation, when, without moving from his privacy, Bartleby, in a singularly mild, firm voice, replied, "I would prefer not to."

I sat awhile in perfect silence, rallying my stunned faculties. Immediately it occurred to me that my ears had deceived me, or Bartleby had entirely misunderstood my meaning. I repeated my request in the clearest tone I could assume; but in quite as clear a one came the previous reply, "I would prefer not to."

"Prefer not to," echoed I, rising in high excitement, and crossing the room with a stride. "What do you mean? Are you moon-struck? I want you to help me compare this sheet here—take it," and I thrust it towards him.

"I would prefer not to," said he.

I looked at him steadfastly. His face was leanly composed; his gray eye dimly calm. Not a wrinkle of agitation rippled him. Had there been the least uneasiness, anger, impatience or impertinence in his manner; in other words, had there been any thing ordinarily human about him, doubtless I should have violently dismissed him from the premises. But as it was, I should have as soon thought of turning my pale plaster-of-paris bust of Cicero out of doors. I stood gazing at him awhile, as he went on with his own writing, and then reseated myself at my desk. This is very strange, thought I. What had one best do? But my business hurried me. I concluded to forget the matter for the present, reserving it for my future leisure. So calling Nippers from the other room, the paper was speedily examined.

A few days after this, Bartleby concluded four lengthy documents, being quadruplicates of a week's testimony taken before me in my High Court of Chancery. It became necessary to examine them. It was an important suit, and great accuracy was imperative. Having all things arranged, I called Turkey, Nippers, and Ginger Nut, from the next room, meaning to place the four copies in the hands of my four clerks, while I should read from the original. Accordingly, Turkey, Nippers, and Ginger Nut had taken their seats in a row, each with his document in his hand, when I called to Bartleby to join this interesting group.

"Bartleby! quick, I am waiting."

I heard a slow scrape of his chair legs on the uncarpeted floor, and soon he appeared standing at the entrance of his hermitage.

"What is wanted?" said he, mildly.

"The copies, the copies," said I, hurriedly. "We are going to examine them. There"—and I held towards him the fourth quadruplicate.

"I would prefer not to," he said, and gently disappeared behind the screen.

For a few moments I was turned into a pillar of salt, standing at the head of my seated column of clerks. Recovering myself, I advanced towards the screen, and demanded the reason for such extraordinary conduct.

"Why do you refuse?"

"I would prefer not to."

With any other man I should have flown outright into a dreadful passion, scorned all further words, and thrust him ignominiously from my presence. But there was something about Bartleby that not only strangely disarmed me, but, in a wonderful manner, touched and disconcerted me. I began to reason with him.

"These are your own copies we are about to examine. It is labor saving to you, because one examination will answer for your four papers. It is common usage. Every copyist is bound to help examine his copy. Is it not so? Will you not speak? Answer!"

"I prefer not to," he replied in a flutelike tone. It seemed to me that, while I had been addressing him, he carefully revolved every statement that I made, fully comprehended the meaning; could not gainsay the irresistible conclusion; but, at the same time, some paramount consideration prevailed with him to reply as he did.

"You are decided, then, not to comply with my request—a request made according to common usage and common sense?"

He briefly gave me to understand, that on that point my judgment was sound. Yes: his decision was irreversible.

It is not seldom the case that, when a man is browbeaten in some unprecedented and violently unreasonable way, he begins to stagger in his own plainest faith. He begins, as it were, vaguely to surmise that, wonderful as it may be, all the justice and all the reason is on the other side. Accordingly, if any disinterested persons are present, he turns to them for some reinforcement of his own faltering mind.

"Turkey," said I, "what do you think of this? Am I not right?"

"With submission, sir," said Turkey, in his blandest tone, "I think that you are."

"Nippers," said I, "what do *you* think of it?"

"I think I should kick him out of the office."

(The reader, of nice perceptions, will here perceive that, it being morning, Turkey's answer is couched in polite and tranquil terms, but Nippers replies in ill-tempered ones. Or, to repeat a previous sentence, Nippers's ugly mood was on duty, and Turkey's off.)

"Ginger Nut," said I, willing to enlist the smallest suffrage in my behalf, "what do *you* think of it?"

"I think, sir, he's a little *luny*," replied Ginger Nut, with a grin.

"You hear what they say," said I, turning towards the screen, "come forth and do your duty."

But he vouchsafed no reply. I pondered a moment in sore perplexity. But once more business hurried me. I determined again to postpone the consideration of this dilemma to my future leisure. With a little trouble we made out to examine the papers without Bartleby, though at every page or two Turkey deferentially dropped his opinion, that this proceeding was quite out of the common; while Nippers, twitching in his chair with a dyspeptic nervousness, ground out, between his set teeth, occasional hissing maledictions against the stubborn oaf behind the screen. And for his (Nippers's) part, this was the first and the last time he would do another man's business without pay.

Meanwhile Bartleby sat in his hermitage, oblivious to everything but his own peculiar business there.

Some days passed, the scrivener being employed upon another lengthy work. His late remarkable conduct led me to regard his ways narrowly. I observed that he never went to dinner; indeed, that he never went anywhere. As yet I had never, of my personal knowledge, known him to be outside of my office. He was a perpetual sentry in the corner. At about eleven o'clock though, in the morning, I noticed that Ginger Nut would advance toward the opening in Bartleby's screen, as if silently beckoned thither by a gesture invisible to me where I sat. The boy would then leave the office, jingling a few pence, and reappear with a handful of ginger-nuts, which he delivered in the hermitage, receiving two of the cakes for his trouble.

He lives, then, on ginger-nuts, thought I; never eats a dinner, properly speaking; he must be a vegetarian, then; but no; he never eats even vegetables, he eats nothing but ginger-nuts. My mind then ran on in reveries concerning the probable effects upon the human constitution of living entirely on ginger-nuts. Ginger-nuts are so called, because they contain ginger as one of their peculiar constituents, and the final flavoring one. Now, what was ginger? A hot, spicy thing. Was Bartleby hot and spicy? Not at all. Ginger, then, had no effect upon Bartleby. Probably he preferred it should have none.

Nothing so aggravates an earnest person as a passive resistance. If the individual so resisted be of a not inhumane temper, and the resisting one perfectly harmless in his passivity, then, in the better moods of the former, he will endeavor charitably to construe to his imagination what proves impossible to be solved by his judgment. Even so, for the most part, I regarded Bartleby and his ways. Poor fellow! thought I, he means no mischief; it is plain he intends no insolence; his aspect sufficiently evinces that his eccentricities are involuntary. He is useful to me. I can get along with him. If I turn him away, the chances are he will fall in with some less-indulgent employer, and then he will be rudely treated, and perhaps driven forth miserably to starve. Yes. Here I can cheaply purchase a delicious self-approval. To befriend Bartleby; to humor him in his strange willfulness, will cost me little or nothing, while I lay up in my soul what will eventually prove a sweet morsel for my conscience. But this mood was not invariable with me. The passiveness of Bartleby sometimes irritated me. I felt strangely goaded on to encounter him in new opposition—to elicit some angry spark from him answerable to my own. But, indeed, I might as well have essayed to strike fire with my knuckles against a bit of Windsor soap. But one afternoon the evil impulse in me mastered me, and the following little scene ensued:

"Bartleby," said I, "when those papers are all copied, I will compare them with you."

"I would prefer not to."

"How? Surely you do not mean to persist in that mulish vagary?"

No answer.

I threw open the folding-doors near by, and, turning upon Turkey and Nippers, exclaimed:

"Bartleby a second time says, he won't examine his papers. What do you think of it, Turkey?"

It was afternoon, be it remembered. Turkey sat glowing like a brass boiler; his bald head steaming; his hands reeling among his blotted papers.

"Think of it?" roared Turkey; "I think I'll just step behind his screen, and black his eyes for him!"

So saying, Turkey rose to his feet and threw his arms into a pugilistic position. He was hurrying away to make good his promise, when I detained him, alarmed at the effect of incautiously rousing Turkey's combativeness after dinner.

"Sit down, Turkey," said I, "and hear what Nippers has to say. What do you think of it, Nippers? Would I not be justified in immediately dismissing Bartleby?"

"Excuse me, that is for you to decide, sir. I think his conduct quite unusual, and, indeed, unjust, as regards Turkey and myself. But it may only be a passing whim."

"Ah," exclaimed I, "you have strangely changed your mind, then—you speak very gently of him now."

"All beer," cried Turkey; "gentleness is effects of beer—Nippers and I dined together to-day. You see how gentle I am, sir. Shall I go and black his eyes?"

"You refer to Bartleby, I suppose. No, not to-day, Turkey," I replied; "pray, put up your fists."

I closed the doors, and again advanced towards Bartleby. I felt additional incentives tempting me to my fate. I burned to be rebelled against again. I remembered that Bartleby never left the office.

"Bartleby," said I, "Ginger Nut is away; just step around to the Post Office, won't you? (it was but a three minutes' walk), and see if there is anything for me."

"I would prefer not to."

"You will not?"

"I prefer not."

I staggered to my desk, and sat there in a deep study. My blind inveteracy returned. Was there any other thing in which I could procure myself to be ignominiously repulsed by this lean, penniless wight?—my hired clerk? What added thing is there, perfectly reasonable, that he will be sure to refuse to do?

"Bartleby!"

No answer.

"Bartleby," in a louder tone.

No answer.

"Bartleby," I roared.

Like a very ghost, agreeably to the laws of magical invocation, at the third summons, he appeared at the entrance of his hermitage.

"Go to the next room, and tell Nippers to come to me."

"I prefer not to," he respectfully and slowly said, and mildly disappeared.

"Very good, Bartleby," said I, in a quiet sort of serenely-severe self-possessed tone, intimating the unalterable purpose of some terrible retribution very close at hand. At the moment I half intended something of the kind. But upon the whole, as it was drawing towards my dinner-hour, I thought it best to put on my hat and walk home for the day, suffering much from perplexity and distress of mind.

Shall I acknowledge it? The conclusion of this whole business was, that it soon became a fixed fact of my chambers, that a pale young scrivener, by the name of Bartleby, had a desk there; that he copied for me at the usual rate of four cents a folio (one hundred words); but he was permanently exempt from examining the work done by him, that duty being transferred to Turkey and Nippers, out of compliment, doubtless, to their superior acuteness; moreover, said Bartleby was never, on any account, to be dispatched on the most trivial errand of any sort; and that even if entreated to take upon him such a matter, it was generally understood that he would "prefer not to"—in other words, that he would refuse point-blank.

As days passed on, I became considerably reconciled to Bartleby. His steadiness, his freedom from all dissipation, his incessant industry (except when he chose to throw himself into a standing revery behind his screen), his great stillness, his unalterableness of demeanor under all circumstances, made him a valuable acquisition. One prime thing was this—*he was always there*—first in the morning, continually through the day, and the last at night. I had a singular confidence in his honesty. I felt my most precious papers perfectly safe in his hands. Sometimes, to be sure, I could not, for the very soul of me, avoid falling into sudden spasmodic passions with him. For it was exceeding difficult to bear in mind all the time those strange peculiarities, privileges, and unheard of exemptions, forming the tacit stipulations on Bartleby's part under which he remained in my office. Now and then, in the eagerness of dispatching pressing business, I would inadvertently summon Bartleby, in a short, rapid tone, to put his finger, say, on the incipient tie of a bit of red tape with which I was about compressing some papers. Of course, from behind the screen the usual answer, "I prefer not to," was sure to come; and then, how could a human creature, with the common infirmities of our nature, refrain from bitterly exclaiming upon such perverseness—such unreasonableness. However, every added repulse of this sort which I received only tended to lessen the probability of my repeating the inadvertence.

Here it must be said, that according to the custom of most legal gentlemen occupying chambers in densely-populated law buildings, there were several keys to my door. One was kept by a woman residing in the attic, which person weekly scrubbed and daily swept and dusted my apartments. Another was kept by Turkey for convenience sake. The third I sometimes carried in my own pocket. The fourth I knew not who had.

Now, one Sunday morning I happened to go to Trinity Church,[4] to hear a celebrated preacher, and finding myself rather early on the ground I thought I would walk around to my chambers for a while. Luckily I had my key with me; but upon applying it to the lock, I found it resisted by something inserted from the inside. Quite surprised, I called out; when to my consternation a key was turned from within; and thrusting his lean visage at me, and holding the door ajar, the apparition of Bartleby appeared, in his shirt sleeves, and otherwise in a strangely tattered deshabille, saying quietly that he was sorry, but he was deeply engaged just then, and—preferred not admitting me at present. In a brief word or two, he moreover added, that perhaps I had better walk around the block two or three times, and by that time he would probably have concluded his affairs.

Now, the utterly unsurmised appearance of Bartleby, tenanting my law-chambers of a Sunday morning, with his cadaverously gentlemanly *nonchalance*, yet withal firm and self-possessed, had such a strange effect upon me, that incontinently I slunk away from my own door, and did as desired. But not without sundry twinges of impotent rebellion against the mild effrontery of this unaccountable scrivener. Indeed, it was his wonderful mildness chiefly, which not only disarmed me, but unmanned me as it were. For I consider that one, for the time, is a sort of unmanned when he tranquilly permits his hired clerk to dictate to him, and order him away from his own premises. Furthermore, I was full of uneasiness as to what Bartleby could possibly be doing in my office in his shirt sleeves, and in an otherwise dismantled condition of a Sunday morning. Was anything amiss going on? Nay, that was out of the question. It was not to be thought of for a moment that Bartleby was an immoral person. But what could he be doing there?—copying? Nay again, whatever might be his eccentricities, Bartleby was an eminently decorous person. He would be the last

man to sit down to his desk in any state approaching to nudity. Besides, it was Sunday; and there was something about Bartleby that forbade the supposition that he would by any secular occupation violate the proprieties of the day.

Nevertheless, my mind was not pacified; and full of a restless curiosity, at last I returned to the door. Without hindrance I inserted my key, opened it, and entered. Bartleby was not to be seen. I looked round anxiously, peeped behind his screen; but it was very plain that he was gone. Upon more closely examining the place, I surmised that for an indefinite period Bartleby must have ate, dressed, and slept in my office, and that, too without plate, mirror, or bed. The cushioned seat of a ricketty old sofa in one corner bore the faint impress of a lean, reclining form. Rolled away under his desk, I found a blanket; under the empty grate, a blacking box and brush; on a chair, a tin basin, with soap and a ragged towel; in a newspaper a few crumbs of ginger-nuts and a morsel of cheese. Yes, thought I, it is evident enough that Bartleby has been making his home here, keeping bachelor's hall all by himself. Immediately then the thought came sweeping across me, what miserable friendlessness and loneliness are here revealed! His poverty is great; but his solitude, how horrible! Think of it. Of a Sunday, Wall Street is deserted as Petra;[5] and every night of every day it is an emptiness. This building, too, which of weekdays hums with industry and life, at nightfall echoes with sheer vacancy, and all through Sunday is forlorn. And here Bartleby makes his home; sole spectator of a solitude which he has seen all populous—a sort of innocent and transformed Marius[6] brooding among the ruins of Carthage!

For the first time in my life a feeling of overpowering stinging melancholy seized me. Before, I had never experienced aught but a not unpleasing sadness. The bond of a common humanity now drew me irresistibly to gloom. A fraternal melancholy! For both I and Bartleby were sons of Adam. I remembered the bright silks and sparkling faces I had seen that day, in gala trim, swan-like sailing down the Mississippi of Broadway; and I contrasted them with the pallid copyist, and thought to myself, Ah, happiness courts the light, so we deem the world is gay; but misery hides aloof, so we deem that misery there is none. These sad fancyings—chimeras, doubtless, of a sick and silly brain—led on to

[4]A fashionable Episcopal Church on Wall Street.

[5]An ancient city in modern Jordan; rediscovered shortly before Melville's lifetime after having been deserted for centuries.

[6]Caius Marius (155–86 B.C.), a general and consul of Rome who was exiled after civil war; he fled to Carthage but was forbidden to land. The allusion is to a message Marius sent to the governor of Carthage.

other and more special thoughts, concerning the eccentricities of Bartleby. Presentiments of strange discoveries hovered round me. The scrivener's pale form appeared to me laid out, among uncaring strangers, in its shivering winding sheet.

Suddenly I was attracted by Bartleby's closed desk, the key in open sight left in the lock.

I mean no mischief, seek the gratification of no heartless curiosity, thought I; besides, the desk is mine, and its contents, too, so I will make bold to look within. Everything was methodically arranged, the papers smoothly placed. The pigeon holes were deep, and removing the files of documents, I groped into their recesses. Presently I felt something there, and dragged it out. It was an old bandanna handkerchief, heavy and knotted. I opened it, and saw it was a savings's bank.

I now recalled all the quiet mysteries which I had noted in the man. I remembered that he never spoke but to answer; that, though at intervals he had considerable time to himself, yet I had never seen him reading—no, not even a newspaper; that for long periods he would stand looking out, at his pale window behind the screen, upon the dead brick wall; I was quite sure he never visited any refectory or eating house; while his pale face clearly indicated that he never drank beer like Turkey, or tea and coffee even, like other men; that he never went anywhere in particular that I could learn, never went out for a walk, unless, indeed, that was the case at present; that he had declined telling who he was, or whence he came, or whether he had any relatives in the world; that though so thin and pale, he never complained of ill health. And more than all, I remembered a certain unconscious air of pallid—how shall I call it?—of pallid haughtiness, say, or rather an austere reserve about him, which had positively awed me into my tame compliance with his eccentricities, when I had feared to ask him to do the slightest incidental thing for me, even though I might know, from his long-continued motionlessness, that behind his screen he must be standing in one of those dead-wall reveries of his.

Revolving all these things, and coupling them with the recently discovered fact, that he made my office his constant abiding place and home, and not forgetful of his morbid moodiness; revolving all these things, a prudential feeling began to steal over me. My first emotions had been those of pure melancholy and sincerest pity; but just in proportion as the forlornness of Bartleby grew and grew to my imagination, did that same melancholy merge into fear, that pity into repulsion. So true it is, and so terrible, too, that up to a certain point the thought or sight of misery enlists our best affections; but, in certain special cases, beyond that point it does not. They err who would assert that invariably this is

owing to the inherent selfishness of the human heart. It rather proceeds from a certain hopelessness of remedying excessive and organic ill. To a sensitive being, pity is not seldom pain. And when at last it is perceived that such pity cannot lead to effectual succor, common sense bids the soul be rid of it. What I saw that morning persuaded me that the scrivener was the victim of innate and incurable disorder. I might give alms to his body; but his body did not pain him; it was his soul that suffered, and his soul I could not reach.

I did not accomplish the purpose of going to Trinity Church that morning. Somehow, the things I had seen disqualified me for the time from church-going. I walked homeward, thinking what I would do with Bartleby. Finally, I resolved upon this—I would put certain calm questions to him the next morning, touching his history, etc., and if he declined to answer them openly and unreservedly (and I supposed he would prefer not), then to give him a twenty dollar bill over and above whatever I might owe him, and tell him his services were no longer required; but that if in any other way I could assist him, I would be happy to do so, especially if he desired to return to his native place, wherever that might be, I would willingly help to defray the expenses. Moreover, if, after reaching home, he found himself at any time in want of aid, a letter from him would be sure of a reply.

The next morning came.

"Bartleby," said I, gently calling to him behind his screen.

No reply.

"Bartleby," said I, in a still gentler tone, "come here; I am not going to ask you to do anything you would prefer not to do—I simply wish to speak to you."

Upon this he noiselessly slid into view.

"Will you tell me, Bartleby, where you were born?"

"I would prefer not to."

"Will you tell me *anything* about yourself?"

"I would prefer not to."

"But what reasonable objection can you have to speak to me? I feel friendly towards you."

He did not look at me while I spoke, but kept his glance fixed upon my bust of Cicero, which, as I then sat, was directly behind me, some six inches above my head.

"What is your answer, Bartleby?" said I, after waiting a considerable time for a reply, during which his countenance remained immovable, only there was the faintest conceivable tremor of the white attenuated mouth.

"At present I prefer to give no answer," he said, and retired into his hermitage.

It was rather weak in me I confess, but his manner, on this occasion, nettled me. Not only did there seem to lurk in it a certain calm disdain, but his perverseness seemed ungrateful, considering the undeniable good usage and indulgence he had received from me.

Again I sat ruminating what I should do. Mortified as I was at his behavior, and resolved as I had been to dismiss him when I entered my office, nevertheless I strangely felt something superstitious knocking at my heart, and forbidding me to carry out my purpose, and denouncing me for a villain if I dared to breathe one bitter word against this forlornest of mankind. At last, familiarly drawing my chair behind his screen, I sat down and said: "Bartleby, never mind, then, about revealing your history; but let me entreat you, as a friend, to comply as far as may be with the usages of this office. Say now, you will help to examine papers to-morrow or next day: in short, say now, that in a day or two you will begin to be a little reasonable:—say so, Bartleby."

"At present I would prefer not to be a little reasonable," was his mildly cadaverous reply.

Just then the folding-doors opened, and Nippers approached. He seemed suffering from an unusually bad night's rest, induced by severer indigestion than common. He overheard those final words of Bartleby.

"*Prefer not,* eh?" gritted Nippers—"I'd *prefer* him, if I were you, sir," addressing me—"I'd *prefer* him; I'd give him preferences, the stubborn mule! What is it, sir, pray, that he *prefers* not to do now?"

Bartleby moved not a limb.

"Mr. Nippers," said I, "I'd prefer that you would withdraw for the present."

Somehow, of late, I had got into the way of involuntarily using this word "prefer" upon all sorts of not exactly suitable occasions. And I trembled to think that my contact with the scrivener had already and seriously affected me in a mental way. And what further and deeper aberration might it not yet produce? This apprehension had not been without efficacy in determining me to summary measures.

As Nippers, looking very sour and sulky, was departing, Turkey blandly and deferentially approached.

"With submission, sir," said he, "yesterday I was thinking about Bartleby here, and I think that if he would but prefer to take a quart of good ale every day, it would do much towards mending him, and enabling him to assist in examining his papers."

"So you have got the word, too," said I, slightly excited.

"With submission, what word, sir?" asked Turkey, respectfully crowding himself into the contracted space behind the screen, and by so doing, making me jostle the scrivener. "What word, sir?"

"I would prefer to be left alone here," said Bartleby, as if offended at being mobbed in his privacy.

"*That's* the word, Turkey," said I—"*that's* it."

"Oh, *prefer*? oh yes—queer word. I never use it myself. But sir, as I was saying, if he would but prefer—"

"Turkey," interrupted I, "you will please withdraw."

"Oh, certainly, sir, if you prefer that I should."

As he opened the folding-door to retire, Nippers at his desk caught a glimpse of me, and asked whether I would prefer to have a certain paper copied on blue paper or white. He did not in the least roguishly accent the word prefer. It was plain that it involuntarily rolled from his tongue. I thought to myself, surely I must get rid of a demented man, who already has in some degree turned the tongues, if not the heads of myself and clerks. But I thought it prudent not to break the dismission at once.

The next day I noticed that Bartleby did nothing but stand at his window in his dead-wall revery. Upon asking him why he did not write, he said that he had decided upon doing no more writing.

"Why, how now? what next?" exclaimed I, "do no more writing?"

"No more."

"And what is the reason?"

"Do you not see the reason for yourself," he indifferently replied.

I looked steadfastly at him, and perceived that his eyes looked dull and glazed. Instantly it occurred to me, that his unexampled diligence in copying by his dim window for the first few weeks of his stay with me might have temporarily impaired his vision.

I was touched. I said something in condolence with him. I hinted that of course he did wisely in abstaining from writing for a while; and urged him to embrace that opportunity of taking wholesome exercise in the open air. This, however, he did not do. A few days after this, my other clerks being absent, and being in a great hurry to dispatch certain letters by the mail, I thought that, having nothing else earthly to do, Bartleby would surely be less inflexible than usual, and carry these letters to the post-office. But he blankly declined. So, much to my inconvenience, I went myself.

Still added days went by. Whether Bartleby's eyes improved or not, I could not say. To all appearance, I thought they did. But when I asked him if they did, he vouchsafed no answer. At all events, he would do no copying. At last, in reply to my urgings, he informed me that he had permanently given up copying.

"What!" exclaimed I; "suppose your eyes should get entirely well—better than ever before—would you not copy then?"

"I have given up copying," he answered, and slid aside.

He remained as ever, a fixture in my chamber. Nay—if that were possible—he became still more of a fixture than before. What was to be done? He would do nothing in the office; why should he stay there? In plain fact, he had now become a millstone to me, not only useless as a necklace, but afflictive to bear. Yet I was sorry for him. I speak less than truth when I say that, on his own account, he occasioned me uneasiness. If he would but have named a single relative or friend, I would instantly have written, and urged their taking the poor fellow away to some convenient retreat. But he seemed alone, absolutely alone in the universe. A bit of wreck in the mid Atlantic. At length, necessities connected with my business tyrannized over all other considerations. Decently as I could, I told Bartleby that in six days time he must unconditionally leave the office. I warned him to take measures, in the interval, for procuring some other abode. I offered to assist him in this endeavor, if he himself would but take the first step towards a removal. "And when you finally quit me, Bartleby," added I, "I shall see that you go not away entirely unprovided. Six days from this hour, remember."

At the expiration of that period, I peeped behind the screen, and lo! Bartleby was there.

I buttoned up my coat, balanced myself; advanced slowly towards him, touched his shoulder, and said, "The time has come; you must quit this place; I am sorry for you; here is money; but you must go."

"I would prefer not," he replied, with his back still towards me.

"You *must*."

He remained silent.

Now I had an unbounded confidence in this man's common honesty. He had frequently restored to me sixpences and shillings carelessly dropped upon the floor, for I am apt to be very reckless in such shirt-button affairs. The proceeding, then, which followed will not be deemed extraordinary.

"Bartleby," said I, "I owe you twelve dollars on account; here are thirty-two; the odd twenty are yours—Will you take it?" and I handed the bills towards him.

But he made no motion.

"I will leave them here, then," putting them under a weight on the table. Then taking my hat and cane and going to the door, I tranquilly turned and added—"After you have removed your things from these offices, Bartleby, you will of course lock the door—since every one is now gone for the day but you—and if you please, slip your key underneath the mat, so that I may have it in the morning. I shall

not see you again, so good-by to you. If, hereafter, in your new place of abode, I can be of any service to you, do not fail to advise me by letter. Good-by, Bartleby, and fare you well."

But he answered not a word; like the last column of some ruined temple, he remained standing mute and solitary in the middle of the otherwise deserted room.

As I walked home in a pensive mood, my vanity got the better of my pity. I could not but highly plume myself on my masterly management in getting rid of Bartleby. Masterly I call it, and such it must appear to any dispassionate thinker. The beauty of my procedure seemed to consist in its perfect quietness. There was no vulgar bullying, no bravado of any sort, no choleric hectoring, and striding to and fro across the apartment, jerking out vehement commands for Bartleby to bundle himself off with his beggarly traps. Nothing of the kind. Without loudly bidding Bartleby depart—as an inferior genius might have done—I *assumed* the ground that depart he must; and upon that assumption built all I had to say. The more I thought over my procedure, the more I was charmed with it. Nevertheless, next morning, upon awakening, I had my doubts—I had somehow slept off the fumes of vanity. One of the coolest and wisest hours a man has, is just after he awakes in the morning. My procedure seemed as sagacious as ever—but only in theory. How it would prove in practice—there was the rub. It was truly a beautiful thought to have assumed Bartleby's departure; but, after all, that assumption was simply my own, and none of Bartleby's. The great point was, not whether I had assumed that he would quit me, but whether he would prefer so to do. He was more a man of preferences than assumptions.

After breakfast, I walked down town, arguing the probabilities pro and con. One moment I thought it would prove a miserable failure, and Bartleby would be found all alive at my office as usual; the next moment it seemed certain that I should find his chair empty. And so I kept veering about. At the corner of Broadway and Canal Street, I saw quite an excited group of people standing in earnest conversation.

"I'll take odds he doesn't," said a voice as I passed.

"Doesn't go?—done!" said I, "put up your money."

I was instinctively putting my hand in my pocket to produce my own, when I remembered that this was an election day. The words I had overheard bore no reference to Bartleby, but to the success or non-success of some candidate for the mayoralty. In my intent frame of mind, I had, as it were, imagined that all Broadway shared in my excitement, and were debating the same question with me. I passed on, very thankful that the uproar of the street screened my momentary absent-mindedness.

As I had intended, I was earlier than usual at my office door. I stood listening for a moment. All was still. He must be gone. I tried the knob. The door was locked. Yes, my procedure had worked to a charm; he indeed must be vanished. Yet a certain melancholy mixed with this: I was almost sorry for my brilliant success. I was fumbling under the door mat for the key, which Bartleby was to have left there for me, when accidentally my knee knocked against a panel, producing a summoning sound, and in response a voice came to me from within—"Not yet; I am occupied."

It was Bartleby.

I was thunderstruck. For an instant I stood like the man who, pipe in mouth, was killed one cloudless afternoon long ago in Virginia, by summer lightning; at his own warm open window he was killed, and remained leaning out there upon the dreamy afternoon, till some one touched him, when he fell.

"Not gone!" I murmured at last. But again obeying that wondrous ascendancy which the inscrutable scrivener had over me, and from which ascendancy, for all my chafing, I could not completely escape, I slowly went down stairs and out into the street, and while walking round the block, considered what I should next do in this unheard-of perplexity. Turn the man out by an actual thrusting I could not; to drive him away by calling him hard names would not do; calling in the police was an unpleasant idea; and yet, permit him to enjoy his cadaverous triumph over me—this, too, I could not think of. What was to be done? or, if nothing could be done, was there anything further that I could *assume* in the matter? Yes, as before I had prospectively assumed that Bartleby would depart, so now I might retrospectively assume that departed he was. In the legitimate carrying out of this assumption, I might enter my office in a great hurry, and pretending not to see Bartleby at all, walk straight against him as if he were air. Such a proceeding would in a singular degree have the appearance of a home-thrust. It was hardly possible that Bartleby could withstand such an application of the doctrine of assumptions. But upon second thoughts the success of the plan seemed rather dubious. I resolved to argue the matter over with him again.

"Bartleby," said I, entering the office, with a quietly severe expression, "I am seriously displeased. I am pained, Bartleby. I had thought better of you. I had imagined you of such a gentlemanly organization, that in any delicate dilemma a slight hint would suffice—in short, an assumption. But it appears I am deceived. Why," I added, unaffectedly

starting, "you have not even touched that money yet," pointing to it, just where I had left it the evening previous.

He answered nothing.

"Will you, or will you not, quit me?" I now demanded in a sudden passion, advancing close to him.

"I would prefer *not* to quit you," he replied, gently emphasizing the *not*.

"What earthly right have you to stay here? Do you pay any rent? Do you pay my taxes? Or is this property yours?"

He answered nothing.

"Are you ready to go on and write now? Are your eyes recovered? Could you copy a small paper for me this morning? or help examine a few lines? or step round to the post-office? In a word, will you do anything at all, to give a coloring to your refusal to depart the premises?"

He silently retired into his hermitage.

I was now in such a state of nervous resentment that I thought it but prudent to check myself at present from further demonstrations. Bartleby and I were alone. I remembered the tragedy of the unfortunate Adams and the still more unfortunate Colt in the solitary office of the latter; and how poor Colt, being dreadfully incensed by Adams, and imprudently permitting himself to get wildly excited, was at unawares hurried into his fatal act—an act which certainly no man could possibly deplore more than the actor himself.[7] Often it had occurred to me in my ponderings upon the subject, that had that altercation taken place in the public street, or at a private residence, it would not have terminated as it did. It was the circumstance of being alone in a solitary office, up stairs, of a building entirely unhallowed by humanizing domestic associations—an uncarpeted office, doubtless, of a dusty, haggard sort of appearance—this it must have been, which greatly helped to enhance the irritable desperation of the hapless Colt.

But when this old Adam of resentment rose in me and tempted me concerning Bartleby, I grappled him and threw him. How? Why, simply by recalling the divine injunction: "A new commandment give I unto you, that ye love one another."[8] Yes, this it was that saved me. Aside from higher considerations, charity often operates as a vastly wise and prudent principle—a great safeguard to its possessor. Men have committed murder for jealousy's sake, and anger's sake, and hatred's sake, and selfishness' sake, and spiritual pride's sake; but no man, that ever I heard of, ever committed a diabolical murder for sweet charity's sake. Mere self-interest, then, if no better motive can be enlisted, should, especially

[7] An actual murder that occurred in 1842.
[8] See John xiii.34.

with high-tempered men, prompt all beings to charity and philanthropy. At any rate, upon the occasion in question, I strove to drown my exasperated feelings towards the scrivener by benevolently construing his conduct. Poor fellow, poor fellow! thought I, he don't mean anything; and besides, he has seen hard times, and ought to be indulged.

I endeavored, also, immediately to occupy myself, and at the same time to comfort my despondency. I tried to fancy, that in the course of the morning, at such time as might prove agreeable to him, Bartleby, of his own free accord, would emerge from his hermitage and take up some decided line of march in the direction of the door. But no. Half-past twelve o'clock came; Turkey began to glow in the face, overturn his inkstand, and become generally obstreperous; Nippers abated down into quietude and courtesy; Ginger Nut munched his noon apple; and Bartleby remained standing at his window in one of his profoundest dead-wall reveries. Will it be credited? Ought I to acknowledge it? That afternoon I left the office without saying one further word to him.

Some days now passed, during which, at leisure intervals I looked a little into "Edwards on the Will," and "Priestley on Necessity." [9] Under the circumstances, those books induced a salutary feeling. Gradually I slid into the persuasion that these troubles of mine, touching the scrivener, had been all predestinated from eternity, and Bartleby was billeted upon me for some mysterious purpose of an allwise Providence, which it was not for a mere mortal like me to fathom. Yes, Bartleby, stay there behind your screen, thought I; I shall persecute you no more; you are harmless and noiseless as any of these old chairs; in short, I never feel so private as when I know you are here. At last I see it, I feel it; I penetrate to the predestinated purpose of my life. I am content. Others may have loftier parts to enact; but my mission in this world, Bartleby, is to furnish you with office-room for such period as you may see fit to remain.

I believe that this wise and blessed frame of mind would have continued with me, had it not been for the unsolicited and uncharitable remarks obtruded upon me by my professional friends who visited the rooms. But thus it often is, that the constant friction of illiberal minds wears out at last the best resolves of the more generous. Though to be sure, when I reflected upon it, it was not strange that people entering my office should be struck by the peculiar aspect of the unaccountable Bartleby, and so be

[9] Jonathan Edwards in *Freedom of the Will* (1754) and Joseph Priestley in *The Doctrine of Philosophic Necessity* (1777) argued for predestination and inevitability but from different perspectives: Edwards supported Calvinism while Priestley rejected it and relied on rationalism.

tempted to throw out some sinister observations concerning him. Sometimes an attorney, having business with me, and calling at my office, and finding no one but the scrivener there, would undertake to obtain some sort of precise information from him touching my whereabouts; but without heeding his idle talk, Bartleby would remain standing immovable in the middle of the room. So after contemplating him in that position for a time, the attorney would depart, no wiser than he came.

Also, when a reference was going on, and the room full of lawyers and witnesses, and business driving fast, some deeply-occupied legal gentleman present, seeing Bartleby wholly unemployed, would request him to run round to his (the legal gentleman's) office and fetch some papers for him. Thereupon, Bartleby would tranquilly decline, and yet remain idle as before. Then the lawyer would give a great stare, and turn to me. And what could I say? At last I was made aware that all through the circle of my professional acquaintance, a whisper of wonder was running round, having reference to the strange creature I kept at my office. This worried me very much. And as the idea came upon me of his possibly turning out a long-lived man, and keep occupying my chambers, and denying my authority; and perplexing my visitors; and scandalizing my professional reputation; and casting a general gloom over the premises; keeping soul and body together to the last upon his savings (for doubtless he spent but half a dime a day), and in the end perhaps outlive me, and claim possession of my office by right of his perpetual occupancy: as all these dark anticipations crowded upon me more and more, and my friends continually intruded their relentless remarks upon the apparition in my room; a great change was wrought in me. I resolved to gather all my faculties together, and forever rid me of this intolerable incubus.

Ere revolving any complicated project, however, adapted to this end, I first simply suggested to Bartleby the propriety of his permanent departure. In a calm and serious tone, I commended the idea to his careful and mature consideration. But, having taken three days to meditate upon it, he apprised me, that his original determination remained the same; in short, that he still preferred to abide with me.

What shall I do? I now said to myself, buttoning up my coat to the last button. What shall I do? what ought I to do? what does conscience say I *should* do with this man, or, rather, ghost. Rid myself of him, I must; go, he shall. But how? You will not thrust him, the poor, pale, passive mortal—you will not thrust such a helpless creature out of your door? you will not dishonor yourself by such cruelty? No, I will not, I cannot do that. Rather would I let him live and die here, and then mason up his remains in the wall. What, then, will you do? For all your coaxing, he will not budge. Bribes he leaves under your own paper-weight on your table; in short, it is quite plain that he prefers to cling to you.

Then something severe, something unusual must be done. What! surely you will not have him collared by a constable, and commit his innocent pallor to the common jail? And upon what ground could you procure such a thing to be done?—a vagrant, is he? What! he a vagrant, a wanderer, who refuses to budge? It is because he will *not* be a vagrant, then, that you seek to count him *as* a vagrant. That is too absurd. No visible means of support: there I have him. Wrong again: for indubitably he *does* support himself, and that is the only unanswerable proof that any man can show of his possessing the means so to do. No more, then. Since he will not quit me, I must quit him. I will change my offices; I will move elsewhere, and give him fair notice, that if I find him on my new premises I will then proceed against him as a common trespasser.

Acting accordingly, next day I thus addressed him: "I find these chambers too far from the City Hall; the air is unwholesome. In a word, I propose to remove my offices next week, and shall no longer require your services. I tell you this now, in order that you may seek another place."

He made no reply, and nothing more was said.

On the appointed day I engaged carts and men, proceeded to my chambers, and, having but little furniture, everything was removed in a few hours. Throughout, the scrivener remained standing behind the screen, which I directed to be removed the last thing. It was withdrawn; and, being folded up like a huge folio, left him the motionless occupant of a naked room. I stood in the entry watching him a moment, while something from within me upbraided me.

I re-entered, with my hand in my pocket—and—and my heart in my mouth.

"Good-by, Bartleby; I am going—good-by, and God some way bless you; and take that," slipping something in his hand. But it dropped upon the floor, and then—strange to say—I tore myself from him whom I had so longed to be rid of.

Established in my new quarters, for a day or two I kept the door locked, and started at every footfall in the passages. When I returned to my rooms, after any little absence, I would pause at the threshold for an instant, and attentively listen, ere applying my key. But these fears were needless. Bartleby never came nigh me.

I thought all was going well, when a perturbed-looking stranger visited me, inquiring whether I was the person who had recently occupied rooms at No. — Wall Street.

Full of forebodings, I replied that I was.

"Then, sir," said the stranger, who proved a lawyer, "you are responsible for the man you left there. He refuses to do any copying; he refuses to do anything; he says he prefers not to; and he refuses to quit the premises."

"I am very sorry, sir," said I, with assumed tranquillity, but an inward tremor, "but, really, the man you allude to is nothing to me—he is no relation or apprentice of mine, that you should hold me responsible for him."

"In mercy's name, who is he?"

"I certainly cannot inform you. I know nothing about him. Formerly I employed him as a copyist; but he has done nothing for me now for some time past."

"I shall settle him, then—good morning, sir."

Several days passed, and I heard nothing more; and, though I often felt a charitable prompting to call at the place and see poor Bartleby, yet a certain squeamishness, of I know not what, withheld me.

All is over with him, by this time, thought I, at last, when, through another week, no further intelligence reached me. But, coming to my room the day after, I found several persons waiting at my door in a high state of nervous excitement.

"That's the man—here he comes," cried the foremost one, whom I recognized as the lawyer who had previously called upon me alone.

"You must take him away, sir, at once," cried a portly person among them, advancing upon me, and whom I knew to be the landlord of No. — Wall Street. "These gentlemen, my tenants, cannot stand it any longer; Mr. B——," pointing to the lawyer, "has turned him out of his room, and he now persists in haunting the building generally, sitting upon the banisters of the stairs by day, and sleeping in the entry by night. Everybody is concerned; clients are leaving the offices; some fears are entertained of a mob; something you must do, and that without delay."

Aghast at this torrent, I fell back before it, and would fain have locked myself in my new quarters. In vain I persisted that Bartleby was nothing to me—no more than to any one else. In vain—I was the last person known to have anything to do with him, and they held me to the terrible account. Fearful, then, of being exposed in the papers (as one person present obscurely threatened), I considered the matter, and, at length, said, that if the lawyer would give me a confidential interview with the scrivener, in his (the lawyer's) own room, I would, that afternoon, strive my best to rid them of the nuisance they complained of.

Going up stairs to my old haunt, there was Bartleby silently sitting upon the banister at the landing.

"What are you doing here, Bartleby?" said I.

"Sitting upon the banister," he mildly replied.

I motioned him into the lawyer's room, who then left us.

"Bartleby," said I, "are you aware that you are the cause of great tribulation to me, by persisting in occupying the entry after being dismissed from the office?"

No answer.

"Now one of two things must take place. Either you must do something, or something must be done to you. Now what sort of business would you like to engage in? Would you like to re-engage in copying for some one?"

"No; I would prefer not to make any change."

"Would you like a clerkship in a dry-goods store?"

"There is too much confinement about that. No, I would not like a clerkship; but I am not particular."

"Too much confinement," I cried, "why you keep yourself confined all the time!"

"I would prefer not to take a clerkship," he rejoined, as if to settle that little item at once.

"How would a bar-tender's business suit you? There is no trying of the eye-sight in that."

"I would not like it at all; though, as I said before, I am not particular."

His unwonted wordiness inspirited me. I returned to the charge.

"Well, then, would you like to travel through the country collecting bills for the merchants? That would improve your health."

"No, I would prefer to be doing something else."

"How, then, would going as a companion to Europe, to entertain some young gentleman with your conversation—how would that suit you?"

"Not at all. It does not strike me that there is anything definite about that. I like to be stationary. But I am not particular."

"Stationary you shall be, then," I cried, now losing all patience, and, for the first time in all my exasperating connection with him, fairly flying into a passion. "If you do not go away from these premises before night, I shall feel bound—indeed, I *am* bound—to—to—to quit the premises myself!" I rather absurdly concluded, knowing not with what possible threat to try to frighten his immobility into compliance. Despairing of all further efforts, I was precipitately leaving him, when a final thought occurred to me—one which had not been wholly unindulged before.

"Bartleby," said I, in the kindest tone I could assume under such exciting circumstances, "will you go home with me now—not to my office, but my dwelling—and remain there till we can conclude upon some convenient arrangement for you at our leisure? Come, let us start now, right away."

"No: at present I would prefer not to make any change at all."

I answered nothing; but, effectually dodging every one by the suddenness and rapidity of my flight, rushed from the building, ran up Wall Street towards Broadway, and, jumping into the first omnibus, was soon removed from pursuit. As soon as tranquillity returned, I distinctly perceived that I had now done all that I possibly could, both in respect to the demands of the landlord and his tenants, and with regard to my own desire and sense of duty, to benefit Bartleby, and shield him from rude persecution. I now strove to be entirely care-free and quiescent; and my conscience justified me in the attempt; though, indeed, it was not so successful as I could have wished. So fearful was I of being again hunted out by the incensed landlord and his exasperated tenants, that, surrendering my business to Nippers, for a few days, I drove about the upper part of the town and through the suburbs, in my rockaway; crossed over to Jersey City and Hoboken, and paid fugitive visits to Manhattanville and Astoria. In fact, I almost lived in my rockaway for the time.

When again I entered my office, lo, a note from the landlord lay upon the desk. I opened it with trembling hands. It informed me that the writer had sent to the police, and had Bartleby removed to the Tombs as a vagrant. Moreover, since I knew more about him than any one else, he wished me to appear at that place, and make a suitable statement of the facts. These tidings had a conflicting effect upon me. At first I was indignant; but, at last, almost approved. The landlord's energetic, summary disposition, had led him to adopt a procedure which I do not think I would have decided upon myself; and yet, as a last resort, under such peculiar circumstances, it seemed the only plan.

As I afterwards learned, the poor scrivener, when told that he must be conducted to the Tombs, offered not the slightest obstacle, but, in his pale, unmoving way, silently acquiesced.

Some of the compassionate and curious bystanders joined the party; and headed by one of the constables arm in arm with Bartleby, the silent procession filed its way through all the noise, and heat, and joy of the roaring thoroughfares at noon.

The same day I received the note, I went to the Tombs, or, to speak more properly, the Halls of Justice. Seeking the right officer, I stated the purpose of my call, and was informed that the individual I described was, indeed, within. I then assured the functionary that Bartleby was a perfectly honest man, and greatly to be compassionated, however unaccountably eccentric. I narrated all I knew, and closed by suggesting the idea of letting him remain in as indulgent confinement as possible, till something less harsh might be done—though, indeed, I hardly knew what. At all events, if nothing else could be decided upon, the alms-house must receive him. I then begged to have an interview.

Being under no disgraceful charge, and quite serene and harmless in all his ways, they had permitted him freely to wander about the prison, and, especially, in the inclosed grass-platted yards thereof. And so I found him there, standing all alone in the quietest of the yards, his face towards a high wall, while all around, from the narrow slits of the jail windows, I thought I saw peering out upon him the eyes of murderers and thieves.

"Bartleby!"

"I know you," he said, without looking round— "and I want nothing to say to you."

"It was not I that brought you here, Bartleby," said I, keenly pained at his implied suspicion. "And to you, this should not be so vile a place. Nothing reproachful attaches to you by being here. And see, it is not so sad a place as one might think. Look, there is the sky, and here is the grass."

"I know where I am," he replied, but would say nothing more, and so I left him.

As I entered the corridor again, a broad meat-like man, in an apron accosted me, and jerking his thumb over his shoulder, said—"Is that your friend?"

"Yes."

"Does he want to starve? If he does, let him live on the prison fare, that's all."

"Who are you?" asked I, not knowing what to make of such an unofficially speaking person in such a place.

"I am the grub-man. Such gentlemen as have friends here, hire me to provide them with something good to eat."

"Is this so?" said I, turning to the turnkey.

He said it was.

"Well, then," said I, slipping some silver into the grub-man's hands (for so they called him), "I want you to give particular attention to my friend there; let him have the best dinner you can get. And you must be as polite to him as possible."

"Introduce me, will you?" said the grub-man, looking at me with an expression which seemed to say he was all impatience for an opportunity to give a specimen of his breeding.

Thinking it would prove of benefit to the scrivener, I acquiesced; and, asking the grub-man his name, went up with him to Bartleby.

"Bartleby, this is a friend; you will find him very useful to you."

"Your sarvant, sir, your sarvant," said the grub-man, making a low salutation behind his apron. "Hope you find it pleasant here, sir; nice grounds— cool apartments—hope you'll stay with us sometime—try to make it agreeable. What will you have for dinner to-day?"

"I prefer not to dine to-day," said Bartleby, turning away. "It would disagree with me; I am unused to dinners." So saying, he slowly moved to the other side of the inclosure, and took up a position fronting the dead-wall.

"How's this?" said the grub-man, addressing me with a stare of astonishment. "He's odd, ain't he?"

"I think he is a little deranged," said I, sadly.

"Deranged? deranged is it? Well, now, upon my word, I thought that friend of yourn was a gentleman forger; they are always pale and genteel-like, them forgers. I can't help pity 'em—can't help it, sir. Did you know Monroe Edwards?" he added, touchingly, and paused. Then, laying his hand piteously on my shoulder, sighed, "he died of consumption at Sing-Sing. So you weren't acquainted with Monroe?"

"No, I was never socially acquainted with any forgers. But I cannot stop longer. Look to my friend yonder. You will not lose by it. I will see you again."

Some few days after this, I again obtained admission to the Tombs, and went through the corridors in quest of Bartleby; but without finding him.

"I saw him coming from his cell not long ago," said a turnkey, "may be he's gone to loiter in the yards."

So I went in that direction.

"Are you looking for the silent man?" said another turnkey, passing me. "Yonder he lies—sleeping in the yard there. 'Tis not twenty minutes since I saw him lie down."

The yard was entirely quiet. It was not accessible to the common prisoners. The surrounding walls, of amazing thickness, kept off all sounds behind them. The Egyptian character of the masonry weighed upon me with its gloom. But a soft imprisoned turf grew under foot. The heart of the eternal pyramids, it seemed, wherein, by some strange magic, through the clefts, grass-seed, dropped by birds, had sprung.

Strangely huddled at the base of the wall, his knees drawn up, and lying on his side, his head touching the cold stones, I saw the wasted Bartleby. But nothing stirred. I paused; then went close up to him; stooped over, and saw that his dim eyes were open; otherwise he seemed profoundly sleeping. Something prompted me to touch him. I felt his hand, when a tingling shiver ran up my arm and down my spine to my feet.

The round face of the grub-man peered upon me now. "His dinner is ready. Won't he dine to-day, either? Or does he live without dining?"

"Lives without dining," said I, and closed the eyes.

"Eh!—He's asleep, ain't he?"

"With kings and counselors," [10] murmured I.

There would seem little need for proceeding further in this history. Imagination will readily supply the meagre recital of poor Bartleby's interment. But, ere parting with the reader, let me say, that if

[10] A synonym for death; see Job iii.14. Job wished to be at rest with kings and counselors.

this little narrative has sufficiently interested him, to awaken curiosity as to who Bartleby was, and what manner of life he led prior to the present narrator's making his acquaintance, I can only reply, that in such curiosity I fully share, but am wholly unable to gratify it. Yet here I hardly know whether I should divulge one little item of rumor, which came to my ear a few months after the scrivener's decease. Upon what basis it rested, I could never ascertain; and hence, how true it is I cannot now tell. But, inasmuch as this vague report has not been without a certain suggestive interest to me, however sad, it may prove the same with some others; and so I will briefly mention it. The report was this: that Bartleby had been a subordinate clerk in the Dead Letter Office at Washington, from which he had been suddenly removed by a change in the administration. When I think over this rumor, hardly can I express the emotions which seize me. Dead letters! does it not sound like dead men? Conceive a man by nature and misfortune prone to a pallid hopelessness, can any business seem more fitted to heighten it than that of continually handling these dead letters, and assorting them for the flames? For by the cart-load they are annually burned. Sometimes from out the folded paper the pale clerk takes a ring—the finger it was meant for, perhaps, moulders in the grave; a bank-note sent in swiftest charity—he whom it would relieve, nor eats nor hungers any more; pardon for those who died despairing; hope for those who died unhoping; good tidings for those who died stifled by unrelieved calamities. On errands of life, these letters speed to death.

Ah, Bartleby! Ah, humanity!

1853

Benito Cereno

Although the story is titled "Benito Cereno," it actually dramatizes the ways in which the three main characters—Cereno, Delano, and Babo—encounter and interpret the human situation. Through his skillful use of irony, ambiguity, and point of view, Melville suggests that each character fails, finally, to comprehend reality. Delano seems to succeed, but in the end he is no more capable of dealing with reality than before: he sails off into a blue sky. Benito Cereno sees only evil and malevolence in the world; he has lost all hope and trust, and thus wastes away physically and psychologically. And although Babo and the slaves have a case for revolt against their white oppressors, their way offers nothing because it leads to violence and death, not to any understanding or solution of a serious social and moral problem. Melville has transformed a bare and matter-of-fact source—Delano's *Narrative of Voyages and Travels in the Northern and Southern Hemispheres* (Boston, 1817)—into a fascinating and complex story. Text: *The Piazza Tales*, ed. Egbert S. Oliver (New York, 1948).

In the year 1799, Captain Amasa Delano, of Duxbury, in Massachusetts, commanding a large sealer and general trader, lay at anchor with a valuable cargo, in the harbor of St. Maria—a small, desert, uninhabited island towards the southern extremity of the long coast of Chili. There he had touched for water.

On the second day, not long after dawn, while lying in his berth, his mate came below, informing him that a strange sail was coming into the bay. Ships were then not so plenty in those waters as now. He rose, dressed, and went on deck.

The morning was one peculiar to that coast. Everything was mute and calm; everything gray. The sea, though undulated into long roods of swells, seemed fixed, and was sleeked at the surface like waved lead that has cooled and set in the smelter's mould. The sky seemed a gray surtout. Flights of troubled gray fowl, kith and kin with flights of troubled gray vapors among which they were mixed, skimmed low and fitfully over the waters, as swallows over meadows before storms. Shadows present, foreshadowing deeper shadows to come.

To Captain Delano's surprise, the stranger, viewed through the glass, showed no colors; though to do so upon entering a haven, however unhabited in its shores, where but a single other ship might be lying, was the custom among peaceful seamen of all nations. Considering the lawlessness and loneliness of the spot, and the sort of stories, at that day, associated with those seas, Captain Delano's surprise might have deepened into some uneasiness had he not been a person of a singularly undistrustful good nature, not liable, except on extraordinary and repeated incentives, and hardly then, to indulge in personal alarms, any way involving the imputation of malign evil in man. Whether, in view of what humanity is capable such a trait implies, along with a benevolent heart, more than ordinary quickness and accuracy of intellectual perception, may be left to the wise to determine.

But whatever misgivings might have obtruded on first seeing the stranger, would almost, in any seaman's mind, have been dissipated by observing that the ship, in navigating into the harbor, was drawing too near the land; a sunken reef making out off her bow. This seemed to prove her a stranger, indeed, not only to the sealer, but the island; consequently, she could be no wonted freebooter on that ocean. With no small interest, Captain Delano continued to watch her—a proceeding not much facilitated by the vapors partly mantling the hull, through which the far matin light from her cabin streamed equivocally enough; much like the sun—by this time hemisphered on the rim of the horizon, and, apparently, in company with the strange ship entering the harbor—which, wimpled by the same low, creeping clouds, showed not unlike a Lima intriguante's one sinister eye peering across the Plaza from the Indian loop-hole of her rusk *saya-y-manta*.[1]

It might have been but a deception of the vapors, but, the longer the stranger was watched the more singular appeared her manoeuvres. Ere long it seemed hard to decide whether she meant to come in or no—what she wanted, or what she was about. The wind, which had breezed up a little during the night, was now extremely light and baffling, which the more increased the apparent uncertainty of her movements.

Surmising, at last, that it might be a ship in distress, Captain Delano ordered his whale-boat to be dropped, and, much to the wary opposition of his mate, prepared to board her, and, at the least, pilot her in. On the night previous, a fishing-party of the seamen had gone a long distance to some detached rocks out of sight from the sealer, and, an hour or two before daybreak, had returned, having met with no small success. Presuming that the stranger might have been long off soundings, the good captain put several baskets of the fish, for presents, into his boat, and so pulled away. From her continuing too near the sunken reef, deeming her in danger, calling to his men, he made all haste to apprise those on board of their situation. But, some time ere the boat came up, the wind, light though it was, having shifted, had headed the vessel off, as well as partly broken the vapors from about her.

Upon gaining a less remote view, the ship, when made signally visible on the verge of the leaden-hued swells, with the shreds of fog here and there raggedly furring her, appeared like a white-washed monastery after a thunderstorm, seen perched upon some dun cliff among the Pyrenees. But it was no purely fanciful resemblance which now, for a moment, almost led Captain Delano to think that nothing less than a ship-load of monks was before him. Peering over the bulwarks were what really seemed, in the hazy distance, throngs of dark cowls; while, fitfully revealed through the open port-holes, other dark moving figures were grimly described, as of Black Friars[2] pacing the cloisters.

Upon a still nigher approach, this appearance was modified, and the true character of the vessel was plain—a Spanish merchantman of the first class, carrying negro slaves, amongst other valuable freight, from one colonial port to another. A very large, and, in its time, a very fine vessel, such as in those days were at intervals encountered along that main; sometimes superseded Acapulco treasure-ships, or retired frigates of the Spanish king's navy, which,

like superannuated Italian palaces, still, under a decline of masters, preserved signs of former state.

As the whale-boat drew more and more nigh, the cause of the peculiar pipe-clayed aspect of the stranger was seen in the slovenly neglect pervading her. The spars, ropes, and great part of the bulwarks, looked woolly, from long unacquaintance with the scraper, tar, and the brush. Her keel seemed laid, her ribs put together, and she launched, from Ezekiel's Valley of Dry Bones.[3]

In the present business in which she was engaged, the ship's general model and rig appeared to have undergone no material change from their original warlike and Froissart[4] pattern. However, no guns were seen.

The tops were large, and were railed about with what had once been octagonal net-work, all now in sad disrepair. These tops hung overhead like three ruinous aviaries, in one of which was seen perched, on a ratlin, a white noddy, a strange fowl, so called from its lethargic, somnambulistic character, being frequently caught by hand at sea. Battered and mouldy, the castellated forecastle seemed some ancient turret, long ago taken by assault, and then left to decay. Toward the stern, two high-raised quarter galleries—the balustrades here and there covered with dry, tindery sea-moss—opening out from the unoccupied state-cabin, whose dead-lights, for all the mild weather, were hermetically closed and calked—these tenantless balconies hung over the sea as if it were the grand Venetian canal. But the principal relic of faded grandeur was the ample oval of the shield-like stern-piece, intricately carved with the arms of Castile and Leon, medallioned about by groups of mythological or symbolical devices; uppermost and central of which was a dark satyr in a mask, holding his foot on the prostrate neck of a writhing figure, likewise masked.

Whether the ship had a figure-head, or only a plain beak, was not quite certain, owing to canvas wrapped about that part, either to protect it while undergoing a re-furbishing, or else decently to hide its decay. Rudely painted or chalked, as in a sailor freak, along the forward side of a sort of pedestal below the canvas, was the sentence, "*Seguid vuestro jefe*" (follow your leader); while upon the tarnished headboards, near by, appeared, in stately capitals, once gilt, the ship's name "SAN DOMINICK," each letter streakingly corroded with tricklings of copper-spike rust; while, like mourning weeds, dark festoons of sea-grass slimily swept to and fro over the name, with every hearse-like roll of the hull.

As, at last, the boat was hooked from the bow along toward the gangway amidship, its keel, while

[1] Lima women wore a loose-fitting robe that concealed their figures and heads. They could peer out, undetected, with one eye, and also, undetected, arrange an "intrigue."

[2] Dominican friars.

[3] See Ezekiel xxxvii.1–10.

[4] Jean Froissart (1337–1410), author of the *Chronicles*. Suggests the ship's ancient design.

yet some inches separated from the hull, harshly grated as on a sunken coral reef. It proved a huge bunch of conglobated barnacles adhering below the water to the side like a wen—a token of baffling airs and long calms passed somewhere in those seas.

Climbing the side, the visitor was at once surrounded by a clamorous throng of whites and blacks, but the latter outnumbering the former more than could have been expected, negro transportation-ship as the stranger in port was. But, in one language, and as with one voice, all poured out a common tale of suffering; in which the negresses, of whom there were not a few, exceeded the others in their dolorous vehemence. The scurvy, together with the fever, had swept off a great part of their number, more especially the Spaniards. Off Cape Horn they had narrowly escaped shipwreck; then, for days together, they had lain tranced without wind; their provisions were low; their water next to none; their lips that moment were baked.

While Captain Delano was thus made the mark of all eager tongues, his one eager glance took in all the faces, with every other object about him.

Always upon first boarding a large and populous ship at sea, especially a foreign one, with a nondescript crew such as Lascars[5] or Manilla men, the impression varies in a peculiar way from that produced by first entering a strange house with strange inmates in a strange land. Both house and ship—the one by its walls and blinds, the other by its high bulwarks like ramparts—hoard from view their interiors till the last moment; but in the case of the ship there is this addition; that the living spectacle it contains, upon its sudden and complete disclosure, has, in contrast with the blank ocean which zones it, something of the effect of enchantment. The ship seems unreal; these strange costumes, gestures, and faces, but a shadowy tableau just emerged from the deep, which directly must receive back what it gave.

Perhaps it was some such influence, as above is attempted to be described, which, in Captain Delano's mind, heightened whatever, upon a staid scrutiny, might have seemed unusual; especially the conspicuous figures of four elderly grizzled negroes, their heads like black, doddered willow tops, who, in venerable contrast to the tumult below them, were couched sphynx-like, one on the starboard cathead, another on the larboard, and the remaining pair face to face on the opposite bulwarks above the main-chains. They each had bits of unstranded old junk in their hands, and, with a sort of stoical self-content, were picking the junk into oakum, a small heap of which lay by their sides. They accompanied the task with a continuous, low, monotonous chant;

[BLACKS]

[5] East Indian sailors.

droning and druling away like so many gray-headed bag-pipers playing a funeral march.

The quarter-deck rose into an ample elevated poop, upon the forward verge of which, lifted, like the oakum-pickers, some eight feet above the general throng, sat along in a row, separated by regular spaces, the cross-legged figures of six other blacks; each with a rusty hatchet in his hand, which, with a bit of brick and a rag, he was engaged like a scullion in scouring; while between each two was a small stack of hatchets, their rusted edges turned forward awaiting a like operation. Though occasionally the four oakum-pickers would briefly address some person or persons in the crowd below, yet the six hatchet-polishers neither spoke to others, nor breathed a whisper among themselves, but sat intent upon their task, except at intervals, when, with the peculiar love in negroes of uniting industry with pastime, two and two they sideways clashed their hatchets together, like cymbals, with a barbarous din. All six, unlike the generality, had the raw aspect of unsophisticated Africans.

[HATCHET BLACKS]

But that first comprehensive glance which took in those ten figures, with scores less conspicuous, rested but an instant upon them, as, impatient of the hubbub of voices, the visitor turned in quest of whomsoever it might be that commanded the ship.

But as if not unwilling to let nature make known her own case among his suffering charge, or else in despair of restraining it for the time, the Spanish captain, a gentlemanly, reserved-looking, and rather young man to a stranger's eye, dressed with singular richness, but bearing plain traces of recent sleepless cares and disquietudes, stood passively by, leaning against the main-mast, at one moment casting a dreary, spiritless look upon his excited people, at the next an unhappy glance toward his visitor. By his side stood a black of small stature, in whose rude face, as occasionally, like a shepherd's dog, he mutely turned it up into the Spaniard's, sorrow and affection were equally blended.

[BENITO]

[BABO]

Struggling through the throng, the American advanced to the Spaniard, assuring him of his sympathies, and offering to render whatever assistance might be in his power. To which the Spaniard returned for the present but grave and ceremonious acknowledgments, his national formality dusked by the saturnine mood of ill-health.

But losing no time in mere compliments, Captain Delano, returning to the gangway, had his basket of fish brought up; and as the wind still continued light, so that some hours at least must elapse ere the ship could be brought to the anchorage, he bade his men return to the sealer, and fetch back as much water as the whale-boat could carry, with whatever soft bread the steward might have, all the remaining pumpkins on board, with a box of sugar, and a dozen of his private bottles of cider.

Not many minutes after the boat's pushing off, to the vexation of all, the wind entirely died away, and the tide turning, began drifting back the ship helplessly seaward. But trusting this would not long last, Captain Delano sought, with good hopes, to cheer up the strangers, feeling no small satisfaction that, with persons in their condition, he could—thanks to his frequent voyages along the Spanish main—converse with some freedom in their native tongue.

While left alone with them, he was not long in observing some things tending to heighten his first impressions; but surprise was lost in pity, both for the Spaniards and blacks, alike evidently reduced from scarcity of water and provisions; while long-continued suffering seemed to have brought out the less good-natured qualities of the negroes, besides, at the same time, impairing the Spaniard's authority over them. But, under the circumstances, precisely this condition of things was to have been anticipated. In armies, navies, cities, or families, in nature herself, nothing more relaxes good order than misery. Still, Captain Delano was not without the idea, that had Benito Cereno been a man of greater energy, misrule would hardly have come to the present pass. But the debility, constitutional or induced by the hardships, bodily and mental, of the Spanish captain, was too obvious to be overlooked. A prey to settled dejection, as if long mocked with hope he would not now indulge it, even when it had ceased to be a mock, the prospect of that day or evening at furthest, lying at anchor, with plenty of water for his people, and a brother captain to counsel and befriend, seemed in no perceptible degree to encourage him. His mind appeared unstrung, if not still more seriously affected. Shut up in these oaken walls, chained to one dull round of command, whose unconditionality cloyed him, like some hypochondriac abbot he moved slowly about, at times suddenly pausing, starting, or staring, biting his lip, biting his finger-nail, flushing, paling, twitching his beard, with other symptoms of an absent or moody mind. This distempered spirit was lodged, as before hinted, in as distempered a frame. He was rather tall, but seemed never to have been robust, and now with nervous suffering was almost worn to a skeleton. A tendency to some pulmonary complaint appeared to have been lately confirmed. His voice was like that of one with lungs half gone—hoarsely suppressed, a husky whisper. No wonder that, as in this state he tottered about, his private servant apprehensively followed him. Sometimes the negro gave his master his arm, or took his handkerchief out of his pocket for him; performing these and similar offices with that affectionate zeal which transmutes into something filial or fraternal acts in themselves

but menial; and which has gained for the negro the repute of making the most pleasing body-servant in the world; one, too, whom a master need be on no stiffly superior terms with, but may treat with familiar trust; less a servant than a devoted companion.

Marking the noisy indocility of the blacks in general, as well as what seemed the sullen inefficiency of the whites, it was not without humane satisfaction that Captain Delano witnessed the steady good conduct of Babo.

But the good conduct of Babo, hardly more than the ill-behavior of others, seemed to withdraw the half-lunatic Don Benito from his cloudy languor. Not that such precisely was the impression made by the Spaniard on the mind of his visitor. The Spaniard's individual unrest was, for the present, but noted as a conspicuous feature in the ship's general affliction. Still, Captain Delano was not a little concerned at what he could not help taking for the time to be Don Benito's unfriendly indifference towards himself. The Spaniard's manner, too, conveyed a sort of sour and gloomy disdain, which he seemed at no pains to disguise. But this the American in charity ascribed to the harassing effects of sickness, since, in former instances, he had noted that there are peculiar natures on whom prolonged physical suffering seems to cancel every social instinct of kindness; as if, forced to black bread themselves, they deemed it but equity that each person coming nigh them should, indirectly, by some slight or affront, be made to partake of their fare.

But ere long Captain Delano bethought him that, indulgent as he was at the first, in judging the Spaniard, he might not, after all, have exercised charity enough. At bottom it was Don Benito's reserve which displeased him; but the same reserve was shown towards all but his faithful personal attendant. Even the formal reports which, according to sea-usage, were, at stated times, made to him by some petty underling, either a white, mulatto or black, he hardly had patience enough to listen to, without betraying contemptuous aversion. His manner upon such occasions was, in its degree, not unlike that which might be supposed to have been his imperial countryman's, Charles V,[6] just previous to the anchoritish retirement of that monarch from the throne.

This splenetic disrelish of his place was evinced in almost every function pertaining to it. Proud as he was moody, he condescended to no personal mandate. Whatever special orders were necessary, their delivery was delegated to his body-servant, who in turn transferred them to their ultimate destination, through runners, alert Spanish boys or slave boys, like pages or pilot-fish within easy call continually

[6] Charles V (1500–1558), Holy Roman Emperor and King of Spain, old and feeble at the time of his retirement.

hovering round Don Benito. So that to have beheld this undemonstrative invalid gliding about, apathetic and mute, no landsman could have dreamed that in him was lodged a dictatorship beyond which, while at sea, there was no earthly appeal.

Thus, the Spaniard, regarded in his reserve, seemed the involuntary victim of mental disorder. But, in fact, his reserve might, in some degree, have proceeded from design. If so, then here was evinced the unhealthy climax of that icy though conscientious policy, more or less adopted by all commanders of large ships, which, except in signal emergencies, obliterates alike the manifestation of sway with every trace of sociality; transforming the man into a block, or rather into a loaded cannon, which, until there is call for thunder, has nothing to say.

Viewing him in this light, it seemed but a natural token of the perverse habit induced by a long course of such hard self-restraint, that, notwithstanding the present condition of his ship, the Spaniard should still persist in a demeanor, which, however harmless, or, it may be, appropriate, in a well-appointed vessel, such as the San Dominick might have been at the outset of the voyage, was anything but judicious now. But the Spaniard, perhaps, thought that it was with captains as with gods: reserve, under all events, must still be their cue. But probably this appearance of slumbering dominion might have been but an attempted disguise to conscious imbecility—not deep policy, but shallow device. But be all this as it might, whether Don Benito's manner was designed or not, the more Captain Delano noted its pervading reserve, the less he felt uneasiness at any particular manifestation of that reserve towards himself.

Neither were his thoughts taken up by the captain alone. Wonted to the quiet orderliness of the sealer's comfortable family of a crew, the noisy confusion of the San Dominick's suffering host repeatedly challenged his eye. Some prominent breaches, not only of discipline but of decency, were observed. These Captain Delano could not but ascribe, in the main, to the absence of those subordinate deck-officers to whom, along with higher duties, is intrusted what may be styled the police department of a populous ship. True, the old oakum-pickers appeared at times to act the part of monitorial constables to their countrymen, the blacks; but though occasionally succeeding in allaying trifling outbreaks now and then between man and man, they could do little or nothing toward establishing general quiet. The San Dominick was in the condition of a transatlantic emigrant ship, among whose multitude of living freight are some individuals, doubtless, as little troublesome as crates and bales; but the friendly remonstrances of such with their ruder companions are of not so much avail as the unfriendly arm of the mate. What the San Dominick wanted was, what the

emigrant ship has, stern superior officers. But on these decks not so much as a fourth-mate was to be seen.

The visitor's curiosity was roused to learn the particulars of those mishaps which had brought about such absenteeism, with its consequences; because, though deriving some inkling of the voyage from the wails which at the first moment had greeted him, yet of the details no clear understanding had been had. The best account would, doubtless, be given by the captain. Yet at first the visitor was loth to ask it, unwilling to provoke some distant rebuff. But plucking up courage, he at last accosted Don Benito, renewing the expression of his benevolent interest, adding, that did he (Captain Delano) but know the particulars of the ship's misfortunes, he would, perhaps, be better able in the end to relieve them. Would Don Benito favor him with the whole story.

Don Benito faltered; then, like some somnambulist suddenly interfered with, vacantly stared at his visitor, and ended by looking down on the deck. He maintained this posture so long that Captain Delano, almost equally disconcerted, and involuntarily almost as rude, turned suddenly from him, walking forward to accost one of the Spanish seamen for the desired information. But he had hardly gone five paces, when, with a sort of eagerness, Don Benito invited him back, regretting his momentary absence of mind, and professing readiness to gratify him.

While most part of the story was being given, the two captains stood on the after part of the main-deck, a privileged spot, no one being near but the servant.

"It is now a hundred and ninety days," began the Spaniard, in his husky whisper, "that this ship, well officered and well manned, with several cabin passengers—some fifty Spaniards in all—sailed from Buenos Ayres bound to Lima, with a general cargo, Paraguay tea and the like—and," pointing forward, "that parcel of negroes, now not more than a hundred and fifty, as you see, but then numbering over three hundred souls. Off Cape Horn we had heavy gales. In one moment, by night, three of my best officers, with fifteen sailors, were lost, with the main-yard; the spar snapping under them in the slings, as they sought, with heavers, to beat down the icy sail. To lighten the hull, the heavier sacks of mata[7] were thrown into the sea, with most of the water-pipes[8] lashed on deck at the time. And this last necessity it was, combined with the prolonged detentions afterwards experienced, which eventually brought about our chief causes of suffering. When—"

Here there was a sudden fainting attack of his cough, brought on, no doubt, by his mental distress. His servant sustained him, and drawing a cordial from his pocket placed it to his lips. He a little

[7] Paraguay tea.
[8] Water casks.

revived. But unwilling to leave him unsupported while yet imperfectly restored, the black with one arm still encircled his master, at the same time keeping his eye fixed on his face, as if to watch for the first sign of complete restoration, or relapse, as the event might prove.

The Spaniard proceeded, but brokenly and obscurely, as one in a dream.

—"Oh, my God! rather than pass through what I have, with joy I would have hailed the most terrible gales; but—"

His cough returned and with increased violence; this subsiding, with reddened lips and closed eyes he fell heavily against his supporter.

"His mind wanders. He was thinking of the plague that followed the gales," plaintively sighed the servant; "my poor, poor master!" wringing one hand, and with the other wiping the mouth. "But be patient, Señor," again turning to Captain Delano, "these fits do not last long; master will soon be himself."

Don Benito reviving, went on; but as this portion of the story was very brokenly delivered, the substance only will here be set down.

It appeared that after the ship had been many days tossed in storms off the Cape, the scurvy broke out, carrying off numbers of the whites and blacks. When at last they had worked round into the Pacific, their spars and sails were so damaged, and so inadequately handled by the surviving mariners, most of whom were become invalids, that, unable to lay her northerly course by the wind, which was powerful, the unmanageable ship, for successive days and nights, was blown northwestward, where the breeze suddenly deserted her, in unknown waters, to sultry calms. The absence of the water-pipes now proved as fatal to life as before their presence had menaced it. Induced, or at least aggravated, by the more than scanty allowance of water, a malignant fever followed the scurvy; with the excessive heat of the lengthened calm, making such short work of it as to sweep away, as by billows, whole families of the Africans, and a yet larger number, proportionably, of the Spaniards, including, by a luckless fatality, every remaining officer on board. Consequently, in the smart west winds eventually following the calm, the already rent sails, having to be simply dropped, not furled, at need, had been gradually reduced to the beggar's rags they were now. To procure substitutes for his lost sailors, as well as supplies of water and sails, the captain, at the earliest opportunity, had made for Baldivia, the southernmost civilized port of Chili and South America; but upon nearing the coast the thick weather had prevented him from so much as sighting that harbor. Since which period, almost without a crew, and almost without canvas and almost without wa-

ter, and, at intervals, giving its added dead to the sea, the San Dominick had been battle-dored about by contrary winds, inveigled by currents, or grown weedy in calms. Like a man lost in woods, more than once she had doubled upon her own track.

"But throughout these calamities," huskily continued Don Benito, painfully turning in the half embrace of his servant, "I have to thank those negroes you see, who, though to your inexperienced eyes appearing unruly, have, indeed, conducted themselves with less of restlessness than even their owner could have thought possible under such circumstances."

Here he again fell faintly back. Again his mind wandered; but he rallied, and less obscurely proceeded.

"Yes, their owner was quite right in assuring me that no fetters would be needed with his blacks; so that while, as is wont in this transportation, those negroes have always remained upon deck—not thrust below, as in the Guinea-men[9]—they have, also, from the beginning, been freely permitted to range within given bounds at their pleasure."

Once more the faintness returned—his mind roved—but, recovering, he resumed:

"But it is Babo here to whom, under God, I owe not only my own preservation, but likewise to him, chiefly, the merit is due, of pacifying his more ignorant brethren, when at intervals tempted to murmurings."

"Ah, master," sighed the black, bowing his face, "don't speak of me; Babo is nothing; what Babo has done was but duty."

"Faithful fellow!" cried Captain Delano. "Don Benito, I envy you such a friend; slave I cannot call him."

As master and man stood before him, the black upholding the white, Captain Delano could not but bethink him of the beauty of that relationship which could present such a spectacle of fidelity on the one hand and confidence on the other. The scene was heightened by the contrast in dress, denoting their relative positions. The Spaniard wore a loose Chili jacket of dark velvet; white small-clothes and stockings, with silver buckles at the knee and instep; a high-crowned sombrero, of fine grass; a slender sword, silver mounted, hung from a knot in his sash—the last being an almost invariable adjunct, more for utility than ornament, of a South American gentleman's dress to this hour. Excepting when his occasional nervous contortions brought about disarray, there was a certain precision in his attire curiously at variance with the unsightly disorder around; especially in the belittered Ghetto, forward the main-mast, wholly occupied by the blacks.

[9] Slave ships trading with Guinea.

The servant wore nothing but wide trowsers, apparently, from their coarseness and patches, made out of some old topsail; they were clean, and confined at the waist by a bit of unstranded rope, which, with his composed, deprecatory air at times, made him look something like a begging friar of St. Francis.

However unsuitable for the time and place, at least in the blunt-thinking American's eyes, and however strangely surviving in the midst of all his afflictions, the toilette of Don Benito might not, in fashion at least, have gone beyond the style of the day among South Americans of his class. Though on the present voyage sailing from Buenos Ayres, he had avowed himself a native and resident of Chili, whose inhabitants had not so generally adopted the plain coat and once plebeian pantaloons; but, with a becoming modification, adhered to their provincial costume, picturesque as any in the world. Still, relatively to the pale history of the voyage, and his own pale face, there seemed something so incongruous in the Spaniard's apparel, as almost to suggest the image of an invalid courtier tottering about London streets in the time of the plague.

The portion of the narrative which, perhaps, most excited interest, as well as some surprise, considering the latitudes in question, was the long calms spoken of, and more particularly the ship's so long drifting about. Without communicating the opinion, of course, the American could not but impute at least part of the detentions both to clumsy seamanship and faulty navigation. Eyeing Don Benito's small, yellow hands, he easily inferred that the young captain had not got into command at the hawse-hole, but the cabin-window; and if so, why wonder at incompetence, in youth, sickness, and gentility united?

But drowning criticism in compassion, after a fresh repetition of his sympathies, Captain Delano, having heard out his story, not only engaged, as in the first place, to see Don Benito and his people supplied in their immediate bodily needs, but, also, now further promised to assist him in procuring a large permanent supply of water, as well as some sails and rigging; and, though it would involve no small embarrassment to himself, yet he would spare three of his best seamen for temporary deck officers; so that without delay the ship might proceed to Conception, there fully to refit for Lima, her destined port.

Such generosity was not without its effect, even upon the invalid. His face lighted up; eager and hectic, he met the honest glance of his visitor. With gratitude he seemed overcome.

"This excitement is bad for master," whispered the servant, taking his arm, and with soothing words gently drawing him aside.

When Don Benito returned, the American was pained to observe that his hopefulness, like the sudden kindling in his cheek, was but febrile and transient.

Ere long, with a joyless mien, looking up towards the poop, the host invited his guest to accompany him there, for the benefit of what little breath of wind might be stirring.

As, during the telling of the story, Captain Delano had once or twice started at the occasional cymballing of the hatchet-polishers, wondering why such an interruption should be allowed, especially in that part of the ship, and in the ears of an invalid; and moreover, as the hatchets had anything but an attractive look, and the handlers of them still less so, it was, therefore, to tell the truth, not without some lurking reluctance, or even shrinking, it may be, that Captain Delano, with apparent complaisance, acquiesced in his host's invitation. The more so, since, with an untimely caprice of punctilio, rendered distressing by his cadaverous aspect, Don Benito, with Castilian bows, solemnly insisted upon his guest's preceding him up the ladder leading to the elevation; where, one on each side of the last step, sat for armorial supporters and sentries two of the ominous file. Gingerly enough stepped good Captain Delano between them, and in the instant of leaving them behind, like one running the gauntlet, he felt an apprehensive twitch in the calves of his legs.

But when, facing about, he saw the whole file, like so many organ-grinders, still stupidly intent on their work, unmindful of everything beside, he could not but smile at his late fidgety panic.

Presently, while standing with his host, looking forward upon the decks below, he was struck by one of those instances of insubordination previously alluded to. Three black boys, with two Spanish boys, were sitting together on the hatches, scraping a rude wooden platter, in which some scanty mess had recently been cooked. Suddenly, one of the black boys, enraged at a word dropped by one of his white companions, seized a knife, and, though called to forbear by one of the oakum-pickers, struck the lad over the head, inflicting a gash from which blood flowed.

In amazement, Captain Delano inquired what this meant. To which the pale Don Benito dully muttered, that it was merely the sport of the lad.

"Pretty serious sport, truly," rejoined Captain Delano. "Had such a thing happened on board the Bachelor's Delight, instant punishment would have followed."

At these words the Spaniard turned upon the American one of his sudden, staring, half-lunatic looks; then, relapsing into his torpor, answered, "Doubtless, doubtless, Señor."

Is it, thought Captain Delano, that this hapless

man is one of those paper captains I've known, who by policy wink at what by power they cannot put down? I know no sadder sight than a commander who has little of command but the name.

"I should think, Don Benito," he now said, glancing towards the oakum-picker who had sought to interfere with the boys, "that you would find it advantageous to keep all your blacks employed, especially the younger ones, no matter at what useless task, and no matter what happens to the ship. Why, even with my little band, I find such a course indispensable. I once kept a crew on my quarter-deck thrumming mats for my cabin, when, for three days, I had given up my ship—mats, men, and all—for a speedy loss, owing to the violence of a gale, in which we could do nothing but helplessly drive before it."

"Doubtless, doubtless," muttered Don Benito.

"But," continued Captain Delano, again glancing upon the oakum-pickers and then at the hatchet-polishers, near by, "I see you keep some, at least, of your host employed."

"Yes," was again the vacant response.

"Those old men there, shaking their pows from their pulpits," continued Captain Delano, pointing to the oakum-pickers, "seem to act the part of old dominies to the rest, little heeded as their admonitions are at times. Is this voluntary on their part, Don Benito, or have you appointed them shepherds to your flock of black sheep?"

"What posts they fill, I appointed them," rejoined the Spaniard in an acrid tone, as if resenting some supposed satiric reflection.

"And these others, these Ashantee conjurors here," continued Captain Delano, rather uneasily eying the brandished steel of the hatchet-polishers, where, in spots, it had been brought to a shine, "this seems a curious business they are at, Don Benito?"

"In the gales we met," answered the Spaniard, "what of our general cargo was not thrown overboard was much damaged by the brine. Since coming into calm weather, I have had several cases of knives and hatchets daily brought up for overhauling and cleaning."

"A prudent idea, Don Benito. You are part owner of ship and cargo, I presume; but none of the slaves, perhaps?"

"I am owner of all you see," impatiently returned Don Benito, "except the main company of blacks, who belonged to my late friend Alexandro Aranda."

As he mentioned this name, his air was heartbroken; his knees shook; his servant supported him.

Thinking he divined the cause of such unusual emotion, to confirm his surmise, Captain Delano, after a pause, said: "And may I ask, Don Benito, whether—since awhile ago you spoke of some cabin passengers—the friend, whose loss so afflicts you, at the outset of the voyage accompanied his blacks?"

"Yes."

"But died of the fever?"

"Died of the fever. Oh, could I but—"

Again quivering, the Spaniard paused.

"Pardon me," said Captain Delano, lowly, "but I think that, by a sympathetic experience, I conjecture, Don Benito, what it is that gives the keener edge to your grief. It was once my hard fortune to lose at sea, a dear friend, my own brother, then supercargo. Assured of the welfare of his spirit, its departure I could have borne like a man; but that honest eye, that honest hand—both of which had so often met mine—and that warm heart; all, all—like scraps to the dogs—to throw all to the sharks! It was then I vowed never to have for fellow-voyager a man I loved, unless, unbeknown to him, I had provided every requisite, in case of a fatality, for embalming his mortal part for interment on shore. Were your friend's remains now on board this ship, Don Benito, not thus strangely would the mention of his name affect you."

"On board this ship?" echoed the Spaniard. Then, with horrified gestures, as directed against some spectre, he unconsciously fell into the ready arms of his attendant, who, with a silent appeal toward Captain Delano, seemed beseeching him not again to broach a theme so unspeakably distressing to his master.

This poor fellow now, thought the pained American, is the victim of that sad superstition which associates goblins with the deserted body of man, as ghosts with an abandoned house. How unlike are we made! What to me, in like case, would have been a solemn satisfaction, the bare suggestion, even, terrifies the Spaniard into this trance. Poor Alexandro Aranda! what would you say could you here see your friend—who, on former voyages, when you, for months, were left behind, has, I dare say, often longed, and longed, for one peep at you—now transported with terror at the least thought of having you anyway nigh him.

At this moment, with a dreary grave-yard toll, betokening a flaw, the ship's forecastle bell, smote by one of the grizzled oakum-pickers, proclaimed ten o'clock, through the leaden calm; when Captain Delano's attention was caught by the moving figure of a gigantic black, emerging from the general crowd below, and slowly advancing towards the elevated poop. An iron collar was about his neck, from which depended a chain, thrice wound round his body; the terminating links padlocked together at a broad band of iron, his girdle.

"How like a mute Atufal moves," murmured the servant.

The black mounted the steps of the poop, and, like a brave prisoner, brought up to receive sentence, stood in unquailing muteness before Don Benito, now recovered from his attack.

At the first glimpse of his approach, Don Benito had started, a resentful shadow swept over his face; and, as with the sudden memory of bootless rage, his white lips glued together.

This is some mulish mutineer, thought Captain Delano, surveying, not without a mixture of admiration, the colossal form of the negro.

"See, he waits your question, master," said the servant.

Thus reminded, Don Benito, nervously averting his glance, as if shunning, by anticipation, some rebellious response, in a disconcerted voice, thus spoke:—

"Atufal, will you ask my pardon now?"

The black was silent.

"Again, master," murmured the servant, with bitter upbraiding eyeing his countryman, "again, master; he will bend to master yet."

"Answer," said Don Benito, still averting his glance, "say but the one word, *pardon*, and your chains shall be off."

Upon this, the black, slowly raising both arms, let them lifelessly fall, his links clanking, his head bowed; as much as to say, "No, I am content."

"Go," said Don Benito, with inkept and unknown emotion.

Deliberately as he had come, the black obeyed.

"Excuse me, Don Benito," said Captain Delano, "but this scene surprises me; what means it, pray?"

"It means that that negro alone, of all the band, has given me peculiar cause of offence. I have put him in chains; I——"

Here he paused; his hand to his head, as if there were a swimming there, or a sudden bewilderment of memory had come over him; but meeting his servant's kindly glance seemed reassured, and proceeded:—

"I could not scourge such a form. But I told him he must ask my pardon. As yet he has not. At my command, every two hours he stands before me."

"And how long has this been?"

"Some sixty days."

"And obedient in all else? And respectful?"

"Yes."

"Upon my conscience, then," exclaimed Captain Delano, impulsively, "he has a royal spirit in him, this fellow."

"He may have some right to it," bitterly returned Don Benito, "he says he was king in his own land."

"Yes," said the servant, entering a word, "those slits in Atufal's ears once held wedges of gold; but poor Babo here, in his own land, was only a poor

slave; a black man's slave was Babo, who now is the white's."

Somewhat annoyed by these conversational familiarities, Captain Delano turned curiously upon the attendant, then glanced inquiringly at his master; but, as if long wonted to these little informalities, neither master nor man seemed to understand him.

"What, pray, was Atufal's offence, Don Benito?" asked Captain Delano; "if it was not something very serious, take a fool's advice, and, in view of his general docility, as well as in some natural respect for his spirit, remit him his penalty."

"No, no, master never will do that," here murmured the servant to himself, "proud Atufal must first ask master's pardon. The slave there carries the padlock, but master here carries the key."

His attention thus directed, Captain Delano now noticed for the first time, that, suspended by a slender silken cord, from Don Benito's neck, hung a key. At once, from the servant's muttered syllables, divining the key's purpose, he smiled and said:— "So, Don Benito—padlock and key—significant symbols, truly."

Biting his lip, Don Benito faltered.

Though the remark of Captain Delano, a man of such native simplicity as to be incapable of satire or irony, had been dropped in playful allusion to the Spaniard's singularly evidenced lordship over the black; yet the hypochondriac seemed in some way to have taken it as a malicious reflection upon his confessed inability thus far to break down, at least, on a verbal summons, the entrenched will of the slave. Deploring this supposed misconception, yet despairing of correcting it, Captain Delano shifted the subject; but finding his companion more than ever withdrawn, as if still sourly digesting the lees of the presumed affront above mentioned, by-and-by Captain Delano likewise became less talkative, oppressed, against his own will, by what seemed the secret vindictiveness of the morbidly sensitive Spaniard. But the good sailor, himself of a quite contrary disposition, refrained, on his part, alike from the appearance as from the feeling of resentment, and if silent, was only so from contagion.

Presently the Spaniard, assisted by his servant, somewhat discourteously crossed over from his guest; a procedure which, sensibly enough, might have been allowed to pass for idle caprice of ill-humor, had not master and man, lingering round the corner of the elevated skylight, began whispering together in low voices. This was unpleasing. And more; the moody air of the Spaniard, which at times had not been without a sort of valetudinarian stateliness, now seemed anything but dignified; while the menial familiarity of the servant lost its original charm of simple-hearted attachment.

In his embarrassment, the visitor turned his face to the other side of the ship. By so doing, his glance accidentally fell on a young Spanish sailor, a coil of rope in his hand, just stepped from the deck to the first round of the mizzenrigging. Perhaps the man would not have been particularly noticed, were it not that, during his ascent to one of the yards, he, with a sort of covert intentness, kept his eye fixed on Captain Delano, from whom, presently, it passed, as if by a natural sequence, to the two whisperers.

His own attention thus redirected to that quarter, Captain Delano gave a slight start. From something in Don Benito's manner just then, it seemed as if the visitor had, at least partly, been the subject of the withdrawn consultation going on—a conjecture as little agreeable to the guest as it was little flattering to the host.

The singular alternations of courtesy and ill-breeding in the Spanish captain were unaccountable, except on one of two suppositions—innocent lunacy, or wicked imposture.

But the first idea, though it might naturally have occurred to an indifferent observer, and, in some respects, had not hitherto been wholly a stranger to Captain Delano's mind, yet, now that, in an incipient way, he began to regard the stranger's conduct something in the light of an intentional affront, of course the idea of lunacy was virtually vacated. But if not a lunatic, what then? Under the circumstances, would a gentleman, nay, any honest boor, act the part now acted by his host? The man was an imposter. Some low-born adventurer, masquerading as an oceanic grandee; yet so ignorant of the first requisites of mere gentlemanhood as to be betrayed into the present remarkable indecorum. That strange ceremoniousness, too, at other times evinced, seemed not uncharacteristic of one playing a part above his real level. Benito Cereno—Don Benito Cereno—a sounding name. One, too, at that period, not unknown, in the surname, to supercargoes and sea captains trading along the Spanish Main, as belonging to one of the most enterprising and extensive mercantile families in all those provinces; several members of it having titles; a sort of Castilian Rothschild, with a noble brother, or cousin, in every great trading town of South America. The alleged Don Benito was in early manhood, about twenty-nine or thirty. To assume a sort of roving cadetship in the maritime affairs of such a house, what more likely scheme for a young knave of talent and spirit? But the Spaniard was a pale invalid. Never mind. For even to the degree of simulating mortal disease, the craft of some tricksters had been known to attain. To think that, under the aspect of infantile weakness, the most savage energies might be

couched—those velvets of the Spaniard but the velvet paw to his fangs.

From no train of thought did these fancies come; not from within, but from without; suddenly, too, and in one throng, like hoar frost; yet as soon to vanish as the mild sun of Captain Delano's good-nature regained its meridian.

Glancing over once again towards his host—whose side-face, revealed above the skylight, was now turned toward him—he was struck by the profile, whose clearness of cut was refined by the thinness, incident to ill-health, as well as ennobled about the chin by the beard. Away with suspicion. He was a true off-shoot of a true hidalgo Cereno.

Relieved by these and other better thoughts, the visitor, lightly humming a tune, now began indifferently pacing the poop, so as not to betray to Don Benito that he had at all mistrusted incivility, much less duplicity; for such mistrust would yet be proved illusory, and by the event; though, for the present, the circumstance which had provoked that distrust remained unexplained. But when that little mystery should have been cleared up, Captain Delano thought he might extremely regret it, did he allow Don Benito to become aware that he had indulged in ungenerous surmises. In short, to the Spaniard's black-letter text, it was best, for a while, to leave open margin.

Presently, his pale face twitching and overcast, the Spaniard, still supported by his attendant, moved over towards his guest, when, with even more than his usual embarrassment, and a strange sort of intriguing intonation in his husky whisper, the following conversation began:—

"Señor, may I ask how long you have lain at this isle?"

"Oh, but a day or two, Don Benito."

"And from what port are you last?"

"Canton."

"And there, Señor, you exchanged your sealskins for teas and silks, I think you said?"

"Yes. Silks, mostly."

"And the balance you took in specie, perhaps?"

Captain Delano, fidgeting a little, answered—

"Yes; some silver, not a very great deal, though."

"Ah—well. May I ask how many men have you, Señor?"

Captain Delano slightly started, but answered—

"About five-and-twenty, all told."

"And at present, Señor, all on board, I suppose?"

"All on board, Don Benito," replied the Captain, now with satisfaction.

"And will be to-night, Señor?"

At this last question, following so many pertinacious ones, for the soul of him Captain Delano could not but look very earnestly at the questioner, who, instead of meeting the glance, with every token of craven discomposure dropped his eyes to the deck; presenting an unworthy contrast to his servant, who, just then, was kneeling at his feet, adjusting a loose shoe-buckle; his disengaged face meantime, with humble curiosity, turned openly up into his master's downcast one.

The Spaniard, still with a guilty shuffle, repeated his question:

"And—and will be to-night Señor?"

"Yes, for aught I know," returned Captain Delano—"but nay," rallying himself into fearless truth, "some of them talked of going off on another fishing party about midnight."

"Your ships generally go—go more or less armed, I believe, Señor?"

"Oh, a six-pounder or two, in case of emergency," was the intrepidly indifferent reply, "with a small stock of muskets, sealing-spears, and cutlasses, you know."

As he thus responded, Captain Delano again glanced at Don Benito, but the latter's eyes were averted; while abruptly and awkwardly shifting the subject, he made some peevish allusion to the calm, and then, without apology, once more, with his attendant, withdrew to the opposite bulwarks, where the whispering was resumed.

At this moment, and ere Captain Delano could cast a cool thought upon what had just passed, the young Spanish sailor, before mentioned, was seen descending from the rigging. In act of stooping over to spring inboard to the deck, his voluminous, unconfined frock, or shirt, of coarse woolen, much spotted with tar, opened out far down the chest, revealing a soiled under garment of what seemed the finest linen, edged, about the neck, with a narrow blue ribbon, sadly faded and worn. At this moment the young sailor's eye was again fixed on the whisperers, and Captain Delano thought he observed a lurking significance in it, as if silent signs, of some Freemason sort, had that instant been interchanged.

This once more impelled his own glance in the direction of Don Benito, and, as before, he could not but infer that himself formed the subject of the conference. He paused. The sound of the hatchet-polishing fell on his ears. He cast another swift side-look at the two. They had the air of conspirators. In connection with the late questionings, and the incident of the young sailor, these things now begat such return of involuntary suspicion, that the singular guilelessness of the American could not endure it. Plucking up a gay and humorous expression, he crossed over to the two rapidly, saying:—"Ha, Don Benito, your black here seems high in your trust; a sort of privy-counsellor, in fact."

Upon this, the servant looked up with a good-natured grin, but the master started as from a venom-

ous bite. It was a moment or two before the Spaniard sufficiently recovered himself to reply; which he did, at last, with cold constraint:—"Yes, Señor, I have trust in Babo."

Here Babo, changing his previous grin of mere animal humor into an intelligent smile, not ungratefully eyed his master.

Finding that the Spaniard now stood silent and reserved, as if involuntarily, or purposely giving hint that his guest's proximity was inconvenient just then, Captain Delano, unwilling to appear uncivil even to incivility itself, made some trivial remark and moved off; again and again turning over in his mind the mysterious demeanor of Don Benito Cereno.

He had descended from the poop, and, wrapped in thought, was passing near a dark hatchway, leading down into the steerage, when, perceiving motion there, he looked to see what moved. The same instant there was a sparkle in the shadowy hatchway, and he saw one of the Spanish sailors, prowling there, hurriedly placing his hand in the bosom of his frock, as if hiding something. Before the man could have been certain who it was that was passing, he slunk below out of sight. But enough was seen of him to make it sure that he was the same young sailor before noticed in the rigging.

What was that which so sparkled? thought Captain Delano. It was no lamp—no match—no live coal. Could it have been a jewel? But how come sailors with jewels?—or with silk-trimmed under-shirts either? Has he been robbing the trunks of the dead cabin-passengers? But if so, he would hardly wear one of the stolen articles on board ship here. Ah, ah—if, now, that was, indeed, a secret sign I saw passing between this suspicious fellow and his captain awhile since; if I could only be certain that, in my uneasiness, my senses did not deceive me, then——

Here, passing from one suspicious thing to another, his mind revolved the strange questions put to him concerning his ship.

By a curious coincidence, as each point was recalled, the black wizards of Ashantee would strike up with their hatchets, as in ominous comment on the white stranger's thoughts. Pressed by such enigmas and portents, it would have been almost against nature, had not, even into the least distrustful heart, some ugly misgivings obtruded.

Observing the ship now helplessly fallen into a current, with enchanted sails, drifting with increased rapidity seaward; and noting that, from a lately intercepted projection of the land, the sealer was hidden, the stout mariner began to quake at thoughts which he barely durst confess to himself. Above all, he began to feel a ghostly dread of Don Benito. And yet, when he roused himself, dilated his chest, felt

REASSURING HIMSELF

himself strong on his legs, and coolly considered it— what did all these phantoms amount to?

Had the Spaniard any sinister scheme, it must have reference not so much to him (Captain Delano) as to his ship (the Bachelor's Delight). Hence the present drifting away of the one ship from the other, instead of favoring any such possible scheme, was, for the time at least, opposed to it. Clearly any suspicion, combining such contradictions, must need be delusive. Beside, was it not absurd to think of a vessel in distress—a vessel by sickness almost dismanned of her crew—a vessel whose inmates were parched for water—was it not a thousand times absurd that such a craft should, at present, be of a piratical character; or her commander, either for himself or those under him, cherish any desire but for speedy relief and refreshment? But then, might not general distress, and thirst in particular, be affected? And might not that same undiminished Spanish crew, alleged to have perished off to a remnant, be at that very moment lurking in the hold? On heart-broken pretence of entreating a cup of cold water, fiends in human form had got into lonely dwellings, nor retired until a dark deed had been done. And among the Malay pirates, it was no unusual thing to lure ships after them into their treacherous harbors, or entice boarders from a declared enemy at sea, by the spectacle of thinly manned or vacant decks, beneath which prowled a hundred spears with yellow arms ready to upthrust them through the mats. Not that Captain Delano had entirely credited such things. He had heard of them—and now, as stories, they recurred. The present destination of the ship was the anchorage. There she would be near his own vessel. Upon gaining that vicinity, might not the San Dominick, like a slumbering volcano, suddenly let loose energies now hid?

SUSPICIONS

He recalled the Spaniard's manner while telling his story. There was a gloomy hesitancy and subterfuge about it. It was just the manner of one making up his tale for evil purposes, as he goes. But if that story was not true, what was the truth? That the ship had unlawfully come into the Spaniard's possession? But in many of its details, especially in reference to the more calamitous parts, such as the fatalities among the seamen, the consequent prolonged beating about, the past sufferings from obstinate calms, and still continued suffering from thirst; in all these points, as well as others, Don Benito's story had corroborated not only the wailing ejaculations of the indiscriminate multitude, white and black, but likewise—what seemed impossible to be counterfeit—by the very expression and play of every human feature, which Captain Delano saw. If Don Benito's story was, throughout, an invention, then every soul on board, down to the youngest negress,

WHAT IS TRUE?...

was his carefully drilled recruit in the plot: an incredible inference. And yet, if there was ground for mistrusting his veracity, that inference was a legitimate one.

But those questions of the Spaniard. There, indeed, one might pause. Did they not seem put with much the same object with which the burglar or assassin, by day-time, reconnoitres the walls of a house? But, with ill purposes, to solicit such information openly of the chief person endangered, and so, in effect, setting him on his guard; how unlikely a procedure was that? Absurd, then, to suppose that those questions had been prompted by evil designs. Thus, the same conduct, which, in this instance, had raised the alarm, served to dispel it. In short, scarce any suspicion or uneasiness, however, apparently reasonable at the time, which was not now, with equal apparent reason, dismissed.

At last he began to laugh at his former forebodings; and laugh at the strange ship for, in its aspect, someway siding with them, as it were; and laugh, too, at the odd-looking blacks, particularly those old scissors-grinders, the Ashantees; and those bed-ridden old knitting women, the oakum-pickers; and almost at the dark Spaniard himself, the central hobgoblin of all.

For the rest, whatever in a serious way seemed enigmatical, was now good-naturedly explained away by the thought that, for the most part, the poor invalid scarcely knew what he was about; either sulking in black vapors, or putting idle questions without sense or object. Evidently, for the present, the man was not fit to be intrusted with the ship. On some benevolent plea withdrawing the command from him, Captain Delano would yet have to send her to Conception, in charge of his second mate, a worthy person and good navigator—a plan not more convenient for the San Dominick than for Don Benito; for, relieved from all anxiety, keeping wholly to his cabin, the sick man, under the good nursing of his servant, would probably, by the end of the passage, be in a measure restored to health, and with that he should also be restored to authority.

Such were the American's thoughts. They were tranquilizing. There was a difference between the idea of Don Benito's darkly pre-ordaining Captain Delano's fate, and Captain Delano's lightly arranging Don Benito's. Nevertheless, it was not without something of relief that the good seaman presently perceived his whale-boat in the distance. Its absence had been prolonged by unexpected detention at the sealer's side, as well as its returning trip lengthened by the continual recession of the goal.

The advancing speck was observed by the blacks. Their shouts attracted the attention of Don Benito, who, with a return of courtesy, approaching Captain

Delano, expressed satisfaction at the coming of some supplies, slight and temporary as they must necessarily prove.

Captain Delano responded; but while doing so, his attention was drawn to something passing on the deck below: among the crowd climbing the landward bulwarks, anxiously watching the coming boat, two blacks, to all appearances accidentally incommoded by one of the sailors, violently pushed him aside, which the sailor someway resenting, they dashed him to the deck, despite the earnest cries of the oakum-pickers.

"Don Benito," said Captain Delano quickly, "do you see what is going on there? Look!"

But, seized by his cough, the Spaniard staggered, with both hands to his face, on the point of falling. Captain Delano would have supported him, but the servant was more alert, who, with one hand sustaining his master, with the other applied the cordial. Don Benito restored, the black withdrew his support, slipping aside a little, but dutifully remaining within call of a whisper. Such discretion was here evinced as quite wiped away, in the visitor's eyes, any blemish of impropriety which might have attached to the attendant, from the indecorous conferences before mentioned; showing, too, that if the servant were to blame, it might be more the master's fault than his own, since, when left to himself, he could conduct thus well.

His glance called away from the spectacle of disorder to the more pleasing one before him, Captain Delano could not avoid again congratulating his host upon possessing such a servant, who, though perhaps a little too forward now and then, must upon the whole be invaluable to one in the invalid's situation.

"Tell me, Don Benito," he added, with a smile— "I should like to have your man here, myself—what will you take for him? Would fifty doubloons be any object?"

"Master wouldn't part with Babo for a thousand doubloons," murmured the black, overhearing the offer, and taking it in earnest, and, with the strange vanity of a faithful slave, appreciated by his master, scorning to hear so paltry a valuation put upon him by a stranger. But Don Benito, apparently hardly yet completely restored, and again interrupted by his cough, made but some broken reply.

Soon his physical distress became so great, affecting his mind, too, apparently, that, as if to screen the sad spectacle, the servant gently conducted his master below.

Left to himself, the American, to while away the time till his boat should arrive, would have pleasantly accosted some one of the few Spanish seamen he saw; but recalling something that Don Benito had said touching their ill conduct, he refrained; as a

shipmaster indisposed to countenance cowardice or unfaithfulness in seamen.

While, with these thoughts, standing with eye directed forward towards that handful of sailors, suddenly he thought that one or two of them returned the glance and with a sort of meaning. He rubbed his eyes, and looked again; but again seemed to see the same thing. Under a new form, but more obscure than any previous one, the old suspicions recurred, but, in the absence of Don Benito, with less of panic than before. Despite the bad account given of the sailors, Captain Delano resolved forthwith to accost one of them. Descending the poop, he made his way through the blacks, his movement drawing a queer cry from the oakum-pickers, prompted by whom, the negroes, twitching each other aside, divided before him; but, as if curious to see what was the object of this deliberate visit to their Ghetto, closing in behind, in tolerable order, followed the white stranger up. His progress thus proclaimed as by mounted kings-at-arms, and escorted as by a Caffre[10] guard of honor, Captain Delano, assuming a good-humored, off-handed air, continued to advance; now and then saying a blithe word to the negroes, and his eye curiously surveying the white faces, here and there sparsely mixed in with the blacks, like stray white pawns venturously involved in the ranks of the chess-men opposed.

While thinking which of them to select for his purpose, he chanced to observe a sailor seated on the deck engaged in tarring the strap of a large block, a circle of blacks squatted round him inquisitively eying the process.

The mean employment of the man was in contrast with something superior in his figure. His hand, black with continually thrusting it into the tar-pot held for him by a negro, seemed not naturally allied to his face, a face which would have been a very fine one but for its haggardness. Whether this haggardness had aught to do with criminality, could not be determined, since, as intense heat and cold, though unlike, produce like sensations, so innocence and guilt, when, through casual association with mental pain, stamping any visible impress, use one seal—a hacked one.

Not again that this reflection occurred to Captain Delano at the time, charitable man as he was. Rather another idea. Because observing so singular a haggardness combined with a dark eye, averted as in trouble and shame, and then, again recalling Don Benito's confessed ill opinion of his crew, insensibly he was operated upon by certain general notions which, while disconnecting pain and abashment from virtue, invariably link them with vice.

If, indeed, there be any wickedness on board this

[10] Kaffir: South African Bantu.

ship, thought Captain Delano, be sure that man there has fouled his hand in it, even as now he fouls it in the pitch. I don't like to accost him. I will speak to this other, this old Jack here on the windlass.

He advanced to an old Barcelona tar, in ragged red breeches and dirty night-cap, cheeks trenched and bronzed, whiskers dense as thorn hedges. Seated between two sleepy-looking Africans, this mariner, like his younger shipmate, was employed upon some rigging—splicing a cable—the sleepy-looking blacks performing the inferior function of holding the outer parts of the ropes for him.

Upon Captain Delano's approach, the man at once hung his head below its previous level; the one necessary for business. It appeared as if he desired to be thought absorbed, with more than common fidelity, in his task. Being addressed, he glanced up, but with what seemed a furtive, diffident air, which sat strangely enough on his weather-beaten visage, much as if a grizzly bear, instead of growling and biting, should simper and cast sheep's eyes. He was asked several questions concerning the voyage—purposely referring to several particulars in Don Benito's narrative, not previously corroborated by those impulsive cries greeting the visitor on first coming on board. The questions were briefly answered, confirming all that remained to be confirmed of the story. The negroes about the windlass joined in with the old sailor; but, as they became talkative, he by degrees became mute, and at length quite glum, seemed morosely unwilling to answer more questions, and yet, all the while, this ursine air was somehow mixed with his sheepish one.

Despairing of getting into unembarrassed talk with such a centaur, Captain Delano, after glancing round for a more promising countenance, but seeing none, spoke pleasantly to the blacks to make way for him; and so, amid various grins and grimaces, returned to the poop, feeling a little strange at first, he could hardly tell why, but upon the whole with regained confidence in Benito Cereno.

How plainly, thought he, did that old whisker-ando yonder betray a consciousness of ill desert. No doubt, when he saw me coming, he dreaded lest I, apprised by his Captain of the crew's general misbehavior, came with sharp words for him, and so down with his head. And yet—and yet, now that I think of it, that very old fellow, if I err not, was one of those who seemed so earnestly eyeing me here awhile since. Ah, these currents spin one's head round almost as much as they do the ship. Ha, there now's a pleasant sort of sunny sight; quite sociable, too.

His attention had been drawn to a slumbering negress, partly disclosed through the lace-work of some rigging, lying, with youthful limbs carelessly disposed, under the lee of the bulwarks, like a doe in the shade of a woodland rock. Sprawling at her lapped breasts, was her wide-awake fawn, stark naked, its black little body half lifted from the deck, crosswise with its dam's; its hands, like two paws, clambering upon her; its mouth and nose ineffectually rooting to get at the mark; and meantime giving a vexatious half-grunt, blending with the composed snore of the negress.

The uncommon vigor of the child at length roused the mother. She started up, at a distance facing Captain Delano. But as if not at all concerned at the attitude in which she had been caught, delightedly she caught the child up, with maternal transports, covering it with kisses.

There's naked nature, now; pure tenderness and love, thought Captain Delano, well pleased.

This incident prompted him to remark the other negresses more particularly than before. He was gratified with their manners: like most uncivilized women, they seemed at once tender of heart and tough of constitution; equally ready to die for their infants or fight for them. Unsophisticated as leopardesses; loving as doves. Ah! thought Captain Delano, there, perhaps, are some of the very women whom Ledyard[11] saw in Africa, and gave such a noble account of.

These natural sights somehow insensibly deepened his confidence and ease. At last he looked to see how his boat was getting on; but it was still pretty remote. He turned to see if Don Benito had returned; but he had not.

To change the scene, as well as to please himself with a leisurely observation of the coming boat, stepping over into the mizzen-chains, he clambered his way into the starboard quarter-gallery—one of those abandoned Venetian-looking water-balconies previously mentioned—retreats cut off from the deck. As his foot pressed the half-damp, half-dry sea-mosses matting the place, and a chance phantom cats-paw—an islet of breeze, unheralded, unfollowed—as this ghostly cats-paw came fanning his cheek; as his glance fell upon the row of small, round dead-lights—all closed like coppered eyes of the coffined—and the state-cabin door, once connecting with the gallery, even as the dead-lights had once looked out upon it, but now calked fast like a sarcophagus lid; and to a purple-black, tarred-over panel, threshold, and post; and he bethought him of the time, when that state-cabin and this state-balcony had heard the voices of the Spanish king's officers, and the forms of the Lima viceroy's daughters had perhaps leaned where he stood—as these and other images flitted through his mind, as the cats-paw through the calm, gradually he felt rising a

[11] John Ledyard (1751–89), a famous American traveler.

dreamy inquietude, like that of one who alone on the prairie feels unrest from the repose of the noon.

He leaned against the carved balustrade, again looking off toward his boat; but found his eye falling upon the ribbon grass, trailing along the ship's waterline, straight as a border of green box; and parterres of seaweed, broad ovals and crescents, floating nigh and far, with what seemed long formal alleys between, crossing the terraces of swells, and sweeping round as if leading to the grottoes below. And overhanging all was the balustrade by his arm, which, partly stained with pitch and partly embossed with moss, seemed the charred ruin of some summer-house in a grand garden long running to waste.

Trying to break one charm, he was but becharmed anew. Though upon the wide sea, he seemed in some far inland country; prisoner in some deserted château, left to stare at empty grounds, and peer out at vague roads, where never wagon or wayfarer passed.

But these enchantments were a little disenchanted as his eye fell on the corroded main-chains. Of an ancient style, massy and rusty in link, shackle and bolt, they seemed even more fit for the ship's present business than the one for which she had been built.

Presently he thought something moved nigh the chains. He rubbed his eyes, and looked hard. Groves of rigging were about the chains; and there, peering from behind a great stay, like an Indian from behind a hemlock, a Spanish sailor, a marlingspike in his hand, was seen, who made what seemed an imperfect gesture towards the balcony, but immediately, as if alarmed by some advancing step along the deck within, vanished into the recesses of the hempen forest, like a poacher.

What meant this? Something the man had sought to communicate, unbeknown to any one, even to his captain. Did the secret involve aught unfavorable to his captain? Were those previous misgivings of Captain Delano's about to be verified? Or, in his haunted mood at the moment, had some random, unintentional motion of the man, while busy with the stay, as if repairing it, been mistaken for a significant beckoning?

Not unbewildered, again he gazed off for his boat. But it was temporarily hidden by a rocky spur of the isle. As with some eagerness he bent forward, watching for the first shooting view of its beak, the balustrade gave way before him like charcoal. Had he not clutched an outreaching rope he would have fallen into the sea. The crash, though feeble, and the fall, though hollow, of the rotten fragments, must have been overheard. He glanced up. With sober curiosity peering down upon him was one of the old oakum-pickers, slipped from his perch to an outside

boom; while below the old negro, and, invisible to him, reconnoitering from a porthole like a fox from the mouth of its den, crouched the Spanish sailor again. From something suddenly suggested by the man's air, the mad idea now darted into Captain Delano's mind, that Don Benito's plea of indisposition, in withdrawing below, was but a pretense; that he was engaged there maturing his plot, of which the sailor, by some means gaining an inkling, had a mind to warn the stranger against; incited, it may be, by gratitude for a kind word on first boarding the ship. Was it from foreseeing some possible interference like this, that Don Benito had, beforehand, given such a bad character of his sailors, while praising the negroes; though, indeed, the former seemed as docile as the latter the contrary? The whites, too, by nature, were the shrewder race. A man with some evil design, would he not be likely to speak well of that stupidity which was blind to his depravity, and malign that intelligence from which it might not be hidden? Not unlikely, perhaps. But if the whites had dark secrets concerning Don Benito, could then Don Benito be any way in complicity with the blacks? But they were too stupid. Besides, who ever heard of a white so far a renegade as to apostatize from his very species almost, by leaguing in against it with negroes? These difficulties recalled former ones. Lost in their mazes, Captain Delano, who had now regained the deck, was uneasily advancing along it, when he observed a new face; an aged sailor seated cross-legged near the main hatchway. His skin was shrunk up with wrinkles like a pelican's empty pouch; his hair frosted; his countenance grave and composed. His hands were full of ropes, which he was working into a large knot. Some blacks were about him obligingly dipping the strands for him here and there, as the exigencies of the operation demanded.

Captain Delano crossed over to him, and stood in silence surveying the knot; his mind, by a not uncongenial transition, passing from its own entanglements to those of the hemp. For intricacy, such a knot he had never seen in an American ship, or indeed any other. The old man looked like an Egyptian priest, making Gordian knots for the temple of Ammon. The knot seemed a combination of double-bowline-knot, treble-crown-knot, back-handed-well-knot, knot-in-and-out-knot, and jamming-knot.

At last, puzzled to comprehend the meaning of such a knot, Captain Delano addressed the knotter:

"What are you knotting there, my man?"

"The knot," was the brief reply, without looking up.

"So it seems; but what is it for?"

"For some one else to undo," muttered back the old man, plying his fingers harder than ever, the knot being now nearly completed.

While Captain Delano stood watching him, suddenly the old man threw the knot towards him, saying in broken English—the first heard in the ship—something to this effect: "Undo it, cut it, quick." It was said lowly, but with such condensation of rapidity, that the long, slow words in Spanish, which had preceded and followed, almost operated as covers to the brief English between.

For a moment, knot in hand, and knot in head, Captain Delano stood mute; while, without further heeding him, the old man was now intent upon other ropes. Presently there was a slight stir behind Captain Delano. Turning, he saw the chained negro, Atufal, standing quietly there. The next moment the old sailor rose, muttering, and, followed by his subordinate negroes, removed to the forward of the ship, where in the crowd he disappeared.

An elderly negro, in a clout like an infant's, and with a pepper and salt head, and a kind of attorney air, now approached Captain Delano. In tolerable Spanish, and with a good-natured, knowing wink, he informed him that the old knotter was simple-witted, but harmless; often playing his old tricks. The negro concluded by begging the knot, for of course the stranger would not care to be troubled with it. Unconsciously, it was handed to him. With a sort of congé, the negro received it, and, turning his back, ferreted into it like a detective custom-house officer after smuggled laces. Soon, with some African word, equivalent to pshaw, he tossed the knot overboard.

All this is very queer now, thought Captain Delano, with a qualmish sort of emotion; but, as one feeling incipient sea-sickness, he strove, by ignoring the symptoms, to get rid of the malady. Once more he looked off for his boat. To his delight, it was now again in view, leaving the rocky spur astern.

The sensation here experienced, after at first relieving his uneasiness, with unforeseen efficacy soon began to remove it. The less distant sight of that well-known boat—showing it, not as before, half blended with the haze, but with outline defined, so that its individuality, like a man's, was manifest; that boat, Rover by name, which, though now in strange seas, had often pressed the beach of Captain Delano's home, and brought to its threshold for repairs, had familiarly lain there, as a Newfoundland dog; the sight of that household boat evoked a thousand trustful associations, which, contrasted with previous suspicions, filled him not only with lightsome confidence, but somehow with half humorous self-reproaches at his former lack of it.

"What, I, Amasa Delano—Jack of the Beach, as they called me when a lad—I, Amasa; the same that, duck-satchel in hand, used to paddle along the waterside to the schoolhouse made from the old hulk—I, little Jack of the Beach, that used to go berrying with cousin Nat and the rest; I to be murdered here at the ends of the earth, on board a haunted pirate-ship by a horrible Spaniard? Too nonsensical to think of! Who would murder Amasa Delano? His conscience is clean. There is some one above. Fie, fie, Jack of the Beach! you are a child indeed; a child of the second childhood, old boy; you are beginning to dote and drule, I'm afraid."

Light of heart and foot, he stepped aft, and there was met by Don Benito's servant, who, with a pleasing expression, responsive to his own present feelings, informed him that his master had recovered from the effects of his coughing fit, and had just ordered him to go present his compliments to his good guest, Don Amasa, and say that he (Don Benito) would soon have the happiness to rejoin him.

There now, do you mark that? again thought Captain Delano, walking the poop. What a donkey I was. This kind gentleman who here sends me his kind compliments, he, but ten minutes ago, dark-lantern in hand, was dodging round some old grindstone in the hold, sharpening a hatchet for me, I thought. Well, well; these long calms have a morbid effect on the mind, I've often heard, though I never believed it before. Ha! glancing towards the boat; there's Rover; good dog; a white bone in her mouth. A pretty big bone though, seems to me.—What? Yes, she has fallen afoul of the bubbling tide-rip there. It sets her the other way, too, for the time. Patience.

It was now about noon, though, from the grayness of everything, it seemed to be getting towards dusk.

The calm was confirmed. In the far distance, away from the influence of land, the leaden ocean seemed laid out and leaded up, its course finished, soul gone, defunct. But the current from landward, where the ship was, increased; silently sweeping her further and further towards the tranced waters beyond.

Still, from his knowledge of those latitudes, cherishing hopes of a breeze, and a fair and fresh one, at any moment, Captain Delano, despite present prospects, buoyantly counted upon bringing the San Dominick safely to anchor ere night. The distance swept over was nothing; since, with a good wind, ten minutes' sailing would retrace more than sixty minutes' drifting. Meantime, one moment turning to mark "Rover" fighting the tide-rip, and the next to see Don Benito approaching, he continued walking the poop.

Gradually he felt a vexation arising from the delay of his boat; this soon merged into uneasiness; and at last—his eye falling continually, as from a stage-box into the pit, upon the strange crowd before and below him, and, by-and-by, recognizing there the face—now composed to indifference—of the Spanish sailor who had seemed to beckon from the main-chains—something of his old trepidations returned.

Ah, thought he—gravely enough—this is like the ague: because it went off, it follows not that it won't come back.

Though ashamed of the relapse, he could not altogether subdue it; and so, exerting his good-nature to the utmost, insensibly he came to a compromise.

Yes, this is a strange craft; a strange history, too, and strange folks on board. But—nothing more.

By way of keeping his mind out of mischief till the boat should arrive, he tried to occupy it with turning over and over, in a purely speculative sort of way, some lesser peculiarities of the captain and crew. Among others, four curious points recurred:

First, the affair of the Spanish lad assailed with a knife by the slave boy; an act winked at by Don Benito. Second, the tyranny in Don Benito's treatment of Atufal, the black; as if a child should lead a bull of the Nile by the ring in his nose. Third, the trampling of the sailor by the two negroes; a piece of insolence passed over without so much as a reprimand. Fourth, the cringing submission to their master of all the ships' underlings, mostly blacks; as if by the least inadvertence they feared to draw down his despotic displeasure.

Coupling these points, they seemed somewhat contradictory. But what then, thought Captain Delano, glancing towards his now nearing boat—what then? Why, Don Benito is a very capricious commander. But he is not the first of the sort I have seen; though it's true he rather exceeds any other. But as a nation—continued he in his reveries—these Spaniards are all an odd set; the very word Spaniard has a curious, conspirator, Guy-Fawkish twang to it. And yet, I dare say, Spaniards in the main are as good folks as any in Duxbury, Massachusetts. Ah good! At last "Rover" has come.

As, with its welcome freight, the boat touched the side, the oakum-pickers, with venerable gestures, sought to restrain the blacks, who, at the sight of three gurried[12] water-casks in its bottom, and a pile of wilted pumpkins in its bow, hung over the bulwarks in disorderly raptures.

Don Benito, with his servant, now appeared; his coming, perhaps, hastened by hearing the noise. Of him Captain Delano sought permission to serve out the water, so that all might share alike, and none injure themselves by unfair excess. But sensible, and, on Don Benito's account, kind as this offer was, it was received with what seemed impatience; as if aware that he lacked energy as a commander, Don Benito, with the true jealousy of weakness, resented as an affront any interference. So, at least, Captain Delano inferred.

[12] Dirty.

In another moment the casks were being hoisted in, when some of the eager negroes accidentally jostled Captain Delano, where he stood by the gangway; so that, unmindful of Don Benito, yielding to the impulse of the moment, with good-natured authority he bade the blacks stand back; to enforce his words making use of a half-mirthful, half-menacing gesture. Instantly the blacks paused, just where they were, each negro and negress suspended in his or her posture, exactly as the word had found them—for a few seconds continuing so—while, as between the responsive posts of a telegraph, an unknown syllable ran from man to man among the perched oakum-pickers. While the visitor's attention was fixed by this scene, suddenly the hatchet-polishers half rose, and a rapid cry came from Don Benito.

Thinking that at the signal of the Spaniard he was about to be massacred, Captain Delano would have sprung for his boat, but paused, as the oakum-pickers, dropping down into the crowd with earnest exclamations, forced every white and every negro back, at the same moment, with gestures friendly and familiar, almost jocose, bidding him, in substance, not to be a fool. Simultaneously the hatchet-polishers resumed their seats, quietly as so many tailors, and at once, as if nothing had happened, the work of hoisting in the casks was resumed, whites and blacks singing at the tackle.

Captain Delano glanced towards Don Benito. As he saw his meagre form in the act of recovering itself from reclining in the servant's arms, into which the agitated invalid had fallen, he could not but marvel at the panic by which himself had been surprised on the darting supposition that such a commander, who, upon a legitimate occasion, so trivial, too, as it now appeared, could lose all self-command, was, with energetic iniquity, going to bring about his murder.

The casks being on deck, Captain Delano was handed a number of jars and cups by one of the steward's aids, who, in the name of his captain, entreated him to do as he had proposed—dole out the water. He complied, with republican impartiality as to this republican element, which always seeks one level, serving the oldest white no better than the youngest black; excepting, indeed, poor Don Benito, whose condition, if not rank, demanded an extra allowance. To him, in the first place, Captain Delano presented a fair pitcher of the fluid; but, thirsting as he was for it, the Spaniard quaffed not a drop until after several grave bows and salutes. A reciprocation of courtesies which the sight-loving Africans hailed with clapping of hands.

Two of the less wilted pumpkins being reserved for the cabin table, the residue were minced up on the spot for the general regalement. But the soft bread, sugar, and bottled cider, Captain Delano would have given the whites alone, and in chief Don Benito; but the latter objected; which disinterestedness not a little pleased the American; and so mouthfuls all around were given alike to whites and blacks; excepting one bottle of cider, which Babo insisted upon setting aside for his master.

Here it may be observed that as, on the first visit of the boat, the American had not permitted his men to board the ship, neither did he now; being unwilling to add to the confusion of the decks.

Not uninfluenced by the peculiar good-humor at present prevailing, and for the time oblivious of any but benevolent thoughts, Captain Delano, who, from recent indications, counted upon a breeze within an hour or two at furthest, dispatched the boat back to the sealer, with orders for all the hands that could be spared immediately to set about rafting casks to the watering-place and filling them. Likewise he bade word be carried to his chief officer, that if, against present expectation, the ship was not brought to anchor by sunset, he need be under no concern; for as there was to be a full moon that night, he (Captain Delano) would remain on board ready to play the pilot, come the wind soon or late.

As the two Captains stood together, observing the departing boat—the servant, as it happened, having just spied a spot on his master's velvet sleeve, and silently engaged in rubbing it out—the American expressed his regrets that the San Dominick had no boats; none, at least, but the unseaworthy old hulk of the long-boat, which, warped as a camel's skeleton in the desert, and almost as bleached, lay potwise inverted amidships, one side a little tipped, furnishing a subterranean sort of den for family groups of the blacks, mostly women and small children; who, squatting on old mats below, or perched above in the dark dome, on the elevated seats, were described, some distance within, like a social circle of bats, sheltering in some friendly cave; at intervals, ebon flights of naked boys and girls, three or four years old, darting in and out of the den's mouth.

"Had you three or four boats now, Don Benito," said Captain Delano, "I think that, by tugging at the oars, your negroes here might help along matters some. Did you sail from port without boats, Don Benito?"

"They were stove in the gales, Señor."

"That was bad. Many men, too, you lost then. Boats and men. Those must have been hard gales, Don Benito."

"Past all speech," cringed the Spaniard.

"Tell me, Don Benito," continued his companion with increased interest, "tell me, were these gales immediately off the pitch of Cape Horn?"

"Cape Horn?—who spoke of Cape Horn?"

"Yourself did, when giving me an account of your voyage," answered Captain Delano, with almost equal astonishment at this eating of his own words, even as he ever seemed eating his own heart, on the part of the Spaniard. "You yourself, Don Benito, spoke of Cape Horn," he emphatically repeated.

The Spaniard turned, in a sort of stooping posture, pausing an instant, as one about to make a plunging exchange of elements, as from air to water.

At this moment a messenger-boy, a white, hurried by, in the regular performance of his function carrying the last expired half-hour forward to the forecastle, from the cabin time-piece, to have it struck at the ship's large bell.

"Master," said the servant, discontinuing his work on the coat sleeve, and addressing the rapt Spaniard with a sort of timid apprehensiveness, as one charged with a duty, the discharge of which, it was foreseen, would prove irksome to the very person who had imposed it, and for whose benefit it was intended, "master told me never mind where he was, or how engaged, always to remind him, to a minute, when shaving-time comes. Miguel has gone to strike the half-hour afternoon. It is *now*, master. Will master go into the cuddy?"

"Ah—yes," answered the Spaniard, starting, as from dreams into realities; then turning upon Captain Delano, he said that ere long he would resume the conversation.

"Then if master means to talk more to Don Amasa," said the servant, "why not let Don Amasa sit by master in the cuddy, and master can talk, and Don Amasa can listen, while Babo here lathers and strops."

"Yes," said Captain Delano, not unpleased with this sociable plan, "yes, Don Benito, unless you had rather not, I will go with you."

"Be it so, Señor."

As the three passed aft, the American could not but think it another strange instance of his host's capriciousness, this being shaved with such uncommon punctuality in the middle of the day. But he deemed it more than likely that the servant's anxious fidelity had something to do with the matter; inasmuch as the timely interruption served to rally his master from the mood which had evidently been coming upon him.

The place called the cuddy was a light deck-cabin formed by the poop, a sort of attic to the large cabin below. Part of it had formerly been the quarters of the officers; but since their death all the partitionings had been thrown down, and the whole interior converted into one spacious and airy marine hall; for absence of fine furniture and picturesque disarray of odd appurtenances, somewhat answering to the wide, cluttered hall of some eccentric bachelor-squire in the country, who hangs his shooting-jacket and tobacco-pouch on deer antlers, and keeps his fishing-rod, tongs, and walking-stick in the same corner.

The similitude was heightened, if not originally suggested, by glimpses of the surrounding sea; since, in one aspect, the country and the ocean seem cousins-german.

The floor of the cuddy was matted. Overhead, four or five old muskets were stuck into horizontal holes along the beams. On one side was a claw-footed old table lashed to the deck; a thumbed missal on it, and over it a small, meagre crucifix attached to the bulk-head. Under the table lay a dented cutlass or two, with a hacked harpoon, among some melancholy old rigging, like a heap of poor friars' girdles. There were also two long, sharp-ribbed settees of Malacca cane, black with age, and uncomfortable to look at as inquisitors' racks, with a large, misshapen arm-chair, which, furnished with a rude barber's crotch at the back, working with a screw, seemed some grotesque engine of torment. A flag locker was in one corner, open, exposing various colored bunting, some rolled up, others half unrolled, still others tumbled. Opposite was a cumbrous washstand, of black mahogany, all of one block, with a pedestal, like a font, and over it a railed shelf, containing combs, brushes, and other implements of the toilet. A torn hammock of stained grass swung near; the sheets tossed, and the pillow wrinkled up like a brow, as if whoever slept here slept but illy, with alternate visitations of sad thoughts and bad dreams.

The further extremity of the cuddy, overhanging the ship's stern, was pierced with three openings, windows or port-holes, according as men or cannon might peer, socially and unsocially, out of them. At present neither men nor cannon were seen, though huge ring-bolts and other rusty iron fixtures of the wood-work hinted of twenty-four-pounders.

Glancing towards the hammock as he entered, Captain Delano said, "You sleep here, Don Benito?"

"Yes, Señor, since we got into mild weather."

"This seems a sort of dormitory, sitting-room, sail-loft, chapel, armory, and private closet all together, Don Benito," added Captain Delano, looking round.

"Yes, Señor; events have not been favorable to much order in my arrangements."

Here the servant, napkin on arm, made a motion as if waiting his master's good pleasure. Don Benito signified his readiness, when, seating him in the Malacca arm-chair, and for the guest's convenience drawing opposite one of the settees, the servant commenced operations by throwing back his master's collar and loosening his cravat.

There is something in the negro which, in a peculiar way, fits him for avocations about one's person.

Most negroes are natural valets and hair-dressers; taking to the comb and brush congenially as to the castinets, and flourishing them apparently with almost equal satisfaction. There is, too, a smooth tact about them in this employment, with a marvelous, noiseless, gliding briskness, not ungraceful in its way, singularly pleasing to behold, and still more so to be the manipulated subject of. And above all is the great gift of good-humor. Not the mere grin or laugh is here meant. Those were unsuitable. But a certain easy cheerfulness, harmonious in every glance and gesture; as though God had set the whole negro to some pleasant tune.

When to all this is added the docility arising from the unaspiring contentment of a limited mind, and that susceptibility of bland attachment sometimes inhering in indisputable inferiors, one readily perceives why those hypochondriacs, Johnson and Byron—it may be, something like the hypochondriac Benito Cereno—took to their hearts, almost to the exclusion of the entire white race, their serving men, the negroes, Barber and Fletcher. But if there be that in the negro which exempts him from the inflicted sourness of the morbid or cynical mind, how, in his most prepossessing aspects, must he appear to a benevolent one? When at ease with respect to exterior things, Captain Delano's nature was not only benign, but familiarly and humorously so. At home, he had often taken rare satisfaction in sitting in his door, watching some free man of color at his work or play. If on a voyage he chanced to have a black sailor, invariably he was on chatty and half-gamesome terms with him. In fact, like most men of a good, blithe heart, Captain Delano took to negroes, not philanthropically, but genially, just as other men to Newfoundland dogs.

Hitherto, the circumstances in which he found the San Dominick had repressed the tendency. But in the cuddy, relieved from his former uneasiness, and, for various reasons, more sociably inclined than at any previous period of the day, and seeing the colored servant, napkin on arm, so debonair about his master, in a business so familiar as that of shaving, too, all his old weakness for negroes returned.

Among other things, he was amused with an odd instance of the African love of bright colors and fine shows, in the black's informally taking from the flag-locker a great piece of bunting of all hues, and lavishly tucking it under his master's chin for an apron.

The mode of shaving among the Spaniards is a little different from what it is with other nations. They have a basin, specifically called a barber's basin, which on one side is scooped out, so as accurately to receive the chin, against which it is closely held in lathering; which is done, not with a brush, but with soap dipped in the water of the basin and rubbed on the face.

In the present instance salt-water was used for lack of better; and the parts lathered were only the upper lip, and low down under the throat, all the rest being cultivated beard.

These preliminaries being somewhat novel to Captain Delano, he sat curiously eying them, so that no conversation took place, nor, for the present, did Don Benito appear disposed to renew any.

Setting down his basin, the negro searched among the razors, as for the sharpest, and having found it, gave it an additional edge by expertly strapping it on the firm, smooth, oily skin of his open palm; he then made a gesture as if to begin, but midway stood suspended for an instant, one hand elevating the razor, the other professionally dabbling among the bubbling suds on the Spaniard's lank neck. Not unaffected by the close sight of the gleaming steel, Don Benito nervously shuddered; his usual ghastliness was heightened by the lather, which lather, again, was intensified in its hue by the contrasting sootiness of the negro's body. Altogether the scene was somewhat peculiar, at least to Captain Delano, nor, as he saw the two thus postured, could he resist the vagary, that in the black he saw a headsman, and in the white a man at the block. But this was one of those antic conceits, appearing and vanishing in a breath, from which, perhaps, the best regulated mind is not always free.

Meantime the agitation of the Spaniard had a little loosened the bunting from around him, so that one broad fold swept curtain-like over the chair-arm to the floor, revealing, amid a profusion of armorial bars and ground-colors—black, blue, and yellow—a closed castle in a blood-red field diagonal with a lion rampant in a white.

"The castle and the lion," exclaimed Captain Delano—"why, Don Benito, this is the flag of Spain you use here. It's well it's only I, and not the King, that sees this," he added, with a smile, "but"—turning towards the black—"it's all one, I suppose, so the colors be gay;" which playful remark did not fail somewhat to tickle the negro.

"Now, master," he said, readjusting the flag, and pressing the head gently further back into the crotch of the chair; "now, master," and the steel glanced nigh the throat.

Again Don Benito faintly shuddered.

"You must not shake so, master. See, Don Amasa, master always shakes when I shave him. And yet master knows I never yet have drawn blood, though it's true, if master will shake so, I may some of these times. Now, master," he continued. "And now, Don Amasa, please go on with your talk about the gale, and all that; master can hear, and between times, master can answer."

"Ah yes, these gales," said Captain Delano; "but the more I think of your voyage, Don Benito, the more I wonder, not at the gales, terrible as they must have been, but at the disastrous interval following them. For here, by your account, have you been these two months and more getting from Cape Horn to St. Maria, a distance which I myself, with a good wind, have sailed in a few days. True, you had calms, and long ones, but to be becalmed for two months, that is, at least, unusual. Why, Don Benito, had almost any other gentleman told me such a story, I should have been half disposed to a little incredulity."

Here an involuntary expression came over the Spaniard, similar to that just before on the deck, and whether it was the start he gave, or a sudden gawky roll of the hull in the calm, or a momentary unsteadiness of the servant's hand, however it was, just then the razor drew blood, spots of which stained the creamy lather under the throat; immediately the black barber drew back his steel, and remaining in his professional attitude, back to Captain Delano, and face to Don Benito, held up the trickling razor, saying, with a sort of half humorous sorrow, "See, master—you shook so—here's Babo's first blood."

No sword drawn before James the First of England, no assassination in that timid King's presence, could have produced a more terrified aspect than was now presented by Don Benito.

Poor fellow, thought Captain Delano, so nervous he can't even bear the sight of barber's blood; and this unstrung, sick man, is it credible that I should have imagined he meant to spill all my blood, who can't endure the sight of one little drop of his own? Surely, Amasa Delano, you have been beside yourself this day. Tell it not when you get home, sappy Amasa. Well, well, he looks like a murderer, doesn't he? More like as if himself were to be done for. Well, well, this day's experience shall be a good lesson.

Meantime, while these things were running through the honest seaman's mind, the servant had taken the napkin from his arm, and to Don Benito had said—"But answer Don Amasa, please, master, while I wipe this ugly stuff off the razor, and strop it again."

As he said the words, his face was turned half round, so as to be alike visible to the Spaniard and the American, and seemed, by its expression, to hint, that he was desirous, by getting his master to go on with the conversation, considerably to withdraw his attention from the recent annoying accident. As if glad to snatch the offered relief, Don Benito resumed, rehearsing to Captain Delano, that not only were the calms of unusual duration, but the ship had fallen in with obstinate currents; and other things he added, some of which were but repetitions of former statements, to explain how it came to pass that the passage from Cape Horn to St. Maria had been so exceedingly long; now and then mingling with his words, incidental praises, less qualified than before, to the blacks, for their general good conduct. These particulars were not given consecutively, the servant, at convenient times, using his razor, and so, between the intervals of shaving, the story and panegyric went on with more than usual huskiness.

To Captain Delano's imagination, now again not wholly at rest, there was something so hollow in the Spaniard's manner, with apparently some reciprocal hollowness in the servant's dusky comment of silence, that the idea flashed across him, that possibly master and man, for some unknown purpose, were acting out, both in word and deed, nay, to the very tremor of Don Benito's limbs, some juggling play before him. Neither did the suspicion of collusion lack apparent support, from the fact of those whispered conferences before mentioned. But then, what could be the object of enacting this play of the barber before him? At last, regarding the notion as a whimsy, insensibly suggested, perhaps, by the theatrical aspect of Don Benito in his harlequin ensign, Captain Delano speedily banished it.

The shaving over, the servant bestirred himself with a small bottle of scented waters, pouring a few drops on the head, and then diligently rubbing; the vehemence of the exercise causing the muscles of his face to twitch rather strangely.

His next operation was with comb, scissors, and brush; going round and round, smoothing a curl here, clipping an unruly whisker-hair there, giving a graceful sweep to the temple-lock, with other impromptu touches evincing the hand of a master; while, like any resigned gentleman in barber's hands, Don Benito bore all, much less uneasily, at least, than he had done the razoring; indeed, he sat so pale and rigid now, that the negro seemed a Nubian sculptor finishing off a white statue-head.

All being over at last, the standard of Spain removed, tumbled up, and tossed back into the flag-locker, the negro's warm breath blowing away any stray hair which might have lodged down his master's neck; collar and cravat readjusted; a speck of lint whisked off the velvet lapel; all this being done; backing off a little space, and pausing with an expression of subdued self-complacency, the servant for a moment surveyed his master, as, in toilet at least, the creature of his own tasteful hands.

Captain Delano playfully complimented him upon his achievement; at the same time congratulating Don Benito.

But neither sweet waters, nor shampooing, nor fidelity, nor sociality, delighted the Spaniard. Seeing him relapsing into forbidding gloom, and still remaining seated, Captain Delano, thinking that his presence was undesired just then, withdrew, on pretense of seeing whether, as he had prophesied, any signs of a breeze were visible.

Walking forward to the main-mast, he stood awhile thinking over the scene, and not without some undefined misgivings, when he heard a noise near the cuddy, and turning, saw the negro, his hand to his cheek. Advancing, Captain Delano perceived that the cheek was bleeding. He was about to ask the cause, when the negro's wailing soliloquy enlightened him.

"Ah, when will master get better from his sickness; only the sour heart that sour sickness breeds made him serve Babo so; cutting Babo with the razor, because, only by accident, Babo had given master one little scratch; and for the first time in so many a day, too. Ah, ah, ah," holding his hand to his face.

Is it possible, thought Captain Delano; was it to wreak in private his Spanish spite against this poor friend of his, that Don Benito, by his sullen manner, impelled me to withdraw? Ah, this slavery breeds ugly passions in man.—Poor fellow!

He was about to speak in sympathy to the negro, but with a timid reluctance he now reentered the cuddy.

Presently master and man came forth; Don Benito leaning on his servant as if nothing had happened.

But a sort of love-quarrel, after all, thought Captain Delano.

He accosted Don Benito, and they slowly walked together. They had gone but a few paces, when the steward—a tall, rajah-looking mulatto, orientally set off with a pagoda turban formed by three or four Madras handkerchiefs wound about his head, tier on tier—approaching with a salaam, announced lunch in the cabin.

On their way thither, the two captains were preceded by the mulatto, who, turning round as he advanced, with continual smiles and bows, ushered them on, a display of elegance which quite completed the insignificance of the small bare-headed Babo, who, as if not unconscious of inferiority, eyed askance the graceful steward. But in part, Captain Delano imputed his jealous watchfulness to that peculiar feeling which the full-blooded African entertains for the adulterated one. As for the steward, his manner, if not bespeaking much dignity or self-respect, yet evidenced his extreme desire to please; which is doubly meritorious, as at once Christian and Chesterfieldian.

Captain Delano observed with interest that while the complexion of the mulatto was hybrid, his physiognomy was European—classically so.

"Don Benito," whispered he, "I am glad to see this usher-of-the-golden-rod of yours; the sight refutes an ugly remark once made to me by a Barbados planter; that when a mulatto has a regular European face, look out for him; he is a devil. But see, your steward here has features more regular than King George's of England; and yet there he nods, and bows, and smiles; a king, indeed—the king of kind hearts and polite fellows. What a pleasant voice he has, too?"

"He has, Señor."

"But, tell me, has he not, so far as you have known him, always proved a good, worthy fellow?" said Captain Delano, pausing, while with a final genuflexion the steward disappeared into the cabin; "come, for the reason just mentioned, I am curious to know."

"Francesco is a good man," rather sluggishly responded Don Benito, like a phlegmatic appreciator, who would neither find fault nor flatter.

"Ah, I thought so. For it were strange, indeed, and not very creditable to us white-skins, if a little of our blood mixed with the African's, should, far from improving the latter's quality, have the sad effect of pouring vitriolic acid into black broth; improving the hue, perhaps, but not the wholesomeness."

"Doubtless, doubtless, Señor, but"—glancing at Babo—"not to speak of negroes, your planter's remark I have heard applied to the Spanish and Indian intermixtures in our provinces. But I know nothing about the matter," he listlessly added.

And here they entered the cabin.

The lunch was a frugal one. Some of Captain Delano's fresh fish and pumpkins, biscuit and salt beef, the reserved bottle of cider, and the San Dominick's last bottle of Canary.

As they entered, Francesco, with two or three colored aids, was hovering over the table giving the last adjustments. Upon perceiving their master they withdrew, Francesco making a smiling congé, and the Spaniard, without condescending to notice it, fastidiously remarking to his companion that he relished not superfluous attendance.

Without companions, host and guest sat down, like a childless married couple, at opposite ends of the table, Don Benito waving Captain Delano to his place, and, weak as he was, insisting upon that gentleman being seated before himself.

The negro placed a rug under Don Benito's feet, and a cushion behind his back, and then stood behind, not his master's chair, but Captain Delano's. At first, this a little surprised the latter. But it was soon evident that, in taking his position, the black was still true to his master; since by facing him he could the more readily anticipate his slightest want.

"This is an uncommonly intelligent fellow of yours, Don Benito," whispered Captain Delano across the table.

"You say true, Señor."

During the repast, the guest again reverted to parts of Don Benito's story, begging further particulars here and there. He inquired how it was that the scurvy and fever should have committed such wholesale havoc upon the whites, while destroying less than half of the blacks. As if this question reproduced the whole scene of plague before the Spaniard's eyes, miserably reminding him of his solitude in a cabin where before he had had so many friends and officers round him, his hand shook, his face became hueless, broken words escaped; but directly the sane memory of the past seemed replaced by insane terrors of the present. With starting eyes he stared before him at vacancy. For nothing was to be seen but the hand of his servant pushing the Canary over towards him. At length a few sips served partially to restore him. He made random reference to the different constitution of races, enabling one to offer more resistance to certain maladies than another. The thought was new to his companion.

Presently Captain Delano, intending to say something to his host concerning the pecuniary part of the business he had undertaken for him, especially—since he was strictly accountable to his owners—with reference to the new suit of sails, and other things of that sort; and naturally preferring to conduct such affairs in private, was desirous that the servant should withdraw; imagining that Don Benito for a few minutes could dispense with his attendance. He, however, waited awhile; thinking that, as the conversation proceeded, Don Benito, without being prompted, would perceive the propriety of the step.

But it was otherwise. At last catching his host's eye, Captain Delano, with a slight backward gesture of his thumb, whispered, "Don Benito, pardon me, but there is an interference with the full expression of what I have to say to you."

Upon this the Spaniard changed countenance; which was imputed to his resenting the hint, as in some way a reflection upon his servant. After a moment's pause, he assured his guest that the black's remaining with them could be of no disservice; because since losing his officers he had made Babo (whose original office, it now appeared, had been captain of the slaves) not only his constant attendant and companion, but in all things his confidant.

After this, nothing more could be said; though, indeed, Captain Delano could hardly avoid some little tinge of irritation upon being left ungratified in so inconsiderable a wish, by one, too, for whom he intended such solid services. But it is only his querulousness, thought he; and so filling his glass he proceeded to business.

The price of the sails and other matters was fixed upon. But while this was being done, the American observed that, though his original offer of assistance had been hailed with hectic animation, yet now when it was reduced to a business transaction, indifference and apathy were betrayed. Don Benito, in fact, appeared to submit to hearing the details more out of regard to common propriety, than from any impression that weighty benefit to himself and his voyage was involved.

Soon, his manner became still more reserved. The effort was vain to seek to draw him into social talk. Gnawed by his splenetic mood, he sat twitching his beard, while to little purpose the hand of his servant, mute as that on the wall, slowly pushed over the Canary.

Lunch being over, they sat down on the cushioned transom; the servant placing a pillow behind his master. The long continuance of the calm had now affected the atmosphere. Don Benito sighed heavily, as if for breath.

"Why not adjourn to the cuddy," said Captain Delano; "there is more air there." But the host sat silent and motionless.

Meantime his servant knelt before him, with a large fan of feathers. And Francesco coming in on tiptoes, handed the negro a little cup of aromatic waters, with which at intervals he chafed his master's brow; smoothing the hair along the temples as a nurse does a child's. He spoke no word. He only rested his eye on his master's, as if, amid all Don Benito's distress, a little to refresh his spirit by the silent sight of fidelity.

Presently the ship's bell sounded two o'clock; and through the cabin windows a slight rippling of the sea was discerned; and from the desired direction.

"There," exclaimed Captain Delano, "I told you so, Don Benito, look!"

He had risen to his feet, speaking in a very animated tone, with a view the more to rouse his companion. But though the crimson curtain of the stern-window near him that moment fluttered against his pale cheek, Don Benito seemed to have even less welcome for the breeze than the calm.

Poor fellow, thought Captain Delano, bitter experience has taught him that one ripple does not make a wind, any more than one swallow a summer. But he is mistaken for once. I will get his ship in for him, and prove it.

Briefly alluding to his weak condition, he urged his host to remain quietly where he was, since he (Captain Delano) would with pleasure take upon himself the responsibility of making the best use of the wind.

Upon gaining the deck, Captain Delano started at the unexpected figure of Atufal, monumentally fixed at the threshold, like one of those sculptured porters of black marble guarding the porches of Egyptian tombs.

But this time the start was, perhaps, purely physical. Atufal's presence, singularly attesting docility even in sullenness, was contrasted with that of the hatchet-polishers, who in patience evinced their industry; while both spectacles showed, that lax as Don Benito's general authority might be, still, whenever he chose to exert it, no man so savage or colossal but must, more or less, bow.

Snatching a trumpet which hung from the bulwarks, with a free step Captain Delano advanced to the forward edge of the poop, issuing his orders in his best Spanish. The few sailors and many negroes, all equally pleased, obediently set about heading the ship towards the harbor.

While giving some directions about setting a lower stu'n'-sail, suddenly Captain Delano heard a voice faithfully repeating his orders. Turning, he saw Babo, now for the time acting, under the pilot, his original part of captain of the slaves. This assistance proved valuable. Tattered sails and warped yards were soon brought into some trim. And no brace or halyard was pulled but to the blithe songs of the inspirited negroes.

Good fellows, thought Captain Delano, a little training would make fine sailors of them. Why see, the very women pull and sing too. These must be some of those Ashantee negresses that make such capital soldiers, I've heard. But who's at the helm? I must have a good hand there.

He went to see.

The San Dominick steered with a cumbrous tiller, with large horizontal pullies attached. At each pulley-end stood a subordinate black, and between them, at the tiller-head, the responsible post, a Spanish seaman, whose countenance evinced his due share in the general hopefulness and confidence at the coming of the breeze.

He proved the same man who had behaved with so shame-faced an air on the windlass.

"Ah,—it is you, my man," exclaimed Captain Delano—"well, no more sheep's-eyes now;—look straight forward and keep the ship so. Good hand, I trust? And want to get into the harbor, don't you?"

The man assented with an inward chuckle, grasping the tiller-head firmly. Upon this, unperceived by the American, the two blacks eyed the sailor intently.

Finding all right at the helm, the pilot went forward to the forecastle, to see how matters stood there.

The ship now had way enough to breast the current. With the approach of evening, the breeze would be sure to freshen.

Having done all that was needed for the present, Captain Delano, giving his last orders to the sailors, turned aft to report affairs to Don Benito in the cabin; perhaps additionally incited to rejoin him by the hope of snatching a moment's private chat while the servant was engaged upon deck.

From opposite sides, there were, beneath the poop, two approaches to the cabin; one further forward than the other, and consequently communicating with a longer passage. Marking the servant still above, Captain Delano, taking the nighest entrance—the one last named, and at whose porch Atufal still stood—hurried on his way, till, arrived at the cabin threshold, he paused an instant, a little to recover from his eagerness. Then, with the words of his intended business upon his lips, he entered. As he advanced toward the seated Spaniard, he heard another footstep, keeping time with his. From the opposite door, a salver in hand, the servant was likewise advancing.

"Confound the faithful fellow," thought Captain Delano; "what a vexatious coincidence."

Possibly, the vexation might have been something different, were it not for the brisk confidence inspired by the breeze. But even as it was, he felt a slight twinge, from a sudden indefinite association in his mind of Babo with Atufal.

"Don Benito," said he, "I give you joy; the breeze will hold, and will increase. By the way, your tall man and time-piece, Atufal, stands without. By your order, of course?"

Don Benito recoiled, as if at some bland satirical touch, delivered with such adroit garnish of apparent good breeding as to present no handle for retort.

He is like one flayed alive, thought Captain Delano; where may one touch him without causing a shrink?

The servant moved before his master, adjusting a cushion; recalled to civility, the Spaniard stiffly replied: "you are right. The slave appears where you saw him, according to my command; which is, that if at the given hour I am below, he must take his stand and abide my coming."

"Ah now, pardon me, but that is treating the poor fellow like an ex-king indeed. Ah, Don Benito," smiling, "for all the license you permit in some things, I fear lest, at bottom, you are a bitter hard master."

Again Don Benito shrank; and this time, as the good sailor thought, from a genuine twinge of his conscience.

Again conversation became constrained. In vain Captain Delano called attention to the now perceptible motion of the keel gently cleaving the sea; with lack-lustre eye, Don Benito returned words few and reserved.

By-and-by, the wind having steadily risen, and still blowing right into the harbor, bore the San Dominick swiftly on. Rounding a point of land, the sealer at distance came into open view.

Meantime Captain Delano had again repaired to the deck, remaining there some time. Having at last altered the ship's course, so as to give the reef a wide berth, he returned for a few moments below.

I will cheer up my poor friend, this time, thought he.

"Better and better, Don Benito," he cried as he blithely re-entered: "there will soon be an end to your cares, at least for awhile. For when, after a long, sad voyage, you know, the anchor drops into the haven, all its vast weight seems lifted from the captain's heart. We are getting on famously, Don Benito. My ship is in sight. Look through this side-light here; there she is; all a-taunt-o![13] The Bachelor's Delight, my good friend. Ah, how this wind braces one up. Come, you must take a cup of coffee with me this evening. My old steward will give you as fine a cup as ever any sultan tasted. What say you, Don Benito, will you?"

At first, the Spaniard glanced feverishly up, casting a longing look towards the sealer, while with mute concern his servant gazed into his face. Suddenly the old ague of coldness returned, and dropping back to his cushions he was silent.

"You do not answer. Come, all day you have been my host; would you have hospitality all on one side?"

"I cannot go," was the response.

"What? It will not fatigue you. The ships will lie together as near as they can, without swinging foul. It will be little more than stepping from deck to deck; which is but as from room to room. Come, come, you must not refuse me."

"I cannot go," decisively and repulsively repeated Don Benito.

Renouncing all but the last appearance of courtesy, with a sort of cadaverous sullenness, and biting his thin nails to the quick, he glanced, almost glared, at his guest, as if impatient that a stranger's presence should interfere with the full indulgence of his morbid hour. Meantime the sound of the parted waters came more and more gurglingly and merrily in at the windows; as reproaching him for his dark spleen; as telling him that, sulk as he might, and go mad with it, nature cared not a jot; since, whose fault was it, pray?

But the foul mood was now at its depth, as the fair wind at its height.

There was something in the man so far beyond any mere unsociality or sourness previously evinced, that even the forbearing good-nature of his guest could no longer endure it. Wholly at a loss to account for such demeanor, and deeming sickness with eccentricity, however extreme, no adequate excuse,

[13] Fully rigged.

well satisfied, too, that nothing in his own conduct could justify it, Captain Delano's pride began to be roused. Himself became reserved. But all seemed one to the Spaniard. Quitting him, therefore, Captain Delano once more went to the deck.

The ship was now within less than two miles of the sealer. The whale-boat was seen darting over the interval.

To be brief, the two vessels, thanks to the pilot's skill, ere long in neighborly style lay anchored together.

Before returning to his own vessel, Captain Delano had intended communicating to Don Benito the smaller details of the proposed services to be rendered. But, as it was, unwilling anew to subject himself to rebuffs, he resolved, now that he had seen the San Dominick safely moored, immediately to quit her, without further allusion to hospitality or business. Indefinitely postponing his ulterior plans, he would regulate his future actions according to future circumstances. His boat was ready to receive him; but his host still tarried below. Well, thought Captain Delano, if he has little breeding, the more need to show mine. He descended to the cabin to bid a ceremonious, and, it may be, tacitly rebukeful adieu. But to his great satisfaction, Don Benito, as if he began to feel the weight of that treatment with which his slighted guest had, not indecorously, retaliated upon him, now supported by his servant, rose to his feet, and grasping Captain Delano's hand, stood tremulous; too much agitated to speak. But the good augury hence drawn was suddenly dashed, by his resuming all his previous reserve, with augmented gloom, as, with half-averted eyes, he silently reseated himself on his cushions. With a corresponding return of his own chilled feelings, Captain Delano bowed and withdrew.

He was hardly midway in the narrow corridor, dim as a tunnel, leading from the cabin to the stairs, when a sound, as of the tolling for execution in some jail-yard, fell on his ears. It was the echo of the ship's flawed bell, striking the hour, drearily reverberated in this subterranean vault. Instantly, by a fatality not to be withstood, his mind, responsive to the portent, swarmed with superstitious suspicions. He paused. In images far swifter than these sentences, the minutest details of all his former distrusts swept through him.

Hitherto, credulous good-nature had been too ready to furnish excuses for reasonable fears. Why was the Spaniard, so superfluously punctilious at times, now heedless of common propriety in not accompanying to the side his departing guest? Did indisposition forbid? Indisposition had not forbidden more irksome exertion that day. His last equivocal demeanor recurred. He had risen to his feet, grasped his guest's hand, motioned toward his hat; then, in an instant, all was eclipsed in sinister muteness and gloom. Did this imply one brief, repentant relenting at the final moment, from some iniquitous plot, followed by remorseless return to it? His last glance seemed to express a calamitous, yet acquiescent farewell to Captain Delano forever. Why decline the invitation to visit the sealer that evening? Or was the Spaniard less hardened than the Jew,[14] who refrained not from supping at the board of him whom the same night he meant to betray? What imported all those day-long enigmas and contradictions, except they were intended to mystify, preliminary to some stealthy blow? Atufal, the pretended rebel, but punctual shadow, that moment lurked by the threshold without. He seemed a sentry, and more. Who, by his own confession, had stationed him there? Was the negro now lying in wait?

The Spaniard behind—his creature before: to rush from darkness to light was the involuntary choice.

The next moment, with clenched jaw and hand, he passed Atufal, and stood unharmed in the light. As he saw his trim ship lying peacefully at anchor, and almost within ordinary call; as he saw his household boat, with familiar faces in it, patiently rising and falling on the short waves by the San Dominick's side; and then, glancing about the decks where he stood, saw the oakum-pickers still gravely plying their fingers; and heard the low, buzzing whistle and industrious hum of the hatchet-polishers, still bestirring themselves over their endless occupation; and more than all, as he saw the benign aspect of nature, taking her innocent repose in the evening; the screened sun in the quiet camp of the west shining out like the mild light from Abraham's tent; as charmed eye and ear took in all these, with the chained figure of the black, clenched jaw and hand relaxed. Once again he smiled at the phantoms which had mocked him, and felt something like a tinge of remorse, that, by indulging them even for a moment, he should, by implication, have betrayed an atheist doubt of the ever-watchful Providence above.

There was a few minutes' delay, while, in obedience to his orders, the boat was being hooked along to the gangway. During this interval, a sort of saddened satisfaction stole over Captain Delano, at thinking of the kindly offices he had that day discharged for a stranger. Ah, thought he, after good actions one's conscience is never ungrateful, however much so the benefited party may be.

Presently, his foot, in the first act of descent into the boat, pressed the first round of the side-ladder, his face presented inward upon the deck. In the same moment, he heard his name courteously

[14] Judas Iscariot.

sounded; and, to his pleased surprise, saw Don Benito advancing—an unwonted energy in his air, as if, at the last moment, intent upon making amends for his recent discourtesy. With instinctive good feeling, Captain Delano, withdrawing his foot, turned and reciprocally advanced. As he did so, the Spaniard's nervous eagerness increased, but his vital energy failed; so that, the better to support him, the servant, placing his master's hand on his naked shoulder, and gently holding it there, formed himself into a sort of crutch.

When the two captains met, the Spaniard again fervently took the hand of the American, at the same time casting an earnest glance into his eyes, but, as before, too much overcome to speak.

I have done him wrong, self-reproachfully thought Captain Delano; his apparent coldness has deceived me; in no instance has he meant to offend.

Meantime, as if fearful that the continuance of the scene might too much unstring his master, the servant seemed anxious to terminate it. And so, still, presenting himself as a crutch, and walking between the two captains, he advanced with them towards the gangway; while still, as if full of kindly contrition, Don Benito would not let go the hand of Captain Delano, but retained it in his, across the black's body.

Soon they were standing by the side, looking over into the boat, whose crew turned up their curious eyes. Waiting a moment for the Spaniard to relinquish his hold, the now embarrassed Captain Delano lifted his foot, to overstep the threshold of the open gangway; but still Don Benito would not let go his hand. And yet, with an agitated tone, he said, "I can go no further; here I must bid you adieu. Adieu, my dear, dear Don Amasa. Go—go!" suddenly tearing his hand loose, "go, and God guard you better than me, my best friend."

Not unaffected, Captain Delano would now have lingered; but catching the meekly admonitory eye of the servant, with a hasty farewell he descended into his boat, followed by the continual adieus of Don Benito, standing rooted in the gangway.

Seating himself in the stern, Captain Delano, making a last salute, ordered the boat shoved off. The crew had their oars on end. The bowsmen pushed the boat a sufficient distance for the oars to be lengthwise dropped. The instant that was done, Don Benito sprang over the bulwarks, falling at the feet of Captain Delano; at the same time, calling towards his ship, but in tones so frenzied, that none in the boat could understand him. But, as if not equally obtuse, three sailors, from three different and distant parts of the ship, splashed into the sea, swimming after their captain, as if intent upon his rescue.

The dismayed officer of the boat eagerly asked what this meant. To which, Captain Delano, turning a disdainful smile upon the unaccountable Spaniard, answered that, for his part, he neither knew nor cared; but it seemed as if Don Benito had taken it into his head to produce the impression among his people that the boat wanted to kidnap him. "Or else—give way for your lives," he wildly added, starting at a clattering hubbub in the ship, above which rang the tocsin of the hatchet-polishers; and seizing Don Benito by the throat he added, "this plotting pirate means murder!" Here, in apparent verification of the words, the servant, a dagger in his hand, was seen on the rail overhead, poised, in the act of leaping, as if with desperate fidelity to befriend his master to the last; while, seemingly to aid the black, the three white sailors were trying to clamber into the hampered bow. Meantime, the whole host of negroes, as if inflamed at the sight of their jeopardized captain, impended in one sooty avalanche over the bulwarks.

All this, with what preceded, and what followed, occurred with such involutions of rapidity, that past, present, and future seemed one.

Seeing the negro coming, Captain Delano had flung the Spaniard aside, almost in the very act of clutching him, and, by the unconscious recoil, shifting his place, with arms thrown up, so promptly grappled the servant in his descent, that with dagger presented at Captain Delano's heart, the black seemed of purpose to have leaped there as to his mark. But the weapon was wrenched away, and the assailant dashed down into the bottom of the boat, which now, with disentangled oars, began to speed through the sea.

At this juncture, the left hand of Captain Delano, on one side, again clutched the half-reclined Don Benito, heedless that he was in a speechless faint, while his right foot, on the other side, ground the prostrate negro; and his right arm pressed for added speed on the after oar, his eye bent forward, encouraging his men to their utmost.

But here, the officer of the boat, who had at last succeeded in beating off the towing sailors, and was now, with face turned aft, assisting the bowsman at his oar, suddenly called to Captain Delano, to see what the black was about; while a Portuguese oarsman shouted to him to give heed to what the Spaniard was saying.

Glancing down at his feet, Captain Delano saw the freed hand of the servant aiming with a second dagger—a small one, before concealed in his wool—with this he was snakishly writhing up from the boat's bottom, at the heart of his master, his countenance lividly vindictive, expressing the centered purpose of his soul; while the Spaniard, half-choked, was vainly shrinking away, with husky words, incoherent to all but the Portuguese.

That moment, across the long-benighted mind of Captain Delano, a flash of revelation swept, illuminating in unanticipated clearness, his host's whole mysterious demeanor, with every enigmatic event of the day, as well as the entire past voyage of the San Dominick. He smote Babo's hand down, but his own heart smote him harder. With infinite pity he withdrew his hold from Don Benito. Not Captain Delano, but Don Benito, the black, in leaping into the boat, had intended to stab.

Both the black's hands were held, as, glancing up towards the San Dominick, Captain Delano, now with scales dropped from his eyes, saw the negroes, not in misrule, not in tumult, not as if frantically concerned for Don Benito, but with mask torn away, flourishing hatchets and knives, in ferocious piratical revolt. Like delirious black dervishes, the six Ashantees danced on the poop. Prevented by their foes from springing into the water, the Spanish boys were hurrying up to the topmost spars, while such of the few Spanish sailors, not already in the sea, less alert, were described, helplessly mixed in, on deck, with the blacks.

Meantime Captain Delano hailed his own vessel, ordering the ports up, and the guns run out. But by this time the cable of the San Dominick had been cut; and the fag-end, in lashing out, whipped away the canvas shroud about the beak, suddenly revealing, as the bleached hull swung round towards the open ocean, death for the figure-head, in a human skeleton; chalky comment on the chalked words below, *"Follow your leader."*

At the sight, Don Benito, covering his face, wailed out: " 'Tis he, Aranda! my murdered, unburied friend!"

Upon reaching the sealer, calling for ropes, Captain Delano bound the negro, who made no resistance, and had him hoisted to the deck. He would then have assisted the now almost helpless Don Benito up the side; but Don Benito, wan as he was, refused to move, or be moved, until the negro should have been first put below out of view. When, presently assured that it was done, he no more shrank from the ascent.

The boat was immediately dispatched back to pick up the three swimming sailors. Meantime, the guns were in readiness, though, owing to the San Dominick having glided somewhat astern of the sealer, only the aftermost one could be brought to bear. With this, they fired six times; thinking to cripple the fugitive ship by bringing down her spars. But only a few inconsiderable ropes were shot away. Soon the ship was beyond the gun's range, steering broad out of the bay; the blacks thickly clustering round the bowsprit, one moment with taunting cries towards the whites, the next with upthrown gestures hailing the now dusky moors of ocean—cawing crows escaped from the hand of the fowler.

The first impulse was to slip the cables and give chase. But, upon second thoughts, to pursue with whale-boat and yawl seemed more promising.

Upon inquiring of Don Benito what fire-arms they had on board the San Dominick, Captain Delano was answered that they had none that could be used; because, in the earlier stages of the mutiny, a cabin-passenger, since dead, had secretly put out of order the locks of what few muskets there were. But with all his remaining strength, Don Benito entreated the American not to give chase, either with ship or boat; for the negroes had already proved themselves such desperadoes, that, in case of a present assault, nothing but a total massacre of the whites could be looked for. But, regarding this warning as coming from one whose spirit had been crushed by misery the American did not give up his design.

The boats were got ready and armed. Captain Delano ordered his men into them. He was going himself when Don Benito grasped his arm.

"What! have you saved my life, Señor, and are you now going to throw away your own?"

The officers also, for reasons connected with their interests and those of the voyage, and a duty owing to the owners, strongly objected against their commander's going. Weighing their remonstrances a moment, Captain Delano felt bound to remain; appointing his chief mate—an athletic and resolute man, who had been a privateer's-man—to head the party. The more to encourage the sailors, they were told, that the Spanish captain considered his ship good as lost; that she and her cargo, including some gold and silver, were worth more than a thousand dubloons. Take her, and no small part should be theirs. The sailors replied with a shout.

The fugitives had now almost gained an offing. It was nearly night; but the moon was rising. After hard, prolonged pulling, the boats came up on the ship's quarters, at a suitable distance laying upon their oars to discharge their muskets. Having no bullets to return, the negroes sent their yells. But, upon the second volley, Indianlike, they hurtled their hatchets. One took off a sailor's fingers. Another struck the whale-boat's bow, cutting off the rope there, and remaining stuck in the gunwale like a woodman's axe. Snatching it, quivering from its lodgment, the mate hurled it back. The returned gauntlet now stuck in the ship's broken quarter-gallery, and so remained.

The negroes giving too hot a reception, the whites kept a more respectful distance. Hovering now just out of reach of the hurtling hatchets, they, with a view to the close encounter which must soon come, sought to decoy the blacks into entirely disarming themselves of their most murderous weapons in a hand-to-hand fight, by foolishly flinging them, as missiles, short of the mark, into the sea. But, ere long, perceiving the stratagem, the negroes desisted, though not before many of them had to replace their lost hatchets with handspikes; an exchange which, as counted upon, proved, in the end, favorable to the assailants.

Meantime, with a strong wind, the ship still clove the water; the boats alternately falling behind, and pulling up, to discharge fresh volleys.

The fire was directed towards the stern, since there, chiefly, the negroes, at present, were clustering. But to kill or maim the negroes was not the object. To take them, with the ship, was the object. To do it, the ship must be boarded; which could not be done by boats while she was sailing so fast.

A thought now struck the mate. Observing the Spanish boys still aloft, high as they could get, he called to them to descend to the yards, and cut adrift the sails. It was done. About this time, owing to causes hereafter to be shown, two Spaniards, in the dress of sailors, and conspicuously showing themselves, were killed; not by volleys, but by deliberate marksman's shots; while, as it afterwards appeared, by one of the general discharges, Atufal, the black, and the Spaniard at the helm likewise were killed. What now, with the loss of the sails, and loss of leaders, the ship became unmanageable to the negroes.

With creaking masts, she came heavily round to the wind; the prow slowly swinging into view of the boats, its skeleton gleaming in the horizontal moonlight, and casting a gigantic ribbed shadow upon the water. One extended arm of the ghost seemed beckoning the whites to avenge it.

"Follow your leader!" cried the mate; and, one on each bow, the boats boarded. Sealing-spears and cutlasses crossed hatchets and hand-spikes. Huddled upon the long-boat amidships, the negresses raised a wailing chant, whose chorus was the clash of the steel.

For a time, the attack wavered; the negroes wedging themselves to beat it back; the half-repelled sailors, as yet unable to gain a footing, fighting as troopers in the saddle, one leg sideways flung over the bulwarks, and one without, plying their cutlasses like carters' whips. But in vain. They were almost overborne, when, rallying themselves into a squad as one man, with a huzza, they sprang inboard, where, entangled, they involuntarily separated again. For a few breaths' space, there was a vague, muffled, inner sound, as of submerged sword-fish rushing hither and thither through shoals of black-fish. Soon, in a reunited band, and joined by the Spanish seamen, the whites came to the surface, irresistibly driving the negroes toward the stern. But a barricade of casks and sacks, from side to side, had been thrown up by the mainmast. Here the negroes faced about, and though scorning peace or truce, yet fain would have had respite. But, without pause, overleaping the barrier, the unflagging sailors again closed. Exhausted, the blacks now fought in despair.

Their red tongues lolled, wolf-like, from their black mouths. But the pale sailors' teeth were set; not a word was spoken; and, in five minutes more, the ship was won.

Nearly a score of the negroes were killed. Exclusive of those by the balls, many were mangled; their wounds—mostly inflicted by the long-edged sealing-spears—resembling those shaven ones of the English at Preston Pans,[15] made by the poled scythes of the Highlanders. On the other side, none were killed, though several were wounded; some severely, including the mate. The surviving negroes were temporarily secured, and the ship, towed back into the harbor at midnight, once more lay anchored.

Omitting the incidents and arrangements ensuing, suffice it that, after two days spent in refitting, the two ships sailed in company for Conception, in Chili, and thence for Lima, in Peru; where, before the vice-regal courts, the whole affair, from the beginning, underwent investigation.

Though, midway on the passage, the ill-fated Spaniard, relaxed from constraint, showed some signs of regaining health with free-will; yet, agreeably to his own foreboding, shortly before arriving at Lima, he relapsed, finally becoming so reduced as to be carried ashore in arms. Hearing of his story and plight, one of the many religious institutions of the City of Kings opened an hospitable refuge to him, where both physician and priest were his nurses, and a member of the order volunteered to be his one special guardian and consoler, by night and by day.

The following extracts, translated from one of the official Spanish documents, will, it is hoped, shed light on the preceding narrative, as well as, in the first place, reveal the true port of departure and true history of the San Dominick's voyage, down to the time of her touching at the island of St. Maria.

But, ere the extracts come, it may be well to preface them with a remark.

The document selected, from among many others, for partial translation, contains the deposition of Benito Cereno; the first taken in the case. Some disclosures therein were, at the time, held dubious for both learned and natural reasons. The tribunal inclined to the opinion that the deponent, not undisturbed in his mind by recent events, raved of some things which could never have happened. But subsequent depositions of the surviving sailors, bearing out the revelations of their captain in several of the strangest particulars, gave credence to the rest. So that the tribunal, in its final decision, rested its capital sentences upon statements which, had they lacked confirmation, it would have deemed it but duty to reject.

---

[15]A battle fought in 1745, where the Scottish Highlanders defeated the English.

I, Don Jose de Abos and Padilla, His Majesty's Notary for the Royal Revenue, and Register of this Province, and Notary Public of the Holy Crusade of this Bishopric, etc.

Do certify and declare, as much as is requisite in law, that, in the criminal cause commenced the twenty-fourth of the month of September, in the year seventeen hundred and ninety-nine, against the negroes of the ship San Dominick, the following declaration before me was made:

Declaration of the first witness, DON BENITO CERENO.

The same day, and month, and year, His Honor, Doctor Juan Martinez de Rozas, Councilor of the Royal Audience of this Kingdom, and learned in the law of this Intendency, ordered the captain of the ship San Dominick, Don Benito Cereno, to appear; which he did in his litter, attended by the monk Infelez; of whom he received the oath, which he took by God, our Lord, and a sign of the Cross; under which he promised to tell the truth of whatever he should know and should be asked;—and being interrogated agreeably to the tenor of the act commencing the process, he said, that on the twentieth of May last, he set sail with his ship from the port of Valparaiso, bound to that of Callao; loaded with the produce of the country beside thirty cases of hardware and one hundred and sixty blacks, of both sexes, mostly belonging to Don Alexandro Aranda, gentleman, of the city of Mendoza; that the crew of the ship consisted of thirty-six men, beside the persons who went as passengers; that the negroes were in part as follows:

Here, in the original, follows a list of some fifty names, descriptions, and ages, compiled from certain recovered documents of Aranda's, and also from recollections of the deponent, from which portions only are extracted.

—One, from about eighteen to nineteen years, named José, and this was the man that waited upon his master, Don Alexandro, and who speaks well the Spanish, having served him four or five years; . . . A mulatto, named Francesco, the cabin steward, of a good person and voice, having sung in the Valparaiso churches, native of the province of Buenos Ayres, aged about thirty-five years. . . . A smart negro, name Dago, who had been for many years a grave-digger among the Spaniards, aged forty-six years. . . . Four old negroes, born in Africa, from sixty to seventy, but sound, calkers by trade, whose names are as follows:—the first was named Muri, and he was killed (as was also his son named Diamelo); the second, Nacta; the third, Yola, likewise killed; the fourth, Ghofan; and six full-grown negroes, aged from thirty to forty-five, all raw, and born among the Ashantees—Matiluqui, Yan, Lecbe, Mapenda, Yambaio, Akim; four of whom were killed; . . . a powerful negro named Atufal, who being supposed to have been a chief in Africa, his owner set great store by him. . . . And a small negro of Senegal, but some years among the Spaniards, aged about thirty, which Negro's name was Babo; . . . that he does not remember the names of the others, but that still expecting the residue of Don Alexandro's papers will be found, will then take due account of them all, and remit to the court; . . . and thirty-nine women and children of all ages.

The catalogue over, the deposition goes on:

. . . That all the negroes slept upon deck, as is customary in this navigation, and none wore fetters, because the owner, his friend Aranda, told him that they were all tractable; . . . that on the seventh day after leaving port, at three o'clock in the morning, all the Spaniards being asleep except the two officers on the watch, who were the boatswain, Juan Robles, and the carpenter, Juan Bautista Gayete, and the helmsman and his boy, the negroes revolted suddenly, wounded dangerously the boatswain and the carpenter, and successively killed eighteen men of those who were sleeping upon deck, some with handspikes and hatchets, and others by throwing them alive overboard, after tying them; that of the Spaniards upon deck, they left about seven, as he thinks, alive and tied, to manoeuvre the ship, and three or four more, who hid themselves, remained also alive. Although in the act of revolt the negroes made themselves masters of the hatchway, six or seven wounded went through it to the cockpit, without any hindrance on their part; that during the act of revolt, the mate and another person, whose name he does not recollect, attempted to come up through the hatchway, but being quickly wounded, were obliged to return to the cabin; that the deponent resolved at break of day to come up the companion-way, where the negro Babo was, being the ringleader, and Atufal, who assisted him, and having spoken to them, exhorted them to cease committing such atrocities, asking them, at the same time, what they wanted and intended to do, offering, himself, to obey their commands; that notwithstanding this, they threw, in his presence, three men, alive and tied, overboard; that they told the deponent to come up, and that they would not kill him; which having done, the negro Babo asked him whether there were in those seas any negro countries where they might be carried, and he answered them, No; that the negro Babo afterwards told him to carry them to Senegal or to the neighbouring islands of St. Nicholas; and he answered, that this was impossible, on account of the great distance, the necessity involved of rounding Cape Horn, the bad condition of the vessel, the want of provisions, sails, and water; but that the negro Babo replied to him he must carry them in any way; that they would do and conform themselves to everything the deponent should require as to eating and drinking; that after a long conference, being absolutely compelled to please them, for they threatened to kill all the whites if they were not, at all events, carried to Senegal, he told them that what was most wanting for the voyage was water; that they would go near the coast to take it, and thence they would proceed on their course; that the negro Babo agreed to it; and the deponent steered towards the intermediate ports, hoping to meet some Spanish or foreign vessel that would save them; that within ten or eleven days they saw the land, and continued by it in the vicinity of Nasca; that the deponent observed that the negroes were now restless and mutinous, because he did not effect the taking in of water, the negro Babo having required, with threats, that it should be done, without fail, the following day; he told him he saw plainly that the coast was steep, and the rivers designated in the maps were not to be found, with other reasons suitable to the circumstances; that the best way would be to go to the island of Santa Maria, where they might water easily, it being a solitary island, as the foreigners did; that the deponent did not go to Pisco, that was near, nor make any other port of the coast, because the negro Babo had intimated to him several times, that he would kill all the whites the very moment he should perceive any city, town, or settlement of any kind on the shores to which they should be carried: that having determined to go to the island of Santa Maria, as the deponent had planned, for the purpose of trying whether, on the passage or near the island itself, they could find any vessel that should favor them, or whether he could escape from it in a boat to the neighboring coast of Arruco, to adopt the necessary means he immediately changed his course, steering for the island; that the negroes Babo and Atufal held daily conferences, in which they discussed what was necessary for their design of returning to Senegal, whether they were to kill all the Spaniards, and particularly the deponent; that eight days after parting from the coast of Nasca, the deponent being on the watch a little after daybreak, and soon after the negroes had their meeting, the negro Babo came to the place where the deponent was, and told him that he had determined to kill his master, Don Alexandro Aranda, both because he and his companions could not otherwise be sure of their liberty, and that to keep the seamen in subjection, he wanted to prepare a warning of what road they should be made to take did they or any of them oppose him; and that, by means of the death of Don Alexandro, that warning would best be given; but, that what this last meant, the deponent did not at the time comprehend, nor could not, further than that the death of Don Alexandro was intended; and moreover the negro Babo proposed to the deponent to call the mate Raneds, who was sleeping in the cabin, before the thing was done, for fear, as the deponent understood it, that the mate, who was a good navigator, should be killed with Don Alexandro and the rest; that the deponent, who was the friend, from youth, of Don Alexandro, prayed and conjured, but all was useless; for the negro Babo answered him that the thing could not be prevented, and that all the Spaniards risked their death if they should attempt to frustrate his will in this matter, or any other; that, in this conflict, the deponent called the mate, Raneds, who was forced to go apart, and immediately the negro Babo commanded the Ashantee Martinqui and the Ashantee Lecbe to go and commit the murder; that those two went down with hatchets to the berth of Don Alexandro; that, yet half alive and mangled, they dragged him on deck; that they were going to throw him overboard in that state, but the negro Babo stopped them, bidding the murder be completed on the deck before him, which was done, when, by his orders, the body was carried below, forward; that nothing more was seen of it by the deponent for three days; . . . that Don Alonzo Sidonia, an old man, long resident at Valparaiso, and lately appointed to a civil office in Peru, whither he had taken passage, was at the time sleeping in the berth opposite Don Alexandro's; that awakening at his cries, surprised by them, and at the sight of the negroes with their bloody hatchets in their hands, he threw himself into the sea through a window which was near him, and was drowned, without it being in the power of the deponent to assist or take him up; . . . that a short time after killing Aranda, they brought upon deck his german-cousin, of middle-age, Don Francisco Masa, of Mendoza, and the young Don Joaquin, Marques de Aramboalaza, then lately from Spain, with his Spanish servant Ponce, and the three young clerks of Aranda, José Mozairi,

Lorenzo Bargas, and Hermenegildo Gandix, all of Cadiz; that Don Joaquin and Hermenegildo Gandix, the negro Babo, for purposes hereafter to appear, preserved alive; but Don Francisco Masa, José Mozairi, and Lorenzo Bargas, with Ponce the servant, beside the boatswain, Juan Robles, the boatswain's mates, Manuel Viscaya and Roderigo Hurta, and four of the sailors, the negro Babo ordered to be thrown alive into the sea, although they made no resistance, nor begged for anything else but mercy; that the boatswain, Juan Robles, who knew how to swim, kept the longest above water, making acts of contrition, and, in the last words he uttered, charged this deponent to cause mass to be said for his soul to our Lady of Succor: . . . that, during the three days which followed, the deponent, uncertain what fate had befallen the remains of Don Alexandro, frequently asked the negro Babo where they were, and, if still on board, whether they were to be preserved for interment ashore, entreating him so to order it; that the negro Babo answered nothing till the fourth day, when at sunrise, the deponent coming on deck, the negro Babo showed him a skeleton, which had been substituted for the ship's proper figure-head—the image of Christopher Colon, the discoverer of the New World; that the negro Babo asked him whose skeleton that was, and whether, from its whiteness, he should not think it a white's; that, upon discovering his face, the negro Babo, coming close, said words to this effect: "Keep faith with the blacks from here to Senegal, or you shall in spirit, as now in body, follow your leader," pointing to the prow; . . . that the same morning the negro Babo took by succession each Spaniard forward, and asked him whose skeleton that was, and whether, from its whiteness, he should not think it a white's; that each Spaniard covered his face; that then to each the negro Babo repeated the words in the first place said to the deponent; . . . that they (the Spaniards), being then assembled aft, the negro Babo harangued them, saying that he had now done all; that the deponent (as navigator for the negroes) might pursue his course, warning him and all of them that they should, soul and body, go the way of Don Alexandro, if he saw them (the Spaniards) speak or plot anything against them (the negroes)— a threat which was repeated every day; that, before the events last mentioned, they had tied the cook to throw him overboard, for it is not known what thing they heard him speak, but finally the negro Babo spared his life, at the request of the deponent; that a few days after, the deponent, endeavoring not to omit any means to preserve the lives of the remaining whites, spoke to the negroes of peace and tranquillity, and agreed to draw up a paper, signed by the deponent and the sailors who could write, as also by the negro Babo, for himself and all the blacks, in which the deponent obliged himself to carry them to Senegal, and they not to kill any more, and he formally to make over to them the ship, with the cargo, with which they were for that time satisfied and quieted. . . . But the next day, the more surely to guard against the sailors' escape, the negro Babo commanded all the boats to be destroyed but the long-boat, which was unseaworthy, and another, a cutter in good condition, which knowing it would yet be wanted for towing the water casks, he had it lowered down into the hold.

Various particulars of the prolonged and perplexed navigation ensuing here follow, with incidents of a

calamitous calm, from which portion one passage is extracted, to wit:

—That on the fifth day of the calm, all on board suffering much from the heat, and want of water, and five having died in fits, and mad, the negroes became irritable, and for a chance gesture, which they deemed suspicious— though it was harmless—made by the mate, Raneds, to the deponent in the act of handing a quadrant, they killed him; but that for this they afterwards were sorry, the mate being the only remaining navigator on board, except the deponent.

. . . .

—That omitting other events, which daily happened, and which can only serve uselessly to recall past misfortunes and conflicts, after seventy-three days' navigation, reckoned from the time they sailed from Nasca, during which they navigated under a scanty allowance of water, and were afflicted with the calms before mentioned, they at last arrived at the island of Santa Maria, on the seventeenth of the month of August, at about six o'clock in the afternoon, at which hour they cast anchor very near the American ship, Bachelor's Delight, which lay in the same bay, commanded by the generous Captain Amasa Delano; but at six o'clock in the morning, they had already described the port, and the negroes became uneasy, as soon as at distance they saw the ship, not having expected to see one there; that the negro Babo pacified them, assuring them that no fear need be had; that straightway he ordered the figure on the bow to be covered with canvas, as for repairs, and had the decks a little set in order; that for a time the negro Babo and the negro Atufal conferred; that the negro Atufal was for sailing away, but the negro Babo would not, and, by himself, cast about what to do; that at last he came to the deponent, proposing to him to say and do all that the deponent declares to have said and done to the American captain;

. . . .

—That the negro Babo warned him that if he varied in the least, or uttered any word, or gave any look that should give the least intimation of the past events or present state, he would instantly kill him, with all his companions, showing a dagger, which he carried hid, saying something which, as he understood it, meant that that dagger would be alert as his eye; that the negro Babo then announced the plan to all his companions, which pleased them; that he then, the better to disguise the truth, devised many expedients, in some of them uniting deceit and defense; that of this sort was the device of the six Ashantees before named, who were his bravoes; that them he stationed on the break of the poop, as if to clean certain hatchets (in cases, which were part of the cargo), but in reality to use them, and distribute them at need, and at a given word he told them; that, among other devices, was the device of presenting Atufal, his right hand man, as chained, though in a moment the chains could be dropped; that in every particular he informed the deponent what part he was expected to enact in every device, and what story he was to tell on every occasion, always threatening him with instant death if he varied in the least; that, conscious that many of the negroes would be turbulent, the negro Babo appointed the four aged negroes, who were calkers, to keep what domestic order they could on the decks; that again and again he harangued the Spaniards and his companions, informing

them of his intent, and of his devices, and of the invented story that this deponent was to tell; charging them lest any of them varied from that story; that these arrangements were made and matured during the interval of two or three hours between their first sighting the ship and the arrival on board of Captain Amasa Delano; that this happened at about half-past seven o'clock in the morning, Captain Amasa Delano coming in his boat, and all gladly receiving him; that the deponent, as well as he could force himself, acting then the part of principal owner, and a free captain of the ship, told Captain Amasa Delano, when called upon, that he came from Buenos Ayres, bound to Lima, with three hundred negroes; that off Cape Horn, and in a subsequent fever, many negroes had died; that also, by similar casualties, all the sea officers and the greatest part of the crew had died.

And so the deposition goes on, circumstantially recounting the fictitious story dictated to the deponent by Babo, and through the deponent imposed upon Captain Delano; and also recounting the friendly offers of Captain Delano, with other things, but all of which is here omitted. After the fictitious story, etc., the deposition proceeds:

—that the generous Captain Amasa Delano remained on board all the day, till he left the ship anchored at six o'clock in the evening, deponent speaking to him always of his pretended misfortunes, under the fore-mentioned principles, without having had it in his power to tell a single word, or give him the least hint, that he might know the truth and state of things; because the negro Babo, performing the office of an officious servant with all the appearance of submission of the humble slave, did not leave the deponent one moment; that this was in order to observe the deponent's actions and words, for the negro Babo understands well the Spanish; and besides, there were thereabout some others who were constantly on the watch, and likewise understood the Spanish; . . . that upon one occasion, while deponent was standing on the deck conversing with Amasa Delano, by a secret sign the negro Babo drew him (the deponent) aside, the act appearing as if originating with the deponent; that then, he being drawn aside, the negro Babo proposed to him to gain from Amasa Delano full particulars about his ship, and crew, and arms; that the deponent asked "For what?" that the negro Babo answered he might conceive; that, grieved at the prospect of what might overtake the generous Captain Amasa Delano, the deponent at first refused to ask the desired questions, and used every argument to induce the negro Babo to give up this new design; that the negro Babo showed the point of his dagger; that, after the information had been obtained the negro Babo again drew him aside, telling him that that very night he (the deponent) would be captain of two ships, instead of one, for that, great part of the American's ship's crew being to be absent fishing, the six Ashantees, without any one else, would easily take it; that at this time he said other things to the same purpose; that no entreaties availed; that, before Amasa Delano's coming on board, no hint had been given touching the capture of the American ship; that to prevent this project the deponent was powerless; . . . —that in some things his memory is confused, he cannot distinctly recall every event; . . . . —that as soon as they had cast anchor at six of the clock in the evening, as has before been stated, the American Captain took leave, to return to his vessel; that upon a sudden impulse, which the deponent believes to have come from God and his angels, he, after the farewell had been said, followed the generous Captain Amasa Delano as far as the gunwale, where he stayed, under pretense of taking leave, until Amasa Delano should have been seated in his boat; that on shoving off, the deponent sprang from the gunwale into the boat, and fell into it, he knows not how, God guarding him; that—

Here, in the original, follows the account of what further happened at the escape, and how the San Dominick was retaken, and of the passage to the coast; including in the recital many expressions of "eternal gratitude" to the "generous Captain Amasa Delano." The deposition then proceeds with recapitulatory remarks, and a partial renumeration of the negroes, making record of their individual part in the past events, with a view to furnishing, according to command of the court, the data whereon to found the criminal sentences to be pronounced. From this portion is the following:

—That he believes that all the negroes, though not in the first place knowing to the design of revolt, when it was accomplished, approved it. . . . That the negro, José, eighteen years old, and in the personal service of Don Alexandro, was the one who communicated the information to the negro Babo, about the state of things in the cabin, before the revolt; that this is known, because, in the preceding midnight, he used to come from his berth, which was under his master's, in the cabin, to the deck where the ringleader and his associates were, and had secret conversations with the negro Babo, in which he was several times seen by the mate; that, one night, the mate drove him away twice; . . . that this same negro José was the one who, without being commanded to do so by the negro Babo, as Lecbe and Martinqui were, stabbed his master, Don Alexandro, after he had been dragged half-lifeless to the deck; . . . that the mulatto steward, Francesco, was of the first band of revolters, that he was, in all things, the creature and tool of the negro Babo; that, to make his court, he, just before a repast in the cabin, proposed, to the negro Babo, poisoning a dish for the generous Captain Amasa Delano; this is known and believed, because the negroes have said it; but that the negro Babo, having another design, forbade Francesco; . . . that the Ashantee Lecbe was one of the worst of them; for that, on the day the ship was retaken, he assisted in the defense of her, with a hatchet in each hand, with one of which he wounded, in the breast, the chief mate of Amasa Delano, in the first act of boarding; this all knew; that, in sight of the deponent, Lecbe struck, with a hatchet, Don Francisco Masa, when, by the negro Babo's orders, he was carrying him to throw him overboard, alive; beside participating in the murder, before mentioned, of Don Alexandro Aranda, and others of the cabin-passengers; that, owing to the fury with which the Ashantees fought in the engagement with the boats, but this Lecbe and Yan survived; that Yan was bad as Lecbe; that Yan was the man who, by Babo's command, willingly prepared the skeleton of Don Alexandro, in a way the negroes afterwards told the depo-

nent, but which he, so long as reason is left him, can never divulge; that Yan and Lecbe were the two who, in a calm by night, riveted the skeleton to the bow; this also the negroes told him; that the negro Babo was he who traced the inscription below it; that the negro Babo was the plotter from first to last; he ordered every murder, and was the helm and keel of the revolt; that Atufal was his lieutenant in all; but Atufal, with his own hand, committed no murder; nor did the negro Babo; . . . that Atufal was shot, being killed in the fight with the boats, ere boarding; . . . that the negresses, of age, were knowing to the revolt, and testified themselves satisfied at the death of their master, Don Alexandro; that, had the negroes not restrained them, they would have tortured to death, instead of simply killing, the Spaniards slain by command of the negro Babo; that the negresses used their utmost influence to have the deponent made away with; that, in the various acts of murder, they sang songs and danced—not gaily, but solemnly; and before the engagement with the boats, as well as during the action, they sang melancholy songs to the negroes, and that this melancholy tone was more inflaming than a different one would have been, and was so intended; that all this is believed because the negroes have said it.
—that of the thirty-six men of the crew, exclusive of the passengers (all of whom are now dead), which the deponent had knowledge of, six only remained alive, with four cabin-boys and ship-boys, not included with the crew; . . .
—that the negroes broke an arm of one of the cabin-boys and gave him strokes with hatchets.

Then follow various random disclosures referring to various periods of time. The following are extracted:

—That during the presence of Captain Amasa Delano on board, some attempts were made by the sailors, and one by Hermenegildo Gandix, to convey hints to him of the true state of affairs; but that these attempts were ineffectual, owing to fear of incurring death, and, furthermore, owing to the devices which offered contradictions to the true state of affairs, as well as owing to the generosity and piety of Amasa Delano incapable of sounding such wickedness; . . . that Luys Galgo, a sailor about sixty years of age, and formerly of the king's navy, was one of those who sought to convey tokens to Captain Amasa Delano; but his intent, though undiscovered, being suspected, he was, on a pretense, made to retire out of sight, and at last into the hold, and there was made away with. This the negroes have since said; . . . that one of the ship-boys feeling, from Captain Amasa Delano's presence, some hopes of release, and not having enough prudence, dropped some chance-word respecting his expectations, which being overheard and understood by a slave-boy with whom he was eating at the time, the latter struck him on the head with a knife, inflicting a bad wound, but of which the boy is now healing; that likewise, not long before the ship was brought to anchor, one of the seamen, steering at the time, endangered himself by letting the blacks remark some expression in his countenance, arising from some cause similar to the above; but this sailor, by his heedful after conduct, escaped; . . . that these statements are made to show the court that from the beginning to the end of the revolt, it was impossible for the deponent and his men to act otherwise than they did; . . .

—that the third clerk, Hermenegildo Gandix, who before had been forced to live among the seamen, wearing a seaman's habit, and in all respects appearing to be one for the time; he, Gandix, was killed by a musket ball fired through mistake from the boats before boarding; having in his fright run up the mizzenrigging, calling to the boats— "don't board," lest upon their boarding the negroes should kill him; that this inducing the Americans to believe he some way favored the cause of the negroes, they fired two balls at him, so that he fell wounded from the rigging, and was drowned in the sea; . . . —that the young Don Joaquin, Marques de Aramboalaza, like Hermenegildo Gandix, the third clerk, was degraded to the office and appearance of a common seaman; that upon one occasion when Don Joaquin shrank, the negro Babo commanded the Ashantee Lecbe to take tar and heat it, and pour it upon Don Joaquin's hands; . . . —that Don Joaquin was killed owing to another mistake of the Americans, but one impossible to be avoided, as upon the approach of the boats, Don Joaquin, with a hatchet tied edge out and upright to his hand, was made by the negroes to appear on the bulwarks; whereupon, seen with arms in his hands and in a questionable attitude, he was shot for a renegade seaman; . . . —that on the person of Don Joaquin was found secreted a jewel, which, by papers that were discovered, proved to have been meant for the shrine of our Lady of Mercy in Lima; a votive offering, beforehand prepared and guarded, to attest his gratitude, when he should have landed in Peru, his last destination, for the safe conclusion of his entire voyage from Spain; . . . —that the jewel, with the other effects of the late Don Joaquin, is in the custody of the brethren of the Hospital de Sacerdotes, awaiting the disposition of the honorable court; . . . —that, owing to the condition of the deponent, as well as the haste in which the boats departed for the attack, the Americans were not forewarned that there were, among the apparent crew, a passenger and one of the clerks, disguised by the negro Babo; . . . —that, beside the negroes killed in the action, some were killed after the capture and re-anchoring at night, when shackled to the ring-bolts on deck; that these deaths were committed by the sailors, ere they could be prevented. That as soon as informed of it, Captain Amasa Delano used all his authority, and, in particular with his own hand, struck down Martinez Gola, who, having found a razor in the pocket of an old jacket of his, which one of the shackled negroes had on, was aiming it at the negro's throat; that the noble Captain Amasa Delano also wrenched from the hand of Bartholomew Barlo a dagger, secreted at the time of the massacre of the whites, with which he was in the act of stabbing a shackled negro, who, the same day, with another negro, had thrown him down and jumped upon him; . . . —that, for all the events, befalling through so long a time, during which the ship was in the hands of the negro Babo, he cannot here give account; but that, what he has said is the most substantial of what occurs to him at present, and is the truth under the oath which he has taken; which declaration he affirmed and ratified, after hearing it read to him.

He said that he is twenty-nine years of age, and broken in body and mind; that when finally dismissed by the court, he shall not return home to Chili, but betake himself to the monastery on Mount Agonia without; and signed with his honor, and crossed himself, and, for the time, departed as he came, in his litter, with the monk Infelez, to the Hospital de Sacerdotes.

BENITO CERENO

DOCTOR ROZAS.

If the Deposition have served as the key to fit into the lock of the complications which precede it, then, as a vault whose door has been flung back, the San Dominick's hull lies open to-day.

Hitherto the nature of this narrative, besides rendering the intricacies in the beginning unavoidable, has more or less required that many things, instead of being set down in the order of occurrence, should be retrospectively, or irregularly given; this last is the case with the following passages, which will conclude the account.

During the long, mild voyage to Lima, there was, as before hinted, a period during which the sufferer a little recovered his health, or, at least in some degree, his tranquillity. Ere the decided relapse which came, the two captains had many cordial conversations—their fraternal unreserve in singular contrast with former withdrawments.

Again and again it was repeated, how hard it had been to enact the part forced on the Spaniard by Babo.

"Ah, my dear friend," Don Benito once said, "at those very times when you thought me so morose and ungrateful, nay, when, as you now admit, you half thought me plotting your murder, at those very times my heart was frozen; I could not look at you, thinking of what, both on board this ship and your own, hung, from other hands, over my kind benefactor. And as God lives, Don Amasa, I know not whether desire for my own safety alone could have nerved me to that leap into your boat, had it not been for the thought that, did you, unenlightened, return to your ship, you, my best friend, with all who might be with you, stolen upon, that night, in your hammocks, would never in this world have wakened again. Do but think how you walked this deck, how you sat in this cabin, every inch of ground mined into honey-combs under you. Had I dropped the least hint, made the least advance towards an understanding between us, death, explosive death—yours as mine—would have ended the scene."

"True, true," cried Captain Delano, starting, "you have saved my life, Don Benito, more than I yours; saved it, too, against my knowledge and will."

"Nay, my friend," rejoined the Spaniard, courteous even to the point of religion, "God charmed your life, but you saved mine. To think of some things you did—those smilings and chattings, rash pointings and gesturings. For less than these, they slew my mate, Raneds; but you had the Prince of Heaven's safe-conduct through all ambuscades."

"Yes, all is owing to Providence, I know; but the temper of my mind that morning was more than commonly pleasant, while the sight of so much suffering, more apparent than real, added to my good-nature, compassion, and charity, happily interweaving the three. Had it been otherwise, doubtless, as you hint, some of my interferences might have ended unhappily enough. Besides, those feelings I spoke of enabled me to get the better of momentary distrust, at times when acuteness might have cost me my life, without saving another's. Only at the end did my suspicions get the better of me, and you know how wide of the mark they then proved."

"Wide, indeed," said Don Benito, sadly; "you were with me all day; stood with me, sat with me, talked with me, looked at me, ate with me, drank with me; and yet, your last act was to clutch for a monster, not only an innocent man, but the most pitiable of all men. To such degree may malign machinations and deceptions impose. So far may even the best man err, in judging the conduct of one with the recesses of whose condition he is not acquainted. But you were forced to it; and you were in time undeceived. Would that, in both respects, it was so ever, and with all men."

"You generalize, Don Benito; and mournfully enough. But the past is passed; why moralize upon it? Forget it. See, yon bright sun has forgotten it all, and the blue sea, and the blue sky; these have turned over new leaves."

"Because they have no memory," he dejectedly replied; "because they are not human."

"But these mild trades that now fan your cheek, do they not come with a human-like healing to you? Warm friends, steadfast friends are the trades."

"With their steadfastness they but waft me to my tomb, Señor," was the foreboding response.

"You are saved," cried Captain Delano, more and more astonished and pained; "you are saved: what has cast such a shadow upon you?"

"The negro."

There was silence, while the moody man sat, slowly and unconsciously gathering his mantle about him, as if it were a pall.

There was no more conversation that day.

But if the Spaniard's melancholy sometimes ended in muteness upon topics like the above, there were others upon which he never spoke at all; on which, indeed, all his old reserves were piled. Pass over the worst, and, only to elucidate, let an item or two of these be cited. The dress so precise and costly, worn by him on the day whose events have been narrated, had not willingly been put on. And that silver-mounted sword, apparent symbol of despotic command, was not, indeed, a sword, but the ghost of one. The scabbard, artificially stiffened, was empty.

As for the black—whose brain, not body, had schemed and led the revolt, with the plot—his slight frame, inadequate to that which it held, had at once yielded to the superior muscular strength of his captor, in the boat. Seeing all was over, he uttered no sound, and could not be forced to. His aspect seemed to say, since I cannot do deeds, I will not speak words. Put in irons in the hold, with the rest, he was carried to Lima. During the passage, Don Benito did not visit him. Nor then, nor at any time after, would he look at him. Before the tribunal he refused. When pressed by the judges he fainted. On the testimony of the sailors alone rested the legal identity of Babo.

Some months after, dragged to the gibbet at the tail of a mule, the black met his voiceless end. The body was burned to ashes; but for many days, the head, that hive of subtlety, fixed on a pole in the Plaza, met, unabashed, the gaze of the whites; and across the Plaza looked towards St. Bartholomew's church, in whose vaults slept then, as now, the recovered bones of Aranda: and across the Rimac bridge looked towards the monastery, on Mount Agonia without; where, three months after being dismissed by the court, Benito Cereno, borne on the bier, did, indeed, follow his leader.

1855

The Portent

John Brown was hanged on December 2, 1859. The contrast between the beautiful, fertile Shenandoah Valley and Brown's death is central to the poem.

The texts of this and the following short poems are from *Collected Poems of Herman Melville*, edited by Howard P. Vincent (Chicago, 1947).

Hanging from the beam,
  Slowly swaying (such the law),
Gaunt the shadow on your green,
  Shenandoah!
The cut is on the crown   5
  (Lo, John Brown),
And the stabs shall heal no more.

Hidden in the cap
  Is the anguish none can draw;
So your future veils its face,   10
  Shenandoah!
But with streaming beard is shown
  (Weird John Brown),
The meteor of the war.
1859   1866

A Utilitarian View of the Monitor's Fight

The subject of the poem is the naval engagement of March 9, 1862, between the Union ironclad *Monitor* and the Confederate *Merrimac* at Hampton Roads. Melville recognizes in the battle the increasingly impersonal and mechanical nature of war.

Plain be the phrase, yet apt the verse,
  More ponderous than nimble;
For since grimed War here laid aside
His painted pomp, 'twould ill befit
    Overmuch to ply   5
  The rhyme's barbaric cymbal.

Hail to victory without the gaud
  Of glory; zeal that needs no fans
Of banners; plain mechanic power
Plied cogently in War now placed—   10
    Where War belongs—
  Among the trades and artisans.

Yet this was battle, and intense—
  Beyond the strife of fleets heroic;
Deadlier, closer, calm 'mid storm;   15
No passion; all went on by crank,
    Pivot, and screw,
  And calculations of caloric.

Needless to dwell; the story's known.
  The ringing of those plates on plates   20
Still ringeth round the world—
The clangor of that blacksmiths' fray.
    The anvil-din
  Resounds this message from the Fates:

War yet shall be, and to the end;   25
  But war-paint shows the streaks of weather;
War yet shall be, but warriors
Are now but operatives; War's made
    Less grand than Peace,
  And a singe runs through lace and feather.   30
                                                      1866

Malvern Hill

Ye elms that wave on Malvern Hill[1]
  In prime of morn and May,
Recall ye how McClellan's men
    Here stood at bay?

Malvern Hill. [1] The site of an 1862 battle that marked the end of General George B. McClellan's unsuccessful peninsular campaign against Richmond.

While deep within yon forest dim   5
  Our rigid comrades lay—
Some with the cartridge in their mouth,
Others with fixed arms lifted South—
    Invoking so
The cypress glades? Ah wilds of woe!   10

The spires of Richmond, late beheld
  Through rifts in musket-haze,
Were closed from view in clouds of dust
    On leaf-walled ways,
Where streamed our wagons in caravan;   15
  And the Seven Nights and Days
Of march and fast, retreat and fight,
Pinched our grimed faces to ghastly plight—
    Does the elm wood
Recall the haggard beards of blood?   20

The battle-smoked flag, with stars eclipsed,
  We followed (it never fell!)—
In silence husbanded our strength—
    Received their yell;
Till on this slope we patient turned   25
  With cannon ordered well;
Reverse we proved was not defeat;
But ah, the sod what thousands meet!—
    Does Malvern Wood
Bethink itself, and muse and brood?   30

    We elms of Malvern Hill!
      Remember every thing;
    But sap the twig will fill:
    Wag the world how it will,
      Leaves must be green in Spring.   35
1862   1866

The Aeolian Harp

At the Surf Inn

List the harp[1] in window wailing
  Stirred by fitful gales from sea:
Shrieking up in mad crescendo—
  Dying down in plaintive key!

Listen: less a strain ideal   5
  Than Ariel's[2] rendering of the Real.
What that Real is, let hint
  A picture stamped in memory's mint.

The Aeolian Harp. [1] The Aeolian harp is a common metaphor for the poet's role in the creative process: the winds of inspiration cause him to sing or say his poem.
[2] The airy spirit in Shakespeare's *The Tempest.*

Braced well up, with beams aslant,
Betwixt the continents sails the *Phocion*, 10
To Baltimore bound from Alicant.
Blue breezy skies white fleeces fleck
Over the chill blue white-capped ocean:
From yard-arm comes—"Wreck ho, a wreck!"

Dismasted and adrift, 15
Long time a thing forsaken;
Overwashed by every wave
Like the slumbering kraken;
Heedless if the billow roar,
Oblivious of the lull, 20
Leagues and leagues from shoal or shore,
It swims—a levelled hull:
Bulwarks gone—a shaven wreck,
Nameless, and a grass-green deck.
A lumberman: perchance, in hold 25
Prostrate pines with hemlocks rolled.

It has drifted, waterlogged,
Till by trailing weeds beclogged:
    Drifted, drifted, day by day,
    Pilotless on pathless way. 30
It has drifted till each plank
Is oozy as the oyster-bank:
    Drifted, drifted, night by night,
    Craft that never shows a light;
Nor ever, to prevent worse knell, 35
Tolls in fog the warning bell.

From collision never shrinking,
Drive what may through darksome smother;
Saturate, but never sinking,
Fatal only to the *other!* 40
    Deadlier than the sunken reef
Since still the snare it shifteth,
    Torpid in dumb ambuscade
Waylayingly it drifteth.

    O, the sailors—O, the sails! 45
    O, the lost crews never heard of!
    Well the harp of Ariel wails
    Thoughts that tongue can tell no word of!
                                    1888

The Maldive Shark

About the Shark, phlegmatical one,
Pale sot of the Maldive sea,[1]
The sleek little pilot-fish, azure and slim,
How alert in attendance be.
From his saw-pit of mouth, from his charnel of
    maw 5

The Maldive Shark. [1] An archipelago in the Indian Ocean.

They have nothing of harm to dread,
But liquidly glide on his ghastly flank
Or before his Gorgonian head;
Or lurk in the port of serrated teeth
In white triple tiers of glittering gates, 10
And there find a haven when peril's abroad,
An asylum in jaws of the Fates!
They are friends; and friendly they guide him to
    prey,
Yet never partake of the treat—
Eyes and brains to the dotard lethargic and dull, 15
Pale ravener of horrible meat.
                                    1888

The Berg

(A Dream)

I saw a ship of martial build
(Her standards set, her brave apparel on)
Directed as by madness mere
Against a stolid iceberg steer, 4
Nor budge it, though the infatuate ship went down.
The impact made huge ice-cubes fall
Sullen, in tons that crashed the deck;
But that one avalanche was all—
No other movement save the foundering wreck.

Along the spurs of ridges pale, 10
Not any slenderest shaft and frail,
A prism over glass-green gorges lone,
Toppled; or lace of traceries fine,
Nor pendant drops in grot or mine
Were jarred, when the stunned ship went down. 15
Nor sole the gulls in cloud that wheeled
Circling one snow-flanked peak afar,
But nearer fowl the floes that skimmed
And crystal beaches, felt no jar.
No thrill transmitted stirred the lock 20
Of jack-straw needle-ice at base;
Towers undermined by waves—the block
Atilt impending—kept their place.
Seals, dozing sleek on sliddery ledges
Slipt never, when by loftier edges 25
Through very inertia overthrown,
The impetuous ship in bafflement went down.

Hard Berg (methought), so cold, so vast,
With mortal damps self-overcast;
Exhaling still thy dankish breath— 30
Adrift dissolving, bound for death;
Though lumpish thou, a lumbering one—
A lumbering lubbard loitering slow,
Impingers rue thee and go down,
Sounding thy precipice below, 35

Nor stir the slimy slug that sprawls
Along thy dead indifference of walls.

                                                    1888

"Healed of my hurt"

This is the seventh and last in a series of epigrams, called
"Pebbles," commenting on Melville's experiences with the
sea.

Healed of my hurt, I laud the inhuman Sea—
Yea, bless the Angels Four[1] that there convene;
For healed I am even by their pitiless breath
Distilled in wholesome dew named rosmarine.[2]

                                                    1888

Art

In placid hours well-pleased we dream
Of many a brave unbodied scheme.
But form to lend, pulsed life create,
What unlike things must meet and mate:
A flame to melt—a wind to freeze;   5
Sad patience—joyous energies;
Humility—yet pride and scorn;
Instinct and study; love and hate;
Audacity—reverence. These must mate,
And fuse with Jacob's[1] mystic heart,   10
To wrestle with the angel—Art.

                                                    1891

FROM *Clarel*

Clarel: A Poem and Pilgrimage in the Holy Land, published in 1876, is based on Melville's own pilgrimage to
Palestine in 1857. It is a long poem, running to 20,000
lines and 150 cantos. "The poem as narrative and symbol
is cast in the form of a quest. It focuses upon Clarel, a
young American ministerial student whose pursuit of theology has raised irritating questions rather than brought
spiritual peace. He meets Ruth, daughter of Nathan, an
American farmer converted to Judaism and Zionism. They
fall in love, but Nathan is killed by Arab bandits, and
Ruth, according to Jewish custom, is required to undergo
a period of retirement. During this interval Clarel becomes one of a group of pilgrims who set out on a ten-day
excursion that takes them to Jericho, the Jordan River, the
Dead Sea, and Siddim Plain, and the Monastery of Mar

Healed. [1] An allusion to Revelation vii.1–3. The four angels
held back the four winds, while another angel admonished
them not to let the earth be harmed by the winds' "pitiless
breath."

[2] Supposedly a restorative that promoted physical and
psychic health; rosemary.

Art. [1] Jacob's victory over the angel earned him a blessing
and a new name; Genesis xxxii.24–29.

Saba in the Mountains of Judah. Here they remain for
three days and then depart for Bethlehem. They return to
Jerusalem at sunrise on Ash Wednesday. In Clarel's absence Ruth has died of grief. His search for a resolution of
faith ends inconclusively." (Cohen, *Selected Poems*)

Text: W. E. Bezanson's edition of *Clarel* (New York,
1960).

II

xxxv. Prelusive

"Melville's reflections on the prints in the sequence 'Imaginary Prisons' of Giovanni Battista Piranesi follow Mortmain's drink from the Dead Sea and are prelusive to his
discussion of the depravities ('not all carnal harlotry,/But
sins refined, crimes of the spirit') which brought about the
destruction of Sodom. Piranesi's set of sixteen etchings was
executed in the 1740's when he was about twenty-five.
Highly romantic and theatrical, they captivated Coleridge,
and his descriptions of them, as recorded in De Quincey's
Confessions of an English Opium Eater (1822), are close in
language and spirit to Melville's. In the Victorian period,
however, interest in Piranesi declined severely. Ruskin ig-
nores him, but Melville found in the 'Imaginary Prisons' a
visual expression of the 'mystery of iniquity' which so
intrigued him." (Cohen, *Selected Poems*)

In Piranezi's rarer prints,
Interiors measurelessly strange,
Where the distrustful thought may range
Misgiving still—what mean the hints?
Stairs upon stairs which dim ascend   5
In series from plunged Bastiles drear—
Pit under pit; long tier on tier
Of shadowed galleries which impend
Over cloisters, cloisters without end;
The height, the depth—the far, the near;   10
Ring-bolts to pillars in vaulted lanes,
And dragging Rhadamanthine[1] chains;
These less of wizard influence lend
Than some allusive chambers closed.
Those wards of hush are not disposed   15
In gibe of goblin fantasy—
Grimace—unclean diablery:
Thy wings, Imagination, span
Ideal truth in fable's seat:
The thing implied is one with man,   20
His penetralia of retreat—
The heart, with labyrinths replete:
In freaks of intimation see
Paul's "mystery of iniquity:"
Involved indeed, a blur of dream;   25
As, awed by scruple and restricted
In first design, or interdicted
By fate and warnings as might seem;
The inventor miraged all the maze,

Clarel. [1] Rhadamanthus, in Greek mythology, was one of the
judges of the dead in Hades.

Obscured it with prudential haze;   30
Nor less, if subject unto question,
The egg left, egg of the suggestion.

    Dwell on those etchings in the night,
Those touches bitten in the steel
By aqua-fortis, till ye feel   35
The Pauline text in gray of light;
Turn hither then and read aright.

    For ye who green or gray retain
Childhood's illusion, or but feign;
As bride and suite let pass a bier—   40
So pass the coming canto here.

xxxvi. Sodom

Full night. The moon has yet to rise;
The air oppresses, and the skies
Reveal beyond the lake afar
One solitary tawny star—
Complexioned so by vapors dim,   5
Whereof some hang above the brim
And nearer waters of the lake,
Whose bubbling air-beads mount and break
As charged with breath of things alive.

    In talk about the Cities Five   10
Engulfed, on beach they linger late.
And he, the quaffer of the brine,
Puckered with that heart-wizening wine
Of bitterness, among them sate
Upon a camel's skull, late dragged   15
From forth the wave, the eye-pits slagged
With crusted salt.—"What star is yon?"
And pointed to that single one
Befogged above the sea afar.
"It might be Mars, so red it shines,"   20
One answered; "duskily it pines
In this strange mist."—"It is the star
Called Wormwood.[2] Some hearts die in thrall
Of waters which yon star makes gall;"
And, lapsing, turned, and made review   25
Of what that wickedness might be
Which down on these ill precincts drew
The flood, the fire; put forth new plea,
Which not with Writ might disagree;
Urged that those malefactors stood   30
Guilty of sins scarce scored as crimes
In any statute known, or code—
Nor now, nor in the former times:
Things hard to prove: decorum's wile,
Malice discreet, judicious guile;   35
Good done with ill intent—reversed:
Best deeds designed to serve the worst;
And hate which under life's fair hue

[2] See Revelation viii.10–11.

Prowls like the shark in sunned Pacific blue.
    He paused, and under stress did bow,   40
Lank hands enlocked across the brow.[3]
        "Nay, nay, thou sea,
'Twas not all carnal harlotry,
But sins refined, crimes of the spirit,
Helped earn that doom ye here inherit: 45
Doom well imposed, though sharp and dread,
In some god's reign, some god long fled.—
Thou gaseous puff of mineral breath
Mephitical; thou swooning flaw
That fann'st me from this pond of death;   50
Wert thou that venomous small thing
Which tickled with the poisoned straw?
Thou, stronger, but who yet couldst start
Shrinking with sympathetic sting,
While willing the uncompunctious dart!   55
Ah, ghosts of Sodom, how ye thrill
About me in this peccant air,
Conjuring yet to spare, but spare!
Fie, fie, that didst in formal will
Plot piously the posthumous snare.   60
And thou, the mud-flow—evil mass
Of surest-footed sluggishness
Swamping the nobler breed—art there?
Moan, Burker[4] of kind heart: all's known
To Him; with thy connivers, moan.—   65
Sinners—expelled, transmuted souls
Blown in these airs, or whirled in shoals
Of gurgles which your gasps send up,
Or on this crater marge and cup
Slavered in slime, or puffed in stench—   70
Not ever on the tavern bench
Ye lolled. Few dicers here, few sots,
Few sluggards, and no idiots.
'Tis *thou* who servedst Mammon's hate
Or greed through forms which holy are—   75
Black slaver steering by a star,
'Tis *thou*—and all like thee in state.
Who knew the world, yet varnished it;
Who traded on the coast of crime
Though landing not; who did outwit   80
Justice, his brother, and the time—
These, chiefly these, to doom submit.
But who the manifold may tell?
And sins there be inscrutable,
Unutterable."   85
        Ending there
He shrank, and like an osprey gray

[3] "Mortmain [the speaker], a tormented Swede, was once an idealistic revolutionary but has been disillusioned to such an extent that he can do little but rail at what strikes him as the evil in men and turn self-destructively upon himself. What hurts Mortmain most is his feeling that the inevitable result of the emulation of Christ on earth is crucifixion." (Cohen)

[4] "William Burke was executed in 1829 for murdering by suffocation in order not to mar a body meant for dissection." (Bezanson)

Peered on the wave. His hollow stare
Marked then some smaller bubbles play
In cluster silvery like spray: 90
"Be these the beads on the wives'-wine,
Tofana-brew?[5]—O fair Medea—
O soft man-eater, furry-fine:
Oh, be thou Jael, be thou Leah[6]—
Unfathomably shallow!—No!   95
Nearer the core than man can go
Or Science get—nearer the slime
Of nature's rudiments and lime
In chyle before the bone. Thee, thee,
In thee the filmy cell is spun—   100
The mould thou art of what men be:
Events are all in thee begun—
By thee, through thee!—Undo, undo,
Prithee, undo, and still renew
The fall forever!"   105
          On his throne
He lapsed; and muffled came the moan
How multitudinous in sound,

[5] Wine from the Tophenna near Constantinople.
[6] Women involved in deceit, treachery, and murder. Medea murdered her rival for Jason and her two children. Jael killed Sisera by hammering a spike through his head while he slept (Judges iv.17-22). Leah was married to Jacob by deception (Genesis xxix.13-30).

From Sodom's wave. He glanced around:
They all had left him, one by one.   110
Was it because he open threw
The inmost to the outward view?
Or did but pain at frenzied thought,
Prompt to avoid him, since but naught
In such case might remonstrance do?   115
But none there ventured idle plea,
Weak sneer, or fraudful levity.

Two spirits, hovering in remove,
Sad with inefficacious love,
Here sighed debate: "Ah Zoima,[7] say;   120
Be it far from me to impute a sin,
But may a sinless nature win
Those deeps he knows?"—"Sin shuns that way;
Sin acts the sin, but flees the thought
That sweeps the abyss that sin has wrought.   125
Innocent be the heart and true—
Howe'er it feed on bitter bread—
That, venturous through the Evil led,
Moves as along the ocean's bed
Amid the dragon's staring crew."   130
          1876

[7] Bezanson guesses that this is a coined name meaning life or life-force.

JOHN GREENLEAF WHITTIER [1807–1892]

BROUGHT UP ON A FARM tilled by his ancestors as far back as 1647, Whittier lived his span of eighty-five years at Haverhill and Amesbury in northeastern Massachusetts. Life meant to him for many years hard toil and poverty, and always frail health, but also the charms of nature, the happiness of human affection, and the consolation of the Quaker faith of his fathers. It meant, too, dedicated service in the cause of abolition of slavery, and the satisfaction of poetic creation.

At the age of fourteen Whittier read Robert Burns and began to scribble verses. Some of them appeared in *The Free Press,* a weekly edited in Newburyport by William Lloyd Garrison. Garrison became interested in his young contributor and urged the boy's parents to send him to Haverhill Academy. There he studied for only two terms; mainly he was self-educated. By turns he was a shoemaker, a teacher, an editor of journals in Boston and Hartford. In 1831 he published his first book, *Legends of New England,* and two years later entered the lists for abolition with a pamphlet on *Justice and Expediency.*

The next three decades, the most vigorous of his life, Whittier gave to his "opinion mill." He was a delegate to the antislavery convention in 1833 in Philadelphia. He was in the Massachusetts legislature in 1835 and 1836. He argued against slavery in prose, verse, and speech, risked his life before hostile mobs, gave up his political career, edited *The*

Pennsylvania Freeman. In 1846 he published *Voices of Freedom,* two years later a collected edition of his *Poems,* and after two more years *Songs of Labor and Other Poems.*

The War of the Secession ended, Whittier settled down to the peaceful years he had earned. *Snow-Bound,* a deservedly popular success, was his first financially rewarding volume. Many other publications followed, including one of his best, *The Pennsylvania Pilgrim,* and at length the Riverside Edition of his verse and prose in seven volumes.

His poetry shows clearly the modern concern with "the near, the low, the common" of which Emerson had spoken. It is largely a poetry of the humble: of the pleasures of labor, of the evil of slavery; a poetry of simple home life on the farm; a poetry of popular, regional legends; a poetry of simple religion, the love of God and of man. The spirit of Whittier was close to that of Burns, Scotland's poet of the people, and to that of John Woolman, the Quaker tailor whose *Journal* he edited. Because his verse was often sentimental and moralistic, as well as facile and diffuse, it now seems to us to have been long overvalued. Yet he rose above his usual mediocrity often enough to achieve a small body of genuine poetry that has latterly been undervalued.

Text: *The Writings of John Greenleaf Whittier,* Riverside Edition, edited by Horace E. Scudder (Boston, 1888–89).

Further reading: Whitman Bennett, *Whittier, Bard of Freedom,* 1941. J. A. Pollard, *Whittier, Friend of Man,* 1949. John B. Pickard, *John Greenleaf Whittier,* 1961. Edward C. Wagenknecht, *John Greenleaf Whittier,* 1967.

First-Day Thoughts

Christian attitudes and allusions enter into many of Whittier's poems, regardless of subject. They also become the subject of a considerable group of poems. In "First-Day Thoughts" we see Whittier take his place in a Quaker meeting. The poem is essentially a prayer.

In calm and cool and silence, once again
  I find my old accustomed place among
  My brethren, where, perchance, no human
      tongue
  Shall utter words; where never hymn is sung,   4
  Nor deep-toned organ blown, nor censer swung,
Nor dim light falling through the pictured pane!
There, syllabled by silence, let me hear
The still small voice which reached the prophet's
      ear;
Read in my heart a still diviner law
Than Israel's leader on his tables saw!   10
There let me strive with each besetting sin,
  Recall my wandering fancies, and restrain
  The sore disquiet of a restless brain;
  And, as the path of duty is made plain,
May grace be given that I may walk therein,   15
  Not like the hireling, for his selfish gain,
With backward glances and reluctant tread,
Making a merit of his coward dread,
  But, cheerful, in the light around me thrown,
  Walking as one to pleasant service led;   20
  Doing God's will as if it were my own,
Yet trusting not in mine, but in His strength alone!

1852

Laus Deo!

"On hearing the bells ring on the passage of the constitutional amendment abolishing slavery."—Whittier's note.

In *Laus Deo!* (Praise be to God!), Whittier's emotion expressed itself in a strongly marked, trochaic meter and in Old Testament echoes: lines 19–20, Job xxxviii.1; line 24, Psalms cvii.16; lines 27–30, Exodus xv.21; lines 34–36, Isaiah xxiii.11; lines 40–41, Numbers xvii.8.

  It is done!
  Clang of bell and roar of gun
Send the tidings up and down.
  How the belfries rock and reel!
  How the great guns, peal on peal,   5
Fling the joy from town to town!

  Ring, O bells!
  Every stroke exulting tells
Of the burial hour of crime.
  Loud and long, that all may hear,   10
  Ring for every listening ear
Of Eternity and Time!

  Let us kneel:
  God's own voice is in that peal,
And this spot is holy ground.   15
  Lord, forgive us! What are we,
  That our eyes this glory see,
That our ears have heard the sound!

  For the Lord
  On the whirlwind is abroad;   20

In the earthquake He has spoken:
He has smitten with His thunder
The iron walls asunder,
And the gates of brass are broken!

Loud and long   25
Lift the old exulting song;
Sing with Miriam by the sea,
He has cast the mighty down;
Horse and rider sink and drown;
"He hath triumphed gloriously!"   30

Did we dare,
In our agony of prayer,
Ask for more than He has done?
When was ever His right hand
Over any time or land   35
Stretched as now beneath the sun?

How they pale,
Ancient myth and song and tale,
In this wonder of our days,
When the cruel rod of war   40
Blossoms white with righteous law,
And the wrath of man is praise!

Blotted out!
All within and all about
Shall a fresher life begin;   45
Freer breathe the universe
As it rolls its heavy curse
On the dead and buried sin!

It is done!
In the circuit of the sun   50
Shall the sound thereof go forth.
It shall bid the sad rejoice,
It shall give the dumb a voice,
It shall belt with joy the earth!

Ring and swing,   55
Bells of joy! On morning's wing
Send the song of praise abroad!
With a sound of broken chains
Tell the nations that He reigns,
Who alone is Lord and God!   60
1865

Snow-Bound

A Winter Idyl

This idyl (little picture) of rural New England has the poetic warmth of a long cherished memory. "Out of his loyalty, not alone to vanished faces, but to the fulfillment of personal relationships which his boyhood home symbolized, he wrote *Snow-Bound* (1866), the finest of his Yankee idyls, a faultless integration of precisely remembered detail and tender devotion. In a general way this poem is the New England analogue of Burns' 'The Cotter's Saturday Night,' with which it compares favorably both for its wealth of homely description and for its genuineness of sentiment. But against the background of a nation fast adapting itself to urban ways the poem appears something more than a cold pastoral. It is a quiet tribute to a form of civilized living that was passing. Here embodied in glowing terms was the Jeffersonian dream of the virtuous small landholder, beholden to no one and winning an honest, laborious livelihood from the soil." (G. F. Whicher in *Literary History of the United States*)

As the Spirits of Darkness be stronger in the dark, so Good Spirits, which be Angels of Light, are augmented not only by the Divine light of the Sun, but also by our common Wood Fire: and as the Celestial Fire drives away dark spirits, so also this our Fire of Wood doth the same—COR. AGRIPPA, *Occult Philosophy*, Book I. ch. v.[1]

Announced by all the trumpets of the sky,
Arrives the snow, and, driving o'er the fields,
Seems nowhere to alight the whited air
Hides hills and woods, the river and the heaven,
And veils the farm-house at the garden's end.
The sled and traveller stopped, the courier's feet
Delayed, all friends shut out, the housemates sit
Around the radiant fireplace, enclosed
In a tumultuous privacy of storm.
—Emerson, *The Snow-Storm*

The sun that brief December day
Rose cheerless over hills of gray,
And, darkly circled, gave at noon
A sadder light than waning moon.
Slow tracing down the thickening sky   5
Its mute and ominous prophecy,
A portent seeming less than threat,
It sank from sight before it set.
A chill no coat, however stout,
Of homespun stuff could quite shut out,   10
A hard, dull bitterness of cold,
That checked, mid-vein, the circling race
Of life-blood in the sharpened face,
The coming of the snow-storm told.
The wind blew east; we heard the roar   15
Of Ocean on his wintry shore,
And felt the strong pulse throbbing there
Beat with low rhythm our inland air.

Meanwhile we did our nightly chores,—
Brought in the wood from out of doors,   20
Littered the stalls, and from the mows
Raked down the herd's-grass for the cows:
Heard the horse whinnying for his corn;

Snow-Bound. [1] Whittier said in his introduction that he had the book (dated 1651) which a local "sorcerer" used as a "conjuring book." It was apparently the work of Henricus Cornelius Agrippa (1486-1535), a scholar and writer about the occult.

And, sharply clashing horn on horn,
Impatient down the stanchion rows 25
The cattle shake their walnut bows;
While, peering from his early perch
Upon the scaffold's pole of birch,
The cock his crested helmet bent
And down his querulous challenge sent. 30

Unwarmed by any sunset light
The gray day darkened into night,
A night made hoary with the swarm
And whirl-dance of the blinding storm,
As zigzag, wavering to and fro, 35
Crossed and recrossed the wingèd snow:
And ere the early bedtime came
The white drift piled the window-frame,
And through the glass the clothes-line posts
Looked in like tall and sheeted ghosts. 40

So all night long the storm roared on:
The morning broke without a sun;
In tiny spherule traced with lines
Of Nature's geometric signs,
In starry flake, and pellicle, 45
All day the hoary meteor fell;
And, when the second morning shone,
We looked upon a world unknown,
On nothing we could call our own.
Around the glistening wonder bent 50
The blue walls of the firmament,
No cloud above, no earth below,—
A universe of sky and snow!
The old familiar sights of ours
Took marvellous shapes; strange domes and towers
Rose up where sty or corn-crib stood, 56
Or garden-wall, or belt of wood;
A smooth white mound the brush-pile showed,
A fenceless drift what once was road;
The bridle-post an old man sat 60
With loose-flung coat and high cocked hat;
The well-curb had a Chinese roof;
And even the long sweep, high aloof,
In its slant splendor, seemed to tell
Of Pisa's leaning miracle. 65

A prompt, decisive man, no breath
Our father wasted: "Boys, a path!"
Well pleased, (for when did farmer boy
Count such a summons less than joy?)
Our buskins on our feet we drew; 70
With mittened hands, and caps drawn low,
To guard our necks and ears from snow,
We cut the solid whiteness through.
And, where the drift was deepest, made
A tunnel walled and overlaid 75
With dazzling crystal: we had read
Of rare Aladdin's wondrous cave,

And to our own his name we gave,
With many a wish the luck were ours
To test his lamp's supernal powers. 80
We reached the barn with merry din,
And roused the prisoned brutes within.
The old horse thrust his long head out,
And grave with wonder gazed about;
The cock his lusty greeting said, 85
And forth his speckled harem led;
The oxen lashed their tails, and hooked,
And mild reproach of hunger looked;
The hornèd patriarch of the sheep,
Like Egypt's Amun roused from sleep, 90
Shook his sage head with gesture mute,
And emphasized with stamp of foot.

All day the gusty north-wind bore
The loosening drift its breath before;
Low circling round its southern zone, 95
The sun through dazzling snow-mist shone.
No church-bell lent its Christian tone
To the savage air, no social smoke
Curled over woods of snow-hung oak.
A solitude made more intense 100
By dreary-voicèd elements,
The shrieking of the mindless wind,
The moaning tree-boughs swaying blind,
And on the glass the unmeaning beat
Of ghostly finger-tips of sleet. 105
Beyond the circle of our hearth
No welcome sound of toil or mirth
Unbound the spell, and testified
Of human life and thought outside.
We minded that the sharpest ear 110
The buried brooklet could not hear,
The music of whose liquid lip
Had been to us companionship,
And, in our lonely life, had grown
To have an almost human tone. 115

As night drew on, and, from the crest
Of wooded knolls that ridged the west,
The sun, a snow-blown traveller, sank
From sight beneath the smothering bank,
We piled, with care, our nightly stack 120
Of wood against the chimney-back,—
The oaken log, green, huge, and thick,
And on its top the stout back-stick;
The knotty forestick laid apart,
And filled between with curious art 125
The ragged brush; then, hovering near,
We watched the first red blaze appear,
Heard the sharp crackle, caught the gleam
On whitewashed wall and sagging beam,
Until the old, rude-furnished room 130
Burst, flower-like, into rosy bloom;
While radiant with a mimic flame

Outside the sparkling drift became,
And through the bare-boughed lilac-tree
Our own warm hearth seemed blazing free. 135
The crane and pendent trammels showed,
The Turks' heads on the andirons glowed:
While childish fancy, prompt to tell
The meaning of the miracle,
Whispered the old rhyme: "*Under the tree,* 140
When fire outdoors burns merrily,
There the witches are making tea."

The moon above the eastern wood
Shone at its full; the hill-range stood
Transfigured in the silver flood, 145
Its blown snows flashing cold and keen,
Dead white, save where some sharp ravine
Took shadow, or the sombre green
Of hemlocks turned to pitchy black
Against the whiteness at their back. 150
For such a world and such a night
Most fitting that unwarming light,
Which only seemed where'er it fell
To make the coldness visible.

Shut in from all the world without, 155
We sat the clean-winged hearth about,
Content to let the north-wind roar
In baffled rage at pane and door,
While the red logs before us beat
The frost-line back with tropic heat; 160
And ever, when a louder blast
Shook beam and rafter as it passed,
The merrier up its roaring draught
The great throat of the chimney laughed;
The house-dog on his paws outspread 165
Laid to the fire his drowsy head,
The cat's dark silhouette on the wall
A couchant tiger's seemed to fall;
And, for the winter fireside meet,
Between the andirons' straddling feet, 170
The mug of cider simmered slow,
The apples sputtered in a row,
And, close at hand, the basket stood
With nuts from brown October's wood.

What matter how the night behaved? 175
What matter how the north-wind raved?
Blow high, blow low, not all its snow
Could quench our hearth-fire's ruddy glow.
O Time and Change!—with hair as gray
As was my sire's that winter day, 180
How strange it seems, with so much gone
Of life and love, to still live on!
Ah, brother![2] only I and thou
Are left of all that circle now,—

The dear home faces whereupon 185
That fitful firelight paled and shone.
Henceforward, listen as we will,
The voices of that hearth are still;
Look where we may, the wide earth o'er
Those lighted faces smile no more. 190
We read the paths their feet have worn,
We sit beneath their orchard trees,
We hear, like them, the hum of bees
And rustle of the bladed corn;
We turn the pages that they read, 195
Their written words we linger o'er,
But in the sun they cast no shade,
No voice is heard, no sign is made,
No step is on the conscious floor!
Yet Love will dream, and Faith will trust, 200
(Since He who knows our need is just,)
That somehow, somewhere, meet we must.
Alas for him who never sees
The stars shine through his cypress-trees!
Who, hopeless, lays his dead away, 205
Nor looks to see the breaking day
Across the mournful marbles play!
Who hath not learned, in hours of faith,
The truth to flesh and sense unknown,
That Life is ever lord of Death, 210
And Love can never lose its own!

We sped the time with stories old,
Wrought puzzles out, and riddles told,
Or stammered from our school-book lore[3]
"The Chief of Gambia's golden shore." 215
How often since, when all the land
Was clay in Slavery's shaping hand,
As if a far-blown trumpet stirred
The languorous sin-sick air, I heard:
"*Does not the voice of reason cry,* 220
Claim the first right which Nature gave,
From the red scourge of bondage fly,
Nor reign to live a burdened slave!"[4]
Our father rode again his ride
On Memphremagog's wooded side; 225
Sat down again to moose and samp
In trapper's hut and Indian camp;
Lived o'er the old idyllic ease
Beneath St. François' hemlock-trees;[5]
Again for him the moonlight shone 230
On Norman cap and bodiced zone;
Again he heard the violin play
Which led the village dance away,

[2] Matthew Franklin Whittier (1812–83), who shared his brother's strong antislavery sentiments.

[3] The book, according to Whittier, was Caleb Bingham's *The American Preceptor.*
[4] The fourth stanza of a poem by Sarah Wentworth Morton called "The African Chief," published in Bingham.
[5] Whittier's father had traveled to Canada as a youth. Memphremagog is a lake between Vermont and Canada. St. Francis is a lake in Quebec.

And mingled in its merry whirl
The grandam and the laughing girl.   235
Or, nearer home, our steps he led
Where Salisbury's level marshes spread
   Mile-wide as flies the laden bee;
Where merry mowers, hale and strong,
Swept, scythe on scythe, their swaths along   240
   The low green prairies of the sea.
We shared the fishing off Boar's Head,
   And round the rocky Isles of Shoals
   The hake-broil on the drift-wood coals;
The chowder on the sand-beach made,   245
Dipped by the hungry, steaming hot,
With spoons of clam-shell from the pot.
We heard the tales of witchcraft old,
And dream and sign and marvel told
To sleepy listeners as they lay   250
Stretched idly on the salted hay,
Adrift along the winding shores,
When favoring breezes deigned to blow
The square sail of the gundelow
And idle lay the useless oars.   255

Our mother, while she turned her wheel
Or run the new-knit stocking-heel,
Told how the Indian hordes came down
At midnight on Cocheco town,
And how her own great-uncle bore   260
His cruel scalp-mark to fourscore.[6]
Recalling, in her fitting phrase,
   So rich and picturesque and free,
   (The common unrhymed poetry
Of simple life and country ways,)   265
The story of her early days,—
She made us welcome to her home;
Old hearths grew wide to give us room;
We stole with her a frightened look
At the gray wizard's conjuring-book,   270
The fame whereof went far and wide
Through all the simple country side;
We heard the hawks at twilight play,
The boat-horn on Piscataqua,[7]
The loon's weird laughter far away;   275
We fished her little trout-brook, knew
What flowers in wood and meadow grew,
What sunny hillsides autumn-brown
She climbed to shake the ripe nuts down,
Saw where in sheltered cove and bay   280
The ducks' black squadron anchored lay,
And heard the wild-geese calling loud
Beneath the gray November cloud.

Then, haply, with a look more grave,
And soberer tone, some tale she gave   285

[6] His mother "was born in the Indian-haunted region of
Somerset, New Hampshire." (Whittier)

[7] A river between New Hampshire and Maine.

From painful Sewel's[8] ancient tome,
Beloved in every Quaker home,
Of faith fire-winged by martyrdom,
Or Chalkley's Journal,[9] old and quaint,—
Gentlest of skippers, rare sea-saint!—   290
Who, when the dreary calms prevailed,
And water-butt and bread-cask failed,
And cruel, hungry eyes pursued
His portly presence mad for food,
With dark hints muttered under breath   295
Of casting lots for life or death,
Offered, if Heaven withheld supplies,
To be himself the sacrifice.
Then, suddenly, as if to save
The good man from his living grave,   300
A ripple on the water grew,
A school of porpoise flashed in view.
"Take, eat," he said, "and be content;
These fishes in my stead are sent
By Him who gave the tangled ram   305
To spare the child of Abraham."

Our uncle, innocent of books,
Was rich in lore of fields and brooks,
The ancient teachers never dumb
Of Nature's unhoused lyceum.   310
In moons and tides and weather wise,
He read the clouds as prophecies,
And foul or fair could well divine,
By many an occult hint and sign,
Holding the cunning-warded keys   315
To all the woodcraft mysteries;
Himself to Nature's heart so near
That all her voices in his ear
Of beast or bird had meanings clear,
Like Apollonius[10] of old,   320
Who knew the tales the sparrows told,
Or Hermes,[11] who interpreted
What the sage cranes of Nilus said;
A simple, guileless, childlike man,
Content to live where life began;   325
Strong only on his native grounds,
The little world of sights and sounds
Whose girdle was the parish bounds,
Whereof his fondly partial pride
The common features magnified,   330
As Surrey hills to mountains grew

[8] William Sewel (1653–1720), a Dutch Quaker historian,
author of *History of the Rise, Increase, and Progress of the . . .
Quakers.*

[9] Thomas Chalkley (1675–1741), a sea captain and Quaker
zealot, describes this incident in his *Journal* (1747).

[10] Probably Apollonius of Tyana, a philosopher of the first
century A.D., who supposedly had magical and wonder-working powers.

[11] Legendary author of Hermetic Books, supposedly the author of all mystical doctrines.

In White of Selborne's[12] loving view,—
He told how teal and loon he shot,
And how the eagle's eggs he got,
The feats on pond and river done,   335
The prodigies of rod and gun;
Till, warming with the tales he told,
Forgotten was the outside cold,
The bitter wind unheeded blew,
From ripening corn the pigeons flew,   340
The partridge drummed i' the wood, the mink
Went fishing down the river-brink;
In fields with bean or clover gay,
The woodchuck, like a hermit gray,
   Peered from the doorway of his cell;   345
The muskrat plied the mason's trade,
And tier by tier his mud-walls laid;
And from the shagbark overhead
   The grizzled squirrel dropped his shell.

Next, the dear aunt, whose smile of cheer   350
And voice in dreams I see and hear,—
The sweetest woman ever Fate
Perverse denied a household mate,
Who, lonely, homeless, not the less
Found peace in love's unselfishness,   355
And welcome whereso'er she went,
A calm and gracious element,
Whose presence seemed the sweet income
And womanly atmosphere of home—
Called up her girlhood memories,   360
The huskings and the apple-bees,
The sleigh-rides and the summer sails,
Weaving through all the poor details
And homespun warp of circumstance
A golden woof-thread of romance.   365
For well she kept her genial mood
And simple faith of maidenhood;
Before her still a cloud-land lay,
The mirage loomed across her way;
The morning dew, that dries so soon   370
With others, glistened at her noon;
Through years of toil and soil and care,
From glossy tress to thin gray hair,
All unprofaned she held apart
The virgin fancies of the heart.   375
Be shame to him of woman born
Who hath for such but thought of scorn.

There, too, our elder sister plied
Her evening task the stand beside;
A full, rich nature, free to trust,   380
Truthful and almost sternly just,
Impulsive, earnest, prompt to act,
And make her generous thought a fact,

Keeping with many a light disguise
The secret of self-sacrifice.   385
O heart sore-tried! thou hast the best
That Heaven itself could give thee,—rest,
Rest from all bitter thoughts and things!
   How many a poor one's blessing went
   With thee beneath the low green tent   390
Whose curtain never outward swings!

As one who held herself a part
Of all she saw, and let her heart
   Against the household bosom lean,
Upon the motley-braided mat   395
Our youngest and our dearest sat,
Lifting her large, sweet, asking eyes,
   Now bathed in the unfading green
And holy peace of Paradise.[13]
Oh, looking from some heavenly hill,   400
   Or from the shade of saintly palms,
   Or silver reach of river calms,
Do those large eyes behold me still?
With me one little year ago:—
The chill weight of the winter snow   405
   For months upon her grave has lain;
And now, when summer south-winds blow
   And brier and harebell bloom again,
I tread the pleasant paths we trod,
I see the violet-sprinkled sod   410
Whereon she leaned, too frail and weak
The hillside flowers she loved to seek,
Yet following me where'er I went
With dark eyes full of love's content.
The birds are glad; the brier-rose fills   415
The air with sweetness; all the hills
Stretch green to June's unclouded sky;
But still I wait with ear and eye
For something gone which should be nigh,
A loss in all familiar things,   420
In flower that blooms, and bird that sings.
And yet, dear heart! remembering thee,
   Am I not richer than of old?
Safe in thy immortality,
   What change can reach the wealth I hold?   425
   What chance can mar the pearl and gold
Thy love hath left in trust with me?
And while in life's late afternoon,
   Where cool and long the shadows grow,
I walk to meet the night that soon   430
   Shall shape and shadow overflow,
I cannot feel that thou art far,
Since near at need the angels are;
And when the sunset gates unbar,
   Shall I not see thee waiting stand,   435
And, white against the evening star,
   The welcome of thy beckoning hand?

---

[12] Gilbert White (1720-93), curate of Selborne, who wrote
The Natural History and Antiquities of Selborne, published
1789.

[13] His younger sister, Elizabeth Hussey Whittier, died in
1864.

Brisk wielder of the birch and rule,
The master of the district school
Held at the fire his favored place,   440
Its warm glow lit a laughing face
Fresh-hued and fair, where scarce appeared
The uncertain prophecy of beard.
He teased the mitten-blinded cat,
Played cross-pins on my uncle's hat,   445
Sang songs, and told us what befalls
In classic Dartmouth's college halls.
Born the wild Northern hills among,
From whence his yeoman father wrung
By patient toil subsistence scant,   450
Not competence and yet not want,
He early gained the power to pay
His cheerful, self-reliant way;
Could doff at ease his scholar's gown
To peddle wares from town to town;   455
Or through the long vacation's reach
In lonely lowland districts teach,
Where all the droll experience found
At stranger hearths in boarding round,
The moonlit skater's keen delight,   460
The sleigh-drive through the frosty night,
The rustic-party, with its rough
Accompaniment of blind-man's-buff,
And whirling-plate, and forfeits paid,
His winter task a pastime made.   465
Happy the snow-locked homes wherein
He tuned his merry violin,
Or played the athlete in the barn,
Or held the good dame's winding-yarn,
Or mirth-provoking versions told   470
Of classic legends rare and old,
Wherein the scenes of Greece and Rome
Had all the commonplace of home,
And little seemed at best the odds
'Twixt Yankee pedlers and old gods;   475
Where Pindus-born Arachthus[14] took
The guise of any grist-mill brook,
And dread Olympus at his will
Became a huckleberry hill.

A careless boy that night he seemed;   480
    But at his desk he had the look
And air of one who wisely schemed,
    And hostage from the future took
    In trainèd thought and lore of book.
Large-brained, clear-eyed, of such as he   485
Shall Freedom's young apostles be,
Who, following in War's bloody trail,
Shall every lingering wrong assail;
All chains from limb and spirit strike,
Uplift the black and white alike;   490
Scatter before their swift advance

The darkness and the ignorance,
The pride, the lust, the squalid sloth,
Which nurtured Treason's monstrous growth,
Made murder pastime, and the hell   495
Of prison-torture possible;
The cruel lie of caste refute,
Old forms remould, and substitute
For Slavery's lash the freeman's will,
For blind routine, wise-handed skill;   500
A school-house plant on every hill,
Stretching in radiate nerve-lines thence
The quick wires of intelligence;
Till North and South together brought
Shall own the same electric thought,   505
In peace a common flag salute,
And, side by side in labor's free
And unresentful rivalry,
Harvest the fields wherein they fought.

Another guest[15] that winter night   510
Flashed back from lustrous eyes the light.
Unmarked by time, and yet not young,
The honeyed music of her tongue
And words of meekness scarcely told
A nature passionate and bold,   515
Strong, self-concentred, spurning guide,
Its milder features dwarfed beside
Her unbent will's majestic pride.
She sat among us, at the best,
A not unfeared, half-welcome guest,   520
Rebuking with her cultured phrase
Our homeliness of words and ways.
A certain pard-like, treacherous grace
Swayed the lithe limbs and drooped the lash,
Lent the white teeth their dazzling flash;   525
And under low brows, black with night,
Rayed out at times a dangerous light;
The sharp heat-lightnings of her face
Presaging ill to him whom Fate
Condemned to share her love or hate.   530
A woman tropical, intense
In thought and act, in soul and sense,
She blended in a like degree
The vixen and the devotee,
Revealing with each freak or feint   535
    The temper of Petruchio's Kate,[16]

[14] A river rising in the Pindus mountains in northern Greece.

[15] Whittier's introduction makes lines 510–589 clear: "Harriet Livermore . . . a young woman of fine natural ability, enthusiastic, eccentric, with slight control over her violent temper. . . : She early embraced the doctrine of the Second Advent, and felt it her duty to proclaim the Lord's speedy coming. With this message she crossed the Atlantic and spent the greater part of a long life in travelling over Europe and Asia. She lived some time with Lady Hester Stanhope, a woman as fantastic and mentally strained as herself, on the slope of Mt. Lebanon. . . ."

[16] In Shakespeare's *The Taming of the Shrew*.

The raptures of Siena's saint.[17]
Her tapering hand and rounded wrist
Had facile power to form a fist;
The warm, dark languish of her eyes   540
Was never safe from wrath's surprise.
Brows saintly calm and lips devout
Knew every change of scowl and pout;
And the sweet voice had notes more high
And shrill for social battle-cry.   545

Since then what old cathedral town
Has missed her pilgrim staff and gown,
What convent-gate has held its lock
Against the challenge of her knock!
Through Smyrna's plague-hushed thoroughfares, 550
Up sea-set Malta's rocky stairs,
Gray olive slopes of hills that hem
    Thy tombs and shrines, Jerusalem,
Or startling on her desert throne
The crazy Queen of Lebanon[18]   555
With claims fantastic as her own,
Her tireless feet have held their way;
And still, unrestful, bowed, and gray,
She watches under Eastern skies,
    With hope each day renewed and fresh,   560
    The Lord's quick coming in the flesh,
Whereof she dreams and prophesies!

Where'er her troubled path may be,
    The Lord's sweet pity with her go!
The outward wayward life we see,   565
    The hidden springs we may not know.
Nor is it given us to discern
    What threads the fatal sisters spun,
    Through what ancestral years has run
The sorrow with the woman born,   570
What forged her cruel chain of moods,
What set her feet in solitudes,
    And held the love within her mute,
What mingled madness in the blood,
    A life-long discord and annoy,   575
    Water of tears with oil of joy,
And hid within the folded bud
    Perversities of flower and fruit.
It is not ours to separate
    The tangled skein of will and fate,   580
To show what metes and bounds should stand
Upon the soul's debatable land,
And between choice and Providence
Divide the circle of events;
But He who knows our frame is just,   585
Merciful and compassionate,
And full of sweet assurances

<hr>

[17] St. Catherine of Siena (1347–86), the greatest of 14th-century Italian mystics.
[18] Lady Hester Stanhope.

And hope for all the language is,
That He remembereth we are dust!

At last the great logs, crumbling low,   590
Sent out a dull and duller glow,
The bull's-eye watch that hung in view,
Ticking its weary circuit through,
Pointed with mutely warning sign
Its black hand to the hour of nine.   595
That sign the pleasant circle broke:
My uncle ceased his pipe to smoke,
Knocked from its bowl the refuse gray,
And laid it tenderly away;
Then roused himself to safely cover   600
The dull red brands with ashes over.
And while, with care, our mother laid
The work aside, her steps she stayed
One moment, seeking to express
Her grateful sense of happiness   605
For food and shelter, warmth and health,
And love's contentment more than wealth,
With simple wishes (not the weak,
Vain prayers which no fulfilment seek,
But such as warm the generous heart,   610
O'er-prompt to do with Heaven its part)
That none might lack, that bitter night,
For bread and clothing, warmth and light.

Within our beds awhile we heard
The wind that round the gables roared,   615
With now and then a ruder shock,
Which made our very bedsteads rock.
We heard the loosened clapboards tost,
The board-nails snapping in the frost;
And on us, through the unplastered wall,   620
Felt the light sifted snow-flakes fall.
But sleep stole on, as sleep will do
When hearts are light and life is new;
Faint and more faint the murmurs grew,
Till in the summer-land of dreams   625
They softened to the sound of streams,
Low stir of leaves, and dip of oars,
And lapsing waves on quiet shores.

Next morn we wakened with the shout
Of merry voices high and clear,   630
And saw the teamsters drawing near
To break the drifted highways out.
Down the long hillside treading slow
We saw the half-buried oxen go,
Shaking the snow from heads uptost,   635
Their straining nostrils white with frost.
Before our door the straggling train
Drew up, an added team to gain.
The elders threshed their hands a-cold,
    Passed, with the cider-mug, their jokes   640
    From lip to lip; the younger folks

Down the loose snow-banks, wrestling, rolled,
Then toiled again the cavalcade
    O'er windy hill, through clogged ravine,
    And woodland paths that wound between   645
Low drooping pine-boughs winter-weighed.
From every barn a team afoot,
At every house a new recruit,
Where, drawn by Nature's subtlest law,
Haply the watchful young men saw   650
Sweet doorway pictures of the curls
And curious eyes of merry girls,
Lifting their hands in mock defence
Against the snow-ball's compliments,
And reading in each missive tost   655
The charm with Eden never lost.

We heard once more the sleigh-bells' sound;
    And, following where the teamsters led,
The wise old Doctor went his round,
Just pausing at our door to say,   660
In the brief autocratic way
Of one who, prompt at Duty's call,
Was free to urge her claim on all,
    That some poor neighbor sick abed
At night our mother's aid would need.   665
For, one in generous thought and deed,
    What mattered in the sufferer's sight
    The Quaker matron's inward light,
The Doctor's mail of Calvin's creed?
All hearts confess the saints elect   670
    Who, twain in faith, in love agree,
And melt not in an acid sect
    The Christian pearl of charity!

So days went on: a week had passed
Since the great world was heard from last.   675
The Almanac we studied o'er,
Read and reread our little store
Of books and pamphlets, scarce a score;
One harmless novel, mostly hid
From younger eyes, a book forbid,   680
And poetry, (or good or bad,
A single book was all we had,)
Where Ellwood's[19] meek, drab-skirted Muse,
    A stranger to the heathen Nine,
    Sang, with a somewhat nasal whine,   685
The wars of David and the Jews.
At last the floundering carrier bore
The village paper to our door.
Lo! broadening outward as we read,
To warmer zones the horizon spread;   690
In panoramic length unrolled
We saw the marvels that it told.
Before us passed the painted Creeks,

And daft McGregor on his raids
    In Costa Rica's everglades.   695
And up Taygetos winding slow
Rode Ypsilanti's Mainote Greeks,
A Turk's head at each saddle-bow![20]
Welcome to us its week-old news,
Its corner for the rustic Muse,   700
    Its monthly gauge of snow and rain,
Its record, mingling in a breath
The wedding bell and dirge of death:
Jest, anecdote, and love-lorn tale,
The latest culprit sent to jail;   705
Its hue and cry of stolen and lost,
Its vendue sales and goods at cost,
    And traffic calling loud for gain.
We felt the stir of hall and street,
The pulse of life that round us beat;   710
The chill embargo of the snow
Was melted in the genial glow;
Wide swung again our ice-locked door,
And all the world was ours once more!

Clasp, Angel of the backward look   715
    And folded wings of ashen gray
    And voice of echoes far away,
The brazen covers of thy book;
The weird palimpsest old and vast,
Wherein thou hid'st the spectral past;   720
Where, closely mingling, pale and glow
The characters of joy and woe;
The monographs of outlived years,
Or smile-illumed or dim with tears,
    Green hills of life that slope to death, 725
And haunts of home, whose vistaed trees
Shade off to mournful cypresses
    With the white amaranths underneath.
Even while I look, I can but heed
    The restless sands' incessant fall,   730
Importunate hours that hours succeed,
Each clamorous with its own sharp need,
    And duty keeping pace with all.
Shut down and clasp the heavy lids;
I hear again the voice that bids   735
The dreamer leave his dream midway
For larger hopes and graver fears;
Life greatens in these later years,
The century's aloe flowers to-day!

Yet, haply, in some lull of life,   740
Some Truce of God, which breaks its strife,
The worldling's eyes shall gather dew,
    Dreaming in throngful city ways
Of winter joys his boyhood knew;

---

[19] Thomas Ellwood (1639–1714), friend of Milton and author of *Davideis* (1712), not to be confused with the better-known *Davideis* (1656) by Abraham Cowley.

[20] Contemporary topical references, no longer very important. Gregor McGregor was an adventurer and pirate; the Ypsilanti were a family of Greeks several of whom were active in movements against Turkish rule and, specifically, in the Greek War of Independence.

And dear and early friends—the few 745
Who yet remain—shall pause to view
These Flemish[21] pictures of old days;
Sit with me by the homestead hearth,
And stretch the hands of memory forth
To warm them at the wood-fire's blaze! 750
And thanks untraced to lips unknown
Shall greet me like the odors blown
From unseen meadows newly mown,
Or lilies floating in some pond,
Wood-fringed, the wayside gaze beyond; 755
The traveller owns the grateful sense
Of sweetness near, he knows not whence,
And, pausing, takes with forehead bare
The benediction of the air.

1866

Abraham Davenport

In blank verse—a form he rarely used—Whittier here
shows a terseness and ironic undertone in keeping with a
New England type of character he evidently relished. It is
a type that much later found a poetic voice in the "wisdom and grace" and "shrewd dry humor" of Robert Frost.
"The famous Dark Day of New England, May 19, 1780,
was a physical puzzle for many years to our ancestors, but
its occurrence brought something more than philosophical
speculation into the minds of those who passed through it.
The incident of Colonel Abraham Davenport's sturdy protest is a matter of history." (Whittier)

In the old days (a custom laid aside
With breeches and cocked hats) the people sent
Their wisest men to make the public laws.
And so, from a brown homestead, where the Sound
Drinks the small tribute of the Mianas, 5
Waved over by the woods of Rippowams,
And hallowed by pure lives and tranquil deaths,
Stamford sent up to the councils of the State
Wisdom and grace in Abraham Davenport.

'Twas on a May-day of the far old year 10
Seventeen hundred eighty, that there fell
Over the bloom and sweet life of the Spring,
Over the fresh earth and the heaven of noon,
A horror of great darkness, like the night
In day of which the Norland sagas tell,— 15
The Twilight of the Gods.[1] The low-hung sky
Was black with ominous clouds, save where its rim
Was fringed with a dull glow, like that which climbs

The crater's sides from the red hell below.
Birds ceased to sing, and all the barn-yard fowls 20
Roosted; the cattle at the pasture bars
Lowed, and looked homeward; bats on leathern
wings
Flitted abroad; the sounds of labor died;
Men prayed, and women wept; all ears grew sharp
To hear the doom-blast of the trumpet[2] shatter 25
The black sky, that the dreadful face of Christ
Might look from the rent clouds, not as he looked
A loving guest at Bethany, but stern
As Justice and inexorable Law. 29

Meanwhile in the old State House, dim as ghosts
Sat the lawgivers of Connecticut,
Trembling beneath their legislative robes.
"It is the Lord's Great Day! Let us adjourn,"
Some said; and then, as if with one accord,
All eyes were turned to Abraham Davenport. 35
He rose, slow cleaving with his steady voice
The intolerable hush. "This well may be
The Day of Judgment which the world awaits;
But be it so or not, I only know
My present duty, and my Lord's command 40
To occupy till He come. So at the post
Where He hath set me in His providence,
I choose, for one, to meet Him face to face,—
No faithless servant frightened from my task,
But ready when the Lord of the harvest calls; 45
And therefore, with all reverence, I would say,
Let God do His work, we will see to ours.
Bring in the candles." And they brought them in.

Then by the flaring lights the Speaker read,
Albeit with husky voice and shaking hands, 50
An act to amend an act to regulate
The shad and alewive fisheries. Whereupon
Wisely and well spake Abraham Davenport,
Straight to the question, with no figures of speech
Save the ten Arab signs,[3] yet not without 55
The shrewd dry humor natural to the man:
His awe-struck colleagues listening all the while,
Between the pauses of his argument,
To hear the thunder of the wrath of God
Break from the hollow trumpet of the cloud. 60

And there he stands in memory to this day,
Erect, self-poised, a rugged face, half seen
Against the background of unnatural dark,
A witness to the ages as they pass,
That simple duty hath no place for fear. 65

1866

---

[21] Refers to Flemish genre painting of domestic subjects.
Abraham Davenport. [1] Or Götterdämmerung, the end of the
world; the time when the gods war with their enemies until
all are dead.

[2] The Judgment Day trumpet.
[3] The Arabic numerals.

HENRY WADSWORTH LONGFELLOW
[1807–1882]

LONGFELLOW'S REPUTATION as a poet has been, by turns, inflated and deflated. It was inflated at least until the end of the nineteenth century. He was the most widely read poet in the English language, and the first American poet to be memorialized by a bust in Westminster Abbey. He was translated into a score of foreign tongues, from Russian to Portuguese. In America he brought poetry home to the people as no other poet had done, while at the same time winning the applause of most of the men of letters of his day. Unfortunately Longfellow's renown rested largely on his inferior work. Among critics generally, his fame rapidly subsided after 1900, and in the rebellious 1920's he was mercilessly attacked as Victorian, genteel, preachy, silly, out of touch with the realities of American life. By the early 1930's a critic like Ludwig Lewisohn was saying: "Am I slaying the thrice slain? Who, except wretched schoolchildren, now reads Longfellow? . . . The thing to establish in America is not that Longfellow was a very small poet, but that he did not partake of the poetic character at all."

Now, however, we should be able to read Longfellow justly: to avoid the excesses of both the nineteenth-century inflation and the twentieth-century deflation, and to focus attention upon what seems, in sober afterthought, to be his best achievement.

Longfellow came from Portland, Maine. His mother was a descendant of John Alden, a *Mayflower* Pilgrim, his father a lawyer and trustee of Bowdoin College, where the boy Henry entered as a sophomore. One of his classmates was Hawthorne. When he graduated in 1825 he had already shown enough ability at writing verse to make him desire a literary career, though his father wished him to enter the law. Bowdoin settled the matter by establishing a professorship in modern languages and sending the young man to Europe for three years to prepare himself. He returned with a knowledge of German, French, Italian, and Spanish, and late in 1829 he joined the faculty at his alma mater. He had been teaching at Bowdoin for six years when Harvard offered him the Smith professorship of modern languages, and after another year of further preparation in Europe, he began his long residence at the "Craigie house" in Cambridge.

The professor was soon a successful author. His early Irvingesque prose work, *Outre-Mer: A Pilgrimage Beyond the Sea*, was followed by the Germanic romance *Hyperion*. In the same year (1839) came his first book of poems, *Voices of the Night*, including the vastly popular "Psalm of Life." Other volumes of poems quickly followed, and the first of his long narrative poems, *Evangeline* By 1854 the poet was chafing at the professor's duties, and he resigned from Harvard after eighteen years of service during which he had introduced thousands of young men to the literatures of Europe. *Hiawatha*, his long Indian poem, appeared in 1855, and three years later *The Courtship of Miles Standish*, in which he used his Puritan background. But the even tenor of his life and writings was tragically broken in 1861 when his wife was burned to death. After bringing out *Tales of a Wayside Inn* (Part I), largely done before his wife's death, he buried himself and his grief in the discipline of translating Dante's *Divina Commedia*. Another trip abroad brought him honorary degrees from Oxford and Cambridge and a private audience with Queen Victoria. The major efforts of his later years went into the second and third parts of the *Tales of a Wayside Inn* and his long-projected trilogy *Christus: A Mystery* (1872), a series of thematically related verse dramas. To Craigie House, as to a shrine, came streams of visitors, notables and schoolchildren alike; and there he died peacefully in his seventy-sixth year.

Text: The Riverside Edition of the *Complete Poetical and Prose Works* (Boston, 1886).
Further reading: Lawrance Thompson, *Young Longfellow*, 1938. H. S. Gorman, *A Victorian American: Henry Wadsworth Longfellow*, 1926. Newton Arvin, *Longfellow: His Life and Work*, 1963. Edward C. Wagenknecht, *Henry Wadsworth Longfellow*, 1966.

The Skeleton in Armor

In his bookish way, Longfellow had "been looking," as he said, "at the old Northern Sagas, and thinking of a series of ballads or a romantic poem on the deeds of the first bold Viking who crossed to this western world." Noting the discovery of the skeleton of a supposed Norseman at Fall River, Massachusetts, Longfellow wrote this ballad. The ballad refers also to the Newport Tower, an old stone tower that, at the time, some people thought might be of Norse origin.

"Speak! speak! thou fearful guest!
Who, with thy hollow breast
Still in rude armor drest,
   Comest to daunt me!
Wrapt not in Eastern balms,   5
But with thy fleshless palms
Stretched, as if asking alms,
   Why dost thou haunt me?"

Then, from those cavernous eyes
Pale flashes seemed to rise,   10
As when the Northern skies
   Gleam in December;
And, like the water's flow
Under December's snow,
Came a dull voice of woe   15
   From the heart's chamber.

"I was a Viking old!
My deeds, though manifold,
No Skald in song has told,
   No Saga taught thee!   20
Take heed, that in thy verse
Thou dost the tale rehearse,
Else dread a dead man's curse;
   For this I sought thee.

"Far in the Northern Land,   25
By the wild Baltic's strand,
I, with my childish hand,
   Tamed the gerfalcon;
And, with my skates fast-bound,
Skimmed the half-frozen Sound,   30
That the poor whimpering hound
   Trembled to walk on.

"Oft to his frozen lair
Tracked I the grisly bear,
While from my path the hare   35
   Fled like a shadow;
Oft through the forest dark
Followed the were-wolf's bark,
Until the soaring lark
   Sang from the meadow.   40

"But when I older grew,
Joining a corsair's crew,
O'er the dark sea I flew
   With the marauders.
Wild was the life we led;   45
Many the souls that sped,
Many the hearts that bled,
   By our stern orders.

"Many a wassail-bout
Wore the long Winter out;   50
Often our midnight shout
   Set the cocks crowing,
As we the Berserk's tale
Measured in cups of ale,
Draining the oaken pail,   55
   Filled to o'erflowing.

"Once as I told in glee
Tales of the stormy sea,
Soft eyes did gaze on me,
   Burning yet tender;   60
And as the white stars shine
On the dark Norway pine,
On the dark heart of mine
   Fell their soft splendor.

"I wooed the blue-eyed maid,   65
Yielding, yet half afraid,
And in the forest's shade
   Our vows were plighted.
Under its loosened vest
Fluttered her little breast,   70
Like birds within their nest
   By the hawk frighted.

"Bright in her father's hall
Shields gleamed upon the wall,
Loud sang the minstrels all,   75
   Chanting his glory;
When of old Hildebrand
I asked his daughter's hand,

Mute did the minstrels stand
  To hear my story.   80

"While the brown ale he quaffed,
Loud then the champion laughed,
And as the wind-gusts waft
  The sea-foam brightly,
So the loud laugh of scorn,   85
Out of those lips unshorn,
From the deep drinking-horn
  Blew the foam lightly.

"She was a Prince's child,
I but a Viking wild,   90
And though she blushed and smiled,
  I was discarded!
Should not the dove so white
Follow the sea-mew's flight,
Why did they leave that night   95
  Her nest unguarded?

"Scarce had I put to sea,
Bearing the maid with me,
Fairest of all was she
  Among the Norsemen!   100
When on the white sea-strand,
Waving his armèd hand,
Saw we old Hildebrand,
  With twenty horsemen.

"Then launched they to the blast,   105
Bent like a reed each mast,
Yet we were gaining fast,
  When the wind failed us;
And with a sudden flaw
Came round the gusty Skaw,   110
So that our foe we saw
  Laugh as he hailed us.

"And as to catch the gale
Round veered the flapping sail,
'Death!' was the helmsman's hail,   115
  'Death without quarter!'
Midships with iron keel
Struck we her ribs of steel;
Down her black hulk did reel
  Through the black water!   120

"As with his wings aslant,
Sails the fierce cormorant,
Seeking some rocky haunt,
  With his prey laden,—
So toward the open main,   125
Beating to sea again,
Through the wild hurricane,
  Bore I the maiden.

"Three weeks we westward bore,
And when the storm was o'er,   130
Cloud-like we saw the shore
  Stretching to leeward;
There for my lady's bower
Built I the lofty tower,
Which, to this very hour,   135
  Stands looking seaward.

"There lived we many years;
Time dried the maiden's tears;
She had forgot her fears,
  She was a mother;   140
Death closed her mild blue eyes,
Under that tower she lies;
Ne'er shall the sun arise
  On such another!

"Still grew my bosom then,   145
Still as a stagnant fen!
Hateful to me were men,
  The sunlight hateful!
In the vast forest here,
Clad in my warlike gear,   150
Fell I upon my spear,
  Oh, death was grateful!

"Thus, seamed with many scars,
Bursting these prison bars,
Up to its native stars   155
  My soul ascended!
There from the flowing bowl
Deep drinks the warrior's soul,
Skoal! to the Northland! *skoal!* "
  Thus the tale ended.   160
1840

Nuremberg

Longfellow visited the old Bavarian city in 1842, and two years later communicated his delight to his readers in the New World.

In the valley of the Pegnitz, where across broad
    meadow-lands
Rise the blue Franconian mountains, Nuremberg,
    the ancient, stands.

Quaint old town of toil and traffic, quaint old town
    of art and song,
Memories haunt thy pointed gables, like the rooks
    that round them throng:

Memories of the Middle Ages, when the emperors,
    rough and bold,   5
Had their dwelling in thy castle, time-defying,
    centuries old;

And thy brave and thrifty burghers boasted, in their
uncouth rhyme,
That their great imperial city stretched its hand
through every clime.

In the court-yard of the castle, bound with many an
iron band,
Stands the mighty linden planted by Queen
Cunigunde's[1] hand;   10

On the square the oriel window, where in old heroic
days
Sat the poet Melchior[2] singing Kaiser Maximilian's
praise,

Everywhere I see around me rise the wondrous
world of Art:
Fountains wrought with richest sculpture standing in
the common mart;

And above cathedral doorways saints and bishops
carved in stone,   15
By a former age commissioned as apostles to our
own.

In the church of sainted Sebald[3] sleeps enshrined his
holy dust,
And in bronze the Twelve Apostles guard from age
to age their trust;

In the church of sainted Lawrence stands a pix of
sculpture rare,[4]
Like the foamy sheaf of fountains, rising through the
painted air.   20

Here, when Art was still religion, with a simple,
reverent heart,
Lived and labored Albrecht Dürer,[5] the Evangelist
of Art;

Hence in silence and in sorrow, toiling still with
busy hand,
Like an emigrant he wandered, seeking for the Better Land.

Nuremberg. [1]Empress and wife of Henry II, the last Saxon
king of Germany (1002–1024).
[2]Melchior Pfinzing was one of the most celebrated poets of
the sixteenth century. The hero of his *Teuerdank* was the
reigning Emperor, Maximilian. [Longfellow's note.]
[3]The tomb of Saint Sebald, in the church which bears his
name, is one of the richest works of art in Nuremberg. [Long-
fellow's note.]
[4]This pix, or tabernacle for the vessels of the sacrament, is
by the hand of Adam Kraft. It is an exquisite piece of
sculpture. [Longfellow's note.]
[5]German painter and engraver (1471–1528), noted for his
engravings and woodcuts of religious subjects.

Emigravit[6] is the inscription on the tomb-stone
where he lies;   25
Dead he is not, but departed,—for the artist never
dies.

Fairer seems the ancient city, and the sunshine
seems more fair,
That he once has trod its pavement, that he once
has breathed its air!

Through these streets so broad and stately, these
obscure and dismal lanes,
Walked of yore the Mastersingers, chanting rude
poetic strains.   30

From remote and sunless suburbs came they to the
friendly guild,
Building nests in Fame's great temple, as in spouts
the swallows build.

As the weaver plied the shuttle, wove he too the
mystic rhyme,
And the smith his iron measures hammered to the
anvil's chime;

Thanking God, whose boundless wisdom makes the
flowers of poesy bloom   35
In the forge's dust and cinders, in the tissues of the
loom.

Here Hans Sachs, the cobbler-poet, laureate of the
gentle craft,
Wisest of the Twelve Wise Masters, in huge folios
sang and laughed.[7]

But his house is now an ale-house, with a nicely
sanded floor,
And a garland in the window, and his face above
the door.   40

Painted by some humble artist, as in Adam Puschman's song,[8]
As the old man gray and dove-like, with his great
beard white and long.

[6]He has departed.
[7]The Twelve Wise Masters was the title of the original
corporation of the Mastersingers. Hans Sachs, the cobbler of
Nuremberg, though not one of the original twelve, was the
most renowned of the Mastersingers, as well as the most
voluminous. [Longfellow's note.]
[8]Adam Puschman, in his poem on the death of Hans Sachs,
describes him as he appears in a vision:—

An old man,
Gray and white, and dove-like,
Who had, in sooth, a great beard,
And read in a fair, great book,
Beautiful with golden clasps.

[Longfellow's note.]

And at night the swart mechanic comes to drown his
    cark and care,
Quaffing ale from pewter tankards, in the master's
    antique chair.

Vanished is the ancient splendor, and before my
    dreamy eye   45
Wave these mingled shapes and figures, like a faded
    tapestry.

Not thy Councils, not thy Kaisers, win for thee the
    world's regard;
But thy painter, Albrecht Dürer, and Hans Sachs thy
    cobbler bard.

Thus, O Nuremberg, a wanderer from a region far
    away,
As he paced thy streets and court-yards, sang in
    thought his careless lay: 50

Gathering from the pavement's crevice, as a flow-
    eret of the soil,
The nobility of labor,—the long pedigree of toil.

1844

The Arsenal at Springfield

On his wedding journey Longfellow passed through Springfield, Massachusetts, and visited the United States arsenal in company with Charles Sumner. "While Mr. Sumner was endeavoring," says S. Longfellow, "to impress upon the attendant that the money expended upon these weapons of war would have been much better spent upon a great library, Mrs. Longfellow pleased her husband by remarking how like an organ looked the ranged and shining gun-barrels which covered the walls from floor to ceiling, and suggesting what mournful music Death would bring from them. 'We grew quite warlike against war,' she wrote, 'and I urged H. to write a peace poem.'"

This is the Arsenal. From floor to ceiling,
    Like a huge organ, rise the burnished arms;
But from their silent pipes no anthem pealing
    Startles the villages with strange alarms.

Ah! what a sound will rise, how wild and dreary,   5
    When the death-angel touches those swift keys!
What loud lament and dismal Miserere[1]
    Will mingle with their awful symphonies!

I hear even now the infinite fierce chorus,
    The cries of agony, the endless groan,   10
Which, through the ages that have gone before us,
    In long reverberations reach our own.

The Arsenal. [1]"Have mercy": a prayer.

On helm and harness rings the Saxon hammer,
    Through Cimbric forest roars the Norseman's
      song,
And loud, amid the universal clamor,   15
    O'er distant deserts sounds the Tartar gong.

I hear the Florentine, who from his palace
    Wheels out his battle-bell with dreadful din,
And Aztec priests upon their teocallis   19
    Beat the wild war-drums made of serpent's skin;

The tumult of each sacked and burning village;
    The shout that every prayer for mercy drowns;
The soldiers' revels in the midst of pillage;
    The wail of famine in beleaguered towns;   24

The bursting shell, the gateway wrenched asunder,
    The rattling musketry, the clashing blade;
And ever and anon, in tones of thunder,
    The diapason of the cannonade.

Is it, O man, with such discordant noises,
    With such accursed instruments as these,   30
Thou drownest Nature's sweet and kindly voices,
    And jarrest the celestial harmonies?

Were half the power, that fills the world with
    terror,
    Were half the wealth, bestowed on camps and
      courts,
Given to redeem the human mind from error,   35
    There were no need of arsenals or forts:

The warrior's name would be a name abhorrèd!
    And every nation, that should lift again
Its hand against a brother, on its forehead
    Would wear forevermore the curse of Cain!   40

Down the dark future, through long generations,
    The echoing sounds grow fainter and then cease;
And like a bell, with solemn, sweet vibrations,
    I hear once more the voice of Christ say,
      "Peace!"

Peace! and no longer from its brazen portals   45
    The blast of War's great organ shakes the skies!
But beautiful as songs of the immortals,
    The holy melodies of love arise.

1844

The Fire of Drift-Wood

Devereux Farm, near Marblehead

Though not widely familiar, this clearly seems to be one of Longfellow's successful poems. It states no obtrusive moral. It manages without the aid of elaborate figures of speech. Within a firmly developed unity, it harmonizes a striking scene, a complex retrospective mood, a sensitively simple diction, and the subdued music of the verse. Less immediately obvious is the use of contrast (the turbulence of sea and wind vs. the quiet talk indoors) and of similarity (the old farmhouse, old wrecks, old times, also the two fires brought together at the end).

We sat within the farm-house old,
    Whose windows, looking o'er the bay,
Gave to the sea-breeze damp and cold,
    An easy entrance, night and day.

Not far away we saw the port,   5
    The strange, old-fashioned, silent town,
The lighthouse, the dismantled fort,
    The wooden houses, quaint and brown.

We sat and talked until the night,
    Descending, filled the little room;   10
Our faces faded from the sight,
    Our voices only broke the gloom.

We spake of many a vanished scene,
    Of what we once had thought and said,
Of what had been, and might have been,   15
    And who was changed, and who was dead;

And all that fills the hearts of friends,
    When first they feel, with secret pain,
Their lives thenceforth have separate ends,
    And never can be one again;   20

The first slight swerving of the heart,
    That words are powerless to express,
And leave it still unsaid in part,
    Or say it in too great excess.

The very tones in which we spake   25
    Had something strange, I could but mark;
The leaves of memory seemed to make
    A mournful rustling in the dark.

Oft died the words upon our lips,
    As suddenly, from out the fire   30
Built of the wreck of stranded ships,
    The flames would leap and then expire.

And, as their splendor flashed and failed,
    We thought of wrecks upon the main,
Of ships dismasted, that were hailed   35
    And sent no answer back again.

The windows, rattling in their frames,
    The ocean, roaring up the beach,
The gusty blast, the bickering flames,
    All mingled vaguely in our speech;   40

Until they made themselves a part
    Of fancies floating through the brain,
The long-lost ventures of the heart,
    That send no answers back again.

O flames that glowed! O hearts that yearned!   45
    They were indeed too much akin,
The drift-wood fire without that burned,
    The thoughts that burned and glowed within.

                              1848

The Jewish Cemetery at Newport

At Newport, Rhode Island, on July 9, 1852, Longfellow wrote in his diary: "Went this morning into the Jewish burying-ground, with a polite old gentleman who keeps the key. There are few graves; nearly all are low tombstones of marble with Hebrew inscriptions, and a few words added in English or Portuguese."

How strange it seems! These Hebrews in their
        graves,
    Close by the street of this fair seaport town,
Silent beside the never-silent waves,
    At rest in all this moving up and down!   4

The trees are white with dust, that o'er their sleep
    Wave their broad curtains in the south-wind's
        breath,
While underneath these leafy tents they keep
    The long, mysterious Exodus of Death.

And these sepulchral stones, so old and brown,
    That pave with level flags their burial-place,   10
Seem like the tablets of the Law, thrown down
    And broken by Moses at the mountain's base.

The very names recorded here are strange,
    Of foreign accent, and of different climes;
Alvares and Rivera interchange   15
    With Abraham and Jacob of old times.

"Blessed be God! for he created Death!"
    The mourners said, "and Death is rest and
        peace;"
Then added, in the certainty of faith,
    "And giveth Life that nevermore shall cease."   20

Closed are the portals of their Synagogue,
    No Psalms of David now the silence break,
No Rabbi reads the ancient Decalogue
    In the grand dialect the Prophets spake.

Gone are the living, but the dead remain,   25
    And not neglected; for a hand unseen,

Scattering its bounty, like a summer rain,
 Still keeps their graves and their remembrance
  green.

How came they here? What burst of Christian hate,
 What persecution, merciless and blind,   30
Drove o'er the sea—that desert desolate—
 These Ishmaels and Hagars of mankind?[1]

They lived in narrow streets and lanes obscure,
 Ghetto and Judenstrass,[2] in mirk and mire;
Taught in the school of patience to endure 35
 The life of anguish and the death of fire.

All their lives long, with the unleavened bread
 And bitter herbs of exile and its fears,
The wasting famine of the heart they fed,
 And slaked its thirst with marah[3] of their tears. 40

Anathema maranatha![4] was the cry
 That rang from town to town, from street to
  street;
At every gate the accursed Mordecai[5]
 Was mocked and jeered, and spurned by Chris-
  tian feet.

Pride and humiliation hand in hand   45
 Walked with them through the world where'er
  they went;
Trampled and beaten were they as the sand,
 And yet unshaken as the continent.

For in the background figures vague and vast
 Of patriarchs and of prophets rose sublime, 50
And all the great traditions of the Past
 They saw reflected in the coming time.

And thus forever with reverted look
 The mystic volume of the world they read,
Spelling it backward, like a Hebrew book, 55
 Till life became a Legend of the Dead.

The Jewish Cemetery. [1]Ishmael was the son of Abraham by
Hagar; cf. Genesis xvi. Both were exiled and hence the names
imply outcast.
 [2]Street of Jews: they lived in restricted areas or ghettos.
 [3]Bitterness.
 [4]Anathema (an accused person or formal curse); Maranatha
(O Lord, come). The combination results in an intensified
curse, calling on God to destroy the Jews. Cf. I Corinthians
xvi.22.
 [5]In the book of Esther, Mordecai (Esther's cousin) sat in
the king's gate and aroused the anger of the king's chief
minister, Haman, by refusing to bow down before him. Haman plotted to kill Mordecai and all the Jews, but Haman
instead was executed. Longfellow's allusion to Mordecai is to
all the persecutions of the Jews.

But ah! what once has been shall be no more!
 The groaning earth in travail and in pain
Brings forth its races, but does not restore,
 And the dead nations never rise again. 60
1852

In the Churchyard at Cambridge

In the village churchyard she lies,
Dust is in her beautiful eyes,
 No more she breathes, nor feels, nor stirs;
At her feet and at her head
Lies a slave to attend the dead,   5
 But their dust is white as hers.

Was she, a lady of high degree,
So much in love with the vanity
 And foolish pomp of this world of ours?
Or was it Christian charity,   10
And lowliness and humility,
 The richest and rarest of all dowers?

Who shall tell us? No one speaks;
No color shoots into those cheeks,
 Either of anger or of pride,   15
At the rude question we have asked;
Nor will the mystery be unmasked
 By those who are sleeping at her side.

Hereafter?—And do you think to look
On the terrible pages of that Book 20
 To find her failings, faults, and errors?
Ah, you will then have other cares,
In your own shortcomings and despairs,
 In your own secret sins and terrors!

1853

My Lost Youth

Longfellow's *Journal:* "March 29, 1855—A day of pain,
cowering over the fire. At night as I lie in bed, a poem
comes into my mind,—a memory of Portland,—my native
town, the city by the sea. . . ." "March 30—Wrote the
poem; and am rather pleased with it, and with the bringing in of the two lines of the old Lapland song:

  A boy's will is the wind's will,
 And the thoughts of youth are long, long thoughts."

These two lines Longfellow translated literally from the
German rendering of the Lapland song by Herder, precur-
sor of the German romantic school.

Often I think of the beautiful town
 That is seated by the sea;

Often in thought go up and down
The pleasant streets of that dear old town,
    And my youth comes back to me.   5
      And a verse of a Lapland song
      Is haunting my memory still:
    "A boy's will is the wind's will,
And the thoughts of youth are long, long thoughts."

I can see the shadowy lines of its trees,   10
    And catch, in sudden gleams,
The sheen of the far-surrounding seas,
And islands that were the Hesperides
    Of all my boyish dreams.
      And the burden of that old song,   15
      It murmurs and whispers still:
    "A boy's will is the wind's will,
And the thoughts of youth are long, long thoughts."

I remember the black wharves and the slips,
    And the sea-tides tossing free;   20
And Spanish sailors with bearded lips,
And the beauty and mystery of the ships,
    And the magic of the sea.
      And the voice of that wayward song
      Is singing and saying still: 25
    "A boy's will is the wind's will,
And the thoughts of youth are long, long thoughts."

I remember the bulwarks by the shore,
    And the fort upon the hill;
The sunrise gun, with its hollow roar,   30
The drum-beat repeated o'er and o'er,
    And the bugle wild and shrill.
      And the music of that old song
      Throbs in my memory still:
    "A boy's will is the wind's will,   35
And the thoughts of youth are long, long thoughts."

I remember the sea-fight far away,[1]
    How it thundered o'er the tide!
And the dead captains, as they lay
In their graves, o'erlooking the tranquil bay,   40
    Where they in battle died.
      And the sound of that mournful song
      Goes through me with a thrill:
    "A boy's will is the wind's will,   44
And the thoughts of youth are long, long thoughts."

I can see the breezy dome of groves,
    The shadows of Deering's Woods;

My Lost Youth. [1] This refers to a naval engagement of the War of 1812, just outside Portland harbor, in which the *Enterprise* (American) defeated the *Boxer* (British); both captains were killed, and were buried side by side in a hillside cemetery in Portland. Longfellow was six years old at the time.

And the friendships old and the early loves
Come back with a Sabbath sound, as of doves
    In quiet neighborhoods.   50
      And the verse of that sweet old song,
      It flutters and murmurs still:
    "A boy's will is the wind's will,
And the thoughts of youth are long, long thoughts."

I remember the gleams and glooms that dart   55
    Across the school-boy's brain;
The song and the silence in the heart,
That in part are prophecies, and in part
    Are longings wild and vain.
      And the voice of that fitful song   60
      Sings on, and is never still:
    "A boy's will is the wind's will,
And the thoughts of youth are long, long thoughts."

There are things of which I may not speak;
    There are dreams that cannot die;   65
There are thoughts that make the strong heart weak,
And bring a pallor into the cheek,
    And a mist before the eye.
      And the words of that fatal song
      Come over me like a chill: 70
    "A boy's will is the wind's will,
And the thoughts of youth are long, long thoughts."

Strange to me now are the forms I meet
    When I visit the dear old town;
But the native air is pure and sweet,   75
And the trees that o'ershadow each well-known
    street,
    As they balance up and down,
      Are singing the beautiful song,
      Are sighing and whispering still:
    "A boy's will is the wind's will,   80
And the thoughts of youth are long, long thoughts."

And Deering's Woods are fresh and fair,
    And with joy that is almost pain
My heart goes back to wander there,
And among the dreams of the days that were,   85
    I find my lost youth again.
      And the strange and beautiful song,
      The groves are repeating it still:
    "A boy's will is the wind's will,   89
And the thoughts of youth are long, long thoughts."
1855

FROM *Tales of a Wayside Inn*

This collection of narrative poems was conceived in the manner of Boccaccio's *Decameron* and Chaucer's *Canterbury Tales.* It was published in three parts, beginning in 1863, and finally as a whole. The stories are told by a group of friends who meet at an old inn (actually the Red Horse Tavern) about twenty miles from Boston.

The Student's Tale

Emma and Eginhard

When Alcuin taught the sons of Charlemagne,[1]
In the free schools of Aix,[2] how kings should reign,
And with them taught the children of the poor
How subjects should be patient and endure,
He touched the lips of some, as best befit,   5
With honey from the hives of Holy Writ;
Others intoxicated with the wine
Of ancient history, sweet but less divine;
Some with the wholesome fruits of grammar fed;
Others with mysteries of the stars o'erhead,   10
That hang suspended in the vaulted sky
Like lamps in some fair palace vast and high.

In sooth, it was a pleasant sight to see
That Saxon monk, with hood and rosary,
With inkhorn at his belt, and pen and book,   15
And mingled love and reverence in his look,
Or hear the cloister and the court repeat
The measured footfalls of his sandaled feet,
Or watch him with the pupils of his school,
Gentle of speech, but absolute of rule.   20

Among them, always earliest in his place,
Was Eginhard,[3] a youth of Frankish race,
Whose face was bright with flashes that forerun
The splendors of a yet unrisen sun.
To him all things were possible, and seemed   25
Not what he had accomplished, but had dreamed,
And what were tasks to others were his play,
The pastime of an idle holiday.

Smaragdo, Abbot of St. Michael's, said,
With many a shrug and shaking of the head,   30
Surely some demon must possess the lad,
Who showed more wit than ever school-boy had,

Emma and Eginhard. [1] Alcuin or Albinus (735–804), theologian and man of letters; collaborated with Charlemagne in educational reforms. Charlemagne (742–814) became king of the Franks in 768 and emperor of the West in 800.
[2] A city in southern France.
[3] Or Einhard (770?–840?), who became a Frankish noble in Charlemagne's service and who later wrote a biography of the emperor. According to false tradition, he was Charlemagne's son-in-law. Longfellow suggests this in the Interlude immediately following the tale:

> Thus ran the Student's pleasant rhyme
> of Eginhard and love and youth;
> Some doubted its historic truth,
> But while they doubted, ne'ertheless,
> Saw in it gleams of truthfulness. . . .

And learned his Trivium thus without the rod;
But Alcuin said it was the grace of God.

Thus he grew up, in Logic point-device,   35
Perfect in Grammar, and in Rhetoric nice;
Science of Numbers, Geometric art,
And lore of Stars, and Music knew by heart;
A Minnesinger, long before the times
Of those who sang their love in Suabian rhymes.   40

The Emperor, when he heard this good report
Of Eginhard much buzzed about the court,
Said to himself, "This stripling seems to be
Purposely sent into the world for me;   44
He shall become my scribe, and shall be schooled
In all the arts whereby the world is ruled."
Thus did the gentle Eginhard attain
To honor in the court of Charlemagne;
Became the sovereign's favorite, his right hand,
So that his fame was great in all the land,   50
And all men loved him for his modest grace
And comeliness of figure and of face.
An inmate of the palace, yet recluse,
A man of books, yet sacred from abuse
Among the armed knights with spur on heel,   55
The tramp of horses and the clang of steel;
And as the Emperor promised he was schooled
In all the arts by which the world is ruled.
But the one art supreme, whose law is fate,
The Emperor never dreamed of till too late.   60

Home from her convent to the palace came
The lovely Princess Emma, whose sweet name,
Whispered by seneschal or sung by bard,
Had often touched the soul of Eginhard.
He saw her from his window, as in state   65
She came, by knights attended through the gate;
He saw her at the banquet of that day,
Fresh as the morn, and beautiful as May;
He saw her in the garden, as she strayed
Among the flowers of summer with her maid,   70
And said to him, "O Eginhard, disclose
The meaning and the mystery of the rose;"
And trembling he made answer: "In good sooth,
Its mystery is love, its meaning youth!"
How can I tell the signals and the signs   75
By which one heart another heart divines?
How can I tell the many thousand ways
By which it keeps the secret it betrays?

O mystery of love! O strange romance!
Among the Peers and Paladins of France,   80
Shining in steel, and prancing on gay steeds,
Noble by birth, yet nobler by great deeds,
The Princess Emma had no words nor looks
But for this clerk, this man of thought and books.

The summer passed, the autumn came; the stalks 85
Of lilies blackened in the garden walks;
The leaves fell, russet-golden and blood-red,
Love-letters thought the poet fancy-led,
Or Jove descending in a shower of gold
Into the lap of Danaë of old;[4] 90
For poets cherish many a strange conceit,
And love transmutes all nature by its heat.
No more the garden lessons, nor the dark
And hurried meetings in the twilight park;
But now the studious lamp, and the delights 95
Of firesides in the silent winter nights,
And watching from his window hour by hour
The light that burned in Princess Emma's tower.

At length one night, while musing by the fire,
O'ercome at last by his insane desire,— 100
For what will reckless love not do and dare?
He crossed the court, and climbed the winding stair,
With some feigned message in the Emperor's name;
But when he to the lady's presence came
He knelt down at her feet, until she laid 105
Her hand upon him, like a naked blade,
And whispered in his ear: "Arise, Sir Knight,
To my heart's level, O my heart's delight."

And there he lingered till the crowing cock,
The Alectryon[5] of the farmyard and the flock, 110
Sang his aubade with lusty voice and clear,
To tell the sleeping world that dawn was near.
And then they parted; but at parting, lo!
They saw the palace courtyard white with snow,
And, placid as a nun, the moon on high 115
Gazing from cloudy cloisters of the sky,
"Alas!" he said, "how hide the fatal line
Of footprints leading from thy door to mine,
And none returning!" Ah, he little knew
What woman's wit, when put to proof, can do! 120

That night the Emperor, sleepless with the cares
And troubles that attend on state affairs,
Had risen before the dawn, and musing gazed
Into the silent night, as one amazed
To see the calm that reigned o'er all supreme, 125
When his own reign was but a troubled dream.
The moon lit up the gables capped with snow,
And the white roofs, and half the court below,
And he beheld a form, that seemed to cower
Beneath a burden, came from Emma's tower,— 130
A woman, who upon her shoulders bore
Clerk Eginhard to his own private door,

[4] Confined to a tower by her father, Danaë was visited
there by Jove (or Zeus) who descended in a shower of gold.
Their son was Perseus.

[5] Sent by Ares to watch for the sun during his night with
Aphrodite, Alectryon fell asleep; Ares and Aphrodite were
discovered, and Ares changed Alectryon into a cock.

And then returned in haste, but still essayed
To tread the footprints she herself had made;
And as she passed across the lighted space, 135
The Emperor saw his daughter Emma's face!

He started not; he did not speak or moan,
But seemed as one who hath been turned to stone;
And stood there like a statue, nor awoke
Out of his trance of pain, till morning broke, 140
Till the stars faded, and the moon went down,
And o'er the towers and steeples of the town
Came the gray daylight; then the sun, who took
The empire of the world with sovereign look,
Suffusing with a soft and golden glow 145
All the dead landscape in its shroud of snow,
Touching with flame the tapering chapel spires,
Windows and roofs, and smoke of household fires,
And kindling park and palace as he came; 149
The stork's nest on the chimney seemed in flame.
And thus he stood till Eginhard appeared,
Demure and modest with his comely beard
And flowing flaxen tresses, come to ask,
As was his wont, the day's appointed task.
The Emperor looked upon him with a smile, 155
And gently said: "My son, wait yet awhile;
This hour my council meets upon some great
And very urgent business of the state.
Come back within the hour. On thy return
The work appointed for thee shalt thou learn." 160

Having dismissed this gallant Troubadour,
He summoned straight his council, and secure
And steadfast in his purpose, from the throne
All the adventure of the night made known;
Then asked for sentence; and with eager breath 165
Some answered banishment, and others death.

Then spake the king: "Your sentence is not mine;
Life is the gift of God, and is divine;
Nor from these palace walls shall one depart
Who carries such a secret in his heart; 170
My better judgment points another way.
Good Alcuin, I remember how one day
When my Pepino asked you, 'What are men?'
You wrote upon his tablets with your pen,
'Guests of the grave and travellers that pass!' 175
This being true of all men, we, alas!
Being all fashioned of the selfsame dust,
Let us be merciful as well as just;
This passing traveller, who hath stolen away
The brightest jewel of my crown to-day, 180
Shall of himself the precious gem restore;
By giving it, I make it mine once more.
Over those fatal footprints I will throw
My ermine mantle like another snow."

Then Eginhard was summoned to the hall, 185
And entered, and in presence of them all,

The Emperor said: "My son, for thou to me
Hast been a son, and evermore shalt be,
Long hast thou served thy sovereign, and thy zeal
Pleads to me with importunate appeal,   190
While I have been forgetful to requite
Thy service and affection as was right.
But now the hour is come, when I, thy Lord,
Will crown thy love with such supreme reward,
A gift so precious kings have striven in vain   195
To win it from the hands of Charlemagne."

Then sprang the portals of the chamber wide,
And Princess Emma entered, in the pride
Of birth and beauty, that in part o'ercame
The conscious terror and the blush of shame.   200
And the good Emperor rose up from his throne,
And taking her white hand within his own
Placed it in Eginhard's, and said: "My son,
This is the gift thy constant zeal hath won;
Thus I repay the royal debt I owe,   205
And cover up the footprints in the snow."

1872

The Sicilian's Tale

The Monk of Casal-Maggiore

Once on a time, some centuries ago,
  In the hot sunshine two Franciscan friars
Wended their weary way, with footsteps slow,
  Back to their convent, whose white walls and
    spires
Gleamed on the hillside like a patch of snow;   5
  Covered with dust they were, and torn by briers,
And bore like sumpter-mules upon their backs
The badge of poverty, their beggar's sacks.

The first was Brother Anthony, a spare
  And silent man, with pallid cheeks and thin,   10
Much given to vigils, penance, fasting, prayer,
  Solemn and gray, and worn with discipline,
As if his body but white ashes were,
  Heaped on the living coals that glowed within;
A simple monk, like many of his day,   15
Whose instinct was to listen and obey.

A different man was Brother Timothy,
  Of larger mould and of a coarser paste;
A rubicund and stalwart monk was he,
  Broad in the shoulders, broader in the waist,   20
Who often filled the dull refectory
  With noise by which the convent was disgraced,
But to the mass-book gave but little heed,
By reason he had never learned to read.

Now, as they passed the outskirts of a wood,   25
  They saw, with mingled pleasure and surprise,
Fast tethered to a tree an ass, that stood
  Lazily winking his large, limpid eyes.
The farmer Gilbert, of that neighborhood,
  His owner was, who, looking for supplies   30
Of fagots, deeper in the wood had strayed,
Leaving his beast to ponder in the shade.

As soon as Brother Timothy espied
  The patient animal, he said: "Good-lack!
Thus for our needs doth Providence provide;   35
  We'll lay our wallets on the creature's back."
This being done, he leisurely untied
  From head and neck the halter of the jack,
And put it round his own, and to the tree
Stood tethered fast as if the ass were he.   40

And, bursting forth into a merry laugh,
  He cried to Brother Anthony: "Away!
And drive the ass before you with your staff;
  And when you reach the convent you may say
You left me at a farm, half tired and half   45
  Ill with a fever, for a night and day,
And that the farmer lent this ass to bear
Our wallets, that are heavy with good fare."

Now Brother Anthony, who knew the pranks
  Of Brother Timothy, would not persuade   50
Or reason with him on his quirks and cranks,
  But, being obedient, silently obeyed;
And, smiting with his staff the ass's flanks,
  Drove him before him over hill and glade,
Safe with his provend to the convent gate,   55
Leaving poor Brother Timothy to his fate.

Then Gilbert, laden with fagots for his fire,
  Forth issued from the wood, and stood aghast
To see the ponderous body of the friar
  Standing where he had left his donkey last.   60
Trembling he stood, and dared not venture nigher,
  But stared, and gaped, and crossed himself full
    fast;
For, being credulous and of little wit,
He thought it was some demon from the pit.

While speechless and bewildered thus he gazed,   65
  And dropped his load of fagots on the ground,
Quoth Brother Timothy: "Be not amazed
  That where you left a donkey should be found
A poor Franciscan friar, half-starved and crazed,
  Standing demure and with a halter bound;   70
But set me free, and hear the piteous story
Of Brother Timothy of Casal-Maggiore.

"I am a sinful man, although you see
  I wear the consecrated cowl and cape;

You never owned an ass, but you owned me,   75
  Changed and transformed from my own natural
    shape
All for the deadly sin of gluttony,
  From which I could not otherwise escape,
Than by this penance, dieting on grass,
And being worked and beaten as an ass.   80

"Think of the ignominy I endured;
  Think of the miserable life I led,
The toil and blows to which I was inured,
  My wretched lodging in a windy shed,
My scanty fare so grudgingly procured,   85
  The damp and musty straw that formed my bed!
But, having done this penance for my sins,
My life as man and monk again begins."

The simple Gilbert, hearing words like these,
  Was conscience-stricken, and fell down apace   90
Before the friar upon his bended knees,
  And with a suppliant voice implored his grace;
And the good monk, now very much at ease,
  Granted him pardon with a smiling face,
Nor could refuse to be that night his guest,   95
It being late, and he in need of rest.

Upon a hillside, where the olive thrives,
  With figures painted on its whitewashed walls,
The cottage stood; and near the humming hives
  Made murmurs as of far-off waterfalls;   100
A place where those who love secluded lives
  Might live content, and, free from noise and
    brawls,
Like Claudian's[1] Old Man of Verona here
Measure by fruits the slow-revolving year.

And, coming to this cottage of content,   105
  They found his children, and the buxom wench
His wife, Dame Cicely, and his father, bent
  With years and labor, seated on a bench,
Repeating over some obscure event
  In the old wars of Milanese and French;   110
All welcomed the Franciscan, with a sense
Of sacred awe and humble reverence.

When Gilbert told them what had come to pass,
  How beyond question, cavil, or surmise,
Good Brother Timothy had been their ass,   115
  You should have seen the wonder in their eyes;
You should have heard them cry, "Alas! alas!"
  Have heard their lamentations and their sighs!
For all believed the story, and began
To see a saint in this afflicted man.   120

The Monk of Casal-Maggiore. [1] Claudius Claudianus (fl. 395–404), the last great poet of Rome.

Forthwith there was prepared a grand repast,
  To satisfy the craving of the friar
After so rigid and prolonged a fast;
  The bustling housewife stirred the kitchen fire;
Then her two barn-yard fowls, her best and last,   125
  Were put to death, at her express desire,
And served up with a salad in a bowl,
And flasks of country wine to crown the whole.

It would not be believed should I repeat
  How hungry Brother Timothy appeared;   130
It was a pleasure but to see him eat,
  His white teeth flashing through his russet beard,
His face aglow and flushed with wine and meat,
  His roguish eyes that rolled and laughed and
    leered!
Lord! how he drank the blood-red country wine   135
As if the village vintage were divine!

And all the while he talked without surcease,
  And told his merry tales with jovial glee
That never flagged, but rather did increase,
  And laughed aloud as if insane were he,   140
And wagged his red beard, matted like a fleece,
  And cast such glances at Dame Cicely
That Gilbert now grew angry with his guest,
And thus in words his rising wrath expressed.

"Good Father," said he, "easily we see   145
  How needful in some persons, and how right,
Mortification of the flesh may be.
  The indulgence you have given it to-night,
After long penance, clearly proves to me
  Your strength against temptation is but slight,   150
And shows the dreadful peril you are in
Of a relapse into your deadly sin.

"Tomorrow morning, with the rising sun,
  Go back unto your convent, nor refrain
From fasting and from scourging, for you run   155
  Great danger to become an ass again,
Since monkish flesh and asinine are one;
  Therefore be wise, nor longer here remain,
Unless you wish the scourge should be applied   160
By other hands, that will not spare your hide."

When this the monk had heard, his color fled
  And then returned, like lightning in the air,
Till he was all one blush from foot to head,
  And even the bald spot on his russet hair
Turned from its usual pallor to bright red!   165
  The old man was asleep upon his chair.
Then all retired, and sank into the deep
And helpless imbecility of sleep.

They slept until the dawn of day drew near,
  Till the cock should have crowed, but did not
    crow,   170

For they had slain the shining chanticleer
    And eaten him for supper, as you know.
The monk was up betimes and of good cheer,
    And, having breakfasted, made haste to go,
As if he heard the distant matin bell,   175
And had but little time to say farewell.

Fresh was the morning as the breath of kine;
    Odors of herbs commingled with the sweet
Balsamic exhalations of the pine;
    A haze was in the air presaging heat;   180
Uprose the sun above the Apennine,
    And all the misty valleys at its feet
Were full of the delirious song of birds,
Voices of men, and bells, and low of herds.

All this to Brother Timothy was naught;   185
    He did not care for scenery, nor here
His busy fancy found the thing it sought;
    But when he saw the convent walls appear,
And smoke from kitchen chimneys upward caught
    And whirled aloft into the atmosphere,   190
He quickened his slow footsteps, like a beast
That scents the stable a league off at least.

And as he entered through the convent gate
    He saw there in the court the ass, who stood
Twirling his ears about, and seemed to wait,   195
    Just as he found him waiting in the wood;
And told the Prior that, to alleviate
    The daily labors of the brotherhood,
The owner, being a man of means and thrift,
Bestowed him on the convent as a gift.   200

And thereupon the Prior for many days
    Revolved this serious matter in his mind,
And turned it over many different ways,
    Hoping that some safe issue he might find;
But stood in fear of what the world would say,   205
    If he accepted presents of this kind,
Employing beasts of burden for the packs
That lazy monks should carry on their backs.

Then, to avoid all scandal of the sort,
    And stop the mouth of cavil, he decreed   210
That he would cut the tedious matter short,
    And sell the ass with all convenient speed,
Thus saving the expense of his support,
    And hoarding something for a time of need.
So he dispatched him to the neighboring Fair,   215
And freed himself from cumber and from care.

It happened now by chance, as some might say,
    Others perhaps would call it destiny,
Gilbert was at the Fair; and heard a bray.
    And nearer came, and saw that it was he,   220
And whispered in his ear, "Ah, lackaday!

Good father, the rebellious flesh, I see,
Has changed you back into an ass again,
And all my admonitions were in vain."

The ass, who felt this breathing in his ear,   225
    Did not turn round to look, but shook his head,
As if he were not pleased these words to hear,
    And contradicted all that had been said.
And this made Gilbert cry in voice more clear,
    "I know you well; your hair is russet-red;   230
Do not deny it; for you are the same
Franciscan friar, and Timothy by name."

The ass, though now the secret had come out,
    Was obstinate, and shook his head again;
Until a crowd was gathered round about   235
    To hear this dialogue between the twain;
And raised their voices in a noisy shout
    When Gilbert tried to make the matter plain,
And flouted him and mocked him all day long
With laughter and with jibes and scraps of song.   240

"If this be Brother Timothy," they cried,
    "Buy him, and feed him on the tenderest grass;
Thou canst not do too much for one so tried
    As to be twice transformed into an ass."
So simple Gilbert bought him, and untied   245
    His halter, and o'er mountain and morass
He led him homeward, talking as he went
Of good behavior and a mind content.   248

The children saw them coming, and advanced,
    Shouting with joy, and hung about his neck,—
Not Gilbert's, but the ass's,—round him danced,
    And wove green garlands wherewithal to deck
His sacred person; for again it chanced
    Their childish feelings, without rein or check,
Could not discriminate in any way   255
A donkey from a friar of Orders Gray.

"O Brother Timothy," the children said,
    "You have come back to us just as before;
We were afraid, and thought that you were dead,
    And we should never see you any more."   260
And then they kissed the white star on his head,
    That like a birth-mark or a badge he wore,
And patted him upon the neck and face,
And said a thousand things with childish grace.

Thenceforward and forever he was known   265
    As Brother Timothy, and led alway
A life of luxury, till he had grown
    Ungrateful, being stuffed with corn and hay,
And very vicious. Then in angry tone,
    Rousing himself, poor Gilbert said one day,   270
"When simple kindness is misunderstood
A little flagellation may do good."

His many vices need not here be told;
  Among them was a habit that he had
Of flinging up his heels at young and old,   275
  Breaking his halter, running off like mad
O'er pasture-lands and meadow, wood and wold,
  And other misdemeanors quite as bad;
But worst of all was breaking from his shed
At night, and ravaging the cabbage-bed.   280

So Brother Timothy went back once more
  To his old life of labor and distress;
Was beaten worse than he had been before;
  And now, instead of comfort and caress,
Came labors manifold and trials sore;   285
  And as his toils increased his food grew less,
Until at last the great consoler, Death,
Ended his many sufferings with his breath.

Great was the lamentation when he died;
  And mainly that he died impenitent;
Dame Cicely bewailed, the children cried,   290
  The old man still remembered the event
In the French war, and Gilbert magnified
  His many virtues, as he came and went,
And said: "Heaven pardon Brother Timothy,   295
And keep us from the sin of gluttony."
1873

Sonnets

Divina Commedia

Longfellow wrote these sonnets during the long labor of translating the *Divine Comedy*. He thinks of Dante's magnificent imaginative structure as the poetic equivalent of a medieval cathedral. Building and poem alike have an architectural grandeur, a correspondence of form and function, a unity dominating an endless variety. At the same time the cathedral image suggests the spiritual refuge which the poem afforded Longfellow, a contemplative retreat from the harsh realities of "the Time" (to be specific, the Civil War and the death of his wife by fire).

The first two sonnets prefaced the *Inferno;* the third and fourth, the *Purgatorio;* the last two, the *Paradiso.*

I

In the quiet of the church, laborer and poet alike will pray and find peace, forgetting the clamor and sorrows of the world. Time yields to the higher reality of the eternal.

Oft have I seen at some cathedral door
A laborer, pausing in the dust and heat,
Lay down his burden, and with reverent feet
Enter, and cross himself, and on the floor
Kneel to repeat his paternoster o'er;   5
Far off the noises of the world retreat;
The loud vociferations of the street

Become an undistinguishable roar.
So, as I enter here from day to day,
And leave my burden at this minster gate,   10
Kneeling in prayer, and not ashamed to pray,
The tumult of the time disconsolate
To inarticulate murmurs dies away,
While the eternal ages watch and wait.

II

The poet is outside the cathedral, marveling at its rich sculptural adornments. The evil of the world is emphasized by the gargoyles, the dead Christ, the thieves, the traitor Judas. In the last six lines Longfellow indicates that the *Divine Comedy,* like the medieval cathedral, was the creation not of one man but of a whole people, a whole age.

How strange the sculptures that adorn these
    towers!   15
This crowd of statues, in whose folded sleeves
Birds build their nests; while canopied with leaves
Parvis and portal bloom like trellised bowers,
And the vast minster seems a cross of flowers!
But fiends and dragons on the gargoyled eaves   20
Watch the dead Christ between the living thieves,
And, underneath, the traitor Judas lowers!
Ah! from what agonies of heart and brain,
What exultations trampling on despair,   24
What tenderness, what tears, what hate of wrong,
What passionate outcry of a soul in pain,
Uprose this poem of the earth and air,
This mediaeval miracle of song!

III

The poet is now in the twilight of the cathedral interior.

I enter, and I see thee in the gloom
Of the long aisles, O poet saturnine!   30
And strive to make my steps keep pace with thine.
The air is filled with some unknown perfume;
The congregation of the dead make room
For thee to pass; the votive tapers shine;
Like rooks that haunt Ravenna's groves of pine   35
The hovering echoes fly from tomb to tomb.
From the confessionals I hear arise
Rehearsals of forgotten tragedies
And lamentations from the crypts below;
And then a voice celestial that begins   40
With the pathetic words, "Although your sins
As scarlet be," and ends with "as the snow."

IV

Longfellow imagines a meeting of Dante with Beatrice. She, whom Dante had loved spiritually, from afar, became, in the *Divine Comedy,* his guide through Paradise.

Divina Commedia. Dante's burial site.

With snow-white veil and garments as of flame,
She stands before thee, who so long ago
Filled thy young heart with passion and the woe   45
From which thy song and all its splendors came;
And while with stern rebuke she speaks thy name,
The ice about thy heart melts as the snow
On mountain heights, and in swift overflow
Comes gushing from thy lips in sobs of shame.   50
Thou makest full confession; and a gleam,
As of the dawn on some dark forest cast,
Seems on thy lifted forehead to increase;
Lethe and Eunoë[2]—the remembered dream
And the forgotten sorrow—bring at last   55
That perfect pardon which is perfect peace.

V

For Longfellow, the glorious windows, one of them rose-shaped, typify this part of Dante's work. The Rose refers to the end of Dante's journey, when he beholds the Trinity and the Blessed in the form of a rose. The elevation of the Host is the supreme moment of the Mass.

I lift mine eyes, and all the windows blaze
With forms of Saints and holy men who died,
Here martyred and hereafter glorified;
And the great Rose upon its leaves displays   60
Christ's Triumph, and the angelic roundelays,
With splendor upon splendor multiplied;
And Beatrice again at Dante's side
No more rebukes, but smiles her words of praise.
And then the organ sounds, and unseen choirs   65
Sing the old Latin hymns of peace and love
And benedictions of the Holy Ghost;
And the melodious bells among the spires
O'er all the house-tops and through heaven above
Proclaim the elevation of the Host!   70

VI

Longfellow describes Dante, the builder of the poetic edifice, as also a poet of freedom and prophet of the soul.

O star of morning and of liberty!
O bringer of the light, whose splendor shines
Above the darkness of the Apennines,
Forerunner of the day that is to be!
The voices of the city and the sea,   75
The voices of the mountains and the pines,
Repeat thy song, till the familiar lines
Are footpaths for the thought of Italy!
Thy flame is blown abroad from all the heights,
Through all the nations, and a sound is heard,   80
As of a mighty wind, and men devout,
Strangers of Rome, and the new proselytes,
In their own language hear thy wondrous word,
And many are amazed and many doubt.
1864–67

[2] Lethe is the river of forgetfulness; Eunoë, the river of good.

Milton

I pace the sounding sea-beach and behold
  How the voluminous billows roll and run,
  Upheaving and subsiding, while the sun
  Shines through their sheeted emerald far unrolled,
And the ninth wave, slow gathering fold by fold   5
  All its loose-flowing garments into one,
  Plunges upon the shore, and floods the dun
  Pale reach of sands, and changes them to gold.
So in majestic cadence rise and fall
  The mighty undulations of thy song,   10
  O sightless bard, England's Maeonides![1]
And ever and anon, high over all
  Uplifted, a ninth wave superb and strong,
  Floods all the soul with its melodious seas.
1873

Venice

White swan of cities, slumbering in thy nest
  So wonderfully built among the reeds
  Of the lagoon, that fences thee and feeds,
  As sayeth thy old historian and thy guest!
White water-lily, cradled and caressed   5
  By ocean streams, and from the silt and weeds
  Lifting thy golden filaments and seeds,
  Thy sun-illumined spires, thy crown and crest!
White phantom city, whose untrodden streets   9
  Are rivers, and whose pavements are the shifting
  Shadows of palaces and strips of sky;
I wait to see thee vanish like the fleets
  Seen in mirage, or towers of cloud uplifting
  In air their unsubstantial masonry.
                                          1875

The Tide Rises, The Tide Falls

The tide rises, the tide falls,
The twilight darkens, the curlew calls;
Along the sea-sands damp and brown
The traveller hastens toward the town,
    And the tide rises, the tide falls.   5

Darkness settles on roofs and walls,
But the sea, the sea in the darkness calls;
The little waves, with their soft, white hands,
Efface the footprints in the sands,
    And the tide rises, the tide falls.   10

The morning breaks; the steeds in their stalls
Stamp and neigh, as the hostler calls;
The day returns, but nevermore
Returns the traveller to the shore,
    And the tide rises, the tide falls.   15
1879

Milton. [1] Homer.

JAMES RUSSELL LOWELL [1819-1891]

LOWELL WAS BORN and bred in Cambridge, and at his pleasant colonial house "Elmwood" spent most of his life. He came of one of the old, distinguished families of New England, and his home was rich in accumulated books. As an undergraduate at Harvard he read, he said, "nearly everything except the books prescribed by the faculty." When a senior he edited the college magazine, *Harvardiana,* and wrote the class poem. After graduation in 1838 he studied law, for no good reason. He was not interested.

Then he engaged to marry Maria White, of Watertown, Mass., who communicated to him her enthusiasms. Miss White wrote good poetry, was an ardent liberal and abolitionist, and inclined to mysticism. "They say," he reported, "that she is 'transcendental.' " Her influence and that of her romantic associates—"the Band"—is clear in two books of verse that Lowell published in the period before their marriage in 1844. Briefly he was an editor of the unsuccessful *Pioneer,* and he did antislavery writing for other periodicals. In 1848 he brought out *Poems* (second series), *The Biglow Papers* (first series), *A Fable for Critics,* and *The Vision of Sir Launfal*—all these in one year. He was now successfully launched as a poet. More than that, he had already written most of his best poetry.

He traveled in Europe, with his wife, two children, a nurse, and a goat, in 1851-52. The next year his wife died. He gave a course of lectures in Boston on the English poets, and this led to his Harvard appointment as Smith professor of French and Spanish and of belles-lettres at age thirty-five. After a second sojourn in Europe, 1855-56, he began the life of a teacher, scholar, critic, and, less frequently, poet. By this time his humanitarian ardors had cooled, and he had moved toward nationalism and a conservative humanism, impressed, as H. H. Clark puts it, with the need of "tradition, permanence, and inner control."

In 1857 he married Frances Dunlap, who had been his daughter's governess, and in the same year was made first editor of the *Atlantic Monthly.* Two years later he shifted to the *North American Review.* During the Civil War he wrote the second series of *The Biglow Papers,* and when the war was over delivered his "Commemoration Ode." Then came his long series of critical essays, beginning with *Among My Books* and *My Study Windows.* Before the middle of the 1870's he had been given honorary degrees by Oxford and Cambridge.

He was appointed Minister to Spain in 1877, as Irving had been thirty-five years before. After three years in Madrid, he was made minister to England, where he served till 1885. "During my reign no ambassador or minister has created so much interest or won so much regard," said Queen Victoria. After 1885 Lowell traveled widely, returned to Elmwood, and died.

It was a good life, and he won fame as poet, critic, essayist, professor, editor, diplomat. But he had never quite integrated his abounding talents.

Like Whittier and Longfellow, Lowell has a diminished reputation. This is partly because he had been overrated, and partly because he does not satisfy twentieth-century attitudes and tastes. Even less than Whittier's and Longfellow's poetry has Lowell's continued to speak across the years. His prose essays on European writers of various periods do impress many readers with his admirable standards and frequent insight. But he is too casual in method greatly to serve the literary intellectuals of today.

Text: *The Writings of James Russell Lowell,* Riverside Edition (Boston, 1890).

Further reading: Leon Howard, *Victorian Knight-Errant,* 1952. Martin Duberman, *James Russell Lowell,* 1966.

FROM *A Fable for Critics*

This piece of high-spirited, often penetrating banter is reminiscent of such earlier satires as Pope's *Dunciad*, Byron's *English Bards and Scotch Reviewers*, and Leigh Hunt's *The Feast of the Poets*, as well as *A Critical Fable* by Amy Lowell in the twentieth century. The "fable" is almost nonexistent. Essentially the poem presents critical sketches of American authors, such as those below.

[Emerson]

"There comes Emerson first, whose rich words, every one,
Are like gold nails in temples to hang trophies on,
Whose prose is grand verse, while his verse, the Lord knows,
Is some of it pr— No, 't is not even prose;
I'm speaking of metres; some poems have welled 5
From those rare depths of soul that have ne'er been excelled;
They're not epics, but that doesn't matter a pin,
In creating, the only hard thing's to begin;
A grass-blade's no easier to make than an oak;
If you've once found the way, you've achieved the grand stroke; 10
In the worst of his poems are mines of rich matter,
But thrown in a heap with a crash and a clatter;
Now it is not one thing nor another alone
Makes a poem, but rather the general tone,
The something pervading, uniting the whole, 15
The before unconceived, unconceivable soul,
So that just in removing this trifle or that, you
Take away, as it were, a chief limb of the statue;
Roots, wood, bark, and leaves singly perfect may be,
But, clapt hodge-podge together, they don't make a tree. 20

"But, to come back to Emerson (whom, by the way,
I believe we left waiting),—his is, we may say,
A Greek head on right Yankee shoulders, whose range
Has Olympus for one pole, for t' other the Exchange;
He seems, to my thinking (although I'm afraid 25
The comparison must, long ere this, have been made),
A Plotinus-Montaigne, where the Egyptian's gold mist
And the Gascon's shrewd wit cheek-by-jowl coexist;
All admire, and yet scarcely six converts he's got
To I don't (nor they either) exactly know what; 30
For though he builds glorious temples, 't is odd
He leaves never a doorway to get in a god.
'T is refreshing to old-fashioned people like me
To meet such a primitive Pagan as he,
In whose mind all creation is duly respected 35
As parts of himself—just a little projected;
And who's willing to worship the stars and the sun,
A convert to—nothing but Emerson.
So perfect a balance there is in his head,
That he talks of things sometimes as if they were dead; 40
Life, nature, love, God, and affairs of that sort,
He looks at as merely ideas; in short,
As if they were fossils stuck round in a cabinet,
Of such vast extent that our earth's a mere dab in it;
Composed just as he is inclined to conjecture her,
Namely, one part pure earth, ninety-nine parts pure lecturer; 46
You are filled with delight at his clear demonstration,
Each figure, word, gesture, just fits the occasion,
With the quiet precision of science he'll sort 'em,
But you can't help suspecting the whole a *post mortem.*° ° ° 50

"He has imitators in scores, who omit
No part of the man but his wisdom and wit,—
Who go carefully o'er the sky-blue of his brain,
And when he has skimmed it once, skim it again;
If at all they resemble him, you may be sure it is 55
Because their shoals mirror his mists and obscurities,
As a mud-puddle seems deep as heaven for a minute,
While a cloud that floats o'er is reflected within it.

[Whittier]

"There is Whittier, whose swelling and vehement heart
Strains the strait-breasted drab of the Quaker apart,
And reveals the live Man, still supreme and erect,
Underneath the bemummying wrappers of sect;
There was ne'er a man born who had more of the swing 5
Of the true lyric bard and all that kind of thing;
And his failures arise (though he seem not to know it)
From the very same cause that has made him a poet,—
A fervor of mind which knows no separation
'Twixt simple excitement and pure inspiration, 10
As my Pythoness erst sometimes erred from not knowing
If't were I or mere wind through her tripod was blowing;
Let his mind once get head in its favorite direction
And the torrent of verse bursts the dams of reflection,
While, borne with the rush of the metre along, 15
The poet may chance to go right or go wrong,
Content with the whirl and delirium of song;

Then his grammar's not always correct, nor his
    rhymes,
And he's prone to repeat his own lyrics sometimes,
Not his best, though, for those are struck off at
    white-heats   20
When the heart in his breast like a trip-hammer
    beats,
And can ne'er be repeated again any more
Than they could have been carefully plotted before:
Like old what's-his-name[1] there at the battle of
    Hastings
(Who, however, gave more than mere rhythmical
    bastings),   25
Our Quaker leads off metaphorical fights
For reform and whatever they call human rights,
Both singing and striking in front of the war,
And hitting his foes with the mallet of Thor;
Anne haec, one exclaims, on beholding his knocks,
Vestis filii tui,[2] O leather-clad Fox?[3]   31
Can that be thy son, in the battle's mid din,
Preaching brotherly love and then driving it in
To the brain of the tough old Goliath of sin,
With the smoothest of pebbles from Castaly's[4]
    spring   35
Impressed on his hard moral sense with a sling?

    "All honor and praise to the right-hearted bard
Who was true to The Voice when such service was
    hard,
Who himself was so free he dared sing for the slave
When to look but a protest in silence was brave;   40
All honor and praise to the women and men
Who spoke out for the dumb and the down-trodden
    then!

[Hawthorne]

    "There is Hawthorne, with genius so shrinking
    and rare
That you hardly at first see the strength that is
    there;
A frame so robust, with a nature so sweet,
So earnest, so graceful, so lithe and so fleet,
Is worth a descent from Olympus to meet;   5
'T is as if a rough oak that for ages had stood,
With his gnarled bony branches like ribs of the
    wood,
Should bloom, after cycles of struggle and scathe,

With a single anemone trembly and rathe;
His strength is so tender, his wildness so meek,   10
That a suitable parallel sets one to seek,—
He's a John Bunyan Fouqué, a Puritan Tieck;[1]
When Nature was shaping him, clay was not granted
For making so full-sized a man as she wanted,
So, to fill out her model, a little she spared   15
From some finer-grained stuff for a woman
    prepared,
And she could not have hit a more excellent plan
For making him fully and perfectly man.

[Poe and Longfellow]

    "There comes Poe, with his raven, like Barnaby
    Rudge,[1]
Three fifths of him genius and two fifths sheer
    fudge,
Who talks like a book of iambs and pentameters,
In a way to make people of common sense damn
    metres,
Who has written some things quite the best of their
    kind,   5
But the heart somehow seems all squeezed out by
    the mind,
Who— But hey-day! What's this? Messieurs
    Mathews[2] and Poe,
You must n't fling mud-balls at Longfellow so,
Does it make a man worse that his character's such
As to make his friends love him (as you think) too
    much?   10
Why, there is not a bard at this moment alive
More willing than he that his fellows should thrive;
While you are abusing him thus, even now
He would help either one of you out of a slough;
You may say that he's smooth and all that till you're
    hoarse,   15
But remember that elegance also is force;
After polishing granite as much as you will,
The heart keeps its tough old persistency still;
Deduct all you can, *that* still keeps you at bay;
Why, he'll live till men weary of Collins and Gray.[3]
I'm not over-fond of Greek metres in English,   21
To me rhyme's a gain, so it be not too jinglish,
And your modern hexameter verses are no more

Whittier. [1] Taillefer, a minstrel in William the Conqueror's army who supposedly encouraged the Normans at the Battle of Hastings by singing of the deeds of Roland.
    [2] Latin version of Genesis xxxvii.32; "Is this thy son's coat?" Asked by Joseph's brothers.
    [3] George Fox (1624-91), founder of the Society of Friends, the Quakers. The allusions suggest that Whittier is Fox's spiritual or Quaker "son."
    [4] Fountain on Mt. Parnassus, sacred to Apollo; the source of poetic inspiration.

Hawthorne. [1] The allusions suggest a contrast between moral intensity and romantic fantasy: John Bunyan (1628-88), Puritan author of *The Pilgrim's Progress*, 1678; Friedrich, Baron de la Motte Fouqué (1777-1843), who published *Undine*, a fairy romance, in 1811; Ludwig Tieck (1773-1853), a German romantic novelist.
    Poe. [1] The title character in the Dickens novel, 1841; Rudge was a murderer, a half-wit, and the owner of a raven.
    [2] Cornelius Mathews (1817-89). Both Poe and Mathews criticized Longfellow's poetry.
    [3] William Collins (1721-59) and Thomas Gray (1716-71), English poets.

Like Greek ones than sleek Mr. Pope[4] is like
    Homer;
As the roar of the sea to the coo of a pigeon is,   25
So, compared to your moderns, sounds old
    Melesigenes;[5]
I may be too partial, the reason, perhaps, o't is
That I've heard the old blind man recite his own
    rhapsodies,
And my ear with that music impregnate may be,
Like the poor exiled shell with the soul of the sea,
Or as one can't bear Strauss when his nature is
    cloven   31
To its deeps within deeps by the stroke of
    Beethoven;
But, set that aside, and 't is truth that I speak,
Had Theocritus[6] written in English, not Greek,
I believe that his exquisite sense would scarce
    change a line   35
In that rare, tender, virgin-like pastoral Evangeline.[7]
That's not ancient nor modern, its place is apart
Where time has no sway, in the realm of pure Art,
'T is a shrine of retreat from Earth's hubbub and
    strife
As quiet and chaste as the author's own life.   40

[Lowell]

"There is Lowell, who's striving Parnassus[1] to
    climb
With a whole bale of *isms* tied together with rhyme,
He might get on alone, spite of brambles and
    boulders,
But he can't with that bundle he has on his
    shoulders,
The top of the hill he will ne'er come nigh reaching
Till he learns the distinction 'twixt singing and
    preaching;   6
His lyre has some chords that would ring pretty
    well,
But he'd rather by half make a drum of the shell,
And rattle away till he's old as Methusalem,   9
At the head of a march to the last new Jerusalem.
    1848

FROM *The Biglow Papers*

Lowell published the First Series of *The Biglow Papers*
(1848) without his own name, as the verses of a young
Yankee farmer, "Hosea Biglow," laboriously edited by
"Homer Wilbur, A.M., Pastor of the First Church in
Jaalam."

[4]Alexander Pope (1688–1744) translated Homer into heroic
couplets.
[5]An ancient epithet for Homer.
[6]A Greek pastoral poet of the third century B.C.
[7]A long narrative poem in hexameter by Longfellow.
Lowell. [1]A mountain in Greece sacred to the Muses.

In these poems Lowell used humor and dialect for
propagandist ends, with great popular success. He found
his verses, he said, "copied everywhere; I saw them
pinned up in workshops; I heard them quoted and their
authorship debated." Whittier declared that the laugh
caused by Hosea Biglow was alone enough to have
"shaken half the walls of Slavery down." There had been
popular "cracker-box philosophers" before, notably Seba
Smith ("Major Downing"), but Lowell showed a grasp of
character and a literary skill that gave his work a deeper
interest.

The First Series concerned the Mexican War and
slavery. Lowell said later: "Thinking the Mexican War, as
I think it still, a national crime committed in behoof of
slavery, our common sin, and wishing to put the feeling of
those who thought as I did in a way that would tell, I
imagined to myself such an up-country man as I had often
seen at antislavery gatherings, capable of district school
English, but always instinctively falling back into the natural stronghold of his homely dialect when heated to the
point of self-forgetfulness. . . .

"In choosing the Yankee dialect, I did not act without
forethought. It had long seemed to me that the great vice
of American writing and speaking was a studied want of
simplicity, that we were in danger of coming to look on
our mother-tongue as a dead language, to be sought in the
grammar and dictionary rather than in the heart, and that
our only chance of escape was by seeking it at its living
sources among those who were, as Scottowe says of Major-
General Gibbons, 'divinely illiterate.' "

A Letter

FROM MR. EZEKIEL BIGLOW OF JAALAM TO THE HON.
  JOSEPH T. BUCKINGHAM, EDITOR OF THE BOSTON
  COURIER, INCLOSING A POEM OF HIS SON, MR.
  HOSEA BIGLOW.

Jaylem, june 1846.

MISTER EDDYTER:—Our Hosea wuz down to Bos-
ton last week, and he see a cruetin Sarjunt[1] a struttin
round as popler as a hen with 1 chicking, with 2
fellers a drummin and fifin arter him like all nater.
the sarjunt he thout Hosea hed n't gut his i teeth cut
cos he looked a kindo's though he'd jest com down,
so he cal'lated to hook him in, but Hosy wood n't
take none o' his sarse for all he hed much as 20
Rooster's tales stuck onto his hat and eenamost enuf
brass a bobbin up and down on his shoulders and
figureed onto his coat and trousis, let alone wut
nater hed sot in his featers, to make a 6 pounder out
on.

wal, Hosea he com home considerabal riled, and
arter I'd gone to bed I heern Him a thrashin round
like a short-tailed Bull in fli-time. The old Woman
ses she to me ses she, Zekle, ses she, our Hosee's gut
the chollery or suthin anuther ses she, don't you Bee

A Letter. [1]Recruiting sergeant. President Polk had been
authorized to employ the militia and call out 50,000
volunteers.

skeered, ses I, he 's oney amakin pottery ses i, he's ollers on hand at that ere busynes like Da & martin,[2] and shure enuf, cum mornin, Hosy he cum down stares full chizzle, hare on eend and cote tales flyin, and sot rite of to go reed his varses to Parson Wilbur bein he haint aney grate shows o' book larnin himself, bimeby he cum back and sed the parson wuz dreffle tickled with 'em as i hoop you will Be, and said they wuz True grit.

Hosea ses taint hardly fair to call 'em hisn now, cos the parson kind o' slicked off sum o' the last varses, but he told Hosee he did n't want to put his ore in to tetch to the Rest on 'em, bein they wuz verry well As thay wuz, and then Hosy ses he sed suthin a nuther about Simplex Mundishes[3] or sum sech feller, but I guess Hosea kind o' did n't hear him, for I never hearn o' nobody o' that name in this villadge, and I've lived here man and boy 76 year cum next tater diggin, and thair aint no wheres a kitting spryer 'n I be.

If you print 'em I wish you'd jest let folks know who hosy's father is, cos my ant Keziah used to say it 's nater to be curus ses she, she aint livin though and he's a likely kind o' lad.

EZEKIEL BIGLOW.

Thrash away, you'll *hev* to rattle
  On them kittle-drums o' yourn,—
'Taint a knowin' kind o' cattle
  Thet is ketched with mouldy corn;
Put in stiff, you fifer feller,   5
  Let folks see how spry you be,—
Guess you 'll toot till you are yeller
  'Fore you git ahold o' me!

Thet air flag's a leetle rotten,
  Hope it aint your Sunday's best;—   10
Fact! it takes a sight o' cotton
  To stuff out a soger's chest:
Sence we farmers hev to pay fer 't,
  Ef you must wear humps like these,
S'posin' you should try salt hay fer't,   15
  It would du ez slick ez grease.

'T would n't suit them Southun fellers,
  They're a dreffle graspin' set,
We must ollers blow the bellers
  Wen they want their irons het;   20
May be it's all right ez preachin',
  But *my* narves it kind o' grates,
Wen I see the overreachin'
  O' them nigger-drivin' States.

[2] Day and Martin: makers of shoe polish, who advertised in verse.
[3] The parson was actually calling him a simpleton.

Them thet rule us, them slave-traders,   25
  Haint they cut a thunderin' swarth
(Helped by Yankee renegaders),
  Thru the vartu o' the North!
We begin to think it's nater
  To take sarse an' not be riled;—   30
Who'd expect to see a tater
  All on eend at bein' biled?

Ez fer war, I call it murder,—
  There you hev it plain an' flat;
I don't want to go no furder   35
  Than my Testyment fer that;
God hez sed so plump an' fairly,
  It's ez long ez it is broad,
An' you've got to git up airly
  Ef you want to take in God.   40

'Taint your eppyletts an' feathers
  Make the thing a grain more right;
'Taint afollerin' your bell-wethers
  Will excuse ye in His sight;
Ef you take a sword an' dror it,   45
  An' go stick a feller thru,
Guv'ment aint to answer for it,
  God 'll send the bill to you.

Wut's the use o' meetin'-goin'
  Every Sabbath, wet or dry,   50
Ef it's right to go amowin'
  Feller-men like oats an' rye?
I dunno but wut it's pooty
  Trainin' round in bobtail coats,—
But it's curus Christian dooty   55
  This 'ere cuttin' folks's throats.

They may talk o' Freedom's airy
  Tell they're pupple in the face,—
It's a grand gret cemetary
  Fer the barthrights of our race;
They jest want this Californy[4]   60
  So's to lug new slave-states in
To abuse ye, an' to scorn ye,
  An' to plunder ye like sin.

Aint it cute to see a Yankee   65
  Take sech everlastin' pains,
All to git the Devil's thankee
  Helpin' on 'em weld their chains?
Wy, it's jest ez clear ez figgers,
  Clear ez one an' one make two,   70
Chaps thet make black slaves o' niggers
  Want to make wite slaves o' you.

[4] The Compromise of 1850 admitted California as a free state.

Tell ye jest the eend I've come to
   Arter cipherin' plaguy smart,
An' it makes a handy sum, tu,   75
   Any gump[5] could larn by heart;
Laborin' man an' laborin' woman
   Hev one glory an' one shame.
Ev'y thin' thet's done inhuman
   Injers all on 'em the same.   80

'Taint by turnin' out to hack folks
   You're agoin' to git your right,
Nor by lookin' down on black folks
   Coz you're put upon by wite;
Slavery aint o' nary color,   85
   'Taint the hide thet makes it wus,
All it keers fer in a feller
   'S jest to make him fill its pus.

Want to tackle *me* in, du ye?
   I expect you'll hev to wait;   90
Wen cold lead puts daylight thru ye
   You'll begin to kal'late;
S'pose the crows wun't fall to pickin'
   All the carkiss from your bones,
Coz you helped to give a lickin'   95
   To them poor half-Spanish drones?

Jest go home an' ask our Nancy
   Wether I'd be sech a goose
Ez to jine ye,—guess you'd fancy
   The etarnal bung wuz loose!   100
She wants me fer home consumption,
   Let alone the hay's to mow,—
Ef you're arter folks o' gumption,
   You've a darned long row to hoe.

Take them editors thet's crowin'   105
   Like a cockerel three months old,—
Don't ketch any on 'em goin',
   Though they *be* so blasted bold;
Aint they a prime lot o' fellers?
   'Fore they think on 't guess they'll sprout   110
(Like a peach thet's got the yellers[6]),
   With the meanness bustin' out.

Wal, go 'long to help 'em stealin'
   Bigger pens to cram with slaves,
Help the men thet's ollers dealin'   115
   Insults on your fathers' graves;
Help the strong to grind the feeble,
   Help the many agin the few,
Help the men thet call your people
   Witewashed slaves an' peddlin' crew!   120

[5] A foolish fellow, a dullard. [Lowell's note.]
[6] A fungus or virus disease.

Massachusetts,[7] God forgive her,
   She's akneelin' with the rest,
She, thet ough' to ha' clung ferever
   In her grand old eagle-nest;
She thet ough' to stand so fearless   125
   W'ile the wracks are round her hurled,
Holdin' up a beacon peerless
   To the oppressed of all the world!

Ha'n't they sold your colored seamen?[8]
   Ha'n't they made your env'ys w'iz?[9]   130
Wut'll make ye act like freemen?
   Wut'll git your dander riz?
Come, I'll tell ye wut I'm thinkin'
   Is our dooty in this fix,
They'd ha' done 't ez quick ez winkin'   135
   In the days o' seventy-six.

Clang the bells in every steeple,
   Call all true men to disown
The tradoocers of our people,
   The enslavers o' their own;   140
Let our dear old Bay State proudly
   Put the trumpet to her mouth,
Let her ring this messidge loudly
   In the ears of all the South:—

"I'll return ye good fer evil   145
   Much ez we frail mortils can,
But I wun't go help the Devil
   Makin' man the cus o' man;
Call me coward, call me traiter,
   Jest ez suits your mean idees,—   150
Here I stand a tyrant-hater,
   An' the friend o' God an' Peace!"

Ef I'd *my* way I hed ruther
   We should go to work an' part,
They take one way, we take t' other,   155
   Guess it wouldn't break my heart;
Man hed ough' to put asunder
   Them thet God has noways jined;
An' I shouldn't gretly wonder
   Ef there's thousands o' my mind.   160

1848

What Mr. Robinson Thinks

In 1847 George Nixon Briggs, Whig governor of Massachusetts, was up for re-election. He was opposed by General Caleb Cushing, the Democratic candidate, then

[7] Two of Massachusetts' representatives supported the bill declaring war.
[8] Several Southern states passed laws preventing free blacks from entering those states. The laws were particularly severe on black seamen.
[9] In 1844 Samuel Hoar and George Hubbard went South to act on behalf of oppressed black citizens of Massachusetts. The two were expelled.

serving in Mexico. John P. Robinson, lawyer and Whig
politician, who had previously supported Briggs, published
an open letter announcing his switch to the Democratic
candidate.

Guvener B. is a sensible man;
　He stays to his home an' looks arter his folks;
He draws his furrer ez straight ez he can,
　An' into nobody's tater-patch pokes;
　　　But John P.　　　　　　　　5
　　　Robinson he
　Sez he wunt vote fer Guvener B.

My! aint it terrible? Wut shall we du?
　We can't never choose him o' course,—thet's flat;
Guess we shall hev to come round, (don't you?)　10
　An' go in fer thunder an' guns, an' all that;
　　　Fer John P.
　　　Robinson he
　Sez he wunt vote fer Guvener B.

Gineral C. is a dreffle smart man:　　　15
　He's ben on all sides thet give places or pelf;
But consistency still wuz a part of his plan,—
　He 's ben true to *one* party,—an' thet is
　　　himself;—
　　　So John P.
　　　Robinson he　　　　　　　20
　Sez he shall vote fer Gineral C.

Gineral C. he goes in fer the war;
　He don't vally princerple more 'n an old cud;
Wut did God make us raytional creeturs fer,
　But glory an' gunpowder, plunder an' blood?　25
　　　So John P.
　　　Robinson he
　Sez he shall vote fer Gineral C.

We were gittin' on nicely up here to our village,
　With good old idees o' wut's right an' wut aint,　30
We kind o' thought Christ went agin war an' pillage,
　An' thet eppyletts worn't the best mark of a saint;
　　　But John P.
　　　Robinson he
　Sez this kind o' thing's an exploded idee.　　35

The side of our country must ollers be took,
　An' Presidunt Polk, you know, *he* is our country.
An' the angel thet writes all our sins in a book
　Puts the *debit* to him, an' to us the *per contry;*
　　　An' John P.　　　　　　　40
　　　Robinson he
　Sez this is his view o' the thing to a T.

Parson Wilbur he calls all these argimunts lies;
　Sez they're nothin' on airth but jest *fee, faw, fum;*
An' thet all this big talk of our destinies　　45
　Is half on it ign'ance, an' t' other half rum;

But John P.
　Robinson he
Sez it aint no sech thing; an', of course, so must
　we.

Parson Wilbur sez *he* never heerd in his life　50
　Thet th' Apostles rigged out in their swaller-tail
　　coats,
An' marched round in front of a drum an' a fife,
　To git some on 'em office, an' some on 'em votes;
　　　But John P.
　　　Robinson he　　　　　　　55
　Sez they didn't know everythin' down in Judee.

Wal, it's a marcy we've gut folks to tell us
　The rights an' the wrongs o' these matters, I
　　vow,—
God sends country lawyers, an' other wise fellers,
　To start the world's team wen it gits in a slough;
　　　Fer John P.　　　　　　　61
　　　Robinson he
　Sez the world 'll go right, ef he hollers out
　　Gee!¹

　　　　　　　　　　　　　　1848

The Courtin'

"The Courtin' " appeared in a brief form in the First
Series. Expanded—as given below—it opened the Second
Series, which was launched fourteen years after the First,
at the time of the Civil War.

God makes sech nights, all white an' still
　Fur 'z you can look or listen,
Moonshine an' snow on field an' hill,
　All silence an' all glisten.

Zekle crep' up quite unbeknown　　　5
　An' peeked in thru' the winder,
An' there sot Huldy all alone,
　'ith no one nigh to hender.

A fireplace filled the room's one side
　With half a cord o' wood in—　　　10
There warn't no stoves (tell comfort died)
　To bake ye to a puddin'.

The wa'nut logs shot sparkles out
　Towards the pootiest, bless her,
An' leetle flames danced all about　　15
　The chiny on the dresser.

Agin the chimbley crook-necks hung,
　An' in amongst 'em rusted

Mr. Robinson. ¹A command to oxen to turn right.

The ole queen's-arm[1] thet gran'ther Young
   Fetched back f'om Concord busted.'   20

The very room, coz she was in,
   Seemed warm f'om floor to ceilin',
An' she looked full ez rosy agin
   Ez the apples she was peelin'.

'T was kin' o' kingdom-come to look   25
   On sech a blessed cretur,
A dogrose blushin' to a brook
   Ain't modester nor sweeter.

He was six foot o' man, A 1,
   Clear grit an' human natur',   30
None couldn't quicker pitch a ton
   Nor dror a furrer straighter.

He'd sparked it with full twenty gals,
   Hed squired 'em, danced 'em, druv 'em,
Fust this one, an' then thet, by spells—   35
   All is, he couldn't love 'em.

But long o' her his veins 'ould run
   All crinkly like curled maple,
The side she breshed felt full o' sun
   Ez a south slope in Ap'il.   40

She thought no v'ice hed sech a swing
   Ez hisn in the choir;
My! when he made Ole Hunderd ring,
   She *knowed* the Lord was nigher.

An' she'd blush scarlit, right in prayer,   45
   When her new meetin'-bunnet
Felt somehow thru' its crown a pair
   O' blue eyes sot upun it.

Thet night, I tell ye, she looked *some!*
   She seemed to 've gut a new soul,   50
For she felt sartin-sure he'd come,
   Down to her very shoe-sole.

She heered a foot, an' knowed it tu,
   A-raspin' on the scraper,—
All ways to once her feelins flew   55
   Like sparks in burnt-up paper.

He kin' o' l'itered on the mat,
   Some doubtfle o' the sekle,
His heart kep' goin' pity-pat,
   But hern went pity Zekle.   60

An' yit she gin her cheer a jerk
   Ez though she wished him furder,

The Courtin'. [1] Musket.

An' on her apples kep' to work,
   Parin' away like murder.

"You want to see my Pa, I s'pose?"   65
   "Wal . . . no . . . I come dasignin' "—
"To see my Ma? She's sprinklin' clo'es
   Agin to-morrer's i'nin'."

To say why gals acts so or so,
   Or don't, 'ould be presumin';   70
Mebby to mean *yes* an' say *no*
   Comes naceral to women.

He stood a spell on one foot fust,
   Then stood a spell on t' other,
An' on which one he felt the wust   75
   He couldn't ha' told ye nuther.

Says he, "I'd better call agin";
   Says she, "Think likely, Mister":
Thet last word pricked him like a pin,
   An' . . . Wal, he up an' kist her.   80

When Ma bimeby upon 'em slips,
   Huldy sot pale ez ashes,
All kin' o' smily roun' the lips
   An' teary roun' the lashes.

For she was jes' the quiet kind   85
   Whose naturs never vary,
Like streams that keep a summer mind
   Snowhid in Jenooary.

The blood clost roun' her heart felt glued
   Too tight for all expressin',   90
Tell mother see how metters stood,
   An' gin 'em both her blessin'.

Then her red come back like the tide
   Down to the Bay o' Fundy,
An' all I know is they was cried[2]   95
   In meetin' come nex' Sunday.

                           1867

Fitz Adam's Story

Lowell prefixed his poem with the following note: "The greater part of this poem was written many years ago as part of a larger one, to be called 'The Nooning,' made up of tales in verse, some of them grave, some comic. It gives me a sad pleasure to remember that I was encouraged in this project by my friend the late Arthur Hugh Clough." Elsewhere he described the intent of his long poem thus: "My plan is this. I am going to bring together a party of

[2] Announcement was made of the couple's intention to marry.

half a dozen old friends at Elmwood. They go down to the river and bathe, and then one proposes that they shall go up into a great willow tree . . . to take their nooning. They agree that each shall tell a story or recite a poem of some sort."

The poem is of particular interest for its adumbration of themes and techniques that would be more fully explored by later writers: e.g., the use of folk or regional materials, anticipating the local colorists; the framework device of the cultivated narrator, widely used by frontier humorists; the Jamesian expatriate; and the mean-souled deacon, almost a prototype of Faulkner's Flem Snopes.

The next whose fortune 't was a tale to tell
Was one whom men, before they thought, loved
  well,
And after thinking wondered why they did,
For half he seemed to let them, half forbid,   4
And wrapped him so in humors, sheath on sheath,
'T was hard to guess the mellow soul beneath;
But, once divined, you took him to your heart,
While he appeared to bear with you as part
Of life's impertinence, and once a year
Betrayed his true self by a smile or tear,   10
Or rather something sweetly-shy and loath,
Withdrawn ere fully shown, and mixed of both.
A cynic? Not precisely: one who thrust
Against a heart too prone to love and trust,
Who so despised false sentiment he knew   15
Scarce in himself to part the false and true,
And strove to hide, by roughening-o'er the skin,
Those cobweb nerves he could not dull within.
Gentle by birth, but of a stem decayed,
He shunned life's rivalries and hated trade;   20
On a small patrimony and larger pride,
He lived uneaseful on the Other Side
(So he called Europe), only coming West
To give his Old-World appetite new zest;
Yet still the New World spooked it in his veins,   25
A ghost he could not lay with all his pains;
For never Pilgrims' offshoot scapes control
Of those old instincts that have shaped his soul.
A radical in thought, he puffed away
With shrewd contempt the dust of usage gray,   30
Yet loathed democracy as one who saw,
In what he longed to love, some vulgar flaw,
And, shocked through all his delicate reserves,
Remained a Tory by his taste and nerves.
His fancy's thrall, he drew all ergoes thence,   35
And thought himself the type of common sense;
Misliking women, not from cross or whim,
But that his mother shared too much in him,
And he half felt that what in them was grace
Made the unlucky weakness of his race.   40
What powers he had he hardly cared to know,
But sauntered through the world as through a show;
A critic fine in his haphazard way,

A sort of mild La Bruyère[1] on half-pay.
For comic weaknesses he had an eye   45
Keen as an acid for an alkali,
Yet you could feel, through his sardonic tone,
He loved them all, unless they were his own.
You might have called him, with his humorous twist,
A kind of human entomologist: 50
As these bring home, from every walk they take,
Their hat-crowns stuck with bugs of curious make,
So he filed all the lining of his head
With characters impaled and ticketed,
And had a cabinet behind his eyes   55
For all they caught of mortal oddities.
He might have been a poet—many worse—
But that he had, or feigned, contempt of verse;
Called it tattooing language, and held rhymes
The young world's lullaby of ruder times.   60
Bitter in words, too indolent for gall,
He satirized himself the first of all,
In men and their affairs could find no law,
And was the ill logic that he thought he saw.

  Scratching a match to light his pipe anew,   65
With eyes half shut some musing whiffs he drew,
And thus began: "I give you all my word,
I think this mock-Decameron absurd;
Boccaccio's[2] garden! how bring that to pass
In our bleak clime save under double glass?   70
The moral east-wind of New England life
Would snip its gay luxuriance like a knife;
Mile-deep the glaciers brooded here, they say,
Through aeons numb; we feel their chill to-day.
These foreign plants are but half-hardy still,   75
Die on a south, and on a north wall chill.
Had we stayed Puritans! *They* had some heat,
(Though whence derived I have my own conceit,)
But you have long ago raked up their fires;
Where they had faith, you've ten sham-Gothic
  spires.   80
Why more exotics? Try your native vines,
And in some thousand years you *may* have wines;
Your present grapes are harsh, all pulps and skins,
And want traditions of ancestral bins   84
That saved for evenings round the polished board
Old lava-fires, the sun-steeped hillside's hoard.
Without a Past, you lack that southern wall
O'er which the vines of Poesy should crawl;
Still they're your only hope; no midnight oil
Makes up for virtue wanting in the soil;   90

Fitz Adam's Story. [1] Jean de la Bruyère (1645-96), a French ethical writer and thus a kind of critic.
[2] Giovanni Boccaccio (1313-75), Italian writer and humanist who wrote *The Decameron*, a collection of tales. In it a group of people, who leave Florence because of the 1348 plague, amuse one another with stories.

Manure them well and prune them; 't won't be
    France,
Nor Spain, nor Italy, but there's your chance.
You have one story-teller worth a score
Of dead Boccaccios,—nay, add twenty more,—
A hawthorn[3] asking spring's most dainty breath,   95
And him you're freezing pretty well to death.
However, since you say so, I will tease
My memory to a story by degrees,
Though you will cry, 'Enough!' I'm wellnigh sure,
Ere I have dreamed through half my overture.   100
Stories were good for men who had no books,
(Fortunate race!) and built their nests like rooks
In lonely towers, to which the Jongleur[4] brought
His pedler's-box of cheap and tawdry thought,
With here and there a fancy fit to see   105
Wrought to quaint grace in golden filigree,—
Some ring that with the Muse's finger yet
Is warm, like Aucassin and Nicolete;[5]
The morning newspaper has spoilt his trade,
(For better or for worse, I leave unsaid,)   110
And stories now, to suit a public nice,
Must be half epigram, half pleasant vice.

    "All tourists know Shebagog County: there
The summer idlers take their yearly stare,
Dress to see Nature in a well-bred way,   115
As 't were Italian opera, or play,
Encore the sunrise (if they're out of bed),
And pat the Mighty Mother on the head:
These have I seen,—all things are good to see,—
And wondered much at their complacency.   120
This world's great show, that took in getting-up
Millions of years, they finish ere they sup;
Sights that God gleams through with soul-tingling
    force
They glance approvingly as things of course,
Say, 'That's a grand rock,' 'This a pretty fall,'   125
Not thinking, 'Are we worthy?' What if all
The scornful landscape should turn round and say,
'This is a fool, and that a popinjay'?
I often wonder what the Mountain thinks   129
Of French boots creaking o'er his breathless brinks,
Or how the Sun would scare the chattering crowd,
If some fine day he chanced to think aloud.
I, who love Nature much as sinners can,
Love her where she most grandeur shows,—in man:
Here find I mountain, forest, cloud, and sun,   135
River and sea, and glows when day is done;
Nay, where she makes grotesques, and moulds in
    jest
The clown's cheap clay, I find unfading zest.

[3] Reference to Nathaniel Hawthorne.
[4] A wandering minstrel in medieval France.
[5] A 13th-century legend of Provence, a love story.

The natural instincts year by year retire,
As deer shrink northward from the settler's fire,   140
And he who loves the wild game-flavor more
Than city-feasts, where every man's a bore
To every other man, must seek it where
The steamer's throb and railway's iron blare
Have not yet startled with their punctual stir   145
The shy, wood-wandering brood of Character.

    "There is a village, once the county town,
Through which the weekly mail rolled dustily down,
Where the courts sat, it may be, twice a year,
And the one tavern reeked with rustic cheer;   150
Cheeshogquesumscot erst, now Jethro hight,
Red-man and pale-face bore it equal spite.
The railway ruined it, the natives say,
That passed unwisely fifteen miles away,
And made a drain to which, with steady ooze,   155
Filtered away law, stage-coach, trade, and news.
The railway saved it; so at least think those
Who love old ways, old houses, old repose.
Of course the Tavern stayed: its genial host
Thought not of flitting more than did the post   160
On which high-hung the fading signboard creaks,
Inscribed, 'The Eagle Inn, by Ezra Weeks.'

    "If in life's journey you should ever find
An inn medicinal for body and mind,
'T is sure to be some drowsy-looking house   165
Whose easy landlord has a bustling spouse:
He, if he like you, will not long forego
Some bottle deep in cobwebbed dust laid low,
That, since the War we used to call the 'Last,'
Has dozed and held its lang-syne memories fast;   170
From him exhales that Indian-summer air
Of hazy, lazy welcome everywhere,
While with her toil the napery is white,
The china dustless, the keen knife-blades bright,
Salt dry as sand, and bread that seems as though   175
'T were rather sea-foam baked than vulgar dough.

    "In our swift country, houses trim and white
Are pitched like tents, the lodging of a night;
Each on its bank of baked turf mounted high
Perches impatient o'er the roadside dry,   180
While the wronged landscape coldly stands aloof,
Refusing friendship with the upstart roof.
Not so the Eagle; on a grass-green swell
That toward the south with sweet concessions fell
It dwelt retired, and half had grown to be   185
As aboriginal as rock or tree.
It nestled close to earth, and seemed to brood
O'er homely thoughts in a half-conscious mood,
As by the peat that rather fades than burns
The smouldering grandam nods and knits by turns,
Happy, although her newest news were old   191

Ere the first hostile drum at Concord[6] rolled.
If paint it e'er had known, it knew no more
Than yellow lichens spattered thickly o'er
That soft lead-gray, less dark beneath the eaves   195
Which the slow brush of wind and weather leaves.
The ample roof slopes backward to the ground,
And vassal lean-tos gathered thickly round,
Patched on, as sire or son had felt the need,
Like chance growths sprouting from the old roof's
        seed,   200
Just as about a yellow-pine-tree spring
Its rough-barked darlings in a filial ring.
But the great chimney was the central thought
Whose gravitation through the cluster wrought;
For 'tis not styles far-fetched from Greece or
        Rome,   205
But just the Fireside, that can make a home;
None of your spindling things of modern style,
Like pins stuck through to stay the card-built pile,
It rose broad-shouldered, kindly, debonair,
Its warm breath whitening in the October air,   210
While on its front a heart in outline showed
The place it filled in that serene abode.

"When first I chanced the Eagle to explore,
Ezra sat listless by the open door;
One chair careened him at an angle meet,   215
Another nursed his hugely-slippered feet;
Upon a third reposed a shirt-sleeved arm,
And the whole man diffused tobacco's charm.
'Are you the landlord?' 'Wahl, I guess I be,'
Watching the smoke, he answered leisurely.   220
He was a stoutish man, and through the breast
Of his loose shirt there showed a brambly chest;
Streaked redly as a wind-foreboding morn,
His tanned cheeks curved to temples closely shorn;
Clean-shaved he was, save where a hedge of gray
Upon his brawny throat leaned every way   226
About an Adam's-apple, that beneath
Bulged like a boulder from a brambly heath.
The Western World's true child and nursling he,
Equipt with aptitudes enough for three: 230
No eye like his to value horse or cow,
Or gauge the contents of a stack or mow;
He could foretell the weather at a word,
He knew the haunt of every beast and bird,
Or where a two-pound trout was sure to lie,   235
Waiting the flutter of his home-made fly;
Nay, once in autumns five, he had the luck
To drop at fair-play range a ten-tined buck;[7]
Of sportsmen true he favored every whim,
But never cockney found a guide in him;   240
A natural man, with all his instincts fresh,
Not buzzing helpless in Reflection's mesh,

Firm on its feet stood his broad-shouldered mind,
As bluffly honest as a northwest wind;   244
Hard-headed and soft-hearted, you'd scarce meet
A kindlier mixture of the shrewd and sweet;
Generous by birth, and ill at saying 'No,'
Yet in a bargain he was all men's foe,
Would yield no inch of vantage in a trade,
And gave away ere nightfall all he made.   250

" 'Can I have lodging here?' once more I said.
He blew a whiff, and, leaning back his head,
'You come a piece through Bailey's woods, I s'pose,
Acrost a bridge where a big swamp-oak grows?
It don't grow, neither: it's ben dead ten year,   255
Nor th' ain't a livin' creetur, fur nor near,
Can tell wut killed it; but I some misdoubt
'T was borers, there's sech heaps on 'em about.
You did n' chance to run ag'inst my son,
A long, slab-sided youngster with a gun?   260
He'd oughto ben back more 'n an hour ago,
An' brought some birds to dress for supper—sho!
There he comes now. 'Say, Obed, wut ye got?
(He'll hev some upland plover like as not.)
Wal, them's real nice uns, an 'll eat A 1,   265
Ef I can stop their bein' over-done;
Nothin' riles me (I pledge my fastin' word)
Like cookin' out the natur' of a bird;
(Obed, you pick 'em out o' sight an' sound,   269
Your ma am don't love no feathers cluttrin' round;)
Jes' scare 'em with the coals,—thet's my idee.'
Then, turning suddenly about on me,
'Wal, Square, I guess so. Callilate[8] to stay?
I'll ask Mis' Weeks; 'bout thet it's hern to say.'

"Well, there I lingered all October through,   275
In that sweet atmosphere of hazy blue,
So leisurely, so soothing, so forgiving,
That sometimes makes New England fit for living.
I watched the landscape, erst so granite glum,
Bloom like the south side of a ripening plum,   280
And each rock-maple on the hillside make
His ten days' sunset doubled in the lake;
The very stone walls draggling up the hills
Seemed touched, and wavered in their roundhead
        wills.
Ah! there's a deal of sugar in the sun!   285
Tap me in Indian summer, I should run
A juice to make rock-candy of,—but then
We get such weather scarce one year in ten.

"There was a parlor in the house, a room
To make you shudder with its prudish gloom.   290
The furniture stood round with such an air,
There seemed an old maid's ghost in every chair,
Which looked as it had scuttled to its place

[6] In the famous battle with the British, April 19, 1775.
[7] A ten-pointed buck.
[8] Calculate.

And pulled extempore a Sunday face,
Too smugly proper for a world of sin,   295
Like boys on whom the minister comes in.
The table, fronting you with icy stare,
Strove to look witless that its legs were bare,
While the black sofa with its horse-hair pall
Gloomed like a bier for Comfort's funeral.   300
Each piece appeared to do its chilly best
To seem an utter stranger to the rest,
As if acquaintanceship were deadly sin,
Like Britons meeting in a foreign inn.   304
Two portraits graced the wall in grimmest truth,
Mister and Mistress W. in their youth,—
New England youth, that seems a sort of pill,
Half wish-I-dared, half Edwards on the Will,
Bitter to swallow, and which leaves a trace
Of Calvinistic colic on the face.   310
Between them, o'er the mantel, hung in state
Solomon's temple, done in copperplate;
Invention pure, but meant, we may presume,
To give some Scripture sanction to the room.
Facing this last, two samplers you might see,   315
Each, with its urn and stiffly-weeping tree,
Devoted to some memory long ago
More faded than their lines of worsted woe;
Cut paper decked their frames against the flies,
Though none e'er dared an entrance who were
          wise,   320
And bushed asparagus in fading green
Added its shiver to the franklin clean.

"When first arrived, I chilled a half-hour there,
Nor dared deflower with use a single chair;
I caught no cold, yet flying pains could find   325
For weeks in me,—a rheumatism of mind.
One thing alone imprisoned there had power
To hold me in the place that long half-hour:
A scutcheon this, a helm-surmounted shield,
Three griffins argent on a sable field;   330
A relic of the shipwrecked past was here,
And Ezra held some Old-World lumber[9] dear.
Nay, do not smile; I love this kind of thing,
These cooped traditions with a broken wing,
This freehold nook in Fancy's pipe-blown ball,   335
This less than nothing that is more than all!
Have I not seen sweet natures kept alive
Amid the humdrum of your business hive,
Undowered spinsters shielded from all harms,
By airy incomes from a coat of arms?"   340

He paused a moment, and his features took
The flitting sweetness of that inward look
I hinted at before; but, scarcely seen,
It shrank for shelter 'neath his harder mien,
And, rapping his black pipe of ashes clear,   345

[9] Miscellaneous stored or discarded articles.

He went on with a self-derisive sneer:
"No doubt we make a part of God's design,
And break the forest-path for feet divine;
To furnish foothold for this grand prevision
Is good, and yet—to be the mere transition,   350
That, you will say, is also good, though I
Scarce like to feed the ogre By-and-by.
Raw edges rasp my nerves; my taste is wooed
By things that are, not going to be, good,   354
Though were I what I dreamed two lustres[10] gone,
I'd stay to help the Consummation on,
Whether a new Rome than the old more fair,
Or a deadflat of rascal-ruled despair;
But *my* skull somehow never closed the suture
That seems to knit yours firmly with the future,   360
So you'll excuse me if I'm sometimes fain
To tie the Past's warm nightcap o'er my brain;
I'm quite aware 'tis not in fashion here,
But then your northeast winds are *so* severe!

"But to my story: though 'tis truly naught   365
But a few hints in Memory's sketchbook caught,
And which may claim a value on the score
Of calling back some scenery now no more.
Shall I confess? The tavern's only Lar[11]   369
Seemed (be not shocked!) its homely-featured bar.
Here dozed a fire of beechen logs, that bred
Strange fancies in its embers golden-red,
And nursed the loggerhead whose hissing dip,
Timed by nice instinct, creamed the mug of flip
That made from mouth to mouth its genial round,
Nor left one nature wholly winter-bound;   376
Hence dropt the tinkling coal all mellow-ripe
For Uncle Reuben's talk-extinguished pipe;
Hence rayed the heat, as from an indoor sun,
That wooed forth many a shoot of rustic fun.   380
Here Ezra ruled as king by right divine;
No other face had such a wholesome shine,
No laugh like his so full of honest cheer;
Above the rest it crowed like Chanticleer.[12]

"In this one room his dame you never saw,   385
Where reigned by custom old a Salic law;[13]
Here coatless lolled he on his throne of oak,
And every tongue paused midway if he spoke.
Due mirth he loved, yet was his sway severe;
No blear-eyed driveller got his stagger here;   390

[10] Lustrum: a five-year period.
[11] *Lar familiaris:* the lord or tutelary spirit of a family, saluted daily by the ancient Romans in an area called the lararium; the bar was apparently either the household lord or the place where the spirit was saluted.
[12] The cock that figures in "Reynard the Fox" and Chaucer's "Nun's Priest's Tale."
[13] A law excluding women from inheriting land or one excluding them from succession in the French and Spanish monarchies.

'Measure was happiness; who wanted more,
Must buy his ruin at the Deacon's store;'
None but his lodgers after ten could stay,
Nor after nine on eves of Sabbath-day.
He had his favorites and his pensioners, 395
The same that gypsy Nature owns for hers:
Loose-ended souls, whose skills bring scanty gold,
And whom the poor-house catches when they're
 old;
Rude country-minstrels, men who doctor kine,
Or graft, and, out of scions ten, save nine; 400
Creatures of genius they, but never meant
To keep step with the civic regiment.
These Ezra welcomed, feeling in his mind
Perhaps some motions of the vagrant kind;
These paid no money, yet for them he drew 405
Special Jamaica[14] from a tap they knew,
And, for their feelings, chalked behind the door
With solemn face a visionary score.
This thawed to life in Uncle Reuben's throat
A torpid shoal of jest and anecdote, 410
Like those queer fish that doze the droughts away,
And wait for moisture, wrapt in sun-baked clay;
This warmed the one-eyed fiddler to his task,
Perched in the corner on an empty cask,
By whose shrill art rapt suddenly, some boor 415
Rattled a double-shuffle on the floor;
'Hull's Victory' was, indeed, the favorite air,
Though 'Yankee Doodle' claimed its proper share.

 " 'T was there I caught from Uncle Reuben's lips,
In dribbling monologue 'twixt whiffs and sips, 420
The story I so long have tried to tell;
The humor coarse, the persons common,—well,
From Nature only do I love to paint,
Whether she send a satyr or a saint;
To me Sincerity's the one thing good, 425
Soiled though she be and lost to maidenhood.
Quompegan is a town some ten miles south
From Jethro, at Nagumscot river-mouth,
A seaport town, and makes its title good
With lumber and dried fish and eastern wood. 430
Here Deacon Bitters dwelt and kept the Store,
The richest man for many a mile of shore;
In little less than everything dealt he,
From meeting-houses to a chest of tea;
So dextrous therewithal a flint to skin, 435
He could make profit on a single pin;
In business strict, to bring the balance true
He had been known to bite a fig in two,
And change a board-nail for a shingle-nail.
All that he had he ready held for sale, 440
His house, his tomb, whate'er the law allows,
And he had gladly parted with his spouse.
His one ambition still to get and get,
He would arrest your very ghost for debt. 444

 [14] Rum, probably.

His store looked righteous, should the Parson come,
But in a dark back-room he peddled rum,
And eased Ma'am Conscience, if she e'er would
 scold,
By christening it with water ere he sold.
A small, dry man he was, who wore a queue,
And one white neckcloth all the week-days
 through,— 450
On Monday white, by Saturday as dun
As that worn homeward by the prodigal son.
His frosted earlocks, striped with foxy brown,
Were braided up to hide a desert crown;
His coat was brownish, black perhaps of yore; 455
In summer-time a banyan loose he wore;
His trousers short, through many a season true,
Made no pretence to hide his stockings blue;
A waistcoat buff his chief adornment was,
Its porcelain buttons rimmed with dusky brass. 460
A deacon he, you saw it in each limb,
And well he knew to deacon-off a hymn,
Or lead the choir through all its wandering woes
With voice that gathered unction in his nose,
Wherein a constant snuffle you might hear, 465
As if with him 't were winter all the year.
At pew-head sat he with decorous pains,
In sermon-time could foot his weekly gains,
Or, with closed eyes and heaven-abstracted air,
Could plan a new investment in long-prayer. 470
A pious man, and thrifty too, he made
The psalms and prophets partners in his trade,
And in his orthodoxy straitened more
As it enlarged the business at his store;
He honored Moses, but, when gain he planned, 475
Had his own notion of the Promised Land.

 "Soon as the winter made the sledding good,
From far around the farmers hauled him wood,
For all the trade had gathered 'neath his thumb.
He paid in groceries and New England rum, 480
Making two profits with a conscience clear,—
Cheap all he bought, and all he paid with dear.
With his own mete-wand measuring every load,
Each somehow had diminished on the road;
An honest cord in Jethro still would fail 485
By a good foot upon the Deacon's scale,
And, more to abate the price, his gimlet eye
Would pierce to cat-sticks that none else could spy;
Yet none dared grumble, for no farmer yet
But New Year found him in the Deacon's debt. 490

 "While the first snow was mealy under feet,
A team drawled creaking down Quompegan street.
Two cords of oak weighed down the grinding sled,
And cornstalk fodder rustled overhead;
The oxen's muzzles, as they shouldered through, 495
Were silver-fringed; the driver's own was blue
As the coarse frock that swung below his knee.

Behind his load for shelter waded he;
His mittened hands now on his chest he beat,
Now stamped the stiffened cowhides of his feet,   500
Hushed as a ghost's; his armpit scarce could hold.
The walnut whipstock slippery-bright with cold.
What wonder if, the tavern as he past,   503
He looked and longed, and stayed his beasts at last,
Who patient stood and veiled themselves in steam
While he explored the bar-room's ruddy gleam?

"Before the fire, in want of thought profound,
There sat a brother-townsman weather-bound:
A sturdy churl, crisp-headed, bristly-eared,
Red as a pepper; 'twixt coarse brows and beard   510
His eyes lay ambushed, on the watch for fools,
Clear, gray, and glittering like two bay-edged pools;
A shifty creature, with a turn for fun,
Could swap a poor horse for a better one,—
He 'd a high-stepper always in his stall;   515
Liked far and near, and dreaded therewithal.
To him the in-comer, 'Perez, how d' ye do?'
'Jest as I'm mind to, Obed; how do you?'
Then, his eyes twinkling such swift gleams as run
Along the levelled barrel of a gun   520
Brought to his shoulder by a man you know
Will bring his game down, he continued, 'So,
I s'pose you're haulin' wood? But you're too late;
The Deacon's off; Old Splitfoot[15] couldn't wait;
He made a bee-line las' night in the storm   525
To where he won't need wood to keep him warm.
'Fore this he's treasurer of a fund to train
Young imps as missionaries; hopes to gain
That way a contract that he has in view
For fireproof pitchforks of a pattern new.   530
It must have tickled him, all drawbacks weighed,
To think he stuck the Old One in a trade;
His soul, to start with, wasn't worth a carrot,
And all he'd left 'ould hardly serve to swear at.'

"By this time Obed had his wits thawed out,   535
And, looking at the other half in doubt,
Took off his fox-skin cap to scratch his head,
Donned it again, and drawled forth, 'Mean he's
     dead?'
'Jesso; he's dead and t' other d that follers
With folks that never love a thing but dollars.   540
He pulled up stakes last evening, fair and square,
And ever since there's been a row Down There.
The minute the old chap arrived, you see,
Comes the Boss-devil to him, and says he,
"What are you good at? Little enough, I fear;   545
We callilate to make folks useful here."
"Well," says old Bitters, "I expect I can
Scale a fair load of wood with e'er a man."
"Wood we don't deal in; but perhaps you'll suit,

[15]The devil. The deacon died and went to hell.

Because we buy our brimstone by the foot: 550
Here, take this measurin'-rod, as smooth as sin,
And keep a reckonin' of what loads comes in.
You'll not want business, for we need a lot
To keep the Yankees that you send us hot;
At firin' up they're barely half as spry   555
As Spaniards or Italians, though they're dry;
At first we have to let the draught on stronger,
But, heat 'em through, they seem to hold it longer."

" 'Bitters he took the rod, and pretty soon
A teamster comes, whistling an ex-psalm tune.   560
A likelier chap you wouldn't ask to see,
No different, but his limp, from you or me'—
'No different, Perez! Don't your memory fail?
Why, where in thunder was his horns and tail?'
'They're only worn by some old-fashioned pokes;
They mostly aim at looking just like folks.   566
Sech things are scarce as queues and top-boots here;
'T would spoil their usefulness to look too queer.
Ef you could always know 'em when they come,
They'd get no purchase on you: now be mum.   570
On come the teamster, smart as Davy Crockett,[16]
Jinglin' the red-hot coppers in his pocket,
And clost behind, ('t was gold-dust, you'd ha'
     sworn,)
A load of sulphur yallower 'n seed-corn;
To see it wasted as it is Down There   575
Would make a Friction-Match Co. tear its hair!
"Hold on!" says Bitters, "stop right where you be;
You can't go in athout a pass from me."
"All right," says t' other, "only step round smart;
I must be home by noon-time with the cart."   580
Bitters goes round it sharp-eyed as a rat,
Then with a scrap of paper on his hat
Pretends to cipher. "By the public staff,   583
That load scarce rises twelve foot and a half."
"There's fourteen foot and over," says the driver,
"Worth twenty dollars, ef it's worth a stiver;
Good fourth-proof brimstone, that'll make 'em
     squirm,—
I leave it to the Headman of the Firm;
After we masure it, we always lay
Some on to allow for settlin' by the way.   590
Imp and full-grown, I've carted sulphur here,
And gi'n fair satisfaction, thirty year."
With that they fell to quarrellin' so loud
That in five minutes they had drawed a crowd,
And afore long the Boss, who heard the row,   595
Comes elbowin' in with "What's to pay here now?"
Both parties heard, the measurin'-rod he takes,
And of the load a careful survey makes.
"Sence I have bossed the business here," says he,
"No fairer load was ever seen by me."   600

[16]Frontier hero and successful politician (1786–1836);
known for his shrewd native intelligence.

Then, turnin' to the Deacon, "You mean cus,
None of your old Quompegan tricks with us!
They won't do here: we're plain old-fashioned folks,
And don't quite understand that kind o' jokes.
I know this teamster, and his pa afore him, 605
And the hard-working Mrs. D. that bore him;
He wouldn't soil his conscience with a lie,
Though he might get the custom-house thereby.
Here, constable, take Bitters by the queue,
And clap him into furnace ninety-two, 610
And try this brimstone on him; if he's bright,
He'll find the masure honest afore night.
He isn't worth his fuel, and I'll bet
The parish oven has to take him yet!" '

"This is my tale, heard twenty years ago 615
From Uncle Reuben, as the logs burned low,
Touching the walls and ceiling with that bloom
That makes a rose's calyx of a room.
I could not give his language, wherethrough ran
The gamy flavor of the bookless man 620
Who shapes a word before the fancy cools,
As lonely Crusoe improvised his tools.
I liked the tale,—'t was like so many told
By Rutebeuf[17] and his brother Trouvères bold;
Nor were the hearers much unlike to theirs, 625
Men unsophisticate, rude-nerved as bears.
Ezra is gone and his large-hearted kind,
The landlords of the hospitable mind;
Good Warriner of Springfield was the last;
An inn is now a vision of the past; 630
One yet-surviving host my mind recalls,—
You'll find him if you go to Trenton Falls."

1867

Emerson the Lecturer

Lowell's informal prose is spontaneous, often infectiously gay, often illuminatingly serious, and abounds in apt allusions and figures of speech. Far from an Emersonian, he yet managed to draw a sympathetic portrait of one of the princes of the Lyceum platform.

This essay was first published in the *Atlantic Monthly* in 1861, as a review of *The Conduct of Life,* and was revised in 1868. It may be compared with Lowell's thumbnail sketch of Emerson in *A Fable for Critics* twenty years earlier.

It is a singular fact, that Mr. Emerson is the most steadily attractive lecturer in America. Into that somewhat cold-waterish region adventurers of the sensational kind come down now and then with a

[17] Thirteenth-century French *trouvère:* i.e. composer of epic narrative poems.

splash, to become disregarded King Logs[1] before the next season. But Mr. Emerson always draws. A lecturer now for something like a third of a century, one of the pioneers of the lecturing system, the charm of his voice, his manner, and his matter has never lost its power over his earlier hearers, and continually winds new ones in its enchanting meshes. What they do not fully understand they take on trust, and listen, saying to themselves, as the old poet of Sir Philip Sidney,—

A sweet, attractive, kind of grace,
A full assurance given by looks,
Continual comfort in a face,
The lineaments of gospel books.

We call it a singular fact, because we Yankees are thought to be fond of the spread-eagle style, and nothing can be more remote from that than his. We are reckoned a practical folk, who would rather hear about a new air-tight stove than about Plato; yet our favorite teacher's practicality is not in the least of the Poor Richard variety.[2] If he have any Buncombe constituency, it is that unrealized commonwealth of philosophers which Plotinus[3] proposed to establish; and if he were to make an almanac his directions to farmers would be something like this "OCTOBER: *Indian Summer;* now is the time to get in your early Vedas."[4] What, then, is his secret? Is it not that he out-Yankees us all? that his range includes us all? that he is equally at home with the potato-disease and original sin, with pegging shoes and the Over-soul? that, as we try all trades, so has he tried all cultures? and above all, that his mysticism gives us a counterpoise to our super-practicality?

There is no man living to whom, as a writer, so many of us feel and thankfully acknowledge so great an indebtedness for ennobling impulses,—none whom so many cannot abide. What does he mean? ask these last. Where is his system? What is the use of it all? What the deuse have we to do with Brahma? I do not propose to write an essay on Emerson at this time. I will only say that one may find grandeur and consolation in a starlit night without caring to ask what it means, save grandeur and consolation;

Emerson the Lecturer. [1] According to Aesop, Jupiter, petitioned by the frogs for a king, cast a log among them, which ruled satisfactorily till the frogs lost their fright and knew the log for what it was.
[2] Refers to *Poor Richard's Almanack* (1733-58), by Benjamin Franklin which presented a great deal of homely wisdom through shrewd maxims and proverbs.
[3] Plotinus (c 203-262), a Neo-Platonic philosopher who wished to convert his disciples to the highest and most spiritual way of life
[4] Four ancient sacred books of the Hindus.

one may like Montaigne,[5] as some ten generations before us have done, without thinking him so systematic as some more eminently tedious (or shall we say tediously eminent?) authors; one may think roses as good in their way as cabbages, though the latter would make a better show in the witness-box, if cross-examined as to their usefulness; and as for Brahma, why, he can take care of himself, and won't bite us at any rate.

The bother with Mr. Emerson is, that, though he writes in prose, he is essentially a poet. If you undertake to paraphrase what he says, and to reduce it to words of one syllable for infant minds, you will make as sad work of it as the good monk with his analysis of Homer in the "Epistolae Obscurorum Virorum."[6] We look upon him as one of the few men of genius whom our age has produced, and there needs no better proof of it than his masculine faculty of fecundating other minds. Search for his eloquence in his books and you will perchance miss it, but meanwhile you will find that it has kindled all your thoughts. For choice and pith of language he belongs to a better age than ours, and might rub shoulders with Fuller[7] and Browne[8]—though he does use that abominable word *reliable*. His eye for a fine, telling phrase that will carry true is like that of a backwoodsman for a rifle; and he will dredge you up a choice word from the mud of Cotton Mather himself. A diction at once so rich and so homely as his I know not where to match in these days of writing by the page; it is like homespun cloth-of-gold. The many cannot miss his meaning, and only the few can find it. It is the open secret of all true genius. It is wholesome to angle in those profound pools, though one be rewarded with nothing more than the leap of a fish that flashes his freckled side in the sun and as suddenly absconds in the dark and dreamy waters again. There is keen excitement, though there be no ponderable acquisition. If we carry nothing home in our baskets, there is ample gain in dilated lungs and stimulated blood. What does he mean, quotha? He means inspiring hints, a divining-rod to your deeper nature. No doubt, Emerson, like all original men, has his peculiar audience, and yet I know none that can hold a promiscuous crowd in pleased attention so long as he. As in all original men, there is something for every palate. "Would you know," says Goethe, "the ripest cherries? Ask the boys and the blackbirds."

[5] Michel Eyquem de Montaigne (1533–92), author of the famous *Essays*.

[6] *Letters of Obscure Men.*

[7] Thomas Fuller (1608–61), well-known preacher, historian, character writer, and essayist; his greatest work: *The History of the Worthies of England*, 1662.

[8] Sir Thomas Browne (1605–82), physician and prose stylist; known best for *Religio Medici* (A Doctor's Religion), 1642.

The announcement that such a pleasure as a new course of lectures by him is coming, to people as old as I am, is something like those forebodings of spring that prepare us every year for a familiar novelty, none the less novel, when it arrives, because it is familiar. We know perfectly well what we are to expect from Mr. Emerson, and yet what he says always penetrates and stirs us, as is apt to be the case with genius, in a very unlooked-for fashion. Perhaps genius is one of the few things which we gladly allow to repeat itself,—one of the few that multiply rather than weaken the force of their impression by iteration? Perhaps some of us hear more than the mere words, are moved by something deeper than the thoughts? If it be so, we are quite right, for it is thirty years and more of "plain living and high thinking" that speak to us in this altogether unique lay-preacher. We have shared in the beneficence of this varied culture, this fearless impartiality in criticism and speculation, this masculine sincerity, this sweetness of nature which rather stimulates than cloys, for a generation long. If ever there was a standing testimonial to the cumulative power and value of Character, (and we need it sadly in these days,) we have it in this gracious and dignified presence. What an antiseptic is a pure life! At sixty-five (or two years beyond his grand climacteric, as he would prefer to call it) he has that privilege of soul which abolishes the calendar, and presents him to us always the unwasted contemporary of his own prime. I do not know if he seem old to his younger hearers, but we who have known him so long wonder at the tenacity with which he maintains himself even in the outposts of youth. I suppose it is not the Emerson of 1868 to whom we listen. For us the whole life of the man is distilled in the clear drop of every sentence, and behind each word we divine the force of a noble character, the weight of a large capital of thinking and being. We do not go to hear what Emerson says so much as to hear Emerson. Not that we perceive any falling-off in anything that ever was essential to the charm of Mr. Emerson's peculiar style of thought or phrase. The first lecture, to be sure, was more disjointed even than common. It was as if, after vainly trying to get his paragraphs into sequence and order, he had at last tried the desperate expedient of *shuffling* them. It was chaos come again, but it was a chaos full of shooting-stars, a jumble of creative forces. The second lecture, on "Criticism and Poetry," was quite up to the level of old times, full of that power of strangely-subtle association whose indirect approaches startle the mind into almost painful attention, of those flashes of mutual understanding between speaker and hearer that are gone ere one can say it lightens. The vice of Emerson's criticism seems to be, that while no man is so sensitive to what is poetical, few men are less sensible than he of what makes a poem. He values the solid meaning of thought above the subtler meaning of style. He would prefer Donne, I suspect, to Spenser, and sometimes mistakes the queer for the original.

To be young is surely the best, if the most precarious, gift of life; yet there are some of us who would hardly consent to be young again, if it were at the cost of our recollection of Mr. Emerson's first lectures during the consulate of Van Buren.[9] We used to walk in from the country to the Masonic Temple (I think it was), through the crisp winter night, and listen to that thrilling voice of his, so charged with subtle meaning and subtle music, as shipwrecked men on a raft to the hail of a ship that came with unhoped-for food and rescue. Cynics might say what they liked. Did our own imaginations transfigure dry remainder-biscuit into ambrosia? At any rate, he brought us *life,* which, on the whole, is no bad thing. Was it all transcendentalism? magic-lantern pictures on mist? As you will. Those, then, were just what we wanted. But it was not so. The delight and the benefit were that he put us in communication with a larger style of thought, sharpened our wits with a more pungent phrase, gave us ravishing glimpses of an ideal under the dry husk of our New England; made us conscious of the supreme and everlasting originality of whatever bit of soul might be in any of us; freed us, in short, from the stocks of prose in which we had sat so long that we had grown wellnigh contented in our cramps. And who that saw the audience will ever forget it, where every one still capable of fire, or longing to renew in himself the half-forgotten sense of it, was gathered? Those faces, young and old, agleam with pale intellectual light, eager with pleased attention, flash upon me once more from the deep recesses of the years with an exquisite pathos. Ah, beautiful young eyes, brimming with love and hope, wholly vanished now in that other world we call the Past, or peering doubtfully through the pensive gloaming of memory, your light impoverishes these cheaper days! I hear again that rustle of sensation, as they turned to exchange glances over some pithier thought, some keener flash of that humor which always played about the horizon of his mind like heat-lightning, and it seems now like the sad whisper of the autumn leaves that are whirling around me. But would my picture be complete if I forgot that ample and vegete countenance of Mr. R—— of W——,—how, from its regular post at the corner of the front bench, it turned in ruddy triumph to the profaner audience as if he were the inexplicably appointed fugleman of appreciation? I was reminded of him by

those hearty cherubs in Titian's[10] Assumption that look at you as who should say, "Did you ever see a Madonna like *that?* Did you ever behold one hundred and fifty pounds of womanhood mount heavenward before like a rocket?"

To some of us that long-past experience remains as the most marvellous and fruitful we have ever had. Emerson awakened us, saved us from the body of this death. It is the sound of the trumpet that the young soul longs for, careless what breath may fill it. Sidney heard it in the ballad of "Chevy Chase," and we in Emerson. Nor did it blow retreat, but called to us with assurance of victory. Did they say he was disconnected? So were the stars, that seemed larger to our eyes, still keen with that excitement, as we walked homeward with prouder stride over the creaking snow. And were *they* not knit together by a higher logic than our mere sense could master? Were we enthusiasts? I hope and believe we were, and am thankful to the man who made us worth something for once in our lives. If asked what was left? what we carried home? we should not have been careful for an answer. It would have been enough if we had said that something beautiful had passed that way. Or we might have asked in return what one brought away from a symphony of Beethoven? Enough that he had set that ferment of wholesome discontent at work in us. There is one, at least, of those old hearers, so many of whom are now in the fruition of that intellectual beauty of which Emerson gave them both the desire and the foretaste, who will always love to repeat:—

> Che in la mente m'è fitta, ed or m'accuora
> La cara e buona immagine paterna
> Di voi, quando nel mondo ad ora ad ora
> M'insegnavaste come l'uom s'eterna.

> [For in my mind is fixed, and touches now
>   My heart, the dear and good paternal image
>   Of you, when in the world from hour to hour
> You taught me how a man becomes eternal.
>   —Dante, Longfellow's translation.]

I am unconsciously thinking, as I write, of the third lecture of the present course, in which Mr. Emerson gave some delightful reminiscences of the intellectual influences in whose movement he had shared. It was like hearing Goethe read some passages of the "Wahrheit aus seinem Leben."[11] Not that there was not a little *Dichtung,*[12] too, here and there, as the lecturer built up so lofty a pedestal under certain figures as to lift them into a prominence of obscurity, and seem to masthead them there. Everybody was asking his neighbor who this or that recondite great man was, in the faint hope that somebody might once have heard of him. There are those who

[9] Martin Van Buren, President 1837–41. Emerson's *Essays, First Series,* based on lectures, was published in 1841.

[10] Venetian painter of the sixteenth century.
[11] Truths from his life.
[12] Poetry.

call Mr. Emerson cold. Let them revise their judgment in presence of this loyalty of his that can keep warm for half a century, that never forgets a friendship, or fails to pay even a fancied obligation to the uttermost farthing. This substantiation of shadows was but incidental, and pleasantly characteristic of the man to those who know and love him. The greater part of the lecture was devoted to reminiscences of things substantial in themselves. He spoke of Everett, fresh from Greece and Germany; of Channing; of the translations of Margaret Fuller, Ripley, and Dwight; of the Dial and Brook Farm.[13] To what he said of the latter an undertone of good-humored irony gave special zest. But what every one of his hearers felt was that the protagonist in the drama was left out. The lecturer was no Aeneas to babble the *quorum magna pars fui*,[14] and, as one of his listeners, I cannot help wishing to say how each of them was commenting the story as it went along, and filling up the necessary gaps in it from his own private store of memories. His younger hearers could not know how much they owed to the benign impersonality, the quiet scorn of everything ignoble, the never-sated hunger of self-culture, that were personified in the man before them. But the older knew how much the country's intellectual emancipation was due to the stimulus of his teaching and example, how constantly he had kept burning the beacon of an ideal life above our lower region of turmoil. To him more than to all other causes together did the young martyrs of our civil war owe the sustaining strength of thoughtful heroism that is so touching in every record of their lives. Those who are grateful to Mr. Emerson, as many of us are, for what they feel to be most valuable in their culture, or perhaps I should say their impulse, are grateful not so much for any direct teachings of his as for that inspiring lift which only genius can give, and without which all doctrine is chaff.

This was something like the *caret* which some of us older boys wished to fill up on the margin of the master's lecture. Few men have been so much to so many, and through so large a range of aptitudes and temperaments, and this simply because all of us value manhood beyond any or all other qualities of character. We may suspect in him, here and there, a certain thinness and vagueness of quality, but let the waters go over him as they list, this masculine fibre of his will keep its lively color and its toughness of texture. I have heard some great speakers and some accomplished orators, but never any that so moved

and persuaded men as he. There is a kind of undertow in that rich baritone of his that sweeps our minds from their foothold into deeper waters with a drift we cannot and would not resist. And how artfully (for Emerson is a long-studied artist in these things) does the deliberate utterance, that seems waiting for the fit word, appear to admit us partners in the labor of thought and make us feel as if the glance of humor were a sudden suggestion, as if the perfect phrase lying written there on the desk were as unexpected to him as to us! In that closely-filed speech of his at the Burns[15] centenary dinner, every word seemed to have just dropped down to him from the clouds. He looked far away over the heads of his hearers, with a vague kind of expectation, as into some private heaven of invention, and the winged period came at last obedient to his spell. "My dainty Ariel!"[16] he seemed murmuring to himself as he cast down his eyes as if in deprecation of the frenzy of approval and caught another sentence from the Sibylline leaves that lay before him, ambushed behind a dish of fruit and seen only by nearest neighbors. Every sentence brought down the house, as I never saw one brought down before,— and it is not so easy to hit Scotsmen with a sentiment that has no hint of native brogue in it. I watched, for it was an interesting study, how the quick sympathy ran flashing from face to face down the long tables, like an electric spark thrilling as it went, and then exploded in a thunder of plaudits. I watched till tables and faces vanished, for I, too, found myself caught up in the common enthusiasm, and my excited fancy set me under the *bema* listening to him who fulmined over Greece. I can never help applying to him what Ben Jonson said of Bacon: "There happened in my time one noble speaker, who was full of gravity in his speaking. His language was nobly censorious. No man ever spake more neatly, more pressly, more weightily, or suffered less emptiness, less idleness, in what he uttered. No member of his speech but consisted of his own graces. His hearers could not cough, or look aside from him, without loss. He commanded where he spoke." Those who heard him while their natures were yet plastic, and their mental nerves trembled under the slightest breath of divine air, will never cease to feel and say:—

> Was never eye did see that face,
>   Was never ear did hear that tongue,
> Was never mind did mind his grace,
>   That ever thought the travail long;
> But eyes, and ears, and every thought,
> Were with his sweet perfections caught.[17]

1861   1868

[13] Edward Everett, probably, (1794–1865), Unitarian minister, Harvard professor of Greek, and editor of the *North American Review*; William Ellery Channing (1818–1901), poet and friend of Emerson's; Margaret Fuller (1810–50), feminist and Transcendentalist; George Ripley (1802–80), who helped found *The Dial* (1840–44; the quarterly publication of the Transcendentalists) and organize Brook Farm.
[14] "In which events I had a great share."
[15] Robert Burns (1759–96), famous Scottish poet.
[16] Compares Emerson to Prospero addressing the spirit Ariel in *The Tempest*.
[17] From Matthew Roydon's elegy to Sir Philip Sidney (1593), the same poem quoted in the opening paragraph of the essay.

OLIVER WENDELL HOLMES [1809–1894]

As DR. JOHNSON felt about London—"When a man is tired of London, he is tired of life"—so did Holmes feel about Boston. "Boston State-House," he said, "is the hub of the solar system." Holmes was his own Boswell, in *The Autocrat of the Breakfast-Table* and its sequels. In poetic taste, he admired Pope, and, like Pope, was fond of Horace, that "wise and charming" ancient Roman. In general, his attitudes and tone resembled those of the Neoclassic Age: he preferred breakfast-table clarity and reason to the "moonlight-genius" of the romantics, though, like some of the eighteenth-century wits, he was also given to tender sentiment. As a contemporary, William J. Stillman, put it, "He was the sublimation of Yankee wit as Lowell was of Yankee humor and human nature, and he made of witticism a study."

His attachment to Boston came naturally. Born in neighboring Cambridge, he enjoyed a distinguished ancestry that included Anne Bradstreet, belonged to that "Brahmin caste of New England" which he described as a "harmless, inoffensive, untitled aristocracy." His father, the Rev. Abiel Holmes, was a defender of Calvinism, a creed that the son decisively rejected. After graduating from Harvard in 1829, he had a year in the law school, and at this time wrote a fiery lyric, "Old Ironsides," that made his name known throughout the country.

Having given up the law, Holmes prepared himself in medicine at Harvard and in Paris. In 1835 he began to practice (he took as his motto "the smallest fevers thankfully received") and wrote and lectured on the side. His first book of poems had been issued in 1833, and he continued to produce occasional verse and essays, as well as medical articles. His most valuable medical contribution was "The Contagiousness of Puerperal Fever." Turning from practice to teaching, Holmes was briefly professor of anatomy at Dartmouth College, and then, in 1847, entered upon thirty-five years of successful teaching as professor of anatomy and physiology in the Harvard Medical School.

In 1831 he had published in the *New England Magazine* two essays called "The Autocrat of the Breakfast-Table." Twenty-six years later, using the same title, he resumed with a new series, in which his first words were: "I was just going to say, when I was interrupted. . . ." In book form, *The Autocrat of the Breakfast-Table* was followed by *The Professor at the Breakfast-Table, The Poet at the Breakfast-Table,* and *Over the Tea-Cups.* Along with these sparkling monologues, he wrote excellent familiar verse, and also several novels, the best known of which was *Elsie Venner: A Romance of Destiny.* Not important as works of art, his "medicated novels" have acquired interest because they foreshadowed psychological attitudes toward crime and punishment typical of the twentieth century. We doctors, he wrote, "have nothing but compassion for a large class of persons condemned as sinners by theologians, but considered by us as invalids."

Further reading: "The Autocrat of the Breakfast-Table," in *Oliver Wendell Holmes: Representative Selections,* ed. S. I. Hayakawa and H. M. Jones, 1939. M. A. DeW. Howe, *Holmes of the Breakfast-Table,* 1939. E. M. Tilton, *Amiable Autocrat,* 1947.

My Aunt

Humor, wit, and sentiment are here gently commingled in a way that was characteristic of Holmes. The texts of this and the following selections are from the Riverside Edition of *The Writings of Oliver Wendell Holmes* (Boston, 1891).

My aunt! my dear unmarried aunt!
    Long years have o'er her flown;
Yet still she strains the aching clasp
    That binds her virgin zone;
I know it hurts her,—though she looks   5
    As cheerful as she can;
Her waist is ampler than her life,
    For life is but a span.

My aunt! my poor deluded aunt!
    Her hair is almost gray;   10
Why will she train that winter curl
    In such a spring-like way?
How can she lay her glasses down,
    And say she reads as well,
When through a double convex lens   15
    She just makes out to spell?

Her father—grandpapa! forgive
    This erring lip its smiles—
Vowed she should make the finest girl
    Within a hundred miles;   20
He sent her to a stylish school;
    'T was in her thirteenth June;
And with her, as the rules required,
    "Two towels and a spoon."

They braced my aunt against a board,   25
    To make her straight and tall;
They laced her up, they starved her down,
    To make her light and small;
They pinched her feet, they singed her hair,
    They screwed it up with pins;—   30
Oh never mortal suffered more
    In penance for her sins.

So, when my precious aunt was done,
    My grandsire brought her back;
(By daylight, lest some rabid youth   35
    Might follow on the track;)
"Ah!" said my grandsire, as he shook
    Some powder in his pan,[1]
"What could this lovely creature do
    Against a desperate man!"   40

Alas! nor chariot, nor barouche,
    Nor bandit cavalcade,

My Aunt. [1] The part of the flintlock that held the firing powder in old guns and pistols.

Tore from the trembling father's arms
    His all-accomplished maid.
For her how happy had it been!   45
    And Heaven had spared to me
To see one sad, ungathered rose
    On my ancestral tree.

    1831

The Last Leaf

The poem was suggested by the figure of Major Thomas Melville (grandfather of Herman Melville), known as "the last of the cocked hats" of the Revolutionary period.

I saw him once before,
As he passed by the door,
    And again
The pavement stones resound,
As he totters o'er the ground   5
    With his cane.

They say that in his prime,
Ere the pruning-knife of Time
    Cut him down,
Not a better man was found   10
By the Crier on his round
    Through the town.

But now he walks the streets,
And he looks at all he meets
    Sad and wan,
And he shakes his feeble head,   15
That it seems as if he said,
    "They are gone."

The mossy marbles rest
On the lips that he has prest
    In their bloom,   20
And the names he loved to hear
Have been carved for many a year
    On the tomb.

My grandmamma has said—   25
Poor old lady, she is dead
    Long ago—
That he had a Roman nose,
And his cheek was like a rose
    In the snow.   30

But now his nose is thin,
And it rests upon his chin
    Like a staff,
And a crook is in his back,
And a melancholy crack   35
    In his laugh.

I know it is a sin
For me to sit and grin
    At him here;
But the old three-cornered hat,   40
And the breeches, and all that,
    Are so queer!

And if I should live to be
The last leaf upon the tree
    In the spring,   45
Let them smile, as I do now,
At the old forsaken bough
    Where I cling.

                                          1831

The Chambered Nautilus

In introducing this poem in *The Autocrat of the Breakfast-Table*, Holmes remarked, somewhat in the manner of Emerson in *Nature*, "Did I not say to you a little while ago that the universe swam in an ocean of similitudes and analogies?" Though Holmes usually made scant use of Emerson's thought, he may have remembered in writing the poem that Emerson, in "Compensation," had compared man's growth to that of the shell-fish which "crawls out of its beautiful but stony case, because it no longer admits of its growth, and slowly forms itself a new house." In Holmes's poem, the shell-fish is the Pearly Nautilus. As it grows it develops its shell, living successively in a series of compartments or chambers, each larger than the one before.

This is the ship of pearl, which, poets feign,
    Sails the unshadowed main,—
    The venturous bark that flings
On the sweet summer wind its purpled wings
In gulfs enchanted, where the Siren sings,   5
    And coral reefs lie bare,
Where the cold sea-maids rise to sun their streaming
        hair.

Its webs of living gauze no more unfurl;
    Wrecked is the ship of pearl!
    And every chambered cell,   10
Where its dim dreaming life was wont to dwell,
As the frail tenant shaped his growing shell,
    Before thee lies revealed,—
Its irised ceiling rent, its sunless crypt unsealed!

Year after year beheld the silent toil   15
    That spread his lustrous coil;
    Still, as the spiral grew,
He left the past year's dwelling for the new,
Stole with soft step its shining archway through,
    Built up its idle door,   20
Stretched in his last-found home, and knew the old
        no more.

Thanks for the heavenly message brought by thee,
    Child of the wandering sea,
    Cast from her lap, forlorn!
From thy dead lips a clearer note is born   25
Than ever Triton blew from wreathèd horn!
    While on mine ear it rings,
Through the deep caves of thought I hear a voice
        that sings:—

Build thee more stately mansions, O my soul,
    As the swift seasons roll!   30
    Leave thy low-vaulted past!
Let each new temple, nobler than the last,
Shut thee from heaven with a dome more vast,
    Till thou at length art free,   34
Leaving thine outgrown shell by life's unresting sea!

                                                 1858

Contentment

"Man wants but little here below."

Little I ask; my wants are few;
    I only wish a hut of stone,
(A *very plain* brown stone will do,)[1]
    That I may call my own;—
And close at hand is such a one,   5
In yonder street that fronts the sun.

Plain food is quite enough for me;
    Three courses are as good as ten;—
If Nature can subsist on three,
    Thank Heaven for three. Amen!   10
I always thought cold victual nice;—
My *choice* would be vanilla-ice.

I care not much for gold or land;—
    Give me a mortgage here and there,—
Some good bank-stock, some note of hand,   15
    Or trifling railroad share,—
I only ask that Fortune send
A *little* more than I shall spend.

Honors are silly toys, I know,
    And titles are but empty names;   20
I would, *perhaps*, be Plenipo,[2]—
    But only near St. James;
I'm very sure I should not care
To fill our Gubernator's chair.

Contentment. [1] Brownstone was then the fashionable building material among the rich.

[2] A diplomat with full power; the most important American plenipotentiary was the minister to the court of St. James in London.

Jewels are baubles; 'tis a sin   25
  To care for such unfruitful things;—
One good-sized diamond in a pin,—
  Some, *not so large,* in rings;—
A ruby, and a pearl, or so,
Will do for me;—I laugh at show.   30

My dame should dress in cheap attire;
  (Good, heavy silks are never dear;)—
I own perhaps I *might* desire
  Some shawls of true Cashmere,—
Some marrowy crapes of China silk,   35
Like wrinkled skins on scalded milk.

I would not have the horse I drive
  So fast that folks must stop and stare;
An easy gait—two, forty-five—
  Suits me; I do not care;—   40
Perhaps, for just a *single spurt,*
Some seconds less would do no hurt.

Of pictures, I should like to own
  Titians and Raphaels three or four,—
I love so much their style and tone,   45
  One Turner,[3] and no more,
(A landscape,—foreground golden dirt,—
The sunshine painted with a squirt.)

Of books but few,—some fifty score
  For daily use, and bound for wear;   50
The rest upon an upper floor;—
  Some *little* luxury *there*
Of red morocco's gilded gleam
And vellum rich as country cream.[4]

Busts, cameos, gems,—such things as these,   55
  Which others often show for pride,
I value for their power to please,
  And selfish churls deride;—
One Stradivarius, I confess,
Two Meerschaums, I would fain possess.   60

Wealth's wasteful tricks I will not learn,
  Nor ape the glittering upstart fool;—
Shall not carved tables serve my turn,
  But *all* must be of buhl?
Give grasping pomp its double share,—   65
I ask but *one* recumbent chair.

Thus humble let me live and die,
  Nor long for Midas' golden touch;
If Heaven more generous gifts deny,
  I shall not miss them *much,* —   70

[3] Joseph M. W. Turner (1775–1851), well-known landscape painter.
[4] Very expensive leather binding and parchment.

Too grateful for the blessing lent
Of simple tastes and mind content!

                      1858

The Deacon's Masterpiece

Or, The Wonderful "One-Hoss Shay"

A LOGICAL STORY

Another poem from Holmes's *Autocrat.* The comic narrative is also a burlesque of the Calvinist theology that persisted in Holmes's day. Like the one-hoss shay, it too should collapse in spite of its apparent internal logic.

Have you heard of the wonderful one-hoss shay,
That was built in such a logical way
It ran a hundred years to a day,
And then, of a sudden, it—ah, but stay,
I'll tell you what happened without delay,   5
Scaring the parson into fits,
Frightening people out of their wits,—
Have you ever heard of that, I say?

Seventeen hundred and fifty-five.
Georgius Secundus[1] was then alive,—   10
Snuffy old drone from the German hive.
That was the year when Lisbon-town
Saw the earth open and gulp her down,[2]
And Braddock's[3] army was done so brown,
Left without a scalp to its crown.   15
It was on the terrible Earthquake-day
That the Deacon finished the one-hoss shay.

Now in building of chaises, I tell you what,
There is always *somewhere* a weakest spot,—
In hub, tire, felloe, in spring or thill,   20
In panel, or crossbar, or floor, or sill,
In screw, bolt, thoroughbrace,—lurking still,
Find it somewhere you must and will,—
Above or below, or within or without,—
And that's the reason, beyond a doubt,   25
That a chaise *breaks down,* but doesn't *wear out.*

But the Deacon swore (as Deacons do,
With an "I dew vum," or an "I tell *yeou,*")
He would build one shay to beat the taown
'n' the keounty 'n' all the kentry raoun';   30
It should be so built that it *couldn'* break daown:
"Fur," said the Deacon, " 't's mighty plain

The Deacon's Masterpiece. [1] George II, King of England 1727–60, was born in Germany.
  [2] The earthquake of November 1, 1755, one of the severest on record, leveled Lisbon, Portugal, and killed between 10,000 and 20,000 people in that city alone.
  [3] General Edward Braddock, killed in 1755 in the French and Indian War.

Thut the weakes' place mus' stan' the strain;
'n' the way t' fix it, uz I maintain,
     Is only jest   35
T' make that place uz strong uz the rest."

So the Deacon inquired of the village folk
Where he could find the strongest oak,
That couldn't be split nor bent nor broke,—
That was for spokes and floor and sills;   40
He sent for lancewood to make the thills;
The crossbars were ash, from the straightest trees,
The panels of white-wood, that cuts like cheese,
But lasts like iron for things like these;
The hubs of logs from the "Settler's ellum,"—   45
Last of its timber,—they couldn't sell 'em,
Never an axe had seen their chips,
And the wedges flew from between their lips,
Their blunt ends frizzled like celery-tips;
Step and prop-iron, bolt and screw,   50
Spring, tire, axle, and linchpin too,
Steel of the finest, bright and blue;
Thoroughbrace bison-skin, thick and wide;
Boot, top, dasher, from tough old hide
Found in the pit when the tanner died.   55
That was the way he "put her through."
"There!" said the Deacon, "naow she'll dew!"

Do! I tell you, I rather guess
She was a wonder, and nothing less!
Colts grew horses, beards turned gray,   60
Deacon and deaconess dropped away,
Children and grandchildren—where were they?
But there stood the stout old one-hoss shay
As fresh as on Lisbon-earthquake-day!

EIGHTEEN HUNDRED;—it came and found   65
The Deacon's masterpiece strong and sound.
Eighteen hundred increased by ten;—
"Hahnsum kerridge" they called it then.
Eighteen hundred and twenty came;—
Running as usual; much the same.   70
Thirty and forty at last arrive,
And then come fifty, and FIFTY-FIVE.

Little of all we value here
Wakes on the morn of its hundredth year
Without both feeling and looking queer.   75
In fact, there's nothing that keeps its youth,

So far as I know, but a tree and truth.
(This is a moral that runs at large;
Take it.—You're welcome.—No extra charge.)

FIRST OF NOVEMBER,—the Earthquake-day,—   80
There are traces of age in the one-hoss shay,
A general flavor of mild decay,
But nothing local, as one may say.
There couldn't be,—for the Deacon's art
Had made it so like in every part   85
That there wasn't a chance for one to start.
For the wheels were just as strong as the thills,
And the floor was just as strong as the sills,
And the panels just as strong as the floor,
And the whipple-tree neither less nor more,   90
And the back-crossbar as strong as the fore,
And spring and axle and hub *encore.*
And yet, *as a whole,* it is past a doubt
In another hour it will be *worn out!*

First of November, 'Fifty-five!   95
This morning the parson takes a drive.
Now, small boys, get out of the way!
Here comes the wonderful one-hoss shay,
Drawn by a rat-tailed, ewe-necked bay.
"Huddup!" said the parson.—Off went they.   100
The parson was working his Sunday's text,—
Had got to *fifthly,* and stopped perplexed
At what the—Moses—was coming next.
All at once the horse stood still,
Close by the meet'n'-house on the hill.   105
First a shiver, and then a thrill,
Then something decidedly like a spill,—
And the parson was sitting upon a rock,
At half past nine by the meet'n'-house clock,—
Just the hour of the Earthquake shock!   110
What do you think the parson found,
When he got up and stared around?
The poor old chaise in a heap or mound,
As if it had been to the mill and ground!
You see, of course, if you're not a dunce,   115
How it went to pieces all at once,—
All at once, and nothing first,—
Just as bubbles do when they burst.

End of the wonderful one-hoss shay.
Logic is logic. That's all I say.   120

                                  1858

WALT WHITMAN [1819–1892]

THE PULSE OF THE NATION beat strong in New York, a city of over half a million souls in 1855 when Whitman published *Leaves of Grass*. But its literary life could not vie with that of Concord and Cambridge. Whitman was its only great writer, and for many years few recognized his greatness. During the late 1850's and early 1860's he fraternized with the "bohemians" who met at Pfaff's restaurant on—or under—Broadway, among them no writers larger than Fitz James O'Brien and William Winter. They were more congenial to Whitman than another group associated with the city: Taylor, Stedman, Stoddard, Aldrich, poets of romanticism in its decline. But in the decades when the romantic impulse was fading away in a tame conventionality, Whitman gave it a last vigorous expression.

Walter Whitman was born at West Hills, Long Island. His ancestors were English and Dutch, some of them Quakers. The Whitmans moved to Brooklyn when Walt was small, and he felt the dual influence of a large city and a pleasant countryside near enough to be always available. He left school at the age of eleven. Office-boy, type-setter, occasional author, he became an itinerant country school teacher in 1836 and continued in this position until 1841 except for one brief flier in newspaper editing. In his spare time he learned the printing business, and in 1841 he definitely cast his lot with journalism in New York.

In five years he rose to be editor of the *Daily Brooklyn Eagle*, but lost his position in 1848 and was glad to accept another on a paper just starting in New Orleans. Three months in the South and he resigned his position and returned, by way of Chicago, to Brooklyn. Here he made his headquarters until 1862, as journalist, proprietor of a book store, builder, and poet. In 1855 he collected the verse he had recently been writing and published it in a thin volume.

Whitman himself seems to have expected *Leaves of Grass* to be a bombshell. The book, however, was scarcely noticed. It received one important comment: Emerson wrote, "I greet you at the beginning of a great career." Whitman used this sentence, without permission, to advertise the second edition published the next year. This edition contained thirty-two poems, twenty more than the first edition. All his life Whitman continued to supplement, rewrite, and revise *Leaves of Grass*.

Late in 1862 he went down to Fredericksburg to care for a younger brother who had been slightly wounded. The next three years he gave freely of his health and heart as a nurse among the wounded in hospitals in and near Washington. He still found time to write vivid accounts of what he saw, and occasional poems. He gathered the poems in *Drum Taps* in 1865. The same year he was forced out of a governmental clerkship because a superior thought his poems indecent. His friends came to his aid,—one of them with a pamphlet entitled *The Good Gray Poet*, a name which stuck to Whitman thereafter— and he was established as a clerk in another department. Whitman never married; toward men he apparently had an abnormal attraction.

In 1873, two years after he had issued *Democratic Vistas*, he was stricken with paralysis and settled in Camden, New Jersey, where he lived nearly twenty years until his death. He revised his work, sent out a few articles, received many letters from friends in Europe and America, and made occasional journeys. In 1891–92 he approved the ninth edition of *Leaves of Grass*, the last which he supervised before his death.

Whitman's ideas and attitudes were chiefly those of the Romantic Movement. In his response to nature, his mystical desire for immediacy of experience, his cultivation of the senses, feelings, and imagination, his subjective individualism, his celebration of the common man, he was akin to such predecessors as Rousseau, Wordsworth, Shelley, and Emerson. To Emerson, in fact, he was deeply indebted, saying, "I was simmering, simmering, simmering; Emerson brought me to a boil." Even more than the author of "The American Scholar" he felt the romantic desire for a native experience, a national genius, and he tried to make himself spokesman for all America. With his nationalistic vision he combined a faith in progress, which in his day seemed to be supported by the theory of evolution. Into his romanticism he fused what were later to be traits of the developing realistic movement, such as his quest of a living speech coming out of American life, his generous inclusion of the commonplace and trivial, his incorporation of the ugly, his frank emphasis on sex and on bold sexual terms, and his hearty acceptance of science (though he was not really impregnated with its spirit).

To communicate all this, Whitman felt it necessary to achieve a new poetic form. He rejected the time-hallowed marks of English verse: rhymes, regular meters, stanza patterns, elaborate similes, frequent allusions to the Bible, the classics, the Middle Ages, etc. Instead, he aimed at a freer verse form based on the organic principle, a form not imposed upon but growing out of content. One of his least successful experiments was the cataloguing method, coordinating his materials as if to reflect the equality of all things or the complex miscellaneity of modern life. Most successful are features suggested by the art of music.

The reputation of Whitman grew after his death, till it reached a high point during the lusty literary movement of the 1920's. For example, Lewis Mumford in *The Golden Day* (1926) said that "he is more than a single writer: he is almost a literature," and that his poems "belong to sacred literature." Most critics would be less sweeping in their praise; but however Whitman is rated, there is no question of his profound influence on twentieth-century poets, obviously in the case of Carl Sandburg and Allen Ginsberg, more subtly in the case of many others, European as well as American. As a rule the influence of Whitman has stemmed more from his poetic technique than from his vision of life.

Text: *Leaves of Grass,* "Deathbed Edition" (Philadelphia, 1891–92). *Complete Prose Works* (Philadelphia, 1892).

Further reading: *Leaves of Grass: Comprehensive Reader's Edition,* ed. Harold Blodgett and Sculley Bradley, 1965. G. W. Allen, *The Solitary Singer: A Critical Biography of Walt Whitman,* 1955 (rev. 1968). James E. Miller, Jr., *Critical Guide to Leaves of Grass,* 1957. Howard Waskow, *Walt Whitman: Explorations in Form,* 1966. Edwin H. Miller, *Walt Whitman's Poetry: A Psychological Journey,* 1968.

FROM *Preface to Leaves of Grass*

(1855)

Leaves of Grass originally contained a dozen untitled poems headed by a long Preface—a ten-page double-column essay. Believing that it was time "to break down the barriers of form between prose and poetry," Whitman wrote poetry with prominent prose qualities, and prose with prominent poetic qualities. Some of the prose of the Preface he actually incorporated later, with slight change, in various poems.

Whether or not the Preface is good prose, it is valuable (like Wordsworth's Preface to *Lyrical Ballads*) as a statement of what the poet was up to: a poetic revolution. The following extracts will prove illuminating, especially if read both before and after the poems. The rows of periods (. . .) are Whitman's, serving a function similar to that of dashes.

The opening paragraphs recall Emerson's desire for a truly American poet and his conception of America as itself a poem (cf. the closing passages of *The Poet*).

America does not repel the past or what it has produced under its forms or amid other politics or the idea of castes or the old religions . . . accepts the lesson with calmness . . . is not so impatient as has been supposed that the slough still sticks to opinions and manners and literature while the life which served its requirements has passed into the new life of the new forms . . . perceives that the corpse is slowly borne from the eating and sleeping rooms of the house . . . perceives that it waits a little while in the door . . . that it was fittest for its days . . . that its action has descended to the stalwart and well-shaped heir who approaches . . . and that he shall be fittest for his days.

The Americans of all nations at any time upon the earth have probably the fullest poetical nature. The United States themselves are essentially the greatest poem. In the history of the earth hitherto the largest and most stirring appear tame and orderly to their ampler largeness and stir. Here at last is something in the doings of man that corresponds with the broadcast doings of the day and night. Here is not merely a nation but a teeming nation of nations. Here is action united from strings necessarily blind to particulars and details magnificently moving in vast masses. Here is the hospitality which forever indicates heroes. . . . Here are the roughs and beards and space and ruggedness and nonchalance that the soul loves. Here the performance disdaining the trivial unapproached in the tremendous audacity of its crowds and groupings and the push of its perspective spreads with crampless and flowing breadth and showers its prolific and splendid extravagance. One sees it must indeed own the riches of the summer and winter, and need never be bankrupt while corn grows from the ground or the orchards drop apples or the bays contain fish or men beget children upon women.

Other states indicate themselves in their deputies . . . but the genius of the United States is not best or most in its executives or legislatures, nor in its ambassadors or authors or colleges or churches or parlors, nor even in its newspapers or inventors . . . but always most in the common people. Their manners speech dress friendships—the freshness and candor of their physiognomy—the picturesque looseness of their carriage . . . their deathless attachment to freedom—their aversion to anything indecorous or soft or mean—the practical acknowledgment of the citizens of one state by the citizens of all other states—the fierceness of their roused resentment—their curiosity and welcome of novelty—their self-esteem and wonderful sympathy—their susceptibility to a slight—the air they have of persons who never knew how it felt to stand in the presence of superiors—the fluency of their speech—their delight in music, the sure symptom of manly tenderness and native elegance of soul . . . their good temper and open-handedness—the terrible significance of their elections—the President's taking off his hat to them not they to him—these too are unrhymed poetry. It

awaits the gigantic and generous treatment worthy of it.

The largeness of nature or the nation were monstrous without a corresponding largeness and generosity of the spirit of the citizen. Not nature nor swarming states nor streets and steamships nor prosperous business nor farms nor capital nor learning may suffice for the ideal of man . . . nor suffice the poet. No reminiscences may suffice either. A live nation can always cut a deep mark and can have the best authority the cheapest . . . namely from its own soul. This is the sum of the profitable uses of individuals or states and of present action and grandeur and of the subjects of poets.—As if it were necessary to trot back generation after generation to the eastern records! As if the beauty and sacredness of the demonstrable must fall behind that of the mythical! As if men do not make their mark out of any times! As if the opening of the western continent by discovery and what has transpired since in North and South America were less than the small theatre of the antique or the aimless sleepwalking of the middle ages! The pride of the United States leaves the wealth and finesse of the cities and all returns of commerce and agriculture and all the magnitude of geography or shows of exterior victory to enjoy the breed of fullsized men or one fullsized man unconquerable and simple.

The American poets are to enclose old and new for America is the race of races. Of them a bard is to be commensurate with a people. To him the other continents arrive as contributions . . . he gives them reception for their sake and his own sake. His spirit responds to his country's spirit . . . he incarnates its geography and natural life and rivers and lakes. Mississippi with annual freshets and changing chutes, Missouri and Columbia and Ohio and Saint Lawrence with the falls and beautiful masculine Hudson, do not embouchure where they spend themselves more than they embouchure into him. The blue breadth over the inland sea of Virginia and Maryland and the sea off Massachusetts and Maine and over Manhattan bay and over Champlain and Erie and over Ontario and Huron and Michigan and Superior, and over the Texan and Mexican and Floridian and Cuban seas and over the seas off California and Oregon, is not tallied by the blue breadth of the waters below more than the breadth of above and below is tallied by him. When the long Atlantic coast stretches longer and the Pacific coast stretches longer he easily stretches with them north or south. He spans between them also from east to west and reflects what is between them. On him rise solid growths that offset the growths of pine and cedar and hemlock and live-oak and locust and chestnut and cypress and hickory and limetree and cotton-wood and tuliptree and cactus and wildvine and tamarind and persimmon . . . and tangles as tangled as any canebrake or swamp . . . and forests coated with transparent ice and icicles hanging from the boughs and crackling in the wind . . . and sides and peaks of mountains . . . and pasturage sweet and free as savannah or upland or prairie . . . with flights and songs and screams that answer those of the wildpigeon and highhold and orchard-oriole and coot and surf-duck and redshouldered-hawk and fish-hawk and white-ibis and indian-hen and cat-owl and water-pheasant and qua-bird and pied-sheldrake and blackbird and mockingbird and buzzard and condor and night-heron and eagle. To him the hereditary countenance descends both mother's and father's. To him enter the essences of the real things and past and present events—of the enormous diversity of temperature and agriculture and mines—the tribes of red aborigines—the weather-beaten vessels entering new ports or making landings on rocky coasts—the first settlements north or south—the rapid stature and muscle—the haughty defiance of '76, and the war and peace and formation of the constitution . . . the union always surrounded by blatherers and always calm and impregnable—the perpetual coming of immigrants—the wharfhem'd cities and superior marine—the unsurveyed interior—the loghouses and clearings and wild animals and hunters and trappers . . . the free commerce—the fisheries and whaling and gold-digging—the endless gestation of new states—the convening of Congress every December, the members duly coming up from all climates and the uttermost parts . . . the noble character of the young mechanics and of all free American workmen and workwomen . . . the general ardor and friendliness and enterprise—the perfect equality of the female with the male . . . the large amativeness—the fluid movement of the population—the factories and mercantile life and laborsaving machinery—the Yankee swap—the New-York firemen and the target excursion—the southern plantation life—the character of the northeast and the northwest and southwest—slavery and the tremulous spreading of hands to protect it, and the stern opposition to it which shall never cease till it ceases or the speaking of tongues and the moving of lips cease. For such the expression of the American poet is to be transcendant and new. It is to be indirect and not direct or descriptive or epic. Its quality goes through these to much more. Let the age and wars of other nations be chanted and their eras and characters be illustrated and that finish the verse. Not so the great psalm of the republic. Here the theme is creative and has vista. Here comes one among the wellbeloved stonecutters and plans with decision and science and sees the solid and beautiful forms of the future where there are now no solid forms. ° ° °

The land and sea, the animals fishes and birds, the sky of heaven and the orbs, the forests mountains and rivers, are not small themes . . . but folks expect of the poet to indicate more than the beauty and dignity which always attach to dumb real objects . . . they expect him to indicate the path between reality and their souls. Men and women perceive the beauty well enough . . . probably as well as he. The passionate tenacity of hunters, woodmen, early risers, cultivators of gardens and orchards and fields, the love of healthy women for the manly form, seafaring persons, drivers of horses, the passion for light and the open air, all is an old varied sign of the unfailing perception of beauty and of a residence of the poetic in outdoor people. They can never be assisted by poets to perceive . . . some may but they never can. The poetic quality is not marshalled in rhyme or uniformity or abstract addresses to things nor in melancholy complaints or good precepts, but is the life of these and much else and is in the soul. The profit of rhyme is that it drops seeds of a sweeter and more luxuriant rhyme, and of uniformity that it conveys itself into its own roots in the ground out of sight. The rhyme and uniformity of perfect poems show the free growth of metrical laws and bud from them as unerringly and loosely as lilacs or roses on a bush, and take shapes as compact as the shapes of chestnuts and oranges and melons and pears, and shed the perfume impalpable to form. The fluency and ornaments of the finest poems or music or orations or recitations are not independent but dependent. All beauty comes from beautiful blood and a beautiful brain. If the greatnesses are in conjunction in a man or woman it is enough . . . the fact will prevail through the universe . . . but the gaggery and gilt of a million years will not prevail. Who troubles himself about his ornaments or fluency is lost. This is what you shall do: Love the earth and sun and the animals, despise riches, give alms to every one that asks, stand up for the stupid and crazy, devote your income and labor to others, hate tyrants, argue not concerning God, have patience and indulgence toward the people, take off your hat to nothing known or unknown or to any man or number of men, go freely with powerful uneducated persons and with the young and with the mothers of families, read these leaves in the open air every season of every year of your life, reexamine all you have been told at school or church or in any book, dismiss whatever insults your own soul, and your very flesh shall be a great poem and have the richest fluency not only in its words but in the silent lines of its lips and face and between the lashes of your eyes and in every motion and joint of your body. . . . The poet shall not spend his time in unneeded work. He shall know that the ground is always ready plowed and manured . . . others may not know it but he shall. He shall go directly to the creation. His trust shall master the trust of everything he touches . . . and shall master all attachment. ° ° °

The art of art, the glory of expression and the sunshine of the light of letters is simplicity. Nothing is better than simplicity . . . nothing can make up for excess or for the lack of definiteness. To carry on the heave of impulse and pierce intellectual depths and give all subjects their articulations are powers neither common nor very uncommon. But to speak in literature with the perfect rectitude and insouciance of the movements of animals and the unimpeachableness of the sentiment of trees in the woods and grass by the roadside is the flawless triumph of art. If you have looked on him who has achieved it you have looked on one of the masters of all nations and times. You shall not contemplate the flight of the graygull over the bay or the mettlesome action of the blood horse or the tall leaning of sunflowers on their stalk or the appearance of the sun journeying through heaven or the appearance of the moon afterward with any more satisfaction than you shall contemplate him. The greatest poet has less a marked style and is more the channel of thoughts and things without increase or diminution, and is the free channel of himself. He swears to his art, I will not be meddlesome, I will not have in my writing any elegance or effect or originality to hang in the way between me and the rest like curtains. I will have nothing hang in the way, not the richest curtains. What I tell I tell for precisely what it is. Let who may exalt or startle or fascinate or soothe I will have purposes as health or heat or snow has and be as regardless of observation. What I experience or portray shall go from my composition without a shred of my composition. You shall stand by my side and look in the mirror with me. ° ° °

The direct trial of him who would be the greatest poet is today. If he does not flood himself with the immediate age as with vast oceanic tides . . . and if he does not attract his own land body and soul to himself and hang on its neck with incomparable love and plunge his semitic muscle into its merits and demerits . . . and if he be not himself the age transfigured . . . and if to him is not opened the eternity which gives similitude to all periods and locations and processes and animate and inanimate forms, and which is the bond of time, and rises up from its inconceivable vagueness and infiniteness in the swimming shape of today, and is held by the ductile anchors of life, and makes the present spot the passage from what was to what shall be, and commits itself to the representation of this wave of an hour and this one of the sixty beautiful children of the wave—let him merge in the general run and wait his development. . . . Still the final test of poems or any character or work remains. The prescient poet projects himself centuries ahead and judges performer or performance after the changes of time. Does it live through them? Does it still hold on untired? Will the same style and the direction of genius to similar points be satisfactory now? Has no new discovery in science or arrival at superior planes of thought and judgment and behaviour fixed him or his so that either can be looked down upon? Have the marches of tens and hundreds and thousands of years made willing detours to the right hand and the left hand for his sake? Is he beloved long and long after he is buried? Does the young man think often of him? and the young woman think often of him? and do the middle-aged and the old think of him?

A great poem is for ages and ages in common and for all degrees and complexions and all departments and sects and for a woman as much as a man and a man as much as a woman. A great poem is no finish to a man or woman but rather a beginning. Has any one fancied he could sit at last under some due authority and rest satisfied with explanations and realize and be content and full? To no such terminus does the greatest poet bring . . he brings neither cessation or sheltered fatness and ease. The touch of him tells in action. Whom he takes he takes with firm sure grasp into live regions previously unattained . . . thenceforward is no rest . . . they see the space and ineffable sheen that turn the old spots and lights into dead vacuums. The companion of him beholds the birth and progress of stars and learns one of the meanings. Now there shall be a man cohered out of tumult and chaos . . . the elder encourages the younger and shows him how . . . they two shall launch off fearlessly together till the new world fits an orbit for itself and looks unabashed on the lesser orbits of the stars and sweeps through the ceaseless rings and shall never be quiet again.

There will soon be no more priests. Their work is done. They may wait awhile . . . perhaps a generation or two . . . dropping off by degrees. A superior breed shall take their place . . . the gangs of kosmos and prophets en masse shall take their place. A new order shall arise and they shall be the priests of man, and every man shall be his own priest. The churches built under their umbrage shall be the churches of men and women. Through the divinity of themselves shall the kosmos and the new breed of poets be interpreters of men and women and of all events and things. They shall find their inspiration in real objects today, symptoms of the past and future . . . They shall not deign to defend immortality or God or the perfection of things or liberty or the exquisite beauty and reality of the soul. They shall arise in America and be responded to from the remainder of the earth.

The English language befriends the grand American expression . . . it is brawny enough and limber and full enough. On the tough stock of a race who through all change of circumstances was never without the idea of political liberty, which is the animus of all liberty, it has attracted the terms of daintier and gayer and subtler and more elegant tongues. It is the powerful language of resistance . . . it is the dialect of common sense. It is the speech of the proud and melancholy races and of all who aspire. It is the chosen tongue to express growth faith self-esteem freedom justice equality friendliness amplitude prudence decision and courage. It is the medium that shall well nigh express the inexpressible.

No great literature nor any like style of behaviour or oratory or social intercourse or household arrangements or public institutions or the treatment by bosses of employed people, nor executive detail or detail of the army or navy, nor spirit of legislation or courts or police or tuition or architecture or songs or amusements of the costumes of young men, can long elude the jealous and passionate instinct of American standards. Whether or no the sign appears from the mouths of the people, it throbs a live interrogation in every freeman's and freewoman's heart after that which passes by or this built to remain. Is it uniform with my country? Are its disposals without ignominious distinctions? Is it for the evergrowing communes of brothers and lovers, large, well-united, proud beyond the old models, generous beyond all models? Is it something grown fresh out of the fields or drawn from the sea for use to me today here? I know that what answers for me an American must answer for any individual or nation that serves for a part of my materials. Does this answer? or is it without reference to universal needs? or sprung of the needs of the less developed society of special ranks? or old needs or pleasure overlaid by modern science and forms? Does this acknowledge liberty with audible and absolute acknowledgement, and set slavery at naught for life and death? Will it help breed one goodshaped and wellhung man, and a woman to be his perfect and independent mate? Does it improve manners? Is it for the nursing of the young of the republic? Does it solve readily with the sweet milk of the nipples of the breasts of the mother of many children? Has it too the old everfresh forbearance and impartiality? Does it look with the same love on the last born and on those hardening toward stature, and on the errant, and on those who disdain all strength of assault outside of their own?

The poems distilled from other poems will probably pass away. The coward will surely pass away. The expectation of the vital and great can only be satisfied by the demeanor of the vital and great. The swarms of the polished deprecating and reflectors and the polite float off and leave no remembrance. America prepares with composure and goodwill for the visitors that have sent word. It is not intellect that is to be their warrant and welcome. The talented, the artist, the ingenious, the editor, the statesman, the erudite . . . they are not unappreciated . . . they fall in their place and do their work. The soul of the nation also does its work. No disguise can pass on it . . . no disguise can conceal from it. It rejects none, it permits all. Only toward as good as itself and toward the like of itself will it advance half-way. An individual is as superb as a nation when he has the qualities which make a superb nation. The soul of the largest and wealthiest and proudest nation may well go half-way to meet that of its poets. The signs are effectual. There is no fear of mistake. If the one is true the other is true. The proof of a poet is that his country absorbs him as affectionately as he has absorbed it.

Song of Myself

The longest of Whitman's poems—here printed unabridged—is a celebration of modern man. For Whitman, modern man is best illustrated by the everyday American, living in democratic comradeship. "Myself" could just as well have been "Yourself." Naturally Whitman often speaks from his own personality and experience, but throughout the poem his object is to picture a typical American, a "divine average" humanity. Why divine? Because the poet has come to see, in the simplest of lives, a limitless grandeur of body and soul. This grandeur was suddenly clear to him in the experience described in section 5, a revelation that transformed the world for him. Now, in his love of all life, he wishes to convert others.

Addressing his audience with evangelistic intent, he says:

"Long enough have you dream'd contemptible
    dreams,
Now I wash the gum from your eyes,
You must habit yourself to the dazzle of the
    light. . . ."

Whitman was doing in this and other poems what Emerson was doing in his lectures. He himself would have tried the direct method of the lyceum platform if he had been a good speaker. Fascinated by the art of oratory, he adopted a mode of writing closely akin to speaking. He is talking "to you, whoever you are," sometimes as in conversation, more generally as in a public address. It is best to try to *hear* him by reading aloud, not stopping at difficulties but leaving them to be cleared up by what is said later. Until one has grasped his spirit and his drift, it is all but useless to inspect his lines closely. Nor is there much point in looking for the outline the speaker is following, for instead of employing thematic progression, Whitman

seems to say, in each of the fifty-two sections, whatever at the moment seems to him to need saying. Aesthetically, the results are not happy: good, bad, and indifferent passages jostle each other, and the bad and indifferent are many. Yet the best passages are superb.

He begins, in the first three lines, by asserting the essential identity of *you* and *me*.

1

I celebrate myself, and sing myself,
And what I assume you shall assume,
For every atom belonging to me as good belongs to you.

IDENTITY OF HIM + READER

I loafe and invite my soul,
I lean and loafe at my ease observing a spear of summer grass.   5

My tongue, every atom of my blood, form'd from this soil, this air,
Born here of parents born here from parents the same, and their parents the same,
I, now thirty-seven years old in perfect health begin,
Hoping to cease not till death.

Creeds and schools in abeyance,   10
Retiring back a while sufficed at what they are, but never forgotten,
I harbor for good or bad, I permit to speak at every hazard,
Nature without check with original energy.

2

Houses and rooms are full of perfumes, the shelves are crowded with perfumes,
I breathe the fragrance myself and know it and like it,   15
The distillation would intoxicate me also, but I shall not let it.

The atmosphere is not a perfume, it has no taste of the distillation, it is odorless,
It is for my mouth forever, I am in love with it,
I will go to the bank by the wood and become undisguised and naked,
I am mad for it to be in contact with me.   20

The smoke of my own breath,
Echoes, ripples, buzz'd whispers, love-root, silk-thread, crotch and vine,
My respiration and inspiration, the beating of my heart, the passing of blood and air through my
        lungs,
The sniff of green leaves and dry leaves, and of the shore and dark-color'd sea-rocks, and of hay in
        the barn,
The sound of the belch'd words of my voice loos'd to the eddies of the wind,   25
A few light kisses, a few embraces, a reaching around of arms,
The play of shine and shade on the trees as the supple boughs wag,
The delight alone or in the rush of the streets, or along the fields and hill-sides,
The feeling of health, the full-noon trill, the song of me rising from bed and meeting the sun.

Have you reckon'd a thousand acres much? have you reckon'd the earth much?   30
Have you practis'd so long to learn to read?
Have you felt so proud to get at the meaning of poems?

Stop this day and night with me and you shall possess the origin of all poems,
You shall possess the good of the earth and sun, (there are millions of suns left,)
You shall no longer take things at second or third hand, nor look through the eyes of the dead, nor
        feed on the spectres in books,   35

You shall not look through my eyes either, nor take things from me,
You shall listen to all sides and filter them from your self

3

I have heard what the talkers were talking, the talk of the beginning and the end,
But I do not talk of the beginning or the end.

There was never any more inception than there is now,   40
Nor any more youth or age than there is now,
And will never be any more perfection than there is now,
Nor any more heaven or hell than there is now.

Urge and urge and urge,
Always the procreant urge of the world.   45

PERPETUAL LIFE-FORCE

Out of the dimness opposite equals advance, always substance and increase, always sex,
Always a knit of identity, always distinction, always a breed of life.

To elaborate is no avail, learn'd and unlearn'd feel that it is so.

Sure as the most certain sure, plumb in the uprights, well entretied, braced in the beams,
Stout as a horse, affectionate, haughty, electrical,   50
I and this mystery here we stand.

← HE IS AT ONE WITH IT

Clear and sweet is my soul, and clear and sweet is all that is not my soul.

Lack one lacks both, and the unseen is proved by the seen,
Till that becomes unseen and receives proof in its turn.

Showing the best and dividing it from the worst age vexes age,   55
Knowing the perfect fitness and equanimity of things, while they discuss I am silent, and go bathe
    and admire myself.

CONTENT

Welcome is every organ and attribute of me, and of any man hearty and clean,
Not an inch nor a particle of an inch is vile, and none shall be less familiar than the rest.

ACCEPTING EVERY PARTICLE OF HIMSELF

I am satisfied—I see, dance, laugh, sing;
As the hugging and loving bed-fellow sleeps at my side through the night, and withdraws at the
    peep of the day with stealthy tread,   60
Leaving the baskets cover'd with white towels swelling the house with their plenty,
Shall I postpone my acceptation and realization and scream at my eyes,
That they turn from gazing after and down the road,
And forthwith cipher and show me to a cent,
Exactly the value of one and exactly the value of two, and which is ahead?   65

4

Trippers and askers surround me,
People I meet, the effect upon me of my early life or the ward and city I live in, or the nation,
The latest dates, discoveries, inventions, societies, authors old and new,
My dinner, dress, associates, looks, compliments, dues,
The real or fancied indifference of some man or woman I love,   70
The sickness of one of my folks or of myself, or ill-doing or loss or lack of money, or depressions or
    exaltations,
Battles, the horrors of fratricidal war, the fever of doubtful news, the fitful events;
These come to me days and nights and go from me again,
But they are not the Me myself.

Apart from the pulling and hauling stands what I am,   75
Stands amused, complacent, compassionating, idle, unitary,
Looks down, is erect, or bends an arm on an impalpable certain rest,
Looking with side-curved head curious what will come next,
Both in and out of the game and watching and wondering at it.

Backward I see in my own days where I sweated through fog with linguists and contenders,   80
I have no mockings or arguments, I witness and wait.   *JUST WAITING...*

                    5 *MYSTIC COMMUNION WITH SELF*

I believe in you my soul, the other I am must not abase itself to you,
And you must not be abased to the other.

Loafe with me on the grass, loose the stop from your throat,
Not words, not music or rhyme I want, not custom or lecture, not even the best,   85
Only the lull I like, the hum of your valvèd voice.

THE UNION

I mind how once we lay such a transparent summer morning,
How you settled your head athwart my hips and gently turn'd over upon me,
And parted the shirt from my bosom-bone, and plunged your tongue to my bare-stript heart,
And reach'd till you felt my beard, and reach'd till you held my feet.   90

THE VISION

Swiftly arose and spread around me the peace and knowledge that pass all the argument of the
      earth,
And I know that the hand of God is the promise of my own,
And I know that the spirit of God is the brother of my own,
And that all the men ever born are also my brothers, and the women my sisters and lovers,
And that a kelson of the creation is love,   95
And limitless are leaves stiff or drooping in the fields,

THE NATURAL FINITE WORLD INCLUDED

And brown ants in the little wells beneath them,
And mossy scabs of the worm fence, heap'd stones, elder, mullein and poke-weed.

                    6 *"WHAT IS THE GRASS..."*

A child said *What is the grass?* fetching it to me with full hands;
How could I answer the child? I do not know what it is any more than he.   100
I guess it must be the flag of my disposition, out of hopeful green stuff woven.

Or I guess it is the handkerchief of the Lord,
A scented gift and remembrancer designedly dropt,
Bearing the owner's name someway in the corners, that we may see and remark, and say *Whose?*

Or I guess the grass is itself a child, the produced babe of the vegetation.   105

Or I guess it is a uniform hieroglyphic,
And it means, Sprouting alike in broad zones and narrow zones,
Growing among black folks as among white,
Kanuck,[1] Tuckahoe,[2] Congressman, Cuff,[3] I give them the same, I receive them the same.
And now it seems to me the beautiful uncut hair of graves.   110

Tenderly will I use you curling grass,
It may be you transpire from the breasts of young men,
It may be if I had known them I would have loved them,

Song of Myself. [1] French Canadian.
[2] Whitman's most recent editors, Blodgett and Bradley, identify Tuckahoe as a "tidewater Virginian who eats tuckahoe."
[3] A Negro.

It may be you are from old people, or from offspring taken soon out of their mothers' laps,
And here you are the mothers' laps. 115

This grass is very dark to be from the white heads of old mothers,
Darker than the colorless beards of old men,
Dark to come from under the faint red roofs of mouths.

O I perceive after all so many uttering tongues,
And I perceive they do not come from the roofs of mouths for nothing. 120

I wish I could translate the hints about the dead young men and women,
And the hints about old men and mothers, and the offspring taken soon out of their laps.

What do you think has become of the young and old men?
And what do you think has become of the women and children?

They are alive and well somewhere,
The smallest sprout shows there is really no death,
And if ever there was it led forward life, and does not wait at the end to arrest it,
And ceas'd the moment life appear'd.

DEATH AS INFINITE PROCESS 125

All goes onward and outward, nothing collapses,
And to die is different from what any one supposed, and luckier. 130

Has any one supposed it lucky to be born?
I hasten to inform him or her it is just as lucky to die, and I know it.

I pass death with the dying and birth with the new-wash'd babe, and am not contain'd between my
     hat and boots,
And peruse manifold objects, no two alike and every one good,
The earth good and the stars good, and their adjuncts all good. 135

I am not an earth nor an adjunct of an earth,
I am the mate and companion of people, all just as immortal and fathomless as myself.
(They do not know how immortal, but I know.)

Every kind for itself and its own, for me mine male and female,
For me those that have been boys and that love women,
For me the man that is proud and feels how it stings to be slighted,
For me the sweet-heart and the old maid, for me mothers and the mothers of mothers,
For me lips that have smiled, eyes that have shed tears,
For me children and the begetters of children.

COMMUNITY WITH ALL 140

Undrape! you are not guilty to me, nor stale nor discarded,
I see through the broadcloth and gingham whether or no,
And am around, tenacious, acquisitive, tireless, and cannot be shaken away.

UNDRAPE! 145

8

The little one sleeps in its cradle,
I lift the gauze and look a long time, and silently brush away flies with my hand.

The youngster and the red-faced girl turn aside up the bushy hill,
I peeringly view them from the top. 150

The suicide sprawls on the bloody floor of the bedroom,
I witness the corpse with its dabbled hair, I note where the pistol has fallen.

The blab of the pave, tires of carts, sluff of boot-soles, talk of the promenaders,
The heavy omnibus, the driver with his interrogating thumb, the clank of the shod horses on the
     granite floor,   155
The snow-sleighs, clinking, shouted jokes, pelts of snow-balls,
The hurrahs for popular favorites, the fury of rous'd mobs,
The flap of the curtain'd litter, a sick man inside borne to the hospital,
The meeting of enemies, the sudden oath, the blows and fall,
The excited crowd, the policeman with his star quickly working his passage to the centre of the
     crowd,   160
The impassive stones that receive and return so many echoes,
What groans of over-fed or half-starv'd who fall sunstruck or in fits,
What exclamations of women taken suddenly who hurry home and give birth to babes,
What living and buried speech is always vibrating here, what howls restrain'd by decorum,
Arrests of criminals, slights, adulterous offers made, acceptances, rejections with convex lips, 165
I mind them or the show or resonance of them—I come and I depart.

9

ENERGY, FREEDOM---
AN IMAGIST POEM

The big doors of the country barn stand open and ready,
The dried grass of the harvest-time loads the slow-drawn wagon,
The clear light plays on the brown gray and green intertinged,
The armfuls are pack'd to the sagging mow.   170

I am there, I help, I came stretch'd atop of the load,
I felt its soft jolts, one leg reclined on the other,
I jump from the cross-beams and seize the clover and timothy,
And roll head over heels and tangle my hair full of wisps.

10

Alone far in the wilds and mountains I hunt,   175
Wandering amazed at my own lightness and glee,
In the late afternoon choosing a safe spot to pass the night,
Kindling a fire and broiling the fresh-kill'd game,
Falling asleep on the gather'd leaves with my dog and gun by my side.

The Yankee clipper is under her sky-sails, she cuts the sparkle and scud,   180
My eyes settle the land, I bend at her prow or shout joyously from the deck.

The boatmen and clam-diggers arose early and stopt for me,
I tuck'd trowser-ends in my boots and went and had a good time;
You should have been with us that day round the chowder-kettle.

I saw the marriage of the trapper in the open air in the far west, the bride was a red girl, 185
Her father and his friends sat near cross-legged and dumbly smoking, they had moccasins to their
     feet and large thick blankets hanging from their shoulders,
On a bank lounged the trapper, he was drest mostly in skins, his luxuriant beard and curls
     protected his neck, he held his bride by the hand,
She had long eyelashes, her head was bare, her coarse straight locks descended upon her
     voluptuous limbs and reach'd to her feet.

The runaway slave came to my house and stopt outside,
I heard his motions crackling the twigs of the woodpile,
Through the swung half-door of the kitchen I saw him limpsy and weak,   190

And went where he sat on a log and led him in and assured him,
And brought water and fill'd a tub for his sweated body and bruis'd feet,
And gave him a room that enter'd from my own, and gave him some coarse clean clothes,
And remember perfectly well his revolving eyes and his awkwardness, 195
And remember putting plasters on the galls of his neck and ankles;
He staid with me a week before he was recuperated and pass'd north,
I had him sit next me at table, my fire-lock lean'd in the corner.

11

Twenty-eight young men bathe by the shore,
Twenty-eight young men and all so friendly; 200
Twenty-eight years of womanly life and all so lonesome.

She owns the fine house by the rise of the bank,
She hides handsome and richly drest aft the blinds of the window.

Which of the young men does she like the best?
Ah the homeliest of them is beautiful to her. 205

Where are you off to, lady? for I see you,
You splash in the water there, yet stay stock still in your room.

Dancing and laughing along the beach came the twenty-ninth bather,
The rest did not see her, but she saw them and loved them.

The beards of the young men glisten'd with wet, it ran from their long hair, 210
Little streams pass'd all over their bodies.

An unseen hand also pass'd over their bodies,
It descended tremblingly from their temples and ribs.

The young men float on their backs, their white bellies bulge to the sun, they do not ask who
 seizes fast to them,
They do not know who puffs and declines with pendant and bending arch, 215
They do not think whom they souse with spray.

12

The butcher-boy puts off his killing-clothes, or sharpens his knife at the stall in the market,
I loiter enjoying his repartee and his shuffle and break-down.

Blacksmiths with grimed and hairy chests environ the anvil,
Each has his main-sledge, they are all out, there is a great heat in the fire. 220

From the cinder-strew'd threshold I follow their movements,
The lithe sheer of their waists plays even with their massive arms,
Overhand the hammers swing, overhand so slow, overhand so sure,
They do not hasten, each man hits in his place.

13

The Negro holds firmly the reins of his four horses, the block swags underneath on its tied-over
 chain,
The Negro that drives the long dray of the stone-yard, steady and tall he stands pois'd on one leg 225
 on the string-piece,
His blue shirt exposes his ample neck and breast and loosens over his hip-band,

His glance is calm and commanding, he tosses the slouch of his hat away from his forehead,
The sun falls on his crispy hair and mustache, falls on the black of his polish'd and perfect limbs.

I behold the picturesque giant and love him, and I do not stop there, 230
I go with the team also.

In me the caresser of life wherever moving, backward as well as forward sluing,
To niches aside and junior bending, not a person or object missing,
Absorbing all to myself and for this song.

Oxen that rattle the yoke and chain or halt in the leafy shade, what is that you express in your
        eyes?
235
It seems to me more than all the print I have read in my life.

My tread scares the wood-drake and wood-duck on my distant and day-long ramble,
They rise together, they slowly circle around.

I believe in those wing'd purposes,
And acknowledge red, yellow, white, playing within me. 240
And consider green and violet and the tufted crown intentional,
And do not call the tortoise unworthy because she is not something else,
And the jay in the woods never studied the gamut, yet trills pretty well to me,
And the look of the bay mare shames silliness out of me.

14

The wild gander leads his flock through the cool night, 245
Ya-honk he says, and sounds it down to me like an invitation,
The pert may suppose it meaningless, but I listening close,
Find its purpose and place up there toward the wintry sky.

The sharp-hoof'd moose of the north, the cat on the house-sill, the chickadee, the prairie-dog,
The litter of the grunting sow as they tug at her teats, 250
The brood of the turkey-hen and she with her half-spread wings,
I see in them and myself the same old law.

The press of my foot to the earth springs a hundred affections,
They scorn the best I can do to relate them.

I am enamour'd of growing out-doors, 255
Of men that live among cattle or taste of the ocean or woods,
Of the builders and steerers of ships and the wielders of axes and mauls, and the drivers of horses,
I can eat and sleep with them week in and week out.

What is commonest, cheapest, nearest, easiest, is Me.
Me going in for my chances, spending for vast returns, 260
Adorning myself to bestow myself on the first that will take me,
Not asking the sky to come down to my good will,
Scattering it freely forever.

(15) *A CATALOG: DEMOCRATIC SYMPATHY,*
ASSOCIATIVE TECHNIQUE

The pure contralto sings in the organ loft,
The carpenter dresses his plank, the tongue of his foreplane whistles its wild ascending lisp, 265
The married and unmarried children ride home to their Thanksgiving dinner,
The pilot seizes the king-pin, he heaves down with a strong arm,
The mate stands braced in the whale-boat, lance and harpoon are ready,
The duck-shooter walks by silent and cautious stretches,

The deacons are ordain'd with cross'd hands at the altar, 270
The spinning-girl retreats and advances to the hum of the big wheel,
The farmer stops by the bars as he walks on a First-day loafe and looks at the oats and rye,
The lunatic is carried at last to the asylum a confirm'd case,
(He will never sleep any more as he did in the cot in his mother's bedroom;)
The jour printer with gray head and gaunt jaws works at his case, 275
He turns his quid of tobacco while his eyes blurr with the manuscript;
The malform'd limbs are tied to the surgeon's table,
What is removed drops horribly in a pail;
The quadroon girl is sold at the auction-stand, the drunkard nods by the bar-room stove,
The machinists rolls up his sleeves, the policeman travels his beat, the gate-keeper marks who pass,
The young fellow drives the express-wagon, (I love him, though I do not know him;) 281
The half-breed straps on his light boots to compete in the race,
The western turkey-shooting draws old and young, some lean on their rifles, some sit on logs,
Out from the crowd steps the marksman, takes his position, levels his piece;
The groups of newly-come immigrants cover the wharf or levee, 285
As the woolly-pates hoe in the sugar-field, the overseer views them from his saddle,
The bugle calls in the ball-room, the gentlemen run for their partners, the dancers bow to each
    other,
The youth lies awake in the cedar-roof'd garret and harks to the musical rain,
The Wolverine sets traps on the creek that helps fill the Huron,
The squaw wrapt in her yellow-hemm'd cloth is offering moccasins and bead-bags for sale, 290
The connoisseur peers along the exhibition-gallery with half-shut eyes bent sideways,
As the deck-hands make fast the steamboat the plank is thrown for the shore-going passengers,
The young sister holds out the skein while the elder sister winds it off in a ball, and stops now and
    then for the knots,
The one-year wife is recovering and happy having a week ago borne her first child,
The clean-hair'd Yankee girl works with her sewing-machine or in the factory or mill, 295
The paving-man leans on his two-handed rammer, the reporter's lead flies swiftly over the note-
    book, the sign-painter is lettering with blue and gold,
The canal boy trots on the tow-path, the book-keeper counts at his desk, the shoe-maker waxes his
    thread,
The conductor beats time for the band and all the performers follow him,
The child is baptized, the convert is making his first professions,
The regatta is spread on the bay, the race is begun, (how the white sails sparkle!) 300
The drover watching his drove sings out to them that would stray,
The pedler sweats with his pack on his back, (the purchaser higgling about the odd cent;)
The bride unrumples her white dress, the minute-hand of the clock moves slowly,
The opium-eater reclines with rigid head and just-open'd lips,
The prostitute draggles her shawl, her bonnet bobs on her tipsy and pimpled neck, 305
The crowd laugh at her blackguard oaths, the men jeer and wink to each other,
(Miserable! I do not laugh at your oaths nor jeer you;)
The President holding a cabinet council is surrounded by the great Secretaries,
On the piazza walk three matrons stately and friendly with twined arms,
The crew of the fish-smack pack repeated layers of halibut in the hold, 310
The Missourian crosses the plains toting his wares and his cattle,
As the fare-collector goes through the train he gives notice by the jingling of loose change,
The floor-men are laying the floor, the tinners are tinning the roof, the masons are calling for
    mortar,
In single file each shouldering his hod pass onward the laborers;
Seasons pursuing each other the indescribable crowd is gather'd, it is the fourth of Seventh-month,
    (what salutes of cannon and small arms!) 315
Seasons pursuing each other the plougher ploughs, the mower mows, and the winter grain falls in
    the ground;
Off on the lakes the pike-fisher watches and waits by the hole in the frozen surface,
The stumps stand thick round the clearing, the squatter strikes deep with his axe,
Flatboatmen make fast towards dusk near the cotton-wood or pecan-trees,

Coon-seekers go through the regions of the Red river or through those drain'd by the Tennessee, or
    through those of the Arkansas,   320
Torches shine in the dark that hangs on the Chattahooche or Altamahaw,[4]
Patriarchs sit at supper with sons and grandsons and great-grandsons around them,
In walls of adobie, in canvas tents, rest hunters and trappers after their day's sport,
The city sleeps and the country sleeps,
The living sleep for their time, the dead sleep for their time,   325
The old husband sleeps by his wife and the young husband sleeps by his wife;
And these tend inward to me, and I tend outward to them,
And such as it is to be of these more or less I am,
And of these one and all I weave the song of myself.

ONE OUT OF MANY (MANY OUT OF ONE); A SONG WEAVED FROM EVERYTHING

16

I am of old and young, of the foolish as much as the wise,   330
Regardless of others, ever regardful of others,
Maternal as well as paternal, a child as well as a man,
Stuff'd with the stuff that is coarse and stuff'd with the stuff that is fine,
One of the Nation of many nations, the smallest the same and the largest the same,
A Southerner soon as a Northerner, a planter nonchalant and hospitable down by the Oconee I
    live,   335
A Yankee bound my own way ready for trade, my joints the limberest joints on earth and the
    sternest joints on earth,
A Kentuckian walking the vale of the Elkhorn in my deer-skin leggings, a Louisianian or Georgian,
A boatman over lakes or bays or along coasts, a Hoosier, Badger, Buckeye;
At home on Kanadian snow-shoes or up in the bush, or with fishermen off Newfoundland,
At home in the fleet of ice-boats, sailing with the rest and tacking,   340
At home on the hills of Vermont or in the woods of Maine, or the Texan ranch,
Comrade of Californians, comrade of free North-Westerners, (loving their big proportions,)
Comrade of raftsmen and coalmen, comrade of all who shake hands and welcome to drink and
    meat,
A learner with the simplest, a teacher of the thoughtfullest,
A novice beginning yet experient of myriads of seasons,   345
Of every hue and caste am I, of every rank and religion,
A farmer, mechanic, artist, gentleman, sailor, quaker,
Prisoner, fancy-man, rowdy, lawyer, physician, priest.

I resist any thing better than my own diversity,
Breathe the air but leave plenty after me,   350
And am not stuck up, and am in my place.

(The moth and the fish-eggs are in their place,
The bright suns I see and the dark suns I cannot see are in their place,
The palpable is in its place and the impalpable is in its place.)

17

These are really the thoughts of all men in all ages and lands, they are not original with me,   355
If they are not yours as much as mine they are nothing, or next to nothing,
If they are not the riddle and the untying of the riddle they are nothing,
If they are not just as close as they are distant they are nothing.

This is the grass that grows wherever the land is and the water is,
This is the common air that bathes the globe.   360

[4] Southern rivers.

18

With music strong I come, with my cornets and my drums,
I play not marches for accepted victors only, I play marches for conquer'd and slain persons.

Have you heard that it was good to gain the day?
I also say it is good to fall, battles are lost in the same spirit in which they are won.

I beat and pound for the dead,   365
I blow through my embouchures my loudest and gayest for them.

Vivas to those who have fail'd!
And to those whose war-vessels sank in the sea!
And to those themselves who sank in the sea!
And to all generals that lost engagements, and all overcome heroes!   370
And the numberless unknown heroes equal to the greatest heroes known!

19

This is the meal equally set, this the meat for natural hunger,
It is for the wicked just the same as the righteous, I make appointments with all
I will not have a single person slighted or left away,
The kept-woman, sponger, thief, are hereby invited,   375
The heavy-lipp'd slave is invited, the venerealee is invited;
There shall be no difference between them and the rest.

ALL ARE ACCEPTABLE TO HIM — DEMOCRATIC LOVE & EQUALITY

This is the press of a bashful hand, this the float and odor of hair,
This is the touch of my lips to yours, this the murmur of yearning,
This the far-off depth and height reflecting my own face,   380
This the thoughtful merge of myself, and the outlet again.

Do you guess I have some intricate purpose?
Well I have, for the Fourth-month showers have, and the mica on the side of a rock has.

Do you take it I would astonish?
Does the daylight astonish? does the early redstart twittering through the woods?   385
Do I astonish more than they?

This hour I tell things in confidence,
I might not tell everybody, but I will tell you.

20

Who goes there? hankering, gross, mystical, nude;
How is it I extract strength from the beef I eat?   390

What is a man anyhow? what am I? what are you?

All I mark as my own you shall offset it with your own,
Else it were time lost listening to me.

I do not snivel that snivel the world over,
That months are vacuums and the ground but wallow and filth.   395

Whimpering and truckling fold with powders for invalids,[5] conformity goes to the fourth-remov'd,
I wear my hat as I please indoors or out.

Why should I pray? why should I venerate and be ceremonious?

Having pried through the strata, analyzed to a hair, counsel'd with doctors and calculated close,
I find no sweeter fat than sticks to my own bones. 400

BLISSFUL EGOTISM ---
UNIVERSALIZED

In all people I see myself, none more and not one a barley-corn less,
And the good or bad I say of myself I say of them.

I know I am solid and sound,
To me the converging objects of the universe perpetually flow,
All are written to me, and I must get what the writing means. 405

I know I am deathless,
I know this orbit of mine cannot be swept by a carpenter's compass,
I know I shall not pass like a child's carlacue cut with a burnt stick at night.

I know I am august,
I do not trouble my spirit to vindicate itself or be understood,
I see that the elementary laws never apologize, 410
(I reckon I behave no prouder than the level I plant my house by, after all.)

I exist as I am, that is enough,   *ABSOLUTE*
If no other in the world be aware I sit content,   *CONTENT*
And if each and all be aware I sit content. 415

One world is aware and by the far largest to me, and that is myself,   *DON'T WORRY —*
And whether I come to my own to-day or in ten thousand or ten million years,   *WE HAVE*
I can cheerfully take it now, or with equal cheerfulness I can wait.   *ETERNITY*

My foothold is tenon'd and mortis'd in granite,
I laugh at what you call dissolution, 420
And I know the amplitude of time.

(21)

I am the poet of the Body and I am the poet of the Soul,   *PHYSICAL &*
The pleasures of heaven are with me and the pains of hell are with me,   *SPIRITUAL*
The first I graft and increase upon myself, the latter I translate into a new tongue.

I am the poet of the woman the same as the man,   *MALE &* 425
And I say it is as great to be a woman as to be a man,   *FEMALE*
And I say there is nothing greater than the mother of men.

I chant the chant of dilation or pride,
We have had ducking and deprecating about enough,
I show that size is only development. 430

Have you outstrip the rest? are you the President?   *ALL MEN'S*
It is a trifle, they will more than arrive there every one, and still pass on.   *INFINITE*
   DESTINY

I am he that walks with the tender and growing night,
I call to the earth and sea half-held by the night.

[5] Physicians then folded doses of powdered medicine in small papers.

Press close bare-bosom'd night—press close magnetic nourishing night!   435
Night of south winds—night of the large few stars!
Still nodding night—mad naked summer night.

Smile O voluptuous cool-breath'd earth!
Earth of the slumbering and liquid trees!
Earth of departed sunset—earth of the mountains misty-topt!   440
Earth of the vitreous pour of the full moon just tinged with blue!
Earth of shine and dark mottling the tide of the river!
Earth of the limpid gray of clouds brighter and clearer for my sake!
Far-swooping elbow'd earth—rich apple-blossom'd earth!
Smile, for your lover comes.   445

Prodigal, you have given me love—therefore I to you give love!
O unspeakable passionate love.

22

You sea! I resign myself to you also—I guess what you mean,
I behold from the beach your crooked inviting fingers,
I believe you refuse to go back without feeling of me,   450
We must have a turn together, I undress, hurry me out of sight of the land,
Cushion me soft, rock me in billowy drowse,
Dash me with amorous wet, I can repay you.

Sea of stretch'd ground-swells,
Sea breathing broad and convulsive breaths,   455
Sea of the brine of life and of unshovell'd yet always-ready graves,
Howler and scooper of storms, capricious and dainty sea,
I am integral with you, I too am of one phase and of all phases.

Partaker of influx and efflux, I, extoller of hate and conciliation,
Extoller of armies and those that sleep in each others' arms.   460

I am he attesting sympathy,
(Shall I make my list of things in the house and skip the house that supports them?)

I am not the poet of goodness only, I do not decline to be the poet of wickedness also.

What blurt is this about virtue and about vice?
Evil propels me and reform of evil propels me, I stand indifferent,   465
My gait is no fault-finder's or rejecter's gait,
I moisten the roots of all that has grown.

Did you fear some scrofula out of the unflagging pregnancy?
Did you guess the celestial laws are yet to be work'd over and rectified?

I find one side a balance and the antipodal side a balance,   470
Soft doctrine as steady help as stable doctrine,
Thoughts and deeds of the present our rouse and early start.

This minute that comes to me over the past decillions,
There is no better than it and now.

What behaved well in the past or behaves well to-day is not such a wonder,   475
The wonder is always and always how there can be a mean man or an infidel.

23

Endless unfolding of words of ages!
And mine a word of the modern, the word En-Masse.

A word of the faith that never balks,
Here or henceforward it is all the same to me, I accept Time absolutely. 480

It alone is without flaw, it alone rounds and completes all,
That mystic baffling wonder alone completes all.

I accept Reality and dare not question it,
Materialism first and last imbuing.

Hurrah for positive science! long live exact demonstration! 485
Fetch stonecrop[6] mixt with cedar and branches of lilac,
This is the lexicographer, this the chemist, this made a grammar of the old cartouches,
These mariners put the ship through dangerous unknown seas,
This is the geologist, this works with the scalpel, and this is a mathematician.

Gentlemen, to you the first honors always! 490
Your facts are useful, and yet they are not my dwelling,
I but enter by them to an area of my dwelling.

Less the reminders of properties told my words,
And more the reminders they of life untold, and of freedom and extrication,
And make short account of neuters and geldings, and favor men and women fully equipt, 495
And beat the gong of revolt, and stop with fugitives and them that plot and conspire.

(24)

Walt Whitman, a kosmos, of Manhattan the son,
Turbulent, fleshy, sensual, eating, drinking and breeding,
No sentimentalist, no stander above men and women or apart from them,
No more modest than immodest. 500

Unscrew the locks from the doors!   *REVOLUTION*
Unscrew the doors themselves from their jambs!

Whoever degrades another degrades me,
And whatever is done or said returns at last to me.

Through me the afflatus surging and surging, through me the current and index. 505

I speak the pass-word primeval, I give the sign of democracy,
By God! I will accept nothing which all cannot have their counterpart of on the same terms.

Through me many long dumb voices,   *SINGER FOR*
Voices of the interminable generations of prisoners and slaves,   *"LONG DUMB*
Voices of the diseas'd and despairing and of thieves and dwarfs,   *VOICES"* 510
Voices of cycles of preparation and accretion,
And of the threads that connect the stars, and of wombs and of the father-stuff,
And of the rights of them the others are down upon,
Of the deform'd, trivial, flat, foolish, despised,   *COSMIC, &*
Fog in the air, beetles rolling balls of dung.   *UTTERLY HUMBLE* 515

[6]A reference to folk medicine practices.

Through me forbidden voices,
Voices of sexes and lusts, voices veil'd and I remove the veil,
Voices indecent by me clarified and transfigur'd.

I do not press my fingers across my mouth,
I keep as delicate around the bowels as around the head and heart,   520
Copulation is no more rank to me than death is.

I believe in the flesh and the appetites,
Seeing, hearing, feeling, are miracles, and each part and tag of me is a miracle.

THE LOWLY, PHYSICAL, RANK— ARE HOLY MIRACLES TO HIM

Divine am I inside and out, and I make holy whatever I touch or am touch'd from,
The scent of these arm-pits aroma finer than prayer,   525
This head more than churches, bibles, and all the creeds.

If I worship one thing more than another it shall be the spread of my own body, or any part of it,
Translucent mould of me it shall be you!
Shaded ledges and rests it shall be you!
Firm masculine colter it shall be you!   530
Whatever goes to the tilth of me it shall be you!
You my rich blood! your milky stream pale strippings of my life!
Breast that presses against other breasts it shall be you!
My brain it shall be your occult convolutions!   534
Root of wash'd sweet-flag! timorous pond-snipe! nest of guarded duplicate eggs! it shall be you!
Mix'd tussled hay of head, beard, brawn, it shall be you!
Trickling sap of maple, fibre of manly wheat, it shall be you!
Sun so generous it shall be you!
Vapors lighting and shading my face it shall be you!
You sweaty brooks and dews it shall be you!   540
Winds whose soft-tickling genitals rub against me it shall be you!
Broad muscular fields, branches of live oak, loving lounger in my winding paths it shall be you!
Hands I have taken, face I have kiss'd, mortal I have ever touch'd, it shall be you.

I dote on myself, there is that lot of me and all so luscious,
Each moment and whatever happens thrills me with joy,   545
I cannot tell how my ankles bend, nor whence the cause of my faintest wish,
Nor the cause of the friendship I emit, nor the cause of the friendship I take again.

That I walk up my stoop, I pause to consider if it really be,
A morning-glory at my window satisfies me more than the metaphysics of books.

To behold the day-break!   550
The little light fades the immense and diaphanous shadows,
The air tastes good to my palate.

Hefts of the moving world at innocent gambols silently rising, freshly exuding,
Scooting obliquely high and low.

Something I cannot see puts upward libidinous prongs,   555
Seas of bright juice suffuse heaven.

The earth by the sky staid with, the daily close of their junction,
The heav'd challenge from the east that moment over my head,
The mocking taunt, See then whether you shall be master!

25

Dazzling and tremendous how quick the sun-rise would kill me,   560
If I could not now and always send sun-rise out of me.

We also ascend dazzling and tremendous as the sun,
We found our own O my soul in the calm and cool of the daybreak.

My voice goes after what my eyes cannot reach,
With the twirl of my tongue I encompass worlds and volumes of worlds.   565

Speech is the twin of my vision, it is unequal to measure itself,
It provokes me forever, it says sarcastically,
Walt you contain enough, why don't you let it out then?

Come now I will not be tantalized, you conceive too much of articulation,
Do you not know O speech how the buds beneath you are folded?   570
Waiting in gloom, protected by frost,
The dirt receding before my prophetical screams,
I underlying causes to balance them at last,
My knowledge my live parts, it keeping tally with the meaning of all things,
Happiness, (which whoever hears me let him or her set out in search of this day.)   575

My final merit I refuse you, I refuse putting from me what I really am,
Encompass worlds, but never try to encompass me,
I crowd your sleekest and best by simply looking toward you.

Writing and talk do not prove me,
I carry the plenum of proof and every thing else in my face,   580
With the hush of my lips I wholly confound the skeptic.

26

Now I will do nothing but listen,
To accrue what I hear into this song, to let sounds contribute toward it.

I hear bravuras of birds, bustle of growing wheat, gossip of flames, clack of sticks cooking my
    meals,
I hear the sound I love, the sound of the human voice,   585
I hear all sounds running together, combined, fused or following,
Sounds of the city and sounds out of the city, sounds of the day and night,
Talkative young ones to those like them, the loud laugh of work-people at their meals,
The angry base of disjointed friendship, the faint tones of the sick,
The judge with hands tight to the desk, his pallid lips pronouncing a death-sentence,   590
The heave'e'yo of stevedores unlading ships by the wharves, the refrain of the anchor-lifters,
The ring of alarm-bells, the cry of fire, the whirr of swift-streaking engines and hose-carts with
    premonitory tinkles and color'd lights,
The steam-whistle, the solid roll of the train of approaching cars,
The slow march play'd at the head of the association marching two and two,
(They go to guard some corpse, the flag-tops are draped with black muslin.)   595

I hear the violoncello, ('tis the young man's heart's complaint,)
I hear the key'd cornet, it glides quickly in through my ears,
It shakes mad-sweet pangs through my belly and breast.

I hear the chorus, it is a grand opera,
Ah this indeed is music—this suits me.   600

A tenor large and fresh as the creation fills me,
The orbic flex of his mouth is pouring and filling me full.

I hear the train'd soprano (what work with hers is this?)
The orchestra whirls me wider than Uranus flies,
It wrenches such ardors from me I did not know I possess'd them,   605
It sails me, I dab with bare feet, they are lick'd by the indolent waves,
I am cut by bitter and angry hail, I lose my breath,
Steep'd amid honey'd morphine, my windpipe throttled in fakes of death,
At length let up again to feel the puzzle of puzzles,
And that we call Being.   610

27

To be in any form, what is that?
(Round and round we go, all of us, and ever come back thither.)
If nothing lay more develop'd the quahaug in its callous shell were enough.

EVOLUTION, CHANGES, LIFE PROCESS ARE A WONDERFUL GAME, BUT EVEN THAT IS NOT NECESSARY —

Mine is no callous shell,
I have instant conductors all over me whether I pass or stop,   615
They seize every object and lead it harmlessly through me.

I merely stir, press, feel with my fingers, and am happy,
To touch my person to some one else's is about as much as I can stand.

TOUCH

28

Is this then a touch? quivering me to a new identity,
Flames and ether making a rush for my veins,   620
Treacherous tip of me reaching and crowding to help them,
My flesh and blood playing out lightning to strike what is hardly different from myself,
On all sides prurient provokers stiffening my limbs,
Straining the udder of my heart for its withheld drip,
Behaving licentious toward me, taking no denial,   625
Depriving me of my best as for a purpose,
Unbuttoning my clothes, holding me by the bare waist,
Deluding my confusion with the calm of the sunlight and pasture-fields,
Immodestly sliding the fellow-senses away,
They bribed to swap off with touch and go and graze at the edges of me,   630
No consideration, no regard for my draining strength or my anger,
Fetching the rest of the herd around to enjoy them a while,
Then all uniting to stand on a headland and worry me.

The sentries desert every other part of me,
They have left me helpless to a red marauder,   635
They all come to the headland to witness and assist against me.

I am given up by traitors,
I talk wildly, I have lost my wits, I and nobody else am the greatest traitor,
I went myself first to the headland, my own hands carried me there.

You villain touch! what are you doing? my breath is tight in its throat,   640
Unclench your floodgates, you are too much for me.

29

Blind loving wrestling touch, sheath'd hooded sharp-tooth'd touch!
Did it make you ache so, leaving me?

Parting track'd by arriving, perpetual payment of perpetual loan,
Rich showering rain, and recompense richer afterward.   645

Sprouts take and accumulate, stand by the curb prolific and vital,
Landscapes projected masculine, full-sized and golden.

30

All truths wait in all things,
They neither hasten their own delivery nor resist it,
They do not need the obstetric forceps of the surgeon,   650
The insignificant is as big to me as any,
(What is less or more than a touch?)

Logic and sermons never convince,
The damp of the night drives deeper into my soul.

(Only what proves itself to every man and woman is so,   655
Only what nobody denies it so.)

A minute and a drop of me settle my brain,
I believe the soggy clods shall become lovers and lamps,
And a compend of compends is the meat of a man or woman,
And a summit and flower there is the feeling they have for each other,   660
And they are to branch boundlessly out of that lesson until it becomes omnific,
And until one and all shall delight us, and we them.

31

I believe a leaf of grass is no less than the journey-work of the stars,
And the pismire is equally perfect, and a grain of sand, and the egg of the wren,
And the tree-toad is a chef-d'oeuvre for the highest,   665
And the running blackberry would adorn the parlors of heaven,
And the narrowest hinge in my hand puts to scorn all machinery,
And the cow crunching with depress'd head surpasses any statue,
And a mouse is miracle enough to stagger sextillions of infidels.

I find I incorporate gneiss, coal, long-threaded moss, fruits, grains, esculent roots,   670
And am stucco'd with quadrupeds and birds all over,
And have distanced what is behind me for good reasons,
But call any thing back again when I desire it.

In vain the speeding or shyness,
In vain the plutonic rocks send their old heat against my approach,   675
In vain the mastodon retreats beneath its own powder'd bones,
In vain objects stand leagues off and assume manifold shapes,
In vain the ocean settling in hollows and the great monsters lying low,
In vain the buzzard houses herself with the sky,
In vain the snake slides through the creepers and logs,   680
In vain the elk takes to the inner passes of the woods,
In vain the razor-bill'd auk sails far north to Labrador,
I follow quickly, I ascend to the nest in the fissure of the cliff.

I think I could turn and live with animals, they are so placid and self-contain'd,
I stand and look at them long and long.   685

They do not sweat and whine about their condition,
They do not lie awake in the dark and weep for their sins,
They do not make me sick discussing their duty to God,
Not one is dissatisfied, not one is demented with the mania of owning things,
Not one kneels to another, nor to his kind that lived thousands of years ago, 690
Not one is respectable or unhappy over the whole earth.

So they show their relations to me and I accept them,
They bring me tokens of myself, they evince them plainly in their possession.

I wonder where they get those tokens,
Did I pass that way huge times ago and negligently drop them? 695

Myself moving forward then and now and forever,
Gathering and showing more always and with velocity,
Infinite and omnigenous, and the like of these among them,
Not too exclusive toward the reachers of my remembrancers.
Picking out here one that I love, and now go with him on brotherly terms. 700

A gigantic beauty of a stallion, fresh and responsive to my caresses,
Head high in the forehead, wide between the ears,
Limbs glossy and supple, tail dusting the ground,
Eyes full of sparkling wickedness, ears finely cut, flexibly moving.

His nostrils dilate as my heels embrace him, 705
His well-built limbs tremble with pleasure as we race around and return.

I but use you a minute, then I resign you, stallion,
Why do I need your paces when I myself out-gallop them?
Even as I stand or sit passing faster than you.

33

Space and Time! now I see it is true, what I guess'd at, 710
What I guess'd when I loaf'd on the grass,
What I guess'd while I lay alone in my bed,
And again as I walk'd the beach under the paling stars of the morning.

My ties and ballasts leave me, my elbows rest in sea-gaps,
I skirt sierras, my palms cover continents, 715
I am afoot with my vision.

By the city's quadrangular houses—in log huts, camping with lumbermen,
Along the ruts of the turnpike, along the dry gulch and rivulet bed,
Weeding my onion-patch or hoeing rows of carrots and parsnips, crossing savannas, trailing in
    forests,
Prospecting, gold-digging, girdling the trees of a new purchase, 720
Scorch'd ankle-deep by the hot sand, hauling my boat down the shallow river,
Where the panther walks to and fro on a limb overhead, where the buck turns furiously at the
    hunter,
Where the rattlesnake suns his flabby length on a rock, where the otter is feeding on fish,
Where the alligator in his tough pimples sleeps by the bayou,
Where the black bear is searching for roots or honey, where the beaver pats the mud with his
    paddle-shaped tail; 725
Over the growing sugar, over the yellow-flower'd cotton plant, over the rice in its low moist field,

Over the sharp-peak'd farm house, with its scallop'd scum and slender shoots[7] from the gutters,
Over the western persimmon, over the long-leav'd corn, over the delicate blue-flower flax,
Over the white and brown buckwheat, a hummer and buzzer there with the rest,
Over the dusky green of the rye as it ripples and shades in the breeze;   730
Scaling mountains, pulling myself cautiously up, holding on by low scragged limbs,
Walking the path worn in the grass and beat through the leaves of the brush,
Where the quail is whistling betwixt the woods and the wheat-lot,
Where the bat flies in the Seventh-month eve, where the great gold-bug drops through the dark,
Where the brook puts out of the roots of the old tree and flows to the meadow,   735
Where cattle stand and shake away flies with the tremulous shuddering of their hides,
Where the cheese-cloth hangs in the kitchen, where andirons straddle the hearth-slab, where
     cobwebs fall in festoons from the rafters;
Where trip-hammers crash, where the press is whirling its cylinders,
Wherever the human heart beats with terrible throes under its ribs,   739
Where the pear-shaped balloon is floating aloft, (floating in it myself and looking composedly
     down,)
Where the life-car[8] is drawn on the slip-noose, where the heat hatches pale-green eggs in the
     dented sand,
Where the she-whale swims with her calf and never forsakes it,
Where the steam-ship trails hind-ways its long pennant of smoke,
Where the fin of the shark cuts like a black chip out of the water,
Where the half-burn'd brig is riding on unknown currents,   745
Where shells grow to her slimy deck, where the dead are corrupting below;
Where the dense-starr'd flag is borne at the head of the regiments,
Approaching Manhattan up by the long-stretching island,
Under Niagara, the cataract falling like a veil over my countenance,
Upon a door-step, upon the horse-block of hard wood outside,   750
Upon the race-course, or enjoying picnics or jigs or a good game of base-ball,
At he-festivals, with blackguard gibes, ironical license, bull-dances, drinking, laughter,
At the cider-mill tasting the sweets of the brown mash, sucking the juice through a straw,
At apple-peelings wanting kisses for all the red fruit I find,
At musters, beach-parties, friendly bees, huskings, house-raisings;   755
Where the mocking-bird sounds his delicious gurgles, cackles, screams, weeps,
Where the hay-rick stands in the barn-yard, where the dry-stalks are scatter'd, where the brood-
     cow waits in the hovel,
Where the bull advances to do his masculine work, where the stud to the mare, where the cock is
     treading the hen,
Where the heifers browse, where geese nip their food with short jerks,
Where sun-down shadows lengthen over the limitless and lonesome prairie,   760
Where herds of buffalo make a crawling spread of the square miles far and near,
Where the humming-bird shimmers, where the neck of the long-lived swan is curving and winding,
Where the laughing-gull scoots by the shore, where she laughs her near-human laugh,
Where bee-hives range on a gray bench in the garden half hid by the high weeds,
Where band-neck'd partridges roost in a ring on the ground with their heads out,   765
Where burial coaches enter the arch'd gates of a cemetery,
Where winter wolves bark amid wastes of snow and icicled trees,
Where the yellow-crown'd heron comes to the edge of the marsh at night and feeds upon small
     crabs,
Where the splash of swimmers and divers cools the warm noon,
Where the katy-did works her chromatic reed on the walnut-tree over the well,   770
Through patches of citrons and cucumbers with silver-wired leaves,
Through the salt-lick or orange glade, or under conical firs,
Through the gymnasium, through the curtain'd saloon, through the office or public hall;
Pleas'd with the native and pleas'd with the foreign, pleas'd with the new and old,

---

[7] Sediment washed down the roof by the rain.
[8] A watertight boat or chamber traveling on a rope and usually used to haul persons through surf too heavy for an open boat.

Pleas'd with the homely woman as well as the handsome, 775
Pleas'd with the quakeress as she puts off her bonnet and talks melodiously,
Pleas'd with the tune of the choir of the whitewash'd church,
Pleas'd with the earnest words of the sweating Methodist preacher, impress'd seriously at the
    camp-meeting;
Looking in at the shop-windows of Broadway the whole forenoon, flatting the flesh of my nose on
    the thick plate glass,
Wandering the same afternoon with my face turn'd up to the clouds, or down a lane or along the
    beach, 780
My right and left arms round the sides of two friends, and I in the middle,
Coming home with the silent and dark-cheek'd bush-boy, (behind me he rides at the drape of the
    day,)
Far from the settlements studying the print of animals' feet, or the moccasin print,
By the cot in the hospital reaching lemonade to a feverish patient,
Nigh the coffin'd corpse when all is still, examining with a candle; 785
Voyaging to every port to dicker and adventure,
Hurrying with the modern crowd as eager and fickle as any,
Hot toward one I hate, ready in my madness to knife him,
Solitary at midnight in my back yard, my thoughts gone from me a long while,
Walking the old hills of Judaea with the beautiful gentle God by my side, 790
Speeding through space, speeding through heaven and the stars,
Speeding amid the seven satellites and the broad ring, and the diameter of eighty thousand miles,
Speeding with tail'd meteors, throwing fire-balls like the rest,
Carrying the crescent child that carries its own full mother in its belly,
Storming, enjoying, planning, loving, cautioning, 795
Backing and filling, appearing and disappearing,
I tread day and night such roads.

I visit the orchards of spheres and look at the product,
And look at quintillions ripen'd and look at quintillions green.

I fly those flights of a fluid and swallowing soul, 800
My course runs below the soundings of plummets.

I help myself to material and immaterial,
No guard can shut me off, no law prevent me.

I anchor my ship for a little while only,
My messengers continually cruise away or bring their returns to me. 805

I go hunting polar furs and the seal, leaping chasms with a pike-pointed staff, clinging to topples of
    brittle and blue.

I ascend to the foretruck,
I take my place late at night in the crow's nest,
We sail the arctic sea, it is plenty light enough,
Through the clear atmosphere I stretch around on the wonderful beauty, 810
The enormous masses of ice pass me and I pass them, the scenery is plain in all directions,
The white-topt mountains show in the distance, I fling out my fancies toward them,
We are approaching some great battle-field in which we are soon to be engaged,
We pass the colossal outposts of the encampment, we pass with still feet and caution,
Or we are entering by the suburbs some vast and ruin'd city, 815
The blocks and fallen architecture more than all the living cities of the globe.

I am a free companion, I bivouac by invading watchfires,
I turn the bridegroom out of bed and stay with the bride myself,
I tighten her all night to my thighs and lips.

My voice is the wife's voice, the screech by the rail of the stairs, 820
They fetch my man's body up dripping and drown'd.

I understand the large hearts of heroes,
The courage of present times and all times,
How the skipper saw the crowded and rudderless wreck of the steam-ship, and Death chasing it up
      and down the storm,
How he knuckled tight and gave not back an inch, and was faithful of days and faithful of nights, 825

And chalk'd in large letters on a board, *Be of good cheer, we will not desert you;*
How he follow'd with them and tack'd with them three days and would not give it up,
How he saved the drifting company at last,
How the lank loose-gown'd women look'd when boated from the side of their prepared graves,
How the silent old-faced infants and the lifted sick, and the sharp-lipp'd unshaven men; 830
All this I swallow, it tastes good, I like it well, it becomes mine,
I am the man, I suffer'd, I was there.

The disdain and calmness of martyrs,
The mother of old, condemn'd for a witch, burnt with dry wood, her children gazing on,
The hounded slave that flags in the race, leans by the fence, blowing, cover'd with sweat, 835
The twinges that sting like needles his legs and neck, the murderous buckshot and the bullets,
All these I feel or am.

I am the hounded slave, I wince at the bite of the dogs,
Hell and despair are upon me, crack and again crack the marksmen,
I clutch the rails of the fence, my gore dribs, thinn'd with the ooze of my skin, 840
I fall on the weeds and stones,
The riders spur their unwilling horses, haul close,
Taunt my dizzy ears and beat me violently over the head with whip-stocks.

Agonies are one of my changes of garments,
I do not ask the wounded person how he feels, I myself become the wounded person, 845
My hurts turn livid upon me as I lean on a cane and observe.

I am the mash'd fireman with breast-bone broken,
Tumbling walls buried me in their debris,
Heat and smoke I inspired, I heard the yelling shouts of my comrades,
I heard the distant click of their picks and shovels, 850
They have clear'd the beams away, they tenderly lift me forth.

I lie in the night air in my red shirt, the pervading hush is for my sake,
Painless after all I lie exhausted but not so unhappy,
White and beautiful are the faces around me, the heads are bared of their firecaps,
The kneeling crowd fades with the light of the torches. 855

Distant and dead resuscitate,
They show as the dial or move as the hands of me, I am the clock myself.

I am an old artillerist, I tell of my fort's bombardment,
I am there again.

Again the long roll of the drummers, 860
Again the attacking cannon, mortars,
Again to my listening ears the cannon responsive.

I take part, I see and hear the whole,
The cries, curses, roar, the plaudits for well-aim'd shots,

The ambulanza slowly passing trailing its red drip, 865
Workmen searching after damages, making indispensable repairs,
The fall of grenades through the rent roof, the fan-shaped explosion,
The whizz of limbs, heads, stone, wood, iron, high in the air.

Again gurgles the mouth of my dying general, he furiously waves with his hand,
He gasps through the clot *Mind not me—mind—the entrenchments.* 870

34

Now I tell what I knew in Texas in my early youth,
(I tell not the fall of Alamo,
Not one escaped to tell the fall of Alamo,
The hundred and fifty are dumb yet at Alamo,)
'Tis the tale of the murder in cold blood of four hundred and twelve young men. 875

Retreating they had form'd in a hollow square with their baggage for breastworks,
Nine hundred lives out of the surrounding enemy's, nine times their number, was the price they
    took in advance.
Their colonel was wounded and their ammunition gone,
They treated for an honorable capitulation, receiv'd writing and seal, gave up their arms and
    march'd back prisoners of war.

They were the glory of the race of rangers, 880
Matchless with horse, rifle, song, supper, courtship,
Large, turbulent, generous, handsome, proud, and affectionate,
Bearded, sunburnt, drest in the free costume of hunters,
Not a single one over thirty years of age.

The second First-day morning they were brought out in squads and massacred, it was beautiful
    early summer,
The work commenced about five o'clock and was over by eight. 885

None obey'd the command to kneel,
Some made a mad and helpless rush, some stood stark and straight,
A few fell at once, shot in the temple or heart, the living and dead lay together,
The maim'd and mangled dug in the dirt, the new-comers saw them there, 890
Some half-kill'd attempted to crawl away,
These were despatch'd with bayonets or batter'd with the blunts of muskets,
A youth not seventeen years old seiz'd his assassin till two more came to release him,
The three were all torn and cover'd with the boy's blood.

At eleven o'clock began the burning of the bodies; 895
That is the tale of the murder of the four hundred and twelve young men.

35

Would you hear of an old-time sea-fight?
Would you learn who won by the light of the moon and stars?
List to the yarn, as my grandmother's father the sailor told it to me.

Our foe was no skulk in his ship I tell you, (said he,) 900
His was the surly English pluck, and there is no tougher or truer, and never was, and never will
    be;
Along the lower'd eve he came horribly raking us.

We closed with him, the yards entangled, the cannon touch'd,
My captain lash'd fast with his own hands.

We had receiv'd some eighteen pound shots under the water,
On our lower-gun-deck two large pieces had burst at the first fire, killing all around and blowing
      up overhead. 905

Fighting at sun-down, fighting at dark,
Ten o'clock at night, the full moon well up, our leaks on the gain, and five feet of water reported,
The master-at-arms loosing the prisoners confined in the after-hold to give them a chance for
      themselves.

The transit to and from the magazine is now stopt by the sentinels, 910
They see so many strange faces they do not know whom to trust.

Our frigate takes fire,
The other asks if we demand quarter?
If our colors are struck and the fighting done?

Now I laugh content, for I hear the voice of my little captain, 915
We have not struck, he composedly cries, *we have just begun our part of the fighting.*

Only three guns are in use,
One is directed by the captain himself against the enemy's main-mast,
Two well serv'd with grape and canister silence his musketry and clear his decks.

The tops alone second the fire of this little battery, especially the main-top, 920
They hold out bravely during the whole of the action.

Not a moment's cease,
The leaks gain fast on the pumps, the fire eats toward the powder-magazine.

One of the pumps has been shot away, it is generally thought we are sinking.

Serene stands the little captain, 925
He is not hurried, his voice is neither high nor low,
His eyes give more light to us than our battle-lanterns.

Toward twelve there in the beams of the moon they surrender to us.

36

Stretch'd and still lies the midnight,
Two great hulls motionless on the breast of the darkness, 930
Our vessel riddled and slowly sinking, preparations to pass to the one we have conquer'd,
The captain on the quarter-deck coldly giving his orders through a countenance white as a sheet,
Near by the corpse of the child that serv'd in the cabin,
The dead face of an old salt with long white hair and carefully curl'd whiskers,
The flames spite of all that can be done flickering aloft and below, 935
The husky voices of the two or three officers yet fit for duty,
Formless stacks of bodies and bodies by themselves, dabs of flesh upon the masts and spars,
Cut of cordage, dangle of rigging, slight shock of the soothe of waves,
Black and impassive guns, litter of powder-parcels, strong scent,
A few large stars overhead, silent and mournful shining, 940
Delicate sniffs of sea-breeze, smells of sedgy grass and fields by the shore, death-messages given in
      charge to survivors,
The hiss of the surgeon's knife, the gnawing teeth of his saw,
Wheeze, cluck, swash of falling blood, short wild scream, and long, dull, tapering groan,
These so, these irretrievable.

37

You laggards there on guard! look to your arms! 945
In at the conquer'd doors they crowd! I am possess'd!
Embody all presences outlaw'd or suffering,
See myself in prison shaped like another man,
And feel the dull unintermitted pain.

For me the keepers of convicts shoulder the carbines and keep watch, 950
It is I let out in the morning and barr'd at night.

Not a mutineer walks handcuff'd to jail but I am handcuff'd to him and walk by his side,
(I am less the jolly one there, and more the silent one with sweat on my twitching lips.)

Not a youngster is taken for larceny but I go up too, and am tried and sentenced.

Not a cholera patient lies at the last gasp but I also lie at the last gasp, 955
My face is ash-color'd, my sinews gnarl, away from me people retreat.

Askers embody themselves in me and I am embodied in them,
I project my hat, sit shame-faced, and beg.

38

Enough! enough! enough!
Somehow I have been stunn'd. Stand back!
Give me a little time beyond my cuff'd head, slumbers, dreams, gaping, 960
I discover myself on the verge of a usual mistake.

That I could forget the mockers and insults!
That I could forget the trickling tears and the blows of the bludgeons and hammers!
That I could look with a separate look on my own crucifixion and bloody crowning. 965

I remember now,
I resume the overstaid fraction,
The grave of rock multiplies what has been confided to it, or to any graves,
Corpses rise, gashes heal, fastenings roll from me.

I troop forth replenish'd with supreme power, one of an average unending procession, 970
Inland and sea-coast we go, and pass all boundary lines,
Our swift ordinances on their way over the whole earth,
The blossoms we wear in our hats the growth of thousands of years.

Eleves,[9] I salute you! come forward!
Continue your annotations, continue your questionings. 975

39

The friendly and flowing savage, who is he?
Is he waiting for civilization, or past it and mastering it?

Is he some Southwesterner rais'd out-doors? is he Kanadian?
Is he from the Mississippi country? Iowa, Oregon, California?
The mountains? prairie-life, bush-life? or sailor from the sea? 980

Wherever he goes men and women accept and desire him,
They desire he should like them, touch them, speak to them, stay with them.

[9] French for pupils or students.

Behavior lawless as snow-flakes, words simple as grass, uncomb'd head, laughter, and naïveté,
Slow-stepping feet, common features, common modes and emanations,
They descend in new forms from the tips of his fingers,   985
They are wafted with the odor of his body or breath, they fly out of the glance of his eyes.

Flaunt of the sunshine I need not your bask—lie over!
You light surfaces only, I force surfaces and depths also.

Earth! you seem to look for something at my hands,
Say, old top-knot,[10] what do you want?   990
Man or woman, I might tell how I like you, but cannot,
And might tell what it is in me and what it is in you, but cannot,
And might tell that pining I have, that pulse of my nights and days.

Behold, I do not give lectures or a little charity,   GIVING HIMSELF,   995
When I give I give myself.   BREATHING LIFE
                                                                            INTO OTHERS

You there, impotent, loose in the knees,
Open your scarf'd chops till I blow grit within you,
Spread your palms and lift the flaps of your pockets.
I am not to be denied, I compel, I have stores plenty and to spare,
And any thing I have I bestow.   1000

I do not ask who you are, that is not important to me,
You can do nothing and be nothing but what I will infold you.

To cotton-field drudge or cleaner of privies I lean,   UNIVERSAL
On his right cheek I put the family kiss,   LOVE
And in my soul I swear I never will deny him.   1005

On women fit for conception I start bigger and nimbler babes,   COSMIC
(This day I am jetting the stuff of far more arrogant republics.)   ORGASM

To any one dying, thither I speed and twist the knob of the door,
Turn the bed-clothes toward the foot of the bed.   RAISING
Let the physician and the priest go home.   THE DYING—   1010

I seize the descending man and raise him with resistless will,
O despairer, here is my neck,
By God, you shall not go down! hang your whole weight upon me.

I dilate you with tremendous breath, I buoy you up,
Every room of the house do I fill with an arm'd force,   1015
Lovers of me, bafflers of graves.

Sleep—I and they keep guard all night,
Not doubt, not decease shall dare to lay finger upon you,
I have embraced you, and henceforth possess you to myself,
And when you rise in the morning you will find what I tell you is so.   1020

41

I am he bringing help for the sick as they pant on their backs,
And for strong upright men I bring yet more needed help.

[10]A comic term for an Indian, because of the tuft of hair on top of the head. The address here, of course, is not to an Indian.

I heard what was said of the universe,
Heard it and heard it of several thousand years;
It is middling well as far as it goes—but is that all? 1025

Magnifying and applying come I,
Outbidding at the start the old cautious hucksters,
Taking myself the exact dimensions of Jehovah,
Lithographing Kronos,[11] Zeus his son, and Hercules his grandson,
Buying drafts of Osiris, Isis, Belus, Brahma, Buddha, 1030
In my portfolio placing Manito loose, Allah on a leaf, the crucifix engraved,
With Odin and the hideous-faced Mexitli and every idol and image,
Taking them all for what they are worth and not a cent more,
Admitting they were alive and did the work of their days,
(They bore mites as for unfledg'd birds who have now to rise and fly and sing for themselves,) 1035
Accepting the rough deific sketches to fill out better in myself, bestowing them freely on each man and woman I see,
Discovering as much or more in a framer framing a house,
Putting higher claims for him there with his roll'd-up sleeves driving the mallet and chisel,
Not objecting to special revelations, considering a curl of smoke or a hair on the back of my hand just as curious as any revelation,
Lads ahold of fire-engines and hook-and-ladder ropes no less to me than the gods of the antique wars, 1040
Minding their voices peal through the crash of destruction,
Their brawny limbs passing safe over charr'd laths, their white foreheads whole and unhurt out of the flames;
By the mechanic's wife with her babe at her nipple interceding for every person born,
Three scythes at harvest whizzing in a row from three lusty angels with shirts bagg'd out at their waists,
The snag-tooth'd hostler with red hair redeeming sins past and to come, 1045
Selling all he possesses, travelling on foot to fee lawyers for his brother and sit by him while he is tried for forgery;
What was strewn in the amplest strewing the square rod about me, and not filling the square rod then,
The bull and the bug never worshipp'd half enough,
Dung and dirt more admirable than was dream'd,
The supernatural of no account, myself waiting my time to be one of the supremes, 1050
The day getting ready for me when I shall do as much good as the best, and be as prodigious;
By my life-lumps! becoming already a creator,
Putting myself here and now to the ambush'd womb of the shadows.

42

A call in the midst of the crowd,
My own voice, orotund sweeping and final. 1055

Come my children,
Come my boys and girls, my women, household and intimates,
Now the performer launches his nerve, he has pass'd his prelude on the reeds within.

Easily written loose-finger'd chords—I feel the thrum of your climax and close.

My head slues round on my neck, 1060
Music rolls, but not from the organ,
Folks are around me, but they are no household of mine.

[11]The list of names suggests gods of all times, places, and religions from the Titan, Kronos, to an Algonquian nature spirit, Manito.

Ever the hard unsunk ground,
Ever the eaters and drinkers, ever the upward and downward sun, ever the air and the ceaseless
    tides,
Ever myself and my neighbors, refreshing, wicked, real,   1065
Ever the old inexplicable query, ever that thorn'd thumb, that breath of itches and thirsts,
Ever the vexer's *hoot! hoot!* till we find where the sly one hides and bring him forth,
Ever love, ever the sobbing liquid of life,
Ever the bandage under the chin, ever the trestles of death.

Here and there with dimes on the eyes walking,   1070
To feed the greed of the belly the brains liberally spooning,
Tickets buying, taking, selling, but in to the feast never once going,
Many sweating, ploughing, thrashing, and then the chaff for payment receiving,
A few idly owning, and they the wheat continually claiming.

This is the city and I am one of the citizens,   1075
Whatever interests the rest interests me, politics, wars, markets, newspapers, schools,
The mayor and councils, banks, tariffs, steamships, factories, stocks, stores, real estate and personal
    estate.

The little plentiful manikins skipping around in collars and tail'd coats,
I am aware who they are, (they are positively not worms or fleas,)
I acknowledge the duplicates of myself, the weakest and shallowest is deathless with me,   1080
What I do and say the same waits for them,
Every thought that flounders in me the same flounders in them.

I know perfectly well my own egotism,
Know my omnivorous lines and must not write any less,
And would fetch you whoever you are flush with myself.   1085

Not words of routine this song of mine,
But abruptly to question, to leap beyond yet nearer bring;
This printed and bound book—but the printer and the printing-office boy?
The well-taken photographs—but your wife or friend close and solid in your arms?
The black ship mail'd with iron, her mighty guns in her turrets—but the pluck of the captain and
    engineers?   1090
In the houses the dishes and fare and furniture—but the host and hostess, and the look out of their
    eyes?
The sky up there—yet here or next door, or across the way?
The saints and sages in history—but you yourself?
Sermons, creeds, theology—but the fathomless human brain,
And what is reason? and what is love? and what is life?   1095

43

I do not despise you priests, all time, the world over,
My faith is the greatest of faiths and the least of faiths,
Enclosing worship ancient and modern and all between ancient and modern,
Believing I shall come again upon the earth after five thousand years,
Waiting responses from oracles, honoring the gods, saluting the sun,   1100
Making a fetich of the first rock or stump, powowing with sticks in the circle of obis,[12]
Helping the llama or brahmin as he trims the lamps of the idols,
Dancing yet through the streets in a phallic procession, rapt and austere in the woods a
    gymnosophist,
Drinking mead from the skull-cup, to Shastas and Vedas admirant, minding the Koran,   1104
Walking the teokallis, spotted with gore from the stone and knife, beating the serpent-skin drum,

[12] "obis," "llama," etc.—references to a variety of religious practices.

Accepting the Gospels, accepting him that was crucified, knowing assuredly that he is divine,
To the mass kneeling or the puritan's prayer rising, or sitting patiently in a pew,
Ranting and frothing in my insane crisis, or waiting dead-like till my spirit arouses me,
Looking forth on pavement and land, or outside of pavement and land,
Belonging to the winders of the circuit of circuits.   1110

One of that centripetal and centrifugal gang I turn and talk like a man leaving charges before a
  journey.

Down-hearted doubters dull and excluded,
Frivolous, sullen, moping, angry, affected, dishearten'd, atheistical,
I know every one of you, I know the sea of torment, doubt, despair and unbelief.

How the flukes splash!   1115
How they contort rapid as lightning, with spasms and spouts of blood!

Be at peace bloody flukes of doubters and sullen mopers,
I take my place among you as much as among any,
The past is the push of you, me, all, precisely the same,
And what is yet untried and afterward is for you, me, all, precisely the same.   1120

I do not know what is untried and afterward,
But I know it will in its turn prove sufficient, and cannot fail.

Each who passes is consider'd, each who stops is consider'd, not a single one can it fail.

It cannot fail the young man who died and was buried,
Nor the young woman who died and was put by his side,   1125
Nor the little child that peep'd in at the door, and then drew back and was never seen again,
Nor the old man who has lived without purpose, and feels it with bitterness worse than gall,
Nor him in the poor house tubercled by rum and the bad disorder,
Nor the numberless slaughter'd and wreck'd, nor the brutish koboo call'd the ordure of humanity,
Nor the sacs merely floating with open mouths for food to slip in,   1130
Nor any thing in the earth, or down in the oldest graves of the earth,
Nor any thing in the myriads of spheres, nor the myriads of myriads that inhabit them,
Nor the present, nor the least wisp that is known.

It is time to explain myself—let us stand up.

What is known I strip away,
I launch all men and women forward with me into the Unknown.   1135

The clock indicates the moment—but what does eternity indicate?

We have thus far exhausted trillions of winters and summers,
There are trillions ahead, and trillions ahead of them.

Births have brought us richness and variety,   1140
And other births will bring us richness and variety.

I do not call one greater and one smaller,
That which fills its period and place is equal to any.

Were mankind murderous or jealous upon you, my brother, my sister?
I am sorry for you, they are not murderous or jealous upon me,   1145

All has been gentle with me, I keep no account with lamentation,
(What have I to do with lamentation?)

I am an acme of things accomplish'd, and I an encloser of things to be.

My feet strike an apex of the apices of the stairs,
On every step bunches of ages, and larger bunches between the steps,
All below duly travel'd, and still I mount and mount. 1150

Rise after rise bow the phantoms behind me,
Afar down I see the huge first Nothing, I know I was even there,
I waited unseen and always, and slept through the lethargic mist,
And took my time, and took no hurt from the fetid carbon. 1155

Long I was hugg'd close—long and long.

Immense have been the preparations for me,
Faithful and friendly the arms that have help'd me.

Cycles ferried my cradle, rowing and rowing like cheerful boatmen,
For room to me stars kept aside in their own rings, 1160
They sent influences to look after what was to hold me.

Before I was born out of my mother generations guided me,
My embryo has never been torpid, nothing could overlay it.

For it the nebula cohered to an orb,
The long slow strata piled to rest it on, 1165
Vast vegetables gave it sustenance,
Monstrous sauroids transported it in their mouths and deposited it with care.

All forces have been steadily employ'd to complete and delight me,
Now on this spot I stand with my robust soul.

45

O span of youth! ever-push'd elasticity. 1170
O manhood, balanced, florid and full.

My lovers suffocate me,
Crowding my lips, thick in the pores of my skin,
Jostling me through streets and public halls, coming naked to me at night,
Crying by day *Ahoy!* from the rocks of the river, swinging and chirping over my head, 1175
Calling my name from flower-beds, vines, tangled underbrush,
Lighting on every moment of my life,
Bussing my body with soft balsamic busses,
Noiselessly passing handfuls out of their hearts and giving them to be mine.

Old age superbly rising! O welcome, ineffable grace of dying days! 1180

Every condition promulges not only itself, it promulges what grows after and out of itself,
And the dark hush promulges as much as any.

I open my scuttle at night and see the far-sprinkled systems,
And all I see multiplied as high as I can cipher edge but the rim of the farther systems.

Wider and wider they spread, expanding, always expanding, 1185
Outward and outward and forever outward.

My sun has his sun and round him obediently wheels,
He joins with his partners a group of superior circuit,
And greater sets follow, making specks of the greatest inside them.

There is no stoppage and never can be stoppage,   1190
If I, you, and the worlds, and all beneath or upon their surfaces, were this moment reduced back
      to a pallid float, it would not avail in the long run,
We should surely bring up again where we now stand,
And surely go as much farther, and then farther and farther.

A few quadrillions of eras, a few octillions of cubic leagues, do not hazard the span or make it
      impatient,
They are but parts, any thing is but a part.   1195

See ever so far, there is limitless space outside of that,
Count ever so much, there is limitless time around that.

My rendezvous is appointed, it is certain,
The Lord will be there and wait till I come on perfect terms,
The great Camerado, the lover true for whom I pine will be there.   1200

I know I have the best of time and space, and was never measured and never will be measured.

I tramp a perpetual journey, (come listen all!)
My signs are a rain-proof coat, good shoes, and a staff cut from the woods,   *[handwritten: THE PUBLIC ROAD, SENDING MEN FORTH]*
No friend of mine takes his ease in my chair,
I have no chair, no church, no philosophy,   1205
I lead no man to a dinner-table, library, exchange,
But each man and each woman of you I lead upon a knoll,   *[handwritten: A ROAD, NOT A PHILOSOPHY OR INSTITUTION]*
My left hand hooking you round the waist,
My right hand pointing to landscapes of continents and the public road.

Not I, not any one else can travel that road for you,   1210
You must travel it for yourself.

It is not far, it is within reach,
Perhaps you have been on it since you were born and did not know,
Perhaps it is everywhere on water and on land.

Shoulder your duds dear son, and I will mine, and let us hasten forth,   1215
Wonderful cities and free nations we shall fetch as we go.

If you tire, give me both burdens, and rest the chuff[13] of your hand on my hip,   *[handwritten: HELPER]*
And in due time you shall repay the same service to me,
For after we start we never lie by again.
This day before dawn I ascended a hill and look'd at the crowded heaven,   1220
And I said to my spirit *When we become the enfolders of those orbs, and the pleasure and*
      knowledge of every thing in them, shall we be fill'd and satisfied then?   *[handwritten: ENDLESS PROCESS]*
And my spirit said *No, we but level that lift to pass and continue beyond.*

You are also asking me questions and I hear you,
I answer that I cannot answer, you must find out for yourself.

[handwritten in left margin: TRAVEL CAN HELP, BUT NOT FIND YOUR OR FIND ANSWERS FOR YOU]

---

[13] The fat part, cheek, or heel of the hand.

Sit a while dear son, 1225
Here are biscuits to eat and here is milk to drink,
But as soon as you sleep and renew yourself in sweet clothes, I kiss you with a good-by kiss and
    open the gate for your egress hence.

Long enough have you dream'd contemptible dreams,
Now I wash the gum from your eyes,
You must habit yourself to the dazzle of the light and of every moment of your life. 1230

Long have you timidly waded holding a plank by the shore,
Now I will you to be a bold swimmer,
To jump off in the midst of the sea, rise again, nod to me, shout, and laughingly dash with your
    hair.

47

I am the teacher of athletes,
He that by me spreads a wider breast than my own proves the width of my own, 1235
He most honors my style who learns under it to destroy the teacher.

The boy I love, the same becomes a man not through derived power, but in his own right,
Wicked rather than virtuous out of conformity or fear,
Fond of his sweetheart, relishing well his steak,
Unrequited love or a slight cutting him worse than sharp steel cuts, 1240
First-rate to ride, to fight, to hit the bull's eye, to sail a skiff, to sing a song or play on the banjo,
Preferring scars and the beard and faces pitted with small-pox over all latherers,
And those well-tann'd to those that keep out of the sun.

I teach straying from me, yet who can stray from me?
I follow you whoever you are from the present hour, 1245
My words itch at your ears till you understand them.

I do not say these things for a dollar or to fill up the time while I wait for a boat,
(It is you talking just as much as myself, I act as the tongue of you,
Tied in your mouth, in mine it begins to be loosen'd.)

I swear I will never again mention love or death inside a house, 1250
And I swear I will never translate myself at all, only to him or her who privately stays with me in
    the open air.

If you would understand me go to the heights or water-shore,
The nearest gnat is an explanation, and a drop or motion of waves a key,
The maul, the oar, the hand-saw, second my words.

No shutter'd room or school can commune with me, 1255
But roughs and little children better than they.

The young mechanic is closest to me, he knows me well,
The woodman that takes his axe and jug with him shall take me with him all day,
The farm-boy ploughing in the field feels good at the sound of my voice,
In vessels that sail my words sail, I go with fishermen and seamen and love them. 1260

The soldier camp'd or upon the march is mine,
On the night ere the pending battle many seek me, and I do not fail them,
On that solemn night (it may be their last) those that know me seek me.

My face rubs to the hunter's face when he lies down alone in his blanket,
The driver thinking of me does not mind the jolt of his wagon, 1265

The young mother and old mother comprehend me,
The girl and the wife rest the needle a moment and forget where they are.
They and all would resume what I have told them.

48

I have said that the soul is not more than the body,
And I have said that the body is not more than the soul,   1270
And nothing, not God, is greater to one than one's self is,
And whoever walks a furlong without sympathy walks to his own funeral drest in his shroud,
And I or you pocketless of a dime may purchase the pick of the earth,
And to glance with an eye or show a bean in its pod confounds the learning of all times,
And there is no trade or employment but the young man following it may become a hero,   1275
And there is no object so soft but it makes a hub for the wheel'd universe,
And I say to any man or woman, Let your soul stand cool and composed before a million
      universes.

And I say to mankind, Be not curious about God,
For I who am curious about each am not curious about God,
(No array of terms can say how much I am at peace about God and about death.)   1280

I hear and behold God in every object, yet understand God not in the least,
Nor do I understand who there can be more wonderful than myself.

Why should I wish to see God better than this day?
I see something of God each hour of the twenty-four, and each moment then,
In the faces of men and women I see God, and in my own face in the glass,   1285
I find letters from God dropt in the street, and every one is sign'd by God's name,
And I leave them where they are, for I know that wheresoe'er I go,
Others will punctually come for ever and ever.

49

And as to you Death, and you bitter hug of mortality, it is idle to try to alarm me.

To his work without flinching the accoucheur comes,   1290
I see the elder-hand pressing receiving supporting,
I recline by the sills of the exquisite flexible doors,
And mark the outlet, and mark the relief and escape.

And as to you Corpse I think you are good manure, but that does not offend me,
I smell the white roses sweet-scented and growing,   1295
I reach to the leafy lips, I reach to the polish'd breasts of melons.

And as to you Life I reckon you are the leavings of many deaths,
(No doubt I have died myself ten thousand times before.)

I hear you whispering there O stars of heaven,
O suns—O grass of graves—O perpetual transfers and promotions,   1300
If you do not say any thing how can I say any thing?

Of the turbid pool that lies in the autumn forest,
Of the moon that descends the steeps of the soughing twilight,
Toss, sparkles of day and dusk—toss on the black stems that decay in the muck,
Toss to the moaning gibberish of the dry limbs.   1305

I ascend from the moon, I ascend from the night,
I perceive that the ghastly glimmer is noonday sunbeams reflected,
And debouch to the steady and central from the offspring great or small.

50

There is that in me—I do not know what it is—but I know it is in me.

Wrench'd and sweaty—calm and cool then my body becomes,   1310
I sleep—I sleep long.

I do not know it—it is without name—it is a word unsaid,
It is not in any dictionary, utterance, symbol.

Something it swings on more than the earth I swing on,
To it the creation is the friend whose embracing awakes me.   1315

Perhaps I might tell more. Outlines! I plead for my brothers and sisters.

Do you see O my brothers and sisters?
It is not chaos or death—it is form, union, plan—it is eternal life—it is Happiness.

51

The past and present wilt—I have fill'd them, emptied them,
And proceed to fill my next fold of the future.   1320

Listener up there! what have you to confide to me?
Look in my face while I snuff the sidle[14] of evening,
(Talk honestly, no one else hears you, and I stay only a minute longer.)
Do I contradict myself?
Very well then I contradict myself,   1325
(I am large, I contain multitudes.)

I concentrate toward them that are nigh, I wait on the door-slab.

Who has done his day's work? who will soonest be through with his supper?
Who wishes to walk with me?

Will you speak before I am gone? will you prove already too late?   1330

52   THE POETS FAREWELL

The spotted hawk swoops by and accuses me, he complains of my gab and my loitering.

I too am not a bit tamed, I too am untranslatable,
I sound my barbaric yawp over the roofs of the world.

The last scud of day holds back for me,
It flings my likeness after the rest and true as any on the shadow'd wilds, 1335
It coaxes me to the vapor and the dusk.

I depart as air, I shake my white locks at the runaway sun,
I effuse my flesh in eddies, and drift it in lacy jags.

I bequeath myself to the dirt to grow from the grass I love,
If you want me again look for me under your boot-soles.   1340

[14]To snuff out the last light of evening. "Sidle": side-light or sidelong.

You will hardly know who I am or what I mean,
But I shall be good health to you nevertheless,
And filter and fibre your blood.

Failing to fetch me at first keep encouraged,
Missing me one place search another,   1345
I stop somewhere waiting for you.

1855, 1881

There Was a Child Went Forth

> Like "Song of Myself," this poem was among the twelve of the first edition
> of *Leaves of Grass*. Here, quite evidently, Whitman is speaking of his own
> experience: his parents, the men and women in the streets, the wonderful
> life of nature inland and by the sea—the shaping influences on the child that
> went forth into the world.

There was a child went forth every day,
And the first object he look'd upon, that object he became
And that object became part of him for the day or a certain part of the day,
Or for many years or stretching cycles of years.

The early lilacs became part of this child,   5
And grass and white and red morning-glories, and white and red clover, and the song of the
      phoebe-bird,
And the Third-month lambs and the sow's pink-faint litter, and the mare's foal and the cow's calf,
And the noisy brood of the barnyard or by the mire of the pond-side,
And the fish suspending themselves so curiously below there, and the beautiful curious liquid,
And the water-plants with their graceful flat heads, all became part of him.   10

The field-sprouts of Fourth-month and Fifth-month became part of him,
Winter-grain sprouts and those of the light-yellow corn, and the esculent roots of the garden,
And the apple-trees cover'd with blossoms and the fruit afterward, and wood-berries, and the
      commonest weeds by the road,
And the old drunkard staggering home from the outhouse of the tavern whence he had lately risen,
And the schoolmistress that pass'd on her way to the school,   15
And the friendly boys that pass'd, and the quarrelsome boys,
And the tidy and fresh-cheek'd girls, and the barefoot negro boy and girl,
And all the changes of city and country wherever he went.

His own parents, he that had father'd him and she that had conceiv'd him in her womb and birth'd
      him,
They gave this child more of themselves than that,   20
They gave him afterward every day, they became part of him.

The mother at home quietly placing the dishes on the supper-table,
The mother with mild words, clean her cap and gown, a wholesome odor falling off her person
      and clothes as she walks by,
The father, strong, self-sufficient, manly, mean, anger'd, unjust,
The blow, the quick loud word, the tight bargain, the crafty lure,   25
The family usages, the language, the company, the furniture, the yearning and swelling heart,
Affection that will not be gainsay'd, the sense of what is real, the thought if after all it should prove
      unreal,
The doubts of day-time and the doubts of night-time, the curious whether and how,
Whether that which appears so is so, or is it all flashes and specks?
Men and women crowding fast in the streets, if they are not flashes and specks what are they?   30

The streets themselves and the façades of houses, and goods in the windows,
Vehicles, teams, the heavy-plank'd wharves, the huge crossing at the ferries,
The village on the highland seen from afar at sunset, the river between,
Shadows, aureola and mist, the light falling on roofs and gables of white or brown two miles off,
The schooner near by sleepily dropping down the tide, the little boat slack-tow'd astern,   35
The hurrying tumbling waves, quick-broken crests, slapping,
The strata of color'd clouds, the long bar of maroon-tint away solitary by itself, the spread of purity
    it lies motionless in,
The horizon's edge, the flying sea-crow, the fragrance of salt marsh and shore mud,
These became part of that child who went forth every day, and who now goes, and will always go
    forth every day.

1855, 1871

The Sleepers

"The Sleepers," another of the twelve poems in the first edition of *Leaves of Grass*, is a deeply personal, confessional poem—a night journey in which the confused and "ill-assorted" adolescent self moves through sexual awareness toward wholeness and maturity. "The landscape, in which obscure symbols disguise the latent content and the universal taboos, and in which the protagonist undergoes sudden and seemingly inexplicable personal and sexual transformations, is dreamlike, even surrealistic at times, because it evokes vague memories of almost forgotten rites of cultures which provided meaningful communal ceremonies to celebrate the individual's journey to adulthood, as a modern industrial society does not. Unlike a dream, the poem does not end inconclusively, but as in a rite of adolescence the protagonist experiences the terrors of anticipated initiation, with its physical pain, as well as the attendant joys of entrance into manhood and into society—except that the drama in Whitman's poem, of necessity, is played out in the protagonist's consciousness, and that the conclusion is sublimation." (Edwin H. Miller)

1

I wander all night in my vision,
Stepping with light feet, swiftly and noiselessly stepping and stopping,
Bending with open eyes over the shut eyes of sleepers,
Wandering and confused, lost to myself, ill-assorted, contradictory,
Pausing, gazing, bending, and stopping.   5

How solemn they look there, stretch'd and still,
How quiet they breathe, the little children in their cradles.

The wretched features of ennuyés, the white features of corpses, the livid faces of drunkards, the
    sick-gray faces of onanists,
The gash'd bodies on battle-fields, the insane in their strong-door'd rooms, the sacred idiots, the
    new-born emerging from gates, and the dying emerging from gates,
The night pervades them and infolds them.   10

The married couple sleep calmly in their bed, he with his palm on the hip of the wife, and she
    with her palm on the hip of the husband,
The sisters sleep lovingly side by side in their bed,
The men sleep lovingly side by side in theirs,
And the mother sleeps with her little child carefully wrapt.

The blind sleep, and the deaf and dumb sleep,   15
The prisoner sleeps well in the prison, the runaway son sleeps,
The murderer that is to be hung next day, how does he sleep?
And the murder'd person, how does he sleep?

The female that loves unrequited sleeps,
And the male that loves unrequited sleeps,   20

The head of the money-maker that plotted all day sleeps.
And the enraged and treacherous dispositions, all, all sleep.

I stand in the dark with drooping eyes by the worst-suffering and the most restless,
I pass my hands soothingly to and fro a few inches from them,
The restless sink in their beds, they fitfully sleep.   25

Now I pierce the darkness, new beings appear,
The earth recedes from me into the night,
I saw that it was beautiful, and I see that what is not the earth is beautiful.

I go from bedside to bedside, I sleep close with the other sleepers each in turn,
I dream in my dream all the dreams of the other dreamers,   30
And I become the other dreamers.

I am a dance—play up there! the fit is whirling me fast!

I am the ever-laughing—it is new moon and twilight,
I see the hiding of douceurs,[1] I see nimble ghosts whichever way I look,
Cache and cache again deep in the ground and sea, and where it is neither ground nor sea.   35

Well do they do their jobs those journeymen divine,
Only from me can they hide nothing, and would not if they could,
I reckon I am their boss and they make me a pet besides,
And surround me and lead me and run ahead when I walk,
To lift their cunning covers to signify me with stretch'd arms, and resume the way;   40
Onward we move, a gay gang of blackguards! with mirth-shouting music and wild-flapping pen-
    nants of joy!

I am the actor, the actress, the voter, the politician,
The emigrant and the exile, the criminal that stood in the box.
He who has been famous and he who shall be famous after to-day,
The stammerer, the well-formed person, the wasted or feeble person.   45

I am she who adorn'd herself and folded her hair expectantly,
My truant lover has come, and it is dark.

Double yourself and receive me darkness,
Receive me and my lover too, he will not let me go without him.

I roll myself upon you as upon a bed, I resign myself to the dusk.   50

He whom I call answers me and takes the place of my lover,
He rises with me silently from the bed.

Darkness, you are gentler than my lover, his flesh was sweaty and panting,
I feel the hot moisture yet that he left me.

My hands are spread forth, I pass them in all directions,   55
I would sound up the shadowy shore to which you are journeying.

Be careful darkness! already what was it touch'd me?
I thought my lover had gone, else darkness and he are one,
I hear the heart-beat, I follow, I fade away.

[1] Sweets.

2

I descend my western course, my sinews are flaccid, 60
Perfume and youth course through me and I am their wake.

It is my face yellow and wrinkled instead of the old woman's,
I sit low in a straw-bottom chair and carefully darn my grandson's stockings.

It is I too, the sleepless widow looking out on the winter midnight,
I see the sparkles of starshine on the icy and pallid earth. 65

A shroud I see and I am the shroud, I wrap a body and lie in the coffin,
It is dark here under ground, it is not evil or pain here, it is blank here, for reasons.

(It seems to me that every thing in the light and air ought to be happy,
Whoever is not in his coffin and the dark grave let him know he has enough.)

3

I see a beautiful gigantic swimmer swimming naked through the eddies of the sea, 70
His brown hair lies close and even to his head, he strikes out with courageous arms, he urges
   himself with his legs,

I see his white body, I see his undaunted eyes,
I hate the swift-running eddies that would dash him head-foremost on the rocks.

What are you doing you ruffianly red-trickled waves?
Will you kill the courageous giant? will you kill him in the prime of his middle age? 75

Steady and long he struggles,
He is baffled, bang'd, bruis'd, he holds out while his strength holds out,
The slapping eddies are spotted with his blood, they bear him away, they roll him, swing him, turn
   him,
His beautiful body is borne in the circling eddies, it is continually bruis'd on rocks,
Swiftly and out of sight is borne the brave corpse. 80

4

I turn but do not extricate myself,
Confused, a past-reading, another, but with darkness yet.

The beach is cut by the razory ice-wind, the wreck-guns sound.
The tempest lulls, the moon comes floundering through the drifts.

I look where the ship helplessly heads end on, I hear the burst as she strikes, I hear the howls of
   dismay, they grow fainter and fainter. 85

I cannot aid with my wringing fingers,
I can but rush to the surf and let it drench me and freeze upon me.

I search with the crowd, not one of the company is wash'd to us alive,
In the morning I help pick up the dead and lay them in rows in a barn.

5

Now of the older war-days, the defeat at Brooklyn, 90
Washington stands inside the lines, he stands on the intrench'd hills amid a crowd of officers,
His face is cold and damp, he cannot repress the weeping drops,

He lifts the glass perpetually to his eyes, the color is blanch'd from his cheeks,
He sees the slaughter of the southern braves confided to him by their parents.

The same at last and at last when peace is declared, 95
He stands in the room of the old tavern, the well-belov'd soldiers all pass through,
The officers speechless and slow draw near in their turns,
The chief encircles their necks with his arm and kisses them on the cheek,
He kisses lightly the wet cheeks one after another, he shakes hands and bids good-by to the army.

6

Now what my mother told me one day as we sat at dinner together, 100
Of when she was a nearly grown girl living home with her parents on the old homestead.

A red squaw came one breakfast-time to the old homestead,
On her back she carried a bundle of rushes for rush-bottoming chairs,
Her hair, straight, shiny, coarse, black, profuse, half-envelop'd her face,
Her step was free and elastic, and her voice sounded exquisitely as she spoke. 105

My mother look'd in delight and amazement at the stranger,
She look'd at the freshness of her tall-borne face and full and pliant limbs,
The more she look'd upon her she loved her,
Never before had she seen such wonderful beauty and purity,
She made her sit on a bench by the jamb of the fireplace, she cook'd food for her, 110
She had no work to give her, but she gave her remembrance and fondness.

The red squaw staid all the forenoon, and toward the middle of the afternoon she went away,
O my mother was loth to have her go away,
All the week she thought of her, she watch'd for her many a month,
She remember'd her many a winter and many a summer, 115
But the red squaw never came nor was heard of there again.

7

A show of the summer softness—a contact of something unseen—an amour of the light and air,
I am jealous and overwhelm'd with friendliness,
And will go gallivant with the light and air myself.

O love and summer, you are in the dreams and in me, 120
Autumn and winter are in the dreams, the farmer goes with his thrift,
The droves and crops increase, the barns are well-fill'd.

Elements merge in the night, ships make tacks in the dreams,
The sailor sails, the exile returns home,
The fugitive returns unharm'd, the immigrant is back beyond months and years, 125
The poor Irishman lives in the simple house of his childhood with the well-known neighbors and
	faces,
They warmly welcome him, he is barefoot again, he forgets he is well off,
The Dutchman voyages home, and the Scotchman and Welshman voyage home, and the native of
	the Mediterranean voyages home,
To every port of England, France, Spain, enter well-fill'd ships,
The Swiss foots it toward his hills, the Prussian goes his way, the Hungarian his way, and the Pole
	his way,
The Swede returns, and the Dane and Norwegian return. 130

The homeward bound and the outward bound,
The beautiful lost swimmer, the ennuyé, the onanist, the female that loves unrequited, the money-
	maker,

The actor and actress, those through with their parts and those waiting to commence,
The affectionate boy, the husband and wife, the voter, the nominee that is chosen and the nominee that has fail'd, 135
The great already known and the great any time after to-day,
The stammerer, the sick, the perfect-form'd, the homely,
The criminal that stood in the box, the judge that sat and sentenced him, the fluent lawyers, the jury, the audience,
The laugher and weeper, the dancer, the midnight widow, the red squaw,
The consumptive, the erysipalite, the idiot, he that is wrong'd, 140
The antipodes, and every one between this and them in the dark,
I swear they are averaged now—one is no better than the other,
The night and sleep have liken'd them and restored them.

I swear they are all beautiful,
Every one that sleeps is beautiful, every thing in the dim light is beautiful, 145
The wildest and bloodiest is over, and all is peace.

Peace is always beautiful,
The myth of heaven indicates peace and night.

The myth of heaven indicates the soul,
The soul is always beautiful, it appears more or it appears less, it comes or it lags behind, 150
It comes from its embower'd garden and looks pleasantly on itself and encloses the world,
Perfect and clean the genitals previously jetting, and perfect and clean the womb cohering,
The head well-grown proportion'd and plumb, and the bowels and joints proportion'd and plumb.

The soul is always beautiful,
The universe is duly in order, every thing is in its place, 155
What has arrived is in its place and what waits shall be in its place,
The twisted skull waits, the watery or rotten blood waits,
The child of the glutton or venerealee waits long, and the child of the drunkard waits long, and the drunkard himself waits long,
The sleepers that lived and died wait, the far advanced are to go on in their turns, and the far behind are to come on in their turns,
The diverse shall be no less diverse, but they shall flow and unite—they unite now. 160

8

The sleepers are very beautiful as they lie unclothed,
They flow hand in hand over the whole earth from east to west as they lie unclothed,
The Asiatic and African are hand in hand, the European and American are hand in hand,
Learn'd and unlearn'd are hand in hand, and male and female are hand in hand,
The bare arm of the girl crosses the bare breast of her lover, they press close without lust, his lips press her neck, 165
The father holds his grown or ungrown son in his arms with measureless love, and the son holds the father in his arms with measureless love,
The white hair of the mother shines on the white wrist of the daughter,
The breath of the boy goes with the breath of the man, friend is inarm'd by friend,
The scholar kisses the teacher and the teacher kisses the scholar, the wrong'd is made right,
The call of the slave is one with the master's call, and the master salutes the slave, 170
The felon steps forth from the prison, the insane becomes sane, the suffering of sick persons is reliev'd,
The sweatings and fevers stop, the throat that was unsound is sound, the lungs of the consumptive are resumed, the poor distress'd head is free,
The joints of the rheumatic move as smoothly as ever, and smoother than ever,
Stiflings and passages open, the paralyzed become supple,

The swell'd and convuls'd and congested awake to themselves in condition,   175
They pass the invigoration of the night and the chemistry of the night, and awake.

I too pass from the night,
I stay a while away O night, but I return to you again and love you.

Why should I be afraid to trust myself to you?
I am not afraid, I have been well brought forward by you,   180
I love the rich running day, but I do not desert her in whom I lay so long,
I know not how I came of you and I know not where I go with you, but I know I came well and
    shall go well.

I will stop only a time with the night, and rise betimes,
I will duly pass the day O my mother, and duly return to you.

1855, 1881

Crossing Brooklyn Ferry

Like "Song of Myself," this poem makes no pretence of developing a logical progress of ideas. But it does have more form. There is a single scene: New York harbor. A single situation: the poet is crossing on the ferry between Manhattan and Brooklyn. And a single dominant idea: the identity of all men—those living in the present and those who will follow in the future. The shared experience of place establishes continuity and the possibility of communication between the poet and others to come after him; their common humanity provides a basic identity; and the inner, spiritual reality Whitman speaks of also joins them.

1

Flood-tide below me! I see you face to face!
Clouds of the west—sun there half an hour high—I see you also face to face.

Crowds of men and women attired in the usual costumes, how curious you are to me!
On the ferry-boats the hundreds and hundreds that cross, returning home, are more curious to me
    than you suppose,
And you that shall cross from shore to shore years hence are more to me, and more in my
    meditations, than you might suppose.   5

2

The impalpable sustenance of me from all things at all hours of the day,
The simple, compact, well-join'd scheme, myself disintegrated, every one disintegrated yet part of
    the scheme,
The similitudes of the past and those of the future,
The glories strung like beads on my smallest sights and hearings, on the walk in the street and the
    passage over the river,
The current rushing so swiftly and swimming with me far away,   10
The others that are to follow me, the ties between me and them,
The certainty of others, the life, love, sight, hearing of others.

Others will enter the gates of the ferry and cross from shore to shore,
Others will watch the run of the flood-tide,
Others will see the shipping of Manhattan north and west, and the heights of Brooklyn to the south
    and east,
Others will see the islands large and small;   15
Fifty years hence, others will see them as they cross, the sun half an hour high,
A hundred years hence, or ever so many hundred years hence, others will see them,
Will enjoy the sunset, the pouring-in of the flood-tide, the falling-back to the sea of the ebb-tide.

3

It avails not, time nor place—distance avails not, 20
I am with you, you men and women of a generation, or ever so many generations hence,
Just as you feel when you look on the river and sky, so I felt,
Just as any of you is one of a living crowd, I was one of a crowd,
Just as you are refresh'd by the gladness of the river and the bright flow, I was refresh'd,
Just as you stand and lean on the rail, yet hurry with the swift current, I stood yet was hurried, 25
Just as you look on the numberless masts of ships and the thick-stemm'd pipes of steamboats, I look'd.

I too many and many a time cross'd the river of old,
Watched the Twelfth-month sea-gulls, saw them high in the air floating with motionless wings, oscillating their bodies,
Saw how the glistening yellow lit up parts of their bodies and left the rest in strong shadow,
Saw the slow-wheeling circles and the gradual edging toward the south, 30
Saw the reflection of the summer sky in the water,
Had my eyes dazzled by the shimmering track of beams,
Look'd at the fine centrifugal spokes of light round the shape of my head in the sunlit water,
Look'd on the haze on the hills southward and south-westward,
Look'd on the vapor as it flew in fleeces tinged with violet, 35
Look'd toward the lower bay to notice the vessels arriving,
Saw their approach, saw aboard those that were near me,
Saw the white sails of schooners and sloops, saw the ships at anchor,
The sailors at work in the rigging or out astride the spars,
The round masts, the swinging motion of the hulls, the slender serpentine pennants, 40
The large and small steamers in motion, the pilots in their pilot-houses,
The white wake left by the passage, the quick tremulous whirl of the wheels,
The flags of all nations, the falling of them at sunset,
The scallop-edged waves in the twilight, the ladled cups, the frolicsome crests and glistening,
The stretch afar growing dimmer and dimmer, the gray walls of the granite storehouses by the docks, 45
On the river the shadowy group, the big steam-tug closely flank'd on each side by the barges, the hay-boat, the belated lighter,
On the neighboring shore the fires from the foundry chimneys burning high and glaringly into the night,
Casting their flicker of black contrasted with wild red and yellow light over the tops of houses and down into the clefts of streets.

4

These and all else were to me the same as they are to you,
I loved well those cities, loved well the stately and rapid river, 50
The men and women I saw were all near to me,
Others the same—others who look back on me because I look'd forward to them,
(The time will come, though I stop here to-day and to-night.)

5

What is it then between us?
What is the count of the scores or hundreds of years between us? 55

Whatever it is, it avails not—distance avails not, and place avails not,
I too lived, Brooklyn of ample hills was mine,
I too walk'd the streets of Manhattan island, and bathed in the waters around it,
I too felt the curious abrupt questionings stir within me,
In the day among crowds of people sometimes they came upon me, 60
In my walks home late at night or as I lay in my bed they came upon me,

I too had been struck from the float forever held in solution,
I too had receiv'd identity by my body,
That I was I knew was of my body, and what I should be I knew I should be of my body.

6

It is not upon you alone the dark patches fall,   65
The dark threw its patches down upon me also,
The best I had done seem'd to me blank and suspicious,
My great thoughts as I supposed them, were they not in reality meagre?
Nor is it you alone who know what it is to be evil,
I am he who knew what it was to be evil,   70
I too knitted the old knot of contrariety,
Blabb'd, blush'd, resented, lied, stole, grudg'd,
Had guile, anger, lust, hot wishes I dared not speak,
Was wayward, vain, greedy, shallow, sly, cowardly, malignant,
The wolf, the snake, the hog, not wanting in me,   75
The cheating look, the frivolous word, the adulterous wish, not wanting,
Refusals, hates, postponements, meanness, laziness, none of these wanting,
Was one with the rest, the days and haps of the rest,
Was call'd my nighest name by clear loud voices of young men as they saw me approaching or
        passing,
Felt their arms on my neck as I stood, or the negligent leaning of their flesh against me as I sat,   80
Saw many I loved in the street or ferry-boat or public assembly, yet never told them a word,
Lived the same life with the rest, the same old laughing, gnawing, sleeping,
Play'd the part that still looks back on the actor or actress,
The same old role, the role that is what we make it, as great as we like,
Or as small as we like, or both great and small.   85

7

Closer yet I approach you,
What thought you have of me now, I had as much of you—I laid in my stores in advance,
I consider'd long and seriously of you before you were born.

Who was to know what should come home to me?
Who knows but I am enjoying this?   90
Who knows, for all the distance, but I am as good as looking at you now, for all you cannot see
        me?

8

Ah, what can ever be more stately and admirable to me than mast-hemm'd Manhattan?
River and sunset and scallop-edg'd waves of flood-tide?
The sea-gulls oscillating their bodies, the hay-boat in the twilight, and the belated lighter?
What gods can exceed these that clasp me by the hand, and with voices I love call me promptly
        and loudly by my nighest name as I approach?   95
What is more subtle than this which ties me to the woman or man that looks in my face?
Which fuses me into you now, and pours my meaning into you?

We understand then do we not?
What I promis'd without mentioning it, have you not accepted?
What the study could not teach—what the preaching could not accomplish is accomplish'd, is it
        not?   100

9

Flow on, river! flow with the flood-tide, and ebb with the ebb-tide!
Frolic on, crested and scallop-edg'd waves!
Gorgeous clouds of the sunset! drench with your splendor me, or the men and women generations
    after me!
Cross from shore to shore, countless crowds of passengers!
Stand up, tall masts of Mannahatta! stand up, beautiful hills of Brooklyn!   105
Throb, baffled and curious brain! throw out questions and answers!
Suspend here and everywhere, eternal float of solution!
Gaze, loving and thirsting eyes, in the house or street or public assembly!
Sound out, voices of young men! loudly and musically call me by my nighest name!
Live, old life! play the part that looks back on the actor or actress!   110
Play the old role, the role that is great or small according as one makes it!
Consider, you who peruse me, whether I may not in unknown ways be looking upon you;
Be firm, rail over the river, to support those who lean idly, yet haste with the hasting current;
Fly on, sea-birds! fly sideways, or wheel in large circles high in the air;
Receive the summer sky, you water, and faithfully hold it till all downcast eyes have time to take it
    from you!   115
Diverge, fine spokes of light, from the shape of my head, or any one's head, in the sunlit water!
Come on, ships from the lower bay! pass up or down, white-sail'd schooners, sloops, lighters!
Flaunt away, flags of all nations! be duly lower'd at sunset!
Burn high your fires, foundry chimneys! cast black shadows at nightfall! cast red and yellow light
    over the tops of the houses!
Appearances, now or henceforth, indicate what you are,   120
You necessary film, continue to envelop the soul,
About my body for me, and your body for you, be hung our divinest aromas,
Thrive, cities—bring your freight, bring your shows, ample and sufficient rivers,
Expand, being than which none else is perhaps more spiritual,
Keep your places, objects than which none else is more lasting.   125

You have waited, you always wait, you dumb, beautiful ministers,
We receive you with free sense at last, and are insatiate henceforward,
Not you any more shall be able to foil us, or withhold yourselves from us,
We use you, and do not cast you aside—we plant you permanently within us,
We fathom you not—we love you—there is perfection in you also,   130
You furnish your parts toward eternity,
Great or small, you furnish your parts toward the soul.

                        1856, 1881

Out of the Cradle Endlessly Rocking

Here we have Whitman at his best, full of his theme, concentrating on an artistic aim from beginning to end, rich in images, sounds, and symbolic meanings, shaping his verse patterns to fit the sense. Psychologically, the poem relates itself to the group of sex poems, "Children of Adam." It is a reminiscence of a boy's inner turmoil, with meanings infused by maturity.

The scene is the seashore of Long Island (Whitman liked its Indian name Paumanok). The time is May to September (he preferred the Quaker Fifth-Month, Ninth-Month). The "characters" are the boy, a pair of mocking-birds, and the sea ("fierce old Mother"). An introduction, a periodic sentence of 22 lines (with the epic predicate "I . . . sing"), lightly touches upon the happenings and significance we are to find in the poem. The poem proper is in two parts. The first part, extending to line 143, gives the story of the birds. The rest, line 143 to the end, interprets the influence of the male bird's song on the "outsetting bard."

Out of the cradle endlessly rocking,
Out of the mocking-bird's throat, the musical shuttle,
Out of the Ninth-month midnight,

Over the sterile sands and the fields beyond, where the child leaving his bed wander'd alone,
      bareheaded, barefoot,
Down from the shower'd halo,
Up from the mystic play of shadows twining and twisting as if they were alive,
Out from the patches of briers and blackberries,
From the memories of the bird that chanted to me,
From your memories sad brother, from the fitful risings and fallings I heard,
From under that yellow half-moon late-risen and swollen as if with tears,
From those beginning notes of yearning and love there in the mist,
From the thousand responses of my heart never to cease,
From the myriad thence-arous'd words
From the word stronger and more delicious than any,
From such as now they start the scene revisiting,
As a flock, twittering, rising, or overhead passing,
Borne hither, ere all eludes me, hurriedly,
A man, yet by these tears a little boy again,
Throwing myself on the sand, confronting the waves,
I, chanter of pains and joys, uniter of here and hereafter,
Taking all hints to use them, but swiftly leaping beyond them,
A reminiscence sing.

Once Paumanok,
When the lilac-scent was in the air and Fifth-month grass was growing,
Up this seashore in some briers,
Two feather'd guests from Alabama, two together,
And their nest, and four light-green eggs spotted with brown,
And every day the he-bird to and fro near at hand,
And every day the she-bird crouch'd on her nest, silent, with bright eyes,
And every day I, a curious boy, never too close, never disturbing them,
Cautiously peering, absorbing, translating.

Shine! shine! shine!
Pour down your warmth, great sun!
While we bask, we two together.

Two together!
Winds blow south, or winds blow north,
Day come white, or night come black,
Home, or rivers and mountains from home,
Singing all time, minding no time,
While we two keep together.

Till of a sudden.
May-be kill'd, unknown to her mate,
One forenoon that she-bird crouch'd not on the nest,
Nor return'd that afternoon, nor the next,
Nor ever appear'd again.

And thenceforward all summer in the sound of the sea,
And at night under the full of the moon in calmer weather,
Over the hoarse surging of the sea,
Or flitting from brier to brier by day,
I saw, I heard at intervals the remaining one, the he-bird,
The solitary guest from Alabama.

Blow! blow! blow!
Blow up sea-winds along Paumanok's shore;
I wait and I wait till you blow my mate to me.

Yes, when the stars glisten'd,
All night long on the prong of a moss-scallop'd stake,
Down almost amid the slapping waves,
Sat the lone singer wonderful causing tears.

He call'd on his mate,
He pour'd forth the meanings which I of all men know.

Yes my brother I know,
The rest might not, but I have treasur'd every note,
For more than once dimly down to the beach gliding,
Silent, avoiding the moonbeams, blending myself with the shadows,
Recalling now the obscure shapes, the echoes, the sounds and sights after their sorts,
The white arms out in the breakers tirelessly tossing,
I, with bare feet, a child, the wind wafting my hair,
Listen'd long and long.

Listen'd to keep, to sing, now translating the notes,
Following you my brother.

Soothe! soothe! soothe!
Close on its wave soothes the wave behind,
And again another behind embracing and lapping, every one close,
But my love soothes not me, not me.

Low hangs the moon, it rose late,
It is lagging—O I think it is heavy with love, with love.

O madly the sea pushes upon the land,
With love, with love.

O night! do I not see my love fluttering out among the breakers?
What is that little black thing I see there in the white?

Loud! loud! loud!
Loud I call to you, my love!
High and clear I shoot my voice over the waves,
Surely you must know who is here, is here,
You must know who I am, my love.

Low-hanging moon!
What is that dusky spot in your brown yellow?
O it is the shape, the shape of my mate!
O moon do not keep her from me any longer.

Land! land! O land!
Whichever way I turn, O I think you could give me my mate back again if you only would,
For I am almost sure I see her dimly whichever way I look.

O rising stars!
Perhaps the one I want so much will rise, will rise with one of you.

O throat! O trembling throat!
Sound clearer through the atmosphere!
Pierce the woods, the earth,
Somewhere listening to catch you must be the one I want.   95

Shake out carols!
Solitary here, the night's carols!
Carols of lonesome love! death's carols!   100
Carols under that lagging, yellow, waning moon!
O under that moon where she droops almost down into the sea!
O reckless despairing carols.

But soft! sink low!   105
Soft! let me just murmur,
And do you wait a moment you husky-nois'd sea,
For somewhere I believe I heard my mate responding to me,
So faint, I must be still, be still to listen,
But not altogether still, for then she might not come immediately to me.   110

Hither my love!
Here I am! here!
With this just-sustain'd note I announce myself to you,
This gentle call is for you my love, for you.

Do not be decoy'd elsewhere,   115
That is the whistle of the wind, it is not my voice,
That is fluttering, the fluttering of the spray,
Those are the shadows of leaves.

O darkness! O in vain!
O I am very sick and sorrowful.   120

O brown halo in the sky near the moon, drooping upon the sea!
O troubled reflection in the sea!
O throat! O throbbing heart!
And singing uselessly, uselessly all the night.

O past! O happy life! O song of joy!   125
In the air, in the woods, over fields,
Loved! loved! loved! loved! loved!
But my mate no more, no more with me!
We two together no more.

The aria sinking,   130
All else continuing, the stars shining,
The winds blowing, the notes of the bird continuous echoing,
With angry moan the fierce old mother incessantly moaning,
On the sands of Paumanok's shore gray and rustling,
The yellow half-moon enlarged, sagging down, drooping, the face of the sea almost touching,   135
The boy ecstatic, with his bare feet the waves, with his hair the atmosphere dallying,
The love in the heart long pent, now loose, now at last tumultuously bursting,
The aria's meaning, the ears, the soul, swiftly depositing,
The strange tears down the cheeks coursing,
The colloquy there, the trio, each uttering,   140
The undertone, the savage old mother incessantly crying,
To the boy's soul's questions sullenly timing, some drown'd secret hissing,
To the outsetting bard.

Demon or bird! (said the boy's soul,)
Is it indeed toward your mate you sing? or is it really to me?   145
For I, that was a child, my tongue's use sleeping, now I have heard you,
Now in a moment I know what I am for, I awake,
And already a thousand singers, a thousand songs, clearer, louder, and more sorrowful than yours,
A thousand warbling echoes have started to life within me, never to die.

O you singer solitary, singing by yourself, projecting me,   150
O solitary me listening, never more shall I cease perpetuating you,
Never more shall I escape, never more the reverberations,
Never more the cries of unsatisfied love be absent from me,
Never again leave me to be the peaceful child I was before what there in the night,
By the sea under the yellow and sagging moon,   155
The messenger there arous'd, the fire, the sweet hell within,
The unknown want, the destiny of me.

O give me the clew! (it lurks in the night here somewhere,)
O if I am to have so much, let me have more!

A word then, (for I will conquer it,)   160
The word final, superior to all,
Subtle, sent up—what is it?—I listen;
Are you whispering it, and have been all the time, you sea-waves?
Is that it from your liquid rims and wet sands?

Whereto answering, the sea,   165
Delaying not, hurrying not,
Whisper'd me through the night, and very plainly before daybreak,
Lisp'd to me the low and delicious word death,
And again death, death, death, death,
Hissing melodious, neither like the bird nor like my arous'd child's heart,   170
But edging near as privately for me rustling at my feet,
Creeping thence steadily up to my ears and laving me softly all over,
Death, death, death, death, death.

Which I do not forget,
But fuse the song of my dusky demon and brother,   175
That he sang to me in the moonlight on Paumanok's gray beach,
With the thousand responsive songs at random,
My own songs awaked from that hour,
And with them the key, the word up from the waves,
The word of the sweetest song and all songs,   180
That strong and delicious word which, creeping to my feet,
(Or like some old crone rocking the cradle, swathed in sweet garments, bending aside,)
The sea whisper'd me.

1859, 1881

As I Ebb'd with the Ocean of Life

This poem is Whitman's classic expression of alienation and despair. In it the poet speaks of his personal insignificance as a man and as a poet; he identifies himself with the meaningless "little wash'd-up drifts" along the shore; and he ends the poem, as he began it, oppressed by his insignificance and by the mystery of nature and death.

1

As I ebb'd with the ocean of life,
As I wended the shores I know,
As I walk'd where the ripples continually wash you Paumanok,
Where they rustle up hoarse and sibilant,
Where the fierce old mother endlessly cries for her castaways,   5
I musing late in the autumn day, gazing off southward,
Held by this electric self out of the pride of which I utter poems,
Was seiz'd by the spirit that trails in the lines underfoot,
The rim, the sediment that stands for all the water and all the land of the globe.

Fascinated, my eyes reverting from the south, dropt, to follow those slender windrows,   10
Chaff, straw, splinters of wood, weeds, and the sea-gluten,
Scum, scales from shining rocks, leaves of salt-lettuce, left by the tide,
Miles walking, the sound of breaking waves the other side of me,
Paumanok there and then as I thought the old thought of likenesses,
These you presented to me you fish-shaped island,   15
As I wended the shores I know,
As I walk'd with that electric self seeking types.

2

As I wend to the shores I know not,
As I list to the dirge, the voices of men and women wreck'd,
As I inhale the impalpable breezes that set in upon me,   20
As the ocean so mysterious rolls toward me closer and closer,
I too but signify at the utmost a little wash'd-up drift,
A few sands and dead leaves to gather,
Gather, and merge myself as part of the sands and drift.

O baffled, balk'd, bent to the very earth,   25
Oppress'd with myself that I have dared to open my mouth,
Aware now that amid all that blab whose echoes recoil upon me I have not once had the least idea
       who or what I am,
But that before all my arrogant poems the real Me stands yet untouch'd, untold, altogether
       unreach'd,
Withdrawn far, mocking me with mock-congratulatory signs and bows,
With peals of distant ironical laughter at every word I have written,   30
Pointing in silence to these songs, and then to the sand beneath.

I perceive I have not really understood any thing, not a single object, and that no man ever can,
Nature here in sight of the sea taking advantage of me to dart upon me and sting me,
Because I have dared to open my mouth to sing at all.

3

You oceans both, I close with you,   35
We murmur alike reproachfully rolling sands and drift, knowing not why,
These little shreds indeed standing for you and me and all.

You friable shore with trails of debris,
You fish-shaped island, I take what is underfoot,
What is yours is mine my father.   40

I too Paumanok,
I too have bubbled up, floated the measureless float, and been wash'd on your shores,

I too am but a trail of drift and debris,
I too leave little wrecks upon you, you fish-shaped island.

I throw myself upon your breast my father, 45
I cling to you so that you cannot unloose me,
I hold you so firm till you answer me something.

Kiss me my father,
Touch me with your lips as I touch those I love,
Breathe to me while I hold you close the secret of the murmuring I envy. 50

4

Ebb, ocean of life, (the flow will return,)
Cease not your moaning you fierce old mother,
Endlessly cry for your castaways, but fear not, deny not me,
Rustle not up so hoarse and angry against my feet as I touch you or gather from you.

I mean tenderly by you and all, 55
I gather for myself and for this phantom looking down where we lead, and following me and mine.

Me and mine, loose windrows, little corpses,
Froth, snowy white, and bubbles,
(See, from my dead lips the ooze exuding at last,
See, the prismatic colors glistening and rolling,) 60
Tufts of straw, sands, fragments,
Buoy'd hither from many moods, one contradicting another,
From the storm, the long calm, the darkness, the swell,
Musing, pondering, a breath, a briny tear, a dab of liquid or soil,
Up just as much out of fathomless workings fermented and thrown, 65
A limp blossom or two, torn, just as much over waves floating, drifted at random,
Just as much for us that sobbing dirge of Nature,
Just as much whence we come that blare of the cloud-trumpets,
We, capricious, brought hither we know not whence, spread out before you,
You up there walking or sitting, 70
Whoever you are, we too lie in drifts at your feet.

1860, 1881

Once I Pass'd Through a Populous City

From the group of poems on the body, sex, and love which Whitman
collected under the title "Children of Adam," this poem has been of more
biographic than poetic interest. In the original unpublished draft, the lover
was not a woman but "the man who wandered with me there," "one rude
and ignorant man."

Once I pass'd through a populous city imprinting my brain for future use with its shows,
    architecture, customs, traditions,
Yet now of all that city I remember only a woman I casually met there who detain'd me for love
    of me,
Day by day and night by night we were together—all else has long been forgotten by me,
I remember I say only that woman who passionately clung to me,
Again we wander, we love, we separate again,
Again she holds me by the hand, I must not go, 5
I see her close beside me with silent lips sad and tremulous.

1860, 1867

When I Heard at the Close of the Day

When I heard at the close of the day how my name had been receiv'd with plaudits in the capitol,
    still it was not a happy night for me that follow'd,
And else when I carous'd, or when my plans were accomplish'd, still I was not happy,
But the day when I rose at dawn from the bed of perfect health, refresh'd, singing, inhaling the
    ripe breath of autumn,
When I saw the full moon in the west grow pale and disappear in the morning light,
When I wander'd alone over the beach, and undressing bathed, laughing with the cool waters, and
    saw the sun rise,   5
And when I thought how my dear friend my lover was on his way coming, O then I was happy,
O then each breath tasted sweeter, and all that day my food nourish'd me more and the beautiful
    day pass'd well,
And the next came with equal joy, and with the next at evening came my friend,
And that night while all was still I heard the waters roll slowly continually up the shores,
I heard the hissing rustle of the liquid and sands as directed to me whispering to congratulate me,   10
For the one I love most lay sleeping by me under the same cover in the cool night,
In the stillness in the autumn moonbeams his face was inclined toward me,
And his arm lay lightly around my breast—and that night I was happy.

                               1860, 1867

A Glimpse

A glimpse through an interstice caught,
Of a crowd of workmen and drivers in a bar-room around the stove late of a winter night, and I
    unremark'd seated in a corner,
Of a youth who loves me and whom I love, silently approaching and seating himself near, that he
    may hold me by the hand,
A long while amid the noises of coming and going, of drinking and oath and smutty jest
There we two, content, happy in being together, speaking little, perhaps not a word.   5

                               1860, 1867

A Noiseless Patient Spider

A noiseless patient spider,
I mark'd where on a little promontory it stood isolated,
Mark'd how to explore the vacant vast surrounding,
It lauch'd forth filament, filament, filament, out of itself,
Ever unreeling them, ever tirelessly speeding them.   5

And you O my soul where you stand,
Surrounded, detached, in measureless oceans of space,
Ceaselessly musing, venturing, throwing, seeking the spheres to connect them,
Till the bridge you will need be form'd, till the ductile anchor hold,
Till the gossamer thread you fling catch somewhere, O my soul.   10

                            1862–63, 1881

When I Heard the Learn'd Astronomer

When I heard the learn'd astronomer,
When the proofs, the figures, were ranged in columns before me,
When I was shown the charts and the diagrams, to add, divide, and measure them,

When I sitting heard the astronomer where he lectured with much applause in the lecture-room,
How soon unaccountable I became tired and sick, 5
Till rising and gliding out I wander'd off by myself,
In the mystical moist night-air, and from time to time,
Look'd up in perfect silence at the stars.

1865, 1867

Cavalry Crossing a Ford

A line in long array where they wind betwixt green islands,
They take a serpentine course, their arms flash in the sun—hark to the musical clank,
Behold the silvery river, in it the splashing horses loitering stop to drink,
Behold the brown-faced men, each group, each person a picture, the negligent rest on the saddles,
Some emerge on the opposite bank, others are just entering the ford—while, 5
Scarlet and blue and snowy white,
The guidon flags flutter gayly in the wind.

1865, 1871

A March in the Ranks Hard-Prest,
and The Road Unknown

A march in the ranks hard prest, and the road unknown,
A route through a heavy wood with muffled steps in the darkness,
Our army foil'd with loss severe, and the sullen remnant retreating,
Till after midnight glimmer upon us the lights of a dim-lighted building,
We come to an open space in the woods, and halt by the dim-lighted building, 5
'Tis a large old church at the crossing roads, now an impromptu hospital,
Entering but for a minute I see a sight beyond all the pictures and poems ever made,
Shadows of deepest, deepest black, just lit by moving candles and lamps,
And by one great pitchy torch stationary with wild red flame and clouds of smoke,
By these, crowds, groups of forms vaguely I see on the floor, some in the pews laid down, 10
At my feet more distinctly a soldier, a mere lad, in danger of bleeding to death, (he is shot in the abdomen,)
I stanch the blood temporarily, (the youngster's face is white as a lily,)
Then before I depart I sweep my eyes o'er the scene fain to absorb it all,
Faces, varieties, postures beyond description, most in obscurity, some of them dead,
Surgeons operating, attendants holding lights, the smell of ether, the odor of blood, 15
The crowd, O the crowd of the bloody forms, the yard outside also fill'd,
Some on the bare ground, some on planks or stretchers, some in the death-spasm sweating,
An occasional scream or cry, the doctor's shouted orders or calls,
The glisten of the little steel instruments catching the glint of the torches,
These I resume as I chant, I see again the forms, I smell the odor, 20
Then hear outside the orders given, *Fall in, my men, fall in;*
But first I bend to the dying lad, his eyes open, a half-smile gives he me,
Then the eyes close, calmly close, and I speed forth to the darkness,
Resuming, marching, ever in darkness marching, on in the ranks,
The unknown road still marching. 25

1865

A Sight in Camp in the Daybreak
Gray and Dim

A sight in camp in the daybreak gray and dim,
As from my tent I emerge so early sleepless,
As slow I walk in the cool fresh air the path near by the hospital tent,

Three forms I see on stretchers lying, brought out there untended lying,
Over each the blanket spread, ample brownish woolen blanket,
Gray and heavy blanket, folding, covering all.

Curious I halt and silent stand,
Then with light fingers I from the face of the nearest the first just lift the blanket;
Who are you elderly man so gaunt and grim, with well-gray'd hair, and flesh all sunken about the
    eyes?
Who are you my dear comrade?

Then to the second I step—and who are you my child and darling?
Who are you sweet boy with cheeks yet blooming?

Then to the third—a face nor child nor old, very calm, as of beautiful yellow-white ivory;
Young man I think I know you—I think this face is the face of the Christ himself,
Dead and divine and brother of all, and here again he lies.

1865

The Wound-Dresser

1

An old man bending I come among new faces,
Years looking backward resuming in answer to children,
Come tell us old man, as from young men and maidens that love me,
(Arous'd and angry, I'd thought to beat the alarum, and urge relentless war,
But soon my fingers fail'd me, my face droop'd and I resign'd myself,
To sit by the wounded and soothe them, or silently watch the dead;)
Years hence of these scenes, of these furious passions, these chances,
Of unsurpass'd heroes, (was one side so brave? the other was equally brave;)
Now be witness again, paint the mightiest armies of earth,
Of those armies so rapid so wondrous what saw you to tell us?
What stays with you latest and deepest? of curious panics,
Of hard-fought engagements or sieges tremendous what deepest remains?

2

O maidens and young men I love and that love me,
What you ask of my days those the strangest and sudden your talking recalls,
Soldier alert I arrive after a long march cover'd with sweat and dust,
In the nick of time I come, plunge in the fight, loudly shout in the rush of successful charge,
Enter the captur'd works—yet lo, like a swift-running river they fade,
Pass and are gone they fade—I dwell not on soldiers' perils or soldiers' joys,
(Both I remember well—many of the hardships, few the joys, yet I was content.)

But in silence, in dreams' projections,
While the world of gain and appearance and mirth goes on,
So soon what is over forgotten, and waves wash the imprints off the sand,
With hinged knees returning I enter the doors, (while for you up there,
Whoever you are, follow without noise and be of strong heart.)

Bearing the bandages, water and sponge,
Straight and swift to my wounded I go,
Where they lie on the ground after the battle brought in,
Where their priceless blood reddens the grass the ground,
Or to the rows of the hospital tent, or under the roof'd hospital,
To the long rows of cots up and down each side I return,

To each and all one after another I draw near, not one do I miss,
An attendant follows holding a tray, he carries a refuse pail,
Soon to be fill'd with clotted rags and blood, emptied, and fill'd again.

I onward go, I stop,
With hinged knees and steady hand to dress wounds,   35
I am firm with each, the pangs are sharp yet unavoidable,
One turns to me his appealing eyes—poor boy! I never knew you,
Yet I think I could not refuse this moment to die for you, if that would save you.

3

On, on I go, (open doors of time! open hospital doors!)
The crush'd head I dress, (poor crazed hand tear not the bandage away,)   40
The neck of the cavalry-man with the bullet through and through I examine,
Hard the breathing rattles, quite glazed already the eye, yet life struggles hard,
(Come sweet death! be persuaded O beautiful death!
In mercy come quickly.)

From the stump of the arm, the amputated hand,   45
I undo the clotted lint, remove the slough, wash off the matter and blood,
Back on his pillow the soldier bends with curv'd neck and side-falling head,
His eyes are closed, his face is pale, he dares not look on the bloody stump,
And has not yet look'd on it.

I dress a wound in the side, deep, deep,   50
But a day or two more, for see the frame all wasted and sinking,
And the yellow-blue countenance see.

I dress the perforated shoulder, the foot with the bullet-wound,
Cleanse the one with a gnawing and putrid gangrene, so sickening, so offensive,
While the attendant stands behind aside me holding the tray and pail.   55

I am faithful, I do not give out,
The fractur'd thigh, the knee, the wound in the abdomen,
These and more I dress with impassive hand, (yet deep in my breast a fire, a burning flame.)

4

Thus in silence in dreams' projections,
Returning, resuming, I thread my way through the hospitals,   60
The hurt and wounded I pacify with soothing hand,
I sit by the restless all the dark night, some are so young,
Some suffer so much, I recall the experience sweet and sad,
(Many a soldier's loving arms about this neck have cross'd and rested,
Many a soldier's kiss dwells on these bearded lips.)   65

1865, 1881

When Lilacs Last in the Dooryard Bloom'd

This is a poem about Lincoln, the best of many in American literature.

In Washington, during the year of Gettysburg, Whitman wrote: "I see the President almost every day, as I happen to live where he passes to or from his lodgings out of town. . . . the deep-cut lines, the eyes, always to me with a deep latent sadness in the expression. We have got so that we exchange bows."

On the second inauguration, March 4, 1865: "I saw him on his return, at three o'clock, after the performance was over. He was in his plain two-horse barouche, and look'd very much worn and tired; . . . yet all the old goodness, tenderness, sadness, and canny shrewdness, underneath the furrows. . . . By his side sat his little boy, of ten years. There were no soldiers."

The next month the President was murdered. It was lilac time in Brooklyn when Whitman heard the news—April 15, early in the morning. "Mother prepared breakfast—and other meals afterward—as usual; but not a mouthful was eaten all day by either of us. We each drank half a cup of coffee; that was all. Little was said. We got every newspaper morning and evening, and the frequent extras of that period, and pass'd them silently to each other." A funeral train left Washington on April 21, carrying Lincoln's body to his home town, Springfield, Illinois, halting on the way at Philadelphia, New York, Chicago, and other cities.

The poem which Whitman was moved to write does not mention Lincoln's name, or dwell upon "the man I love." Instead, it unites two broad themes that absorbed him: America, "my land" (typified by its great President) and death, the "dark mother" of all of us. The solemn sense of bereavement that runs through the poem and the remarkable song to "lovely and soothing death" are not so much personal as national. As the funeral train moves on, and the bells toll in cities draped in black, the poet's emotion is that of a people, his tribute only his "sprig of lilac."

The poem is developed largely through three symbols: the star (Lincoln), the lilac (love), the hermit thrush (the poet singing of death). They keep reappearing, like themes in a musical recitative, and at the end are brought together in one phrase—"Lilac and star and bird."

1

When lilacs last in the dooryard bloom'd
And the great star early droop'd in the western sky in the night,
I mourn'd, and yet shall mourn with ever-returning spring.

Ever-returning spring, trinity sure to me you bring,
Lilac blooming perennial and drooping star in the west,   5
And thought of him I love.

2

O powerful western fallen star!
O shades of night!—O moody, tearful night!
O great star disappear'd—O the black murk that hides the star!
O cruel hands that hold me powerless—O helpless soul of me!   10
O harsh surrounding cloud that will not free my soul.

3

In the dooryard fronting an old farm-house near the white-wash'd palings,
Stands the lilac-bush tall-growing with heart-shaped leaves of rich green,
With many a pointed blossom rising delicate, with the perfume strong I love,
With every leaf a miracle—and from this bush in the dooryard,   15
With delicate-color'd blossoms and heart-shaped leaves of rich green,
A sprig with its flower I break.

4

In the swamp in secluded recesses,
A shy and hidden bird is warbling a song.

Solitary the thrush,   20
The hermit withdrawn to himself, avoiding the settlements,
Sings by himself a song.

Song of the bleeding throat,
Death's outlet song of life, (for well dear brother I know,
If thou wast not granted to sing thou would'st surely die.)   25

5

Over the breast of the spring, the land, amid cities,
Amid lanes and through old woods, where lately the violets peep'd from the ground, spotting the
    gray debris,
Amid the grass in the fields each side of the lanes, passing the endless grass,
Passing the yellow-spear'd wheat, every grain from its shroud in the dark-brown fields uprisen,
Passing the apple-tree blows of white and pink in the orchards,
Carrying a corpse to where it shall rest in the grave,
Night and day journeys a coffin.

6

Coffin that passes through lanes and streets,
Through day and night with the great cloud darkening the land,
With the pomp of the inloop'd flags with the cities draped in black,
With the show of the States themselves as of crape-veil'd women standing,   35
With processions long and winding and the flambeaus of the night,
With the countless torches lit, with the silent sea of faces and the unbared heads,
With the waiting depot, the arriving coffin, and the sombre faces,
With dirges through the night, with the thousand voices rising strong and solemn,   40
With all the mournful voices of the dirges pour'd around the coffin,
The dim-lit churches and the shuddering organs—where amid these you journey,
With the tolling tolling bells' perpetual clang,
Here, coffin that slowly passes,
I give you my sprig of lilac.   45

7

(Nor for you, for one alone,
Blossoms and branches green to coffins all I bring,
For fresh as the morning, thus would I chant a song for you O sane and sacred death.

All over bouquets of roses,
O death, I cover you over with roses and early lilies,   50
But mostly and now the lilac that blooms the first,
Copious I break, I break the sprigs from the bushes,
With loaded arms I come, pouring for you,
For you and the coffins all of you O death.)

8

O western orb sailing the heaven,   55
Now I know what you must have meant as a month since I walk'd,
As I walk'd in silence the transparent shadowy night,
As I saw you had something to tell as you bent to me night after night,
As you droop'd from the sky low down as if to my side, (while the other stars all look'd on,)
As we wander'd together the solemn night, (for something I know not what kept me from sleep,)
As the night advanced, and I saw on the rim of the west how full you were of woe,   61
As I stood on the rising ground in the breeze in the cool transparent night,
As I watch'd where you pass'd and was lost in the netherward black of the night,
As my soul in its trouble dissatisfied sank, as where you sad orb,
Concluded, dropt in the night, and was gone.   65

9

Sing on there in the swamp,
O singer bashful and tender, I hear your notes, I hear your call,
I hear, I come presently, I understand you,

But a moment I linger, for the lustrous star has detain'd me,
The star my departing comrade holds and detains me.   70

10

O how shall I warble myself for the dead one there I loved?
And how shall I deck my song for the large sweet soul that has gone?
And what shall my perfume be for the grave of him I love?

Sea-winds blown from east and west,
Blown from the Eastern sea and blown from the Western sea, till there on the prairies meeting,   75
These and with these and the breath of my chant,
I'll perfume the grave of him I love.

11

O what shall I hang on the chamber walls?
And what shall the pictures be that I hang on the walls,
To adorn the burial-house of him I love?   80

Pictures of growing spring and farms and homes,
With the Fourth-month eve at sundown, and the gray smoke lucid and bright,
With floods of the yellow gold of the gorgeous indolent, sinking sun, burning, expanding the air,
With the fresh sweet herbage under foot, and the pale green leaves of the trees prolific,
In the distance the flowing glaze, the breast of the river, with a wind-dapple here and there,   85
With ranging hills on the banks, with many a line against the sky, and shadows,
And the city at hand with dwellings so dense, and stacks of chimneys,
And all the scenes of life and the workshops, and the workmen homeward returning.

12

Lo, body and soul—this land,
My own Manhattan with spires, and the sparkling and hurrying tides, and the ships,   90
The varied and ample land, the South and the North in the light, Ohio's shores and flashing
    Missouri,
And ever the far-spreading prairies cover'd with grass and corn.

Lo, the most excellent sun so calm and haughty,
The violet and purple morn with just-felt breezes,
The gentle soft-brown measureless light,   95
The miracle spreading bathing all, the fulfill'd noon,
The coming eve delicious, the welcome night and the stars,
Over my cities shining all, enveloping man and land.

13

Sing on, sing on you gray-brown bird,
Sing from the swamps, the recesses, pour your chant from the bushes,   100
Limitless out of the dusk, out of the cedars and pines.

Sing on dearest brother, warble your reedy song,
Loud human song, with voice of uttermost woe.

O liquid and free and tender!
O wild and loose to my soul—O wondrous singer!   105
You only I hear—yet the star holds me, (but will soon depart,)
Yet the lilac with mastering odor holds me.

14

Now while I sat in the day and look'd forth,
In the close of the day with its light and the fields of spring, and the farmers preparing their crops,
In the large unconscious scenery of my land with its lakes and forests,
In the heavenly aerial beauty, (after the perturb'd winds and the storms,) 110
Under the arching heavens of the afternoon swift passing, and the voices of children and women,
The many-moving sea-tides, and I saw the ships how they sail'd,
And the summer approaching with richness, and the fields all busy with labor,
And the infinite separate houses, how they all went on, each with its meals and minutia of daily
     usages, 115
And the streets how their throbbings throbb'd, and the cities pent—lo, then and there,
Falling upon them all and among them all, enveloping me with the rest,
Appear'd the cloud, appear'd the long black trail,
And I knew death, its thought, and the sacred knowledge of death.

Then with the knowledge of death as walking one side of me, 120
And the thought of death close-walking the other side of me,
And I in the middle as with companions, and as holding the hands of companions,
I fled forth to the hiding receiving night that talks not,
Down to the shores of the water, the path by the swamp in the dimness,
To the solemn shadowy cedars and ghostly pines so still. 125

And the singer so shy to the rest receiv'd me,
The gray-brown bird I know receiv'd us comrades three,
And he sang the carol of death, and a verse for him I love.

From deep secluded recesses,
From the fragrant cedars and the ghostly pines so still,
Came the carol of the bird. 130

And the charm of the carol rapt me,
As I held as if by their hands my comrades in the night,
And the voice of my spirit tallied the song of the bird.

Come lovely and soothing death, 135
Undulate round the world, serenely arriving, arriving,
In the day, in the night, to all, to each,
Sooner or later delicate death.

Prais'd be the fathomless universe,
For life and joy, and for objects and knowledge curious, 140
And for love, sweet love—but praise! praise! praise!
For the sure-enwinding arms of cool-enfolding death.

Dark mother always gliding near with soft feet,
Have none chanted for thee a chant of fullest welcome?
Then I chant it for thee, I glorify thee above all, 145
I bring thee a song that when thou must indeed come, come unfalteringly.

Approach strong deliveress,
When it is so, when thou hast taken them I joyously sing the dead,
Lost in the loving floating ocean of thee,
Laved in the flood of thy bliss O death. 150

From me to thee glad serenades,
Dances for thee I propose saluting thee, adornments and feastings for thee,

And the sights of the open landscape and the high-spread sky are fitting,
And life and the fields, and the huge and thoughtful night.

The night in silence under many a star,   155
The ocean shore and the husky whispering wave whose voice I know,
And the soul turning to thee O vast and well-veil'd death,
And the body gratefully nestling close to thee.

Over the tree-tops I float thee a song,
Over the rising and sinking waves, over the myriad fields and the prairies wide, 160
Over the dense-pack'd cities all and the teeming wharves and ways,
I float this carol with joy, with joy to thee O death.

15

To the tally of my soul,
Loud and strong kept up the gray-brown bird,
With pure deliberate notes spreading filling the night.   165

Loud in the pines and cedars dim,
Clear in the freshness moist and swamp-perfume,
And I with my comrades there in the night.

While my sight that was bound in my eyes unclosed,
As to long panoramas of visions.   170

And I saw askant the armies,
I saw as in noiseless dreams hundreds of battle-flags,
Borne through the smoke of the battles and pierc'd with missiles I saw them,
And carried hither and yon through the smoke, and torn and bloody,
And at last but a few shreds left on the staffs, (and all in silence,) 175
And the staffs all splinter'd and broken.

I saw battle-corpses, myriads of them,
And the white skeletons of young men, I saw them,
I saw the debris and debris of all the slain soldiers of the war,
But I saw they were not as was thought,   180
They themselves were fully at rest, they suffer'd not,
The living remain'd and suffer'd, the mother suffer'd,
And the wife and the child and the musing comrade suffer'd,
And the armies that remain'd suffer'd.

16

Passing the visions, passing the night,   185
Passing, unloosing the hold of my comrades' hands,
Passing the song of the hermit bird and the tallying song of my soul,
Victorious song, death's outlet song, yet varying ever-altering song,
As low and wailing, yet clear the notes, rising and falling, flooding the night,
Sadly sinking and fainting, as warning and warning, and yet again bursting with joy, 190
Covering the earth and filling the spread of the heaven,
As that powerful psalm in the night I heard from recesses,
Passing, I leave thee lilac with heart-shaped leaves,
I leave thee there in the door-yard, blooming, returning with spring.

I cease from my song for thee,   195
From my gaze on thee in the west, fronting the west, communing with thee,
O comrade lustrous with silver face in the night.

Yet each to keep and all, retrievements out of the night,
The song, the wondrous chant of the gray-brown bird,
And the tallying chant, the echo arous'd in my soul,   200
With the lustrous and drooping star with the countenance full of woe,
With the holders holding my hand hearing the call of the bird,
Comrades mine and I in the midst, and their memory ever to keep, for the dead I loved so well,
For the sweetest, wisest soul of all my days and lands—and this for his dear sake,
Lilac and star and bird twined with the chant of my soul,   205
There in the fragrant pines and the cedars dusk and dim.

1865-66, 1881

On the Beach at Night

On the beach at night,
Stands a child with her father,
Watching the east, the autumn sky.

Up through the darkness,
While ravening clouds, the burial clouds, in black masses spreading,   5
Lower sullen and fast athwart and down the sky,
Amid a transparent clear belt of ether yet left in the east,
Ascends large and calm the lord-star Jupiter,
And nigh at hand, only a very little above,
Swim the delicate sisters the Pleiades.   10

From the beach the child holding the hand of her father,
Those burial clouds that lower victorious soon to devour all,
Watching, silently weeps.

Weep not, child,
Weep not, my darling,   15
With these kisses let me remove your tears,
The ravening clouds shall not long be victorious,
They shall not long possess the sky, they devour the stars only in apparition,
Jupiter shall emerge, be patient, watch again another night, the Pleiades shall emerge,
They are immortal, all those stars both silvery and golden shall shine out again,   20
The great stars and the little ones shall shine out again, they endure,
The vast immortal suns and the long-enduring pensive moons shall again shine.

Then dearest child mournest thou only for Jupiter?
Considerest thou alone the burial of the stars?

Something there is,   25
(With my lips soothing thee, adding I whisper,
I give thee the first suggestion, the problem and indirection,)
Something there is more immortal even than the stars,
(Many the burials, many the days and nights, passing away,)
Something that shall endure longer even than lustrous Jupiter,   30
Longer than sun or any revolving satellite,
Or the radiant sisters the Pleiades.

1871

Passage to India

The main technological achievements Whitman speaks of in this poem are the opening of the Suez Canal, the completion of the transcontinental railroad, and the laying of the transoceanic cable—each an achievement in communications, primarily. Whitman also alludes to many other names, places, and events, both past and present; all develop the main themes of the poem—circumnavigation of the world, journey into the past, journey beyond the past and history.

The burden of the poem, Whitman once remarked, is "evolution—. . . the unfolding of cosmic purposes." For him, evolution meant far more than material development. The world has been welded together

> "not for trade or transportation only,
> But in God's name, and for thy sake O soul."

Far in the past, India led the way in poetry and religion. This will be the way of the future. The world will be circumnavigated by the soul. "Finally shall come the poet worthy that name." He it is who will show how truly, how deeply, the world is one, that Spirit and Matter, Nature and Men, are one. In section 8 we see Whitman taking ship, launching out on trackless seas in an ecstatic adventure of the soul, a voyage to far more than India, more than stars or suns, a voyage whose destination is God.

1

Singing my days,
Singing the great achievements of the present,
Singing the strong light works of engineers,
Our modern wonders, (the antique ponderous Seven outvied,)
In the Old World the east the Suez canal, 5
The New by its mighty railroad spann'd,
The seas inlaid with eloquent gentle wires;
Yet first to sound, and ever sound, the cry with thee O soul,
The Past! the Past! the Past!

The Past—the dark unfathom'd retrospect! 10
The teeming gulf—the sleepers and the shadows!
The past—the infinite greatness of the past!
For what is the present after all but a growth out of the past?
(As a projectile form'd, impell'd, passing a certain line, still keeps on,
So the present, utterly form'd, impell'd by the past,) 15

2

Passage O soul to India!
Eclaircise the myths Asiatic, the primitive fables.

Not you alone proud truths of the world,
Nor you alone ye facts of modern science,
But myths and fables of eld, Asia's, Africa's fables, 20
The far-darting beams of the spirit, the unloos'd dreams,
The deep diving bibles and legends,
The daring plots of the poets, the elder religions;
O you temples fairer than lilies pour'd over by the rising sun!
O you fables spurning the known, eluding the hold of the known, mounting to heaven! 25
You lofty and dazzling towers, pinnacled, red as roses, burnish'd with gold!
Towers of fables immortal fashion'd from mortal dreams!
You too I welcome and fully the same as the rest!
You too with joy I sing.

Passage to India! 30
Lo, soul, seest thou not God's purpose from the first?
The earth to be spann'd, connected by network,
The races, neighbors, to marry and be given in marriage,
The oceans to be cross'd, the distant brought near,
The lands to be welded together. 35

A worship new I sing,
You captains, voyagers, explorers, yours,
You engineers, you architects, machinists, yours,

You, not for trade or transportation only,
But in God's name, and for thy sake O soul.   40

3

Passage to India!
Lo soul for thee of tableaus twain,
I see in one the Suez canal initiated, open'd,
I see the procession of steamships, the Empress Eugenie's leading the van,
I mark from on deck the strange landscape, the pure sky, the level sand in the distance,   45
I pass swiftly the picturesque groups, the workmen gather'd,
The gigantic dredging machines.

In one again, different, (yet thine, all thine, O soul, the same,)
I see over my own continent the Pacific railroad surmounting every barrier,
I see continual trains of cars winding along the Platte carrying freight and passengers,   50
I hear the locomotives rushing and roaring, and the shrill steam-whistle,
I hear the echoes reverberate through the grandest scenery in the world,
I cross the Laramie plains, I note the rocks in grotesque shapes, the buttes,
I see the plentiful larkspur and wild onions, the barren, colorless, sage-deserts,
I see in glimpses afar or towering immediately above me the great mountains, I see the Wind river
   and the Wahsatch mountains,   55
I see the Monument mountain and the Eagle's Nest, I pass the Promontory, I ascend the Nevadas,
I scan the noble Elk mountain and wind around its base,
I see the Humboldt range, I thread the valley and cross the river,
I see the clear waters of lake Tahoe, I see forests of majestic pines,
Or crossing the great desert, the alkaline plains, I behold enchanting mirages of waters and
   meadows,   60
Marking through these and after all, in duplicate slender lines,
Bridging the three or four thousand miles of land travel,
Tying the Eastern to the Western sea,
The road between Europe and Asia.

(Ah Genoese thy dream! thy dream!   65
Centuries after thou art laid in thy grave,
The shore thou foundest verifies thy dream.)

4

Passage to India!
Struggles of many a captain, tales of many a sailor dead,
Over my mood stealing and spreading they come,   70
Like clouds and cloudlets in the unreach'd sky.

Along all history, down the slopes,
As a rivulet running, sinking now, and now again to the surface rising,
A ceaseless thought, a varied train—lo, soul, to thee, thy sight, they rise
The plans, the voyages again, the expeditions;   75
Again Vasco de Gama sails forth,
Again the knowledge gain'd, the mariner's compass,
Lands found and nations born, thou born America,
For purpose vast, man's long probation fill'd,
Thou rondure of the world at last accomplish'd.   80

5

O vast Rondure, swimming in space,
Cover'd all over with visible power and beauty,

Alternate light and day and the teeming spiritual darkness,
Unspeakable high processions of sun and moon and countless stars above,
Below, the manifold grass and waters, animals, mountains, trees,
With inscrutable purpose, some hidden prophetic intention,
Now first it seems my thought begins to span thee.

Down from the gardens of Asia descending radiating,
Adam and Eve appear, then their myriad progeny after them,
Wandering, yearning, curious, with restless explorations,
With questionings, baffled, formless, feverish, with never-happy hearts,
With that sad incessant refrain, *Wherefore unsatisfied soul? and Whither O mocking life?*

Ah who shall soothe these feverish children?
Who justify these restless explorations?
Who speak the secret of impassive earth?
Who bind it to us? what is this separate Nature so unnatural?
What is this earth to our affections? (unloving earth, without a throb to answer ours,
Cold earth, the place of graves.)

Yet soul be sure the first intent remains, and shall be carried out,
Perhaps even now the time has arrived.

After the seas are all cross'd, (as they seem already cross'd,)
After the great captains and engineers have accomplish'd their work,
After the noble inventors, after the scientists, the chemist, the geologist, ethnologist,
Finally shall come the poet worthy that name,
The true son of God shall come singing his songs.

Then not your deeds only O voyagers, O scientists and inventors, shall be justified,
All these hearts as of fretted children shall be sooth'd,
All affection shall be fully responded to, the secret shall be told,
All these separations and gaps shall be taken up and hook'd and link'd together,
The whole earth, this cold, impassive, voiceless earth, shall be completely justified,
Trinitas divine shall be gloriously accomplish'd and compacted by the true son of God, the poet,
(He shall indeed pass the straits and conquer the mountains,
He shall double the cape of Good Hope to some purpose,)
Nature and Man shall be disjoin'd and diffused no more,
The true son of God shall absolutely fuse them.

6

Year at whose wide-flung door I sing!
Year of the purpose accomplish'd!
Year of the marriage of continents, climates and oceans!
(No mere doge of Venice now wedding the Adriatic,)
I see O year in you the vast terraqueous globe given and giving all,
Europe to Asia, Africa join'd, and they to the New World,
The lands, geographies, dancing before you, holding a festival garland,
As brides and bridegrooms hand in hand.

Passage to India!
Cooling airs from Caucasus far, soothing cradle of man,
The river Euphrates flowing, the past lit up again.

Lo soul, the retrospect brought forward,
The old, most populous, wealthiest of earth's lands,
The streams of the Indus and the Ganges and their many affluents

(I my shores of America walking to-day behold, resuming all,)   130
The tale of Alexander on his warlike marches suddenly dying,
On one side China and on the other side Persia and Arabia,
To the south the great seas and the bay of Bengal,
The flowing literatures, tremendous epics, religions, castes,
Old occult Brahma interminably far back, the tender and junior Buddha,   135
Central and southern empires and all their belongings, possessors,
The wars of Tamerlane, the reign of Aurungzebe,
The traders, rulers, explorers, Moslems, Venetians, Byzantium, the Arabs, Portuguese,
The first travelers famous yet, Marco Polo, Batouta the Moor,
Doubts to be solv'd, the map incognita, blanks to be fill'd,   140
The foot of man unstay'd, the hands never at rest,
Thyself O soul that will not brook a challenge.

The mediaeval navigators rise before me.
The world of 1492, with its awaken'd enterprise,
Something swelling in humanity now like the sap of the earth in spring,   145
The sunset splendor of chivalry declining.

And who art thou sad shade?
Gigantic, visionary, thyself a visionary,
With majestic limbs and pious beaming eyes,
Spreading around with every look of thine a golden world,   150
Enhuing it with gorgeous hues.

As the chief histrion,
Down to the footlights walks in some great scena,
Dominating the rest I see the Admiral himself,
(History's type of courage, action, faith,)   155
Behold him sail from Palos leading his little fleet,
His voyage behold, his return, his great fame,
His misfortunes, calumniators, behold him a prisoner, chain'd,
Behold his dejection, poverty, death.

(Curious in time I stand, noting the efforts of heroes,   160
Is the deferment long? bitter the slander, poverty, death?
Lies the seed unreck'd for centuries in the ground? lo, to God's due occasion,
Uprising in the night, it sprouts, blooms,
And fills the earth with use and beauty.)

7

Passage indeed O soul to primal thought,   165
Not lands and seas alone, thy own clear freshness,
The young maturity of brood and bloom,
To realms of budding bibles.

O soul, repressless, I with thee and thou with me,
Thy circumnavigation of the world begin,   170
Of man, the voyage of his mind's return,
To reason's early paradise,
Back, back to wisdom's birth, to innocent intuitions,
Again with fair creation.

8

O we can wait no longer,   175
We too take ship O soul,

Joyous we too launch out on trackless seas,
Fearless for unknown shores on waves of ecstasy to sail,
Amid the wafting winds, (thou pressing me to thee, I thee to me, O soul,)
Caroling free, singing our song of God,
Chanting our chant of pleasant exploration. 180

With laugh and many a kiss,
(Let others deprecate, let others weep for sin, remorse, humiliation,)
O soul thou pleasest me, I thee.

Ah more than any priest O soul we too believe in God, 185
But with the mystery of God we dare not dally.

O soul thou pleasest me, I thee.
Sailing these seas or on the hills, or waking in the night,
Thoughts, silent thoughts, of Time and Space and Death, like waters flowing,
Bear me indeed as through the regions infinite, 190
Whose air I breathe, whose ripples hear, lave me all over,
Bathe me O God in thee, mounting to thee,
I and my soul to range in range of thee.

O Thou transcendent,
Nameless, the fibre and the breath, 195
Light of the light, shedding forth universes, thou centre of them,
Thou mightier centre of the true, the good, the loving,
Thou moral, spiritual fountain—affection's source—thou reservoir,
(O pensive soul of me—O thirst unsatisfied—waitest not there?
Waitest not haply for us somewhere there the Comrade perfect?) 200
Thou pulse—thou motive of the stars, suns, systems,
That, circling, move in order, safe, harmonious,
Athwart the shapeless vastnesses of space,
How should I think, how breathe a single breath, how speak, if, out of myself,
I could not launch, to those, superior universes? 205

Swiftly I shrivel at the thought of God,
At Nature and its wonders, Time and Space and Death,
But that I, turning, call to thee O soul, thou actual Me,
And lo, thou gently masterest the orbs,
Thou matest Time, smilest content at Death, 210
And fillest, swellest full the vastnesses of Space.

Greater than stars or suns,
Bounding O soul thou journeyest forth;
What love than thine and ours could wider amplify?
What aspirations, wishes, outvie thine and ours O soul? 215
What dreams of the ideal? what plans of purity, perfection, strength?
What cheerful willingness for others' sake to give up all?
For others' sake to suffer all?

Reckoning ahead O soul, when thou, the time achiev'd,
The seas all cross'd, weather'd the capes, the voyage done, 220
Surrounded, copest, frontest God, yieldest, the aim attain'd,
As fill'd with friendship, love complete, the Elder Brother found,
The Younger melts in fondness in his arms.

9

Passage to more than India!
Are thy wings plumed indeed for such far flights?
O soul, voyagest thou indeed on voyages like those?   225
Disportest thou on waters such as those?
Soundest below the Sanscrit and the Vedas?
Then have thy bent unleash'd.

Passage to you, your shores, ye aged fierce enigmas!   230
Passage to you, to mastership of you, ye strangling problems!
You, strew'd with the wrecks of skeletons, that, living, never reach'd you.

Passage to more than India!
O secret of the earth and sky!
Of you O waters of the sea! O winding creeks and rivers!   235
Of you O woods and fields! of you strong mountains of my land!
Of you O prairies! of you gray rocks!
O morning red! O clouds! O rain and snows!
O day and night, passage to you!

O sun and moon and all you stars! Sirius and Jupiter!   240
Passage to you!

Passage, immediate passage! the blood burns in my veins!
Away O soul! hoist instantly the anchor!
Cut the hawsers—haul out—shake out every sail!
Have we not stood here like trees in the ground long enough?   245
Have we not grovel'd here long enough, eating and drinking like mere brutes?
Have we not darken'd and dazed ourselves with books long enough?

Sail forth—steer for the deep waters only,
Reckless O soul, exploring, I with thee, and thou with me,
For we are bound where mariner has not yet dared to go,   250
And we will risk the ship, ourselves and all.

O my brave soul!
O farther farther sail!
O daring joy, but safe! are they not all the seas of God?
O farther, farther, farther sail!   255

1871

Song of the Redwood-Tree

1

A California song,
A prophecy and indirection, a thought impalpable to breathe as air,
A chorus of dryads, fading, departing, or hamadryads departing,
A murmuring, fateful, giant voice, out of the earth and sky,
Voice of a mighty dying tree in the redwood forest dense.   5

Farewell my brethren,
Farewell O earth and sky, farewell ye neighboring waters,
My time has ended, my term has come.

Along the northern coast,
Just back from the rock-bound shore and the caves,   10
In the saline air from the sea in the Mendocino country,
With the surge for base and accompaniment low and hoarse,
With crackling blows of axes sounding musically driven by strong arms,
Riven deep by the sharp tongues of the axes, there in the redwood forest dense,
I heard the mighty tree its death-chant chanting.   15

The choppers heard not, the camp shanties echoed not,
The quick-ear'd teamsters and chain and jack-screw men heard not,
As the wood-spirits came from their haunts of a thousand years to join the refrain,
But in my soul I plainly heard.

Murmuring out of its myriad leaves,   20
Down from its lofty top rising two hundred feet high,
Out of its stalwart trunk and limbs, out of its foot-thick bark,
That chant of the seasons and time, chant not of the past only but the future.

You untold life of me,
And all you venerable and innocent joys,   25
Perennial hardy life of me with joys and rain and many a summer sun,
And the white snows and night and the wild winds;
O the great patient rugged joys, my soul's strong joys unreck'd by man,
(For know I bear the soul befitting me, I too have consciousness, identity,
And all the rocks and mountains have, and all the earth,)   30
Joys of the life befitting me and brothers mine,
Our time, our term has come.

Nor yield we mournfully majestic brothers,
We who have grandly fill'd our time;
With Nature's calm content, with tacit huge delight,   35
We welcome what we wrought for through the past,
And leave the field for them.

For them predicted long,
For a superber race, they too to grandly fill their time,
For them we abdicate, in them ourselves ye forest kings!   40
In them these skies and airs, these mountain peaks, Shasta, Nevadas,
These huge precipitous cliffs, the amplitude, these valleys, far Yosemite,
To be in them absorb'd, assimilated.

Then to a loftier strain,
Still prouder, more ecstatic rose the chant,   45
As if the heirs, the deities of the West,
Joining with master-tongue bore part.

Not wan from Asia's fetiches,
Nor red from Europe's old dynastic slaughter-house,
(Area of murder-plots of thrones, with scent left yet of wars and scaffolds everywhere,)   50
But come from Nature's long and harmless throes, peacefully builded thence,
These virgin lands, lands of the Western shore,
To the new culminating man, to you, the empire new,
You promis'd long, we pledge, we dedicate.

You occult deep volitions,   55
You average spiritual manhood, purpose of all, pois'd on yourself, giving not taking law.

You womanhood divine, mistress and source of all, whence life and love and aught that comes from
    life and love,
You unseen moral essence of all the vast materials of America, (age upon age working in death the
    same as life,)
You that, sometimes known, oftener unknown, really shape and mould the New World, adjusting it
    to Time and Space,
You hidden national will lying in your abysms, conceal'd but ever alert,   60
You past and present purposes tenaciously pursued, may-be unconscious of yourselves,
Unswerv'd by all the passing errors, perturbations of the surface;
You vital, universal, deathless germs, beneath all creeds, arts, statutes, literatures,
Here build your homes for good, establish here, these areas entire, lands of the Western shore,
We pledge, we dedicate to you.   65

For man of you, your characteristic race,
Here may be hardy, sweet, gigantic grow, here tower proportionate to Nature,
Here climb the vast pure spaces unconfined, unchek'd by wall or roof,
Here laugh with storm or sun, here joy, here patiently inure,
Here heed himself, unfold himself, (not others' formulas heed,) here fill his time,   70
To duly fall, to aid, unreck'd at last,
To disappear, to serve.

Thus on the northern coast,
In the echo of teamsters' calls and the clinking chains, and the music of choppers' axes,
The falling trunk and limbs, the crash, the muffled shriek, the groan,   75
Such words combined from the redwood-tree, as of voices ecstatic, ancient and rustling,
The century-lasting, unseen dryads, singing, withdrawing,
All their recesses of forests and mountains leaving,
From the Cascade range to the Wahsatch, or Idaho far, or Utah,
To the deities of the modern henceforth yielding,   80
The chorus and indications, the vistas of coming humanity, the settlements, features all,
In the Mendocino woods I caught.

2

The flashing and golden pageant of California,
The sudden and gorgeous drama, the sunny and ample lands,
The long and varied stretch from Puget sound to Colorado south,   85
Lands bathed in sweeter, rarer, healthier air, valley and mountain cliffs,
The fields of Nature long prepared and fallow, the silent, cyclic chemistry,
The slow and steady ages plodding, the unoccupied surface ripening, the rich ores forming
    beneath;
At last the New arriving, assuming, taking possession,
A swarming and busy race settling and organizing everywhere,   90
Ships coming in from the whole round world, and going out to the whole world,
To India and China and Australia and the thousand island paradises of the Pacific,
Populous cities, the latest inventions, the steamers on the rivers, the railroads, with many a thrifty
    farm, with machinery,
And wool and wheat and the grape, and diggings of yellow gold.

3

But more in you than these, lands of the Western shore,   95
(These but the means, the implements, the standing-ground,)
I see in you, certain to come, the promise of thousands of years, till now deferr'd,
Promis'd to be fulfill'd, our common kind, the race.

The new society at last, proportionate to Nature,

In man of you, more than your mountain peaks or stalwart trees imperial,   100
In woman more, far more, than all your gold or vines, or even vital air.

Fresh come, to a new world indeed, yet long prepared,
I see the genius of the modern, child of the real and ideal,
Clearing the ground for broad humanity, the true America, heir of the past so grand,
To build a grander future.   105

1874, 1881

Prayer of Columbus

In "Passage to India," lines 152–159, Whitman had described Columbus as falling upon evil days—misfortunes, imprisonment, dejection, poverty, death. Only two years after the publication of that poem, he himself, in his middle fifties, fell upon evil days. His mother, ever touchingly close to him, died in his presence. This was not long after he had his first paralytic stroke. Lonely, getting about with difficulty, he lived at his brother's in Camden, New Jersey, unable to resume his clerkship in Washington. Facing a dark future. Whitman remembered the sorrows of Columbus. He proceeded to represent his own, not through direct self-pity, but by imaginatively identifying himself with the great Admiral on the island of Jamaica, "a batter'd, wreck'd old man." The "Prayer of Columbus" may be read as the prayer of Walt Whitman.

A batter'd, wreck'd old man,
Thrown on this savage shore, far, far from home,
Pent by the sea and dark rebellious brows, twelve dreary months,
Sore, stiff with many toils, sicken'd and nigh to death,
I take my way along the island's edge,   5
Venting a heavy heart.

I am too full of woe!
Haply I may not live another day;
I cannot rest O God, I cannot eat or drink or sleep,
Till I put forth myself, my prayer, once more to Thee,   10
Breathe, bathe myself once more in Thee, commune with Thee,
Report myself once more to Thee.

Thou knowest my years entire, my life,
My long and crowded life of active work, not adoration merely;
Thou knowest the prayers and vigils of my youth,   15
Thou knowest my manhood's solemn and visionary meditations,
Thou knowest how before I commenced I devoted all to come to Thee,
Thou knowest I have in age ratified all those vows and strictly kept them,
Thou knowest I have not once lost nor faith nor ecstasy in Thee,
In shackles, prison'd, in disgrace, repining not,   20
Accepting all from Thee, as duly come from Thee.

All my emprises have been fill'd with Thee,
My speculations, plans, begun and carried on in thoughts of Thee,
Sailing the deep or journeying the land for Thee;
Intentions, purports, aspirations mine, leaving results to Thee.   25

O I am sure they really came from Thee,
The urge, the ardor, the unconquerable will,
The potent, felt, interior command, stronger than words,
A message from the Heavens whispering to me even in sleep,
These sped me on.   30

By me and these the work so far accomplish'd,
By me earth's elder cloy'd and stifled lands uncloy'd, unloos'd,
By me the hemispheres rounded and tied, the unknown to the known.

The end I know not, it is all in Thee,
Or small or great I know not—haply what broad fields, what lands, 35
Haply the brutish measureless human undergrowth I know,
Transplanted there may rise to stature, knowledge worthy Thee,
Haply the swords I know may there indeed be turn'd to reaping-tools,
Haply the lifeless cross I know, Europe's dead cross, may bud and blossom there.

One effort more, my altar this bleak sand; 40
That Thou O God my life hast lighted,
With ray of light, steady, ineffable, vouchsafed of Thee,
Light rare untellable, lighting the very light,
Beyond all signs, descriptions, languages;
For that O God, be it my latest word, here on my knees, 45
Old, poor, and paralyzed, I thank Thee.

My terminus near,
The clouds already closing in upon me,
The voyage balk'd, the course disputed, lost,
I yield my ships to Thee. 50

My hands, my limbs grow nerveless,
My brain feels rack'd, bewilder'd,
Let the old timbers part, I will not part,
I will cling fast to Thee, O God, though the waves buffet me,
Thee, Thee at least I know. 55

Is it the prophet's thought I speak, or am I raving?
What do I know of life? what of myself?
I know not even my own work past or present,
Dim ever-shifting guesses of it spread before me,
Of newer better worlds, their mighty parturition, 60
Mocking, perplexing me.

And these things I see suddenly, what mean they?
As if some miracle, some hand divine unseal'd my eyes,
Shadowy vast shapes smile through the air and sky,
And on the distant waves sail countless ships, 65
And anthems in new tongues I hear saluting me.

1874

To a Locomotive in Winter

Thee for my recitative,
Thee in the driving storm even as now, the snow, the winter-day declining,
Thee in thy panoply, thy measur'd dual throbbing and thy beat convulsive,
Thy black cylindric body, golden brass and silvery steel,
Thy ponderous side-bars, parallel and connecting rods, gyrating, shuttling at thy sides, 5
Thy metrical, now swelling pant and roar, now tapering in the distance,
Thy great protruding head-light fix'd in front,
Thy long, pale, floating vapor-pennants, tinged with delicate purple,
The dense and murky clouds out-belching from thy smoke-stack,
Thy knitted frame, thy springs and valves, the tremulous twinkle of thy wheels, 10

Thy train of cars behind, obedient, merrily following,
Through gale or calm, now swift, now slack, yet steadily careering;
Type of the modern—emblem of motion and power—pulse of the continent,
For once come serve the Muse and merge in verse, even as here I see thee,
With storm and buffeting gusts of wind and falling snow,   15
By day thy warning ringing bell to sound its notes,
By night thy silent signal lamps to swing.

Fierce-throated beauty!
Roll through my chant with all thy lawless music, thy swinging lamps at night,
Thy madly-whistled laughter, echoing, rumbling like an earthquake, rousing all,   20
Law of thyself complete, thine own track firmly holding,
(No sweetness debonair of tearful harp or glib piano thine,)
Thy trills of shrieks by rocks and hills return'd,
Launch'd o'er the prairies wide, across the lakes,
To the free skies unpent and glad and strong.   25

                                                                          1876

To the Man-of-War-Bird

*At the close Whitman departs, in a striking manner, from the
romantic tendency to treat nature as equal or superior to man.*

Thou who has slept all night upon the storm,
Waking renew'd on thy prodigious pinions,
(Burst the wild storm? above it thou ascended'st,
And rested on the sky, thy slave that cradled thee,)
Now a blue point, far, far in heaven floating,   5
As to the light emerging here on deck I watch thee,
(Myself a speck, a point on the world's floating vast.)

Far, far at sea,
After the night's fierce drifts have strewn the shore with wrecks,
With re-appearing day as now so happy and serene,   10
The rosy and elastic dawn, the flashing sun,
The limpid spread of air cerulean,
Thou also re-appearest.

Thou born to match the gale, (thou art all wings,)
To cope with heaven and earth and sea and hurricane,   15
Thou ship of air that never furl'st thy sails,
Days, even weeks untired and onward, through spaces, realms gyrating,
At dusk that look'st on Senegal, at morn America,
That sport'st amid the lightning-flash and thunder-cloud,
In them, in thy experiences, had'st thou my soul,   20
What joys! what joys were thine!

                                                                    1876, 1881

The Dalliance of the Eagles

Skirting the river road, (my forenoon walk, my rest,)
Skyward in air a sudden muffled sound, the dalliance of the eagles,
The rushing amorous contact high in space together,
The clinching interlocking claws, a living, fierce, gyrating wheel,
Four beating wings, two beaks, a swirling mass tight grappling,   5

In tumbling turning clustering loops, straight downward falling,
Till o'er the river pois'd, the twain yet one, a moment's lull,
A motionless still balance in the air, then parting, talons loosing,
Upward again on slow-firm pinions slanting, their separate diverse flight,
She hers, he his, pursuing.

10

1880, 1881

The Dismantled Ship

In some unused lagoon, some nameless bay,
On sluggish, lonesome waters, anchor'd near the shore,
An old, dismasted, gray and batter'd ship, disabled, done,
After free voyages to all the seas of earth, haul'd up at last and hawser'd tight,
Lies rusting, mouldering.

5

1888

FROM *Democratic Vistas*

After the Civil War, the moral corruption of politics and business, and the low tone of life generally, might well have disillusioned a romantic like Whitman. Instead, he sharply characterized what he saw around him, and bravely offered his specifications for a mature democracy in the future.

[American Democracy, Actual and Ideal]

We had best look our times and lands searchingly in the face, like a physician diagnosing some deep disease. Never was there, perhaps, more hollowness at heart than at present, and here in the United States. Genuine belief seems to have left us. The underlying principles of the States are not honestly believ'd in, (for all this hectic glow, and these melodramatic screamings,) nor is humanity itself believ'd in. What penetrating eye does not everywhere see through the mask? The spectacle is appalling. We live in an atmosphere of hypocrisy throughout. The men believe not in the women, nor the women in the men. A scornful superciliousness rules in literature. The aim of all the *littérateurs* is to find something to make fun of. A lot of churches, sects, etc., the most dismal phantasms I know, usurp the name of religion. Conversation is a mass of badinage. From deceit in the spirit, the mother of all false deeds, the offspring is already incalculable. An acute and candid person, in the revenue department in Washington, who is led by the course of his employment to regularly visit the cities, north, south and west, to investigate frauds, has talk'd much with me about his discoveries. The depravity of the business classes of our country is not less than has been supposed, but infinitely greater. The official services of America, national, state, and municipal, in all their branches and departments, except the judiciary, are saturated in corruption, bribery, falsehood, maladministration; and the judiciary is tainted. The great cities reek with respectable as much as non-respectable robbery and scoundrelism. In fashionable life, flippancy, tepid amours, weak infidelism, small aims, or no aims at all, only to kill time. In business, (this all-devouring modern word, business,) the one sole object is, by any means, pecuniary gain. The magician's serpent in the fable ate up all the other serpents; and money-making is our magician's serpent, remaining to-day sole master of the field. The best class we show, is but a mob of fashionably dress'd speculators and vulgarians. True, indeed, behind this fantastic farce, enacted on the visible stage of society, solid things and stupendous labors are to be discover'd, existing crudely and going on in the background, to advance and tell themselves in time. Yet the truths are none the less terrible. I say that our New World democracy, however great a success in uplifting the masses out of their sloughs, in materialistic development, products, and in certain highly-deceptive superficial popular intellectuality, is, so far, an almost complete failure in its social aspects, and in really grand religious, moral, literary, and esthetic results. In vain do we march with unprecedented strides to empire so colossal, outvying the antique, beyond Alexander's, beyond the proudest sway of Rome. In vain have we annex'd Texas, California, Alaska, and reach north for Canada and south for Cuba. It is as if we were somehow being endow'd with a vast and more and more thoroughly-appointed body, and then left with little or no soul.

Let me illustrate further, as I write, with current observations, localities, etc. The subject is important, and will bear repetition. After an absence, I am now again (September, 1870) in New York city and Brooklyn, on a few weeks' vacation. The splendor, picturesqueness, and oceanic amplitude and rush of these great cities, the unsurpass'd situation, rivers and bay, sparkling sea-tides, costly and lofty new buildings, façades of marble and iron, of original grandeur and elegance of design, with the masses of gay color, the preponderance of white and blue, the flags flying, the endless ships, the tumultuous streets, Broadway, the heavy, low, musical roar, hardly ever intermitted, even at night; the jobbers' houses, the rich shops, the wharves, the great Central Park, and the Brooklyn Park of hills, (as I wander among them this beautiful fall weather, musing, watching, absorbing)—the assemblages of the citizens in their groups, conversations, trades, evening amusements, or along the by-quarters—these, I say, and the like of these, completely satisfy my senses of power, fulness, motion, etc., and give me, through such senses and appetites, and through my esthetic conscience, a continued exaltation and absolute fulfilment. Always and more and more, as I cross the East and North rivers, the ferries, or with the pilots in their pilot-houses, or pass an hour in Wall street, or the gold exchange, I realize, (if we must admit such partialisms,) that not Nature alone is great in her fields of freedom and the open air, in her storms, the shows of night and day, the mountains, forests, seas—but in the artificial, the work of man too is equally great—in this profusion of teeming humanity—in these ingenuities, streets, goods, houses, ships—these hurrying, feverish, electric crowds of men, their complicated business genius, (not least among the geniuses,) and all this mighty, many-threaded wealth and industry concentrated here.

But sternly discarding, shutting our eyes to the glow and grandeur of the general superficial effect, coming down to what is of the only real importance, Personalities, and examining minutely, we question, we ask, Are there, indeed, *men* here worthy the name? Are there athletes? Are there perfect women, to match the generous material luxuriance? Is there a pervading atmosphere of beautiful manners? Are there crops of fine youths, and majestic old persons? Are there arts worthy freedom and a rich people? Is there a great moral and religious civilization—the only justification of a great material one? Confess that to severe eyes, using the moral miscroscope upon humanity, a sort of dry and flat Sahara appears, these cities, crowded with petty grotesques, malformations, phantoms, playing meaningless antics. Confess that everywhere, in shop, street, church, theatre, barroom, official chair, are pervading flippancy and vulgarity, low cunning, infidelity—everywhere the youth puny, impudent, foppish, prematurely ripe—everywhere an abnormal libidinous-

ness, unhealthy forms, male, female, painted, padded, dyed, chignon'd, muddy complexions, bad blood, the capacity for good motherhood deceasing or deceas'd, shallow notions of beauty, with a range of manners, or rather lack of manners, (considering the advantages enjoy'd,) probably the meanest to be seen in the world.

Of all this, and these lamentable conditions, to breathe into them the breath recuperative of sane and heroic life, I say a new founded literature, not merely to copy and reflect existing surfaces, or pander to what is called taste—not only to amuse, pass away time, celebrate the beautiful, the refined, the past, or exhibit technical, rhythmic, or grammatical dexterity—but a literature underlying life, religious, consistent with science, handling the elements and forces with competent power, teaching and training men—and, as perhaps the most precious of its results, achieving the entire redemption of woman out of these incredible holds and webs of silliness, millinery, and every kind of dyspeptic depletion—and thus insuring to the States a strong and sweet Female Race, a race of perfect Mothers—is what is needed.

And now, in the full conception of these facts and points, and all that they infer, pro and con—with yet unshaken faith in the elements of the American masses, the composites, of both sexes, and even consider'd as individuals—and ever recognizing in them the broadest bases of the best literary and esthetic appreciation—I proceed with my speculations, Vistas.

First, let us see what we can make out of a brief, general, sentimental consideration of political democracy, and whence it has arisen, with regard to some of its current features, as an aggregate, and as the basic structure of our future literature and authorship. We shall, it is true, quickly and continually find the origin-idea of the singleness of man, individualism, asserting itself, and cropping forth, even from the opposite ideas. But the mass, or lump character, for imperative reasons, is to be ever carefully weigh'd, borne in mind, and provided for. Only from it, and from its proper regulation and potency, comes the other, comes the chance of individualism. The two are contradictory, but our task is to reconcile them.

The political history of the past may be summ'd up as having grown out of what underlies the words, order, safety, caste, and especially out of the need of some prompt deciding authority, and of cohesion at all cost. Leaping time, we come to the period within the memory of people now living, when, as from some lair where they had slumber'd long, accumulating wrath, sprang up and are yet active, (1790, and on even to the present, 1870,) those noisy eructations, destructive iconoclasms, a fierce sense of wrongs, amid which moves the form, well known in modern history, in the old world, stain'd with much blood, and mark'd by savage reactionary clamors and demands. These bear, mostly, as on one inclosing point of need.

For after the rest is said—after the many time-honor'd and really true things for subordination, experience, rights of property, etc., have been listen'd to and acquiesced in—after the valuable and well-settled statement of our duties and relations in society is thoroughly conn'd over and exhausted—it remains to bring forward and modify everything else with the idea of that Something a man is, (last precious consolation of the drudging poor,) standing apart from all else, divine in his own right, and a woman in hers, sole and untouchable by any canons of authority, or any rule derived from precedent, state-safety, the acts of legislatures, or even from what is called religion, modesty, or art. The radiation of this truth is the key of the most significant doings of our immediately preceding three centuries, and has been the political genesis and life of America. Advancing visibly, it still more advances invisibly. Underneath the fluctuations of the expressions of society, as well as the movements of the politics of the leading nations of the world, we see steadily pressing ahead and strengthening itself, even in the midst of immense tendencies toward aggregation, this image of completeness in separatism, of individual personal dignity, of a single person, either male or female, characterized in the main, not from extrinsic acquirements or position, but in the pride of himself or herself alone; and, as an eventual conclusion and summing up, (or else the entire scheme of things is aimless, a cheat, a crash,) the simple idea that the last, best dependence is to be upon humanity itself, and its own inherent, normal, full-grown qualities, without any superstitious support whatever.° ° °

[What Is an American?]

And, if we think of it, what does civilization itself rest upon—and what object has it, with its religions, arts, schools, etc., but rich, luxuriant, varied personalism? To that, all bends; and it is because toward such result democracy alone, on anything like Nature's scale, breaks up the limitless fallows of humankind, and plants the seed, and gives fair play, that its claims now precede the rest. The literature, songs, esthetics, etc., of a country are of importance principally because they furnish the materials and suggestions of personality for the women and men of that country, and enforce them in a thousand effective ways. As the topmost claim of a strong consoli-

dating of the nationality of these States, is, that only by such powerful compaction can the separate States secure that full and free swing within their spheres, which is becoming to them, each after its kind, so will individuality, with unimpeded branchings, flourish best under imperial republican forms.

Assuming Democracy to be at present in its embryo condition, and that the only large and satisfactory justification of it resides in the future, mainly through the copious production of perfect characters among the people, and through the advent of a sane and pervading religiousness, it is with regard to the atmosphere and spaciousness fit for such characters, and of certain nutriment and cartoon-draftings proper for them, and indicating them for New World purposes, that I continue the present statement—an exploration, as of new ground, wherein, like other primitive surveyors, I must do the best I can, leaving it to those who come after me to do much better. (The service, in fact, if any, must be to break a sort of first path or track, no matter how rude and ungeometrical.)

We have frequently printed the word Democracy. Yet I cannot too often repeat that it is a word the real gist of which still sleeps, quite unawaken'd, notwithstanding the resonance and the many angry tempests out of which its syllables have come, from pen or tongue. It is a great word, whose history, I suppose, remains unwritten, because that history has yet to be enacted. It is, in some sort, younger brother of another great and often-used word, Nature, whose history also waits unwritten. As I perceive, the tendencies of our day, in the States, (and I entirely respect them,) are toward those vast and sweeping movements, influences, moral and physical, of humanity, now and always current over the planet, on the scale of the impulses of the elements. Then it is also good to reduce the whole matter to the consideration of a single self, a man, a woman, on permanent grounds. Even for the treatment of the universal, in politics, metaphysics, or anything, sooner or later we come down to one single, solitary soul.

There is, in sanest hours, a consciousness, a thought that rises, independent, lifted out from all else, calm, like the stars, shining eternal. This is the thought of identity—yours for you, whoever you are, as mine for me. Miracle of miracles, beyond statement, most spiritual and vaguest of earth's dreams, yet hardest basic fact, and only entrance to all facts. In such devout hours, in the midst of the significant wonders of heaven and earth, (significant only because of the Me in the centre,) creeds, conventions, fall away and become of no account before this simple idea. Under the luminousness of real vision, it alone takes possession, takes value. Like the shadowy dwarf in the fable, once liberated and look'd upon, it expands over the whole earth, and spreads to the roof of heaven.

The quality of BEING, in the object's self, according to its own central idea and purpose, and of growing therefrom and thereto—not criticism by other standards, and adjustments thereto—is the lesson of Nature. True, the full man wisely gathers, culls, absorbs; but if, engaged disproportionately in that, he slights or overlays the precious idiocrasy and special nativity and intention that he is, the man's self, the main thing, is a failure, however wide his general cultivation. Thus, in our times, refinement and delicatesse are not only attended to sufficiently but threaten to eat us up, like a cancer. Already, the democratic genius watches, ill-pleased, these tendencies. Provision for a little healthy rudeness, savage virtue, justification of what one has in one's self, whatever it is, is demanded. Negative qualities, even deficiencies, would be a relief. Singleness and normal simplicity and separation, amid this more and more complex, more and more artificialized state of society—how pensively we yearn for them! how we would welcome their return!

In some direction, then—at any rate enough to preserve the balance—we feel called upon to throw what weight we can, not for absolute reasons, but current ones. To prune, gather, trim, conform, and ever cram and stuff, and be genteel and proper, is the pressure of our days. While aware that much can be said even in behalf of all this, we perceive that we have not now to consider the question of what is demanded to serve a half-starved and barbarous nation, or set of nations, but what is most applicable, most pertinent, for numerous congeries of conventional, over-corpulent societies, already becoming stifled and rotten with flatulent, infidelistic literature, and polite conformity and art. In addition to establish'd sciences, we suggest a science as it were of healthy average personalism, on original-universal grounds, the object of which should be to raise up and supply through the States a copious race of superb American men and women, cheerful, religious, ahead of any yet known.

America has yet morally and artistically originated nothing. She seems singularly unaware that the models of persons, books, manners, etc., appropriate for former conditions and for European lands, are but exiles and exotics here. No current of her life, as shown on the surfaces of what is authoritatively called her society, accepts or runs into social or esthetic democracy; but all the currents set squarely against it. Never, in the Old World, was thoroughly upholster'd exterior appearance and show, mental and other, built entirely on the idea of caste, and on the sufficiency of mere outside acquisition—never were glibness, verbal intellect, more the test, the emulation—more loftily elevated as head and

sample—than they are on the surface of our republican States this day. The writers of a time hint the mottoes of its gods. The word of the modern, say these voices, is the word Culture.

We find ourselves abruptly in close quarters with the enemy. This word Culture, or what it has come to represent, involves, by contrast, our whole theme, and has been, indeed, the spur, urging us to engagement. Certain questions arise. As now taught, accepted and carried out, are not the processes of culture rapidly creating a class of supercilious infidels, who believe in nothing? Shall a man lose himself in countless masses of adjustments, and be so shaped with reference to this, that, and the other, that the simply good and healthy and brave parts of him are reduced and clipp'd away, like the bordering of box in a garden? You can cultivate corn and roses and orchards—but who shall cultivate the mountain peaks, the ocean, and the tumbling gorgeousness of the clouds? Lastly—is the readily-given reply that culture only seeks to help, systematize, and put in attitude, the elements of fertility and power, a conclusive reply?

I do not so much object to the name, or word, but I should certainly insist, for the purposes of these States, on a radical change of category, in the distribution of precedence. I should demand a programme of culture, drawn out, not for a single class alone, or for the parlors or lecture-rooms, but with an eye to practical life, the west, the working-men, the facts of farms and jack-planes and engineers, and of the broad range of the women also of the middle and working strata, and with reference to the perfect equality of women, and of a grand and powerful motherhood. I should demand of this programme or theory a scope generous enough to include the widest human area. It must have for its spinal meaning the formation of a typical personality of character, eligible to the uses of the high average of men—and *not* restricted by conditions ineligible to the masses. The best culture will always be that of the manly and courageous instincts, and loving perceptions, and of self-respect—aiming to form, over this continent, an idiocrasy of universalism, which, true child of America, will bring joy to its mother, returning to her in her own spirit, recruiting myriads of offspring, able, natural, perceptive, tolerant, devout believers in her, America, and with some definite instinct why and for what she has arisen, most vast, most formidable of historic births, and is, now and here, with wonderful step, journeying through Time.

The problem, as it seems to me, presented to the New World, is, under permanent law and order, and after preserving cohesion, (ensemble-Individuality,) at all hazards, to vitalize man's free play of special Personalism, recognizing in it something that calls ever more to be consider'd, fed, and adopted as the substratum for the best that belongs to us, (government indeed is for it,) including the new esthetics of our future.

To formulate beyond this present vagueness—to help line and put before us the species, or a specimen of the species, of the democratic ethnology of the future, is a work toward which the genius of our land, with peculiar encouragement, invites her well-wishers. Already certain limnings, more or less grotesque, more or less fading and watery, have appear'd. We too, (repressing doubts and qualms,) will try our hand.

Attempting, then, however crudely, a basic model or portrait of personality for general use for the manliness of the States, (and doubtless that is most useful which is most simple and comprehensive for all, and toned low enough,) we should prepare the canvas well beforehand. Parentage must consider itself in advance. (Will the time hasten when fatherhood and motherhood shall become a science—and the noblest science?) To our model, a clear-blooded, strong-fibred physique, is indispensable; the questions of food, drink, air, exercise, assimilation, digestion, can never be intermitted. Out of these we descry a well-begotten selfhood—in youth, fresh, ardent, emotional, aspiring, full of adventure; at maturity, brave, perceptive, under control, neither too talkative nor too reticent, neither flippant nor sombre; of the bodily figure, the movements easy, the complexion showing the best blood, somewhat flush'd, breast expanded, an erect attitude, a voice whose sound outvies music, eyes of calm and steady gaze, yet capable also of flashing—and a general presence that holds its own in the company of the highest. (For it is native personality, and that alone, that endows a man to stand before presidents or generals, or in any distinguish'd collection, with *aplomb*—and *not* culture, or any knowledge or intellect whatever.)

With regard to the mental-educational part of our model, enlargement of intellect, stores of cephalic knowledge, etc., the concentration thitherward of all the customs of our age, especially in America, is so over-weening, and provides so fully for that part, that, important and necessary as it is, it really needs nothing from us here—except, indeed, a phrase of warning and restraint. Manners, costumes, too, though important, we need not dwell upon here. Like beauty, grace of motion, etc., they are results. Causes, original things, being attended to, the right manners unerringly follow. Much is said, among artists, of "the grand style," as if it were a thing by itself. When a man, artist or whoever, has health, pride, acuteness, noble aspirations, he has the motive-elements of the grandest style. The rest is but manipulation, (yet that is no small matter.)

Leaving still unspecified several sterling parts of any model fit for the future personality of America, I must not fail, again and ever, to pronounce myself on one, probably the least attended to in modern times—a hiatus, indeed, threatening its gloomiest consequences after us. I mean the simple, unsophisticated Conscience, the primary moral element. If I were asked to specify in what quarter lie the grounds of darkest dread, respecting the America of our hopes, I should have to point to this particular. I should demand the invariable application to individuality, this day and any day, of that old, ever-true plumb-rule of persons, eras, nations. Our triumphant modern civilizee, with his all-schooling and his wondrous appliances, will still show himself but an amputation while this deficiency remains. Beyond, (assuming a more hopeful tone,) the vertebration of the manly and womanly personalism of our western world, can only be, and is, indeed to be, (I hope,) its all penetrating Religiousness.

The ripeness of Religion is doubtless to be looked for in this field of individuality, and is a result that no organization or church can ever achieve. As history is poorly retain'd by what the technists call history, and is not given out from their pages, except the learner has in himself the sense of the well-wrapt, never yet written, perhaps impossible to be written, history—so Religion, although casually arrested, and, after a fashion, preserv'd in the churches and creeds, does not depend at all upon them, but is a part of the identified soul, which, when greatest, knows not bibles in the old way, but in new ways,—the identified soul, which can really confront Religion when it extricates itself entirely from the churches, and not before.

Personalism fuses this, and favors it. I should say, indeed that only in the perfect uncontamination and solitariness of individuality may the spirituality of religion positively come forth at all. Only here, and on such terms, the meditation, the devout ecstasy, the soaring flight. Only here, communion with the mysteries, the eternal problems, whence? whither? Alone, and identity, and the mood—and the soul emerges, and all statements, churches, sermons, melt away like vapors. Alone, and silent thought and awe, and aspiration—and then the interior consciousness, like a hitherto unseen inscription, in magic ink, beams out its wondrous lines to the sense. Bibles may convey, and priests expound, but it is exclusively for the noiseless operation of one's isolated Self, to enter the pure ether of veneration, reach the divine levels, and commune with the unutterable.

To practically enter into politics is an important part of American personalism. To every young man, north and south, earnestly studying these things, I should here, as an offset to what I have said in former pages, now also say, that may-be to views of very largest scope, after all, perhaps the political, (perhaps the literary and sociological,) America goes best about its development its own way—sometimes, to temporary sight, appalling enough. It is the fashion among dilettants and fops (perhaps I myself am not guiltless,) to decry the whole formulation of the active politics of America, as beyond redemption, and to be carefully kept away from. See you that you do not fall into this error. America, it may be, is doing very well upon the whole, notwithstanding these antics of the parties and their leaders, these half-brain'd nominees, the many ignorant ballots, and many elected failures and blatherers. It is the dilettants, and all who shirk their duty, who are not doing well. As for you, I advise you to enter more strongly yet into politics. I advise every young man to do so. Always inform yourself; always do the best you can; always vote. Disengage yourself from parties. They have been useful, and to some extent remain so; but the floating, uncommitted electors, farmers, clerks, mechanics, the masters of parties—watching aloof, inclining victory this side or that side—such are the ones most needed, present and future. For America, if eligible at all to downfall and ruin, is eligible within herself, not without; for I see clearly that the combined foreign world could not beat her down. But these savage, wolfish parties alarm me. Owning no law but their own will, more and more combative, less and less tolerant of the idea of ensemble and of equal brotherhood, the perfect equality of the States, the ever-over-arching American ideas, it behooves you to convey yourself implicitly to no party, nor submit blindly to their dictators, but steadily hold yourself judge and master over all of them.

So much, (hastily toss'd together, and leaving far more unsaid), for an ideal, or intimations of an ideal, toward American manhood. But the other sex, in our land, requires at least a basis of suggestion.

I have seen a young American woman, one of a large family of daughters, who, some years since, migrated from her meagre country home to one of the northern cities, to gain her own support. She soon became an expert seamstress, but finding the employment too confining for health and comfort, she went boldly to work for others, to house-keep, cook, clean, etc. After trying several places, she fell upon one where she was suited. She told me that she finds nothing degrading in her position; it is not inconsistent with personal dignity, self-respect, and the respect of others. She confers benefits and receives them. She has good health; her presence itself is healthy and bracing; her character is unstain'd; she has made herself understood, and preserves her independence, and has been able to help her parents, and educate and get places for her sisters; and her course of life is not without opportunities for mental improvement. and of much quiet, uncosting happiness and love.

I have seen another woman who, from taste and necessity conjoin'd, has gone into practical affairs, carries on a mechanical business, partly works at it herself, dashes out more and more into real hardy life, is not abash'd by the coarseness of the contact, knows how to be firm and silent at the same time, holds her own with unvarying coolness and decorum, and will compare, any day, with superior carpenters, farmers, and even boatmen and drivers. For all that, she has not lost the charm of the womanly nature, but preserves and bears it fully, though through such rugged presentation.

Then there is the wife of a mechanic, mother of two children, a woman of merely passable English education, but of fine wit, with all her sex's grace and intuitions, who exhibits, indeed, such a noble female personality, that I am fain to record it here. Never abnegating her own proper independence, but always genially preserving it, and what belongs to it—cooking, washing, child-nursing, house-tending—she beams sunshine out of all these duties, and make them illustrious. Physiologically sweet and sound, loving work, practical, she yet knows that there are intervals, however few, devoted to recreation, music, leisure, hospitality—and affords such intervals. Whatever she does, and wherever she is, that charm, that indescribable perfume of genuine womanhood attends her, goes with her, exhales from her, which belongs of right to all of the sex, and is, or ought to be, the invariable atmosphere and common aureola of old as well as young.

My dear mother once described to me a resplendent person, down on Long Island, whom she knew in early days. She was known by the name of the Peacemaker. She was well toward eighty years old, of happy and sunny temperament, had always lived on a farm, and was very neighborly, sensible and discreet, an invariable and welcom'd favorite, especially with young married women. She had numerous children and grandchildren. She was uneducated, but possess'd a native dignity. She had come to be a tacitly agreed upon domestic regulator, judge, settler of difficulties, shepherdess, and reconciler in the land. She was a sight to draw near and look upon, with her large figure, her profuse snow-white hair, (uncoif'd by any head-dress or cap,) dark eyes, clear complexion, sweet breath, and peculiar personal magnetism.

The foregoing portraits, I admit, are frightfully out of line from these imported models of womanly personality—the stock feminine characters of the current novelist, or of the foreign court poems,

(Ophelias, Enids, princesses, or ladies of one thing or another,) which fill the envying dreams of so many poor girls, and are accepted by our men, too, as supreme ideals of feminine excellence to be sought after. But I present mine just for a change.

Then there are mutterings, (we will not now stop to heed them here, but they must be heeded,) of something more revolutionary. The day is coming when the deep questions of woman's entrance amid the arenas of practical life, politics, the suffrage, etc., will not only be argued all around us, but may be put to decision, and real experiment.

Of course, in these States, for both man and woman, we must entirely recast the types of highest personality from what the oriental, feudal, ecclesiastical worlds bequeath us, and which yet possess the imaginative and esthetic fields of the United States, pictorial and melo-dramatic, not without use as studies, but making sad work, and forming a strange anachronism upon the scenes and exigencies around us. Of course, the old undying elements remain. The task is, to successfully adjust them to new combinations, our own days. Nor is this so incredible. I can conceive a community, to-day and here, in which, on a sufficient scale, the perfect personalities without noise meet; say in some pleasant western settlement or town, where a couple of hundred best men and women, of ordinary worldly status, have by luck been drawn together, with nothing extra of genius or wealth, but virtuous, chaste, industrious, cheerful, resolute, friendly and devout. I can conceive such a community organized in running order, powers judiciously delegated—farming, building, trade, courts, mails, schools, elections, all attended to; and then the rest of life, the main thing, freely branching and blossoming in each individual, and bearing golden fruit. I can see there, in every young and old man, after his kind, and in every woman after hers, a true personality, develop'd, exercised proportionately in body, mind, and spirit. I can imagine this case as one not necessarily rare or difficult, but in buoyant accordance with the municipal and general requirements of our times. And I can realize in it the culmination of something better than any stereotyped *eclat* of history or poems. Perhaps, unsung, undramatized, unput in essays or biographies—perhaps even some such community already exists, in Ohio, Illinois, Missouri, or somewhere, practically fulfilling itself, and thus outvying, in cheapest vulgar life, all that has been hitherto shown in best ideal pictures.

In short, and to sum up, America, betaking herself to formative action, (as it is about time for more solid achievement, and less windy promise,) must, for her purposes, cease to recognize a theory of character grown of feudal aristocracies, or form'd by merely literary standards, or from any ultramarine, full-dress formulas of culture, polish, caste, etc., and must sternly promulgate her own new standard, yet old enough, and accepting the old, the perennial elements, and combining them into groups, unities, appropriate to the modern, the democratic, the west, and to the practical occasions and needs of our own cities, and of the agricultural regions. Ever the most precious in the common.°°°

[An American Literature]

What is the reason our time, our lands, that we see no fresh local courage, sanity, of our own—the Mississippi, stalwart Western men, real mental and physical facts, Southerners, etc., in the body of our literature? especially the poetic part of it. But always, instead, a parcel of dandies and ennuyees, dapper little gentlemen from abroad, who flood as with their thin sentiment of parlors, parasols, piano-songs, tinkling rhymes, the five-hundredth importation—or whimpering and crying about something, chasing one aborted conceit after another, and forever occupied in dyspeptic amours with dyspeptic women. While, current and novel, the grandest events and revolutions, and stormiest passions of history, are crossing to-day with unparallel'd rapidity and magnificence over the stages of our own and all the continents, offering new materials, opening new vistas, with largest needs, inviting the daring launching forth of conceptions in literature, inspired by them, soaring in highest regions, serving art in its highest, (which is only the other name for serving God, and serving humanity,) where is the man of letters, where is the book, with any nobler aim than to follow in the old track, repeat what has been said before—and, as its utmost triumph, sell well, and be erudite or elegant?

Mark the roads, the processes, through which these States have arrived, standing easy, henceforth ever-equal, ever-compact, in their range to-day. European adventures? the most antique? Asiatic or African? old history—miracles—romances? Rather, our own unquestion'd facts. They hasten, incredible, blazing bright as fire. From the deeds and days of Columbus down to the present, and including the present—and especially the late Secession war—when I con them, I feel, every leaf, like stopping to see if I have not made a mistake, and fall'n on the splendid figments of some dream. But it is no dream. We stand, live, move, in the huge flow of our age's materialism—in its spirituality. We have had founded for us the most positive of lands. The founders have pass'd to other spheres—but what are these terrible duties they have left us?

Their politics the United States have, in my opinion, with all their faults, already substantially establish'd, for good, on their own native, sound, long-vista'd principles, never to be overturn'd, offering a sure basis for all the rest. With that, their future religious forms, sociology, literature, teachers, schools, costumes, etc., are of course to make a compact whole, uniform, on tallying principles. For how can we remain, divided, contradicting ourselves, this way? I say we can only attain harmony and stability by consulting ensemble and the ethic purports, and faithfully building upon them. For the New World, indeed, after two grand stages of preparation-strata, I perceive that now a third stage, being ready for, (and without which the other two were useless,) with unmistakable signs appears. The First stage was the planning and putting on record the political foundation rights of immense masses of people—indeed all people—in the organization of republican National, State, and municipal governments, all constructed with reference to each, and each to all. This is the American programme, not for classes, but for universal man, and is embodied in the compacts of the Declaration of Independence, and, as it began and has now grown, with its amendments, the Federal Constitution—and in the State governments, with all their interiors, and with general suffrage; those having the sense not only of what is in themselves, but that their certain several things started, planted, hundreds of others in the same direction duly arise and follow. The Second stage relates to material prosperity, wealth, produce, labor-saving machines, iron, cotton, local, State and continental railways, intercommunication and trade with all lands, steamships, mining, general employment, organization of great cities, cheap appliances for comfort, numberless technical schools, books, newspapers, a currency for money circulation, etc. The Third stage, rising out of the previous ones, to make them and all illustrious, I, now, for one, promulge, announcing a native expression-spirit, getting into form, adult, and through mentality, for these States, self-contain'd, different from others, more expansive, more rich and free, to be evidenced by original authors and poets to come, by American personalities, plenty of them, male and female traversing the States, none excepted—and by native superber tableaux and growths of language, songs, operas, orations, lectures, architecture—and by a sublime and serious Religious Democracy sternly taking command, dissolving the old, sloughing off surfaces, and from its own interior and vital principles, reconstructing, democratizing society.°°°

America demands a poetry that is bold, modern, and all-surrounding and kosmical, as she is herself. It must in no respect ignore science or the modern, but inspire itself with science and the modern. It must bend its vision toward the future, more than the past. Like America, it must extricate itself from even the greatest models of the past, and, while courteous to them, must have entire faith in itself, and the products of its own democratic spirit only. Like her, it must place in the van, and hold up at all hazards, the banner of the divine pride of man in himself, (the radical foundation of the new religion.) Long enough have the People been listening to poems in which common humanity, deferential, bends low, humiliated, acknowledging superiors. But America listens to no such poems. Erect, inflated, and fully self-esteeming be the chant; and then America will listen with pleased ears.°°°

In the prophetic literature of these States (the reader of my speculations will miss their principal stress unless he allows well for the point that a new Literature, perhaps a new Metaphysics, certainly a new Poetry, are to be, in my opinion, the only sure and worthy supports and expressions of the American Democracy,) Nature, true Nature, and the true idea of Nature, long absent, must, above all, become full restored, enlarged and must furnish the pervading atmosphere to poems, and the test of all high literary and esthetic compositions. I do not mean the smooth walks, trimm'd hedges, poseys and nightingales of the English poets, but the whole orb, with its geologic history, the kosmos, carrying fire and snow, that rolls through the illimitable areas, light as a feather, though weighing billions of tons. Furthermore, as by what we now partially call Nature is intended, at most, only what is entertainable by the physical conscience, the sense of matter, and of good animal health—on these it must be distinctly accumulated, incorporated, that man, comprehending these, has, in towering super-addition, the moral and spiritual consciences, indicating his destination beyond the ostensible, the mortal.

To the heights of such estimate of Nature indeed ascending, we proceed to make observations for our Vistas, breathing rarest air. What is I believe called Idealism seems to me to suggest, (guarding against extravagance, and ever modified even by its opposite,) the course of inquiry and desert of favor for our New World metaphysics, their foundation of and in literature, giving hue to all.

The elevating and etherealizing ideas of the unknown and of unreality must be brought forward with authority, as they are the legitimate heirs of the known, and of reality, and at least as great as their parents. Fearless of scoffing, and of the ostent, let us take our stand, our ground, and never desert it, to confront the growing excess and arrogance of realism. To the cry, now victorious—the cry of sense, science, flesh, incomes, farms, merchandise, logic, intellect, demonstrations, solid perpetuities, buildings of brick and iron, or even the facts of the shows of trees, earth, rocks, etc., fear not, my brethren, my sisters, to sound out with equally determin'd voice, that conviction brooding within the recesses of every envision'd soul—illusions! apparitions! figments all! True, we must not condemn the show, neither absolutely deny it, for the indispensability of its meanings; but how clearly we see that, migrate in soul to what we can already conceive of superior and spiritual points of view, and palpable as it seems under present relations, it all and several might, nay certainly would, fall apart and vanish.

I hail with joy the oceanic, variegated, intense practical energy, the demand for facts, even the business materialism of the current age, our States. But wo to the age or land in which these things, movements, stopping at themselves, do not tend to ideas. As fuel to flame, and flame to the heavens, so must wealth, science, materialism—even this democracy of which we make so much—unerringly feed the highest mind, the soul. Infinitude the flight: fathomless the mystery. Man, so diminutive, dilates beyond the sensible universe, competes with, out-

copes space and time, meditating even one great idea. Thus, and thus only, does a human being, his spirit, ascend above, and justify, objective Nature, which, probably nothing in itself, is incredibly and divinely serviceable, indispensable, real, here. And as the purport of objective Nature is doubtless folded, hidden, somewhere here—as somewhere here is what this globe and its manifold forms, and the light of day, and night's darkness, and life itself, with all its experiences, are for—it is here the great literature, especially verse, must get its inspiration and throbbing blood. Then may we attain to a poetry worthy the immortal soul of man, and which, while absorbing materials, and, in their own sense, the shows of Nature, will, above all, have, both directly and indirectly, a freeing, fluidizing, expanding, religious character, exulting with science, fructifying the moral elements, and stimulating aspirations, and meditations on the unknown.

1871

A House Divided

HENRY TIMROD [1828–1867]

TIMROD WAS a member of the Charleston literary group that flourished in the decade before the war and included the novelist William Gilmore Simms and the poets Paul Hamilton Hayne and J. M. Legaré. In general their views were those common in the Romantic Movement, with a significant exception. Convinced defenders of the slave system and the Southern way of life, they did not share in the aspirations toward the reform or basic renewal of society characteristic of such writers as Wordsworth and Shelley, Emerson and Lowell.

Timrod was a native of Charleston. He studied for a year and a half at the University of Georgia, read enough law to convince him that he was unsuited to the legal profession, then supported himself for several years as a tutor on a Carolina plantation while writing poetry. A book of poems emerged in 1860. He enlisted as a volunteer in the armies of the Confederacy, but his frail constitution soon forced him out of service. He was editing a newspaper in Columbia, S. C., when Sherman's army arrived. His fortunes and his health ruined, he died of tuberculosis two years later.

In the "mood of exalted devotion which characterized the Confederacy at its best" (to use J. B. Hubbell's phrase) Timrod quickly matured as a poet. What he had written by 1860 was thinly romantic; his best poems came in the few years left to him. They showed a fine sensibility, at once passionate and controlled. They endure, as F. O. Matthiessen has said, with a classic hardness.

Further reading: J. B. Hubbell, *The South in American Literature*, 1954, pp. 466-74. Edd Winfield Parks, *Henry Timrod*, 1964.

Ethnogenesis

The Greek title means "The Birth of a Nation." Written in February 1861 while the First Confederate Congress was in session at Montgomery, Alabama, this poem reflects the spirit of the South on the verge of armed conflict. Fort Sumter was bombarded April 12.

This and the following poems are reprinted from the Memorial Edition of *Poems of Henry Timrod* (Richmond, 1901).

I

Hath not the morning dawned with added light?
And shall not evening call another star
Out of the infinite regions of the night,
To mark this day in Heaven? At last, we are
A nation among nations; and the world   5
Shall soon behold in many a distant port
    Another flag unfurled!
Now, come what may, whose favor need we court?
And, under God, whose thunder need we fear?
    Thank him who placed us here   10
Beneath so kind a sky—the very sun
Takes part with us; and on our errands run
All breezes of the ocean; dew and rain
Do noiseless battle for us; and the Year,
And all the gentle daughters in her train,   15
March in our ranks, and in our service wield
    Long spears of golden grain!
A yellow blossom as her fairy shield,
June flings her azure banner to the wind,
    While in the order of their birth   20
Her sisters pass, and many an ample field
Grows white beneath their steps, till now, behold,
    Its endless sheets unfold
THE SNOW OF SOUTHERN SUMMERS! Let the earth
Rejoice! beneath those fleeces soft and warm   25
Our happy land shall sleep
In a repose as deep
As if we lay intrenched behind
Whole leagues of Russian ice and Arctic storm!

II

And what if, mad with wrongs themselves have
        wrought,
    In their own treachery caught,   30
    By their own fears made bold,
    And leagued with him of old,
Who long since in the limits of the North

Set up his evil throne, and warred with God—[1]   35
What if, both mad and blinded in their rage,
Our foes should fling us down their mortal gage,
And with a hostile step profane our sod!
We shall not shrink, my brothers, but go forth
To meet them, marshaled by the Lord of Hosts,   40
And overshadowed by the mighty ghosts
Of Moultrie and of Eutaw[2]—who shall foil
Auxiliars such as these? Not these alone,
    But every stock and stone
    Shall help us; but the very soil,   45
And all the generous wealth it gives to toil,
And all for which we love our noble land,
Shall fight beside, and through us; sea and strand,
    The heart of woman, and her hand,
Tree, fruit, and flower, and every influence,   50
    Gentle, or grave, or grand;
    The winds in our defence
Shall seem to blow; to us the hills shall lend
    Their firmness and their calm;
And in our stiffened sinews we shall blend   55
    The strength of pine and palm!

III

Nor would we shun the battleground,
    Though weak as we are strong;
Call up the clashing elements around,
    And test the right and wrong!   60
On one side, creeds that dare to teach
What Christ and Paul refrained to preach;
Codes built upon a broken pledge,
And Charity that whets a poniard's edge;
Fair schemes that leave the neighboring poor   65
To starve and shiver at the schemer's door,
While in the world's most liberal ranks enrolled,
He turns some vast philanthropy to gold;
Religion, taking every mortal form
But that a pure and Christian faith makes warm,   70
Where not to vile fanatic passion urged,
Or not in vague philosophies submerged,
Repulsive with all Pharisaic leaven,
And making laws to stay the laws of Heaven!
And on the other, scorn of sordid gain,   75
Unblemished honor, truth without a stain,
Faith, justice, reverence, charitable wealth,
And, for the poor and humble, laws which give,
Not the mean right to buy the right to live,
    But life, and home, and health!   80

Ethnogenesis. [1] Refers to Satan in Milton's *Paradise Lost.*
[2] Revolutionary War conflicts.

To doubt the end were want of trust in God,
   Who, if he has decreed
   That we must pass a redder sea[3]
Than that which rang to Miriam's holy glee,
   Will surely raise at need   85
   A Moses with his rod!

IV

But let our fears—if fears we have—be still,
And turn us to the future! Could we climb
Some mighty Alp, and view the coming time,
   The rapturous sight would fill   90
   Our eyes with happy tears!
Not only for the glories which the years
Shall bring us; not for lands from sea to sea,
And wealth, and power, and peace, though these
        shall be;
But for the distant peoples we shall bless,   95
And the hushed murmurs of a world's distress:
For, to give labor to the poor,
   The whole sad planet o'er,
And save from want and crime the humblest door,
Is one among the many ends for which   100
   God makes us great and rich!
The hour perchance is not yet wholly ripe
When all shall own it, but the type
Whereby we shall be known in every land
Is that vast gulf[4] which lips our Southern strand, 105
And through the cold, untempered ocean pours
Its genial streams, that far off Arctic shores
May sometimes catch upon the softened breeze
Strange tropic warmth and hints of summer seas.

                     1861, 1862

The Cotton Boll

While I recline
At ease beneath
This immemorial pine,
Small sphere!
(By dusky fingers brought this morning here   5
And shown with boastful smiles),
I turn thy cloven sheath,
Through which the soft white fibres peer,
That, with their gossamer bands,
Unite, like love, the sea-divided lands,   10
And slowly, thread by thread,
Draw forth the folded strands,
Than which the trembling line,
By whose frail help yon startled spider fled
Down the tall spear-grass from his swinging bed, 15
Is scarce more fine;

[3] Cf. Exodus xiv.15.
[4] Gulf stream.

And as the tangled skein
Unravels in my hands,
Betwixt me and the noonday light,
A veil seems lifted, and for miles and miles   20
The landscape broadens on my sight,
As, in the little boll, there lurked a spell
Like that which, in the ocean shell,
With mystic sound,   24
Breaks down the narrow walls that hem us round,
And turns some city lane
Into the restless main,
With all his capes and isles!

Yonder bird,
Which floats, as if at rest,   30
In those blue tracts above the thunder, where
No vapors cloud the stainless air,
And never sound is heard,
Unless at such rare time
When, from the City of the Blest,   35
Rings down some golden chime,
Sees not from his high place
So vast a cirque of summer space
As widens round me in one mighty field,
Which, rimmed by seas and sands,   40
Doth hail its earliest daylight in the beams
Of gray Atlantic dawns;
And, broad as realms made up of many lands,
Is lost afar
Behind the crimson hills and purple lawns   45
Of sunset, among plains which roll their streams
Against the Evening Star!
And lo!
To the remotest point of sight,
Although I gaze upon no waste of snow,   50
The endless field is white;
And the whole landscape glows,
For many a shining league away,
With such accumulated light
As Polar lands would flash beneath a tropic day! 55
Nor lack there (for the vision grows,
And the small charm within my hands—
More potent even than the fabled one,
Which oped whatever golden mystery
Lay hid in fairy wood or magic vale,   60
The curious ointment of the Arabian tale—
Beyond all mortal sense
Doth stretch my sight's horizon, and I see,
Beneath its simple influence,
As if with Uriel's crown,   65
I stood in some great temple of the Sun,
And looked, as Uriel, down!)
Nor lack there pastures rich and fields all green
With all the common gifts of God,
For temperate airs and torrid sheen   70
Weave Edens of the sod;
Through lands which look one sea of billowy gold

Broad rivers wind their devious ways;
A hundred isles in their embraces fold
A hundred luminous bays;   75
And through yon purple haze
Vast mountains lift their plumed peaks cloud-
        crowned;
And, save where up their sides the plowman creeps
An unhewn forest girds them grandly round,
In whose dark shades a future navy sleeps!   80
Ye Stars, which, though unseen, yet with me gaze
Upon this loveliest fragment of the earth!
Thou Sun, that kindlest all thy gentlest rays
Above it, as to light a favorite hearth!
Ye Clouds, that in your temples in the West   85
See nothing brighter than its humblest flowers!
And you, ye Winds, that on the ocean's breast
Are kissed to coolness ere ye reach its bowers!
Bear witness with me in my song of praise,
And tell the world that, since the world began,   90
No fairer land hath fired a poet's lays,
Or given a home to man!

But these are charms already widely blown!
His be the meed whose pencil's trace
Hath touched our very swamps with grace,   95
And round whose tuneful way
All Southern laurels bloom;
The Poet of "The Woodlands,"[1] unto whom
Alike are known
The flute's low breathing and the trumpet's tone,
And the soft west wind's sighs;   101
But who shall utter all the debt,
O land wherein all powers are met
That bind a people's heart,
The world doth owe thee at this day,   105
And which it never can repay,
Yet scarcely deigns to own!
Where sleeps the poet who shall fitly sing
The source wherefrom doth spring
That mighty commerce which, confined   110
To the mean channels of no selfish mart,
Goes out to every shore
Of this broad earth, and throngs the sea with ships
That bear no thunders; hushes hungry lips
In alien lands;   115
Joins with a delicate web remotest strands;
And gladdening rich and poor,
Doth gild Parisian domes,
Or feed the cottage-smoke of English homes,
And only bounds its blessings by mankind!   120
In offices like these, thy mission lies,
My Country! and it shall not end
As long as rain shall fall and Heaven bend
In blue above thee; though thy foes be hard

The Cotton Boll. [1] The country estate of William Gilmore
Simms, novelist and poet.

And cruel as their weapons, it shall guard   125
Thy hearth-stones as a bulwark; make thee great
In white and bloodless state;
And haply, as the years increase—
Still working through its humbler reach
With that large wisdom which the ages teach—   130
Revive the half-dead dream of universal peace!
As men who labor in that mine
Of Cornwall, hollowed out beneath the bed
Of ocean, when a storm rolls overhead,
Hear the dull booming of the world of brine   135
Above them, and a mighty muffled roar
Of winds and waters, yet toil calmly on,
And split the rock and pile the massive ore,
Or carve a niche, or shape the archèd roof;
So I, as calmly, weave my woof   140
Of song, chanting the days to come,
Unsilenced, though the quiet summer air
Stirs with the bruit of battles, and each dawn
Wakes from its starry silence to the hum
Of many gathering armies. Still,   145
In that we sometimes hear,
Upon the Northern winds, the voice of woe
Not wholly drowned in triumph, though I know
The end must crown us, and a few brief years
Dry all our tears,   150
I may not sing too gladly. To thy will
Resigned, O Lord! we cannot all forget
That there is much even Victory must regret.
And, therefore, not too long
From the great burthen of our country's wrong   155
Delay our just release!
And, if it may be, save
These sacred fields of peace
From stain of patriot or of hostile blood!
Oh, help us, Lord! to roll the crimson flood   160
Back on its course, and while our banners wing
Northward, strike with us! till the Goth shall cling
To his own blasted altar-stones, and crave
Mercy; and we shall grant it, and dictate
The lenient future of his fate   165
There, where some rotting ships and crumbling
        quays
Shall one day mark the Port which ruled the West-
        ern seas.
                                                         1861

Charleston

Calm as that second summer which precedes
    The first fall of the snow,
In the broad sunlight of heroic deeds,
    The City bides the foe.

As yet, behind their ramparts stern and proud,   5
    Her bolted thunders sleep—

Dark Sumter like a battlemented cloud,
  Looms o'er the solemn deep.

No Calpe[1] frowns from lofty cliff or scar
  To guard the holy strand;   10
But Moultrie holds in leash her dogs of war
  Above the level sand.

And down the dunes a thousand guns lie couched
  Unseen, beside the flood,
Like tigers in some Orient jungle crouched,   15
  That wait and watch for blood.

Meanwhile, through streets still echoing with trade,
  Walk grave and thoughtful men,
Whose hands may one day wield the patriot's blade
  As lightly as the pen.   20

And maidens with such eyes as would grow dim
  Over a bleeding hound,
Seem each one to have caught the strength of him
  Whose sword she sadly bound.

Charleston. [1] Gibraltar.

Thus girt without and garrisoned at home,   25
  Day patient following day,
Old Charleston looks from roof, and spire, and
    dome,
  Across her tranquil bay.

Ships, through a hundred foes, from Saxon lands
  And spicy Indian ports,   30
Bring Saxon steel and iron to her hands,
  And Summer to her courts.

But still, along yon dim Atlantic line,
  The only hostile smoke
Creeps like a harmless mist above the brine,   35
  From some frail, floating oak.

Shall the Spring dawn, and she still clad in smiles,
  And with an unscathed brow,
Rest in the strong arms of her palm-crowned isles,
  As fair and free as now?   40

We know not; in the temple of the Fates
  God has inscribed her doom;
And, all untroubled in her faith, she waits
  The triumph or the tomb.

          1862

FREDERICK DOUGLASS [1817?–1895]

SON OF AN UNKNOWN white father and a black mother from whom he was separated in infancy, Frederick Augustus Washington Bailey was born into slavery on a plantation at Tuckahoe, Maryland. When he was about eight years old he was sent to Baltimore to be house-boy in the home of relatives of his master. His new mistress kindly yielded to his plea to be taught to read, though it was illegal to instruct slaves and the lessons ended abruptly when the master of the household discovered what was going on. But the seed had been sown: the child now understood what gave the white man his power over the black man, and saw that education was the pathway to freedom. Secretly, painfully, he persevered with his reading and taught himself to write.

Returned to plantation life at fifteen, he showed an independence of spirit that induced his master to turn him over to a "slave-breaker" named Covey, with whom he spent a year that hardened his determination to escape to freedom. After one unsuccessful attempt, he managed in 1838 to reach New York, and then New Bedford, Massachusetts, where he found work as a laborer. To mark his entry on the life of a free man, he now took the name of Douglass, after the fugitive chieftain in Scott's *The Lady of the Lake.*

The public career of Frederick Douglass began in 1841. While attending an antislavery convention at Nantucket, the young ex-slave was unexpectedly called upon to speak, and though trembling with stage-fright before the audience of distinguished New Englanders, he spoke so movingly that the Massachusetts Anti-Slavery Society at once offered him a position as lecturer and agent. From that time on, Douglass committed himself to the antislavery cause, as speaker, writer, and founder and editor of several newspapers and periodicals. He was a naturally endowed orator—six feet tall, broad-shouldered, with fine strong features, a melodious voice, an eloquent command of language, and a sincerity and conviction stemming from twenty-one bitter years of bondage. Because many people found it hard to believe that the literate, polished speaker was actually a fugitive slave, he wrote and published the *Narrative of the Life of Frederick Douglass* in 1845, naming names, dates, and places—and indeed so exposing himself that he found it expedient to spend the next two years in England to avoid possible re-enslavement. Members of the Society of Friends arranged the purchase of his freedom, and in 1847 he returned to America, moving to Rochester, New York. In 1859 he again fled the country to avoid arrest for alleged complicity in John Brown's raid.

Returning to the United States in 1860, he supported Lincoln and was thereafter active in Republican Party counsels and in national affairs. Among other honors and offices, he served as Marshal of the District of Columbia and as Minister to Haiti. No gradualist and no theorist, he fought Jim Crow practices and racism in the same practical, hard-line terms that he had fought slavery. In assessing his career, his most recent biographer, Benjamin Quarles, quotes from a *Memorial* by Albion W. Tourgée, published the year after Douglass's death: "Three classes of the American people are under special obligation to him: the colored bondman whom he helped to free from the chains which he himself had worn; the free persons of color whom he had helped make citizens; the white people of the United States whom he sought to free from the bondage of caste and relieve from the odium of slavery."

Further reading: *Narrative of the Life of Frederick Douglass, an American Slave, written by himself,* ed. Benjamin Quarles (The John Harvard Library), 1960. Benjamin Quarles, *Frederick Douglass,* 1948.

FROM ## *Narrative of the Life of Frederick Douglass*

Douglass twice rewrote his autobiography, and brought it up to date, in *My Bondage and My Freedom* (1855) and the *Life and Times of Frederick Douglass* (1882). The selection given here is from the first edition (Boston, 1845).

Chapter X

I left Master Thomas's[1] house, and went to live with Mr. Covey, on the 1st of January, 1833. I was now, for the first time in my life, a field hand. In my new employment, I found myself even more awkward than a country boy appeared to be in a large city. I had been at my new home but one week before Mr. Covey gave me a very severe whipping, cutting my back, causing the blood to run, and raising ridges on my flesh as large as my little finger. The details of this affair are as follows: Mr. Covey sent me, very early in the morning of one of our coldest days in the month of January, to the woods, to get a load of wood. He gave me a team of unbro-

[1] Thomas Auld of St. Michael's, Talbot County, Maryland.

ken oxen. He told me which was the in-hand ox, and which the off-hand one. He then tied the end of a large rope around the horns of the in-hand ox, and gave me the other end of it, and told me, if the oxen started to run, that I must hold on upon the rope. I had never driven oxen before, and of course I was very awkward. I, however, succeeded in getting to the edge of the woods with little difficulty; but I had got a very few rods into the woods, when the oxen took fright, and started full tilt, carrying the cart against trees, and over stumps, in the most frightful manner. I expected every moment that my brains would be dashed out against the trees. After running thus for a considerable distance, they finally upset the cart, dashing it with great force against a tree, and threw themselves into a dense thicket. How I escaped death, I do not know. There I was, entirely alone, in a thick wood, in a place new to me. My cart was upset and shattered, my oxen were entangled among the young trees, and there was none to help me. After a long spell of effort, I succeeded in getting my cart righted, my oxen disentangled, and again yoked to the cart. I now proceeded with my team to the place where I had, the day before, been chopping wood, and loaded my cart pretty heavily, thinking in this way to tame my oxen. I then proceeded on my way home. I had now consumed one half of the day. I got out of the woods safely, and now felt out of danger. I stopped my oxen to open the woods gate; and just as I did so, before I could get hold of my ox-rope, the oxen again started, rushed through the gate, catching it between the wheel and the body of the cart, tearing it to pieces, and coming within a few inches of crushing me against the gate-post. Thus twice, in one short day, I escaped death by the merest chance. On my return, I told Mr. Covey what had happened, and how it happened. He ordered me to return to the woods again immediately. I did so, and he followed on after me. Just as I got into the woods, he came up and told me to stop my cart, and that he would teach me how to trifle away my time, and break gates. He then went to a large gum-tree, and with his axe cut three large switches, and, after trimming them up neatly with his pocket-knife, he ordered me to take off my clothes. I made him no answer, but stood with my clothes on. He repeated his order. I still made him no answer, nor did I move to strip myself. Upon this he rushed at me with the fierceness of a tiger, tore off my clothes, and lashed me till he had worn out his switches, cutting me so savagely as to leave the marks visible for a long time after. This whipping was the first of a number just like it, and for similar offences.

I lived with Mr. Covey one year. During the first six months, of that year, scarce a week passed without his whipping me. I was seldom free from a sore back. My awkwardness was almost always his excuse for whipping me. We were worked fully up to the point of endurance. Long before day we were up, our horses fed, and by the first approach of day we were off to the field with our hoes and ploughing teams. Mr. Covey gave us enough to eat, but scarce time to eat it. We were often less than five minutes taking our meals. We were often in the field from the first approach of day till its last lingering ray had left us; and at saving-fodder time, midnight often caught us in the field binding blades.

Covey would be out with us. The way he used to stand it, was this. He would spend the most of his afternoons in bed. He would then come out fresh in the evening, ready to urge us on with his words, example, and frequently with the whip. Mr. Covey was one of the few slaveholders who could and did work with his hands. He was a hard-working man. He knew by himself just what a man or a boy could do. There was no deceiving him. His work went on in his absence almost as well as in his presence; and he had the faculty of making us feel that he was ever present with us. This he did by surprising us. He seldom approached the spot where we were at work openly, if he could do it secretly. He always aimed at taking us by surprise. Such was his cunning, that we used to call him, among ourselves, "the snake." When we were at work in the cornfield, he would sometimes crawl on his hands and knees to avoid detection, and all at once he would rise nearly in our midst, and scream out, "Ha, ha! Come, come! Dash on, dash on!" This being his mode of attack, it was never safe to stop a single minute. His comings were like a thief in the night. He appeared to us as being ever at hand. He was under every tree, behind every stump, in every bush, and at every window, on the plantation. He would sometimes mount his horse, as if bound to St. Michael's, a distance of seven miles, and in half an hour afterwards you would see him coiled up in the corner of the wood-fence, watching every motion of the slaves. He would, for this purpose, leave his horse tied up in the woods. Again, he would sometimes walk up to us, and give us orders as though he was upon the point of starting on a long journey, turn his back upon us, and make as though he was going to the house to get ready; and, before he would get half way thither, he would turn short and crawl into a fence-corner, or behind some tree, and there watch us till the going down of the sun.

Mr. Covey's *forte* consisted in his power to deceive. His life was devoted to planning and perpetrating the grossest deceptions. Every thing he possessed in the shape of learning or religion, he made conform to his disposition to deceive. He seemed to think himself equal to deceiving the Almighty. He would make a short prayer in the morning, and a long prayer at night; and, strange as it may seem, few men would at times appear more devotional than he. The exercises of his family devotions were always commenced with singing; and, as he was a very poor singer himself, the duty of raising the hymn generally came upon me. He would read his hymn, and nod at me to commence. I would at times do so; at others, I would not. My non-compliance would almost always produce much confusion. To show himself independent of me, he would start and stagger through with his hymn in the most discordant manner. In this state of mind, he prayed with more than ordinary spirit. Poor man! such was his disposition, and success at deceiving, I do verily believe that he sometimes deceived himself into the solemn belief, that he was a sincere worshipper of the most high God; and this, too, at a time when he may be said to have been guilty of compelling his woman slave to commit the sin of adultery. The facts in the case are these: Mr. Covey was a poor man; he was just commencing in life; he was only able to buy one slave; and, shocking as is the fact, he bought her, as he said, for *a breeder*. This woman was named Caroline. Mr. Covey bought her from Mr. Thomas Lowe, about six miles from St. Michael's. She was a large, able-bodied woman, about twenty years old. She had already given birth to one child, which proved her to be just what he wanted. After buying her, he hired a married man of Mr. Samuel Harrison, to live with him one year; and him he used to fasten up with her every night! The result was, that, at the end of the year, the miserable woman gave birth to twins. At this result Mr. Covey seemed to be highly pleased, both with the man and the wretched woman. Such was his joy, and that of his wife, that nothing they could do for Caroline during her confinement was too good, or too hard, to be done. The children were regarded as being quite an addition to his wealth.

If at any one time of my life more than another, I was made to drink the bitterest dregs of slavery, that time was during the first six months of my stay with Mr. Covey. We were worked in all weathers. It was never too hot or too cold; it could never rain, blow, hail, or snow, too hard for us to work in the field. Work, work, work, was scarcely more the order of the day than of the night. The longest days were too short him, and the shortest nights too long for him. I was somewhat unmanageable when I first went there, but a few months of this discipline tamed me. Mr. Covey succeeded in breaking me. I was broken in body, soul, and spirit. My natural elasticity was crushed, my intellect languished, the disposition to read departed, the cheerful spark that lingered about my eye died; the dark night of slavery closed in upon me; and behold a man transformed into a brute!

Sunday was my only leisure time. I spent this in a sort of beast-like stupor, between sleep and wake, under some large tree. At times I would rise up, a flash of energetic freedom would dart through my soul, accompanied with a faint beam of hope, that flickered for a moment, and then vanished. I sank down again, mourning over my wretched condition. I was sometimes prompted to take my life, and that of Covey, but was prevented by a combination of hope and fear. My sufferings on this plantation seem now like a dream rather than a stern reality.

Our house stood within a few rods of the Chesapeake Bay, whose broad bosom was ever white with sails from every quarter of the habitable globe. Those beautiful vessels, robed in purest white, so delightful to the eye of freemen, were to me so many shrouded ghosts, to terrify and torment me with thoughts of my wretched condition. I have often, in the deep stillness of a summer's Sabbath, stood all alone upon the lofty banks of that noble bay, and traced, with saddened heart and tearful eye, the countless number of sails moving off to the mighty ocean. The sight of these always affected me powerfully. My thoughts would compel utterance; and there, with no audience but the Almighty, I would pour out my soul's complaint, in my rude way, with an apostrophe to the moving multitude of ships:—

"You are loosed from your moorings, and are free; I am fast in my chains, and am a slave! You move merrily before the gentle gale, and I sadly before the bloody whip! You are freedom's swift-winged angels, that fly round the world; I am confined in bands of iron! O that I were free! O, that I were on one of your gallant decks, and under your protecting wing! Alas! betwixt me and you, the turbid waters roll. Go on, go on. O that I could also go! Could I but swim! If I could fly! O, why was I born a man, of whom to make a brute! The glad ship is gone; she hides in the dim distance. I am left in the hottest hell of unending slavery. O God, save me! God, deliver me! Let me be free! Is there any God? Why am I a slave? I will run away. I will not stand it. Get caught, or get clear, I'll try it. I had as well die with ague as the fever. I have only one life to lose. I had as well be killed running as die standing. Only think of it; one hundred miles straight north, and I am free! Try it? Yes! God helping me, I will. It cannot be that I shall live and die a slave. I will take to the water. This very bay shall yet bear me into freedom. The steamboats steered in a north-east course from North Point. I will do the same; and when I get to the head of the bay, I will turn my canoe adrift, and walk straight through Delaware into Pennsylvania. When I get there, I shall not be required to have a pass; I can travel without being disturbed. Let but the first opportunity offer, and, come what will, I am off. Meanwhile, I will try to bear up under the yoke. I am not the only slave in the world. Why should I fret? I can bear as much as any of them. Besides, I am but a boy, and all boys are bound to some one. It may be that my misery in slavery will only increase my happiness when I get free. There is a better day coming."

Thus I used to think, and thus I used to speak to myself; goaded almost to madness at one moment, and at the next reconciling myself to my wretched lot.

I have already intimated that my condition was much worse, during the first six months of my stay at Mr. Covey's, than in the last six. The circumstances leading to the change in Mr. Covey's course toward me form an epoch in my humble history. You have seen how a man was made a slave; you shall see how a slave was made a man. On one of the hottest days of the month of August, 1833, Bill Smith, William Hughes, a slave named Eli, and myself, were engaged in fanning wheat. Hughes was clearing the fanned wheat from before the fan, Eli was turning, Smith was feeding, and I was carrying wheat to the fan. The work was simple, requiring strength rather than intellect; yet, to one entirely unused to such work, it came very hard. About three o'clock of that day, I broke down; my strength failed me; I was seized with a violent aching of the head, attended with extreme dizziness; I trembled in every limb. Finding what was coming, I nerved myself up, feeling it would never do to stop work. I stood as long as I could stagger to the hopper with grain. When I could stand no longer, I fell, and felt as if held down by an immense weight. The fan of course stopped; every one had his own work to do; and no one could do the work of the other, and have his own go on at the same time.

Mr. Covey was at the house, about one hundred yards from the treading-yard where we were fanning. On hearing the fan stop, he left immediately, and came to the spot where we were. He hastily inquired what the matter was. Bill answered that I was sick, and there was no one to bring wheat to the fan. I had by this time crawled away under the side of the post and rail-fence by which the yard was enclosed, hoping to find relief by getting out of the sun. He then asked where I was. He was told by one of the hands. He came to the spot, and, after looking at me awhile, asked me what was the matter. I told him as well as I could, for I scarce had strength to speak. He then gave me a savage kick in the side, and told me to get up. I tried to do so, but fell back in the attempt. He gave me another kick, and again told me to rise. I again tried, and succeeded in gaining my feet; but, stooping to get the tub with which I was feeding the fan, I again staggered and fell. While down in this situation, Mr. Covey took up the hickory slat with which Hughes had been striking off the half-bushel measure, and with it gave me a heavy blow upon the head, making a large wound, and the blood ran freely; and with this again told me to get up. I made no effort to comply, having now made up my mind to let him do his worst. In a short time after receiving this blow, my head grew better. Mr. Covey had now left me to my fate. At this moment I resolved, for the first time, to go to my master, enter a complaint, and ask his protection. In order to do this, I must that afternoon walk seven miles; and this, under the circumstances, was truly a severe undertaking. I was exceedingly feeble; made so as much by the kicks and blows which I received, as by the severe fit of sickness to which I had been subjected. I, however, watched my chance, while Covey was looking in an opposite direction, and started for St. Michael's. I succeeded in getting a considerable distance on my way to the woods, when Covey discovered me, and called after me to come back, threatening what he would do if I did not come. I disregarded both his calls and his threats, and made my way to the woods as fast as my feeble state would allow; and thinking I might be overhauled by him if I kept the road, I walked through the woods, keeping far enough from the road to avoid detection, and near enough to prevent losing my way. I had not gone far before my little strength again failed me. I could go no farther. I fell down, and lay for a considerable time. The blood was yet oozing from the wound on my head. For a time I thought I should bleed to death; and think now that I should have done so, but that the blood so matted my hair as to stop the wound. After lying there about three quarters of an hour, I nerved myself up again, and started on my way, through bogs and briers, barefooted and bareheaded, tearing my feet sometimes at nearly every step; and after a journey of about seven miles, occupying some five hours to perform it, I arrived at master's store. I then presented an appearance enough to affect any but a heart of iron. From the crown of my head to my feet, I was covered with blood. My hair was all clotted with dust and blood; my shirt was stiff with blood. My legs and feet were torn in sundry places with briers and thorns, and were also covered with blood. I suppose I looked like a man who had escaped a den of wild beasts, and barely escaped them. In this state I appeared before my master, humbly entreating him to interpose his authority for my protection. I told him all the circumstances as well as I could, and it seemed, as I spoke, at times to affect him. He would then walk the floor, and seek to justify Covey by saying he expected I deserved it. He asked me what I wanted. I told him, to let me get a new home; that as sure as I lived with Mr. Covey again, I should live with but to die with him; that Covey would surely kill me; he was in a fair way for it. Master Thomas ridiculed the idea that there was any danger of Mr. Covey's killing me, and said that he knew Mr. Covey; that he was a good man, and that he could not think of taking me from him; that, should he do so, he would lose the whole year's wages; that I belonged to Mr. Covey for one year, and that I must go back to him, come what might; and that I must not trouble him with any more stories, or that he would himself *get hold of me.* After threatening me thus, he gave me a very large dose of salts, telling me that I might remain in St. Michael's that night, (it being quite late,) but that I must be off back to Mr. Covey's early in the morning; and that if I did not, he would *get hold of me,* which meant that he would whip me. I remained all night, and, according to his orders, I started off to Covey's in the morning, (Saturday morning,) wearied in body and broken in spirit. I got no supper that night, or breakfast that morning. I reached Covey's about nine o'clock; and just as I was getting over the fence that divided Mrs. Kemp's fields from ours, out ran Covey with his cowskin, to give me another whipping. Before he could reach me, I succeeded in getting to the cornfield; and as the corn was very high, it afforded me the means of

Frederick Douglass | 811

hiding. He seemed very angry, and searched for me a long time. My behavior was altogether unaccountable. He finally gave up the chase, thinking, I suppose, that I must come home for something to eat; he would give himself no further trouble in looking for me. I spent that day mostly in the woods, having the alternative before me,—to go home and be whipped to death, or stay in the woods and be starved to death. That night, I fell in with Sandy Jenkins, a slave with whom I was somewhat acquainted. Sandy had a free wife who lived about four miles from Mr. Covey's; and it being Saturday, he was on his way to see her. I told him my circumstances, and he very kindly invited me to go home with him. I went home with him, and talked this whole matter over, and got his advice as to what course it was best for me to pursue. I found Sandy an old adviser. He told me, with great solemnity, I must go back to Covey; but that before I went, I must go with him into another part of the woods, where there was a certain *root*, which, if I would take some of it with me, carrying it *always on my right side*, would render it impossible for Mr. Covey, or any other white man, to whip me. He said he had carried it for years; and since he had done so, he had never received a blow, and never expected to while he carried it. I at first rejected the idea, that the simple carrying of a root in my pocket would have any such effect as he had said, and was not disposed to take it; but Sandy impressed the necessity with much earnestness, telling me it could do no harm, if it did no good. To please him, I at length took the root, and, according to his direction, carried it upon my right side. This was Sunday morning. I immediately started for home; and upon entering the yard gate, out came Mr. Covey on his way to meeting. He spoke to me very kindly, bade me drive the pigs from a lot near by, and passed on towards the church. Now, this singular conduct of Mr. Covey really made me begin to think that there was something in the *root* which Sandy had given me; and had it been on any other day than Sunday, I could have attributed the conduct to no other cause than the influence of that root; and as it was, I was half inclined to think the *root* to be something more than I at first had taken it to be. All went well till Monday morning. On this morning, the virtue of the *root* was fully tested. Long before daylight, I was called to go and rub, curry, and feed, the horses. I obeyed, and was glad to obey. But whilst thus engaged, whilst in the act of throwing down some blades from the loft, Mr. Covey entered the stable with a long rope; and just as I was half out of the loft, he caught hold of my legs, and was about tying me. As soon as I found what he was up to, I gave a sudden spring, and as I did so, he holding to my legs, I was brought sprawling on the stable floor.

Mr. Covey seemed now to think he had me, and could do what he pleased; but at this moment—from whence came the spirit I don't know—I resolved to fight; and suiting my action to the resolution, I seized Covey hard by the throat; and as I did so, I rose. He held on to me, and I to him. My resistance was so entirely unexpected, that Covey seemed taken all aback. He trembled like a leaf. This gave me assurance, and I held him uneasy, causing the blood to run where I touched him with the ends of my fingers. Mr. Covey soon called out to Hughes for help. Hughes came, and, while Covey held me, attempted to tie my right hand. While he was in the act of doing so, I watched my chance, and gave him a heavy kick close under the ribs. This kick fairly sickened Hughes, so that he left me in the hands of Mr. Covey. This kick had the effect of not only weakening Hughes, but Covey also. When he saw Hughes bending over with pain, his courage quailed. He asked me if I meant to persist in my resistance. I told him I did, come what might; that he had used me like a brute for six months, and that I was determined to be used so no longer. With that, he strove to drag me to a stick that was lying just out of the stable door. He meant to knock me down. But just as he was leaning over to get the stick, I seized him with both hands by his collar, and brought him by a sudden snatch to the ground. By this time, Bill came. Covey called upon him for assistance. Bill wanted to know what he could do. Covey said, "Take hold of him, take hold of him!" Bill said his master hired him out to work, and not to help whip me; so he left Covey and myself to fight our own battle out. We were at it for nearly two hours. Covey at length let me go, puffing and blowing at a great rate, saying that if I had not resisted, he would not have whipped me half so much. The truth was, that he had not whipped me at all. I considered him as getting entirely the worst end of the bargain; for he had drawn no blood from me, but I had from him. The whole six months afterwards, that I spent with Mr. Covey, he never laid the weight of his finger upon me in anger. He would occasionally say, he didn't want to get hold of me again. "No," thought I, "you need not; for you will come off worse than you did before."

This battle with Mr. Covey was the turning-point in my career as a slave. It rekindled the few expiring embers of freedom, and revived within me a sense of my own manhood. It recalled the departed self-confidence, and inspired me again with a determination to be free. The gratification afforded by the triumph was a full compensation for whatever else might follow, even death itself. He only can understand the deep satisfaction which I experienced, who has himself repelled by force the bloody arm of slavery. I felt as I never felt before. It was a glorious resurrection, from the tomb of slavery, to the heaven of freedom. My long-crushed spirit rose, cowardice departed, bold defiance took its place; and I now resolved that, however long I might remain a slave in form, the day had passed forever when I could be a slave in fact. I did not hesitate to let it be known of me, that the white man who expected to succeed in whipping, must also succeed in killing me.

From this time I was never again what might be called fairly whipped, though I remained a slave four years afterwards. I had several fights, but was never whipped.

It was for a long time a matter of surprise to me why Mr. Covey did not immediately have me taken by the constable to the whipping-post, and there regularly whipped for the crime of raising my hand against a white man in defence of myself. And the only explanation I can now think of does not entirely satisfy me; but such as it is, I will give it. Mr. Covey enjoyed the most unbounded reputation for being a first-rate overseer and negro-breaker. It was of considerable importance to him. That reputation was at stake; and had he sent me—a boy about sixteen years old—to the public whipping-post, his reputation would have been lost; so, to save his reputation, he suffered me to go unpunished.°°°

On the first of January, 1834, I left Mr. Covey, and went to live with Mr. William Freeland, who lived about three miles from St. Michael's. I soon found Mr. Freeland a very different man from Mr. Covey. Though not rich, he was what would be called an educated southern gentleman. Mr. Covey, as I have shown, was a well-trained negro-breaker and slavedriver. The former (slaveholder though he was) seemed to possess some regard for honor, some reverence for justice, and some respect for humanity. The latter seemed totally insensible to all such sentiments. Mr. Freeland had many of the faults peculiar to slaveholders, such as being very passionate and fretful; but I must do him the justice to say, that he was exceedingly free from those degrading vices to which Mr. Covey was constantly addicted. The one was open and frank, and we always knew where to find him. The other was a most artful deceiver, and could be understood only by such as were skilful enough to detect his cunningly-devised frauds. Another advantage I gained in my new master was, he made no pretensions to, or profession of, religion; and this, in my opinion, was truly a great advantage. I assert most unhesitatingly, that the religion of the south is a mere covering for the most horrid crimes,—a justifier of the most appalling barbarity,—a sanctifier of the most hateful frauds,—and a dark shelter under which the darkest, foulest, grossest, and most infernal deeds of slaveholders find the strongest protection. Were I to be again reduced to the chains of slavery, next to that enslavement, I should regard being the slave of a religious master the greatest calamity that could befall me.°°°

Mr. Freeland was himself the owner of but two slaves. Their names were Henry Harris and John Harris. The rest of his hands he hired. These consisted of myself, Sandy Jenkins,[2] and Handy Caldwell. Henry and John were quite intelligent, and in a very little while after I went there, I succeeded in creating in them a strong desire to learn how to read. This desire soon sprang up in the others also. They very soon mustered up some old spelling-books, and nothing would do but that I must keep a Sabbath school. I agreed to do so, and accordingly devoted my Sundays to teaching these my loved fellow-slaves how to read. Neither of them knew his letters when I went there. Some of the slaves of the neighboring farms found what was going on, and also availed themselves of this little opportunity to learn to read. It was understood, among all who came, that there must be as little display about it as possible. It was necessary to keep our religious masters at St. Michael's unacquainted with the fact, that, instead of spending the Sabbath in wrestling, boxing, and drinking whisky, we were trying to learn how to read the will of God; for they had much rather see us engaged in those degrading sports, than to see us behaving like intellectual, moral, and accountable beings. My blood boils as I think of the bloody manner in which Messrs. Wright Fairbanks and Garrison West, both class-leaders, in connection with many others, rushed in upon us with sticks and stones, and broke up our virtuous little Sabbath school, at St. Michael's—all calling themselves Christians! humble followers of the Lord Jesus Christ! But I am again digressing.

I held my Sabbath school at the house of a free colored man, whose name I deem it imprudent to mention; for should it be known, it might embarrass him greatly, though the crime of holding the school was committed ten years ago. I had at one time over forty scholars, and those of the right sort, ardently desiring to learn. They were of all ages, though mostly men and women. I look back to those Sundays with an amount of pleasure not to be expressed. They were great days to my soul. The work of instructing my dear fellow-slaves was the sweetest engagement with which I was ever blessed. We loved each other, and to leave them at the close of the Sabbath was a severe cross indeed. When I think that these precious souls are to-day shut up in the prison-house of slavery, my feelings overcome me, and I am almost ready to ask, "Does a righteous God govern the universe? and for what does he hold

[2] This is the same man who gave me the roots to prevent my being whipped by Mr. Covey. [Douglass's note.]

the thunders in his right hand, if not to smite the oppressor, and deliver the spoiled out of the hand of the spoiler?" These dear souls came not to Sabbath school because it was popular to do so, nor did I teach them because it was reputable to be thus engaged. Every moment they spent in that school, they were liable to be taken up, and given thirty-nine lashes. They came because they wished to learn. Their minds had been starved by their cruel masters. They had been shut up in mental darkness. I taught them, because it was the delight of my soul to be doing something that looked like bettering the condition of my race. I kept up my school nearly the whole year I lived with Mr. Freeland; and, beside my Sabbath school, I devoted three evenings in the week, during the winter, to teaching the slaves at home. And I have the happiness to know, that several of those who came to Sabbath school learned how to read; and that one, at least, is now free through my agency.

The year passed off smoothly. It seemed only about half as long as the year which preceded it. I went through it without receiving a single blow. I will give Mr. Freeland the credit of being the best master I ever had, *till I became my own master.* For the ease with which I passed the year, I was, however, somewhat indebted to the society of my fellow-slaves. They were noble souls; they not only possessed loving hearts, but brave ones. We were linked and interlinked with each other. I loved them with a love stronger than any thing I have experienced since. It is sometimes said that we slaves do not love and confide in each other. In answer to this assertion, I can say, I never loved any or confided in any people more than my fellow-slaves, and especially those with whom I lived at Mr. Freeland's. I believe we would have died for each other. We never undertook to do any thing, of any importance, without a mutual consultation. We never moved separately. We were one; and as much so by our tempers and dispositions, as by the mutual hardships to which we were necessarily subjected by our condition as slaves.

At the close of the year 1834, Mr. Freeland again hired me of my master, for the year 1835. But, by this time, I began to want to live *upon free land* as well as *with Freeland;* and I was no longer content, therefore, to live with him or any other slaveholder. I began, with the commencement of the year, to prepare myself for a final struggle, which should decide my fate one way or the other. My tendency was upward. I was fast approaching manhood, and year after year had passed, and I was still a slave. These thoughts roused me—I must do something. I therefore resolved that 1835 should not pass without witnessing an attempt, on my part, to secure my liberty. But I was not willing to cherish this determi-

nation alone. My fellow-slaves were dear to me. I was anxious to have them participate with me in this, my life-giving determination. I therefore, though with great prudence, commenced early to ascertain their views and feelings in regard to their condition, and to imbue their minds with thoughts of freedom. I bent myself to devising ways and means for our escape, and meanwhile strove, on all fitting occasions, to impress them with the gross fraud and inhumanity of slavery. I went first to Henry, next to John, then to the others. I found, in them all, warm hearts and noble spirits. They were ready to hear, and ready to act when a feasible plan should be proposed. This was what I wanted. I talked to them of our want of manhood, if we submitted to our enslavement without at least one noble effort to be free. We met often, and consulted frequently, and told our hopes and fears, recounted the difficulties, real and imagined, which we should be called on to meet. At times we were almost disposed to give up, and try to content ourselves with our wretched lot; at others, we were firm and unbending in our determination to go. Whenever we suggested any plan, there was shrinking—the odds were fearful. Our path was beset with the greatest obstacles; and if we succeeded in gaining the end of it, our right to be free was yet questionable—we were yet liable to be returned to bondage. We could see no spot, this side of the ocean, where we could be free. We knew nothing about Canada. Our knowledge of the north did not extend farther than New York; and to go there, and be forever harassed with the frightful liability of being returned to slavery—with the certainty of being treated tenfold worse than before—the thought was truly a horrible one, and one which it was not easy to overcome. The case sometimes stood thus: At every gate through which we were to pass, we saw a watchman—at every ferry a guard—on every bridge a sentinel—and in every wood a patrol. We were hemmed in upon every side. Here were the difficulties, real or imagined—the good to be sought, and the evil to be shunned. On the one hand, there stood slavery, a stern reality, glaring frightfully upon us,—its robes already crimsoned with the blood of millions, and even now feasting itself greedily upon our own flesh. On the other hand, away back in the dim distance, under the flickering light of the north star, behind some craggy hill or snow-covered mountain, stood a doubtful freedom—half frozen—beckoning us to come and share its hospitality. This in itself was sometimes enough to stagger us; but when we permitted ourselves to survey the road, we were frequently appalled. Upon either side we saw grim death, assuming the most horrid shapes. Now it was starvation, causing us to eat our own flesh;—now we were contending with the waves, and were drowned;—now we were overtaken, and torn to pieces by the fangs of the terrible bloodhound. We were stung by scorpions, chased by wild beasts, bitten by snakes, and finally, after having nearly reached the desired spot,—after swimming rivers, encountering wild beasts, sleeping in the woods, suffering hunger and nakedness,—we were overtaken by our pursuers, and, in our resistance, we were shot dead upon the spot! I say, this picture sometimes appalled us, and made us

> "rather bear those ills we had,
> Than fly to others, that we knew not of."[3]

In coming to a fixed determination to run away, we did more than Patrick Henry, when he resolved upon liberty or death. With us it was a doubtful liberty at most, and almost certain death if we failed. For my part, I should prefer death to hopeless bondage.

Sandy, one of our number, gave up the notion, but still encouraged us. Our company then consisted of Henry Harris, John Harris, Henry Bailey, Charles Roberts, and myself. Henry Bailey was my uncle, and belonged to my master. Charles married my aunt: he belonged to my master's father-in-law, Mr. William Hamilton.

The plan we finally concluded upon was, to get a large canoe belonging to Mr. Hamilton, and upon the Saturday night previous to Easter holidays, paddle directly up the Chesapeake Bay. On our arrival at the head of the bay, a distance of seventy or eighty miles from where we lived, it was our purpose to turn our canoe adrift, and follow the guidance of the north star till we got beyond the limits of Maryland. Our reason for taking the water route was, that we were less liable to be suspected as runaways; we hoped to be regarded as fishermen; whereas, if we should take the land route, we should be subjected to interruptions of almost every kind. Any one having a white face, and being so disposed, could stop us, and subject us to examination.

The week before our intended start, I wrote several protections, one for each of us. As well as I can remember, they were in the following words, to wit:—

"THIS is to certify that I, the undersigned, have given the bearer, my servant, full liberty to go to Baltimore, and spend the Easter holidays. Written with mine own hand, &c., 1835.

"WILLIAM HAMILTON,
"Near St. Michael's, in Talbot county, Maryland."

We were not going to Baltimore; but, in going up

[3] Shakespeare, *Hamlet* III.i.81–82.

the bay, we went toward Baltimore, and these protections were only intended to protect us while on the bay.

As the time drew near for our departure, our anxiety became more and more intense. It was truly a matter of life and death with us. The strength of our determination was about to be fully tested. At this time, I was very active in explaining every difficulty, removing every doubt, dispelling every fear, and inspiring all with the firmness indispensable to success in our undertaking; assuring them that half was gained the instant we made the move; we had talked long enough; we were now ready to move; if not now, we never should be; and if we did not intend to move now, we had as well fold our arms, sit down, and acknowledge ourselves fit only to be slaves. This, none of us were prepared to acknowledge. Every man stood firm; and at our last meeting, we pledged ourselves afresh, in the most solemn manner, that, at the time appointed, we would certainly start in pursuit of freedom. This was in the middle of the week, at the end of which we were to be off. We went, as usual, to our several fields of labor, but with bosoms highly agitated with thoughts of our truly hazardous undertaking. We tried to conceal our feelings as much as possible; and I think we succeeded very well.

After a painful waiting, the Saturday morning, whose night was to witness our departure, came. I hailed it with joy, bring what of sadness it might. Friday night was a sleepless one for me. I probably felt more anxious than the rest, because I was, by common consent, at the head of the whole affair. The responsibility of success or failure lay heavily upon me. The glory of the one, and the confusion of the other, were alike mine. The first two hours of that morning were such as I never experienced before, and hope never to again. Early in the morning, we went, as usual, to the field. We were spreading manure; and all at once, while thus engaged, I was overwhelmed with an indescribable feeling, in the fulness of which I turned to Sandy, who was near by, and said, "We are betrayed!" "Well," said he, "that thought has this moment struck me." We said no more. I was never more certain of any thing.

The horn was blown as usual, and we went up from the field to the house for breakfast. I went for the form, more than for want of any thing to eat that morning. Just as I got to the house, in looking out at the lane gate, I saw four white men, with two colored men. The white men were on horseback, and the colored ones were walking behind, as if tied. I watched them a few moments till they got up to our lane gate. Here they halted, and tied the colored men to the gate-post. I was not yet certain as to what the matter was. In a few moments, in rode Mr. Hamilton, with a speed betokening great excitement. He came to the door, and inquired if Master William was in. He was told he was at the barn. Mr. Hamilton, without dismounting, rode up to the barn with extraordinary speed. In a few moments, he and Mr. Freeland returned to the house. By this time, the three constables rode up, and in great haste dismounted, tied their horses, and met Master William and Mr. Hamilton returning from the barn; and after talking awhile, they all walked up to the kitchen door. There was no one in the kitchen but myself and John. Henry and Sandy were up at the barn. Mr. Freeland put his head in at the door, and called me by name, saying, there were some gentlemen at the door who wished to see me. I stepped to the door, and inquired what they wanted. They at once seized me, and, without giving me any satisfaction, tied me—lashing my hands closely together. I insisted upon knowing what the matter was. They at length said, that they had learned I had been in a "scrape," and that I was to be examined before my master; and if their information proved false, I should not be hurt.

In a few moments, they succeeded in tying John. They then turned to Henry, who had by this time returned, and commanded him to cross his hands. "I won't!" said Henry, in a firm tone, indicating his readiness to meet the consequences of his refusal. "Won't you?" said Tom Graham, the constable. "No, I won't!" said Henry, in a still stronger tone. With this, two of the constables pulled out their shining pistols and swore, by their Creator, that they would make him cross his hands or kill him. Each cocked his pistol, and, with fingers on the trigger, walked up to Henry, saying, at the same time, if he did not cross his hands, they would blow his damned heart out. "Shoot me, shoot me!" said Henry; "you can't kill me but once. Shoot, shoot,—and be damned! *I won't be tied!*" This he said in a tone of loud defiance; and at the same time, with a motion as quick as lightning, he with one single stroke dashed the pistols from the hand of each constable. As he did this, all hands fell upon him, and, after beating him some time, they finally overpowered him, and got him tied.

During the scuffle, I managed, I know not how, to get my pass out, and, without being discovered, put it into the fire. We were all now tied; and just as we were to leave for Easton jail, Betsy Freeland, mother of William Freeland, came to the door with her hands full of biscuits, and divided them between Henry and John. She then delivered herself of a speech, to the following effect:—addressing herself to me, she said, "*You devil! You yellow devil!* it was you that put it into the heads of Henry and John to run away. But for you, you long-legged mulatto dev-

il! Henry nor John would never have thought of such a thing." I made no reply, and was immediately hurried off towards St. Michael's. Just a moment previous to the scuffle with Henry, Mr. Hamilton suggested the propriety of making search for the protections which he had understood Frederick had written for himself and the rest. But, just at the moment he was about carrying his proposal into effect, his aid was needed in helping to tie Henry; and the excitement attending the scuffle caused him either to forget, or to deem it unsafe, under the circumstances, to search. So we were not yet convicted of the intention to run away.

When we got about half way to St. Michael's while the constables having us in charge were looking ahead, Henry inquired of me what he should do with his pass. I told him to eat it with his biscuit, and own nothing; and we passed the word around, "*Own nothing;*" and "*Own nothing!*" said we all. Our confidence in each other was unshaken. We were resolved to succeed or fail together, after the calamity had befallen us as much as before. We were now prepared for any thing. We were to be dragged that morning fifteen miles behind horses, and then to be placed in the Easton jail. When we reached St. Michael's, we underwent a sort of examination. We all denied that we ever intended to run away. We did this more to bring out the evidence against us, than from any hope of getting clear of being sold; for, as I have said, we were ready for that. The fact was, we cared but little where we went, so we went together. Our greatest concern was about separation. We dreaded that more than any thing this side of death. We found the evidence against us to be the testimony of one person; our master would not tell who it was; but we came to a unanimous decision among ourselves as to who their informant was. We were sent off to the jail at Easton. When we got there, we were delivered up to the sheriff, Mr. Joseph Graham, and by him placed in jail. Henry, John, and myself, were placed in one room together—Charles, and Henry Bailey, in another. Their object in separating us was to hinder concert.

We had been in jail scarcely twenty minutes, when a swarm of slave traders, and agents for slave traders, flocked into jail to look at us, and to ascertain if we were for sale. Such a set of beings I never saw before! I felt myself surrounded by so many fiends from perdition. A band of pirates never looked more like their father, the devil. They laughed and grinned over us, saying, "Ah, my boys! we have got you, haven't we?" And after taunting us in various ways, they one by one went into an examination of us, with intent to ascertain our value. They would impudently ask us if we would not like to have them for our masters. We would make them no answer, and leave them to find out as best they could. Then they would curse and swear at us, telling us that they could take the devil out of us in a very little while, if we were only in their hands.

While in jail, we found ourselves in much more comfortable quarters than we expected when we went there. We did not get much to eat, nor that which was very good; but we had a good clean room, from the windows of which we could see what was going on in the street, which was very much better than though we had been placed in one of the dark, damp cells. Upon the whole, we got along very well, so far as the jail and its keeper were concerned. Immediately after the holidays were over, contrary to all our expectations, Mr. Hamilton and Mr. Freeland came up to Easton, and took Charles, the two Henrys, and John, out of jail, and carried them home, leaving me alone. I regarded this separation as a final one. It caused me more pain than any thing else in the whole transaction. I was ready for any thing rather than separation. I supposed that they had consulted together, and had decided that, as I was the whole cause of the intention of the others to run away, it was hard to make the innocent suffer with the guilty; and that they had, therefore, concluded to take the others home, and sell me, as a warning to the others that remained. It is due to the noble Henry to say, he seemed almost as reluctant at leaving the prison as at leaving home to come to the prison. But we knew we should, in all probability, be separated, if we were sold; and since he was in their hands, he concluded to go peaceably home.

I was now left to my fate. I was all alone; and within the walls of a stone prison. But a few days before, and I was full of hope. I expected to have been safe in a land of freedom; but now I was covered with gloom, sunk down to the utmost despair. I thought the possibility of freedom was gone. I was kept in this way about one week, at the end of which Captain Auld, my master, to my surprise and utter astonishment, came up, and took me out, with the intention of sending me, with a gentleman of his acquaintance, into Alabama. But, from some cause or other, he did not send me to Alabama, but concluded to send me back to Baltimore, to live again with his brother Hugh, and to learn a trade.°°°

1845

FROM *Fourth of July Oration, 1852*

Speaking in the sonorous cadences of the nineteenth-century American oratorical tradition, yet varying this at times with an almost conversational tone, Douglass confronted his audience, in Corinthian Hall, Rochester, with the question: What could the Fourth of July mean to the black American, slave or free? The text is from the pamphlet publication of the address, Rochester, N. Y., 1852.

°°°My business, if I have any here to-day, is with the present. The accepted time with God and his cause is the ever-living now.

> "Trust no future, howe'er pleasant,
>   Let the dead past bury its dead;
> Act, act in the living present,
>   Heart within, and God o'erhead." [1]

We have to do with the past only as we can make it useful to the present and to the future. To all inspiring motives, to noble deeds which can be gained from the past, we are welcome. But now is the time, the important time. Your fathers have lived, died, and have done their work, and have done much of it well. You live and must die, and you must do your work. You have no right to enjoy a child's share in the labor of your fathers, unless your children are to be blest by your labors. You have no right to wear out and waste the hard-earned fame of your fathers to cover your indolence. Sydney Smith tells us that men seldom eulogize the wisdom and virtues of their fathers, but to excuse some folly or wickedness of their own. This truth is not a doubtful one. There are illustrations of it near and remote, ancient and modern. It was fashionable, hundreds of years ago, for the children of Jacob to boast, we have "Abraham to our father," [2] when they had long lost Abraham's faith and spirit. That people contented themselves under the shadow of Abraham's great name, while they repudiated the deeds which made his name great. Need I remind you that a similar thing is being done all over this country to-day? Need I tell you that the Jews are not the only people who built the tombs of the prophets, and garnished the sepulchres of the righteous? Washington could not die till he had broken the chains of his slaves. Yet his monument is built up by the price of human blood, and the traders in the bodies and souls of men, shout—"We have Washington to *our father*."—Alas! that it should be so; yet so it is.

> "The evil that men do, lives after them,
>   The good is oft interred with their bones." [3]

Fellow-citizens, pardon me, allow me to ask, why am I called upon to speak here to-day? What have I, or those I represent, to do with your national independence? Are the great principles of political freedom and of natural justice, embodied in that Declaration of Independence, extended to us? and am I, therefore, called upon to bring our humble

[1] Longfellow, "A Psalm of Life."
[2] Luke iii.8.
[3] Shakespeare, *Julius Caesar* III.ii.80–81.

offering to the national altar, and to confess the benefits and express devout gratitude for the blessings resulting from your independence to us?

Would to God, both for your sakes and ours, that an affirmative answer could be truthfully returned to these questions! Then would my task be light, and my burden easy and delightful. For *who* is there so cold, that a nation's sympathy could not warm him? Who so obdurate and dead to the claims of gratitude, that would not thankfully acknowledge such priceless benefits? Who so stolid and selfish, that would not give his voice to swell the hallelujahs of a nation's jubilee, when the chains of servitude had been torn from his limbs? I am not that man. In a case like that, the dumb might eloquently speak, and the "lame man leap as an hart."[4]

But, such is not the state of the case. I say it with a sad sense of the disparity between us. I am not included within the pale of this glorious anniversary! Your high independence only reveals the immeasurable distance between us. The blessings in which you, this day, rejoice, are not enjoyed in common.— The rich inheritance of justice, liberty, prosperity and independence, bequeathed by your fathers, is shared by you, not by me. The sunlight that brought life and healing to you, has brought stripes and death to me. This Fourth July is *yours,* not *mine.* *You* may rejoice, *I* must mourn. To drag a man in fetters into the grand illuminated temple of liberty, and call upon him to join you in joyous anthems, were inhuman mockery and sacrilegious irony. Do you mean, citizens, to mock me, by asking me to speak to-day? If so, there is a parallel to your conduct. And let me warn you that it is dangerous to copy the example of a nation whose crimes, towering up to heaven, were thrown down by the breath of the Almighty, burying that nation in irrecoverable ruin! I can to-day take up the plaintive lament of a peeled and woe-smitten people!

"By the rivers of Babylon, there we sat down. Yea! we wept when we remembered Zion. We hanged our harps upon the willows in the midst thereof. For there, they that carried us away captive, required of us a song; and they who wasted us required of us mirth, saying, Sing us one of the songs of Zion. How can we sing the Lord's song in a strange land? If I forget thee, O Jerusalem, let my right hand forget her cunning. If I do not remember thee, let my tongue cleave to the roof of my mouth."[5]

Fellow citizens; above your national, tumultous joy, I hear the mournful wail of millions! whose chains, heavy and grievous yesterday, are, to-day, rendered more intolerable by the jubilee shouts that reach them. If I do forget, if I do not faithfully remember those bleeding children of sorrow this day, "may my right hand forget her cunning, and may my tongue cleave to the roof of my mouth!" To forget them, to pass lightly over their wrongs, and to chime in with the popular theme, would be treason most scandalous and shocking, and would make me a reproach before God and the world. My subject, then, fellow-citizens, is AMERICAN SLAVERY. I shall see, this day, and its popular characteristics, from the slave's point of view. Standing, there, identified with the American bondman, making his wrongs mine, I do not hesitate to declare, with all my soul, that the character and conduct of this nation never looked blacker to me than on this 4th of July! Whether we turn to the declarations of the past, or to the professions of the present, the conduct of the nation seems equally hideous and revolting. America is false to the past, false to the present, and solemnly binds herself to be false to the future. Standing with God and the crushed and bleeding slave on this occasion, I will, in the name of humanity which is outraged, in the name of liberty which is fettered, in the name of the constitution and the Bible, which are disregarded and trampled upon, dare to call in question and to denounce, with all the emphasis I can command, everything that serves to perpetuate slavery—the great sin and shame of America! "I will not equivocate; I will not excuse;"[6] I will use the severest language I can command; and yet not one word shall escape me that any man, whose judgment is not blinded by prejudice, or who is not at heart a slaveholder, shall not confess to be right and just.

But I fancy I hear some one of my audience say, it is just in this circumstance that you and your brother abolitionists fail to make a favorable impression on the public mind. Would you argue more, and denounce less, would you persuade more, and rebuke less, your cause would be much more likely to succeed. But, I submit, where all is plain there is nothing to be argued. What point in the anti-slavery creed would you have me argue? On what branch of the subject do the people of this country need light? Must I undertake to prove that the slave is a man? That point is conceded already. Nobody doubts it. The slaveholders themselves acknowledge it in the enactment of laws for their government. They acknowledge it when they punish disobedience on the part of the slave. There are seventy-two crimes in the State of Virginia, which, if committed by a black man, (no matter how ignorant he be,) subject him to the punishment of death; while only two of the same crimes will subject a white man to the like punishment.—What is this but the acknowledgement that the slave is a moral, intellec-

[4] Isaiah xxxv.6.
[5] Psalms cxxxvii.1-6.

[6] William Lloyd Garrison, in the Salutory of *The Liberator.*

tual and responsible being. The manhood of the slave is conceded. It is admitted in the fact that Southern statute books are covered with enactments forbidding, under severe fines and penalties, the teaching of the slave to read or to write.—When you can point to any such laws, in reference to the beasts of the field, then I may consent to argue the manhood of the slave. When the dogs in your streets, when the fowls of the air, when the cattle on your hills, when the fish of the sea, and the reptiles that crawl, shall be unable to distinguish the slave from a brute, *then* will I argue with you that the slave is a man!

For the present, it is enough to affirm the equal manhood of the negro race. Is it not astonishing that, while we are ploughing, planting and reaping, using all kinds of mechanical tools, erecting houses, constructing bridges, building ships, working in metals of brass, iron, copper, silver and gold; that, while we are reading, writing and cyphering, acting as clerks, merchants and secretaries, having among us lawyers, doctors, ministers, poets, authors, editors, orators and teachers; that, while we are engaged in all manner of enterprises common to other men, digging gold in California, capturing the whale in the Pacific, feeding sheep and cattle on the hill-side, living, moving, acting, thinking, planning, living in families as husbands, wives and children, and, above all, confessing and worshipping the Christian's God, and looking hopefully for life and immortality beyond the grave, we are called upon to prove that we are men!

Would you have me argue that man is entitled to liberty? that he is the rightful owner of his own body? You have already declared it. Must I argue the wrongfulness of slavery? Is that a question for Republicans? Is it to be settled by the rules of logic and argumentation, as a matter beset with great difficulty, involving a doubtful application of the principle of justice, hard to be understood? How should I look to-day, in the presence of Americans dividing, and subdividing a discourse, to show that men have a natural right to freedom? speaking of it relatively, and positively, negatively, and affirmatively. To do so, would be to make myself ridiculous, and to offer an insult to your understanding.— There is not a man beneath the canopy of heaven, that does not know that slavery is wrong *for him.*

What, am I to argue that it is wrong to make men brutes, to rob them of their liberty, to work them without wages, to keep them ignorant of their relations to their fellow men, to beat them with sticks, to flay their flesh with the lash, to load their limbs with irons, to hunt them with dogs, to sell them at auction, to sunder their families, to knock out their teeth, to burn their flesh, to starve them into obedience and submission to their masters? Must I argue that a system thus marked with blood, and stained with pollution, is *wrong?* No! I will not. I have better employment for my time and strength, than such arguments would imply.

What, then, remains to be argued? Is it that slavery is not divine; that God did not establish it; that our doctors of divinity are mistaken? There is blasphemy in the thought. That which is inhuman, cannot be divine! *Who* can reason on such a proposition? They that can, may; I cannot. The time for such argument is past.

At a time like this, scorching irony, not convincing argument, is needed. O! had I the ability, and could I reach the nation's ear, I would, to day, pour out a fiery stream of biting ridicule, blasting reproach, withering sarcasm, and stern rebuke. For it is not light that is needed, but fire; it is not the gentle shower, but thunder. We need the storm, the whirlwind, and the earthquake. The feeling of the nation must be quickened; the conscience of the nation must be roused; the propriety of the nation must be startled; the hypocrisy of the nation must be exposed; and its crimes against God and man must be proclaimed and denounced.

What, to the American slave, is your 4th of July? I answer; a day that reveals to him, more than all other days in the year, the gross injustice and cruelty to which he is the constant victim. To him, your celebration is a sham; your boasted liberty, an unholy license; your national greatness, swelling vanity; your sounds of rejoicing are empty and heartless; your denunciations of tyrants, brass fronted impudence; your shouts of liberty and equality, hollow mockery; your prayers and hymns, your sermons and thanksgivings, with all your religious parade, and solemnity, are, to him, mere bombast, fraud, deception, impiety, and hypocrisy—a thin veil to cover up crimes which would disgrace a nation of savages. There is not a nation on the earth guilty of practices, more shocking and bloody, than are the people of these United States, at this very hour.

Go where you may, search where you will, roam through all the monarchies and despotisms of the old world, travel through South America, search out every abuse, and when you have found the last, lay your facts by the side of the every day practices of this nation, and you will say with me, that, for revolting barbarity and shameless hypocrisy, America reigns without a rival.°°°

1852

ABRAHAM LINCOLN [1809–1865]

To THE WELL-KNOWN FACTS of Lincoln's biography—his Kentucky birth, his youth in Indiana, his young manhood in backwoods Illinois, his training in law, his tenure in the state and national legislatures—one might add a few pertinent details. There was the senatorial campaign of 1858, the great debates with Stephen A. Douglas. Lincoln lost the election, but when the Republican national convention met in Chicago two years later he was nominated for the Presidency on the third ballot. With 180 electoral votes to his opponents' 123, he was elected to the office and began four stormy years in the White House.

Lincoln's part in the war need not be discussed here. When the result of the conflict was still in doubt, he was re-elected to the Presidency by an overwhelming majority in the electoral college. Inaugurated March 4, 1865, he had served little more than a month of his second term when an assassin's bullet ended his life.

Lincoln has won a place in American letters by salient ideas expressed in a style free of the bombastic oratory of the frontier, a style that ranged from the simply direct to the quietly firm or the harmoniously elevated.

Text: *The Collected Works of Abraham Lincoln,* Rutgers Edition, (New Brunswick, N. J., 1953).

Further reading: Carl Sandburg, *Abraham Lincoln: The Prairie Years and the War Years* (one-volume abridgement of his six-volume work), 1954. David Donald, *Lincoln Reconsidered,* 1956.

Reply to Horace Greeley

EXECUTIVE MANSION, WASHINGTON,
August 22, 1862

HON. HORACE GREELEY.

Dear Sir: I have just read yours of the 19th addressed to myself through the New-York *Tribune.* If there be in it any statement, or assumptions of fact, which I may know to be erroneous, I do not, now and here, controvert them. If there be in it any inferences which I may believe to be falsely drawn, I do not, now and here, argue against them. If there be perceptible in it an impatient and dictatorial tone, I waive it in deference to an old friend, whose heart I have always supposed to be right.

As to the policy I "seem to be pursuing," as you say, I have not meant to leave any one in doubt.

I would save the Union. I would save it the shortest way under the Constitution. The sooner the national authority can be restored, the nearer the Union will be "the Union as it was." If there be

those who would not save the Union, unless they could at the same time *save* slavery, I do not agree with them. If there be those who would not save the Union unless they could at the same time *destroy* slavery, I do not agree with them. My paramount object in this struggle *is* to save the Union, and is *not* either to save or to destroy slavery. If I could save the Union without freeing *any* slave, I would do it; and if I could save it by freeing *all* the slaves, I would do it; and if I could save it by freeing some and leaving others alone, I would also do that. What I do about slavery, and the colored race, I do because I believe it helps to save the Union; and what I forbear, I forbear because I do *not* believe it would help to save the Union. I shall do *less* whenever I shall believe what I am doing hurts the cause, and I shall do *more* whenever I shall believe doing more will help the cause. I shall try to correct errors when shown to be errors, and I shall adopt new views so fast as they shall appear to be the true views.

I have here stated my purpose according to my view of *official* duty; and I intend no modification of my oft-expressed *personal* wish that all men every where could be free.

Yours,
A. LINCOLN

Gettysburg Address

"In a photographer's studio eleven days before delivering the speech at Gettysburg, Lincoln had held in his hands the lengthy address of Edward Everett, the designated orator of the day, the printed two-hour discourse covering nearly two sides of a one-sheet supplement of a Boston newspaper. To a young newspaper correspondent from California he said his own speech at Gettysburg would be 'short, short, short'—as it proved to be, ten sentences spoken in less than five minutes. In its implicative qualities, it stands among the supreme utterances of democratic peoples of the world." (Carl Sandburg, in *Literary History of the United States.*)

Four score and seven years ago our fathers brought forth on this continent, a new nation, conceived in liberty, and dedicated to the proposition that all men are created equal.

Now we are engaged in a great civil war, testing whether that nation, or any nation so conceived and so dedicated, can long endure. We are met on a great battle-field of that war. We have come to dedicate a portion of that field, as a final resting place for those who here gave their lives that that nation might live. It is altogether fitting and proper that we should do this.

But, in a larger sense, we cannot dedicate—we cannot consecrate—we cannot hallow—this ground. The brave men, living and dead, who struggled here, have consecrated it, far above our poor power to add or detract. The world will little note, nor long remember what we say here, but it can never forget what they did here. It is for us the living, rather, to be dedicated here to the unfinished work which they who fought here have thus far so nobly advanced. It is rather for us to be here dedicated to the great task remaining before us—that from these honored dead we take increased devotion to that cause for which they gave the last full measure of devotion—that we here highly resolve that these dead shall not have died in vain—that this nation, under God, shall have a new birth of freedom—and that government of the people, by the people, for the people, shall not perish from the earth.

1863

Letter to Mrs. Bixby

"The War Department records showed a Boston woman to have lost five sons in combat actions. The number was less than five, as later research revealed, but Lincoln spoke through her to all families that had lost a boy or man in the war." (Sandburg)

EXECUTIVE MANSION, WASHINGTON,
November 21, 1864

MRS. BIXBY, Boston, Massachusetts.

Dear Madam,—I have been shown in the files of the War Department a statement of the Adjutant General of Massachusetts that you are the mother of five sons who have died gloriously on the field of battle.

I feel how weak and fruitless must be any words of mine which should attempt to beguile you from the grief of a loss so overwhelming. But I cannot refrain from tendering to you the consolation that may be found in the thanks of the Republic they died to save.

I pray that our Heavenly Father may assuage the anguish of your bereavement, and leave you only the cherished memory of the loved and lost, and the solemn pride that must be yours to have laid so costly a sacrifice upon the altar of Freedom.

Yours, very sincerely and respectfully,
ABRAHAM LINCOLN

Second Inaugural Address

FELLOW-COUNTRYMEN: At this second appearing to take the oath of the presidential office, there is less occasion for an extended address than there was at the first. Then a statement, somewhat in detail, of a course to be pursued, seemed fitting and proper. Now, at the expiration of four years, during which public declarations have been constantly called forth on every point and phase of the great contest which still absorbs the attention and engrosses the energies of the nation, little that is new could be presented. The progress of our arms, upon which all else chiefly depends, is as well known to the public as to myself; and it is, I trust, reasonably satisfactory and encouraging to all. With high hope for the future, no prediction in regard to it is ventured.

On the occasion corresponding to this four years ago, all thoughts were anxiously directed to an impending civil war. All dreaded it—all sought to avert it. While the inaugural address was being delivered from this place, devoted altogether to *saving* the Union without war, insurgent agents were in the city seeking to *destroy* it without war—seeking to dissolve the Union, and divide effects, by negotiation. Both parties deprecated war; but one of them would *make* war rather than let the nation survive; and the other would *accept* war rather than let it perish. And the war came.

One eighth of the whole population were colored

slaves, not distributed generally over the Union, but localized in the Southern part of it. These slaves constituted a peculiar and powerful interest. All knew that this interest was, somehow, the cause of the war. To strengthen, perpetuate, and extend this interest was the object for which the insurgents would rend the Union, even by war; while the government claimed no right to do more than to restrict the territorial enlargement of it. Neither party expected for the war, the magnitude, or the duration, which it has already attained. Neither anticipated that the *cause* of the conflict might cease with, or even before, the conflict itself should cease. Each looked for an easier triumph, and a result less fundamental and astounding. Both read the same Bible, and pray to the same God; and each invokes His aid against the other. It may seem strange that any men should dare to ask a just God's assistance in wringing their bread from the sweat of other men's faces; but let us judge not that we be not judged. The prayers of both could not be answered; that of neither has been answered fully. The Almighty has his own purposes. "Woe unto the world because of offences! for it must needs be that offences come; but woe to that man by whom the offence cometh!" If we shall suppose that American Slavery is one of those offences which, in the providence of God, must needs come, but which, having continued through His appointed time, He now wills to remove, and that He gives to both North and South this terrible war, as the woe due to those by whom the offence came, shall we discern therein any departure from those divine attributes which the believers in a Living God always ascribe to him? Fondly do we hope—fervently do we pray—that this mighty scourge of war may speedily pass away. Yet, if God wills that it continue, until all the wealth piled by the bound-man's two hundred and fifty years of unrequited toil shall be sunk, and until every drop of blood drawn with the lash, shall be paid by another drawn with the sword, as was said three thousand years ago, so still it must be said, "the judgments of the Lord are true and righteous altogether."

With malice toward none; with charity for all; with firmness in the right, as God gives us to see the right, let us strive on to finish the work we are in; to bind up the nation's wounds; to care for him who shall have borne the battle, and for his widow, and his orphan—to do all which may achieve and cherish a just, and a lasting peace, among ourselves, and with all nations.

1865

Index of Authors and Titles